BARRON'S

COMPACT GUIDE TO COLLEGES

17th Edition

D0724542

**Compiled and Edited by the College
Division of Barron's Educational Series, Inc.**

© Copyright 2010, 2008, 2006, 2004, 2002, 2000, 1998, 1996, 1994, 1992, 1990, 1988, 1986, 1984, 1983, 1980, 1978 by Barron's Educational Series, Inc.

Opinions and details expressed in articles and profiles in this publication are those of the individual writers and the schools, and do not necessarily reflect those of the publisher.

All inquiries should be addressed to:
Barron's Educational Series, Inc.
250 Wireless Boulevard
Hauppauge, New York 11788
www.barronseduc.com

ISBN-13: 978-0-7641-4487-5
ISBN-10: 0-7641-4487-1
International Standard Serial No. 1065-5018

PRINTED IN THE UNITED STATES OF AMERICA

9 8 7 6 5 4 3 2 1

CONTENTS

PREFACE

The seventeenth edition of Barron's *Compact Guide to Colleges* offers an abridged version of our very popular Barron's *Profiles of American Colleges*. Now in its twenty-ninth edition, *Profiles* presents extensive descriptions of all regionally accredited four-year colleges and universities in the United States as well as colleges in Canada and abroad. As the number of colleges has grown, so has this collection of profiles; today, the book has information on more than 1650 schools.

We realize that many students are only interested in highly competitive colleges. For this reason we have attempted to present, in this compact volume, those schools that have Selector Ratings of Most Competitive, Highly Competitive, and Very Competitive. We have also included some schools that are rated Special, usually because of art or music programs or because they have unique academic programs. Finally, we have included those institutions with the largest undergraduate enrollments. Their Selector Ratings range from Most Competitive to Noncompetitive, according to Barron's College Admission Selector, and represent all levels of admissions competitiveness. (For a complete description of the Selector, see the latter part of the section An Explanation of the College Entries.) Omission of a school does not mean that the college is in any way inferior to those included.

For each of the colleges included in this book, we present a capsule of basic information—most notably, enrollment and tuition data, along with the Selector Rating of admission competitiveness—and sections that describe the environment surrounding the college, student life (including housing and sports), the programs of study offered, admissions information and procedures, financial aid and computer facilities and availability. For in-depth descriptions of the colleges presented here and other colleges, we refer you to Barron's *Profiles of American Colleges*, available at your local bookseller.

As with all our college directories, we are grateful to the college admissions officers who supplied the data. We also are grateful to the many students, parents, and high school advisers who send us their comments and suggestions.

Start your college search positively. Start with the knowledge that there are many schools out there that want you. Start with the idea that there are many good college choices for every student. Too often these days, articles on college admission make students and their parents apprehensive. You can have choices. You can get financial aid. You can have a happy, successful college career.

When you begin to think about college, you are embarking on a major research project. You have many choices available to you in order to get the best possible education for which you are qualified. This article is intended to help you think of some of the important variables in your college search.

Let us help make the book work for you!

THE CURRENT ADMISSION SCENE

Today there are approximately 1650 accredited four-year colleges and universities. Most existing institutions have grown larger, and many have expanded their programs, offering master's and doctoral degrees as well as bachelor's.

The total of graduate and undergraduate students has also grown, from under 4 million in 1960 to more than 16 million today. In fact, between 2000 and 2013 total enrollment at U.S. colleges and universities is expected to rise 19 percent, to 18.2 million students. Almost 40 percent are part-time students, including many working adults. Part-time enrollments are mostly concentrated in the two-year colleges, which enroll about a third of all students.

What does this all mean to you? There is good news and bad news. The good news is that most of the colleges you will read about in this book are colleges you can get into! In other words, the vast majority of colleges in the U.S. admit more than 70 percent of those who apply. Many hundreds admit all of those who apply. So, on one level, you shouldn't worry that you won't be able to get a college education. The bad news is for the student with extremely high grades who seeks admission to the 50 or so most competitive colleges in the country. These "brand name" colleges have many times more candidates than they admit. Even incredibly qualified students are sometimes denied admission.

The key to good college planning is, as mentioned above, research. Find out about what makes one college different from another. Find out what students say about their experiences. Rely on many sources of information—many people, many books, many web sites, and so on. There are lots of people and materials available to help you. This book is one of them. Let the information be your guide. But also let your instincts and your sense of what's best for you play a part. The higher education opportunities in the U.S. are unlimited. The opportunity to let education help pave the way to achieving your dreams is a worthy goal of your college search.

MAKING A SHORT LIST

You have probably already started a list of colleges you know about from friends or relatives who have attended them, from recommendations by counselors or teachers, or by their academic or social reputations. This list will grow as you read the Profiles, receive college mailings, and attend college fairs. If you are interested in preparing for a very specific career, such as engineering, agriculture, nursing, or architecture, you should add only institutions that offer that program. If you want to study business, teacher education, or the arts and sciences, almost every college can provide a suitable major. Either way, your list will soon include dozens of institutions. Most students apply to between four and seven colleges. To narrow your list, you should keep the following process in mind:

- As you explore, be attuned to the admission requirements. You will want to have colleges on your list that span the admission selectivity continuum—from "reach" colleges (those where your grades, test scores, etc., suggest less chance of admission) to "safety" schools (those where your credentials are a bit better than the average student admitted), eliminating colleges at which you clearly would not qualify for admission.
- You also will want to keep an eye on cost. You want to consider colleges that are generally in line with your family's ability to finance your education. Be very cautious as you do this. Literally millions of dollars are available each year for students. There is both "need-based" aid (aid based on your family's ability to pay) and "merit-based" aid (aid based on such things as grades, test scores, and leadership ability).
- Screen the list according to your preferences, such as size, academic competitiveness, religious focus, and location.
- Make quality judgments, using published information and campus visits, to decide which colleges can give you the best quality and value.

The following sections are organized around the factors most important in researching a college. Discussion of admission competitiveness and cost comes first. After that, a wide range of factors important to consider as you evaluate colleges is examined. These include size, housing, the faculty, academic programs, internships, accreditation, libraries and computer technology, and religious/racial considerations. The final two sections are a discussion of campus visits and, finally, a checklist of 25 important questions to ask about each of the colleges you are exploring.

In the end, you must allow yourself to be a good decision maker. You will have to make some quality judgments. It is not as difficult as you may think. You have to be willing to read the information in this book and the literature that the schools make available, to visit a few campuses, and to ask plenty of questions. Usually you can ask questions of the admissions office by regular mail, e-mail, or in person during a campus visit. Because colleges sincerely are interested in helping you make the right choice, they generally will welcome your questions and answer them politely and honestly. In addition, your high school counselor is a key person who can offer advice and guidance. Finally, there are many resources available, in printed form and on the web, to help you.

GETTING THE MOST FROM YOUR CAMPUS VISIT

It is best not to eliminate any options without at least visiting a few campuses of different types to judge their feeling and style first hand.

To learn everything important about a college, you need more than the standard presentation and tour given to visiting students and parents. Plan your visit for a weekday during the school term. This will let you see how classes are taught and how students live. It also is the best time to meet faculty and staff members. If the college does not schedule group presentations or tours at the time you want, call the office of admissions to arrange for an individual tour and interview. (This is more likely at a small college.) At the same time, ask the admissions office to make appointments with people you want to meet.

To find out about a specific academic program, ask to meet the department chairperson or a professor. If you are interested in athletics, religion, or music, arrange to meet with the coach, the chaplain, or the conductor of the orchestra. Your parents will also want to talk to a financial aid counselor about scholarships, grants, and loans. The office of academic affairs can help with your questions about courses or the faculty. The office of student affairs is in charge of residence halls, health services, and extracurricular activities. Each of these areas has a dean or vice president and a number of assistants, so you should be able to get your questions answered even if you go in without an appointment.

Take advantage of a group presentation and tour if one is scheduled on the day of your visit. Much of what you learn may be familiar, but other students and parents will ask about some of the same things you want to know. Student tour guides are also good sources of information. They love to talk about their own courses, professors, and campus experiences.

Finally, explore the campus on your own. Check the condition of the buildings and the grounds. If they appear well maintained, the college probably has good overall management. If they look run down, the college may have financial problems that also make it scrimp on the book budget or laboratory supplies. Visit a service office, such as the registrar, career planning, or academic advising. Observe whether they treat students courteously and seem genuinely interested in helping them. Look at bulletin boards for signs of campus activities.

And, perhaps most importantly, talk to some of the students who are already enrolled at the college. They will usually speak frankly about weekend activities, whether they find it easy to talk to professors out of class, and how much drinking or drug abuse there is on campus. Most importantly, meeting other students will help you discover how friendly the campus is and whether the college will suit you socially and intellectually.

More than buildings and courses of study, a college is a community of people. Only during a campus visit can you experience the human environment in which you will live and work during four critical years.

25 CRITICAL QUESTIONS

The following questions form a checklist to evaluate each college or university you are considering. Use the profiles, material from the colleges, and your own inquiries and observations to get the answers.

1. Do I have a reasonable chance of being admitted?
2. Can my family manage the costs?
3. Is the overall size of the school right for my personality?
4. Is the location right? (Consider such specifics as region, distance from a major city, distance from home, and weather.)

5. Are class sizes right for my learning style and my need for involvement in class?
6. Will I be comfortable with the setting of the campus?
7. Are the housing and food services suitable?
8. Does the college offer the program I want to study? (Or, often more importantly, does the college offer people and classes that will help me decide what I want to study?)
9. Will the college push me academically, but not shove me?
10. Do the best professors teach undergraduate courses?
11. Can I change majors easily, if I need to?
12. Do students say the majority of classes are taught by fun, stimulating, interesting professors?
13. Is the library collection adequate and accessible?
14. Are computer facilities readily available and are campus networking opportunities up-to-date?
15. Is the connection to the Internet adequate?
16. Are there resources for career development?
17. Do the people in the financial aid, housing, and other service offices seem attentive and genuinely interested in helping students?
18. Will I find activities that meet my interests?
19. Does the campus seem well maintained and managed?
20. Will the college meet my religious and/or ethnic needs?
    And, finally, the five most critical questions:
21. Is there a good chance I will be academically successful there?
22. Will I be happy as a student there?
23. Do I seem compatible with the student population? Do they seem to enjoy what I enjoy?
24. Does the student life seem in sync with my personality and my goals? Is the student life what I'm looking for in a college?
25. Does the college "feel" right for me?

Steven R. Antonoff
Sheldon Halpern
Barbara Aronson

AN EXPLANATION OF THE COLLEGE ENTRIES

The descriptions of the schools are presented in alphabetical order. For each school, the following information is presented. Bear in mind that, occasionally, certain data are not available or are not applicable. Also be aware that certain types of information, such as tuition, change continually,

THE HEADING

Name of the College
City, State, Zip Code   Phone and Fax Numbers

THE CAPSULE

The capsule of each profile provides basic information about the college at a glance. Wherever "n/av" is used in the capsule, it means the information was not available.

COMPLETE NAME OF SCHOOL
(Former Name, if any)
City, State, Zip Code   **Fax and Phone Numbers**
(Accreditation Status, if a candidate)

Full-time: Full-time undergraduate enrollment
Part-time: Part-time undergraduate enrollment
Graduate: Graduate enrollment
Year: Semesters, quarters, summer sessions
Application Deadline: Fall admission deadline
Freshman Class: Number of students who applied, number accepted, number enrolled
SAT: Median Critical Reading, Math, Writing (abbreviated CR/M/W)
ACT: Median composite ACT
Faculty: Number of full-time faculty; AAUP category of school, salary-level symbol
Ph.D.s: Percentage of faculty holding Ph.D.
Student/Faculty: Full-time student/full-time faculty ratio
Tuition: Yearly tuition and fees (out-of-state if different)
Room & Board: Yearly room-and-board costs
                                             ADMISSIONS SELECTOR RATING

Full-time, Part-time, Graduate

Enrollment figures are the clearest indication of the size of a college, and show whether or not it is coeducational and what the male-female ratio is. Graduate enrollment is presented to give a better idea of the size of the entire student body; some schools have far more graduate students enrolled than undergraduates.

Year

Some of the more innovative college calendars include the 4-1-4, 3-2-3, 3-3-1, and 1-3-1-4-3 terms. College administrators sometimes utilize various intersessions or interims—special short terms—for projects, independent study, short courses, or travel programs. The early semester calendar, which allows students to finish spring semesters earlier than those of the traditional semester calendar, gives students a head start on finding summer jobs. A modified semester (4-1-4) system provides a January or winter term, approximately four weeks long, for special projects that usually earn the same credit as one semester-long course. The trimester calendar divides the year into three equal parts; students may attend college during all three but generally take a vacation during any one. The quarter calendar divides the year into four equal parts; students usually attend for three quarters each year. The capsule also indicates schools that offer a summer session.

Application Deadline

Indicated here is the deadline for applications for admission to the fall semester. If there are no specific deadlines, it will say "open." Application deadlines for admission to other semesters are, where available, given in the admissions section of the profile.

Faculty

The first number given refers to the number of full-time faculty members at the college or university.

The Roman numeral and symbol that follow represent the salary level of faculty at the entire institution as compared with faculty salaries nationally. This information is based on the salary report* published by the American Association of University Professors (AAUP). The Roman numeral refers to the AAUP category to which the particular college or university is assigned. (This allows for comparison of faculty salaries at the same types of schools.) Category I includes "institutions that offer the doctorate degree, and that conferred in the most recent three years an annual average of fifteen or more earned doctorates covering a minimum of three nonrelated disciplines." Category IIA includes "institutions awarding degrees above the baccalaureate, but not included in Category I." Category IIB includes "institutions awarding only the baccalaureate or equivalent degree." Category III includes "institutions with academic ranks, mostly two-year institutions." Category IV includes "institutions without academic ranks." (With the exception of a few liberal arts colleges, this category includes mostly two-year institutions.)

The symbol that follows the Roman numeral indicates into which percentile range the average salary of professors, associate professors, assistant professors, and instructors at the school falls, as compared with other schools in the same AAUP category. The symbols used in this book represent the following:

++$	95th percentile and above
+$	80th–94.9th percentile
av$	60th–79.9th percentile
–$	40th–59.9th percentile
––$	39.9th percentile and below

If the school is not a member of AAUP, nothing will appear.

Ph.D.s

The figure here indicates the percentage of full-time faculty who have Ph.D.s or the highest terminal degree.

Student/Faculty

Student/faculty ratios may be deceptive because the faculties of many large universities include scholars and scientists who do little or no teaching. Nearly every college has some large lecture classes, usually in required or popular subjects, and many small classes in advanced or specialized fields. Here, the ratio reflects full-time students and full-time faculty, and some colleges utilize the services of a large part-time faculty. In general, a student/faculty ratio of 10 to 1 is very good.

---

*Source: Annual Report on the Economic Status of the Profession published in the March-April 2009 issue of *Academe: Bulletin of the AAUP*, 1012 Fourteenth St. N.W., Suite 500, Washington, D.C. 20005.

If the faculty and student body are both mostly part-time, the entry will say "n/app."

Tuition

It is important to remember that tuition costs change continually and that in many cases, these changes are substantial. Particularly heavy increases have occurred recently and will continue to occur. On the other hand, some smaller colleges are being encouraged to lower tuitions, in order to make higher education more affordable. Students are therefore urged to contact individual colleges for the most current tuition figures.

The figure given here includes tuition and student fees for the school's standard academic year. If costs differ for state residents and out-of-state residents, the figure for nonresidents is given in parentheses. Where tuition costs are listed per credit hour (p/c), per course (p/course), or per unit (p/unit), student fees are not included. In some university systems, tuition is the same for all schools. However, student fees, and therefore the total tuition figure, may vary from school to school.

Room and Board

It is suggested that students check with individual schools for the most current room-and-board figures because, like tuition figures, they increase continually. The room-and-board figures given here represent the annual cost of a double room and all meals. The word "none" indicates that the college does not charge for room and board; "n/app" indicates that room and board are not provided.

Freshman Class

The numbers apply to the number of students who applied, were accepted, and enrolled in the 2009–2010 freshman class or in a recent class.

SAT, ACT

Whenever available, the median SAT scores—Critical Reading, Math, and Writing—and the median ACT composite score for the 2009–2010 freshman class are given. If the school has not reported median SAT or ACT scores, the capsule indicates whether the SAT or ACT is required. NOTE: Test scores are reported for mainstream students.

Admissions Selector Rating

The College Admissions Selector Rating indicates the degree of competitiveness of admission to the college.

THE GENERAL DESCRIPTION

The Introductory Paragraph

This paragraph indicates, in general, what types of programs the college offers, when it was founded, whether it is public or private, and its religious affiliation. Baccalaureate program accreditation and information on the size of the school's library collection are also provided. Special facilities such as a museum, radio or TV station, and Internet access are also described in this paragraph.

Programs of Study

Listed here are the bachelor's degrees granted, strongest and most popular majors, and whether associate, master's, and doctoral degrees are awarded. Major areas of study have been included under broader general areas (shown in capital letters in the profiles) for quicker reference; however, the general areas do not necessarily correspond to the academic divisions of the college or university but are more career-oriented.

Special

Special programs are described here. Students at almost every college now have the opportunity to study abroad, either through their college or through other institutions. Internships with businesses, schools, hospitals, and public agencies permit students to gain work experience as they learn. The pass/fail grading option, now quite prevalent, allows students to take courses in unfamiliar areas without threatening their academic average. Many schools offer students the opportunity to earn a combined B.A.-B.S. degree, pursue a general studies (no major) degree, or design their own major. Frequently students may take advantage of a cooperative program offered by two or more universities. Such a program might be referred to, for instance, as a 3-2 engineering program; a student in this program would spend three years at one institution and two at another. The number of national honor societies represented on campus is included. Schools also may conduct honors programs for qualified students, either university-wide or in specific major fields, and these also are listed.

Admissions

The admissions section gives detailed information on standards so you can evaluate your chances for acceptance. Where the SAT or ACT scores of the 2009–2010 freshman class are broken down, you may compare your own scores. Because the role of standardized tests in the admissions process has been subject to criticism, more colleges are considering other factors such as recommendations from high school officials, leadership record, special talents, extracurricular activities, and advanced placement or honors courses completed. A few schools may consider education of parents, ability to pay for college, and relationship to alumni. Some give preference to state residents; others seek a geographically diverse student body.

Requirements

This subsection specifies the minimum high school class rank and GPA, if any, required by the college for freshman applicants. It indicates what standardized tests (if any) are required, whether an essay, interview, or audition is necessary, and if AP*/CLEP credit is given. If a college accepts applications on computer disk or on-line, those facts are so noted and described. Other factors used by the school in the admissions decision are also listed.

---

* Advanced Placement and AP are registered trademarks owned by the College Entrance Examination Board. No endorsement of this product is implied or given.

Procedure

This subsection indicates when you should take entrance exams, the application deadlines for various sessions, the application fee, and when students are notified of the admissions decision. Some schools note that their application deadlines are open; this can mean either that they will consider applications until a class is filled, or that applications are considered right up until registration for the term in which the student wishes to enroll. If a waiting list is an active part of the admissions procedure, the college may indicate the number of applicants placed on that list and the number of wait-listed applicants accepted.

Financial Aid

This paragraph in each profile describes the availability of financial aid. It includes the percentage of freshmen and continuing students who receive aid, the average freshman award, and average and maximum amounts for various types of need-based and non-need-based financial aid. Aid application deadlines and required forms are also given.

Computers

This section details the scope of computerized facilities that are available for academic use. Limitations (if any) on student use of computer facilities are outlined. It also gives information on the required or recommended ownership of a PC.

THE COLLEGE ADMISSIONS SELECTOR

The College Admissions *Selector Rating* groups the colleges and universities listed in *Profiles of American Colleges* according to degree of admissions competitiveness. The *Selector* is not a rating of colleges by academic standards or quality of education; it is rather an attempt to describe, in general terms, the situation a prospective student will meet when applying for admission. It includes seven categories: Most Competitive, Highly Competitive, Very Competitive, Competitive, Less Competitive, Noncompetitive, and Special. Most of the institutions in this book are in one of the top three categories.

The factors used in determining the category for each college are median entrance examination scores for the 2009–2010 freshman class (the SAT score is derived by averaging the median critical reading, math, and writing scores; the ACT score is the median composite score); percentages of 2009–2010 freshmen scoring 500 and above and 600 and above on the critical reading, math, and writing sections of the SAT; percentages of 2009–2010 freshmen scoring 21 and above and 27 and above on the ACT; percentage of 2009–2010 freshmen who ranked in the upper fifth of their high school class and percentage who ranked in the upper two fifths; minimum class rank and grade point average (GPA) required for admission; and percentage of applicants to the 2009–2010 freshman class who were accepted. The *Selector* cannot and does not take into account all the other factors that each college considers when making admissions decisions. Colleges place varying degrees of emphasis on the factors within each of these categories.

State-supported institutions have been classified according to the requirements for state residents, but standards for admission of out-of-state students are usually higher. Colleges that are experimenting with the admission of students of high potential but lower achievement may appear in a less competitive category because of this fact.

A word of caution: The *Selector* is intended primarily for preliminary screening, to eliminate the majority of colleges that are not suitable for a particular student. Be sure to examine the admissions policies spelled out in the Admissions section of each profile. And remember that many colleges have to reject *qualified* students; the *Selector* will tell you what your chances are, not which colleges will accept you.

The following descriptions spell out the requirements for each category, but only in a general sense. A school that has very high test scores, for example, may also have low class rank and GPA requirements, which may place that school in a category lower than the scores would indicate.

Most Competitive

Even superior students will encounter a great deal of competition for admission to the colleges in this category. In general, these colleges require high school rank in the top 10% to 20% and grade averages of A to B+. Median freshman test scores at these categories are generally between 655 and 800 on the SAT and 29 and above on the ACT. In addition, many of these colleges admit only a small percentage of those who apply—usually fewer than one third.

Highly Competitive

Colleges in this group generally look for students with grade averages of B+ to B and accept most of their students from the top 20% to 35% of the high school class. Median freshman test scores at these colleges generally range from 620 to 654 on the SAT and 27 to 28 on the ACT. These schools generally accept between one third and one half of their applicants.

To provide for finer distinctions within this admissions category, a plus (+) symbol has been placed before some entries. These are colleges with median freshman scores of 645 or more on the SAT or 28 or above on the ACT (depending on which test the college prefers), and colleges that accept fewer than one quarter of their applicants.

Very Competitive

The colleges in this category generally admit students whose averages are no less than B– and who rank in the top 35% to 50% of their graduating class. They generally report median freshman test scores in the 573 to 619 range on the SAT and from 24 to 26 on the ACT. The schools in this category generally accept between one half and three quarters of their applicants.

The plus (+) has been placed before colleges with median freshman scores of 610 or above on the SAT or 26 or above on the ACT (depending on which test the college prefers), and colleges that accept fewer than one third of their applicants.

Competitive

This category is a very broad one, covering colleges that generally have median freshman test scores between 500 and 572 on the SAT and between 21 and 23 on the ACT. Most of these colleges require that students have high school averages in the C range. Generally, these colleges prefer students in the top 50% to 65% of the graduating class and accept between 75% and 85% of their applicants.

Colleges with a plus (+) are those with median SAT scores of 563 or more or median ACT scores of 24 or above (depending on which test the college prefers), and those that admit fewer that half of their applicants.

Less Competitive

Included in this category are colleges with median freshman test scores generally below 500 on the SAT and below 21 on the ACT; some colleges that require entrance examinations but do not report median scores; and colleges that admit students with averages generally below C who rank in the top 65% of the graduating class. These colleges usually admit 85% or more of their applicants.

Noncompetitive

The colleges in this category generally only require evidence of graduation from an accredited high school (although they may also require the completion of a certain number of high school units) or an equivalency degree. Some require that entrance examinations be taken for placement purposes only, or only by graduates of unaccredited high schools or only by out-of-state students. In some cases, insufficient capacity may compel a college in this category to limit the number of students that are accepted; generally, however, if a college accepts 98% or more of its applicants, or all of its in-state applicants, it automatically falls in this category.

Special

Listed here are colleges whose programs of study are specialized; professional schools of nursing, art, music, and other disciplines, or those oriented toward working adults. In general, the admissions requirements are not based primarily on academic criteria, but on evidence of talent or special interest in the field. Many other colleges and universities offer special-interest programs *in addition to* regular academic curricula, but such institutions have been given a regular competitive rating based on academic criteria.

KEY TO ABBREVIATIONS

DEGREES

A.A.—Associate of Arts
A.A.S.—Associate of Applied Science
A.B. or B.A.—Bachelor of Arts
A.B.J.—Bachelor of Arts in Journalism
A.S.—Associate of Science

B.A.—Bachelor of Arts
B.A.A.—Bachelor of Applied Arts
B.A.A.S. or B.Applied A.S.—Bachelor of Applied Arts and Sciences
B.Ac. or B.Acc.—Bachelor of Accountancy
B.A.C.—Bachelor of Science in Air Commerce

B.A.C.V.I.—Bachelor of Arts in Computer and Video Imaging
B.A.E. or B.A.Ed.—Bachelor of Arts in Education
B.A.G.E.—Bachelor of Arts in General Education
B.Agri.—Bachelor of Agriculture
B.A.G.S.—Bachelor of Arts in General Studies
B.A.J.S.—Bachelor of Arts in Judaic Studies
B.A.M.—Bachelor of Arts in Music
B.Applied Sc.—Bachelor of Applied Science
B.A.R.—Bachelor of Religion
B.Arch.—Bachelor of Architecture
B.Arch.Hist.—Bachelor of Architectural History
B.Arch.Tech.—Bachelor of Architectural Technology
B.Ar.Sc.—Baccalaurium Artium et Scientiae (honors college degree) (Bachelor of Arts & Sciences)
B.Art.Ed.—Bachelor of Art Education
B.A.S.—Bachelor of Applied Science
B.A.S.—Bachelor of Arts and Sciences
B.A.Sec.Ed.—Bachelor of Arts in Secondary Ed.
B.A.S.W.—Bachelor of Arts in Social Work
B.A.T.—Bachelor of Arts in Teaching
B.B. or B.Bus.—Bachelor of Business
B.B.A.—Bachelor of Business Administration
B.B.E.—Bachelor of Business Education
B.C. or B.Com. or B.Comm.—Bachelor of Commerce
B.C.A.—Bachelor of Creative Arts
B.C.E.—Bachelor of Civil Engineering
B.C.E.—Bachelor of Computer Engineering
B.Ch. or B.Chem.—Bachelor of Chemistry
B.Ch.E.—Bachelor of Chemical Engineering
B.C.J.—Bachelor of Criminal Justice
B.C.M.—Bachelor of Christian Ministries
B.Church Mus.—Bachelor of Church Music
B.C.S.—Bachelor of College Studies
B.E.—Bachelor of English
B.E. or B.Ed.—Bachelor of Education
B.E.—Bachelor of Engineering
B.E.D.—Bachelor of Environmental Design
B.E.E.—Bachelor of Electrical Engineering
B.En. or B.Eng.—Bachelor of Engineering
B.E.S. or B.Eng.Sc.—Bachelor of Engineering Science
B.E.T.—Bachelor of Engineering Technology
B.F.A.—Bachelor of Fine Arts
B.G.S.—Bachelor of General Studies
B.G.S.—Bachelor of Geological Sciences
B.H.E.—Bachelor of Health Education
B.H.P.E.—Bachelor of Health and Physical Education
B.H.S.—Bachelor of Health Science
B.I.D.—Bachelor of Industrial Design
B.I.M.—Bachelor of Industrial Management
B.Ind.Tech.—Bachelor of Industrial Technology
B.Int.Arch.—Bachelor of Interior Architecture
B.Int.Design—Bachelor of Interior Design
B.I.S.—Bachelor of Industrial Safety
B.I.S.—Bachelor of Interdisciplinary Studies
B.J.—Bachelor of Journalism
B.J.S.—Bachelor of Judaic Studies
B.L.A. or B.Lib.Arts—Bachelor of Liberal Arts
B.L.A. or B.Land.Arch.—Bachelor in Landscape Architecture
B.L.I.—Bachelor of Literary Interpretation
B.L.S.—Bachelor of Liberal Studies
B.M. or B.Mus. or Mus.Bac.—Bachelor of Music
B.M.E.—Bachelor of Mechanical Engineering

B.M.E. or B.M.Ed. or B.Mus.Ed.—Bachelor of Music Education

B.Med.Lab.Sc.—Bachelor of Medical Laboratory Science

B.Min—Bachelor of Ministry

B.M.P. or B.Mu.—Bachelor of Music in Performance

B.Mus.A.—Bachelor of Applied Music

B.M.T.—Bachelor of Music Therapy

B.O.T.—Bachelor of Occupational Therapy

B.P.A.—Bachelor of Public Administration

B.P.E.—Bachelor of Physical Education

B.Perf.Arts—Bachelor of Performing Arts

B.Ph.—Bachelor of Philosophy

B.Pharm.—Bachelor of Pharmacy

B.Phys.Hlth.Ed.—Bachelor of Physical Health Education

B.P.S.—Bachelor of Professional Studies

B.P.T.—Bachelor of Physical Therapy

B.R.E.—Bachelor of Religious Education

B.R.T.—Bachelor of Respiratory Therapy

B.S. or B.Sc. or S.B.—Bachelor of Science

B.S.A. or B.S.Ag. or B.S.Agr.—Bachelor of Science in Agriculture

B.Sacred Mus.—Bachelor of Sacred Music

B.Sacred Theol.—Bachelor of Sacred Theology

B.S.A.E.—Bachelor of Science in Agricultural Engineering

B.S.A.E. or B.S.Art Ed.—Bachelor of Science in Art Education

B.S.Ag.E.—Bachelor of Science in Agricultural Engineering

B.S.A.S.—Bachelor of Science in Administrative Sciences

B.S.A.T.—Bachelor of Science in Athletic Training

B.S.B.—Bachelor of Science (business)

B.S.B.A. or B.S.Bus. Adm.—Bachelor of Science in Business Administration

B.S.Bus.—Bachelor of Science in Business

B.S.Bus.Ed.—Bachelor of Science in Business Education

B.S.C.—Bachelor of Science in Commerce

B.S.C.E. or B.S.C.I.E.—Bachelor of Science in Civil Engineering

B.S.C.E.T—Bachelor of Science in Computer Engineering Technology

B.S.Ch. or B.S.Chem. or B.S. in Ch.—Bachelor of Science in Chemistry

B.S.C.H.—Bachelor of Science in Community Health

B.S.Ch.E.—Bachelor of Science in Chemical Engineering

B.S.C.I.S.—Bachelor of Science in Computer Information Sciences

B.S.C.J.—Bachelor of Science in Criminal Justice

B.S.C.L.S.—Bachelor of Science in Clinical Laboratory Science

B.S.Comp.Eng.—Bachelor of Science in Computer Engineering

B.S.Comp.Sci. or B.S.C.S.—Bachelor of Science in Computer Science

B.S.Comp.Soft—Bachelor of Science in Computer Software

B.S.Comp.Tech.—Bachelor of Science in Computer Technology

B.Sc.(P.T.)—Bachelor of Science in Physical Therapy

B.S.C.S.T.—Bachelor of Science in Computer Science Technology

B.S.D.H.—Bachelor of Science in Dental Hygiene

B.S.Die—Bachelor of Science in Dietetics

B.S.E. or B.S.Ed. or B.S.Educ.—Bachelor of Science in Education

B.S.E. or B.S in E. or B.S. in Eng.—Bachelor of Science in Engineering

B.S.E.E.—Bachelor of Science in Electrical Engineering

B.S.E.E.T.—Bachelor of Science in Electrical Engineering Technology
B.S.E.H.—Bachelor of Science in Environmental Health
B.S.Elect.T.—Bachelor of Science in Electronics Technology
B.S.El.Ed. or B.S. in Elem. Ed.—Bachelor of Science in Elementary Education
B.S.E.P.H.—Bachelor of Science in Environmental and Public Health
B.S.E.S.—Bachelor of Science in Engineering Science
B.S.E.S.—Bachelor of Science in Environmental Studies
B.S.E.T.—Bachelor of Science in Engineering Technology
B.S.F.—Bachelor of Science in Forestry
B.S.F.R.—Bachelor of Science in Forestry Resources
B.S.F.W.—Bachelor of Science in Fisheries and Wildlife
B.S.G.—Bachelor of Science in Geology
B.S.G.—Bachelor of Science in Gerontology
B.S.G.E.—Bachelor of Science in Geological Engineering
B.S.G.S.—Bachelor of Science in General Studies
B.S.H.C.A.—Bachelor of Science in Health Care Administration
B.S.H.E.—Bachelor of Science in Home Economics
B.S.H.F.—Bachelor of Science in Health Fitness
B.S.H.M.S.—Bachelor of Science in Health Management Systems
B.S.H.S.—Bachelor of Science in Health Sciences
B.S.H.S.—Bachelor of Science in Human Services
B.S.I.A.—Bachelor of Science in Industrial Arts
B.S.I.E.—Bachelor of Science in Industrial Engineering
B.S.I.M.—Bachelor of Science in Industrial Management
B.S. in Biomed.Eng.—Bachelor of Science in Biomedical Engineering
B.S. in C.D.—Bachelor of Science in Communication Disorders
B.S.Ind.Ed.—Bachelor of Science in Industrial Education
B.S.Ind.Tech.—Bachelor of Science in Industrial Technology
B.S. in Sec.Ed.—Bachelor of Science in Secondary Education
B.S.I.S.—Bachelor of Science in Interdisciplinary Studies
B.S.I.T.—Bachelor of Science in Industrial Technology
B.S.J.—Bachelor of Science in Journalism
B.S.L.E.—Bachelor of Science in Law Enforcement
B.S.M.—Bachelor of Science in Management
B.S.M.—Bachelor of Science in Music
B.S.M.E.—Bachelor of Science in Mechanical Engineering
B.S.Med.Tech. or B.S.M.T.—Bachelor of Science in Medical Technology
B.S.Met.E.—Bachelor of Science in Metallurgical Engineering
B.S.M.R.A.—Bachelor of Science in Medical Records Administration
B.S.M.T.—Bachelor of Science in Medical Technology
B.S.M.T.—Bachelor of Science in Music Therapy
B.S.Mt.E.—Bachelor of Science in Materials Engineering
B.S.Mus.Ed.—Bachelor of Science in Music Education
B.S.N.—Bachelor of Science in Nursing
B.S.Nuc.T.—Bachelor of Science in Nuclear Technology
B.S.O.A.—Bachelor of Science in Office Administration
B.S.O.E.—Bachelor of Science in Occupational Education
B.S.O.T.—Bachelor of Science in Occupational Therapy
B.S.P. or B.S.Pharm—Bachelor of Science in Pharmacy
B.S.P.A.—Bachelor of Science in Public Administration
B.S.Pcs.—Bachelor of Science in Physics
B.S.P.E.—Bachelor of Science in Physical Education
B.S.P.T.—Bachelor of Science in Physical Therapy

B.S.Rad.Tech.—Bachelor of Science in Radiation Technology
B.S.R.C.—Bachelor of Science in Respiratory Care
B.S.R.S.—Bachelor of Science in Radiological Science
B.S.R.T.T.—Bachelor of Science in Radiation Therapy Technology
B.S.S.—Bachelor of Science in Surveying
B.S.S.—Bachelor of Special Studies
B.S.S.A.—Bachelor of Science in Systems Analysis
B.S.Soc. Work or B.S.S.W.—Bachelor of Science in Social Work
B.S.Sp.—Bachelor of Science in Speech
B.S.S.T.—Bachelor of Science in Surveying and Topography
B.S.T. or B.S.Tech.—Bachelor of Science in Technology
B.S.S.W.E.—Bachelor of Science in Software Engineering
B.S.V.T.E.—Bachelor of Science in Vocational Technical Education
B.S.W.—Bachelor of Social Work
B.T. or B.Tech.—Bachelor of Technology
B.Th.—Bachelor of Theology
B.T.S.—Bachelor of Technical Studies
B.U.S.—Bachelor of Urban Studies
B.V.M.—Bachelor of Veterinarian Medicine
B.Voc.Arts or B.V.A.—Bachelor of Vocational Arts
B.V.E.D. or B.Voc.Ed.—Bachelor of Vocational Education

D.D.S.—Doctor of Dental Surgery

Ed.S.—Education Specialist
J.D.—Doctor of Jurisprudence

LL.B.—Bachelor of Laws

M.A.—Master of Arts
M.A.Ed.—Master of Arts in Education
M.A.T.—Master of Arts in Teaching
M.B.A.—Master of Business Administration
M.D.—Doctor of Medicine
M.F.A.—Master of Fine Arts
M.P.A.—Master of Public Administration
M.S.—Master of Science
Mus.B. or Mus.Bac.—Bachelor of Music

Ph.D.—Doctor of Philosophy

R.N.—Registered Nurse

S.B. or B.S. or B.Sc.—Bachelor of Science

OTHER ABBREVIATIONS

AABC—Accrediting Association of Bible Colleges
AACN—American Association of Colleges of Nursing
AACSB—American Assembly of Collegiate Schools of Business
AAFCS—American Association of Family and Consumer Sciences
AALE—American Academy for Liberal Education
AALS—Association of American Law Schools
AAMFT—American Association for Marriage and Family Therapy
ABA—American Bar Association
ABET—Accreditation Board for Engineering and Technology

ABFSE—American Board of Funeral Service Education
ABHES—Accrediting Bureau of Health Education Schools
ACBSP—Association of Collegiate Business Schools and Programs
ACCE—American Council for Construction Education
ACE HSA—Accrediting Commission on Education for Health Services Administration
ACE JMC—American Council on Education in Journalism and Mass Communication
ACOTE—American Council for Occupational Therapy Education
ACPE—Association for Clinical Pastoral Education, Inc.
ACPE—American Council on Pharmaceutical Education
ACS—American Chemical Society
ACT—American College Testing Program
ADA—American Dietetic Association
ADA—American Dental Association
ADDA—American Design Drafting Association
AFSA—Application for Federal Student Aid
AHEA—American Home Economics Association
AHIMA—American Health Information Management Association
ALA—American Library Association
ALIGU—American Language Institute of Georgetown University
AMAC AHEA—American Medical Association Committee on Allied Health Education and Accreditation
AOA—American Osteopathic Association
AOA—American Optometric Association
AOTA—American Occupational Therapy Association
AP—Advanced Placement
APA—American Podiatry Association
APA—American Psychological Association
APET—Asset Placement Evaluation Test
APIEL—Advance Placement International English Language Exam
APTA—American Physical Therapy Association
ASHA—American School Health Association
ASLA—American Society of Landscape Architects
ASLHA—American Speech-Language-Hearing Association
ATSUSC—Association of Theological Schools in the United States and Canada
AUCC—Association of Universities and Colleges of Canada
AVMA—American Veterinary Medical Association

BEOG—Basic Educational Opportunity Grant (now Pell Grant)

CAA—Council on Aviation Accreditation
CAADE—California Association for Alcohol/Drug Educators
CAAHEP—Commission on Accreditation of Allied Health Education Programs
CAAP—College Achievement Admission Program
CACREP—Council for Accreditation of Counseling and Related Educational Programs
CADE—Commission on Accreditation for Dietetics Education
CAPTE—Commission on Accreditation in Physical Therapy Education
CAS—Certificate of Advanced Study
CCE—Council on Chiropractic Education
CCNE—Commission on Collegiate Nursing Education

CCTE—California Commission on Teacher Credentialing
CDN—Canadian
CED—Council for Education of the Deaf
CEEB—College Entrance Examination Board
CELT—Comprehensive English Language Test
CEPH—Council on Education for Public Health
CLAST—College Level Academic Skills Test
CLEP—College-Level Examination Program
COE—Council on Occupational Education
CRDA—Candidates Reply Date Agreement
CRE—Council on Rehabilitation Education
CSAB—Computing Science Accreditation Board
CSS—College Scholarship Service
CSS/Profile—College Scholarship Service Financial Aid
   Profile
CSWE—Council on Social Work Education
CWS—College Work-Study

EESL—Examination of English as a Second Language
ELPT—English Language Proficiency Test (SAT II)
ELS/ALA—English Language Services/American
   Language Academy
EMH—Educable Mentally Handicapped
EOP—Equal Opportunity Program
ESL—English as a Second Language
ETS—Educational Testing Service

FAFSA—Free Application for Federal Student Aid
FET—Full-time equivalent
FFS—Family Financial Statement
FIDER—Foundation for Interior Design Education Research
FISL—Federally Insured Student Loan
FTE—Full-Time Equivalent

GED—General Educational Development (high school
   equivalency examination)
GPA—Grade Point Average
GRE—Graduate Record Examination
GSLP—Guaranteed Student Loan Program
G-STEP—Georgia State Test for English Proficiency

HEOP—Higher Equal Opportunity Program
HPER—Health, Physical Education, and Recreation

IACBE—International Assembly for Collegiate Business
   Education
IAME—International Association for Management
   Education
IB—International Baccalaureate
IELTS—International English Language Testing System

JRCERT—Joint Review Committee on Education in
   Radiologic Technology
JRCNMT—Joint Review Committee on Educational Programs
   in Nuclear Medicine Technology

LCME—Liaison Committee on Medical Education

MAPS—Multiple Assessment Program/Services
MELAB—Michigan English Language Assessment Battery
MUSIC—Multi-User System for Interactive Computing

NAAB—National Architectural Accrediting Board

NAACLS—National Accrediting Agency for Clinical Laboratory Educators
NAIT—National Association of Industrial Technology
NAPNES—National Association for Practical Nurse Education and Service
NASAD—National Association of Schools of Art and Design
NASD—National Association of Schools of Dance
NASDTEC—National Association of State Development Teacher Education
NASM—National Association of Schools of Music
NASPAA—National Association of Schools of Public Affairs and Administration
NASPE—National Association of Sport and Physical Education
NAST—National Association of Schools of Theatre
NCATE—National Council for Accreditation of Teacher Education
NCCAA—National Christian College Athletic Association
NCOPE—National Commission on Orthotic and Prosthetic Education
NDEA—National Defense Education Act
NLN—National League for Nursing
NRPA—National Recreation and Park Association

PCS—Parents' Confidential Statement
PAIR—PHEAA Aid Information Request
PEP—Proficiency Examination Program
PHEAA—Pennsylvania Higher Education Assistance Agency
PSAT/NMSQT—Preliminary Scholastic Aptitude Test/National Merit Scholarship Qualifying Test

ROTC—Reserve Officers Training Corps
RSE—Regents Scholarship Examination (New York State)

SAAC—Student Aid Application for California
SACU—Service for Admission to College and University (Canada)
SAF—Society of American Foresters
SAM—Single Application Method
SAR—Student Aid Report
SAT—Scholastic Assessment Testing (formerly ATP–Admissions Testing Program)
SCAT—Scholastic College Aptitude Test
SCS—Students' Confidential Statement
SEOG—Supplementary Educational Opportunity Grant
SOA—Society of Actuaries

TAP—Tuition Assistance Program (New York State)
TDD—Telecommunication Device for the Deaf
TEAC—Teacher Education Accreditation Council
TOEFL—Test of English as a Foreign Language
TTY—Talking Typewriter

UAP—Undergraduate Assessment Program
UP—Undergraduate Program (area tests)

VFAF—Virginia Financial Assistance Form

WPCT—Washington Pre-College Test

INDEX BY STATE

DELAWARE
University of Delaware, **666**

DISTRICT OF COLUMBIA
American University, **37**
Catholic University of America, **129**
Gallaudet University, **252**
George Washington University, **257**
Georgetown University, **258**

FLORIDA
Eckerd College, **225**
Flagler College, **237**
Florida Atlantic University, **238**
Florida Institute of Technology, **240**
Florida International University, **241**
Florida State University, **243**
New College of Florida, **425**
Rollins College, **501**
Stetson University, **590**
University of Central Florida, **653**
University of Florida, **671**
University of Miami, **696**
University of North Florida, **725**
University of South Florida, **756**

GEORGIA
Agnes Scott College, **29**
Art Institute of Atlanta, **44**
Berry College, **77**
Covenant College, **199**
Emory University, **232**
Georgia Institute of Technology, **260**
Georgia Southern University, **261**
Georgia State University, **263**
Kennesaw State University, **333**
Mercer University, **392**
Oglethorpe University, **447**
Savannah College of Art and
    Design, **544**
Southern Polytechnic State
    University, **566**
Spelman College, **569**
University of Georgia, **673**

HAWAII
Brigham Young University/Hawaii, **96**
University of Hawaii at Manoa, **675**

ILLINOIS
Augustana College, **51**
Bradley University, **91**
Illinois Institute of Technology, **306**
Illinois State University, **307**
Illinois Wesleyan University, **309**
Knox College, **341**
Lake Forest College, **344**
Loyola University Chicago, **361**
North Central College, **435**

Northwestern University, **441**
Principia College, **478**
Roosevelt University, **502**
School of the Art Institute of
    Chicago, **545**
Shimer College, **552**
University of Chicago, **655**
University of Illinois at Chicago, **679**
University of Illinois at
    Urbana-Champaign, **681**
University of Saint Francis, **746**
Wheaton College, **823**

INDIANA
Butler University, **104**
DePauw University, **206**
Earlham College, **222**
Goshen College, **269**
Hanover College, **284**
Indiana University Bloomington, **311**
Indiana University-Purdue University
    Indianapolis, **313**
Purdue University/West
    Lafayette, **481**
Rose-Hulman Institute of
    Technology, **504**
Saint Mary's College, **523**
Taylor University, **601**
University of Evansville, **669**
University of Notre Dame, **728**
Wabash College, **796**

IOWA
Central College, **133**
Coe College, **153**
Cornell College, **195**
Dordt College, **211**
Drake University, **212**
Grinnell College, **275**
Iowa State University, **317**
Luther College, **366**
Maharishi University of
    Management, **372**
Simpson College, **559**
University of Iowa, **683**
Wartburg College, **802**

KANSAS
Benedictine College, **69**
Bethel College, **78**
Kansas State University, **332**
Ottawa University, **457**
University of Kansas, **685**

KENTUCKY
Asbury University, **48**
Bellarmine University, **64**
Berea College, **74**

Centre College, **135**
Murray State University, **421**
Transylvania University, **614**
University of Louisville, **687**

LOUISIANA
Centenary College of Louisiana, **132**
Dillard University, **210**
Louisiana State University and Agricultural and Mechanical College, **357**
Loyola University New Orleans, **364**
Tulane University, **623**
University of New Orleans, **717**

MAINE
Bates College, **61**
Bowdoin College, **89**
Colby College, **155**
College of the Atlantic, **167**

MARYLAND
Goucher College, **271**
Hood College, **301**
Johns Hopkins University, **325**
Loyola University in Maryland, **363**
Maryland Institute College of Art, **381**
McDaniel College, **391**
Saint John's College, **514**
Saint Mary's College of Maryland, **524**
Towson University, **613**
United States Naval Academy, **632**
University of Maryland/Baltimore County, **690**
University of Maryland/College Park, **691**
University of Maryland/University College, **693**
Washington College, **807**

MASSACHUSETTS
Amherst College, **39**
Art Institute of Boston at Lesley University, **45**
Babson College, **56**
Bentley University, **72**
Berklee College of Music, **76**
Boston College, **86**
Boston University, **87**
Brandeis University, **93**
Cambridge College, **120**
Clark University, **147**
College of the Holy Cross, **169**
Elms College, **228**
Emerson College, **231**
Gordon College, **268**

Hampshire College, **283**
Harvard University/Harvard College, **287**
Hellenic College/Holy Cross Greek Orthodox School of Theology, **291**
Massachusetts College of Art and Design, **387**
Massachusetts College of Pharmacy and Health Sciences, **388**
Massachusetts Institute of Technology, **389**
Mount Holyoke College, **418**
Northeastern University, **437**
Simmons College, **556**
Simon's Rock College of Bard, **558**
Smith College, **561**
Stonehill College, **593**
Tufts University, **621**
University of Massachusetts Amherst, **694**
Wellesley College, **812**
Wheaton College, **825**
Williams College, **831**
Worcester Polytechnic Institute, **835**

MICHIGAN
Albion College, **30**
Alma College, **35**
Calvin College, **118**
College for Creative Studies, **158**
Concordia University, Ann Arbor, **186**
Grand Valley State University, **273**
Hillsdale College, **295**
Hope College, **303**
Kalamazoo College, **329**
Kettering University, **338**
Lawrence Technological University, **346**
Madonna University, **371**
Michigan State University, **400**
Michigan Technological University, **402**
Northern Michigan University, **439**
Oakland University, **443**
University of Michigan/Ann Arbor, **698**
University of Michigan/Dearborn, **700**

MINNESOTA
Bethel University, **80**
Carleton College, **123**
College of Saint Benedict, **166**
Gustavus Adolphus College, **278**
Hamline University, **281**
Macalester College, **369**

22

New York Institute of Technology, **430**
New York University, **431**
Pace University, **459**
Parsons New School for Design, **464**
Polytechnic Institute of New York University, **471**
Pratt Institute, **474**
Rensselaer Polytechnic Institute, **491**
Rochester Institute of Technology, **499**
Saint Lawrence University, **519**
Sarah Lawrence College, **543**
School of Visual Arts, **546**
Siena College, **553**
State University of New York at Binghamton /Binghamton University, **571**
State University of New York at Fredonia, **573**
State University of New York at Oswego, **575**
State University of New York/College at Brockport, **577**
State University of New York/College at Geneseo, **579**
State University of New York/College at Oneonta, **580**
State University of New York/College of Environmental Science and Forestry, **582**
State University of New York/Empire State College, **584**
State University of New York/University at Albany, **585**
State University of New York/University at Stony Brook, **587**
Syracuse University, **598**
Union College, **626**
United States Merchant Marine Academy, **630**
United States Military Academy, **631**
University at Buffalo/State University of New York, **634**
University of Rochester, **744**
Vassar College, **789**
Wagner College, **797**
Webb Institute, **811**
Wells College, **813**
Yeshiva University, **840**

NORTH CAROLINA
Appalachian State University, **40**
Davidson College, **203**
Duke University, **218**
Elon University, **229**
North Carolina State University, **433**

Queens University of Charlotte, **483**
Salem College, **532**
University of North Carolina at Asheville, **718**
University of North Carolina at Chapel Hill, **720**
University of North Carolina at Wilmington, **722**
Wake Forest University, **799**
Warren Wilson College, **800**

NORTH DAKOTA
University of North Dakota, **723**

OHIO
Baldwin-Wallace College, **57**
Case Western Reserve University, **127**
Cedarville University, **130**
College of Mount Saint Joseph, **160**
College of Wooster, **174**
Columbus College of Art and Design, **185**
Denison University, **205**
Franciscan University of Steubenville, **246**
Hiram College, **296**
John Carroll University, **323**
Kent State University, **335**
Kenyon College, **337**
Malone University, **373**
Miami University, **398**
Oberlin College, **444**
Ohio Northern University, **449**
Ohio State University, **450**
University of Cincinnati, **656**
University of Dayton, **664**
Xavier University, **837**

OKLAHOMA
Northeastern State University, **436**
Oklahoma Baptist University, **452**
Oklahoma City University, **454**
Oklahoma State University, **455**
University of Oklahoma, **730**
University of Science and Arts of Oklahoma, **752**
University of Tulsa, **770**

OREGON
Art Institute of Portland, **47**
Corban College, **194**
George Fox University, **253**
Lewis & Clark College, **353**
Linfield College, **354**
Reed College, **490**
University of Oregon, **732**
University of Portland, **738**

Willamette University, **828**

ABILENE CHRISTIAN UNIVERSITY

Abilene, TX 79699-9000 (325) 674-2650
(800) 460-6228; (325) 674-2130

Full-time: 1674 men, 1917 women	**Faculty:** 227; IIA, --$
Part-time: 124 men, 201 women	**Ph.D.s:** 81%
Graduate: 375 men, 522 women	**Student/Faculty:** 16 to 1
Year: semesters, summer session	**Tuition:** $20,290
Application Deadline: February 15	**Room & Board:** $7510
Freshman Class: 3712 applied, 1823 accepted, 983 enrolled	
SAT CR/M: 545/558	**ACT:** 24 **VERY COMPETITIVE**

Abilene Christian University, founded in 1906, is a private nonprofit institution affiliated with the Churches of Christ. The university offers a wide range of programs through the colleges of Biblical Studies, Business Administration, Arts and Sciences and Education and Human Services, Honors and the schools of Information Technology and Computing, Social Work, and the Patty Hanks School of Nursing. There are 8 undergraduate schools and 10 graduate schools. In addition to regional accreditation, ACU has baccalaureate program accreditation with AACSB, ACEJMC, CSWE, FIDER, and NASM. The library contains 530,254 volumes, 1.2 million microform items, and 64,533 audio/video tapes/CDs/DVDs, and subscribes to 1,195 periodicals including electronic. Computerized library services include interlibrary loans, database searching, Internet access, and laptop Internet portals. Special learning facilities include an art gallery, planetarium, radio station, TV station, and a volunteer and service learning center. The 208-acre campus is in an urban area 150 miles west of the Dallas-Fort Worth metroplex. Including any residence halls, there are 41 buildings.

Programs of Study: ACU confers B.A., B.S., B.B.A., B.F.A., B.M., and B.S.N. degrees. Associate, master's, and doctoral degrees are also awarded. Bachelor's degrees are awarded in AGRICULTURE (agricultural business management and animal science), BIOLOGICAL SCIENCE (biochemistry, biology/biological science, and nutrition), BUSINESS (accounting, banking and finance, electronic business, management science, and marketing/retailing/merchandising), COMMUNICATIONS AND THE ARTS (advertising, art, broadcasting, communications, design, dramatic arts, English, fine arts, graphic design, journalism, music, public relations, and Spanish), COMPUTER AND PHYSICAL SCIENCE (chemistry, computer science, information sciences and systems, mathematics, and physics), EDUCATION (art education, early childhood education, elementary education, foreign languages education, middle school education, music education, physical education, science education, secondary education, and special education), ENGINEERING AND ENVIRONMENTAL DESIGN (engineering and applied science, environmental science, and interior design), HEALTH PROFESSIONS (nursing, predentistry, premedicine, and speech pathology/audiology), SOCIAL SCIENCE (biblical studies, criminal justice, family/consumer studies, history, international relations, ministries, missions, political science/government, prelaw, psychology, religion, social work, and sociology). Biology, chemistry, accounting, and physics are the strongest academically. Elementary education, management, and psychology are the largest.

Special: ACU offers cross-registration with Hardin-Simmons and McMurry Universities and study abroad in 3 countries. Double majors and credit for military training are available. Internships are possible in most majors, as are B.A.-B.S. degrees in biology, bio-chemistry, communication, and mathematics. A 3-2 engineering degree is offered with the University of Texas at Arlington and an admissions agreement with Texas Tech for applied physics MS program. Student designed majors (interdisciplinary studies) are available. The applied studies program enables degree completion for adult students. There are 19 national honor societies and there is an Honors College for all majors across campus.

Admissions: 49% of the 2009-2010 applicants were accepted. The SAT scores for the 2009-2010 freshman class were: Critical Reading--32% below 500, 39% between 500 and 599, 22% between 600 and 700, and 7% above 700; Math--26% below 500, 40% between 500 and 599, 28% between 600 and 700, and 6% above 700. The ACT scores were 21% below 21, 25% between 21 and 23, 24% between 24 and 26, 13% between 27 and 28, and 17% above 28. 42% of the current freshmen were in the top fifth of their class; 69% were in the top two fifths. There were 9 National Merit finalists. 18 freshmen graduated first in their class.

Requirements: The SAT is recommended, with a satisfactory SAT or ACT score. Applicants must be graduates of an accredited secondary school or have the GED and have completed 22 academic credits, including 4 in English, 2 each in math and science, and 1 each in history and social studies. 2 years of the same foreign language are required. Art majors need to submit a portfolio, and music and theater majors must audition. ACU requires applicants to be in the upper 50% of their class. AP and CLEP credits are accepted. Important factors in the admissions decision are leadership record, recommendations by alumni, and advanced placement or honors courses.

Procedure: Freshmen are admitted to all sessions. Entrance exams should be taken by February of the senior year. Applications should be filed by February 15 for fall entry, along with a $50 fee. Notifications are sent February 15. Applications are accepted on-line.

Financial Aid: In 2009-2010, 98% of all full-time freshmen and 90% of continuing full-time students received some form of financial aid. 70% of all full-time freshmen and 64% of continuing full-time students received need-based aid. The average freshman award was $18,543. Need-based scholarships or need-based grants averaged $5,416 ; need-based self-help aid (loans and jobs) averaged $7,107; non-need-based athletic scholarships averaged $11,576; and other non-need-based awards and non-need-based scholarships averaged $7,798. 18% of undergraduate students work part-time. Average annual earnings from campus work are $2000. The average financial indebtedness of the 2009 graduate was $35,453. The FAFSA is required. The deadline for filing freshman financial aid applications for fall entry is March 1.

Computers: Wireless access is available. All residence halls and most departments have a PC lab with approximately 700 available PCs. All areas and buildings (interior and exterior)of the main campus have full wireless Internet access. All students may access the system 24-hours-a-day. There are no time limits and no fees.

Decatur, GA 30030 (404) 471-6423
(800) 868-8602; (404) 471-6414

Full-time: 8 men, 802 women	**Faculty:** 83; IIB, av$
Part-time: 1 man, 31 women	**Ph.D.s:** 100%
Graduate: 5 men, 21 women	**Student/Faculty:** 10 to 1
Year: semesters, summer session	**Tuition:** $30,105
Application Deadline: March 1	**Room & Board:** $9850
Freshman Class: 1984 applied, 918 accepted, 237 enrolled	
SAT CR/M/W: 590/560/580	**ACT:** 25 **HIGHLY COMPETITIVE**

Agnes Scott College, founded in 1889, is an independent liberal arts college for women and is affiliated with the Presbyterian Church (U.S.A.). There is 1 graduate school. The library contains 231,399 volumes, 33,562 microform items, and 22,815 audio/video tapes/CDs/DVDs, and subscribes to 26,956 periodicals including electronic. Computerized library services include interlibrary loans, database searching, Internet access, and laptop Internet portals. Special learning facilities include a learning resource center, art gallery, planetarium, TV station, an educational technology center, multimedia classrooms, and centers for writing and speaking. The 100-acre campus is in an urban area 6 miles from downtown Atlanta. Including any residence halls, there are 27 buildings.

Programs of Study: Agnes Scott confers B.A. degrees. Master's degrees are also awarded. Bachelor's degrees are awarded in BIOLOGICAL SCIENCE (biochemistry, biology/biological science, and neurosciences), COMMUNICATIONS AND THE ARTS (art, art history and appreciation, classical languages, classics, dance, dramatic arts, English, English literature, fine arts, French, German, music, and Spanish), COMPUTER AND PHYSICAL SCIENCE (astrophysics, chemistry, mathematics, and physics), SOCIAL SCIENCE (African studies, anthropology, classical/ancient civilization, economics, history, international relations, philosophy, political science/government, psychology, religion, sociology, and women's studies). Psychology, English literature-creative writing, sociology and anthropology are the largest.

Special: There is cross-registration through ARCHE (a 19-member consortium), and more than 300 credit and noncredit internships are available. There is a 3-2 engineering program with the Georgia Institute of Technology, and the college offers dual, student-designed, and interdisciplinary majors. Pass/fail options are also available. Opportunities for study abroad include exchange programs, a Global Awareness program, and Global Connections. Also offered are a Washington semester, an Atlanta semester, the PLEN Public Policy Semester, the Mills College Exchange, a 3-4 architecture degree with Washington University, a 3-2 nursing program with Emory University, and work-study programs. B.A. degree requirements may be completed in 3 years. There are 13 national honor societies, including Phi Beta Kappa.

Admissions: 46% of the 2009-2010 applicants were accepted. The SAT scores for the 2009-2010 freshman class were: Critical Reading--15% below 500, 38% between 500 and 599, 34% between 600 and 700, and 13% above 700; Math--27% below 500, 42% between 500 and 599, 23% between 600 and 700, and 8% above 700; Writing--21% below 500, 37% between 500 and 599, 31% between 600 and 700, and 11% above 700. The ACT scores were 12% below 21, 26% between 21 and 23, 29% between 24 and 26, 11% between 27 and 28, and 21% above 28. 52% of the current freshmen were in the top fifth of their class; 87%

were in the top two fifths. There were 3 National Merit finalists. 7 freshmen graduated first in their class.

Requirements: The SAT or ACT is recommended. In addition, applicants (except early admission) must graduate from an accredited secondary school or have a GED. A total of 16 academic credits is recommended, including 4 years of English, 3 of math, and 2 each of a foreign language, science, and social studies. An essay is required and an interview is recommended. An audition is required for those seeking a music scholarship. AP credits are accepted. Important factors in the admissions decision are advanced placement or honors courses, recommendations by school officials, and leadership record.

Procedure: Freshmen are admitted fall and spring. Entrance exams should be taken late in the junior year or by January of the senior year. There are early decision and deferred admissions plans. Early decision applications should be filed by November 15 and regular applications should be filed by March 1 for fall entry and November 1 for spring entry, along with a $35 fee. Notification of early decision is sent December 15, regular decision, March 1. Applications are accepted on-line. A waiting list is maintained.

Financial Aid: In a recent year, all full-time freshmen received some form of financial aid. 70% of all full-time freshmen and 72% of continuing full-time students received need-based aid. The average freshman award was $30,031. Need-based scholarships or need-based grants averaged $24,448; need-based self-help aid (loans and jobs) averaged $5,139. 90% of undergraduate students work part-time. Average annual earnings from campus work are $2000. The average financial indebtedness of the 2009 graduate was $23,176. Agnes Scott is a member of CSS. The FAFSA, the college's own financial statement, and previous year's tax return are required. The priority date for freshman financial aid applications for fall entry is February 15. The deadline for filing freshman financial aid applications for fall entry is May 1.

Computers: Wireless access is available. Internet access is available for course work, recreation, and personal use. 38 of 52 (science labs are not included in the classroom total) are equipped with a presentation system that includes a personal computer and a variety of A/V equipment. All residence hall rooms have information outlet (data/voice/CATA) per bed. Wireless access is available in all residence halls. There are 250 computers in computer and teaching labs throughout the campus. All students may access the system. There are no time limits and no fees.

ALBION COLLEGE
Albion, MI 49224　　　　　　　　　　　　　　　　　**(517) 629-0321**
　　　　　　　　　　　　　　　　(800) 858-6770; (517) 629-0569

Full-time: 813 men, 896 women	**Faculty:** 124
Part-time: none	**Ph.D.s:** 94%
Graduate: none	**Student/Faculty:** 14 to 1
Year: semesters, summer session	**Tuition:** $30,482
Application Deadline: open	**Room & Board:** $8510
Freshman Class: 1781 applied, 1412 accepted, 434 enrolled	
SAT CR/M/W: 580/610/547	**ACT:** 25　　**VERY COMPETITIVE**

Albion College, established in 1835, is a private institution affiliated with the United Methodist Church and offering undergraduate degrees in liberal arts curricula. There is 1 undergraduate school. In addition to regional accreditation, Albion has baccalaureate program accreditation with NASM. The library contains 354,678 volumes, 51,673 microform items, and 11,597 audio/video tapes/CDs/

DVDs, and subscribes to 19,910 periodicals including electronic. Computerized library services include interlibrary loans, database searching, and Internet access. Special learning facilities include a learning resource center, art gallery, planetarium, radio station, nature center, equestrian center, women's center, observatory, and honors program center. The 225-acre campus is in a small town 90 miles west of Detroit and 175 miles east of Chicago. Including any residence halls, there are 30 buildings.

Programs of Study: Albion confers B.A. and B.F.A. degrees. Bachelor's degrees are awarded in BIOLOGICAL SCIENCE (biology/biological science), COMMUNICATIONS AND THE ARTS (art, art history and appreciation, English, French, German, music, Spanish, speech/debate/rhetoric, and visual and performing arts), COMPUTER AND PHYSICAL SCIENCE (chemistry, computer science, earth science, geoscience, mathematics, and physics), EDUCATION (athletic training and physical education), HEALTH PROFESSIONS (predentistry and premedicine), SOCIAL SCIENCE (American studies, anthropology, economics, ethnic studies, gender studies, history, international studies, philosophy, political science/government, psychology, public affairs, religion, sociology, and women's studies). English, economics, biology are the strongest academically. Economics, English, and psychology are the largest.

Special: Albion offers work-study and internship programs, study abroad in 35 countries, a Washington semester, and study in New York City, Philadelphia, Oak Ridge, Chicago, and the Virgin Islands. Students may earn a 3-2 engineering degree in conjunction with Columbia, Case Western, or Michigan Technological Universities or the University of Michigan. Student-designed majors, dual and interdisciplinary majors, including computational math, speech communication and theater, math/physics, and math/economics, and pass/fail grading are possible. There are 4 national honor societies, including Phi Beta Kappa, a freshman honors program, and 18 departmental honors programs.

Admissions: 79% of the 2009-2010 applicants were accepted. The SAT scores for the 2009-2010 freshman class were: Critical Reading--18% below 500, 39% between 500 and 599, 29% between 600 and 700, and 14% above 700; Math--7% below 500, 32% between 500 and 599, 36% between 600 and 700, and 25% above 700; Writing--11% below 500, 37% between 500 and 599, 33% between 600 and 700, and 19% above 700. The ACT scores were 12% below 21, 24% between 21 and 23, 30% between 24 and 26, 16% between 27 and 28, and 18% above 28. There were 2 National Merit finalists.

Requirements: The SAT or ACT is required. In addition, applicants must graduate from an accredited secondary school or earn a GED. Completion of 15 Carnegie credits is required. A strong background in English, math, and lab and social sciences is recommended. A GPA of 3.0 is required. AP and CLEP credits are accepted. Important factors in the admissions decision are advanced placement or honors courses, extracurricular activities record, and personality/intangible qualities.

Procedure: Freshmen are admitted fall and spring. Entrance exams should be taken in April or June of the junior year. There are early admissions, deferred admissions, and rolling admissions plans. Check with the school for current application deadlines. The application fee is $40. Notification is sent on a rolling basis. Applications are accepted on-line at the Albion web site via CollegeNet and Common App.

Financial Aid: In 2009-2010, 98% of all full-time freshmen and 98% of continuing full-time students received some form of financial aid. 71% of all full-time freshmen and 65% of continuing full-time students received need-based aid. The average freshman award was $25,800. Need-based scholarships or need-based

grants averaged $19,748 ($38,100 maximum), and need-based self-help aid (loans and jobs) averaged $5774 ($9000 maximum). 45% of undergraduate students work part-time. Average annual earnings from campus work are $1062. The average financial indebtedness of the 2009 graduate was $30,149. The CSS/Profile and FAFSA are required. The deadline for filing freshman financial aid applications for fall entry is March 1.

Computers: More than 80% of the campus has wireless access. All students may access the system. There are no time limits and no fees. It is strongly recommended that all students have a personal computer.

ALFRED UNIVERSITY
Alfred, NY 14802-1205

(607) 871-2115
(800) 541-9229; (607) 871-2198

Full-time: 896 men, 931 women	**Faculty:** 165
Part-time: 34 men, 48 women	**Ph.D.s:** 91%
Graduate: 122 men, 288 women	**Student/Faculty:** 11 to 1
Year: semesters, summer session	**Tuition:** $25,246
Application Deadline: February 1	**Room & Board:** $11,174
Freshman Class: 2579 applied, 1816 accepted, 465 enrolled	
SAT CR/M/W: 540/560/530	**ACT:** 24 **VERY COMPETITIVE**

Alfred University, founded in 1836, is composed of the privately endowed College of Business, College of Liberal Arts and Sciences, and New York State College of Ceramics (Inamori School of Engineering and School of Art and Design). Bachelor's, master's, and doctoral degrees and certificates of advanced study are awarded. There are 4 undergraduate schools and 1 graduate school. In addition to regional accreditation, AU has baccalaureate program accreditation with AACSB, ABET, ACS, CAAHEP, and NASAD. The 2 libraries contain 297,996 volumes, 86,536 microform items, and 176,336 audio/video tapes/CDs/DVDs, and subscribe to 48,886 periodicals including electronic. Computerized library services include interlibrary loans, database searching, and Internet access. Special learning facilities include a learning resource center, art gallery, radio station, TV station, and an observatory. The 232-acre campus is in a rural area 70 miles south of Rochester. Including any residence halls, there are 57 buildings.

Programs of Study: AU confers B.A., B.S., and B.F.A. degrees. Master's and doctoral degrees are also awarded. Bachelor's degrees are awarded in BIOLOGICAL SCIENCE (biology/biological science), BUSINESS (accounting, business administration and management, management science, and marketing/retailing/merchandising), COMMUNICATIONS AND THE ARTS (art history and appreciation, ceramic art and design, communications, dramatic arts, English, fine arts, French, German, glass, performing arts, and Spanish), COMPUTER AND PHYSICAL SCIENCE (chemistry, geology, mathematics, physics, and science), EDUCATION (art education, athletic training, business education, early childhood education, mathematics education, science education, secondary education, and social studies education), ENGINEERING AND ENVIRONMENTAL DESIGN (ceramic engineering, electrical/electronics engineering, environmental science, materials engineering, and mechanical engineering), SOCIAL SCIENCE (criminal justice, crosscultural studies, economics, gerontology, history, interdisciplinary studies, philosophy, political science/government, psychology, public administration, and sociology). Ceramic engineering, electrical engineering, and mechanical engineering are the strongest academically. Art and design, business administration, and ceramic engineering are the largest.

Special: There are cooperative programs in engineering and business with Duke, Clarkson, and Columbia Universities and SUNY/Brockport. There is cross-registration with the SUNY College of Technology and a 5-year program in environmental management/forestry with Duke. Alfred offers internships in all programs, extensive study abroad, Washington and Albany semesters, work-study, a general studies degree, student-designed majors, dual majors, credit by exam, and pass/fail options. There are 16 national honor societies, including Phi Beta Kappa, and a freshman honors program.

Admissions: 70% of the 2009-2010 applicants were accepted. The SAT scores for the 2009-2010 freshman class were: Critical Reading--26% below 500, 46% between 500 and 599, 23% between 600 and 700, and 5% above 700; Math--20% below 500, 49% between 500 and 599, 25% between 600 and 700, and 6% above 700; Writing--34% below 500, 44% between 500 and 599, 21% between 600 and 700, and 1% above 700. The ACT scores were 12% below 21, 31% between 21 and 23, 27% between 24 and 26, 13% between 27 and 28, and 17% above 28. 40% of the current freshmen were in the top fifth of their class; 76% were in the top two fifths. There were 3 National Merit finalists. 10 freshmen graduated first in their class.

Requirements: The SAT or ACT is required. A GED is accepted. In addition, a minimum of 16 Carnegie units is required, including 4 years of English and 2 to 3 years each of math, history/social studies, and science. The remaining units may be either in a foreign language or any of the previously mentioned fields. An essay is required, and applicants to B.F.A. programs must submit a portfolio. Interviews are encouraged. AP credits are accepted. Important factors in the admissions decision are advanced placement or honors courses, personality/intangible qualities, and extracurricular activities record.

Procedure: Freshmen are admitted fall and spring. Entrance exams should be taken in the junior year. There are early decision, deferred admissions and rolling admissions plans. Early decision applications should be filed by December 1; regular applications, by February 1 for fall entry and December 1 for spring entry, along with a $50 fee. Notification of early decision is sent December 15; regular decision, on a rolling basis. 33 early decision candidates were accepted for the 2009-2010 class. Applications are accepted on-line.

Financial Aid: In 2009-2010, 84% of all full-time students received some form of financial aid. 78% of all full-time freshmen and 76% of continuing full-time students received need-based aid. Need-based scholarships or need-based grants averaged $17,882; need-based self-help aid (loans and jobs) averaged $6471; and other non-need-based awards and non-need-based scholarships averaged $8755. 50% of undergraduate students work part-time. Average annual earnings from campus work are $1500. The average financial indebtedness of the 2009 graduate was $24,665. AU is a member of CSS. The FAFSA, the college's own financial statement, the business/farm supplement, and the noncustodial parent statement are required. The deadline for filing freshman financial aid applications for fall entry is May 1.

Computers: Wireless access is available. Each dorm room is wired; wireless is available in libraries, the campus center, and some classrooms. There are approximately 400 PCs available across campus for student use. All students may access the system 24 hours a day, 7 days a week. There are no time limits and no fees.

Meadville, PA 16335

(814) 332-4351
(800) 521-5293; (814) 337-0431

Full-time: 948 men, 1146 women	**Faculty:** 152; IIB, av$
Part-time: 15 men, 23 women	**Ph.D.s:** 93%
Graduate: none	**Student/Faculty:** 14 to 1
Year: semesters	**Tuition:** $33,560
Application Deadline: February 15	**Room & Board:** $8440
Freshman Class: 3916 applied, 2594 accepted, 580 enrolled	
SAT CR/M/W: 607/601/600	**ACT:** 26 **HIGHLY COMPETITIVE**

Allegheny College, founded in 1815, is a private liberal arts institution affiliated with the United Methodist Church. The library contains 935,113 volumes, 494,192 microform items, and 9,69 audio/video tapes/CDs/DVDs, and subscribes to 21,752 periodicals including electronic. Computerized library services include interlibrary loans, database searching, Internet access, and laptop Internet portals. Special learning facilities include a learning resource center, planetarium, radio station, TV station, observatory, 283-acre experimental research reserve, art studio, 80-acre protected forest, dance studio, Geographic Information Systems Learning Laboratory, language learning center, science complex, seismographic network station, and the Center for Political Participation. The 565-acre campus is in a suburban area 90 minutes north of Pittsburg. Including any residence halls, there are 36 buildings.

Programs of Study: Allegheny confers B.A. and B.S. degrees. Bachelor's degrees are awarded in AGRICULTURE (environmental studies), BIOLOGICAL SCIENCE (biochemistry, biology/biological science, and neurosciences), COMMUNICATIONS AND THE ARTS (art, art history and appreciation, communications, dramatic arts, English, French, German, music, Spanish, and studio art), COMPUTER AND PHYSICAL SCIENCE (chemistry, computer science, environmental geology, geology, mathematics, physics, and software engineering), ENGINEERING AND ENVIRONMENTAL DESIGN (environmental science), SOCIAL SCIENCE (economics, history, international studies, philosophy, political science/government, psychology, religion, and women's studies). Physical and biological sciences, political science, and economics are the strongest academically. Biology, economics, and psychology are the largest.

Special: Allegheny offers a Washington semester, internships, dual majors, student-designed majors, study abroad in 14 countries, work study, and co-op programs. A 3-2 engineering degree is available with Case Western Reserve, Columbia, Duke, Pittsburgh, and Washington Universities. Accelerated programs, preprofessional programs, independent study, a marine biology study program, and an experiential learning term are also available. There are 15 national honor societies, including Phi Beta Kappa, and 18 departmental honors programs.

Admissions: 66% of the 2009-2010 applicants were accepted. The SAT scores for the 2009-2010 freshman class were: Critical Reading--8% below 500, 32% between 500 and 599, 46% between 600 and 700, and 14% above 700; Math--9% below 500, 33% between 500 and 599, 51% between 600 and 700, and 7% above 700; Writing--12% below 500, 38% between 500 and 599, 40% between 600 and 700, and 10% above 700. The ACT scores were 10% below 21, 22% between 21 and 23, 20% between 24 and 26, 17% between 27 and 28, and 31% above 28. 69% of the current freshmen were in the top fifth of their class; 92% were in the top two fifths. 25 freshmen graduated first in their class.

Requirements: The SAT or ACT is required. In addition, graduation from an accredited secondary school is required for admission. Students must have 16 Carnegie units, including 4 years of English, 3 years each of math, science, and social studies, and 2 years of a foreign language. An essay is required, and an interview is recommended. The GED is accepted. A college prep program and 2 letters of recommendation (1 from a guidance counselor, 1 from a teacher) are required. AP and CLEP credits are accepted.

Procedure: Freshmen are admitted fall and spring. Entrance exams should be taken by January of the senior year. There are early decision, early admissions, and deferred admissions plans. Early decision applications should be filed by November 15; regular applications, by February 15 for fall entry; and November 1 for spring entry, along with a $35 fee. Notification of early decision is sent December 15; regular decision, April 1. 61 early decision candidates were accepted for the 2009-2010 class. 327 applicants were on the 2009 waiting list; 6 were admitted. Applications are accepted on-line.

Financial Aid: In 2009-2010, 99% of all full-time freshmen and 98% of continuing full-time students received some form of financial aid. 69% of all students received need-based aid. The average freshman award was $25,950. Need-based scholarships or need-based grants averaged $21,029 ($42,000 maximum); need-based self-help aid (loans and jobs) averaged $6590 ($8700 maximum); other non-need-based awards and non-need-based scholarships averaged $13,523 ($27,500 maximum); and other forms of aid, including tuition remission to students without regard to financial need, averaged $30,354 ($33,240 maximum). 59% of undergraduate students work part-time. Average annual earnings from campus work are $1315. The average financial indebtedness of the 2009 graduate was $20,771. The FAFSA is required. The priority date for freshman financial aid applications for fall entry is February 15.

Computers: Wireless access is available. 185 PCs are networked and available for students to use in the library, residence halls, the campus center, academic buildings, and computer services. The wireless system can accommodate approximately 500 simultaneous users. Wireless access is available in residence hall lounges and patios, the library, campus center, and food court area, plus there is 1 residence complex with total wireless capability. All students may access the system 24 hours per day. There are no time limits and no fees. It is strongly recommended that all students have a personal computer. An Intel/Windows model is recommended.

ALMA COLLEGE
Alma, MI 48801-1599

(989) 463-7139
(800) 321-ALMA; (989) 463-7057

Full-time: 616 men, 761 women	**Faculty:** 85; IIB, av$
Part-time: 25 men, 42 women	**Ph.D.s:** 89%
Graduate: none	**Student/Faculty:** 14 to 1
Year: see profile	**Tuition:** $26,068
Application Deadline: open	**Room & Board:** $8518
Freshman Class: 1822 applied, 1334 accepted, 461 enrolled	
SAT CR/M/W: 581/565/567	**ACT:** 24 **VERY COMPETITIVE**

Alma College, established in 1886, is a private baccalaureate liberal arts college committed to academic excellence and development of responsible leaders. Alma offers challenging academic programs in a small-college environment emphasizing active, collaborative learning and close student-faculty interaction. There is 1 undergraduate school. In addition to regional accreditation, Alma has baccalaureate program accreditation with NASM. The library contains 279,901 volumes, 246,449 microform items, and 10,758 audio/video tapes/CDs/DVDs, and subscribes to 1500 periodicals including electronic. Computerized library services include interlibrary loans, database searching, and Internet access. Special learning facilities include a learning resource center, art gallery, planetarium, radio station, audio-visual center, and writing lab. The 125-acre campus is in a small town 50 miles north of Lansing. Including any residence halls, there are 26 buildings.

Programs of Study: Alma confers B.A., B.S., B.M., and B.F.A. degrees. Bachelor's degrees are awarded in BIOLOGICAL SCIENCE (biochemistry and biology/biological science), BUSINESS (business administration and management and international business management), COMMUNICATIONS AND THE ARTS (art, communications, design, dramatic arts, English, French, German, music, and Spanish), COMPUTER AND PHYSICAL SCIENCE (chemistry, computer science, mathematics, and physics), EDUCATION (athletic training, elementary education, and secondary education), HEALTH PROFESSIONS (exercise science and health science), SOCIAL SCIENCE (anthropology, economics, history, philosophy, political science/government, psychology, religion, and sociology). Exercise and health science, business administration, and biology are the strongest academically.

Special: Alma offers internships in many fields, study abroad in 18 countries, experiential learning program at the Philadelphia Center, and a Washington semester at American University. There are work-study programs, dual majors, B.A.-B.S. degrees, and student-designed majors in a wide variety of subjects. The college confers 3-2 engineering degrees in conjunction with the University of Michigan and Michigan Technological University. Nondegree study may be pursued, and students have a pass/fail grading option. A 4-week spring term provides intensive study in 1 course, often combined with travel. There are 4 national honor societies, including Phi Beta Kappa, a freshman honors program, and 16 departmental honors programs.

Admissions: 73% of the 2009-2010 applicants were accepted. The SAT scores for the 2009-2010 freshman class were: Critical Reading--36% below 500, 14% between 500 and 599, 18% between 600 and 700, and 32% above 700; Math--32% below 500, 27% between 500 and 599, 32% between 600 and 700, and 9% above 700; Writing--23% below 500, 32% between 500 and 599, 23% between 600 and 700, and 24% above 700. The ACT scores were 26% below 21, 20% between 21 and 23, 29% between 24 and 26, 12% between 27 and 28, and 13% above 28. 50% of the current freshmen were in the top fifth of their class; 79% were in the top two fifths. There were 7 National Merit finalists. 20 freshmen graduated first in their class.

Requirements: The SAT or ACT is required; the ACT is preferred. In addition, applicants must have graduated from an accredited secondary school and have earned 16 Carnegie units, including 4 years of English and 3 each of math, science, and social studies, with 2 of a foreign language recommended. Alma prefers applicants in the upper 25% of their class. Portfolio and audition are required for performing arts scholarships. A GPA of 3.0 is required. AP credits are accepted. Important factors in the admissions decision are advanced placement or honors courses, leadership record, and recommendations by school officials.

Procedure: Freshmen are admitted fall, winter, and spring. Entrance exams should be taken in the spring of the junior year or as late as the winter of the senior year. There are deferred admissions and rolling admissions plans. Application deadlines are open. Application fee is $25. Notification is sent on a rolling basis. Applications are accepted on-line (no fee).

Financial Aid: In 2009-2010, 99% of all full-time freshmen and 99% of continuing full-time students received some form of financial aid. 83% of all full-time freshmen and 81% of continuing full-time students received need-based aid. The average freshman award was $15,385. Need-based scholarships or need-based grants averaged $19,894 ($25,838 maximum); need-based self-help aid (loans and jobs) averaged $4156 ($7500 maximum). 31% of undergraduate students work part-time. Average annual earnings from campus work are $1675. The average financial indebtedness of the 2009 graduate was $31,476. The FAFSA is required. The priority date for freshman financial aid applications for fall entry is March 1.

Computers: Wireless access is available. Alma has 357 PCs accessible by students located in general, departmental, and residence hall labs. All students may access the system during all hours. There are no time limits and no fees. It is strongly recommended that all students have a personal computer.

AMERICAN UNIVERSITY
Washington, DC 20016-8001   (202) 885-6000; (202) 885-1025

Full-time: 2204 men, 3581 women	**Faculty:** 578; I, av$
Part-time: 110 men, 151 women	**Ph.D.s:** 94%
Graduate: 2015 men, 2143 women	**Student/Faculty:** 14 to 1
Year: semesters, summer session	**Tuition:** $34,973
Application Deadline: January 15	**Room & Board:** $12,930
Freshman Class: 14969 applied, 7978 accepted, 1641 enrolled	
SAT CR/M: 640/620	**ACT:** 28 **HIGHLY COMPETITIVE+**

American University, founded in 1893, is a private liberal arts institution affiliated with the United Methodist Church. There are 5 undergraduate schools and 6 graduate schools. In addition to regional accreditation, AU has baccalaureate program accreditation with AACSB, ACEJMC, NASDTEC, NASM, and NCATE. The library contains 1.0 million volumes, 1.1 million microform items, and 60,870 audio/video tapes/CDs/DVDs, and subscribes to 23,955 periodicals including electronic. Computerized library services include interlibrary loans, database searching, Internet access, and laptop Internet portals. Special learning facilities include a learning resource center, art gallery, radio station, TV station, state-of-the-art language resource center, multimedia design and development labs, science and computer science labs, and buildings for art and the performing arts. The 84-acre campus is in an urban area 5 miles northwest of downtown Washington D.C. Including any residence halls, there are 41 buildings.

Programs of Study: AU confers B.A., B.F.A., B.S., and B.S.B.A. degrees. Associates, master's, and doctoral degrees are also awarded. Bachelor's degrees are awarded in AGRICULTURE (environmental studies), BIOLOGICAL SCIENCE (biochemistry, biology/biological science, and marine science), BUSINESS (business administration and management and international business management), COMMUNICATIONS AND THE ARTS (Arabic, art history and appreciation, audio technology, communications, dramatic arts, film arts, fine arts, graphic design, journalism, literature, multimedia, music, musical theater, performing arts, public relations, and studio art), COMPUTER AND PHYSICAL SCIENCE (applied mathematics, chemistry, computer science, mathematics, physics, and statistics), EDUCATION (elementary education, foreign languages education, and secondary education), ENGINEERING AND ENVIRONMENTAL DESIGN (environmental science), HEALTH PROFESSIONS (health science), SOCIAL SCIENCE (American studies, anthropology, area studies, criminal justice, economics, French studies, gender studies, German area studies, history, interdisciplinary studies, international studies, Judaic studies, Latin American studies, law, philosophy, political science/government, psychology, Russian and Slavic studies, sociology, Spanish studies, and women's studies). International studies, business administration, and political science are the strongest academically and the largest.

Special: AU offers co-op programs and internships in all majors, study abroad in more than 40 countries, and a Washington semester program. Work-study is available on campus and with local community service agencies. Dual majors, interdisciplinary programs, student-designed majors, 3-2 engineering degrees, and B.A.-B.S. degrees are also available. Combined bachelor's/master's programs are available in most majors. Cross-registration may be arranged through the Consortium of Universities of the Washington Metropolitan Area. Credit for life experience, nondegree study, and pass/fail options are available. There are preprofessional programs in dentistry, engineering, law, medicine, optometry, osteopathy, pharmacy, and veterinary medicine. There are 12 national honor societies, including Phi Beta Kappa, and a freshman honors program.

Admissions: 53% of the 2009-2010 applicants were accepted. The SAT scores for the 2009-2010 freshman class were: Critical Reading--4% below 500, 25% between 500 and 599, 46% between 600 and 700, and 25% above 700; Math--6% below 500, 30% between 500 and 599, 48% between 600 and 700, and 17% above 700. The ACT scores were 1% below 21, 8% between 21 and 23, 29% between 24 and 26, 23% between 27 and 28, and 40% above 28. 71% of the current freshmen were in the top fifth of their class; 95% were in the top two fifths.

Requirements: The SAT or ACT is required. The ACT Optional Writing test is also required. In addition, students must have graduated from an accredited secondary school with at least 16 Carnegie units, including at least 4 units in English, 3 units in college preparatory math (including the equivalent of 2 units in algebra), 2 units in social sciences, and 2 units in foreign language(s). Applicants who have satisfactory scores on the GED may also apply. All students must submit an essay and 2 letters of recommendation. Interviews are recommended. AP and CLEP credits are accepted. Important factors in the admissions decision are advanced placement or honors courses, recommendations by school officials, and extracurricular activities record.

Procedure: Freshmen are admitted to all sessions. Entrance exams should be taken in the spring of the junior year or the fall of the senior year. There are early decision and deferred admissions plans. Early decision applications should be filed by November 15; regular applications, by January 15 for fall entry, December 1 for spring entry, and April 1 for summer entry, along with a $60 fee. Notification of early decision is sent December 31; regular decision, April 1. Applications are accepted on-line. 1225 applicants were on a recent waiting list.

Financial Aid: In 2009-2010, 83% of all full-time freshmen and 78% of continuing full-time students received some form of financial aid. The average freshmen award was $29,771. 7% of undergraduate students work part-time. The average financial indebtedness of the 2009 graduate was $20,444. The FAFSA and the college's own financial statement are required. The deadline for filing freshman financial aid applications for fall entry is February 15.

Computers: Wireless access is available. Computing resources are delivered via a fiber optic network as well as a wireless network. Wireless access for laptop computers and other devices is available everywhere on campus with appropriate hardware. AU is a T-Mobile HotSpot, which provides high-speed Wi-Fi wireless Internet access in public on campus locations such as residence halls, classrooms, the library, and the quad. In addition, there are more than 20 computer labs with approximately 700 computers available. All students may access the system.

There are no time limits and no fees. It is strongly recommended that all students have a personal computer.

AMHERST COLLEGE

Amherst, MA 01002-5000	(413) 542-8417; (413) 542-2040
Full-time: 850 men,800 women	**Faculty:** IIB, ++$
Part-time: none	**Ph.D.s:** 94%
Graduate: none	**Student/Faculty:** n/av
Year: semesters	**Tuition:** $35,000
Application Deadline: see profile	**Room & Board:** $10,000
Freshman Class: n/av	
SAT or ACT: required	**MOST COMPETITIVE**

Amherst College, founded in 1821, is a private liberal arts institution. Figures in the above capsule and in this profile are approximate. The 5 libraries contain 1 million volumes, 530,038 microform items, and 60,826 audio/video tapes/CDs/DVDs, and subscribe to 5,563 periodicals including electronic. Computerized library services include interlibrary loans, database searching, and Internet access. Special learning facilities include a learning resource center, art gallery, natural history museum, planetarium, radio station, an observatory, the Emily Dickinson Museum, and the Amherst Center for Russian Culture. The 1015-acre campus is in a small town 90 miles west of Boston. Including any residence halls, there are 75 buildings.

Programs of Study: Amherst confers B.A. degrees. Bachelor's degrees are awarded in BIOLOGICAL SCIENCE (biology/biological science and neurosciences), COMMUNICATIONS AND THE ARTS (classics, dance, dramatic arts, English, fine arts, French, German, Greek, Latin, music, Russian, and Spanish), COMPUTER AND PHYSICAL SCIENCE (astronomy, chemistry, computer science, geology, mathematics, and physics), SOCIAL SCIENCE (African American studies, American studies, anthropology, Asian/Oriental studies, economics, European studies, history, interdisciplinary studies, law, philosophy, political science/government, psychology, religion, sociology, and women's studies). English, psychology, and economics are the largest.

Special: Students may cross-register through the Five College Consortium, the other members of which are all within 10 miles of Amherst, or through the Twelve College Exchange Program. A number of interterm and summer internships are available, as is study-abroad in 40 countries. Dual majors, student-designed interdisciplinary majors based on independent study as of junior or senior year, and work-study programs are possible. There are limited pass/fail options. There are 2 national honor societies, including Phi Beta Kappa, and 30 departmental honors programs.

Requirements: The SAT or ACT is required. In addition, plus 2 SAT: Subject tests are required for admission. Amherst strongly recommends that applicants take 4 years of English, math through calculus, 3 or 4 years of a foreign language, 2 years of history and social science, and at least 2 years of natural science, including a lab science. 2 essays are required. Important factors in the admissions decision are advanced placement or honors courses, recommendations by school officials, and evidence of special talent.

Procedure: Freshmen are admitted fall. Entrance exams should be taken no later than December of the senior year. There are early decision and deferred admissions plans. Check with the school for current application deadlines and fees. Applications are accepted on-line.

Financial Aid: The CSS/Profile and FAFSA are required. Check with the school for current application deadlines.

Computers: Wireless access is available. All dorm rooms provide Internet access as well as libraries and academic buildings. All libraries and academic resource centers provide wireless Internet along with a handful of outdoor areas. There are approximately 270 PC terminals available for student use. All students may access the system 24 hours a day.

APPALACHIAN STATE UNIVERSITY
Boone, NC 28608   **(828) 262-2120; (828) 262-3296**

Full-time: 6884 men, 7232 women	**Faculty:** IIA, av$
Part-time: 310 men, 446 women	**Ph.D.s:** 76%
Graduate: 641 men, 1455 women	**Student/Faculty:** n/av
Year: semesters, summer session	**Tuition:** $4491 ($15,112)
Application Deadline: open	**Room & Board:** $6400
Freshman Class: 13039 applied, 8224 accepted, 2743 enrolled	
SAT CR/M/W: 574/584/558	**ACT:** 24 **VERY COMPETITIVE**

Appalachian State University, founded in 1899 and a member of the University of North Carolina system, is a comprehensive university offering undergraduate and graduate programs in the arts and sciences, business, teacher education, fine and applied arts, and music. There are 5 undergraduate schools and 1 graduate school. In addition to regional accreditation, App State has baccalaureate program accreditation with AACSB, CSAB, CSWE, NASAD, NASM, NCATE, and NRPA. The 2 libraries contain 955,717 volumes, 1.7 million microform items, and 43,900 audio/video tapes/CDs/DVDs, and subscribe to 7,488 periodicals including electronic. Computerized library services include interlibrary loans, database searching, and Internet access. Special learning facilities include a learning resource center, art gallery, planetarium, radio station, and an Appalachian cultural center. The 1300-acre campus is in a rural area in northwest North Carolina. Including any residence halls, there are 94 buildings.

Programs of Study: App State confers B.A., B.S., B.F.A., B.M., B.S.B.A., B.S.C.J., B.S.N., and B.S.W. degrees. Master's and doctoral degrees are also awarded. Bachelor's degrees are awarded in BIOLOGICAL SCIENCE (biology/biological science, ecology, and nutrition), BUSINESS (accounting, banking and finance, hospitality management services, insurance and risk management, marketing/retailing/merchandising, and recreational facilities management), COMMUNICATIONS AND THE ARTS (advertising, art, arts administration/management, communications, dramatic arts, English, French, graphic design, journalism, music business management, music performance, public relations, Spanish, and studio art), COMPUTER AND PHYSICAL SCIENCE (chemistry, computer science, geology, information sciences and systems, mathematics, physics, and statistics), EDUCATION (art education, business education, drama education, elementary education, health education, middle school education, music education, physical education, secondary education, social science education, and special education), ENGINEERING AND ENVIRONMENTAL DESIGN (construction technology, electrical/electronics engineering technology, environmental science, graphic arts technology, industrial engineering technology, and interior design), HEALTH PROFESSIONS (clinical science, exercise science, health care administration, health science, and music therapy), SOCIAL SCIENCE (anthropology, child psychology/development, criminal justice, economics, family/consumer studies, geography, history, interdisciplinary studies, philosophy, political science/government, psychology, religion, social work, and sociology). Elementary education, psychology, and management are the largest.

Special: App State offers a 3-2 engineering degree with Clemson and Auburn Universities, internships, work-study programs, B.A.-B.S. degrees, dual majors, study abroad, and student-designed majors. There are 21 national honor societies, a freshman honors program, and 20 departmental honors programs.

Admissions: 63% of the 2009-2010 applicants were accepted. The SAT scores for the 2009-2010 freshman class were: Critical Reading--12% below 500, 50% between 500 and 599, 34% between 600 and 700, and 4% above 700; Math--8% below 500, 49% between 500 and 599, 40% between 600 and 700, and 3% above 700; Writing--17% below 500, 53% between 500 and 599, 27% between 600 and 700, and 3% above 700. The ACT scores were 14% below 21, 31% between 21 and 23, 32% between 24 and 26, 13% between 27 and 28, and 10% above 28. 50% of the current freshmen were in the top fifth of their class; 85% were in the top two fifths.

Requirements: The SAT or ACT is required. In addition, applicants must be graduates of an accredited secondary school; the GED is accepted under certain circumstances. Applicants must have completed 4 course units in high school English and math, 3 in science, and 2 in foreign languages and social studies. AP and CLEP credits are accepted. Important factors in the admissions decision are advanced placement or honors courses, extracurricular activities record, and evidence of special talent.

Procedure: Freshmen are admitted to all sessions. Entrance exams should be taken by November 15, if possible. There is a rolling admissions plan. Application deadlines are open. Application fee is $50. Applications are accepted on-line. 1646 applicants were on a recent waiting list.

Financial Aid: In 2008-2009, 34% of all full-time freshmen and 46% of continuing full-time students received some form of financial aid. 29% of all full-time freshmen and 40% of continuing full-time students received need-based aid. Need-based scholarships or need-based grants averaged $6,422; need-based self-help aid (loans and jobs) averaged $2,494; non-need based athletic scholarships averaged $10,260. 21% of undergraduate students work part-time. Average annual earnings from campus work are $2200. The average financial indebtedness of the 2009 graduate was $15,080. The FAFSA is required. The priority date for freshman financial aid applications for fall entry is March 31.

Computers: Wireless access is available. All students may access the system. There are no time limits and no fees.

ARIZONA STATE UNIVERSITY

Tempe, AZ 85287-0112	(480) 965-7788; (480) 965-3610
Full-time: 22240 men, 23357 women	**Faculty:** I, -$
Part-time: 4231 men, 4449 women	**Ph.D.s:** n/av
Graduate: 6534 men, 7253 women	**Student/Faculty:** n/av
Year: semesters, summer session	**Tuition:** $6334 ($18,919)
Application Deadline: February 1	**Room & Board:** $9210
Freshman Class: 9344 enrolled	
SAT CR/M: 530/540	**ACT:** 23 COMPETITIVE

Arizona State University, founded in 1885, is a public institution comprising four distinctive campuses, including the Tempe campus, West campus, Polytechnic campus, and the Downtown Phoenix campus. Its research is inspired by real-world application, blurring the boundaries that traditionally separate academic disciplines. There are 14 undergraduate schools and 15 graduate schools. In addition to regional accreditation, ASU has baccalaureate program accreditation with AABI, AACSB, ABET, ACCE, ACEJMC, ADA, CCNE, CIDA, CSWE, LAAB, NAACLS, NASAD, NASM, NRPA, and PBA. The 8 libraries contain 4.4 million volumes, 7.6 million microform items, and 1.6 million audio/video tapes/CDs/DVDs, and subscribe to 87,566 periodicals including electronic. Computerized library services include interlibrary loans, database searching, and Internet access. Special learning facilities include a learning resource center, art gallery, planetarium, radio station, TV station, museums, galleries, collections, and dance studios. The 1964-acre campus is in an urban area in metropolitan Phoenix. The Tempe and Polytechnic campuses are located in the southeast valley, the Downtown campus is in the heart of Phoenix, and the West campus is in northwest Phoenix. Including any residence halls, there are 394 buildings.

Programs of Study: ASU confers B.A., B.S., B.A.E., B.F.A., B.I.S., B.L.S., B.M., B.S.D., B.S.E., B.S.N., B.S.L.A., B.S.P., and B.S.W. degrees. Master's and doctoral degrees are also awarded. Bachelor's degrees are awarded in AGRICULTURE (agricultural business management and environmental studies), BIOLOGICAL SCIENCE (biochemistry, biology/biological science, life science, microbiology, molecular biology, and nutrition), BUSINESS (accounting, banking and finance, business administration and management, business economics, international business management, management science, marketing/retailing/merchandising, nonprofit/public organization management, real estate, recreation and leisure services, recreational facilities management, supply chain management, and tourism), COMMUNICATIONS AND THE ARTS (art, communications, dance, design, English, film arts, fine arts, French, German, graphic design, industrial design, Italian, journalism, literature, music, music theory and composition, performing arts, Russian, Spanish, technical and business writing, and theater management), COMPUTER AND PHYSICAL SCIENCE (applied mathematics, applied science, chemistry, computer management, computer mathematics, computer programming, computer science, earth science, geology, mathematics, physics, systems analysis, and web technology), EDUCATION (early childhood education, education, elementary education, music education, secondary education, and special education), ENGINEERING AND ENVIRONMENTAL DESIGN (aeronautical engineering, aeronautical technology, air traffic control, architecture, bioengineering, chemical engineering, civil engineering, computer engineering, construction engineering, electrical/electronics engineering, electrical/electronics engineering technology, engineering, engineering and applied science, environmental design, environmental engineering technology, environmental science, industrial engineering, interior design, landscape architecture/design, manufacturing technology, materials science, mechanical engineering, mechanical engineering technology, and urban planning technology), HEALTH PROFESSIONS (clinical science, community health work, exercise science, music therapy, nursing, public health, and speech pathology/audiology), SOCIAL SCIENCE (African American studies, American Indian studies, American studies, anthropology, applied psychology, Asian/Oriental studies, behavioral science, counseling/psychology, criminal justice, economics, ethnic studies, gender studies, geography, history, human development, interdisciplinary studies, international studies, law enforcement and corrections, liberal arts/general studies, Mexican-American/Chicano studies, parks and recreation management, philosophy, philosophy and religion, political science/government, psychology, public history/archives, religion, science and society, social science, social work, sociology, urban studies, and women's studies). Engineering, architecture, and business are the strongest academically. Interdisciplinary studies, psychology, and communication are the largest.

Special: ASU offers internships in many disciplines, study abroad in 60 countries, work-study programs, accelerated degree programs, and a variety of interdisciplinary undergraduate programs. Students may participate in educational programs supported by several institutes and centers, such as the Eyring Center, the American Indian Policy Institute, and the Arizona Center for Medieval and Renaissance Studies. Also available are continuing education programs and a summer math and science program for high school students. There are 16 national honor societies, including Phi Beta Kappa, and a freshman honors program. The students who attend Barrett, the Honors College, can choose from more than 250 majors at ASU.

Admissions: The SAT scores for the 2009-2010 freshman class were: Critical Reading--34% below 500, 41% between 500 and 599, 19% between 600 and 700, and 5% above 700; Math--31% below 500, 38% between 500 and 599, 26% between 600 and 700, and 6% above 700. The ACT scores were 25% below 21, 26% between 21 and 23, 25% between 24 and 26, 11% between 27 and 28, and 13% above 28. 49% of the current freshmen were in the top fifth of their class; 75% were in the top two fifths. There were 156 National Merit finalists.

Requirements: The SAT or ACT is required. The minimum composite score on the ACT is 22 for in-state students and 24 for out-of-state students. The minimum composite score on the SAT is 1040 (Critical Reading and Math) for in-state students and 1110 for out-of-state students. Graduation from an accredited secondary school must include 4 years each of English and math, 3 years of lab science, 2 years each of social science (including American history) and the same foreign language, and 1 year of fine arts. ASU requires applicants to be in the upper 25% of their class (top 26% to 50% considered). A GPA of 3.0 is required (GPA of 2.5 to 2.99 considered). AP and CLEP credits are accepted.

Procedure: Freshmen are admitted fall, spring, and summer. There is a rolling admissions plan. Early decision applications should be filed by December 1; regular applications, by February 1 for fall entry, December 1 for spring entry, and June 1 for summer entry, along with a $50 fee ($65 for nonresidents). Notification of regular decision is sent on a rolling basis. Applications are accepted online.

Financial Aid: The FAFSA is required. The priority date for freshman financial aid applications for fall entry is March 1.

Computers: Wireless access is available. Students can connect to the ASU Network and can browse the Internet or access any of ASU's applications, My ASU, or other online resources. ASU offers wireless access across all 4 campuses. Computing sites are available to students, faculty, and staff, with a variety of computing equipment and services available. All students may access the system. There are no time limits and no fees.

ART CENTER COLLEGE OF DESIGN

Pasadena, CA 91103	**(626) 396-2373; (626) 795-0578**

Full-time: 780 men, 530 women	**Faculty:** 85
Part-time: 123 men, 85 women	**Ph.D.s:** n/av
Graduate: 73 men, 57 women	**Student/Faculty:** n/av
Year: trimesters, summer session	**Tuition:** $31,310
Application Deadline: open	**Room & Board:** n/app
Freshman Class: 1153 applied, 811 accepted, 554 enrolled	
SAT CR/M: 545/574	**ACT:** required **SPECIAL**

Art Center College of Design, founded in 1930, is a private institution offering programs in fine arts and design. There is 1 graduate school. In addition to regional accreditation, Art Center has baccalaureate program accreditation with NASAD. The library contains 64,000 volumes, 60,000 microform items, and 4000 audio/video tapes/CDs/DVDs, and subscribes to 400 periodicals including electronic. Computerized library services include database searching and Internet access. Special learning facilities include an art gallery. The 175-acre campus is in a suburban area 10 miles northwest of Los Angeles. There are 2 buildings.

Programs of Study: Art Center confers B.S. and B.F.A. degrees. Master's degrees are also awarded. Bachelor's degrees are awarded in COMMUNICATIONS AND THE ARTS (advertising, design, film arts, fine arts, graphic design, illustration, industrial design, and photography), ENGINEERING AND ENVIRONMENTAL DESIGN (environmental design). Illustration, graphic design, and industrial design are the largest.

Special: The college offers cross-registration with Occidental College, the California Institute of Technology, and the Southern California Institute of Architecture, internships, nondegree study, and study abroad in Sweden, Japan, and Germany.

Admissions: 70% of the 2009-2010 applicants were accepted.

Requirements: The SAT or ACT is required. The ACT Optional Writing test is also required. In addition, applicants must be graduates of an accredited secondary school or have a GED. Official transcripts and a portfolio must be submitted. An interview is recommended. AP credits are accepted. Important factors in the admissions decision are evidence of special talent, advanced placement or honors courses, and extracurricular activities record.

Procedure: Freshmen are admitted fall, spring, and summer. Entrance exams should be taken in the senior year. There is a rolling admissions plan. Application deadlines are open. the application fee is $50.

Financial Aid: In 2009-2010, 73% of all full-time freshmen and 76% of continuing full-time students received some form of financial aid. 70% of all full-time freshmen and 74% of continuing full-time students received need-based aid. The average freshmen award was $12,000, with $7000 ($10,000 maximum) from need-based scholarships or need-based grants and $5500 ($8600 maximum) from need-based self-help aid (loans and jobs). 30% of undergraduate students work part-time. Average annual earnings from campus work is $1500. The average financial indebtedness of the 2009 graduate was $70,000. Art Center is a member of CSS. The FAFSA is required. The deadline for filing freshman financial aid applications for fall entry is March 1.

Computers: Wireless access is available. All students may access the system. There are no time limits and no fees. It is strongly recommended that all students have a personal computer. A Mac is recommended.

ART INSTITUTE OF ATLANTA

Atlanta, GA 30328

(770) 394-8300
(800) 275-4242; (770) 394-0008

Full-time: 1250 men, 1105 women	**Faculty:** n/av
Part-time: 180 men, 185 women	**Ph.D.s:** 51%
Graduate: none	**Student/Faculty:** n/av
Year: trimesters, summer session	**Tuition:** $17,000
Application Deadline: open	**Room & Board:** $7000
Freshman Class: n/av	
SAT or ACT: not required	SPECIAL

The Art Institute of Atlanta, founded in 1949, is a private institution that offers bachelor's degree programs in advertising, media arts and animation, digital media production, game art and design, graphic design, interior design, multimedia and web design, photographic imaging, and culinary arts management. Figures in the above capsule and this capsule are approximate. In addition to regional accreditation, the Art Institute has baccalaureate program accreditation with FIDER. The library contains 38,780 volumes and 6,100 audio/video tapes/CDs/DVDs, and subscribes to 135 periodicals including electronic. Computerized library services include interlibrary loans, database searching, and Internet access. Special learning facilities include a learning resource center, art gallery, and academic support center. The 7-acre campus is in a suburban area in the metro-Atlanta community of Dunwoody, approximately 5 miles north of the city limits. There are 2 buildings.

Programs of Study: The Art Institute confers B.A., B.S., and B.F.A. degrees. Associate degrees are also awarded. Bachelor's degrees are awarded in COMMUNICATIONS AND THE ARTS (advertising, animation, graphic design, multimedia, photography, and video), ENGINEERING AND ENVIRONMENTAL DESIGN (computer graphics and interior design), SOCIAL SCIENCE (culinary arts). Graphic design, culinary arts, and video production are the largest.

Special: Internships in all programs, independent study, work-study programs, and study abroad are possible. There is 1 departmental honors program.

Requirements: Students must submit SAT, ACT, ASSET, or COMPASS test scores. (COMPASS testing is offered free at the college to any applicant needing it). Preference is given to applicants with GPAs of 3.0 or above; a minimum GPA of 2.5 for bachelor's degree applicants is highly recommended. An official transcript showing high school GPA is required; the GED is accepted. An essay and an interview are required. AP and CLEP credits are accepted.

Procedure: Freshmen are admitted to all sessions. Entrance exams should be taken prior to the application closing date. There are early admissions, deferred admissions, and rolling admissions plans. Application deadlines are open. The fall 2009 application fee was $50. Applications are accepted on-line.

Financial Aid: The FAFSA and the state aid form are required. Check with the school for current application deadlines.

Computers: All students may access the system. There are no time limits and no fees.

ART INSTITUTE OF BOSTON AT LESLEY UNIVERSITY

Boston, MA 02215-2598
(617) 585-6710
(800) 773-0494, ext. 6706; (617) 585-6720

Full-time: 301 men, 903 women	**Faculty:** n/a
Part-time: 18 men, 45 women	**Ph.D.s:** 43%
Graduate: none	**Student/Faculty:** n/av
Year: semesters, summer session	**Tuition:** $27,330
Application Deadline: February 15	**Room & Board:** $12,400
Freshman Class: 2523 applied, 1639 accepted, 328 enrolled	**SPECIAL**

The Art Institute of Boston at Lesley University, founded in 1912, is a private institution offering undergraduate visual art programs leading to baccalaureate degrees, 3-year diplomas, and advanced professional certificates, as well as continuing and professional education, intensive workshops, and precollege courses. There are 2 undergraduate schools and 1 graduate school. In addition to regional accreditation, AIB has baccalaureate program accreditation with NASAD. The 2 libraries contain 124,022 volumes, 878,938 microform items, and 42,680 audio/video tapes/CDs/DVDs, and subscribe to 3,935 periodicals including electronic.

Computerized library services include interlibrary loans, database searching, Internet access, and laptop Internet portals. Special learning facilities include a learning resource center, art gallery, computer labs, state-of-the-art animation lab, print-making studio, clay studio, wood-working studio, photo lab, and digital-printing lab. The 2-acre campus is in an urban area in the Kenmore Square area of Boston. Including any residence halls, there are 53 buildings.

Programs of Study: AIB confers B.F.A. degrees. Master's degrees are also awarded. Bachelor's degrees are awarded in COMMUNICATIONS AND THE ARTS (design, fine arts, illustration, and photography). Design and photography are the strongest academically. Illustration/animation is the largest.

Special: There is cross-registration with Lesley University. Internships are required for design majors and encouraged for all other majors. Accelerated degree programs in all majors, study abroad in 6 countries and dual majors in fine art/illustration, design/illustration, illustration/animation, and art education are offered. There is a freshman honors program and 2 departmental honors programs.

Admissions: 65% of the 2009-2010 applicants were accepted. The SAT scores for the 2009-2010 freshman class were: Critical Reading--27% below 500, 47% between 500 and 599, 24% between 600 and 700, and 2% above 700; Math--41% below 500, 46% between 500 and 599, 12% between 600 and 700, and 1% above 700; Writing--27% below 500, 50% between 500 and 599, 20% between 600 and 700, and 3% above 700. The ACT scores were 9% below 21, 50% between 21 and 23, 13% between 24 and 26, 24% between 27 and 28, and 4% above 28. 38% of the current freshmen were in the top fifth of their class; 70% were in the top two fifths.

Requirements: Applicants must submit an official high school transcript, an essay, and do a portfolio review. Letters of recommendation and a campus tour are encouraged. AP and CLEP credits are accepted. Important factors in the admissions decision are evidence of special talent, personality/intangible qualities, and advanced placement or honors courses.

Procedure: Freshmen are admitted fall and spring. Entrance exams should be taken by February 15. There is a deferred admissions plan. Applications should be filed by February 15 for fall entry and November 15 for spring entry. The fall 2009 application fee was $40. Applications are accepted on-line. A waiting list is maintained.

Financial Aid: In 2009-2010, 72% of all full-time freshmen received some form of financial aid. 72% of all full-time freshmen received need-based aid. The average freshmen award was $20,328. 18% of undergraduate students work part-time. Average annual earnings from campus work are $2000. The average financial indebtedness of the 2009 graduate was $14,000. The FAFSA and the college's own financial statement are required. The priority date for freshman financial aid applications for fall entry is February 15.

Computers: The university offers students 12 computer labs, each with an average of 15 computers. In addition, Internet access is provided in all classroom dorms, and lounge areas, and wireless access is available in 50% of all classrooms. A campus-wide network gives all students access to course and extracurricular activity information free of charge. All students may access the system. There are no time limits and no fees.

ART INSTITUTE OF PORTLAND

Portland, OR 97209-2911

(503) 228-6528
(888) 228-6528; (503) 227-1945

Full-time: 470 men, 535 women	**Faculty:** n/av
Part-time: 150 men, 175 women	**Ph.D.s:** n/av
Graduate: none	**Student/Faculty:** 37 to 1
Year: trimesters, summer session	**Tuition:** $21,000
Application Deadline: open	**Room & Board:** $7980
Freshman Class: n/av	
SAT or ACT: recommended	**SPECIAL**

The Art Institute of Portland is a private institution offering undergraduate programs in interior, graphic, and apparel design; media arts and animation; and multimedia and web design, game art and design, digital media production, and advertising. There is 1 undergraduate school. Enrollment figures in the above capsule and figures in this profile are approximate. The library contains 22,289 volumes and 1000 audio/video tapes/CDs/DVDs, and subscribes to 200 periodicals including electronic. Computerized library services include interlibrary loans, database searching, and Internet access. Special learning facilities include a learning resource center. The 1-acre campus is in an urban area in downtown Portland. Including any residence halls, there are 2 buildings.

Programs of Study: AIPD confers B.S. and B.F.A. degrees. Associates degrees are also awarded. Bachelor's degrees are awarded in COMMUNICATIONS AND THE ARTS (advertising, animation, apparel design, graphic design, media arts, and multimedia), ENGINEERING AND ENVIRONMENTAL DESIGN (interior design). Interior design is the strongest academically. Graphic design is the largest.

Special: Accelerated degree programs and field trips to San Francisco and annually to Europe are available. Internships are required for most programs.

Requirements: The SAT or ACT is recommended. A high school diploma or GED is required. An interview with an admissions officer and an essay are required. A GPA of 2.5 is required. AP and CLEP credits are accepted. Important factors in the admissions decision are evidence of special talent, personality/intangible qualities, and recommendations by school officials.

Procedure: Freshmen are admitted to all sessions. There are deferred admissions and rolling admissions plans. Application deadlines are open. Application fee is $50. Notification is sent on a rolling basis. Applications are accepted on-line.

Financial Aid: AIPD is a member of CSS. The FAFSA is required. Check with the school for current application deadlines.

Computers: All students may access the system weekdays and weekends, daytime and evening. There are no time limits and no fees. It is strongly recommended that all students have a personal computer.

Wilmore, KY 40390-1198   **(859) 858-3511**
                                              (800) 888-1818; (859) 858-3921

Full-time: 518 men, 860 women	**Faculty:** 81; IIB, --$
Part-time: 60 men, 61 women	**Ph.D.s:** 71%
Graduate: 30 men, 108 women	**Student/Faculty:** 15 to 1
Year: semesters, summer session	**Tuition:** $22,413
Application Deadline: open	**Room & Board:** $5414

Freshman Class: 1563 applied, 872 accepted, 315 enrolled
SAT CR/M: 584/558   **ACT:** 25   **VERY COMPETITIVE**

Asbury University, formerly Asbury College, founded in 1890, is an independent nondenominational liberal arts institution committed to academic excellence and spiritual vitality. There are 2 graduate schools. In addition to regional accreditation, Asbury has baccalaureate program accreditation with CSWE, NASM, and NCATE. The library contains 150,965 volumes, 25,462 microform items, and 9,534 audio/video tapes/CDs/DVDs, and subscribes to 545 periodicals including electronic. Computerized library services include interlibrary loans, database searching, Internet access, and laptop Internet portals. Special learning facilities include a learning resource center, art gallery, radio station, TV station, and media and fine arts centers. The 65-acre campus is in a small town 20 miles south of Lexington. Including any residence halls, there are 30 buildings.

Programs of Study: Asbury confers B.A., B.S. degrees. Associate and master's degrees are also awarded. Bachelor's degrees are awarded in AGRICULTURE (equine science), BIOLOGICAL SCIENCE (biochemistry and biology/biological science), BUSINESS (accounting, business administration and management, recreation and leisure services, and sports management), COMMUNICATIONS AND THE ARTS (art, broadcasting, classical languages, communications, creative writing, dramatic arts, English, French, journalism, music, and Spanish), COMPUTER AND PHYSICAL SCIENCE (applied mathematics, chemistry, mathematics, and physical sciences), EDUCATION (art education, elementary education, English education, foreign languages education, mathematics education, middle school education, music education, physical education, science education, secondary education, and social studies education), HEALTH PROFESSIONS (exercise science, health science, and prephysical therapy), SOCIAL SCIENCE (biblical languages, biblical studies, history, ministries, missions, philosophy, political science/government, psychology, religion, social work, and sociology). Broadcast/media communications, education, and communication arts are the largest.

Special: For-credit internships are available in several academic areas as are opportunities for study abroad in 14 countries. There is a Washington semester through the American Studies Program. 3-2 engineering degrees are offered with the University of Kentucky. There are 6 national honor societies.

Admissions: 56% of the 2009-2010 applicants were accepted. The SAT scores for the 2009-2010 freshman class were: Critical Reading--15% below 500, 38% between 500 and 599, 37% between 600 and 700, and 1% above 700; Math--27% below 500, 39% between 500 and 599, 27% between 600 and 700, and 7% above 700. The ACT scores were 19% below 21, 24% between 21 and 23, 24% between 24 and 26, 16% between 27 and 28, and 17% above 28. 76% of the current freshmen were in the top fifth of their class; 84% were in the top two fifths. There were 5 National Merit finalists. 12 freshmen graduated first in their class.

Requirements: The SAT or ACT is required. In addition, an official high school transcript or the GED is required for all new students and for transfer students with fewer than 30 college credit hours. Applicants should have completed 15 high school academic credits, including 4 units of English, 3 of math, and 2 each of lab science, social studies, and a foreign language. Either the SAT or ACT is required. A GPA of 2.5 is required. AP and CLEP credits are accepted.

Procedure: Freshmen are admitted to all sessions. Entrance exams should be taken in the junior year or in the first semester of the senior year. There are early admissions, deferred admissions, and rolling admissions plans. Application deadlines are open. Application fee is $30. Notification is sent on a rolling basis. Applications are accepted on-line. A waiting list is maintained.

Financial Aid: In 2009-2010, 78% of all full-time freshmen and 74% of continuing full-time students received some form of financial aid. 67% of all full-time freshmen and 65% of continuing full-time students received need-based aid. The average freshman award was $19,835. Need-based scholarships or need-based grants averaged $13,646; need-based self-help aid (loans and jobs) averaged $3,841; non-need based athletic scholarships averaged $4,571; and other non-need based awards and non-need based scholarships averaged $10,501. 54% of undergraduate students work part-time. Average annual earnings from campus work are $991. The average financial indebtedness of the 2009 graduate was $26,150. The FAFSA and the college's own financial statement are required. The priority date for freshman financial aid applications for fall entry is March 1. The deadline for filing freshman financial aid applications for fall entry is May 1.

Computers: Wireless access is available. High speed Internet connections are available in all dorms, and e-mail accounts are provided for all students. There are 200 computers for use in classrooms, computer labs, the student center, and the library. All students may access the system. There are no time limits and no fees. It is strongly recommended that all students have a personal computer.

AUBURN UNIVERSITY
Auburn, AL 36849-5145   (334) 844-4080; (334) 844-4773

Full-time: 9372 men, 9015 women	**Faculty:** I, -$
Part-time: 922 men, 617 women	**Ph.D.s:** 88%
Graduate: 2296 men, 2380 women	**Student/Faculty:** n/av
Year: semesters, summer session	**Tuition:** $6972 ($19,452)
Application Deadline: open	**Room & Board:** $8972
Freshman Class: 14862 applied, 11816 accepted, 3918 enrolled	
SAT CR/M/W: 570/600/570	**ACT:** 26 **VERY COMPETITIVE+**

Auburn University, founded in 1856, is a state-supported land grant institution offering undergraduate, first professional, and graduate degrees in agriculture, business, education, engineering, liberal arts, sciences and math, veterinary medicine, architecture/design and construction, forestry, human sciences, nursing, and pharmacy. There are 11 undergraduate schools and 1 graduate school. In addition to regional accreditation, Auburn has baccalaureate program accreditation with AACSB, ABET, ACEJMC, ACPE, ADA, AHEA, ASLA, CSAB, CSWE, FIDER, NAAB, NASAD, NASM, NCATE, NLN, and SAF. The 3 libraries contain 3.1 million volumes, 2.7 million microform items, and 235,671 audio/video tapes/CDs/DVDs, and subscribe to 39,318 periodicals including electronic. Computerized library services include interlibrary loans, database searching, Internet access, and laptop Internet portals. Special learning facilities include a learning resource center, art gallery, radio station, TV station, nuclear science center, arboretum, electron microscope laboratory, and museum of fine arts. The 1875-acre campus is in a small town 110 miles southwest of Atlanta, Georgia. Including any residence halls, there are 307 buildings.

Programs of Study: Auburn confers B.A., B.S., B.A.E., B.Arch., B.B.E., B.C.E., B.Che.E., B.E.E., B.F.A., B.Int.Arch., B.Int Design, B.I.S.E., B.M.E., B.Mus.ED., B.Mtl.E., B.P.F.E., B.Sw.E., B.W.E.degrees. Master's and doctoral degrees are also awarded. Bachelor's degrees are awarded in AGRICULTURE (agricultural business management, agriculture, animal science, fishing and fisheries, forest engineering, forestry production and processing, horticulture, poultry science, and soil science), BIOLOGICAL SCIENCE (biochemistry, biology/ biological science, botany, marine biology, microbiology, molecular biology, nutrition, wildlife biology, and zoology), BUSINESS (accounting, banking and finance, business administration and management, business economics, fashion merchandising, hotel/motel and restaurant management, international business management, marketing/retailing/merchandising, personnel management, and transportation management), COMMUNICATIONS AND THE ARTS (communications, design, dramatic arts, English, French, German, industrial design, journalism, languages, public relations, Spanish, and speech/debate/rhetoric), COMPUTER AND PHYSICAL SCIENCE (applied mathematics, chemistry, computer science, geology, mathematics, and physics), EDUCATION (business education, early childhood education, elementary education, English education, foreign languages education, health education, home economics education, industrial arts education, mathematics education, middle school education, physical education, science education, secondary education, social science education, special education, and vocational education), ENGINEERING AND ENVIRONMENTAL DESIGN (aeronautical engineering, agricultural engineering, architecture, aviation administration/management, chemical engineering, civil engineering, computer engineering, construction management, electrical/electronics engineering, environmental science, interior design, landscape architecture/design, mechanical engineering, and textile engineering), HEALTH PROFESSIONS (health care administration, medical laboratory technology, nursing, predentistry, premedicine, preoptometry, preveterinary science, and speech pathology/audiology), SOCIAL SCIENCE (anthropology, criminology, economics, food science, geography, history, home furnishings and equipment management/production/services, human development, philosophy, physical fitness/movement, political science/ government, psychology, public administration, social work, sociology, and textiles and clothing). Engineering, business, education, and architecture are the strongest academically. Liberal arts, business, and engineering are the largest.

Special: Opportunities are available for co-op programs, internships, work-study, and dual majors on a program-by-program basis; students should contact their advisers for specific information. 3-2 engineering degrees are offered with numerous other liberal arts colleges or with Auburn's colleges of Agriculture, Liberal Arts, or Sciences and Mathematics. Other options available to students include study abroad in more than 47 countries, credit by exam, non degree study, and pass/fail grading on select courses. There are 46 national honor societies, including Phi Beta Kappa, a freshman honors program, and 26 departmental honors programs.

Admissions: 80% of the 2009-2010 applicants were accepted. The SAT scores for the 2009-2010 freshman class were: Critical Reading--13% below 500, 47% between 500 and 599, 32% between 600 and 700, and 8% above 700; Math--7% below 500, 40% between 500 and 599, 43% between 600 and 700, and 10% above 700; Writing--17% below 500, 47% between 500 and 599, 31% between 600 and 700, and 5% above 700. The ACT scores were 5% below 21, 21% between 21 and 23, 30% between 24 and 26, 15% between 27 and 28, and 29%

above 28. 59% of the current freshmen were in the top fifth of their class; 84% were in the top two fifths. There were 65 National Merit finalists.

Requirements: The SAT or ACT is required. Favorable consideration for admission will be given to accredited secondary school graduates whose college ability test scores and high school grades give promise of the greatest level of success in college courses. Secondary school students planning to apply for admission are required to complete 4 years of English, 3 years each of social studies and math, and 2 years of science. Applicants of a mature age who are not high school graduates may be considered for admission if their educational attainments are shown through testing to be equivalent to those of high school graduates. Tests include the USAFI General Education Development Test, the American College Test, or other tests recommended by the Admissions Committee. AP credits are accepted.

Procedure: Freshmen are admitted to all sessions. There are deferred admissions and rolling admissions plans. Application deadlines are open. Application fee is $40. Notification is sent on a rolling basis. Applications are accepted on-line.

Financial Aid: In 2009-2010, 69% of all full-time freshmen and 60% of continuing full-time students received some form of financial aid. 27% of all full-time freshmen and 30% of continuing full-time students received need-based aid. The average freshman award was $9,182. Need-based scholarships or need-based grants averaged $5,555; need-based self-help aid (loans and jobs) averaged $4,153); non-need based athletic scholarships averaged $17,730; and other non-need based awards and non-need based scholarships averaged $4,427. 15% of undergraduate students work part-time. Average annual earnings from campus work are $4500. The average financial indebtedness of the 2009 graduate was $31,152. Auburn is a member of CSS. The FAFSA is required. The deadline for filing freshman financial aid applications for fall entry is March 1.

Computers: Wireless access is available. All students may access the system 24 hours a day. There are no time limits and no fees.

AUGUSTANA COLLEGE
Rock Island, IL 61201-2296

(309) 794-7341
(800) 798-8100; (309) 794-7422

Full-time: 1056 men, 1390 women	**Faculty:** 174; IIB, -$
Part-time: 16 men, 13 women	**Ph.Ds:** 96%
Graduate: none	**Student/Faculty:** 14 to 1
Year: quarters, summer session	**Tuition:** $31,326
Application Deadline: open	**Room & Board:** $7950
Freshman Class: 3636 applied, 2647 accepted, 616 enrolled	
ACT: 26	**SAT:** recommended

HIGHLY COMPETITIVE

Augustana College, founded in 1860, is a private liberal arts institution affiliated with the Evangelical Lutheran Church in America. In addition to regional accreditation, Augustana has baccalaureate program accreditation with NASM and NCATE. The 3 libraries contain 209,688 volumes, 78,666 microform items, and 2748 audio/video tapes/CDs/DVDs, and subscribe to 3067 periodicals including electronic. Computerized library services include interlibrary loans, database searching, Internet access, and laptop Internet portals. Special learning facilities include a learning resource center, art gallery, natural history museum, radio station, preschool, center for communicative disorders, geology museum, planetarium/observatory, U.S. Geological Survey map repository, Swedish immigration research center, 3 outdoor environmental labs, and educational technology building. The 115-acre campus is in a suburban area 165 miles west of Chicago. Including any residence halls, there are 47 buildings.

Programs of Study: Augustana confers B.A. degrees. Bachelor's degrees are awarded in BIOLOGICAL SCIENCE (biochemistry and biology/biological science), BUSINESS (accounting, business administration and management, and international business management), COMMUNICATIONS AND THE ARTS (art, art history and appreciation, classics, communications, dramatic arts, English, French, German, music, music performance, Scandinavian languages, Spanish, speech/debate/rhetoric, and studio art), COMPUTER AND PHYSICAL SCIENCE (chemistry, computer science, earth science, geology, mathematics, and physics), EDUCATION (art education, elementary education, music education, physical education, and secondary education), ENGINEERING AND ENVIRONMENTAL DESIGN (engineering physics, landscape architecture/design, and preengineering), HEALTH PROFESSIONS (occupational therapy, premedicine, and speech pathology/audiology), SOCIAL SCIENCE (anthropology, Asian/Oriental studies, economics, geography, history, philosophy, political science/government, psychology, public administration, religion, social work, sociology, and women's studies). Premedicine, business/accounting, and biology are the largest.

Special: Cooperative degree programs are offered in engineering, environmental management, forestry, landscape architecture, and occupational therapy with Duke, Iowa State, Northwestern, Purdue, and Washington (St. Louis) Universities and the University of Illinois (Urbana-Champaign). Domestic and international internships are offered. Study abroad is possible in 17 countries, including China, Peru, Sweden, Germany, and France, as is fall term study in East Asia, Europe, and Latin America. Interdisciplinary majors are offered in earth science, teaching, Asian studies, and public administration. A B.A.-B.S. degree in occupational therapy is offered, as well as 3-2 engineering programs with the University of Illinois and Purdue, Washington (St. Louis), and Iowa State Universities. Work-study programs, double majors, phys ed credits, and pass/fail options are available. There are 13 national honor societies, including Phi Beta Kappa, a freshman honors program, and 12 departmental honors programs.

Admissions: 73% of the 2009-2010 applicants were accepted. The ACT scores were 8% below 21, 23% between 21 and 23, 28% between 24 and 26, 18% between 27 and 28, and 23% above 28. 58% of the current freshmen were in the top fifth of their class; 83% were in the top two fifths.

Requirements: The SAT or ACT is recommended. In addition, applicants should be graduates of an accredited secondary school with 16 academic credits, including 4 in English, 3 in math, 2 each in science and social studies, 1 in foreign language, and other science and math courses for appropriate majors. An audition for music majors and an interview are recommended. The GED is accepted. Students who choose not to submit ACT or SAT scores must interview and submit a photocopy of a graded high school paper. AP credits are accepted. Important factors in the admissions decision are advanced placement or honors courses, evidence of special talent, and recommendations by school officials.

Procedure: Freshmen are admitted fall, winter, and spring. Entrance exams should be taken by fall of the senior year. There are early admissions, deferred admissions, and rolling admissions plans. Application deadlines are open. The fall 2009 application fee was $35. Notification is sent on a rolling basis. Applications are accepted on-line. A waiting list is maintained.

Financial Aid: In 2009-2010, 96% of all full-time students received some form of financial aid. 68% of all full-time freshmen and 66% of continuing full-time students received need-based aid. The average freshman award was $24,505.

80% of undergraduate students work part-time. Average annual earnings from campus work are $900. The average financial indebtedness of the 2009 graduate was $16,716. Augustana is a member of CSS. The FAFSA and the college's own financial statement are required. The deadline for filing freshman financial aid applications for fall entry is April 5.

Computers: An extensive campus network provides intranet services, including e-mail accounts and Internet access. Residence hall rooms have jacks for each resident. Wireless access is provided in selected buildings, including the library. An educational technology building provides computer classrooms and labs, including specialized equipment for multimedia applications. Computers for student access to the network are widespread on campus. All students may access the system. There are no time limits and no fees. It is strongly recommended that all students have a personal computer.

AUGUSTANA COLLEGE
Sioux Falls, SD 57197

(605) 274-5516
(800) 727-2844; (605) 274-5518

Full-time: 608 men, 1058 women	**Faculty:** 118; IIB, --$
Part-time: 48 men, 57 women	**Ph.D.s:** 77%
Graduate: 12 men, 10 women	**Student/Faculty:** 13 to 1
Year: 4-1-4, summer session	**Tuition:** n/av
Application Deadline: n/av	**Room & Board:** $6,190
Freshman Class: 1284 applied, 1037 accepted, 431 enrolled	
SAT: required	**ACT:** 25 **VERY COMPETITIVE**

Augustana College, founded in 1860, is a private, liberal arts institution affiliated with the Evangelical Lutheran Church in America. There are no undergraduate schools. In addition to regional accreditation, Augie has baccalaureate program accreditation with CSWE, NASM, and NCATE. The library contains 200,000 volumes, 35,117 microform items, 4,491 audio/video tapes/CDs/DVDs, and subscribes to 5,000 periodicals including electronic. Computerized library services include interlibrary loans, database searching, Internet access, and laptop Internet portals. Special learning facilities include an art gallery, natural history museum, radio station, and a Center for Western Studies. The 100-acre campus is in an urban area Sioux Falls, South Dakota. Including any residence halls, there are 27 buildings.

Programs of Study: Augie confers B.A. degrees. Master's degrees are also awarded. Bachelor's degrees are awarded in BIOLOGICAL SCIENCE (biology/biological science), BUSINESS (accounting, business administration and management, entrepreneurial studies, management information systems, management science, marketing and distribution, and sports management), COMMUNICATIONS AND THE ARTS (American Sign Language, art, communications, dramatic arts, English, French, German, journalism, modern language, music, and Spanish), COMPUTER AND PHYSICAL SCIENCE (chemistry, computer science, mathematics, and physics), EDUCATION (athletic training, drama education, education of the deaf and hearing impaired, elementary education, music education, physical education, social studies education, and special education), ENGINEERING AND ENVIRONMENTAL DESIGN (engineering management and engineering physics), HEALTH PROFESSIONS (exercise science, nursing, and speech pathology/audiology), SOCIAL SCIENCE (anthropology, economics, history, international studies, philosophy, physical fitness/movement, political science/government, psychology, religion, social work, and sociology). Biology, nursing, and education are the largest.

Special: Cross-registration with Upper Midwest Association for Intercultural Education and Higher Education Consortium for Urban Affairs is available. Internships (both national and local), study abroad in 40 countries, and a 3-2 engineering degree with Columbia University, Washington University in St. Louis, or University of Minnesota are offered. A Washington semester with Lutheran College Washington Consortium or American University is offered. Credit for life experience is possible. There are 12 national honor societies, a freshman honors program, and 3 departmental honors programs.

Admissions: 81% of the 2009-2010 applicants were accepted. The ACT scores were 13% below 21, 23% between 21 and 23, 28% between 24 and 26, 18% between 27 and 28, and 18% above 28. 52% of the current freshmen were in the top fifth of their class; 80% were in the top two fifths. 32 freshmen graduated first in their class.

Requirements: The SAT or ACT is required. In addition, applications must have graduated from an accredited secondary school; however, a GED will be accepted. Applicants should have completed 4 years of high school English, 3 each of math and science, and 2 each of a foreign language and history. An essay, a transcript, and a recommendation are required. An interview is recommended. Augie requires applicants to be in the upper 50% of their class. A GPA of 2.8 is required. AP and CLEP credits are accepted. Important factors in the admissions decision are leadership record, extracurricular activities record, and advanced placement or honors courses.

Procedure: Freshmen are admitted to all sessions. Entrance exams should be taken in the spring of the junior year or early fall of the senior. There are deferred admissions and rolling admissions plans. Application deadlines are open. Notification is sent on a rolling basis. Applications are accepted on-line.

Financial Aid: In 2009-2010, 99% of all full-time freshmen and 99% of continuing full-time students received some form of financial aid. 74% of all full-time freshmen and 70% of continuing full-time students received need-based aid. The average freshmen award was $22,350, with $16,594 ($19,000 maximum) from need-based scholarships or need-based grants; $5,725 ($10,300 maximum) from need-based self-help aid (loans and jobs); and $8,200 ($22,000 maximum) from non-need-based athletic scholarships. 32% of undergraduate students work part-time. Average annual earnings from campus work are $1800. The average financial indebtedness of the 2009 graduate was $21,944. The FAFSA is required. The priority date for freshman financial aid applications for fall entry is March 1.

Computers: Wireless access is available. Each residence hall and academic building has a computer lab(s) for student use. All residence hall rooms are wired with Internet access and access to the Augustana system. Students are also able to check out laptops for wireless use in the library. All academic buildings and Morrison Commons have wireless Internet. All students may access the system.

AUSTIN COLLEGE

Sherman, TX 75090-4400

(903) 813-3000
(800) 442-5363; (903) 813-3198

Full-time: 606 men, 719 women	**Faculty:** 90; IIB, av$
Part-time: 4 men, 6 women	**Ph.D.s:** 96%
Graduate: 8 men, 21 women	**Student/Faculty:** 15 to 1
Year: 4-1-4, summer session	**Tuition:** $27,850
Application Deadline: March 1	**Room & Board:** $9090
Freshman Class: 1678 applied, 1190 accepted, 334 enrolled	
SAT CR/M/W: 620/610/600	**ACT:** 25 **HIGHLY COMPETITIVE**

Austin College, founded in 1849, is a private liberal arts institution affiliated with the Presbyterian Church (U.S.A.) and offering programs in business, liberal arts, and health fields. There is 1 graduate school. The library contains 230,222 volumes, 120,702 microform items, and 6,368 audio/video tapes/CDs/DVDs, and subscribes to 10,352 periodicals including electronic. Computerized library services include interlibrary loans, database searching, Internet access, and laptop Internet portals. Special learning facilities include a learning resource center, a social science lab, television studios for media instruction, environmental research areas near Lake Texoma, and a facility for advanced computing and 3-D graphics. The 70-acre campus is in a suburban area 60 miles north of Dallas. Including any residence halls, there are 34 buildings.

Programs of Study: AC confers B.A. degrees. Master's degrees are also awarded. Bachelor's degrees are awarded in BIOLOGICAL SCIENCE (biochemistry and biology/biological science), BUSINESS (business administration and management and international economics), COMMUNICATIONS AND THE ARTS (art, classics, communications, English, French, German, Latin, music, and Spanish), COMPUTER AND PHYSICAL SCIENCE (chemistry, computer science, mathematics, and physics), SOCIAL SCIENCE (American studies, economics, history, interdisciplinary studies, international studies, Latin American studies, philosophy, political science/government, psychology, religion, and sociology). Biology, psychology, and political science are the strongest academically. Business administration and psychology are the largest.

Special: AC offers study abroad in 58 countries, internships during the January and summer terms, and fall, spring, and summer internships in Washington, D.C. Work-study, accelerated degree programs in all majors, and dual and student-designed majors are available. There is a 3-2 engineering degree program in conjunction with the University of Texas at Dallas and Washington University in St. Louis, as well as cooperative agreements with Columbia University and Texas A&M University. There are 14 national honor societies, including Phi Beta Kappa.

Admissions: 71% of the 2009-2010 applicants were accepted. The SAT scores for the 2009-2010 freshman class were: Critical Reading--7% below 500, 32% between 500 and 599, 48% between 600 and 700, and 13% above 700; Math--8% below 500, 37% between 500 and 599, 46% between 600 and 700, and 9% above 700; Writing--13% below 500, 36% between 500 and 599, 40% between 600 and 700, and 11% above 700. The ACT scores were 13% below 21, 20% between 21 and 23, 35% between 24 and 26, 12% between 27 and 28, and 20% above 28. 62% of the current freshmen were in the top fifth of their class; 90% were in the top two fifths. There were 8 National Merit finalists.

Requirements: The SAT or ACT is required. The ACT Optional Writing test is also required. In addition, applicants must be graduates of an accredited secondary school, home school, or have a GED. The minimum recommended academic requirements are 4 credits in English, 3 each in math and science, 2 each in social studies and foreign language, and 1 in art/music/theater. An essay and recommendation are required. AP and CLEP credits are accepted. Important factors in the admissions decision are advanced placement or honors courses, leadership record, and extracurricular activities record.

Procedure: Freshmen are admitted fall and summer. Entrance exams should be taken in the junior year or the fall of the senior year. There are deferred admissions and rolling admissions plans. Applications should be filed by March 1 for fall entry, along with a $35 fee. Notifications are sent April 1. Applications are accepted on-line. 22 applicants were on a recent waiting list, 7 were accepted.

Financial Aid: In 2009-2010, 98% of all full-time freshmen and 96% of continuing full-time students received some form of financial aid. 68% of all full-time freshmen and 61% of continuing full-time students received need-based aid. Need-based scholarships or need-based grants averaged $21,036; need-based self-help aid (loans and jobs) averaged $5,530; and other non-need based awards and non-need based scholarships averaged $16,020. 35% of undergraduate students work part-time. Average annual earnings from campus work are $1164. AC is a member of CSS. The FAFSA is required. The priority date for freshman financial aid applications for fall entry is March 1. The deadline for filing freshman financial aid applications for fall entry is April 1.

Computers: Wireless access is available. Wireless access is available to all students in all student buildings on campus and most academic buildings. All students may access the system 24 hours a day in some locations. There are no time limits and no fees.

BABSON COLLEGE
Babson Park, MA 02457

(781) 239-5522
(800) 488-3696; (781) 239-4135

Full-time: 1070 men, 730 women	**Faculty:** n/av
Part-time: none	**Ph.D.s:** 72%
Graduate: 1200 men, 440 women	**Student/Faculty:** n/av
Year: semesters, summer session	**Tuition:** $39,040
Application Deadline: see profile	**Room & Board:** $12,900
Freshman Class: n/av	
SAT or ACT: required	**HIGHLY COMPETITIVE**

Babson College, founded in 1919, is a private business school. All students start their own businesses during their freshman year with money loaned by the college. Figures in the above capsule and this capsule are approximate. There is 1 graduate school. In addition to regional accreditation, Babson has baccalaureate program accreditation with AACSB. The library contains 132,024 volumes, 346,941 microform items, and 4645 audio/video tapes/CDs/DVDs, and subscribes to 511 periodicals including electronic. Computerized library services include interlibrary loans, database searching, and Internet access. Special learning facilities include a learning resource center, art gallery, radio station, performing arts theater, and centers for entrepreneurial studies, management, language and culture, writing, math, visual arts, executive education, and women's leadership. The 370-acre campus is in a suburban area 14 miles west of Boston. Including any residence halls, there are 53 buildings.

Programs of Study: Babson confers B.S.M. degrees. Master's degrees are also awarded. Bachelor's degrees are awarded in BUSINESS (business administration and management).

Special: There is cross-registration with Brandeis University, Wellesley College, and F.W. Olin College of Engineering. Internships and study abroad in 27 countries are available. There is a freshman honors program and 10 departmental honors programs.

Requirements: The SAT or ACT is required. In addition, applicants must be graduates of an accredited secondary school or have a GED. 16 academic courses are required, including 4 credits of English, 3 of math, 2 of social studies, and 1 of science. A fourth year of math is strongly recommended. Essays are required. SAT Subject tests in math are recommended. AP credits are accepted. Important factors in the admissions decision are advanced placement or honors courses, evidence of special talent, and leadership record.

Procedure: Freshmen are admitted fall. Entrance exams should be taken prior to application (SAT or ACT). There are early decision, early admissions and deferred admissions plans. Check with the school for current application deadlines. The fall 2009 application fee was $60. Applications are accepted on-line. A waiting list is maintained.

Financial Aid: In a recent year, 4% of all full-time freshmen and 41% of continuing full-time students received some form of financial aid. 45% of all full-time freshmen and 41% of continuing full-time students received need-based aid. The average freshman award was $26,171. 32% of undergraduate students work part-time. Average annual earnings from campus work was $1580. The average financial indebtedness of a recent graduate was $24,900. The CSS/Profile, the FAFSA, and tax returns are required. Check with the school for current application deadlines.

Computers: Wireless access is available. All students may access the system. There are no time limits and no fees. It is strongly recommended that all students have a personal computer. An IBM ThinkPad is recommended.

BALDWIN-WALLACE COLLEGE

Berea, OH 44017-2088	(440) 826-2222; (440) 826-3830
Full-time: 1396 men, 1770 women	**Faculty:** 161; IIB, av$
Part-time: 125 men, 270 women	**Ph.D.s:** 81%
Graduate: 271 men, 417 women	**Student/Faculty:** 22 to 1
Year: semesters, summer session	**Tuition:** $24,230
Application Deadline: May 1	**Room & Board:** $7960
Freshman Class: 2676 applied, 2335 accepted, 755 enrolled	
SAT CR/M: 540/560	**ACT:** 24 **VERY COMPETITIVE**

Baldwin-Wallace College, established in 1845, is a private liberal arts institution that blends the hallmarks of the liberal arts with an emphasis on profession and career preparation through undergraduate and graduate degree programs. There is one undergraduate school and 2 graduate schools. In addition to regional accreditation, B-W has baccalaureate program accreditation with NASM and NCATE. The 3 libraries contain 200,000 volumes, 103,000 microform items, and 0 audio/video tapes/CDs/DVDs, and subscribe to 45,000 periodicals including electronic. Computerized library services include interlibrary loans, database searching, and Internet access. Special learning facilities include a learning resource center, art gallery, radio station, a neuroscience lab, and an observatory. . The 100-acre campus is in a suburban area 14 miles southwest of Cleveland, OH. Including any residence halls, there are 78 buildings.

Programs of Study: B-W confers B.A., B.S., B.M., B.M.E., and B.S.Ed. degrees. Master's degrees are also awarded. Bachelor's degrees are awarded in BIOLOGICAL SCIENCE (biology/biological science and neurosciences), BUSINESS (accounting, banking and finance, business administration and management, human resources, international business management, management science, marketing management, organizational leadership and management, and sports management), COMMUNICATIONS AND THE ARTS (art history and appreciation, broadcasting, communications, creative writing, English, film arts, French, German, music, music history and appreciation, music performance, music theory and composition, musical theater, public relations, Spanish, studio art, theater design, and voice), COMPUTER AND PHYSICAL SCIENCE (chemistry, computer science, mathematics, physics, systems analysis, and web technology), EDUCATION (art education, athletic training, early childhood education, health education, middle school education, music education, physical education, science education, and specific learning disabilities), ENGINEERING AND ENVIRONMENTAL DESIGN (preengineering), HEALTH PROFESSIONS (exercise science, health care administration, music therapy, physical therapy, predentistry, premedicine, prephysical therapy, and preveterinary science), SOCIAL SCIENCE (criminal justice, economics, history, interdisciplinary studies, international studies, philosophy, political science/government, prelaw, psychology, religion, and sociology). Business, education, and music are the strongest academically and the largest.

Special: Special academic programs include internships that can qualify for credit, work-study programs, student teaching in England, and study abroad. There is cross-registration with 9 participating institutions within the Greater Cleveland area, as well as a 3-2 program in social work with Case Western Reserve University, 3-2 master's program in accounting, human resources, and computer science/information systems, and a 3-2 program in engineering with Case Western Reserve and Columbia University. B-W also offers the Consortium for Music Therapy, accelerated degree programs, a general studies degree, a B.A.-B.S. degree, dual and student-designed majors, credit for life, military, and work experience, and pass/fail options. The Continuing Education Program offers degrees through evening and weekend colleges. Concentrations in business include accounting, banking and finance, human resources, international, and marketing. There are 5 national honor societies and a freshman honors program.

Admissions: 87% of the 2009-2010 applicants were accepted. The SAT scores for the 2009-2010 freshman class were: Critical Reading--29% below 500, 41% between 500 and 599, 27% between 600 and 700, and 4% above 700; Math--29% below 500, 40% between 500 and 599, 25% between 600 and 700, and 7% above 700. The ACT scores were 28% below 21, 25% between 21 and 23, 22% between 24 and 26, 18% between 27 and 28, and 8% above 28. 54% of the current freshmen were in the top fifth of their class; 81% were in the top two fifths. There were 3 National Merit finalists. 19 freshmen graduated first in their class.

Requirements: In addition, applicants must be graduates of an accredited secondary school or have earned a GED. Applicants must have completed 16 academic credits, including 4 in English, 3 each in math, natural science, and social science, and 2 in a foreign language; however, alternative distributions are considered. A teacher's recommendation is required. B-W does not require students to submit test scores for admission consideration. B-W requires applicants to be in the upper 50% of their class. A GPA of 2.8 is required. AP and CLEP credits are accepted. Important factors in the admissions decision are leadership record, advanced placement or honors courses, and extracurricular activities record.

Procedure: Freshmen are admitted to all sessions. Entrance exams should be taken during the junior year or early in the senior year. There are deferred admissions and rolling admissions plans. Applications should be filed by May 1 for fall entry; March 15 for spring entry; and June 15 for summer entry, along with a $25 fee. Applications are accepted on-line.

Financial Aid: In 2009-2010, 99% of all full-time freshmen and 99% of continuing full-time students received some form of financial aid. 82% of all full-time freshmen and 82% of continuing full-time students received need-based aid. The average freshman award was $21,833. Need-based scholarships or need-based grants averaged $14,273 ($24,230 maximum); need-based self-help aid (loans and jobs) averaged $7,993 ($9,150 maximum); and other non-need-based awards and non-need-based scholarships averaged $7,210 ($15,600 maximum). 60% of undergraduate students work part-time. Average annual earnings from campus work are $1088. The average financial indebtedness of the 2009 graduate was $19,586. The FAFSA is required. The priority date for freshman financial aid applications for fall entry is April 1. The deadline for filing freshman financial aid applications for fall entry is September 1.

Computers: Wireless access is available. There are 767 lab systems. All students may access the system. 24 hours a day. There are no time limits and no fees.

BARD COLLEGE

Annandale-on-Hudson, NY 12504-5000　　(845) 758-7472
　　　　　　　　　　　　　　　　　　　　　　　　　　　(845) 758-5208

Full-time: 799 men, 1067 women	**Faculty:** 145; IIB, +$
Part-time: 36 men, 37 women	**Ph.D.s:** 96%
Graduate: 114 men, 181 women	**Student/Faculty:** 13 to 1
Year: 4-1-4	**Tuition:** $39,880
Application Deadline: January 15	**Room & Board:** $11,300
Freshman Class: 5510 applied, 1826 accepted, 505 enrolled	

VERY COMPETITIVE+

Bard College, founded in 1860, is an independent liberal arts and sciences institution affiliated historically with the Association of Episcopal Colleges. Discussion-oriented seminars and independent study are encouraged, tutorials are on a one-to-one basis, and most classes are kept small. There are 2 undergraduate schools and 8 graduate schools. The library contains 351,163 volumes, 7,995 microform items, and 3,916 audio/video tapes/CDs/DVDs, and subscribes to 32,413 periodicals including electronic. Computerized library services include interlibrary loans, database searching, Internet access, and laptop Internet portals. Special learning facilities include a learning resource center, art gallery, radio station, an ecology field station, the Levy Economics Institute, the Institute for Writing and Thinking, the Institute for Advanced Theology, the Center for Curatorial Studies and Art in Contemporary Culture, and an archeological station. The 600-acre campus is in a rural area 100 miles north of New York City. Including any residence halls, there are 70 buildings.

Programs of Study: Bard confers B.A. and B.S. degrees. Associate, master's, and doctoral degrees are also awarded. Bachelor's degrees are awarded in BIOLOGICAL SCIENCE (biochemistry, biology/biological science, cell biology, ecology, microbiology, and molecular biology), COMMUNICATIONS AND THE ARTS (American literature, art history and appreciation, Chinese, classical languages, classics, creative writing, dance, dramatic arts, drawing, English, English literature, film arts, French, German, Germanic languages and literature, Italian, music history and appreciation, music performance, music theory and composition, painting, photography, Russian, sculpture, and Spanish), COMPUTER AND PHYSICAL SCIENCE (chemistry, mathematics, natural sciences, and physics), ENGINEERING AND ENVIRONMENTAL DESIGN (environmental science), HEALTH PROFESSIONS (predentistry and premedicine), SO-CIAL SCIENCE (African studies, American studies, anthropology, archeology, area studies, Asian/Oriental studies, British studies, Celtic studies, clinical psychology, developmental psychology, Eastern European studies, economics, European studies, French studies, history, history of philosophy, history of science, human development, interdisciplinary studies, Italian studies, Judaic studies, Latin American studies, medieval studies, philosophy, political science/government, prelaw, religion, Russian and Slavic studies, social psychology, social science, sociology, and Spanish studies). Social studies, visual and/performing arts, and languages and literature are the largest.

Special: Bard offers opportunities for study abroad, internships (no academic credit), Washington and New York semesters, dual majors, student-designed majors, accelerated degree programs, and pass/fail options. A 3-2 engineering degree is available with the Columbia University, Washington University (St. Louis), and Dartmouth College Schools of Engineering. Other 3-2 degrees are available in forestry and environmental studies, social work, architecture, city and regional planning, public health, and business administration. There are also opportunities for independent study, multicultural and ethnic studies, area studies, human rights, and globalization and international affairs.

Admissions: 33% of the 2009-2010 applicants were accepted.

Requirements: Bard places strong emphasis on the academic background and intellectual curiosity of applicants, as well as indications of the student's commitment to social and environmental concerns, independent research, volunteer work, and other important extracurricular activities. Students applying for admission are expected to have graduated from an accredited secondary school (the GED is accepted) and must submit written essays with the application. The high school record should include a full complement of college-preparatory courses. Honors and advanced placement courses are also considered. A GPA of 3.0 is required. AP credits are accepted. Important factors in the admissions decision are advanced placement or honors courses, recommendations by school officials, and extracurricular activities record.

Procedure: Freshmen are admitted fall. There are early admissions and deferred admissions plans. Applications should be filed by January 15 for fall entry and November 1 for spring entry, along with a $50 fee. Notifications are sent April 1. Applications are accepted on-line. 235 applicants were on a recent waiting list, 10 were accepted.

Financial Aid: In 2009-2010, 72% of all full-time freshmen and 66% of continuing full-time students received some form of financial aid. 66% of all full-time freshmen and 60% of continuing full-time students received need-based aid. The average freshman award was $31,959.$31,540. Need-based scholarships or need-based grants averaged $31,540 ($39,540) and need-based self-help aid (loans and jobs) averaged $4949 ($6,650 maximum). 38% of undergraduate students work part-time. Average annual earnings from campus work are $1200. The average financial indebtedness of the 2009 graduate was $26,131. Bard is a member of CSS. The CSS/Profile, FAFSA, the state aid form, and Non-custodial Profile and/or Business/Farm supplement if applicable are required. The priority date for freshman financial aid applications for fall entry is February 1. The deadline for filing freshman financial aid applications for fall entry is February 15.

Computers: Wireless access is available. All students may access the system. There are no time limits and no fees.

BATES COLLEGE

Lewiston, ME 04240　　　　　**(207) 786-6330; (207) 786-6484**

Full-time: 800 men, 860 women	**Faculty:** 179; IIB, ++$
Part-time: none	**Ph.D.s:** 100%
Graduate: none	**Student/Faculty:** n/av
Year: 4-1-4	**Tuition:** $51,300
Application Deadline: January 1	**Room & Board:** see profile
Freshman Class: n/av	
SAT or ACT: not required	**MOST COMPETITIVE**

Bates College, founded in 1855, is a small, private, liberal arts institution dedicated to the principle of active agreement, offering undergraduate programs in humanities, social sciences, and natural sciences. Students are charged a comprehensive fee of $51,300 annually, which includes tuition, room and board, and required fees. Some figures in the above capsule and in this profile are approximate. The library contains 620,000 volumes, 290,000 microform items, and 35,000 audio/video tapes/CDs/DVDs, and subscribes to 27,000 periodicals including electronic. Computerized library services include interlibrary loans, database searching, and Internet access. Special learning facilities include a learning resource center, art gallery, planetarium, radio station, TV station, a 654-acre mountain conservation area, an observatory, a language resource center, and the Edmund S. Muskie archives. The 109-acre campus is in a small town 35 miles north of Portland. Including any residence halls, there are 79 buildings.

Programs of Study: Bates confers B.A. and B.S. degrees. Bachelor's degrees are awarded in AGRICULTURE (environmental studies), BIOLOGICAL SCIENCE (biochemistry, biology/biological science, and neurosciences), COMMUNICATIONS AND THE ARTS (art, Chinese, dramatic arts, English, French, German, Japanese, music, Russian, Spanish, and speech/debate/rhetoric), COMPUTER AND PHYSICAL SCIENCE (chemistry, geology, mathematics, and physics), ENGINEERING AND ENVIRONMENTAL DESIGN (engineering), SOCIAL SCIENCE (African American studies, American studies, anthropology, classical/ ancient civilization, East Asian studies, economics, gender studies, history, interdisciplinary studies, medieval studies, philosophy, political science/government, psychology, religion, sociology, and women's studies). Psychology, political science, and economics are the largest.

Special: Co-op programs in engineering, internships, research apprenticeships, work-study programs, study abroad, and a Washington semester are possible. Dual, student-designed, and interdisciplinary majors, and a 3-2 engineering degree with Columbia University, Dartmouth College, Case Western Reserve University, Rensselaer Polytechnic Institute, and Washington University in St. Louis are available. Students in any major may graduate in 3 years, and a B.A.-B.S. is possible in all majors. Students may also participate in the Williams-Mystic Seaport program in marine biology and maritime history, and exchanges with Spelman College, Morehouse College, Washington and Lee University, and McGill University are possible. There are 2 national honor societies, including Phi Beta Kappa, and 100 departmental honors programs.

Admissions: 30% of a recent year's applicants were accepted. 81% of a recent year's freshmen were in the top fifth of their class; 98% were in the top two fifths.

Requirements: Candidates for admission should have completed at least 4 years of English, 3 each of math, social science, and a foreign language, and 2 of lab science. Essays are required, and an interview on or off campus is strongly recommended. The submission of test scores is optional. AP credits are accepted. Important factors in the admissions decision are advanced placement or honors courses, evidence of special talent, and leadership record.

Procedure: Freshmen are admitted fall and winter. There are early decision and deferred admissions plans. Early decision applications should be filed by November 15; regular applications, by January 1 for fall entry, along with a $60 fee. Notification of early decision is sent December 20; regular decision, March 31. 180 early decision candidates were accepted for a recent class. A waiting list is maintained. Applications are accepted on-line.

Financial Aid: In a recent year, 41% of all full-time freshmen and 43% of continuing full-time students received some form of financial aid, including need-based aid. The average freshman award was $27,686. 50% of undergraduate students work part-time. Average annual earnings from campus work are $1600. The average financial indebtedness of a recent year's graduate was $13,947. Bates is a member of CSS. The CSS/Profile, FAFSA, and parent and student tax returns and W-2 forms are required. Check with the school for current application deadlines.

Computers: Wireless access is available. There are 100 MB network connections in residence halls for each student, network access in every classroom and wireless in some, plus 400 open ports on campus. More than 400 college-owned computers are available for student use. All students may access the system. There are no time limits and no fees.

BAYLOR UNIVERSITY

Waco, TX 76798 (254) 710-3435; (800) BAYLOR-U

Full-time: 4926 men, 6979 women	**Faculty:** I, --$
Part-time: 115 men, 129 women	**Ph.D.s:** 80%
Graduate: 1308 men, 1157 women	**Student/Faculty:** n/av
Year: semesters, , summer session	**Tuition:** $27,910
Application Deadline: February 1	**Room & Board:** $7971
Freshman Class: n/av	
SAT or ACT required	**VERY COMPETITIVE+**

Baylor University, founded in 1845, is an independent institution affiliated with the Baptist Church and offering undergraduate programs in liberal arts and sciences, business, computer science, education, engineering, music, nursing, social work, and an honors college. There are 8 undergraduate schools and 10 graduate schools. In addition to regional accreditation, Baylor has baccalaureate program accreditation with AACSB, AALE, ABET, ACEJMC, ADA, AHEA, APTA, CSWE, FIDER, NASM, and NCATE. The 7 libraries contain 446,201 volumes, 2.1 million microform items, and 92,362 audio/video tapes/CDs/DVDs, and subscribe to 60,348 periodicals including electronic. Computerized library services include interlibrary loans, database searching, and Internet access. Special learning facilities include a learning resource center, art gallery, natural history museum, radio station, TV station, and a speech/hearing clinic. The 508-acre campus is in an urban area 100 miles south of Dallas/Fort Worth. Including any residence halls, there are 115 buildings.

Programs of Study: Baylor confers B.A., B.S., B.B.A., B.F.A., B.M., B.M.E., B.S.Av.Sc., B.S.C., B.S.C.S., B.S.E., B.S.E.C.E., B.S.Ed., B.S.F.C.S., B.S.I., B.S.M.E., B.S.N., and B.S.W. degrees. Master's and doctoral degrees are also awarded. Bachelor's degrees are awarded in AGRICULTURE (forestry and related sciences and soil science), BIOLOGICAL SCIENCE (biochemistry, bioinformatics, biology/biological science, life science, neurosciences, and nutrition),

BUSINESS (accounting, banking and finance, business administration and management, business economics, business statistics, business systems analysis, entrepreneurial studies, fashion merchandising, human resources, insurance, international business management, management information systems, marketing/retailing/merchandising, personnel management, real estate, and sports marketing), COMMUNICATIONS AND THE ARTS (applied music, art, art history and appreciation, broadcasting, choral music, classics, communications, creative writing, dramatic arts, English, French, German, Greek (classical), journalism, languages, Latin, literature, music, music history and appreciation, music performance, music theory and composition, performing arts, Russian, Spanish, speech/debate/rhetoric, studio art, telecommunications, and theater design), COMPUTER AND PHYSICAL SCIENCE (applied mathematics, chemistry, computer science, earth science, geology, geophysics and seismology, information sciences and systems, mathematics, and physics), EDUCATION (art education, athletic training, business education, computer education, drama education, elementary education, English education, foreign languages education, health education, home economics education, journalism education, mathematics education, museum studies, music education, physical education, reading education, recreation education, science education, secondary education, social science education, social studies education, and special education), ENGINEERING AND ENVIRONMENTAL DESIGN (airline piloting and navigation, architecture, computer engineering, electrical/electronics engineering, engineering, environmental science, interior design, and mechanical engineering), HEALTH PROFESSIONS (community health work, health science, medical laboratory technology, nursing, optometry, predentistry, premedicine, speech pathology/audiology, and speech therapy), SOCIAL SCIENCE (American studies, anthropology, archeology, Asian/Oriental studies, biblical languages, child care/child and family studies, dietetics, economics, family/consumer studies, fashion design and technology, forensic studies, geography, history, interdisciplinary studies, international public service, Latin American studies, philosophy, physical fitness/movement, political science/government, psychology, public administration, religion, religious education, religious music, Russian and Slavic studies, social work, sociology, and urban studies). Business, biology, and psychology are the largest.

Special: Baylor offers cooperative programs in architecture, business, dentistry, medicine, and optometry internships in each school, study abroad and student exchange in more than 30 countries, and pass/fail options. There are also honors and university scholars programs and faculty exchange with 4 schools in China and 1 each in Japan, Thailand, and Russia. There are 36 national honor societies, including Phi Beta Kappa, and a freshman honors program.

Admissions: 64% of the current freshmen were in the top fifth of their class; 89% were in the top two fifths. There were 68 National Merit finalists.

Requirements: The SAT or ACT is required. The ACT Optional Writing test is also required. In addition, applicants must be graduates of an accredited secondary school. An interview is recommended. Baylor requires applicants to be in the upper 50% of their class. AP and CLEP credits are accepted.

Procedure: Freshmen are admitted fall, spring, and summer. Entrance exams should be taken in spring of the junior year or fall of the senior year. There are early admissions and rolling admissions plans. Applications should be filed by February 1 for fall entry, along with a $50 fee. Applications are accepted on-line. There is no application fee for on-line applications. A waiting list is maintained.

Financial Aid: In 2009-2010, 95% of all full-time freshmen and 86% of continuing full-time students received some form of financial aid. 64% of all full-time freshmen and 51% of continuing full-time students received need-based aid. The

average freshman award was $20,838. Need-based scholarships or need-based grants averaged $16,907 ($38,272 maximum); need-based self-help aid (loans and jobs) averaged $5,369 ($9,300 maximum); non-need based athletic scholarships averaged $25,821 ($38,540 maximum); and other non-need based awards and non-need based scholarships averaged $8,735 ($33,170 maximum). 14% of undergraduate students work part-time. Average annual earnings from campus work are $1456. The FAFSA is required. The priority date for freshman financial aid applications for fall entry is February 15. The deadline for filing freshman financial aid applications for fall entry is May 1.

Computers: Wireless access is available. All students may access the system. Most systems are accessible 24 hours a day, 7 days per week. There are no time limits and no fees. It is strongly recommended that all students have a personal computer. Students enrolled in Baylor Interdisciplinary Core (BIC) and MBA programs must have a personal computer.

BELLARMINE UNIVERSITY
Louisville, KY 40205

(502) 452-8131
(800) 274-4723; (502) 452-8002

Full-time: 749 men, 1298 women	**Faculty:** 125; IIA, --$
Part-time: 92 men, 278 women	**Ph.D.s:** 80%
Graduate: 229 men, 444 women	**Student/Faculty:** 16 to 1
Year: semesters, summer session	**Tuition:** $28,900
Application Deadline: February 1	**Room & Board:** $8400
Freshman Class: 6021 applied, 3214 accepted, 602 enrolled	
SAT CR/M: 545/550	**ACT:** 25 **VERY COMPETITIVE**

Bellarmine University, founded in 1950, is an independent Catholic university offering undergraduate and graduate programs in the liberal arts and professional studies. There are 6 undergraduate schools and 6 graduate schools. In addition to regional accreditation, Bellarmine has baccalaureate program accreditation with AACSB and NCATE. The library contains 126,164 volumes, 333,829 microform items, and 5,337 audio/video tapes/CDs/DVDs, and subscribes to 514 periodicals including electronic. Computerized library services include interlibrary loans, database searching, Internet access, and laptop Internet portals. Special learning facilities include a learning resource center, art gallery, radio station, the Thomas Merton Center, and a collection of materials by and about Thomas Merton. The 135-acre campus is in a suburban area in Louisville. Including any residence halls, there are 32 buildings.

Programs of Study: Bellarmine confers B.A., B.S., B.H.S., and B.S.N. degrees. Master's and doctoral degrees are also awarded. Bachelor's degrees are awarded in BIOLOGICAL SCIENCE (biochemistry, biology/biological science, biophysics, and molecular biology), BUSINESS (accounting, banking and finance, and business administration and management), COMMUNICATIONS AND THE ARTS (arts administration/management, communications, English, fine arts, languages, music, music technology, Spanish, speech/debate/rhetoric, and studio art), COMPUTER AND PHYSICAL SCIENCE (actuarial science, chemistry, computer science, mathematics, and physics), EDUCATION (elementary education, middle school education, and special education), ENGINEERING AND ENVIRONMENTAL DESIGN (computer engineering, computer technology, and preengineering), HEALTH PROFESSIONS (clinical science, exercise science, medical technology, nursing, predentistry, premedicine, prephysical therapy, preveterinary science, and respiratory therapy), SOCIAL SCIENCE (criminal justice, economics, history, interdisciplinary studies, international studies, liberal arts/general studies, philosophy, political science/government, psychology, sociology, and theological studies). Preprofessional programs, nursing, and accounting are the strongest academically.

Special: Cross-registration may be arranged through Kentuckiana Metroversity, a consortium of colleges in Kentucky and southern Indiana. Bellarmine also offers study abroad in more than 50 countries, internships in most majors, a Washington semester, a liberal studies degree, dual majors, accelerated degree programs, credit for life experience, pass/fail options during the junior and senior years, and a marine biology program in the Bahamas. There is also an honors program and the Brown Leadership Program. There are 5 national honor societies and a freshman honors program.

Admissions: 53% of the 2009-2010 applicants were accepted. The SAT scores for the 2009-2010 freshman class were: Critical Reading--30% below 500, 44% between 500 and 599, 25% between 600 and 700, and 1% above 700; Math--22% below 500, 47% between 500 and 599, and 31% between 600 and 700. The ACT scores were 9% below 21, 28% between 21 and 23, 32% between 24 and 26, 14% between 27 and 28, and 17% above 28. 38% of the current freshmen were in the top fifth of their class; 75% were in the top two fifths.

Requirements: The SAT or ACT is required. In addition, high school courses should include 4 years of English, 3 years of math, and 2 years each of science and social studies. 2 years of foreign language is recommended. The GED is accepted. An essay may be requested. A GPA of 2.5 is required. AP and CLEP credits are accepted. Important factors in the admissions decision are recommendations by school officials, advanced placement or honors courses, and extracurricular activities record.

Procedure: Freshmen are admitted fall, spring, and summer. Entrance exams should be taken by December of the senior year. There is a deferred admissions plan. Applications should be filed by February 1 for fall entry, along with a $25 fee. Applications are accepted on-line.

Financial Aid: In 2009-2010, all full-time freshmen and 98% of continuing full-time students received some form of financial aid. 78% of all full-time freshmen and 69% of continuing full-time students received need-based aid. The average freshman award was $22,285. 90% of undergraduate students work part-time. Average annual earnings from campus work are $1722. The average financial indebtedness of the 2009 graduate was $19,055. The FAFSA is required. The priority date for freshman financial aid applications for fall entry is March 1. The deadline for filing freshman financial aid applications for fall entry is May 1.

Computers: Wireless access is available. All students may access the system. There are no time limits. There is a fee.

BELMONT UNIVERSITY

Nashville, TN 37212-3757 (615) 460-6785
(800) 56E-NROL; (615) 460-5434

Full-time: 1742 men, 2293 women	**Faculty:** 238; IIA, av$
Part-time: 130 men, 213 women	**Ph.D.s:** 80%
Graduate: 348 men, 698 women	**Student/Faculty:** 17 to 1
Year: semesters, summer session	**Tuition:** $22,360
Application Deadline: August 1	**Room & Board:** $8590
Freshman Class: 3220 applied, 2466 accepted, 991 enrolled	
SAT CR/M: 580/584	**ACT:** 25 **VERY COMPETITIVE**

Belmont University, founded in 1890, is a private, Christian liberal arts university. There are 7 undergraduate schools and 6 graduate schools. In addition to regional accreditation, Belmont has baccalaureate program accreditation with AACSB, CSWE, NASM, NCATE, and NLN. The library contains 220,637 volumes, 24,529 microform items, and 31,109 audio/video tapes/CDs/DVDs, and subscribes to 1,072 periodicals including electronic. Computerized library services include interlibrary loans, database searching, and Internet access. Special learning facilities include a learning resource center, art gallery, radio station, TV station, and 19th century antebellum mansion. The 69-acre campus is in an urban area in Nashville, TN. Including any residence halls, there are 37 buildings.

Programs of Study: Belmont confers B.A., B.S., B.B.A., B.F.A., B.M., and B.S.N. degrees. Master's and doctoral degrees are also awarded. Bachelor's degrees are awarded in BIOLOGICAL SCIENCE (biology/biological science and environmental biology), BUSINESS (accounting, business administration and management, hotel/motel and restaurant management, management science, and marketing/retailing/merchandising), COMMUNICATIONS AND THE ARTS (communications, and English, French, music, music business management, music performance, and public relations), COMPUTER AND PHYSICAL SCIENCE (chemistry, computer science, mathematics, and physics), EDUCATION (elementary education, physical education, and science education), HEALTH PROFESSIONS (nursing), SOCIAL SCIENCE (economics, history, liberal arts/general studies, philosophy, political science/government, psychology, religion, and social work). Music, business, and humanities are the strongest academically. Business, music, nursing, and music business management are the largest.

Special: Belmont offers study abroad, student-designed majors, and dual majors in math, physics, and chemistry. Dual degree programs are available with Auburn University and the University of Tennessee at Knoxville. Programs require 3 years of study at Belmont followed by 2 years at the other institution. There are 11 national honor societies, a freshman honors program, and 1 departmental honors program.

Admissions: 77% of the 2009-2010 applicants were accepted. The SAT scores for the 2009-2010 freshman class were: Critical Reading--9% below 500, 50% between 500 and 599, 36% between 600 and 700, and 6% above 700; Math--12% below 500, 47% between 500 and 599, 36% between 600 and 700, and 5% above 700. The ACT scores were 3% below 21, 24% between 21 and 23, 34% between 24 and 26, 19% between 27 and 28, and 20% above 28. 64% of the current freshmen were in the top fifth of their class; 86% were in the top two fifths. 42 freshmen graduated first in their class.

Requirements: The ACT is required, the SAT is recommended. The university expects a composite score of at least 21 on the ACT and a satisfactory score on the SAT. Applicants should be high school graduates or hold the GED. Secondary preparation should include 4 units of English, 3 of math, and 2 each of a foreign language, history, science, and social studies. Potential music majors must audition. Belmont requires applicants to be in the upper 50% of their class. A GPA of 3.0 is required. AP and CLEP credits are accepted. Important factors in the admissions decision are advanced placement or honors courses, recommendations by school officials, and evidence of special talent.

Procedure: Freshmen are admitted fall, spring, and summer. Entrance exams should be taken during the junior or senior year. There are early admissions and rolling admissions plans. Applications should be filed by August 1 for fall entry and December 1 for spring entry, along with a $50 fee. Notification is sent on a rolling basis. Applications are accepted on-line.

Financial Aid: In 2009-2010, 79% of all full-time freshmen and 70% of continuing full-time students received some form of financial aid. 36% of all full-time freshmen and 27% of continuing full-time students received need-based aid. The

average freshman award was $6,204. Need-based scholarships or need-based grants averaged $5,175; need-based self-help aid (loans and jobs) averaged $3,602; non-need based athletic scholarships averaged $17,204; and other non-need based awards and non-need based scholarships averaged $5,839. 17% of undergraduate students work part-time. Average annual earnings from campus work are $2500. The average financial indebtedness of the 2009 graduate was $18,851. The FAFSA is required. The deadline for filing freshman financial aid applications for fall entry is March 1.

Computers: Wireless access is available. There are 500 PCs in student labs and 98% wireless accessible. All students may access the system. There are no time limits and no fees.

BELOIT COLLEGE
Beloit, WI 53511-5595

(608) 363-2500
(800) 9-BELOIT; (608) 363-2075

Full-time: 567 men, 749 women	**Faculty:** 123; IIB, -$
Part-time: 2 men, 5 women	**Ph.D.s:** 94%
Graduate: none	**Student/Faculty:** 11 to 1
Year: semesters, summer session	**Tuition:** $33,418
Application Deadline: January 15	**Room & Board:** $6830
Freshman Class: 1962 applied, 1429 accepted, 332 enrolled	
SAT CR/M: 640/610	**ACT:** 27 **HIGHLY COMPETITIVE**

Beloit College, founded in 1846, is a private liberal arts institution. The library contains 631,140 volumes, 7198 microform items, and 8243 audio/video tapes/CDs/DVDs, and subscribes to 1148 periodicals including electronic. Computerized library services include interlibrary loans, database searching, and Internet access. Special learning facilities include a learning resource center, art gallery, natural history museum, planetarium, radio station, TV station, a comprehensive language lab, an observatory, and a theater complex. The 44-acre campus is in a small town 50 miles south of Madison. Including any residence halls, there are 70 buildings.

Programs of Study: Beloit confers B.A. and B.S. degrees. Bachelor's degrees are awarded in BIOLOGICAL SCIENCE (biochemistry, biology/biological science, cell biology, ecology, and environmental biology), BUSINESS (business administration and management), COMMUNICATIONS AND THE ARTS (art history and appreciation, classical languages, comparative literature, creative writing, dramatic arts, East Asian languages and literature, English, French, German, literature, modern language, music, Russian, Spanish, speech/debate/rhetoric, and studio art), COMPUTER AND PHYSICAL SCIENCE (applied physics, chemistry, computer science, environmental geology, geology, mathematics, and physics), EDUCATION (art education and education), ENGINEERING AND ENVIRONMENTAL DESIGN (environmental science), HEALTH PROFESSIONS (predentistry, premedicine, and preveterinary science), SOCIAL SCIENCE (anthropology, classical/ancient civilization, economics, history, interdisciplinary studies, international relations, philosophy, political science/government, prelaw, psychology, religion, sociology, and women's studies). Anthropology, creative writing, and sociology are the strongest academically. Anthropology, psychology, and international relations are the largest.

Special: Beloit offers cross-registration with the University of Wisconsin/Madison, internships, study abroad in more than 38 countries, and a Washington semester. Dual majors, student-designed and interdisciplinary majors, and nondegree study are available. Students may take a 2-2 nursing program and a 3-2 medical technology program with Rush University. A 3-2 engineering degree is offered with 9 institutions, and co-op programs are available in social services, forestry and environmental management, engineering, nursing, medical technology, and business administration. An intensive summer language program is offered in Russian, Arabic, Japanese, and Chinese. There are 6 national honor societies, including Phi Beta Kappa.

Admissions: 73% of the 2009-2010 applicants were accepted. The SAT scores for the 2009-2010 freshman class were: Critical Reading--12% below 500, 22% between 500 and 599, 37% between 600 and 700, and 28% above 700; Math--12% below 500, 30% between 500 and 599, 42% between 600 and 700, and 16% above 700. The ACT scores were 5% below 21, 15% between 21 and 23, 24% between 24 and 26, 17% between 27 and 28, and 40% above 28. 56% of the current freshmen were in the top fifth of their class; 82% were in the top two fifths. There were 2 National Merit finalists. 10 freshmen graduated first in their class.

Requirements: The SAT or ACT is required. Beloit does not use the SAT writing test for either admissions or placement decisions. Applicants must be graduates of an accredited secondary school or homeschool program, with 4 years of English, 3 each of math, science, and history/social sciences, and 2 of foreign language. The GED is accepted. An essay and a letter of recommendation are required, and an interview is strongly recommended. AP and CLEP credits are accepted. Important factors in the admissions decision are advanced placement or honors courses, recommendations by school officials, and leadership record.

Procedure: Freshmen are admitted fall and spring. Entrance exams should be taken before the end of the first semester of the senior year. There are early admissions, deferred admissions, and rolling admissions plans. Early decision applications should be filed by December 1; regular applications, by January 15 for fall entry, along with a $35 fee. Notification of early decision is sent January 15, regular decision, March 15. 52 applicants were on the 2009 waiting list; 9 were admitted. Applications are accepted on-line. 52 applicants were on a recent waiting list, 8 were accepted.

Financial Aid: In 2009-2010, 94% of all full-time freshmen and 90% of continuing full-time students received some form of financial aid. 65% of all full-time freshmen and 64% of continuing full-time students received need-based aid. The average freshman award was $28,126. Need-based scholarships or need-based grants averaged $23,727 (full-tuition maximum); need-based self-help aid (loans and jobs) averaged $2833 ($8500 maximum); and other non-need-based awards and non-need-based scholarships averaged $14,291 (full-tuition maximum). 79% of undergraduate students work part-time. Average annual earnings from campus work are $1636. The average financial indebtedness of the 2009 graduate was $17,909. Beloit is a member of CSS. The FAFSA and the college's own financial statement are required. The deadline for filing freshman financial aid applications for fall entry is March 1.

Computers: Wireless access is available. Most academic and cultural buildings on campus feature wireless access. The wired campus network is accessible from every campus building. Terminal access includes more than 300 computers (PC and Mac) in the library, specific academic department labs, and 24-hour labs in academic and residential buildings. Every residence hall room includes data ports. All students may access the system at any time. There are no time limits and no fees.

BENEDICTINE COLLEGE

Atchison, KS 66002

(913) 367-5340
(800) 467-5340; (913) 367-6102

Full-time: 696 men, 774 women	**Faculty:** 78
Part-time: 159 men, 187 women	**Ph.D.s:** 82%
Graduate: 34 men, 27 women	**Student/Faculty:** 19 to 1
Year: semesters, summer session	**Tuition:** $19,500
Application Deadline: open	**Room & Board:** $6455
Freshman Class: 1478 applied, 474 accepted, 428 enrolled	
ACT: 24	**VERY COMPETITIVE+**

Benedictine College, established in 1971 by a merger of St. Benedict's College and Mount Saint Scholastics College, is a liberal arts, Catholic, Benedictine institution. There are 2 graduate schools. In addition to regional accreditation, Benedictine has baccalaureate program accreditation with NASM and NCATE. The library contains 277,528 volumes, 36,346 microform items, and 1,032 audio/video tapes/CDs/DVDs, and subscribes to 449 periodicals including electronic. Computerized library services include interlibrary loans and database searching. Special learning facilities include a learning resource center. The 225-acre campus is in a small town 45 miles north of Kansas City. Including any residence halls, there are 18 buildings.

Programs of Study: Benedictine confers B.A., B.S., and B.Mus.Ed. degrees. Associate and master's degrees are also awarded. Bachelor's degrees are awarded in BIOLOGICAL SCIENCE (biochemistry and biology/biological science), BUSINESS (accounting and business administration and management), COMMUNICATIONS AND THE ARTS (art, dramatic arts, English, French, journalism, music, Spanish, and theater management), COMPUTER AND PHYSICAL SCIENCE (astronomy, chemistry, computer science, mathematics, natural sciences, and physics), EDUCATION (athletic training, elementary education, music education, physical education, secondary education, and special education), SOCIAL SCIENCE (economics, history, liberal arts/general studies, philosophy, political science/government, psychology, religion, social science, sociology, and youth ministry). Biology and education are the strongest academically. Business and theology are the largest.

Special: Benedictine offers cross-registration with the 14 other members of the Kansas City Regional Council for Higher Education and study abroad in several countries. The school also offers a 3-2 occupational therapy program with Washington University of St. Louis and a 3-2 engineering degree. Internships, work-study programs, dual majors, B.A.-B.S. degrees in chemistry and biology, an interdisciplinary music marketing major, student-designed majors, pass/fail options, and nondegree study are also available. There are 4 national honor societies and 4 departmental honors programs.

Admissions: 32% of the 2009-2010 applicants were accepted. The ACT scores were 31% below 21, 18% between 21 and 23, 17% between 24 and 26, 18% between 27 and 28, and 14% above 28.; 37% were in the top two fifths.

Requirements: The ACT is required. In addition, Applicants should graduate in the upper 50% of their class at an accredited secondary school. Students should have 16 academic units, including 4 in English, 3 to 4 in math, 2 to 4 in foreign language and science, 2 in social science, and 1 in history. An interview is recommended. Counselor recommendations are required. A GPA of 2.0 is required. AP and CLEP credits are accepted. Important factors in the admissions decision are

69

advanced placement or honors courses, recommendations by school officials, and recommendations by alumni.

Procedure: Freshmen are admitted to all sessions. Entrance exams should be taken before the July following graduation from high school. There are deferred admissions and rolling admissions plans. Application deadlines are open. Application fee is $25. Notification is sent on a rolling basis. Applications are accepted on-line.

Financial Aid: In a recent year, all full-time freshmen and 99% of continuing full-time students received some form of financial aid. 66% of all full-time freshmen and 61% of continuing full-time students received need-based aid. The average freshman award was $20,908. Need-based scholarships or need-based grants averaged $2,057 ($17,051 maximum; need-based self-help aid (loans and jobs) averaged $3,193 ($9,500 maximum); non-need based athletic scholarships averaged $4,010 ($24,770 maximum); and other non-need based awards and non-need based scholarships averaged $9,469 ($36,270 maximum). 41% of undergraduate students worked part-time. Average annual earnings from campus work were $900. The average financial indebtedness of the 2009 graduate was $22,954. Benedictine is a member of CSS. The FAFSA and the college's own financial statement are required. The deadline for filing freshman financial aid applications for fall entry is April 1.

Computers: All students may access the system 24 hours a day in residence halls, and 7:45 A.M. to 11 P.M. weekdays, with shorter hours on weekends. There are no time limits and no fees.

BENNINGTON COLLEGE
Bennington, VT 05201

(802) 440-4312
(800) 833-6845; (802) 440-4320

Full-time: 218 men, 442 women	**Faculty:** 62
Part-time: 2 men, 2 women	**Ph.D:** 73%
Graduate: 39 men, 105 women	**Student/Faculty:** 11 to 1
Year: see profile	**Tuition:** $39,760
Application Deadline: January 3	**Room & Board:** $11,100
Freshman Class: 1054 applied, 696 accepted, 197 enrolled	
SAT CR/M/W: 670/600/665	**ACT:** 29 **HIGHLY COMPETITIVE+**

Bennington College, founded in 1932, is a private liberal arts institution characterized by cross-disciplinary learning, a close working relationship between student and teacher, a self-directed academic planning process, and a connection to the world through it's winter internship term. There are 4 graduate schools. The 2 libraries contain 160,391 volumes, and 16,867 audio/video tapes/CDs/DVDs, and subscribe to 35,667 periodicals including electronic. Computerized library services include interlibrary loans, database searching, Internet access, and laptop Internet portals. Special learning facilities include a learning resource center, art gallery, radio station, a computer center and media labs; digital arts lab; art gallery; architecture, drawing, painting, printmaking, and sculpture studios; ceramics studio and kilns; photography darkrooms; film and video editing studio; several fully equipped professional theaters; dance studios and archives; scripts library; costume shop; electronic music and sound recording studios; music practice rooms and music library; fitness center; student center; observatory; greenhouse, and 470 acres of forest, ponds, wetlands, and fields for recreation and scientific study. The 470-acre campus is in a small town 160 miles north of New York City and 150 miles west of Boston. Including any residence halls, there are 65 buildings.

Programs of Study: Bennington confers B.A. degrees. Master's degrees are also awarded. Bachelor's degrees are awarded in AGRICULTURE (environmental studies), BIOLOGICAL SCIENCE (biology/biological science, botany, ecology, environmental biology, evolutionary biology, and zoology), COMMUNICATIONS AND THE ARTS (American literature, animation, art, ceramic art and design, Chinese, comparative literature, creative writing, dance, design, dramatic arts, drawing, English, English literature, film arts, fine arts, French, Germanic languages and literature, illustration, Italian, Japanese, jazz, journalism, languages, literature, multimedia, music, music performance, music theory and composition, painting, performing arts, photography, piano/organ, playwriting/screenwriting, printmaking, sculpture, Spanish, strings, studio art, theater design, video, visual and performing arts, and voice), COMPUTER AND PHYSICAL SCIENCE (astronomy, chemistry, computer science, digital arts/technology, mathematics, physical sciences, physics, and science), EDUCATION (drama education, early childhood education, education, elementary education, foreign languages education, middle school education, and secondary education), ENGINEERING AND ENVIRONMENTAL DESIGN (architecture and environmental science), HEALTH PROFESSIONS (premedicine), SOCIAL SCIENCE (American studies, anthropology, child psychology/development, European studies, history, humanities, humanities and social science, interdisciplinary studies, international relations, international studies, Judaic studies, Latin American studies, liberal arts/general studies, philosophy, political science/government, prelaw, psychology, social psychology, social science, sociology, and women's studies). Literature, languages, and visual and performing arts are the strongest academically. Literature, visual and performing arts, and interdisciplinary studies are the largest.

Special: 7-week work/internships (during January and February) are required each year in residence. Cross-registration with Southern Vermont and Williams Colleges, and Massachusetts College of Liberal Arts is possible. In addition, study abroad, dual, and student-designed majors are offered.Students receive narrative evaluations with the option of letter grades. A B.A./M.A.T. program is offered for teacher certification.

Admissions: 66% of the 2009-2010 applicants were accepted. The SAT scores for the 2009-2010 freshman class were: Critical Reading--1% below 500, 15% between 500 and 599, 46% between 600 and 700, and 38% above 700; Math--10% below 500, 37% between 500 and 599, 45% between 600 and 700, and 8% above 700; Writing--5% below 500, 13% between 500 and 599, 56% between 600 and 700, and 26% above 700. The ACT scores were 3% between 21 and 23, 23% between 24 and 26, 23% between 27 and 28, and 50% above 28. 52% of the current freshmen were in the top fifth of their class; 80% were in the top two fifths. 2 freshmen graduated first in their class.

Requirements: Bennington admits students who have demonstrated a passion for learning and academic excellence. The Common Application as well as the Bennington Supplement (an essay, a graded analytic paper and the option to submit supplementary materials) are required. Submission of standardized test scores is optional. A majority of applicants are interviewed in person or by phone.

Procedure: Freshmen are admitted fall and spring. Entrance exams should be taken during the spring of the junior year or the fall of the senior year. There are early decision, early admissions and deferred admissions plans. Early decision applications should be filed by November 15 and January 3; regular applications January 3 for fall entry and November 15 for spring entry, along with a $60 fee. Notification of early decision is sent December 15; regular decision, April 1. Applications are accepted on-line. 78 applicants were on a recent waiting list, 14 were accepted.

Financial Aid: In 2009-2010, 81% of all full-time freshmen and 80% of continuing full-time students received some form of financial aid. 71% of all full-time freshmen and 69% of continuing full-time students received need-based aid. The average freshman award was $32,427. Need based scholarships or need-based grants averaged $29,549; need-based self-help aid (loans and jobs) averaged $4,177; and other non-need based awards and non-need based scholarships averaged $10,166. The average financial indebtedness of the 2009 graduate was $22,402. Bennington is a member of CSS. The CSS/Profile, FAFSA, the college's own financial statement, and student and parent tax returns and W-2s are required. The priority date for freshman financial aid applications for fall entry is January 1. The deadline for filing freshman financial aid applications for fall entry is March 1.

Computers: Wireless access is available. Student housing on campus is fully networked and students may access the network with their own computers. There is also wireless networking available in all academic buildings. In addition, computer labs are available in the Computer Center, Isabelle Kaplan Center for Languages and Culture, Commons, Visual and Performing Arts Center, and Crossett Library, with full access to the Internet and Web. All students may access the system. There are no time limits and no fees. It is strongly recommended that all students have a personal computer.

BENTLEY UNIVERSITY
Bentley College

Waltham, MA 02452-4705

(781) 891-2244
(800) 523-2354; (781) 891-3414

Full-time: 2389 men, 1641 women	**Faculty:** 231; IIA, ++$
Part-time: 133 men, 72 women	**Ph.D.s:** 82%
Graduate: 772 men, 609 women	**Student/Faculty:** 17 to 1
Year: semesters, summer session	**Tuition:** $35,828
Application Deadline: January 15	**Room & Board:** $11,740
Freshman Class: 6675 applied, 2842 accepted, 949 enrolled	
SAT CR/M/W: 580/650/600	**ACT:** 26 **HIGHLY COMPETITIVE**

Bentley University, formerly Bentley College, is a private institution that offers advanced business education along with a strong foundation in the arts and sciences. There is 1 graduate school. In addition to regional accreditation, Bentley has baccalaureate program accreditation with AACSB. The library contains 170,300 volumes, 3,700 microform items, and 9,500 audio/video tapes/CDs/DVDs, and subscribes to 39,000 periodicals including electronic. Computerized library services include interlibrary loans, database searching, Internet access, and laptop Internet portals. Special learning facilities include a learning resource center, art gallery, radio station, TV station, Academic Technology Center, Accounting Center (ACELAB), Alliance for Ethics and Social Responsibility, Valente Center for Arts and Sciences, Center for Business Ethics (CBE), Center for International Students and Scholars (CISS), Center for Languages and International Collaboration (CLIC), Center for Marketing Technology (CMT), Cronin International Center, Cyberlaw Center, Design and Usability Center (DUC), Enterprise Risk Management Program, Hughey Center for Financial Services, Library, Service-Learning Center, Trading Room, and Women's Leadership Institute. The 163-acre campus is in a suburban area Waltham, Massachusetts. Including any residence halls, there are 38 buildings.

Programs of Study: Bentley confers B.A., B.S., B.S.MBA, B.A.MBA, B.S.MS, B.A.MS. degrees. Associate, master's, and doctoral degrees are also awarded. Bachelor's degrees are awarded in BUSINESS (accounting, banking and finance, management information systems, management science, and marketing and distribution), COMMUNICATIONS AND THE ARTS (design and media arts), COMPUTER AND PHYSICAL SCIENCE (information sciences and systems and mathematics), ENGINEERING AND ENVIRONMENTAL DESIGN (computer technology), SOCIAL SCIENCE (economics, history, international studies, liberal arts/general studies, and philosophy). Management, finance, and marketing are the strongest academically.

Special: There is cross-registration with Regis College and Brandeis University, and internships are available in business and public service. The college offers study abroad in 24 countries, work-study programs, accelerated degree programs, student-designed majors, credit by exam, and nondegree study. There is also liberal studies major through which business majors can broaden their exposure to the arts and sciences, and arts and science majors can minor in business or interdisciplinary topics. There are 2 national honor societies, a freshman honors program, and 11 departmental honors programs.

Admissions: 43% of the 2009-2010 applicants were accepted. The SAT scores for the 2009-2010 freshman class were: Critical Reading--8% below 500, 47% between 500 and 599, 39% between 600 and 700, and 6% above 700; Math--3% below 500, 18% between 500 and 599, 63% between 600 and 700, and 16% above 700; Writing--9% below 500, 41% between 500 and 599, 43% between 600 and 700, and 7% above 700. The ACT scores were 1% below 21, 13% between 21 and 23, 36% between 24 and 26, 28% between 27 and 28, and 22% above 28. 67% of the current freshmen were in the top fifth of their class; 93% were in the top two fifths. 7 freshmen graduated first in their class.

Requirements: The SAT or ACT is required. In addition, applicants must be graduates of an accredited high school or have a GED. Recommended high school preparation is 4 units each in English and math, geometry, and a senior-year math course; 3 units science; 3 units in a foreign language; 3 units in history; and 2 additional units in English, math, social science or lab science, foreign language, or speech. AP and CLEP credits are accepted. Important factors in the admissions decision are recommendations by school officials, extracurricular activities record, and leadership record.

Procedure: Freshmen are admitted fall and spring. Scores must be received by January 15. There are early decision and deferred admissions plans. Early decision applications should be filed by November 1; regular applications, by January 15 for fall entry; and November 1 for spring entry, along with a $50 fee. Notification of early decision is sent December 18; regular decision, April 1. 148 early decision candidates were accepted for the 2009-2010 class. 410 applicants were on the 2009 waiting list; 118 were admitted. Applications are accepted on-line.

Financial Aid: In 2009-2010, 79% of all full-time freshmen and 76% of continuing full-time students received some form of financial aid. 42% of all full-time freshmen and 43% of continuing full-time students received need-based aid. The average freshman award was $29,106. Need-based scholarships or need-based grants averaged $20,801; need-based self-help aid (loans and jobs) averaged $5,479; non-need-based athletic scholarships averaged $31,526; and other non-need-based awards and non-need-based scholarships averaged $17,052. 28% of undergraduate students work part-time. Average annual earnings from campus work are $1477. The average financial indebtedness of the 2009 graduate was $33,079. Bentley is a member of CSS. The CSS/Profile, FAFSA, and federal tax returns, including all schedules for parents and student are required. The deadline for filing freshman financial aid applications for fall entry is February 1.

Computers: Wireless access is available. The entire campus including resident halls, is fully covered with 802.11n wireless access utilizing WPA2 enterprise encryption. Additionally, approximately 500 desktop computers are available for student usage in specialty classroom laboratories and public areas such as the library. Wired network ports are also available throughout the campus. All students may access the system 24/7. There are no time limits and no fees. All students are required to have a personal computer. All undergraduate students are provided an HP6930p Elitebook notebook computer.

BEREA COLLEGE

Berea, KY 40404

(859) 985-3500
(800) 326-5948; (859) 985-3512

Full-time: 614 men, 887 women	**Faculty:** 130; IIB, av$
Part-time: 26 men, 21 women	**Ph.D.s:** 91%
Graduate: none	**Student/Faculty:** 10 to 1
Year: 4-1-4, summer session	**Tuition:** $876
Application Deadline:	**Room & Board:** $5,768
Freshman Class: 2745 applied, 516 accepted, 392 enrolled	
SAT CR/M/W: 560/540/550	**ACT:** 24 **VERY COMPETITIVE+**

Berea College, founded in 1855, is a private liberal arts institution. Berea combines college, federal, and state grants, as well as outside scholarships earned by students, to provide every admitted student with a 4-year, full-tuition scholarship. As part of these scholarship agreements, each student is required to work on campus at least 10 hours weekly while carrying a normal academic load. Room, board, and fees are assessed on a sliding scale. In addition to regional accreditation, Berea has baccalaureate program accreditation with NCATE. The library contains 381,418 volumes, 147,680 microform items, 413,273 audio/video tapes/CDs/DVDs, and subscribes to 1879 periodicals including electronic. Computerized library services include interlibrary loans, database searching, and Internet access. Special learning facilities include a learning resource center, art gallery, planetarium, and a geology museum. The 140-acre campus is in a suburban area 40 miles south of Lexington. Including any residence halls, there are 45 buildings.

Programs of Study: Berea confers B.A. and B.S. degrees. Bachelor's degrees are awarded in AGRICULTURE (agriculture), BIOLOGICAL SCIENCE (biology/biological science), BUSINESS (business administration and management), COMMUNICATIONS AND THE ARTS (art, dramatic arts, English, French, German, music, Spanish, and speech/debate/rhetoric), COMPUTER AND PHYSICAL SCIENCE (chemistry, computer science, mathematics, and physics), EDUCATION (education, elementary education, and physical education), ENGINEERING AND ENVIRONMENTAL DESIGN (industrial engineering technology), HEALTH PROFESSIONS (nursing), SOCIAL SCIENCE (African studies, African American studies, Asian/Oriental studies, child care/child and family studies, economics, history, philosophy, political science/government, psychology, religion, sociology, and women's studies). Business administration, technology, and industrial arts are the largest.

Special: Students may study abroad in many countries. They can also participate in internships, independent, and team-initiated studies. Student-designed majors are available. A 3-2 engineering degree is offered with Washington University and the University of Kentucky. All students must participate in an on-campus work program 10 to 15 hours per week. There are 18 national honor societies.

Admissions: 19% of the 2009-2010 applicants were accepted. The SAT scores for the 2009-2010 freshman class were: Critical Reading--22% below 500, 43% between 500 and 599, 27% between 600 and 700, and 8% above 700; Math--33% below 500, 46% between 500 and 599, and 21% between 600 and 700; Writing--19% below 500, 56% between 500 and 599, 18% between 600 and 700, and 3% above 700. The ACT scores were 22% below 21, 28% between 21 and 23, 32% between 24 and 26, 10% between 27 and 28, and 9% above 28. 56% of the current freshmen were in the top fifth of their class; 88% were in the top two fifths. 7 freshmen graduated first in their class.

Requirements: The SAT or ACT is required. In addition, applicants should be graduates of an accredited secondary school. The GED is accepted. Home-schooled students are also encouraged to apply. Financial need is a requirement for admission. Berea recommends 4 units in English, 3 in math, and 2 each in foreign language, science, and social studies. AP and CLEP credits are accepted. Important factors in the admissions decision are ability to finance college education, geographical diversity, and advanced placement or honors courses.

Procedure: Freshmen are admitted fall and spring. Entrance exams should be taken during the junior year or early in the senior year. There is a rolling admissions plan. Application deadlines are open. Notification is sent on a rolling basis beginning November 1. There is a $50 enrollment deposit. Applications are accepted on-line.

Financial Aid: In 2009-2010, all full-time freshmen and all continuing full-time students received need-based aid. The average freshman award was $23,840. Need-based scholarships or need-based grants averaged $31,341; and need-based self-help aid (loans and jobs) averaged $1472. All undergraduate students work part-time. Average annual earnings from campus work are $2248. The average financial indebtedness of the 2009 graduate was $8133. The FAFSA is required. The priority date for freshman financial aid applications for fall entry is March 15. The deadline for filing freshman financial aid applications for fall entry is April 1.

Computers: Wireless access is available. The college provides a laptop for every student. Students have access to campus network resources and the Internet through network ports located in residence hall rooms, classrooms, offices, and public spaces. Wireless network access is available in central campus classroom buildings and the library, as well as the snack bar, post office, and dining hall areas. A 65 Mbps connection links the campus network to the Internet. Departmental computer labs offer access to specialized functions such as video editing and graphical production. All students may access the system. 24 hours a day, 7 days a week. There are no time limits. The fee is $300.

BERKLEE COLLEGE OF MUSIC
Boston, MA 02215-3693　　　　　　**(617) 266-1400, ext. 2222**
　　　　　　　　　　　　　　　　　　(800) BERKLEE; (617) 747-2047

Full-time: 3740 men and somen	**Faculty:** n/av
Part-time: 355 men and women	**Ph.Ds:** 12%
Graduate: none	**Student/Faculty:** n/av
Year: semesters, summer session	**Tuition:** $31,300
Application Deadline: see profile	**Room & Board:** $15,800
Freshman Class: n/av	
SAT or ACT: required	**SPECIAL**

Berklee College of Music, founded in 1945, is a private institution offering programs in music production and engineering, film scoring, music business/management, composition, music synthesis, music education, music therapy, performance, contemporary writing and production, jazz composition, songwriting, and professional music. Figures in the above capsule and this profile are approximate. The library contains 47,993 volumes and 36,214 audio/video tapes/CDs/DVDs, and subscribes to 1232 periodicals including electronic. Computerized library services include interlibrary loans, database searching, Internet access, and laptop Internet portals. Special learning facilities include a learning resource center, a radio station, 12 recording studios, 5 performance venues, and film scoring, music synthesis, and songwriting labs. The campus is in an urban area in the Fenway Cultural District, Back Bay, Boston. Including any residence halls, there are 20 buildings.

Programs of Study: Berklee confers B.M. degrees. Master's degrees are also awarded. Bachelor's degrees are awarded in COMMUNICATIONS AND THE ARTS (film arts, jazz, music, music business management, music performance, music technology, and music theory and composition), EDUCATION (music education), HEALTH PROFESSIONS (music therapy). Performance, professional music, and music production and engineering are the largest.

Special: Berklee offers cross-registration with the Pro-Arts Consortium, study abroad in the Netherlands, internships in music education, music therapy, and music production and engineering, 5-year dual majors, and a 4-year professional (nondegree) diploma program. Work-study programs, an accelerated degree program, student-designed majors, and credit by exam are available.

Requirements: The SAT or ACT is required. The ACT Optional Writing test is also required. In addition, applicants must be graduates of an accredited secondary school that has a college preparatory program or have their GED. An audition and interview are recommended. Applicants must also submit a detailed reference letter regarding their training and experience in music and a letter from a private instructor, school music director, or professional musician. A GPA of 2.0 is required. AP credits are accepted. Important factors in the admissions decision are evidence of special talent, extracurricular activities record, and recommendations by alumni.

Procedure: Freshmen are admitted to all sessions. Entrance exams should be taken in the fall of the senior year of high school. There are early decision, deferred admissions and rolling admissions plans. Check with the school for current application deadlines. The fall 2009 application fee was $150. Applications are accepted on-line. A waiting list is maintained.

Financial Aid: In a recent year, 57% of all full-time freshmen and 38% of continuing full-time students received some form of financial aid. 26% of undergraduate students work part-time. Average annual earnings from campus work are

$1880. Berklee is a member of CSS. The CSS/Profile, the FFS, and the college's own financial statement are required. Check with the school for current application deadlines.

Computers: Wireless access is available. All students may access the system. There are no time limits and no fees. All students are required to have a personal computer. An Apple Mac Book Pro is recommended.

BERRY COLLEGE
Mount Berry, GA 30149-0159

(706) 236-2215
(800) BERRYGA; (706) 290-2178

Full-time: 540 men, 1197 women	**Faculty:** 145; IIA, -$
Part-time: 19 men, 21 women	**Ph.D.s:** 86%
Graduate: 48 men, 97 women	**Student/Faculty:** 12 to 1
Year: semesters, summer session	**Tuition:** $23,360
Application Deadline: February 1	**Room & Board:** $8340
Freshman Class: 2412 applied, 1616 accepted, 569 enrolled	
SAT CR/M/W: 580/560/560	**ACT:** 25 **HIGHLY COMPETITIVE**

Berry College, founded in 1902, is a private nonsectarian college offering programs in fine and liberal arts and preprofessional programs in education and business. There are 4 undergraduate schools and 2 graduate schools. In addition to regional accreditation, Berry has baccalaureate program accreditation with AACSB, ACS, NASM, and NCATE. The library contains 347,056 volumes, 528,747 microform items, and 5,183 audio/video tapes/CDs/DVDs, and subscribes to 2,059 periodicals including electronic. Computerized library services include interlibrary loans, database searching, Internet access, and laptop Internet portals. Special learning facilities include a learning resource center, art gallery, an observatory, an equine center, a forestry center, beef-and-dairy-cattle operations, BOLD (Berry Outdoor Leadership Development), Wildlife Management Area, Longleaf Pine Project, student-only campsites, and a trail system for hiking, biking, and horseback riding. The 26,000-acre campus is in a suburban area north of Rome on U.S. 27 in northwest Georgia, 72 miles northwest of Atlanta. Including any residence halls, there are 39 buildings.

Programs of Study: Berry confers B.A., B.S., and B.Mu. degrees. Master's degrees are also awarded. Bachelor's degrees are awarded in AGRICULTURE (animal science), BIOLOGICAL SCIENCE (biology/biological science), BUSINESS (accounting, banking and finance, business administration and management, and marketing management), COMMUNICATIONS AND THE ARTS (art, communications, dramatic arts, English, French, German, music, music business management, Spanish, and studio art), COMPUTER AND PHYSICAL SCIENCE (chemistry, computer science, mathematics, and physics), EDUCATION (art education, early childhood education, mathematics education, middle school education, music education, and physical education), ENGINEERING AND ENVIRONMENTAL DESIGN (environmental science), HEALTH PROFESSIONS (exercise science), SOCIAL SCIENCE (economics, history, interdisciplinary studies, international studies, philosophy, political science/government, psychology, religion, social science, and sociology). Animal science, psychology, and communication are the largest.

Special: The college offers internships, study abroad in more than 20 countries, work-study programs, student-designed majors, co-op programs, cross-registration with Shorter College, dual majors, credit by exam, and nondegree study. There are 3-2 engineering degrees and dual-degree programs in several fields with the Georgia Institute of Technology. There is also a dual-degree program in nursing with Emory University. There are 12 national honor societies, a freshman honors program, and 20 departmental honors programs.

Admissions: 67% of the 2009-2010 applicants were accepted. The SAT scores for the 2009-2010 freshman class were: Critical Reading--10% below 500, 48% between 500 and 599, 33% between 600 and 700, and 9% above 700; Math--20% below 500, 49% between 500 and 599, 28% between 600 and 700, and 3% above 700; Writing--19% below 500, 46% between 500 and 599, 30% between 600 and 700, and 5% above 700. The ACT scores were 8% below 21, 28% between 21 and 23, 26% between 24 and 26, 15% between 27 and 28, and 23% above 28. 85% of the current freshmen were in the top fifth of their class; all were in the top two fifths. 12 freshmen graduated first in their class.

Requirements: The SAT or ACT is required. In addition, applicants should be graduates of an accredited high school or have a GED. 20 academic credits are required, including 4 units each of English and math (including algebra I, algebra II, and either geometry or trigonometry), 3 each of science and social studies, and 2 of a foreign language. AP credits are accepted. Important factors in the admissions decision are advanced placement or honors courses, leadership record, and recommendations by school officials.

Procedure: Freshmen are admitted to all sessions. Entrance exams should be taken by the fall of the senior year. There is a rolling admissions plan. Applications should be filed by February 1 for fall entry, along with a $50 fee. Notifications are sent November 1. Applications are accepted on-line.

Financial Aid: In 2009-2010, all full-time freshmen and 99% of continuing full-time students received some form of financial aid. 73% of all full-time freshmen and 67% of continuing full-time students received need-based aid. The average freshman award was $21,292. Need-based scholarships or need-based grants averaged $17,105; need-based self-help aid (loans and jobs) averaged $5310; and other non-need-based awards and non-need-based scholarships averaged $10,627. 82% of undergraduate students work part-time. Average annual earnings from campus work are $2334. The average financial indebtedness of the 2009 graduate was $15,645. The FAFSA is required. The priority date for freshman financial aid applications for fall entry is April 1.

Computers: Wireless access is available. All residence halls have one 100-Mbps network outlet per student. There are 4 general-use computer labs with 140 workstations. Wireless is available in all academic buildings plus Memorial Library, the Krannert student building, the main administrative building, and the Cage athletic facility. There are more than 280 wireless access points. All students may access the system. There are no time limits and no fees. It is strongly recommended that all students have a personal computer.

BETHEL COLLEGE

North Newton, KS 67117

(316) 284-5230
(800) 522-1887, ext. 230; (316) 284-5870

Full-time: 209 men, 207 women	**Faculty:** 40; IIB, --$
Part-time: 13 men, 8 women	**Ph.D.s:** 50%
Graduate: none	**Student/Faculty:** 9 to 1
Year: 4-1-4, summer session	**Tuition:** $19,990
Application Deadline: open	**Room & Board:** $6770
Freshman Class: n/av	
SAT CR/M/W: 500/565/505	**ACT:** 26 **VERY COMPETITIVE+**

Bethel College, established in 1887, is a private liberal arts institution affiliated with the Mennonite Church U.S.A. In addition to regional accreditation, Bethel

78

has baccalaureate program accreditation with CSWE and NCATE. The 2 libraries contain 147,965 volumes, 14,377 microform items, and 7,113 audio/video tapes/CDs/DVDs, and subscribe to 32,765 periodicals including electronic. Computerized library services include interlibrary loans, database searching, Internet access, and laptop Internet portals. Special learning facilities include a learning resource center, art gallery, natural history museum, radio station, TV station, an observatory. The 90-acre campus is in a suburban area 25 miles north of Wichita. Including any residence halls, there are 21 buildings.

Programs of Study: Bethel confers B.A., B.S., B.S.N., B.S.S.W. degrees. Bachelor's degrees are awarded in BIOLOGICAL SCIENCE (biology/biological science), BUSINESS (business administration and management), COMMUNICATIONS AND THE ARTS (art, communications, English, and music), COMPUTER AND PHYSICAL SCIENCE (chemistry, computer science, mathematics, and natural sciences), EDUCATION (athletic training, elementary education, and health education), HEALTH PROFESSIONS (nursing), SOCIAL SCIENCE (history, psychology, religion, and social work). English, biology, and psychology are the strongest academically. Nursing, elementary education, and biology are the largest.

Special: Students may cross-register with Associated Colleges of Central Kansas (ACCK) institutions and Hesston College. Internships are required in many majors. Work-study programs, study abroad, dual majors, and a Washington semester are available. The college offers a 3-2 engineering degree with University of Kansas, Kansas State University, and Wichita State University.

Admissions: The SAT scores for the 2009-2010 freshman class were: Critical Reading--50% below 500, 20% between 500 and 599, 10% between 600 and 700, and 20 above 700; Math--30% below 500, 40% between 500 and 599, 10% between 600 and 700, and 20 above 700; Writing--50% below 500, 20% between 500 and 599, 20% between 600 and 700, and 10 above 700. The ACT scores were 22% below 21, 15% between 21 and 23, 21% between 24 and 26, 14% between 27 and 28, and 28% above 28. There were 1 National Merit finalists. 15 freshmen graduated first in their class.

Requirements: The SAT or ACT is required. In addition, applicants should present a satisfactory score for SAT and ACT, with a minimum GPA of 2.5 for automatic admission. The GED is accepted. Auditions are required of candidates applying for some scholarships, and interviews are recommended for all applicants. Specific departmental requirements may vary. CLEP, AP, and International Baccalaureate credit may be awarded. A GPA of 2.0 is required. AP and CLEP credits are accepted. Important factors in the admissions decision are evidence of special talent, recommendations by alumni, and parents or siblings attended your school.

Procedure: Freshmen are admitted to all sessions. Entrance exams should be taken by the fall of the senior year. There is a rolling admissions plan. Application deadlines are open. Application fee is $20. Notification is sent on a rolling basis. Applications are accepted on-line.

Financial Aid: In 2009-2010, all full-time freshmen and 84% of continuing full-time students received some form of financial aid. 69% of all full-time freshmen and 56% of continuing full-time students received need-based aid. The average freshman award was $23,440. Need-based scholarships or need-based grants averaged $5,675; need-based self-help aid (loans and jobs) averaged $7,715; and non-need based athletic scholarships averaged $3,102. 2% of undergraduate students work part-time. Average annual earnings from campus work are $787. The average financial indebtedness of the 2009 graduate was $24,241. The FAFSA is required. The priority date for freshman financial aid applications for fall entry is August 15.

Computers: Wireless access is available. Students have 2 network jacks in their dorm rooms which are high speed connection to the Internet. File storage is available on the network along with an e-mail account. The wireless network covers most of the campus and all of the areas where students congregate to work and play. There are 2 computer labs with a total of 28 PCs. The library also has public use PCs. All students may access the system 18 hours a day. There are no time limits and no fees.

BETHEL UNIVERSITY
St. Paul, MN 55112

(651) 638-6242
(800) 255-8706; (651) 635-1490

Full-time: 1131 men, 1642 women	**Faculty:** 188; IIB, -$
Part-time: 191 men, 457 women	**Ph.D.s:** 78%
Graduate: 994 men, 1023 women	**Student/Faculty:** 15 to 1
Year: 4-1-4, summer session	**Tuition:** $27,020
Application Deadline: open	**Room & Board:** $7920
Freshman Class: 2179 applied, 1734 accepted, 727 enrolled	
SAT CR/M: 590/580	**ACT:** 25 **VERY COMPETITIVE**

Bethel University, established in 1871, is a private liberal arts university affiliated with the Converge Worldwide (Baptist General Conference). There are 2 undergraduate schools and 2 graduate schools. In addition to regional accreditation, Bethel has baccalaureate program accreditation with CSWE and TEAC. The library contains 194,196 volumes, 195,650 microform items, and 15,503 audio/video tapes/CDs/DVDs, and subscribes to 38,080 periodicals including electronic. Computerized library services include interlibrary loans, database searching, Internet access, and laptop Internet portals. Special learning facilities include a learning resource center, art gallery, and radio station. The 247-acre campus is in a suburban area 10 miles north of Minneapolis/St. Paul. Including any residence halls, there are 39 buildings.

Programs of Study: Bethel confers B.A., B.S., B.Mus., and B.Mus.Ed degrees. Associates, master's, and doctoral degrees are also awarded. Bachelor's degrees are awarded in AGRICULTURE (environmental studies), BIOLOGICAL SCIENCE (biochemistry, biology/biological science, and molecular biology), BUSINESS (accounting, banking and finance, and business administration and management), COMMUNICATIONS AND THE ARTS (art, communications, dramatic arts, English, English literature, French, journalism, multimedia, music, music performance, Spanish, and visual and performing arts), COMPUTER AND PHYSICAL SCIENCE (applied physics, chemistry, computer science, mathematics, and physics), EDUCATION (athletic training, business education, early childhood education, education, elementary education, English education, foreign languages education, health education, mathematics education, middle school education, music education, physical education, science education, secondary education, social studies education, and teaching English as a second/foreign language (TESOL/TEFOL)), ENGINEERING AND ENVIRONMENTAL DESIGN (engineering and applied science and environmental science), HEALTH PROFESSIONS (community health work, exercise science, and nursing), SOCIAL SCIENCE (biblical studies, economics, history, international relations, philosophy, political science/government, psychology, religious music, social studies, social work, theological studies, Third World studies, and youth ministry). Physics, chemisty, and nursing are the strongest academically. Business, education, and nursing are the largest.

Special: Cross-registration is available through the Council for Christian Colleges and Universities. Students may arrange internships and study abroad in various countries. Students may design their own major and earn a 3-2 engineering degree. An adult degree completion program is offered. There are 6 national honor societies, a freshman honors program, and 6 departmental honors programs.

Admissions: 80% of the 2009-2010 applicants were accepted. The SAT scores for the 2009-2010 freshman class were: Critical Reading--20% below 500, 31% between 500 and 599, 30% between 600 and 700, and 19% above 700; Math--20% below 500, 39% between 500 and 599, 28% between 600 and 700, and 14% above 700. The ACT scores were 17% below 21, 23% between 21 and 23, 26% between 24 and 26, 14% between 27 and 28, and 21% above 28. 45% of the current freshmen were in the top fifth of their class; 74% were in the top two-fifths. 31 freshmen graduated first in their class.

Requirements: The SAT or ACT is required. The PSAT is accepted. An interview is recommended. Requirements include a personal statement, contact information for an academic or spiritual reference, and an official transcript and class ranking from an accredited secondary school (GED is accepted). Bethel requires applicants to be in the upper 50% of their class. A GPA of 2.5 is required. AP and CLEP credits are accepted. Important factors in the admissions decision are advanced placement or honors courses, extracurricular activities record, and personality/intangible qualities.

Procedure: Freshmen are admitted fall and spring. Entrance exams should be taken spring of junior year. There is a rolling admissions plan. Application deadlines are open. Notification is sent on a rolling basis beginning October 1. Applications are accepted on-line. 43 applicants were on a recent waiting list, 10 were accepted.

Financial Aid: In 2009-2010, 99% of all full-time freshmen and 94% of continuing full-time students received some form of financial aid. 71% of all full-time freshmen and 68% of continuing full-time students received need-based aid. The average freshmen award was $19,129, with $7041 ($27,794 maximum) from need-based scholarships or need-based grants; $3753 ($8700 maximum) from need-based self-help aid (loans and jobs); and $8335 ($31,020 maximum) from other non-need-based awards and non-need-based scholarships. 56% of undergraduate students work part-time. Average annual earnings from campus work are $1500. The average financial indebtedness of the 2009 graduate was $30,496. Bethel is a member of CSS. The FAFSA and the college's own financial statement are required. The priority date for freshman financial aid applications for fall entry is April 15.

Computers: Wireless access is available. In addition to many wired network ports throughout campus, wireless Internet is available in all academic buildings. More than 500 computers in labs, departments, and the library are available for student use. All students may access the system 24 hours a day. There are no time limits and no fees.

La Mirada, CA 90639-0001

(562) 903-4752
(800) OK-BIOLA; (562) 903-4709

Full-time: 1305 men, 2147 women	**Faculty:** ; IIA, av$
Part-time: 155 men, 196 women	**Ph.D.s:** 78%
Graduate: 1154 men, 720 women	**Student/Faculty:** n/av
Year: 4-1-4, summer session	**Tuition:** $24,998
Application Deadline: see profile	**Room & Board:** $7632
Freshman Class: 2309 applied, 1886 accepted, 810 enrolled	
SAT CR/M/W: 560/546/556	**ACT:** 24 **VERY COMPETITIVE**

Biola University, founded in 1908, is a private, interdenominational Christian institution offering undergraduate and graduate degrees in arts and sciences, psychology, theology, intercultural studies, and business. There are 6 undergraduate schools and 6 graduate schools. In addition to regional accreditation, Biola has baccalaureate program accreditation with ACBSP, NASAD, NASM, and NLN. The library contains 315,000 volumes, 580,000 microform items, and 9232 audio/video tapes/CDs/DVDs, and subscribes to 30,000 periodicals including electronic. Computerized library services include interlibrary loans, database searching, and Internet access. Special learning facilities include a learning resource center, art gallery, radio station, TV station, film studio, 3-D art facility, MIDI lab for music composition majors, electronic piano lab, listening lab with music archives, physical science labs, and scanning electron microscope. The 95-acre campus is in a suburban area 22 miles southeast of Los Angeles. Including any residence halls, there are 39 buildings.

Programs of Study: Biola confers B.A., B.S., and B.M. degrees. Master's and doctoral degrees are also awarded. Bachelor's degrees are awarded in BIOLOGICAL SCIENCE (biochemistry and biology/biological science), BUSINESS (accounting, business administration and management, management science, and marketing management), COMMUNICATIONS AND THE ARTS (art, broadcasting, communications, English, journalism, music, music performance, music theory and composition, and Spanish), COMPUTER AND PHYSICAL SCIENCE (applied mathematics, computer science, information sciences and systems, mathematics, and physical sciences), EDUCATION (Christian education, mathematics education, music education, and physical education), HEALTH PROFESSIONS (nursing and speech pathology/audiology), SOCIAL SCIENCE (anthropology, biblical studies, crosscultural studies, history, humanities, liberal arts/general studies, philosophy, psychology, social science, and sociology). Business administration, biological science, and chemistry are the strongest academically. Business, psychology, and liberal studies are the largest.

Special: Cross-registration with the Au Sable Institute of Environmental Studies is possible. Biola offers internships, summer travel tours, study abroad in 11 countries, and an American studies program in Washington D.C., sponsored by the Christian College Coalition. Special programs include L.A. Film Studies, a semester in Hollywood working in the film industry; Biola Baja, a 3-week program at Vermillion Sea Field, Baja; a family studies course at Focus on the Family Institute in Colorado Springs; a China studies program at Fudan University in Shanghai, China; and a development theory studies program in Honduras. Also available are on- and off-campus work-study programs, a B.A.- B.S. degree, a 3-2 engineering degree with the University of Southern California, dual majors, and nondegree study. There are several preprofessional programs available, including prelaw, prephysical therapy, and prechiropractic. A 3-1 program with Los

82

Angeles College of Chiropractic is offered. Students can also attend a semester at Martha's Vineyard with the Contemporary Music Center and explore the many areas of the Christian music industry. There are 2 national honor societies, a freshman honors program, and 7 departmental honors programs.

Admissions: 82% of the 2009-2010 applicants were accepted. The SAT scores for the 2009-2010 freshman class were: Critical Reading--23% below 500, 40% between 500 and 599, 31% between 600 and 700, and 6% above 700; Math--28% below 500, 40% between 500 and 599, 29% between 600 and 700, and 3% above 700; Writing--21% below 500, 45% between 500 and 599, 31% between 600 and 700, and 3% above 700. The ACT scores were 22% below 21, 23% between 21 and 23, 27% between 24 and 26, and 13% between 27 and 28.

Requirements: The SAT or ACT is required. In addition, applicants need not be graduates of an accredited secondary school. The GED is accepted. Students should have completed 15 academic credits, including 4 years of English and foreign language, 3 years of math, and 2 each of social studies and science. All students must be evangelical Christians who can demonstrate Christian character, leadership ability, and the aptitude for possible success in college. Applicants must submit 2 personal references: 1 from their pastor or someone on the pastoral staff and 1 from the school last attended or from an employer if they have been out of school for a year and have been working. An essay and an interview are required. A GPA of 3.0 is required. AP and CLEP credits are accepted. Important factors in the admissions decision are personality/intangible qualities, recommendations by school officials, and leadership record.

Procedure: Freshmen are admitted to all sessions. There is a rolling admissions plan. Applications should be filed by March 1 for spring entry, along with a $45 fee. Notification is sent February 15. Applications are accepted on-line.

Financial Aid: In 2009-2010, 80% of all full-time freshmen and 77% of continuing full-time students received some form of financial aid. 81% of all full-time freshmen and 80% of continuing full-time students received need-based aid. The average freshmen award was $17,410, with $2655 ($6000 maximum) from need-based scholarships or need-based grants; $4920 ($5625 maximum) from need-based self-help aid (loans and jobs); $2121 ($20,932 maximum) from non-need-based athletic scholarships; and $2779 ($7000 maximum) from other non-need-based awards and non-need-based scholarships. 34% of undergraduate students work part-time. Average annual earnings from campus work are $2235. The average financial indebtedness of the 2009 graduate was $28,007. Biola is a member of CSS. The FAFSA and the college's own financial statement are required. California residents should also submit the Cal Grant GPA verification form. The deadline for filing freshman financial aid applications for fall entry is May 15.

Computers: All students may access the system every day. There are no time limits and no fees.

BIRMINGHAM-SOUTHERN COLLEGE

Birmingham, AL 35254

(205) 226-4696
(800) 523-5793; (205) 523-3074

Full-time: 740 men, 732 women	**Faculty:** 111; IIB, av$
Part-time: 16 men, 20 women	**Ph.D:s:** 92%
Graduate: 19 men, 22 women	**Student/Faculty:** 12 to 1
Year: 4-1-4, summer session	**Tuition:** $26,746
Application Deadline: January 15	**Room & Board:** $9236
Freshman Class: 1638 applied, 1486 accepted, 424 enrolled	
SAT CR/M/W: 570/570/570	**ACT:** 26 **VERY COMPETITIVE+**

Birmingham-Southern College, founded in 1856, is a private liberal arts college affiliated with the United Methodist Church. There is 1 graduate school. In addition to regional accreditation, BSC has baccalaureate program accreditation with AACSB, NASM, and NCATE. The library contains 263,024 volumes, 90,675 microform items, and 38,261 audio/video tapes/CDs/DVDs, and subscribes to 40,000 periodicals including electronic. Computerized library services include interlibrary loans, database searching, Internet access, and laptop Internet portals. Special learning facilities include a learning resource center, art gallery, planetarium, environmental center, and outdoor educational center. The 192-acre campus is in an urban area 3 miles west of downtown Birmingham. Including any residence halls, there are 45 buildings.

Programs of Study: BSC confers B.A., B.F.A., B.Mus., B.Mus.Ed., and B.S. degrees. Master's degrees are also awarded. Bachelor's degrees are awarded in AGRICULTURE (environmental studies), BIOLOGICAL SCIENCE (biology/biological science), BUSINESS (accounting, business administration and management, and international business management), COMMUNICATIONS AND THE ARTS (art history and appreciation, dance, dramatic arts, English, French, German, music, musical theater, painting, photography, printmaking, sculpture, Spanish, and studio art), COMPUTER AND PHYSICAL SCIENCE (chemistry, computer science, mathematics, and physics), EDUCATION (art education, collaborative education, dance education, education services, music education, and secondary education), SOCIAL SCIENCE (Asian/Oriental studies, biopsychology, economics, history, interdisciplinary studies, international studies, Latin American studies, philosophy, political science/government, psychology, religion, and sociology). Biology, English, and psychology are the strongest academically. Business administration, accounting, and history are the largest.

Special: There is cross-registration with the University of Alabama at Birmingham, Miles College, the University of Montevallo, and Samford University. Student-designed, dual, and interdisciplinary majors, internships, work-study programs, and study abroad are offered. There is a 3-2 nursing program with Vanderbilt University and a 3-2 environmental studies program wih Duke University. A 3-2 engineering degree is offered with the University of Alabama at Birmingham, Auburn University, Columbia University, and Washington University. There are 19 national honor societies, including Phi Beta Kappa, a freshman honors program, and 5 departmental honors programs.

Admissions: 91% of the 2009-2010 applicants were accepted. The SAT scores for the 2009-2010 freshman class were: Critical Reading--14% below 500, 48% between 500 and 599, 26% between 600 and 700, and 12% above 700; Math--17% below 500, 43% between 500 and 599, 34% between 600 and 700, and 6% above 700; Writing--16% below 500, 45% between 500 and 599, 28% between 600 and 700, and 12% above 700. The ACT scores were 4% below 21, 25% between 21 and 23, 30% between 24 and 26, 17% between 27 and 28, and 24% above 28. 50% of the current freshmen were in the top fifth of their class; 75% were in the top two fifths. There were 8 National Merit finalists. 19 freshmen graduated first in their class.

Requirements: The SAT or ACT is required. The minimum SAT score should be 970 combined and the minimum ACT score, 21. Applicants should have graduated from an accredited secondary school with 4 courses in English, 4 each in math, science, and social studies, and a recommended 2 in foreign language. The GED is also accepted. An essay is required and an interview is recommended. Fine arts majors are advised to submit a portfolio or arrange an interview with the fine arts department. BSC requires applicants to be in the upper 50% of their class. A GPA of 2.3 is required. AP and CLEP credits are accepted. Important factors in the admissions decision are advanced placement or honors courses, leadership record, and recommendations by school officials.

Procedure: Freshmen are admitted fall, spring, and summer. Entrance exams should be taken in the spring of the junior year. There are early admissions, deferred admissions, and rolling admissions plans. Applications should be filed by January 15 for fall entry, December 15 for winter entry, January 15 for spring entry, and May 1 for summer entry, along with a $40 fee. Notification is sent on a rolling basis. Applications are accepted on-line.

Financial Aid: In 2009-2010, 99% of all full-time freshmen and 98% of continuing full-time students received some form of financial aid. 62% of all full-time freshmen and 46% of continuing full-time students received need-based aid. The average freshmen award was $26,234, with $5019 ($5350 maximum) from need-based scholarships or need-based grants; $3143 ($5500 maximum) from need-based self-help aid (loans and jobs); and $18,008 ($39,810 maximum) from other non-need-based awards and non-need-based scholarships. 37% of undergraduate students work part-time. Average annual earnings from campus work are $1843. The average financial indebtedness of the 2009 graduate was $27,058. The FAFSA is required. The priority date for freshman financial aid applications for fall entry is March 1.

Computers: Wireless access is available. Connectivity for student-owned machines is available in all residence halls, sororities, fraternities, and academic buildings. Lab facilities include 11 computer classroom labs and 5 small departmental labs, and there are computers in all science labs. There are 58 classrooms with ceiling-mounted computer/video projectors and computers. A high-speed connection provides Internet access to all members of the college community. All students receive an e-mail account. All students may access the system 24 hours a day. There are no time limits. The fee is $556 per semester. It is strongly recommended that all students have a personal computer.

Chestnut Hill, MA 02467 | **(617) 552-3100**
| **(800) 360-2522; (617) 552-0798**

Full-time: 4369 men, 4691 women	**Faculty:** I, +$
Part-time: none	**Ph.D.s:** 98%
Graduate: 2118 men, 2725 women	**Student/Faculty:** n/av
Year: semesters, summer session	**Tuition:** $39,130
Application Deadline: January 1	**Room & Board:** $12,909
Freshman Class: 30,845 applied, 8093 accepted, 2167 enrolled	
SAT CR/M/W: 655/685/665	**ACT:** 30 **MOST COMPETITIVE**

Boston College, founded in 1863, is an independent institution affiliated with the Roman Catholic Church and the Jesuit Order. It offers undergraduate programs in the arts and sciences, business, nursing, and education as well as graduate and professional programs. There are 4 undergraduate schools and 7 graduate schools. In addition to regional accreditation, BC has baccalaureate program accreditation with AACSB, CSWE, NCATE, and NLN. The 8 libraries contain 2.5 million volumes, 4.2 million microform items, and 2099 audio/video tapes/CDs/DVDs, and subscribe to 31,644 periodicals including electronic. Computerized library services include interlibrary loans, database searching, and Internet access. Special learning facilities include a learning resource center, art gallery, radio station, and TV station. The 386-acre campus is in a suburban area 6 miles west of Boston. Including any residence halls, there are 137 buildings.

Programs of Study: BC confers B.A. and B.S. degrees. Master's and doctoral degrees are also awarded. Bachelor's degrees are awarded in BIOLOGICAL SCIENCE (biochemistry and biology/biological science), BUSINESS (accounting, banking and finance, business administration and management, business economics, human resources, management science, marketing/retailing/merchandising, and operations research), COMMUNICATIONS AND THE ARTS (art history and appreciation, classics, communications, dramatic arts, English, film arts, French, Italian, linguistics, music, romance languages and literature, and studio art), COMPUTER AND PHYSICAL SCIENCE (chemistry, computer science, geology, geophysics and seismology, information sciences and systems, mathematics, and physics), EDUCATION (early childhood education, elementary education, secondary education, and special education), ENGINEERING AND ENVIRONMENTAL DESIGN (environmental science), HEALTH PROFESSIONS (nursing), SOCIAL SCIENCE (classical/ancient civilization, economics, German area studies, Hispanic American studies, history, human development, philosophy, political science/government, psychology, Russian and Slavic studies, sociology, and theological studies). Finance, economics, and chemistry are the strongest academically. Finance, communications, and English are the largest.

Special: There are internship programs in management and in arts and sciences. Students may cross-register with Boston University, Brandeis University, Hebrew College, Pine Manor College, Regis College, and Tufts University. BC also offers a Washington semester in cooperation with American University, work-study programs with nonprofit agencies, study abroad in 28 countries, and dual and student-designed majors. Students may pursue a 3-2 engineering program with Boston University and accelerated 5-year programs in social work and education. There are 12 national honor societies, including Phi Beta Kappa, a freshman honors program, and 4 departmental honors programs.

Admissions: 26% of the 2009-2010 applicants were accepted. The SAT scores for the 2009-2010 freshman class were: Critical Reading--3% below 500, 15%

between 500 and 599, 53% between 600 and 700, and 29 above 700; Math--2% below 500, 11% between 500 and 599, 45% between 600 and 700, and 42 above 700; Writing--2% below 500, 13% between 500 and 599, 48% between 600 and 700, and 37 above 700. 62% of ACT scores were above 28. 95% of the current freshmen were in the top fifth of their class; 99% were in the top two fifths.

Requirements: The SAT or ACT is required. Students may take either the SAT test with Writing and 2 Subject tests of their choice or the ACT test with Writing. Applicants must be graduates of an accredited high school, completing 4 units each of English, foreign language, science, and math. Those students applying to the school of nursing must complete at least 2 years of a lab science including 1 unit of chemistry. Applicants to the school of management are strongly encouraged to take 4 years of college preparatory math. An essay is required. AP credits are accepted.

Procedure: Freshmen are admitted fall and spring. Entrance exams should be taken no later than January of the senior year. There are early decision, early action and deferred admissions plans. Early decision applications should be filed by November 1; regular applications, by January 1 for fall entry and November 1 for spring entry, along with a $70 fee. Early action notifications are sent December 25; regular decision, April 15. 2300 applicants were on the 2009 waiting list; 317 were admitted. Applications are accepted on-line.

Financial Aid: In 2009-2010, 42% of all full-time freshmen and 42% of continuing full-time students received some form of financial aid. 39% of all full-time freshmen and 40% of continuing full-time students received need-based aid. The average freshman award was $29,349. Need-based scholarships or need-based grants averaged $26,241; need-based self-help aid (loans and jobs) averaged $5014; non-need-based athletic scholarships averaged $39,975; and other non-need-based awards and non-need-based scholarships averaged $14,828. 26% of undergraduate students work part time. Average annual earnings from campus work are $1700. The average financial indebtedness of the 2009 graduate was $19,358. BC is a member of CSS. The CSS/Profile, FAFSA, federal IRS income tax form, W-2s, and Divorced/Separated Statement (when applicable) are required. The deadline for filing freshman financial aid applications for fall entry is February 1.

Computers: Wireless access is available. All dorm rooms are wired for the college's network, and wireless coverage is available in most buildings on campus, including classrooms, cafeterias, and administration buildings. All students may access the system at all times. There are no time limits and no fees. It is strongly recommended that all students have a personal computer. BC offers special network-ready bundles through both Dell and Apple.

BOSTON UNIVERSITY
Boston, MA 02215   **(617) 353-2300; (617) 353-9695**

Full-time: 7100 men, 10300 women	**Faculty:** I, av$
Part-time: 675 men, 640 women	**Ph.D.s:** 85%
Graduate: 5665 men, 6610 women	**Student/Faculty:** n/av
Year: semesters, summer session	**Tuition:** $39,850
Application Deadline: see profile	**Room & Board:** $12,000
Freshman Class: n/av	
SAT or ACT: required	**HIGHLY COMPETITIVE+**

Boston University, founded in 1839, is a private institution offering undergraduate and graduate programs in basic studies, liberal arts, communication, hotel and food administration, allied health education management, and fine arts. Figures in the above capsule and this capsule are approximate. There are 11 undergraduate schools and 15 graduate schools. In addition to regional accreditation, BU has baccalaureate program accreditation with ABET and NASM. The 23 libraries contain 2.4 million volumes, 4.5 million microform items, and 72,542 audio/video tapes/CDs/DVDs, and subscribe to 34,214 periodicals including electronic. Computerized library services include interlibrary loans and database searching. Special learning facilities include a learning resource center, art gallery, planetarium, radio station, TV station, astronomy observatory, 20th-century archives, theater and theater company in residence, scientific computing and visualization lab, the Geddes language lab, speech, language, and hearing clinic, hotel/food administration culinary center, performance center, multimedia center, center for photonics research, center for remote sensing, and the Metcalf Center for Science and Engineering. The 132-acre campus is in an urban area on the Charles River in Boston's Back Bay. Including any residence halls, there are 349 buildings.

Programs of Study: BU confers B.A., B.S., B.F.A., B.L.S., B.Mus., and B.S.B.A. degrees. Master's and doctoral degrees are also awarded. Bachelor's degrees are awarded in AGRICULTURE (environmental studies), BIOLOGICAL SCIENCE (biochemistry, biology/biological science, ecology, environmental biology, neurosciences, nutrition, and physiology), BUSINESS (accounting, banking and finance, business administration and management, entrepreneurial studies, hotel/motel and restaurant management, international business management, management information systems, management science, marketing/retailing/merchandising, operations research, and organizational behavior), COMMUNICATIONS AND THE ARTS (apparel design, classics, communications, dramatic arts, East Asian languages and literature, English, film arts, French, German, Germanic languages and literature, graphic design, Greek (classical), Greek (modern), Italian, journalism, Latin, linguistics, music, music history and appreciation, music performance, music theory and composition, painting, performing arts, public relations, sculpture, Spanish, theater design, and theater management), COMPUTER AND PHYSICAL SCIENCE (astronomy, astrophysics, chemistry, computer science, earth science, geophysics and seismology, mathematics, physics, and planetary and space science), EDUCATION (art education, athletic training, bilingual/bicultural education, drama education, early childhood education, education, education of the deaf and hearing impaired, elementary education, English education, foreign languages education, mathematics education, music education, physical education, science education, social studies education, and special education), ENGINEERING AND ENVIRONMENTAL DESIGN (aeronautical engineering, biomedical engineering, computer engineering, electrical/electronics engineering, engineering, environmental science, manufacturing engineering, and mechanical engineering), HEALTH PROFESSIONS (exercise science, health, health science, physical therapy, rehabilitation therapy, and speech pathology/audiology), SOCIAL SCIENCE (American studies, anthropology, archeology, Asian/Oriental studies, classical/ancient civilization, East Asian studies, Eastern European studies, economics, French studies, geography, Hispanic American studies, history, interdisciplinary studies, international relations, Italian studies, Japanese studies, Latin American studies, philosophy, physical fitness/movement, political science/government, psychology, religion, sociology, and urban studies). The University Professors Program, accelerated medical and dental programs, and the management honors program are the strongest academically. Communications, business, and marketing are the largest.

Special: Cross-registration is permitted with Brandeis University, Tufts University, Boston College, and Hebrew College in Massachusetts. Opportunities are provided for internships, co-op programs in engineering, a Washington semester, on-

and off-campus work-study, accelerated degree programs, B.A.-B.S. degrees, dual majors, student-designed majors, credit by exam, nondegree studies, pass/fail options, and study abroad in 18 countries. A 3-2 engineering degree is offered with 16 schools and 2-2 engineering agreements with 6 schools, plus 107 other 2-2 agreements. The University Professors Program offers a creative cross-disciplinary approach, and the College of Basic Studies offers team teaching. There are 16 national honor societies, a freshman honors program, and 6 departmental honors programs.

Requirements: The SAT or ACT is required. The ACT Optional Writing test is also required. Applicants are evaluated on an individual basis. Evidence of strong academic performance in a college prep curriculum, including 4 years of English, at least 3 years of math (through precalculus), 3 years of lab sciences, and 3 years of social studies/history with at least 2 years of a foreign language, is the most important aspect of a student's application review. Subject tests in chemistry and math (level 2) are required for the accelerated medical and dental programs. Students planning to take the SAT are required to submit the SAT with the writing section along with 2 SAT Subject tests in different subject areas of their choice. Students selected as finalists in the accelerated programs in medicine and dentistry will be invited to interview in Boston. Candidates for the College of Fine Arts must present a portfolio or participate in an audition. AP and CLEP credits are accepted. Important factors in the admissions decision are advanced placement or honors courses.

Procedure: Freshmen are admitted fall and spring. Entrance exams should be taken in the junior year or early in the senior year. There are early decision, early admissions and deferred admissions plans. Check with the school for current application deadlines. The fall 2009 application fee was $70. Applications are accepted on-line. A waiting list is maintained.

Financial Aid: BU is a member of CSS. The CSS/Profile and FAFSA are required. Check with the school for current application deadlines.

Computers: Wireless access is available. A shared cluster of UNIX systems consisting of several IBM RS/600 machines support the approximately 40,000 users. The BU campus network provides direct access to the Internet, e-mail, the Web, and many other resources. Tens of thousands of ports support communications that are available throughout the campus, including residence halls. All students may access the system 24 hours a day. Students enrolled in the School of Management and the College of Engineerin must have a personal computer.

BOWDOIN COLLEGE
Brunswick, ME 04011　　　　　　　　**(207) 725-3100; (207) 725-3101**

Full-time: 867 men, 904 women	**Faculty:** 177; IIB, ++$
Part-time: 4 men, 2 women	**Ph.D.s:** 98%
Graduate: none	**Student/Faculty:** 9 to 1
Year: semesters	**Tuition:** $40,020
Application Deadline: January 1	**Room & Board:** $10,880
Freshman Class: 5940 applied, 1153 accepted, 494 enrolled	
SAT CR/M/W: 710/710/710	**ACT:** 32　　**MOST COMPETITIVE**

Bowdoin College, established in 1794, is a private liberal arts institution.. The 5 libraries contain 1 million volumes, 122,698 microform items, and 29,499 audio/video tapes/CDs/DVDs, and subscribe to 15,307 periodicals including electronic. Computerized library services include interlibrary loans, database searching, Internet access, and laptop Internet portals. Special learning facilities include a learning resource center, art gallery, radio station, TV station, a museum of art, arctic museum, language media center, women's resource center, electronic classroom, coastal studies center, African American center, the craft center ceramics studio and photography darkroom, scientific station, located in the Bay of Fundy, educational research and development program, theaters, music hall, community service resource center, environmental studies center, and visual arts center. The 205-acre campus is in a small town 25 miles northeast of Portland. Including any residence halls, there are 116 buildings.

Programs of Study: Bowdoin confers A.B. degrees. Bachelor's degrees are awarded in BIOLOGICAL SCIENCE (biochemistry, biology/biological science, and neurosciences), COMMUNICATIONS AND THE ARTS (art history and appreciation, classics, dramatic arts, English, French, German, music, romance languages and literature, Russian, Spanish, and visual and performing arts), COMPUTER AND PHYSICAL SCIENCE (chemical physics, chemistry, computer science, geochemistry, geology, geophysics and seismology, mathematics, and physics), ENGINEERING AND ENVIRONMENTAL DESIGN (environmental science), SOCIAL SCIENCE (African studies, anthropology, archeology, Asian/Oriental studies, classical/ancient civilization, Eastern European studies, economics, history, interdisciplinary studies, Latin American studies, philosophy, political science/government, psychology, religion, sociology, and women's studies). Biology, economics, government and legal studies are the strongest academically and the largest.

Special: A.B. offers degrees in 43 majors, with single, coordinate, double and self-designed major options, and Plus (+) and minus (-) grading system, with credit/D/fail option. Dean's list, Latin Honors and departmental honors are awarded. First-year seminars, intermediate and advanced independent study, student research and close work with faculty advisors is strongly emphasized. Study abroad during the junior year is encouraged. Academic support programs include the Baldwin Program, the Quantitative Skills Program, and the Engineering, Legal Studies, Health Professions Advising and Teacher Certification. There is 1 national honor society, including Phi Beta Kappa, and all departments have honors programs.

Admissions: 19% of the 2009-2010 applicants were accepted. The SAT scores for the 2009-2010 freshman class were: Critical Reading-- 9% between 500 and 599, 34% between 600 and 700, and 57% above 700; Math-- 7% between 500 and 599, 35% between 600 and 700, and 58% above 700; Writing-- 8% between 500 and 599, 36% between 600 and 700, and 56% above 700. The ACT scores were % below 21, 3% between 21 and 23, 7% between 24 and 26, 9% between 27 and 28, and 81% above 28. 93% of the current freshmen were in the top fifth of their class; 98% were in the top two fifths. There were 39 National Merit finalists. 55 freshmen graduated first in their class.

Requirements: There are no specific academic requirements, but typical applicants for admission will have 4 years each of English, social studies, foreign language, and math, 3 1/2 years of science, and 1 course each in art, music, and history. A high school record, 2 teacher recommendations, and an essay are required. AP credits are accepted.

Procedure: Freshmen are admitted in the fall. Entrance exams should be taken by the late summer before the freshman year. There are early decision and deferred admissions plans. Early decision applications should be filed by November 15; regular applications, by January 1 for fall entry, along with a $60 fee. Notification of early decision is sent December 15; regular decision, April 5. Applications are accepted on-line. A waiting list is maintained.

Financial Aid: In 2009-2010, 44% of all full-time freshmen and 44% of continuing full-time students received some form of financial aid. 40% of all full-time

freshmen and 40% of continuing full-time students received need-based aid. The average freshmen award was $36,316, with $35,492 ($53,800 maximum) from need-based scholarships or need-based grants; $1,724 ($2,000 maximum) from need-based self-help aid (loans and jobs); and $1,000 ($2,000 maximum) from other non-need-based awards and non-need-based scholarships. 51% of undergraduate students work part-time. Average annual earnings from campus work are $1525. The average financial indebtedness of the 2009 graduate was $18,135. Bowdoin is a member of CSS. The CSS/Profile and FAFSA, and Noncustodial PROFILE and Business/Farm Supplement are required. The deadline for filing freshman financial aid applications for fall entry is February 15.

Computers: Wireless access is available. Computer equipment and network and Internet access are available to all students in computer labs (150 stations), all residence halls, the library (250 stations), the student center and classrooms (500 stations). Students have access to the wireless network, available in all libraries, some classrooms, computer labs and some residence halls. Students may check out laptops and wireless cards. All students may access the system 24 hours a day. There are no time limits and no fees. It is strongly recommended that all students have a personal computer.

BRADLEY UNIVERSITY

Peoria, IL 61625
(309) 677-1000
(800) 447-6460; (309) 677-2797

Full-time: 2210 men, 2591 women	**Faculty:** 345; II A, av$
Part-time: 107 men, 153 women	**Ph.D.s:** 83%
Graduate: 372 men, 367 women	**Student/Faculty:** 13 to 1
Year: semesters, summer session	**Tuition:** $24,224
Application Deadline: open	**Room & Board:** $7650
Freshman Class: 6221 applied, 4573 accepted, 1106 enrolled	
SAT CR/M: 540/570	**ACT:** 25 **VERY COMPETITIVE**

Bradley University, founded in 1897, is an independent, privately endowed institution offering a full range of baccalaureate and graduate-level programs. There are 5 undergraduate schools and one graduate school. In addition to regional accreditation, Bradley has baccalaureate program accreditation with AACSB, ABET, ACCE, ADA, NASAD, NASM, NCATE, and NLN. The library contains 511,000 volumes, 86,504 microform items, and 13,774 audio/video tapes/CDs/DVDs, and subscribes to 41,689 periodicals including electronic. Computerized library services include interlibrary loans, database searching, Internet access, and laptop Internet portals. Special learning facilities include a learning resource center, art gallery, radio station, and TV station. The 85-acre campus is in an urban area 160 miles southwest of Chicago. Including any residence halls, there are 44 buildings.

Programs of Study: Bradley confers B.A., B.F.A., B.M., B.S., B.S.C., B.S.C.E., B.S.E.E., B.S.I.E., B.S.M.E., B.S.M.F.E., B.S.M.F.E.T., and B.S.N. degrees. Master's and doctoral degrees are also awarded. Bachelor's degrees are awarded in BIOLOGICAL SCIENCE (biochemistry, biology/biological science, and molecular biology), BUSINESS (accounting, banking and finance, business administration and management, entrepreneurial studies, international business management, management information systems, and marketing/retailing/merchandising), COMMUNICATIONS AND THE ARTS (art history and appreciation, communications, dramatic arts, English, French, German, graphic design, multimedia, music, music business management, music performance, music theory and composition, Spanish, and studio art), COMPUTER AND PHYSICAL SCIENCE (actuarial science, chemistry, computer science, information sciences and systems, mathematics, and physics), EDUCATION (art education, drama education, early childhood education, elementary education, music education, and special education), ENGINEERING AND ENVIRONMENTAL DESIGN (civil engineering, construction engineering, electrical/electronics engineering, engineering physics, environmental science, industrial engineering, manufacturing engineering, manufacturing technology, and mechanical engineering), HEALTH PROFESSIONS (health science, medical technology, and nursing), SOCIAL SCIENCE (criminal justice, dietetics, economics, family/consumer studies, history, international studies, liberal arts/general studies, philosophy, political science/government, psychology, religion, social work, and sociology). Business, engineering, and natural sciences are the strongest academically. Communication, elementary education, and psychology are the largest.

Special: Special academic programs include an honors program, co-op programs, internships, a Washington semester, work-study programs, study abroad in 30 countries, B.A.-B.S. degrees in most majors, dual and student-designed majors, and leadership fellowships. There are 31 national honor societies and a freshman honors program.

Admissions: 74% of the 2009-2010 applicants were accepted. The SAT scores for the 2009-2010 freshman class were: Critical Reading--27% below 500, 44% between 500 and 599, 23% between 600 and 700, and 6% above 700; Math--20% below 500, 38% between 500 and 599, 34% between 600 and 700, and 8% above 700. The ACT scores were 12% below 21, 23% between 21 and 23, 30% between 24 and 26, 17% between 27 and 28, and 17% above 28. 51% of the current freshmen were in the top fifth of their class; 83% were in the top two fifths. There were 5 National Merit finalists. 41 freshmen graduated first in their class.

Requirements: The SAT or ACT is required. A GPA of 2.0 is required. AP and CLEP credits are accepted. Important factors in the admissions decision are advanced placement or honors courses, extracurricular activities record, and evidence of special talent.

Procedure: Freshmen are admitted to all sessions. Entrance exams should be taken in the spring of the junior year or the fall of the senior year. There is a rolling admissions plan. Application deadlines are open. Application fee is $35. Applications are accepted on-line. A waiting list is maintained.

Financial Aid: 64% of all full-time freshmen and 57% of continuing full-time students received need-based aid. The average freshman award was $20,164, with $14,179 ($23,950 maximum) from need-based scholarships or need-based grants; $4,660 ($7,000 maximum) from need-based self-help aid (loans and jobs); $15,700 ($31,894 maximum) from non-need-based athletic scholarships; and $8,388 ($23,950 maximum) from other non-need-based awards and non-need-based scholarships. 22% of undergraduate students work part-time. Average annual earnings from campus work are $1142. Bradley is a member of CSS. The FAFSA is required. The deadline for filing freshman financial aid applications for fall entry is March 1.

Computers: Students have access to high-speed wired networking from residence halls, the library, and other public spaces such as meeting rooms. There are approximately 2,000 computers available for student use in public and academic labs. All students may access the system. 24 hours a day. There are no time limits and no fees.

Waltham, MA 02454

(781) 736-3500
(800) 622-0622; (781) 736-3536

Full-time: 1425 men, 1795 women	**Faculty:** I, av$
Part-time: 5 men, 15 women	**Ph.D.s:** 96%
Graduate: 1055 men, 1050 women	**Student/Faculty:** n/av
Year: semesters, summer session	**Tuition:** $40,500
Application Deadline: see profile	**Room & Board:** $11,200
Freshman Class: n/av	
SAT or ACT: required	**MOST COMPETITIVE**

Brandeis University, founded in 1948, is a private liberal arts institution. Figures in the above capsule and this profile are approximate. There are 4 graduate schools. The 3 libraries contain 1.2 million volumes, 950,610 microform items, and 39,201 audio/video tapes/CDs/DVDs, and subscribe to 38,393 periodicals including electronic. Computerized library services include interlibrary loans, database searching, Internet access, and laptop Internet portals. Special learning facilities include a learning resource center, art gallery, radio station, TV station, astronomical observatory, cultural center, treasure hall, art museum, and audiovisual center. The 235-acre campus is in a suburban area 10 miles west of Boston. Including any residence halls, there are 88 buildings.

Programs of Study: Brandeis confers B.A. and B.S. degrees. Master's and doctoral degrees are also awarded. Bachelor's degrees are awarded in AGRICULTURE (environmental studies), BIOLOGICAL SCIENCE (biochemistry, biology/biological science, biophysics, and neurosciences), COMMUNICATIONS AND THE ARTS (American literature, art history and appreciation, classics, comparative literature, dramatic arts, English literature, French, German, Greek (classical), linguistics, music, Russian languages and literature, and Spanish), COMPUTER AND PHYSICAL SCIENCE (chemistry, computer science, mathematics, and physics), HEALTH PROFESSIONS (health science), SOCIAL SCIENCE (African American studies, American studies, anthropology, classical/ancient civilization, East Asian studies, economics, European studies, history, interdisciplinary studies, international studies, Islamic studies, Italian studies, Judaic studies, Latin American studies, Middle Eastern studies, Near Eastern studies, philosophy, political science/government, psychology, sociology, and women's studies). Biology, history, and politics are the strongest academically. Economics, psychology, and international studies are the largest.

Special: Students may pursue interdepartmental programs in 18 different fields. Students may cross-register with Boston, Wellesley, Babson, and Bentley Colleges and Boston and Tufts Universities. Study abroad is possible in 69 countries. Internships are available in virtually every field, and work-study is also available. Dual and student-designed majors can be arranged. The university also offers credit by exam, nondegree study, and pass/fail options. Opportunities for early acceptance to area medical schools are offered. There are 4 national honor societies, including Phi Beta Kappa, a freshman honors program, and 51 departmental honors programs.

Admissions: There were 32 National Merit finalists in a recent year. 19 freshmen graduated first in their class.

Requirements: The SAT or ACT is required. In addition, Brandeis requires the SAT Reasoning test with Writing and 2 SAT Subject tests of different subjects. Students may submit the ACT with writing as a substitute for the SAT Reasoning test and SAT Subject tests. Applicants should prepare with 4 years of high school

English, 3 each of foreign language and math, and at least 1 each of science and social studies. An essay is required, and an interview is recommended. AP credits are accepted. Important factors in the admissions decision are advanced placement or honors courses, recommendations by school officials, and extracurricular activities record.

Procedure: Freshmen are admitted fall and spring. Entrance exams should be taken by January of the senior year. There are early decision and deferred admissions plans. Check with the school for current application deadlines. The fall 2009 application fee was $55. Applications are accepted on-line. A waiting list is maintained.

Financial Aid: In a recent year, 53% of all full-time freshmen and 47% of continuing full-time students received some form of financial aid. 41% of all full-time freshmen and 45% of continuing full-time students received need-based aid. The average freshman award was $27,354. 40% of undergraduate students work part-time. Average annual earnings from campus work are $1588. The average financial indebtedness of a recent graduate was $22,381. Brandeis is a member of CSS. The CSS/Profile, the FAFSA, and copies of student and parent income tax returns for matriculating students are required. Check with the school for current application deadlines.

Computers: Wireless access is available. Wireless connectivity is campus-wide. All students may access the system. There are no time limits and no fees.

BRIGHAM YOUNG UNIVERSITY

Provo, UT 84602	(801) 422-2500; (801) 422-0005
Full-time: 26,910 men and women	**Faculty:** n/av
Part-time: 2670 men and women	**Ph.D.s:** 98%
Graduate: 2000 men, 1300 women	**Student/Faculty:** n/av
Year: quarters, summer session	**Tuition:** $4400 ($8800)
Application Deadline: see profile	**Room & Board:** $6800
Freshman Class: n/av	
ACT: required	**VERY COMPETITIVE**

Brigham Young University, founded in 1875, is a private university affiliated with the Church of Jesus Christ of Latter-day Saints. The university follows a semester calendar with spring and summer terms. Tuition figures in the above capsule apply to members of the Latter-day Saints community; the parenthetical figure applies to nonmembers. Figures in the above capsule and this profile are approximate. There are 10 undergraduate schools and 1 graduate school. In addition to regional accreditation, BYU has baccalaureate program accreditation with AACSB, ABET, ACCE, ACEJMC, ADA, ASLA, CSAB, CSWE, NASAD, NASDTEC, NASM, NCATE, NLN, and NRPA. The 2 libraries contain 3.5 million volumes, 3.3 million microform items, and 195,431 audio/video tapes/CDs/DVDs, and subscribe to 198,871 periodicals including electronic. Computerized library services include interlibrary loans, database searching, Internet access, and laptop Internet portals. Special learning facilities include a learning resource center, art gallery, natural history museum, planetarium, radio station, TV station, archeological museum, earth science museum, reading and writing labs, and math, language, and computer labs. The 557-acre campus is in a suburban area 45 miles south of Salt Lake City. Including any residence halls, there are 330 buildings.

Programs of Study: BYU confers B.A., B.S., B.F.A., B.G.S., B.M., and B.Mus. degrees. Master's and doctoral degrees are also awarded. Bachelor's degrees are awarded in AGRICULTURE (agricultural business management, environmental studies, plant science, and wildlife management), BIOLOGICAL SCIENCE (biochemistry, bioinformatics, biology/biological science, biophysics, biotechnology, botany, microbiology, molecular biology, neurosciences, nutrition, physiology, plant genetics, and plant physiology), BUSINESS (accounting, business administration and management, management information systems, management science, marketing management, recreation and leisure services, and tourism), COMMUNICATIONS AND THE ARTS (advertising, animation, art, art history and appreciation, audio technology, Chinese, classical languages, classics, communications, comparative literature, dance, dramatic arts, English, fine arts, French, German, graphic design, Greek, illustration, industrial design, Italian, Japanese, jazz, Korean, Latin, linguistics, literature, media arts, music, music performance, music technology, music theory and composition, musical theater, performing arts, photography, Portuguese, public relations, Russian, Spanish, studio art, and visual and performing arts), COMPUTER AND PHYSICAL SCIENCE (actuarial science, astronomy, chemistry, computer science, geology, information sciences and systems, mathematics, physics, and statistics), EDUCATION (art education, dance education, drama education, early childhood education, elementary education, English education, home economics education, mathematics education, music education, science education, social science education, special education, and technical education), ENGINEERING AND ENVIRONMENTAL DESIGN (chemical engineering, city/community/regional planning, civil engineering, computer engineering, construction management, electrical/electronics engineering, electrical/electronics engineering technology, environmental design, food services technology, landscape architecture/design, manufacturing engineering, manufacturing technology, and mechanical engineering), HEALTH PROFESSIONS (clinical science, exercise science, health science, nursing, and speech pathology/audiology), SOCIAL SCIENCE (American studies, anthropology, archeology, Asian/American studies, Asian/Oriental studies, classical/ancient civilization, dietetics, economics, family/consumer studies, food science, geography, history, human development, humanities, international relations, Latin American studies, Middle Eastern studies, Near Eastern studies, philosophy, political science/government, psychology, social work, and sociology). Engineering, accounting, and business are the strongest academically. Business, communications, and exercise science are the largest.

Special: Brigham Young offers cooperative programs, national and international internships, study abroad in 55 countries, a Washington semester, dual majors, nondegree study, and credit for life and work experience. There are 22 national honor societies, including Phi Beta Kappa, a freshman honors program, and 100 departmental honors programs.

Requirements: The ACT is required. In addition, applicants must be graduates of an accredited secondary school. The GED is accepted. The school recommends that applicants complete 4 years of English, 3 years of math, and 2 courses in foreign language, lab science, history, and literature or writing. Essays and letters of recommendation are required with the application. AP and CLEP credits are accepted. Important factors in the admissions decision are advanced placement or honors courses, recommendations by school officials, and evidence of special talent.

Procedure: Freshmen are admitted to all sessions. Entrance exams should be taken by December of the senior year. There are early admissions, deferred admissions, and rolling admissions plans. Check with the school for current application deadlines. The application fee is $35. Applications are accepted on-line.

Financial Aid: The FAFSA is required. Contact the school for current application deadlines.

Computers: Wireless access is available. 4658 computers are available for student use, 847 of which are universally available for student use; the rest are controlled by colleges or departments. Students also have access to 5 supercomputers for research purposes. All students may access the system any time. There are no time limits and no fees. Students enrolled in accounting, business, and law school must have a personal computer.

BRIGHAM YOUNG UNIVERSITY/HAWAII
Laie, HI 96762   **(808) 675-3731; (808) 675-3741**

Full-time: 950 men, 1205 women	**Faculty:** n/av
Part-time: 100 men, 155 women	**Ph.D.s:** 60%
Graduate: none	**Student/Faculty:** n/av
Year: semesters, summer session	**Tuition:** $6496
Application Deadline: see profile	**Room & Board:** $7234
Freshman Class: n/av	
SAT: recommended	**ACT:** 23 **VERY COMPETITIVE**

BYU-Hawai'I is a private, comprehensive undergraduate institution that educates 2,400 students each year from 70 countries in Asia, the Pacific, the U.S., and other parts of the world. The figures in the above capsule and in this profile are approximate. There are 4 undergraduate schools. In addition to regional accreditation, BYU - Hawai'i has baccalaureate program accreditation with NCATE. The library contains 21,004 volumes, 450,000 microform items, and 9,538 audio/video tapes/CDs/DVDs, and subscribes to 17,000 periodicals including electronic. Computerized library services include interlibrary loans, database searching, Internet access, and laptop Internet portals. Special learning facilities include a learning resource center, art gallery, natural history museum, the nearby Polynesian Cultural Center, which houses an art collection and an artifact collection, provides valuable research opportunities for students in related programs. The 200-acre campus is in a rural area 38 miles from Honolulu. Including any residence halls, there are 42 buildings.

Programs of Study: BYU - Hawai'i confers B.A., B.S., B.F.A., and B.S.W. degrees. Bachelor's degrees are awarded in BIOLOGICAL SCIENCE (biology/biological science), BUSINESS (accounting, hospitality management services, international business management, and tourism), COMMUNICATIONS AND THE ARTS (art, English, fine arts, and music), COMPUTER AND PHYSICAL SCIENCE (computer science, information sciences and systems, and mathematics), EDUCATION (art education, business education, elementary education, English education, mathematics education, science education, social science education, special education, and teaching English as a second/foreign language (TESOL/TEFOL)), HEALTH PROFESSIONS (predentistry and premedicine), SOCIAL SCIENCE (Hawaiian studies, history, interdisciplinary studies, international studies, Pacific area studies, physical fitness/movement, political science/government, psychology, and social work). International business management, accounting, hospitality and tourism management are the largest.

Special: BYUH offers work-study programs with the Polynesian Cultural Center, internships, cooperative programs in most majors, non-degree study, student-designed majors in interdisciplinary studies, and pass/fail options. There are 5 national honor societies and a freshman honors program.

Requirements: The ACT is required. The SAT is recommended. In addition, applicants should be high school graduates. Home-schooled and other non-traditional students should call for more information. A GPA of 2.0 is required. AP and CLEP credits are accepted. Important factors in the admissions decision are geographical diversity, recommendations by alumni, and personality/intangible qualities.

Procedure: Freshmen are admitted to all sessions. Entrance exams should be taken prior to the application deadline. There is a deferred admissions plan. Applications should be filed by February 15 for fall entry, October 1 for winter entry, February 15 for spring entry, and February 15 for summer entry, along with a $35 fee. Notifications are sent April 1. Applications are accepted on-line.

Financial Aid: The FAFSA is required. Check with the school for current application deadlines.

Computers: Wireless access is available. All students may access the system. The system is available 24 hours a day via personally owned computers. The main computing labs are open until midnight. There are no time limits and no fees.

BROWN UNIVERSITY
Providence, RI 02912 (401) 863-2378; (401) 863-9300

Full-time: 2858 men, 3138 women	**Faculty:** 686; I, +$
Part-time: 10 men, 7 women	**Ph.D.s:** 95%
Graduate: 952 men, 880 women	**Student/Faculty:** 9 to 1
Year: semesters, summer session	**Tuition:** $38,848
Application Deadline: January 1	**Room & Board:** $10,280
Freshman Class: 24,988 applied, 2790 accepted, 1495 enrolled	
SAT CR/M/W: 710/720/720	**ACT:** 32 **MOST COMPETITIVE**

Brown University, founded in 1764, is a coeducational liberal arts institution and a member of the Ivy League. There are 2 graduate schools. In addition to regional accreditation, Brown has baccalaureate program accreditation with ABET. The 6 libraries contain 3.6 million volumes, 1 million microform items, and 28,000 audio/video tapes/CDs/DVDs, and subscribe to 16,000 periodicals including electronic. Computerized library services include interlibrary loans, database searching, and Internet access. Special learning facilities include a learning resource center, art gallery, planetarium, radio station, TV station, and an anthropology museum. The 140-acre campus is in an urban area 45 miles south of Boston. Including any residence halls, there are 243 buildings.

Programs of Study: Brown confers A.B. and Sc.B. degrees. Master's and doctoral degrees are also awarded. Bachelor's degrees are awarded in BIOLOGICAL SCIENCE (biochemistry, biology/biological science, biophysics, marine biology, molecular biology, and neurosciences), BUSINESS (entrepreneurial studies), COMMUNICATIONS AND THE ARTS (American literature, art, art history and appreciation, classics, comparative literature, English, linguistics, media arts, music, performing arts, Portuguese, and visual and performing arts), COMPUTER AND PHYSICAL SCIENCE (applied mathematics, chemical physics, chemistry, computer science, geology, mathematics, physics, and statistics), EDUCATION (education), ENGINEERING AND ENVIRONMENTAL DESIGN (architectural history, architectural technology, architecture, computational sciences, engineering, and environmental science), HEALTH PROFESSIONS (biomedical science and community health work), SOCIAL SCIENCE (African studies, African American studies, American studies, anthropology, archeology, classical/ancient civilization, cognitive science, developmental psychology, East Asian studies, economics, ethnic studies, French studies, gender studies, German area studies, Hispanic American studies, history, human development, international relations, Italian studies, Judaic studies, Latin American studies, medieval studies, Middle Eastern studies, philosophy, political science/government, psychology, public administration, religion, Russian and Slavic studies, science and society, sociology, South Asian studies, and urban studies). Biological sciences, international relations, and history are the largest.

Special: Students may cross-register with Rhode Island School of Design or study abroad in any of 50 programs in 15 countries. A combined A.B.-S.C.B. degree is possible in any major field with 5 years of study. Dual and student-designed majors, community internships, and pass/fail options are available. Students may pursue 5-year programs in the arts or sciences or the 8-year program in the liberal medical education continuum or the Brown/RISD dual degree program. There is a Phi Beta Kappa honors program.

Admissions: 11% of the 2009-2010 applicants were accepted. The SAT scores for the 2009-2010 freshman class were: Critical Reading--1% below 500, 9% between 500 and 599, 30% between 600 and 700; and 60% above 700; Math--7% between 500 and 599, 30% between 600 and 700, and 63% above 700; Writing--1% below 500, 5% between 500 and 599, 29% between 600 and 700; and 65% above 700. The ACT scores were 1% between 21 and 23, 9% between 24 and 26, 12% between 27 and 28, and 78% above 29. 97% of the current freshmen were in the top fifth of their class; 100% were in the top two fifths. 152 freshmen graduated first in their class.

Requirements: The SAT or ACT is required. The ACT Optional Writing test is also required, along with any 2 SAT Subject tests. The ACT may be substituted for both the SAT Reasoning and Subject tests. Applicants must be graduates of accredited high schools. Secondary preparation is expected to include courses in English, foreign language, math, lab science, the arts (music or art), and history. A personal essay is required. The high school transcript is a most important criterion for admission. AP credits are accepted. Important factors in the admissions decision are advanced placement or honors courses, evidence of special talent, and recommendations by school officials.

Procedure: Freshmen are admitted in the fall. Entrance exams should be taken in the junior or senior year. There are early decision, early admissions and deferred admissions plans. Early decision applications should be filed by November 1; regular applications, by January 1 for fall entry, along with a $75 fee. Notification of early decision is sent December 15; regular decision, April 1. 563 early decision applications were accepted in 2009-2010. 450 applicants were on the 2009 waiting list; 82 were admitted. Applications are accepted on-line. A waiting list is maintained.

Financial Aid: In 2009-2010, 56% of all full-time freshmen received need-based financial aid. Brown is a member of CSS. The CSS/Profile, FAFSA, and some state forms are required. The priority date for freshman financial aid applications for fall entry is November 1. The deadline for filing freshman financial aid applications for fall entry is February 1.

Computers: Wireless access is available. There are 400 workstations on campus for student use. All students have access to the mainframe. All students may access the system at any time. There are no time limits and no fees.

BRYANT UNIVERSITY

Smithfield, RI 02917-1284

(401) 232-6100
(800) 622-7001; (401) 232-6741

Full-time: 1909 men, 1438 women	**Faculty:** IIB, ++$
Part-time: 64 men, 63 women	**Ph.D.s:** n/av
Graduate: 186 men, 96 women	**Student/Faculty:** n/av
Year: semesters, summer session	**Tuition:** $32,106
Application Deadline: February 1	**Room & Board:** $11,757
Freshman Class: 6253 applied, 2822 accepted, 911 enrolled	
SAT or ACT: required	**HIGHLY COMPETITIVE**

Bryant University, a private, primarily residential institution founded in 1863, offers degrees in business, liberal arts, and technology. There are 2 undergraduate schools and 1 graduate school. In addition to regional accreditation, Bryant has baccalaureate program accreditation with AACSB. The library contains 153,000 volumes, 14,500 microform items, and 1279 audio/video tapes/CDs/DVDs, and subscribes to 30,300 periodicals including electronic. Computerized library services include interlibrary loans, database searching, Internet access, and laptop Internet portals. Special learning facilities include a learning resource center, a communication complex housing an all-digital television studio and radio station, a learning/language lab, a writing center, an academic center, a center for international business, a center for information and technology, and a financial market trading floor. The 420-acre campus is in a suburban area 12 miles northwest of Providence. Including any residence halls, there are 46 buildings.

Programs of Study: Bryant confers B.A, B.S., B.S.B.A., B.Sc.I.T., and B.S.I.B. degrees. Master's degrees are also awarded. Bachelor's degrees are awarded in BUSINESS (accounting, banking and finance, business administration and management, international business management, management science, and marketing management), COMMUNICATIONS AND THE ARTS (communications and English), COMPUTER AND PHYSICAL SCIENCE (actuarial science, computer security and information assurance, and information sciences and systems), SOCIAL SCIENCE (economics, history, international studies, political science/government, psychology, and sociology). Marketing, management, and accounting are the largest.

Special: Bryant offers internships, study abroad in 21 countries, on-campus work-study programs, dual majors, credit for military experience, and minors in 16 liberal arts disciplines and 6 business disciplines. There are 4 national honor societies and a freshman honors program.

Admissions: 45% of the 2009-2010 applicants were accepted.

Requirements: The SAT or ACT is required. In addition, applicants must be graduates of an accredited secondary school or have a GED certificate. A total of 16 Carnegie units is required, including 4 years of English, 4 of math (minimum of 1 year beyond algebra II), and 2 years each of social studies, lab science, and foreign language. An essay is required. A GPA of 3.3 is required. AP and CLEP credits are accepted.

Procedure: Freshmen are admitted fall and spring. Entrance exams should be taken before January of the senior year. There are early decision, early admissions, and deferred admissions plans. Early decision applications should be filed by November 15; regular applications, by February 1 for fall entry. The fall 2009 application fee was $50. Notification of early decision is sent January 2; regular decision, in mid-March. 140 early decision candidates were accepted for the 2009-2010 class. 720 applicants were on the 2009 waiting list; 162 were admitted. Applications are accepted on-line. 720 applicants were on a recent waiting list, 162 were accepted.

Financial Aid: In 2009-2010, 67% of all full-time freshmen and 66% of continuing full-time students received some form of financial aid. 56% of all full-time freshmen and 58% of continuing full-time students received need-based aid. The average freshman award was $21,021. Need-based scholarships or need-based grants averaged $11,097; need-based self-help aid (loans and jobs) averaged $5619; non-need-based athletic scholarships averaged $10,906; and other non-need-based awards and non-need-based scholarships averaged $11,870. 20% of undergraduate students work part-time. Average annual earnings from campus work are $1580. The average financial indebtedness of the 2009 graduate was $34,628. Bryant is a member of CSS. The FAFSA is required. The deadline for filing freshman financial aid applications for fall entry is February 15.

Computers: Wireless access is available. All freshmen are provided with a wireless labtop and can access the Internet, e-mail, Blackboard (course management), Banner (financial), and web services at anytime. These services can also be accessed on any of the 539 accessible PCs on campus or a student-owned computer. All students may access the system. There are no time limits and no fees. An IBM labtop is provided to all freshmen.

BRYN MAWR COLLEGE

Bryn Mawr, PA 19010-2899   **(610) 526-5152**
                                          (800) 262-1885; (610) 526-7471

Full-time: 1283 women	**Faculty:** 153; IIA, +$
Part-time: 24 women	**Ph.D.s:** 83%
Graduate: 99 men, 365 women	**Student/Faculty:** 8 to 1
Year: semesters, summer session	**Tuition:** $38,934
Application Deadline: January 15	**Room & Board:** $12,000
Freshman Class: 2276 applied, 1107 accepted, 362 enrolled	
SAT CR/M/W: 660/630/660	**ACT:** 28 **MOST COMPETITIVE**

Bryn Mawr College, founded in 1885, is an independent liberal arts institution, primarily for women. The Graduate School of Social Work and Research, the Graduate School of the Arts and Sciences, and the postbaccalaureate premedical programs are coed. There are 2 graduate schools. The 4 libraries contain 1.2 million volumes, 157,522 microform items, and 5652 audio/video tapes/CDs/DVDs, and subscribe to 1712 periodicals including electronic. Computerized library services include interlibrary loans, database searching, and Internet access. Special learning facilities include a learning resource center, art gallery, radio station, archeological museum, and language learning center with audio, video, and computer technology. The 136-acre campus is in a suburban area 11 miles west of Philadelphia. Including any residence halls, there are 57 buildings.

Programs of Study: Bryn Mawr confers A.B. degrees. Master's and doctoral degrees are also awarded. Bachelor's degrees are awarded in BIOLOGICAL SCIENCE (biology/biological science), COMMUNICATIONS AND THE ARTS (art history and appreciation, classical languages, classics, comparative literature, English, fine arts, French, German, Greek, Italian, Latin, linguistics, music, romance languages and literature, Russian, and Spanish), COMPUTER AND PHYSICAL SCIENCE (astronomy, chemistry, computer science, geology, mathematics, and physics), SOCIAL SCIENCE (anthropology, archeology, East Asian studies, economics, history, philosophy, political science/government, psychology, religion, sociology, and urban studies). English, psychology, and math are the largest.

Special: Students may cross-register with Haverford and Swarthmore Colleges and the University of Pennsylvania. Bryn Mawr sponsors more than 100 grants and internships for summer study in a wide range of disciplines and sponsors/cosponsors study abroad in 27 countries. Student-designed and dual majors are possible. Pass/fail options, work-study programs, a 3-2 degree in engineering with the California Institute of Technology, and a 3-2 degree in city and regional planning with the University of Pennsylvania are offered.

Admissions: 49% of the 2009-2010 applicants were accepted. The SAT scores for the 2009-2010 freshman class were: Critical Reading--2% below 500, 19% between 500 and 599, 51% between 600 and 700, and 28% above 700; Math--2% below 500, 29% between 500 and 599, 48% between 600 and 700, and 21% above 700; Writing--19% between 500 and 599, 50% between 600 and 700, and 31% above 700. The ACT scores were 2% below 21, 3% between 21 and 23, 24% between 24 and 26, 23% between 27 and 28, and 48% above 28. 80% of the current freshmen were in the top fifth of their class; 97% were in the top two fifths.

Requirements: The SAT is required. The ACT may be substituted for the SAT. Requirements for admission are 4 years of English, at least 3 years of math (2 of algebra and 1 of geometry), 3 years of a foreign language or 2 years of 2 languages, and 1 year each of science and history. Most applicants have taken at least 3 lab science courses and trigonometry. An essay is required. An interview is strongly recommended. AP credits are accepted. Important factors in the admissions decision are advanced placement or honors courses, evidence of special talent, and extracurricular activities record.

Procedure: Freshmen are admitted fall. Entrance exams should be taken in the spring of the junior year or the fall of the senior year. There are early decision and deferred admissions plans. Early decision applications should be filed by November 15; regular applications, by January 15 for fall entry, along with a $50 fee. Notification of early decision is sent December 15; regular decision, in April. 68 early decision candidates were accepted for the 2009-2010 class. 213 applicants were on the 2009 waiting list; 39 were admitted. Applications are accepted on-line.

Financial Aid: In 2009-2010, 77% of all full-time freshmen and 58% of continuing full-time students received some form of financial aid. 69% of all full-time freshmen and 53% of continuing full-time students received need-based aid. The average freshman award was $36,562. Need-based scholarships or need-based grants averaged $33,108 ; need-based self-help aid (loans and jobs) averaged $4068; and other non-need-based awards and non-need-based scholarships averaged $5700. 74% of undergraduate students work part-time. Average annual earnings from campus work are $1500. The average financial indebtedness of the 2009 graduate was $20,156. Bryn Mawr is a member of CSS. The CSS/Profile, the FAFSA, the prior year's tax returns, the noncustodial parent statement, and the business/farm supplement are required. The deadline for filing freshman financial aid applications for fall entry is February 2.

Computers: Wireless access is available. The libraries, campus center, computing center, some academic buildings, and many dorm living rooms have campus wireless networking. All public, academic, and residential buildings on campus are Ethernet wired to provide students with a connection to the campus network and the Internet. All students may access the system every day. There are no time limits and no fees.

BUCKNELL UNIVERSITY

Lewisburg, PA 17837   **(570) 577-1101; (570) 577-3538**

Full-time: 1719 men, 1804 women	**Faculty:** 345; IIA, +$
Part-time: 10 men, 10 women	**Ph.D.s:** 97%
Graduate: 46 men, 84 women	**Student/Faculty:** 10 to 1
Year: semesters, , summer session	**Tuition:** $40,816
Application Deadline: January 15	**Room & Board:** $9504
Freshman Class: 7572 applied, 2263 accepted, 920 enrolled	
SAT CR/M/W: 640/670/660	**ACT:** 29 **MOST COMPETITIVE**

Bucknell University, established in 1846, is a private independent institution offering undergraduate and graduate programs in arts, music, education, humanities, management, engineering, sciences, and social sciences. There are 2 undergraduate schools and one graduate school. In addition to regional accreditation, Bucknell has baccalaureate program accreditation with ABET, CSAB, and NASM. The library contains 818,837 volumes, 49,958 microform items, and 22,427 audio/video tapes/CDs/DVDs, and subscribes to 36,242 periodicals including electronic. Computerized library services include interlibrary loans, database searching, Internet access, and laptop Internet portals. Special learning facilities include a learning resource center, art gallery, radio station, an outdoor natural area, greenhouse, primate facility, observatory, photography lab, race and gender resource center, library resources training lab, electronic classroom, multimedia lab, conference center, performing arts center, and multicultural, writing, craft, and poetry centers, herbarium, and engineering structural test lab. The 450-acre campus is in a small town 75 miles north of Harrisburg. Including any residence halls, there are 123 buildings.

Programs of Study: Bucknell confers B.A., B.S., B.S.B.A., B.S.B.E., B.S.C.E., B.S.Ch.E., B.S.C.S.E., B.S.Ed., B.S.E.E., and B.Mus. degrees. Master's degrees are also awarded. Bachelor's degrees are awarded in AGRICULTURE (animal science), BIOLOGICAL SCIENCE (biochemistry, biology/biological science, cell biology, and neurosciences), BUSINESS (accounting and business administration and management), COMMUNICATIONS AND THE ARTS (art, art history and appreciation, classics, dramatic arts, English, fine arts, French, German, music, music history and appreciation, music performance, music theory and composition, Russian, Spanish, and visual and performing arts), COMPUTER AND PHYSICAL SCIENCE (chemistry, computer science, geology, mathematics, physics, and quantitative methods), EDUCATION (early childhood education, education, educational statistics and research, elementary education, music education, and secondary education), ENGINEERING AND ENVIRONMENTAL DESIGN (biomedical engineering, chemical engineering, civil engineering, computer engineering, electrical/electronics engineering, engineering, environmental science, and mechanical engineering), SOCIAL SCIENCE (anthropology, East Asian studies, economics, geography, history, humanities, interdisciplinary studies, international relations, Latin American studies, philosophy, political science/government, psychology, religion, sociology, and women's studies). Humanities, biology, engineering, and English are the strongest academically. Biology, management, and mechanical engineering are the largest.

Special: Bucknell offers internships, study abroad in more than 60 countries, a Washington semester, a 5-year B.A.-B.S. degree in arts and engineering, a 3-2 engineering degree, and dual and student-designed majors. An interdisciplinary major in animal behavior is offered through the biology and psychology departments. Nondegree study is possible, and a pass/fail grading option is offered in some courses. The Residential College program offers opportunities for an academic-residential mix and faculty-student collaborative learning. Undergraduate research opportunities are available in the humanities/social sciences and the sciences and engineering. There are 23 national honor societies, including Phi Beta Kappa, and 55 departmental honors programs.

Admissions: 30% of the 2009-2010 applicants were accepted. The SAT scores for the 2009-2010 freshman class were: Critical Reading--2% below 500, 21% between 500 and 599, 57% between 600 and 700, and 20 above 700; Math--2% below 500, 10% between 500 and 599, 54% between 600 and 700, and 34 above 700; Writing--3% below 500, 18% between 500 and 599, 54% between 600 and 700, and 25 above 700. The ACT scores were 1% below 21, 4% between 21 and 23, 15% between 24 and 26, 21% between 27 and 28, and 59% above 28. 80% of the current freshmen were in the top fifth of their class.

Requirements: The SAT or ACT is required. The ACT Optional Writing test is also required. In addition, applicants must graduate from an accredited secondary school or have a GED. 16 units must be earned, including 4 in English, 3 in math, and 2 each in history, science, social studies, and a foreign language. An essay is required, and an interview is recommended. Music applicants are required to audition. A portfolio is recommended for art applicants. AP and CLEP credits are accepted. Important factors in the admissions decision are advanced placement or honors courses, evidence of special talent, and extracurricular activities record.

Procedure: Freshmen are admitted fall. Entrance exams should be taken before January 1. There are early decision, deferred admissions plan. Early decision applications should be filed by November 15; regular applications, by January 15 for fall entry. The fall 2008 application fee was $60. Notification of early decision is sent December 15; regular decision, April 1. Applications are accepted online. 2073 applicants were on a recent waiting list, 23 were accepted.

Financial Aid: In 2009-2010, 59% of all full-time freshmen and 51% of continuing full-time students received some form of financial aid. 47% of all full-time freshmen and 46% of continuing full-time students received need-based aid. The average freshmen award was $26,900. 40% of undergraduate students work part-time. Average annual earnings from campus work are $1500. The average financial indebtedness of the 2009 graduate was $18,800. Bucknell is a member of CSS. The CSS/Profile and FAFSA, and noncustodial parent's statement are required. The deadline for filing freshman financial aid applications for fall entry is January 1.

Computers: Wireless access is available. All spaces in academic, administrative, and co-curricular locations (such as lounges) in residence halls and most outdoor spaces are wireless. There are 970 student accessible PCs throughout campus, some of which are located in 42 labs and classrooms. All students may access the system. 24 hours per day, 7 days per week. There are no time limits and no fees. It is strongly recommended that all students have a personal computer.

BUTLER UNIVERSITY

Indianapolis, IN 46208

(317) 940-8100
(888) 940-8100; (317) 940-8150

Full-time: 1518 men, 2379 women	**Faculty:** 288; IIA, -$
Part-time: 27 men, 33 women	**Ph.D.s:** 78%
Graduate: 268 men, 280 women	**Student/Faculty:** 14 to 1
Year: semesters, summer session	**Tuition:** $29,246
Application Deadline: open	**Room & Board:** $9740
Freshman Class: 6246 applied, 4928 accepted, 945 enrolled	
SAT CR/M/W: 570/600/570	**ACT:** 28 **VERY COMPETITIVE+**

Butler University, founded in 1855, is an independent, private institution offering programs in liberal arts and sciences, business administration, fine arts, pharmacy, health sciences, and education. There are 5 undergraduate schools and 5 graduate schools. In addition to regional accreditation, Butler has baccalaureate program accreditation with AACSB, ACPE, NASM, and NCATE. The 2 libraries contain 339,944 volumes, 90,000 microform items, and 17,536 audio/video tapes/CDs/DVDs, and subscribe to 33,627 periodicals including electronic. Computerized library services include interlibrary loans and database searching. Special learning facilities include a learning resource center, planetarium, TV station, and observatory. The 290-acre campus is in a suburban area 5 miles from downtown Indianapolis. Including any residence halls, there are 19 buildings.

Programs of Study: Butler confers B.A., B.S., B.F.A., B.M., B.S.H.S., and B.S.P. degrees. Master's degrees are also awarded. Bachelor's degrees are awarded in BIOLOGICAL SCIENCE (biology/biological science), BUSINESS (accounting, banking and finance, international business management, management information systems, and marketing/retailing/merchandising), COMMUNICATIONS AND THE ARTS (arts administration/management, communications, dance, dramatic arts, English, French, German, Greek, journalism, Latin, media arts, music, music business management, music performance, music theory and composition, performing arts, Spanish, and speech/debate/rhetoric), COMPUTER AND PHYSICAL SCIENCE (actuarial science, chemistry, computer science, mathematics, physics, and software engineering), EDUCATION (elementary education, music education, and secondary education), HEALTH PROFESSIONS (health science, pharmacy, and speech pathology/audiology), SOCIAL SCIENCE (anthropology, criminal justice, economics, history, international studies, philosophy, political science/government, psychology, religion, science and society, sociology, and urban studies). Pharmacy, chemistry, and biology are the strongest academically. Business, education, and pharmacy are the largest.

Special: Butler offers cross-registration with the 4 other members of the Consortium for Urban Education, co-op programs in business administration, and internships in pharmacy, arts administration, and business programs. A 3-2 degree program in engineering with Purdue University, extensive study-abroad programs, and work-study programs are available. There are dual majors including French, German, and Spanish combined with business studies, student-designed majors, a general studies degree, pass/fail options, and nondegree study. There are 5 national honor societies and a freshman honors program.

Admissions: 79% of the 2009-2010 applicants were accepted. The SAT scores for the 2009-2010 freshman class were: Critical Reading--15% below 500, 46% between 500 and 599, 32% between 600 and 700, and 7% above 700; Math--11% below 500, 38% between 500 and 599, 42% between 600 and 700, and 9% above 700; Writing--16% below 500, 47% between 500 and 599, 32% between 600 and

700, and 5% above 700. The ACT scores were 3% below 21, 12% between 21 and 23, 24% between 24 and 26, 23% between 27 and 28, and 38% above 28. 72% of the current freshmen were in the top fifth of their class; 94% were in the top two fifths. There were 5 National Merit finalists. 56 freshmen graduated first in their class.

Requirements: The SAT or ACT is required. In addition, applicants should be graduates of an accredited secondary school, but Butler will consider talented or gifted students without a diploma. Students should have earned at least 17 academic units, based on 4 years of English, 3 each of math and lab science, 2 each of a foreign language and history/social science, and the rest of electives. An audition is required for dance, music, and theater majors, and an interview is required for radio/TV majors. Butler requires applicants to be in the upper 50% of their class. A GPA of 2.0 is required. AP and CLEP credits are accepted. Important factors in the admissions decision are advanced placement or honors courses, evidence of special talent, and leadership record.

Procedure: Freshmen are admitted to all sessions. Entrance exams should be taken during the junior year. There are deferred admissions and rolling admissions plans. Application deadlines are open. The application fee is $35. Notification is sent on a rolling basis. Applications are accepted on-line. 54 applicants were on a recent waiting list, 10 were accepted.

Financial Aid: 40% of undergraduate students work part-time. Average annual earnings from campus work are $1200. Butler is a member of CSS. The FAFSA and the college's own financial statement are required. The deadline for filing freshman financial aid applications for fall entry is March 1.

Computers: Wireless access is available. All students may access the system 24 hours a day. There are no time limits and no fees. It is strongly recommended that all students have a personal computer.

CALIFORNIA COLLEGE OF THE ARTS

San Francisco, CA 94107   (415) 703-9523
(800) 447-1ART; (415) 703-9539

Full-time: 495 men, 794 women	**Faculty:** 81
Part-time: 47 men, 68 women	**Ph.D.s:** 67%
Graduate: 166 men, 261 women	**Student/Faculty:** 16 to 1
Year: semesters, summer session	**Tuition:** $33,254
Application Deadline: February 1	**Room & Board:** $9650
Freshman Class: 988 applied, 884 accepted, 212 enrolled	
SAT CR/M/W: 530/540/520	**ACT:** 22 SPECIAL

California College of the Arts, founded in 1907, offers 20 undergraduate programs and 7 graduate majors in the areas of fine arts, architecture, design, and writing. There are no undergraduate schools and 7 graduate schools. In addition to regional accreditation, CCA has baccalaureate program accreditation with FIDER, NAAB, and NASAD. The 2 libraries contain 39,000 volumes, 50 microform items, and 520 audio/video tapes/CDs/DVDs, and subscribe to 340 periodicals including electronic. Computerized library services include interlibrary loans and database searching. Special learning facilities include a learning resource center, art gallery, and material resource center. The 4-acre campus is in an urban area. Including any residence halls, there are 18 buildings.

Programs of Study: CCA confers B.A., B.Arch, and B.F.A. degrees. Master's degrees are also awarded. Bachelor's degrees are awarded in COMMUNICATIONS AND THE ARTS (art, ceramic art and design, creative writing, film arts, glass, graphic design, illustration, industrial design, metal/jewelry, painting, pho-

tography, printmaking, sculpture, and visual and performing arts), ENGINEER-
ING AND ENVIRONMENTAL DESIGN (architecture, furniture design, and interior design), SOCIAL SCIENCE (fashion design and technology and textiles
and clothing). Graphic design, illustration, and architecture are the largest.

Special: Cross-registration is permitted with Mills and Holy Names Colleges in
Oakland. Internships are required for some majors and strongly encouraged for
others. Study abroad in 11 countries, student-designed majors, and nondegree
study are possible. The Association of Independent Colleges of Art and Design
Mobility Program is also offered.

Admissions: 89% of the 2009-2010 applicants were accepted. The SAT scores
for the 2009-2010 freshman class were: Critical Reading--33% below 500, 35%
between 500 and 599, 29% between 600 and 700, and 3 above 700; Math--30%
below 500, 40% between 500 and 599, 24% between 600 and 700, and 6 above
700; Writing--39% below 500, 37% between 500 and 599, 19% between 600 and
700, and 5 above 700.

Requirements: Graduation from an accredited secondary school is required; a
GED is accepted. An essay, portfolio, and 2 letters of recommendation are required. An interview is optional. A GPA of 2.0 is required. AP credits are accepted. Important factors in the admissions decision are evidence of special talent,
recommendations by school officials, and extracurricular activities record.

Procedure: Freshmen are admitted fall and spring. There is a rolling admissions
plan. Applications should be filed by February 1 for fall entry and October 1 for
spring entry, along with a $60 fee. Notification is sent on a rolling basis. Applica-
tions are accepted on-line.

Financial Aid: In 2009-2010, 77% of all full-time freshmen received some form
of financial aid. 59% of all full-time freshmen received need-based aid. The average freshmen award was $24,315. All undergraduate students work part-time.
Average annual earnings from campus work are $1882. The average financial in-
debtedness of the 2009 graduate was $34,518. The FAFSA and the college's own
financial statement are required. The deadline for filing freshman financial aid
applications for fall entry is March 1.

Computers: Wireless access is available. There are 295 workstations available
for student use, and the campuses support a wireless network. All students may
access the system. There are no time limits and no fees. A MacBook Pro is recommended.

CALIFORNIA INSTITUTE OF TECHNOLOGY
Pasadena, CA 91125   (626) 395-6341; (626) 683-3026

Full-time: 610 men, 311 women	**Faculty:** 332
Part-time: none	**Ph.D.s:** 98%
Graduate: 842 men, 363 women	**Student/Faculty:** 3 to 1
Year: quarters	**Tuition:** $36,984
Application Deadline: January 1	**Room & Board:** $10,755
Freshman Class: 674 accepted, 252 enrolled	
SAT or ACT: required	**MOST COMPETITIVE**

California Institute of Technology, founded in 1891, is a private institution offering programs in engineering, science, and math. There are 6 graduate schools. In
addition to regional accreditation, Caltech has baccalaureate program accreditation with ABET. The 5 libraries contain 624,136 volumes, 10,586 microform
items, and 3,033 audio/video tapes/CDs/DVDs, and subscribe to 2,641 periodicals including electronic. Computerized library services include interlibrary
loans, database searching, and Internet access. Special learning facilities include

a learning resource center. The 124-acre campus is in a suburban area 12 miles northeast of Los Angeles. Including any residence halls, there are 105 buildings.

Programs of Study: Caltech confers B.S. degrees. Master's and doctoral degrees are also awarded. Bachelor's degrees are awarded in BIOLOGICAL SCIENCE (biology/biological science), BUSINESS (business administration and management), COMPUTER AND PHYSICAL SCIENCE (applied mathematics, astrophysics, chemistry, computer mathematics, computer science, geochemistry, geology, geophysics and seismology, mathematics, physics, and planetary and space science), ENGINEERING AND ENVIRONMENTAL DESIGN (chemical engineering, computer engineering, electrical/electronics engineering, engineering and applied science, materials science, and mechanical engineering), HEALTH PROFESSIONS (environmental health science), SOCIAL SCIENCE (economics, history, history of science, philosophy, and political science/government). Engineering, applied science, and physical sciences are the largest.

Special: Caltech offers cross-registration with Scripps College, Occidental College, and Art Center College of Design, various work-study programs, including those with NASA's Jet Propulsion Laboratory, dual majors in any major, and independent studies degrees with faculty-approved student-designed majors. A 3-2 engineering degree is possible with several institutions. Pass/fail options are available for freshmen. A summer undergraduate research fellowship program is offered. Study abroad at University College in London, Cambridge University, and University of Copenhagen, in Denmark is available.

Admissions: The SAT scores for the 2009-2010 freshman class were: Critical Reading--1% between 500 and 599, 23% between 600 and 700, and 76% above 700; Math--100% above 700; Writing--1% between 500 and 599, 28% between 600 and 700, and 71% above 700. The ACT scores were 100% above 28. All off the current freshmen were in the top fifth of their class; all were in the top two fifths. There were 53 National Merit finalists. 85 freshmen graduated first in their class.

Requirements: The SAT or ACT is required. In addition, SAT II: Subject tests in writing, math level II, and one in physics, biology, or chemistry are required. Applicants should have completed 4 years of high school math, 3 of English, 1 each of chemistry and history, and 5 units from other concentrations. Important factors in the admissions decision are advanced placement or honors courses, recommendations by school officials, and evidence of special talent.

Procedure: Freshmen are admitted in the fall. Entrance exams should be taken through December of the senior year. There are early decision and deferred admissions plans,and a non-binding early action plan. Applications should be filed November 1 for early decion; January 1 for fall entry, along with a $65 fee. Notifications are sent Decenber 15 for early decison; April 1, regular decision. Applications are accepted on-line. 556 applicants were on a recent waiting list.

Financial Aid: In 2009-2010, 75% of all full-time freshmen and 67% of continuing full-time students received some form of financial aid. 57% of all full-time freshmen and 55% of continuing full-time students received need-based aid. The average freshmen award was $30,960, with $28,991 ($51,041 maximum) from need-based scholarships or need-based grants and $3,273 ($5,500 maximum) from need-based self-help aid (loans and jobs). The average financial indebtedness of the 2009 graduate was $8,218. Caltech is a member of CSS. The CSS/Profile, FAFSA, the state aid form, and the college's own financial statement are required. The deadline for filing freshman financial aid applications for fall entry is January 15.

Computers: All students may access the system any time. There are no time limits and no fees. It is strongly recommended that all students have a personal computer.

CALIFORNIA INSTITUTE OF THE ARTS
Valencia, CA 91355
(661) 255-1050
(800) 545-ARTS; (661) 253-7710

Full-time: 455 men, 427 women	**Faculty:** n/av
Part-time: 2 men, 4 women	**Ph.D.s:** n/av
Graduate: 229 men, 275 women	**Student/Faculty:** n/av
Year: semesters	**Tuition:** $35406
Application Deadline: January 5	**Room & Board:** $9293
Freshman Class: 3151 applied, 1094 accepted, 506 enrolled	**SPECIAL**

California Institute of the Arts, founded in 1961, is a private, institution offering undergraduate and graduate programs in art, dance, film and video, music, and theater, and graduate majors in directing, integrated media, and writing. There are 6 undergraduate schools and 6 graduate schools. In addition to regional accreditation, Cal-Arts has baccalaureate program accreditation with NASAD and NASM. The library contains 199,935 volumes, 5,124 microform items, and 31,411 audio/ video tapes/CDs/DVDs, and subscribes to 679 periodicals including electronic. Computerized library services include interlibrary loans, database searching, and Internet access. Special learning facilities include a learning resource center, art gallery, radio station, TV station, movie theater, sound stages, scenery construction shops, and slide and film libraries. The 60-acre campus is in a suburban area 30 miles north of Los Angeles. Including any residence halls, there are 3 buildings.

Programs of Study: Cal-Arts confers B.F.A. degrees. Master's degrees are also awarded. Bachelor's degrees are awarded in COMMUNICATIONS AND THE ARTS (animation, dance, film arts, fine arts, graphic design, music, and theater design). Art, music, and acting are the strongest academically. Art, film/video, and theater are the largest.

Special: Cal Arts offers internships with local and national companies, student-designed majors, interdisciplinary studies, study abroad in 6 countries, and a co-operative education program.

Admissions: 35% of the 2009-2010 applicants were accepted.

Requirements: In addition, applicants must be graduates of an accredited secondary school or have a GED certificate. They must submit an official transcript and an essay. Portfolios and auditions are required and an interview is recommended for some programs. AP credits are accepted. Important factors in the admissions decision are evidence of special talent and advanced placement or honors courses.

Procedure: Freshmen are admitted fall and spring. Applications should be filed by January 5 for fall entry and November 15 for spring entry, along with a $70 fee. Notifications are sent April 1. 209 applicants were on a recent waiting list, 60 were accepted.

Financial Aid: In 2009-2010, 77% of all full-time freshmen and 78% of continuing full-time students received some form of financial aid. 66% of all full-time freshmen and 67% of continuing full-time students received need-based aid. The average freshmen award was $30,145, with $14,031 ($34,830 maximum) from need-based scholarships or need-based grants and $6,063 ($12,000 maximum) from need-based self-help aid (loans and jobs). 29% of undergraduate students work part-time. Average annual earnings from campus work are $1230. The average financial indebtedness of the 2009 graduate was $39,286. Cal-Arts is a member of CSS. The FAFSA is required. The priority date for freshman financial aid applications for fall entry is March 2.

Computers: Wireless access is available. Students have access to the Institute network from their dorm rooms, studios, and in the library. They also have access to wireless in key locations within the main building of the Institute. All students may access the system. There are no time limits and no fees. Students enrolled in graphic design must have a personal computer.

CALIFORNIA POLYTECHNIC STATE UNIVERSITY

San Luis Obispo, CA 93407-0005 (805) 756-2311
(805) 756-5400

Full-time: 9899 men, 7724 women	**Faculty:** 824; IIA, +$
Part-time: 397 men, 282 women	**Ph.D.s:** 82%
Graduate: 541 men, 482 women	**Student/Faculty:** 21 to 1
Year: quarters	**Tuition:** $6198 ($17,358)
Application Deadline: November 30	**Room & Board:** $9623
Freshman Class: 31489 applied, 11737 accepted, 3908 enrolled	
SAT or ACT: required	**HIGHLY COMPETITIVE**

California Polytechnic State University, founded in 1901, is a public institution that is part of the California State University system. It offers programs in agriculture, architecture and environmental design, business, education, engineering, liberal arts, sciences and math, and preprofessional studies. There are 6 undergraduate schools. In addition to regional accreditation, Cal Poly has baccalaureate program accreditation with AACSB, ABET, ACCE, ADA, ASLA, NAAB, NASAD, NASM, NRPA, and SAF. The library contains 634,400 volumes, 1.3 million microform items, and 48,300 audio/video tapes/CDs/DVDs, and subscribes to 99,700 periodicals including electronic. Computerized library services include interlibrary loans, database searching, and Internet access. Special learning facilities include a learning resource center, art gallery, radio station, and TV station. The 6000-acre campus is in a suburban area 200 miles north of Los Angeles and 230 miles south of San Francisco. Including any residence halls, there are 106 buildings.

Programs of Study: Cal Poly confers B.A., B.S.,B.Arch, B.F.A., and B.L.A. degrees. Master's degrees are also awarded. Bachelor's degrees are awarded in AGRICULTURE (agricultural business management, agriculture, animal science, dairy science, forestry and related sciences, horticulture, natural resource management, and soil science), BIOLOGICAL SCIENCE (biochemistry, biology/biological science, microbiology, and nutrition), BUSINESS (business administration and management and recreation and leisure services), COMMUNICATIONS AND THE ARTS (communications, dramatic arts, English, fine arts, graphic design, journalism, modern language, and music), COMPUTER AND PHYSICAL SCIENCE (chemistry, computer science, earth science, mathematics, physics, software engineering, and statistics), ENGINEERING AND ENVIRONMENTAL DESIGN (aeronautical engineering, agricultural engineering, architectural engineering, architecture, biomedical engineering, bioresource engineering, city/community/regional planning, civil engineering, computer engineering, construction management, electrical/electronics engineering, engineering, environmental engineering, environmental science, industrial engineering, industrial engineering technology, landscape architecture/design, manufacturing engineering, materials engineering, and mechanical engineering), HEALTH PROFESSIONS (exercise science), SOCIAL SCIENCE (anthropology, child psychology/development, economics, ethnic studies, food science, history, interdisciplinary studies, liberal arts/general studies, philosophy, political science/government, psychology, social science, and sociology).

Special: Cal Poly offers work-study programs, co-op programs in numerous majors, study abroad in 8 countries, and dual majors. Credit for military experience and pass/fail options are available. There is a freshman honors program.

Admissions: 37% of the 2009-2010 applicants were accepted. The SAT scores for the 2009-2010 freshman class were: Critical Reading--13% below 500, 45% between 500 and 599, 36% between 600 and 700, and 6% above 700; Math--5% below 500, 29% between 500 and 599, 49% between 600 and 700, and 16% above 700.

Requirements: The SAT or ACT is required. In addition, applicants must be graduates of an accredited high school or have a GED. 15 academic credits are required including 4 years of English, 3 each of math and science (1 a lab), 2 of social sciences and a foreign language, and 1 each of history, visual and performing arts, and electives. AP and CLEP credits are accepted.

Procedure: Freshmen are admitted in the fall. Entrance exams should be taken mid-June every year. There are early decision and early admissions plans. Early decision applications should be filed by October 31; regular applications should be filed by November 30 for fall entry and February 28 for summer entry, along with a $55 fee. Notification of early decision is sent December 15; regular decision, April 1. Applications are accepted on-line. 425 applicants were on a recent waiting list, 33 were accepted.

Financial Aid: The FAFSA is required. The priority date for freshman financial aid applications for fall entry is March 21.

Computers: Wireless access is available. Students log on wirelessly on campus with their usernames (e-mail address). Computers are available for general student use in the library, University Union, and various college/department labs. All students may access the system. There are no time limits and no fees. It is strongly recommended that all students have a personal computer. Students enrolled in Construction Management must have a personal computer.

CALIFORNIA STATE POLYTECHNIC UNIVERSITY, POMONA

Pomona, CA 91768-4019   **(909) 869-3258; (909) 869-4529**

Full-time: 9341 men, 7300 women	**Faculty:** ; IIA, +$
Part-time: 2158 men, 1337 women	**Ph.D.s:** %
Graduate: 960 men, 1177 women	**Student/Faculty:** n/av
Year: quarters, summer session	**Tuition:** $4551 ($15,711)
Application Deadline: November 1	**Room & Board:** $9570
Freshman Class: 20759 applied, 12731 accepted, 1261 enrolled	
SAT CR/M: 487/523	**ACT:** 20 **COMPETITIVE**

California State Polytechnic University, Pomona, an occupationally oriented institution founded in 1938, is part of the state-supported university system. It offers undergraduate and graduate programs in agriculture, liberal arts and sciences, business, engineering, and technical and professional training. There are 8 undergraduate schools and 7 graduate schools. In addition to regional accreditation, Cal Poly Pomona has baccalaureate program accreditation with AACSB, ABET, ADA, ASLA, CSAB, and NAAB. The library contains 757,460 volumes, 1.4 million microform items, and 11,280 audio/video tapes/CDs/DVDs, and subscribes to 8445 periodicals including electronic. Computerized library services include interlibrary loans, database searching, and Internet access. Special learning facilities include a learning resource center, art gallery, TV station, and interactive TV studio. The 1438-acre campus is in a suburban area 30 miles east of Los Angeles. Including any residence halls, there are 80 buildings.

Programs of Study: Cal Poly Pomona confers B.A., B.S., BArch., and B.F.A. degrees. Master's degrees are also awarded. Bachelor's degrees are awarded in AGRICULTURE (agricultural business management, agriculture, agronomy, animal science, and horticulture), BIOLOGICAL SCIENCE (biology/biological science, biotechnology, botany, microbiology, plant physiology, and zoology), BUSINESS (apparel and accessories marketing, business administration and management, hotel/motel and restaurant management, human resources, and international business management), COMMUNICATIONS AND THE ARTS (art, communications, dramatic arts, English, graphic design, music, and Spanish), COMPUTER AND PHYSICAL SCIENCE (chemistry, computer science, geology, information sciences and systems, mathematics, and physics), ENGINEERING AND ENVIRONMENTAL DESIGN (architecture, chemical engineering, civil engineering, computer technology, construction technology, electrical/electronics engineering, engineering technology, industrial engineering, landscape architecture/design, manufacturing engineering, materials engineering, mechanical engineering, and urban planning technology), SOCIAL SCIENCE (anthropology, behavioral science, economics, food science, geography, history, liberal arts/general studies, philosophy, physical fitness/movement, political science/government, psychology, social science, sociology, and urban studies). Engineering, architecture, and business are the strongest academically. Civil engineering, management and human resources, and mechanical engineering are the largest.

Special: Cross-registration is possible with any California State University school. Internships and co-op programs are available in agriculture, business, environmental design, engineering, science, political science, behavioral science, and phys ed. An international study program in 17 countries, work-study programs, B.A.-B.S. degrees, a liberal studies degree, credit for military experience, an external degree program, and credit/no credit options are offered. Nondegree study is possible. There are 30 national honor societies and a freshman honors program.

Admissions: 61% of the 2009-2010 applicants were accepted. The SAT scores for the 2009-2010 freshman class were: Critical Reading--42% below 500, 42% between 500 and 599, 14% between 600 and 700, and 2 above 700; Math--28% below 500, 37% between 500 and 599, 28% between 600 and 700, and 7 above 700. The ACT scores were 30% below 21, 26% between 21 and 23, 25% between 24 and 26, 12% between 27 and 28, and 7% above 28.

Requirements: In addition, applicants must be graduates of an accredited secondary school or have a GED equivalent. Secondary school courses must include 4 years of high school English, 3 each of math and electives, 2 of foreign language, and 1 each of science, history, and art. A GPA of 2.0 is required. AP and CLEP credits are accepted.

Procedure: Freshmen are admitted to all sessions. Entrance exams should be taken during the fall of the senior year. There is a rolling admissions plan. Applications should be filed by November 1 for fall entry, June 1 for winter entry, August 1 for spring entry, and February 1 for summer entry, along with a $55 fee. Notification is sent on a rolling basis. Applications are accepted on-line.

Financial Aid: In 2009-2010, 49% of all full-time freshmen and 51% of continuing full-time students received some form of financial aid. 42% of all full-time freshmen and 46% of continuing full-time students received need-based aid. The

average freshmen award was $8197. Average annual earnings from campus work are $2000. The average financial indebtedness of the 2009 graduate was $14,035. The FAFSA is required. The deadline for filing freshman financial aid applications for fall entry is March 2.

Computers: All students may access the system, 24 hours per day. There are no time limits and no fees. Students enrolled in environmental design must have a personal computer.

CALIFORNIA STATE UNIVERSITY, FULLERTON

Fullerton, CA 92834 (657) 278-2371; (657) 278-2356

Full-time: 9696 men, 13,266 women	**Faculty:** 887; IIA, av$
Part-time: 3338 men, 4437 women	**Ph.D.s:** 82%
Graduate: 2046 men, 3479 women	**Student/Faculty:** 24 to 1
Year: semesters, summer session	**Tuition:** $4622 ($15,782)
Application Deadline: November 30	**Room & Board:** $9082
Freshman Class: 30612 applied, 16865 accepted, 4065 enrolled	
SAT CR/M: 480/500	**ACT:** 21 COMPETITIVE

California State University, Fullerton, founded in 1957, is part of the California State University system. The school offers programs in the arts, business and economics, communications, engineering and computer science, education, health and human development, humanities and social science, natural science, math, and nursing. The institution provides a comprehensive teaching credential program. There are 8 undergraduate schools and 8 graduate schools. In addition to regional accreditation, Cal State Fullerton has baccalaureate program accreditation with AACSB, ABET, ACEJMC, NASAD, NASM, NCATE, and NLN, among others. The library contains 1.3 million volumes, 1.1 million microform items, and 32,781 audio/video tapes/CDs/DVDs, and subscribes to 10,917 periodicals including electronic. Computerized library services include interlibrary loans, database searching, Internet access, and laptop Internet portals. Special learning facilities include a learning resource center, art gallery, radio station, TV station, wildlife sanctuary, arboretum, desert studies center, demographic research center, and a number of centers for studies in economics and business, the environment, aging, education, land use, oral and public history, and religion in American life. The 236-acre campus is in a suburban area 30 miles southeast of Los Angeles. Including any residence halls, there are 27 buildings.

Programs of Study: Cal State Fullerton confers B.A., B.S., B.F.A., and B.M. degrees. Master's degrees are also awarded. Bachelor's degrees are awarded in BIOLOGICAL SCIENCE (biochemistry and biology/biological science), BUSINESS (accounting, banking and finance, business administration and management, business economics, entrepreneurial studies, international business management, management information systems, management science, marketing/retailing/merchandising, and tourism), COMMUNICATIONS AND THE ARTS (advertising, animation, art, art history and appreciation, broadcasting, communications, comparative literature, dance, dramatic arts, English, French, German, Japanese, journalism, linguistics, music, music performance, performing arts, public relations, Spanish, speech/debate/rhetoric, and studio art), COMPUTER AND PHYSICAL SCIENCE (applied mathematics, chemistry, computer science, geology, information sciences and systems, mathematics, physics, and statistics), EDUCATION (music education and physical education), ENGINEERING AND ENVIRONMENTAL DESIGN (civil engineering, computer engineering, electrical/electronics engineering, engineering, engineering and applied science, and mechanical engineering), HEALTH PROFESSIONS (health science, nursing, and speech pathology/audiology), SOCIAL SCIENCE (African American studies, American studies, anthropology, Asian/American studies, child psychology/development, criminal justice, economics, European studies, geography, history, human services, Latin American studies, liberal arts/general studies, Mexican-American/Chicano studies, philosophy, political science/government, psychology, public administration, religion, sociology, and women's studies). Business and economics, teacher credential programs, and drama and musical theater are the strongest academically. Business and economics, humanities and social sciences, and health and human development are the largest.

Special: The university offers cross-registration with other schools in the California State University system, the University of California, and California community colleges, internships and co-op programs in 45 academic areas, study abroad in 18 countries, and work-study programs both on and off campus. A B.A.-B.S. degree in chemistry, dual majors, and pass/fail options are also available. There are 16 national honor societies, a freshman honors program, and 5 departmental honors programs.

Admissions: 55% of the 2009-2010 applicants were accepted. The SAT scores for the 2009-2010 freshman class were: Critical Reading--54% below 500, 36% between 500 and 599, 9% between 600 and 700, and 1% above 700; Math--47% below 500, 37% between 500 and 599, 15% between 600 and 700, and 1% above 700. The ACT scores were 48% below 21, 30% between 21 and 23, 15% between 24 and 26, 5% between 27 and 28, and 3% above 28. 36% of the current freshmen were in the top fifth of their class; 77% were in the top two fifths.

Requirements: The SAT or ACT is required. In addition, applicants must be graduates of an accredited secondary school or have a GED certificate. Secondary school courses must include 4 years of English, 3 of math, 2 each of a foreign language, science, and history, and 1 of visual or performing arts. Admission is based on the Qualifiable Eligibility Index, a combination of the high school GPA and either the SAT or ACT score. Auditions are required for music majors. Cal State Fullerton requires applicants to be in the upper 75% of their class. A GPA of 2.0 is required. AP and CLEP credits are accepted. Important factors in the admissions decision are advanced placement or honors courses, ability to finance college education, and geographical diversity.

Procedure: Freshmen are admitted fall. Entrance exams should be taken during the senior year of high school. There is a rolling admissions plan. Applications should be filed by November 30 for fall entry, along with a $55 fee. Notification is sent on a rolling basis. Applications are accepted on-line.

Financial Aid: In 2009-2010, 39% of all full-time freshmen and 32% of continuing full-time students received some form of financial aid. 36% of all full-time freshmen and 22% of continuing full-time students received need-based aid. The average financial indebtedness of the 2009 graduate was $14,626. The FAFSA is required. The priority date for freshman financial aid applications for fall entry is March 2. The deadline for filing freshman financial aid applications for fall entry is May 23.

Computers: Wireless access is available. Approximately 2000 computers for general student use are located in the library, computer labs, the student center, and housing facilities. Wireless network connectivity is provided throughout the campus. All students may access the system 24 hours a day. There are no time limits and no fees.

CALIFORNIA STATE UNIVERSITY, LONG BEACH

Long Beach, CA 90840-0106   (562) 985-4141; (562) 985-4973

Full-time: 9490 men, 14,205 women	**Faculty:** 1021; IIA, +$
Part-time: 2228 men, 2953 women	**Ph.D.s:** 85%
Graduate: 2352 men, 3979 women	**Student/Faculty:** 23 to 1
Year: semesters, summer session	**Tuition:** $4370 ($15,530)
Application Deadline: November 30	**Room & Board:** $10,832
Freshman Class: 45,771 applied, 14,543 accepted, 3551 enrolled	
SAT CR/M: 500/520	**ACT:** 21 **COMPETITIVE+**

California State University, Long Beach, founded in 1949, is a nonprofit institution that is part of the California State University system. The commuter university offers undergraduate programs through the Colleges of Health and Human Services, Liberal Arts, Natural Sciences and Math, Business Administration, Engineering, the Arts, and Education. There are 7 undergraduate schools and 7 graduate schools. In addition to regional accreditation, CSULB has baccalaureate program accreditation with AACSB, ABET, ACEJMC, AHEA, APTA, CSWE, FIDER, NASAD, NASM, NLN, and NRPA. The library contains 1.9 million volumes, 1.5 million microform items, and 104,622 audio/video tapes/CDs/DVDs, and subscribes to 35,860 periodicals including electronic. Computerized library services include interlibrary loans, database searching, and Internet access. Special learning facilities include a learning resource center, art gallery, radio station, and TV station. The 322-acre campus is in a suburban area 25 miles southeast of Los Angeles. Including any residence halls, there are 84 buildings.

Programs of Study: CSULB confers B.A., B.S., B.F.A., B.M., and B.Voc.Ed. degrees. Master's degrees are also awarded. Bachelor's degrees are awarded in BIOLOGICAL SCIENCE (biochemistry, biology/biological science, botany, cell biology, ecology, physiology, and zoology), BUSINESS (accounting, banking and finance, business administration and management, international business management, management information systems, marketing/retailing/merchandising, and personnel management), COMMUNICATIONS AND THE ARTS (art, communications, comparative literature, dance, design, dramatic arts, English, film arts, French, German, Japanese, journalism, music, and Spanish), COMPUTER AND PHYSICAL SCIENCE (applied mathematics, chemistry, computer science, earth science, geology, mathematics, physics, and statistics), EDUCATION (elementary education, mathematics education, science education, and special education), ENGINEERING AND ENVIRONMENTAL DESIGN (aerospace studies, chemical engineering, civil engineering, computer engineering, electrical/electronics engineering, engineering technology, and mechanical engineering), HEALTH PROFESSIONS (health care administration and health science), SOCIAL SCIENCE (African American studies, anthropology, Asian/Oriental studies, economics, geography, Hispanic American studies, history, human development, interdisciplinary studies, international studies, philosophy, political science/government, psychology, religion, sociology, and women's studies). Art, biological sciences, and music are the strongest academically. Business administration, psychology, and liberal studies are the largest.

Special: The university offers cross-registration with California State University, Dominguez Hills for courses not offered at CSULB. Internships, study abroad in 22 countries, dual majors in engineering, a 3-2 engineering degree, student-designed majors, and pass/fail options are also available. There are 23 national honor societies, including Phi Beta Kappa, and a freshman honors program.

Admissions: 32% of the 2009-2010 applicants were accepted. The SAT scores for the 2009-2010 freshman class were: Critical Reading--47% below 500, 40% between 500 and 599, 12% between 600 and 700; and 2% above 700; Math--39% below 500, 36% between 500 and 599, 22% between 600 and 700, and 2% above 700.

Requirements: The SAT or ACT is required. In addition, applicants must be graduates of an accredited secondary school and have completed 4 years of English, 3 years each of math and electives, 2 years of foreign language, and 1 year each of lab science, U.S. history or U.S. history and government, and 1 visual and performing arts. Students are admitted on the basis of the eligibility index, which is computed from the secondary school GPA and SAT or ACT scores. California residents with a minimum 3.0 GPA are automatically admissible. A portfolio is required for art and design students. An audition is required for dance, music, and theater students. A GPA of 2.0 is required. AP and CLEP credits are accepted.

Procedure: Freshmen are admitted fall and spring. Entrance exams should be taken during the fall semester of the senior year. There is a rolling admissions plan. Applications should be filed by November 30 for fall entry; August 31 for spring entry, along with a $55 fee. Applications are accepted on-line.

Financial Aid: CSULB is a member of CSS. The FAFSA is required. Check with the school for current application deadlines.

Computers: All students may access the system during open lab hours, which vary across campus. There are no time limits and no fees.

CALIFORNIA STATE UNIVERSITY, NORTHRIDGE

Northridge, CA 91330	(818) 677-3700; (818) 677-3766
Full-time: 8135 men, 11510 women	**Faculty:** IIA, +$
Part-time: 2435 men, 3455 women	**Ph.D.s:** n/av
Graduate: 2505 men, 5005 women	**Student/Faculty:** n/av
Year: semesters, summer session	**Tuition:** $4000 ($9500)
Application Deadline: see profile	**Room & Board:** $7000
Freshman Class: n/av	
SAT or ACT: required	**LESS COMPETITIVE**

California State University, Northridge, founded in 1958, is part of the state-supported university system offering degree programs in the liberal arts and sciences, business administration, education, engineering, music, health fields, and fine arts. The figures given in the above capsule and in this profile are approximate. There are 8 undergraduate schools and 1 graduate school. In addition to regional accreditation, CSUN has baccalaureate program accreditation with AACSB, ABET, ACEJMC, AHEA, APTA, CAHEA, CSAB, NASAD, NASM, NCATE, and NRPA. The library contains 1.3 million volumes, 3.1 million microform items, and 17,677 audio/video tapes/CDs/DVDs, and subscribes to 16,973 periodicals including electronic. Computerized library services include interlibrary loans and database searching. Special learning facilities include a learning resource center, art gallery, planetarium, radio station, TV station, observatory, anthropological museum, botanical gardens, urban archives center, Natural Center on Deafness, and Center for the Study of Cancer and Development Biology. The 353-acre campus is in a suburban area 25 miles north of Los Angeles. Including any residence halls, there are 76 buildings.

Programs of Study: CSUN confers B.A., B.S., and B.M. degrees. Master's degrees are also awarded. Bachelor's degrees are awarded in BIOLOGICAL SCI-

ENCE (biochemistry, biology/biological science, environmental biology, and microbiology), BUSINESS (accounting, banking and finance, business administration and management, management information systems, marketing/retailing/merchandising, and recreation and leisure services), COMMUNICATIONS AND THE ARTS (art, dance, dramatic arts, English, film arts, French, German, journalism, linguistics, music, Spanish, and speech/debate/rhetoric), COMPUTER AND PHYSICAL SCIENCE (astrophysics, chemistry, computer science, earth science, geology, mathematics, physics, and radiological technology), EDUCATION (business education, education of the deaf and hearing impaired, home economics education, and physical education), ENGINEERING AND ENVIRONMENTAL DESIGN (engineering), HEALTH PROFESSIONS (biomedical science, exercise science, health, health care administration, medical laboratory technology, nursing, physical therapy, recreation therapy, and speech pathology/audiology), SOCIAL SCIENCE (African American studies, anthropology, Asian/American studies, child psychology/development, criminology, economics, family/consumer studies, geography, history, humanities, liberal arts/general studies, Mexican-American/Chicano studies, philosophy, political science/government, psychology, sociology, urban studies, and women's studies). Liberal studies is the strongest academically. Business administration and economics, social and behavioral sciences, and arts, media and communication are the largest.

Special: Cross-registration is offered through the Intra System Visitor Program. Study abroad in 16 countries, internships, university work-study programs, dual majors, student-designed majors, credit for military experience, and pass/fail options for elective courses are offered. There are 4 national honor societies, a freshman honors program, and 5 departmental honors programs.

Requirements: The SAT or ACT is required for students with a GPA below 3.0 (3.6 for nonresidents). Applicants should have completed 4 years of high school English, 3 each of math and academic electives, 2 of foreign language, and 1 each of lab science, U.S. history/government, and visual/performing arts. A GPA of 2.0 is required. AP and CLEP credits are accepted. Important factors in the admissions decision are recommendations by school officials, evidence of special talent, and leadership record.

Procedure: Freshmen are admitted fall and spring. Entrance exams should be taken by December of the senior year. There are early decisions and a rolling admissions plan. Check with the school for current application deadlines. The fall 2009 application fee was $55. Notification is sent on a rolling basis. Applications are accepted on-line.

Financial Aid: CSUN is a member of CSS. Check with the school for current application deadlines.

Computers: All students may access the system 24 hours a day, 7 days a week.

CALIFORNIA STATE UNIVERSITY, SACRAMENTO

Sacramento, CA 95819-6048

(916) 278-7362
(800) 722-4748; (916) 278-5603

Full-time: 7525 men, 10375 women	**Faculty:** IIA, av$
Part-time: 2310 men, 2860 women	**Ph.D.s:** n/av
Graduate: 1580 men, 3360 women	**Student/Faculty:** n/av
Year: semesters, summer session	**Tuition:** $4500 ($14,500)
Application Deadline: November 30	**Room & Board:** $8500
Freshman Class: n/av	
SAT or ACT: required	**COMPETITIVE**

California State University/Sacramento, founded in 1947, is part of the state-supported university system. The school offers graduate and undergraduate programs in the liberal arts and sciences, business administration, education, engineering, music, health and human services, natural sciences, math, and social sciences. The figures given in the above capsule and in this profile are approximate. There are 8 undergraduate schools and 7 graduate schools. In addition to regional accreditation, Sac State has baccalaureate program accreditation with AACSB, ABET, ACBSP, ACCE, ADA, AHEA, APTA, ASLA, CSWE, FIDER, NASAD, NASM, NCATE, NLN, NRPA, and TEAC. The library contains 1.3 million volumes, 2.3 million microform items, and 53,515 audio/video tapes/CDs/DVDs, and subscribes to 3,761 periodicals including electronic. Computerized library services include interlibrary loans, database searching, and Internet access. Special learning facilities include a learning resource center, art gallery, radio station, TV station, an aquatic center, and an anthropology museum. The 300-acre campus is in a suburban area 90 miles northeast of San Francisco. Including any residence halls, there are 51 buildings.

Programs of Study: Sac State confers B.A., B.S., B.M., and B.V.E degrees. Master's and doctoral degrees are also awarded. Bachelor's degrees are awarded in BIOLOGICAL SCIENCE (biology/biological science and microbiology), BUSINESS (accounting, banking and finance, business administration and management, insurance, international business management, management information systems, marketing/retailing/merchandising, and real estate), COMMUNICATIONS AND THE ARTS (communications, dramatic arts, English, French, German, journalism, music, and Spanish), COMPUTER AND PHYSICAL SCIENCE (chemistry, computer science, geology, mathematics, physical sciences, and physics), EDUCATION (business education, early childhood education, and health education), ENGINEERING AND ENVIRONMENTAL DESIGN (civil engineering, computer engineering, electrical/electronics engineering, engineering technology, and mechanical engineering), HEALTH PROFESSIONS (environmental health science, medical laboratory technology, nursing, physical therapy, and speech pathology/audiology), SOCIAL SCIENCE (anthropology, criminal justice, economics, geography, history, international relations, parks and recreation management, philosophy, psychology, public administration, social science, social work, and sociology). Nursing, criminal justice, and business administration are the strongest academically. Business administration, communications, and criminal justice. are the largest.

Special: The university offers cross-registration with other California State University schools, co-op programs in many academic programs, internships, a Washington semester, study abroad in 12 countries, and dual and student-designed majors. A joint Ph.D. program in public history is available with the university of California at Santa Barbara. There are 3 national honor societies, including Phi Beta Kappa, a freshman honors program, and 26 departmental honors programs.

Requirements: he SAT or ACT is required of applicants with a high school GPA below 3.0. Applicants should have completed 4 years of high school English, 3 years of math, 2 years of a foreign language, 1 year each of lab science, history, and visual/performing arts and 3 years of college preparatory electives. A GPA of 2.0 is required. AP and CLEP credits are accepted.

Procedure: Freshmen are admitted fall and spring. Entrance exams should be taken before December of the senior year. There are deferred admissions and rolling admissions plans. Applications should be filed by November 30 for fall entry. The fall 2009 application fee was $55. Notifications are sent November 1. Applications are accepted on-line.

Financial Aid: Sac State is a member of CSS. The FAFSA and SAAC is required. Check with the school for current application deadlines.

Computers: Wireless access is available. All students may access the system. There are no fees. It is strongly recommended that all students have a personal computer.

CALVIN COLLEGE
Grand Rapids, MI 49546   (616) 526-6106
                                   (800) 688-0122; (616) 526-6777

Full-time: 1797 men, 2086 women	**Faculty:** 326; IIB, av$
Part-time: 59 men, 73 women	**Ph.D.s:** 82%
Graduate: 25 men, 52 women	**Student/Faculty:** 12 to 1
Year: 4-1-4, summer session	**Tuition:** $24,035
Application Deadline: August 15	**Room & Board:** $8275
Freshman Class: 2529 applied, 2346 accepted, 945 enrolled	
SAT CR/M: 600/600	**ACT:** 26 **VERY COMPETITIVE+**

Calvin College, established in 1876, is a private institution affiliated with the Christian Reformed Church, offering undergraduate and graduate degrees in liberal arts and in some professional programs. In addition to regional accreditation, Calvin has baccalaureate program accreditation with ABET, CSWE, NASM, and NCATE. The library contains 493,218 volumes, 808,547 microform items, and 3,694 audio/video tapes/CDs/DVDs, and subscribes to 22,183 periodicals including electronic. Computerized library services include interlibrary loans, database searching, Internet access, and laptop Internet portals. Special learning facilities include a learning resource center, art gallery, a TV studio, an ecosystem preserve, an interpretive center, an electron microscope lab, an observatory with a 16-inch telescope, a greenhouse, and an audiology and speech pathology clinic. The 390-acre campus is in a suburban area 7 miles southeast of downtown Grand Rapids. Including any residence halls, there are 40 buildings.

Programs of Study: Calvin confers B.A., B.S., B.A.S.P.A., B.C.S., B.F.A., B.M.E., B.S.A., B.S.E., B.S.N., B.S.P.A., B.S.R., and B.S.W. degrees. Master's degrees are also awarded. Bachelor's degrees are awarded in BIOLOGICAL SCIENCE (biochemistry, biology/biological science, and biotechnology), BUSINESS (accounting, business administration and management, business communications, and recreation and leisure services), COMMUNICATIONS AND THE ARTS (art, art history and appreciation, classical languages, classics, communications, dramatic arts, Dutch, English, film arts, French, German, Greek, Latin, media arts, music, Spanish, and voice), COMPUTER AND PHYSICAL SCIENCE (chemistry, computer science, digital arts/technology, geology, information sciences and systems, mathematics, and physics), EDUCATION (art education, elementary education, music education, physical education, secondary education, and special education), ENGINEERING AND ENVIRONMENTAL DESIGN (chemical engineering, civil engineering, electrical/electronics engineering, engineering, environmental science, and mechanical engineering), HEALTH PROFESSIONS (nursing, occupational therapy, predentistry, premedicine, prepharmacy, preveterinary science, and speech pathology/audiology), SOCIAL SCIENCE (area studies, Asian/Oriental studies, economics, geography, history, international studies, philosophy, political science/government, prelaw, psychology, religion, social work, and sociology). Natural sciences, history, and English are the strongest academically. Education, engineering, and psychology are the largest.

Special: Dual and student-designed majors are available, as well as a combined curriculum program in occupational therapy. Students may study abroad in numerous countries and enroll in a Washington semester. Cooperative programs include Los Angeles film studies, the Au Sable Institute, the Chicago Metropolitan program, Oregon extension, Latin American, Middle East, Chinese, and Russian studies, and programs in business. Internships, work-study programs, and cross-registration at Grand Valley State University in special education, in occupational therapy at Washington University, and in religion at Reformed Bible College are also available. There are 6 national honor societies, a freshman honors program, and 25 departmental honors programs.

Admissions: 93% of the 2009-2010 applicants were accepted. The SAT scores for the 2009-2010 freshman class were: Critical Reading--17% below 500, 32% between 500 and 599, 34% between 600 and 700, and 17% above 700; Math--11% below 500, 34% between 500 and 599, 40% between 600 and 700, and 15% above 700. The ACT scores were 11% below 21, 18% between 21 and 23, 24% between 24 and 26, 18% between 27 and 28, and 28% above 28. 49% of the current freshmen were in the top fifth of their class; 74% were in the top two fifths. There were 28 National Merit finalists. 33 freshmen graduated first in their class.

Requirements: The ACT is required. In addition, in selecting students for admission, Calvin College looks for evidence of Christian commitment and for the capacity and desire to learn. Students who are interested in the Christian perspective and curriculum of Calvin, and who show interest in its aims, are eligible for consideration. Although the prospect of academic success is of primary consideration, the aspirations of the applicant, the recommendation of a high school counselor, teacher, or principal, and the ability of Calvin to be of service, will also be considered. A GPA of 2.5 is required. AP and CLEP credits are accepted. Important factors in the admissions decision are recommendations by school officials, leadership record, and extracurricular activities record.

Procedure: Freshmen are admitted fall, spring, and summer. Entrance exams should be taken during the spring of the junior year or fall of the senior year. There are deferred admissions and rolling admissions plans. Applications should be filed by August 15 for fall entry and January 15 for spring entry, along with a $35 fee. Applications are accepted on-line.

Financial Aid: In 2009-2010, 98% of all full-time freshmen and 97% of continuing full-time students received some form of financial aid. 69% of all full-time freshmen and 63% of continuing full-time students received need-based aid. The average freshman award was $12,500. Need-based scholarships or need-based grants averaged $10,800 ($28,000 maximum); need-based self-help aid (loans and jobs) averaged $5200 ($10,000 maximum); and other non-need-based awards and non-need-based scholarships averaged $4000 ($20,000 maximum). 80% of undergraduate students work part-time. Average annual earnings from campus work are $1200. The average financial indebtedness of the 2009 graduate was $28,500. The FAFSA and the college's own financial statement are required. The priority date for freshman financial aid applications for fall entry is February 15. The deadline for filing freshman financial aid applications for fall entry is August 1.

Computers: Wireless access is available. Calvin provides resident students with high-speed Internet connections, telephones, cable television, access to fax machines, and Helpdesk support services. All students enjoy access to more than 800 computers in campus labs and classrooms. Wireless access is available in all dorms and apartments as well as the library and other academic buildings on campus. All students may access the system at any time. There are no time limits and no fees.

CAMBRIDGE COLLEGE
Cambridge, MA 02138

(617) 868-1000
800-877-4723; (617) 349-3561

Full-time: 214 men, 191 women	**Faculty:** n/av
Part-time: 587 men, 253 women	**Ph.D.s:** 63%
Graduate: 2135 men, 982 women	**Student/Faculty:** n/av
Year: semesters, summer session	**Tuition:** $13,280
Application Deadline: open	**Room & Board:** n/app
Freshman Class: 375 applied, 256 accepted, 188 enrolled	
SAT or ACT: not required	**SPECIAL**

Founded in 1971, Cambridge College is a private, non-profit commuter institution dedicated to providing educational opportunities for working adults and underserved learners. Cambridge College is approved and accredited to offer programs through its main campus and 8 regional centers in Springfield and Lawrence, MA; Chesapeake and South Boston, VA; Augusta, GA; San Juan, PR; Ontario, CA; and Memphis, TN. There is 1 undergraduate school and 3 graduate schools. Computerized library services include interlibrary loans, database searching, Internet access, and laptop Internet portals. Special learning facilities include a learning resource center. The campus is in an urban area in Cambridge. Including any residence halls, there are 3 buildings.

Programs of Study: Cambridge College confers B.A. and B.S. degrees. Master's and doctoral degrees are also awarded. Bachelor's degrees are awarded in BUSINESS (management science) and SOCIAL SCIENCE (human services, interdisciplinary studies, and psychology). Multidisciplinary studies, management, and psychology are the strongest academically and the largest.

Admissions: 68% of the 2009-2010 applicants were accepted.

Requirements: CLEP credits are accepted.

Procedure: Freshmen are admitted to all sessions. There are deferred admissions and rolling admissions plans. Application deadlines are open. The fall 2008 application fee was $30. Applications are accepted on-line.

Financial Aid: In 2009-2010, 61% of all full-time freshmen and 72% of continuing full-time students received some form of financial aid. At least 61% of all full-time freshmen and 72% of continuing full-time students received need-based aid. The average freshman award was $3478. Need-based scholarships or need-based grants averaged $5092, and need-based self-help aid (loans and jobs) averaged $3574. The FAFSA and the college's own financial statement are required.

Computers: Wireless access is available. All students may access the system.

Buffalo, NY 14208

(716) 888-2200
(800) 843-1517; (716) 888-3230

Full-time: 1444 men, 1606 women	**Faculty:** 223; IIA, av$
Part-time: 81 men, 65 women	**Ph.D.s:** 92%
Graduate: 634 men, 944 women	**Student/Faculty:** 11 to 1
Year: semesters, summer session	**Tuition:** $29,512
Application Deadline: March 1	**Room & Board:** $10,556
Freshman Class: 3996 applied, 3084 accepted, 708 enrolled	
SAT CR/M: 549/569	**ACT:** 24 **VERY COMPETITIVE**

Canisius College, founded in 1870, is a private Roman Catholic college in the Jesuit tradition. It offers undergraduate programs in the liberal arts and sciences, business, education, and human services. There are 3 undergraduate schools and 3 graduate schools. In addition to regional accreditation, Canisius has baccalaureate program accreditation with AACSB, CAHEA, and NCATE. The library contains 353,617 volumes, 599,947 microform items, and 11,361 audio/video tapes/CDs/DVDs, and subscribes to 37,240 periodicals including electronic. Computerized library services include interlibrary loans, database searching, Internet access, and laptop Internet portals. Special learning facilities include a learning resource center, art gallery, radio station, a television studio, foreign language lab, 87 media-assisted classrooms, digital media lab, and musical instrument digital interface classroom. The 36-acre campus is in an urban area in Buffalo. Including any residence halls, there are 51 buildings.

Programs of Study: Canisius confers B.A. and B.S., B.A.Ed., and B.S.Ed. degrees. Master's degrees are also awarded. Bachelor's degrees are awarded in BIOLOGICAL SCIENCE (biochemistry, bioinformatics, biology/biological science, environmental biology, and zoology), BUSINESS (accounting, banking and finance, business administration and management, business communications, business economics, entrepreneurial studies, fashion merchandising, international business management, investments and securities, management information systems, management science, marketing management, and marketing/retailing/merchandising), COMMUNICATIONS AND THE ARTS (art history and appreciation, communications, digital communications, English, French, German, media arts, modern language, music, Spanish, and speech/debate/rhetoric), COMPUTER AND PHYSICAL SCIENCE (chemistry, computer science, information sciences and systems, mathematics, and physics), EDUCATION (athletic training, early childhood education, elementary education, English education, foreign languages education, mathematics education, middle school education, physical education, science education, social studies education, and special education), ENGINEERING AND ENVIRONMENTAL DESIGN (environmental science and preengineering), HEALTH PROFESSIONS (medical laboratory technology, predentistry, premedicine, prepharmacy, preveterinary science, and sports medicine), SOCIAL SCIENCE (anthropology, criminal justice, European studies, history, humanities and social science, international relations, liberal arts/general studies, philosophy, prelaw, psychology, sociology, and urban studies). Accounting, biology, and chemistry are the strongest academically. Psychology, biology, and communications studies are the largest.

Special: Canisius offers internships, credit by exam, pass/fail options, dual majors, a Washington semester, work-study programs, and study abroad in 13 countries. Cooperative programs are available with the Fashion Institute of Technology in New York City. Cross-registration is permitted with 14 schools in the

Western New York Consortium of Higher Education. Canisius also offers early assurance and joint degree programs, with SUNY health professions schools in Buffalo and Syracuse, and a 3-2 MBA. There are 9 national honor societies, a freshman honors program, and 5 departmental honors programs.

Admissions: 77% of the 2009-2010 applicants were accepted. The SAT scores for the 2009-2010 freshman class were: Critical Reading--24% below 500, 48% between 500 and 599, 25% between 600 and 700, and 3% above 700; Math--19% below 500, 43% between 500 and 599, 33% between 600 and 700, and 5% above 700. The ACT scores were 8% below 21, 17% between 21 and 23, 22% between 24 and 26, 23% between 27 and 28, and 30% above 28. 51% of the current freshmen were in the top fifth of their class; 78% were in the top two fifths. 4 freshmen graduated first in their class.

Requirements: The SAT or ACT is required. In addition, all students must submit official high school transcript (or GED) and SAT or ACT results. College preparatory course work should include 4 units each of English and social science, 3 units each of math, science, and foreign language. Students with a B+ average and a satisfactory SAT score are most competitive. An essay and an interview are recommended. A GPA of 2.0 is required. AP and CLEP credits are accepted. Important factors in the admissions decision are leadership record, recommendations by school officials, and advanced placement or honors courses.

Procedure: Freshmen are admitted fall, spring, and summer. Entrance exams should be taken during the junior or senior year. There are deferred admissions and rolling admissions plans. Applications should be filed by March 1 for fall entry, along with a $40 fee. Notification is sent on a rolling basis. Applications are accepted on-line.

Financial Aid: In 2009-2010, 98% of all full-time freshmen and 94% of continuing full-time students received some form of financial aid. 82% of all full-time freshmen and 75% of continuing full-time students received need-based aid. The average freshman award was $26,843. Need-based scholarships or need-based grants averaged $9,552 ($36,848 maximum); need-based self-help aid (loans and jobs) averaged $4,471 ($7,300 maximum); non-need-based athletic scholarships averaged $19,919 ($42,636 maximum); and other non-need-based awards and non-need-based scholarships averaged $13,582 ($40,418 maximum). 24% of undergraduate students work part-time. Average annual earnings from campus work are $1676. The average financial indebtedness of the 2009 graduate was $33,645. Canisius is a member of CSS. The FAFSA is required. The priority date for freshman financial aid applications for fall entry is February 15.

Computers: Wireless access is available. Students may access more than 527 PCs throughout campus including kiosk stations in academic buildings. All computers are connected to the Internet and have access to extensive on-line research database provided by the library. Laptops with wireless access are available for use in the library. All students may access the system. The web can be accessed at any time. There are no time limits and no fees. It is strongly recommended that all students have a personal computer.

CARLETON COLLEGE

Northfield, MN 55057

(507) 222-4190
(800) 995-CARL; (507) 222-4526

Full-time: 963 men, 1023 women	**Faculty:** 217; IIB, ++$
Part-time: none	**Ph.D.s:** 94%
Graduate: none	**Student/Faculty:** 9 to 1
Year: trimesters	**Tuition:** $39,777
Application Deadline: January 15	**Room & Board:** $10,428
Freshman Class: 4784 applied, 1459 accepted, 529 enrolled	
SAT or ACT: required	**MOST COMPETITIVE**

Carleton College, founded in 1866, is a private liberal arts college. The library contains 957,655 volumes, 203,313 microform items, and 792 audio/video tapes/CDs/DVDs, and subscribes to 14,435 periodicals including electronic. Computerized library services include interlibrary loans, database searching, and Internet access. Special learning facilities include a learning resource center, art gallery, radio station, an observatory, and an 850-acre arboretum. The 955-acre campus is in a small town 35 miles south of Minneapolis-St. Paul. Including any residence halls, there are 46 buildings.

Programs of Study: Carleton confers B.A. degrees. Bachelor's degrees are awarded in AGRICULTURE (environmental studies), BIOLOGICAL SCIENCE (biology/biological science), COMMUNICATIONS AND THE ARTS (art history and appreciation, classics, English, French, German, Greek, Latin, media arts, music, romance languages and literature, Russian, Spanish, and studio art), COMPUTER AND PHYSICAL SCIENCE (chemistry, computer science, geology, mathematics, and physics), SOCIAL SCIENCE (African studies, African American studies, American studies, anthropology, Asian/Oriental studies, classical/ancient civilization, economics, history, international relations, Latin American studies, philosophy, political science/government, psychology, religion, sociology, and women's studies). Social sciences and history, physical sciences, and biological life are the largest.

Special: Students may cross-register with Saint Olaf College and pursue a variety of internships. The college offers study abroad in 53 countries. Dual majors in all areas and student-designed majors are available. Students may earn a 3-2 engineering degree with Washington or Columbia Universities, a 3-2 degree in nursing, and a 3-3 degree in law. Pass/fail options are offered. There are 3 national honor societies, including Phi Beta Kappa.

Admissions: 30% of the 2009-2010 applicants were accepted. The SAT scores for 2009-2010 were; Critical Reading--6% between 500-599, 33% between 600-700, and 59% above 700; Math--1% below 500, 4% between 500-599, 44% between 600-700, and 51% above 700; Writing--7% between 500-599, 36% between 600-700, and 56% above 700. The SAT scores were 4% between 18-23, 28% between 24-29, and 67% above 29. 88% of the current freshmen were in the top fifth of their class; 99% were in the top two fifths. There were 76 National Merit finalists.

Requirements: The SAT or ACT is required. The ACT Optional Writing test is also required. There are no secondary school requirements, but it is recommended that applicants have completed 4 years of English, 3 years each of math and a foreign language, 2 years each of history and science, and 1 year of social studies. An essay and 2 teacher recommendations are required. AP credits are accepted. Important factors in the admissions decision are advanced placement or honors courses, personality/intangible qualities, and evidence of special talent.

Procedure: Freshmen are admitted in the fall. Entrance exams should be taken before February 15. There are early decision, early admissions, and deferred admissions plans. Early decision applications should be filed by November 15; regular applications by January 15 for fall entry, along with a $30 fee. Notification of early decision is sent December 15; regular decision, April 15. Applications are accepted on-line. 331 applicants were on a recent waiting list.

Financial Aid: In 2009-2010, 77% of all full-time freshmen and 86% of continuing full-time students received some form of financial aid. 58% of all full-time freshmen and 55% of continuing full-time students received need-based aid. The average freshman award was $31,789. Need-based scholarships or need-based grants averaged $28,868; need-based self-help aid (loans and jobs) averaged $5,034; and other non-need based awards and non-need based scholarships averaged $1,962. 81% of undergraduate students work part-time. Average annual earnings from campus work are $1744. The average financial indebtedness of the 2009 graduate was $18,601. Carleton is a member of CSS. The CSS/Profile and FAFSA are required. The deadline for filing freshman financial aid applications for fall entry is February 15.

Computers: Wireless access is available. Dorms offer hard-wired or wireless hookups. There are 32 computer labs, with 247 general purpose computers available in 14 general purpose labs. All students may access the system 24 hours a day. There are no time limits and no fees.

CARNEGIE MELLON UNIVERSITY
Pittsburgh, PA 15213   **(412) 268-2082; (412) 268-7838**

Full-time: 3430 men, 2432 women	**Faculty:** I, +$
Part-time: 65 men, 36 women	**Ph.D.s:** 96%
Graduate: 3789 men, 1631 women	**Student/Faculty:** 7 to 1
Year: semesters, summer session	**Tuition:** $40,920
Application Deadline: see profile	**Room & Board:** $10,340
Freshman Class: 14,153 applied, 5132 accepted, 1423 enrolled	
SAT CR/M/W: 670/730/680	**ACT:** 31 **MOST COMPETITIVE**

Carnegie Mellon University, established in 1900, is a private nonsectarian institution offering undergraduate programs in liberal arts and science and technology. There are 6 undergraduate schools and 7 graduate schools. In addition to regional accreditation, Carnegie Mellon has baccalaureate program accreditation with AACSB, ABET, NAAB, NASAD, and NASM. The 4 libraries contain 1.1 million volumes, 1.1 million microform items, and 30,729 audio/video tapes/CDs/ DVDs, and subscribe to 1955 periodicals including electronic. Computerized library services include interlibrary loans, database searching, Internet access, and laptop Internet portals. Special learning facilities include a learning resource center, art gallery, radio station, and TV station. The 145-acre campus is in a suburban area 4 miles from downtown Pittsburgh. Including any residence halls, there are 80 buildings.

Programs of Study: Carnegie Mellon confers B.A., B.S., B.A.H., B.Arch., B.F.A., and B.S.A. degrees. Master's and doctoral degrees are also awarded. Bachelor's degrees are awarded in BIOLOGICAL SCIENCE (biology/biological science), BUSINESS (business administration and management, business economics, and marketing/retailing/merchandising), COMMUNICATIONS AND THE ARTS (communications, design, dramatic arts, English, fine arts, French, German, journalism, languages, music, and Spanish), COMPUTER AND PHYSICAL SCIENCE (chemistry, computer programming, computer science, information sciences and systems, mathematics, physics, and statistics), EDUCATION (music education), ENGINEERING AND ENVIRONMENTAL DESIGN (chemical engineering, civil engineering, computer engineering, electrical/electronics engineering, engineering, and mechanical engineering), SOCIAL SCIENCE (economics, history, philosophy, political science/government, psychology, public administration, social science, and urban studies). Computer science, engineering, and business administration are the strongest academically. Engineering is the largest.

Special: Students may cross-register with other Pittsburgh Council of Higher Education institutions. Also available are internships, work-study programs, study abroad in 49 countries, a Washington semester, accelerated degrees, B.A.-B.S. degrees, co-op programs, dual majors, and limited student-designed majors. There are 10 national honor societies, including Phi Beta Kappa, and a freshman honors program.

Admissions: 36% of the 2009-2010 applicants were accepted. The SAT scores for the 2009-2010 freshman class were: Critical Reading--1% below 500, 14% between 500 and 599, 16% between 600 and 700, and 69% above 700; Math--1% below 500, 5% between 500 and 599, 28% between 600 and 700, and 66% above 700; Writing--1% below 500, 13% between 500 and 599, 47% between 600 and 700, and 39% above 700. The ACT scores were 2% below 21, 3% between 21 and 23, 6% between 24 and 26, 11% between 27 and 28, and 78% above 28. 88% of the current freshmen were in the top fifth of their class; 97% were in the top two fifths. 69 freshmen graduated first in their class.

Requirements: The SAT or ACT is required. SAT Subject tests are not required for drama, design, art, or music applicants. All other applicants must take appropriate tests, preferably by December but no later than January. Applicants must graduate from an accredited secondary school or have a GED. They must earn 16 Carnegie units and must have completed 4 years of English. Applicants to the Carnegie Institute of Technology and the Mellon College of Science must take 4 years of math and 1 year each of biology, chemistry, and physics. Essays are required, and interviews are recommended. Art and design applicants must submit a portfolio. Drama and music applicants must audition. AP credits are accepted.

Procedure: Freshmen are admitted in the fall. Entrance exams should be taken be received by Jan 1 (Dec 15 for College of Fine Arts). There are early decision, early admissions and deferred admissions plans. Check with the school for current application deadlines. The fall 2009 application fee was $70. Applications are accepted on-line. A waiting list is maintained.

Financial Aid: In 2009-2010, 76% of all full-time freshmen and 67% of continuing full-time students received some form of financial aid. 53% of all full-time freshmen and 47% of continuing full-time students received need-based aid. The average freshmen award was $28,678. 31% of undergraduate students work part-time. The average financial indebtedness of the 2009 graduate was $29,546. Carnegie Mellon is a member of CSS. The FAFSA and the college's own financial statement, and parent and student federal tax returns and W-2 forms are required. Check with the school for current application deadlines.

Computers: Wireless access is available. There are 444 computers in public clusters available to students. All students may access the system 24 hours per day. There are no time limits and no fees.

CARSON-NEWMAN COLLEGE

Jefferson City, TN 37760

(865) 471-2000
(800) 678-9061; (865) 471-3502

Full-time: 820 men, 980 women	**Faculty:** IIB, --$
Part-time: 55 men, 105 women	**Ph.D.s:** n/av
Graduate: 45 men, 130 women	**Student/Faculty:** n/av
Year: semesters, summer session	**Tuition:** $19,600
Application Deadline: see profile	**Room & Board:** $6400
Freshman Class: n/av	
SAT or ACT: required	**VERY COMPETITIVE**

Carson-Newman College, founded in 1851, is a private liberal arts college affiliated with the Tennessee Baptist Convention. Figures in the above capsule are approximate. There are 2 graduate schools. In addition to regional accreditation, Carson-Newman has baccalaureate program accreditation with ADA, AHEA, NASAD, NASM, NCATE, and NLN. The library contains 300,000 volumes, 221,960 microform items, and 15,000 audio/video tapes/CDs/DVDs, and subscribes to 2000 periodicals including electronic. Computerized library services include interlibrary loans, database searching, and Internet access. Special learning facilities include a learning resource center, art gallery, natural history museum, radio station, and TV station. The 100-acre campus is in a small town 27 miles northeast of Knoxville. Including any residence halls, there are 27 buildings.

Programs of Study: Carson-Newman confers B.A., B.S., B.M., B.S.M., and B.S.N. degrees. Associates and master's degrees are also awarded. Bachelor's degrees are awarded in BIOLOGICAL SCIENCE (biology/biological science), BUSINESS (accounting, business administration and management, and business economics), COMMUNICATIONS AND THE ARTS (communications, English, fine arts, French, languages, music, and Spanish), EDUCATION (art education, early childhood education, elementary education, foreign languages education, health education, home economics education, middle school education, music education, science education, and secondary education), HEALTH PROFESSIONS (nursing and physical therapy), SOCIAL SCIENCE (economics, history, philosophy, psychology, religion, social science, and sociology). Nursing, music, and biology are the strongest academically. Nursing, business, and education are the largest.

Special: The college offers internships, study in England, France, Japan, Hong Kong, and Spain, a Washington semester, on-campus work-study programs, B.A.-B.S. degrees, dual majors, a general studies degree, student-designed majors, and pass/fail options. Students may receive credit for life, military, or work experience. There is 1 national honor society, a freshman honors program, and 16 departmental honors programs.

Admissions: There were 3 National Merit finalists in a recent year. 10 freshmen graduated first in their class.

Requirements: The SAT or ACT is required. Applicants should be graduates of an accredited secondary school. The GED is accepted. 20 academic credits are required, including 4 units of English and 2 units each of history, math, science, and social studies. An essay, a portfolio, an audition, and an interview are recommended. A GPA of 2.3 is required. AP and CLEP credits are accepted. Important factors in the admissions decision are advanced placement or honors courses, leadership record, and parents or siblings attended your school.

126

Procedure: Freshmen are admitted to all sessions. Entrance exams should be taken in the fall of the senior year or the spring of the junior year. There are deferred admissions and rolling admissions plans. Check with the school for current application deadlines. The fall 2009 application fee was $25. Applications are accepted on-line.

Financial Aid: Carson-Newman is a member of CSS. The FAFSA and the college's own financial statement are required. Check with the school for current application deadlines.

Computers: Wireless access is available. All students may access the system until the lab closes at 11 P.M. There are no time limits. The fee is $380. It is strongly recommended that all students have a personal computer.

CASE WESTERN RESERVE UNIVERSITY
Cleveland, OH 44106   (216) 368-4450; (216) 368-5111

Full-time: 2334 men, 1761 women	**Faculty:** 581; I, av$
Part-time: 52 men, 81 women	**Ph.D.s:** 95%
Graduate: 2644 men, 2866 women	**Student/Faculty:** 10 to 1
Year: semesters, summer session	**Tuition:** $36,608
Application Deadline: January 15	**Room & Board:** $10,890
Freshman Class: 7998 applied, 5599 accepted, 966 enrolled	
SAT CR/M/W: 645/690/640	**ACT:** 30 **MOST COMPETITIVE**

Case Western Reserve University, founded in 1826, is a private institution offering undergraduate, graduate, and professional programs in arts and sciences, dentistry, engineering, law, management, medicine, nursing, and social work. There are 4 undergraduate schools and 8 graduate schools. In addition to regional accreditation, Case has baccalaureate program accreditation with AACSB, ABET, CAHEA, CSAB, NASM, and NLN. The 7 libraries contain 2.5 million volumes, 2.6 million microform items, and 59,980 audio/video tapes/CDs/DVDs, and subscribe to 18,422 periodicals including electronic. Computerized library services include interlibrary loans, database searching, Internet access, and laptop Internet portals. Special learning facilities include a learning resource center, art gallery, natural history museum, planetarium, radio station, and a biology field station. The 155-acre campus is in an urban area 4 miles east of downtown Cleveland, OH. Including any residence halls, there are 130 buildings.

Programs of Study: Case confers B.A., B.S., B.S.E., and B.S.N. degrees. Master's and doctoral degrees are also awarded. Bachelor's degrees are awarded in BIOLOGICAL SCIENCE (biochemistry, biology/biological science, evolutionary biology, and nutrition), BUSINESS (accounting and business administration and management), COMMUNICATIONS AND THE ARTS (art history and appreciation, classics, comparative literature, dramatic arts, English, French, German, music, and Spanish), COMPUTER AND PHYSICAL SCIENCE (applied mathematics, astronomy, chemistry, computer science, fluid and thermal science, geology, mathematics, natural sciences, physics, polymer science, and statistics), EDUCATION (art education, education, and music education), ENGINEERING AND ENVIRONMENTAL DESIGN (aeronautical engineering, architecture, biomedical engineering, chemical engineering, civil engineering, computer engineering, electrical/electronics engineering, engineering, engineering physics, environmental science, materials science, mechanical engineering, and systems engineering), HEALTH PROFESSIONS (nursing and speech pathology/audiology), SOCIAL SCIENCE (American studies, anthropology, Asian/Oriental studies, cognitive science, economics, French studies, German area studies, gerontology, history, history of science, international studies, Japanese studies, philosophy, political science/government, psychology, religion, sociology, systems science, and women's studies). Engineering, biology, and music are the strongest academically. Engineering, nursing, and biology are the largest.

Special: Case offers co-op programs with more than 160 employers, and students may alternate classroom study with full-time employment. Cross-registration with 13 institutions in the Cleveland area is available, as well as internships in government, corporations, and nonprofit agencies. Students may participate in study abroad, a Washington semester, work-study programs, and accelerated-degree programs. B.A.-B.S. degrees, dual and student-designed majors, 3-2 engineering degrees, non-degree study, independent study, and pass/fail options are possible. There are extensive opportunities for undergraduates to work with faculty on research projects. Pre-profesional Scholars Programs in medicine, dental medicine, social work, and law are available. Interdisciplinary majors, such as environmental geology and a double major in pre-architecture, and intradisciplinary majors, such as nutritional biochemistry and metabolism, are available. There are 3 national honor societies, including Phi Beta Kappa, and 16 departmental honors programs.

Admissions: 70% of the 2009-2010 applicants were accepted. The SAT scores for the 2009-2010 freshman class were: Critical Reading--5% below 500, 21% between 500 and 599, 49% between 600 and 700, and 25% above 700; Math--1% below 500, 7% between 500 and 599, 46% between 600 and 700, and 46% above 700; Writing--3% below 500, 24% between 500 and 599, 53% between 600 and 700, and 20% above 700. The ACT scores were 1% below 21, 2% between 21 and 23, 14% between 24 and 26, 14% between 27 and 28, and 70% above 28. 82% of the current freshmen were in the top fifth of their class; 96% were in the top two fifths. There were 48 National Merit finalists. 78 freshmen graduated first in their class.

Requirements: The SAT or ACT is required. The ACT Optional Writing test is also required. In addition, SAT Subject tests in writing plus 2 others of the student's choice are strongly recommended for students who take the SAT. Applicants must be graduates of an accredited secondary school. However, the GED is accepted. 16 high school academic credits are required, including 4 years of English, 3 of math, (4 for science, math, and engineering majors), and 2 of lab science (3 for science and math majors and premedical students). 2 to 4 years of foreign language are strongly recommended. Engineering, math, and science students should take the SAT: Subject tests in math I/IC or IIC and physics and/or chemistry. A writing sample of the student's choice is required, and an interview is recommended. AP credits are accepted. Important factors in the admissions decision are advanced placement or honors courses, leadership record, and recommendations by school officials.

Procedure: Freshmen are admitted fall, spring, and summer. Entrance exams should be taken by the fall of the senior year. There is a deferred admissions plan. Applications should be filed by January 15 for fall entry. Notifications are sent March 1. Applications are accepted on-line. 188 applicants were on a recent waiting list.

Financial Aid: In 2009-2010, 84% of all full-time freshmen and 90% of continuing full-time students received some form of financial aid. 62% of all full-time freshmen and 65% of continuing full-time students received need-based aid. The average freshmen award was $35,215, with $23,434 ($48,633 maximum) from need-based scholarships or need-based grants and $9,879 ($34,500 maximum) from need-based self-help aid (loans and jobs). 45% of undergraduate students work part-time. Average annual earnings from campus work are $3200. The average financial indebtedness of the 2009 graduate was $37,207. Case is a member of CSS. The FAFSA and the college's own financial statement, and Parent and student income tax returns and W-2 forms are required. The priority date for freshman financial aid applications for fall entry is February 1.

Computers: Wireless access is available. All residence halls, classrooms, libraries, and lounges feature a switched gig-to-the desktop network, providing short download times, wireless access, and high-performance networking at speeds about 1,000 times faster than the typical home broadband network. All students may access the system. 24 hours a day. There are no time limits and no fees. It is strongly recommended that all students have a personal computer. A Windows and Mac models configured to use Case's network is recommended.

CATHOLIC UNIVERSITY OF AMERICA
Washington, DC 20064

(202) 319-5305
(800) 673-2772; (202) 319-6171

Full-time: 1250 men, 1550 women	**Faculty:** I, -$
Part-time: 85 men, 175 women	**Ph.D.s:** 98%
Graduate: 1500 men, 1595 women	**Student/Faculty:** n/av
Year: semesters, summer session	**Tuition:** $28,000
Application Deadline: see profile	**Room & Board:** $10,000
Freshman Class: n/av	
SAT or ACT: required	**VERY COMPETITIVE**

Catholic University of America, founded in 1887 and affiliated with the Roman Catholic Church, offers undergraduate programs in arts and sciences, engineering, architecture, nursing, philosophy, and music and through the Metropolitan College. Figures in the above capsule are approximate. There are 7 undergraduate schools and 11 graduate schools. In addition to regional accreditation, CUA has baccalaureate program accreditation with ABET, ACPE, CSWE, NAAB, NASM, NCATE, and NLN. The 3 libraries contain 1.6 million volumes, 1.2 million microform items, and 40,697 audio/video tapes/CDs/DVDs, and subscribe to 10,448 periodicals including electronic. Computerized library services include interlibrary loans, database searching, Internet access, and laptop Internet portals. Special learning facilities include a learning resource center, art gallery, radio station, archeology lab, rare book collection, and electronic/computer classrooms. The 193-acre campus is in an urban area in Washington, D.C. Including any residence halls, there are 52 buildings.

Programs of Study: CUA confers B.A., B.S., B.A.G.S., B. Arch, B.B.E., B.C.E., B.E.E., B.M., B.M.E., B. S. Arch, and B.S.N., degrees. Master's and doctoral degrees are also awarded. Bachelor's degrees are awarded in BIOLOGICAL SCIENCE (biochemistry and biology/biological science), BUSINESS (accounting, banking and finance, business administration and management, international economics, and management science), COMMUNICATIONS AND THE ARTS (art, art history and appreciation, classics, communications, dramatic arts, English, French, German, Latin, music, music history and appreciation, music performance, music theory and composition, musical theater, painting, piano/organ, sculpture, Spanish, and voice), COMPUTER AND PHYSICAL SCIENCE (chemistry, computer science, elementary particle physics, mathematics, and physics), EDUCATION (art education, drama education, early childhood education, education, elementary education, English education, mathematics education, music education, and secondary education), ENGINEERING AND ENVIRONMENTAL DESIGN (architecture, biomedical engineering, civil engineering, electrical/electronics engineering, engineering, environmental science, and mechanical engineering), HEALTH PROFESSIONS (medical laboratory technology and nursing), SOCIAL SCIENCE (anthropology, economics, history, liberal arts/general studies, medieval studies, philosophy, political science/government, psychology, religion, social work, and sociology). Politics is the strongest academically. Architecture is the largest.

Special: Cross-registration is available with the Consortium of Universities of the Washington Metropolitan Area. Opportunities are also provided for internships, accelerated degree programs, dual majors, B.A.-B.S. degrees, work study, pass/fail options, and study abroad in 13 countries. There are 15 national honor societies, including Phi Beta Kappa, and a freshman honors program.

Requirements: The SAT or ACT is required. In addition, applicants must be graduates of an accredited secondary school. Students should present 17 academic credits, including 4 each in English and social studies, 3 each in math and science, 2 in foreign languages, and 1 in fine arts or humanities. An essay is required. An audition is required for music applicants, and a portfolio for architecture applicants is recommended. A GPA of 3.0 is required. AP credits are accepted. Important factors in the admissions decision are extracurricular activities record, leadership record, and advanced placement or honors courses.

Procedure: Freshmen are admitted fall and spring. Entrance exams should be taken by February of the senior year of high school. There is early decision and deferred admissions plans. Check with the school for current application deadlines. The fall 2009 application fee was $55. Applications are accepted on-line.

Financial Aid: CUA is a member of CSS. The FAFSA is required. Check with the school for current application deadlines.

Computers: Wireless access is available. There are 500 PCs located around campus for student use. All students may access the system 24 hours a day, 7 days a week. There are no time limits and no fees. It is strongly recommended that all students have a personal computer. A Dell or Gateway is recommended.

CEDARVILLE UNIVERSITY
Cedarville, OH 45314-0601 (937) 766-7700
(800) CEDARVILLE; (937) 766-2760

Full-time: 1285 men, 1595 women	**Faculty:** IIB, -$
Part-time: 60 men, 70 women	**Ph.D.s:** n/av
Graduate: none	**Student/Faculty:** n/av
Year: semesters, summer session	**Tuition:** $23,500
Application Deadline: open	**Room & Board:** $5100
Freshman Class: n/av	
SAT or ACT: required	**VERY COMPETITIVE+**

Cedarville University, founded in 1887, is a private Baptist college of arts and sciences offering programs in engineering, nursing, accounting, computer information systems, and education. Figures in the above capsule are approximate. In addition to regional accreditation, Cedarville has baccalaureate program accreditation with ABET and NLN. The library contains 195,949 volumes, 20,698 microform items, and 7320 audio/video tapes/CDs/DVDs, and subscribes to 15,707 periodicals including electronic. Computerized library services include interlibrary loans, database searching, Internet access, and laptop Internet portals. Special learning facilities include a learning resource center, radio station, media resource center, and observatory. The 400-acre campus is in a small town 12 miles south of Springfield. Including any residence halls, there are 45 buildings.

Programs of Study: Cedarville confers B.A., B.S., B.M., B.M.E., B.S.E.E., B.S.M.E., B.S.N., and Cp.E. degrees. Master's degrees are also awarded. Bachelor's degrees are awarded in BIOLOGICAL SCIENCE (biology/biological science), BUSINESS (accounting, banking and finance, business administration and management, management information systems, marketing/retailing/ merchandising, and sports management), COMMUNICATIONS AND THE ARTS (communications, dramatic arts, English, graphic design, multimedia, music, Spanish, and technical and business writing), COMPUTER AND PHYSICAL SCIENCE (chemistry, computer science, information sciences and systems, mathematics, and physics), EDUCATION (athletic training, Christian education, early childhood education, English education, foreign languages education, mathematics education, middle school education, music education, physical education, science education, social studies education, and special education), ENGINEERING AND ENVIRONMENTAL DESIGN (computer engineering, electrical/ electronics engineering, and mechanical engineering), HEALTH PROFESSIONS (exercise science and nursing), SOCIAL SCIENCE (American studies, biblical studies, criminal justice, history, international studies, missions, pastoral studies, philosophy, political science/government, prelaw, psychology, public administration, religious music, social work, and sociology). Biblical education, business administration, and education are the largest.

Special: Internships, study abroad in 97 countries, a Washington semester, dual majors, student-designed majors, B.A.-B.S. degrees in biology, physics, chemistry, and math, and work-study programs with the college are available. Cross-registration with the Southwest Ohio Consortium for Higher Education and the Ohio Learning Network is possible. There are 6 national honor societies, a freshman honors program, and 5 departmental honors programs.

Admissions: In a recent year, there were 4 National Merit finalists. 51 freshmen graduated first in their class.

Requirements: The SAT or ACT (preferred) is required, with scores above the national average preferred. The college recommends that applicants have 4 years of English, 3 to 4 of math, and 3 each of social studies, math, science, and a foreign language. The GED is accepted. Recommendations from a local pastor and a high school counselor are required. An interview is recommended. Cedarville requires applicants to be in the upper 50% of their class. A GPA of 3.0 is required. AP and CLEP credits are accepted. Important factors in the admissions decision are personality/intangible qualities, recommendations by school officials, and advanced placement or honors courses.

Procedure: Freshmen are admitted to all sessions. Entrance exams should be taken by late junior year or early senior year. There are early admissions, deferred admissions, and rolling admissions plans. Application deadlines are open. The application fee is $30. Applications are accepted on-line. A waiting list is maintained.

Financial Aid: In a recent year, 93% of all full-time freshmen and 89% of continuing full-time students received some form of financial aid. 78% of all full-time freshmen and 69% of continuing full-time students received need-based aid. The average freshmen award was $15,462, with $5380 ($15,860 maximum) from need-based scholarships or need-based grants; $4073 ($10,000 maximum) from need-based self-help aid (loans and jobs); $4081 ($19,680 maximum) from non-need-based athletic scholarships; and $11,227 ($29,261 maximum) from other non-need-based awards and non-need-based scholarships. 54% of undergraduate students work part-time. Average annual earnings from campus work are $798. The average financial indebtedness of a recent graduate was $40,796. The FAFSA and the college's own financial statement are required. Check with the school for current application deadlines.

Computers: Wireless access is available. There are 2600 university-owned computers on campus, including university-owned computers and printers in every dorm room, and over 150 software packages available on the network. Cedarville University is a participant in the Internet 2, grid-computing project available for student research, gigabit connectivity to other Ohio universities, and on-line access to 4000 full-text journals. All students may access the system 24 hours a day for dorm rooms or up to 93 hours a week in the labs. There are no time limits and no fees.

CENTENARY COLLEGE OF LOUISIANA
Shreveport, LA 71104
(318) 869-5131
(800) 234-4448; (318) 869-5005

Full- and part-time: 370 men, 500 women	**Faculty:** 72; IIB, -$
	Ph.D.s: 94%
Graduate: 50 men, 100 women	**Student/Faculty:** n/av
Year: semesters, summer session	**Tuition:** $22,880
Application Deadline: see profile	**Room & Board:** $8400
Freshman Class: n/av	
SAT or ACT: required	**VERY COMPETITIVE**

Centenary College of Louisiana, founded in 1825, is a private institution affiliated with the United Methodist Church offering degrees in the liberal arts, music, business, sciences, and education. There are 2 graduate schools. Figures in the above capsule and in this profile are approximate. In addition to regional accreditation, Centenary has baccalaureate program accreditation with NASM. The 2 libraries contain 180,000 volumes, 310,600 microform items, and 400 audio/video tapes/CDs/DVDs, and subscribe to 900 periodicals including electronic. Computerized library services include interlibrary loans and database searching. Special learning facilities include a radio station, a theater, and an art museum. The 65-acre campus is in an urban area in the northwest corner of Louisana, 180 miles East of Dallas, Texas. Including any residence halls, there are 23 buildings.

Programs of Study: Centenary confers B.A., B.S., and B.M. degrees. Master's degrees are also awarded. Bachelor's degrees are awarded in BIOLOGICAL SCIENCE (biochemistry, biology/biological science, biophysics, and neurosciences), BUSINESS (accounting, banking and finance, business administration and management, and business economics), COMMUNICATIONS AND THE ARTS (art, communications, dance, dramatic arts, English, French, German, Latin, music, music performance, and Spanish), COMPUTER AND PHYSICAL SCIENCE (chemistry, geology, mathematics, and physics), EDUCATION (elementary education, foreign languages education, music education, physical education, and social studies education), ENGINEERING AND ENVIRONMENTAL DESIGN (environmental science), HEALTH PROFESSIONS (exercise science), SOCIAL SCIENCE (economics, history, interdisciplinary studies, liberal arts/general studies, philosophy, political science/government, psychology, religion, religious music, and sociology). Physical sciences, life sciences, and political science are the strongest academically. Business, biology, and psychology are the largest.

Special: Centenary offers study abroad in 7 countries, cross-registration with Associated Colleges of the South, internships in all majors, a Washington semester, and a work-study program within the college. A 3-1 communications disorders degree with Louisiana State University Medical Center is possible, as is a 3-2 engineering degree with Washington University in St. Louis, the University of Southern California, Columbia, Texas A&M, and Case Western Reserve Universities, and Louisiana Tech. A 3-2 applied science preprofessional degree combines with health administration or medical school. Preveterinary studies, general studies and interdisciplinary degrees, and student-designed majors are available. There are 7 national honor societies and 15 departmental honors programs.

Requirements: A satisfactory score is required on the SAT or ACT. In addition, applicants should be high school graduates. Secondary school preparation should include 15 academic credits, including 4 of English, 3 each of math and science, 2 each of a foreign language and history, 1 of social studies, and electives. Music students must audition; art students are advised to present a portfolio. A GPA of 2.0 is required. AP credits are accepted. Important factors in the admissions decision are advanced placement or honors courses, extracurricular activities record, and personality/intangible qualities.

Procedure: Freshmen are admitted fall, spring, and summer. Entrance exams should be taken by the fall of the senior year. There are early decision, early admissions and rolling admissions plans. Early decision applications should be filed by December 1. Check with the school for other current application deadlines. Notification of early decision is sent January 1. Applications are accepted on-line.

Financial Aid: The FAFSA and the college's own financial statement are required. Check with the school for current financial aid deadlines.

Computers: Wireless access is available. All students may access the system. There are no time limits. Check with the school for current fees. It is strongly recommended that all students have a personal computer.

CENTRAL COLLEGE
Pella, IA 50219

(641) 628-5285
(877) 462-3687; (641) 628-5316

Full-time: 752 men, 845 women	**Faculty:** 88; IIB, -$
Part-time: 16 men, 23 women	**Ph.D.s:** 88%
Graduate: none	**Student/Faculty:** 17 to 1
Year: semesters, summer session	**Tuition:** $25,010
Application Deadline: March 1	**Room & Board:** $8368
Freshman Class: 2451 applied, 1823 accepted, 443 enrolled	
SAT: required	**ACT:** 24 **VERY COMPETITIVE**

Central College, founded in 1853, is a private institution affiliated with the Reformed Church in America. The college offers undergraduate degree programs in applied arts, behavioral sciences, cross-cultural studies, fine arts, humanities, and natural sciences. There is 1 undergraduate school. In addition to regional accreditation, Central has baccalaureate program accreditation with NASM and NCATE. The 3 libraries contain 197,672 volumes, 51,906 microform items, and 10,986 audio/video tapes/CDs/DVDs, and subscribe to 11,206 periodicals including electronic. Computerized library services include interlibrary loans, database searching, Internet access, and laptop Internet portals. Special learning facilities include a learning resource center, art gallery, and radio station. The 169-acre campus is in a suburban area 45 miles southeast of Des Moines. Including any residence halls, there are 50 buildings.

Programs of Study: Central confers B.A. degrees. Bachelor's degrees are awarded in BIOLOGICAL SCIENCE (biology/biological science), BUSINESS (accounting, business administration and management, and international business management), COMMUNICATIONS AND THE ARTS (communications, dramatic arts, English, fine arts, French, German, languages, linguistics, music, and Spanish), COMPUTER AND PHYSICAL SCIENCE (actuarial science, chemistry, computer science, mathematics, and physics), EDUCATION (athletic training, elementary education, music education, and secondary education), ENGINEERING AND ENVIRONMENTAL DESIGN (environmental science),

HEALTH PROFESSIONS (exercise science), SOCIAL SCIENCE (anthropology, economics, history, international studies, philosophy, political science/government, psychology, religion, and sociology). Business management, elementary education, and exercise science are the largest.

Special: Nearly half the students participate in study abroad programs in London, Paris, Vienna, Mexico, Spain, Wales, China, and the Netherlands. Central also offers a Washington, D.C. semester, a Chicago program, numerous internship opportunities, and work-study. A 3-2 engineering degree is available with Washington, Iowa State, and Iowa Universities. General studies and individualized interdisciplinary majors are also available. There is 1 national honor society and a freshman honors program.

Admissions: 74% of the 2009-2010 applicants were accepted. The ACT scores were 23% below 21, 25% between 21 and 23, 27% between 24 and 26, 14% between 27 and 28, and 11% above 28. 54% of the current freshmen were in the top fourth of their class; 84% were in the top half. 25 freshmen graduated first in their class.

Requirements: The SAT or ACT is required. In addition, applicants must be graduates of an accredited secondary school or have earned a GED. Central requires 16 academic credits and recommends including 4 years of English, 3 each of lab science, social studies, and math, including 2 in algebra and 1 in geometry, and 2 of foreign language. An interview and an essay is recommended. Central requires applicants to be in the upper 50% of their class. A GPA of 2.7 is required. AP and CLEP credits are accepted.

Procedure: Freshmen are admitted to all sessions. Entrance exams should be taken in the spring of the junior year. There are deferred admissions and rolling admissions plans. Applications should be filed by March 1 for fall entry, November 1 for spring entry, and May 1 for summer entry, along with a $25 fee. Notification is sent on a rolling basis. Applications are accepted on-line.

Financial Aid: In 2009-2010, 89% of all full-time freshmen and 82% of continuing full-time students received some form of financial aid. At least 89% of all full-time freshmen and at least 82% of continuing full-time students received need-based aid. The average freshman award was $23,302. Need-based scholarships or need-based grants averaged $17,284; need-based self-help aid (loans and jobs) averaged $5273; and non-need-based awards and non-need-based scholarships averaged $12,169. 63% of undergraduate students work part-time. Average annual earnings from campus work are $722. The average financial indebtedness of the 2009 graduate was $15,811. Central is a member of CSS. The FAFSA is required. The priority date for freshman financial aid applications for fall entry is March 15.

Computers: Wireless access is available. There are 700 computers serving the academic program and distributed across campus, of which nearly 500 are reserved for student use. Residential rooms are equipped with dedicated high-speed network connections. All students may access the system. There are no time limits. The fee is $90 per semester. It is strongly recommended that all students have a personal computer.

Danville, KY 40422

(859) 238-5350
(800) 423-6236; (859) 238-5373

Full-time: 500 men, 600 women	**Faculty:** 102; IIB, av$
Part-time: 3 men and women	**Ph.D.s:** 98%
Graduate: none	**Student/Faculty:** 12 to 1
Year: 4-1-4	**Tuition:** see profile
Application Deadline: see profile	**Room & Board:** see profile
Freshman Class: n/av	
SAT or ACT: required	**HIGHLY COMPETITIVE+**

Centre College, founded in 1819 by the Presbyterian Church (U.S.A.), is a private liberal arts and sciences institution. A comprehensive fee of $40,750 per year includes tuition, room, and board. Some figures in the above capsule and in this profile are approximate. The library contains 361,500 volumes, 56,700 microform items, and 4,300 audio/video tapes/CDs/DVDs, and subscribes to 19,300 periodicals including electronic. Computerized library services include interlibrary loans, database searching, Internet access, and laptop Internet portals. Special learning facilities include a learning resource center, art gallery, natural history museum, radio station, TV station, and performing arts center. The 150-acre campus is in a small town 35 miles southwest of Lexington and 80 miles southeast of Louisville. Including any residence halls, there are 67 buildings.

Programs of Study: Centre confers B.A. and B.S. degrees. Bachelor's degrees are awarded in BIOLOGICAL SCIENCE (biochemistry, biology/biological science, and molecular biology), COMMUNICATIONS AND THE ARTS (art history and appreciation, dramatic arts, English, fine arts, French, German, music, and Spanish), COMPUTER AND PHYSICAL SCIENCE (chemical physics, chemistry, computer science, mathematics, physical chemistry, and physics), EDUCATION (elementary education), SOCIAL SCIENCE (anthropology, classical/ancient civilization, economics, history, international relations, philosophy, political science/government, psychobiology, psychology, religion, and sociology). Biology, history, and psychology are the strongest academically and have the largest enrollments.

Special: Centre offers internships, study abroad in 12 countries, a Washington semester through American University, work-study, and a 3-2 engineering degree with Vanderbilt University, Washington University at St. Louis, Columbia University, and the University of Kentucky. Student-designed majors, interdisciplinary majors including chemical physics, secondary education certification, and prelaw, prebusiness, and premedicine programs are available. Pass/fail options also are available. There are 8 national honor societies including Phi Beta Kappa.

Admissions: 61% of a recent year's applicants were accepted. The SAT scores for a recent year's freshman class were: Critical Reading--6% below 500, 31% between 500 and 599, 38% between 600 and 700, and 25% above 700; Math--6% below 500, 28% between 500 and 599, 56% between 600 and 700, and 10% above 700. The ACT scores were 2% below 21, 6% between 21 and 23, 25% between 24 and 26, 22% between 27 and 28, and 45% above 28. 79% of recent freshmen were in the top fifth of their class; 95% were in the top two fifths. There were 8 National Merit finalists. 29 freshmen graduated first in their class.

Requirements: The SAT or ACT are required, and the ACT writing test is recommended. No minimum test scores are required. Students should have completed a minimum of 15 academic credits, including 4 years each in English and math, 3 years each in science and social studies, 2 years in foreign language, and

1 year in an art- or music-related course. An essay is required, and an interview is strongly recommended. AP credits are accepted. Important factors in the admissions decision are advanced placement or honors courses, extracurricular activities record, and recommendations by school officials.

Procedure: Freshmen are admitted in the fall. Entrance exams should be taken by February of the senior year. There is a deferred admissions plan. Check with the school for current application deadlines and fee. Applications are accepted on-line. 186 applicants were on a recent waiting list, 19 were accepted.

Financial Aid: In a recent year, 95% of all full-time freshmen and 96% of continuing full-time students received some form of financial aid. 58% of all full-time freshmen and 56% of continuing full-time students received need-based aid. The average freshman award was $22,193. Need-based scholarships or need-based grants averaged $19,673 ($28,000 maximum); and need-based self-help aid (loans and jobs) averaged $4,599 ($5,300 maximum). 24% of undergraduate students work part-time. Average annual earnings from campus work are $1750. The average financial indebtedness of a recent graduate was $15,700. Centre is a member of CSS. The FAFSA and the college's own financial statement are required. Check with the school for current deadlines.

Computers: Wireless access is available. All students may access the system. There are no time limits and no fees.

CHAMPLAIN COLLEGE
Burlington, VT 05402-0670

(802) 860-2727
(800) 570-5858; (802) 860-2767

Full-time: 1155 men, 850 women	**Faculty:** n/av
Part-time: 330 men, 355 women	**Ph.D.s:** 40%
Graduate: 70 men, 45 women	**Student/Faculty:** n/av
Year: semesters, summer session	**Tuition:** $27,200
Application Deadline: see profile	**Room & Board:** $12,000
Freshman Class: n/av	
SAT or ACT: required	**VERY COMPETITIVE**

Champlain College, founded in 1878, is a private school that offers professional training in a liberal arts setting. Students earn their bachelor's degree, with an embedded associate's degree, in one of 24 majors. Internship opportunities are built into the curriculum. Champlain also offers 2 on-line master's degrees. Figures in the above capsule and this profile are approximate. There is 1 undergraduate school. The library contains 40,213 volumes, 1020 microform items, and 1175 audio/video tapes/CDs/DVDs, and subscribes to 27,045 periodicals including electronic. Computerized library services include interlibrary loans, database searching, and Internet access. Special learning facilities include a learning resource center, a video production studio, and several multimedia and graphic design studios. The 21-acre campus is in a suburban area in the Hill section of Burlington. Including any residence halls, there are 38 buildings.

Programs of Study: Champlain confers B.S. degrees. Associate and master's degrees are also awarded. Bachelor's degrees are awarded in BUSINESS (accounting, business administration and management, electronic business, hospitality management services, hotel/motel and restaurant management, international business management, management science, marketing management, and tourism), COMMUNICATIONS AND THE ARTS (advertising, broadcasting, communications technology, graphic design, journalism, media arts, multimedia, public relations, technical and business writing, and telecommunications), COMPUTER AND PHYSICAL SCIENCE (computer security and information assurance, information sciences and systems, radiological technology, software engineering, and web services), EDUCATION (early childhood education, elementary education, middle school education, and secondary education), SOCIAL SCIENCE (applied psychology, criminal justice, forensic studies, liberal arts/general studies, paralegal studies, psychology, and social work). Information security, software engineering, and electronic game and interactive development are the strongest academically. Business and multimedia/graphic design are the largest.

Special: Cross-registration with St. Michael's College, co-op programs with the Walt Disney World College Program, Federal Law Enforcement Training Center, and Vermont police academy, student teaching, internships, and study abroad through school-sponsored programs in England, France, Sweden, and Switzerland are available. Study abroad in other countries is also available. Dual majors are possible through the professional studies and computer information systems programs. Accelerated degree programs, such as the 5-year B.S./M.B.A. with Clarkson and Southern New Hampshire Universities, and student-designed majors are also available. There is a freshman honors program and 99 departmental honors programs.

Requirements: The SAT or ACT is required. In addition, applicants must be graduates of an accredited high school or the equivalent. AP and CLEP credits are accepted. Important factors in the admissions decision are advanced placement or honors courses, recommendations by school officials, and leadership record.

Procedure: Freshmen are admitted fall and spring. Entrance exams should be taken prior to applying. There are early decision and deferred admissions plans. Application deadlines are open. Notifications are sent March 25. Applications are accepted on-line.

Financial Aid: In a recent year, 77% of all full-time freshmen and all continuing full-time students received some form of financial aid. 63% of all full-time freshmen and all continuing full-time students received need-based aid. The average freshman award was $4869. 70% of undergraduate students work part-time. Average annual earnings from campus work are $1190. The FAFSA and the college's own financial statement are required. Check with the school for current application deadlines.

Computers: Wireless access is available. All students may access the system. There are no time limits and no fees. It is strongly recommended that all students have a personal computer. Students enrolled in multimedia graphic design must have a personal computer. A Mac is recommended.

CHAPMAN UNIVERSITY

| Orange, CA 92866 | (714) 997-6711 |
| | (888) CU-APPLY; (714) 997-6713 |

Full-time: 1790 men, 2474 women	**Faculty:** 291; IIA, ++$
Part-time: 100 men, 112 women	**Ph.D.s:** 91%
Graduate: 849 men, 1073 women	**Student/Faculty:** 15 to 1
Year: 4-1-4, summer session	**Tuition:** $36,764
Application Deadline: January 15	**Room & Board:** $12,832
Freshman Class: 6159 applied, 3468 accepted, 1032 enrolled	
SAT CR/M/W: 604/623/614	**ACT:** 27 **VERY COMPETITIVE+**

Chapman University, founded in 1861, is one of the oldest private universities in California. There are 6 undergraduate schools and 6 graduate schools. In addition to regional accreditation, Chapman has baccalaureate program accreditation with AACSB and NASM. The 2 libraries contain 242,910 volumes, 685,188 microform items, and 13,523 audio/video tapes/CDs/DVDs, and subscribe to 1630 periodicals including electronic. Computerized library services include interlibrary loans, database searching, Internet access, and laptop Internet portals. Special learning facilities include a learning resource center, art gallery, radio station, food science sensory lab, and economic sciences lab. The 76-acre campus is in a suburban area 35 miles southeast of Los Angeles. Including any residence halls, there are 40 buildings.

Programs of Study: Chapman confers B.A., B.S., B.F.A., B.M. degrees. Master's and doctoral degrees are also awarded. Bachelor's degrees are awarded in BIOLOGICAL SCIENCE (biochemistry and biology/biological science), BUSINESS (accounting and business administration and management), COMMUNICATIONS AND THE ARTS (art, art history and appreciation, broadcasting, communications, creative writing, dance, dramatic arts, English, film arts, French, graphic design, music, music performance, music theory and composition, playwriting/screenwriting, public relations, Spanish, and studio art), COMPUTER AND PHYSICAL SCIENCE (chemistry, computer science, information sciences and systems, and mathematics), EDUCATION (athletic training and music education), ENGINEERING AND ENVIRONMENTAL DESIGN (environmental science), HEALTH PROFESSIONS (health science and music therapy), SOCIAL SCIENCE (economics, history, liberal arts/general studies, peace studies, philosophy, political science/government, psychology, religion, and sociology). Business is the strongest academically. Business, film, and communication studies are the largest.

Special: Internship programs are available. Students may study abroad for a semester or spend a semester in Washington, D.C. Dual and student-designed majors are possible. A general studies degree, B.A.-B.S. degrees, nondegree study options, and pass/fail options are also permitted. A 3-2 engineering degree with the University of California, Irvine, is possible. There are 3 national honor societies and a freshman honors program.

Admissions: 56% of the 2009-2010 applicants were accepted. The SAT scores for the 2009-2010 freshman class were: Critical Reading--4% below 500, 45% between 500 and 599, 43% between 600 and 700, and 8% above 700; Math--2% below 500, 34% between 500 and 599, 50% between 600 and 700, and 14% above 700; Writing--3% below 500, 39% between 500 and 599, 47% between 600 and 700, and 11% above 700. The ACT scores were 1% below 21, 16% between 21 and 23, 34% between 24 and 26, 22% between 27 and 28, and 27% above 28.

Requirements: The SAT or ACT is required. The ACT Optional Writing test is also required. In addition, applicants should be graduates of accredited high schools or have earned the GED. Secondary preparation should include 4 years of English, 3 each of math and social science or electives, and 2 each of science and a foreign language. Prospective art or music majors should show some preparation in those fields. A personal essay is required. An on-campus interview is recommended. Entry to the film school requires portfolio acceptance. Dance performance and theater performance require audition. A GPA of 2.8 is required. AP and CLEP credits are accepted. Important factors in the admissions decision are advanced placement or honors courses, evidence of special talent, and leadership record.

Procedure: Freshmen are admitted fall and spring. Entrance exams should be taken by fall of the senior year. Applications should be filed by January 15 for fall entry and November 1 for spring entry, along with a $55 fee. Notification is sent January 15. Applications are accepted on-line. A waiting list is maintained.

Financial Aid: In 2007-2008, 90% of all full-time freshmen and 86% of continuing full-time students received some form of financial aid. 56% of all full-time freshmen and 59% of continuing full-time students received need-based aid. The average freshman award was $25,481. Need-based scholarships or need-based grants averaged $22,290; need-based self-help aid (loans and jobs) averaged $6452; and other non-need-based awards and non-need-based scholarships averaged $18,040. The average financial indebtedness of the 2009 graduate was $22,955. Chapman is a member of CSS. The FAFSA and the state aid form are required. The priority date for freshman financial aid applications for fall entry is March 2.

Computers: Wireless access is available. Wireless access covers the entire campus, and Internet access is available in dorms. PC stations are available for general student use in dorms, libraries, and labs. There are Mac labs for the film production and graphic design programs. All students may access the system 24 hours a day, 7 days a week. There are no time limits and no fees. It is strongly recommended that all students have a personal computer.

CHRISTENDOM COLLEGE
Front Royal, VA 22630

(540) 636-2900
(800) 877-5456; (540) 636-1655

Full-time: 185 men, 210 women	**Faculty:** n/av
Part-time: 5 men, 10 women	**Ph.D.s:** 65%
Graduate: 35 men, 35 women	**Student/Faculty:** n/av
Year: semesters	**Tuition:** $19,500
Application Deadline: see profile	**Room & Board:** $7500
Freshman Class: n/av	
SAT or ACT: required	**VERY COMPETITIVE**

Christendom College, founded in 1977, is a private liberal arts institution affiliated with the Roman Catholic Church. Figures in the above capsule and this profile are approximate. There is 1 graduate school. The library contains 68,314 volumes, 860 microform items, and 1345 audio/video tapes/CDs/DVDs, and subscribes to 279 periodicals including electronic. Computerized library services include interlibrary loans and database searching. Special learning facilities include a learning resource center and a writing center. The 100-acre campus is in a rural area 65 miles west of Washington, D.C. Including any residence halls, there are 19 buildings.

Programs of Study: Christendom confers B.A. degrees. Associate and master's degrees are also awarded. Bachelor's degrees are awarded in COMMUNICATIONS AND THE ARTS (English), SOCIAL SCIENCE (classical/ancient civilization, history, philosophy, political science/government, and theological studies). Political science is the strongest academically. Philosophy is the largest.

Special: Christendom offers summer internships in Washington, D.C. for political science students and also sponsors a semester in Rome during the junior year. Students may pursue dual majors. There is a work-study program with the college. There are 5 departmental honors programs.

Requirements: The SAT or ACT is required, with a total score of 1650 on the SAT or 24 on the ACT. The SAT is preferred. Applicants need not be graduates of an accredited secondary school. GED certificates are accepted. Essays and letters of recommendation are required. A campus visit and a meeting with the Admissions Director are highly recommended. Christendom requires applicants to be in the upper 50% of their class. A GPA of 3.0 is required. AP credits are accepted.

Procedure: Freshmen are admitted fall and spring. Entrance exams should be taken in the spring of the junior year or fall of the senior year. There is an early admissions plan. Check with the school for current application deadlines. The application fee is $25 (waived for on-line applications). Applications are accepted on-line.

Financial Aid: In a recent year, 78% of all full-time freshmen and 66% of continuing full-time students received some form of financial aid. 53% of all full-time freshmen and 52% of continuing full-time students received need-based aid. The average freshman award was $10,845. 40% of undergraduate students work part-time. Average annual earnings from campus work are $1750. The average financial indebtedness of a recent graduate was $13,570. The the college's own financial statement is required. Check with the school for current application deadlines.

Computers: All students may access the system. There are no time limits and no fees.

CHRISTIAN BROTHERS UNIVERSITY

Memphis, TN 38104-5581
(901) 321-4213
(800) 288-7576; (901) 321-3202

Full-time: 577 men, 683 women	**Faculty:** 91; IIB, --$
Part-time: 53 men, 112 women	**Ph.D.s:** 87%
Graduate: 194 men, 257 women	**Student/Faculty:** 13 to 1
Year: semesters, summer session	**Tuition:** $23,730
Application Deadline: August 1	**Room & Board:** $6140
Freshman Class: 1912 applied, 936 accepted, 302 enrolled	
ACT: 24	**HIGHLY COMPETITIVE**

Christian Brothers University, founded in 1871, is a private Catholic university providing undergraduate educational opportunities in the arts, business, engineering, the sciences, and teacher education and specialized graduate programs. There are 4 undergraduate schools and 3 graduate schools. In addition to regional accreditation, CBU has baccalaureate program accreditation with ABET and NCATE. The library contains 165,204 volumes and 1818 audio/video tapes/CDs/DVDs, and subscribes to 18,377 periodicals including electronic. Computerized library services include interlibrary loans, database searching, Internet access, and laptop Internet portals. Special learning facilities include a learning resource center, art gallery, and radio station. The 75-acre campus is in an urban area in Memphis. Including any residence halls, there are 25 buildings.

Programs of Study: CBU confers B.A., B.F.A., and B.S. degrees. Master's degrees are also awarded. Bachelor's degrees are awarded in BIOLOGICAL SCIENCE (biochemistry and biology/biological science), BUSINESS (accounting and business administration and management), COMMUNICATIONS AND THE ARTS (English and studio art), COMPUTER AND PHYSICAL SCIENCE (chemistry, computer science, mathematics, natural sciences, and physics), EDUCATION (early childhood education and special education), ENGINEERING AND ENVIRONMENTAL DESIGN (chemical engineering, civil engineering, electrical/electronics engineering, engineering management, engineering physics, and mechanical engineering), SOCIAL SCIENCE (applied psychology, history, liberal arts/general studies, philosophy and religion, and psychology). Engineering and biology are the strongest academically. Psychology, business, and electrical and mechanical engineering are the largest.

Special: Special academic programs include on-campus work study, study abroad in 4 countries, and internships for all juniors and seniors. There is cross-registration with the Greater Memphis Consortium, Rhodes College, and the University of Memphis. An accelerated degree program is available to all business and psychology majors through the professional studies program, and a general studies degree is offered. Up to 36 hours of nondegree study is possible, as are dual majors, an honors program, and pass/fail options. Numerous teacher licensure programs are also offered. There are 9 national honor societies and a freshman honors program.

Admissions: 49% of the 2009-2010 applicants were accepted. The ACT scores were 10% below 21, 39% between 21 and 23, 28% between 24 and 26, 10% between 27 and 28, and 13% above 28. 57% of the current freshmen were in the top fifth of their class; 84% were in the top two fifths. 4 freshmen graduated first in their class.

Requirements: The ACT is required, with a score of 20. Other admissions requirements include graduation from an accredited secondary school with a college-preparatory curriculum recommended. The GED is also accepted. An interview is advised. A GPA of 2.5 is required. AP and CLEP credits are accepted. Important factors in the admissions decision are advanced placement or honors courses, leadership record, and recommendations by school officials.

Procedure: Freshmen are admitted to all sessions. Entrance exams should be taken by the end of the junior year. There are deferred admissions and rolling admissions plans. Applications should be filed by August 1 for fall entry, December 1 for spring entry, and May 1 for summer entry, along with a $25 fee. Notifications are sent December 1. Applications are accepted on-line.

Financial Aid: In 2009-2010, 79% of all full-time freshmen and 75% of continuing full-time students received some form of financial aid. 97% of undergraduate students work part-time. Average annual earnings from campus work are $1199. The average financial indebtedness of the 2009 graduate was $28,259. The FAFSA is required. Check with the school for current application deadlines.

Computers: Wireless access is available. All students may access the system during the 93 1/2 hours per week of computer center operation; 24-hour dial-in phone access is available. There are no time limits and no fees.

CHRISTOPHER NEWPORT UNIVERSITY
Newport News, VA 23606-2998

(757) 594-7015
(800) 333-4268; (757) 594-7333

Full-time: 2010 men, 2450 women	**Faculty:** IIB, +$
Part-time: 105 men, 130 women	**Ph.D.s:** 85%
Graduate: 70 men, 125 women	**Student/Faculty:** n/av
Year: semesters, summer session	**Tuition:** $8500 ($18,000)
Application Deadline: see profile	**Room & Board:** $9000
Freshman Class: n/av	
SAT or ACT: required	**VERY COMPETITIVE**

Christopher Newport University, founded in 1960, is a comprehensive public university offering undergraduate programs in business and economics, arts and humanities, social science and professional studies, and science and technology. Figures in the above capsule and this profile are approximate. There are 2 undergraduate schools and 1 graduate school. In addition to regional accreditation, CNU has baccalaureate program accreditation with AACSB, ABET, CSWE, and NASM. The library contains 399,557 volumes, 198,744 microform items, and 9679 audio/video tapes/CDs/DVDs, and subscribes to 906 periodicals including electronic. Computerized library services include interlibrary loans, database searching, Internet access, and laptop Internet portals. Special learning facilities include a learning resource center, art gallery, radio station, the Ferguson Center for the Arts, and the Mariner's Museum Library. The 260-acre campus is in a suburban area 20 miles northwest of Norfolk and 20 miles southeast of Williamsburg. Including any residence halls, there are 20 buildings.

Programs of Study: CNU confers B.A., B.S., B.M., B.S.B.A., and B.S.I.S. degrees. Master's degrees are also awarded. Bachelor's degrees are awarded in AGRICULTURE (horticulture), BIOLOGICAL SCIENCE (biology/biological science and environmental biology), BUSINESS (accounting, banking and finance, business administration and management, business economics, and marketing management), COMMUNICATIONS AND THE ARTS (art history and appreciation, classical languages, communications, creative writing, dramatic arts, English, English literature, fine arts, French, German, journalism, language arts, literature, music, music history and appreciation, music performance, music theory and composition, musical theater, performing arts, romance languages and literature, Spanish, studio art, technical and business writing, theater design, and theater management), COMPUTER AND PHYSICAL SCIENCE (applied physics, chemistry, computer science, information sciences and systems, mathematics, and physics), EDUCATION (music education), ENGINEERING AND ENVIRONMENTAL DESIGN (computer engineering and environmental science), HEALTH PROFESSIONS (predentistry, premedicine, preoptometry, prepharmacy, prephysical therapy, and preveterinary science), SOCIAL SCIENCE (American studies, anthropology, criminology, history, interdisciplinary studies, philosophy, political science/government, prelaw, psychology, religion, social work, and sociology). Business, psychology, and biology are the largest.

Special: CNU offers cross-registration with Thomas Nelson Community College and Hampton and Old Dominion Universities, dual majors, various B.A.-B.S. degrees, a student-designed interdisciplinary studies major internship, and study abroad in 23 countries. Special course offerings include the Honors Program, President's Leadership Program, and Freshman Learning Communities. There are 20 national honor societies, a freshman honors program, and 16 departmental honors programs.

Admissions: 2 freshmen graduated first in their class in a recent year.

Requirements: The SAT or ACT is required. In addition, VA's Advanced Studies Diploma or a similar college preparatory diploma from an accredited high school with a satisfactory score on the SAT or ACT are required. The GED is accepted. A total of 24 academic credits is recommended, including 4 units of English, 3 each of social science, math, and science, and either 3 units of 1 foreign language (preferred) or 2 years of 2 foreign languages. An essay and a personal statement are required. SAT or ACT scores are not required for students with a 3.5 or higher high school GPA. A GPA of 3.0 is required. AP credits are accepted. Important factors in the admissions decision are recommendations by school officials, extracurricular activities record, and evidence of special talent.

Procedure: Freshmen are admitted fall and spring. Entrance exams should be taken in the junior year. There are deferred admissions and rolling admissions plans. Check with the school for current application deadlines. The application fee is $45. Applications are accepted on-line. 500 applicants were on a recent waiting list, 35 were accepted.

Financial Aid: In a recent year, 66% of all full-time freshmen and 59% of continuing full-time students received some form of financial aid. 37% of all full-time freshmen and 32% of continuing full-time students received need-based aid. The average freshman award was $7304. Need-based scholarships or need-based grants averaged $3964 ($5400 maximum); need-based self-help aid (loans and jobs) averaged $2551 ($5000 maximum); and other non-need-based awards and non-need-based scholarships averaged $789 ($5000 maximum). 24% of undergraduate students work part-time. Average annual earnings from campus work are $1532. The average financial indebtedness of a recent graduate was $14,801. The FAFSA is required. Check with the school for current application deadlines.

Computers: Wireless access is available. The university has 20 computer classroom/labs with approximately 325 computers; there are computer workrooms in 3 freshman residence halls; the library has 50 computers in classrooms and 60 in the open areas; and the student union has 12 computers. All computers have access to the Internet. All students may access the system 24 hours a day, 7 days a week. There are no time limits and no fees.

CITY UNIVERSITY OF NEW YORK/BARUCH COLLEGE

New York, NY 10010-5585   (646) 312-1400; (646) 312-1361

Full-time: 4750 men, 4880 women	**Faculty:** IIA, ++$
Part-time: 1420 men, 1860 women	**Ph.D.s:** n/av
Graduate: 1550 men, 1700 women	**Student/Faculty:** n/av
Year: semesters, summer session	**Tuition:** $5400 ($9900)
Application Deadline: February 1	**Room & Board:** n/app
Freshman Class: n/av	
SAT or ACT: required	**VERY COMPETITIVE**

Baruch College was founded in 1919 and became a separate unit of the City University of New York in 1968. It offers undergraduate programs in business and public administration and liberal arts and sciences. The figures in the above capsule and in this profile are approximate. There are 3 undergraduate schools and 3 graduate schools. In addition to regional accreditation, Baruch has baccalaureate program accreditation with AACSB. The library contains 456,132 volumes, 2.1 million microform items, and 1,246 audio/video tapes/CDs/DVDs, and subscribes to 15,860 periodicals including electronic. Computerized library services include interlibrary loans, database searching, and Internet access. Special learning facilities include an art gallery and radio station. The 39-acre campus is in an urban area Manhattan. Including any residence halls, there are 6 buildings.

Programs of Study: Baruch confers B.A., B.S., and B.B.A. degrees. Master's and doctoral degrees are also awarded. Bachelor's degrees are awarded in BUSINESS (accounting, investments and securities, management science, marketing management, marketing/retailing/merchandising, operations research, personnel management, and real estate), COMMUNICATIONS AND THE ARTS (advertising, communications, English, journalism, music, and Spanish), COMPUTER AND PHYSICAL SCIENCE (actuarial science, information sciences and systems, mathematics, and statistics), SOCIAL SCIENCE (economics, history, industrial and organizational psychology, philosophy, political science/government, psychology, public affairs, and sociology). Economics, English, and math are the strongest academically. Accounting, finance, and computer information systems are the largest.

Special: Students may take courses at all CUNY schools. The college offers internships and study abroad in Great Britain, France, Germany, Mexico, and Israel. Students may design their own liberal arts major. A federal work-study program is available, and pass/fail options are permitted for liberal arts majors. Students may combine any undergraduate major with a master's in accountancy. There are 7 national honor societies, a freshman honors program, and 3 departmental honors programs.

143

Requirements: The SAT or ACT is required. In addition, applicants must present an official high school transcript (a GED will be accepted) indicating a minimum average grade of 81% in academic subjects (minimum of 14 credits). A GPA of 80.0 is required. AP and CLEP credits are accepted.

Procedure: Freshmen are admitted fall and spring. There are early decision admission plans. Entrance exams should be taken March 1. Applications should be filed by February 1 for fall entry and October 1 for spring entry. The fall 2009 application fee was $65.

Financial Aid: The FAFSA is required. Check with the school for current application deadlines.

Computers: Wireless access is available. All students receive a network account upon acceptance. They may use it for both wired and wireless network access. There are 1300 PCs in the 25 computer labs plus kiosks in high-traffic areas. All students may access the system. There are no time limits and no fees.

CITY UNIVERSITY OF NEW YORK/HUNTER COLLEGE

New York, NY 10065	(212) 772-4490; (800) 772-4000
Full-time: 3820 men, 7352 women	**Faculty:** 686; IIA, ++$
Part-time: 1462 men, 3226 women	**Ph.D.s:** 88%
Graduate: 1421 men, 4867 women	**Student/Faculty:** 15 to 1
Year: semesters, summer session	**Tuition:** $4999 ($10,359)
Application Deadline: open	**Room & Board:** $3500
Freshman Class: n/av	
SAT CR/M: 557/575	**VERY COMPETITIVE**

Hunter College, a comprehensive, nonprofit institution established in 1870, is part of the City University of New York and is both city- and state-supported. Primarily a commuter college, it emphasizes liberal arts in its undergraduate and graduate programs. There are 3 undergraduate schools and 4 graduate schools. In addition to regional accreditation, Hunter has baccalaureate program accreditation with ADA, APTA, ASLA, CSWE, NCATE, and NLN. The library contains 815,668 volumes, 1.2 million microform items, and 14,982 audio/video tapes/CDs/DVDs, and subscribes to 5749 periodicals including electronic. Computerized library services include database searching. Special learning facilities include a learning resource center, art gallery, radio station, geography/geology lab, on-campus elementary and secondary schools, and theater. The 3-acre campus is in an urban area in New York City. Including any residence halls, there are 6 buildings.

Programs of Study: Hunter confers B.A., B.S., B.F.A., B.Mus., and B.S.Ed degrees. Master's degrees are also awarded. Bachelor's degrees are awarded in BIOLOGICAL SCIENCE (biology/biological science and nutrition), BUSINESS (accounting), COMMUNICATIONS AND THE ARTS (Chinese, classics, comparative literature, creative writing, dance, dramatic arts, English, English literature, film arts, fine arts, French, German, Greek, Hebrew, Italian, languages, Latin, media arts, music, Russian, and Spanish), COMPUTER AND PHYSICAL SCIENCE (chemistry, computer science, mathematics, physics, and statistics), EDUCATION (art education, early childhood education, elementary education, foreign languages education, health education, middle school education, music education, science education, and secondary education), ENGINEERING AND ENVIRONMENTAL DESIGN (energy management technology, environmental science, and preengineering), HEALTH PROFESSIONS (medical laboratory technology, nursing, physical therapy, predentistry, premedicine, and public health), SOCIAL SCIENCE (African American studies, anthropology, archeology, economics, geography, Hispanic American studies, history, international relations, Judaic studies, Latin American studies, philosophy, political science/government, prelaw, psychology, religion, social science, sociology, urban studies, and women's studies). Nursing is the strongest academically. Psychology is the largest.

Special: Special academic programs include internships, student-designed majors, work-study, study abroad in 24 countries, and dual majors. There is cross-registration with the Brooklyn School of Law, Marymount Manhattan College, and the YIVO Institute. Through the National Student Exchange Program, Hunter students can study for 1 or 2 semesters at any of 150 U.S. campuses. Accelerated degree programs are offered in anthropology, biopharmacology, economics, English, history, math, physics, sociology, and social research. Exchange programs in Paris or Puerto Rico are possible. There are 2 national honor societies, including Phi Beta Kappa, a freshman honors program, and 19 departmental honors programs.

Admissions: The SAT scores for the 2009-2010 freshman class were: Critical Reading--21% below 500, 55% between 500 and 599, 24% between 600 and 700, and % above 700; Math--12% below 500, 51% between 500 and 599, 30% between 600 and 700, and 7% above 700.

Requirements: The SAT is required. Admission is based on a combination of high school grade average, high school academic credits, including English and math, and SAT scores. AP and CLEP credits are accepted.

Procedure: Freshmen are admitted fall and spring. Entrance exams should be taken by October of the junior year. There are early admissions, deferred admissions, and rolling admissions plans. Application deadlines are open. The application fee is $65. Notification of early decision is sent December 15; regular decision, January 1. 4 early decision candidates were accepted for the 2009-2010 class. Applications are accepted on-line.

Financial Aid: The FAFSA and the college's own financial statement are required. The deadline for filing freshman financial aid applications for fall entry is May 1.

Computers: All students may access the system 24 hours a day. There are no time limits and no fees.

CLAREMONT MCKENNA COLLEGE
Claremont, CA 91711-6425   (909) 621-8088; (909) 621-8516

Full-time: 625 men, 525 women	**Faculty:** IIB, ++$
Part-time: none	**Ph.D.s:** n/av
Graduate: none	**Student/Faculty:** n/av
Year: semesters	**Tuition:** $36,000
Application Deadline: January 2	**Room & Board:** $12,000
Freshman Class: n/av	
SAT: required	**MOST COMPETITIVE**

Claremont McKenna College, founded in 1946, is a liberal arts college with a curricular emphasis on economics, government, international relations, public affairs, and leadership. The figures given in the above capsule and in this profile are approximate. The 5 libraries contain 2.5 million volumes, 1.5 million microform items, and 10,861 audio/video tapes/CDs/DVDs, and subscribe to 15,995 periodicals including electronic. Computerized library services include interlibrary loans, database searching, Internet access, and laptop Internet portals. Special learning facilities include a learning resource center, art gallery, radio station,

TV station, and 11 research institutes. The 50-acre campus is in a small town 35 miles east of downtown Los Angeles. Including any residence halls, there are 31 buildings.

Programs of Study: CMC confers B.A. degrees. Bachelor's degrees are awarded in AGRICULTURE (environmental studies), BIOLOGICAL SCIENCE (biochemistry, biology/biological science, ecology, molecular biology, and neurosciences), BUSINESS (management engineering), COMMUNICATIONS AND THE ARTS (English literature, film arts, French, literature, media arts, and Spanish), COMPUTER AND PHYSICAL SCIENCE (chemistry, mathematics, physics, and science technology), ENGINEERING AND ENVIRONMENTAL DESIGN (environmental science), SOCIAL SCIENCE (American studies, Asian/ Oriental studies, economics, history, interdisciplinary studies, international relations, law, philosophy, political science/government, psychology, and religion). Economics, government, and international relations are strongest academically and have the largest enrollments.

Special: CMC students may cross-register at any of the Claremont Colleges and may participate in exchange programs with Haverford, Spelman, or Colby Colleges. Students may study abroad in 39 countries or spend a semester in Washington, D.C. Part-time and full-time internships and dual and student-designed majors are available. There is a 3-2 economics-engineering program with Harvey Mudd College and a 3-2 management-engineering program. A multidisciplinary program in leadership studies and an interdisciplinary program in legal studies are offered. There are limited pass/fail options. There are 5 national honor societies, including Phi Beta Kappa.

Requirements: The SAT is required. The ACT Optional Writing test is also required. In addition, applicants must be graduates of an accredited high school or have earned the GED. Secondary preparation must include 4 years of English, 3 years (preferably 4) of math, at least 3 years of a foreign language , 2 years (preferably 3) of science, and 1 year of history. A personal essay is required. AP credits are accepted. Important factors in the admissions decision are advanced placement or honors courses, leadership record, and extracurricular activities record.

Procedure: Freshmen are admitted fall and spring. Entrance exams should be taken during the junior year or between October and January of the senior year. There are early decisions; applications should be filed by November 15; regular applications by January 2 for fall entry and November 1 for spring entry, along with a $60 fee. Notification of early decision is sent December 15; regular decision, April 1. Applications are accepted on-line. A waiting list is maintained.

Financial Aid: In a recent year, 64% of all full-time freshmen and 66% of continuing full-time students received some form of financial aid. 48% of all full-time freshmen and 46% of continuing full-time students received need-based aid. The average freshmen award was $35,972, with $32,126 ($41,670 maximum) from need-based scholarships or need-based grants and $3,550 ($5,200 maximum) from need-based self-help aid (loans and jobs). 52% of undergraduate students worked part-time. Average annual earnings from campus work were $2139. The average financial indebtedness of the 2009 graduate was $11,769. CMC is a member of CSS. The CSS/Profile and FAFSA are required. Check with the school for current application deadlines.

Computers: Wireless access is available. Poppa Lab hosts 32 PC and 3 Mac workstations and is open 24 hours a day with support staff typically available between 8 A.M. and midnight. It provides students with high-capacity black-and-white and color laser printing. South Lab, also open 24 hours a day, hosts 14 PC workstations, as well as a high-capacity black-and-white printer. Bauer Technology Classroom is open evenings as a student lab, with 16 PC workstations. It offers students the opportunity to work collectively on group projects and is staffed by technology assistants selected to provide advanced drop-in support on more complex software packages and technical tasks. All students may access the system. There are no time limits and no fees.

CLARK UNIVERSITY
Worcester, MA 01610-1477
(508) 793-7431
(800) 462-5275; (508) 793-8821

Full-time: 860 men, 1634 women	**Faculty:** 187; IIA, +$
Part-time: 49 men, 78 women	**Ph.D.s:** 96%
Graduate: 494 men, 589 women	**Student/Faculty:** 13 to 1
Year: semesters, summer session	**Tuition:** $35,220
Application Deadline: January 15	**Room & Board:** $6750
Freshman Class: 4271 applied, 2741 accepted, 550 enrolled	
SAT CR/M/W: 600/590/600	**ACT:** 26 **HIGHLY COMPETITIVE**

Clark University, founded in 1887, is an independent liberal arts and research institution. There are 2 undergraduate schools and 3 graduate schools. In addition to regional accreditation, Clark has baccalaureate program accreditation with AACSB and NASDTEC. The 6 libraries contain 617,838 volumes, 60,363 microform items, and 1372 audio/video tapes/CDs/DVDs, and subscribe to 1303 periodicals including electronic. Computerized library services include interlibrary loans, database searching, Internet access, and laptop Internet portals. Special learning facilities include a learning resource center, art gallery, radio station, TV studio, campus cable network, center for music with 2 studios for electronic music, 2 theaters, and magnetic resonance imaging facility. The 50-acre campus is in an urban area 50 miles west of Boston. Including any residence halls, there are 69 buildings.

Programs of Study: Clark confers B.A. degrees. Master's and doctoral degrees are also awarded. Bachelor's degrees are awarded in BIOLOGICAL SCIENCE (biochemistry and biology/biological science), BUSINESS (business administration and management), COMMUNICATIONS AND THE ARTS (art history and appreciation, communications, comparative literature, dramatic arts, English, film arts, fine arts, French, languages, music, romance languages and literature, Spanish, studio art, and visual and performing arts), COMPUTER AND PHYSICAL SCIENCE (chemistry, computer science, mathematics, and physics), ENGINEERING AND ENVIRONMENTAL DESIGN (environmental science), HEALTH PROFESSIONS (predentistry and premedicine), SOCIAL SCIENCE (classical/ancient civilization, economics, geography, history, international relations, international studies, philosophy, political science/government, prelaw, psychology, sociology, and women's studies). Psychology, government/international, and biology are the largest.

Special: For-credit internships are available in all disciplines with private corporations and small businesses, medical centers, and government agencies. There is cross-registration with members of the Worcester Consortium, including 9 other colleges and universities. Clark also offers study abroad in 16 countries, a Washington semester with American University, work-study programs, accelerated degree programs, dual and student-designed majors, pass/no record options, and a 3-2 engineering degree with Columbia University. A gerontology certificate is offered with the Worcester Consortium for Higher Education. There are 8 national honor societies, including Phi Beta Kappa, and 21 departmental honors programs.

Admissions: 64% of the 2009-2010 applicants were accepted. The SAT scores for the 2009-2010 freshman class were: Critical Reading--11% below 500, 37% between 500 and 599, 40% between 600 and 700, and 12% above 700; Math--12% below 500, 42% between 500 and 599, 38% between 600 and 700, and 8% above 700; Writing--10% below 500, 37% between 500 and 599, 44% between 600 and 700, and 9% above 700. The ACT scores were 6% below 21, 15% between 21 and 23, 31% between 24 and 26, 17% between 27 and 28, and 31% above 28. 60% of the current freshmen were in the top fifth of their class; 91% were in the top two fifths. 2 freshmen graduated first in their class.

Requirements: The SAT or ACT is required. In addition, the SAT Writing test is also recommended. Applicants must graduate from an accredited secondary school or have a GED. 16 Carnegie units are required, including 4 years of English, 3 each of math and science, and 2 each of foreign language and social studies, including history. An interview is recommended. AP credits are accepted. Important factors in the admissions decision are advanced placement or honors courses, recommendations by alumni, and recommendations by school officials.

Procedure: Freshmen are admitted fall and spring. Entrance exams should be taken by November of the senior year. There ae early decision and deferred admissions plans. Early decision applications should be filed by November 15; regular applications, by January 15 for fall entry and November 15 for spring entry, along with a $55 fee. Notification of early decision is sent January 1; regular decision, April 1. 56 early decision candidates were accepted for the 2009-2010 class. 35 applicants were on the 2009 waiting list; 12 were admitted. Applications are accepted on-line.

Financial Aid: In 2009-2010, 91% of all full-time freshmen and 82% of continuing full-time students received some form of financial aid. 56% of all full-time freshmen and 56% of continuing full-time students received need-based aid. The average freshman award was $20,962. Need-based scholarships or need-based grants averaged $20,705; need-based self-help aid (loans and jobs) averaged $4844; and non-need-based awards and non-need-based scholarships averaged $34,900. 75% of undergraduate students work part-time. Average annual earnings from campus work are $1901. The average financial indebtedness of the 2009 graduate was $21,925. Clark is a member of CSS. The CSS/Profile and FAFSA are required. The deadline for filing freshman financial aid applications for fall entry is January 15.

Computers: Wireless access is available. All students may access the system 7 days per week. There are no time limits and no fees. It is strongly recommended that all students have a personal computer.

CLARKSON COLLEGE
Omaha, NE 68131

(402) 552-3041
(800) 647-5500; (402) 552-6057

Full-time: 505 men and women	**Faculty:** n/av
Part-time: 205 men and women	**Ph.D.s:** n/av
Graduate: 140 men and women	**Student/Faculty:** n/av
Year: semesters, summer session	**Tuition:** $11,300
Application Deadline: open	**Room & Board:** $5000
Freshman Class: n/av	
SAT or ACT: required	**VERY COMPETITIVE**

Clarkson College, established in 1888 and affiliated with the Episcopal Church, offers undergraduate and graduate degrees in the health care professions and business. The figures in the above capsule and in this profile are approximate. There are 3 undergraduate schools and 2 graduate schools. In addition to regional accreditation, Clarkson has baccalaureate program accreditation with NLN. The library contains 7,613 volumes, and 698 audio/video tapes/CDs/DVDs, and subscribes to 217 periodicals including electronic. Computerized library services include interlibrary loans, database searching, and Internet access. Special learning facilities include a learning resource center, regional medical center. The 3-acre campus is in an urban area in Omaha. Including any residence halls, there are 4 buildings.

Programs of Study: Clarkson confers B.S. and B.S.N. degrees. Associates and master's degrees are also awarded. Bachelor's degrees are awarded in BUSINESS (business administration and management), COMPUTER AND PHYSICAL SCIENCE (radiological technology), HEALTH PROFESSIONS (nursing and radiograph medical technology). Radiological technology and nursing are the strongest academically. Nursing is the largest.

Special: A co-op program in nursing, work-study programs, and dual majors are available. Credit is given for military experience, and nondegree study is possible. The distance education option allows advanced placement students living a distance from the campus to complete their studies at home. There is 1 national honor society.

Requirements: The SAT or ACT is require, with a minimum composite score of 20 on the ACT or a satisfactory score on the SAT. The ACT is preferred. Tests are not required for applicants more than 2 years out of high school. Applicants must be graduates of an accredited secondary school, with 3 years of English and 2 each of social science, algebra, and science (including lab science). The GED is accepted. Clarkson requires applicants to be in the upper 50% of their class. A GPA of 2.5 is required. AP and CLEP credits are accepted. Important factors in the admissions decision are advanced placement or honors courses, extracurricular activities record, and evidence of special talent.

Procedure: Freshmen are admitted to all sessions. Entrance exams should be taken during the junior year or first semester of the senior year. There is a deferred admissions plan. Application deadlines are open. Application fee is $35. Notifications are sent June 1. A waiting list is maintained.

Financial Aid: In a recent year, 90% of all full-time freshmen and 90% of continuing full-time students received some form of financial aid. 75% of continuing full-time students received need-based aid. Clarkson is a member of CSS. The FAFSA and the college's own financial statement are required. Check with the school for current application deadlines.

Computers: Wireless access is available. Students have several computer labs with extended hours. Wireless campus includes residence halls. All students may access the system 7 A.M. to 8:30 P.M. There are no time limits and no fees.

CLARKSON UNIVERSITY

Potsdam, NY 13699
(315) 268-6480; (315) 268-7647

Full-time: 1979 men, 756 women
Part-time: 7 men, 4 women
Graduate: 302 men, 139 women
Year: semesters, summer session
Application Deadline: January 15
Freshman Class: 4054 applied, 2945 accepted, 777 enrolled
SAT CR/M: 550/610

Faculty: 178; I, -$
Ph.D.s: 87%
Student/Faculty: 15 to 1
Tuition: $32,910
Room & Board: $11,118

ACT: 25   **VERY COMPETITIVE**

Clarkson University, founded in 1896, is a private nationally ranked research institute offering undergraduate programs in engineering, business, science, and the humanities, and graduate programs in engineering, business, science, and health sciences. There are 3 undergraduate schools and 3 graduate schools. In addition to regional accreditation, Clarkson has baccalaureate program accreditation with AACSB, ABET, and APTA. The 2 libraries contain 338,321 volumes, 262,705 microform items, and 2,079 audio/video tapes/CDs/DVDs, and subscribe to 3,127 periodicals including electronic. Computerized library services include interlibrary loans, database searching, Internet access, and laptop Internet portals. Special learning facilities include a learning resource center, radio station, and TV station. The 640-acre campus is in a rural area 70 miles north of Watertown and 75 miles south of Ottawa, Canada. Including any residence halls, there are 43 buildings.

Programs of Study: Clarkson confers B.S. and B.P.S. degrees. Master's and doctoral degrees are also awarded. Bachelor's degrees are awarded in BIOLOGICAL SCIENCE (biology/biological science and molecular biology), BUSINESS (business administration and management, business systems analysis, electronic business, entrepreneurial studies, management information systems, and supply chain management), COMMUNICATIONS AND THE ARTS (communications and technical and business writing), COMPUTER AND PHYSICAL SCIENCE (applied mathematics, chemistry, computer science, digital arts/technology, information sciences and systems, mathematics, physics, science, and software engineering), ENGINEERING AND ENVIRONMENTAL DESIGN (aeronautical engineering, chemical engineering, civil engineering, computer engineering, electrical/electronics engineering, engineering management, environmental engineering, environmental science, and mechanical engineering), SOCIAL SCIENCE (American studies, history, humanities, interdisciplinary studies, political science/government, psychology, social science, and sociology). Engineering, business, and interdisciplinary engineering and management are the strongest academically.

Special: Clarkson offers cross-registration with the SUNY Potsdam, SUNY Canton, and St. Lawrence University. Co-op programs in all academic areas, dual majors in business and liberal arts, interdisciplinary majors, internships, accelerated degree programs, student-designed majors in the B.P.S. degree program, and study abroad in England, Italy, New Zealand, Sweden, Germany, Australia, France, Austria, China, Korea, Mexico, Slovenia, Croatia, Spain, and Ireland are possible. There are 3-2 engineering programs with many institutions in the United States. Students who participate take the first 3 years of the prescribed program at a 4-year liberal arts institution and then transfer with junior standing into one of Clarkson's 4-year engineering curricula. There are 9 national honor societies, a freshman honors program, and 12 departmental honors programs.

Admissions: 73% of the 2009-2010 applicants were accepted. The SAT scores for the 2009-2010 freshman class were: Critical Reading--22% below 500, 47% between 500 and 599, 27% between 600 and 700, and 4% above 700; Math--7% below 500, 34% between 500 and 599, 50% between 600 and 700, and 9% above 700; Writing--28% below 500, 51% between 500 and 599, 18% between 600 and 700, and 3% above 700. The ACT scores were 9% below 21, 23% between 21 and 23, 35% between 24 and 26, 18% between 27 and 28, and 15% above 28. 59% of the current freshmen were in the top fifth of their class; 90% were in the top two fifths. 13 freshmen graduated first in their class.

Requirements: The SAT or ACT is required. In addition, SAT Subject tests are also recommended. Applicants must have graduated from an accredited secondary school or have the GED. A campus visit and interview are also recommended. SAT or ACT scores are required. AP and CLEP credits are accepted. Important factors in the admissions decision are advanced placement or honors courses, recommendations by school officials, and extracurricular activities record.

Procedure: Freshmen are admitted fall and spring. Entrance exams should be taken by November. There is an early decision and a deferred admissions plan. Early decision applications should be filed by December 1; regular applications, by January 15 for fall entry and December 1 for spring entry, along with a $50 fee. Notification of early decision is sent December 15; regular decision, February 1. Applications are accepted on-line. 143 applicants were on a recent waiting list, 20 were accepted.

Financial Aid: In 2009-2010, 99% of all full-time freshmen and 95% of continuing full-time students received some form of financial aid. 82% of all full-time freshmen and 76% of continuing full-time students received need-based aid. The average freshmen award was $30,422, with $24,416 ($35,300 maximum) from need-based scholarships or need-based grants; $6,458 ($16,907 maximum) from need-based self-help aid (loans and jobs); $30,212 ($44,828 maximum) from non-need-based athletic scholarships; $14,715 ($32,910 maximum) from other non-need-based awards and non-need-based scholarships; and $2,243 from other forms of aid. 25% of undergraduate students work part-time. Average annual earnings from campus work are $914. The average financial indebtedness of the 2009 graduate was $32,125. The FAFSA is required. The deadline for filing freshman financial aid applications for fall entry is February 15.

Computers: Wireless access is available. The campus has 350 lab PCs, distributed between 8 public-access computer labs and 4 department labs. All campus computers (both wired and wireless) have unrestricted access to the Internet for both academic and recreational use. All students may access the system. There are no time limits and no fees. It is strongly recommended that all students have a personal computer.

CLEMSON UNIVERSITY

Clemson, SC 29634-5124	(864) 656-2287; (864) 656-0622
Full-time: 7393 men, 6387 women	**Faculty:** 952; I, --$
Part-time: 588 men, 345 women	**Ph.D.s:** 83%
Graduate: 1883 men, 1721 women	**Student/Faculty:** 14 to 1
Year: semesters, summer session	**Tuition:** $11,478 ($25,788)
Application Deadline: May 1	**Room & Board:** $6774
Freshman Class: 16282 applied, 10224 accepted, 3386 enrolled	
SAT CR/M/W: 600/630/540	**ACT:** 27 **HIGHLY COMPETITIVE**

Clemson University, founded in 1889, is a public institution with programs in agriculture, architecture, commerce and industry, education, engineering, forest and recreation resources, liberal arts, nursing, and sciences. There are 5 undergraduate schools and one graduate school. In addition to regional accreditation, Clemson has baccalaureate program accreditation with AACSB, ABET, CSAB, NAAB, NCATE, NLN, and NRPA. The 3 libraries contain 1.2 million volumes, 1.2 million microform items, and 140,000 audio/video tapes/CDs/DVDs, and subscribe to 11,400 periodicals including electronic. Computerized library services include interlibrary loans, database searching, Internet access, and laptop Internet portals. Special learning facilities include a learning resource center, art gallery, natural history museum, planetarium, radio station, TV station, geology museum, experimental forest, research park, and state botanical gardens. The 1400-acre campus is in a small town 32 miles west of Greenville. Including any residence halls, there are 587 buildings.

Programs of Study: Clemson confers B.A., B.S., B.F.A., and B.L.A. degrees. Master's and doctoral degrees are also awarded. Bachelor's degrees are awarded in AGRICULTURE (agriculture, animal science, forestry production and processing, forestry and related sciences, horticulture, and soil science), BIOLOGICAL SCIENCE (biochemistry, biology/biological science, and microbiology), BUSINESS (accounting, banking and finance, business administration and management, management science, and marketing/retailing/merchandising), COMMUNICATIONS AND THE ARTS (communications, design, English, fine arts, French, German, modern language, and Spanish), COMPUTER AND PHYSICAL SCIENCE (chemistry, computer science, geology, information sciences and systems, mathematics, and physics), EDUCATION (agricultural education, early childhood education, elementary education, industrial arts education, secondary education, and special education), ENGINEERING AND ENVIRONMENTAL DESIGN (agricultural engineering, ceramic engineering, chemical engineering, civil engineering, computer engineering, construction management, electrical/electronics engineering, graphic arts technology, industrial administration/management, industrial engineering, landscape architecture/design, mechanical engineering, and textile technology), HEALTH PROFESSIONS (medical laboratory technology, nursing, predentistry, premedicine, prepharmacy, preveterinary science, and speech pathology/audiology), SOCIAL SCIENCE (economics, food science, history, parks and recreation management, philosophy, political science/government, prelaw, psychology, and sociology). Engineering, architecture, and biological sciences are the strongest academically. Marketing and engineering are the largest.

Special: Co-op programs are available in all majors except nursing. Work-study programs and study abroad in 39 countries are offered. There are 24 national honor societies, including Phi Beta Kappa, a freshman honors program, and 40 departmental honors programs.

Admissions: 63% of the 2009-2010 applicants were accepted. The SAT scores for the 2009-2010 freshman class were: Critical Reading--8% below 500, 41% between 500 and 599, 42% between 600 and 700, and 9% above 700; Math--4% below 500, 25% between 500 and 599, 54% between 600 and 700, and 17% above 700; Writing--24% below 500, 49% between 500 and 599, 23% between 600 and 700, and 2% above 700. The ACT scores were 8% below 21, 15% between 21 and 23, 31% between 24 and 26, 15% between 27 and 28, and 31% above 28. 69% of the current freshmen were in the top fifth of their class; 97% were in the top two fifths. There were 24 National Merit finalists. 179 freshmen graduated first in their class.

Requirements: The SAT or ACT is required. The ACT Optional Writing test is also required. In addition, applicants should be graduates of an accredited secondary school. The GED is accepted. AP and CLEP credits are accepted. Important

152

factors in the admissions decision are advanced placement or honors courses, parents or siblings attended your school, and evidence of special talent.

Procedure: Freshmen are admitted fall, spring, and summer. Entrance exams should be taken during spring of the junior year or fall of the senior year. Applications should be filed by May 1 for fall entry and December 15 for spring entry. The fall 2009 application fee was $60. Notifications are sent February 15. Applications are accepted on-line. 164 applicants were on a recent waiting list, 86 were accepted.

Financial Aid: In 2009-2010, 87% of all full-time freshmen and 71% of continuing full-time students received some form of financial aid. 28% of all full-time freshmen and 31% of continuing full-time students received need-based aid. The average freshmen award was $9,147, with $3,264 ($7,500 maximum) from need-based scholarships or need-based grants; $3,394 ($7,125 maximum) from need-based self-help aid (loans and jobs); $11,925 ($25,409 maximum) from non-need-based athletic scholarships; and $7,075 ($24,426 maximum) from other non-need-based awards and non-need-based scholarships. 57% of undergraduate students work part-time. Average annual earnings from campus work are $2302. The average financial indebtedness of the 2009 graduate was $14,307. The FAFSA is required. The priority date for freshman financial aid applications for fall entry is April 1.

Computers: Wireless access is available almost everywhere on campus, including at several outdoor locations. All students may access the system. There are no time limits and no fees. All students are required to have a personal computer. A Dell E6500 is recommended.

COE COLLEGE
Cedar Rapids, IA 52402

(319) 399-8500
(877) CALL-COE; (319) 399-8816

Full-time: 510 men, 670 women	**Faculty:** IIB, av$
Part-time: 55 men, 60 women	**Ph.D.s:** 95%
Graduate: 5 men, 25 women	**Student/Faculty:** n/av
Year: semesters, summer session	**Tuition:** $30,700
Application Deadline: see profile	**Room & Board:** $7300
Freshman Class: n/av	
SAT or ACT: required	**VERY COMPETITIVE**

Coe College, founded in 1851, is a private liberal arts institution affiliated with the Presbyterian Church (U.S.A.). Figures in the above capsule and this profile are approximate. There is 1 graduate school. In addition to regional accreditation, Coe has baccalaureate program accreditation with NASM and NLN. The 2 libraries contain 216,699 volumes, 5828 microform items, and 9044 audio/video tapes/CDs/DVDs, and subscribe to 1380 periodicals including electronic. Computerized library services include interlibrary loans, database searching, and Internet access. Special learning facilities include a learning resource center, art gallery, radio station, and ornithological wing. The 53-acre campus is in an urban area 225 miles west of Chicago. Including any residence halls, there are 22 buildings.

Programs of Study: Coe confers B.A., B.Mus., and B.S.N. degrees. Master's degrees are also awarded. Bachelor's degrees are awarded in BIOLOGICAL SCIENCE (biochemistry, biology/biological science, and molecular biology), BUSINESS (accounting and business administration and management), COMMUNICATIONS AND THE ARTS (art, dramatic arts, English, French, German, literature, music, public relations, and Spanish), COMPUTER AND

PHYSICAL SCIENCE (chemistry, computer science, mathematics, physics, and science), EDUCATION (athletic training, elementary education, music education, physical education, and secondary education), ENGINEERING AND ENVIRONMENTAL DESIGN (environmental science and preengineering), HEALTH PROFESSIONS (medical laboratory technology, nursing, physical therapy, predentistry, and premedicine), SOCIAL SCIENCE (African American studies, American studies, Asian/Oriental studies, classical/ancient civilization, economics, history, human services, interdisciplinary studies, philosophy, political science/government, prelaw, psychology, religion, sociology, and women's studies). Chemistry, physics, and psychology are the strongest academically. Business administration, psychology, and biology are the largest.

Special: Coe offers cross-registration with nearby Mount Mercy College and the University of Iowa, a cooperative program in architecture, Washington and New York semesters, and study abroad in 17 countries. Nondegree study and dual and student-designed majors also are possible. Practicum experience is required. Core course instructors serve as students' mentors. There are 8 national honor societies, including Phi Beta Kappa, a freshman honors program, and 100 departmental honors programs.

Admissions: 15 freshmen graduated first in their class in a recent year.

Requirements: The SAT or ACT is required. In addition, Coe recommends that applicants have 4 years in English, 3 each in math, history, science, and social studies, and 2 in foreign language. All students must submit an essay. In addition, fine arts students need a portfolio or audition. The GED is accepted. A GPA of 2.8 is required. AP and CLEP credits are accepted. Important factors in the admissions decision are advanced placement or honors courses, recommendations by school officials, and extracurricular activities record.

Procedure: Freshmen are admitted fall and spring. Entrance exams should be taken in the spring of the junior year or the fall of the senior year. There is a deferred admissions plan. Check with the school for current application deadlines and fee. Applications are accepted on-line.

Financial Aid: In a recent year, 98% of all full-time freshmen and 95% of continuing full-time students received some form of financial aid. 80% of all full-time freshmen and 79% of continuing full-time students received need-based aid. The average freshman award was $19,879. Need-based scholarships or need-based grants averaged $14,657 ($21,280 maximum); need-based self-help aid (loans and jobs) averaged $5492 ($8225 maximum); and other non-need-based awards and non-need-based scholarships averaged $9396 ($13,000 maximum). 43% of undergraduate students work part-time. Average annual earnings from campus work are $1400. The average financial indebtedness of a recent graduate was $22,157. The FAFSA is required. Check with the school for current application deadlines.

Computers: All students may access the system 24 hours a day. There are no time limits and no fees.

COLBY COLLEGE

Waterville, ME 04901-8841

(207) 859-4800
(800) 723-3032; (207) 859-4828

Full-time: 800 men, 1000 women	**Faculty:** 160; IIB, ++$
Part-time: none	**Ph.D.s:** 96%
Graduate: none	**Student/Faculty:** n/av
Year: 4-1-4	**Tuition:** $51,990
Application Deadline: January 1	**Room & Board:** see profile
Freshman Class: n/av	
SAT or ACT: required	**MOST COMPETITIVE**

Colby College, founded in 1813, is a private liberal arts college. Students are charged a comprehensive fee of $51,990 annually, which includes tuition, room and board, and required fees. Some of the figures in the above capsule and in this profile are approximate. In addition to regional accreditation, Colby has baccalaureate program accreditation with ACS. The 3 libraries contain 1.0 million volumes, 402,000 microform items, and 22,779 audio/video tapes/CDs/DVDs, and subscribe to 17,840 periodicals including electronic. Computerized library services include interlibrary loans, database searching, Internet access, and laptop Internet portals. Special learning facilities include a learning resource center, art gallery, radio station, observatory, astronomy classroom, arboretum, state wildlife management area, and electronic-research classroom. The 714-acre campus is in a small town 75 miles north of Portland. Including any residence halls, there are 60 buildings.

Programs of Study: Colby confers B.A. degrees. Bachelor's degrees are awarded in BIOLOGICAL SCIENCE (biochemistry, biology/biological science, and neurosciences), COMMUNICATIONS AND THE ARTS (art history and appreciation, classics, creative writing, English, Germanic languages and literature, music, performing arts, Russian languages and literature, Spanish, and studio art), COMPUTER AND PHYSICAL SCIENCE (applied mathematics, chemistry, computer science, geology, geoscience, mathematics, physics, and science technology), ENGINEERING AND ENVIRONMENTAL DESIGN (environmental science), SOCIAL SCIENCE (African American studies, American studies, anthropology, classical/ancient civilization, East Asian studies, economics, French studies, history, international studies, Latin American studies, philosophy, political science/government, psychology, religion, sociology, and women's studies). Chemistry, economics, and biology are the strongest academically. Biology, economics, and government are the largest.

Special: Colby offers study abroad in numerous countries. Colby also offers Washington semester programs through American University and the Washington Center, on-campus work-study, exchange programs with various colleges and universities, a 3-2 engineering degree with Dartmouth College, and maritime and oceanographic studies programs. Dual and student-designed majors are possible. There are 9 national honor societies, including Phi Beta Kappa, and 26 departmental honors programs.

Admissions: 32% of a recent year's applicants were accepted. 81% of a recent year's freshmen were in the top fifth of their class; 96% were in the top two fifths. 19 freshmen graduated first in their class in a recent year.

Requirements: The SAT or ACT is required. In addition, candidates should be high school graduates with a recommended academic program of 4 years of English, 3 each of foreign language and math, and 2 each of science (including lab work), social studies/history, and other college preparatory courses. AP credits are accepted. Important factors in the admissions decision are advanced placement or honors courses, recommendations by school officials, and extracurricular activities record.

Procedure: Freshmen are admitted fall and spring. Entrance exams should be taken by January of the senior year. There are early decision and deferred admissions plan. Early decision applications should be filed by November 15; regular applications, by January 1 for fall entry, along with a $65 fee. Notification of early decision is sent December 15; regular decision, April 1. 192 early decision candidates were accepted for a recent class. 396 applicants were on a recent year's waiting list; 4 were admitted. Applications are accepted on-line.

Financial Aid: In a recent year, 39% of all full-time freshmen and 38% of continuing full-time students received some form of financial aid, including need-based aid. The average freshmen award was $29,231. Need-based scholarships or need-based grants averaged $28,134; need-based self-help aid (loans and jobs) averaged $13,531. 67% of undergraduate students work part-time. Average annual earnings from campus work are $1290. The average financial indebtedness of a recent year's graduate was $19,222. Colby is a member of CSS. The CSS/Profile, FAFSA, and the college's own financial statement are required. Check with the school for current application deadlines.

Computers: Wireless access is available in all dorm rooms and in many public locations. More than 350 public/student lab computers with Internet access are available. A computer loaner pool is available only to faculty and staff. All students may access the system 24 hours a day. There are no time limits and no fees. It is strongly recommended that all students have a personal computer.

COLGATE UNIVERSITY
Hamilton, NY 13346   **(315) 228-7401; (315) 228-7544**

Full-time: 1313 men, 1487 women	**Faculty:** 266; IIB, ++$
Part-time: 10 men, 15 women	**Ph.D.s:** 96%
Graduate: 4 men, 8 women	**Student/Faculty:** 11 to 1
Year: semesters	**Tuition:** $41,020
Application Deadline: January 15	**Room & Board:** $9910
Freshman Class: 7816 applied, 2464 accepted, 750 enrolled	
SAT CR/M: 661/680	**ACT:** 30 **MOST COMPETITIVE**

Colgate University, founded in 1819, is a private liberal arts institution. There is 1 graduate school. The 2 libraries contain 734,812 volumes, 593,646 microform items, and subscribe to 36,752 periodicals including electronic. Computerized library services include interlibrary loans, database searching, Internet access, and laptop Internet portals. Special learning facilities include a learning resource center, art gallery, radio station, TV station, anthropology museum, and observatory. The 515-acre campus is in a rural area 45 miles southeast of Syracuse and 35 miles southwest of Utica. Including any residence halls, there are 87 buildings.

Programs of Study: Colgate confers B.A. degrees. Master's degrees are also awarded. Bachelor's degrees are awarded in BIOLOGICAL SCIENCE (biochemistry, biology/biological science, molecular biology, and neurosciences), COMMUNICATIONS AND THE ARTS (art history and appreciation, Chinese, classics, dramatic arts, English, French, German, Greek, Japanese, Latin, music, Russian, Spanish, and studio art), COMPUTER AND PHYSICAL SCIENCE (astronomy, astrophysics, chemistry, computer science, geology, geophysics and seismology, mathematics, natural sciences, physical sciences, and physics), EDUCATION (education), ENGINEERING AND ENVIRONMENTAL DESIGN (environmental science), SOCIAL SCIENCE (African studies, Asian/Oriental studies, economics, geography, history, humanities, international relations, Latin American studies, Native American studies, peace studies, philosophy, political science/government, psychology, religion, Russian and Slavic studies, social science, sociology, and women's studies). English, economics, and history are the largest.

Special: Colgate offers various internships, semester and summer research opportunities with faculty, work-study, study abroad in 22 countries, accelerated degree programs, dual majors, and student-designed majors. A 3-2 engineering degree with Columbia and Washington Universities and Rensselaer Polytechnic Institute, an early assurance medical program with George Washington University, credit by exam, and pass/fail options are available. There are 12 national honor societies, including Phi Beta Kappa, and 10 departmental honors programs.

Admissions: 32% of the 2009-2010 applicants were accepted. The SAT scores for the 2009-2010 freshman class were: Critical Reading--4% below 500, 12% between 500 and 599, 47% between 600 and 700, and 37% above 700; Math--2% below 500, 11% between 500 and 599, 45% between 600 and 700, and 42% above 700. The ACT scores were 1% below 21, 3% between 21 and 23, 9% between 24 and 26, 13% between 27 and 28, and 76% above 28. 86% of the current freshmen were in the top fifth of their class; 98% were in the top two-fifths. 23 freshmen graduated first in their class.

Requirements: The SAT or ACT is required. In addition, 2 teacher recommendations and a counselor's report are required. An interview, though not evaluated, is recommended. Students should present 16 or more Carnegie credits, based on 4 years each of English and math and at least 3 of lab science, social science, and a foreign language, with electives in the arts. AP credits are accepted. Important factors in the admissions decision are advanced placement or honors courses, recommendations by school officials, and leadership record.

Procedure: Freshmen are admitted in the fall. Entrance exams should be taken in time for score reports to reach the university by January 15. There are early decision and deferred admissions plans. Early decision applications should be filed by November 15; regular applications, by January 15 for fall entry, along with a $55 fee. Notification of early decision is sent December 15; regular decision, April 1. Applications are accepted on-line. 709 applicants were on a recent waiting list, 22 were accepted.

Financial Aid: In 2009-2010, 34% of all full-time freshmen and 35% of continuing full-time students received some form of financial aid, including need-based aid. The average freshmen award was $39,758. The average financial indebtedness of the 2009 graduate was $14,170. Colgate is a member of CSS. The CSS/Profile and FAFSA are required. International students need the International Student's Financial Aid Application. The deadline for filing freshman financial aid applications for fall entry is January 15.

Computers: Wireless access is available. A general appropriate use policy exists for students using the university's network. Colgate provides 53 computer labs for students with an average of 16 computers in each lab. All classrooms allow for both wired and wireless connectivity to the Internet. All students may access the system. There are no time limits and no fees. It is strongly recommended that all students have a personal computer.

COLLEGE FOR CREATIVE STUDIES

Detroit, MI 48202-4034　　　　　　　　　　　**(313) 664-7425**
　　　　　　　　　　　　　　　　　(800) 952-ARTS; (313) 872-2739

Full-time: 661 men, 521 women	**Faculty:** 51
Part-time: 102 men, 98 women	**Ph.D.s:** 76%
Graduate: 13 men, 5 women	**Student/Faculty:** 11 to 1
Year: semesters, summer session	**Tuition:** $31275
Application Deadline: August 1	**Room & Board:** $5400

Freshman Class: 1434 applied, 556 accepted, 126 enrolled
SAT or ACT: required　　　　　　　　　　　　　　**SPECIAL**

The College for Creative Studies, established in 1906, is a private, independent institution offering comprehensive 4-year B.F.A programs in animation and digital media, crafts, fine arts, communication design, industrial design, interior design, and photography, as well as teacher certification in art education. There are no undergraduate schools. In addition to regional accreditation, CCS has baccalaureate program accreditation with NASAD. The library contains 21,000 volumes and subscribes to 100 periodicals including electronic. Special learning facilities include a learning resource center, and art gallery. The 11-acre campus is in an urban area 3 miles from downtown Detroit. Including any residence halls, there are 6 buildings.

Programs of Study: CCS confers B.F.A degrees. Bachelor's degrees are awarded in COMMUNICATIONS AND THE ARTS (advertising, animation, ceramic art and design, fine arts, glass, graphic design, illustration, industrial design, metal/jewelry, painting, photography, printmaking, and sculpture), COMPUTER AND PHYSICAL SCIENCE (digital arts/technology), EDUCATION (art education), ENGINEERING AND ENVIRONMENTAL DESIGN (interior design), SOCIAL SCIENCE (textiles and clothing). Industrial design and communication design is the strongest academically. Animation and digital media is the largest.

Special: Internships are available within the student's departmental major. Credit for internships and dual majors are available. Study abroad is possible.

Admissions: 39% of the 2009-2010 applicants were accepted.

Requirements: The SAT or ACT is required. In addition, applicants must graduate from an accredited secondary school or earn a GED. A portfolio of representative work and an essay are required. A general college preparatory program is recommended. A GPA of 2.5 is required. AP and CLEP credits are accepted. Important factors in the admissions decision are advanced placement or honors courses and evidence of special talent.

Procedure: Freshmen are admitted fall and winter. There are deferred admissions and rolling admissions plans. Applications should be filed by August 1 for fall entry, along with a $35 fee. Notifications are sent September 15. A waiting list is maintained. Applications are accepted on-line.

Financial Aid: The average financial indebtedness of the 2009 graduate was $54,000. The FAFSA is required. The priority date for freshman financial aid applications for fall entry is July 1.

Computers: All students may access the system. There are no time limits and no fees. It is strongly recommended that all students have a personal computer.

COLLEGE OF CHARLESTON

Charleston, SC 29424   **(843) 953-5670; (843) 953-6322**

Full-time: 3349 men, 5985 women	**Faculty:** 518; IIA, -$
Part-time: 345 men, 468 women	**Ph.D.s:** 87%
Graduate: 283 men, 1342 women	**Student/Faculty:** 18 to 1
Year: semesters, summer session	**Tuition:** $8988 ($21,846)
Application Deadline: April 1	**Room & Board:** $9411
Freshman Class: 11,083 applied, 7703 accepted, 2143 enrolled	
SAT CR/M: 606/605	**ACT:** 25 **VERY COMPETITIVE**

The College of Charleston, founded in 1770, is a state-assisted institution offering liberal arts programs, including business and education. There are 6 undergraduate schools and 1 graduate school. In addition to regional accreditation, C of C has baccalaureate program accreditation with AACSB, CSAB, NASM, and NCATE. The 2 libraries contain 762,034 volumes, 879,998 microform items, and 8815 audio/video tapes/CDs/DVDs, and subscribe to 3075 periodicals including electronic. Computerized library services include interlibrary loans, database searching, and Internet access. Special learning facilities include a learning resource center, art gallery, natural history museum, radio station, TV station, observatory, communications museum, marine lab, African American research center, and bronze sculpture foundry. The 52-acre campus is in an urban area in the center of Charleston. Including any residence halls, there are 133 buildings.

Programs of Study: C of C confers B.A., B.S., A.B., B.S.D., and B.S.M. degrees. Master's degrees are also awarded. Bachelor's degrees are awarded in BIOLOGICAL SCIENCE (biochemistry, biology/biological science, and marine biology), BUSINESS (accounting, business administration and management, hospitality management services, and international business management), COMMUNICATIONS AND THE ARTS (art history and appreciation, arts administration/management, classics, communications, dramatic arts, English, French, German, historic preservation, music, and Spanish), COMPUTER AND PHYSICAL SCIENCE (astronomy, astrophysics, chemistry, computer science, geology, information sciences and systems, mathematics, and physics), EDUCATION (athletic training, early childhood education, elementary education, middle school education, physical education, secondary education, and special education), SOCIAL SCIENCE (anthropology, economics, history, Latin American studies, philosophy, political science/government, psychology, religion, sociology, and urban studies). Sciences and business are the strongest academically. Business and communication are the largest.

Special: Cross-registration is possible with the Medical University of South Carolina, Trident Technical College, and The Citadel. Co-op programs and internships in all majors, a Washington semester, study abroad in 39 countries, workstudy programs, B.A.-B.S. degrees, and dual majors are offered. The B.S.D. and B.S.M. degrees provide 3 years in predentistry or premedicine, with the fourth year of completion at a medical school. Engineering degrees are available with Case Western Reserve University, Clemson University, Georgia Institute of Technology, University of South Carolina, and Washington University of St. Louis. A 2-2 program in allied health, biometry, or nursing is offered with the Medical University of South Carolina. The college's 3-week Maymester session offers unconventional courses and programs using alternative methods of instruction. There is an interdisciplinary honors program available to talented students. There are 10 national honor societies, a freshman honors program, and 10 departmental honors programs.

Admissions: 70% of the 2009-2010 applicants were accepted. The SAT scores for the 2009-2010 freshman class were: Critical Reading--2% below 500, 44% between 500 and 599, 45% between 600 and 700, and 9% above 700; Math--2% below 500, 40% between 500 and 599, 52% between 600 and 700, and 6% above 700. The ACT scores were 7% below 21, 28% between 21 and 23, 40% between 24 and 26, 15% between 27 and 28, and 10% above 28. 58% of the current freshmen were in the top fifth of their class; 87% were in the top two fifths. There were 8 National Merit finalists. 79 freshmen graduated first in their class.

Requirements: The SAT or ACT is required. In addition, applicants should have completed 4 units of high school English, 3 each of math, lab science, and social science (including 1 unit of U.S. history and 1/2 unit each of economics and government), 2 of foreign language, and 1 of phys ed. Students should also have 1 unit of advanced math or computer science or a combination of these, or 1 unit of world history, world geography, or Western civilization. The GED is accepted. An essay is required. A GPA of 2.0 is required of in-state residents, 2.3 for out-of-state. AP and CLEP credits are accepted. Important factors in the admissions decision are ability to finance college education, leadership record, and evidence of special talent.

Procedure: Freshmen are admitted fall and spring. Entrance exams should be taken by March 1. There are early decision, early admissions, deferred admissions, and rolling admissions plans. Early decision applications should be filed by November 1; regular applications, by April 1 for fall entry and November 1 for spring entry, along with a $45 fee. Notification of early decision is sent December 15; regular decision, April 1. 290 applicants were on the 2009 waiting list; 27 were admitted. Applications are accepted on-line. 290 applicants were on a recent waiting list, 27 were accepted.

Financial Aid: The FAFSA is required. The priority date for freshman financial aid applications for fall entry is March 1.

Computers: Wireless access is available. All students may access the system 24 hours a day. There are no time limits. The fee is $35.

COLLEGE OF MOUNT SAINT JOSEPH

Cincinnati, OH 45233-1670
(513) 244-4531
(800) 654-9314; (513) 244-4851

Full-time: 525 men, 825 women	**Faculty:** IIA, --$
Part-time: 100 men, 490 women	**Ph.D.s:** 73%
Graduate: 65 men, 280 women	**Student/Faculty:** n/av
Year: semesters, summer session	**Tuition:** $22,800
Application Deadline: see profile	**Room & Board:** $7300
Freshman Class: n/av	
SAT or ACT: required	**VERY COMPETITIVE**

The College of Mount St. Joseph, founded in 1920, is a private Catholic college offering 34 undergraduate and 5 graduate degree programs. Figures in the above capsule are approximate. There is 1 graduate school. In addition to regional accreditation, the Mount has baccalaureate program accreditation with CSWE, NASM, NLN, and TEAC. The library contains 97,583 volumes, 366,000 microform items, and 3741 audio/video tapes/CDs/DVDs, and subscribes to 8619 periodicals including electronic. Computerized library services include interlibrary loans, database searching, Internet access, and laptop Internet portals. Special learning facilities include a learning resource center and art gallery. The 92-acre campus is in a suburban area 7 miles west of downtown Cincinnati. Including any residence halls, there are 9 buildings.

Programs of Study: The Mount confers B.A., B.S., B.F.A., and B.S.N. degrees. Associates, master's, and doctoral degrees are also awarded. Bachelor's degrees are awarded in BIOLOGICAL SCIENCE (biochemistry and biology/biological science), BUSINESS (accounting, business administration and management, and sports management), COMMUNICATIONS AND THE ARTS (art, communications, English, fine arts, graphic design, and music), COMPUTER AND PHYSICAL SCIENCE (chemistry, mathematics, and natural sciences), EDUCATION (art education, athletic training, early childhood education, elementary education, middle school education, and special education), ENGINEERING AND ENVIRONMENTAL DESIGN (interior design), HEALTH PROFESSIONS (nursing), SOCIAL SCIENCE (criminology, history, liberal arts/general studies, paralegal studies, pastoral studies, psychology, religion, religious education, social work, and sociology). Nursing, business administration, and athletic training are the strongest academically. Business administration, nursing, and graphic design are the largest.

Special: The college offers co-op programs in all majors, cross-registration with the Greater Cincinnati Consortium of Colleges and Universities, internships, credit for experiential learning, and study abroad in 3 countries. Also available are work-study programs, accelerated degree programs in 11 majors, dual majors, cultural immersion courses in the United States and abroad, a dual enrollment program (for transfer students), service learning, and off-campus study for RNs in area hospitals. The Mount also has a program for students with learning disabilities (Project EXCEL). There are 12 national honor societies and a freshman honors program.

Admissions: 2 freshmen graduated first in their class in a recent year.

Requirements: The SAT or ACT is required. In addition, the Mount conducts a comprehensive and individualized review of every candidate's credentials for admission including but not limited to the following: a college prep high school curriculum, strong GPA, standardized test scores, evidence of leadership, and extracurricular involvement. An ACT score at or above the national average is recommended. In addition, students' personal background, attributes, and individual life circumstances are taken into consideration. A GPA of 2.5 is required. AP and CLEP credits are accepted.

Procedure: Freshmen are admitted to all sessions. There is a rolling admissions plan. Check with the school for current application deadlines. The application fee is $25. Notification is sent on a rolling basis. Applications are accepted on-line.

Financial Aid: In a recent year, 99% of all students received some form of financial aid. 81% of all full-time freshmen and 78% of continuing full-time students received need-based aid. The average freshmen award was $17,320, with $12,857 ($28,070 maximum) from need-based scholarships or need-based grants; $4872 ($7000 maximum) from need-based self-help aid (loans and jobs); and $5766 ($15,160 maximum) from other non-need-based awards and non-need-based scholarships. 8% of undergraduate students work part-time. Average annual earnings from campus work are $1392. The average financial indebtedness of a recent graduate was $18,752. The FAFSA is required. Check with the school for current application deadlines.

Computers: Wireless access is available. Students may use the network, including access to e-mail and the Internet, throughout the campus via their own wireless laptop computer, from 1 of 40 available loaner wireless laptop computers, or from any of the computers located in the library or computer labs. All students may access the system 24 hours a day. There are no time limits. The fee is $150 per semester. All students are required to have a personal computer. A Gateway is recommended.

COLLEGE OF NEW JERSEY

Ewing, NJ 08628-0718

(609) 771-2131
(800) 624-0967; (609) 637-5174

Full-time: 2519 men, 3561 women	**Faculty:** 347; IIA, +$
Part-time: 62 men, 95 women	**Ph.D.s:** 88%
Graduate: 150 men, 593 women	**Student/Faculty:** 18 to 1
Year: semesters, summer session	**Tuition:** $12,722 ($21,408)
Application Deadline: January 15	**Room & Board:** $9996

Freshman Class: 9238 applied, 1284 accepted, 4267 enrolled
SAT CR/M/W: 630/660/630 **MOST COMPETITIVE**

The College of New Jersey, founded in 1855, is a public institution offering programs in the liberal arts, sciences, business, engineering, nursing, and education. There are 7 undergraduate schools and 1 graduate school. In addition to regional accreditation, TCNJ has baccalaureate program accreditation with AACSB, ABET, NASM, NCATE, and NLN. The library contains 561,250 volumes, 18,204 microform items, and 33,464 audio/video tapes/CDs/DVDs, and subscribes to 6194 periodicals including electronic. Computerized library services include interlibrary loans, database searching, Internet access, and laptop Internet portals. Special learning facilities include a learning resource center, art gallery, planetarium, radio station, TV station, electron microscopy lab, nuclear magnetic resonance lab, optical spectroscopy lab, observatory, planetarium, and greenhouse. The 289-acre campus is in a suburban area between Princeton and Trenton. Including any residence halls, there are 61 buildings.

Programs of Study: TCNJ confers B.A., B.S., B.A.B.M.E., B.F.A., B.M., B.S.C.E., B.S.Co.E., B.S.E.E., B.S.M.E., and B.S.N. degrees. Master's degrees are also awarded. Bachelor's degrees are awarded in BIOLOGICAL SCIENCE (biology/biological science), BUSINESS (accounting and business administration and management), COMMUNICATIONS AND THE ARTS (art, art history and appreciation, communications, English, fine arts, graphic design, multimedia, music, and Spanish), COMPUTER AND PHYSICAL SCIENCE (chemistry, computer science, digital arts/technology, mathematics, and physics), EDUCATION (art education, early childhood education, education of the deaf and hearing impaired, elementary education, English education, health education, mathematics education, music education, physical education, science education, social science education, social studies education, special education, and technical education), ENGINEERING AND ENVIRONMENTAL DESIGN (biomedical engineering, civil engineering, computer engineering, electrical/electronics engineering, engineering and applied science, and mechanical engineering), HEALTH PROFESSIONS (exercise science and nursing), SOCIAL SCIENCE (criminal justice, economics, history, international studies, philosophy, political science/government, psychology, sociology, and women's studies). Biology, education, and engineering are the strongest academically. Psychology, biology, and elementary education are the largest.

Special: TCNJ offers cross-registration with the New Jersey Marine Science Consortium, a limited number of overseas internship possibilities, numerous internships in the public and private sectors, a Washington semester, and study abroad in more than a dozen countries. Pass/fail options and some dual majors are possible. Specially designed research courses allow students to participate in collaborative scholarly projects with members of the faculty, and the Bonner Center offers opportunities for community-engaged initiatives. Combined advanced and accelerated degree programs are offered in education of the deaf and hard of hearing, special education, medicine, and optometry. There are 16 national honor societies, including Phi Beta Kappa, a freshman honors program, and 40 departmental honors programs.

Admissions: 14% of the 2009-2010 applicants were accepted. The SAT scores for the 2009-2010 freshman class were: Critical Reading--2% below 500, 31% between 500 and 599, 53% between 600 and 700, and 15% above 700; Math--1% below 500, 16% between 500 and 599, 62% between 600 and 700, and 22% above 700; Writing--1% below 500, 26% between 500 and 599, 59% between 600 and 700, and 14% above 700. 87% of the current freshmen were in the top fifth of their class; 98% were in the top two fifths. 13 freshmen graduated first in their class.

Requirements: The SAT is required. In addition, applicants must have earned 16 academic credits in high school, consisting of 4 in English, 3 each in math and science, 2 each in foreign language and social studies, and 6 others distributed among math, science, social studies, and a foreign language. An essay is required. Art majors must submit a portfolio, and music majors must audition. The GED is accepted. A GPA of 2.0 is required. AP and CLEP credits are accepted. Important factors in the admissions decision are advanced placement or honors courses, leadership record, and evidence of special talent.

Procedure: Freshmen are admitted fall and spring. Entrance exams should be taken by the end of the junior year or early in the senior year. There are early decision and rolling admissions plans. Early decision applications should be filed by November 15; regular applications, by January 15 for fall entry and November 1 for spring entry, along with a $70 fee. Notification of early decision is sent December 15; other notifications are sent on a rolling basis beginning January 15. 288 early decision candidates were accepted for the 2009-2010 class. 550 applicants were on the 2009 waiting list; 288 were admitted. Applications are accepted on-line.

Financial Aid: In 2009-2010, 86% of all full-time freshmen and 72% of continuing full-time students received some form of financial aid. 42% of all full-time freshmen and 40% of continuing full-time students received need-based aid. The average freshmen award was $11,258, with $3912 ($8000 maximum) from need-based self-help aid (loans and jobs) and $7255 ($35,172 maximum) from other non-need-based awards and non-need-based scholarships. 21% of undergraduate students work part-time. Average annual earnings from campus work are $1863. The average financial indebtedness of the 2009 graduate was $22,088. TCNJ is a member of CSS. The FAFSA and copies of students' and parents' tax returns as applicable are required. The priority date for freshman financial aid applications for fall entry is March 1. The deadline for filing freshman financial aid applications for fall entry is October 1.

Computers: There are 631 computers in 30 computer labs on campus, classrooms, and the library. All classrooms are connected to the college network. The majority of TCNJ's campus is wireless. All residence hall rooms have access to the college network. All students may access the system. There are no time limits. The fee is $189. It is strongly recommended that all students have a personal computer.

COLLEGE OF NEW ROCHELLE

New Rochelle, NY 10805-2339

(914) 654-5452
(800) 933-5923; (914) 654-5464

Full-time: 25 men, 605 women	**Faculty:** IIA, av$
Part-time: 60 men, 335 women	**Ph.Ds:** n/av
Graduate: 105 men, 930 women	**Student/Faculty:** n/av
Year: semesters, summer session	**Tuition:** $24,600
Application Deadline: August 15	**Room & Board:** $9000
Freshman Class: n/av	
SAT: required	**VERY COMPETITIVE**

The College of New Rochelle was founded in 1904 by the Ursuline order as the first Catholic college for women in New York State. Now independent, there are 3 undergraduate schools. The School of Arts and Sciences offers liberal arts baccalaureate education for women only; the School of Nursing is coeducational. The School of New Resources is described in a separate profile. The figures in the above profile and in this capsule are approximate. There are 3 undergraduate schools and 1 graduate school. In addition to regional accreditation, CNR has baccalaureate program accreditation with CSWE and NLN. The library contains 224,000 volumes, 277 microform items, and 5,700 audio/video tapes/CDs/DVDs, and subscribes to 1,432 periodicals including electronic. Computerized library services include interlibrary loans, database searching, and Internet access. Special learning facilities include a learning resource center, art gallery, and the Learning Center for Nursing. The 20-acre campus is in a suburban area 12 miles north of New York City. Including any residence halls, there are 20 buildings.

Programs of Study: CNR confers B.A., B.S., B.F.A., and B.S.N. degrees. Master's degrees are also awarded. Bachelor's degrees are awarded in AGRICULTURE (environmental studies), BIOLOGICAL SCIENCE (biology/biological science), BUSINESS (business administration and management), COMMUNICATIONS AND THE ARTS (art history and appreciation, classics, communications, English, French, and Spanish), COMPUTER AND PHYSICAL SCIENCE (chemistry and mathematics), EDUCATION (art education), HEALTH PROFESSIONS (art therapy and nursing), SOCIAL SCIENCE (economics, history, international studies, philosophy, political science/government, psychology, religion, social work, sociology, and women's studies). Nursing, art, and psychology are the largest.

Special: CNR provides cooperative programs in all disciplines, work-study programs, dual majors in all majors, interdisciplinary studies, an accelerated degree program in nursing, a Washington semester, internships, study abroad in 9 countries, nondegree study, pass/fail options, student-designed majors, and a general studies degree. There is 1 national honor society and a freshman honors program.

Requirements: The SAT is required. In addition, graduation from an accredited secondary school is required; the GED is accepted. Applicants must have completed 15 academic credits, with 4 in English, 3 each in math, science, and social studies, and 2 in a foreign language. A portfolio is required for art majors. An essay and interview are recommended. AP and CLEP credits are accepted. Important factors in the admissions decision are advanced placement or honors courses, recommendations by school officials, and leadership record.

Procedure: Freshmen are admitted to all sessions. Entrance exams should be taken in the junior year or fall of the senior year. There are early admissions, deferred admissions, and rolling admissions plans. Applications should be filed by

August 15 for fall entry and January 10 for spring entry. The fall 2009 application fee was $20. Notification is sent on a rolling basis.

Financial Aid: The FAFSA, CCS/Profile, FFS or SFS, the college's own financial statement, and income documentation are required. Check with the school for current application deadlines.

Computers: Wireless access is available. All students may access the system 24 hours per day. There are no time limits and no fees. It is strongly recommended that all students have a personal computer.

COLLEGE OF NEW ROCHELLE - SCHOOL OF NEW RESOURCES

New Rochelle, NY 10805-2339

(914) 654-5526
(800) 288-4767; (914) 654-5664

Full-time: 405 men, 3505 women	**Faculty:** IIA,av$
Part-time: 50 men, 400 women	**Ph.D.s:** n/av
Graduate: none	**Student/Faculty:** n/av
Year: semesters, summer session	**Tuition:** n/av
Application Deadline: August 15	**Room & Board:** n/a
Freshman Class: n/av	**SPECIAL**

The College of New Rochelle's School of New Resources is a liberal arts institution serving adult baccalaureate students. The figures in the above capsule and in this profile are approximate. There are no undergraduate schools. The library contains 224,000 volumes, 277 microform items, and 5,700 audio/video tapes/CDs/DVDs, and subscribes to 1,432 periodicals including electronic. Computerized library services include interlibrary loans, database searching, and Internet access. Special learning facilities include a learning resource center, art gallery, TV station, Access Centers to assist students in improving writing, reading, and math skills. The -acre campus is in an urban area 12 miles north of New York City. Five additional campuses are located within the city. Including any residence halls, there are 20 buildings.

Programs of Study: SNR confers B.A. degrees. Bachelor's degrees are awarded in SOCIAL SCIENCE (liberal arts/general studies).

Special: SNR provides a voluntary work-study program. Student-designed internships, courses, and degree plans are available. Credit for prior learning may be obtained.

Requirements: In addition, Enrolling students must be age 21 or older, have a high school diploma or its equivalent, and have successfully completed an English assessment. Test scores are not required. New students are expected to attend an orientation workshop. AP and CLEP credits are accepted.

Procedure: Freshmen are admitted to all sessions. Entrance exams should be taken in the junior year or fall of the senior year. There is a rolling admissions plan. Applications should be filed by August 15 for fall entry and January 10 for spring entry. Notification is sent on a rolling basis.

Financial Aid: The FAFSA and the college's own financial statement, and income documentation are required. The deadline for filing freshman financial aid applications for fall entry is open.

Computers: All students may access the system. from 8:30 A.M. to 11 P.M. daily. Students are limited to 2 hours during peak usage. There are no fees.

COLLEGE OF SAINT BENEDICT
St. Joseph, MN 56374-2099   (320) 363-2196
                                              (800) 544-1489; (320) 363-3206

Full-time: 2057 women	**Faculty:** 159; IIB, av$
Part-time: 49 women	**Ph.D.s:** 84%
Graduate: none	**Student/Faculty:** 12 to 1
Year: semesters	**Tuition:** $29,936
Application Deadline: open	**Room & Board:** $8608
Freshman Class: 1604 applied, 1369 accepted, 551 enrolled	
ACT: 25	**SAT:** required
	VERY COMPETITIVE

The College of Saint Benedict, established in 1913, is a private, Catholic Benedictine institution offering undergraduate liberal arts study for women in partnership with St. John's University, a Catholic Benedictine institution for men. The coordinate institutions share an academic calendar, academic curriculum, and many combined extracurricular activities. In addition to regional accreditation, St. Benedict has baccalaureate program accreditation with ADA, CSWE, NASM, and NCATE. The 2 libraries contain 658,438 volumes, 121,244 microform items, and 40,637 audio/video tapes/CDs/DVDs, and subscribe to 71,720 periodicals including electronic. Computerized library services include interlibrary loans, database searching, Internet access, and laptop Internet portals. Special learning facilities include a learning resource center, a pottery studio, an arboretum, an observatory, a greenhouse, an herbarium, a labyrinth, natural history museum, and the Hill Manuscript library available for CSB students to access at St. John's University. The 800-acre campus is in a small town 70 miles northwest of Minneapolis and 10 miles west of St. Cloud. Including any residence halls, there are 34 buildings.

Programs of Study: St. Benedict confers B.A. and B.S.N. degrees. Bachelor's degrees are awarded in AGRICULTURE (environmental studies), BIOLOGICAL SCIENCE (biochemistry, biology/biological science, and nutrition), BUSINESS (management science), COMMUNICATIONS AND THE ARTS (art, classics, communications, dramatic arts, English, French, German, music, and Spanish), COMPUTER AND PHYSICAL SCIENCE (chemistry, computer science, mathematics, natural sciences, and physics), EDUCATION (elementary education), ENGINEERING AND ENVIRONMENTAL DESIGN (preengineering), HEALTH PROFESSIONS (nursing, occupational therapy, predentistry, premedicine, preoptometry, prepharmacy, prephysical therapy, and preveterinary science), SOCIAL SCIENCE (dietetics, economics, gender studies, history, humanities, liberal arts/general studies, pastoral studies, peace studies, philosophy, political science/government, prelaw, psychology, social science, sociology, theological studies, and women's studies). Chemistry, economics, and biology are the strongest academically. Biology, nursing, and psychology are the largest.

Special: Students may cross-register with St. Cloud State University. There are study-abroad programs in Australia, Austria, Chile, China, England, France, Guatemala, Greece, Ireland, Italy, Japan, South Africa, and Spain. Internships, student-designed majors, preprofessional programs, and liberal studies degrees may be pursued. A 3-2 engineering program is offered through the University of Minnesota as is a 3-1 program in dentistry. Nondegree study and a pass/fail grading option are also available. There is 1 national honor society, Phi Beta Kappa, and a freshman honors program.

Admissions: 85% of the 2009-2010 applicants were accepted. The SAT scores for the 2009-2010 freshman class were: Critical Reading--19% below 500, 39% between 500 and 599, 29% between 600 and 700, and 13% above 700; Math--22% below 500, 36% between 500 and 599, 29% between 600 and 700, and 13% above 700; Writing--23% below 500, 28% between 500 and 599, 34% between 600 and 700, and 15% above 700. The ACT scores were 7% below 21, 22% between 21 and 23, 30% between 24 and 26, 18% between 27 and 28, and 24% above 28. 67% of the current freshmen were in the top fifth of their class; 91% were in the top two fifths. 30 freshmen graduated first in their class.

Requirements: The SAT or ACT is required. In addition, students should be graduates of an accredited secondary school. Academic preparation should include 15 units, including 4 of English, 3 of math, 2 each of a lab science and social studies, and 4 electives. A foreign language is recommended. The GED is accepted. An essay is required. Home-schooled applicants are not required to have a high school diploma but are required to provide appropriate documentation of college preparatory curriculum. St. Benedict requires applicants to be in the upper 50% of their class. A GPA of 3.0 is required. AP and CLEP credits are accepted. Important factors in the admissions decision are advanced placement or honors courses, leadership record, and extracurricular activities record.

Procedure: Freshmen are admitted fall and spring. Entrance exams should be taken during the spring of the junior year or fall of the senior year. There is a deferred admissions plan. Application deadlines are open. Notifications are sent April 1. Applications are accepted on-line. A waiting list is maintained.

Financial Aid: In 2009-2010, 94% of all full-time freshmen and 95% of continuing full-time students received some form of financial aid. 68% of all full-time freshmen and 66% of continuing full-time students received need-based aid. The average freshman award was $24,818. Need-based scholarships or need-based grants averaged $20,136; need-based self-help aid (loans and jobs) averaged $5,586; and other non-need-based awards and non-need-based scholarships averaged $11,985. 60% of undergraduate students work part-time. Average annual earnings from campus work are $2600. St. Benedict is a member of CSS. The FAFSA and the college's own financial statement and federal tax returns and W-2s are required. The priority date for freshman financial aid applications for fall entry is March 15.

Computers: Wireless access is available. Students are not required to own a computer, but network connections are available for all students in their residence hall. Students can access computers in computer labs, libraries, student centers, and residence halls. All students may access the system 24 hours per day. There are no time limits. The fee is $220.

COLLEGE OF THE ATLANTIC
Bar Harbor, ME 04609 (207) 288-5015
(800) 528-0025; (207) 288-4126

Full-time: 101 men, 220 women	**Faculty:** 25
Part-time: 7 men, 17 women	**Ph.D.s:** 90%
Graduate: 2 men, 3 women	**Student/Faculty:** 11 to 1
Year: varies	**Tuition:** $33,060
Application Deadline: February 15	**Room & Board:** $8490
Freshman Class: 307 applied, 244 accepted, 76 enrolled	
SAT CR/M/W: 642/565/622	**ACT:** 25 **VERY COMPETITIVE**

College of the Atlantic, founded in 1969, is a private liberal arts college dedicated to the study of human ecology. The library contains 40,500 volumes, 274 microform items, and subscribes to 600 periodicals including electronic. Computerized library services include interlibrary loans, database searching, Internet access, and laptop Internet portals. Special learning facilities include a learning resource center, art gallery, natural history museum, writing center, taxidermy lab, photography lab, sculpture and painting studio, ceramics studio, marine mammal research center, 2 greenhouses, 80-acre organic farm (12 miles off campus), and 2 offshore research centers. The 35-acre campus is in a small town 45 miles southeast of Bangor, along the Atlantic Ocean shoreline. Including any residence halls, there are 15 buildings.

Programs of Study: COA confers B.A. degrees. Master's degrees are also awarded. Bachelor's degrees are awarded in SOCIAL SCIENCE (human ecology).

Special: Students may cross-register with the University of Maine and other local nautical schools. Eco League exchanges are available with Alaska Pacific University, and Green Mountain, Antioch, Northland, and Prescott colleges. COA offers study abroad programs in Mexico, the Czech Republic, France, and Guatemala. A 10-week internship is a requirement of graduation, and students are assisted in finding internships in the US and abroad in an area of interest. All students design their own path to completion of their B.A. in human ecology.

Admissions: 79% of the 2009-2010 applicants were accepted. The SAT scores for the 2009-2010 freshman class were: Critical Reading--3% below 500, 14% between 500 and 599, 63% between 600 and 700, and 20% above 700; Math--20% below 500, 46% between 500 and 599, 34% between 600 and 700, and % above 700; Writing--5% below 500, 23% between 500 and 599, 61% between 600 and 700, and 11% above 700. The ACT scores were 10% below 21, 20% between 21 and 23, 40% between 24 and 26, 10% between 27 and 28, and 20% above 28. 54% of the current freshmen were in the top fifth of their class; 83% were in the top two fifths. 1 freshman graduated first in the class.

Requirements: In addition, Candidates for admission must be high school graduates who have completed 4 years of English, 3 to 4 of math, 2 to 3 of science, 2 of a foreign language, and 1 of history. AP and CLEP credits are accepted. Important factors in the admissions decision are personality/intangible qualities, extracurricular activities record, and advanced placement or honors courses.

Procedure: Freshmen are admitted fall, winter, and spring. Entrance exams should be taken in the junior or senior year. There are early decision and deferred admissions plans. Early decision applications should be filed by December 1; regular applications, by February 15 for fall entry; November 15 for winter entry; and February 15 for spring entry, along with a $45 fee. Notification of early decision is sent December 15; regular decision, April 1. 28 early decision candidates were accepted for the 2009-2010 class. 12 applicants were on the 2009 waiting list; 1 was admitted. Applications are accepted on-line.

Financial Aid: In 2009-2010, 89% of all full-time freshmen and 85% of continuing full-time students received some form of financial aid. 88% of all full-time freshmen and 83% of continuing full-time students received need-based aid. The average freshman award was $32,034. Need-based scholarships or need-based grants averaged $30,543 ($43,230 maximum); and need-based self-help aid (loans and jobs) averaged $5,134 ($7,701 maximum). 78% of undergraduate students work part-time. Average annual earnings from campus work are $1800. The average financial indebtedness of the 2009 graduate was $23,760. COA is a member of CSS. The FAFSA and the college's own financial statement are required. The deadline for filing freshman financial aid applications for fall entry is February 15.

Computers: 16 public computers (13 PCs and 3 Macs) are available for use in various areas. In addition, 4 notebook computers are available for use within the library. All computers are connected to the campus network and have access to e-mail and Internet. Most campus locations (dorms, classrooms and public spaces) have wireless access and all dormitory rooms have wired access to the campus network. In addition, 11 library study carrels are equipped with network connections for notebook computers. All students may access the system 24 hours a day. There are no time limits and no fees. It is strongly recommended that all students have a personal computer.

COLLEGE OF THE HOLY CROSS

Worcester, MA 01610

(508) 793-2443
(800) 442-2421; (508) 793-3888

Full-time: 1315 men, 1582 women	**Faculty:** 244; IIB, +$
Part-time: 21 men, 15 women	**Ph.D.s:** 98%
Graduate: none	**Student/Faculty:** 12 to 1
Year: semesters	**Tuition:** $38,722
Application Deadline: January 15	**Room & Board:** $10,620
Freshman Class: 6652 applied, 2426 accepted, 747 enrolled	
SAT CR/M: 634/647	**ACT:** 28 **MOST COMPETITIVE**

The College of the Holy Cross is the only liberal arts college that embraces a Catholic, Jesuit identity. And of the 28 Jesuit colleges and universities in the United States, Holy Cross stands alone in its exclusive commitment to undergraduate education. Students enjoy a full array of athletic facilities, a state-of the-art fitness center, and outstanding arts spaces. The 4 libraries contain 627,742 volumes, 16,518 microform items, and 30,320 audio/video tapes/CDs/DVDs, and subscribe to 1,334 periodicals including electronic. Computerized library services include interlibrary loans, database searching, Internet access, and laptop Internet portals. Special learning facilities include a learning resource center, art gallery, radio station, greenhouses, facilities for aquatic research, and a multimedia resource center. The 174-acre campus is in a suburban area 45 miles west of Boston. Including any residence halls, there are 34 buildings.

Programs of Study: Holy Cross confers A.B. degrees. Bachelor's degrees are awarded in AGRICULTURE (environmental studies), BIOLOGICAL SCIENCE (biology/biological science), BUSINESS (accounting), COMMUNICATIONS AND THE ARTS (art history and appreciation, classics, dramatic arts, English, French, German, Italian, literature, music, Russian, Spanish, and studio art), COMPUTER AND PHYSICAL SCIENCE (chemistry, computer science, mathematics, and physics), EDUCATION (agricultural education), ENGINEERING AND ENVIRONMENTAL DESIGN (architecture), SOCIAL SCIENCE (anthropology, Asian/Oriental studies, economics, German area studies, history, medieval studies, philosophy, political science/government, psychology, religion, Russian and Slavic studies, and sociology). Economics, English, and psychology are the largest.

Special: Academic internships are available through the Center for Interdisciplinary and Special Studies. Student-designed majors, dual majors including economics-accounting major, a Washington semester, and study abroad in approximately 17 countries are possible. There is a 3-2 engineering program with Columbia University or Dartmouth College, internships, and an accelerated degree program. Students may cross-register with other universities in the Colleges of Worcester Consortium. There are 2 national honor societies, including Phi Beta Kappa, and 5 departmental honors programs.

Admissions: 36% of the 2009-2010 applicants were accepted. The SAT scores for the 2009-2010 freshman class were: Critical Reading--3% below 500, 21% between 500 and 599, 57% between 600 and 700, and 19% above 700; Math--3% below 500, 16% between 500 and 599, 61% between 600 and 700, and 20% above 700. 89% of the current freshmen were in the top fifth of their class; 99% were in the top two fifths. There was 1 National Merit finalist. 13 freshmen graduated first in their class.

Requirements: Applicants should be graduates of an accredited secondary school or hold the GED. Recommended preparatory courses include English, foreign language, history, math, and science. An essay is required. Students have the option to submit standardized test scores if they believe the results represent a fuller picture of their achievements and potential; students who opt not to submit scores will not be at any disadvantage in admissions decisions. An interview is recommended. AP credits are accepted. Important factors in the admissions decision are extracurricular activities record, recommendations by school officials, and advanced placement or honors courses.

Procedure: Freshmen are admitted in the fall. Entrance exams should be taken no later than January 15th of the senior year. There is an early decision and a deferred admissions plan. Early decision applications should be filed by December 15; regular applications by January 15 for fall entry. The fall 2009 application fee was $60. Notification of early decision is sent January 1; regular decision, April 1. Applications are accepted on-line. 526 applicants were on a recent waiting list.

Financial Aid: In 2009-2010, 64% of all full-time freshmen and 58% of continuing full-time students received some form of financial aid. 62% of all full-time freshmen and 57% of continuing full-time students received need-based aid. The average freshman award was $32,441. Need-based scholarships or need-based grants averaged $25,182 ($48,800 maximum); need-based self-help aid (loans and jobs) averaged $7,091 ($7,500 maximum); non-need based athletic scholarships averaged $49,748 ($48,800 maximum); and other non-need based awards and non-need based scholarships averaged $29,105 ($38,180 maximum). 45% of undergraduate students work part-time. Average annual earnings from campus work are $1800. The average financial indebtedness of the 2009 graduate was $23,785. Holy Cross is a member of CSS. The CSS/Profile, FAFSA, and student and parent federal tax returns are required. The deadline for filing freshman financial aid applications for fall entry is February 1.

Computers: Wireless access is available. Students have full access to the college's computer network system, including broadband Internet access in all residential rooms and common areas as well as 485 college-provided PCs and Macs located throughout the campus. All students may access the system 24 hours per day. There are no time limits and no fees.

COLLEGE OF THE OZARKS

Point Lookout, MO 65726

(417) 334-6411, ext. 4219
(800) 222-0525; (417) 335-2618

Full-time: 575 men, 740 women	**Faculty:** IIB, --$
Part-time: 20 men, 25 women	**Ph.D.s:** 58%
Graduate: none	**Student/Faculty:** 15 to 1
Year: semesters	**Tuition:** $305
Application Deadline: see profile	**Room & Board:** $5300
Freshman Class: n/av	
ACT: required	**VERY COMPETITIVE**

College of the Ozarks, founded in 1906, is a private liberal arts college affiliated with the Presbyterian Church (U.S.A.). Instead of paying tuition, students work a total of 560 hours in campus jobs and are responsible only for room and board, books, personal expenses, and an acceptance fee of $305. Figures in the above capsule and this profile are approximate. In addition to regional accreditation, C of O has baccalaureate program accreditation with ADA. The library contains 117,125 volumes, 31,210 microform items, and 5764 audio/video tapes/CDs/DVDs, and subscribes to 1,756,059 periodicals including electronic. Computerized library services include interlibrary loans, database searching, and Internet access. Special learning facilities include a learning resource center, art gallery, radio station, museum, grist mill, weaving studio, firehouse, print shop, orchid greenhouses, fruitcake/jelly kitchens, day care center, and 3 farm operations. The 1000-acre campus is in a small town 40 miles south of Springfield, adjacent to the resort town of Branson. Including any residence halls, there are 82 buildings.

Programs of Study: C of O confers B.A. and B.S. degrees. Bachelor's degrees are awarded in AGRICULTURE (agricultural business management, agriculture, agronomy, animal science, conservation and regulation, and horticulture), BIO-LOGICAL SCIENCE (biology/biological science), BUSINESS (accounting, business administration and management, business economics, hotel/motel and restaurant management, international business management, and marketing management), COMMUNICATIONS AND THE ARTS (art, broadcasting, communications, dramatic arts, English, journalism, media arts, music, music business management, musical theater, performing arts, public relations, Spanish, studio art, and theater design), COMPUTER AND PHYSICAL SCIENCE (chemistry, computer science, information sciences and systems, and mathematics), EDUCA-TION (agricultural education, art education, business education, early childhood education, elementary education, English education, foreign languages education, mathematics education, music education, physical education, recreation education, secondary education, social studies education, and vocational education), ENGINEERING AND ENVIRONMENTAL DESIGN (graphic arts technology and preengineering), HEALTH PROFESSIONS (health, medical technology, nursing, premedicine, prepharmacy, and preveterinary science), SOCIAL SCI-ENCE (child psychology/development, clothing and textiles management/production/services, corrections, criminal justice, criminology, dietetics, family/consumer studies, food science, gerontology, history, home economics, interdisciplinary studies, law enforcement and corrections, philosophy, prelaw, psychology, religion, religious music, social work, and sociology). Sciences, history, and education are the strongest academically. Business administration, education, and criminal justice are the largest.

Special: The college offers co-op programs, cross-registration with Focus on the Family Institute, internships, a 3-2 engineering degree program, and independent study/practicum courses. All students are required to work as part of the work education program. There are 6 national honor societies, a freshman honors program, and 7 departmental honors programs.

Admissions: 9 freshmen graduated first in their class in a recent year.

Requirements: The ACT is required. In addition, applicants must be graduates of accredited secondary schools, have a GED, or have an ACT score of 19 or better. A physical exam, financial aid application, 2 recommendations (preferably from school personnel), and an interview are required. C of O requires applicants to be in the upper 50% of their class. A GPA of 3.0 is required. AP and CLEP credits are accepted. Important factors in the admissions decision are ability to finance college education, leadership record, and advanced placement or honors courses.

Procedure: Freshmen are admitted fall and spring. Entrance exams should be taken in October or December of the senior year. There is a rolling admissions plan. Check with the school for current application deadlines. Applications are accepted on-line. A waiting list is maintained.

Financial Aid: In a recent year, all full-time students received some form of financial aid. 90% of all full-time students received need-based aid. The average freshmen award was $14,900. Need-based scholarships or need-based grants averaged $10,379 ($12,260 maximum); need-based self-help aid (loans and jobs) averaged $43,640 (maximum); and non-need-based athletic scholarships averaged $2361 ($4400 maximum). All undergraduate students work part-time. Average annual earnings from campus work are $3640. The average financial indebtedness of a recent graduate was $6013. The FAFSA is required. Check with the school for current application deadlines.

Computers: Wireless access is available. Computer labs, dorm rooms and lobbies, and the College Center have wireless Internet access. All students may access the system 24 hours a day, 7 days a week. There are no time limits and no fees.

COLLEGE OF WILLIAM & MARY
Williamsburg, VA 23187-8795   (757) 221-4223; (757) 221-1242

Full-time: 2628 men, 3132 women	**Faculty:** I, av$
Part-time: 33 men, 43 women	**Ph.D.s:** n/av
Graduate: 988 men, 1050 women	**Student/Faculty:** n/av
Year: semesters, summer session	**Tuition:** $10,800 ($30,964)
Application Deadline: January 1	**Room & Board:** $8382
Freshman Class: 12110 applied, 4058 accepted, 1391 enrolled	
SAT or ACT: required	**MOST COMPETITIVE**

The College of William & Mary, founded in 1693, is the second-oldest college in the United States. The public institution offers undergraduate degrees in the arts and sciences. Graduate programs are offered in arts and sciences, law, business, education, and marine science. There are 3 undergraduate schools and 5 graduate schools. In addition to regional accreditation, William & Mary has baccalaureate program accreditation with AACSB and NCATE. The 5 libraries contain 227,720 volumes, 452,588 microform items, and 38,246 audio/video tapes/CDs/DVDs, and subscribe to 89,845 periodicals including electronic. Computerized library services include interlibrary loans, database searching, Internet access, and laptop Internet portals. Special learning facilities include a learning resource center, art gallery, radio station, anthropology museum, art studio, greenhouse, the Center for Archaeological Research, and the Omohundro Institute of Early American History and Culture. The 1200-acre campus is in a small town 50 miles southeast of Richmond. Including any residence halls, there are 195 buildings.

Programs of Study: William & Mary confers B.A., B.S., and B.B.A. degrees. Master's and doctoral degrees are also awarded. Bachelor's degrees are awarded in BIOLOGICAL SCIENCE (biology/biological science), BUSINESS (business administration and management), COMMUNICATIONS AND THE ARTS (art, art history and appreciation, dramatic arts, English, French, German, and music), COMPUTER AND PHYSICAL SCIENCE (chemistry, computer science, geology, mathematics, and physics), HEALTH PROFESSIONS (health science), SOCIAL SCIENCE (American studies, anthropology, classical/ancient civilization, economics, Hispanic American studies, history, interdisciplinary studies, international relations, international studies, philosophy, political science/government, psychology, public affairs, religion, and sociology). Business, interdisciplinary studies, and English are the largest.

Special: William & Mary offers a forestry/environmental science program with Duke University. Also available are internships, study abroad in more than 40 countries, dual and student-designed majors, work-study programs, an accelerated degree in computer science, a Washington semester, nondegree study, and pass/fail options. There are 34 national honor societies, including Phi Beta Kappa, a freshman honors program, and 34 departmental honors programs.

Admissions: 34% of the 2009-2010 applicants were accepted. 95% of the current freshmen were in the top fifth of their class; 100% were in the top two fifths. There were 59 National Merit finalists. 510 freshmen graduated first in their class.

Requirements: The SAT or ACT is required. Also required are the Common App, the William & Mary Supplement to the Common App, a secondary school report form complete with a high school transcript and counselor letter of recommendation, a midyear school report form, and an official report of standardized test scores. AP credits are accepted. Important factors in the admissions decision are advanced placement or honors courses, extracurricular activities record, and recommendations by school officials.

Procedure: Freshmen are admitted fall and spring. Entrance exams should be taken in spring of the junior year or fall of the senior year. There are early decision and deferred admissions plans. Early decision applications should be filed by November 1; regular applications, by January 1 for fall entry; and November 1 for spring entry. The fall 2009 application fee was $60. Notification of early decision is sent December 1; regular decision, April 1. 508 early decision candidates were accepted for the 2009-2010 class. 1273 applicants were on the 2009 waiting list; 17 were admitted. Applications are accepted on-line. 1273 applicants were on a recent waiting list, 17 were accepted.

Financial Aid: In 2009-2010, 41% of all full-time freshmen and 34% of continuing full-time students received some form of financial aid. 24% of all students received need-based aid. The average freshman award was $15,715. Need-based scholarships or need-based grants averaged $15,302 ($39,466 maximum); need-based self-help aid (loans and jobs) averaged $4413 ($8700 maximum); non-need-based athletic scholarships averaged $18,737 ($40,099 maximum); and other non-need-based awards and non-need-based scholarships averaged $4974 ($42,500 maximum). The average financial indebtedness of the 2009 graduate was $16,765. The FAFSA is required, and the CSS Profile is also required for early decision enrollees. The deadline for filing freshman financial aid applications for fall entry is March 1.

Computers: Wireless access is available. Students may use the network to access the Internet and Blackboard and store data. All lab machines include software.

All students may access the system. There are no time limits and no fees. All students are required to have a personal computer.

COLLEGE OF WOOSTER
Wooster, OH 44691
(330) 263-2322
(800) 877-9905; (330) 263-2621

Full-time: 860 men, 950 women	**Faculty:** IIB, -$
Part-time: 5 men, 5 women	**Ph.D.s:** 91%
Graduate: none	**Student/Faculty:** n/av
Year: semesters, summer session	**Tuition:** $45,600
Application Deadline: see profile	**Room & Board:** $7000
Freshman Class: n/av	
SAT or ACT: required	**VERY COMPETITIVE**

The College of Wooster, founded in 1866, is a private liberal arts college. Figures in the above capsule are approximate. In addition to regional accreditation, Wooster has baccalaureate program accreditation with NASM. The 3 libraries contain 622,672 volumes, 210,094 microform items, and 24,149 audio/video tapes/CDs/DVDs, and subscribe to 6696 periodicals including electronic. Computerized library services include interlibrary loans and database searching. Special learning facilities include a learning resource center, art gallery, and radio station. The 240-acre campus is in a suburban area 55 miles southwest of Cleveland. Including any residence halls, there are 37 buildings.

Programs of Study: Wooster confers B.A., B.Mus., and B.Mus.Ed. degrees. Bachelor's degrees are awarded in BIOLOGICAL SCIENCE (biochemistry and biology/biological science), BUSINESS (business economics), COMMUNICATIONS AND THE ARTS (communications, comparative literature, dramatic arts, English, fine arts, French, German, Greek (classical), Latin, music, and Spanish), COMPUTER AND PHYSICAL SCIENCE (chemistry, computer science, geology, mathematics, and physics), SOCIAL SCIENCE (African American studies, anthropology, archeology, area studies, economics, history, interdisciplinary studies, international relations, philosophy, political science/government, psychology, religion, Russian and Slavic studies, sociology, urban studies, and women's studies). Chemistry, history, and English are the strongest academically. History, English, and sociology are the largest.

Special: A 3-2 engineering degree is offered in conjunction with Case Western Reserve and Washington Universities. A B.A.-B.S. degree is offered in music/music education. Cross-registration is possible with off-campus programs of the Great Lakes Colleges Association. Internships are available in American politics in Washington, D.C., the Ohio State Legislature, and the U.S. State Department, as well as in professional theater and economics. Student-designed majors, dual majors, study abroad in 50 countries, a Washington semester, accelerated degree programs, nondegree study, and pass/fail options for a limited number of courses are available. All seniors participate in a 2-term independent-study project in the major. The student chooses the topic and works on a one-to-one basis with a faculty mentor. A sophomore research program is available by application. There are 12 national honor societies, including Phi Beta Kappa.

Requirements: The SAT or ACT is required. In addition, applicants should be graduates of an accredited secondary school. The GED is accepted. Students should have completed a minimum of 17 high school academic credits. The school also requires an essay and recommends an interview. AP credits are accepted. Important factors in the admissions decision are advanced placement or honors courses, recommendations by school officials, and leadership record.

Procedure: Freshmen are admitted fall and winter. Entrance exams should be taken in the fall of the senior year. There are early decision, early admissions and deferred admissions plans. Check with the school for current application deadlines. The application fee is $40. Applications are accepted on-line. A waiting list is maintained.

Financial Aid: Wooster is a member of CSS. The CSS/Profile, FAFSA, and the college's own financial statement are required. Check with the school for current application deadlines.

Computers: All students may access the system any time.

COLORADO CHRISTIAN UNIVERSITY
Lakewood, CO 80226-7499

(303) 963-3207
(800) 44 FAITH; (303) 963-3401

Full-time: 425 men, 700 women	**Faculty:** n/av
Part-time: 175 men, 175 women	**Ph.D.s:** 85%
Graduate: 55 men, 80 women	**Student/Faculty:** n/av
Year: semesters, summer session	**Tuition:** $20,000
Application Deadline: see profile	**Room & Board:** $7500
Freshman Class: n/av	
SAT or ACT: required	**VERY COMPETITIVE**

Colorado Christian University, founded in 1914, is a private, Christian interdenominational institution offering undergraduate and graduate programs in the arts and sciences, biblical studies, music, and education. Figures in the above capsule are approximate. There are 4 undergraduate schools and 3 graduate schools. The library contains 53,532 volumes, 281,234 microform items, and 3917 audio/video tapes/CDs/DVDs, and subscribes to 415 periodicals including electronic. Computerized library services include interlibrary loans, database searching, and Internet access. Special learning facilities include a learning resource center and art gallery. The 29-acre campus is in a suburban area 10 miles west of Denver. Including any residence halls, there are 21 buildings.

Programs of Study: CCU confers B.A., B.S., and B.M. degrees. Associates and master's degrees are also awarded. Bachelor's degrees are awarded in BIOLOGICAL SCIENCE (biology/biological science), BUSINESS (accounting, business administration and management, human resources, management information systems, and management science), COMMUNICATIONS AND THE ARTS (art, communications, English, and music), COMPUTER AND PHYSICAL SCIENCE (computer management and science), EDUCATION (elementary education, music education, and secondary education), SOCIAL SCIENCE (biblical studies, history, liberal arts/general studies, psychology, social science, theological studies, and youth ministry). Science, biology, and education are the strongest academically. Human resources management, computer/information technology, and liberal arts are the largest.

Special: The school offers an ROTC program in cooperation with CU Boulder, cross-registration with the Focus on the Family Institute, internships, study abroad in 7 countries, a Washington semester, and work-study programs. Accelerated degree programs are available in Christian leadership, organizational management, and management of information systems. Dual and student-designed majors, nondegree study, pass/fail options, and credit for life, military, and work experience are also available. There are 2 national honor societies, a freshman honors program, and 1 departmental honors programs.

Requirements: The SAT or ACT is required. In addition, applicants must be graduates of an accredited secondary school. The GED is accepted. An essay is required. A campus visit is recommended. A GPA of 2.8 is required. AP and CLEP credits are accepted.

Procedure: Freshmen are admitted to all sessions. There are deferred admissions and rolling admissions plans. Check with the school for current application deadlines. The fall 2009 application fee was $40. Applications are accepted on-line.

Financial Aid: The FAFSA is required. Check with the school for current application deadlines.

Computers: All students may access the system.

COLORADO COLLEGE
Colorado Springs, CO 80903

(719) 389-6344
(800) 542-7214; (719) 389-6816

Full-time: 923 men, 1043 women	**Faculty:** 162; IIB, +$
Part-time: 11 men, 23 women	**Ph.D.s:** 98%
Graduate: 13 men, 19 women	**Student/Faculty:** 12 to 1
Year: see profile, summer session	**Tuition:** $37,278
Application Deadline: January 15	**Room & Board:** $9624
Freshman Class: 4941 applied, 1600 accepted, 527 enrolled	
SAT CR/M/W: 660/660/660	**ACT:** 29 **MOST COMPETITIVE**

Colorado College, founded in 1874, is an independent liberal arts and sciences institution. The academic year is based on a block plan, under which students take only 1 course during each of the 8 3-1/2-week-long blocks of study; there is also a 9-week 3-block summer session. There is one graduate school. The library contains 550,622 volumes, 131,070 microform items, and 37,802 audio/video tapes/CDs/DVDs, and subscribes to 41,724 periodicals including electronic. Computerized library services include interlibrary loans and database searching. Special learning facilities include a learning resource center, art gallery, radio station, an electronic music studio, a telescope dome, a multimedia computer lab, the Colorado College Press, an herbarium, a Fourier transform nuclear magnetic resonance spectrometer, a scanning electronic microscope and transmission electronic microscope, an environmental service van equipped for field research, petrographic microscopes, an X-ray diffractometer, a sedimentology lab, metabolic equipment, hydrostatic weighing equipment, and a cadaver study in sports science. The 90-acre campus is in an urban area 70 miles south of Denver. Including any residence halls, there are 70 buildings.

Programs of Study: CC confers B.A. degrees. Master's degrees are also awarded. Bachelor's degrees are awarded in BIOLOGICAL SCIENCE (biochemistry, biology/biological science, and neurosciences), BUSINESS (international economics), COMMUNICATIONS AND THE ARTS (art history and appreciation, classics, comparative literature, creative writing, dance, dramatic arts, English, film arts, French, Germanic languages and literature, Italian, music, romance languages and literature, Russian languages and literature, and studio art), COMPUTER AND PHYSICAL SCIENCE (chemistry, computer mathematics, computer science, geology, mathematics, and physics), ENGINEERING AND ENVIRONMENTAL DESIGN (environmental science), SOCIAL SCIENCE (anthropology, Asian/Oriental studies, economics, French studies, Hispanic American studies, history, history of philosophy, liberal arts/general studies, philosophy, political science/government, psychology, religion, Russian and Slavic studies, sociology, Southwest American studies, Spanish studies, and women's studies). Economics, biology, and political science are the largest.

Special: CC offers co-op programs with Columbia University School of Law, study abroad in 47 countries, internships, a Washington semester, work-study programs, dual and student-designed majors, and 3-2 engineering degrees with Columbia University, Rensselaer Polytechnic Institute, University of Southern California, and Washington University. There are 13 national honor societies, including Phi Beta Kappa, and a freshman honors program.

Admissions: 32% of the 2009-2010 applicants were accepted. The SAT scores for the 2009-2010 freshman class were: Critical Reading--1% below 500, 15% between 500 and 599, 54% between 600 and 700, and 31% above 700; Math--1% below 500, 15% between 500 and 599, 54% between 600 and 700, and 30% above 700; Writing--2% below 500, 16% between 500 and 599, 53% between 600 and 700, and 30% above 700. The ACT scores were 1% below 21, 5% between 21 and 23, 10% between 24 and 26, 20% between 27 and 28, and 64% above 28. 83% of the current freshmen were in the top fifth of their class; 97% were in the top two fifths. 19 freshmen graduated first in their class.

Requirements: The SAT or ACT is required. In addition, applicants should have completed at least 16 (18 to 20 recommended) high school academic credits. The GED is accepted. An essay is required. AP credits are accepted. Important factors in the admissions decision are advanced placement or honors courses, extracurricular activities record, and evidence of special talent.

Procedure: Freshmen are admitted fall and winter. Entrance exams should be taken by January 15 for fall entry. There are early decision, early admissions, and deferred admissions plans. Early decision applications should be filed by November 15; regular applications should be filed by January 15 for fall entry and November 1 for winter entry, along with a $50 fee. Notifications of early decision are sent December 20; regular decision, April 1. Applications are accepted online. 324 applicants were on a recent waiting list, 24 were accepted.

Financial Aid: In 2009-2010, 48% of all full-time freshmen and 61% of continuing full-time students received some form of financial aid. 31% of all full-time freshmen and 46% of continuing full-time students received need-based aid. The average freshman award was $27,220. Average annual earnings from campus work are $1697. The average financial indebtedness of the 2009 graduate was $16,172. CC is a member of CSS. The CSS/Profile, FAFSA, and noncustodial parents' form, parent and student tax return are required. The priority date for regular freshman financial aid applications for fall entry is February 15; for early applicants, November 15. The deadline for filing freshman financial aid applications for fall entry is February 15.

Computers: Wireless access is available. The campus has 53 computer labs and classrooms that are accessible by undergarduate students with an average of 10 computers per lab. 95% of classrooms allow wired connectivity student and 98% allow wireless connectivity. Network access is available across campus and nearly all campus-owned buildings have wireless access. All students may access the system. There are no time limits and no fees. It is strongly recommended that all students have a personal computer.

COLORADO SCHOOL OF MINES

Golden, CO 80401-1842

(303) 273-3220
(888) 446-9489; (303) 273-3509

Full-time: 2125 men, 590 women
Part-time: 470 men, 135 women
Graduate: 635 men, 270 women
Year: semesters, summer session
Application Deadline: see profile
Freshman Class: n/av
SAT or ACT: required

Faculty: I, av$
Ph.D.s: 90%
Student/Faculty: n/av
Tuition: $10,500 ($23,500)
Room & Board: $7500

HIGHLY COMPETITIVE

The Colorado School of Mines, founded in 1874, is a public institution offering programs in math, science, economics, and engineering. Figures in the above capsule are approximate. In addition to regional accreditation, Mines has baccalaureate program accreditation with ABET. The library contains 356,000 volumes and 236,000 microform items, and subscribes to 2700 periodicals including electronic. Computerized library services include interlibrary loans, database searching, and Internet access. The 373-acre campus is in a small town 20 miles west of Denver. Including any residence halls, there are 40 buildings.

Programs of Study: Mines confers B.S. degrees. Master's and doctoral degrees are also awarded. Bachelor's degrees are awarded in COMPUTER AND PHYSICAL SCIENCE (chemistry, mathematics, and physics), ENGINEERING AND ENVIRONMENTAL DESIGN (chemical engineering, engineering, geological engineering, geophysical engineering, metallurgical engineering, mining and mineral engineering, and petroleum/natural gas engineering), SOCIAL SCIENCE (economics). Chemical engineering, geological engineering, and petroleum engineering are the strongest academically. General engineering, chemical engineering, and engineering physics are the largest.

Special: Co-op programs, internships in the humanities, accelerated degree programs in all majors, dual majors, study abroad in 20 countries, and nondegree study are offered. There is 1 national honor society, a freshman honors program, and 3 departmental honors programs.

Admissions: 75 freshmen graduated first in their class in a recent year.

Requirements: The SAT or ACT is required. In addition, applicants must be graduates of an accredited secondary school. The GED is accepted. Students should have completed 16 high school academic credits, including 4 credits each of English and math, 3 of science, 2 of social studies, and 3 academic electives. AP credits are accepted. Important factors in the admissions decision are advanced placement or honors courses, leadership record, and recommendations by school officials.

Procedure: Freshmen are admitted to all sessions. Entrance exams should be taken by late in the junior year or early in the senior year. There are deferred admissions and rolling admissions plans. Check with the school for current application deadlines. The fall 2009 application fee was $45. Applications are accepted online.

Financial Aid: In a recent year, 85% of all students received some form of financial aid. 74% of students received need-based aid. The average freshmen award was $15,540. 70% of undergraduate students work part-time. Average annual earnings from campus work are $900. The average financial indebtedness of a recent graduate was $18,500. Mines is a member of CSS. The FAFSA is required. Check with the school for current application deadlines.

Computers: Wireless access is available. Several hundred PCs are located around campus for student use. All residence hall rooms are wired for direct access to campus network and the Internet. Many buildings have wireless access. All students may access the system 24 hours a day. There are no time limits and no fees.

COLORADO STATE UNIVERSITY-FORT COLLINS

Fort Collins, CO 80523-1062	**(970) 491-6909; (970) 491-7799**

Full-time: 9483 men, 10236 women	**Faculty:** 944; I, -$
Part-time: 825 men, 660 women	**Ph.D.s:** 99%
Graduate: 1896 men, 2313 women	**Student/Faculty:** 21 to 1
Year: semesters, summer session	**Tuition:** $6318 ($22,240)
Application Deadline: February 1	**Room & Board:** $8378
Freshman Class: 15,142 applied, 10,976 accepted, 4285 enrolled	
SAT CR/M/W: 560/580/540	**ACT:** 24 **VERY COMPETITIVE**

Colorado State University, founded in 1870 and part of the Colorado State University system, is a public, land-grant institution offering 78 undergraduate majors in 52 departments within 8 colleges. There are 8 undergraduate schools and 1 graduate school. In addition to regional accreditation, Colorado State has baccalaureate program accreditation with AACSB, AAVLD, ABET, ACCE, ACEJMC, ADA, ASLA, CSWE, FIDER, IFT, LAAB, NASM, NCATE, NEHSPAC, NRPA, SAF, and SRM. The 3 libraries contain 2.4 million volumes, 1.2 million microform items, and 1,766 audio/video tapes/CDs/DVDs, and subscribe to 52,433 periodicals including electronic. Computerized library services include interlibrary loans, database searching, Internet access, and laptop Internet portals. Special learning facilities include a learning resource center, art gallery, radio station, TV station, a concert hall, a theater, a music hall, an art museum, an engineering research center, an equine center, a veterinary teaching hospital, an environmental learning center, and a plant environmental research center. The 582-acre campus is in a suburban area about 65 miles north of Denver. Including any residence halls, there are 155 buildings.

Programs of Study: Colorado State confers B.A., B.S., B.F.A., and B.M. degrees. Master's and doctoral degrees are also awarded. Bachelor's degrees are awarded in AGRICULTURE (agricultural business management, agricultural economics, agronomy, animal science, equine science, fishing and fisheries, forestry and related sciences, horticulture, natural resource management, range/farm management, and soil science), BIOLOGICAL SCIENCE (biochemistry, biology/biological science, botany, ecology, microbiology, nutrition, wildlife biology, and zoology), BUSINESS (accounting, apparel and accessories marketing, banking and finance, business administration and management, hotel/motel and restaurant management, marketing/retailing/merchandising, real estate, and recreational facilities management), COMMUNICATIONS AND THE ARTS (apparel design, art, art history and appreciation, communications, creative writing, dance, dramatic arts, English, fine arts, French, German, journalism, metal/jewelry, music, music performance, music theory and composition, performing arts, public relations, Spanish, and speech/debate/rhetoric), COMPUTER AND PHYSICAL SCIENCE (actuarial science, applied mathematics, chemistry, computer science, geology, information sciences and systems, mathematics, natural sciences, physical sciences, physics, and statistics), EDUCATION (agricultural education, art education, education, English education, foreign languages education, mathematics education, and music education), ENGINEERING AND EN-

VIRONMENTAL DESIGN (chemical engineering, civil engineering, computer engineering, construction management, electrical/electronics engineering, engineering, engineering and applied science, engineering physics, environmental engineering, interior design, landscape architecture/design, and mechanical engineering), HEALTH PROFESSIONS (biomedical science, environmental health science, and exercise science), SOCIAL SCIENCE (anthropology, criminal justice, economics, family/consumer studies, fire services administration, history, human development, interdisciplinary studies, international studies, liberal arts/general studies, philosophy, political science/government, psychology, social work, sociology, and water resources). Engineering and applied science, chemistry, and microbiology are the strongest academically. Business, health and exercise science, and psychology are the largest.

Special: Colorado State participates in a cooperative program with Aims Community College. Study abroad, a semester at sea, work-study programs, internships, B.A.-B.S. degrees, dual majors, and pass/fail options are available. Teaching certification students receive a bachelor's degree in their chosen subject and also complete a certification sequence through the School of Education. There are 35 national honor societies, including Phi Beta Kappa, a freshman honors program, and 19 departmental honors programs.

Admissions: 72% of the 2009-2010 applicants were accepted. The SAT scores for the 2009-2010 freshman class were: Critical Reading--21% below 500, 46% between 500 and 599, 29% between 600 and 700, and 4% above 700; Math--20% below 500, 39% between 500 and 599, 36% between 600 and 700, and 5% above 700; Writing--27% below 500, 47% between 500 and 599, 24% between 600 and 700, and 2% above 700. The ACT scores were 13% below 21, 27% between 21 and 23, 31% between 24 and 26, 16% between 27 and 28, and 13% above 28. 41% of the current freshmen were in the top fifth of their class; 74% were in the top two fifths. There were 11 National Merit finalists. 79 freshmen graduated first in their class.

Requirements: The SAT or ACT is required. In addition, graduation from secondary school is required, but the GED is accepted. Priority consideration is given to those with a minimum 3.25 GPA and 18 recommended high school credits, to include 4 English, 4 math (algebra I and II, geometry, and an advanced math), 3 natural sciences (at least 2 must include a lab), 3 social studies (at least 1 must be U.S. history or Western civilization), 2 foreign language (must be the same language), and 2 academic electives. Applicants who have a GPA below 2.5 and/or who do not meet the recommended high school units are encouraged to apply as all applicants receive a careful, holistic review. An essay (minimum 250 words) and 1 recommendation are required. The typical entering freshman carries a GPA between 3.2 and 3.8 and has an ACT composite between 22 and 26 or a combined SAT (Critical Reading and Math) between 1020 and 1220. AP and CLEP credits are accepted. Important factors in the admissions decision are advanced placement or honors courses, leadership record, and recommendations by school officials.

Procedure: Freshmen are admitted to all sessions. Entrance exams should be taken during the junior year or early fall of the senior year. There is a rolling admissions plan. Applications should be filed by February 1 for fall entry and December 1 for spring entry, along with a $50 fee. Notification is sent on a rolling basis. Applications are accepted on-line.

Financial Aid: In 2009-2010, 69% of all full-time freshmen and 55% of continuing full-time students received some form of financial aid. 40% of all full-time freshmen and 42% of continuing full-time students received need-based aid. Need-based scholarships or need-based grants averaged $6728; need-based self-help aid (loans and jobs) averaged $4572; non-need-based athletic scholarships averaged $15,801; and other non-need-based awards and non-need-based scholarships averaged $2970. 32% of undergraduate students work part-time. Average annual earnings from campus work are $3189. The average financial indebtedness of the 2009 graduate was $20,432. The FAFSA is required. The deadline for filing freshman financial aid applications for fall entry is March 1.

Computers: Wireless access is available. Students can change personal information; view billing, records, and grades; access the Web and e-mail; take on-line courses; and register for courses. There are approximately 2700 PCs in 90 labs, classrooms, dorms, and student centers. The new computer science building houses several 24-hour labs. All students may access the system 24 hours a day. There are no time limits and no fees.

COLUMBIA UNIVERSITY
New York, NY 10027　　　　　　(212) 854-2522; (212) 854-1209

Full-time: 3005 men, 2700 women	**Faculty:** I, ++$
Part-time: none	**Ph.D.s:** n/av
Graduate: none	**Student/Faculty:** n/av
Year: semesters, summer session	**Tuition:** $38,000
Application Deadline: January 2	**Room & Board:** $10,000
Freshman Class: n/av	
SAT or ACT: required	**MOST COMPETITIVE**

Columbia University in the City of New York was founded in 1754. 4,100 undergraduates study liberal arts and science programs in Columbia College and 1,400 major in The Fu Foundation School of Engineering and Applied Science. Students also have access to our more than a dozen graduate and professional schools, a traditional college campus in the neighborhood of Morningside Heights, and all that New York City has to offer professionally, socially, and culturally. The figures in the above capsule and in this profile are approximate. The 25 libraries contain 9.5 million volumes. Computerized library services include interlibrary loans, database searching, Internet access, and laptop Internet portals. Special learning facilities include an art gallery, planetarium, radio station, TV station, and an observatory. The 36-acre campus is in an urban area New York City. Including any residence halls, there are 50 buildings.

Programs of Study: Columbia confers A.B. degrees. Bachelor's degrees are awarded in BIOLOGICAL SCIENCE (biochemistry, biology/biological science, biophysics, environmental biology, and neurosciences), BUSINESS (operations research), COMMUNICATIONS AND THE ARTS (art history and appreciation, classics, comparative literature, dance, dramatic arts, English, film arts, French, German, Germanic languages and literature, Greek, Latin, linguistics, music, Russian, Spanish, and visual and performing arts), COMPUTER AND PHYSICAL SCIENCE (applied mathematics, applied physics, astronomy, astrophysics, chemistry, computer science, earth science, geochemistry, geology, geophysics and seismology, mathematics, physics, and statistics), EDUCATION (education), ENGINEERING AND ENVIRONMENTAL DESIGN (architecture, biomedical engineering, chemical engineering, civil engineering, computer engineering, electrical/electronics engineering, engineering management, engineering mechanics, environmental science, industrial engineering technology, materials science, mechanical engineering, metallurgical engineering, and mining and mineral engineering), SOCIAL SCIENCE (African American studies, American studies, anthropology, archeology, area studies, Asian/American studies, classical/ancient civilization, East Asian studies, economics, Hispanic American studies, history,

Italian studies, Latin American studies, medieval studies, Middle Eastern studies, philosophy, political science/government, psychology, religion, Russian and Slavic studies, sociology, urban studies, and women's studies). Political science, economics, biomedical engineering, history, operations research, and mechanical engineering are the largest.

Special: There is a study abroad program at more than 100 locations, including France, Oxford and Cambridge Universities in England, and the Kyoto Center for Japanese Studies in Japan. Cross-registration is possible with the Juilliard School and Barnard College. Combined B.A.-B.S. degrees are offered via 3-2 or 4-1 engineering programs. A 3-2 engineering degree is offered with Columbia's Fu Foundation School of Engineering and Applied Science. There is also a 5-year B.A./M.I.A. with Columbia's School of International and Public Affairs. The college offers work-study, internships, credit by exam, pass/fail options, and dual, student-designed, and interdisciplinary majors, including regional studies and ancient studies. There are 31 departmental honors programs.

Requirements: The SAT or ACT is required. The ACT Optional Writing test is also required. AP credits are accepted.

Procedure: Freshmen are admitted fall. Entrance exams should be taken by October or November of the senior year. There are early decision and deferred admissions plans. Early decision applications should be filed by November 1; regular applications, by January 2 for fall entry. The fall 2009 application fee was $70. Notification of early decision is sent December 15; regular decision, April 1. Applications are accepted on-line. A waiting list is maintained.

Financial Aid: In a recent year, 63% of all full-time freshmen and 53% of continuing full-time students received some form of financial aid. 51% of all full-time freshmen and 48% of continuing full-time students received need-based aid. The average freshmen award was $34,577. The average financial indebtedness of the 2009 graduate was $17,144. Columbia is a member of CSS. The CSS/Profile, FAFSA, the college's own financial statement, federal tax returns, the business/farm supplement, and/or the divorced/separated parents statement, if applicable, are required. Check with the school for current application deadlines.

Computers: Wireless access is available. There are computer labs and stand-alone terminals throughout the campus and computer clusters in residence halls. Every dorm room has an Ethernet connection. All students may access the system. 24 hours a day, 7 days a week. There are no time limits. There is a fee.

COLUMBIA UNIVERSITY/BARNARD COLLEGE

New York, NY 10027-6598	(212) 854-5262; (212) 854-6220
Full-time: 2300 women	**Faculty:** n/av
Part-time: 55 women	**Ph.D.s:** n/av
Graduate: none	**Student/Faculty:** n/av
Year: semesters	**Tuition:** $29,000
Application Deadline: January 1	**Room & Board:** $12,000
Freshman Class: n/av	
SAT or ACT: required	**MOST COMPETITIVE**

Barnard College, founded in 1889, is an independent affiliate of Columbia University. It is an undergraduate womens' liberal arts college. Figures in the above capsule and in this profile are approximate. The library contains 204,906 volumes, 17,705 microform items, and 17,448 audio/video tapes/CDs/DVDs, and subscribes to 543 periodicals including electronic. Computerized library services include interlibrary loans, database searching, and Internet access. Special learning facilities include a learning resource center, art gallery, radio station, TV station, a greenhouse, history of physics lab, child development research and study center, dance studio, modern theater, womens' research archives within a womens' center, and multimedia labs and classrooms. The 4-acre campus is in an urban area occupying 4 city blocks of Manhattan's Upper West Side. Including any residence halls, there are 15 buildings.

Programs of Study: Barnard College confers B.A. degrees. Bachelor's degrees are awarded in BIOLOGICAL SCIENCE (biochemistry and biology/biological science), COMMUNICATIONS AND THE ARTS (art history and appreciation, classics, comparative literature, dance, dramatic arts, English, film arts, French, German, Greek, Italian, Latin, linguistics, music, Russian, and Spanish), COMPUTER AND PHYSICAL SCIENCE (astronomy, chemistry, computer science, mathematics, physics, and statistics), ENGINEERING AND ENVIRONMENTAL DESIGN (architecture and environmental science), SOCIAL SCIENCE (American studies, anthropology, biopsychology, classical/ancient civilization, East Asian studies, economics, European studies, history, international studies, medieval studies, Middle Eastern studies, philosophy, political science/government, psychology, religion, sociology, urban studies, and women's studies). English, psychology, and economics and have the largest enrollments.

Special: Barnard offers cross-registration with Columbia University, more than 2500 internships with New York City firms and institutions, and study abroad worldwide. A 3-2 engineering program with the Columbia School of Engineering and double-degree programs with the Columbia University Schools of International and Public Affairs, Law, and Dentistry, the Juilliard School, and the Jewish Theological Seminary are possible. The college offers dual and student-designed majors and multidisciplinary majors, including economic history. There is 1 national honor society and Phi Beta Kappa.

Requirements: The SAT or ACT is required. If taking the SAT, an applicant must also take 3 SAT Subject tests, one of which must be in writing or literature. A GED is accepted. Applicants should prepare with 4 years of English, 3 of math and science, 3 or 4 of a foreign language, 2 of a lab science, and 1 of history. An interview is recommended. AP credits are accepted. Important factors in the admissions decision are advanced placement or honors courses, evidence of special talent, and extracurricular activities record.

Procedure: Freshmen are admitted fall. Entrance exams should be taken by January of the senior year. There are early decision, early admissions and deferred admissions plans. Early decision applications should be filed by November 15; regular applications, by January 1 for fall entry, along with a $55 fee. Notification of early decision is sent December 15; regular decision, April 1. Applications are accepted on-line. A waiting list is maintained.

Financial Aid: In a recent year, 44% of all full-time freshmen and 44% of continuing full-time students received some form of financial aid. 41% of all full-time freshmen and 42% of continuing full-time students received need-based aid. The average freshmen award was $30,644. 46% of undergraduate students worked part-time. The average financial indebtedness of the 2009 graduate was $17,630. Barnard College is a member of CSS. The CSS/Profile, FAFSA, the state aid form, the college's own financial statement, the parents' and student's federal tax returns, and the business and/or farm supplement are required. Check with the school for current application deadlines.

Computers: All students may access the system. There are no time limits and no fees. It is strongly recommended that all students have a personal computer.

COLUMBIA UNIVERSITY/SCHOOL OF GENERAL STUDIES

New York, NY 10027

(212) 854-2772
(800) 895-1169; (212) 854-6316

Full-time: 445 men, 367 women	**Faculty:** I, ++$
Part-time: 229 men, 310 women	**Ph.D.s:** 99%
Graduate: none	**Student/Faculty:** n/av
Year: semesters, summer session	**Tuition:** $36,058
Application Deadline: June 1	**Room & Board:** $14,066
Freshman Class: n/av	
SAT or ACT: recommended	**MOST COMPETITIVE**

The School of General Studies of Columbia University, founded in 1947, offers liberal arts degree programs and postgraduate studies for adult men and women whose post-high school education has been interrupted or postponed by at least 1 year. The 22 libraries contain 9.5 million volumes, 5.9 million microform items, and 107,850 audio/video tapes/CDs/DVDs, and subscribe to 117,264 periodicals including electronic. Computerized library services include interlibrary loans, database searching, Internet access, and laptop Internet portals. Special learning facilities include a learning resource center, art gallery, radio station, and TV station. The 36-acre campus is in an urban area on the upper west side of Manhattan in New York City.

Programs of Study: GS confers B.A. and B.S. degrees. Bachelor's degrees are awarded in BIOLOGICAL SCIENCE (biology/biological science), COMMUNICATIONS AND THE ARTS (art history and appreciation, classics, comparative literature, dance, dramatic arts, English literature, film arts, French, German, Italian, literature, music, Slavic languages, Spanish, and visual and performing arts), COMPUTER AND PHYSICAL SCIENCE (applied mathematics, astronomy, chemistry, computer science, geoscience, mathematics, physics, and statistics), ENGINEERING AND ENVIRONMENTAL DESIGN (architecture and environmental science), SOCIAL SCIENCE (African American studies, anthropology, archeology, classical/ancient civilization, East Asian studies, economics, French studies, German area studies, Hispanic American studies, history, Italian studies, Latin American studies, Middle Eastern studies, philosophy, political science/government, psychology, religion, sociology, urban studies, and women's studies). Political science, economics, and English are the largest.

Special: Preprofessional studies in allied health and medical fields and interdisciplinary majors, minors, and concentrations are offered. Internships in New York City, work-study programs on campus, study abroad, a 3-2 engineering degree at Columbia University School of Engineering and Applied Science, B.A.-B.S. degrees, and dual majors are available. There is a Phi Beta Kappa honors program.

Requirements: The SAT or ACT is recommended. SAT, ACT, or Columbia's General Studies Admissions Exam scores should be submitted along with high school and all college transcripts. An autobiographical statement is required. An interview is encouraged. AP credits are accepted. Important factors in the admissions decision are personality/intangible qualities, extracurricular activities record, and evidence of special talent.

Procedure: Freshmen are admitted to all sessions. Entrance exams should be taken as early as possible. There is a deferred admissions plan. Early decision applications should be filed by March 1 for fall entry and October 1 for spring entry. Regular decision applications should be filed by June 1 for fall entry, November

1 for pring entry, and April 1 for summer entry. The application fee is $65. Applications are accepted on-line. A waiting list is maintained.

Financial Aid: In 2009-2010, the average freshmen award was $8000. 75% of undergraduate students work part-time. Average annual earnings from campus work are $2500. The average financial indebtedness of the 2009 graduate was $65,000. GS is a member of CSS. The FAFSA and the college's own financial statement are required. Check with the school for current application deadlines.

Computers: Wireless access is available. There are computer facilities in more than 65 buildings. All students may access the system. Students are limited to 1 hour. There are no fees. It is strongly recommended that all students have a personal computer.

COLUMBUS COLLEGE OF ART AND DESIGN

Columbus, OH 43215	**(614) 222-3261**
	(877) 997-CCAD; (614) 232-8344

Full-time: 660 men, 690 women	**Faculty:** n/av
Part-time: 200 men, 205 women	**Ph.D.s:** 47%
Graduate: none	**Student/Faculty:** n/av
Year: semesters, summer session	**Tuition:** $24,800
Application Deadline: open	**Room & Board:** $7000
Freshman Class: n/av	
SAT or ACT: required	**SPECIAL**

Columbus College of Art and Design, founded in 1879, is a private institution offering undergraduate programs in art and fine arts. Figures in the above capsule are approximate. In addition to regional accreditation, CCAD has baccalaureate program accreditation with NASAD. The library contains 41,396 volumes and 13,475 microform items, and subscribes to 254 periodicals including electronic. Computerized library services include database searching. Special learning facilities include a learning resource center, art gallery, and art museum. The 17-acre campus is in an urban area in Columbus. Including any residence halls, there are 15 buildings.

Programs of Study: CCAD confers B.F.A. degrees. Bachelor's degrees are awarded in COMMUNICATIONS AND THE ARTS (advertising, fine arts, graphic design, illustration, industrial design, and media arts), ENGINEERING AND ENVIRONMENTAL DESIGN (interior design), SOCIAL SCIENCE (fashion design and technology). Media arts and fine arts are the largest.

Special: Cross-registration is offered with Franklin, Ohio State, and Capital Universities, Ohio Dominican, Otterbein, and Pontifical Colleges, Columbus State Community College, Mount Carmel College of Nursing, and DeVry Institute of Technology. Internships are available, as are on-campus work-study, dual majors, and nondegree study.

Requirements: The SAT or ACT is required. In addition, applicants should be graduates of an accredited secondary school or have the GED. A portfolio of artwork indicative of abilities must be submitted. An interview is advised. A GPA of 2.0 is required. AP credits are accepted. Important factors in the admissions decision are evidence of special talent, recommendations by school officials, and recommendations by alumni.

Procedure: Freshmen are admitted fall and spring. There is a rolling admissions plan. Application deadlines are open. The fall 2009 application fee was $25. Applications are accepted on-line.

Financial Aid: CCAD is a member of CSS. The FAFSA and the college's own financial statement are required. Check with the school for current application deadlines.

Computers: All students may access the system during scheduled lab hours and class time. There are no time limits and no fees.

CONCORDIA UNIVERSITY, ANN ARBOR

Ann Arbor, MI 48105

(734) 995-7311
(800) 253-0680; (734) 995-4610

Full-time: 186 men, 242 women	**Faculty:** 39
Part-time: 53 men, 40 women	**Ph.D.s:** 60%
Graduate: 154 men, 400 women	**Student/Faculty:** 11 to 1
Year: semesters, summer session	**Tuition:** $19,870
Application Deadline: open	**Room & Board:** $7,350
Freshman Class: 429 applied, 281 accepted, 94 enrolled	
SAT CR/M/W: 575/550/560	**ACT:** 22 **VERY COMPETITIVE**

Concordia University, established in 1963, is a private institution affiliated with the Missouri Synod of the Lutheran Church, offering undergraduate and graduate degrees in the arts and sciences, business, education, and human services. There are 4 undergraduate schools and 2 graduate schools. In addition to regional accreditation, Concordia has baccalaureate program accreditation with NCATE. The library contains 117,000 volumes, 300,000 microform items, 1,400 audio/video tapes/CDs/DVDs, and subscribes to 660 periodicals including electronic. Computerized library services include interlibrary loans, database searching, Internet access, and laptop Internet portals. Special learning facilities include a learning resource center and an art gallery. The 187-acre campus is in a suburban area 40 miles west of Detroit. Including any residence halls, there are 30 buildings.

Programs of Study: Concordia confers B.A. degrees. Associates and master's degrees are also awarded. Bachelor's degrees are awarded in BIOLOGICAL SCIENCE (biology/biological science), BUSINESS (business administration and management and hospitality management services), COMMUNICATIONS AND THE ARTS (art, communications, dramatic arts, English, Greek, journalism, language arts, music, and Spanish), COMPUTER AND PHYSICAL SCIENCE (chemistry, mathematics, physical sciences, physics, and science), EDUCATION (early childhood education, elementary education, health education, physical education, and secondary education), ENGINEERING AND ENVIRONMENTAL DESIGN (preengineering), HEALTH PROFESSIONS (predentistry and premedicine), SOCIAL SCIENCE (biblical languages, criminal justice, family/consumer studies, history, philosophy, psychology, religion, religious music, safety management, social studies, and sociology). Education, business, and family life are the strongest academically. Business administration, teacher education, and English are the largest.

Special: Internships are available in most academic majors. Cross-registration is available with Eastern Michigan and Kettering Universities, Schoolcraft College, Henry Ford Community College, Michigan State Police Training Division, and Michigan Academy of Emergency Services. Students may study abroad in 6 countries. Accelerated degree programs are available in business administration, criminal justice administration, communication, hospitality management, and public safety. The college confers credit for life, military, and work experience through the School of Adult and Continuing Education. Nondegree study, dual majors in many combinations, student-designed majors, a 3-2 engineering degree with Kettering University, and a pass/fail grading option are available.

Admissions: 66% of the 2009-2010 applicants were accepted. The SAT scores for the 2009-2010 freshman class were: Critical Reading--36% below 500, 21% between 500 and 599, 21% between 600 and 700, and 22 above 700; Math--28% below 500, 43% between 500 and 599, 29% between 600 and 700, and above 700; Writing--43% below 500, 7% between 500 and 599, 29% between 600 and 700, and 21 above 700. The ACT scores were 36% below 21, 20% between 21 and 23, 27% between 24 and 26, 11% between 27 and 28, and 6% above 28.

Requirements: The SAT or ACT is required. However, the ACT is preferred. Applicants must graduate from an accredited secondary school or have the GED. 20 Carnegie units are recommended, including 4 units in English, 3 in math, and 2 each in science, social studies, and foreign language. AP and CLEP credits are accepted. Important factors in the admissions decision are leadership record, advanced placement or honors courses, and evidence of special talent.

Procedure: Freshmen are admitted fall and spring. There are deferred admissions and rolling admissions plans. Application deadlines are open. The fall 2008 application fee was $25. Notification is sent on a rolling basis. Applications are accepted on-line.

Financial Aid: In 2009-2010, 100% of all full-time freshmen and 100% of continuing full-time students received some form of financial aid. 65% of all full-time freshmen and 69% of continuing full-time students received need-based aid. The average freshmen award was $18,392, with $5,047 ($13,505 maximum) from need-based scholarships or need-based grants; $7,766 ($9,000 maximum) from need-based self-help aid (loans and jobs); $8,274 ($17,500 maximum) from non-need-based athletic scholarships; and $6,500 ($19,700 maximum) from other non-need-based awards and non-need-based scholarships. 42% of undergraduate students work part-time. Average annual earnings from campus work are $1781. The average financial indebtedness of the 2009 graduate was $25,000. The FAFSA and the college's own financial statement are required. The deadline for filing freshman financial aid applications for fall entry is March 1.

Computers: Wireless access is available. Every student living on campus has access to the university's network. Virus protection and firewall protection are required. Access is from the dorm room, library, or computer lab. All students may access the system. 8 A.M. to midnight, with 24-hour access from dorm rooms. There are no time limits and no fees. It is strongly recommended that all students have a personal computer.

CONCORDIA UNIVERSITY NEBRASKA
Seward, NE 68434

(402) 643-7233
(800) 535-5494; (402) 643-4073

Full-time: 1050 men and women	**Faculty:** IIB, --$
Part-time: 35 men and women	**Ph.D.s:** n/av
Graduate: 205 men and women.	**Student/Faculty:** n/av
Year: semesters, summer session	**Tuition:** $20,000
Application Deadline: see profile	**Room & Board:** $6000
Freshman Class: n/av	
SAT or ACT: required	**VERY COMPETITIVE**

Concordia University Nebraska, founded in 1894, is a private university owned and operated by the Lutheran Church-Missouri Synod, with degree programs in professional education and liberal arts. Among Concordia's major programs are those for professional work in the Lutheran Church: teacher education, director of Christian education, preseminary pastoral training, and church music. The figures in the above capsule and in this profile are approximate. There is 1 graduate school. In addition to regional accreditation, Concordia has baccalaureate program accreditation with NCATE. The 3 libraries contain 177,683 volumes, 10,719 microform items, and 13,214 audio/video tapes/CDs/DVDs, and subscribe to 545 periodicals including electronic. Computerized library services include database searching. Special learning facilities include a learning resource center, art gallery, natural history museum, and an observatory. The 120-acre campus is in a small town 25 miles west of Lincoln. Including any residence halls, there are 26 buildings.

Programs of Study: Concordia confers B.A., B.S., B.F.A., B.S.Med.Tech., B.Mus., and B. Sacred Music degrees. Master's degrees are also awarded. Bachelor's degrees are awarded in BIOLOGICAL SCIENCE (biology/biological science), BUSINESS (accounting, business administration and management, and sports management), COMMUNICATIONS AND THE ARTS (communications, dramatic arts, English, fine arts, music, speech/debate/rhetoric, and studio art), COMPUTER AND PHYSICAL SCIENCE (chemistry, computer science, mathematics, natural sciences, and physical sciences), EDUCATION (business education, Christian education, early childhood education, elementary education, home economics education, industrial arts education, middle school education, music education, physical education, science education, secondary education, and special education), HEALTH PROFESSIONS (exercise science, health, medical laboratory technology, predentistry, and premedicine), SOCIAL SCIENCE (behavioral science, geography, history, physical fitness/movement, prelaw, psychology, and theological studies). Education, business, and art are the strongest academically. Education is the largest.

Special: Concordia offers cross-registration with the University of Nebraska in Lincoln. Internships are available in education, business, and Christian education. B.A.-B.S. degrees, student-designed majors, dual majors, study abroad in England and China, nondegree studies, and pass/fail options are available. There is an accelerated degree program in organizational management. There is a freshman honors program.

Requirements: The SAT or ACT is required. A minimum composite score of 18 is recommended for the ACT. Applicants need not be graduates of an accredited secondary school. The GED is accepted. The school strongly encourages high school courses in art, English, foreign language, history, math, music, phys ed, science, and social studies. An interview is recommended. A GPA of 2.8 is required. AP and CLEP credits are accepted. Important factors in the admissions decision are ability to finance college education, leadership record, and recommendations by alumni.

Procedure: Freshmen are admitted to all sessions. Entrance exams should be taken in the junior or senior year. There is a rolling admissions plan. Application deadlines are open. Applications are accepted on-line.

Financial Aid: In a recent year, 98% of all full-time freshmen received some form of financial aid. The FAFSA and the college's own financial statement are required. Check with the school for current application deadlines.

Computers: All students may access the system. There are no time limits and no fees. It is strongly recommended that all students have a personal computer.

CONCORDIA UNIVERSITY WISCONSIN

Mequon, WI 53097   **(414) 243-4305; (414) 243-4545**

Full-time: 2330 men and women	**Faculty:** 99; IIB, -$
Part-time: 1757 men and women	**Ph.D.s:** 75%
Graduate: 3091 men and women	**Student/Faculty:** 11 to 1
Year: 4-1-4, summer session	**Tuition:** $20,990 ($28,980)
Application Deadline: August 1	**Room & Board:** $7990
Freshman Class: 1130 accepted, 402 enrolled	
SAT: required	**ACT:** 22 **VERY COMPETITIVE**

Concordia University Wisconsin, established in 1881, is a private institution affiliated with the Lutheran Church-Missouri Synod. There are 4 undergraduate schools and 1 graduate school. In addition to regional accreditation, CUW has baccalaureate program accreditation with NLN. The library contains 120,000 volumes, 270,602 microform items, and 4,152 audio/video tapes/CDs/DVDs, and subscribes to 37,000 periodicals including electronic. Computerized library services include interlibrary loans, database searching, and Internet access. Special learning facilities include a learning resource center, art gallery, radio station, a curriculum library for education students, and health and fitness facility. The 155-acre campus is in a suburban area 15 miles north of Milwaukee. Including any residence halls, there are 17 buildings.

Programs of Study: CUW confers B.A., B.S., and B.S.N. degrees. Associate and master's degrees are also awarded. Bachelor's degrees are awarded in BIOLOGICAL SCIENCE (biology/biological science), BUSINESS (accounting, banking and finance, business administration and management, management science, and marketing/retailing/merchandising), COMMUNICATIONS AND THE ARTS (art, communications, English, graphic design, music, Spanish, speech/debate/rhetoric, and telecommunications), COMPUTER AND PHYSICAL SCIENCE (mathematics and radiological technology), EDUCATION (athletic training, early childhood education, elementary education, physical education, and secondary education), ENGINEERING AND ENVIRONMENTAL DESIGN (interior design), HEALTH PROFESSIONS (nursing, occupational therapy, and sports medicine), SOCIAL SCIENCE (biblical languages, criminal justice, history, humanities, ministries, paralegal studies, pastoral studies, psychology, religion, religious music, social science, social work, and theological studies). Education, business, and health sciences are the strongest academically.

Special: Internships, study abroad, pass/fail options, and credit for life, military, and work experience are available. Concordia offers a general studies degree, dual, student-designed, and interdisciplinary majors, including justice and public policy, and nondegree study. Accelerated degree programs are available in several fields. There is 1 national honor society.

Requirements: The SAT or ACT is required, with a satisfactory score on the SAT or on the ACT. Applicants must be graduates of an accredited secondary school, having completed 16 academic credits, including 3 of English and 2 each of math, science, and social studies. The GED is accepted. A GPA of 2.5 is required. AP and CLEP credits are accepted. Important factors in the admissions decision are leadership record, recommendations by school officials, and personality/intangible qualities.

Procedure: Freshmen are admitted to all sessions. Entrance exams should be taken in the junior year. There is a rolling admissions plan. Applications should be filed by August 1 for fall entry. The fall 2008 application fee was $35.

Financial Aid: The CSS/Profile, FAFSA, the college's own financial statement, and income tax forms are required. The deadline for filing freshman financial aid applications for fall entry is April 30.

Computers: All students may access the system. There are no time limits and no fees.

CONNECTICUT COLLEGE
New London, CT 06320-4196   (860) 439-2200; (860) 439-4301

Full-time: 710 men, 1129 women	**Faculty:** 177; IIB, +$
Part-time: 38 men, 29 women	**Ph.D.s:** 91%
Graduate: no men, 5 women	**Student/Faculty:** 9 to 1
Year: varies	**Tuition:** $42335
Application Deadline: January 1	**Room & Board:** $8780
Freshman Class: 4733 applied, 1732 accepted, 503 enrolled	
SAT CR/M/W: 660/650/660*	**ACT:** 27 **MOST COMPETITIVE**

Connecticut College, founded in 1911, is a private institution offering degree programs in the liberal arts and sciences. There are no undergraduate schools and one graduate school. The 2 libraries contain 616,590 volumes, 151,979 microform items, and 98,432 audio/video tapes/CDs/DVDs, and subscribe to 5,599 periodicals including electronic. Computerized library services include interlibrary loans, database searching, Internet access, and laptop Internet portals. Special learning facilities include an art gallery, radio station, an observatory, and an arboretum. The 750-acre campus is in a small town midway between Boston and New York City. Including any residence halls, there are 51 buildings.

Programs of Study: Connecticut College confers B.A. degrees. Master's degrees are also awarded. Bachelor's degrees are awarded in BIOLOGICAL SCIENCE (biochemistry, biology/biological science, botany, and neurosciences), COMMUNICATIONS AND THE ARTS (art, art history and appreciation, Chinese, classics, dance, dramatic arts, English, film arts, French, German, Japanese, music, and music technology), COMPUTER AND PHYSICAL SCIENCE (astrophysics, chemistry, mathematics, and physics), ENGINEERING AND ENVIRONMENTAL DESIGN (architecture and environmental science), SOCIAL SCIENCE (African studies, American studies, anthropology, East Asian studies, economics, gender studies, Hispanic American studies, history, human development, international relations, Italian studies, Latin American studies, philosophy, political science/government, psychology, religion, Russian and Slavic studies, sociology, and urban studies). Economics, English, and government are the largest.

Special: Cross-registration with 12 area colleges, internships in government, human services, and other fields, a Washington semester at American University, dual majors, student-designed majors, a 3-2 engineering degree with Washington University in St. Louis and Boston University, non-degree study, and satisfactory/unsatisfactory options are available. One third of the junior class studies abroad. An international studies certificate program is available, which combines competency in a foreign language, an internship, and study abroad. There are also certificate programs in museum studies, community action and public policy, conservation biology and environmental studies, arts and technology, and teaching. There are 5 national honor societies, including Phi Beta Kappa, and a freshman honors program.

Admissions: 37% of the 2009-2010 applicants were accepted. The SAT scores for the 2009-2010 freshman class were: Critical Reading--2% below 500, 17% between 500 and 599, 49% between 600 and 700, and 32% above 700; Math--1%

below 500, 17% between 500 and 599, 61% between 600 and 700, and 21% above 700; Writing--3% below 500, 10% between 500 and 599, 54% between 600 and 700, and 33% above 700.

Requirements: In addition, the submission of standardized tests are optional, although students whose primary language is not English are required to submit the TOEFL or its equivalent. In addition, applicants must be graduates of an accredited secondary school. An essay is required and an interview is recommended. AP credits are accepted.

Procedure: Freshmen are admitted fall and spring. Entrance exams should be taken by January of the senior year. There is a early decision, and deferred admissions plans. Early decision applications should be filed by November 15, regular application January 1 for fall entry and December 1 for spring entry, along with a $60 fee. Notification of early decision is sent December 15, regular decision, April 1. Applications are accepted on-line. 367 applicants were on a recent waiting list, 49 were accepted.

Financial Aid: In 2009-2010, 40% of continuing full-time students received some form of financial aid. 45% of continuing full-time students received need-based aid. The average freshmen award was $31,457. The average financial indebtedness of the 2009 graduate was $22,038. Connecticut College is a member of CSS. The CSS/Profile and FAFSA, and parent and student tax forms, including noncustodial parent's statement are required. The deadline for filing freshman financial aid applications for fall entry is January 15.

Computers: Wireless access is available. The campus has 84 wireless access points in academic buildings and all residence halls, with 3100 network drops. The college owns and supports about 1600 computers, some for faculty/staff, others in student labs. All students may access the system 24 hours a day. There are no time limits and no fees. It is strongly recommended that all students have a personal computer.

CONVERSE COLLEGE
Spartanburg, SC 29302

(864) 596-9040
(800) 766-1125; (864) 596-9225

Full-time: 605 women	**Faculty:** 68
Part-time: 120 women	**Ph.D.s:** 89%
Graduate: 65 men, 380 women	**Student/Faculty:** 9 to 1
Year: 4-1-4, summer session	**Tuition:** $25,230
Application Deadline: see profile	**Room & Board:** $7760
Freshman Class: n/av	
SAT or ACT: recommended	**VERY COMPETITIVE**

Converse College, founded in 1889, is a private women's liberal arts college. Men are admitted to the graduate programs. There are 2 undergraduate schools and 2 graduate schools. Enrollment figures in the above capsule and figures in this profile are approximate. In addition to regional accreditation, Converse has baccalaureate program accreditation with NASM. The library contains 150,000 volumes, 310 microform items, and 12,000 audio/video tapes/CDs/DVDs, and subscribes to 700 periodicals including electronic. Computerized library services include interlibrary loans and database searching. Special learning facilities include a learning resource center, art gallery, and natural history museum. The 72-acre campus is in an urban area 80 miles southwest of Charlotte. Including any residence halls, there are 27 buildings.

Programs of Study: Converse confers B.A., B.S., B.F.A., and B.Mus. degrees. Master's degrees are also awarded. Bachelor's degrees are awarded in BIOLOGI-

CAL SCIENCE (biology/biological science), BUSINESS (accounting and business administration and management), COMMUNICATIONS AND THE ARTS (English, fine arts, French, languages, modern language, music, and Spanish), COMPUTER AND PHYSICAL SCIENCE (chemistry, computer science, and mathematics), EDUCATION (art education, early childhood education, elementary education, foreign languages education, music education, science education, and secondary education), ENGINEERING AND ENVIRONMENTAL DESIGN (interior design), HEALTH PROFESSIONS (art therapy, predentistry, and premedicine), SOCIAL SCIENCE (economics, history, political science/government, prelaw, psychology, and religion). English, politics, and biology are the strongest academically. Music, education, and business are the largest.

Special: There are co-op programs and cross-registration with Wofford College. Internships, study abroad, a work-study program, accelerated degree programs, B.A.-B.S. degrees in business, economics, sociology, biology, and chemistry, and dual and student-designed majors are offered. There are 10 national honor societies, a freshman honors program, and honors programs in all departments.

Requirements: The SAT or ACT is recommended. In addition, applicants should be graduates of an accredited secondary school, having completed 20 Carnegie units, including 4 years of English, 3 of math, 2 each of foreign language, science, and social studies, and 1 of history. The GED is accepted. An interview is recommended for all students, and an audition is recommended for music students. A GPA of 2.0 is required. AP and CLEP credits are accepted. Important factors in the admissions decision are advanced placement or honors courses, recommendations by school officials, and leadership record.

Procedure: Freshmen are admitted to all sessions. Entrance exams should be taken by the senior year of high school. There are early decision and rolling admissions plans. Early decision applications should be filed by November; check with the school for other current application deadlines and fee. Notification of early decision is sent in November; regular decision, sent on a rolling basis. Applications are accepted on-line.

Financial Aid: The FAFSA is required. Check with the school for current deadlines.

Computers: All students may access the system. There are no time limits and no fees. It is strongly recommended that all students have a personal computer. A Compaq is recommended.

COOPER UNION FOR THE ADVANCEMENT OF SCIENCE AND ART

New York, NY 10003-7120　　　　　(212) 353-4120; (212) 353-4342

Full-time: 561 men, 336 women	**Faculty:** 53; II B, ++$
Part-time: 1 men, no women	**Ph.D.s:** 89%
Graduate: 77 men, 11 women	**Student/Faculty:** 17 to 1
Year: semesters, summer session	**Tuition:** $1600
Application Deadline: January 1	**Room & Board:** $13,500
Freshman Class: 3387 applied, 249 accepted, 193 enrolled	
SAT CR/M: 660/720	**ACT:** 33　　**MOST COMPETITIVE**

The Cooper Union for the Advancement of Science and Art, is an all honors college that provides full-tuition scholarships (estimated value $ 35000) to all undergradutes accepted. It offers degrees in architecture, art, and engineering. There are 3 undergraduate schools and one graduate school. In addition to regional accreditation, Cooper Union has baccalaureate program accreditation with ABET, NAAB, and NASAD. The library contains 104,000 volumes, 25,000 microform items, and 1,472 audio/video tapes/CDs/DVDs, and subscribes to 2,471 periodicals including electronic. Computerized library services include interlibrary loans, database searching, and Internet access. Special learning facilities include a learning resource center, art gallery, a center for speaking and writing, an electronic resources center, and a visual resources center. The campus is in an urban area located in the heart of lower Manhattan. Including any residence halls, there are 5 buildings.

Programs of Study: Cooper Union confers B.S., B.Arch., B.E., and B.F.A. degrees. Master's degrees are also awarded. Bachelor's degrees are awarded in COMMUNICATIONS AND THE ARTS (fine arts and graphic design), ENGINEERING AND ENVIRONMENTAL DESIGN (architecture, chemical engineering, civil engineering, electrical/electronics engineering, engineering, and mechanical engineering). Engineering is the strongest academically and the largest.

Special: Cross-registration with New School University, internships, study abroad for art students in 15 countries, and for engineering students in 12 countries, and some pass/fail options are available. Nondegree study is possible. An accelerated degree in engineering is also available (combined bachelors and masters degree program). There are 4 national honor societies and 1 departmental honors program.

Admissions: 7% of the 2009-2010 applicants were accepted. The SAT scores for the 2009-2010 freshman class were: Critical Reading--4% below 500, 22% between 500 and 599, 40% between 600 and 700, and 34% above 700; Math--7% below 500, 17% between 500 and 599, 21% between 600 and 700, and 5% above 700. The ACT scores were 25% between 27 and 28 and 75% above 28. 90% of the current freshmen were in the top fifth of their class; 98% were in the top two fifths. There were 8 National Merit finalists. 5 freshmen graduated first in their class.

Requirements: The SAT is required. In addition, engineering applicants must take SAT Subject Tests in mathematics I or II and physics or chemistry. Graduation from an approved secondary school is required. Applicants should have completed 16 to 18 high school academic credits, depending on their major. An essay is part of the application process. Art students must submit a portfolio. Art and architecture applicants must complete a project called the home test. AP credits are accepted. Important factors in the admissions decision are evidence of special talent, advanced placement or honors courses, and personality/intangible qualities.

Procedure: Freshmen are admitted in the fall. Entrance exams should be taken before February 1. There are early decision and deferred admissions plans. Early decision applications should be filed by December 1; regular applications, by January 1 for fall entry. The fall 2008 application fee was $65. Notification of early decision is sent February 1; regular decision, April 1. Applications are accepted on-line. 50 applicants were on a recent waiting list, 3 were accepted.

Financial Aid: In 2009-2010, all full-time freshmen and all of continuing full-time students received some form of financial aid. 36% of all full-time freshmen and 35% of continuing full-time students received need-based aid. The average freshmen award was $35,000, with $3,249 ($5,000 maximum) from need-based scholarships or need-based grants; $2,084 ($3,000 maximum) from need-based self-help aid (loans and jobs); and $35,000 ($35,000 maximum) from other non-need-based awards and non-need-based scholarships. 47% of undergraduate students work part-time. Average annual earnings from campus work are $1001. The average financial indebtedness of the 2009 graduate was $9,900. Cooper Union is a member of CSS. The CSS/Profile and FAFSA are required. The priority date for freshman financial aid applications for fall entry is April 15. The deadline for filing freshman financial aid applications for fall entry is May 1.

Computers: Wireless access is available. All students may access the system whenever the Engineering Building is open. There are no time limits and no fees.

CORBAN COLLEGE
Salem, OR 97301-9392

(503) 375-7005
(800) 845-3005; (503) 585-4316

Full-time: 298 men, 460 women	**Faculty:** 35
Part-time: 60 men, 70 women	**Ph.D.s:** 39%
Graduate: 73 men, 139 women	**Student/Faculty:** 22 to 1
Year: semesters, summer session	**Tuition:** $23,220
Application Deadline: August 1	**Room & Board:** $7520
Freshman Class: 907 applied, 518 accepted, 215 enrolled	
SAT CR/M/W: 560/545/535	**ACT:** 23　**VERY COMPETITIVE**

Corban College is a Christian, liberal arts institution offering degrees in biblical-theological studies, business administration, education, humanities, math, phys ed, social sciences, psychology, intercultural studies, and youth work. There is 1 undergraduate schools. The library contains 82,000 volumes, 4100 microform items, and 4532 audio/video tapes/CDs/DVDs, and subscribes to 552 periodicals including electronic. Computerized library services include interlibrary loans, database searching, and Internet access. Special learning facilities include a learning resource center and an archaeological museum. The 140-acre campus is in a suburban area in Salem. Including any residence halls, there are 22 buildings.

Programs of Study: Corban confers B.A., B.S., and Th.B. degrees. Associate degrees are also awarded. Bachelor's degrees are awarded in BUSINESS (accounting and business administration and management), COMMUNICATIONS AND THE ARTS (communications, English, and music), COMPUTER AND PHYSICAL SCIENCE (computer science and mathematics), EDUCATION (education and physical education), HEALTH PROFESSIONS (health science), SOCIAL SCIENCE (biblical studies, counseling/psychology, crosscultural studies, history, humanities, ministries, psychology, and social science). Education, psychology, and business are the largest.

Special: Corban offers a preseminary co-op program, cross-registration with Oregon Independent Colleges, study abroad in 4 countries, a Washington semester, internships with the approval of a program adviser, accelerated programs in management and communication and in family studies, and student-designed majors with adviser approval. There is a freshman honors program and 3 departmental honors programs.

Admissions: 57% of the 2009-2010 applicants were accepted. The SAT scores for the 2009-2010 freshman class were: Critical Reading--23% below 500, 41% between 500 and 599, 30% between 600 and 700, and 4% above 700; Math--24% below 500, 44% between 500 and 599, 26% between 600 and 700, and 4% above 700; Writing--33% below 500, 42% between 500 and 599, 19% between 600 and 700, and 3% above 700. The ACT scores were 24% below 21, 20% between 21 and 23, 31% between 24 and 26, 9% between 27 and 28, and 16% above 28. 46% of the current freshmen were in the top fifth of their class; 76% were in the top two fifths. 14 freshmen graduated first in their class.

Requirements: The SAT or ACT is required, as is an essay. A GPA of 2.7 is required. AP and CLEP credits are accepted. Important factors in the admissions decision are extracurricular activities record, leadership record, and evidence of special talent.

Procedure: Freshmen are admitted fall and spring. There is a rolling admissions plan. Applications should be filed by August 1 for fall entry and December 1 for spring entry, along with a $35 fee. Notification is sent on a rolling basis. Applications are accepted on-line.

Financial Aid: In 2009-2010, 98% of all full-time freshmen and 97% of continuing full-time students received some form of financial aid. 83% of all full-time freshmen and 87% of continuing full-time students received need-based aid. The average freshman award was $19,888. 30% of undergraduate students work part-time. Average annual earnings from campus work are $1000. The average financial indebtedness of the 2009 graduate was $19,000. The FAFSA is required. The deadline for filing freshman financial aid applications for fall entry is March 1.

Computers: Wireless access is available. All students have access through the 2 computer labs on campus. Students may use personal computers in their rooms. The wireless network is available throughout campus. All students may access the system 7 days per week/24 hours per day. There are no time limits and no fees. It is strongly recommended that all students have a personal computer. Students enrolled in business information systems and computer science must have a personal computer.

CORNELL COLLEGE
Mount Vernon, IA 52314-1098　　　　　　　　**(319) 895-4215**
(800) 747-1112; (319) 895-4451

Full-time: 536 men, 585 women	**Faculty:** 87; IIB, av$
Part-time: 4 men, 8 women	**Ph.D.s:** 95%
Graduate: none	**Student/Faculty:** 13 to 1
Year: see profile	**Tuition:** $29,580
Application Deadline: February 1	**Room & Board:** $7500
Freshman Class: 3208 applied, 1411 accepted, 340 enrolled	
SAT CR/M/W: 610/610/570	**ACT:** 26　**HIGHLY COMPETITIVE**

Cornell College, founded in 1853, is private institution affiliated with the United Methodist Church. Its emphases are on the liberal arts and on student service and leadership. Cornell has a 1-course-at-a-time calendar in which the year is divided into nine 3 1/2 week terms. The library contains 202,794 volumes, 75,514 microform items, and 8,827 audio/video tapes/CDs/DVDs, and subscribes to 477 periodicals including electronic. Computerized library services include interlibrary loans, database searching, Internet access, and laptop Internet portals. Special learning facilities include a learning resource center, art gallery, natural history museum, and radio station. The 129-acre campus is in a small town 15 miles east of Cedar Rapids and 3 hours west of Chicago, Il. Including any residence halls, there are 44 buildings.

Programs of Study: Cornell confers B.A., B.Mus., B.Ph., and B.S.S. degrees. Bachelor's degrees are awarded in BIOLOGICAL SCIENCE (biochemistry and biology/biological science), BUSINESS (business economics), COMMUNICATIONS AND THE ARTS (art history and appreciation, dramatic arts, English, fine arts, French, German, languages, music, Russian, Spanish, and studio art), COMPUTER AND PHYSICAL SCIENCE (chemistry, computer science, geology, mathematics, and physics), EDUCATION (art education, elementary education, foreign languages education, music education, science education, and secondary education), ENGINEERING AND ENVIRONMENTAL DESIGN (environmental science), SOCIAL SCIENCE (archeology, classical/ancient civilization, economics, ethnic studies, history, international relations, Latin American studies, medieval studies, philosophy, political science/government, psychology, religion, Russian and Slavic studies, sociology, and women's studies). Politics, chemistry, and, art are the strongest academically. Psychology, biology, and business economics are the largest.

Special: Special academic programs include study abroad in 25 to 30 countries, internships including a Washington semester, double majors, student-designed majors, and interdisciplinary majors in biochemistry and molecular biology, environmental studies, classical studies, ethnic studies, Latin American studies, Russian studies, anthropolgy and sociology, international relations, and women's studies. A cooperative degree program in Medical Technology with St. Luke's Methodist Hospital, a degree program in Nursing and Allied Health Science with Rush University, a 3-2 engineering program with the University of Minnesota, and a 3-4 architecture program with Washington University, and a 3-2 forestry or environmental management program with Duke University are also available. There are 12 national honor societies, including Phi Beta Kappa.

Admissions: 44% of the 2009-2010 applicants were accepted. The SAT scores for the 2009-2010 freshman class were: Critical Reading--8% below 500, 36% between 500 and 599, 36% between 600 and 700, and 20% above 700; Math--7% below 500, 35% between 500 and 599, 40% between 600 and 700, and 18% above 700; Writing--14% below 500, 43% between 500 and 599, 32% between 600 and 700, and 11% above 700. The ACT scores were 8% below 21, 14% between 21 and 23, 29% between 24 and 26, 16% between 27 and 28, and 32% above 28. 52% of the current freshmen were in the top fifth of their class; 79% were in the top two fifths. There were 3 National Merit finalists. 17 freshmen graduated first in their class.

Requirements: The SAT or ACT is required. In addition, applicants should be graduates of an accredited secondary school, with a recommended 4 years each of English, 3 or more years of math and science, and social studies, 2 or more years of a foreign language. An essay and a secondary school report are required, and an interview is advised. The GED is accepted. AP credits are accepted. Important factors in the admissions decision are advanced placement or honors courses, evidence of special talent, and leadership record.

Procedure: Freshmen are admitted in the fall. There are early decision, early admissions, and deferred admissions plans. Early decision applications should be filed by November 1, regular applications should be filed by February 1 for fall entry, along with a $30 fee. Notification of early decision is sent December 20; regular decision, March 20. Applications are accepted on-line. 142 applicants were on a recent waiting list, 50 were accepted.

Financial Aid: In a recent year, 93% of all full-time freshmen and 95% of continuing full-time students received some form of financial aid. 65% of all full-time freshmen and 69% of continuing full-time students received need-based aid. The average freshman award was $19,675. Need-based scholarships or need-based grants averaged $13,135 ($20,000 maximum); need-based self-help aid (loans and jobs) averaged $2,750 ($7,500 maximum); and other non-need based awards and non-need based scholarships averaged $10,250 ($20,000 maximum). 61% of undergraduate students worked part-time. Average annual earnings from campus work were $1200. The average financial indebtedness of the 2009 graduate was $25,645. Cornell is a member of CSS. The FAFSA and the college's own financial statement are required. Check with the school for current application deadlines.

Computers: Wireless access is available. Wired Internet access is available in all residence halls, academic buildings, the student union, and the library. Wireless network access is available in all classrooms, the student union, library, and dining areas. Wireless is available in the common areas of each residence hall. All students may access the system. There are no time limits and no fees.

CORNELL UNIVERSITY
Ithaca, NY 14850 (607) 255-5241

Full-time: 7050 men, 6881 women	**Faculty:** 1432; I, +$
Part-time: none	**Ph.D.s:** 93%
Graduate: 3837 men, 2865 women	**Student/Faculty:** 10 to 1
Year: semesters, summer session	**Tuition:** $50,114
Application Deadline: January 1	**Room & Board:** $12,160
Freshman Class: 34371 applied, 6565 accepted, 3181 enrolled	
SAT or ACT: required	**MOST COMPETITIVE**

Cornell University was founded in 1865 as a land-grant institution. This private institution has undergraduate divisions that include the College of Architecture, Art, and Planning, the College of Arts and Sciences, the College of Engineering, and the School of Hotel Administration. State-assisted undergraduate divisions include the College of Agriculture and Life Sciences, the College of Human Ecology, and the School of Industrial and Labor Relations. There are 7 undergraduate schools and 4 graduate schools. In addition to regional accreditation, Cornell has baccalaureate program accreditation with AACSB, ABET, ASLA, and NAAB. The 19 libraries contain 7.5 million volumes, 8.5 million microform items, and 140,997 audio/video tapes/CDs/DVDs, and subscribe to 93,000 periodicals including electronic. Computerized library services include interlibrary loans, database searching, Internet access, and laptop Internet portals. Special learning facilities include a learning resource center, art gallery, planetarium, radio station, biotechnology institute, woods sanctuary, 4 designated national resource centers, 2 local optical observatories, Africana Studies and research center, arboretum, particle accelerator, supercomputers, national research centers, performing arts center, lab of ornithology, vertebrates museum, living and learning communities, campus orchard, dairy pilot plant, mineralogical museum, animal teaching hospital, 2 agricultural experiment stations, and a marine laboratory. The 745-acre campus is in a rural area 60 miles south of Syracuse, NY. Including any residence halls, there are 770 buildings.

Programs of Study: Cornell confers B.A., B.S., B.Arch., and B.F.A. degrees. Master's and doctoral degrees are also awarded. Bachelor's degrees are awarded in AGRICULTURE (agricultural business management, agricultural economics, agriculture, animal science, horticulture, international agriculture, natural resource management, plant protection (pest management), plant science, and soil science), BIOLOGICAL SCIENCE (biochemistry, biology/biological science, ecology, entomology, microbiology, neurosciences, nutrition, plant genetics, and plant pathology), BUSINESS (hotel/motel and restaurant management and operations research), COMMUNICATIONS AND THE ARTS (art history and appreciation, Chinese, classics, communications, comparative literature, dance, dramatic arts, English, film arts, fine arts, French, German, Italian, linguistics, music, Russian, and Spanish), COMPUTER AND PHYSICAL SCIENCE (astronomy, atmospheric sciences and meteorology, chemistry, computer science, earth science, geology, information sciences and systems, mathematics, physics, science technology, and statistics), EDUCATION (education, home economics education, and science education), ENGINEERING AND ENVIRONMENTAL DESIGN (agricultural engineering, architectural history, architecture, bioengineering, chemical engineering, city/community/regional planning, civil engineering, computer engineering, electrical/electronics engineering, engineering physics, environmental engineering technology, environmental science, industrial administration/management, landscape architecture/design, materials science, and mechanical engineering), SOCIAL SCIENCE (African studies, American studies, anthropology, archeology, Asian/Oriental studies, classical/ancient civilization, consumer services, economics, family/consumer studies, food production/management/services, food science, gender studies, German area studies, history, human development, human services, Near Eastern studies, philosophy, political science/government, psychology, public affairs, religion, rural sociology, Russian and Slavic studies, sociology, textiles and clothing, urban studies, and women's studies). Engineering, business, and agriculture are the largest.

Special: Cornell's colleges and schools offer nearly unlimited opportunities for international study internships and exchanges. There are opportunities for dual-majors, dual-degrees, and minors throughout the university. Refer to information provided by the individual schools, colleges, and programs for details. There are 47 national honor societies and including Phi Beta Kappa.

Admissions: 19% of the 2009-2010 applicants were accepted. The SAT scores for the 2009-2010 freshman class were: Critical Reading--1% below 500, 13% between 500 and 599, 44% between 600 and 700, and 42% above 700; Math--1% below 500, 6% between 500 and 599, 33% between 600 and 700, and 60% above 700. The ACT scores were % below 21, 2% between 21 and 23, 9% between 24 and 26, 11% between 27 and 28, and 78% above 28. 97% of the current freshmen were in the top fifth of their class; 100% were in the top two fifths.

Requirements: The SAT or ACT is required. The ACT Optional Writing test is also required. In addition, an essay is required as part of the application process. Other requirements vary by division or program, including specific SAT Subject tests and selection of courses within the minimum 16 secondary-school academic units needed. An interview and/or portfolio is required for specific majors. AP credits are accepted. Important factors in the admissions decision are advanced placement or honors courses, evidence of special talent, and leadership record.

Procedure: Freshmen are admitted fall and spring. Entrance exams should be taken by December of the senior year. There are early decision, early admissions and deferred admissions plans. Early decision applications should be filed by November 1; regular applications, by January 1 for fall entry and October 1 for spring entry. The fall 2009 application fee was $70. Notification of early decision is sent in December. Notifications are sent in April. Applications are accepted online. 1949 applicants were on a recent waiting list.

Financial Aid: In 2009-2010, 60% of all full-time freshmen and 64% of continuing full-time students received some form of financial aid. 52% of all full-time freshmen and 46% of continuing full-time students received need-based aid. The average freshmen award was $36,062. The average financial indebtedness of the 2009 graduate was $21,549. The CSS/Profile, FAFSA, and the college's own financial statement, and The IRS form is required after enrollment are required. The deadline for filing freshman financial aid applications for fall entry is January 2.

Computers: Wireless access is available. Students have access to campus wide PC centers and more than 30 departmental facilities with more than 2000 PCs, as well as networks in residence halls. Wireless connections are available in most campus locations. All networks are connected to the Internet. All students may access the system. There are no time limits and no fees. It is strongly recommended that all students have a personal computer. Students enrolled in engineering must have a personal computer.

COVENANT COLLEGE

Lookout Mountain, GA 30750

(706) 820-2398
(888) 451-2683; (706) 820-0893

Full-time: 421 men, 544 women	**Faculty:** 58; IIB, -$
Part-time: 17 men, 16 women	**Ph.D.s:** 88%
Graduate: 25 men, 38 women	**Student/Faculty:** 16 to 1
Year: semesters, summer session	**Tuition:** $25,270
Application Deadline: May 1	**Room & Board:** $7170
●Freshman Class: 1078 applied, 649 accepted, 277 enrolled	
SAT CR/M/W: 603/565/587	**ACT:** 25 **VERY COMPETITIVE**

Covenant College, founded in 1955, is a private liberal arts college affiliated with the Presbyterian Church in America (P.C.A.). There is one undergraduate schls and one graduate school. The library contains 80,250 volumes, 125,000 microform items, and 7,540 audio/video tapes/CDs/DVDs, and subscribes to 400 periodicals including electronic. Computerized library services include interlibrary loans, database searching, and Internet access. Special learning facilities include a radio station. The 300-acre campus is in a suburban area 12 miles southwest of Chattanooga, Tennessee. Including any residence halls, there are 13 buildings.

Programs of Study: Covenant confers B.A., B.S., and B.Mus. degrees. Associates and master's degrees are also awarded. Bachelor's degrees are awarded in BIOLOGICAL SCIENCE (biology/biological science), BUSINESS (business administration and management), COMMUNICATIONS AND THE ARTS (art, dramatic arts, English, music, and music performance), COMPUTER AND PHYSICAL SCIENCE (chemistry, computer science, mathematics, physical sciences, and physics), EDUCATION (elementary education, English education, mathematics education, and science education), SOCIAL SCIENCE (biblical studies, economics, history, interdisciplinary studies, philosophy, psychology, religion, social science, and sociology). Community development, education, and Biblical and theological studies are the largest.

Special: Cross-registration is possible with the Council for Christian Colleges and Universities (CCCU) as are internships in business, psychology, and biology. Students may study abroad in 9 countries or spend a semester in Washington. There is a 3-2 engineering program with Georgia Tech and other universities and technical institutes, and a 13-month degree-completion program for students with 2 years of previous college experience. Juniors and seniors may take classes on a pass/fail basis. There are 2 national honor societies, a freshman honors program, and 2 departmental honors programs.

Admissions: 60% of the 2009-2010 applicants were accepted. The SAT scores for the 2009-2010 freshman class were: Critical Reading--14% below 500, 30% between 500 and 599, 40% between 600 and 700, and 17% above 700; Math--20% below 500, 44% between 500 and 599, 32% between 600 and 700, and 5% above 700; Writing--16% below 500, 39% between 500 and 599, 36% between 600 and 700, and 10% above 700. The ACT scores were 12% below 21, 21% between 21 and 23, 25% between 24 and 26, 19% between 27 and 28, and 22% above 28. 50% of the current freshmen were in the top fifth of their class; 68% were in the top two fifths. 5 freshmen graduated first in their class.

Requirements: The SAT or ACT is required, with a minimum satisfactory score on the SAT or 21 on the ACT. Applicants must graduate from an accredited high school or have a GED. Applicants should have 16 total units, including 4 years of high school English, 3 years of math, and 2 years each of foreign language, history, science, and social studies. An essay and an interview are required. A

GPA of 2.5 is required. AP and CLEP credits are accepted. Important factors in the admissions decision are advanced placement or honors courses, extracurricular activities record, and leadership record.

Procedure: Freshmen are admitted fall and spring. Entrance exams should be taken by January of the senior year. There is a rolling admissions plan. Applications should be filed by May 1 for fall entry and November 1 for spring entry, along with a $35 fee.

Financial Aid: In 2009-2010, 100% of all full-time freshmen and 99% of continuing full-time students received some form of financial aid. 76% of all full-time freshmen and 64% of continuing full-time students received need-based aid. The average freshmen award was $19,824, with $15,627 ($27,050 maximum) from need-based scholarships or need-based grants; $5,297 ($24,240 maximum) from need-based self-help aid (loans and jobs); and $10,770 ($24,000 maximum) from other non-need-based awards and non-need-based scholarships. 50% of undergraduate students work part-time. Average annual earnings from campus work are $2715. The average financial indebtedness of the 2009 graduate was $17,824. The FAFSA and the college's own financial statement are required. The priority date for freshman financial aid applications for fall entry is March 1. The deadline for filing freshman financial aid applications for fall entry is March 31.

Computers: Wireless access is available. The wireles network is available in all college-owned housing, library, computer labs, and some classrooms. All students may access the system 8 A.M. to 12 A.M. Monday through Thursday and Saturday and 8 A.M. to 6 P.M. on Friday. There are no time limits. The fee is $80.

CREIGHTON UNIVERSITY
Omaha, NE 68178-0001

(402) 280-2703
(800) 282-5835; (402) 280-2685

Full-time: 1573 men, 2296 women	**Faculty:** 300; IIA, av$
Part-time: 108 men, 156 women	**Ph.D.s:** 83%
Graduate: 1499 men, 1753 women	**Student/Faculty:** 13 to 1
Year: semesters, summer session	**Tuition:** $29,544
Application Deadline: August 1	**Room & Board:** $8814
Freshman Class: 4752 applied, 3886 accepted, 1054 enrolled	
SAT CR/M/W: 580/600/580	**ACT:** 26 **VERY COMPETITIVE+**

Creighton University, founded in 1878, is a private Jesuit Catholic institution offering undergraduate programs in arts and sciences, business administration, and nursing as well as graduate, dental, medical, law, pharmacy, physical therapy, and occupational therapy programs. There are 3 undergraduate schools and 5 graduate schools. In addition to regional accreditation, Creighton has baccalaureate program accreditation with AACSB, ACPE, CSWE, NCATE, and NLN. The 3 libraries contain 925,385 volumes, 1.8 million microform items, and 21,005 audio/video tapes/CDs/DVDs, and subscribe to 42,374 periodicals including electronic. Computerized library services include interlibrary loans, database searching, Internet access, and laptop Internet portals. Special learning facilities include a learning resource center, art gallery, and TV station. The 108-acre campus is in an urban area near downtown Omaha. Including any residence halls, there are 51 buildings.

Programs of Study: Creighton confers B.A., B.S., B.F.A., B.S. Atmospheric Science, B.S.B.A., B.S.Chem., B.S. Computer Science, B.S. Environmental Science, B.S. Mathematics, B.S.N., B.S. Physics, B.S.Soc., and B.S.W. degrees. Associate, master's, and doctoral degrees are also awarded. Bachelor's degrees are awarded in BIOLOGICAL SCIENCE (biology/biological science), BUSINESS (accounting, banking and finance, business administration and management, international business management, management information systems, management science, and marketing/retailing/merchandising), COMMUNICATIONS AND THE ARTS (art, communications, dance, dramatic arts, English, fine arts, French, German, Greek, journalism, Latin, music, Spanish, speech/debate/rhetoric, and theater design), COMPUTER AND PHYSICAL SCIENCE (atmospheric sciences and meteorology, chemistry, computer science, mathematics, and physics), EDUCATION (elementary education and secondary education), ENGINEERING AND ENVIRONMENTAL DESIGN (environmental science), HEALTH PROFESSIONS (emergency medical technologies, exercise science, health care administration, and nursing), SOCIAL SCIENCE (African studies, American studies, anthropology, classical/ancient civilization, economics, history, Native American studies, peace studies, philosophy, political science/government, psychology, social work, sociology, and theological studies). Business, science/health science, and nursing are the strongest academically and the largest.

Special: The university offers study abroad in 41 countries, a Washington semester, and numerous internship opportunities. Students may take an accelerated degree program in organizational communication and creative writing. B.A.-B.S. degrees and dual majors are possible as well as a 3-2 engineering degree with Marquette University and the University of Detroit Mercy. There are 14 national honor societies and a freshman honors program; the College of Arts and Sciences sponsors the honors program.

Admissions: 82% of the 2009-2010 applicants were accepted. The SAT scores for the 2009-2010 freshman class were: Critical Reading--18% below 500, 38% between 500 and 599, 34% between 600 and 700, and 11% above 700; Math--13% below 500, 36% between 500 and 599, 38% between 600 and 700, and 13% above 700. The ACT scores were 6% below 21, 16% between 21 and 23, 27% between 24 and 26, 18% between 27 and 28, and 33% above 28. 66% of the current freshmen were in the top fifth of their class; 87% were in the top two fifths. 49 freshmen graduated first in their class.

Requirements: The SAT or ACT is required. In addition, applicants must be graduates of an accredited secondary school. The GED is accepted. Students should have completed 16 credits including 4 credits in English, 3 each in math and electives, and 2 each in foreign language, science, and social studies. Homeschooled students are welcome. A GPA of 2.5 is required. AP and CLEP credits are accepted. Important factors in the admissions decision are leadership record, extracurricular activities record, and recommendations by school officials.

Procedure: Freshmen are admitted to all sessions. Entrance exams should be taken prior to May 1 of the senior year. There are deferred admissions and rolling admissions plans. Applications should be filed by August 1 for fall entry and January 1 for spring entry, along with a $40 fee. Notification is sent on a rolling basis. 87 applicants were on the 2009 waiting list; 18 were admitted. Applications are accepted on-line.

Financial Aid: In a recent year, 88% of all full-time freshmen and 87% of continuing full-time students received some form of financial aid. 59% of all full-time freshmen and 51% of continuing full-time students received need-based aid. The average freshman award was $28,401. Need-based scholarships or need-based grants averaged $15,389; need-based self-help aid (loans and jobs) averaged $7477; non-need-based athletic scholarships averaged $19,452; and other non-need-based awards and non-need-based scholarships averaged $10,623. 52% of undergraduate students work part-time. The average financial indebtedness of a recent graduate was $29,074. The FAFSA is required. The priority date for freshman financial aid applications for fall entry is March 1. The deadline for filing freshman financial aid applications for fall entry is April 1.

Computers: Wireless access is available. All residence halls offer student connectivity 24/7. In addition, other areas of the campus, including some classrooms, offer wireless and hard-wire connectivity. All students may access the system any time. There are no time limits and no fees. It is strongly recommended that all students have a personal computer.

DARTMOUTH COLLEGE

Hanover, NH 03755   **(603) 646-2875; (603) 646-1216**

Full-time: 2064 men, 2037 women	**Faculty:** 482
Part-time: 25 men, 21 women	**Ph.D.s:** n/av
Graduate: 988 men, 713 women	**Student/Faculty:** 8 to 1
Year: quarters, summer session	**Tuition:** $36,690
Application Deadline: January 1	**Room & Board:** $10,779
Freshman Class: 16538 applied, 2228 accepted, 1095 enrolled	
SAT or ACT: required	**MOST COMPETITIVE**

Dartmouth College, chartered in 1769, is a private liberal arts institution offering a wide range of graduate and undergraduate programs. There is a year-round academic calendar of 4 10-week terms. There are 4 graduate schools. The 10 libraries contain 2.5 million volumes, 2.6 million microform items, and 772,660 audio/video tapes/CDs/DVDs, and subscribe to 42,116 periodicals including electronic. Computerized library services include interlibrary loans, database searching, Internet access, and laptop Internet portals. Special learning facilities include a learning resource center, art gallery, radio station, creative and performing arts center, life sciences lab, physical and social sciences centers, and observatory. The 265-acre campus is in a rural area 140 miles northwest of Boston. Including any residence halls, there are 100 buildings.

Programs of Study: Dartmouth confers B.A. and B.Eng. degrees. Master's and doctoral degrees are also awarded. Bachelor's degrees are awarded in AGRICULTURE (environmental studies), BIOLOGICAL SCIENCE (biochemistry, biology/biological science, genetics, and neurosciences), COMMUNICATIONS AND THE ARTS (Arabic, art history and appreciation, Chinese, classical languages, classics, comparative literature, dramatic arts, English, film arts, French, German, Italian, linguistics, music, Portuguese, romance languages and literature, Russian, Spanish, and studio art), COMPUTER AND PHYSICAL SCIENCE (astrophysics, chemistry, computer science, earth science, mathematics, and physics), ENGINEERING AND ENVIRONMENTAL DESIGN (engineering and applied science, engineering physics, and environmental science), SOCIAL SCIENCE (African American studies, anthropology, Asian/Oriental studies, classical/ancient civilization, cognitive science, economics, French studies, geography, German area studies, history, Latin American studies, Middle Eastern studies, Native American studies, philosophy, psychology, religion, Russian and Slavic studies, sociology, Spanish studies, and women's studies). Economics, government, and psychological and brain sciences are the largest.

Special: Students may design programs using the college's unique Dartmouth Plan, which divides the academic calendar into 4 10-week terms, based on the seasons. The plan permits greater flexibility for vacations and for the 45 study-abroad programs in 23 countries in Latin America, Europe, Asia, and Africa. Cross-registration is offered through the Twelve College Exchange Network. Exchange programs also exist with the University of California at San Diego, Stanford, Oxford, and McGill Universities, selected German universities, Keio University in Tokyo, and Beijing Normal University in China. Students may design their own interdisciplinary majors involving multiple departments, take dual majors in all fields, or create a modified major involving 2 departments, with emphasis in 1. Hands-on computer science education, internships, and work-study programs also are available. A 3-2 engineering degree is offered with Dartmouth's Thayer School of Engineering. There are 3 national honor societies, including Phi Beta Kappa.

Admissions: 13% of the 2009-2010 applicants were accepted. 95% of the current freshmen were in the top fifth of their class; all were in the top two fifths. 323 freshmen graduated first in their class.

Requirements: The SAT or ACT is required. The ACT Optional Writing test is also required. In addition, as are 2 SAT subject tests. Evidence of intellectual capacity, motivation, and personal integrity are important factors in the highly competitive admissions process, which also considers talent, accomplishment, and involvement in nonacademic areas. Course requirements are flexible, but students are urged to take English, foreign language, math, lab science, and history. The GED is accepted. AP credits are accepted.

Procedure: Freshmen are in the admitted fall. Entrance exams should be taken no later than November or January of the senior year. There is a early decision and deferred admissions plans. Early decision applications should be filed by November 1; regular applications, by January 1 for fall entry. The fall 2009 application fee was $70. Notification of early decision is sent December 15; regular decision, April 1. 958 applicants were on the 2009 waiting list; 95 were admitted. Applications are accepted on-line.

Financial Aid: In 2009-2010, 49% of all full-time freshmen and 53% of continuing full-time students received some form of financial aid. 49% of all full-time freshmen and 53% of continuing full-time students received need-based aid. The average freshman award was $37,055. The average financial indebtedness of the 2009 graduate was $18,095. Dartmouth is a member of CSS. The CSS/Profile, FAFSA, and parents' and student's federal income tax returns are required. The deadline for filing freshman financial aid applications for fall entry is February 1.

Computers: Wireless access is available. All students may access the system 24 hours daily. There are no time limits and no fees. All students are required to have a personal computer.

DAVIDSON COLLEGE
Davidson, NC 28035-5000

(704) 894-2230
(800) 768-0380; (704) 894-2016

Full-time: 858 men, 887 women	**Faculty:** 164; IIB, +$
Part-time: none	**Ph.D.s:** 97%
Graduate: none	**Student/Faculty:** 11 to 1
Year: semesters	**Tuition:** $35,124
Application Deadline: January 2	**Room & Board:** $9906
Freshman Class: 4494 applied, 1185 accepted, 491 enrolled	
SAT CR/M/W: 670/670/680	**ACT:** 30 **MOST COMPETITIVE**

Davidson College, founded in 1837, is a private liberal arts institution affiliated with the Presbyterian Church (U.S.A.). In addition to regional accreditation, Davidson has baccalaureate program accreditation with NCATE. The 3 libraries contain 630,349 volumes, 556,896 microform items, and 16,979 audio/video tapes/CDs/DVDs, and subscribe to 4,869 periodicals including electronic. Computerized library services include interlibrary loans, database searching, and Internet access. Special learning facilities include a learning resource center, art gallery, radio station, arboretum. The 450-acre campus is in a small town 19 miles north of Charlotte. Including any residence halls, there are 98 buildings.

Programs of Study: Davidson confers A.B. and B.S. degrees. Bachelor's degrees are awarded in BIOLOGICAL SCIENCE (biology/biological science), COMMUNICATIONS AND THE ARTS (art, classics, dramatic arts, English, French, German, music, and Spanish), COMPUTER AND PHYSICAL SCIENCE (chemistry, mathematics, and physics), SOCIAL SCIENCE (anthropology, economics, history, interdisciplinary studies, philosophy, political science/government, psychology, religion, and sociology). English, history, and biology are the largest.

Special: Davidson offers interdisciplinary international and South Asian studies programs and study abroad in 12 countries as well as through other schools' study-abroad programs. A 3-2 engineering program may be arranged with Georgia Institute of Technology and Columbia, Duke, North Carolina State, and Washington (St. Louis) Universities. Students may design their own majors and cross-register with any college in the Charlotte Area Educational Consortium. There are 15 national honor societies, including Phi Beta Kappa, and 20 departmental honors programs.

Admissions: 26% of the 2009-2010 applicants were accepted. The SAT scores for the 2009-2010 freshman class were: Critical Reading--1% below 500, 11% between 500 and 599, 49% between 600 and 700, and 39% above 700; Math--10% between 500 and 599, 57% between 600 and 700, and 32% above 700; Writing--1% below 500, 12% between 500 and 599, 49% between 600 and 700, and 38% above 700. The ACT scores were 2% between 21 and 23, 8% between 24 and 26, 15% between 27 and 28, and 75% above 28. 96% of the current freshmen were in the top fifth of their class; 99% were in the top two fifths. 26 freshmen graduated first in their class.

Requirements: The SAT or ACT is required. In addition, SAT Subject Tests are strongly recommended. At least 16 high school units are required, although 20 units are recommended. These should include 4 units of English, 3 units of math, 2 units of the same foreign language, 2 units of science, and 2 units of history/social studies. It is strongly recommended that high school students continue for the third and fourth years in science and in the same foreign language, continue math through calculus, and take additional courses in history. AP credits are accepted. Important factors in the admissions decision are advanced placement or honors courses, recommendations by school officials, and leadership record.

Procedure: Freshmen are admitted in the fall. Entrance exams should be taken by the end of the junior year. There are early decision and deferred admissions plans. Early decision applications should be filed by November 15; regular applications, by January 2 for fall entry. The fall 2009 application fee was $50. Notification of early decision is sent December 15; regular decision, April 1. 235 early decision candidates were accepted for the 2009-2010 class. 1103 applicants were on the 2009 waiting list; 121 were admitted. Applications are accepted on-line.

Financial Aid: 30% of undergraduate students work part-time. The CSS/Profile, FAFSA, and the college's own financial statement are required. The deadline for filing freshman financial aid applications for fall entry is February 15.

Computers: Wireless access is available. All students may access the system 24 hours per day. There are no time limits and no fees.

DENISON UNIVERSITY

Granville, OH 43023

(740) 587-6276
(800) DENISON; (740) 587-6306

Full-time: 979 men, 1257 women	**Faculty:** 197; IIB, +$
Part-time: 4 men	**Ph.D.s:** 9%
Graduate: none	**Student/Faculty:** 11 to 1
Year: semesters	**Tuition:** $36,560
Application Deadline: January 15	**Room & Board:** $9160
Freshman Class: 5002 applied, 2509 accepted, 649 enrolled	
SAT CR/M: 630/620	**ACT:** 28 **HIGHLY COMPETITIVE+**

Denison University, founded in 1831, is a private independent institution of liberal arts and sciences. The library contains 459,565 volumes, 123,029 microform items, and 26,000 audio/video tapes/CDs/DVDs, and subscribes to 21,805 periodicals including electronic. Computerized library services include interlibrary loans, database searching, Internet access, and laptop Internet portals. Special learning facilities include a learning resource center, art gallery, planetarium, radio station, TV station, observatory, multimedia MIX lab, field research station in a 350-acre biological reserve, high-resolution spectrometer, economics computer lab, and modern languages lab. The 900-acre campus is in a small town 30 miles east of Columbus. Including any residence halls, there are 62 buildings.

Programs of Study: Denison confers B.A. and B.S. degrees. Bachelor's degrees are awarded in AGRICULTURE (environmental studies), BIOLOGICAL SCIENCE (biochemistry and biology/biological science), COMMUNICATIONS AND THE ARTS (art history and appreciation, communications, dance, dramatic arts, English, film arts, fine arts, French, German, languages, Latin, media arts, music, Spanish, speech/debate/rhetoric, and studio art), COMPUTER AND PHYSICAL SCIENCE (chemistry, computer science, geology, mathematics, and physics), EDUCATION (education and physical education), SOCIAL SCIENCE (African American studies, anthropology, classical/ancient civilization, East Asian studies, economics, history, international studies, Latin American studies, philosophy, political science/government, psychology, religion, sociology, Western European studies, and women's studies). Psychology, biology, and sociology/anthropology are the strongest academically. Communication, biology, and economics are the largest.

Special: Work-study programs, a Washington semester, study-abroad programs in more than 35 countries, student-designed majors, a dual major in education and various other majors, a philosophy, political science, and economics interdisciplinary major, and pass/fail options are available. A 3-2 engineering program is offered with Rensselaer Polytechnic Institute and Case Western Reserve, Columbia, and Washington Universities. A May-term internship is available at more than 200 U.S. locations. A B.A.-B.S. degree, accelerated degree programs, a media technology and arts interdisciplinary major, and nondegree study are possible. There are 15 national honor societies, including Phi Beta Kappa.

Admissions: 50% of the 2009-2010 applicants were accepted. The SAT scores for the 2009-2010 freshman class were: Critical Reading--2% below 500, 28% between 500 and 599, 47% between 600 and 700, and 23% above 700; Math--3% below 500, 29% between 500 and 599, 52% between 600 and 700, and 16% above 700. The ACT scores were 13% below 21, 13% between 21 and 23, 37% between 24 and 26, 7% between 27 and 28, and 30% above 28. 76% of the current freshmen were in the top fifth of their class; 95% were in the top two-fifths. There were 32 National Merit finalists. 55 freshmen graduated first in their class.

Requirements: Applicants should have completed 19 Carnegie units, including 4 each in English, math, and science, 3 in foreign language, 2 in social studies, and 1 each in history and academic electives. An essay is part of the application process. An interview is advised, and a portfolio or an audition is recommended for art and music majors, respectively. AP and CLEP credits are accepted. Important factors in the admissions decision are personality/intangible qualities, evidence of special talent, and advanced placement or honors courses.

Procedure: Freshmen are admitted in the fall. Entrance exams should be taken by December of the senior year. There are early decision, early admissions and deferred admissions plans. Early decision applications should be filed by December 1; regular applications, by January 15 for fall entry, along with a $40 fee. Notification of early decision is sent January 1; regular decision, April 1. Applications are accepted on-line. 466 applicants were on a recent waiting list.

Financial Aid: In 2009-2010, 93% of all full-time freshmen and 92% of continuing full-time students received some form of financial aid. 50% of all full-time freshmen and 44% of continuing full-time students received need-based aid. The average freshmen award was $26,152. 45% of undergraduate students work part-time. Average annual earnings from campus work are $2430. The average financial indebtedness of the 2009 graduate was $13,902. The FAFSA is required. The deadline for filing freshman financial aid applications for fall entry is February 15.

Computers: Wireless access is available. The wireless network is available throughout the campus. All students may access the system 24 hours a day. There are no time limits and no fees.

DEPAUW UNIVERSITY
Greencastle, IN 46135

(765) 658-4006
(800) 447-2495; (765) 658-4007

Full-time: 1028 men, 1334 women	**Faculty:** IIB, +$
Part-time: 21 men, 15 women	**Ph.D.s:** 91%
Graduate: none	**Student/Faculty:** n/av
Year: 4-1-4	**Tuition:** $33,250
Application Deadline: February 1	**Room & Board:** $8740
Freshman Class: 4347 applied, 2877 accepted, 717 enrolled	
SAT CR/M/W: 580/600/580	**ACT:** 27 **VERY COMPETITIVE+**

DePauw University, founded in 1837, is a private institution affiliated with the United Methodist Church offering programs in the fields of liberal arts and music. There are 2 undergraduate schools. In addition to regional accreditation, DePauw has baccalaureate program accreditation with NASM and NCATE. The 3 libraries contain 818,618 volumes, 381,066 microform items, and 34,325 audio/video tapes/CDs/DVDs, and subscribe to 29,188 periodicals including electronic. Computerized library services include interlibrary loans, database searching, and Internet access. Special learning facilities include a learning resource center, art gallery, natural history museum, radio station, TV station, an observatory, an arboretum, a digital video studio, and a digital media lab. The 175-acre campus is in a small town 45 miles west of Indianapolis. Including any residence halls, there are 81 buildings.

Programs of Study: DePauw confers B.A., B.M.A., B.M.E., and B.Mu. degrees. Bachelor's degrees are awarded in BIOLOGICAL SCIENCE (biochemistry and biology/biological science), COMMUNICATIONS AND THE ARTS (art history and appreciation, classical languages, communications, English, English literature, French, German, Greek, Latin, music, music business management, music

206

performance, music theory and composition, romance languages and literature, Spanish, and studio art), COMPUTER AND PHYSICAL SCIENCE (chemistry, computer science, earth science, geology, mathematics, and physics), EDUCATION (elementary education and music education), ENGINEERING AND ENVIRONMENTAL DESIGN (environmental science and preengineering), SOCIAL SCIENCE (African American studies, anthropology, classical/ancient civilization, East Asian studies, economics, geography, history, interdisciplinary studies, peace studies, philosophy, physical fitness/movement, political science/government, psychology, religion, Russian and Slavic studies, sociology, and women's studies). English, economics, and communications are the largest.

Special: DePauw offers dual majors in any 2 disciplines, student-designed majors, internships for honors programs and winter-term projects, unlimited study-abroad options through cooperative arrangements with other universities, a Washington semester, pass/fail options, and credit by departmental examination. Also available are 3-2 engineering degrees with Case Western Reserve, Columbia, and Washington Universities and a 3-2 nursing program with Rush University Hospital in Chicago. The Media Fellows, Management Fellows, and Science Research Fellows programs offer majors in any discipline, plus a semester-long internship. There are 13 national honor societies, including Phi Beta Kappa, a freshman honors program, and 12 departmental honors programs.

Admissions: 66% of the 2009-2010 applicants were accepted. The SAT scores for the 2009-2010 freshman class were: Critical Reading--14% below 500, 40% between 500 and 599, 35% between 600 and 700, and 10% above 700; Math--8% below 500, 36% between 500 and 599, 41% between 600 and 700, and 14% above 700; Writing--13% below 500, 42% between 500 and 599, 37% between 600 and 700, and 7% above 700.

Requirements: The SAT or ACT is required. In addition, Graduation from an accredited secondary school or a GED is required for admission. Course distribution should include 4 each in English and math, 3 to 4 each in social studies, and science (2 or more with lab), and 2 to 4 in a foreign language. An essay is required, and an interview is strongly recommended. Applicants for the School of Music must audition. AP credits are accepted. Important factors in the admissions decision are advanced placement or honors courses, recommendations by school officials, and personality/intangible qualities.

Procedure: Freshmen are admitted fall and spring. Entrance exams should be taken as early as possible. There are early decision, early admissions and deferred admissions plans. Early decision applications should be filed by November 1; regular applications, by February 1 for fall entry and December 1 for spring entry. The fall 2009 application fee was $40. Notification of early decision is sent January 1; regular decision, April 1. 3 applicants were on the 2009 waiting list; none were admitted. Applications are accepted on-line.

Financial Aid: DePauw is a member of CSS. The CSS/Profile, FAFSA, and the college's own financial statement are required. The priority date for freshman financial aid applications for fall entry is February 15.

Computers: Wireless access is available. All students may access the system 24 hours a day.

DICKINSON COLLEGE
Carlisle, PA 17013

(717) 245-1231
(800) 644-1773; (717) 245-1442

Full-time: 1025 men, 1315 women	**Faculty:** 193; IIB, +$
Part-time: 17 men, 19 women	**Ph.D.s:** 93%
Graduate: none	**Student/Faculty:** 12 to 1
Year: semesters, summer session	**Tuition:** $40,114
Application Deadline: February 1	**Room & Board:** $10,080
Freshman Class: 5026 applied, 2459 accepted, 582 enrolled	
SAT CR/M: 650/640	**ACT: 28 HIGHLY COMPETITIVE+**

Dickinson College, founded in 1783, is a private institution offering a liberal arts curriculum that includes international education and science. There are no undergraduate schools. The library contains 501,043 volumes, 168,649 microform items, 25,546 audio/video tapes/CDs/DVDs, and subscribes to 2,451 periodicals including electronic. Computerized library services include interlibrary loans, database searching, and Internet access. Special learning facilities include an art gallery, planetarium, radio station, fiber-optic and satellite telecommunications networks, a telescope observatory, and an archival collection. The 308-acre campus is in a suburban area about 20 miles west of Harrisburg, PA and 2 hours from Washington, D.C. Including any residence halls, there are 141 buildings.

Programs of Study: Dickinson confers B.A. and B.S. degrees. Bachelor's degrees are awarded in BIOLOGICAL SCIENCE (biochemistry, biology/biological science, and neurosciences), BUSINESS (international business management), COMMUNICATIONS AND THE ARTS (classical languages, dance, dramatic arts, English, fine arts, French, German, Greek, Latin, music, Russian, and Spanish), COMPUTER AND PHYSICAL SCIENCE (chemistry, computer science, geology, mathematics, and physics), ENGINEERING AND ENVIRONMENTAL DESIGN (environmental science), HEALTH PROFESSIONS (environmental health science), SOCIAL SCIENCE (African studies, American studies, anthropology, archeology, classical/ancient civilization, East Asian studies, economics, history, international studies, Italian studies, Judaic studies, law, medieval studies, Middle Eastern studies, philosophy, political science/government, psychology, public affairs, religion, sociology, and women's studies). International education/foreign languages, natural sciences, and preprofessional programs are the strongest academically. International business and management/international studies, political science, and psychology are the largest.

Special: Students may cross-register with Central Pennsylvania Consortium Colleges. 32 academic year or summer study-abroad programs are offered in 24 countries. A Washington semester, work-study, and accelerated degree programs are available, as are dual majors, student-designed majors, non-degree study, pass/fail options, and a 3-3 law degree with the Dickinson School of Law of Pennsylvania State University. There are 3-2 engineering degrees offered with Case Western Reserve University, Rensselaer Polytechnic Institute, and the University of Pennsylvania. Instruction in 12 languages is available. There is a certification program in Latin American studies. Through an articulation agreement with the University of East Anglia, graduates of Dickinson can pursue a M.A. in the Humanities, and through a direct admission agreement program can begin a MBA program with the Simon School of Business at the University of Rochester.There are 15 national honor societies, including Phi Beta Kappa, and 33 departmental honors programs.

Admissions: 49% of the 2009-2010 applicants were accepted. The SAT scores for the 2009-2010 freshman class were: Critical Reading--3% below 500, 22% between 500 and 599, 54% between 600 and 700, and 21% above 700; Math--4% below 500, 23% between 500 and 599, 57% between 600 and 700, and 16% above 700; Writing--4% below 500, 22% between 500 and 599, 52% between 600 and 700, and 22% above 700. The ACT scores were 1% below 21, 5% between 21 and 23, 23% between 24 and 26, 28% between 27 and 28, and 43% above 28. 63% of the current freshmen were in the top fifth of their class; 90% were in the top two fifths.

Requirements: In addition, the SAT and ACT Subject Tests are optional submissions. The GED is accepted. Applicants should have completed 16 academic credits, including 4 years of English, 3 each of math and science, 2 (preferably 3) of foreign language, 2 of social studies, and 2 additional courses drawn from the above areas. An essay is required, and an interview is recommended. AP credits are accepted. Important factors in the admissions decision are advanced placement or honors courses, extracurricular activities record, and recommendations by school officials.

Procedure: Freshmen are admitted fall. Entrance exams should be taken in the spring of the junior year or the fall of the senior year. There are early decision, early admissions and deferred admissions plans. Early decision applications should be filed by January 15; regular applications, by February 1 for fall entry. The fall 2008 application fee was $65. Notification of early decision is sent February 15; regular decision, March 31. Applications are accepted on-line. 297 applicants were on a recent waiting list, 65 were accepted.

Financial Aid: In 2009-2010, 64% of all full-time freshmen and 61% of continuing full-time students received some form of financial aid. 56% of all full-time freshmen and 51% of continuing full-time students received need-based aid. The average freshmen award was $32,037, with $29,286 ($52,884 maximum) from need-based scholarships or need-based grants; $5,723 ($7,700 maximum) from need-based self-help aid (loans and jobs); and $10,941 from other forms of aid. 47% of undergraduate students work part-time. Average annual earnings from campus work are $1218. The average financial indebtedness of the 2009 graduate was $23,224. Dickinson is a member of CSS. The CSS/Profile, FAFSA, and the state aid form, and noncustodial parent statement, and business farm supplement are required. The deadline for filing freshman financial aid applications for fall entry is February 1.

Computers: Wireless access is available. The library hosts more than 100 computers equipped with the Microsoft Office suite and other applications, as well as laptop computers that may be borrowed by students. The campus has a range of computer labs with approximately 390 Windows and 271 Mac computers for student use. Laser printers are available. The campus is completely networked, and every student room has at least 1 Ethernet network connection. Students may access the Internet from any location on campus through wired Ethernet connections or through the wireless network in the Waider-Spahr Library, the Quarry, and the Holland Union Building. All students may access the system. There are no time limits and no fees.

DILLARD UNIVERSITY

New Orleans, LA 70122

(504) 816-4670
(800) 216-6637; (504) 816-4895

Full- and part-time: 270 men and 740 women	**Faculty:** 104
Graduate: none	**Ph.D.s:** 62%
Year: semesters, summer session	**Student/Faculty:** n/av
Application Deadline: see profile	**Tuition:** $13,000
Freshman Class: n/av	**Room & Board:** $8300
SAT or ACT: required	**VERY COMPETITIVE**

Dillard University, established in 1930, is an independent, nonsectarian, liberal arts institution affiliated with the United Church of Christ and the United Methodist Church. It offers undergraduate programs in business, education, humanities, natural sciences, nursing, and social sciences. There are 6 undergraduate schools. Figures in the above capsule and in this profile are approximate. In addition to regional accreditation, Dillard has baccalaureate program accreditation with NLN. The library contains 104,600 volumes, 21,600 microform items, and 400 audio/video tapes/CDs/DVDs, and subscribes to 290 periodicals including electronic. Computerized library services include interlibrary loans and database searching. Special learning facilities include a learning resource center, art gallery, and radio station. The 55-acre campus is in an urban area in New Orleans. Including any residence halls, there are 21 buildings.

Programs of Study: Dillard confers B.A., B.S., and B.S.N. degrees. Bachelor's degrees are awarded in BIOLOGICAL SCIENCE (biology/biological science), BUSINESS (accounting and business administration and management), COMMUNICATIONS AND THE ARTS (art, communications, English, French, languages, music, music business management, music performance, and Spanish), COMPUTER AND PHYSICAL SCIENCE (chemistry, computer science, mathematics, and physics), EDUCATION (elementary education, secondary education, and special education), HEALTH PROFESSIONS (nursing and public health), SOCIAL SCIENCE (African studies, economics, history, Japanese studies, political science/government, psychology, sociology, and urban studies). Biological sciences are the largest.

Special: Opportunities are provided for internships, work-study programs, credit by exam, nondegree study, and pass/fail options. All social science majors are encouraged to pursue a double major. There is a 4-year co-op degree in music therapy with Loyola University, a clinical public health curriculum with Howard University, a 5-year joint degree in urban studies with Columbia University, and preengineering dual degree programs with the Georgia Institute of Technology and Auburn and Columbia Universities. There are 3 national honor societies.

Requirements: The SAT or ACT is required, including the writing component of either test. In addition, graduation from an accredited secondary school is required; a GED will be accepted. Applicants must submit an academic record of 20 units, distributed as follows: 4 units in English, 3 each in math, natural sciences, and social studies, and 6 in academic electives. Recommendations from a high school teacher and the principal or a student counselor are required. AP credits are accepted. Important factors in the admissions decision are recommendations by school officials, leadership record, and personality/intangible qualities.

Procedure: Freshmen are admitted fall and spring. Entrance exams should be taken between April of the junior year and December of the senior year. There are early admissions, deferred admissions, and rolling admissions plans. Check with the school for current application deadlines and fee. Notification is sent on a rolling basis. Applications are accepted on-line.

Financial Aid: Dillard is a member of CSS. The FAFSA and the college's own financial statement are required. Check with the school for current financial aid deadlines.

Computers: There are no time limits. Check with the school for current fees. It is strongly recommended that all students have a personal computer.

DORDT COLLEGE

Sioux Center, IA 51250

(712) 722-6080
(800) 34-DORDT; (712) 722-1967

Full-time: 565 men, 675 women	**Faculty:** IIB, --$
Part-time: 30 men, 30 women	**Ph.D.s:** 85%
Graduate: 35 men, 60 women	**Student/Faculty:** n/av
Year: semesters	**Tuition:** $21,720
Application Deadline: see profile	**Room & Board:** $6000
Freshman Class: n/av	
SAT or ACT: required	**VERY COMPETITIVE**

Dordt College, founded in 1955, is a private institution affiliated with the Christian Reformed Church. The curriculum, which is designed to reflect the principles of the Christian faith, leads to degrees in liberal arts, agriculture, art, music, business, engineering, and teaching preparation. Figures in the above capsule and this profile are approximate. In addition to regional accreditation, Dordt has baccalaureate program accreditation with ABET and CSWE. The library contains 185,000 volumes, 14,819 microform items, and 5000 audio/video tapes/CDs/DVDs, and subscribes to 700 periodicals including electronic. Computerized library services include interlibrary loans. Special learning facilities include a learning resource center, planetarium, radio station, and 2 observatories, as well as a 160-acre agriculture stewardship center just north of the campus. The 110-acre campus is in a rural area 42 miles north of Sioux City. Including any residence halls, there are 22 buildings.

Programs of Study: Dordt confers B.A., B.S., B.S.N., and B.S.W. degrees. Associate and master's degrees are also awarded. Bachelor's degrees are awarded in BIOLOGICAL SCIENCE (biology/biological science), BUSINESS (accounting and business administration and management), COMMUNICATIONS AND THE ARTS (broadcasting, communications, dramatic arts, Dutch, English, fine arts, German, graphic design, journalism, languages, music, Spanish, and speech/debate/rhetoric), COMPUTER AND PHYSICAL SCIENCE (chemistry, computer programming, computer science, information sciences and systems, mathematics, and physics), EDUCATION (art education, business education, elementary education, foreign languages education, music education, and secondary education), ENGINEERING AND ENVIRONMENTAL DESIGN (chemical engineering, electrical/electronics engineering, engineering, environmental science, and mechanical engineering), HEALTH PROFESSIONS (health science, medical laboratory technology, nursing, predentistry, and premedicine), SOCIAL SCIENCE (criminal justice, history, philosophy, political science/government, prelaw, psychology, religion, social science, social work, sociology, and youth ministry). Engineering, business administration, and social work are the strongest academically. Education is the largest.

Special: Students may study abroad in 10 countries. Dordt also offers a Washington semester, a Chicago metro semester, a joint nursing degree program with St. Luke's School of Nursing, a B.S.N. with Briar Cliff University, B.A.-B.S. degrees in engineering and agriculture, and numerous internships in all majors. Dual majors, student-designed majors, and pass/fail options are available. There is a freshman honors program.

Requirements: The SAT or ACT is required. In addition, applicants must be graduates of accredited secondary schools or have earned a GED. The college requires 18 academic credits, including 4 in English and 2 each in foreign language, math, science, and social studies. A GPA of 2.3 is required. AP and CLEP credits are accepted. Important factors in the admissions decision are advanced placement or honors courses, evidence of special talent, and leadership record.

Procedure: Freshmen are admitted fall and spring. Entrance exams should be taken by October of the senior year and no later than April. There is a rolling admissions plan. Check with the school for current application deadlines. The fall 2009 application fee was $25. Applications are accepted on-line.

Financial Aid: The FAFSA and the college's own financial statement are required. Check with the school for current application deadlines.

Computers: All students may access the system. There are no time limits and no fees.

DRAKE UNIVERSITY
Des Moines, IA 50311

(515) 271-3181
(800) 44-DRAKE; (515) 271-2831

Full-time: 1370 men, 1835 women	**Faculty:** n/av
Part-time: 120 men, 120 women	**Ph.D.s:** 95%
Graduate: 815 men, 1370 women	**Student/Faculty:** n/av
Year: semesters, summer session	**Tuition:** $26,960
Application Deadline: see profile	**Room & Board:** $8130
Freshman Class: n/av	
SAT or ACT: required	**VERY COMPETITIVE**

Drake University, founded in 1881, is a private institution offering undergraduate and graduate programs in arts and sciences, business and public administration, pharmacy and health sciences, journalism and mass communication, education, fine arts, and law. Figures in the above capsule and this profile are approximate. There are 5 undergraduate schools and 1 graduate school. In addition to regional accreditation, Drake has baccalaureate program accreditation with AACSB, ACEJMC, ACPE, NASAD, and NASM. The 2 libraries contain 501,567 volumes, 1.9 million microform items, and 2766 audio/video tapes/CDs/DVDs, and subscribe to 15,000 periodicals including electronic. Computerized library services include interlibrary loans, database searching, and Internet access. Special learning facilities include a learning resource center, art gallery, radio station, TV station, observatory, and the Henry G. Harmon Fine Arts Center. The 120-acre campus is in an urban area in Des Moines. Including any residence halls, there are 49 buildings.

Programs of Study: Drake confers B.A., B.S., B.A.Journ. and Mass Comm., B.F.A., B.Mus., B.Mus.Ed., B.S.B.A., and B.S.Ed. degrees. Master's and doctoral degrees are also awarded. Bachelor's degrees are awarded in BIOLOGICAL SCIENCE (biology/biological science and neurosciences), BUSINESS (accounting, banking and finance, business administration and management, international business management, management science, and marketing management), COMMUNICATIONS AND THE ARTS (advertising, art history and appreciation, broadcasting, communications, dramatic arts, English, graphic design, journalism, music, music business management, music performance, printmaking, public relations, speech/debate/rhetoric, and studio art), COMPUTER AND PHYSI-

CAL SCIENCE (actuarial science, chemistry, computer science, information sciences and systems, mathematics, and physics), EDUCATION (elementary education, mathematics education, music education, and secondary education), ENGINEERING AND ENVIRONMENTAL DESIGN (environmental science), HEALTH PROFESSIONS (pharmacy), SOCIAL SCIENCE (economics, ethics, politics, and social policy, history, international relations, philosophy, political science/government, psychology, religion, and sociology). Actuarial science, pharmacy, and physics/astronomy are the strongest academically. Pharmacy, marketing, and actuarial science are the largest.

Special: Study abroad is available in 60 countries and at sea. The university offers cross-registration with Des Moines area colleges, including Grand View, internships, a Washington semester, cooperative programs in computer science, and work-study programs. Dual majors, B.A.-B.S. degrees, a 3-2 engineering degree with Washington University, student-designed majors, credit for military experience, and nondegree study are possible. Students may take a maximum of 12 hours of course work on a credit/no credit basis. There are 25 national honor societies, including Phi Beta Kappa, a freshman honors program, and 19 departmental honors programs.

Admissions: There were 7 National Merit finalists in a recent year. 50 freshmen graduated first in their class.

Requirements: The SAT or ACT is required. In addition, applicants must be graduates of an accredited secondary school. The GED is accepted. Students should have completed 4 years of English, 3 years of math, and 9 other units to be selected from English, foreign languages, social studies, math, lab sciences, and others. A portfolio is required for art majors and for those seeking scholarship consideration. An audition is necessary for admission to the music and theatre programs. Tapes are accepted. A GPA of 3.3 is required. AP and CLEP credits are accepted. Important factors in the admissions decision are advanced placement or honors courses, recommendations by school officials, and extracurricular activities record.

Procedure: Freshmen are admitted to all sessions. Entrance exams should be taken during the spring of the junior year or early fall of the senior year. There are deferred admissions and rolling admissions plans. Check with the school for current application deadlines. The application fee is $25. Applications are accepted on-line.

Financial Aid: In a recent year, 95% of all full-time freshmen and 93% of continuing full-time students received some form of financial aid. 61% of all full-time freshmen and 59% of continuing full-time students received need-based aid. The average freshman award was $20,436. 28% of undergraduate students work part-time. Average annual earnings from campus work are $1556. The average financial indebtedness of a recent graduate was $19,951. Drake is a member of CSS. The FAFSA is required. Check with the school for current application deadlines.

Computers: Wireless access is available. All students may access the system. There are no time limits. There is a fee. It is strongly recommended that all students have a personal computer.

DREW UNIVERSITY/COLLEGE OF LIBERAL ARTS

Madison, NJ 07940   (973) 408-DREW; (973) 408-3068

Full-time: 640 men, 975 women	**Faculty:** IIA, +$
Part-time: 25 men, 45 women	**Ph.D.s:** n/av
Graduate: 350 men, 420 women	**Student/Faculty:** n/av
Year: semesters, summer session	**Tuition:** $35,600
Application Deadline: February 15	**Room & Board:** $10,000
Freshman Class: n/av	**VERY COMPETITIVE**

The College of Liberal Arts was added to Drew University in 1928 and is part of an educational complex that includes a theological school and a graduate school. Drew is a private, nonprofit, independent institution. The figures in the above capsule and in this profile are approximate. There are 2 graduate schools. The library contains 571,850 volumes, 485,288 microform items, and 2,611 audio/video tapes/CDs/DVDs, and subscribes to 21,997 periodicals including electronic. Computerized library services include interlibrary loans, database searching, Internet access, and laptop Internet portals. Special learning facilities include a learning resource center, art gallery, radio station, TV station, observatory, photography gallery, and TV satellite dish. The 186-acre campus is in a small town 30 miles west of New York City. Including any residence halls, there are 57 buildings.

Programs of Study: Drew confers B.A. degrees. Master's and doctoral degrees are also awarded. Bachelor's degrees are awarded in BIOLOGICAL SCIENCE (biochemistry, biology/biological science, and neurosciences), COMMUNICATIONS AND THE ARTS (art, art history and appreciation, Chinese, classics, dramatic arts, English, French, German, music, and Spanish), COMPUTER AND PHYSICAL SCIENCE (chemistry, computer science, mathematics, and physics), SOCIAL SCIENCE (African studies, anthropology, behavioral science, economics, history, philosophy, political science/government, psychology, religion, sociology, and women's studies). Psychology, political science, and English are the largest.

Special: Drew offers co-op programs with Duke University, as well as cross-registration with the College of Saint Elizabeth and Fairleigh Dickinson University. There are also dual majors, study abroad, a Wall Street semester, a Washington semester, student-designed majors, internships, 3-2 engineering programs with Washington University in St. Louis, the Stevens Institute of Technology, and Columbia University in New York City, and a 7-year B.A.-M.D. program in medicine with UMDNJ. There are 11 national honor societies, including Phi Beta Kappa, and 12 departmental honors programs.

Requirements: The university strongly recommends 18 academic credits or Carnegie units, including 4 in English, 3 in math, and 2 each in foreign language, science, social studies, and history, with the remaining 3 in additional academic courses. An essay is also required, and an interview is recommended. AP and CLEP credits are accepted. Important factors in the admissions decision are ability to finance college education, advanced placement or honors courses, and extracurricular activities record.

Procedure: Freshmen are admitted fall and spring. Entrance exams should be taken by January of the senior year. There are early decision, early admissions and deferred admissions plans. Early decision applications should be filed by December 1; regular applications, by February 15 for fall entry and December 1 for spring entry, along with a $50 fee. Notification of early decision is sent December 24; regular decision, March 15. Applications are accepted on-line. A waiting list is maintained.

Financial Aid: In a recent year, 51% of all full-time freshmen and 49% of continuing full-time students received some form of financial aid. 51% of all full-time freshmen and 48% of continuing full-time students received need-based aid. The average freshmen award was $23,523. 29% of undergraduate students worked part-time. Average annual earnings from campus work were $1200. The average financial indebtedness of the 2009 graduate was $18,275. Drew is a member of CSS. The CSS/Profile and FAFSA are required. Check with the school for current application deadlines.

Computers: Wireless access is available. All students may access the system. There are no time limits and no fees. A IBM thinkpad is recommended.

DREXEL UNIVERSITY
Philadelphia, PA 19104   **(215) 895-2400**
                                         (800) 2-DREXEL; (215) 895-5939

Full-time: 6244 men, 4573 women	**Faculty:** 729; I, -$
Part-time: 1209 men, 1458 women	**Ph.D.s:** 84%
Graduate: 3685 men, 5324 women	**Student/Faculty:** 15 to 1
Year: quarters, summer session	**Tuition:** $31,835
Application Deadline: March 1	**Room & Board:** $12,681
Freshman Class: 39,827 applied, 21,729 accepted, 2346 enrolled	
SAT CR/M/W: 580/620/580	**VERY COMPETITIVE**

Drexel University, established in 1891, is a private institution with undergraduate programs in business and administration, engineering, information studies, design arts, and arts and sciences. There are 9 undergraduate schools and 12 graduate schools. In addition to regional accreditation, Drexel has baccalaureate program accreditation with AACSB, ABET, ADA, APA, CSAB, FIDER, and NAAB. The 2 libraries contain 643,869 volumes, 18,070 microform items, and 3443 audio/video tapes/CDs/DVDs, and subscribe to 27,399 periodicals including electronic. Computerized library services include interlibrary loans, database searching, Internet access, and laptop Internet portals. Special learning facilities include a learning resource center, art gallery, radio station, and TV station. The 94-acre campus is in an urban area near the center of Philadelphia. Including any residence halls, there are 98 buildings.

Programs of Study: Drexel confers B.A., B.S., and B.Arch. degrees. Master's and doctoral degrees are also awarded. Bachelor's degrees are awarded in BIOLOGICAL SCIENCE (biology/biological science and nutrition), BUSINESS (business administration and management, fashion merchandising, hotel/motel and restaurant management, and marketing/retailing/merchandising), COMMUNICATIONS AND THE ARTS (communications, creative writing, design, film arts, graphic design, literature, music, photography, and video), COMPUTER AND PHYSICAL SCIENCE (chemistry, computer science, digital arts/technology, information sciences and systems, mathematics, physics, and science), EDUCATION (education), ENGINEERING AND ENVIRONMENTAL DESIGN (architectural engineering, architecture, biomedical engineering, chemical engineering, civil engineering, computer engineering, construction management, electrical/electronics engineering, environmental engineering, environmental science, interior design, materials engineering, and mechanical engineering), HEALTH PROFESSIONS (predentistry and premedicine), SOCIAL SCIENCE (fashion design and technology, food production/management/services, history, international studies, political science/government, prelaw, psychology, and sociology). Engineering, business, and design arts are the strongest academically. Business, mechanical engineering, and biological sciences are the largest.

Special: The Drexel Plan of Cooperative Education enables students to alternate periods of full-time classroom studies and full-time employment with university-approved employers. Participation in cooperative education is mandatory for most students. Cross-registration is available with Indiana University of Pennsylvania and Lincoln University. Drexel also offers study abroad, internships, accelerated degrees, 3-3 engineering degrees, dual majors, nondegree study, and credit/no credit options. There is 1 national honor society, a freshman honors program, and 3 departmental honors programs.

Admissions: 55% of the 2009-2010 applicants were accepted. The SAT scores for the 2009-2010 freshman class were: Critical Reading--9% below 500, 47% between 500 and 599, 38% between 600 and 700, and 6% above 700; Math--3% below 500, 32% between 500 and 599, 53% between 600 and 700, and 12% above 700; Writing--12% below 500, 46% between 500 and 599, 36% between 600 and 700, and 6% above 700. 54% of the current freshmen were in the top fifth of their class; 83% were in the top two fifths.

Requirements: The SAT or ACT is required; the SAT I is preferred. In addition, applicants must be graduates of an accredited secondary school. The GED is accepted. An interview is recommended. A GPA of 2.0 is required. AP and CLEP credits are accepted. Important factors in the admissions decision are advanced placement or honors courses, evidence of special talent, and recommendations by school officials.

Procedure: Freshmen are admitted fall. There are deferred admissions and rolling admissions plans. Applications should be filed by March 1 for fall entry, along with a $75 fee (no fee for on-line applications). Notification is sent on a rolling basis. 3849 applicants were on the 2009 waiting list; 924 were admitted. Applications are accepted on-line.

Financial Aid: The FAFSA is required. The deadline for filing freshman financial aid applications for fall entry is February 15.

Computers: Wireless access is available. Drexel provides both wireless and wired Internet and Internet2 access across the entire campus, including all residence halls and classrooms. The campus network includes more than 24,000 active Gigabit Ethernet connections of which about 2500 are available for ''plug and play'' use. The wireless network Dragonfly connects more than 8000 devices, including laptops, game consoles, and mobile phones. All students may access the system 24 hours a day. There are no time limits and no fees. All students are required to have a personal computer.

DRURY UNIVERSITY
Springfield, MO 65802

(417) 873-7614
(800) 922-2274; (417) 866-3873

Full-time: 717 men, 801 women	**Faculty:** 131; II B, --$
Part-time: 16 men, 16 women	**Ph.D.s:** 92%
Graduate: 131 men, 395 women	**Student/Faculty:** 12 to 1
Year: semesters, summer session	**Tuition:** $19,015
Application Deadline: August 1	**Room & Board:** $7364
Freshman Class: 1184 applied, 832 accepted, 338 enrolled	
ACT: 25	**SAT:** required
	VERY COMPETITIVE

Drury University, founded in 1873, is a private university with degree programs emphasizing the liberal arts, architecture, business, communications, economics, education, and health sciences. There are 3 undergraduate schools and 8 graduate schools. In addition to regional accreditation, Drury has baccalaureate program accreditation with ACBSP, NAAB, NASM, and NCATE. The library contains 189,895 volumes, 19,771 microform items, and 4774 audio/video tapes/CDs/DVDs, and subscribes to 11,760 periodicals including electronic. Computerized library services include interlibrary loans, database searching, Internet access, and laptop Internet portals. Special learning facilities include an art gallery, radio station, TV station, astronomical observatory, greenhouse, teleconference facility, art and architecture slide collection, speech communication center, and writing center. The 80-acre campus is in an urban area 200 miles southwest of St. Louis and 150 miles southeast of Kansas City. Including any residence halls, there are 40 buildings.

Programs of Study: Drury confers B.A., B.Arch., B.M.E., B.M.T., and B.S.Ed. degrees. Master's degrees are also awarded. Bachelor's degrees are awarded in AGRICULTURE (environmental studies), BIOLOGICAL SCIENCE (biology/biological science), BUSINESS (accounting, banking and finance, business administration and management, marketing management, and sports management), COMMUNICATIONS AND THE ARTS (advertising, art history and appreciation, arts administration/management, communications, dramatic arts, English, fine arts, French, German, journalism, media arts, music, public relations, Spanish, and speech/debate/rhetoric), COMPUTER AND PHYSICAL SCIENCE (chemistry, computer science, information sciences and systems, mathematics, and physics), EDUCATION (elementary education, mathematics education, music education, physical education, and secondary education), ENGINEERING AND ENVIRONMENTAL DESIGN (architecture and environmental science), HEALTH PROFESSIONS (exercise science, music therapy, predentistry, premedicine, preoptometry, preosteopathy, prepharmacy, prephysical therapy, and preveterinary science), SOCIAL SCIENCE (American studies, criminology, economics, history, international studies, philosophy, political science/government, prelaw, psychology, religion, and sociology). Premedicine, business, and architecture are the strongest academically. Psychology, business/marketing, and biology are the largest.

Special: Drury offers study abroad in Volos, Greece, and 19 other countries as well as cross-registration with colleges in 8 countries; 45% of students study abroad. Premedical early admission arrangements with St. Louis University, the University of Missouri, and Kirksville College of Osteopathic Medicine and a 3-2 engineering dual-degree program in conjunction with the University of Missouri and Washington University are available. Co-op programs include computer information systems and arts administration. 75% of students complete a professional internship; options include public and private sectors and a Washington semester. Work study, credit by exam, nondegree study, dual majors in most majors, and satisfactory/unsatisfactory options are also possible. There are 11 national honor societies, including Phi Beta Kappa, a freshman honors program, and 8 departmental honors programs.

Admissions: 70% of the 2009-2010 applicants were accepted. The ACT scores were 11% below 21, 25% between 21 and 23, 27% between 24 and 26, 12% between 27 and 28, and 26% above 28. 61% of the current freshmen were in the top fifth of their class; 84% were in the top two fifths. 31 freshmen graduated first in their class.

Requirements: The SAT or ACT is required. In addition, applicants must be graduates of an accredited secondary school or have a GED certificate. Recommended high school credits include 4 units of English and at least 3 each of math through algebra II, natural science, and social studies. An essay and a reference from the high school counselor or principal are required. A GPA of 2.7 is required. AP and CLEP credits are accepted. Important factors in the admissions decision are advanced placement or honors courses, extracurricular activities record, and leadership record.

Procedure: Freshmen are admitted to all sessions. Entrance exams should be taken in the spring of the junior year or fall of the senior year. There are deferred admissions and rolling admissions plans. Applications should be filed by August 1 for fall entry; December 1 for spring entry, along with a $25 fee. Notifications are sent October 1. Applications are accepted on-line.

Financial Aid: In 2009-2010, 88% of all full-time freshmen and 93% of continuing full-time students received some form of financial aid. 83% of all full-time freshmen and 87% of continuing full-time students received need-based aid. The average freshman award was $7985. Need-based scholarships or need-based grants averaged $6990 ; need-based self-help aid (loans and jobs) averaged $6850; non-need-based athletic scholarships averaged $9795; and other non-need-based awards and non-need-based scholarships averaged $3585. 87% of undergraduate students work part-time. Average annual earnings from campus work are $3000. The average financial indebtedness of the 2009 graduate was $20,500. Drury is a member of CSS. The FAFSA and the college's own financial statement are required. The deadline for filing freshman financial aid applications for fall entry is March 15.

Computers: Wireless access is available on 100% of the campus; 389 PCs are available in labs. Residence halls are equipped with 1 network port per student. All students may access the system 24 hours a day, 7 days a week in technology centers. There are no time limits and no fees.

DUKE UNIVERSITY
Durham, NC 27706   (919) 684-3214; (919) 681-8941

Full-time: 3270 men, 2980 women	**Faculty:** I, ++$
Part-time: 10 men, 5 women	**Ph.D.s:** 97%
Graduate: 3845 men, 3375 women	**Student/Faculty:** n/av
Year: semesters, summer session	**Tuition:** $39,080
Application Deadline: see profile	**Room & Board:** $11,170
Freshman Class: n/av	
SAT or ACT: required	**MOST COMPETITIVE**

Duke University, founded in 1838, is a private institution affiliated with the United Methodist Church and offering undergraduate programs in arts and sciences and engineering. Figures in the above capsule are approximate. There are 2 undergraduate schools and 8 graduate schools. In addition to regional accreditation, Duke has baccalaureate program accreditation with AACSB, ABET, ACPE, AHEA, APTA, NCATE, NLN, and SAF. The 9 libraries contain 5.5 million volumes, 4.2 million microform items, and 61,281 audio/video tapes/CDs/DVDs, and subscribe to 33,934 periodicals including electronic. Computerized library services include interlibrary loans, database searching, and Internet access. Special learning facilities include a learning resource center, art gallery, radio station, TV station, marine lab at Beaufort, primate center, center for international studies, nuclear lab, free electron laser, science research center, institutes of the arts, statistics and decision sciences, policy sciences and public affairs, and centers for teaching and learning, community service, geometric computing, culture, and women. The 9727-acre campus is in a suburban area 285 miles southwest of Washington, D.C. Including any residence halls, there are 208 buildings.

Programs of Study: Duke confers B.S., A.B., and B.S.E. degrees. Master's and doctoral degrees are also awarded. Bachelor's degrees are awarded in BIOLOGICAL SCIENCE (anatomy and biology/biological science), COMMUNICATIONS AND THE ARTS (African languages, art history and appreciation, classical languages, dramatic arts, English, Germanic languages and literature, linguistics, literature, music, Slavic languages, Spanish, and visual and performing arts), COMPUTER AND PHYSICAL SCIENCE (chemistry, computer science, geology, mathematics, and physics), ENGINEERING AND ENVIRONMENTAL DESIGN (biomedical engineering, civil engineering, electrical/electronics engineering, environmental science, materials science, and mechanical engineering), SOCIAL SCIENCE (African studies, African American studies, anthropology, area studies, Asian/Oriental studies, Canadian studies, classical/ancient civilization, economics, French studies, history, Italian studies, medieval studies, philosophy, political science/government, psychology, public affairs, religion, sociology, and women's studies). Public policy studies, political science, and economics are the strongest academically. Biology, psychology, and history are the largest.

Special: Duke offers cross-registration with the University of North Carolina/Chapel Hill and North Carolina State and North Carolina Central Universities. Also available are internships through the Career Development Center, study abroad in 36 countries, and a Washington semester. An accelerated degree program is possible, achieving graduation in 3 years or combining the senior year with the first graduate year of the law, business, or environment schools. Several 3-2 and 4-1 medical technology programs (degree completed at Duke) are available. Project Calc, an innovative program in calculus, is also offered. Dual majors of any combination, student-designed majors, nondegree study, and pass/fail options are possible. There are 4 national honor societies, including Phi Beta Kappa, and 38 departmental honors programs.

Requirements: The SAT or ACT is required. The ACT Optional Writing test is also required. In addition, 3 SAT: Subject tests, including writing, are required. Applicants must be graduates of an accredited secondary school and have completed 15 academic credits, with 4 in English and 3 each in math, science, and foreign language; an additional 2 in social studies or history are recommended. Engineering students must have 4 credit units in math and 1 in physics or chemistry. An essay is required and an interview is recommended. A portfolio or audition is advised in appropriate instances. AP credits are accepted. Important factors in the admissions decision are advanced placement or honors courses, recommendations by school officials, and extracurricular activities record.

Procedure: Freshmen are admitted fall and spring. Entrance exams should be taken in October of the junior year for early decision applicants and by January of the senior year for regular decision. There are early decision, early admissions and deferred admissions plans. Check with the school for current application deadlines. The application fee is $75. A waiting list is maintained.

Financial Aid: The CSS/Profile and FAFSA are required. Check with the school for current deadlines.

Computers: All students may access the system. 24 hours a day. There are no time limits and no fees. It is strongly recommended that all students have a personal computer.

Pittsburgh, PA 15282-0201   **(412) 396-6222**
(800) 456-0590; (412) 396-5644

Full-time: 2406 men, 3142 women	**Faculty:** 435; IIA, +$
Part-time: 105 men, 117 women	**Ph.D.s:** 85%
Graduate: 1811 men, 2692 women	**Student/Faculty:** 13 to 1
Year: semesters, summer session	**Tuition:** $26,468
Application Deadline: July 1	**Room & Board:** $9200

Freshman Class: 6626 applied, 5054 accepted, 1432 enrolled
SAT CR/M/W: 559/568/553   **ACT:** 25   **VERY COMPETITIVE**

Duquesne University, founded in 1878 by the Spiritan Congregation, is a private Roman Catholic institution offering programs in liberal arts, natural and environmental sciences, nursing, health sciences, pharmacy, business, music, teacher preparation, preprofessional training, law, and leadership and professional development. There are 9 undergraduate schools and 10 graduate schools. In addition to regional accreditation, Duquesne has baccalaureate program accreditation with AACSB, ACPE, NASM, and NCATE. The library contains 715,518 volumes, 292,871 microform items, and 31,060 audio/video tapes/CDs/DVDs, and subscribes to 0 periodicals including electronic. Computerized library services include interlibrary loans, database searching, Internet access, and laptop Internet portals. Special learning facilities include a learning resource center, art gallery, radio station, TV station, and 160 multimedia-enhanced teaching facilities. The 49-acre campus is in an urban area on a private, self-contained campus in the center of Pittsburgh. Including any residence halls, there are 31 buildings.

Programs of Study: Duquesne confers B.A., B.S., B.M., B.S.A.T., B.S.B.A., B.S.Ed., B.S.H.M.S., B.S.H.S., B.S.N., and B.S.P.S. degrees. Master's and doctoral degrees are also awarded. Bachelor's degrees are awarded in BIOLOGICAL SCIENCE (biochemistry and biology/biological science), BUSINESS (accounting, banking and finance, business administration and management, business communications, business economics, business law, entrepreneurial studies, international business management, investments and securities, management information systems, management science, marketing/retailing/merchandising, nonprofit/public organization management, organizational leadership and management, sports marketing, and supply chain management), COMMUNICATIONS AND THE ARTS (advertising, art history and appreciation, classical languages, communications, dramatic arts, English, Greek (classical), journalism, Latin, literature, media arts, modern language, multimedia, music performance, music technology, Spanish, and speech/debate/rhetoric), COMPUTER AND PHYSICAL SCIENCE (chemistry, computer science, computer security and information assurance, mathematics, physics, and web technology), EDUCATION (athletic training, early childhood education, education, elementary education, English education, foreign languages education, mathematics education, music education, secondary education, and special education), ENGINEERING AND ENVIRONMENTAL DESIGN (environmental science), HEALTH PROFESSIONS (health care administration, music therapy, nursing, occupational therapy, pharmaceutical science, physical therapy, physician's assistant, premedicine, and speech pathology/audiology), SOCIAL SCIENCE (classical/ancient civilization, criminal justice, economics, history, international relations, liberal arts/general studies, philosophy, political science/government, prelaw, psychology, sociology, and theological studies). Pharmacy, nursing, and psychology are the largest.

Special: The university offers cross-registration through the Pittsburgh Council on Higher Education, internships, study abroad in 26 countries, and a Washington semester. Also available are B.A.-B.S. degrees, accelerated degree programs, dual and student-designed majors, a 3-2 engineering program with Case Western Reserve University and University of Pittsburgh, a 3-3 law degree and a 3-2 business degree, pass/fail options, and credit for life, military, and work experience. There are 22 national honor societies, a freshman honors program, and all departments have honors programs.

Admissions: 76% of the 2009-2010 applicants were accepted. The SAT scores for the 2009-2010 freshman class were: Critical Reading--16% below 500, 56% between 500 and 599, 26% between 600 and 700, and 2% above 700; Math--15% below 500, 50% between 500 and 599, 32% between 600 and 700, and 3% above 700; Writing--19% below 500, 53% between 500 and 599, 26% between 600 and 700, and 2% above 700. The ACT scores were 3% below 21, 27% between 21 and 23, 35% between 24 and 26, 19% between 27 and 28, and 16% above 28. 46% of the current freshmen were in the top fifth of their class; 79% were in the top two fifths. 28 freshmen graduated first in their class.

Requirements: The SAT or ACT is required. The ACT Optional Writing test is also required. In addition, students should have either a high school diploma or the GED. Applicants are required to have 16 academic credits, including 4 each in English and academic electives, and 8 combined in social studies, language, math, and science. An audition is required for music majors. An essay is required, and an interview is recommended. A GPA of 3.0 is required. AP and CLEP credits are accepted.

Procedure: Freshmen are admitted to all sessions. Entrance exams should be taken during the spring of the junior year or the fall of the senior year. There are early decision, early admissions, deferred admissions, and rolling admissions plans. Early decision applications should be filed by November 1; regular applications, by July 1 for fall entry, December 1 for spring entry, and April 1 for summer entry, along with a $50 fee. Notification of early decision is sent December 15; regular decision, sent on a rolling basis. Applications are accepted online.

Financial Aid: In 2009-2010, 100% of all full-time freshmen and 96% of continuing full-time students received some form of financial aid. 67% of all full-time freshmen and 67% of continuing full-time students received need-based aid. The average freshmen award was $24,945, with $16,252 ($21,632 maximum) from need-based scholarships or need-based grants; $10,124 ($34,735 maximum) from need-based self-help aid (loans and jobs); $15,113 ($42,940 maximum) from non-need-based athletic scholarships; and $7,168 ($24,356 maximum) from other non-need-based awards and non-need-based scholarships. The FAFSA and the college's own financial statement are required. The deadline for filing freshman financial aid applications for fall entry is May 1.

Computers: Wireless access is available. The campus is covered by a 7,000-node Ethernet network, a wireless network, and more than 850 computers in computer labs. All students may access the system. There are no time limits and no fees. It is strongly recommended that all students have a personal computer. A Dell or Apple is recommended.

EARLHAM COLLEGE

Richmond, IN 47374

(765) 983-1600
(800) 327-5426; (765) 983-1560

Full-time: 498 men, 607 women	**Faculty:** 89; IIB, av$
Part-time: 7 men, 15 women	**Ph.D.s:** 98%
Graduate: 57 men, 109 women	**Student/Faculty:** 16 to 1
Year: semesters	**Tuition:** $35,164
Application Deadline: February 15	**Room & Board:** $7160
Freshman Class: 1668 applied, 1272 accepted, 292 enrolled	
SAT CR/M: 640/590	**ACT:** 27 **VERY COMPETITIVE+**

Earlham College, established in 1847 by the Society of Friends, is a private liberal arts college that emphasizes Quaker values. It offers undergraduate programs in humanities, fine arts, social sciences and natural sciences. There is 1 undergraduate school and 2 graduate schools. The 2 libraries contain 406,423 volumes, 223,603 microform items, and 7333 audio/video tapes/CDs/DVDs, and subscribe to 20,673 periodicals including electronic. Computerized library services include interlibrary loans, database searching, Internet access, and laptop Internet portals. Special learning facilities include a learning resource center, art gallery, natural history museum, planetarium, radio station, observatory, herbarium, and greenhouse. The 800-acre campus is in a small town 70 miles east of Indianapolis and 40 miles west of Dayton, Ohio. Including any residence halls, there are 56 buildings.

Programs of Study: Earlham confers B.A. degrees. Master's degrees are also awarded. Bachelor's degrees are awarded in AGRICULTURE (environmental studies), BIOLOGICAL SCIENCE (biochemistry and biology/biological science), BUSINESS (business administration and management), COMMUNICATIONS AND THE ARTS (art, dramatic arts, English, French, German, languages, linguistics, music, and Spanish), COMPUTER AND PHYSICAL SCIENCE (chemistry, computer science, geoscience, mathematics, and physics), ENGINEERING AND ENVIRONMENTAL DESIGN (environmental science), HEALTH PROFESSIONS (premedicine), SOCIAL SCIENCE (African American studies, anthropology, classical/ancient civilization, economics, history, human development, international studies, Japanese studies, Latin American studies, peace studies, philosophy, political science/government, psychobiology, psychology, religion, sociology, and women's studies). Psychology, biology, and English are the largest.

Special: Opportunities are provided for dual majors, cross-registration with Indiana University East, internships, accelerated degree programs, nondegree study, and student-designed majors. Study off-campus is available through 20 foreign and domestic programs. Preprofessional and professional options are offered in law and medicine. There is a 3-2 engineering degree with Case Western Reserve University, Columbia University, University of Rochester, Rensselaer Polytechnic Institute, and Washington University. There are 2 national honor societies, including Phi Beta Kappa.

Admissions: 76% of the 2009-2010 applicants were accepted. The SAT scores for the 2009-2010 freshman class were: Critical Reading--13% below 500, 20% between 500 and 599, 41% between 600 and 700, and 26% above 700; Math--13% below 500, 46% between 500 and 599, 32% between 600 and 700, and 9% above 700; Writing--12% below 500, 31% between 500 and 599, 40% between 600 and 700, and 17% above 700. There were 7 National Merit finalists. 9 freshmen graduated first in their class.

Requirements: The SAT or ACT is required. The ACT Optional Writing test is also required. In most cases, graduation from an accredited secondary school is required; a GED will be accepted. Home-schooled students are not required to take the GED or have a high school diploma. Students must have completed at least 15 academic credits, including 4 years of English, 3¨of math, and 2 each of science, history or social studies, and a foreign language. Students are required to submit an essay and letters of recommendation from a teacher and guidance counselor. An interview is recommended. AP credits are accepted. Important factors in the admissions decision are advanced placement or honors courses, evidence of special talent, and extracurricular activities record.

Procedure: Freshmen are admitted fall and spring. Entrance exams should be taken during the spring of the junior year or early fall of the senior year. There are early decision, early admissions, and deferred admissions plans. Early decision applications should be filed by December 1, regular applications, by February 15 for fall entry, and November 15 for winter or spring entry. The fall 2009 application fee was $30. Notification of early decision is senr December 15; regular decision, March 15. 28 early decision candidates were accepted for the 2009-2010 class. 29 applicants were on the 2009 waiting list; 12 were admitted. Applications are accepted on-line.

Financial Aid: In 2009-2010, 94% of all full-time freshmen and 90% of continuing full-time students received some form of financial aid. 57% of all full-time freshmen and 56% of continuing full-time students received need-based aid. The average freshman award was $24,092. Need-based scholarships or need-based grants averaged $19,900 ($37,200 maximum); need-based self-help aid (loans and jobs) averaged $5420 ($8320 maximum); and non-need-based awards and non-need-based scholarships averaged $8625 ($12,000 maximum). 60% of undergraduate students work part-time. Average annual earnings from campus work are $1104. The average financial indebtedness of the 2009 graduate was $19,688. Earlham is a member of CSS. The FAFSA and the college's own financial statement are required. The deadline for filing freshman financial aid applications for fall entry is March 1.

Computers: Wireless access is available. 9 computing labs provide 122 Dell computers and 42 Macs for student use. 2 of these labs, located in the library, are open 24 hours providing a total of 17 PCs, 12 Macs, 2 printers, and a scanner. There also are 12 other discipline-specific labs throughout the campus providing an additional 72 computers. In addition, undergraduates with their own units can connect to the campus network from ports in their residence hall rooms or via the wireless network from 101 access points around campus. All students may access the system 24 hours per day. There are no time limits and no fees.

EASTERN MENNONITE UNIVERSITY

Harrisonburg, VA 22802-2462
(540) 432-4118
(800) 368-2665; (540) 432-4444

Full-time: 350 men, 525 women	**Faculty:** IIA, --$
Part-time: 20 men, 20 women	**Ph.D.s:** 71%
Graduate: 110 men, 310 women	**Student/Faculty:** n/av
Year: semesters, summer session	**Tuition:** $25,200
Application Deadline: open	**Room & Board:** $8100
Freshman Class: n/av	
SAT or ACT: required	**VERY COMPETITIVE**

Eastern Mennonite University, founded in 1917, is a private Christian liberal arts university affiliated with the Mennonite Church. The university offers programs in the arts and sciences, education, biology, and nursing. EMU also offers master's degrees in several areas. EMU's Lancaster site provides some programs in Lancaster, Pennsylvania.Figures in the above capsule and this profile are approximate. There are 2 graduate schools. In addition to regional accreditation, EMU has baccalaureate program accreditation with ACPE, CSWE, NCATE, and NLN. The library contains 167,242 volumes, 92,096 microform items, and 3723 audio/video tapes/CDs/DVDs, and subscribes to 1056 periodicals including electronic. Computerized library services include interlibrary loans, database searching, Internet access, and laptop Internet portals. Special learning facilities include a learning resource center, art gallery, natural history museum, planetarium, radio station, arboretum and greenhouse, and nursing lab. The 93-acre campus is in a small town 110 miles southwest of Washington, D.C. Including any residence halls, there are 44 buildings.

Programs of Study: EMU confers B.A. and B.S. degrees. Associate and master's degrees are also awarded. Bachelor's degrees are awarded in AGRICULTURE (international agriculture), BIOLOGICAL SCIENCE (biochemistry and biology/biological science), BUSINESS (accounting, business administration and management, international business management, and recreational facilities management), COMMUNICATIONS AND THE ARTS (art, communications, dramatic arts, English, French, German, music, and Spanish), COMPUTER AND PHYSICAL SCIENCE (chemistry, computer management, computer science, and mathematics), EDUCATION (early childhood education, elementary education, physical education, secondary education, and special education), ENGINEERING AND ENVIRONMENTAL DESIGN (environmental science), HEALTH PROFESSIONS (medical laboratory technology and nursing), SOCIAL SCIENCE (biblical studies, development economics, economics, history, liberal arts/general studies, ministries, peace studies, philosophy, psychology, religion, social science, social work, sociology, and theological studies). Business, education, and nursing are the largest.

Special: EMU offers study-abroad programs each semester and during the summer at a variety of locations around the world. Students may also choose to study 1 or 2 semesters in Washington, D.C. There are internships in a variety of majors, dual majors, a student-designed major, and a 2 year general studies degree. There is 1 national honor society and a freshman honors program.

Requirements: The SAT or ACT is required, with a minimum composite score on 20 the ACT or a satisfactory score on the SAT. Applicants must be graduates of an accredited secondary school or have a GED certificate. The university recommends that students have completed 4 credits of English, 3 each of math, science, and social studies, 2 or more of foreign language and chemistry for nursing majors. A personal reference is required and an interview is recommended. A GPA of 2.2 is required. AP and CLEP credits are accepted. Important factors in the admissions decision are leadership record, extracurricular activities record, and recommendations by school officials.

Procedure: Freshmen are admitted fall and spring. Entrance exams should be taken in the spring of the junior year or the fall of the senior year. There are deferred admissions and rolling admissions plans. Application deadlines are open. The application fee is $75. Applications are accepted on-line.

Financial Aid: EMU is a member of CSS. The FAFSA and the state aid form are required. Check with the school for current application deadlines.

Computers: Wireless access is available. There are 2 public computer labs for student use. Residential students may connect their PC to the network in specified locations. There are several wireless locations for labtop users. All students may access the system day and evening. There are no time limits and no fees.

ECKERD COLLEGE

St. Petersburg, FL 33711

(727) 864-8331
(800) 456-9009; (727) 866-2304

Full-time: 770 men, 1040 women	**Faculty:** IIB, av$
Part-time: 10 men, 15 women	**Ph.D.s:** 95%
Graduate: none	**Student/Faculty:** n/av
Year: 4-1-4, summer session	**Tuition:** $33,230
Application Deadline: see profile	**Room & Board:** $9330
Freshman Class: n/av	
SAT or ACT: required	**VERY COMPETITIVE**

Eckerd College, founded in 1958, is a private liberal arts institution affiliated with the Presbyterian Church (U.S.A.). Interdisciplinary programs are an important part of the school's curriculum, thus faculty are organized into collegia, rather than into traditional departments. Figures in the above capsule are approximate. The library contains 113,850 volumes, 14,606 microform items, and 1941 audio/video tapes/CDs/DVDs, and subscribes to 3009 periodicals including electronic. Computerized library services include interlibrary loans and database searching. Special learning facilities include an art gallery, radio station, and TV station. The 188-acre campus is in a suburban area on 1 1/4 miles of waterfront, 5 miles south of St. Petersburg. Including any residence halls, there are 46 buildings.

Programs of Study: Eckerd confers B.A. and B.S. degrees. Bachelor's degrees are awarded in AGRICULTURE (environmental studies), BIOLOGICAL SCIENCE (biochemistry, biology/biological science, and marine science), BUSINESS (business administration and management, international business management, and management science), COMMUNICATIONS AND THE ARTS (communications, comparative literature, creative writing, dramatic arts, French, literature, modern language, music, Spanish, and visual and performing arts), COMPUTER AND PHYSICAL SCIENCE (chemistry, computer science, mathematics, and physics), HEALTH PROFESSIONS (predentistry and premedicine), SOCIAL SCIENCE (American studies, anthropology, East Asian studies, economics, history, human development, humanities, international relations, philosophy, political science/government, prelaw, psychology, religion, sociology, and women's studies). Marine science, management, and environmental studies are the largest.

Special: Eckerd offers internships, study abroad, work-study programs, and dual majors in all subjects, interdisciplinary majors in international relations and environmental studies, student-designed majors, nondegree study, and pass/fail options. Students may earn B.A.-B.S. degrees in biology, chemistry, and marine science. A 3-2 engineering degree is offered with Auburn, Washington, and Columbia Universities and the University of Miami. There are 8 national honor societies, including Phi Beta Kappa, and a freshman honors program.

Admissions: 4 freshmen graduated first in their class in a recent year.

Requirements: The SAT or ACT is required. In addition, graduation from an accredited secondary school or satisfactory scores on the GED is required. High school courses must include 4 years of English, 3 each of math and science, 2 each of a foreign language and social studies, and 1 of history. SAT: Subject tests in writing, literature, and math are recommended. An essay is required, and an interview is recommended. A GPA of 2.0 is required. AP and CLEP credits are accepted. Important factors in the admissions decision are advanced placement or honors courses, leadership record, and personality/intangible qualities.

Procedure: Freshmen are admitted fall, winter, and spring. Entrance exams should be taken in October, November, or December. There are deferred admissions and rolling admissions plans. Check with the school for current application deadlines. The fall 2009 application fee was $35. A waiting list is maintained.

Financial Aid: The FAFSA is required. Check with the school for current application deadlines.

Computers: Wireless access is available. Numerous computers labs are available to students. All students may access the system at any time. There are no time limits and no fees. It is strongly recommended that all students have a personal computer.

ELIZABETHTOWN COLLEGE

Elizabethtown, PA 17022   (717) 361-1400; (717) 361-1365

Full-time: 686 men, 1200 women	**Faculty:** 123
Part-time: 158 men, 278 women	**Ph.D.s:** 99%
Graduate: 5 men, 40 women	**Student/Faculty:** 15 to 1
Year: semesters, summer session	**Tuition:** $31,800
Application Deadline: open	**Room & Board:** $8150
Freshman Class: 3323 applied, 2488 accepted, 568 enrolled	
SAT CR/M: 560/580	**ACT:** 24 **VERY COMPETITIVE**

Elizabethtown College, founded in 1899, is a private college founded by members of the Church of the Brethren. It offers nearly 50 majors and 70 minors with concentrations in the arts, sciences, humanities, and professional programs, and a master's program in occupational therapy. In addition to regional accreditation, E-town has baccalaureate program accreditation with ABET, ACBSP, CSWE, and NASM. The library contains 260,037 volumes, 23,614 microform items, and 4,474 audio/video tapes/CDs/DVDs, and subscribes to 40,003 periodicals including electronic. Computerized library services include interlibrary loans, database searching, Internet access, and laptop Internet portals. Special learning facilities include a learning resource center, art gallery, radio station, TV station, and the Young Center for Anabaptist and Pietist Studies, a nationally unique academic research facility. The 201-acre campus is in a small town 10 minutes from Hershey and 25 minutes from Lancaster and Harrisburg. Including any residence halls, there are 26 buildings.

Programs of Study: E-town confers B.A., B.S., and B.M. degrees. Associates and master's degrees are also awarded. Bachelor's degrees are awarded in AGRICULTURE (forestry and related sciences), BIOLOGICAL SCIENCE (biochemistry, biology/biological science, and biotechnology), BUSINESS (accounting, business administration and management, business economics, business systems analysis, entrepreneurial studies, international business management, and marketing management), COMMUNICATIONS AND THE ARTS (art, communications, dramatic arts, English, English literature, French, German, Japanese, modern language, music, and Spanish), COMPUTER AND PHYSICAL SCIENCE (actuarial science, chemistry, computer science, information sciences and systems, mathematics, and physics), EDUCATION (early childhood education, elementary education, English education, mathematics education, music education, science education, secondary education, and social studies education), ENGINEERING AND ENVIRONMENTAL DESIGN (computer engineering, engineering, environmental science, industrial engineering, and preengineering), HEALTH PROFESSIONS (allied health, music therapy, occupational therapy, and premedicine), SOCIAL SCIENCE (criminal justice, economics, history, philosophy, political science/government, psychology, religion, social studies, social work, and sociology). Business administration, communications, and elementary education are the largest.

Special: Students can participate in short-term, semester-long, and year-long study-abroad experiences in 18 different locations worldwide. Also available are work-study programs, internships, a Washington semester, accelerated degrees, and dual majors, including sociology and anthropology. There is a 3-2 engineering degree with Pennsylvania State University; a 3-3 allied health degree and a 3-3 physical therapy degree with Thomas Jefferson University, Widener University, and the University of Maryland/Baltimore County; and a 3-2 forestry or environmental management degree with Duke University. There are 19 national honor societies, a freshman honors program, and 100 departmental honors programs.

Admissions: 75% of the 2009-2010 applicants were accepted. The SAT scores for the 2009-2010 freshman class were: Critical Reading--19% below 500, 50% between 500 and 599, 27% between 600 and 700, and 4 above 700; Math--18% below 500, 40% between 500 and 599, 37% between 600 and 700, and 5 above 700. The ACT scores were 29% below 21, 21% between 21 and 23, 23% between 24 and 26, 12% between 27 and 28, and 15% above 28. 54% of the current freshmen were in the top fifth of their class; 85% were in the top two fifths. 11 freshmen graduated first in their class.

Requirements: The SAT or ACT is required. Recommended composite scores for the SAT range from 1030 to 1230; for the ACT, 21 to 27. Applicants must be graduates of an accredited secondary school or have earned a GED. The college encourages completion of 18 academic credits, based on 4 years of English, 3 of math, 2 each of lab science, social studies, and consecutive foreign language, and 5 additional college preparatory units. An audition is required for music majors and an interview is required for occupational therapy majors. AP and CLEP credits are accepted. Important factors in the admissions decision are advanced placement or honors courses, recommendations by school officials, and extracurricular activities record.

Procedure: Freshmen are admitted to all sessions. Entrance exams should be taken in spring of the junior year or fall of the senior year. There are deferred admissions and rolling admissions plans. Application deadlines are open. Application fee is $30. Applications are accepted on-line. 80 applicants were on a recent waiting list, 0 were accepted.

Financial Aid: In 2009-2010, 99% of all full-time freshmen and 96% of continuing full-time students received some form of financial aid. 74% of all full-time freshmen and 73% of continuing full-time students received need-based aid. The average freshmen award was $23,278, with $19,243 ($32,020 maximum) from need-based scholarships or need-based grants and $4,926 ($8,000 maximum) from need-based self-help aid (loans and jobs). All undergraduate students work part-time. Average annual earnings from campus work are $1109. E-town is a member of CSS. The FAFSA, the college's own financial statement, and family federal tax returns are required. The deadline for filing freshman financial aid applications for fall entry is March 15.

Computers: All students are provided with Internet access and e-mail service. PCs are available in computer centers and labs, residence halls, the library, and the student center. There are open, wired network connections in the library, computer labs, and elsewhere on campus. All of the college-owned and college-operated housing units are wired for high-speed Internet access. Some areas of the campus have wireless access. All students may access the system. any time. There are no time limits and no fees. It is strongly recommended that all students have a personal computer.

Chicopee, MA 01013　　　　　　　　　　　　**(413) 592-3189**
　　　　　　　　　　　　　　　　　　　　(800) 255-ELMS; (413) 594-2781

Full-time: 65 men, 360 women	**Faculty:** n/av
Part-time: 25 men, 190 women	**Ph.D.s:** 76%
Graduate: 20 men, 80 women	**Student/Faculty:** n/av
Year: semesters	**Tuition:** $14,100
Application Deadline: open	**Room & Board:** $9800
Freshman Class: n/av	
SAT or ACT: required	**VERY COMPETITIVE**

Elms College, founded in 1928 as College of Our Lady of the Elms, is a Roman Catholic institution offering undergraduate degrees in liberal arts and sciences and graduate degrees in liberal arts, education, and theology. Figures in the above capsule and this profile are approximate. In addition to regional accreditation, Elms has baccalaureate program accreditation with CSWE and NLN. The library contains 103,136 volumes, 77,784 microform items, and 2208 audio/video tapes/CDs/DVDs, and subscribes to 695 periodicals including electronic. Computerized library services include interlibrary loans and database searching. Special learning facilities include a learning resource center, art gallery, radio station, TV station, and rare books collection. The 32-acre campus is in a suburban area 2 miles north of Springfield and 90 miles west of Boston. Including any residence halls, there are 11 buildings.

Programs of Study: Elms confers B.A. and B.S. degrees. Associate and master's degrees are also awarded. Bachelor's degrees are awarded in BIOLOGICAL SCIENCE (biology/biological science), BUSINESS (accounting, business administration and management, international business management, and marketing/retailing/merchandising), COMMUNICATIONS AND THE ARTS (English, fine arts, and Spanish), COMPUTER AND PHYSICAL SCIENCE (chemistry, computer science, mathematics, and natural sciences), EDUCATION (bilingual/bicultural education, early childhood education, elementary education, foreign languages education, middle school education, science education, secondary education, special education, and teaching English as a second/foreign language (TESOL/TEFOL)), HEALTH PROFESSIONS (health science, medical laboratory technology, nursing, predentistry, premedicine, and speech pathology/audiology), SOCIAL SCIENCE (American studies, international studies, paralegal studies, prelaw, psychology, religion, social work, and sociology). Nursing, education, and biology are the strongest academically. Education, business, and nursing are the largest.

Special: Students may cross-register at any of the Cooperating Colleges of Greater Springfield or Consortium of Sisters of St. Joseph Colleges. Internships are available with local hospitals, businesses, and schools. Study abroad, student-designed interdepartmental majors, accelerated degree programs, work-study, dual majors, nondegree study, and pass/fail options are offered. There are 5 national honor societies, including Phi Beta Kappa, and a freshman honors program.

Requirements: The SAT or ACT is required. In addition, applicants should be graduates of accredited high schools or have earned the GED. Secondary preparation should include 4 units of English, 3 each of math and science, and 2 each of foreign language, history, and social studies. A personal essay is required; an interview is recommended. A GPA of 2.5 is required. AP and CLEP credits are accepted. Important factors in the admissions decision are advanced placement or honors courses, recommendations by school officials, and extracurricular activities record.

Procedure: Freshmen are admitted fall and spring. Entrance exams should be taken no later than November of the senior year. There are early admissions, deferred admissions, and rolling admissions plans. Application deadlines are open. The fall 2009 application fee was $30. Applications are accepted on-line.

Financial Aid: Elms is a member of CSS. The FAFSA and the college's own financial statement are required. Check with the school for current application deadlines.

Computers: All students may access the system 8 A.M. to 10 P.M. Monday through Friday and 12 noon to 9 P.M. Saturday and Sunday. Residence hall labs are open 24 hours. There are no time limits and no fees.

ELON UNIVERSITY
Elon, NC 27244-2010

(336) 278-3566
(800) 334-8448; (336) 278-7699

Full-time: 1996 men, 2877 women	**Faculty:** 316; II A, av$
Part-time: 45 men, 77 women	**Ph.D.s:** 85%
Graduate: 315 men, 356 women	**Student/Faculty:** 15 to 1
Year: 4-1-4, summer session	**Tuition:** $25,489
Application Deadline: January 10	**Room & Board:** $8236
Freshman Class: 9041 applied, 4367 accepted, 1291 enrolled	
SAT CR/M/W: 611/614/618	**ACT:** 27 **HIGHLY COMPETITIVE**

Elon University, founded in 1889 by the United Church of Christ, is a selective private institution that offers programs in the liberal arts and sciences and professional programs. There are 4 undergraduate schools and 4 graduate schools. In addition to regional accreditation, Elon has baccalaureate program accreditation with AACSB, ACEJMC, CAHEA, and NCATE. The library contains 302,630 volumes, 951,791 microform items, and 23,915 audio/video tapes/CDs/DVDs, and subscribes to 32,442 periodicals including electronic. Computerized library services include interlibrary loans, database searching, Internet access, and laptop Internet portals. Special learning facilities include a learning resource center, art gallery, radio station, TV station, writing center, botanical preserve, and observatory. The 575-acre campus is in a suburban area adjacent to Burlington and 17 miles east of Greensboro. Including any residence halls, there are 120 buildings.

Programs of Study: Elon confers B.A., B.S., and B.F.A. degrees. Master's and doctoral degrees are also awarded. Bachelor's degrees are awarded in BIOLOGICAL SCIENCE (biology/biological science), BUSINESS (accounting, banking and finance, business administration and management, entrepreneurial studies, management information systems, marketing and distribution, and sports management), COMMUNICATIONS AND THE ARTS (art, broadcasting, communications, creative writing, dance, dramatic arts, English, film arts, French, journalism, literature, music, music performance, music technology, musical theater, Spanish, and theater design), COMPUTER AND PHYSICAL SCIENCE (applied mathematics, chemistry, computer science, information sciences and systems, mathematics, and physics), EDUCATION (elementary education, foreign languages education, health education, mathematics education, middle school education, music education, physical education, science education, secondary education, social science education, and special education), ENGINEERING AND ENVIRONMENTAL DESIGN (engineering, engineering physics, environmental science, and military science), HEALTH PROFESSIONS (medical technology and sports medicine), SOCIAL SCIENCE (anthropology, economics, history, human services, international studies, philosophy, political science/government, psychology, public administration, religion, and sociology). Business, education, and music theater are the strongest academically. Business, education, and journalism and communication are the largest.

Special: Elon offers co-op programs in most majors, dual majors, student-designed majors, cross-registration with 6 other colleges and universities in North Carolina, paid and unpaid internships, study abroad in 65 countries, a Washington semester, work-study programs, pass/fail options, and 3-2 dual engineering degree programs. The 3-week January term includes extensive international study opportunities and courses with domestic travel components. There are 26 national honor societies, including Phi Beta Kappa, a freshman honors program, and 23 departmental honors programs.

Admissions: 48% of the 2009-2010 applicants were accepted. The SAT scores for the 2009-2010 freshman class were: Critical Reading--6% below 500, 35% between 500 and 599, 48% between 600 and 700, and 11% above 700; Math--6% below 500, 31% between 500 and 599, 51% between 600 and 700, and 12% above 700; Writing--5% below 500, 31% between 500 and 599, 49% between 600 and 700, and 15% above 700. The ACT scores were 6% below 21, 11% between 21 and 23, 31% between 24 and 26, 23% between 27 and 28, and 29% above 28. 61% of the current freshmen were in the top fifth of their class; 86% were in the top two fifths. There was 1 National Merit finalist. 12 freshmen graduated first in their class.

Requirements: The SAT or ACT is required. The ACT Optional Writing test is also required. In addition, students must be graduates of an accredited secondary school or have a GED certificate. They should have completed 4 credits in English, 3 or more in math, 2 or more in a foreign language, 2 or more in science, including at least 1 lab science, and 2 or more in social studies, including U.S. history. A GPA of 2.7 is required. AP and CLEP credits are accepted.

Procedure: Freshmen are admitted in the fall. Entrance exams should be taken in the spring of the junior year and the fall of the senior year. There are early decision, early admissions and deferred admissions plans. Early decision applications should be filed by November 1; regular applications, by January 10 for fall entry, along with a $50 fee. Notification of early decision is sent December 1; regular decision, March 15. 2810 applicants were on the 2009 waiting list; 148 were admitted. Applications are accepted on-line.

Financial Aid: In 2009-2010, 77% of all full-time freshmen and 73% of continuing full-time students received some form of financial aid. 32% of all full-time freshmen and 31% of continuing full-time students received need-based aid. The average freshman award was $13,266, with $10,071 ($30,400 maximum) from need-based scholarships or need-based grants; $5,590 ($9,000 maximum) from need-based self-help aid (loans and jobs); $21,349 ($37,297 maximum) from non-need-based athletic scholarships; and $6,035 ($30,659 maximum) from other non-need-based awards and non-need-based scholarships. 30% of undergraduate students work part-time. Average annual earnings from campus work are $3000. The average financial indebtedness of the 2009 graduate was $22,939. Elon is a member of CSS. The CSS/Profile, FAFSA, and the college's own financial statement are required. The priority date for freshman financial aid applications for fall entry is February 15.

Computers: All of the campus is wireless; all dorm rooms are wired and wireless; Elon has 750 PCs for student use. All students may access the system 24 hours a day. It is strongly recommended that all students have a personal computer.

EMERSON COLLEGE

Boston, MA 02116-4624　　　　(617) 824-8600; (617) 824-8609

Full-time: 1402 men, 2020 women	**Faculty:** 141; IIA, av$
Part-time: 78 men, 196 women	**Ph.D.s:** 72%
Graduate: 213 men, 637 women	**Student/Faculty:** 24 to 1
Year: semesters, summer session	**Tuition:** $30,080
Application Deadline: January 5	**Room & Board:** $12,280

Freshman Class: 6943 applied, 2926 accepted, 766 enrolled
SAT CR/M/W: 623/592/622　　　　**ACT:** 26　**HIGHLY COMPETITIVE**

Founded in 1880, Emerson is one of the premier colleges in the United States for the study of communication and the arts. There are 2 undergraduate schools and 2 graduate schools. The library contains 179,380 volumes, 9899 microform items, and 11,596 audio/video tapes/CDs/DVDs, and subscribes to 23,446 periodicals including electronic. Computerized library services include interlibrary loans, database searching, Internet access, and laptop Internet portals. Special learning facilities include a learning resource center, art gallery, radio station, TV station, sound-treated television studios, film production facilities and digital production labs, speech-language-hearing clinics, a proscenium stage theater, 2 radio stations, marketing research suite, and digital newsroom. The 8-acre campus is in an urban area on Boston Common in the Theater District. Including any residence halls, there are 10 buildings.

Programs of Study: Emerson confers B.A., B.S., and B.F.A. degrees. Master's and doctoral degrees are also awarded. Bachelor's degrees are awarded in BUSINESS (marketing management), COMMUNICATIONS AND THE ARTS (advertising, broadcasting, communications, creative writing, dramatic arts, film arts, journalism, media arts, musical theater, performing arts, public relations, publishing, radio/television technology, speech/debate/rhetoric, theater design, and theater management), HEALTH PROFESSIONS (speech pathology/audiology), SOCIAL SCIENCE (interdisciplinary studies). Visual and media arts, writing, and literature are the strongest academically. Visual and media arts, performing arts, and communication are the largest.

Special: Student-designed, interdisciplinary, and dual majors are available. Cross-registration is offered with the 6-member Boston ProArts consortium and Suffolk University. Nearly 800 internships are possible, 600 in Boston and 200 in Los Angeles. Internships bear credit and are graded. Emerson has nondegree study as well as study abroad in the Netherlands, Taiwan, Czech Republic, and a summer film program in Prague. There is 1 national honor society and a freshman honors program.

Admissions: 42% of the 2009-2010 applicants were accepted. The SAT scores for the 2009-2010 freshman class were: Critical Reading--4% below 500, 31% between 500 and 599, 48% between 600 and 700, and 17% above 700; Math--7% below 500, 44% between 500 and 599, 43% between 600 and 700, and 6% above 700; Writing--4% below 500, 30% between 500 and 599, 51% between 600 and 700, and 15% above 700. The ACT scores were 4% below 21, 17% between 21 and 23, 32% between 24 and 26, 21% between 27 and 28, and 26% above 28. 77% of the current freshmen were in the top fifth of their class; 98% were in the top two fifths. 5 freshmen graduated first in their class.

Requirements: The SAT or ACT is required. The ACT Optional Writing test is also required. Emerson is a member of the Common Application and requires an Application Supplement. Candidates must have graduated from high school (or have a GED) and present 4 years of English and 3 each in science, social studies, foreign language, and math. Candidates for performing arts programs are required to submit a theater-related resume and either audition or interview, or submit a portfolio or an essay. Candidates for film are required to submit either a 5- to 8-minute video sample and statement, or a 5- to 10-page script. AP and CLEP credits are accepted. Important factors in the admissions decision are advanced placement or honors courses, evidence of special talent, and recommendations by school officials.

Procedure: Freshmen are admitted fall and spring. Entrance exams should be taken before December of the senior year. There are early decision and deferred admissions plan. Early decision applications should be filed by November 1; regular applications, by January 5 for fall entry and November 1 for spring entry, along with a $65 fee. Notifications of early decision are sent December 15, regular decision, April 1. 798 applicants were on the 2009 waiting list; 104 were admitted. Applications are accepted on-line.

Financial Aid: In 2009-2010, 63% of all full-time freshmen and 55% of continuing full-time students received some form of financial aid. 53% of all full-time freshmen and 43% of continuing full-time students received need-based aid. The average freshman award was $15,685. Need-based scholarships or need-based grants averaged $14,243; need-based self-help aid (loans and jobs) averaged $4394; and other non-need-based awards and non-need-based scholarships averaged $12,396. 60% of undergraduate students work part-time. Average annual earnings from campus work are $1600. The average financial indebtedness of the 2009 graduate was $15,262. The CSS/Profile and FAFSA are required. The priority date for freshman financial aid applications for fall entry is March 1.

Computers: Wireless access is available. There are very few restrictions on network or wireless access with more than 3000 ports on campus. All students may access the system 24 hours a day. There are no time limits and no fees. It is strongly recommended that all students have a personal computer.

EMORY UNIVERSITY
Atlanta, GA 30322 (404) 727-6036

Full-time: 2400 men, 3230 women	**Faculty:** I, +$
Part-time: 15 men, 30 women	**Ph.D.s:** 100%
Graduate: 2250 men, 3030 women	**Student/Faculty:** n/av
Year: semesters, summer session	**Tuition:** $35,000
Application Deadline: see profile	**Room & Board:** $10,000
Freshman Class: n/av	
SAT or ACT: recommended	**MOST COMPETITIVE**

Emory University, founded in 1836, is a private institution affiliated with the United Methodist Church. Figures in the above capsule and this profile are approximate. There are 4 undergraduate schools and 7 graduate schools. The 8 libraries contain 3.0 million volumes, 272,000 microform items, and 53,575 audio/video tapes/CDs/DVDs, and subscribe to 54,000 periodicals including electronic. Computerized library services include interlibrary loans, database searching, Internet access, and laptop Internet portals. Special learning facilities include a learning resource center, art gallery, planetarium, radio station, TV station, the Michael C. Carlos Museum, and the Carter Center. The 634-acre campus is in a suburban area 5 miles northeast of downtown Atlanta. Including any residence halls, there are 150 buildings.

Programs of Study: Emory confers B.A., B.S., B.B.A., and B.S.N. degrees. Associate, master's, and doctoral degrees are also awarded. Bachelor's degrees are awarded in AGRICULTURE (environmental studies), BIOLOGICAL SCIENCE (biology/biological science and neurosciences), BUSINESS (accounting, banking and finance, business administration and management, business economics, and marketing/retailing/merchandising), COMMUNICATIONS AND THE ARTS (art, art history and appreciation, Chinese, classics, comparative literature, creative writing, dance, dramatic arts, English, film arts, fine arts, French, Greek, Italian, Japanese, journalism, Latin, linguistics, music, Russian languages and literature, and Spanish), COMPUTER AND PHYSICAL SCIENCE (chemistry, computer science, mathematics, and physics), EDUCATION (educational statistics and research), HEALTH PROFESSIONS (nursing), SOCIAL SCIENCE (African studies, African American studies, American studies, anthropology, Asian/American studies, Asian/Oriental studies, Caribbean studies, classical/ancient civilization, economics, French studies, German area studies, history, interdisciplinary studies, international studies, Italian studies, Judaic studies, Latin American studies, medieval studies, Middle Eastern studies, philosophy, political science/government, psychology, religion, Russian and Slavic studies, sociology, and women's studies). Business administration, psychology, and economics are the largest.

Special: Special academic programs include cross-registration with Atlanta area colleges and universities, departmental internships, work-study programs, dual majors, 3-2 and 4-2 engineering degrees with Georgia Tech, and pass/fail options. A Washington semester and B.A.-B.S. degrees are available, and students may study abroad in many countries. There are accelerated degree programs offered in biology, chemistry, math, physics, English, history, philosophy, political science, sociology, and computer science. There are 30 national honor societies and Phi Beta Kappa.

Requirements: Students must submit a hight school transcript. Students may submit SAT or ACT results, but they are not required unless a student is homeschooled. A recommendation from a high school counselor and up to 2 additional letters of recommendation are required. The student must have acquired 16 academic credits in secondary school, including 4 years of English, 3 years of math, and 2 years each of history, science, and foreign language. AP credits are accepted. Important factors in the admissions decision are advanced placement or honors courses, recommendations by school officials, and extracurricular activities record.

Procedure: Freshmen are admitted fall. Entrance exams should be taken prior to applying. There are early decision, early admissions and deferred admissions plans. Check with the school for current application deadlines. The application fee is $50. Applications are accepted on-line. A waiting list is maintained.

Financial Aid: Emory is a member of CSS. The CSS/Profile and FAFSA are required. Check with the school for current application deadlines.

Computers: Wireless access is available. All students may access the system 24 hours a day. There are no time limits and no fees.

EUGENE LANG COLLEGE NEW SCHOOL FOR LIBERAL ARTS

New York, NY 10011-8963   (212) 229-5665; (212) 229-5166

Full-time: 380 men, 855 women	**Faculty:** n/av
Part-time: 30 men, 45 women	**Ph.D.s:** n/av
Graduate: none	**Student/Faculty:** n/av
Year: semesters	**Tuition:** $35,421
Application Deadline: February 1	**Room & Board:** $12,000
Freshman Class: n/av	**HIGHLY COMPETITIVE**

Eugene Lang College, established in 1978, is the liberal arts undergraduate division of the New School. The figures in the above capsule and in this profile are approximate. The 3 libraries contain 2.4 million volumes, 13,000 microform items, and 14,275 audio/video tapes/CDs/DVDs, and subscribe to 33,320 periodicals including electronic. Computerized library services include interlibrary loans, database searching, Internet access, a -acrnd laptop Internet portals. Special learning facilities include an art gallery and a writing center. The campus is in an urban area Greenwich Village, Manhattan. Including any residence halls, there are 14 buildings.

Programs of Study: Eugene Lang College confers B.A. degrees. Bachelor's degrees are awarded in AGRICULTURE (environmental studies), COMMUNICATIONS AND THE ARTS (creative writing, dramatic arts, English, and literature), EDUCATION (education), SOCIAL SCIENCE (crosscultural studies, economics, history, philosophy, political science/government, psychology, religion, social science, sociology, urban studies, and women's studies). Creative writing, history, urban studies, and education are the strongest academically. Writing and cultural studies are the largest.

Special: Lang College offers a concentration rather than a traditional major; there is no core curriculum and students are instructed in small seminars. Students may cross-register with other New School divisions. A large variety of internships for credit, study abroad, B.A./M.A. and B.A./M.S.T. options, a B.A./B.F.A. degree with Parsons The New School for Design and The New School for Jazz and Contemporary Music Program, student-designed majors, and nondegree study are available.

Requirements: The SAT or ACT is required. In addition, applicants must be enrolled in a strong college preparatory program. The GED is accepted. An essay and an interview are required. Art students must present a portfolio and complete a home exam. Jazz students are required to audition. AP credits are accepted. Important factors in the admissions decision are personality/intangible qualities, recommendations by school officials, and advanced placement or honors courses.

Procedure: Freshmen are admitted fall and spring. Entrance exams should be taken in May of the junior year or October of the senior year. There are early decision,–deferred admissions plan. Early decision applications should be filed by November 15; regular applications, by February 1 for fall entry and November 15 for spring entry, along with a $50 fee. Notification of early decision is sent December 15; regular decision, April 1. Applications are accepted on-line. A waiting list is maintained.

Financial Aid: In a recent year, 63% of all full-time freshmen and 64% of continuing full-time students received some form of financial aid. 61% of all full-time freshmen and 65% of continuing full-time students received need-based aid. The average freshmen award was $23,622, with $12,438 ($30,660 maximum) from need-based scholarships or need-based grants and $3,280 ($5,500 maximum) from need-based self-help aid (loans and jobs). Average annual earnings from campus work were $2000. The average financial indebtedness of the 2009 graduate was $14,770. Eugene Lang College is a member of CSS. The FAFSA, the state aid form, and the college's own financial statement are required. Check with the school for current application deadlines.

Computers: Wireless access is available. All students may access the system. There are no time limits and no fees.

FAIRFIELD UNIVERSITY
Fairfield, CT 06824-5195 — (203) 254-4100; (203) 254-4199

Full-time: 1395 men, 1935 women	**Faculty:** 229; IIA, +$
Part-time: 263 men, 302 women	**Ph.D.s:** 93%
Graduate: 403 men, 828 women	**Student/Faculty:** 14 to 1
Year: semesters, summer session	**Tuition:** $37,490
Application Deadline: January 15	**Room & Board:** $11,270
Freshman Class: 8316 applied, 5376 accepted, 849 enrolled	
SAT CR/M/W: 570/570/580	**ACT:** 25 **VERY COMPETITIVE**

Fairfield University, founded by the Jesuits in 1942, is a private, Roman Catholic Jesuit institution. There are 5 undergraduate schools and 5 graduate schools. In addition to regional accreditation, Fairfield has baccalaureate program accreditation with AACSB, ABET, and NLN. The library contains 394,588 volumes, 881,677 microform items, and 12,788 audio/video tapes/CDs/DVDs, and subscribes to 34,405 periodicals including electronic. Computerized library services include interlibrary loans, database searching, Internet access, and laptop Internet portals. Special learning facilities include an art gallery, radio station, TV station, media center, 750-seat concert hall/theater, a rehearsal and improvisation theater, language learning lab, Business Education Simulation Training (BEST) classroom, and SIM/simulated hospital environment and human patient simulators in the nursing facility. The 200-acre campus is in a suburban, residential community 60 miles northeast of New York City. Including any residence halls, there are 42 buildings.

Programs of Study: Fairfield confers B.A. and B.S. degrees. Associate and master's degrees are also awarded. Bachelor's degrees are awarded in BIOLOGICAL SCIENCE (biochemistry and biology/biological science), BUSINESS (accounting, banking and finance, business administration and management, international business management, management information systems, and marketing/retailing/merchandising), COMMUNICATIONS AND THE ARTS (art history and appreciation, communications, dramatic arts, English, fine arts, French, German, Italian, music, Spanish, studio art, and visual and performing arts), COMPUTER AND PHYSICAL SCIENCE (chemistry, computer science, information sciences and systems, mathematics, physics, and software engineering), ENGINEERING AND ENVIRONMENTAL DESIGN (computer engineering, electrical/electronics engineering, and mechanical engineering), HEALTH PROFESSIONS (nursing), SOCIAL SCIENCE (American studies, economics, history, international studies, philosophy, political science/government, psychology, religion, and sociology). Finance, marketing, and nursing are the strongest academically. Finance, communications, and biology are the largest.

Special: Fairfield administers its own study abroad program in several countries and has affiliations with 17 programs, a Washington semester, a federal work-study program, B.A.-B.S. degrees in economics, international studies, and psychology, student-designed majors, and dual majors in all subjects. A 3-2 engineering degree is offered with the University of Connecticut, Rensselaer Polytechnic Institute, Columbia University, and Stevens Institute of Technology. A general studies degree and credit for life and work experience are available through Continuing Studies at University College. Internships, both credit and noncredit, are offered at area corporations, publications, banks, and other organizations. Interdisciplinary minors include women's studies, marine science, Black studies, environmental studies, jazz, classical performance, Italian studies, Russian and Eastern European studies, Catholic and Judaic studies, applied ethics, Asian studies, Irish studies, Latin American and Caribbean studies, and peace and justice. There are 18 national honor societies, including Phi Beta Kappa, a freshman honors program, and 1 departmental honors program.

Admissions: 65% of the 2009-2010 applicants were accepted. The SAT scores for the 2009-2010 freshman class were: Critical Reading--16% below 500, 49% between 500 and 599, 28% between 600 and 700, and 2% above 700; Math--12% below 500, 42% between 500 and 599, 36% between 600 and 700, and 4% above 700; Writing--12% below 500, 40% between 500 and 599, 37% between 600 and 700, and 6% above 700. The ACT scores were 12% below 21, 19% between 21 and 23, 43% between 24 and 26, 16% between 27 and 28, and 11% above 28. 71% of the current freshmen were in the top fifth of their class; 92% were in the top two fifths.

Requirements: Fairfield has test optional admission. Students who choose to apply without test scores must submit a second essay and are encouraged to complete an on-campus interview. A B average is required. Students should have completed 15 academic credits, including 4 credits of English, 3 to 4 credits each of history, math, and lab science, and 2 to 4 credits of a foreign language. The school recommends SAT Subject tests in language and math, and, for nursing and science majors, in the sciences. A GPA of 3.0 is required. AP and CLEP credits are accepted. Important factors in the admissions decision are advanced placement or honors courses, leadership record, and evidence of special talent.

Procedure: Freshmen are admitted in the fall. Entrance exams should be taken in the spring of the junior year or fall of the senior year. There are early admissions and deferred admissions plans. Applications should be filed by January 15 for fall entry. The fall 2009 application fee was $60. Notifications are sent April 1. 1196 applicants were on the 2009 waiting list; 91 were admitted. Applications are accepted on-line.

Financial Aid: In 2009-2010, 70% of all full-time freshmen and 68% of continuing full-time students received some form of financial aid. 50% of all full-time freshmen and 50% of continuing full-time students received need-based aid. The average freshman award was $29,123, with $24,000 ($43,200 maximum) from need-based scholarships or need-based grants; $5,392 ($7,000 maximum) from need-based self-help aid (loans and jobs); $20,286 ($51,040 maximum) from non-need-based athletic scholarships; and $17,000 ($20,000 maximum) from other non-need-based awards and non-need-based scholarships. 11% of undergraduate students work part-time. Average annual earnings from campus work are $1109. The average financial indebtedness of the 2009 graduate was $35,161. Fairfield is a member of CSS. The CSS/Profile and FAFSA, parent and student federal tax returns, and all schedules and W-2 forms are required. The deadline for filing freshman financial aid applications for fall entry is February 15.

Computers: Wireless access is available. Students have access to grades and scheduling on the Internet. All students may access the system daily until midnight. There are no time limits and no fees. It is strongly recommended that all students have a personal computer.

FLAGLER COLLEGE

St. Augustine, FL 32084

(904) 829-6481
(800) 304-4208; (904) 826-0094

Full-time: 1070 men, 1570 women	**Faculty:** 95; IIB, --$
Part-time: 25 men, 51 women	**Ph.D.s:** 58%
Graduate: none	**Student/Faculty:** 28 to 1
Year: semesters, summer session	**Tuition:** $13,300
Application Deadline: March 1	**Room & Board:** $7190
Freshman Class: 1585 applied, 1149 accepted, 564 enrolled	
SAT CR/M/W: 550/540/540	**ACT:** 23 **VERY COMPETITIVE**

Flagler College, founded in 1968, is an independent liberal arts college that emphasizes undergraduate education in select liberal and preprofessional studies. There is 1 undergraduate school. The library contains 187,956 volumes, 1857 microform items, and 4745 audio/video tapes/CDs/DVDs, and subscribes to 533 periodicals including electronic. Computerized library services include interlibrary loans, database searching, Internet access, and laptop Internet portals. Special learning facilities include a learning resource center, art gallery, and radio station. The 30-acre campus is in a small town 35 miles south of Jacksonville and 45 miles north of Daytona Beach. Including any residence halls, there are 28 buildings.

Programs of Study: Flagler confers B.A., B.S., and B.F.A. degrees. Bachelor's degrees are awarded in BUSINESS (accounting, business administration and management, and sports management), COMMUNICATIONS AND THE ARTS (communications, dramatic arts, English, fine arts, graphic design, and Spanish), EDUCATION (art education, education of the deaf and hearing impaired, education of the exceptional child, elementary education, and secondary education), SOCIAL SCIENCE (economics, history, Latin American studies, liberal arts/general studies, philosophy, political science/government, psychology, public administration, religion, and sociology). Business, liberal studies, and arts are the strongest academically. Business, communications, and education are the largest.

Special: The school offers internships, work-study, and dual majors. Students may participate in study-abroad programs in almost any country. Students majoring in deaf education can work directly with students at the Florida State School for the Deaf and Blind. There are 8 national honor societies and 6 departmental honors programs.

Admissions: 72% of the 2009-2010 applicants were accepted. The SAT scores for the 2009-2010 freshman class were: Critical Reading--13% below 500, 63% between 500 and 599, 22% between 600 and 700, and 2% above 700; Math--15% below 500, 64% between 500 and 599, 20% between 600 and 700, and 1% above 700; Writing--20% below 500, 65% between 500 and 599, 13% between 600 and 700, and 2% above 700. The ACT scores were 14% below 21, 47% between 21 and 23, 27% between 24 and 26, 9% between 27 and 28, and 3% above 28. 43% of the current freshmen were in the top fifth of their class; 84% were in the top two fifths. 1 freshman graduated first in the class.

Requirements: The SAT or ACT is required. In addition, student must have graduated from an accredited secondary school or have a satisfactory score on the GED. Students must have a total of 19 academic credits. High school courses must include 4 credits of English, 3 credits each of math and science, and 2 credits of a foreign language. An essay is required, and an interview is recommended. AP and CLEP credits are accepted. Important factors in the admissions decision are advanced placement or honors courses, leadership record, and extracurricular activities record.

Procedure: Freshmen are admitted fall and spring. Entrance exams should be taken during the fall of the senior year at the latest. There are early decision and deferred admissions plans. Early decision applications should be filed by January 15; regular applications, by March 1 for fall entry and December 15 for spring entry, along with a $40 fee. Notificationsof early decision are sent February 1; regular decision, March 15. 389 early decision candidates were accepted for the 2009-2010 class. 519 applicants were on the 2009 waiting list; 44 were admitted. Applications are accepted on-line.

Financial Aid: In 2009-2010, 92% of all full-time freshmen and 87% of continuing full-time students received some form of financial aid. 56% of all full-time freshmen and 44% of continuing full-time students received need-based aid. The average freshman award was $10,185. Need-based scholarships or need-based grants averaged $5339 ($11,900 maximum); need-based self-help aid (loans and jobs) averaged $3492 ($8900 maximum); non-need-based athletic scholarships averaged $6310 ($21,490 maximum); and other non-need-based awards and non-need-based scholarships averaged $9073 ($25,390 maximum). 69% of undergraduate students work part-time. Average annual earnings from campus work are $1400. The average financial indebtedness of the 2009 graduate was $16,304. The FAFSA and the college's own financial statement are required. The deadline for filing freshman financial aid applications for fall entry is April 1.

Computers: There are 166 PCs and 70 Macs in the library for student use. All are Internet accessible. All students have access to all computer labs and to the wireless network, which is available in most areas of campus. All dorm rooms have wired and wireless connections to the Internet and Intranet. All students may access the system. The labs are available during library hours. There are no time limits and no fees.

FLORIDA ATLANTIC UNIVERSITY
Boca Raton, FL 33431-0991
(561) 297-3040
(800) 299-4FAU; (561) 297-2758

Full-time: 5815 men, 7281 women	**Faculty:** 1084; I, --$
Part-time: 3611 men, 5601 women	**Ph.D.s:** 86%
Graduate: 2022 men, 3370 women	**Student/Faculty:** 18 to 1
Year: semesters, summer session	**Tuition:** $4187 ($17,532)
Application Deadline: June 1	**Room & Board:** $9582
Freshman Class: 14532 applied, 6745 accepted, 2535 enrolled	
SAT CR/M/W: 531/538/517	**ACT:** 23 **COMPETITIVE+**

Florida Atlantic University, founded in 1961, is a publicly funded liberal arts institution in the state university system of Florida. There are 9 undergraduate schools and 8 graduate schools. In addition to regional accreditation, FAU has baccalaureate program accreditation with AACSB, ABET, CSAB, CSWE, NAAB, NASM, NCATE, and NLN. The 4 libraries contain 206,615 volumes, 2.1 million microform items, and 22,414 audio/video tapes/CDs/DVDs, and subscribe to 12,549 periodicals including electronic. Computerized library services include interlibrary loans, database searching, Internet access, and laptop Internet portals. Special learning facilities include a learning resource center, art gallery, radio station, TV station, engineering research labs, a marine sciences research center, a K-12 developmental research school, a nonnative fish research lab, and an environmental sciences center. The 850-acre campus is in a suburban area 17 miles north of Ft. Lauderdale, 45 miles north of Miami, and 22 miles south of Palm Beach. Including any residence halls, there are 120 buildings.

Programs of Study: FAU confers B.A., B.S., B.A.E., B.Arch., B.B.A., B.E.C.E. B.F.A., B.H.S., B.I.E.T., B.Mus., B.P.M., B.S.C.E., B.S.C.V., B.S.E., B.S.E.E., B.S.G.E., B.S.H.S., B.S.M.E., B.S.M.T., B.S.N., B.S.O.E., B.S.W., and B.U.R.P. degrees. Associate, master's, and doctoral degrees are also awarded. Bachelor's degrees are awarded in BIOLOGICAL SCIENCE (biology/biological science and marine biology), BUSINESS (accounting, banking and finance, business administration and management, business economics, hospitality management services, human resources, international business management, management information systems, marketing/retailing/merchandising, real estate, and small business management), COMMUNICATIONS AND THE ARTS (art, communications, dramatic arts, English, fine arts, French, German, graphic design, Italian, jazz, journalism, linguistics, media arts, multimedia, music, Spanish, and visual and performing arts), COMPUTER AND PHYSICAL SCIENCE (chemistry, computer science, computer security and information assurance, geology, information sciences and systems, mathematics, and physics), EDUCATION (education of the exceptional child, elementary education, English education, foreign languages education, physical education, and special education), ENGINEERING AND ENVIRONMENTAL DESIGN (architecture, civil engineering, computer engineering, electrical/electronics engineering, engineering, mechanical engineering, ocean engineering, and urban planning technology), HEALTH PROFESSIONS (health care administration, health science, medical laboratory technology, and nursing), SOCIAL SCIENCE (anthropology, criminal justice, economics, geography, history, interdisciplinary studies, Judaic studies, liberal arts/general studies, philosophy, political science/government, psychobiology, psychology, public administration, social psychology, social science, social work, and sociology). Engineering, education, and business are the strongest academically. Elementary education, biological science, and accounting are the largest.

Special: FAU offers cooperative programs and internships in most majors. Work-study programs, dual and student-designed majors, a general studies degree, credit for military experience, nondegree study, and pass/fail options are available. The school offers a Washington semester, study abroad through all state university system of Florida programs. There are 21 national honor societies, a freshman honors program, and 9 departmental honors programs.

Admissions: 46% of the 2009-2010 applicants were accepted. The SAT scores for the 2009-2010 freshman class were: Critical Reading--32% below 500, 51% between 500 and 599, 15% between 600 and 700, and 2% above 700; Math--30% below 500, 51% between 500 and 599, 18% between 600 and 700, and 2% above 700; Writing--39% below 500, 48% between 500 and 599, 11% between 600 and 700, and 2% above 700. The ACT scores were 18% below 21, 44% between 21 and 23, 24% between 24 and 26, 8% between 27 and 28, and 7% above 28. 44% of the current freshmen were in the top fifth of their class; 74% were in the top two fifths. There were 2 National Merit finalists.

Requirements: The SAT or ACT is required, with a satisfactory score on the SAT Critical Reading and Math sections or on the ACT. In addition, graduation from an accredited secondary school or satisfactory scores on the GED are required. Students must have 19 academic credits, including 4 units of English, 3 each of math (algebra I and higher), science (including 2 with substantial lab work), and social studies, and 2 of a foreign language, plus 4 of electives in computer science, fine arts, or humanities. A portfolio or an audition may be requested by individual departments. An essay and an interview are required. A GPA of 2.0 is required. AP and CLEP credits are accepted. Important factors in the admissions decision are advanced placement or honors courses, evidence of special talent, and recommendations by school officials.

Procedure: Freshmen are admitted fall, spring, and summer. Entrance exams should be taken by June. There are early decision, early admissions, deferred admissions, and rolling admissions plans. Applications should be filed by June 1 for fall entry, October 15 for spring entry, and March 15 for summer entry, along with a $30 fee. Applications are accepted on-line.

Financial Aid: Need-based scholarships or need-based grants averaged $6,740; need-based self-help aid (loans and jobs) averaged $3,065. FAU is a member of CSS. The FAFSA is required. The deadline for filing freshman financial aid applications for fall entry is March 1.

Computers: Wireless access is available. The FAU wireless network allows you to connect to the FAU network via a portable computing device, such as a laptop. That means that you not only have network access, but access to those resources that are available only via the FAU network, such as shared drives. All students may access the system. Hours vary depending on the lab. There are no time limits and no fees.

FLORIDA INSTITUTE OF TECHNOLOGY
Melbourne, FL 32901-6975

(321) 674-8030
(800) 888-4348; (321) 723-9468

Full-time: 1715 men, 700 women	**Faculty:** n/av
Part-time: 115 men, 75 women	**Ph.D.s:** 89%
Graduate: 1540 men, 990 women	**Student/Faculty:** n/av
Year: semesters, summer session	**Tuition:** $26,500
Application Deadline: open	**Room & Board:** $8000
Freshman Class: n/av	
SAT or ACT: required	**VERY COMPETITIVE**

Florida Institute of Technology, founded in 1958, offers undergraduate degrees in engineering, science, business, psychology, liberal arts, and aeronautics. Figures in the above capsule are approximate. There are 5 undergraduate schools and 6 graduate schools. In addition to regional accreditation, Florida Tech has baccalaureate program accreditation with ABET and CSAB. The library contains 425,251 volumes, 318,552 microform items, and 9167 audio/video tapes/CDs/DVDs, and subscribes to 25,474 periodicals including electronic. Computerized library services include interlibrary loans, database searching, Internet access, and laptop Internet portals. Special learning facilities include a learning resource center, radio station, and TV station. The 130-acre campus is in a suburban area 70 miles east of Orlando. Including any residence halls, there are 75 buildings.

Programs of Study: Florida Tech confers B.A. and B.S. degrees. Master's and doctoral degrees are also awarded. Bachelor's degrees are awarded in AGRICULTURE (environmental studies), BIOLOGICAL SCIENCE (biochemistry, biology/biological science, ecology, marine biology, and molecular biology), BUSINESS (accounting, business administration and management, electronic business, international business management, and management information systems), COMMUNICATIONS AND THE ARTS (communications), COMPUTER AND PHYSICAL SCIENCE (applied mathematics, astronomy, atmospheric sciences and meteorology, chemistry, computer science, oceanography, physics, planetary and space science, and software engineering), EDUCATION (mathematics education, middle school education, and science education), ENGINEERING AND ENVIRONMENTAL DESIGN (aeronautical engineering, aeronautical science, aviation administration/management, aviation computer technology, chemical engineering, civil engineering, computer engineering, construction engineering, electrical/electronics engineering, environmental science, mechanical engineering, military science, and ocean engineering), HEALTH PROFESSIONS (premedicine), SOCIAL SCIENCE (forensic studies, humanities, interdisciplinary studies, and psychology). Engineering, science, and aeronautics are the strongest academically. Aerospace engineering, mechanical engineering, and aviation are the largest.

Special: Florida Tech offers co-op programs in all majors. Students may choose to pursue more than 1 degree by completing degree requirements for each major. Internships are available in the senior year for many majors, including psychology, engineering, and aeronautics. Study abroad and work-study programs are available. There are 8 national honor societies and 1 departmental honors program.

Admissions: 6 freshmen graduated first in their class in a recent year.

Requirements: The SAT or ACT is required. In addition, applicants must be graduates of an accredited secondary school or have a GED certificate. At least 18 academic credits or Carnegie units are required, including 4 years each of English, math, and science. An experiential essay is required and an interview is recommended. A GPA of 2.8 is required. AP and CLEP credits are accepted. Important factors in the admissions decision are advanced placement or honors courses, recommendations by school officials, and extracurricular activities record.

Procedure: Freshmen are admitted fall and spring. Entrance exams should be taken during the junior year or the beginning of the senior year of high school. There are deferred admissions and rolling admissions plans. Application deadlines are open. The application fee is $50 (paper) or $40 (online). Applications are accepted on-line.

Financial Aid: The FAFSA is required. Check with the school for current application deadlines.

Computers: Wireless access is available. All students may access the system 24 hours per day. There are no time limits and no fees.

FLORIDA INTERNATIONAL UNIVERSITY
Miami, FL 33199   (305) 348-3675; (305) 348-3648

Full-time: 10107 men, 12472 women	**Faculty:** I, -$
Part-time: 4019 men, 5192 women	**Ph.D.s:** n/av
Graduate: 3111 men, 4817 women	**Student/Faculty:** n/av
Year: semesters, summer session	**Tuition:** $4580
Application Deadline:	**Room & Board:** $11,946
Freshman Class: 15978 applied, 5591 accepted, 2013 enrolled	
SAT CR/M/W: 582/575/571*	**ACT:** 26 **VERY COMPETITIVE+**

Florida International University, founded in 1965, is part of the State University System of Florida. Undergraduate degrees are offered through the Colleges of Architecture, the Arts, Arts and Sciences, Business Administration, Education, Engineering and Computing, Honors, Nursing and Health, Sciences, Social Work, Justice and Public Affairs, and the School of Accounting, Architecture, Art and Art History, Computing and Information Sciences, Criminal Justice, Hospitality and Tourism Management, Journalism and Mass Communication, Music, Public Administration, Public Health, Social Work, Theatre, Dance and Speech Communication. The Biscayne Bay and University Park campuses are in Miami. There are 10 undergraduate schools. In addition to regional accreditation, FIU has baccalaureate program accreditation with AACSB, ABET, ACCE, ACE-

JMC, APTA, ASLA, CSAB, CSWE, NAAB, NASAD, NASM, NCATE, NLN, and NRPA. The 2 libraries contain 2.1 million volumes, 3.6 million microform items, and 163,715 audio/video tapes/CDs/DVDs, and subscribe to 52,511 periodicals including electronic. Computerized library services include interlibrary loans, database searching, Internet access, and laptop Internet portals. Special learning facilities include a learning resource center, radio station, and an art museum. The 573-acre campus is in an urban area 10 miles west of downtown Miami. Including any residence halls, there are 76 buildings.

Programs of Study: FIU confers B.A., B.S., B.Ac., B.B.A., B.F.A., B.H.S.A., B.M., B.P.A., and B.S.N. degrees. Master's and doctoral degrees are also awarded. Bachelor's degrees are awarded in AGRICULTURE (environmental studies), BIOLOGICAL SCIENCE (biology/biological science and marine biology), BUSINESS (accounting, banking and finance, business administration and management, hospitality management services, international business management, management information systems, management science, marketing/retailing/merchandising, personnel management, and real estate), COMMUNICATIONS AND THE ARTS (art, art history and appreciation, communications, dance, dramatic arts, English, fine arts, French, German, music, Portuguese, Spanish, telecommunications, and visual and performing arts), COMPUTER AND PHYSICAL SCIENCE (applied mathematics, chemistry, computer science, geology, information sciences and systems, mathematics, physics, and statistics), EDUCATION (art education, early childhood education, education, education of the emotionally handicapped, education of the mentally handicapped, elementary education, English education, foreign languages education, health education, home economics education, mathematics education, music education, physical education, science education, social studies education, special education, and specific learning disabilities), ENGINEERING AND ENVIRONMENTAL DESIGN (architecture, biomedical engineering, chemical engineering, civil engineering, computer engineering, construction management, electrical/electronics engineering, environmental engineering, environmental science, industrial engineering, interior design, landscape architecture/design, and mechanical engineering), HEALTH PROFESSIONS (exercise science, health care administration, health science, nursing, and occupational therapy), SOCIAL SCIENCE (Asian/Oriental studies, criminal justice, dietetics, economics, geography, history, humanities, international relations, Italian studies, liberal arts/general studies, parks and recreation management, philosophy, political science/government, psychology, public administration, religion, social work, sociology, and women's studies). Business administration, psychology, and biology are the strongest academically.

Special: FIU offers co-op and work-study programs, and study abroad in 34 countries. Accelerated degree programs, nondegree study, dual majors, and B.A.-B.S. degrees in chemistry, environmental studies, and geology may also be arranged. There are 40 national honor societies, including Phi Beta Kappa, and a freshman honors program.

Admissions: 35% of the 2009-2010 applicants were accepted. The SAT scores for the 2009-2010 freshman class were: Critical Reading--5% below 500, 55% between 500 and 599, 37% between 600 and 700, and 2% above 700; Math--9% below 500, 55% between 500 and 599, 34% between 600 and 700, and 2% above 700; Writing--9% below 500, 58% between 500 and 599, 32% between 600 and 700, and 2% above 700. The ACT scores were 1% below 21, 21% between 21 and 23, 43% between 24 and 26, 22% between 27 and 28, and 12% above 28.

Requirements: The SAT or ACT is required. In addition, applicants must be graduates of an accredited secondary school or have a GED certificate. The required academic courses include 4 units in English, 3 each in math, natural science, and social studies, 2 in a foreign language, and 4 in academic electives. The university's placement tests must be taken the semester before attending. An interview may be required. A GPA of 2.0 is required. AP and CLEP credits are accepted. Important factors in the admissions decision are advanced placement or honors courses, evidence of special talent, and recommendations by school officials.

Procedure: Freshmen are admitted fall, spring, and summer. Entrance exams should be taken during the spring of the junior year. There are deferred admissions and rolling admissions plans. Application deadlines are open. Application fee is $30. Applications are accepted on-line.

Financial Aid: FIU is a member of CSS. The FAFSA is required. The deadline for filing freshman financial aid applications for fall entry is March 1.

Computers: Wireless access is available. FIU provides students with instructional and "open" computer labs. These labs are equipped with state of the art workstations that allow students access to software applications, internet access and printing capabilities. There are more than 1,900 stations around the campus in computer labs and at the library. All students may access the system. 8 A.M. to 4 A.M. There are no time limits and no fees.

FLORIDA STATE UNIVERSITY

Tallahassee, FL 32306-　　　　(850) 644-6200; (850) 644-0197

Full-time: 12,350 men, 15,630 women	**Faculty:** I, --$
Part-time: 1705 men, 1920 women	**Ph.D.s:** 91%
Graduate: 3315 men, 4535 women	**Student/Faculty:** n/av
Year: semesters, summer session	**Tuition:** $4110 ($18,960)
Application Deadline: see profile	**Room & Board:** $8000
Freshman Class: n/av	
SAT or ACT: required	**VERY COMPETITIVE**

Florida State University, a public institution founded in 1851, is a residential university designated as a Doctoral Research (Extensive) University by the Carnegie Foundation for the Advancement of Teaching. Figures in the above capsule are approximate. There are 15 undergraduate schools and 16 graduate schools. In addition to regional accreditation, FSU has baccalaureate program accreditation with AACSB, ABET, ADA, AHEA, ASLA, CSWE, FIDER, NASM, NCATE, NLN, and NRPA. The 6 libraries contain 2.9 million volumes, 9.1 million microform items, and 250,484 audio/video tapes/CDs/DVDs, and subscribe to 29,485 periodicals including electronic. Computerized library services include interlibrary loans, database searching, and Internet access. Special learning facilities include a learning resource center, art gallery, planetarium, radio station, TV station, nuclear accelerator, x-ray emission lab, marine lab, supercomputers, and the National High Magnetic Field Laboratory. The 451-acre campus is in a suburban area 163 miles west of Jacksonville. Including any residence halls, there are 224 buildings.

Programs of Study: FSU confers B.A., B.S., B.S.N., B.F.A, B.M., and B.M.Ed. degrees. Associates, master's, and doctoral degrees are also awarded. Bachelor's degrees are awarded in AGRICULTURE (environmental studies and plant science), BIOLOGICAL SCIENCE (biochemistry, biology/biological science, cell biology, ecology, evolutionary biology, genetics, marine biology, molecular biology, nutrition, physiology, and zoology), BUSINESS (accounting, banking and finance, business administration and management, entrepreneurial studies, fashion merchandising, hotel/motel and restaurant management, insurance and risk management, international business management, management science, marketing/retailing/merchandising, personnel management, recreation and leisure services, recreational facilities management, small business management, and sports management), COMMUNICATIONS AND THE ARTS (advertising, American literature, apparel design, art history and appreciation, broadcasting, classics, communications, creative writing, dance, dramatic arts, English, fiber/textiles/weaving, film arts, French, German, Greek, Italian, jazz, Latin, linguistics, music, music history and appreciation, music performance, music theory and composition, musical theater, piano/organ, public relations, Russian, Spanish, speech/debate/rhetoric, strings, studio art, theater design, voice, and winds), COMPUTER AND PHYSICAL SCIENCE (actuarial science, applied mathematics, atmospheric sciences and meteorology, chemical technology, chemistry, computer science, geology, information sciences and systems, mathematics, physics, and statistics), EDUCATION (art education, athletic training, early childhood education, education of the emotionally handicapped, education of the mentally handicapped, education of the visually handicapped, elementary education, English education, foreign languages education, health education, home economics education, mathematics education, music education, physical education, reading education, science education, social science education, and specific learning disabilities), ENGINEERING AND ENVIRONMENTAL DESIGN (bioengineering, biomedical engineering, chemical engineering, civil engineering, computer engineering, electrical/electronics engineering, environmental engineering, environmental science, graphic arts technology, industrial engineering, interior design, materials engineering, and mechanical engineering), HEALTH PROFESSIONS (community health work, music therapy, nursing, predentistry, premedicine, preoptometry, prepharmacy, preveterinary science, rehabilitation therapy, speech pathology/audiology, and sports medicine), SOCIAL SCIENCE (American studies, anthropology, Asian/Oriental studies, Caribbean studies, child care/child and family studies, classical/ancient civilization, clothing and textiles management/production/services, criminology, dietetics, Eastern European studies, economics, family/consumer studies, fashion design and technology, food science, geography, history, home economics, humanities, international relations, Latin American studies, philosophy, political science/government, prelaw, psychology, religion, Russian and Slavic studies, social science, social work, sociology, and women's studies). Biology, meteorology, and physics are the strongest academically. Biology, psychology, and business are the largest.

Special: Cross-registration with Florida Agricultural and Mechanical University and Tallahassee Community College is possible, as is study at FSU centers in London or Florence and in programs in Costa Rica, France, Russia, Spain, Switzerland, and Vietnam, among other countries. FSU offers cooperative programs in engineering, computer science, business, and communication, work-study programs, general studies and combined B.A.-B.S. degrees, dual majors, and accelerated degree programs. Internships are required in criminology, human science, education, nursing, and social work. There are preprofessional programs in health and law. There are 47 national honor societies, including Phi Beta Kappa, a freshman honors program, and 60 departmental honors programs.

Admissions: There were 14 National Merit finalists in a recent year.

Requirements: The SAT or ACT is required. In addition, it is recommended that in-state students have at least an A-/B+ weighted average and a satisfactory SAT or ACT score. Out-of-state students must meet higher standards. Applicants should have at least the following high school units; 4 in English, 3 in math, natural science, and social science, and 2 in a foreign language. Other factors include the number of honors, AP, and IB classes, strength of academic curriculum, class rank, among others. AP and CLEP credits are accepted. Important factors in the admissions decision are advanced placement or honors courses, evidence of special talent, and recommendations by school officials.

Procedure: Freshmen are admitted fall, spring, and summer. Entrance exams should be taken beginning in the second semester of the junior year. There is a rolling admissions plan. Check with the school for current application deadlines. The fall 2009 application fee was $20. Applications are accepted on-line.

Financial Aid: In a recent year, 96% of all full-time freshmen and 81% of continuing full-time students received some form of financial aid. 29% of all full-time freshmen and 33% of continuing full-time students received need-based aid. The average freshmen award was $2,670. 3% of undergraduate students work part-time. Average annual earnings from campus work are $2200. The average financial indebtedness of a recent graduate was $16,636. The FAFSA and the college's own financial statement are required. Check with the school for current application deadlines.

Computers: Wireless access is available. All students may access the system, although use of some machines is restricted to particular majors or graduate students. There are no time limits and no fees. It is strongly recommended that all students have a personal computer. Students enrolled in engineering programs must have a personal computer.

FORDHAM UNIVERSITY

Bronx, NY 10458

(718) 817-4000
(800) FORDHAM; (718) 367-9404

Full-time: 4000 men, 4035 women	**Faculty:** I, av$
Part-time: 200 men, 330 women	**Ph.D.s:** n/av
Graduate: 2645 men, 4170 women	**Student/Faculty:** n/av
Year: semesters, summer session	**Tuition:** $33,500
Application Deadline: see profile	**Room & Board:** $13,000
Freshman Class: n/av	
SAT or ACT: required	**HIGHLY COMPETITIVE**

Fordham University, founded in 1841, is a private institution offering an education based on the Jesuit tradition, with 2 campuses in New York: 1 in the Bronx and 1 in Manhattan near Lincoln Center. The figures in the above capsule and in this profile are approximate. There are 3 undergraduate schools and 6 graduate schools. In addition to regional accreditation, has baccalaureate program accreditation with AACSB and NCATE. The 4 libraries contain 2 million volumes, 3.1 million microform items, and 19,295 audio/video tapes/CDs/DVDs, and subscribe to 15,940 periodicals including electronic. Computerized library services include interlibrary loans, database searching, and Internet access. Special learning facilities include a learning resource center, radio station, a seismic station, an archeological site, and a biological field station. The 85-acre campus is in an urban area adjacent to the Bronx Zoo and New York Botanical Garden. Including any residence halls, there are 32 buildings.

Programs of Study: confers B.A., B.S., and B.F.A. degrees. Master's and doctoral degrees are also awarded. Bachelor's degrees are awarded in BIOLOGICAL SCIENCE (biology/biological science), BUSINESS (accounting, business administration and management, business economics, international business management, and marketing management), COMMUNICATIONS AND THE ARTS (art history and appreciation, broadcasting, classical languages, communications, comparative literature, dance, dramatic arts, English, film arts, fine arts, French, German, Italian, journalism, music, performing arts, Spanish, and visual and performing arts), COMPUTER AND PHYSICAL SCIENCE (chemistry, computer science, information sciences and systems, mathematics, physics, and science), ENGINEERING AND ENVIRONMENTAL DESIGN (engineering physics), SOCIAL SCIENCE (African studies, African American studies, American studies, anthropology, classical/ancient civilization, economics, French studies, German area studies, history, international studies, Italian studies, Latin American studies, medieval studies, Middle Eastern studies, philosophy, political science/government, psychology, religion, social science, social work, sociology, Spanish studies, theological studies, urban studies, and women's studies). Communications, social sciences, and English are the strongest academically. Business, psychology, and biology are the largest.

Special: Fordham University offers career-oriented internships in communications and other majors during the junior or senior year with New York City companies and institutions. A combined 3-2 engineering program is available with Columbia and Case Western Reserve Universities. Study abroad, a Washington semester, accelerated degrees, dual and student-designed majors, and pass/fail options are available. There are 6 national honor societies, including Phi Beta Kappa, and a freshman honors program.

Requirements: The SAT or ACT is required. In addition, applicants should have completed 4 years of high school English and 3 each of math, science, social studies, history, and foreign language. Applicants should submit the Common Application, which includes an essay. A guidance counselor recommendation is also required. Auditions are required for theater and dance majors. AP credits are accepted. Important factors in the admissions decision are advanced placement or honors courses, extracurricular activities record, and recommendations by school officials.

Procedure: Freshmen are admitted fall and spring. Entrance exams should be taken by December of the senior year. There is a deferred admissions plan. Applications should be filed by November 1 for spring entry, along with a $50 fee. Notifications are sent April 1. Applications are accepted on-line. A waiting list is maintained.

Financial Aid: In a recent year, 63% of all full-time freshmen and 63% of continuing full-time students received some form of financial aid. 62% of all full-time freshmen and 61% of continuing full-time students received need-based aid. The average freshmen award was $20,521. The average financial indebtedness of the 2009 graduate was $17,004. is a member of CSS. The CSS/Profile and FAFSA are required. Check with the school for current application deadlines.

Computers: All students may access the system. There are no time limits and no fees.

FRANCISCAN UNIVERSITY OF STEUBENVILLE

Steubenville, OH 43952-1763

(740) 283-6226
(800) 783-6220; (740) 284-5456

Full-time: 760 men, 1135 women	**Faculty:** IIA, --$
Part-time: 60 men, 85 women	**Ph.D.s:** 71%
Graduate: 165 men, 240 women	**Student/Faculty:** n/av
Year: semesters, summer session	**Tuition:** $20,320
Application Deadline: open	**Room & Board:** $7000
Freshman Class: n/av	
SAT or ACT: required	**VERY COMPETITIVE**

Franciscan University of Steubenville, founded in 1946 by the Franciscan Friars, is a private liberal arts institution committed to the Catholic Church and its renewal. Figures in the above capsule are approximate. There are 7 graduate schools. In addition to regional accreditation, Franciscan University has baccalaureate program accreditation with CSWE and NLN. The library contains 235,387 volumes, 250,968 microform items, and 892 audio/video tapes/CDs/DVDs, and subscribes to 5874 periodicals including electronic. Computerized library services include interlibrary loans, database searching, and Internet access. Special learning facilities include an art gallery and radio station. The 220-acre campus is in a small town 40 miles west of Pittsburgh. Including any residence halls, there are 25 buildings.

Programs of Study: Franciscan University confers B.A., B.S., and B.S.N. degrees. Associates and master's degrees are also awarded. Bachelor's degrees are awarded in BIOLOGICAL SCIENCE (biology/biological science), BUSINESS (accounting and business administration and management), COMMUNICATIONS AND THE ARTS (classics, communications, dramatic arts, English, French, German, and Spanish), COMPUTER AND PHYSICAL SCIENCE (chemistry, computer science, information sciences and systems, and mathematics), EDUCATION (elementary education), HEALTH PROFESSIONS (mental health/human services and nursing), SOCIAL SCIENCE (anthropology, economics, history, humanities and social science, law, philosophy, political science/government, psychology, religious music, social work, sociology, and theological studies). Theology, catechetics, and nursing are the strongest academically and the largest.

Special: Dual majors and internships for up to 6 credit hours are available in most majors. A humanities and Catholic culture major in Western tradition and minors in human life studies, film studies, Franciscan studies, and music are offered. Study abroad is offered through the university's course location in Gaming, Austria, where students spend a semester studying humanities as well as traveling through Europe. There are 5 national honor societies, a freshman honors program, and 25 departmental honors programs.

Admissions: 10 freshmen graduated first in their class in a recent year.

Requirements: The SAT or ACT is required. In addition, applicants should have completed 15 academic high school units, including 10 in 4 of the 5 following areas: English, foreign language, social science, math, and natural sciences. The GED is accepted. An essay is required and an interview is recommended. A GPA of 2.4 is required. AP and CLEP credits are accepted. Important factors in the admissions decision are advanced placement or honors courses, evidence of special talent, and leadership record.

Procedure: Freshmen are admitted fall, spring, and summer. Entrance exams should be taken in the spring of the junior year or the fall of the senior year. There is a rolling admissions plan. Application deadlines are open. The application fee is $20. Notification is sent on a rolling basis. Applications are accepted on-line. A waiting list is maintained.

Financial Aid: The FAFSA is required. Check with the school for current application deadlines.

Computers: All students may access the system. There are no time limits and no fees.

FRANKLIN AND MARSHALL COLLEGE

Lancaster, PA 17604-3003
      (717) 291-3953
(877) 678-9111; (717) 291-4389

Full-time: 1043 men, 1016 women	**Faculty:** 184; IIB, +$
Part-time: 21 men, 24 women	**Ph.D.s:** 97%
Graduate: none	**Student/Faculty:** 11 to 1
Year: semesters, summer session	**Tuition:** $36,480
Application Deadline: February 1	**Room & Board:** $9,174
Freshman Class: 5018 applied, 1873 accepted, 570 enrolled	
SAT CR/M: 641/654	**MOST COMPETITIVE**

Franklin and Marshall College, founded in 1787, is a private liberal arts institution. There are no undergraduate schools. The 2 libraries contain 436,822 volumes, 230,755 microform items, 9,982 audio/video tapes/CDs/DVDs, and subscribe to 2,980 periodicals including electronic. Computerized library services include inter-library loans, database searching, and Internet access. Special learning facilities include an art gallery, natural history museum, planetarium, radio station, TV station, academic technology services, advanced language lab, writing center, and student newspaper. The 209-acre campus is in a suburban area 60 miles west of Philadelphia. Including any residence halls, there are 45 buildings.

Programs of Study: F & M confers B.A. degrees. Bachelor's degrees are awarded in AGRICULTURE (environmental studies), BIOLOGICAL SCIENCE (biochemistry, biology/biological science, and neurosciences), BUSINESS (business administration and management), COMMUNICATIONS AND THE ARTS (art history and appreciation, classics, dramatic arts, English, fine arts, French, German, Greek, Latin, music, Spanish, and studio art), COMPUTER AND PHYSICAL SCIENCE (astronomy, astrophysics, chemistry, geology, mathematics, and physics), ENGINEERING AND ENVIRONMENTAL DESIGN (environmental science), SOCIAL SCIENCE (African studies, American studies, anthropology, economics, history, interdisciplinary studies, philosophy, political science/government, psychology, religion, and sociology). Chemistry, geosciences, and psychology are the strongest academically. Government, business, organizations and society are the largest.

Special: There is a 3-2 degree program in forestry and environmental studies with Duke University as well as 3-2 degree programs in engineering with the Pennsylvania State University College of Engineering, Columbia University, Rensselaer Polytechnic Institute, Case Western Reserve, and Washington University at St. Louis. Cross-registration is possible with the Lancaster Theological Seminary, the Central Pennsylvania Consortium, and Millersville University allows students to study at nearby Dickinson College or Gettysburg College. Students may also study architecture and urban planning at Columbia University, studio art at the School of Visual Arts in New York City, theater in Connecticut, oceanography in Massachusetts, and American studies at American University. There are study-abroad programs in England, France, Germany, Greece, Italy, Denmark, India, Japan, and other countries. There are internships for credit, joint majors, many minors, dual majors, student-designed majors, independent study, interdisciplinary studies, optional first-year seminars, collaborative projects, pass/fail options, and non-degree study. There are 12 national honor societies and including Phi Beta Kappa.

Admissions: 37% of the 2009-2010 applicants were accepted. The SAT scores for the 2009-2010 freshman class were: Critical Reading--% below 500, 23% between 500 and 599, 55% between 600 and 700, and 22 above 700; Math--1% below 500, 13% between 500 and 599, 63% between 600 and 700, and 23 above 700. 83% of the current freshmen were in the top fifth of their class; 96% were in the top two fifths.

Requirements: In addition, standardized tests are optional for students; if this option is selected, 2 recent graded writing samples are required. Applicants must be graduates of accredited secondary schools. Recommended college preparatory study includes 4 years each of English and math, 3 or 4 of foreign language, 3 each of lab science and history/social studies, and 1 or 2 courses in art or music. All students must also submit their high school transcripts, recommendations from a teacher and a counselor, and a personal essay. An interview is recommended. AP and CLEP credits are accepted. Important factors in the admissions decision are advanced placement or honors courses, recommendations by school officials, and extracurricular activities record.

Procedure: Freshmen are admitted fall and spring. Entrance exams should be taken by December of the senior year. There early decision, deferred admissions plan. Early decision applications should be filed by November 15; regular applications, by February 1 for fall entry, along with a $50 fee. Notification of early decision is sent December 15; regular decision, April 1. Applications are accepted on-line. 511 applicants were on a recent waiting list, 52 were accepted.

Financial Aid: In 2009-2010, 69% of all full-time freshmen and 70% of continuing full-time students received some form of financial aid. 45% of all full-time freshmen and 41% of continuing full-time students received need-based aid. The average freshmen award was $19,861. 44% of undergraduate students work part-time. The average financial indebtedness of the 2009 graduate was $24,752. F & M is a member of CSS. The CSS/Profile, FAFSA, and the college's own financial statement, and If applicable, the business/farm supplement and noncustodial parents statement are required. are required. The deadline for filing freshman financial aid applications for fall entry is February 1.

Computers: Wireless access is available. All students may access the system. 24 hours a day, 7 days a week. There are no time limits and no fees. It is strongly recommended that all students have a personal computer. An Apple is recommended.

FREED-HARDEMAN UNIVERSITY
Henderson, TN 38340

(731) 989-6651
(800) 630-3480; (731) 989-6047

Full-time: 615 men, 755 women	**Faculty:** IIA, --$
Part-time: 50 men, 65 women	**Ph.D.s:** 69%
Graduate: 200 men, 335 women	**Student/Faculty:** n/av
Year: semesters, summer session	**Tuition:** $15,000
Application Deadline: open	**Room & Board:** $7000
Freshman Class: n/av	
ACT: required	**VERY COMPETITIVE**

Freed-Hardeman University, founded in 1869, is a private, liberal arts institution associated with Churches of Christ. Figures in the above capsule are approximate. There are 6 undergraduate schools and 4 graduate schools. In addition to regional accreditation, FHU has baccalaureate program accreditation with ACBSP, CSWE, and NCATE. The library contains 175,748 volumes, 240,000 microform items, and 43,000 audio/video tapes/CDs/DVDs, and subscribes to 1650 periodicals including electronic. Computerized library services include interlibrary loans, database searching, and Internet access. Special learning facilities include a learning resource center, art gallery, radio station, TV station, aand undergraduate research center. The 120-acre campus is in a small town 85 miles east of Memphis and 13 miles south of Jackson. Including any residence halls, there are 39 buildings.

Programs of Study: FHU confers B.A., B.S., B.B.A., and B.S.W. degrees. Associates and master's degrees are also awarded. Bachelor's degrees are awarded in BIOLOGICAL SCIENCE (biochemistry and biology/biological science), BUSINESS (accounting, banking and finance, and business administration and management), COMMUNICATIONS AND THE ARTS (art, broadcasting, communications, dramatic arts, English, fine arts, journalism, public relations, and speech/debate/rhetoric), COMPUTER AND PHYSICAL SCIENCE (chemistry, computer programming, computer science, information sciences and systems, mathematics, and physical sciences), EDUCATION (art education, early childhood education, elementary education, health education, middle school education, music education, physical education, science education, secondary education, and special education), ENGINEERING AND ENVIRONMENTAL DESIGN (preengineering), HEALTH PROFESSIONS (predentistry, premedicine, preoptometry, prepharmacy, and preveterinary science), SOCIAL SCIENCE (biblical studies, child care/child and family studies, criminal justice, family/consumer studies, history, ministries, psychology, and social work). Premedicine, preengineering, and business are the strongest academically. Business, Bible, and elementary education are the largest.

Special: FHU offers study abroad in Belgium and Italy, a B.A.-B.S. degree in Bible, biology, communication, and arts and humanities, co-op programs, a dual major, field practicum opportunities in several majors, student-designed majors, 3-2 engineering degrees with 6 universities, and nondegree study. There are 4 national honor societies, a freshman honors program, and 13 departmental honors programs.

Requirements: The ACT is required, with a minimum composite score of 19. Candidates for admission should be graduates of an accredited secondary school. An interview is recommended. A GPA of 2.25 is required. AP and CLEP credits are accepted. Important factors in the admissions decision are personality/intangible qualities, recommendations by school officials, and leadership record.

Procedure: Freshmen are admitted fall, spring, and summer. Entrance exams should be taken in early fall or summer before senior year. There are early admissions and rolling admissions plans. Application deadlines are open. Applications are accepted on-line.

Financial Aid: The FAFSA is required. Check with the school for current application deadlines.

Computers: All students may access the system.

FURMAN UNIVERSITY
Greenville, SC 29613   (864) 294-2034; (864) 294-2018

Full-time: 1122 men, 1500 women	**Faculty:** 229; IIB, +$
Part-time: 64 men, 68 women	**Ph.D.s:** 96%
Graduate: 37 men, 173 women	**Student/Faculty:** 11 to 1
Year: semesters, summer session	**Tuition:** $36,656
Application Deadline: January 15	**Room & Board:** $9170
Freshman Class: 4538 applied, 3080 accepted, 656 enrolled	
SAT CR/M/W: 635/640/630	**ACT:** 28 **HIGHLY COMPETITIVE+**

Founded in 1826, Furman University is an independent liberal arts institution offering undergraduate and graduate programs. In addition to regional accreditation, Furman has baccalaureate program accreditation with NASM and NCATE.

The 3 libraries contain 526,690 volumes, 862,324 microform items, and 9200 audio/video tapes/CDs/DVDs, and subscribe to 13,200 periodicals including electronic. Computerized library services include interlibrary loans, database searching, Internet access, and laptop Internet portals. Special learning facilities include a learning resource center, art gallery, planetarium, radio station, observatory, and cable TV with on-campus broadcasting. The 750-acre campus is in a suburban area 5 miles north of Greenville. Including any residence halls, there are 69 buildings.

Programs of Study: Furman confers B.A., B.S., B.L.A., and B.M. degrees. Master's degrees are also awarded. Bachelor's degrees are awarded in BIOLOGICAL SCIENCE (biology/biological science and neurosciences), BUSINESS (accounting and business administration and management), COMMUNICATIONS AND THE ARTS (art, classics, communications, dramatic arts, English, French, German, Greek, Latin, music, music performance, music theory and composition, and Spanish), COMPUTER AND PHYSICAL SCIENCE (chemistry, computer science, information sciences and systems, mathematics, and physics), EDUCATION (education, elementary education, and music education), ENGINEERING AND ENVIRONMENTAL DESIGN (environmental science and preengineering), HEALTH PROFESSIONS (exercise science), SOCIAL SCIENCE (Asian/Oriental studies, economics, history, philosophy, political science/government, psychology, religion, religious music, sociology, and urban studies). Chemistry, biology, and music are the strongest academically. Political science, history, and business administration are the largest.

Special: A 3-2 engineering degree is offered with the Georgia Institute of Technology, Clemson, North Carolina State, and Auburn and Washington Universities. Internships, study abroad in at least 17 countries, a Washington semester with an internship in a government agency or political organization, and work-study programs are offered. B.A.-B.S. degrees, dual majors, interdisciplinary majors such as computer science-math, math-economics, and computing-business, and student-designed majors are available. A bachelor of general studies degree is granted in the evening division. Nondegree study and pass/fail options are possible. Furman features student/faculty research programs. There are 20 national honor societies, including Phi Beta Kappa.

Admissions: 68% of the 2009-2010 applicants were accepted. The SAT scores for the 2009-2010 freshman class were: Critical Reading--3% below 500, 25% between 500 and 599, 48% between 600 and 700, and 24% above 700; Math--5% below 500, 20% between 500 and 599, 57% between 600 and 700, and 18% above 700; Writing--5% below 500, 25% between 500 and 599, 52% between 600 and 700, and 18% above 700. The ACT scores were 3% below 21, 9% between 21 and 23, 26% between 24 and 26, 17% between 27 and 28, and 45% above 28. 81% of the current freshmen were in the top fifth of their class; 95% were in the top two-fifths. There were 28 National Merit finalists. 33 freshmen graduated first in their class.

Requirements: Applicants must be high school graduates or hold a GED. Students should have earned at least 20 units in high school, including 4 of English, 3 each of history, math, and science, and 2 each of social studies and foreign language. A portfolio or an audition, where appropriate, is required. AP credits are accepted. Important factors in the admissions decision are advanced placement or honors courses, extracurricular activities record, and leadership record.

Procedure: Freshmen are admitted in the fall. Entrance exams should be taken by late junior or early senior year. There is an early decision admissions plan. Early decision applications should be filed by November 15; regular applications, by January 15 for fall entry. Notification of early decision is sent December 15;

regular decision, March 15. Applications are accepted on-line. 212 applicants were on a recent waiting list, 38 were accepted.

Financial Aid: In 2009-2010, 85% of all full-time freshmen and 83% of continuing full-time students received some form of financial aid. 53% of all full-time freshmen and 47% of continuing full-time students received need-based aid. The average freshmen award was $26,700. 47% of undergraduate students work part-time. Average annual earnings from campus work are $2400. The average financial indebtedness of the 2009 graduate was $27,300. Furman is a member of CSS. The CSS/Profile, FAFSA, and the state aid form are required. The deadline for filing freshman financial aid applications for fall entry is February 15.

Computers: Wireless access is available. 98% of students have PCs (mostly laptops); all have wired connections to the network; 100% of classrooms and public spaces have wireless access. All students may access the system 24 hours a day. There are no time limits and no fees.

GALLAUDET UNIVERSITY
Washington, DC 20002-3695

(202) 651-5750
(800) 995-0550; (202) 651-5744

Full-time: 485 men, 575 women	**Faculty:** IIA, ++$
Part-time: 105 men, 105 women	**Ph.Ds:** 66%
Graduate: 100 men, 335 women	**Student/Faculty:** n/av
Year: semesters, summer session	**Tuition:** $12,000
Application Deadline: open	**Room & Board:** $10,000
Freshman Class: n/av	
SAT or ACT: recommended	**SPECIAL**

Gallaudet University, founded in 1864 as a university designed exclusively for deaf and hard-of-hearing students, offers programs in liberal and fine arts, teacher preparation, and professional training. Figures in the above capsule are approximate. There are 4 undergraduate schools and 4 graduate schools. In addition to regional accreditation, Gallaudet has baccalaureate program accreditation with CSWE and NCATE. The library contains 215,500 volumes, 371,000 microform items, and 4530 audio/video tapes/CDs/DVDs, and subscribes to 1415 periodicals including electronic. Computerized library services include interlibrary loans and database searching. Special learning facilities include a learning resource center, TV station, child development center, national and international centers on deafness, and research institute on deafness. The 99-acre campus is in an urban area in Washington, D.C. Including any residence halls, there are 30 buildings.

Programs of Study: Gallaudet confers B.A. and B.S. degrees. Associate, master's, and doctoral degrees are also awarded. Bachelor's degrees are awarded in BIOLOGICAL SCIENCE (biology/biological science), BUSINESS (accounting, business administration and management, entrepreneurial studies, management science, and recreation and leisure services), COMMUNICATIONS AND THE ARTS (apparel design, art history and appreciation, communications, dramatic arts, English, French, German, graphic design, media arts, Russian, Spanish, and studio art), COMPUTER AND PHYSICAL SCIENCE (chemical technology, chemistry, computer science, mathematics, and physics), EDUCATION (art education, early childhood education, elementary education, home economics education, physical education, and secondary education), ENGINEERING AND ENVIRONMENTAL DESIGN (engineering technology), HEALTH PROFESSIONS (recreation therapy), SOCIAL SCIENCE (child care/child and family studies, economics, family/consumer studies, history, interpreter for the deaf, parks and recreation management, philosophy, political science/government, psychology, religion, and social work).

Special: Gallaudet offers co-op programs, cross-registration with the Consortium of Universities of the Washington Metropolitan Area, and a 3-2 engineering degree with George Washington University. Internships, study abroad, dual majors, work-study programs, and B.A.-B.S. degrees are available. There is a Phi Beta Kappa honors program and a freshman honors program.

Requirements: Applicants must submit a recent audiogram. SAT or ACT scores may be submitted. High school transcripts, letters of recommendation, and writing samples are required. The GED is accepted. AP and CLEP credits are accepted. Important factors in the admissions decision are advanced placement or honors courses, recommendations by school officials, and leadership record.

Procedure: Freshmen are admitted fall and spring. Entrance exams should be taken in October or November of the senior year. There are deferred admissions and rolling admissions plans. Application deadlines are open. The fall 2009 application fee was $35.

Financial Aid: The FAFSA and the college's own financial statement are required. Check with the school for current application deadlines.

Computers: All students may access the system 24 hours a day. There are no time limits and no fees.

GEORGE FOX UNIVERSITY
Newberg, OR 97132

(503) 554-2240
(800) 765-4369; (503) 554-3110

Full-time: 672 men, 1007 women	**Faculty:** 114; IIA, --$
Part-time: 115 men, 173 women	**Ph.D.s:** 67%
Graduate: 625 men, 796 women	**Student/Faculty:** 15 to 1
Year: semesters, summer session	**Tuition:** $26,180
Application Deadline: February 1	**Room & Board:** $8320
Freshman Class: 1528 applied, 1052 accepted, 413 enrolled	
SAT CR/M/W: 550/540/520	**ACT:** 23 **VERY COMPETITIVE**

George Fox University, founded in 1891, is a Christian university of the humanities, sciences, and professional studies. There are 5 undergraduate schools and 4 graduate schools. In addition to regional accreditation, George Fox has baccalaureate program accreditation with ABET, CSWE, NASM, and NCATE. The 2 libraries contain 218,240 volumes, 211,676 microform items, and 7266 audio/video tapes/CDs/DVDs, and subscribe to 5374 periodicals including electronic. Computerized library services include interlibrary loans, database searching, Internet access, and laptop Internet portals. Special learning facilities include a learning resource center, art gallery, radio station, television production studio, pottery kiln, and the 77-acre Tilikum Retreat Center located 7 miles from campus. The 85-acre campus is in a small town 23 miles southwest of Portland. Including any residence halls, there are 80 buildings.

Programs of Study: George Fox confers B.A., B.S., B.S.A.T., and B.S.W. degrees. Master's and doctoral degrees are also awarded. Bachelor's degrees are awarded in BIOLOGICAL SCIENCE (biology/biological science), BUSINESS (accounting, business administration and management, business communications, management information systems, management science, and organizational leadership and management), COMMUNICATIONS AND THE ARTS (art, communications, creative writing, dramatic arts, film arts, literature, multimedia, music, and Spanish), COMPUTER AND PHYSICAL SCIENCE (chemistry, computer science, information sciences and systems, and mathematics), EDUCATION (athletic training, elementary education, and music education), ENGINEERING AND ENVIRONMENTAL DESIGN (engineering and applied science), HEALTH PROFESSIONS (allied health, health, health care administration, nursing, predentistry, premedicine, and preveterinary science), SOCIAL SCIENCE (behavioral science, biblical studies, cognitive science, economics, family/consumer studies, history, international studies, ministries, philosophy, political science/government, prelaw, psychology, religion, social science, social work, and sociology). Business, nursing, and elementary education are the largest.

Special: There is a 3-2 engineering degree with the University of Portland, Oregon State University, and Washington University in St. Louis and cross-registration through the Oregon Independent College Association. George Fox also offers a 3-1 cooperative degree program with the Fashion Institute of Design and Merchandising (FIDM) in Los Angeles. Students can complete a semester at the Contemporary Music Center in Martha's Vineyard or the Los Angeles Film Studies Center. George Fox offers internships with area companies, study abroad, and a Washington semester through the Council of Christian Colleges and Universities. Work-study programs, accelerated degrees, dual and student-designed interdisciplinary majors, and pass/fail options in upper-division courses outside of the major also are offered. There are 3 national honor societies and a freshman honors program.

Admissions: 69% of the 2009-2010 applicants were accepted. The SAT scores for the 2009-2010 freshman class were: Critical Reading--27% below 500, 43% between 500 and 599, 25% between 600 and 700, and 5% above 700; Math--33% below 500, 37% between 500 and 599, 26% between 600 and 700, and 4% above 700; Writing--32% below 500, 46% between 500 and 599, 19% between 600 and 700, and 3% above 700. The ACT scores were 22% below 21, 35% between 21 and 23, 20% between 24 and 26, 11% between 27 and 28, and 12% above 28. 30% of the current freshmen were in the top fifth of their class; 46% were in the top two fifths. 26 freshmen graduated first in their class.

Requirements: The SAT or ACT is required. In addition, applicants need 16 academic credits or 14 Carnegie units, including a suggested 4 units of English, 3 units of social studies, 2 units each of a foreign language, math, and science, and 1 unit of health and phys ed. An essay and 2 personal recommendations are required; a portfolio, audition, and interview are recommended in certain majors. A GPA of 2.6 is required. AP and CLEP credits are accepted. Important factors in the admissions decision are advanced placement or honors courses, extracurricular activities record, and leadership record.

Procedure: Freshmen are admitted fall and spring. Entrance exams should be taken in fall or winter. There are early admissions, deferred admissions, and rolling admissions plans. Applications should be filed by February 1 for fall entry and December 1 for spring entry. The fall 2009 application fee was $40. Notification is sent on a rolling basis. Applications are accepted on-line.

Financial Aid: In 2009-2010, 99% of all full-time freshmen and 96% of continuing full-time students received some form of financial aid. 78% of all full-time freshmen and 73% of continuing full-time students received need-based aid. The average freshman award was $22,829. Average annual earnings from campus work are $3715. The average financial indebtedness of the 2009 graduate was $23,540. George Fox is a member of CSS. The FAFSA and the state aid form are required. The priority date for freshman financial aid applications for fall entry is February 1.

Computers: All full-time undergraduates are provided with a laptop computer as part of their tuition. The wireless network is accessible in all academic classrooms, the library, the outdoor quad, meeting areas, the student union, and dorm lobbies. All students may access the system. There are no time limits and no fees.

GEORGE MASON UNIVERSITY
Fairfax, VA 22030-4444   **(703) 993-2400; (703) 993-4622**

Full-time: 7147 men, 8042 women	**Faculty:** 1041; I, -$
Part-time: 2203 men, 2310 women	**Ph.D.s:** 90%
Graduate: 5117 men, 7248 women	**Student/Faculty:** 15 to 1
Year: semesters, summer session	**Tuition:** $8024 ($24,008)
Application Deadline: January 15	**Room & Board:** $7700
Freshman Class: 13732 applied, 8691 accepted, 2656 enrolled	
SAT CR/M: 560/570	**ACT:** 25 **VERY COMPETITIVE**

George Mason University, founded in 1972, is an entrepreneurial public institution with national distinction in a range of academic fields. The university has undergraduate and graduate degree programs in engineering, information technology, biotechnology, and health care. There are 8 undergraduate schools and 11 graduate schools. In addition to regional accreditation, Mason has baccalaureate program accreditation with AACSB, ABET, CSAB, CSWE, NASM, and NCATE. The 5 libraries contain 1.9 million volumes, 3.2 million microform items, and 43,289 audio/video tapes/CDs/DVDs, and subscribe to 56,433 periodicals including electronic. Computerized library services include interlibrary loans, database searching, Internet access, and laptop Internet portals. Special learning facilities include a learning resource center, art gallery, radio station, TV station, astronomy observatory, and the Smithsonian Conservation and Research Center. The 806-acre campus is in a suburban area in the Greater Washington Metropolitan area, 21 miles southwest of Washington, D.C. Including any residence halls, there are 115 buildings.

Programs of Study: Mason confers B.A., B.S., B.F.A., B.I.S., B.S.E.D., and B.S.N. degrees. Master's and doctoral degrees are also awarded. Bachelor's degrees are awarded in AGRICULTURE (environmental studies), BIOLOGICAL SCIENCE (biology/biological science and neurosciences), BUSINESS (accounting, banking and finance, business administration and management, marketing/retailing/merchandising, operations management, and tourism), COMMUNICATIONS AND THE ARTS (art history and appreciation, communications, communications technology, dance, dramatic arts, English, film arts, French, music, Spanish, video, and visual and performing arts), COMPUTER AND PHYSICAL SCIENCE (astronomy, chemistry, computer science, earth science, geology, information sciences and systems, mathematics, physics, science and management, and software engineering), EDUCATION (athletic training and physical education), ENGINEERING AND ENVIRONMENTAL DESIGN (civil engineering, computational sciences, computer engineering, electrical/electronics engineering, industrial engineering, and systems engineering), HEALTH PROFESSIONS (community health work, health science, medical technology, and nursing), SOCIAL SCIENCE (anthropology, criminal justice, economics, geography, history, interdisciplinary studies, international relations, Latin American studies, parks and recreation management, philosophy, political science/government, psychology, public administration, religion, Russian and Slavic studies, social work, and sociology). Accounting, biology, and psychology are the largest.

Special: Mason offers internships through academic departments and on-campus work-study programs. Also available are dual and student-designed majors, accelerated degrees, non-degree study, and pass/fail options. New Century College is an integrated program of study that emphasizes collaboration, experimental learning, and self-reflection. Mason also offers the Smithsonian Semester, a 16-credit resident program in conservation studies at the Smithsonian Conservation and Research Center in Front Royal, Virginia. There are 4 national honor societies, a freshman honors program, several departmental honors programs, and a universitywide honors program.

Admissions: 63% of the 2009-2010 applicants were accepted. The SAT scores for the 2009-2010 freshman class were: Critical Reading--15% below 500, 52% between 500 and 599, 28% between 600 and 700, and 6% above 700; Math--12% below 500, 49% between 500 and 599, 34% between 600 and 700, and 5% above 700. The ACT scores were 4% below 21, 30% between 21 and 23, 37% between 24 and 26, 15% between 27 and 28, and 14% above 28. 44% of the current freshmen were in the top fifth of their class; 83% were in the top two fifths.

Requirements: The ACT is recommended. A score-optional review of applications allows applicants to be considered for admission without submitting test scores. Applicants must be graduates of an accredited secondary school or have a GED certificate. A minimum high school GPA of 3.5 is recommended. A minimum of 18 academic credits is required, including 4 years of English, 3 each of math, science, lab science, social studies, and academic electives, and 2 of foreign language. A written personal statement is required. A GPA of 2.0 is required. AP and CLEP credits are accepted. Important factors in the admissions decision are advanced placement or honors courses, evidence of special talent, and recommendations by school officials.

Procedure: Freshmen are admitted fall, spring, and summer. Entrance exams should be taken during the spring of the junior year. There are early action and deferred admissions plan. Applications should be filed by January 15 for fall entry and October 15 for spring entry. The fall 2009 application fee was $75. Notifications are sent April 1. Applications are accepted on-line ($55 fee). A waiting list is maintained.

Financial Aid: In 2009-2010, 67% of all full-time freshmen and 61% of continuing full-time students received some form of financial aid. 43% of all full-time freshmen and 44% of continuing full-time students received need-based aid. The average freshman award was $12,012. Need-based scholarships or need-based grants averaged $7182 ($24,800 maximum); need-based self-help aid (loans and jobs) averaged $3660 ($8500 maximum); non-need-based athletic scholarships averaged $16,156 ($36,533 maximum); and other non-need-based awards and non-need-based scholarships averaged $5940 ($33,540 maximum). The average financial indebtedness of the 2009 graduate was $19,582. The FAFSA is required. The priority date for freshman financial aid applications for fall entry is March 1.

Computers: Wireless access is available. Information regarding computer lab locations and hours of operation, quantity of PCs, and the university's wireless system is available at GMU's Classroom Technologies web site. All students may access the system 24 hours per day. There are no time limits and no fees. Students in some programs are encouraged to have a personal computer.

Full-time: 4240 men, 5515 women	**Faculty:** I, +$
Part-time: 505 men, 520 women	**Ph.D.s:** n/av
Graduate: 6120 men, 7230 women	**Student/Faculty:** n/av
Year: semesters, summer session	**Tuition:** $39,500
Application Deadline: see profile	**Room & Board:** $11,500
Freshman Class: n/av	
SAT or ACT: required	**MOST COMPETITIVE**

George Washington University, founded in 1821, is a private institution providing degree programs in arts and sciences, business, engineering, international affairs, health sciences, education, law, and public health. Figures in the above capsule are approximate. There are 7 undergraduate schools and 9 graduate schools. In addition to regional accreditation, GW has baccalaureate program accreditation with AACSB, ABET, CAHEA, CSAB, NASAD, NASM, and NCATE. Computerized library services include interlibrary loans and database searching. Special learning facilities include a learning resource center, art gallery, radio station, and TV station. The 37-acre campus is in an urban area 3 blocks west of the White House. Including any residence halls, there are 123 buildings.

Programs of Study: GW confers B.A., B.S., B.Accy., B.B.A., B.Mus., B.S.C.E., B.S.C.Eng., B.S.C.S., B.S.E.E., B.S.H.S., B.S.M.E., and B.S.S.A. degrees. Associates, master's, and doctoral degrees are also awarded. Bachelor's degrees are awarded in BIOLOGICAL SCIENCE (biology/biological science), BUSINESS (accounting, banking and finance, business administration and management, business economics, human resources, international business management, marketing management, and tourism), COMMUNICATIONS AND THE ARTS (art history and appreciation, broadcasting, Chinese, classics, communications, dance, dramatic arts, English, fine arts, French, German, Japanese, journalism, literature, multimedia, music, music performance, public relations, Russian, and Spanish), COMPUTER AND PHYSICAL SCIENCE (applied mathematics, chemistry, computer science, geology, information sciences and systems, mathematics, physics, statistics, and systems analysis), ENGINEERING AND ENVIRONMENTAL DESIGN (civil engineering, computer engineering, electrical/electronics engineering, environmental science, and mechanical engineering), HEALTH PROFESSIONS (clinical science, emergency medical technologies, medical laboratory technology, nuclear medical technology, physician's assistant, premedicine, radiological science, and speech pathology/audiology), SOCIAL SCIENCE (American studies, anthropology, archeology, criminal justice, East Asian studies, economics, European studies, geography, history, human services, humanities, interdisciplinary studies, international relations, Judaic studies, Latin American studies, liberal arts/general studies, Middle Eastern studies, philosophy, physical fitness/movement, political science/government, psychology, religion, and sociology). Political communication, international affairs, and biological sciences are the strongest academically. Psychology, political science, and international affairs are the largest.

Special: Cross-registration is available through the Consortium of Colleges and Universities. There are co-op programs in education, business, engineering, arts and sciences, and international affairs and internships in the Washington metropolitan area. Study abroad in locations throughout the world, work-study programs, dual majors, student-designed majors, and a 3-2 engineering degree program with 8 colleges are also available. Nondegree study, a general studies degree, credit by exam, and pass/fail options are possible. There are 12 national honor societies, including Phi Beta Kappa, a freshman honors program, and 21 departmental honors programs.

Requirements: The SAT or ACT is required. In addition, students must have successfully completed a strong academic program in high school. SAT: Subject tests are strongly recommended. An essay, 1 teacher recommendation, and 1 counselor recommendation are required. An interview is encouraged. AP and CLEP credits are accepted. Important factors in the admissions decision are advanced placement or honors courses, recommendations by school officials, and leadership record.

Procedure: Freshmen are admitted to all sessions. Entrance exams should be taken in the junior year or the fall semester of the senior year. There are early decision and deferred admissions plans. Check with the school for current application deadlines. The fall 2009 application fee was $60. Applications are accepted online. A waiting list is maintained.

Financial Aid: GW is a member of CSS. The CSS/Profile and FAFSA are required. Check with the school for current application deadlines.

Computers: All students may access the system at any time. There are no time limits and no fees. It is strongly recommended that all students have a personal computer. A IBM, Mac, Dell, or Compaq is recommended.

GEORGETOWN UNIVERSITY
Washington, DC 20057   (202) 687-3600; (202) 687-5084

Full-time: 3202 men, 3913 women	**Faculty:** I, +$
Part-time: 135 men, 183 women	**Ph.D.s:** 74%
Graduate: 4647 men, 4357 women	**Student/Faculty:** 11 to 1
Year: semesters, summer session	**Tuition:** $39,036
Application Deadline: January 10	**Room & Board:** $8745
Freshman Class: 18619 applied, 3683 accepted, 1558 enrolled	
SAT or ACT: required	**MOST COMPETITIVE**

Georgetown University, founded in 1789, is a private institution affiliated with the Roman Catholic Church and offers programs in arts and sciences, business administration, foreign service, languages and linguistics, and nursing. There are 4 undergraduate schools and 3 graduate schools. In addition to regional accreditation, Georgetown has baccalaureate program accreditation with AACSB. The 6 libraries contain 3.0 million volumes, 4.0 million microform items, and 54,513 audio/video tapes/CDs/DVDs, and subscribe to 61,257 periodicals including electronic. Computerized library services include interlibrary loans, database searching, Internet access, and laptop Internet portals. Special learning facilities include a learning resource center, art gallery, planetarium, radio station, and TV station. The 104-acre campus is in an urban area 1.5 miles northwest of downtown Washington D.C. Including any residence halls, there are 64 buildings.

Programs of Study: Georgetown confers A.B., B.S., B.A.L.S., B.S.B.A., B.S.F.S., and B.S.N. degrees. Master's and doctoral degrees are also awarded. Bachelor's degrees are awarded in BIOLOGICAL SCIENCE (biochemistry and biology/biological science), BUSINESS (accounting, banking and finance, business administration and management, international business management, and marketing/retailing/merchandising), COMMUNICATIONS AND THE ARTS (Arabic, Chinese, classics, comparative literature, English, fine arts, French, German, Italian, Japanese, linguistics, Portuguese, Russian, and Spanish), COMPUTER AND PHYSICAL SCIENCE (chemistry, computer science, mathematics, and physics), HEALTH PROFESSIONS (health and nursing), SOCIAL SCIENCE (American studies, anthropology, economics, history, interdisciplinary studies, international relations, philosophy, political science/government, psychology, religion, and sociology). International affairs, government, and international politics are the largest.

Special: Cross-registration is available with a consortium of universities in the Washington metropolitian area. Opportunities are provided for internships, study abroad in 30 countries, work-study programs, student-designed majors, and dual majors. A liberal studies degree, B.A. and B.S. degrees, non-degree study, credit by examination, and pass/fail options are also offered. There is a chapter of Phi Beta Kappa and a freshman honors program.

Admissions: 20% of the 2009-2010 applicants were accepted. The SAT scores for the 2009-2010 freshman class were: Critical Reading--1% below 500, 10% between 500 and 599, 43% between 600 and 700, and 46% above 700; Math--1% below 500, 8% between 500 and 599, 42% between 600 and 700, and 50% above 700. The ACT scores were 1% below 21, 10% between 21 and 23, 10% between 24 and 26, 16% between 27 and 28, and 63% above 28.

Requirements: The SAT or ACT is required. In addition, graduation from an accredited secondary school is required, including 4 years of English, a minimum of 2 each of a foreign language, math, and social studies, and 1 of natural science. An additional 2 years each of math and science is required for students intending to major in math, science, nursing, or business. SAT subject tests are strongly recommended. AP credits are accepted. Important factors in the admissions decision are evidence of special talent and leadership record.

Procedure: Freshmen are admitted in the fall. Entrance exams should be taken in the junior year and again at the beginning of the senior year. There is a deferred admissions plan. Applications should be filed by January 10 for fall entry, along with a $65 fee. Notifications are sent April 1. 2425 applicants were on a recent waiting list, 158 were accepted.

Financial Aid: Average annual earnings from campus work are $3000. The average financial indebtedness of the 2009 graduate was $27,117. Georgetown is a member of CSS. The CSS/Profile and FAFSA, and non-custodial profile, business/farm supplement, and tax returns are required. The deadline for filing freshman financial aid applications for fall entry is February 1.

Computers: There is a campuswide wired network in all of the dorms. One network jack per dorm resident in the room is guaranteed. The campus wireless network is available in all identified common areas of the university where individuals congregate and work collaboratively, and in select locations to facilitate teaching, research, and learning. There are 11 computer labs and print stations across campus open to students, containing a variety of Windows and Apple computers. All students may access the system. There are no time limits and no fees.

GEORGIA INSTITUTE OF TECHNOLOGY

Atlanta, GA 30332   **(404) 894-4154; (404) 894-9511**

Full-time: 8624 men, 3798 women	**Faculty:** I, +$
Part-time: 799 men, 294 women	**Ph.D.s:** 96%
Graduate: 5096 men, 1680 women	**Student/Faculty:** 20 to 1
Year: semesters, summer session	**Tuition:** $14,781 (32,386)
Application Deadline: January 15	**Room & Board:** $8516

Freshman Class: 11432 applied, 6721 accepted, 2645 enrolled
SAT CR/M/W: 640/689/632   **ACT:** required

HIGHLY COMPETITIVE+

Georgia Institute of Technology, founded in 1885, is a public technological institution offering programs in architecture, management, policy, international affairs, engineering, computing, and science. There are 6 undergraduate schools and 6 graduate schools. In addition to regional accreditation, Georgia Tech has baccalaureate program accreditation with AACSB, ABET, ACCE, NAAB, and NASAD. The 2 libraries contain 2.5 million volumes, 4.6 million microform items, and 317,523 audio/video tapes/CDs/DVDs, and subscribe to 44,875 periodicals including electronic. Computerized library services include interlibrary loans, database searching, Internet access, and laptop Internet portals. Special learning facilities include a learning resource center, art gallery, radio station, and TV station. The 450-acre campus is in an urban area Atlanta. Including any residence halls, there are 223 buildings.

Programs of Study: Georgia Tech confers B.S. degrees. Master's and doctoral degrees are also awarded. Bachelor's degrees are awarded in BIOLOGICAL SCIENCE (biology/biological science), BUSINESS (business administration and management and international economics), COMMUNICATIONS AND THE ARTS (industrial design), COMPUTER AND PHYSICAL SCIENCE (applied mathematics, applied physics, chemistry, computer science, earth science, mathematics, physics, and polymer science), ENGINEERING AND ENVIRONMENTAL DESIGN (aeronautical engineering, architecture, biomedical engineering, chemical engineering, civil engineering, computer engineering, construction management, electrical/electronics engineering, environmental engineering, industrial engineering, materials engineering, materials science, mechanical engineering, nuclear engineering, and technology and public affairs), SOCIAL SCIENCE (economics, history of science, international relations, psychology, and public affairs). Engineering, management, and computer science. are the strongest academically. Mechanical engineering, management, and industrial engineering are the largest.

Special: Extensive co-op programs, cross-registration with other Atlanta-area colleges, and internships are available. Study abroad in 30 countries is possible. An engineering transfer program is offered within the university system, and a liberal arts-engineering dual degree program serves area colleges and institutions nationwide. Students have access to multidisciplinary and certificate programs outside their major field of study. The Georgia Tech Regional Engineering Program (GTREP) offers undergraduate and graduate degrees in collaboration with Armstrong Atlantic State, Georgia Southern, and Savannah State Universities. There are 23 national honor societies and a freshman honors program.

Admissions: 59% of the 2009-2010 applicants were accepted. The SAT scores for the 2009-2010 freshman class were: Critical Reading--2% below 500, 23% between 500 and 599, 58% between 600 and 700, and 17% above 700; Math--1% below 500, 7% between 500 and 599, 51% between 600 and 700, and 42% above

700; Writing--2% below 500, 27% between 500 and 599, 52% between 600 and 700, and 19% above 700. The ACT scores were 1% below 21, 3% between 21 and 23, 17% between 24 and 26, 23% between 27 and 28, and 56% above 28. 87% of the current freshmen were in the top fifth of their class; 99% were in the top two fifths. There were 105 National Merit finalists.

Requirements: The SAT or ACT is required. The ACT Optional Writing test is also required. In addition, candidates for admission must have completed 4 units each of English and math, 3 units of social studies, 3 units of science, including 3 units of lab sciences, and 2 units of foreign language. An essay is required. AP credits are accepted. Important factors in the admissions decision are advanced placement or honors courses, evidence of special talent, and parents or siblings attended your school.

Procedure: Freshmen are admitted fall and summer. Entrance exams should be taken by the end of the junior year. There is an early admissions plan. Applications should be filed by January 15 for fall entry and January 15 for summer entry, along with a $65 fee. Notifications are sent March 15. Applications are accepted on-line. 450 applicants were on a recent waiting list, 123 were accepted.

Financial Aid: In 2009-2010, 44% of all full-time freshmen and 41% of continuing full-time students received some form of financial aid. 31% of all full-time freshmen and 27% of continuing full-time students received need-based aid. The average freshmen award was $11,216. The average financial indebtedness of the 2009 graduate was $13,445. Georgia Tech is a member of CSS. The FAFSA and the college's own financial statement are required. The deadline for filing freshman financial aid applications for fall entry is March 1.

Computers: Wireless access is available. All students have access to the network and wireless system, which can be accessed in locations such as labs, classrooms, the library, the student center, and dorms. Georgia Tech also has a mandatory computer ownership program. All students have a personally owned laptop. All students may access the system. There are no time limits and no fees. All students are required to have a personal computer. Students enrolled in all must have a personal computer. A minimum general requirements include at least 1 GB of RAM is recommended.

GEORGIA SOUTHERN UNIVERSITY
Statesboro, GA 30460　　　　　**(912) 479-5391; (912) 479-7240**

Full-time: 7650 men, 7149 women	**Faculty:** 645; IIA, --$
Part-time: 848 men, 839 women	**Ph.Ds:** 81%
Graduate: 880 men, 1720 women	**Student/Faculty:** 21 to 1
Year: semesters, summer session	**Tuition:** $5640
Application Deadline: May 1	**Room & Board:** $7900
Freshman Class: 9214 applied, 5154 accepted, 3539 enrolled	
SAT CR/M/W: 540/550/530*	**ACT:** 22　　　**COMPETITIVE**

Georgia Southern University, founded in 1906, is a member of the University System of Georgia and offers undergraduate degree programs in education, business, liberal arts and social sciences, information technology, science and technology, and health and human sciences. Graduate degrees in a variety of disciplines are also offered. There are 7 undergraduate schools and one graduate school. In addition to regional accreditation, Georgia Southern has baccalaureate program accreditation with AACSB, ABET, ACCE, NASAD, NASM, NCATE, and NRPA. The library contains 607,542 volumes, 895,643 microform items, and 29,429 audio/video tapes/CDs/DVDs, and subscribes to 49,100 periodicals including electronic. Computerized library services include interlibrary loans, database searching, Internet access, and laptop Internet portals. Special learning facilities include a learning resource center, art gallery, natural history museum, planetarium, radio station, TV station, an electron microscope, woodland nature preserve, eagle sanctuary, national tick collection, wildlife education center, raptor center, botanical garden, family life center, international studies center, institute for anthropology and parasitology, performing arts center, and the black box theater. The 700-acre campus is in a small town 1 hour from Savannah, 2 hours from Florida, and about 3 hours from metropolitan Atlanta. Including any residence halls, there are 158 buildings.

Programs of Study: Georgia Southern confers B.A., B.S., B.B.A., B.F.A., B.G.S., B.M., B.S.B., B.S.C.E.T., B.S.Chem., B.S.Cons., B.S.Ed., B.S.E.E.T., B.S.G.C.M., B.S.H.S., B.S.I.T., B.S.J.S., B.S.K., B.S.Manu., B.S.M.A.T., B.S.M.E.T., B.S.M.T., B.S.N., B.S.N.C., and B.S.P. degrees. Master's and doctoral degrees are also awarded. Bachelor's degrees are awarded in BIOLOGICAL SCIENCE (biology/biological science and nutrition), BUSINESS (accounting, banking and finance, fashion merchandising, hotel/motel and restaurant management, human resources, international economics, logistics, management science, marketing and distribution, marketing/retailing/merchandising, recreation and leisure services, and sports management), COMMUNICATIONS AND THE ARTS (art, broadcasting, communications, dramatic arts, English, French, German, journalism, linguistics, music, music theory and composition, performing arts, and public relations), COMPUTER AND PHYSICAL SCIENCE (chemistry, computer science, geology, information sciences and systems, mathematics, and physics), EDUCATION (art education, business education, early childhood education, English education, foreign languages education, health education, home economics education, mathematics education, middle school education, music education, and special education), ENGINEERING AND ENVIRONMENTAL DESIGN (civil engineering technology, construction management, electrical/electronics engineering technology, engineering technology, industrial administration/management, interior design, and mechanical engineering technology), HEALTH PROFESSIONS (community health work, exercise science, health, medical technology, and nursing), SOCIAL SCIENCE (anthropology, child care/child and family studies, criminal justice, economics, family/consumer studies, food production/management/services, food science, geography, history, international studies, philosophy, political science/government, psychology, and sociology). Biology, nursing, and psychology are the largest.

Special: GSU offers opportunities for study abroad, internships, work-study programs, B.A.-B.S. degrees, cooperative programs, a general studies degree, cross-registration with Georgia Tech and East Georgia College, a 3-2 engineering degree with Georgia Institute of Technology, pass/fail options, credit for military service, and non-degree study. There are 17 national honor societies and a freshman honors program.

Admissions: 56% of the 2009-2010 applicants were accepted. The SAT scores for the 2009-2010 freshman class were: Critical Reading--17% below 500, 63% between 500 and 599, 19% between 600 and 700, and 1% above 700; Math--15% below 500, 60% between 500 and 599, 23% between 600 and 700, and 2% above 700; Writing--30% below 500, 56% between 500 and 599, 13% between 600 and 700, and 1% above 700. The ACT scores were 10% below 21, 54% between 21 and 23, 25% between 24 and 26, 7% between 27 and 28, and 4% above 28. 33% of the current freshmen were in the top fifth of their class; 62% were in the top two fifths.

Requirements: The SAT or ACT is required. The ACT Optional Writing test is also required. In addition, applicants must have a high school diploma or the equivalent is required. A minimum of 16 credits in college preparatory courses should include 4 each in English and math, 3 each in social studies and science, 2 in a foreign language, and 2 additional courses. A GPA of 2.0 is required. AP and CLEP credits are accepted.

Procedure: Freshmen are admitted to all sessions. Entrance exams should be taken during the junior year. There are deferred admissions and rolling admissions plans. Applications should be filed by May 1 for fall entry, December 1 for spring entry, and April 1 for summer entry. The fall 2009 application fee was $30. Notification is sent on a rolling basis. Applications are accepted on-line.

Financial Aid: In 2009-2010, 87% of all full-time freshmen and 82% of continuing full-time students received some form of financial aid. 44% of all full-time freshmen and 42% of continuing full-time students received need-based aid. The average freshmen award was $7,646. Average annual earnings from campus work are $2142. The average financial indebtedness of the 2009 graduate was $18,618. Georgia Southern is a member of CSS. The FAFSA is required. The priority date for freshman financial aid applications for fall entry is April 20.

Computers: Wireless access is available. All students can access the Internet in campus computing labs or their residence hall rooms. There are approximately 2,385 lab computers available for student use on campus. Currently, there are 11 wireless buildings on campus. All students may access the system. 24 hours a day. There are no time limits and no fees.

GEORGIA STATE UNIVERSITY

Atlanta, GA 30302-3999   **(404) 413-2500; (404) 413-2002**

Full-time: 5455 men, 8305 women	**Faculty:** I, --$
Part-time: 2020 men, 3195 women	**Ph.D.s:** 85%
Graduate: 2880 men, 4110 women	**Student/Faculty:** n/av
Year: semesters, summer session	**Tuition:** $5000 ($16,000)
Application Deadline: see profile	**Room & Board:** $7000
Freshman Class: n/av	
SAT or ACT: required	**VERY COMPETITIVE**

Georgia State University, founded in 1913 and a part of the University System of Georgia, is a public residential university offering programs in liberal arts and sciences, business administration, education, law, health sciences, and public policy. Figures in the above capsule and this profile are approximate. There are 5 undergraduate schools and 6 graduate schools. In addition to regional accreditation, Georgia State has baccalaureate program accreditation with AACSB, ADA, APTA, CAHEA, CSWE, NASAD, NASM, NCATE, and NLN. The 2 libraries contain 1.4 million volumes, 1.7 million microform items, and 22,551 audio/ video tapes/CDs/DVDs, and subscribe to 7788 periodicals including electronic. Computerized library services include interlibrary loans, database searching, Internet access, and laptop Internet portals. Special learning facilities include a learning resource center, art gallery, radio station, TV station, digital arts lab, observatory, instructional technology center, and distance learning classrooms. The 33-acre campus is in an urban area in downtown Atlanta. Including any residence halls, there are 46 buildings.

Programs of Study: Georgia State confers B.A., B.S., B.B.A., B.F.A., B.I.S., B.M., B.S.Ed., and B.S.W. degrees. Master's and doctoral degrees are also awarded. Bachelor's degrees are awarded in BIOLOGICAL SCIENCE (biology/ biological science and nutrition), BUSINESS (accounting, banking and finance, business administration and management, business economics, hospitality management services, insurance and risk management, management information systems, marketing/retailing/merchandising, office supervision and management, and real estate), COMMUNICATIONS AND THE ARTS (art, art history and appreciation, classics, English, film arts, fine arts, French, German, journalism, music, music business management, Spanish, speech/debate/rhetoric, and studio art), COMPUTER AND PHYSICAL SCIENCE (actuarial science, chemistry, computer science, geology, mathematics, physics, and statistics), EDUCATION (art education, early childhood education, and physical education), HEALTH PROFESSIONS (exercise science, nursing, and respiratory therapy), SOCIAL SCIENCE (African American studies, anthropology, criminal justice, economics, geography, history, interdisciplinary studies, philosophy, political science/government, psychology, religious education, social work, sociology, urban studies, and women's studies). Biological sciences, psychology, and management are the largest.

Special: There is cross-registration with the Atlanta Regional Consortium for Higher Education (ARCHE). Internships with numerous employers and government agencies can be arranged. Study abroad is available in various countries. Work-study, an accelerated degree program in nursing, and dual majors are available. The Summer Scholar program allows high school seniors to take college-level course work. There is a freshman honors program.

Requirements: The SAT or ACT is required. The ACT Optional Writing test is also required. In addition, applicants must graduate from a regionally accredited high school. A total of 16 academic credits is required. Students should prepare with 4 years each of English and math, 3 years each of science and social science, and 2 years of the same foreign language. They must have a minimum 2.80 high school GPA calculated on the 16 courses listed above. A GPA of 2.8 is required. AP and CLEP credits are accepted. Important factors in the admissions decision are evidence of special talent, advanced placement or honors courses, and extracurricular activities record.

Procedure: Freshmen are admitted fall, spring, and summer. Entrance exams should be taken during the first semester of the senior year. There is a rolling admissions plan. Check with the school for current application deadlines. The fall 2009 application fee was $50. Applications are accepted on-line.

Financial Aid: The FAFSA is required. Check with the school for current application deadlines.

Computers: Wireless access is available. The Georgia State University Wireless Communication Infrastructure (CatChat) is designed and implemented as an adjunct to the existing wired data network. Georgia State's open access computer labs are available to all Georgia State faculty, staff, and students. Users are required to use their Novell user ID/password to gain access to the workstation and the campus network. There are open access PC labs in 6 buildings. Additionally, Georgia State maintains 15 classrooms with PC workstations. These rooms have between 27 to 54 PCs installed for student use during class. All students may access the system 24 hours per day. There are no time limits and no fees. It is strongly recommended that all students have a personal computer. Students enrolled in Computer Information Systems (CIS) must have a personal computer.

GETTYSBURG COLLEGE

Gettysburg, PA 17325-1484   **(717) 337-6100**
(800) 431-0803; (717) 337-6145

Full-time: 1172 men, 1297 women	**Faculty:** IIB, +$
Part-time: 12 men, 16 women	**Ph.D.s:** 95%
Graduate: none	**Student/Faculty:** n/av
Year: semesters	**Tuition:** $35,990
Application Deadline: February 1	**Room & Board:** $8,630
Freshman Class: 6126 applied, 2180 accepted, 695 enrolled	
SAT or ACT: required	**HIGHLY COMPETITIVE**

Gettysburg College, founded in 1832, is a nationally ranked college offering programs in the liberal arts and sciences. There are no undergraduate schools. The library contains 484,357 volumes, 75,067 microform items, 21,128 audio/video tapes/CDs/DVDs, and subscribes to 23,208 periodicals including electronic. Computerized library services include inter-library loans, database searching, Internet access, and laptop Internet portals. Special learning facilities include an art gallery, planetarium, radio station, TV station, electron microscopes, spectrometers, an optics lab, plasma physics lab, greenhouse, observatory, child study lab, fine and performing arts facilities, and a challenge course. The 200-acre campus is in a suburban area 30 miles south of Harrisburg, 55 miles from Baltimore, MD, and 80 miles from Washington, D.C. Including any residence halls, there are 63 buildings.

Programs of Study: Gettysburg confers B.A., B.S., and B.M. (Performance) and B.S. (Music Education) degrees. Bachelor's degrees are awarded in BIOLOGICAL SCIENCE (biochemistry and biology/biological science), BUSINESS (business administration and management), COMMUNICATIONS AND THE ARTS (art history and appreciation, classics, dramatic arts, English, French, German, Greek, Latin, music, Spanish, and studio art), COMPUTER AND PHYSICAL SCIENCE (chemistry, computer science, mathematics, and physics), EDUCATION (elementary education, foreign languages education, music education, science education, and secondary education), ENGINEERING AND ENVIRONMENTAL DESIGN (environmental science), HEALTH PROFESSIONS (health science, predentistry, and premedicine), SOCIAL SCIENCE (anthropology, economics, history, international relations, Japanese studies, philosophy, political science/government, prelaw, psychology, religion, sociology, and women's studies). The sciences, psychology, and history are the strongest academically. Management, political science, and psychology are the largest.

Special: The college offers cross-registration with the Central Pennsylvania Consortium, and an extensive study-abroad program and has special centers worldwide. There are summer internships and a Washington semester with American University. Cross-registration is possible with members of the Central Pennsylvania Consortium. There is a United Nations semester at Drew University, and a 3-2 engineering program with Columbia University, Rensselaer Polytechnic, and Washington University in St. Louis. There are also joint programs in optometry with the Pennsylvania College of Optometry, and forestry and environmental studies with Duke University. The college also offers double majors, student-designed majors, and B.A.-B.S. degrees in biology, chemistry, physics, biochemistry, and molecular biology, environmental studies and health and exercise sciences. Education certification is also available. There are 16 national honor societies, including Phi Beta Kappa.

Admissions: 36% of the 2009-2010 applicants were accepted. The SAT scores for the 2009-2010 freshman class were: Critical Reading--% below 500, 18% between 500 and 599, 63% between 600 and 700, and 19 above 700; Math--% below 500, 25% between 500 and 599, 65% between 600 and 700, and 10 above 700. 81% of the current freshmen were in the top fifth of their class; 99% were in the top two fifths.

Requirements: The SAT or ACT is required. In addition, an essay is required. Art students can submit a portfolio, and music students must audition. An interview and SAT Subject tests are recommended. A GPA of 3.0 is required. AP credits are accepted. Important factors in the admissions decision are evidence of special talent, recommendations by school officials, and advanced placement or honors courses.

Procedure: Freshmen are admitted fall and spring. Entrance exams should be taken by the January testing date of the senior year. There are early decision and deferred admissions plan. Early decision applications should be filed by November 15; regular applications, by February 1 for fall entry, along with a $55 fee. Notifications are sent April 1. Applications are accepted on-line. A waiting list is maintained.

Financial Aid: In 2009-2010, 52% of all full-time freshmen and 63% of continuing full-time students received some form of financial aid. 51% of all full-time freshmen and 55% of continuing full-time students received need-based aid. The average freshmen award was $24,487. 46% of undergraduate students work part-time. Average annual earnings from campus work are $1500. The average financial indebtedness of the 2009 graduate was $21,810. Gettysburg is a member of CSS. The CSS/Profile and FAFSA are required. The deadline for filing freshman financial aid applications for fall entry is February 15.

Computers: Wireless access is available. All students may access the system. 24 hours a day. There are no time limits and no fees. It is strongly recommended that all students have a personal computer. A discounted laptop purchase program is offered.

GONZAGA UNIVERSITY
Spokane, WA 99258-0001

(509) 323-6591
(800) 322-2584; (509) 324-5780

Full-time: 2000 men, 2260women	**Faculty:** n/av
Part-time: 65 men, 85 women	**Ph.D.s:** 86%
Graduate: 1080 men, 1415 women	**Student/Faculty:** n/av
Year: semesters, summer session	**Tuition:** $27,000
Application Deadline: see profile	**Room & Board:** $8000
Freshman Class: n/av	
SAT CR/M: 580/600	**ACT:** 26 **HIGHLY COMPETITIVE**

Gonzaga University, founded in 1887, is a private, liberal arts institution affiliated with the Roman Catholic Church and the Society of Jesus (Jesuits). The university offers undergraduate and graduate degrees in arts and sciences, business, education, engineering, and professional studies. The figures in the above capsule and in this profile are approximate. There are 5 undergraduate schools and 5 graduate schools. In addition to regional accreditation, Gonzaga has baccalaureate program accreditation with AACSB, ABET, NCATE, and NLN. The 2 libraries contain 594,689 volumes, 49,577 microform items, and 5,936 audio/video tapes/CDs/DVDs, and subscribe to 4,753 periodicals including electronic. Computerized library services include interlibrary loans, database searching, Internet access, and laptop Internet portals. Special learning facilities include a learning resource center, art gallery, radio station, and TV station. The 108-acre campus is in an urban area near downtown Spokane. Including any residence halls, there are 87 buildings.

Programs of Study: Gonzaga confers B.A., B.S., B.B.A., B.Ed., B.G.S., and B.S.N. degrees. Master's and doctoral degrees are also awarded. Bachelor's degrees are awarded in BIOLOGICAL SCIENCE (biochemistry and biology/ biological science), BUSINESS (accounting, business administration and management, and business economics), COMMUNICATIONS AND THE ARTS (art, broadcasting, communications, dramatic arts, English, French, German, journalism, literature, music, public relations, Spanish, and speech/debate/rhetoric), COMPUTER AND PHYSICAL SCIENCE (chemistry, computer science, mathematics, and physics), EDUCATION (music education, physical education, and special education), ENGINEERING AND ENVIRONMENTAL DESIGN (civil engineering, computer engineering, electrical/electronics engineering, and mechanical engineering), HEALTH PROFESSIONS (exercise science and nursing), SOCIAL SCIENCE (classical/ancient civilization, criminal justice, economics, history, interdisciplinary studies, international studies, Italian studies, liberal arts/ general studies, philosophy, political science/government, psychology, religion, and sociology). Engineering and business administration are the strongest academically. Business, engineering, and liberal arts are the largest.

Special: Cross-registration with Whitworth College and the Intercollegiate Consortium for Nursing Education, internships, study abroad in 9 countries, a Washington semester, and on-and off-campus work-study programs are offered. High school juniors and seniors may take 6 credits per semester. There is a limited pass/fail option, and an accelerated general studies degree and dual majors are possible. There are 12 national honor societies and a freshman honors program.

Requirements: The SAT or ACT is required. In addition, applicants should be graduates of an accredited secondary school. They must have completed 17 academic credits consisting of 4 years of English, 3 to 4 years of math, 2 to 3 years of the same foreign language; world language preferred, ASL accepted, 3 years of history and/or social science, and 3 to 4 years of natural or physical laboratory science. An essay and letters of recommendation are required. An interview is optional but recommended for students with a GPA lower than 3.1 or a satisfactory SAT score or 23 ACT Composite. A GPA of 3.1 is required. AP and CLEP credits are accepted. Important factors in the admissions decision are advanced placement or honors courses, leadership record, and extracurricular activities record.

Procedure: Freshmen are admitted fall and spring. Entrance exams should be taken by May of the junior year. There are early admissions and deferred admissions plans. Applications should be filed by February 1 for fall entry and November 1 for spring entry, along with a $50 fee. Notifications are sent April 1. Applications are accepted on-line. 200 applicants were on a recent waiting list, 169 were accepted.

Financial Aid: In a recent year, 97% of all full-time freshmen and 95% of continuing full-time students received some form of financial aid. 55% of all full-time freshmen and 56% of continuing full-time students received need-based aid. The average freshmen award was $23,971, with $12,768 ($17,500 maximum) from need-based scholarships or need-based grants; $6,205 ($10,400 maximum) from need-based self-help aid (loans and jobs); $19,283 ($35,237 maximum) from non-need-based athletic scholarships; and $7,052 ($37,685 maximum) from other non-need-based awards and non-need-based scholarships. 41% of undergraduate students work part-time. Average annual earnings from campus work are $2059. The average financial indebtedness of the 2009 graduate was $23,971.

Gonzaga is a member of CSS. The FAFSA is required. Check with the school for current application deadlines.

Computers: Wireless access is available. All students may access the system. 24 hours per day. There are no time limits and no fees. It is strongly recommended that all students have a personal computer.

GORDON COLLEGE
Wenham, MA 01984

(978) 867-4218
(866) 464-6736; (978) 867-4682

Full-time: 582 men, 972 women	**Faculty:** 97; IIB, av$
Part-time: 11 men, 21 women	**Ph.D.s:** 75%
Graduate: 15 men, 80 women	**Student/Faculty:** 16 to 1
Year: semesters	**Tuition:** $28,352
Application Deadline: March 1	**Room & Board:** $7720
Freshman Class: 1664 applied, 1106 accepted, 382 enrolled	
SAT CR/M/W: 588/567/586	**ACT:** 26 **VERY COMPETITIVE+**

Gordon College, founded in 1889, is a private, nondenominational Christian college offering liberal arts and sciences. There are 2 graduate schools. In addition to regional accreditation, Gordon has baccalaureate program accreditation with CSWE, NASDTEC, and NASM. The library contains 191,404 volumes, 31,666 microform items, and 5225 audio/video tapes/CDs/DVDs, and subscribes to 510 periodicals including electronic. Computerized library services include interlibrary loans, database searching, Internet access, and laptop Internet portals. Special learning facilities include a learning resource center and art gallery. The 440-acre campus is in a small town 25 miles north of Boston. Including any residence halls, there are 30 buildings.

Programs of Study: Gordon confers B.A., B.S., and B.Mu. degrees. Master's degrees are also awarded. Bachelor's degrees are awarded in BIOLOGICAL SCIENCE (biology/biological science), BUSINESS (accounting, banking and finance, business administration and management, and recreation and leisure services), COMMUNICATIONS AND THE ARTS (art, communications, dramatic arts, English, French, German, languages, music, music performance, and Spanish), COMPUTER AND PHYSICAL SCIENCE (chemistry, computer science, mathematics, and physics), EDUCATION (early childhood education, elementary education, middle school education, music education, secondary education, and special education), SOCIAL SCIENCE (biblical studies, economics, history, international studies, philosophy, political science/government, psychology, social work, sociology, and youth ministry). English, biology, and psychology are the strongest academically. English, psychology, and communications are the largest.

Special: Gordon offers cooperative education, internships, and cross-registration with other institutions in the Northeast Consortium of Colleges and Universities in Massachusetts. There is a 3-2 engineering program with the University of Massachusetts at Lowell and a 2-2 program in allied health with the Thomas Jefferson College of Allied Health Science in Philadelphia. B.A.-B.S. degrees, dual majors, student-designed majors, nondegree study, and pass/fail options are available. A 3-2 engineering degree is available with the University of Massachusetts at Lowell. Off-campus study opportunities include a Washington semester, the Christian College Consortium Visitor Program, the LaVida Wilderness Expedition, and study abroad in Europe, the Middle East, and China. There are 2 national honor societies and 12 departmental honors programs.

Admissions: 66% of the 2009-2010 applicants were accepted. The SAT scores for the 2009-2010 freshman class were: Critical Reading--15% below 500, 38% between 500 and 599, 36% between 600 and 700, and 11% above 700; Math--21% below 500, 36% between 500 and 599, 35% between 600 and 700, and 6% above 700; Writing--14% below 500, 39% between 500 and 599, 36% between 600 and 700, and 11% above 700. 50% of the current freshmen were in the top fifth of their class; 75% were in the top two fifths. There were 3 National Merit finalists.

Requirements: The SAT or ACT is required. The ACT Optional Writing test is also required. In addition, applicants must graduate from an accredited secondary school or have a GED. A minimum of 17 Carnegie units is required, including 4 English courses and 2 courses each in math, science, and social studies. Foreign language is a recommended elective. An essay, a personal reference, and an interview are required. Music majors must audition. Art majors must submit a portfolio for acceptance to the program. AP credits are accepted. Important factors in the admissions decision are advanced placement or honors courses, leadership record, and personality/intangible qualities.

Procedure: Freshmen are admitted fall and spring. Entrance exams should be taken in the spring of the junior year or the fall of the senior year. There are early decision, deferred admissions and rolling admissions plans. Early decision applications should be filed by November 15; regular applications, by March 1 for fall entry and November 1 for spring entry, along with a $50 fee. Notification of early decision is sent December 15; regular decision, January 1. Applications are accepted on-line.

Financial Aid: In 2009-2010, 94% of all full-time freshmen and 91% of continuing full-time students received some form of financial aid. 63% of all full-time freshmen and 66% of continuing full-time students received need-based aid. The average freshman award was $17,040. 48% of undergraduate students work part-time. Average annual earnings from campus work are $1830. The average financial indebtedness of the 2009 graduate was $33,332. Gordon is a member of CSS. The CSS/Profile and FAFSA are required. The deadline for filing freshman financial aid applications for fall entry is March 1.

Computers: Wireless access is available. Most of the campus is wireless, including common areas. All residence hall rooms are wired. All students may access the system at any time. There are no time limits and no fees.

GOSHEN COLLEGE

Goshen, IN 46526

(574) 535-7535
(800) 348-7422; (574) 535-7609

Full-time: 320 men, 470 women	**Faculty:** IIB, --$
Part-time: 40 men, 100 women	**Ph.D.s:** 59%
Graduate: none	**Student/Faculty:** n/av
Year: semesters, summer session	**Tuition:** $24,500
Application Deadline: see profile	**Room & Board:** $8300
Freshman Class: n/av	
SAT or ACT: required	**VERY COMPETITIVE**

Goshen College, founded in 1894, is a private liberal arts institution affiliated with the Mennonite Church. Figures in the above capsule and this profile are approximate. In addition to regional accreditation, Goshen has baccalaureate program accreditation with CSWE, NCATE, and NLN. The library contains 120,000 volumes, 140,000 microform items, and 1500 audio/video tapes/CDs/DVDs, and subscribes to 900 periodicals including electronic. Computerized library services include interlibrary loans and database searching. Special learning facilities include a learning resource center, art gallery, and radio station. The 135-acre campus is in a small town 120 miles east of Chicago. Including any residence halls, there are 25 buildings.

Programs of Study: Goshen confers B.A., B.S., and B.S.N. degrees. Bachelor's degrees are awarded in BIOLOGICAL SCIENCE (biology/biological science and molecular biology), BUSINESS (accounting, business administration and management, institutional management, and management information systems), COMMUNICATIONS AND THE ARTS (American Sign Language, communications, dramatic arts, English, music, and Spanish), COMPUTER AND PHYSICAL SCIENCE (chemistry, computer programming, information sciences and systems, mathematics, and physics), EDUCATION (art education, business education, elementary education, foreign languages education, middle school education, music education, physical education, science education, and secondary education), ENGINEERING AND ENVIRONMENTAL DESIGN (environmental science and preengineering), HEALTH PROFESSIONS (nursing, predentistry, premedicine, prepharmacy, and preveterinary science), SOCIAL SCIENCE (biblical studies, history, peace studies, psychology, religion, social work, and sociology). Nursing, elementary education, and biology are the largest.

Special: A semester-abroad internship in the required Study Service Term is possible in China, Indonesia, Germany, the Ivory Coast, Cuba, and the Dominican Republic. Cross-registration is offered with member colleges of the Northern Indiana Consortium for Education. A Washington semester, dual majors, student-designed majors, and a 3-2 engineering degree with the University of Illinois, Washington University in St. Louis, and Case Western Reserve University are available. Credit for life experience, pass/fail options, and nondegree study are possible. There is 1 national honor society, a freshman honors program, and 1 departmental honors program.

Requirements: The SAT or ACT is required. In addition, applicants should be graduates of an accredited secondary school or have a GED equivalent, with 4 years of high school English, 2 to 4 years of math, and 2 years each of foreign language, science, history, and social studies. An interview is recommended. AP and CLEP credits are accepted. Important factors in the admissions decision are advanced placement or honors courses, recommendations by school officials, and recommendations by alumni.

Procedure: Freshmen are admitted to all sessions. Entrance exams should be taken by fall of the senior year. There are deferred admissions and rolling admissions plans. Check with the school for current application deadlines. The application fee is $25. Notification is sent on a rolling basis. Applications are accepted on-line.

Financial Aid: Goshen is a member of CSS. The FAFSA and the college's own financial statement are required. Check with the school for current application deadlines.

Computers: All students may access the system. There are no time limits and no fees.

Baltimore, MD 21204   **(410) 337-6100**
                                         (800) 468-2437; (410) 337-6354

Full-time: 455 men, 991 women	**Faculty:** 129; IIB, av$
Part-time: 15 men, 20 women	**Ph.D.s:** n/av
Graduate: 164 men, 634 women	**Student/Faculty:** 10 to 1
Year: semesters	**Tuition:** $33,785
Application Deadline: February 1	**Room & Board:** $10,006
Freshman Class: 3651 applied, 2664 accepted, 400 enrolled	
SAT CR/M/W: 620/570/600	**ACT:** 26 **VERY COMPETITIVE+**

Goucher College, founded in 1885, is an independent, coeducational institution offering programs based on the interdisciplinary traditions of the liberal arts with an international perspective. The college offers 30 majors, many minors, and emphasizes international and intercultural awareness throughout the curriculum. There is 1 one graduate school. In addition to regional accreditation, Goucher has baccalaureate program accreditation with NCATE. The library contains 280,000 volumes, 22,268 microform items, and 45,660 audio/video tapes/CDs/DVDs, and subscribes to 25,200 periodicals including electronic. Computerized library services include interlibrary loans, database searching, and Internet access. Special learning facilities include a learning resource center, art gallery, radio station, TV station, TV studio, theater, technology/learning center, international technology and media center, and centers for writing, math, and politics. The 287-acre campus is in a suburban area 8 miles north of Baltimore. Including any residence halls, there are 20 buildings.

Programs of Study: Goucher confers B.A. degrees. Master's degrees are also awarded. Bachelor's degrees are awarded in BIOLOGICAL SCIENCE (biology/biological science), BUSINESS (international business management), COMMUNICATIONS AND THE ARTS (art, communications, dance, English, French, music, Russian, Spanish, and theater management), COMPUTER AND PHYSICAL SCIENCE (chemistry, computer science, mathematics, and physics), EDUCATION (elementary education and special education), SOCIAL SCIENCE (American studies, anthropology, economics, history, interdisciplinary studies, international relations, peace studies, philosophy, political science/government, psychology, religion, sociology, and women's studies). Biology, chemistry, and history are the strongest academically. Communication, psychology, and English are the largest.

Special: Goucher offers internships, study abroad in 27 countries, and other off-campus experiences. The college also collaborates with many of the 22 other colleges in the Baltimore Collegetown Network (*www.colltown.org*). Students may cross-register with Johns Hopkins, Towson University, College of Notre Dame, Peabody Institute, Villa Julie College, Coppin State College, University of Maryland Baltimore, University of Maryland Baltimore County, Loyola College, and Maryland Institute College of Art. An advanced degree program with the Monterey Institute for International Studies, and a 3-2 engineering degree with Johns Hopkins University are offered. Dual majors are an option, and student-designed majors and pass/no pass options are also available. There is 1 national honor society, including Phi Beta Kappa.

Admissions: 73% of the 2009-2010 applicants were accepted. The SAT scores for the 2009-2010 freshman class were: Critical Reading--11% below 500, 34% between 500 and 599, 39% between 600 and 700, and 16% above 700; Math--21% below 500, 42% between 500 and 599, 31% between 600 and 700, and 6%

above 700; Writing--14% below 500, 35% between 500 and 599, 38% between 600 and 700, and 13% above 700.

Requirements: Applicants should be graduates of an accredited high school or have earned the GED. Secondary preparation should include at least 16 academic units, preferably 4 in English, 3 in math (algebra I and II and geometry) and social studies, and 2 each in the same foreign language, lab science, and electives. A personal essay is required, and an interview is recommended. Prospective arts majors are urged to seek an audition or submit a portfolio. AP credits are accepted. Important factors in the admissions decision are extracurricular activities record, recommendations by school officials, and advanced placement or honors courses.

Procedure: Freshmen are admitted fall and spring. Entrance exams should be taken in spring of the junior year or fall of the senior year. There is a deferred admissions plan. Applications should be filed by February 1 for fall entry and December 1 for spring entry, along with a $55 fee. Notifications are sent April 1. Applications are accepted on-line. 192 applicants were on a recent waiting list, 23 were accepted.

Financial Aid: In 2009-2010, 82% of all full-time freshmen and 83% of continuing full-time students received some form of financial aid. 74% of all full-time freshmen and 62% of continuing full-time students received need-based aid. Need-based scholarships or need-based grants averaged $3,816; need-based self-help aid (loans and jobs) averaged $3,994 and other non-need based awards and non-need based scholarships averaged $13,046. 46% of undergraduate students work part-time. Average annual earnings from campus work are $1300. The average financial indebtedness of the 2009 graduate was $14,783. Goucher is a member of CSS. The CSS/Profile, FAFSA, and the college's own financial statement are required. The deadline for filing freshman financial aid applications for fall entry is February 15.

Computers: Wireless access is available. Goucher has 193 public computer workstations, some of which are located within 24-hour computer labs. There are wireless network Internet capabilities in most locations throughout the campus. All students may access the system. Some facilities are available around the clock. There are no time limits and no fees.

GRAND CANYON UNIVERSITY
Phoenix, AZ 85017-3030   **(877) 860-3951**

Full-time: 536 men, 1178 women	**Faculty:** n/av
Part-time: 852 men, 2258 women	**Ph.D.s:** 32%
Graduate: 2286 men, 6325 women	**Student/Faculty:** n/av
Year: semesters, summer session	**Tuition:** $14,420
Application Deadline: open	**Room & Board:** $7896
Freshman Class: n/av	
SAT or ACT: recommended	**VERY COMPETITIVE**

Grand Canyon University, founded in 1949, is a small, private, publically traded nonsectarian liberal arts institution. There are 5 undergraduate schools and 4 graduate schools. In addition to regional accreditation, GCU has baccalaureate program accreditation with ACBSP and NLN. The library contains 140,456 volumes, 53,459 microform items, and 527 audio/video tapes/CDs/DVDs, and subscribes to 9502 periodicals including electronic. Computerized library services include interlibrary loans, database searching, Internet access, and laptop Internet portals. Special learning facilities include an art gallery. The 90-acre campus is in a suburban area in Phoenix. Including any residence halls, there are 42 buildings.

Programs of Study: GCU confers B.A., B.S., and B.S.N. degrees. Master's degrees are also awarded. Bachelor's degrees are awarded in BIOLOGICAL SCIENCE (biology/biological science), BUSINESS (accounting, business administration and management, management science, and marketing/retailing/merchandising), COMMUNICATIONS AND THE ARTS (communications and English), COMPUTER AND PHYSICAL SCIENCE (chemistry and mathematics), EDUCATION (athletic training, Christian education, elementary education, physical education, recreation education, and secondary education), HEALTH PROFESSIONS (health science, medical science, and nursing), SOCIAL SCIENCE (Christian studies, criminal justice, history, interdisciplinary studies, physical fitness/movement, psychology, safety management, and sociology). Education, business, and nursing are the strongest academically and have the largest enrollments.

Special: Internships are ofered for most majors through organizatons, corporations, and agencies in the Phoenix area. Study abroad in 5 countries and a Washington semester are possible. There are 3 national honor societies and a freshman honors program.

Requirements: The SAT or ACT is recommended. In addition, applicants need to be graduates of an accredited high school or have a GED. A GPA of 2.3 is required. AP and CLEP credits are accepted. Important factors in the admissions decision are evidence of special talent, extracurricular activities record, and leadership record.

Procedure: Freshmen are admitted to all sessions. Entrance exams should be taken during the junior or senior year of high school. There are early decision and rolling admissions plans. Application deadlines are open. Application fee is $100. Applications are accepted on-line.

Financial Aid: In 2009-2010, 70% of all full-time freshmen and 81% of continuing full-time students received some form of financial aid. The average freshman award was $7602. 14% of undergraduate students work part-time. Average annual earnings from campus work are $4800. The FAFSA is recommended. Check with the school for current application deadlines.

Computers: Wireless access is available. Students with their own systems have wireless access in the dorms, apartments, and the student labs (PC lab and library). Students without their own systems can use the approximately 50 PCs in the PC lab or the 15 PCs in the library at no charge. All students may access the system, typically during waking hours. There are no time limits and no fees.

GRAND VALLEY STATE UNIVERSITY

Allendale, MI 49401-9403

(616) 331-5000
(800) 748-0246; (616) 331-2000

Full-time: 7587 men, 10861 women	**Faculty:** 1024; IIA, --$
Part-time: 966 men, 1436 women	**Ph.D.s:** 67%
Graduate: 1197 men, 2361 women	**Student/Faculty:** 17 to 1
Year: semesters, summer session	**Tuition:** $8630 ($12,944)
Application Deadline: July 23	**Room & Board:** $7478
Freshman Class: 13,051 applied, 10,520 accepted, 3727 enrolled	
SAT: required	**ACT:** 24 **VERY COMPETITIVE**

Grand Valley State University, founded in 1960, is a comprehensive public institution offering graduate and undergraduate liberal arts and professional education. There are 8 undergraduate schools and 7 graduate schools. In addition to regional accreditation, GVSU has baccalaureate program accreditation with AACSB, ABET, APTA, CSWE, NASAD, NASM, NCATE, and NLN. The 2 libraries contain 708,000 volumes, 868,850 microform items, and 19,804 audio/ video tapes/CDs/DVDs, and subscribe to 73,759 periodicals including electronic. Computerized library services include interlibrary loans, database searching, Internet access, and laptop Internet portals. Special learning facilities include a learning resource center, art gallery, radio station, TV station, a cadaver lab, 2 Great Lakes research vessels, a performance auditorium, and dance studios. The 1275-acre campus is in a small town 12 miles west of Grand Rapids. Including any residence halls, there are 72 buildings.

Programs of Study: GVSU confers B.A., B.S., B.B.A., B.F.A., B.M., B.M.E., B.S.E., B.S.N., and B.S.W. degrees. Master's and doctoral degrees are also awarded. Bachelor's degrees are awarded in AGRICULTURE (natural resource management), BIOLOGICAL SCIENCE (biology/biological science and cell biology), BUSINESS (accounting, banking and finance, business administration and management, business economics, hotel/motel and restaurant management, international business management, management science, marketing/retailing/merchandising, and personnel management), COMMUNICATIONS AND THE ARTS (advertising, art, art history and appreciation, broadcasting, Chinese, classics, communications, creative writing, dance, design, dramatic arts, English, film arts, fine arts, French, German, journalism, languages, music, photography, and Spanish), COMPUTER AND PHYSICAL SCIENCE (chemistry, computer science, earth science, geochemistry, geology, information sciences and systems, mathematics, physics, science, and statistics), EDUCATION (art education, athletic training, elementary education, foreign languages education, middle school education, music education, science education, secondary education, and special education), ENGINEERING AND ENVIRONMENTAL DESIGN (engineering, industrial engineering technology, and occupational safety and health), HEALTH PROFESSIONS (biomedical science, clinical science, exercise science, health science, medical laboratory technology, nursing, physical therapy, physician's assistant, predentistry, premedicine, and recreation therapy), SOCIAL SCIENCE (anthropology, behavioral science, biopsychology, criminal justice, economics, geography, history, international relations, law, liberal arts/general studies, philosophy, political science/government, prelaw, psychology, public administration, Russian and Slavic studies, social science, social work, and sociology). Health sciences, English, and psychology are the largest.

Special: Many programs offer dual majors and internships, and most majors qualify for B.A.-B.S. degrees. There is an engineering cooperative program, a student-designed major in liberal studies, and many work-study programs. Outside opportunities include study abroad in 10 countries and a Washington semester. There are 14 national honor societies, a freshman honors program, and 12 departmental honors programs.

Admissions: 81% of the 2009-2010 applicants were accepted. The ACT scores were 15% below 21, 32% between 21 and 23, 28% between 24 and 26, 13% between 27 and 28, and 12% above 28. 45% of the current freshmen were in the top fifth of their class; 80% were in the top two fifths. 18 freshmen graduated first in their class.

Requirements: Michigan residents must submit ACT test scores; nonresidents, either ACT or SAT scores. In addition, high school transcripts should indicate 4 years of English with 1 composition course, 3 each of math (including 2 years of algebra), science (including 1 lab), and social studies, and 2 of a foreign language. Applicants who graduated from high school more than 3 years ago need not show test results. The GED is accepted. A GPA of 3.0 is required. AP and

CLEP credits are accepted. Important factors in the admissions decision are extracurricular activities record, recommendations by school officials, and advanced placement or honors courses.

Procedure: Freshmen are admitted to all sessions. Entrance exams should be taken during the junior year. There is a rolling admissions plan. Applications should be filed by July 23 for fall entry, along with a $30 fee. Notification is sent on a rolling basis. Applications are accepted on-line.

Financial Aid: In 2009-2010, 60% of all full-time freshmen and 59% of continuing full-time students received some form of financial aid. 49% of all full-time freshmen and 40% of continuing full-time students received need-based aid. The average freshman award was $9,553. Need-based scholarships or need-based grants averaged $6600 and need-based self-help aid (loans and jobs) averaged $4814. 15% of undergraduate students work part-time. Average annual earnings from campus work are $2500. The average financial indebtedness of the 2009 graduate was $23,993. GVSU is a member of CSS. The FAFSA is required. The deadline for filing freshman financial aid applications for fall entry is February 15.

Computers: Wireless access is available. All students may access the system. There are no time limits and no fees. It is strongly recommended that all students have a personal computer.

GRINNELL COLLEGE

Grinnell, IA 50112
(641) 269-3600
(800) 247-0113; (641) 269-4937

Full-time: 764 men, 863 women	**Faculty:** 157; IIB, +$
Part-time: 2 men, 1 women	**Ph.D.s:** 97%
Graduate: none	**Student/Faculty:** 10 to 1
Year: semesters	**Tuition:** $36,476
Application Deadline: January 2	**Room & Board:** $8536
Freshman Class: 3298 applied, 1108 accepted, 378 enrolled	
SAT or ACT: required	**HIGHLY COMPETITIVE**

Grinnell College, founded in 1846, is a private institution that offers undergraduate degree programs in the arts and sciences. There is 1 undergraduate school. The 3 libraries contain 649,916 volumes, 416,593 microform items, and 34,144 audio/video tapes/CDs/DVDs, and subscribe to 22,059 periodicals including electronic. Computerized library services include interlibrary loans, database searching, Internet access, and laptop Internet portals. Special learning facilities include a learning resource center, art gallery, radio station, observatory, physics museum, and print and drawing gallery. The 120-acre campus is in a small town 55 miles east of Des Moines. Including any residence halls, there are 64 buildings.

Programs of Study: Grinnell confers B.A. degrees. Bachelor's degrees are awarded in BIOLOGICAL SCIENCE (biochemistry and biology/biological science), COMMUNICATIONS AND THE ARTS (art, Chinese, classics, dramatic arts, English, French, German, music, Russian, and Spanish), COMPUTER AND PHYSICAL SCIENCE (chemistry, computer science, mathematics, physics, and science), SOCIAL SCIENCE (anthropology, economics, history, philosophy, political science/government, psychology, religion, sociology, and women's studies). Economics, psychology, and political science are the largest.

Special: Students may participate in 63 study-abroad programs in 33 countries or in off-campus study at selected locations in the United States. Grinnell offers cooperative programs in architecture with Washington University in St. Louis and a 3-2 engineering program with California Institute of Technology, Columbia

University, Washington University, and Rensselaer Polytechnic Institute. There is also an extensive internship program, a Washington semester, a general studies degree in science, student-designed majors, and S/D/F grading options in selected courses. Grinnell's special "plus-2" option permits students to add 2 credits to a regular course through independent study. Students may pursue one of 11 interdisciplinary concentrations in addition to their major. Accelerated degree programs of 6 to 7 semesters may be approved on an individual basis. There are 2 national honor societies, including Phi Beta Kappa.

Admissions: 34% of the 2009-2010 applicants were accepted. The SAT scores for the 2009-2010 freshman class were: Critical Reading--7% below 500, 15% between 500 and 599, 36% between 600 and 700, and 42% above 700; Math--5% below 500, 15% between 500 and 599, 43% between 600 and 700, and 37% above 700. 93% of current freshmen were in the top quarter of their class. 33 freshmen graduated first in their class.

Requirements: The SAT or ACT is required. In addition, applicants must be graduates of accredited secondary schools. The college recommends 20 Carnegie units, 4 each in English and math and 3 to 4 each in lab science, social studies or history, and a foreign language. An essay is required and an interview is recommended. AP credits are accepted. Important factors in the admissions decision are advanced placement or honors courses, extracurricular activities record, and leadership record.

Procedure: Freshmen are admitted in fall. Entrance exams should be taken during the second semester of the junior year or early in the fall semester of the senior year. There are early decision, early admissions, and deferred admissions plans. Early decision applications should be filed by November 15; regular applications, by January 2 for fall entry, along with a $30 fee. Notification of early decision is sent December 15; regular decision, April 1. 145 early decision candidates were accepted for the 2009-2010 class. 1026 applicants were on the 2009 waiting list; 71 were accepted. Applications are accepted on-line.

Financial Aid: In 2009-2010, 84% of all full-time freshmen and 85% of continuing full-time students received some form of financial aid. 71% of all full-time freshmen and 64% of continuing full-time students received need-based aid. Need-based scholarships or need-based grants averaged $28,905; need-based self-help aid (loans and jobs) averaged $3904; and non-need-based awards and non-need-based scholarships averaged $9269. The average financial indebtedness of the 2009 graduate was $19,540. The FAFSA, the college's own financial statement, and a noncustodial profile are required. Check with the school for current deadlines.

Computers: Wireless access is available. All students may access the system 24 hours a day. There are no time limits and no fees.

GROVE CITY COLLEGE
Grove City, PA 16127-2104   (724) 458-2100; (724) 458-3395

Full-time: 1257 men, 1242 women	**Faculty:** 128
Part-time: 20 men, 11 women	**Ph.D.s:** 92%
Graduate: none	**Student/Faculty:** 20 to 1
Year: semesters	**Tuition:** $12,590
Application Deadline: February 1	**Room & Board:** $6824
Freshman Class: 1761 applied, 1123 accepted, 633 enrolled	
SAT CR/M: 630/629	**ACT:** 28 **HIGHLY COMPETITIVE+**

Grove City College, founded in 1876, is a private, liberal arts and science Christian college that is committed to providing rigorous academics within a Christian environment at an amazing value. There are 2 undergraduate schools. In addition to regional accreditation, Grove City has baccalaureate program accreditation with ABET. The library contains 135,100 volumes, 117,862 microform items, and 2,905 audio/video tapes/CDs/DVDs, and subscribes to 36,992 periodicals including electronic. Computerized library services include interlibrary loans, database searching, Internet access, and laptop Internet portals. Special learning facilities include an art gallery, radio station, TV station, and research grade observatory. The 150-acre campus is in a small town 60 miles north of Pittsburgh. Including any residence halls, there are 30 buildings.

Programs of Study: Grove City confers B.A., B.S., B.Mus., B.S.E.E., and B.S.M.E. degrees. Bachelor's degrees are awarded in BIOLOGICAL SCIENCE (biochemistry and biology/biological science), BUSINESS (accounting, banking and finance, business administration and management, entrepreneurial studies, international business management, management information systems, and marketing/retailing/merchandising), COMMUNICATIONS AND THE ARTS (communications, English, French, music, music business management, music performance, and Spanish), COMPUTER AND PHYSICAL SCIENCE (chemistry, computer science, mathematics, and physics), EDUCATION (elementary education, music education, science education, and secondary education), ENGINEERING AND ENVIRONMENTAL DESIGN (electrical/electronics engineering, industrial administration/management, and mechanical engineering), HEALTH PROFESSIONS (predentistry and premedicine), SOCIAL SCIENCE (economics, history, philosophy, political science/government, prelaw, psychology, religion, and religious music). Engineering, computer science, and premedicine are the strongest academically. Mechanical engineering, biology, and English are the largest.

Special: The college offers study abroad, accelerated and double major degrees, summer internships, student-designed interdisciplinary majors, and a Washington semester. There are 9 national honor societies.

Admissions: 64% of the 2009-2010 applicants were accepted. The SAT scores for the 2009-2010 freshman class were: Critical Reading--1% below 500, 27% between 500 and 599, 44% between 600 and 700, and 21% above 700; Math--2% below 500, 27% between 500 and 599, 53% between 600 and 700, and 18% above 700. The ACT scores were 2% below 21, 10% between 21 and 23, 22% between 24 and 26, 25% between 27 and 28, and 41% above 28. 77% of the current freshmen were in the top fifth of their class; 93% were in the top two fifths. There were 21 National Merit finalists. 57 freshmen graduated first in their class.

Requirements: The SAT or ACT is required. In addition, the academic or college preparatory course is highly recommended, including 4 units each of English, history, math, science, and a foreign language. An essay is required of all applicants, and an audition is required of music students. An interview is highly recommended. AP and CLEP credits are accepted. Important factors in the admissions decision are advanced placement or honors courses, personality/intangible qualities, and extracurricular activities record.

Procedure: Freshmen are admitted fall and spring. Entrance exams should be taken in the spring of the junior year or the fall of the senior year. There are early admissions and deferred admissions plans. Early decision applications should be filed by November 15; regular applications should be filed by February 1 for fall entry and December 15 for spring entry, along with a $50 fee. Notification of early decision is sent December 15; regular notifications, March 15. 331 early decision candidates were accepted for the 2008-2009 class. 176 applicants were on the 2009 waiting list; 61 were admitted. Applications are accepted on-line.

Financial Aid: In 2009-2010, 43% of all full-time freshmen and 38% of continuing full-time students received some form of financial aid. 43% of all full-time freshmen and 38% of continuing full-time students received need-based aid. The average freshman award was $6,024. Need-based scholarships or need-based grants averaged $6,024. 40% of undergraduate students work part-time. Average annual earnings from campus work are $1000. The average financial indebtedness of the 2009 graduate was $24,895. The the college's own financial statement is required. The deadline for filing freshman financial aid applications for fall entry is April 15.

Computers: Wireless access is available. All students are provided a tablet PC and have access to the network via their residence hall rooms and wireless areas on campus. All students may access the system any time. There are no time limits and no fees. All students are required to have a personal computer. All freshmen receive an HP Tablet PC.

GUSTAVUS ADOLPHUS COLLEGE
St. Peter, MN 56082-1498

(507) 933-7676
(800) GUSTAVU; (507) 933-6270

Full-time: 1065 men, 1410 women	**Faculty:** 199; IIB, av$
Part-time: 19 men, 22 women	**Ph.D.s:** 97%
Graduate: none	**Student/Faculty:** 12 to 1
Year: 4-1-4	**Tuition:** $32,110
Application Deadline: November 1	**Room & Board:** $7900

Freshman Class: 2984 applied, 2088 accepted, 606 enrolled
ACT: 26   **HIGHLY COMPETITIVE**

Gustavus Adolphus College, founded in 1862, is a private liberal arts college affiliated with the ELCA. In addition to regional accreditation, Gustavus has baccalaureate program accreditation with NASM, NCATE, and NLN. The 2 libraries contain 307,502 volumes, 36,013 microform items, and 17,026 audio/video tapes/CDs/DVDs, and subscribe to 32,840 periodicals including electronic. Computerized library services include interlibrary loans, database searching, Internet access, and laptop Internet portals. Special learning facilities include a learning resource center, art gallery, radio station, TV station, an arboretum, observatory, greenhouse, bronze-casting facility, geology museum, and many specialized laboratories. The 340-acre campus is in a small town 65 miles southwest of Minneapolis. Including any residence halls, there are 55 building

Programs of Study: Gustavus confers B.A. degrees. Bachelor's degrees are awarded in AGRICULTURE (environmental studies), BIOLOGICAL SCIENCE (biochemistry and biology/biological science), BUSINESS (accounting, business administration and management, business economics, and international business management), COMMUNICATIONS AND THE ARTS (classics, communications, dance, dramatic arts, English, fine arts, French, music, Russian, Scandinavian languages, Spanish, and speech/debate/rhetoric), COMPUTER AND PHYSICAL SCIENCE (chemistry, computer science, geology, mathematics, and physics), EDUCATION (art education, business education, elementary education, foreign languages education, health education, middle school education, music education, science education, and secondary education), HEALTH PROFESSIONS (nursing, physical therapy, predentistry, and premedicine), SOCIAL SCIENCE (anthropology, economics, geography, history, philosophy, political science/government, prelaw, psychology, religion, social science, sociology, and women's studies). Physical science and social science are the strongest academically. Business, biology, and communication studies are the largest.

Special: Co-op programs in nursing with St. Olaf College and cross-registration with Minnesota State University are available. The college offers internships, a Washington semester, study abroad in 22 countries, student-designed majors, nondegree study, work-study, and pass/fail options for some courses. A 3-2 engineering degree program with the University of Minnesota and Minnesota State University, Mankato is offered. The Curriculum II core offers a 12-course interdisciplinary program. There are 16 national honor societies, including Phi Beta Kappa, and 12 departmental honors programs.

Admissions: 70% of the 2009-2010 applicants were accepted. The ACT scores were 8% below 21, 22% between 21 and 23, 28% between 24 and 26, 18% between 27 and 28, and 24% above 28. 63% of the current freshmen were in the top fifth of their class; 88% were in the top two fifths. There were 5 National Merit finalists. 62 freshmen graduated first in their class.

Requirements: Applicants must have completed 4 years of English, 3 each of math and science, and 2 each of a foreign language, history, and social studies. AP credits are accepted. Important factors in the admissions decision are advanced placement or honors courses and evidence of special talent.

Procedure: Freshmen are admitted fall, winter, and spring. Entrance exams should be taken in the fall of the senior year. There are deferred admissions and rolling admissions plans. Applications should be filed by November 1 for fall entry, December 1 for winter entry, and January 1 for spring entry. Notifications are sent in November. Applications are accepted on-line. A waiting list is maintained.

Financial Aid: In 2009-2010, 93% of all full-time freshmen and 92% of continuing full-time students received some form of financial aid. 69% of all full-time freshmen and 65% of continuing full-time students received need-based aid. The average freshman award was $24,447. Need-based scholarships or need-based grants averaged $18,326 ($40,010 maximum); need-based self-help aid (loans and jobs) averaged $6,121 ($9,500 maximum). 71% of undergraduate students work part-time. Average annual earnings from campus work are $1539. The average financial indebtedness of the 2009 graduate was $24,300. Gustavus is a member of CSS. The CSS/Profile, FAFSA, and the college's own financial statement are required. The priority date for freshman financial aid applications for fall entry is January 1. The deadline for filing freshman financial aid applications for fall entry is April 15.

Computers: Wireless access is available. All residence halls and most academic buildings are wireless-capable. Computer labs (containing approximately 400 PCs) are in every residence hall and academic building. In addition to wireless, Internet access is available via Ethernet connection in every dorm room. All students may access the system. There are no time limits and no fees. It is strongly recommended that all students have a personal computer.

HAMILTON COLLEGE

Clinton, NY 13323

(315) 859-4421
(800) 843-2655; (315) 859-4457

Full-time: 870 men, 981 women	**Faculty:** 177; IIB, ++$
Part-time: 12 men, 19 women	**Ph.D.s:** 97%
Graduate: none	**Student/Faculty:** 10 to 1
Year: semesters	**Tuition:** $39,760
Application Deadline: January 1	**Room & Board:** $10,100
Freshman Class: 4661 applied, 1390 accepted, 466 enrolled	
SAT CR/M: 710/690	**ACT:** 30 **MOST COMPETITIVE**

Hamilton College, chartered in 1812, is a private, nonsectarian, liberal arts school offering undergraduate programs in the arts and sciences. The 3 libraries contain 617,080 volumes, 433,824 microform items, and 62,655 audio/video tapes/CDs/DVDs, and subscribe to 3800 periodicals including electronic. Computerized library services include interlibrary loans, database searching, and Internet access. Special learning facilities include an art gallery, radio station, and observatory. The 1300-acre campus is in a rural area 9 miles southwest of Utica. Including any residence halls, there are 104 buildings.

Programs of Study: Hamilton confers B.A. degrees. Bachelor's degrees are awarded in AGRICULTURE (environmental studies), BIOLOGICAL SCIENCE (biochemistry, biology/biological science, and neurosciences), COMMUNICATIONS AND THE ARTS (art, art history and appreciation, Chinese, classics, communications, comparative literature, creative writing, dance, dramatic arts, English, English literature, French, languages, music, Spanish, and studio art), COMPUTER AND PHYSICAL SCIENCE (chemical physics, chemistry, computer science, geoscience, mathematics, and physics), SOCIAL SCIENCE (African studies, American studies, anthropology, archeology, Asian/Oriental studies, economics, German area studies, history, interdisciplinary studies, international relations, philosophy, political science/government, psychobiology, psychology, public affairs, religion, Russian and Slavic studies, sociology, and women's studies). Government, economics, and psychology are the largest.

Special: Cross-registration is permitted with Colgate University and Utica College. Opportunities are provided for a Washington semester. Student-designed majors and study abroad in many countries are available, and 3-2 engineering degrees are offered with Washington University, Rensselaer Polytechnic Institute, and Columbia University. There are 7 national honor societies, including Phi Beta Kappa.

Admissions: 30% of the 2009-2010 applicants were accepted. The SAT scores for the 2009-2010 freshman class were: Critical Reading--3% below 500, 8% between 500 and 599, 31% between 600 and 700, and 59% above 700; Math--2% below 500, 8% between 500 and 599, 45% between 600 and 700, and 45% above 700; Writing--2% below 500, 6% between 500 and 599, 37% between 600 and 700, and 54% above 700. The ACT scores were 5% between 21 and 23, 4% between 24 and 26, 12% between 27 and 28, and 78% above 28. 94% of the current freshmen were in the top fifth of their class; 99% were in the top two fifths. 24 freshmen graduated first in their class.

Requirements: The SAT or ACT is required. Although graduation from an accredited secondary school or a GED is desirable, and a full complement of college-preparatory courses is recommended, Hamilton will consider all highly recommended candidates who demonstrate an ability and desire to perform at intellectually demanding levels. Students can fulfill test requirements with the

SAT, ACT, 3 SAT Subject tests, 3 AP exams, or any combination of these. An essay is required, and an interview is recommended. AP credits are accepted. Important factors in the admissions decision are advanced placement or honors courses, recommendations by school officials, and parents or siblings attended your school.

Procedure: Freshmen are admitted fall. Entrance exams should be taken prior to February of the senior year. There are early decision, early admissions and deferred admissions plans. Early decision applications should be filed by november 15; regular applications, by January 1 for fall entry. The fall 2008 application fee was $75. Notification of early decision is sent December 15; regular decision, April 1. Applications are accepted on-line. 1096 applicants were on a recent waiting list, 17 were accepted.

Financial Aid: In 2009-2010, 45% of all full-time freshmen and 42% of continuing full-time students received some form of financial aid. 44% of all full-time freshmen and 40% of continuing full-time students received need-based aid. The average freshman award was $36,931. 56% of undergraduate students work part-time. Average annual earnings from campus work are $1300. The average financial indebtedness of the 2009 graduate was $19,466. The CSS/Profile, the FAFSA, the state aid form, and the college's own financial statement are required. The deadline for filing freshman financial aid applications for fall entry is February 8.

Computers: Wireless access is available. All students may access the system. There are no time limits and no fees.

HAMLINE UNIVERSITY
St. Paul, MN 55104
(651) 523-2207
(800) 753-9753; (651) 523-2458

Full-time: 830 men, 1155 women	**Faculty:** n/av
Part-time: 40 men, 85 women	**Ph.D.s:** 87%
Graduate: 860 men, 1850 women	**Student/Faculty:** n/av
Year: 4-1-4, summer session	**Tuition:** $32,600
Application Deadline: see profile	**Room & Board:** $8000
Freshman Class: n/av	
SAT or ACT: required	**VERY COMPETITIVE**

Hamline University, founded in 1854, is a private liberal arts and sciences university affiliated with the United Methodist Church. Figures in the above capsule and this profile are approximate and include the law school. There are 5 graduate schools. In addition to regional accreditation, Hamline has baccalaureate program accreditation with NASM and NCATE. The 2 libraries contain 335,010 volumes, 1.0 million microform items, and 5045 audio/video tapes/CDs/DVDs, and subscribe to 4312 periodicals including electronic. Computerized library services include interlibrary loans, database searching, Internet access, and laptop Internet portals. Special learning facilities include a learning resource center, art gallery, radio station, centers for environmental education and applied research, the Jewish History Society Archives, and the Center for Excellence in Urban Teaching. The 57-acre campus is in an urban area between the downtowns of Minneapolis and St. Paul. Including any residence halls, there are 27 buildings.

Programs of Study: Hamline confers B.A. degrees. Master's and doctoral degrees are also awarded. Bachelor's degrees are awarded in BIOLOGICAL SCIENCE (biology/biological science), BUSINESS (business administration and management and international business management), COMMUNICATIONS AND THE ARTS (art, art history and appreciation, communications, dramatic arts, English, fine arts, French, German, music, and Spanish), COMPUTER AND PHYSICAL SCIENCE (chemistry, mathematics, and physics), EDUCATION (athletic training, elementary education, foreign languages education, physical education, science education, and secondary education), ENGINEERING AND ENVIRONMENTAL DESIGN (environmental science), HEALTH PROFESSIONS (predentistry and premedicine), SOCIAL SCIENCE (anthropology, criminal justice, East Asian studies, economics, European studies, history, international relations, Latin American studies, paralegal studies, peace studies, philosophy, political science/government, prelaw, psychology, religion, social science, sociology, urban studies, and women's studies). Prelaw, premedicine, and international relations are the strongest academically. Psychology, English, and political science are the largest.

Special: Cross-registration with Augsburg, Macalester, Saint Catherine Colleges and the University of Saint Thomas is possible. Students may select cooperative programs, study abroad, a Washington semester with American University, dual majors, student-designed majors, and pass/fail options. Students may earn a 3-2 or 4-2 engineering degree at the University of Minnesota or Washington University. On-campus work-study is available, as are extensive internship opportunities on and off campus. There are 18 national honor societies, including Phi Beta Kappa, a freshman honors program, and 10 departmental honors programs.

Admissions: There were 3 National Merit finalists in a recent year. 18 freshmen graduated first in their class.

Requirements: The SAT or ACT is required. In addition, it is recommended that candidates for admission complete 4 years of English with 1 year of college preparatory writing, 4 years of social studies, 4 years of academic electives, 3 years each of math, lab science, and social science, and 2 years of a foreign language. The GED is accepted. AP and CLEP credits are accepted. Important factors in the admissions decision are advanced placement or honors courses, recommendations by school officials, and leadership record.

Procedure: Freshmen are admitted fall. Entrance exams should be taken by February of the senior year. There are deferred admissions and rolling admissions plans. Application deadlines are open. Applications are accepted on-line. A waiting list is maintained.

Financial Aid: In a recent year, 97% of all full-time freshmen and 85% of continuing full-time students received some form of financial aid. 74% of all full-time freshmen and 73% of continuing full-time students received need-based aid. The average freshman award was $23,116. Need-based scholarships or need-based grants averaged $14,059 ($30,194 maximum); need-based self-help aid (loans and jobs) averaged $5943 ($9300 maximum); and other non-need-based awards and non-need-based scholarships averaged $8183 ($27,560 maximum). 115% of undergraduate students work part-time. Average annual earnings from campus work are $2300. The average financial indebtedness of a recent graduate was $32,058. The FAFSA is required. Check with the school for current application deadlines.

Computers: Wireless access is available. All students may access the system 24 hours a day, year-round. There are no time limits and no fees. It is strongly recommended that all students have a personal computer.

HAMPSHIRE COLLEGE

Amherst, MA 01002　　　　　　　**(413) 559-5471; (413) 559-5631**

Full-time: 570 men, 780 women	**Faculty:** IIB, +$
Part-time: none	**Ph.D.s:** 90%
Graduate: none	**Student/Faculty:** n/av
Year: 4-1-4	**Tuition:** $39,000
Application Deadline: see profile	**Room & Board:** $10,500
Freshman Class: n/av	
SAT or ACT: not required	**HIGHLY COMPETITIVE**

Hampshire College, founded in 1965, is a private institution offering a liberal arts education with an emphasis on independent research, creative work, and multidisciplinary study. Figures in the above capsule and this profile are approximate. The library contains 124,710 volumes, 4534 microform items, and 8727 audio/video tapes/CDs/DVDs, and subscribes to 731 periodicals including electronic. Computerized library services include interlibrary loans and database searching. Special learning facilities include an art gallery, multimedia center, farm center, music and dance studios, optics lab, electronics shop, integrated greenhouse, aquaculture facility, fabrication shop, and performing arts center. The 800-acre campus is in a rural area 20 miles north of Springfield. Including any residence halls, there are 28 buildings.

Programs of Study: Hampshire confers B.A. degrees. Bachelor's degrees are awarded in AGRICULTURE (agriculture and animal science), BIOLOGICAL SCIENCE (biology/biological science, botany, ecology, marine biology, nutrition, and physiology), COMMUNICATIONS AND THE ARTS (art history and appreciation, communications, comparative literature, creative writing, dance, dramatic arts, film arts, fine arts, journalism, linguistics, literature, media arts, music, performing arts, photography, and video), COMPUTER AND PHYSICAL SCIENCE (chemistry, computer science, geology, mathematics, physics, and science), EDUCATION (education), ENGINEERING AND ENVIRONMENTAL DESIGN (architecture, environmental design, and environmental science), HEALTH PROFESSIONS (health science and premedicine), SOCIAL SCIENCE (African studies, African American studies, American studies, anthropology, Asian/Oriental studies, cognitive science, crosscultural studies, economics, family/consumer studies, geography, history, humanities, international relations, international studies, Judaic studies, Latin American studies, law, Middle Eastern studies, peace studies, philosophy, political science/government, psychology, religion, sociology, urban studies, and women's studies). Film/photography/video is the strongest academically. Social sciences is the largest.

Special: Cross-registration is possible with other members of the Five College Consortium (Amherst College, the University of Massachusetts, Smith College, and Mount Holyoke). Internships, multidisciplinary dual majors, and study abroad (in the ISEP program, Tibetan Center, or a Costa Rica semester) are offered. All majors are student-designed. Students may complete their programs in fewer than 4 years.

Requirements: Applicants must submit all transcripts from ninth grade on or GED/state equivalency exam results. Students are required to submit a personal statement and an analytic essay or academic paper. An interview is recommended. AP credits are accepted. Important factors in the admissions decision are personality/intangible qualities, evidence of special talent, and extracurricular activities record.

Procedure: Freshmen are admitted fall and spring. There are early decision, early admissions and deferred admissions plans. Check with the school for current application deadlines. The fall 2009 application fee was $55. Applications are accepted on-line. A waiting list is maintained.

Financial Aid: Hampshire is a member of CSS. The CSS/Profile, the FAFSA, the college's own financial statement, and noncustodial parent statement are required. Check with the school for current application deadlines.

Computers: All students may access the system 24 hours per day via their own PCs or at designated hours in the labs, generally 8 A.M. to midnight, but up to 24 hours at semester's end.

HANOVER COLLEGE
Hanover, IN 47243

(812) 866-7022
(800) 213-2178; (812) 866-7098

Full-time: 423 men, 509 women	**Faculty:** 91
Part-time: 4 men, 2 women	**Ph.D.s:** 96%
Graduate: none	**Student/Faculty:** 10 to 1
Year: 4-1-4	**Tuition:** $26,350
Application Deadline: March 1	**Room & Board:** $7900
Freshman Class: 3019 applied, 1830 accepted, 293 enrolled	
SAT CR/M: 550/560	**ACT:** 25 **VERY COMPETITIVE**

Hanover College, founded in 1827 and the oldest private college in Indiana, is a liberal arts school affiliated with the United Presbyterian Church. In addition to regional accreditation, Hanover has baccalaureate program accreditation with NCATE. The library contains 222,782 volumes, 44,951 microform items, and 10,015 audio/video tapes/CDs/DVDs, and subscribes to 1,667 periodicals including electronic. Computerized library services include interlibrary loans, database searching, Internet access, and laptop Internet portals. Special learning facilities include a learning resource center, art gallery, planetarium, radio station, TV station, and a geology museum. The 650-acre campus is in a rural area 45 miles north of Louisville, Kentucky. Including any residence halls, there are 36 buildings.

Programs of Study: Hanover confers B.A. degrees. Bachelor's degrees are awarded in BIOLOGICAL SCIENCE (biology/biological science), COMMUNICATIONS AND THE ARTS (art, art history and appreciation, classics, communications, dramatic arts, English, French, German, music, and Spanish), COMPUTER AND PHYSICAL SCIENCE (chemistry, computer science, geology, mathematics, and physics), EDUCATION (elementary education), HEALTH PROFESSIONS (exercise science), SOCIAL SCIENCE (anthropology, economics, history, international studies, Latin American studies, medieval studies, philosophy, political science/government, psychology, sociology, and theological studies). Arts and sciences and interdisciplinary studies are the strongest academically. Psychology and biology are the largest.

Special: Internships, study abroad, a Washington semester, an experiential program at the Philadelphia Center, and student-designed majors in international studies and Latin American studies along with self-designed majors including 2 or more disciplines, are offered. The Center for Business Preparation provides preparation for a career in business, built on a liberal art foundation. There are 8 national honor societies, a freshman honors program, and 8 departmental honors programs.

Admissions: 61% of the 2009-2010 applicants were accepted. The SAT scores for the 2009-2010 freshman class were: Critical Reading--26% below 500, 44%

between 500 and 599, 26% between 600 and 700, and 4% above 700; Math--23% below 500, 43% between 500 and 599, 32% between 600 and 700, and 2% above 700; Writing--32% below 500, 50% between 500 and 599, 17% between 600 and 700, and 1% above 700. The ACT scores were 8% below 21, 37% between 21 and 23, 21% between 24 and 26, 14% between 27 and 28, and 20% above 28. 59% of the current freshmen were in the top fifth of their class; 91% were in the top two fifths. 3 freshmen graduated first in their class.

Requirements: The SAT or ACT is required. Admission is competitive, based on the applicant pool. The college requires 18 academic credits, including 4 years of English and 2 each of a foreign language, math, science, and either history or social studies. The GED is accepted. The college also requires a foreign language achievement test for those who wish to meet their world language requirement in the language they studied in high school, as well as an essay; an interview is recommended. AP credits are accepted. Important factors in the admissions decision are recommendations by school officials, advanced placement or honors courses, and extracurricular activities record.

Procedure: Freshmen are admitted fall and winter. Entrance exams should be taken late in the spring of the junior year. There are deferred admissions and rolling admissions plans. Applications should be filed by March 1 for fall entry, along with a $40 fee. Notifications are sent March 1. Applications are accepted on-line. A waiting list is maintained.

Financial Aid: In 2009-2010, 99% of all full-time freshmen and 97% of continuing full-time students received some form of financial aid. 73% of all full-time freshmen and 74% of continuing full-time students received need-based aid. The average freshman award was $21,628. Need-based scholarships or need-based grants averaged $18,947; need-based self-help aid (loans and jobs) averaged $3,709; and other non-need based awards and non-need based scholarships averaged $11,818. 33% of undergraduate students work part-time. Average annual earnings from campus work are $1566. Hanover is a member of CSS. The FAFSA is required. The priority date for freshman financial aid applications for fall entry is December 20. The deadline for filing freshman financial aid applications for fall entry is March 1.

Computers: Wireless access is available. All students may access the system in computer labs, 8 A.M. to 11 P.M. Monday through Thursday. There are no time limits and no fees.

HARDING UNIVERSITY
Searcy, AR 72149-0001

(501) 279-4407
(800) 477-4407; (501) 279-4129

Full-time: 1786 men, 2042 women	**Faculty:** 212
Part-time: 138 men, 120 women	**Ph.D.s:** 65%
Graduate: 686 men, 1712 women	**Student/Faculty:** 18 to 1
Year: semesters, summer session	**Tuition:** $13,580
Application Deadline: June 1	**Room & Board:** $5814
Freshman Class: 1970 applied, 1430 accepted, 955 enrolled	
SAT CR/M/W: 550/560/540	**ACT:** 24 **VERY COMPETITIVE**

Harding University, founded in 1924, is a private Christian institution comprised of the Colleges of Arts and Humanities, Sciences, Bible and Religion, Business, Communication, Education, Nursing, and Pharmacy. There are 7 undergraduate schools and 6 graduate schools. In addition to regional accreditation, Harding has baccalaureate program accreditation with ABET, ACBSP, CSWE, NASM, NCATE, and NLN. The library contains 422,727 volumes, 247,829 microform items, and 10,665 audio/video tapes/CDs/DVDs, and subscribes to 24,048 periodicals including electronic. Computerized library services include interlibrary loans, database searching, Internet access, and laptop Internet portals. Special learning facilities include a learning resource center, art gallery, radio station, and TV station. The 275-acre campus is in a small town 50 miles northeast of Little Rock and 105 miles west of Memphis, Tenn. Including any residence halls, there are 46 buildings.

Programs of Study: Harding confers B.A., B.S., B.B.A., B.F.A., B.M.E., B.M.N., B.Mus., B.S.M.T., B.S.N., B.S.W., and B.T.H. degrees. Master's and doctoral degrees are also awarded. Bachelor's degrees are awarded in BIOLOGICAL SCIENCE (biochemistry and biology/biological science), BUSINESS (accounting, banking and finance, business administration and management, fashion merchandising, human resources, international business management, marketing/retailing/merchandising, and sports management), COMMUNICATIONS AND THE ARTS (advertising, art, broadcasting, communications, design, dramatic arts, English, fine arts, French, graphic design, journalism, media arts, music, painting, and Spanish), COMPUTER AND PHYSICAL SCIENCE (chemistry, computer science, information sciences and systems, mathematics, and physics), EDUCATION (athletic training, Christian education, early childhood education, elementary education, foreign languages education, music education, and secondary education), ENGINEERING AND ENVIRONMENTAL DESIGN (computer engineering, electrical/electronics engineering, interior design, and mechanical engineering), HEALTH PROFESSIONS (exercise science, health, health care administration, medical technology, nursing, and speech pathology/audiology), SOCIAL SCIENCE (American studies, biblical languages, biblical studies, child care/child and family studies, criminal justice, dietetics, economics, history, home economics, humanities, international studies, liberal arts/general studies, ministries, missions, political science/government, psychology, public administration, religion, social science, social work, and youth ministry). Business, premedicine, and nursing are the strongest academically. Business, nursing, and education are the largest.

Special: The Harding campus in Florence, Italy, and programs in Greece, England, Latin America, France, Switzerland, Australia, and Zambia offer international studies. Internships are given in social work, teaching, nursing, and international missions. Co-op programs in all majors, work-study programs, dual majors, a general studies degree, and non-degree study are available. There are 12 national honor societies and a freshman honors program.

Admissions: 73% of the 2009-2010 applicants were accepted. The SAT scores for the 2009-2010 freshman class were: Critical Reading--26% below 500, 41% between 500 and 599, 24% between 600 and 700, and 9% above 700; Math--27% below 500, 36% between 500 and 599, 30% between 600 and 700, and 7% above 700; Writing--33% below 500, 41% between 500 and 599, 23% between 600 and 700, and 3% above 700. The ACT scores were 18% below 21, 24% between 21 and 23, 23% between 24 and 26, 14% between 27 and 28, and 20% above 28. 43% of the current freshmen were in the top fifth of their class; 69% were in the top two fifths. There were 11 National Merit finalists. 41 freshmen graduated first in their class.

Requirements: The SAT or ACT is required. A lower GPA can be offset by higher test scores. Applicants should be graduates of an accredited secondary school and have completed 15 high school hours, including 4 in English, 3 each in math, and social studies, 3 in art, history, or music, and 2 in a science. An interview is highly recommended. A GPA of 3.0 is required. AP and CLEP credits are accepted. Important factors in the admissions decision are leadership record, recommendations by school officials, and advanced placement or honors courses.

Procedure: Freshmen are admitted to all sessions. Entrance exams should be taken in the junior year or early in the senior year. There are deferred admissions and rolling admissions plans. Applications should be filed by June 1 for fall entry; November 1 for spring entry, along with a $40 fee. Notifications are sent May 1. Applications are accepted on-line.

Financial Aid: In 2009-2010, 95% of all full-time freshmen and 92% of continuing full-time students received some form of financial aid. 32% of undergraduate students work part-time. Average annual earnings from campus work are $1223. The average financial indebtedness of the 2009 graduate was $31,100. The FAFSA is required. The deadline for filing freshman financial aid applications for fall entry is April 1.

Computers: Wireless access is available. All students may access the system. There are no time limits. The fee is $220. It is strongly recommended that all students have a personal computer.

HARVARD UNIVERSITY/HARVARD COLLEGE

Cambridge, MA 02138 (617) 495-1551; (617) 495-8821

Full-time: 3510 men, 3140 women	**Faculty:** I, ++$
Part-time: 10 men, 10 women	**Ph.D.s:** n/av
Graduate: 5565 men, 5350 women	**Student/Faculty:** n/av
Year: semesters, summer session	**Tuition:** $37,000
Application Deadline: see profile	**Room & Board:** $12,000
Freshman Class: n/av	
SAT or ACT: required	**MOST COMPETITIVE**

Harvard College is the undergraduate college of Harvard University. Harvard College was founded in 1636. Harvard University also has 10 graduate schools. Figures in the above capsule and this profile are approximate. In addition to regional accreditation, Harvard has baccalaureate program accreditation with ABET. The 97 libraries contain 15.0 million volumes and subscribe to 100,000 periodicals including electronic. Computerized library services include interlibrary loans and database searching. Special learning facilities include a learning resource center, art gallery, natural history museum, planetarium, and radio station. The 380-acre campus is in an urban area across the Charles River from Boston. Including any residence halls, there are 400 buildings.

Programs of Study: Harvard confers A.B. and S.B. degrees. Master's and doctoral degrees are also awarded. Bachelor's degrees are awarded in BIOLOGICAL SCIENCE (biochemistry, biology/biological science, and biophysics), COMMUNICATIONS AND THE ARTS (art history and appreciation, Chinese, classics, creative writing, English, fine arts, folklore and mythology, French, German, Greek, Hebrew, Italian, Japanese, Latin, linguistics, literature, music, Portuguese, Russian, and Spanish), COMPUTER AND PHYSICAL SCIENCE (applied mathematics, astronomy, chemistry, computer science, geology, geophysics and seismology, mathematics, physical sciences, physics, and statistics), ENGINEERING AND ENVIRONMENTAL DESIGN (engineering, environmental design, environmental science, and preengineering), SOCIAL SCIENCE (African American studies, American studies, anthropology, Asian/Oriental studies, economics, European studies, history, humanities, Middle Eastern studies, philosophy, political science/government, psychology, religion, Russian and Slavic studies, Sanskrit and Indian studies, social science, social studies, sociology, and women's studies). Economics, government, and biology are the largest.

Special: Students may cross-register with MIT and with other schools within the university and may design their own concentrations or enroll for nondegree study. Internships and study abroad may be arranged. Accelerated degree programs, dual majors, a 3-2 engineering degree, and a combined A.B.-S.B. in engineering are offered. There are pass/fail options. There is a Phi Beta Kappa honors program.

Requirements: The SAT or ACT is required, as well as 3 SAT Subject tests. Applicants need not be high school graduates but are expected to be well prepared academically. An essay and an interview are required, in addition to a transcript, a counselor report, and 2 teacher recommendations from academic disciplines. AP credits are accepted. Important factors in the admissions decision are evidence of special talent, personality/intangible qualities, and recommendations by school officials.

Procedure: Freshmen are admitted fall. Entrance exams should be taken by January of the senior year. There is a deferred admissions plan. Check with the school for current application deadlines. The fall 2009 application fee was $65. Applications are accepted on-line. A waiting list is maintained.

Financial Aid: Harvard is a member of CSS. The CSS/Profile, FAFSA, the college's own financial statement, and federal tax forms are required. Check with the school for current application deadlines.

Computers: All students may access the system 24 hours per day. There are no time limits and no fees.

HARVEY MUDD COLLEGE
Claremont, CA 91711　　　　　　　　　(909) 621-8011; (909) 607-7046

Full-time: 483 men, 273 women	**Faculty:** IIB, ++$
Part-time: 1 woman	**Ph.D.s:** 100%
Graduate: none	**Student/Faculty:** n/av
Year: semesters	**Tuition:** $38,467
Application Deadline: January 2	**Room & Board:** $12,570
Freshman Class: n/av	
SAT: required	**MOST COMPETITIVE**

Harvey Mudd College, founded in 1955, is one of the Claremont Colleges. It is a private college specializing in a math, science, and engineering education within a liberal arts tradition. There are 5 undergraduate schools and 2 graduate schools. In addition to regional accreditation, Harvey Mudd has baccalaureate program accreditation with ABET. The 2 libraries contain 2 million volumes and 1 million microform items, and subscribe to 6000 periodicals including electronic. Computerized library services include interlibrary loans, database searching, and Internet access. Special learning facilities include a learning resource center, art gallery, planetarium, and radio station. The 30-acre campus is in a suburban area 35 miles east of Los Angeles. Including any residence halls, there are 20 buildings.

Programs of Study: Harvey Mudd confers B.S. degrees. Bachelor's degrees are awarded in BIOLOGICAL SCIENCE (biology/biological science), COMPUTER AND PHYSICAL SCIENCE (chemistry, computer science, mathematics, and physics), ENGINEERING AND ENVIRONMENTAL DESIGN (engineering). Engineering, math, and computer science are the strongest academically. Engineering and computer science are the largest.

Special: Students may cross-register at any of the other Claremont Colleges. Internships are available for engineering and math majors. Study abroad, a Washington semester, work-study, computer science/math, math/biology majors, and biology/chemistry majors, and student-designed majors are available. A 3-2 engineering degree with Claremont McKenna College or Scripps College is possible. Some courses may be audited. The first semester for freshmen is taken on a pass/fail basis; thereafter, only 1 noncore and nonmajor course per semester may be taken on that basis. There is 1 national honor society and 7 departmental honors programs.

Admissions: There were 51 National Merit finalists in a recent year. 33 freshmen graduated first in their class.

Requirements: The SAT is required. The ACT Optional Writing test is also required. The ACT is recommended. In addition, applicants must be graduates of an accredited secondary school and have completed 4 years each of English and math (including algebra, demonstrative and analytic geometry, trigonometry, and calculus) and 1 year each of physics and chemistry. The college strongly recommends that applicants take 2 years of a foreign language and 1 year each of history and biology. SAT Subject tests in math (level 2) and 1 other subject are required. Letters of recommendation are required from the student's counselor, a math or science teacher, and an English, social science, or foreign language teacher. Applicants must submit 2 personal essays and are encouraged to seek an interview. AP credits are accepted. Important factors in the admissions decision are advanced placement or honors courses, recommendations by school officials, and leadership record.

Procedure: Freshmen are admitted fall. Entrance exams should be taken by January of the senior year. There are early decisions and deferred admissions plans. Early decision applications should be filed by November 15; regular applications, January 2 for fall entry, along with a $60 fee. Notification of early decision is sent December 15; regular decision, April 1. Applications are accepted on-line. 186 applicants were on a recent waiting list.

Financial Aid: In a recent year, 87% of all full-time freshmen and 81% of continuing full-time students received some form of financial aid. 54% of all full-time freshmen and 53% of continuing full-time students received need-based aid. The average freshman award was $25,550. Need-based scholarships or need-based grants averaged $23,359 ($39,735 maximum); and need-based self-help aid (loans and jobs) averaged $4144 ($9575 maximum). 20% of undergraduate students worked part-time. Average annual earnings from campus work were $920. The average financial indebtedness of a recent graduate was $16,078. Harvey Mudd is a member of CSS. The CSS/Profile and FAFSA are required. The deadline for filing freshman financial aid applications for fall entry is February 1.

Computers: Wireless access is available. All students may access the system 24 hours a day. There are no time limits and no fees. It is strongly recommended that all students have a personal computer.

Haverford, PA 19041-1392   (610) 896-1350; (610) 896-1338

Full-time: 538 men, 652 women	**Faculty:** 121; IIB, +$
Part-time: none	**Ph.D.s:** 97%
Graduate: none	**Student/Faculty:** 10 to 1
Year: semesters	**Tuition:** $39,085
Application Deadline: January 15	**Room & Board:** $11,890
Freshman Class: 3403 applied, 862 accepted, 323 enrolled	
SAT CR/M/W: 710/690/700	**ACT:** required

MOST COMPETITIVE

Haverford College, founded in 1833, is a private liberal arts college. The 4 libraries contain 595,855 volumes, 6,752 microform items, and 14,727 audio/video tapes/CDs/DVDs, and subscribe to 6,246 periodicals including electronic. Computerized library services include interlibrary loans, database searching, Internet access, and laptop Internet portals. Special learning facilities include an art gallery, radio station, observatory, and arboretum. The 200-acre campus is in a suburban area 10 miles west of Philadelphia. Including any residence halls, there are 72 buildings.

Programs of Study: Haverford confers B.A. and B.S. degrees. Bachelor's degrees are awarded in BIOLOGICAL SCIENCE (biology/biological science), COMMUNICATIONS AND THE ARTS (art history and appreciation, classics, comparative literature, English, fine arts, French, German, Greek, Italian, Latin, linguistics, music, romance languages and literature, Russian, Spanish, and visual and performing arts), COMPUTER AND PHYSICAL SCIENCE (astronomy, chemistry, computer science, geology, information sciences and systems, mathematics, and physics), SOCIAL SCIENCE (anthropology, archeology, East Asian studies, economics, history, interdisciplinary studies, liberal arts/general studies, philosophy, political science/government, psychology, religion, sociology, and urban studies). Natural and physical sciences, English, and history are the strongest academically. Biology, political science, and economics are the largest.

Special: Haverford offers internship programs, cross-registration with Bryn Mawr and Swarthmore Colleges, study abroad in 35 countries, dual majors, and student-designed majors. Pass/fail options are limited to 4 in 4 years. There is 1 national honor society, Phi Beta Kappa, and 28 departmental honors programs.

Admissions: 25% of the 2009-2010 applicants were accepted. The SAT scores for the 2009-2010 freshman class were: Critical Reading--7% between 500 and 599, 40% between 600 and 700, and 53% above 700; Math--11% between 500 and 599, 47% between 600 and 700, and 41% above 700; Writing--6% between 500 and 599, 45% between 600 and 700, and 49% above 700. 98% of the current freshmen were in the top fifth of their class; all were in the top two fifths.

Requirements: First-year applicants must take the SAT (all 3 tests, including Writing) or the ACT and 2 SAT subject tests before the deadline for the decision plan chosen. Candidates for admission must be graduates of an accredited secondary school and have taken 4 courses in English, 3 each in a foreign language and math, 2 in social studies, and 1 in science. The GED is accepted. An essay is required, and an interview is recommended. AP credits are accepted. Important factors in the admissions decision are advanced placement or honors courses, leadership record, and recommendations by school officials.

Procedure: Freshmen are admitted in the fall. Entrance exams should be taken by January 15. There are early decision, early admissions and deferred admissions plans. Early decision applications should be filed by November 15; regular applications, by January 15 for fall entry, along with a $60 fee. Notification of early decision is sent December 15; regular decision, April 15. Applications are accepted on-line. 311 applicants were on a recent waiting list, 13 were accepted.

Financial Aid: In 2009-2010, 48% of all full-time freshmen and 48% of continuing full-time students received some form of financial aid. 45% of all full-time freshmen and 44% of continuing full-time students received need-based aid. The average freshman award was $33,575. The average financial indebtedness of the 2009 graduate was $16,500. Haverford is a member of CSS. The CSS/Profile and FAFSA are required. The deadline for filing freshman financial aid applications for fall entry is January 31.

Computers: Wireless access is available. All students may access the system. There are no time limits and no fees.

HELLENIC COLLEGE/HOLY CROSS GREEK ORTHODOX SCHOOL OF THEOLOGY

Brookline, MA 02445	(617) 731-3500, ext.1260; (617) 850-1460
Full-time: 50 men, 35 women	**Faculty:** 13
Part-time: none	**Ph.D.s:** 90%
Graduate: 110 men, 17 women	**Student/Faculty:** 7 to 1
Year: semesters	**Tuition:** $18,850
Application Deadline: May 1	**Room & Board:** $11,780
Freshman Class: 61 applied, 44 accepted, 35 enrolled	
SAT or ACT: required	**VERY COMPETITIVE**

Hellenic College, founded in 1937, is a private college affiliated with the Greek Orthodox Church. It offers programs in the classics, elementary education, religious studies, human development, management and leadership, and literature and history. There is 1 graduate school. In addition to regional accreditation, HCHC has baccalaureate program accreditation with NASDTEC. The library contains 75,000 volumes, 863 microform items, and 2,849 audio/video tapes/CDs/DVDs, and subscribes to 721 periodicals including electronic. Computerized library services include interlibrary loans, database searching, and Internet access. The 59-acre campus is in an urban area 4 miles southwest of Boston. Including any residence halls, there are 7 buildings.

Programs of Study: HCHC confers B.A. degrees. Master's degrees are also awarded. Bachelor's degrees are awarded in BUSINESS (business administration and management), COMMUNICATIONS AND THE ARTS (classics and literature), EDUCATION (elementary education), SOCIAL SCIENCE (history, human development, and religion). Religious studies and elementary education are the strongest academically. Religious studies and human development are the largest.

Special: The college offers cross-registration with Boston Theological Institute, Newbury College, and Boston College, credit by examination, and study abroad in Greece. There is a freshman honors program.

Admissions: 72% of the 2009-2010 applicants were accepted. The SAT scores for the 2009-2010 freshman class were: Critical Reading--50% below 500, 25% between 500 and 599, 15% between 600 and 700; and 10% above 700; Math--50% below 500, 40% between 500 and 599, and 10% between 600 and 700; Writing--50% below 500, 25% between 500 and 599, 15% between 600 and 700; and 10% above 700. The ACT scores were 10% below 21, 60% between 21 and 23, 20% between 24 and 26, and 10% between 27 and 28.

Requirements: The SAT or ACT is required. In addition, applicants should graduate from an accredited secondary school or have a GED. 15 academic credits are required, including 4 units of English, 2 each of math, foreign language, and social studies, and 1 of science. An essay is required. A GPA of 2.5 is required. AP and CLEP credits are accepted. Important factors in the admissions decision are recommendations by school officials, advanced placement or honors courses, and recommendations by alumni.

Procedure: Freshmen are admitted fall and spring. There are early decision, deferred, and rolling admissions plans. Early decision applications should be filed by December 1; regular applications, by May 1 for fall entry and December 1 for spring entry. The fall 2009 application fee was $50. Notification of early decision is sent February 1; regular decision, June 15.

Financial Aid: In a recent year, 95% of all full-time students received some form of financial aid, including need-based aid. 33% of undergraduate students work part-time. Average annual earnings from campus work are $1600. The average financial indebtedness of the 2009 graduate was $31,000. The FAFSA and the college's own financial statement are required. The priority date for freshman financial aid applications for fall entry is April 1. The deadline for filing freshman financial aid applications for fall entry is July 1.

Computers: Wireless access is available. All students may access the system. There are no time limits and no fees.

HENDERSON STATE UNIVERSITY
Arkadelphia, AR 71999-0001   (870) 230-5028; (870) 230-5066

Full-time: 1259 men, 1504 women	**Faculty:** 170
Part-time: 161 men, 179 women	**Ph.D.s:** 69%
Graduate: 135 men, 336 women	**Student/Faculty:** 18 to 1
Year: semesters, summer session	**Tuition:** $5083 ($9163)
Application Deadline: open	**Room & Board:** $4964
Freshman Class: 1659 accepted, 643 enrolled	
SAT M/W: 527/520	**ACT:** 22 **VERY COMPETITIVE**

Henderson State University, founded in 1890 as Arkadelphia Methodist College, became a state institution in 1929 and offers liberal arts courses. There are 3 undergraduate schools and 1 graduate school. In addition to regional accreditation, HSU has baccalaureate program accreditation with AACSB, NASM, NCATE, and NLN. Computerized library services include interlibrary loans, database searching, and Internet access. Special learning facilities include an art gallery, planetarium, radio station, and TV station. The 151-acre campus is in a small town 60 miles southwest of Little Rock. Including any residence halls, there are 29 buildings.

Programs of Study: HSU confers B.A., B.S., B.B.A., B.F.A., B.G.S., B.M., B.S.E., and B.S.N. degrees. Associate and master's degrees are also awarded. Bachelor's degrees are awarded in BIOLOGICAL SCIENCE (biology/biological science), BUSINESS (accounting, business administration and management, and recreation and leisure services), COMMUNICATIONS AND THE ARTS (communications, dramatic arts, English, music, Spanish, and studio art), COMPUTER AND PHYSICAL SCIENCE (chemistry, computer science, information sciences and systems, mathematics, and physics), EDUCATION (art education, athletic training, early childhood education, education, middle school education, music education, physical education, social science education, and technical education), ENGINEERING AND ENVIRONMENTAL DESIGN (aviation administration/management), HEALTH PROFESSIONS (medical technology and nursing), SOCIAL SCIENCE (family/consumer studies, history, human services, political science/government, psychology, public administration, and sociology). Education, business administration, and nursing are the largest.

Special: HSU offers co-op programs and cross-registration with Ouachita Baptist University, internships in business, psychology, political science, recreation, and education, work-study programs, credit for military experience, nondegree study, and pass/fail options. There are 11 national honor societies and a freshman honors program.

Admissions: The SAT scores for the 2009-2010 freshman class were: Math-- 34% below 500, 44% between 500 and 599, 19% between 600 and 700, and 3% above 700; Writing--50% below 500, 25% between 500 and 599, and 25% between 600 and 700. The ACT scores were 37% below 21, 21% between 21 and 23, 22% between 24 and 26, 14% between 27 and 28, and 6% above 28. 42% of the current freshmen were in the top fifth of their class; 76% were in the top two fifths. 10 freshmen graduated first in their class.

Requirements: The ACT is required. In addition, applicants need at least 15 academic credits or 15 Carnegie units. Students with a predicted GPA of 1.5 or below will be admitted conditionally. 4 units of English, 3 of history, civics, or American government, 2 each of natural science, math, and foreign language, and a half unit of computer science are recommended. A GPA of 3.2 is required. AP and CLEP credits are accepted.

Procedure: Freshmen are admitted fall, spring, and summer. Entrance exams should be taken during the senior year. There is a rolling admissions plan. Application deadlines are open. Applications are accepted on-line.

Financial Aid: In 2009-2010, need-based scholarships and need-based grants averaged $11,558; need-based self-help aid (loans and jobs) averaged $3500; non-need-based athletic scholarships averaged $2816; and other non-need-based awards and non-need-based scholarships averaged $9354. The FAFSA and FFS are required. Check with the school for current application deadlines.

Computers: Wireless access is available. All students may access the system. There are no time limits and no fees.

HENDRIX COLLEGE
Conway, AR 72032

(501) 450-1362
(800) 277-9017; (501) 450-3843

Full-time: 627 men, 815 women	**Faculty:** 92; IIB, av$
Part-time: 9 men, 5 women	**Ph.D.s:** 97%
Graduate: 2 men, 5 women	**Student/Faculty:** 13 to 1
Year: semesters	**Tuition:** $30,270
Application Deadline:	**Room & Board:** $8664
Freshman Class: 1572 applied, 1278 accepted, 412 enrolled	
SAT CR/M: 635/617	**ACT:** 29 **HIGHLY COMPETITIVE+**

Hendrix College, founded in 1876, is a private (not for profit) liberal arts college affiliated with the United Methodist Church. There are no undergraduate schools and one graduate school. In addition to regional accreditation, Hendrix has baccalaureate program accreditation with NASM and NCATE. The library contains 218,390 volumes, 186,042 microform items, and 1,899 audio/video tapes/CDs/ DVDs, and subscribes to 35,524 periodicals including electronic. Computerized library services include interlibrary loans, database searching, and Internet access. Special learning facilities include an art gallery, radio station, and a writing lab. The 65-acre campus is in a suburban area 25 miles northwest of Little Rock, AR. Including any residence halls, there are 48 buildings.

Programs of Study: Hendrix confers B.A. degrees. Master's degrees are also awarded. Bachelor's degrees are awarded in AGRICULTURE (environmental studies), BIOLOGICAL SCIENCE (biochemistry), BUSINESS (accounting and business economics), COMMUNICATIONS AND THE ARTS (art, dramatic arts, English, French, German, music, and Spanish), COMPUTER AND PHYSICAL SCIENCE (chemical physics, chemistry, computer science, mathematics, and physics), EDUCATION (early childhood education and elementary education), HEALTH PROFESSIONS (allied health and exercise science), SOCIAL SCIENCE (American studies, economics, history, interdisciplinary studies, international relations, philosophy, political science/government, psychology, religion, and sociology). Psychology, chemistry, and philosophy are the strongest academically. Psychology, biology, and english are the largest.

Special: Internships and work-study may be arranged in all fields. The college offers 3-2 engineering programs with Columbia, Vanderbilt, and Washington Universities. Also available are a Washington semester, study abroad, dual majors, and student-designed interdisciplinary studies. Students can pursue minors in all academic departments, as well as gender studies and cultural anthropology. There are 12 national honor societies, including Phi Beta Kappa.

Admissions: 81% of the 2009-2010 applicants were accepted. The SAT scores for the 2009-2010 freshman class were: Critical Reading--6% below 500, 24% between 500 and 599, 49% between 600 and 700, and 21% above 700; Math--7% below 500, 31% between 500 and 599, 49% between 600 and 700, and 13% above 700. The ACT scores were 2% below 21, 5% between 21 and 23, 17% between 24 and 26, 19% between 27 and 28, and 57% above 28. 70% of the current freshmen were in the top fifth of their class; 90% were in the top two fifths. There were 8 National Merit finalists. 28 freshmen graduated first in their class.

Requirements: The SAT or ACT is required. In addition, Hendrix recommends that applicants have completed 4 high school units in English, 3 to 4 each in math and social studies, 2 to 3 in science, and 2 in a foreign language. The GED is accepted. AP and CLEP credits are accepted. Important factors in the admissions decision are extracurricular activities record, advanced placement or honors courses, and leadership record.

Procedure: Freshmen are admitted fall and spring. Entrance exams should be taken during the junior and senior years. There are deferred admissions and rolling admissions plans. Application deadlines are open. Application fee is $40. Notification is sent on a rolling basis. Applications are accepted on-line. 36 applicants were on a recent waiting list, 26 were accepted.

Financial Aid: In 2009-2010, 100% of all full-time freshmen and 100% of continuing full-time students received some form of financial aid. 64% of all full-time freshmen and 59% of continuing full-time students received need-based aid. The average freshmen award was $27,069, with $2,373 ($19,000 maximum) from need-based scholarships or need-based grants; $3,547 ($7,000 maximum) from need-based self-help aid (loans and jobs); and $21,150 ($38,934 maximum) from other non-need-based awards and non-need-based scholarships. 35% of undergraduate students work part-time. Average annual earnings from campus work are $905. The average financial indebtedness of the 2009 graduate was $17,641. The FAFSA and the college's own financial statement are required. The priority date for freshman financial aid applications for fall entry is February 15.

Computers: Wireless access is available. All students may access the system 24 hours a day, 7 days a week. There are no time limits and no fees.

HILLSDALE COLLEGE

Hillsdale, MI 49242　　　　　　　　　　**(517) 607-2327; (517) 607-2223**

Full-time: 616 men, 668 women	**Faculty:** 110
Part-time: 16 men, 26 women	**Ph.D.s:** 90%
Graduate: none	**Student/Faculty:** 12 to 1
Year: semesters, summer session	**Tuition:** $19,090
Application Deadline: February 15	**Room & Board:** $7,350
Freshman Class: 1401 applied, 900 accepted, 358 enrolled	
SAT CR/M/W: 670/630/650	**ACT:** 28 **HIGHLY COMPETITIVE+**

Hillsdale College, founded in 1844, is a private liberal arts college emphasizing classical liberal arts, pre-professional, business, education, science and humanities. There are no undergraduate schools. The 3 libraries contain 220,000 volumes, 76,000 microform items, 12,000 audio/video tapes/CDs/DVDs, and subscribe to 1,200 periodicals including electronic. Computerized library services include interlibrary loans, database searching, and Internet access. Special learning facilities include a learning resource center, a media center, an early childhood education lab, an arboretum, a 3000-book economics library, and a rare books room. The 250-acre campus is in a small town 120 miles southwest of Detroit. Including any residence halls, there are 60 buildings.

Programs of Study: Hillsdale confers B.A. and B.S. degrees. Bachelor's degrees are awarded in BIOLOGICAL SCIENCE (biology/biological science), BUSINESS (accounting, banking and finance, business administration and management, international business management, and marketing/retailing/merchandising), COMMUNICATIONS AND THE ARTS (classics, comparative literature, dramatic arts, English, fine arts, French, German, music, Spanish, and speech/debate/rhetoric), COMPUTER AND PHYSICAL SCIENCE (chemistry, mathematics, and physics), EDUCATION (art education, early childhood education, elementary education, foreign languages education, middle school education, music education, physical education, science education, and secondary education), HEALTH PROFESSIONS (predentistry, premedicine, and preveterinary science), SOCIAL SCIENCE (American studies, Christian studies, economics, European studies, history, political science/government, prelaw, psychology, religion, social science, and sociology). History, economics, and classics are the strongest academically. Business, history, and biology are the largest.

Special: Special academic programs include the Washington Journalism Internship at the National Journalism Center and the Washington-Hillsdale Intern Program (WHIP), which places students in congressional or government offices. Students may study abroad in France, Germany, or Spain, and qualified students are chosen to attend Oxford University for a year. A business internship is offered in London at Regents College. The Thomas Professional Sales Intern program is also available. The college offers an accelerated degree; interdisciplinary majors, including political economy combining economics, history, and political science; 3-2 and 2-2 engineering degrees; and work-study programs at the city radio station WCSR and the city newspaper, the Hillsdale Daily News. There are 24 national honor societies, a freshman honors program, and 24 departmental honors programs.

Admissions: 64% of the 2009-2010 applicants were accepted. The SAT scores for the 2009-2010 freshman class were: Critical Reading--1% below 500, 12% between 500 and 599, 46% between 600 and 700, and 40% above 700; Math--4% below 500, 27% between 500 and 599, 53% between 600 and 700, and 16% above 700; Writing--2% below 500, 20% between 500 and 599, 52% between 600 and

700, and 26 above 700. The ACT scores were 2% below 21, 13% between 21 and 23, 23% between 24 and 26, 23% between 27 and 28, and 39% above 28. 77% of the current freshmen were in the top fifth of their class; 92% were in the top two fifths. There were 13 National Merit finalists. 35 freshmen graduated first in their class.

Requirements: The SAT or ACT is required. In addition, applicants must be a high school graduate or have earned a GED, and must have completed 4 years of English, 3 each of math and science, and 2 each of history, social studies, and foreign language. The college requires 2 letters of recommendation and an essay. An interview is also recommended. For music majors, an audition is required for a scholarship. The school recommends taking SAT: Subject tests. Hillsdale requires applicants to be in the upper 50% of their class. A GPA of 3.2 is required. AP and CLEP credits are accepted. Important factors in the admissions decision are advanced placement or honors courses, leadership record, and extracurricular activities record.

Procedure: Freshmen are admitted fall, spring, and summer. Entrance exams should be taken in the spring of the junior year and/or the fall of the senior year. There are early decision and deferred admissions plans. Early decision applications should be filed by November 15; regular applications, by February 15 for fall entry, December 15 for spring entry, and May 1 for summer entry, along with a $35 fee. Notification of early decision is sent November 15; regular decision, April 1. Applications are accepted on-line. 40 applicants were on a recent waiting list, 5 were accepted.

Financial Aid: In 2009-2010, 85% of all full-time freshmen and 87% of continuing full-time students received some form of financial aid. 75% of all full-time freshmen and 83% of continuing full-time students received need-based aid. The average freshmen award was $13,500. 65% of undergraduate students work part-time. Average annual earnings from campus work are $1300. The average financial indebtedness of the 2009 graduate was $15,000. Hillsdale is a member of CSS. The college's own financial statement is required. The priority date for freshman financial aid applications for fall entry is February 1. The deadline for filing freshman financial aid applications for fall entry is April 1.

Computers: Wireless access is available. All students may access the system. at any time. There are no time limits and no fees.

HIRAM COLLEGE
Hiram, OH 44234

(330) 569-5169
(800) 362-5280; (330) 569-5944

Full-time: 555 men, 634 women	**Faculty:** 72; IIB, --$
Part-time: 54 men, 124 women	**Ph.D.s:** 92%
Graduate: 6 men, 22 women	**Student/Faculty:** 17 to 1
Year: see profile, summer session	**Tuition:** $27,135
Application Deadline: open	**Room & Board:** $9010
Freshman Class: 1269 applied, 1112 accepted, 293 enrolled	
SAT CR/M: 526/521	**ACT:** 23 **VERY COMPETITIVE**

Hiram College, founded in 1850, is a private, residential liberal arts and sciences institution. In addition to regional accreditation, Hiram has baccalaureate program accreditation with NASM. The library contains 506,792 volumes, 131 microform items, and 22,786 audio/video tapes/CDs/DVDs, and subscribes to 8890 periodicals including electronic. Computerized library services include interlibrary loans, database searching, and Internet access. Special learning facilities include a learning resource center, art gallery, planetarium, radio station, a 260-acre biological field station, and a field station in the Upper Peninsula of Michigan. The 110-acre campus is in a rural area 35 miles southeast of Cleveland. Including any residence halls, there are 39 buildings.

Programs of Study: Hiram confers B.A., B.S.N. degrees. Master's degrees are also awarded. Bachelor's degrees are awarded in BIOLOGICAL SCIENCE (biochemistry, biology/biological science, and neurosciences), BUSINESS (accounting and management science), COMMUNICATIONS AND THE ARTS (art, communications, creative writing, dramatic arts, English, French, music, Spanish, and studio art), COMPUTER AND PHYSICAL SCIENCE (chemistry, computer science, mathematics, and physics), EDUCATION (education), ENGINEERING AND ENVIRONMENTAL DESIGN (environmental science), HEALTH PROFESSIONS (biomedical science and nursing), SOCIAL SCIENCE (economics, history, philosophy, political science/government, psychology, religion, social studies, and sociology). Management, accounting, and biology are the largest.

Special: There is cross-registration through the Cleveland Commission on Higher Education and a 3-2 engineering program with Case Western Reserve and Washington Universities. There is a Washington semester and study abroad in many countries with courses taught by Hiram faculty. Double majors and individually arranged internships in all fields, student-designed majors, and pass/no credit options are possible. An accelerated degree program in biomedical humanities is possible. There are 6 national honor societies, including Phi Beta Kappa. In addition, all departments have honors programs.

Admissions: 88% of the 2009-2010 applicants were accepted. The SAT scores for the 2009-2010 freshman class were: Critical Reading--39% below 500, 35% between 500 and 599, 21% between 600 and 700; and 4% above 700; Math--39% below 500, 36% between 500 and 599, 22% between 600 and 700, and 2% above 700. 38% of the current freshmen were in the top fifth of their class.

Requirements: The SAT or ACT is required. In addition, applicants should have completed 16 academic units or the GED equivalent. An essay is required. A portfolio, audition, and interview are recommended. A GPA of 2.6 is required. AP and CLEP credits are accepted.

Procedure: Freshmen are admitted fall and spring. Entrance exams should be taken no later than the fall of the senior year. There are deferred admissions and rolling admissions plans. Application deadlines are open. Notification is sent on a rolling basis. Applications are accepted on-line.

Financial Aid: In 2009-2010, 94% of all full-time freshmen and 93% of continuing full-time students received some form of financial aid. 82% of all full-time students received need-based aid. The average financial indebtedness of the 2009 graduate was $20,381. Hiram is a member of CSS. The FAFSA is required. The deadline for filing freshman financial aid applications for fall entry is March 1.

Computers: Wireless access is available. Students can use wireless networking in the classrooms, academic buildings, and residence halls. Hiram has 120 wireless access points. All students may access the system 24 hours a day, 7 days per week. There are no time limits and no fees. All students are required to have a personal computer. Dell laptops are recommended.

HOBART AND WILLIAM SMITH COLLEGES

Geneva, NY 14456-3397 · **H: (315) 781-3622; (315) 781-3471**

Full-time: 875 men, 1010 women	**Faculty:** IIB, +$
Part-time: 3 men and women	**Ph.D.s:** n/av
Graduate: none	**Student/Faculty:** n/av
Year: semesters	**Tuition:** $34,000
Application Deadline: February 1	**Room & Board:** $9000
Freshman Class: n/av	
SAT or ACT: required	**VERY COMPETITIVE**

Hobart College, a men's college founded in 1822, shares campus, classes, and faculty with William Smith College, a women's college founded in 1908. Together, these coordinate colleges offer degree programs in the liberal arts. Figures in the above capsule and in this profile are approximate. The library contains 375,762 volumes, 77,396 microform items, and 9,600 audio/video tapes/CDs/DVDs, and subscribes to 1,926 periodicals including electronic. Computerized library services include interlibrary loans, database searching, and Internet access. Special learning facilities include a learning resource center, art gallery, radio station, a 100-acre natural preserve, and a 70-foot research vessel. The 170-acre campus is in a small town 50 miles west of Syracuse and 50 miles east of Rochester, on the north shore of Seneca Lake. Including any residence halls, there are 95 buildings.

Programs of Study: HWS confers B.A. and B.S. degrees. Master's degrees are also awarded. Bachelor's degrees are awarded in BIOLOGICAL SCIENCE (biology/biological science), COMMUNICATIONS AND THE ARTS (art history and appreciation, classics, comparative literature, dance, English, fine arts, French, modern language, music, and studio art), COMPUTER AND PHYSICAL SCIENCE (chemistry, computer science, geoscience, mathematics, and physics), ENGINEERING AND ENVIRONMENTAL DESIGN (architecture and environmental science), SOCIAL SCIENCE (African studies, American studies, anthropology, Asian/Oriental studies, economics, European studies, history, international relations, Latin American studies, philosophy, political science/government, psychology, religion, Russian and Slavic studies, sociology, Spanish studies, urban studies, and women's studies). Natural sciences, environmental studies, and creative writing are the strongest academically. English, economics, and political science are the largest.

Special: Students are encouraged to spend at least 1 term in a study-abroad program, offered in more than 29 countries and locales within the United States. Options include a United Nations term, a Washington semester, an urban semester, and prearchitecture semesters in New York, Paris, Florence, or Copenhagen. HWS offers dual and student-designed majors, internships, credit for life/military/work experience, nondegree study, and pass/fail options. There are also advanced business degree programs with Clarkson University and Rochester Institute of Technology and 3-2 engineering degrees with Columbia University, Rensselaer Polytechnic Institute, and Dartmouth College. There are 9 national honor societies, including Phi Beta Kappa, and 100 departmental honors programs.

Requirements: The SAT or ACT is required. SAT: Subject tests are not required but will be considered if taken. A GED may be is accepted. A total of 19 academic credits is required, including 4 years of English, 3 of math, and at least 3 each of lab science, foreign language, and history. An essay is required; an interview is recommended. AP credits are accepted. Important factors in the admissions decision are advanced placement or honors courses, evidence of special talent, and leadership record.

Procedure: Freshmen are admitted fall. Entrance exams should be taken no later than December of the senior year. There are early decision, early admissions and deferred admissions plans. Early decision applications should be filed by November 15; regular applications, by February 1 for fall entry, along with a $45 fee. Notification of early decision is sent December 15; regular decision, sent in March. Applications are accepted on-line. A waiting list is maintained.

Financial Aid: HWS is a member of CSS. The CSS/Profile and FAFSA are required. Check with the school for current application deadlines.

Computers: All students may access the system from 8 A.M. to 1 A.M., 7 days a week. There are no time limits and no fees. It is strongly recommended that all students have a personal computer. A Gateway Solo Laptop is recommended.

HOFSTRA UNIVERSITY
Hempstead, NY 11549

(516) 463-6700
(800) HOFSTRA; (516) 463-7660

Full-time: 3505 men, 3822 women	**Faculty:** 420; I, av$
Part-time: 318 men, 274 women	**Ph.D.s:** 91%
Graduate: 1586 men, 2563 women	**Student/Faculty:** 17 to 1
Year: 4-1-4, summer session	**Tuition:** $30,130
Application Deadline: open	**Room & Board:** $11,330
Freshman Class: 20,829 applied, 11,801 accepted, 1568 enrolled	
SAT CR/M: 580/600	**ACT:** 26 **VERY COMPETITIVE+**

Hofstra University, founded in 1935, is an independent institution offering programs in liberal arts and sciences, business, communications, education, health and human services, honors studies, and law. There are 7 undergraduate schools and 6 graduate schools. In addition to regional accreditation, Hofstra has baccalaureate program accreditation with AACSB, ABA, ABET, ACEJMC, ACS, APA, ARC-PA, CAATE, and TEAC. The 3 libraries contain 1.1 million volumes, 3.5 million microform items, and 16,215 audio/video tapes/CDs/DVDs, and subscribe to 11,353 periodicals including electronic. Computerized library services include interlibrary loans, database searching, Internet access, and laptop Internet portals. Special learning facilities include a learning resource center, art gallery, radio station, TV station, financial trading room, comprehensive media production facility, converged newsroom learning center, career center, writing center, linux beowolf cluster, digital language lab, technology, science, and engineering labs, a rooftop observatory, 7 theaters, assessment centers for child observation and counseling, child care institute, a cultural center, a museum, an arboretum, and a bird sanctuary. The 240-acre campus is in a suburban area 25 miles east of New York City. Including any residence halls, there are 115 buildings.

Programs of Study: Hofstra confers B.A., B.S., B.B.A., B.E., B.F.A., and B.S.Ed. degrees. Master's and doctoral degrees are also awarded. Bachelor's degrees are awarded in AGRICULTURE (environmental studies), BIOLOGICAL SCIENCE (biochemistry, biology/biological science, and ecology), BUSINESS (accounting, banking and finance, business administration and management, business law, entrepreneurial studies, international business management, labor studies, management information systems, and marketing management), COMMUNICATIONS AND THE ARTS (American literature, art history and appreciation, audio technology, ceramic art and design, Chinese, classics, comparative literature, creative writing, dance, design, dramatic arts, English literature, film arts, fine arts, French, German, Hebrew, Italian, jazz, journalism, linguistics, media arts, metal/jewelry, music, music business management, music history and appreciation, music performance, music theory and composition, painting, photography, public relations, publishing, radio/television technology, Russian, Spanish, speech/debate/rhetoric, theater design, theater management, video, and visual and performing arts), COMPUTER AND PHYSICAL SCIENCE (applied mathematics, applied physics, chemistry, computer science, geology, mathematics, natural sciences, and physics), EDUCATION (art education, athletic training, business education, dance education, early childhood education, elementary education, English education, foreign languages education, health education, mathematics education, music education, physical education, science education, secondary education, and social studies education), ENGINEERING AND ENVIRONMENTAL DESIGN (biomedical engineering, civil engineering, computer engineering, electrical/electronics engineering, environmental engineering, industrial engineering, manufacturing engineering, and mechanical engineering), HEALTH PROFESSIONS (allied health, community health work, exercise science, health science, physician's assistant, predentistry, premedicine, preoptometry, preosteopathy, prepodiatry, preveterinary science, and speech pathology/audiology), SOCIAL SCIENCE (African studies, American studies, anthropology, Asian/Oriental studies, Caribbean studies, economics, forensic studies, geography, Hispanic American studies, history, humanities, interdisciplinary studies, Judaic studies, Latin American studies, liberal arts/general studies, philosophy, political science/government, psychology, social science, sociology, and women's studies). Accounting, biology, and English are the strongest academically. Accounting, biology, and education are the largest.

Special: Internships in numerous career fields, a Washington semester, an Albany State Assembly internship, study abroad in 16 countries, and dual and student-designed majors are offered. Credit for prior learning and credit by exam are given with proper credentials. Hofstra offers nondegree study and pass/fail options. There are 32 national honor societies, including Phi Beta Kappa, a freshman honors program, and 35 departmental honors programs.

Admissions: 57% of the 2009-2010 applicants were accepted. The SAT scores for the 2009-2010 freshman class were: Critical Reading--7% below 500, 50% between 500 and 599, 39% between 600 and 700, and 5% above 700; Math--4% below 500, 44% between 500 and 599, 47% between 600 and 700, and 4% above 700. The ACT scores were 3% below 21, 20% between 21 and 23, 38% between 24 and 26, 20% between 27 and 28, and 19% above 28. 49% of the current freshmen were in the top fifth of their class; 78% were in the top two fifths. 8 freshmen graduated first in their class.

Requirements: The SAT or ACT is required for some programs. In addition, applicants should graduate from an accredited secondary school or have a GED. Preparatory work should include 4 years of English, 3 each of history and social studies, math, and science, and 2 of foreign language. Engineering students are required to have 4 years of math and 1 each of chemistry and physics. An essay is required. Interviews are recommended. 1 counselor or teacher recommendation is recommended. AP and CLEP credits are accepted. Important factors in the admissions decision are advanced placement or honors courses, recommendations by school officials, and geographical diversity.

Procedure: Freshmen are admitted fall and spring. Entrance exams should be taken in the junior or senior year. There are early admissions, deferred admissions, and rolling admissions plans. Early decision applications should be filed by December 15; deadlines for regular applications are rolling. Application fee is $70. Notification of early decision is sent January 15; regular decision, February 1. 296 applicants were on the 2009 waiting list; 90 were admitted. Applications are accepted on-line.

Financial Aid: In 2009-2010, 89% of all full-time freshmen and 82% of continuing full-time students received some form of financial aid. 63% of all full-time freshmen and 57% of continuing full-time students received need-based aid. The average freshman award was $15,283. Need-based scholarships or need-based grants averaged $13,189 ($52,122 maximum); need-based self-help aid (loans and jobs) averaged $7,002 ($15,300 maximum); non-need-based athletic scholarships averaged $27,119 ($48,394 maximum); and other non-need-based awards and non-need-based scholarships averaged $10,589 ($33,100 maximum). 41% of undergraduate students work part-time. Average annual earnings from campus work are $3100. The FAFSA and the state aid form are required. The priority date for freshman financial aid applications for fall entry is February 15.

Computers: Wireless access is available. Students have access to 1628 PCs in labs and classrooms. These computers are all connected to the campus network and have access to the Internet and Internet2. Students can use the extensive network of wireless hot spots or plug into public ports to gain access to the campus network and the Internet using their laptops. Residence hall rooms have wireless and a high-speed port per student for access to the network. All students may access the system. There are no time limits. The fee is $105. It is strongly recommended that all students have a personal computer. A Lenovo or Mac laptop (for certain majors) is recommended.

HOOD COLLEGE

Frederick, MD 21701-8575
(301) 696-3400
(800) 922-1599; (301) 696-3819

Full-time: 400 men, 859 women	**Faculty:** 80; IIA, --$
Part-time: 54 men, 119 women	**Ph.D.s:** 98%
Graduate: 319 men, 742 women	**Student/Faculty:** 15 to 1
Year: semesters, summer session	**Tuition:** $28,170
Application Deadline: February 15	**Room & Board:** $9,440
Freshman Class: 1622 applied, 1166 accepted, 251 enrolled	
SAT CR/M/W: 551/535/542	**ACT:** 23 **VERY COMPETITIVE**

Hood College, founded in 1893, is an independent, comprehensive college that offers an integration of the liberal arts and professional preparation, as well as undergraduate majors in the natural sciences. There are no undergraduate schools and one graduate school. In addition to regional accreditation, Hood has baccalaureate program accreditation with CSWE. The library contains 208,950 volumes, 743,691 microform items, 5,696 audio/video tapes/CDs/DVDs, and subscribes to 339 periodicals including electronic. Computerized library services include interlibrary loans, database searching, Internet access, and laptop Internet portals. Special learning facilities include a learning resource center, art gallery, radio station, aquatic center, a child development lab, an observatory, and information technology center. The 50-acre campus is in a suburban area 45 miles northwest of Washington, D.C. and 45 miles west of Baltimore. Including any residence halls, there are 31 buildings.

Programs of Study: Hood confers B.A. and B.S. degrees. Master's degrees are also awarded. Bachelor's degrees are awarded in BIOLOGICAL SCIENCE (biochemistry and biology/biological science), BUSINESS (business administration and management and management science), COMMUNICATIONS AND THE ARTS (art, communications, English, French, German, music, and Spanish), COMPUTER AND PHYSICAL SCIENCE (chemistry, computer science, and mathematics), EDUCATION (early childhood education, elementary education, English education, foreign languages education, mathematics education, science education, secondary education, and special education), ENGINEERING AND ENVIRONMENTAL DESIGN (environmental science), SOCIAL SCIENCE (archeology, economics, history, Latin American studies, law, philosophy, political science/government, psychology, religion, social work, and sociology). Biology, art, and archaeology are the strongest academically. Management, psychology, and biology are the largest.

Special: The college offers a Washington semester with American University, dual majors, student-designed majors, a B.A.-B.S. degree in engineering/math, credit for life experience, nondegree study, an accelerated degree program, pass/fail options, and cross-registration with area colleges and the Duke University Marine Sciences Education Consortium. Internships of up to 15 credits are available in all majors at more than 100 sites throughout the United States and abroad. Students may study abroad in the Dominican Republic, Japan, Spain, France, and other countries. There is a 4-year honors program featuring 1 interdisciplinary course per semester and special co-curricular activities. There are 14 national honor societies, a freshman honors program, and 14 departmental honors programs.

Admissions: 72% of the 2009-2010 applicants were accepted. The SAT scores for the 2009-2010 freshman class were: Critical Reading--29% below 500, 41% between 500 and 599, 22% between 600 and 700, and 8 above 700; Math--38% below 500, 39% between 500 and 599, 20% between 600 and 700, and 3 above 700; Writing--30% below 500, 44% between 500 and 599, 23% between 600 and 700, and 3 above 700. The ACT scores were 29% below 21, 33% between 21 and 23, 19% between 24 and 26, 6% between 27 and 28, and 13% above 28. 41% of the current freshmen were in the top fifth of their class; 71% were in the top two fifths. 3 freshmen graduated first in their class.

Requirements: The SAT or ACT is required. In addition, applicants should be graduates of an accredited secondary school. The GED is accepted. Hood recommends the completion of at least 16 academic credits in high school, including courses in English, social sciences, natural sciences, foreign languages, and math. A GPA of 2.5 is required. AP and CLEP credits are accepted. Important factors in the admissions decision are advanced placement or honors courses, leadership record, and extracurricular activities record.

Procedure: Freshmen are admitted fall and spring. Entrance exams should be taken in spring of the junior year or fall of the senior year. There are early admissions, deferred admissions, and rolling admissions plans. Applications should be filed by February 15 for fall entry and December 31 for spring entry. The fall 2008 application fee was $35. Applications are accepted on-line.

Financial Aid: In 2009-2010, 98% of all full-time freshmen and 99% of continuing full-time students received some form of financial aid. 76% of all full-time freshmen and 81% of continuing full-time students received need-based aid. The average freshmen award was $25,347, with $20,993 ($27,910 maximum) from need-based scholarships or need-based grants; $3,673 ($10,300 maximum) from need-based self-help aid (loans and jobs); and $21,810 ($28,170 maximum) from other non-need-based awards and non-need-based scholarships. 18% of undergraduate students work part-time. Average annual earnings from campus work are $1700. The average financial indebtedness of the 2009 graduate was $17,382. Hood is a member of CSS. The FAFSA is required. The priority date for freshman financial aid applications for fall entry is February 15.

Computers: Wireless access is available. The campus Whitaker Center, the library, and residence halls are wireless. There are 2 labs and 5 simple machines for students to access in those locations, plus 4 to 5 per residence halls. There are more than 150 computers in labs available for student use. All students may access the system. 24 hours per day, 7 days a week. There are no time limits and no fees. It is strongly recommended that all students have a personal computer. A Pentium 4 class machine with WinXP Pro, 256 MB memory is recommended.

HOPE COLLEGE
Holland, MI 49422-9000

(616) 395-7850
(800) 968-7850; (616) 395-7130

Full-time: 1222 men, 1892 women	**Faculty:** 230; IIB, av$
Part-time: 64 men, 52 women	**Ph.D.s:** 72%
Graduate: none	**Student/Faculty:** 14 to 1
Year: semesters, summer session	**Tuition:** $25,660
Application Deadline: open	**Room & Board:** $7870
Freshman Class: 2481 applied, 2275 accepted, 801 enrolled	
SAT CR/M: 585/597	**ACT:** 26 **VERY COMPETITIVE+**

Hope College, founded by Dutch pioneers in 1866, is a private liberal arts institution affiliated with the Reformed Church in America. In addition to regional accreditation, Hope has baccalaureate program accreditation with ABET, CSWE, NASAD, NASM, and NCATE. The 2 libraries contain 368,864 volumes, 394,159 microform items, and 15,846 audio/video tapes/CDs/DVDs, and subscribe to 10,500 periodicals including electronic. Computerized library services include interlibrary loans, database searching, Internet access, and laptop Internet portals. Special learning facilities include a learning resource center, art gallery, planetarium, radio station, TV station, academic support center, and modern and classical language lab. The 120-acre campus is in an urban area 26 miles southwest of Grand Rapids and 5 miles east of Lake Michigan. Including any residence halls, there are 130 buildings.

Programs of Study: Hope confers B.A., B.S., B.Mus., and B.S.N. degrees. Bachelor's degrees are awarded in BIOLOGICAL SCIENCE (biology/biological science), BUSINESS (accounting and business administration and management), COMMUNICATIONS AND THE ARTS (communications, dance, dramatic arts, English, fine arts, French, German, Latin, music, and Spanish), COMPUTER AND PHYSICAL SCIENCE (chemistry, computer science, geology, mathematics, and physics), EDUCATION (art education, elementary education, foreign languages education, music education, science education, secondary education, and special education), ENGINEERING AND ENVIRONMENTAL DESIGN (engineering), HEALTH PROFESSIONS (nursing), SOCIAL SCIENCE (economics, history, international studies, philosophy, physical fitness/movement, political science/government, psychology, religion, social work, and sociology). Chemistry, biological sciences, and psychology are the strongest academically. Management, communications, and psychology are the largest.

Special: The college offers internships in all academic areas as well as on-campus work-study programs, student-designed majors, study abroad in more than 57 countries, and Washington, Chicago, New York, and Philadelphia semesters. Students may have dual majors. There are 20 national honor societies, including Phi Beta Kappa, and 1 departmental honors program.

Admissions: 92% of the 2009-2010 applicants were accepted. The SAT scores for the 2009-2010 freshman class were: Critical Reading--17% below 500, 38% between 500 and 599, 34% between 600 and 700, and 10% above 700; Math--14% below 500, 34% between 500 and 599, 37% between 600 and 700, and 14% above 700. The ACT scores were 8% below 21, 20% between 21 and 23, 30%

between 24 and 26, 176% between 27 and 28, and 26% above 28. 57% of the current freshmen were in the top fifth of their class; 84% were in the top two fifths. There were 8 National Merit finalists.

Requirements: The SAT or ACT is required. The college requires a high school transcript, which must include 4 years of English, 2 each of math, a foreign language, and social science, and 1 year of a lab science, as well as 5 other academic courses. The college requires submission of an essay and recommends an interview. A portfolio or audition is required for certain majors. The GED is considered. AP and CLEP credits are accepted. Important factors in the admissions decision are advanced placement or honors courses, evidence of special talent, and leadership record.

Procedure: Freshmen are admitted fall and spring. Entrance exams should be taken during spring of the junior year or fall of the senior year. There are deferred admissions and rolling admissions plans. Application deadlines are open. The fall 2008 application fee was $35. Applications are accepted on-line. A waiting list is maintained.

Financial Aid: In 2009-2010, 96% of all full-time freshmen and 90% of continuing full-time students received some form of financial aid. 67% of all full-time freshmen and 60% of continuing full-time students received need-based aid. The average freshman award was $22,808. 50% of undergraduate students work part-time. Average annual earnings from campus work are $1206. The average financial indebtedness of the 2009 graduate was $17,794. Hope is a member of CSS. The FAFSA and the college's own financial statement are required. The priority date for freshman financial aid applications for fall entry is March 1.

Computers: Wireless access is available. Unfiltered network and Internet access is provided in all resident rooms, classrooms, study areas, and libraries. Public PCs are located in residence halls, academic buildings, student centers, classrooms, and libraries. All students may access the system 24 hours a day. There are no time limits and no fees.

HOUGHTON COLLEGE
Houghton, NY 14744

(585) 567-9353
(800) 777-2556; (585) 567-9522

Full-time: 428 men, 824 women	**Faculty:** 88
Part-time: 28 men, 31 women	**Ph.D.s:** 88%
Graduate: 13 men, 12 women	**Student/Faculty:** 14 to 1
Year: semesters	**Tuition:** $24,440
Application Deadline: open	**Room & Board:** $7000
Freshman Class: 1000 applied, 889 accepted, 287 enrolled	
SAT CR/M/W: 600/578/582	**ACT:** 26 **VERY COMPETITIVE+**

Houghton College, founded in 1883, provides a residential educational experience integrating academic instruction with Christian faith. In addition to regional accreditation, Houghton has baccalaureate program accreditation with NASM. The library contains 230,070 volumes, 46,858 microform items, and 14,227 audio/video tapes/CDs/DVDs, and subscribes to 27,151 periodicals including electronic. Computerized library services include interlibrary loans, database searching, Internet access, and laptop Internet portals. Special learning facilities include a learning resource center, art gallery, radio station, an equestrian center, a ropes course, and a digital media lab. The 1300-acre campus is in a rural area 65 miles southeast of Buffalo and 70 miles southwest of Rochester. Including any residence halls, there are 20 buildings.

Programs of Study: Houghton confers B.A., B.S., and B.Mus. degrees. Associate and master's degrees are also awarded. Bachelor's degrees are awarded in BIOLOGICAL SCIENCE (biochemistry and biology/biological science), BUSINESS (accounting, business administration and management, and recreation and leisure services), COMMUNICATIONS AND THE ARTS (art, communications, English, music performance, music theory and composition, and Spanish), COMPUTER AND PHYSICAL SCIENCE (chemistry, computer science, information sciences and systems, mathematics, physics, and science), EDUCATION (elementary education, music education, physical education, science education, secondary education, and teaching English as a second/foreign language (TESOL/TEFOL)), ENGINEERING AND ENVIRONMENTAL DESIGN (environmental science), HEALTH PROFESSIONS (medical technology), SOCIAL SCIENCE (biblical studies, crosscultural studies, history, humanities, international relations, ministries, philosophy, political science/government, psychology, religion, and sociology). Biology, religion, and music are the strongest academically. Education, biology, and business are the largest.

Special: Students may cross-register with members of the Western New York Consortium, the Christian College Consortium, and the Five College Committee. Internships are available in psychology, social work, business, educational ministries, physical fitness, political science, graphic design, communication, athletic training, recreation, English, and Christian education. Study abroad in 25 countries, a Washington semester, dual majors, and a 3-2 engineering degree with Clarkson and Washington Universities are available. Credit for military experience and nondegree study are possible. There are 2 national honor societies and a freshman honors program.

Admissions: 89% of the 2009-2010 applicants were accepted. The SAT scores for the 2009-2010 freshman class were: Critical Reading--15% below 500, 38% between 500 and 599, 31% between 600 and 700, and 16% above 700; Math--17% below 500, 42% between 500 and 599, 33% between 600 and 700, and 8% above 700; Writing--17% below 500, 39% between 500 and 599, 33% between 600 and 700, and 11% above 700. The ACT scores were 12% below 21, 24% between 21 and 23, 22% between 24 and 26, 14% between 27 and 28, and 28% above 28. 57% of the current freshmen were in the top fifth of their class; 83% were in the top two fifths. There was 1 National Merit finalist. 16 freshmen graduated first in their class.

Requirements: The SAT or ACT is required. In addition, applicants must graduate from an accredited secondary school, be homeschooled, or have a GED. A total of 16 academic credits is recommended, including 4 of English, 3 of social studies, and 2 each of foreign language, math, and science. An essay is required. Music students must audition. An interview is recommended. Houghton requires applicants to be in the upper 50% of their class. A GPA of 2.5 is required. AP and CLEP credits are accepted. Important factors in the admissions decision are personality/intangible qualities, recommendations by school officials, and advanced placement or honors courses.

Procedure: Freshmen are admitted fall and spring. Entrance exams should be taken in the spring of the junior year or fall of the senior year. There are deferred admissions and rolling admissions plans. Application deadlines are open. Application fee is $40. Notification is sent January 1. Applications are accepted online.

Financial Aid: In 2009-2010, 99% of all full-time freshmen and 98% of continuing full-time students received some form of financial aid. 97% of all full-time freshmen and 89% of continuing full-time students received need-based aid. The average freshman award was $22,000. Need-based scholarships or need-based

grants averaged $8599 ($25,440 maximum); need-based self-help aid (loans and jobs) averaged $5819 ($9750 maximum); non-need-based athletic scholarships averaged $5764 ($15,220 maximum); and other non-need-based awards and non-need-based scholarships averaged $5786 ($21,250 maximum). 43% of undergraduate students work part-time. Average annual earnings from campus work are $888. The average financial indebtedness of the 2009 graduate was $32,580. Houghton is a member of CSS. The FAFSA is required. The priority date for freshman financial aid applications for fall entry is March 1.

Computers: The campus is fully wired and has wireless capabilities. All students are provided with network access. All students may access the system. There are no time limits and no fees. It is strongly recommended that all students have a personal computer. The required model and make change from year to year.

ILLINOIS INSTITUTE OF TECHNOLOGY

Chicago, IL 60616
(312) 567-3025
(800) 448-2329; (312) 567-6939

Full-time: 1710 men, 630 women	**Faculty:** n/av
Part-time: 190men, 65 women	**Ph.D.s:** 88%
Graduate: 3030 men, 1810women	**Student/Faculty:** n/av
Year: semesters, summer session	**Tuition:** $26,000
Application Deadline: open	**Room & Board:** $9000
Freshman Class: n/av	
ACT: 28	**HIGHLY COMPETITIVE+**

Founded in 1890, IIT is a Ph.D.-granting university with more than 7,300 students in engineering, sciences, architecture, psychology, design, humanities, business and law. IIT's interprofessional, technology-focused curriculum is designed to advance knowledge through research and scholarship, to cultivate invention improving the human condition, and to prepare students from throughout the world for a life of professional achievement, service to society, and individual fulfillment. The figures in the above capsule and in this profile are approximate. There are 6 undergraduate schools and 8 graduate schools. In addition to regional accreditation, IIT has baccalaureate program accreditation with ABET and NAAB. The 3 libraries contain 1.3 million volumes, 4,256 audio/video tapes/CDs/DVDs, and subscribe to 24,596 periodicals including electronic. Computerized library services include interlibrary loans, database searching, Internet access, and laptop Internet portals. Special learning facilities include a learning resource center, art gallery, and radio station. The 120-acre campus is in an urban area 3 miles south of downtown Chicago. Including any residence halls, there are 33 buildings.

Programs of Study: IIT confers B.A., B.S. degrees. Master's and doctoral degrees are also awarded. Bachelor's degrees are awarded in BIOLOGICAL SCIENCE (biochemistry, biology/biological science, biophysics, and molecular biology), COMMUNICATIONS AND THE ARTS (technical and business writing), COMPUTER AND PHYSICAL SCIENCE (applied mathematics, chemistry, computer science, information sciences and systems, physics, and web technology), ENGINEERING AND ENVIRONMENTAL DESIGN (aeronautical engineering, architectural engineering, architecture, chemical engineering, civil engineering, computer engineering, electrical/electronics engineering, engineering management, industrial administration/management, manufacturing technology, materials science, mechanical engineering, and metallurgical engineering), SOCIAL SCIENCE (humanities, political science/government, and psychology). Architecture, engineering, and science and letters are the largest.

Special: Co-op programs and internships are available to all majors. All countries are eligible for study abroad. Dual majors may include a variety of majors. Cross-registration available. There are 3 national honor societies.

Requirements: The SAT or ACT are required for some programs. In addition, graduation from an accredited secondary school is required for admission. 17 academic credits are required for admission: 4 units of English; 4 units of math: 3 units of science, of these, 2 units must be laboratory science; 2 units of social studies and 2 units of history. In addition, 2 units of foreign language and 1 unit of computer science are recommended. AP credits are accepted. Important factors in the admissions decision are recommendations by school officials, leadership record, and advanced placement or honors courses.

Procedure: Freshmen are admitted fall and spring. There are deferred admissions and rolling admissions plans. Application deadlines are open. Notification is sent on a rolling basis. Applications are accepted on-line. Check with the school for current application fees.

Financial Aid: In a recent year, all full-time freshmen and 98% of continuing full-time students received some form of financial aid. 70% of all full-time freshmen and 58% of continuing full-time students received need-based aid. The average freshmen award was $19,472. 37% of undergraduate students worked part-time. Average annual earnings from campus work were $2021. The average financial indebtedness of the 2009 graduate was $21,326. IIT is a member of CSS. The FAFSA is required. Check with the school for current application deadlines.

Computers: Wireless access is available. ITT provides wired and wireless network access. Most main campus buildings have wired Internet access except the graduate apartments, which have wireless only. Wireless is available in all residence halls, the campus center, library and all academic buildings. There are over 375 PCs in computer labs located throughout the campus. All students may access the system 24 hours/day, 7 days/week. There are no time limits and no fees. It is strongly recommended that all students have a personal computer. A Dell and Apple are preferred vendors, but not required.

ILLINOIS STATE UNIVERSITY
Normal, IL 61761
(309) 438-2181
(800) 366-2478; (309) 438-3932

Full-time: 7628 men, 9662 women	**Faculty:** 876; I, --$
Part-time: 488 men, 611 women	**Ph.D.s:** 83%
Graduate: 982 men, 1813 women	**Student/Faculty:** 19 to 1
Year: semesters, summer session	**Tuition:** $8280 (14,310)
Application Deadline: March 1	**Room & Board:** $7882
Freshman Class: 14,114 applied, 8711 accepted, 3033 enrolled	
ACT: 24	**VERY COMPETITIVE**

Illinois State University, founded in 1857, is a public institution offering instruction through schools of applied science and technology, arts and sciences, business, education, fine arts, and nursing. There are 6 undergraduate schools and one graduate school. In addition to regional accreditation, ISU has baccalaureate program accreditation with AACSB, ADA, AHEA, CSWE, NASAD, NASM, NCATE, NLN, and NRPA. The library contains 1.6 million volumes, 1.9 million microform items, and 24,716 audio/video tapes/CDs/DVDs, and subscribes to 12,254 periodicals including electronic. Computerized library services include interlibrary loans and database searching. Special learning facilities include a learning resource center, art gallery, planetarium, radio station, TV station, and a distance-learning classroom. The 850-acre campus is in an urban area 125 miles south of Chicago and 180 miles north of St. Louis. Including any residence halls, there are 153 buildings.

Programs of Study: ISU confers B.A., B.F.A., B.Mu., B.Mu.E., B.M.Ed., B.S., B.S.Ed., and B.S.W. degrees. Master's and doctoral degrees are also awarded. Bachelor's degrees are awarded in AGRICULTURE (agriculture), BIOLOGICAL SCIENCE (biochemistry and biology/biological science), BUSINESS (accounting, banking and finance, business administration and management, insurance, international business management, management science, and marketing/retailing/merchandising), COMMUNICATIONS AND THE ARTS (art, communications, dramatic arts, English, French, German, journalism, music, music performance, public relations, Spanish, speech/debate/rhetoric, and telecommunications), COMPUTER AND PHYSICAL SCIENCE (chemistry, computer science, digital arts/technology, geology, information sciences and systems, mathematics, and physics), EDUCATION (athletic training, business education, early childhood education, elementary education, health education, middle school education, music education, physical education, social science education, and special education), ENGINEERING AND ENVIRONMENTAL DESIGN (industrial engineering technology), HEALTH PROFESSIONS (environmental health science, exercise science, health care administration, medical laboratory technology, nursing, and speech pathology/audiology), SOCIAL SCIENCE (anthropology, criminal justice, economics, family/consumer studies, fashion design and technology, geography, history, home economics, interdisciplinary studies, parks and recreation management, philosophy, political science/government, psychology, safety management, social science, social work, and sociology). Elementary education, business administration, and special education are the largest.

Special: There are numerous cooperative programs and internships, dual majors, student-designed majors, and work-study programs both on campus and with nonprofit organizations. There is also a general studies degree, a 3-2 engineering program with the University of Illinois, a BS/MPA, and study abroad in 16 countries. Pass/fail options are available and credit is given for military experience. ISU is part of the National Student Exchange, enabling qualifying juniors and seniors to study for up to 1 year at one of several hundred colleges around the country. There are 25 national honor societies, including Phi Beta Kappa, a freshman honors program, and 34 departmental honors programs.

Admissions: 62% of the 2009-2010 applicants were accepted. The ACT scores were 8% below 21, 33% between 21 and 23, 38% between 24 and 26, 12% between 27 and 28, and 8% above 28. There were 3 National Merit finalists. 2 freshmen graduated first in their class.

Requirements: The ACT is required. In addition, applicants must be graduates of an accredited secondary school or have a GED. Admission is based on a combination of factors, including class rank and ACT or SAT score. AP and CLEP credits are accepted.

Procedure: Freshmen are admitted to all sessions. Entrance exams should be taken in the fall of the junior year. There is a rolling admissions plan. Applications should be filed by March 1 for fall entry, along with a $40 fee. 254 applicants were on the 2009 waiting list; 240 were admitted. Applications are accepted online.

Financial Aid: In 2009-2010, 46% of all full-time freshmen and 47% of continuing full-time students received some form of financial aid. 27% of all full-time freshmen and 27% of continuing full-time students received need-based aid. The average freshman award was $10,408. Average annual earnings from campus work are $2841. The average financial indebtedness of the 2009 graduate was

$18,854. The CCS/Profile, FAFSA, FFS, or SFS is required. The deadline for filing freshman financial aid applications for fall entry is March 1.

Computers: Wireless access is available. Ulabs at Illinois State is comprised of seven computer labs containing a total of over 400 seats around campus open to Illinois State University students. These labs are located in Milner Library, Stevenson 250, Vrooman Center, Watterson Towers, and Whitten Hall. Supported by Computer Infrastructure Support Services, the labs are equipped with state-of-the-art computers, printers, and copy machines. All students may access the system 24 hours a day. There are no time limits and no fees. All students are required to have a personal computer.

ILLINOIS WESLEYAN UNIVERSITY

Bloomington, IL 61702-2900　　　　**(309) 556-3031; (800) 332-2498**

Full-time: 836 men, 1216 women	**Faculty:** IIB, av$
Part-time: 5 men, 2 women	**Ph.D.s:** 85%
Graduate: none	**Student/Faculty:** n/av
Year: see profile	**Tuition:** $30,750
Application Deadline: March 1	**Room & Board:** $7030
Freshman Class: 3321 applied, 1785 accepted, 518 enrolled	
SAT CR/M: 630/660	**ACT:** 28　　**VERY COMPETITIVE+**

Illinois Wesleyan University, founded in 1850, is a private institution offering major programs in liberal arts, fine arts, and nursing. Tuition figures in the above capsule are approximate. There are 5 undergraduate schools. In addition to regional accreditation, Illinois Wesleyan has baccalaureate program accreditation with NASM. The library contains 330,736 volumes, 4311 microform items, and 13,904 audio/video tapes/CDs/DVDs, and subscribes to 17,785 periodicals including electronic. Computerized library services include interlibrary loans, database searching, Internet access, and laptop Internet portals. Special learning facilities include a learning resource center, art gallery, radio station, TV station, observatory, multicultural center, and 20-acre tract of virgin timberland. The 80-acre campus is in a suburban area 130 miles from Chicago and 160 miles from St. Louis, Missouri. Including any residence halls, there are 52 buildings.

Programs of Study: Illinois Wesleyan confers B.A., B.S., B.F.A., B.Mus., B.Mus.Ed., and B.S.N. degrees. Bachelor's degrees are awarded in AGRICULTURE (environmental studies), BIOLOGICAL SCIENCE (biology/biological science), BUSINESS (accounting, business administration and management, insurance and risk management, and international business management), COMMUNICATIONS AND THE ARTS (dramatic arts, English, French, German, music, music theory and composition, musical theater, piano/organ, Spanish, visual and performing arts, and voice), COMPUTER AND PHYSICAL SCIENCE (chemistry, computer science, mathematics, and physics), HEALTH PROFESSIONS (nursing), SOCIAL SCIENCE (American studies, anthropology, economics, Hispanic American studies, history, interdisciplinary studies, international studies, philosophy, political science/government, psychology, religion, sociology, and women's studies). Business administration/accounting, English, and psychology are the largest.

Special: There are several combined degree programs, including a 3-2 degree in forestry and environmental studies with Duke University and a 2-2 engineering degree with the University of Illinois. Students may study abroad in many locations throughout the world through the Institute for the International Education of Students (IES), Pembroke College, Keio University, the University of Oxford, Arcadia University Center for Study Abroad, and other programs. Illinois Wesleyan also offers its own semester-long programs in London and Madrid. The university also offers on-campus work-study, both credit and noncredit internships, Washington and United Nations semesters, B.A.-B.S. degress, dual and student-designed majors, pass/fail options, and an honors research program for upperclass students. There are 25 national honor societies, including Phi Beta Kappa, and 44 departmental honors programs.

Admissions: 54% of the 2009-2010 applicants were accepted. There were 5 National Merit finalists. 15 freshmen graduated first in their class.

Requirements: The SAT or ACT is required. In addition, applicants should graduate from an accredited secondary school; a GED may be accepted. 15 academic credits are required. It is strongly recommended that these include 4 units of English, 3 each of natural science, math, and a foreign language, and 2 of social studies. An audition is required for theater and music majors and a portfolio for art majors. A GPA of 3.0 is required. AP credits are accepted. Important factors in the admissions decision are advanced placement or honors courses, evidence of special talent, and personality/intangible qualities.

Procedure: Freshmen are admitted fall and spring. Entrance exams should be taken in the spring of the junior year. There are early admissions, deferred admissions, and rolling admissions plans. Early decision applications should be filed by November 1; regular applications, by March 1 for fall entry; and November 1 for spring entry. Notification of early decision is sent November 1; regular decision, on a rolling basis. 78 applicants were on the 2009 waiting list; 26 were admitted. Applications are accepted on-line.

Financial Aid: In 2009-2010, 67% of all full-time freshmen and 56% of continuing full-time students received some form of financial aid, including need-based aid. The average freshman award was $25,359. Need-based scholarships or need-based grants averaged $19,231; need-based self-help aid (loans and jobs) averaged $6142; and other non-need-based awards and non-need-based scholarships averaged $13,460. The average financial indebtedness of the 2009 graduate was $26,458. Illinois Wesleyan is a member of CSS. The CSS/Profile, the FAFSA, and the college's own financial statement are required. The deadline for filing freshman financial aid applications for fall entry is March 1.

Computers: Wireless access is available. Students have access to more than 400 networked public access computers in various academic buildings. All classrooms, offices, residence halls, and sorority/fraternity houses are wired to the campus network. Secure wireless network access is available in the library, student center, public areas, and many classrooms. Laptop computers may be checked out for use within the library. Digital cameras may also be checked out from the library. Digital video stations are provided for students working on video projects and e-portfolios. All students may access the system. There are no time limits and no fees.

INDIANA UNIVERSITY BLOOMINGTON

Bloomington, IN 47405-7000   (812) 855-0661; (812) 855-5102

Full-time: 15604 men, 15457 women   **Faculty:** I, -$
Part-time: 768 men, 661 women   **Ph.D.s:** 81%
Graduate: 5008 men, 4849 women   **Student/Faculty:** n/av
Year: semesters, summer session   **Tuition:** $8613 ($26,160)
Application Deadline: February 1   **Room & Board:** $7546
Freshman Class: 33011 applied, 23975 accepted, 7327 enrolled
SAT CR/M/W: 570/600/560   **ACT:** 27   **HIGHLY COMPETITIVE**

Indiana University Bloomington, founded in 1820, is a comprehensive institution that is part of the Indiana University system. The university offers undergraduate programs in arts and sciences, allied health sciences, business, dentistry, education, health, physical education, recreation, journalism, music, nursing, optometry, public and environmental affairs, social work, and informatics. There are 17 undergraduate schools. In addition to regional accreditation, IU has baccalaureate program accreditation with AACSB, ACBSP, ACEJMC, ADA, APTA, ASLA, CAHEA, CSWE, FIDER, NASAD, NASM, NCATE, and NLN. The 19 libraries contain 8.5 million volumes, 5.1 million microform items, and 376,613 audio/video tapes/CDs/DVDs, and subscribe to 84,933 periodicals including electronic. Computerized library services include interlibrary loans and database searching. Special learning facilities include a learning resource center, art gallery, natural history museum, radio station, TV station, an observatory, arboretum, museum of world cultures, garden and nature center, musical arts center, and more than 70 research centers. The 1937-acre campus is in a small town 50 miles southwest of Indianapolis. Including any residence halls, there are 520 buildings.

Programs of Study: IU confers B.A., B.S., B.F.A., B.G.S., B.M., B.S.E., B.S.N., B.S.P.A., B.S.P.H., and B.S.W. degrees. Associate, master's, and doctoral degrees are also awarded. Bachelor's degrees are awarded in AGRICULTURE (environmental studies), BIOLOGICAL SCIENCE (biochemistry, biology/biological science, biotechnology, microbiology, and nutrition), BUSINESS (accounting, apparel and accessories marketing, banking and finance, business administration and management, business economics, entrepreneurial studies, international business management, labor studies, management information systems, management science, marketing/retailing/merchandising, nonprofit/public organization management, operations management, real estate, recreation and leisure services, sports management, supply chain management, and tourism), COMMUNICATIONS AND THE ARTS (art history and appreciation, arts administration/management, ballet, ceramic art and design, choral music, classics, communications, comparative literature, dance, dramatic arts, East Asian languages and literature, English, folklore and mythology, French, German, graphic design, Greek, guitar, Italian, jazz, journalism, Latin, linguistics, media arts, metal/jewelry, music, music history and appreciation, music performance, music theory and composition, musicology/ethnomusicology, painting, percussion, photography, piano/organ, Portuguese, printmaking, public relations, sculpture, Slavic languages, Spanish, speech/debate/rhetoric, sports media, strings, studio art, telecommunications, visual and performing arts, voice, and winds), COMPUTER AND PHYSICAL SCIENCE (astronomy, chemistry, computer science, digital arts/technology, geology, geoscience, information sciences and systems, mathematics, physics, and statistics), EDUCATION (athletic training, early childhood education, education, educational media, elementary education, health education, music education, physical education, secondary education, social studies education, and special education), ENGINEERING AND ENVIRONMENTAL DE-SIGN (environmental science, geological engineering, interior design, and occupational safety and health), HEALTH PROFESSIONS (environmental health science, exercise science, health science, nursing, public health, recreation therapy, and speech pathology/audiology), SOCIAL SCIENCE (African American studies, American studies, anthropology, Asian/Oriental studies, classical/ancient civilization, cognitive science, criminal justice, dietetics, East Asian studies, economics, family/consumer studies, gender studies, geography, history, human development, human ecology, international studies, Judaic studies, law, liberal arts/general studies, Near Eastern studies, parks and recreation management, philosophy, philosophy and religion, physical fitness/movement, political science/government, psychology, public administration, public affairs, religion, social work, sociology, and textiles and clothing).

Special: IU offers cooperative programs with universities in many countries, including China, a variety of internships, and study abroad in more than 25 countries. A Washington semester, work-study programs, B.A.-B.S. degrees in the sciences and liberal arts, dual majors, and the general studies degree through the School of Continuing Studies are available. Student-designed majors through the Individualized Major Program, credit for military experience, nondegree study through the School of Continuing Studies, and pass/fail options are also available. There are 18 national honor societies and a freshman honors program.

Admissions: 73% of the 2009-2010 applicants were accepted. The SAT scores for the 2009-2010 freshman class were: Critical Reading--15% below 500, 45% between 500 and 599, 34% between 600 and 700, and 6% above 700; Math--10% below 500, 38% between 500 and 599, 42% between 600 and 700, and 10% above 700; Writing--19% below 500, 45% between 500 and 599, 32% between 600 and 700, and 5% above 700. The ACT scores were 6% below 21, 13% between 21 and 23, 31% between 24 and 26, 19% between 27 and 28, and 32% above 28. 59% of the current freshmen were in the top fifth of their class; 88% were in the top two fifths.

Requirements: The SAT or ACT is required. In addition, applicants must be graduates of an accredited secondary high school or have a GED certificate. SAT: Subject tests are recommended for credit and placement. Auditions for music majors are required. An interview is recommended for information purposes. AP and CLEP credits are accepted. Important factors in the admissions decision are advanced placement or honors courses, parents or siblings attended your school, and recommendations by school officials.

Procedure: Freshmen are admitted to all sessions. Entrance exams should be taken late in the junior year or early in the senior year. There are deferred admissions and rolling admissions plans. Applications should be filed by February 1 for fall entry, November 1 for spring entry, and February 1 for summer entry. The fall 2008 application fee was $55. Applications are accepted on-line.

Financial Aid: In 2009-2010, 78% of all full-time freshmen and 94% of continuing full-time students received some form of financial aid. 41% of all full-time freshmen and 35% of continuing full-time students received need-based aid. The average freshman award was $10,480. Need-based scholarships or need-based grants averaged $8,980; need-based self-help aid (loans and jobs) averaged $3,730; non-need based athletic scholarships averaged $18,114; other non-need based awards and non-need based scholarships averaged $5,823. The average financial indebtedness of the 2009 graduate was $22,015. The FAFSA is required. The priority date for freshman financial aid applications for fall entry is March 1. The deadline for filing freshman financial aid applications for fall entry is March 10.

Computers: Wireless access is available. All students may access the system 24 hours a day. There are no time limits. The fee is $392. It is strongly recommended that all students have a personal computer. Students enrolled in computer science must have a personal computer.

INDIANA UNIVERSITY-PURDUE UNIVERSITY INDIANAPOLIS

Indianapolis, IN 46202-5143	(317) 274-4591; (317) 278-1862
Full-time: 6575 men, 9121 women	**Faculty:** IIA, av$
Part-time: 2789 men, 3634 women	**Ph.D.s:** 83%
Graduate: 3534 men, 4730 women	**Student/Faculty:** n/av
Year: semesters, summer session	**Tuition:** $7523 ($22,420)
Application Deadline: open	**Room & Board:** $7944
Freshman Class: 9641 applied, 6414 accepted, 3019 enrolled	
SAT CR/M/W: 490/500/470	**ACT:** 21 **COMPETITIVE**

Indiana University-Purdue University Indianapolis is an urban research and academic health sciences campus, with 21 schools and academic units that grant degrees in more than 200 programs from both Indiana University and Purdue University. IUPUI was created in 1969 as a partnership by and between Indiana and Purdue Universities, with IU as the managing partner. IUPUI is IU's home campus for state-wide programs in medicine, law, dentistry, nursing, health and rehabilitation science, and social work and extends its program offerings through IUPU Columbus. There are 21 undergraduate schools. In addition to regional accreditation, IUPUI has baccalaureate program accreditation with AACSB, ABET, ACCE, ACEJMC, ADA, APTA, CAHEA, CSWE, NASAD, NASM, NCATE, and NLN. The 5 libraries contain 1.3 million volumes, 1.2 million microform items, and 152,400 audio/video tapes/CDs/DVDs, and subscribe to 36,000 periodicals including electronic. Computerized library services include database searching. Special learning facilities include an art gallery, an 85-acre medical center, and an electronic classroom. The 509-acre campus is in an urban area near downtown Indianapolis. Including any residence halls, there are 129 buildings.

Programs of Study: IUPUI confers B.A., B.S., B.A.E., B.F.A., B.G.S., B.S.E., B.S.E.E., B.S.M.E., and B.S.W. degrees. Associate, master's, and doctoral degrees are also awarded. Bachelor's degrees are awarded in BIOLOGICAL SCIENCE (biology/biological science and biotechnology), BUSINESS (accounting, banking and finance, business administration and management, business economics, human resources, labor studies, marketing and distribution, marketing/retailing/merchandising, nonprofit/public organization management, organizational leadership and management, sports management, supply chain management, and tourism), COMMUNICATIONS AND THE ARTS (American Sign Language, ceramic art and design, communications, English, fine arts, French, German, journalism, media arts, music technology, painting, photography, printmaking, public relations, sculpture, Spanish, and visual design), COMPUTER AND PHYSICAL SCIENCE (chemistry, computer science, geology, information sciences and systems, mathematics, and physics), EDUCATION (elementary education, English education, foreign languages education, mathematics education, physical education, science education, secondary education, and social studies education), ENGINEERING AND ENVIRONMENTAL DESIGN (biomedical engineering, biomedical equipment technology, computer engineering, computer graphics, computer technology, construction technology, electrical/electronics engineering, electrical/electronics engineering technology, engineering, engineering mechanics, engineering technology, environmental science, furniture design, interior design, mechanical engineering, and mechanical engineering technology), HEALTH PROFESSIONS (clinical science, cytotechnology, dental hygiene, environmental health science, exercise science, health care administration, health science, medical laboratory technology, nuclear medical technology, nursing, premedicine, prephysical therapy, public health, radiation therapy, rehabilitation therapy, and respiratory therapy), SOCIAL SCIENCE (anthropology, criminal justice, economics, forensic studies, geography, history, interdisciplinary studies, international studies, liberal arts/general studies, philosophy, political science/government, prelaw, psychology, public administration, public affairs, religion, social work, and sociology). Engineering and technology, nursing, and education are the largest.

Special: There is a metropolitan studies program for career work in the city and cross-registration with the Consortium for Urban Education. IUPUI also offers study abroad, combined B.A.-B.S. degree programs, internships, work-study programs, dual and student-designed majors, nondegree study, nontraditional programs for adult learners, and interdisciplinary majors such as business economics and public policy, health occupations education, and interdisciplinary engineering. There is a freshman honors program.

Admissions: 67% of the 2009-2010 applicants were accepted. The SAT scores for the 2009-2010 freshman class were: Critical Reading--52% below 500, 37% between 500 and 599, 11% between 600 and 700, and 1% above 700; Math--46% below 500, 38% between 500 and 599, 15% between 600 and 700, and 1% above 700; Writing--59% below 500, 32% between 500 and 599, and 9% between 600 and 700. The ACT scores were 41% below 21, 29% between 21 and 23, 17% between 24 and 26, 8% between 27 and 28, and 4% above 28. 32% of the current freshmen were in the top fifth of their class; 71% were in the top two fifths.

Requirements: The SAT or ACT is required for recent high school graduates. The SAT is preferred. Applicants should be graduates of an accredited high school, rank in the upper half of their class, and have completed 14 Carnegie units, including 4 in English, 3 in math, 2 in social studies, and 1 in lab science. 2 units of a foreign language are recommended. The GED is accepted. AP and CLEP credits are accepted.

Procedure: Freshmen are admitted to all sessions. Entrance exams should be taken by the end of junior year or fall of senior year. There are deferred admissions and rolling admissions plans. Application deadlines are open. The fall 2008 application fee was $50. Notification is sent on a rolling basis.

Financial Aid: In 2009-2010, 84% of all full-time freshmen and 81% of continuing full-time students received some form of financial aid. 61% of all full-time freshmen and 43% of continuing full-time students received need-based aid. The average freshman award was $8,331. Need-based scholarships or need-based grants averaged $7,393; need-based self-help aid (loans and jobs) averaged $3,048; non-need based athletic scholarships averaged $7,214; other non-need based awards and non-need based scholarships averaged $4,564. The average financial indebtedness of the 2009 graduate was $27,062. The FAFSA is required. The priority date for freshman financial aid applications for fall entry is March 1. The deadline for filing freshman financial aid applications for fall entry is March 10.

Computers: All students may access the system up to 24 hours a day in some clusters. There are no time limits and no fees.

New Rochelle, NY 10801-1890

(914) 633-2503
(800) 231-IONA; (914) 633-2642

Full-time: 1406 men, 1839 women	**Faculty:** 183; IIA, +$
Part-time: 50 men, 49 women	**Ph.D.s:** 92%
Graduate: 342 men, 562 women	**Student/Faculty:** 18 to 1
Year: semesters, summer session	**Tuition:** $27,500
Application Deadline: February 15	**Room & Board:** $11,300
Freshman Class: 7313 applied, 4242 accepted, 789 enrolled	
SAT required	**ACT:** recommended
	VERY COMPETITIVE

Iona College, founded in 1940, is a private college offering programs through schools of general studies, arts and science, and business. It has a graduate campus in Rockland County in addition to the main campus in New Rochelle. There are 2 undergraduate schools and 2 graduate schools. In addition to regional accreditation, Iona has baccalaureate program accreditation with AACSB, ABET, ACEJMC, CSWE, and NCATE.The 3 libraries contain 272,014 volumes, 510,100 microform items, and 3,922 audio/video tapes/CDs/DVDs, and subscribe to 475 periodicals including electronic. Computerized library services include interlibrary loans, database searching, Internet access, and laptop Internet portals. Special learning facilities include a learning resource center, art gallery, radio station, TV station, an electron microscope, and a speech and hearing clinic. The 35-acre campus is in a suburban area 20 miles northeast of New York City. Including any residence halls, there are 37 buildings.

Programs of Study: Iona confers B.A., B.S., B.B.A., and B.P.S. degrees. Master's degrees are also awarded. Bachelor's degrees are awarded in BIOLOGICAL SCIENCE (biochemistry and biology/biological science), BUSINESS (accounting, business administration and management, international business management, management science, and marketing management), COMMUNICATIONS AND THE ARTS (advertising, communications, English, French, Italian, Spanish, and speech/debate/rhetoric), COMPUTER AND PHYSICAL SCIENCE (chemistry, computer science, mathematics, and physics), EDUCATION (early childhood education, elementary education, foreign languages education, middle school education, science education, and secondary education), HEALTH PROFESSIONS (medical technology and speech pathology/audiology), SOCIAL SCIENCE (behavioral science, criminal justice, economics, history, international studies, liberal arts/general studies, philosophy, political science/government, psychology, religion, social work, and sociology). Accounting, computer science, and mass communications are the strongest academically. Mass communications, psychology, and criminal justice are the largest.

Special: There are internships for upperclassmen. Study abroad is available in 9 countries. There is work-study in Iona offices and academic departments. Students may earn a combined B.A.-B.S. degree in economics, psychology, childhood education, early adolescence education, and math education. There is a joint B.S./M.S. program with New York Medical College in physical therapy. 5-year programs are offered in computer science, psychology, history, and English. There are 23 national honor societies, a freshman honors program, and all departments have honors programs.

Admissions: 58% of the 2009-2010 applicants were accepted. The SAT scores for the 2009-2010 freshman class were: Critical Reading--43% below 500, 46% between 500 and 599, 9% between 600 and 700, and 2% above 700; Math--44%

below 500, 44% between 500 and 599, 10% between 600 and 700, and 2% above 700; Writing--43% below 500, 46% between 500 and 599, 9% between 600 and 700, and 2% above 700. The ACT scores were 10% below 21, 36% between 21 and 23, 33% between 24 and 26, and 21% between 27 and 28. 49% of the current freshmen were in the top fifth of their class; 81% were in the top two fifths.

Requirements: The SAT is required. In addition, applicants must complete 16 academic credits, including 4 units of English, 3 of math, 2 of foreign language, and 1 each of history, science, and social studies. A GED is accepted. An essay is required, and an interview is recommended. A GPA of 2.5 is required. AP and CLEP credits are accepted. Important factors in the admissions decision are recommendations by school officials, leadership record, and advanced placement or honors courses.

Procedure: Freshmen are admitted fall and spring. Entrance exams should be taken in the spring of the junior year. There are early admissions and deferred admissions plans. Applications should be filed by February 15 for fall entry and January 1 for spring entry. The fall 2008 application fee was $50. Notifications are sent March 20. Applications are accepted on-line. 600 applicants were on a recent waiting list, 79 were accepted.

Financial Aid: In 2009-2010, 98% of all full-time freshmen and 95% of continuing full-time students received some form of financial aid. 67% of all full-time freshmen and 56% of continuing full-time students received need-based aid. The average freshman award was $27,510. Need-based scholarships or need-based grants averaged $6,068 ($13,100 maximum); need-based self-help aid (loans and jobs) averaged $3,777 ($7,600 maximum); non-need based athletic scholarships averaged $14,146 ($43,482 maximum); and other non-need based awards and non-need based scholarships averaged $16,878 ($42,202 maximum). 20% of undergraduate students work part-time. Average annual earnings from campus work are $1125. The average financial indebtedness of the 2009 graduate was $24,212. Iona is a member of CSS. The FAFS, the college's own financial statement, and the TAP (Tuition Assistance Program) form are required. The priority date for freshman financial aid applications for fall entry is February 15. The deadline for filing freshman financial aid applications for fall entry is April 15.

Computers: Wireless access is available. The campus WAN consists of 85 servers (57 NT, 15 LINUX, and 2 UNIX, 9VM, and 2 Apple OSx). There are 1500 college and student owned, high-end, wired and wireless Pentium systems available in computing labs, classrooms, residence halls, libraries, and the student center for student use. The entire college campus is wireless, all students may bring laptops and access the network. There is unlimited access. There are no time limits and no fees. It is strongly recommended that all students have a personal computer. The college negotiates discount pricing on laptops for our students with Dell, Lenovo, and Apple.

Ames, IA 50011-2011

(515) 294-5836
(800) 262-3810; (515) 294-2592

Full-time: 11,000 men, 9000 women	**Faculty:** I, -$
Part-time: 750 men, 605 women	**Ph.D.s:** 88%
Graduate: 2820 men, 2215 women	**Student/Faculty:** n/av
Year: semesters, summer session	**Tuition:** $6100 ($17,660)
Application Deadline: see profile	**Room & Board:** $7600
Freshman Class: n/av	
SAT or ACT: required	**COMPETITIVE**

Iowa State University, established in 1858, is a public land-grant institution offering undergraduate and graduate programs in agriculture, business, design, engineering, human sciences, liberal arts and sciences, and veterinary medicine. Figures in the above capsule and this profile are approximate. There are 7 undergraduate schools and 1 graduate school. In addition to regional accreditation, Iowa State has baccalaureate program accreditation with AACSB, ABET, ACEJMC, ADA, AHEA, ASLA, CSAB, FIDER, NAAB, NASM, and SAF. The library contains 2.4 million volumes, 3.4 million microform items, and 64,524 audio/video tapes/CDs/DVDs, and subscribes to 29,850 periodicals including electronic. Computerized library services include interlibrary loans and database searching. Special learning facilities include a learning resource center, art gallery, natural history museum, planetarium, radio station, and TV station. The 1788-acre campus is in an urban area 30 miles north of Des Moines. Including any residence halls, there are 284 buildings.

Programs of Study: Iowa State confers B.A., B.S., B.Arch., B.B.A., B.F.A., B.L.A., B.L.S., and B.Mus. degrees. Master's and doctoral degrees are also awarded. Bachelor's degrees are awarded in AGRICULTURE (agricultural business management, agriculture, agronomy, animal science, dairy science, forestry and related sciences, horticulture, international agriculture, plant protection (pest management), and plant science), BIOLOGICAL SCIENCE (biochemistry, biology/biological science, biophysics, entomology, genetics, microbiology, nutrition, and plant pathology), BUSINESS (accounting, banking and finance, business administration and management, fashion merchandising, hotel/motel and restaurant management, international business management, management science, marketing/retailing/merchandising, and transportation management), COMMUNICATIONS AND THE ARTS (advertising, communications, design, English, fine arts, French, German, graphic design, journalism, linguistics, music, Russian, Spanish, and speech/debate/rhetoric), COMPUTER AND PHYSICAL SCIENCE (atmospheric sciences and meteorology, chemistry, computer science, earth science, geology, mathematics, physics, and statistics), EDUCATION (agricultural education, early childhood education, elementary education, health education, industrial arts education, music education, physical education, and secondary education), ENGINEERING AND ENVIRONMENTAL DESIGN (aeronautical engineering, agricultural engineering, architecture, chemical engineering, city/community/regional planning, civil engineering, computer engineering, construction engineering, electrical/electronics engineering, engineering, engineering technology, environmental science, industrial engineering technology, interior design, landscape architecture/design, materials engineering, and mechanical engineering), SOCIAL SCIENCE (anthropology, child care/child and family studies, child psychology/development, dietetics, economics, family/consumer resource management, family/consumer studies, fashion design and technology, food science, history, international relations, liberal arts/general studies, philosophy, political science/government, psychology, religion, sociology, and textiles and clothing). Engineering, agriculture, and statistics are the strongest academically. Engineering, business, and agriculture are the largest.

Special: Iowa State offers cooperative programs in engineering, forestry, agronomy, chemistry, computer science, economics, agricultural systems technology, business administration, industrial technology, and performing arts and cross-registration with the Universities of Iowa and Northern Iowa. Internships, study abroad in 38 countries, dual majors, the B.A.-B.S. degree, student-designed majors, and accelerated degree programs are available. Interdisciplinary studies include agricultural biochemistry, agricultural systems technology, animal ecology, public service and administration in agriculture, and engineering operations. There are work-study programs, a Washington semester, nondegree study, and pass/no pass options. There are 16 national honor societies, including Phi Beta Kappa, and a freshman honors program.

Requirements: The SAT or ACT is required. In addition, applicants must graduate from an accredited secondary school. The GED is accepted. For admission to freshman standing, students must have completed 4 years of English, 3 each of math and science, and 2 to 3 of social studies. For the College of Liberal Arts and Sciences, 2 years of a single foreign language are also required. Iowa State requires applicants to be in the upper 50% of their class. AP and CLEP credits are accepted.

Procedure: Freshmen are admitted to all sessions. Entrance exams should be taken during the spring of the junior year or the fall of the senior year. There are deferred admissions and rolling admissions plans. Check with the school for current application deadlines. The fall 2009 application fee was $30. Applications are accepted on-line.

Financial Aid: The FAFSA is required. Check with the school for current application deadlines.

Computers: Wireless access is available. All students may access the system at any time. There are no time limits and no fees.

ITHACA COLLEGE
Ithaca, NY 14850-7000   (607) 274-3124
(800) 429-4274; (607) 274-1900

Full-time: 2749 men, 3621 women	**Faculty:** 463; IIA, av$
Part-time: 32 men, 38 women	**Ph.D.s:** 92%
Graduate: 139 men, 315 women	**Student/Faculty:** 12 to 1
Year: semesters, summer session	**Tuition:** $32,060
Application Deadline: February 1	**Room & Board:** $11,780
Freshman Class: 11917 applied, 9471 accepted, 2027 enrolled	
SAT CR/M/W: 580/580/580	**ACT:** required

VERY COMPETITIVE

Ithaca College, founded in 1892, is a private college offering undergraduate and graduate programs in business, communications, health science and human performance, humanities, sciences, music, and interdisciplinary and international studies. There are 6 undergraduate schools and 1 graduate school. In addition to regional accreditation, Ithaca has baccalaureate program accreditation with AACSB, APTA, NASM, and NRPA. The library contains 304,015 volumes, 34,440 microform items, and 34,160 audio/video tapes/CDs/DVDs, and subscribes to 44,425 periodicals including electronic. Computerized library services include interlibrary loans, database searching, Internet access, and laptop Internet portals.

Special learning facilities include an art gallery, a radio station, a TV station, digital audio and video labs, speech, hearing, wellness, and physical therapy clinics, a greenhouse, a financial "trading room," an observatory, and electroacoustic music studios. The 650-acre campus is in a small town 250 miles northwest of New York City. Including any residence halls, there are 86 buildings.

Programs of Study: Ithaca confers B.A., B.S., B.F.A., and Mus.B. degrees. Master's and doctoral degrees are also awarded. Bachelor's degrees are awarded in BIOLOGICAL SCIENCE (biochemistry and biology/biological science), BUSINESS (accounting, banking and finance, business administration and management, business economics, human resources, international business management, management science, marketing management, marketing/retailing/merchandising, organizational behavior, personnel management, recreation and leisure services, and sports management), COMMUNICATIONS AND THE ARTS (art, art history and appreciation, audio technology, broadcasting, communications, creative writing, dramatic arts, English, film arts, fine arts, French, German, jazz, journalism, languages, media arts, modern language, music, music performance, music theory and composition, musical theater, performing arts, photography, public relations, Spanish, speech/debate/rhetoric, sports media, studio art, telecommunications, theater design, theater management, video, and visual and performing arts), COMPUTER AND PHYSICAL SCIENCE (chemistry, computer mathematics, computer science, information sciences and systems, mathematics, and physics), EDUCATION (art education, athletic training, education, education of the deaf and hearing impaired, educational media, English education, foreign languages education, health education, mathematics education, middle school education, music education, physical education, secondary education, social studies education, speech correction, and sports studies), ENGINEERING AND ENVIRONMENTAL DESIGN (environmental science), HEALTH PROFESSIONS (allied health, clinical science, community health work, exercise science, health, health science, hospital administration, occupational therapy, physical therapy, predentistry, premedicine, public health, recreation therapy, rehabilitation therapy, speech pathology/audiology, speech therapy, and sports medicine), SOCIAL SCIENCE (anthropology, economics, German area studies, gerontology, history, industrial and organizational psychology, interdisciplinary studies, Italian studies, liberal arts/general studies, philosophy, physical fitness/movement, political science/government, prelaw, psychology, social studies, and sociology). Physical therapy, theater, and music are the strongest academically. Music, business administration, and television/radio are the largest.

Special: Cross-registration is available with Cornell University and Wells College. Opportunities are also provided for internships, study abroad in more than 9 countries, a Washington semester, work-study programs, accelerated degree programs, dual majors, nondegree study, pass/fail options, and student-designed majors. A 3-2 engineering degree with Cornell University, Clarkson University, Rensselaer Polytechnic Institute, and SUNY Binghamton is available. There is also a 4-1 B.S./M.B.A. program, a 3-1 optometry program, a pre-law advisory program, and a 1-semester program in marine biology with Duke University and the Sea Education Association. There are 25 national honor societies, a freshman honors program, and 16 departmental honors programs.

Admissions: 79% of the 2009-2010 applicants were accepted. The SAT scores for the 2009-2010 freshman class were: Critical Reading--13% below 500, 46% between 500 and 599, 34% between 600 and 700, and 7% above 700; Math--14% below 500, 42% between 500 and 599, 40% between 600 and 700, and 4% above 700; Writing--14% below 500, 45% between 500 and 599, 35% between 600 and 700, and 6% above 700. 58% of the current freshmen were in the top fifth of their class; 88% were in the top two fifths. There were 4 National Merit finalists. 12 freshmen graduated first in their class.

Requirements: The SAT or ACT is required. The ACT Optional Writing test is also required. In addition, In addition, applicants should be graduates of an accredited secondary school with a minimum of 16 Carnegie units, including 4 years of English, 3 each of math, science, and social studies, 2 of foreign language, and other college-preparatory electives. The GED is accepted. An essay is required, as is an audition for music and theater students. In some majors, a portfolio and an interview are recommended. AP and CLEP credits are accepted.

Procedure: Freshmen are admitted fall and spring. Entrance exams should be taken in spring of the junior year or fall of the senior year. There are early decision, early admissions, deferred admissions, and rolling admissions plans. Early decision applications should be filed by November 1; regular applications, by February 1 for fall entry; and December 1 for spring entry, along with a $60 fee. Notification of early decision is sent December 15; regular decision, April 15. Applications are accepted on-line.

Financial Aid: In 2009-2010, 96% of all full-time freshmen and 89% of continuing full-time students received some form of financial aid. 74% of all full-time freshmen and 67% of continuing full-time students received need-based aid. The average freshman award was $30,905. Need-based scholarships or need-based grants averaged $19,799 ($45,185 maximum); need-based self-help aid (loans and jobs) averaged $7,585 ($15,900 maximum); and other non-need-based awards and non-need-based scholarships averaged $6,204 ($46,562 maximum). 45% of undergraduate students work part-time. Average annual earnings from campus work are $2400. Ithaca is a member of CSS. The CSS/Profile and FAFSA are required. The deadline for filing freshman financial aid applications for fall entry is February 1.

Computers: Wireless access is available. Students may access Ithaca College's network from any of the approximately 640 computers available for general student use in labs, classrooms, and the library as well as via wireless networks in campus residence halls and many other areas on campus. All students may access the system 24 hours a day. There are no time limits and no fees. Students enrolled in the School of Business should have a Windows laptop; School of Communications students should have a Mac laptop.

JAMES MADISON UNIVERSITY

Harrisonburg, VA 22807	(540) 568-5681; (540) 568-3332
Full-time: 6584 men, 9905 women	**Faculty:** 840; IIA, -$
Part-time: 399 men, 393 women	**Ph.D.s:** 78%
Graduate: 495 men, 1195 women	**Student/Faculty:** 20 to 1
Year: semesters, summer session	**Tuition:** $7244 ($19,376)
Application Deadline: January 15	**Room & Board:** $7386
Freshman Class: 21189 applied, 11991 accepted, 4220 enrolled	
SAT CR/M/W: 560/580/570	**ACT:** 24 **VERY COMPETITIVE**

James Madison University, founded in 1908, is a public institution with programs in science and math, business, education, arts and letters, visual and performing arts, and integrated science and technology. There are 7 undergraduate schools and one graduate school. In addition to regional accreditation, JMU has baccalaureate program accreditation with AACSB, ABET, ADA, AHEA, CSWE, FIDER, NASAD, NASM, and NCATE. The 3 libraries contain 645,740 volumes, 1.1 million microform items, and 42,676 audio/video tapes/CDs/DVDs, and subscribe to 12,662 periodicals including electronic. Computerized library services include interlibrary loans, database searching, and Internet access. Special learning facilities include a learning resource center, art gallery, planetarium, radio station, arboretum, music library, CISAT Library Services, mineral museum, and Science on a Sphere. The 712-acre campus is in a small town 123 miles southwest of Washington, D.C. Including any residence halls, there are 111 buildings.

Programs of Study: JMU confers B.A., B.S., B.B.A., B.F.A., B.I.S., B.M., B.S.N., and B.S.W. degrees. Master's and doctoral degrees are also awarded. Bachelor's degrees are awarded in BIOLOGICAL SCIENCE (biology/biological science and biotechnology), BUSINESS (accounting, banking and finance, business administration and management, business economics, hospitality management services, international business management, marketing/retailing/merchandising, recreation and leisure services, and tourism), COMMUNICATIONS AND THE ARTS (art, art history and appreciation, communications, communications technology, dance, dramatic arts, English, fine arts, media arts, modern language, music, and speech/debate/rhetoric), COMPUTER AND PHYSICAL SCIENCE (chemistry, computer science, geology, information sciences and systems, mathematics, physics, quantitative methods, science technology, and statistics), EDUCATION (athletic training), ENGINEERING AND ENVIRONMENTAL DESIGN (engineering), HEALTH PROFESSIONS (health care administration, health science, nursing, and speech pathology/audiology), SOCIAL SCIENCE (anthropology, criminal justice, dietetics, economics, geography, history, international studies, liberal arts/general studies, philosophy, physical fitness/movement, political science/government, psychology, public administration, religion, social science, social work, and sociology). Interdisciplinary liberal studies, health science, and kinesiology are the largest.

Special: JMU offers internships, work-study programs, a Washington semester, and study abroad in London, Antwerp, Florence, and Salamanca. There is a combined program in forestry with Virginia Tech. An individualized study degree, nondegree study, pass/fail options, and credit for life, military, and work experience are available. There are 28 national honor societies, including Phi Beta Kappa, a freshman honors program, and 82 departmental honors programs.

Admissions: 57% of the 2009-2010 applicants were accepted. The SAT scores for the 2009-2010 freshman class were: Critical Reading--14% below 500, 52% between 500 and 599, 30% between 600 and 700, and 4% above 700; Math--11% below 500, 47% between 500 and 599, 38% between 600 and 700, and 4% above 700. The ACT scores were 11% below 21, 27% between 21 and 23, 36% between 24 and 26, 16% between 27 and 28, and 10% above 28. 21 freshmen graduated first in their class.

Requirements: The SAT or ACT is required. In addition, applicants must be graduates of an accredited secondary school. They must show solid achievement in 4 or more academic courses each year of high school including some honors or advanced course work. A personal statement is optional. Art students must present a portfolio. Theater, dance, and music students must audition. Nursing students must apply to the nursing department in addition to applying for undergraduate admission. AP credits are accepted. Important factors in the admissions decision are advanced placement or honors courses, recommendations by school officials, and extracurricular activities record.

Procedure: Freshmen are admitted in the fall. Entrance exams should be taken in the spring of the junior year or the fall of the senior year. There are early admissions and deferred admissions plans. Applications should be filed by January 15 for fall entry. The fall 2009 application fee was $50. Notification is sent April 1. Applications are accepted on-line. 1341 applicants were on a recent waiting list, 499 were accepted.

Financial Aid: In 2009-2010, 32% of all full-time freshmen and 33% of continuing full-time students received some form of financial aid. 35% of all full-time freshmen and 31% of continuing full-time students received need-based aid. The average freshman award was $8,389. Need-based scholarships or need-based grants averaged $7,029 ($14,900 maximum); need-based self-help aid (loans and jobs) averaged $3,698 ($5,500 maximum); non-need-based athletic scholarships averaged $14,858 ($27,066 maximum); and other non-need-based awards and non-need-based scholarships averaged $3,614 ($10,000 maximum). 20% of undergraduate students work part-time. Average annual earnings from campus work are $1885. The average financial indebtedness of the 2009 graduate was $18,183. The FAFSA is required. The deadline for filing freshman financial aid applications for fall entry is March 1.

Computers: Wireless access is available. Students have access from their residence hall rooms to our network from their own PC. All students may access the system 24 hours a day. There are no time limits and no fees. It is strongly recommended that all students have a personal computer. Students enrolled in business and integrated science and technology must have a personal computer. Recommended configurations for Dell or Apple are available on line at *www.jmu.edu/computing/purchase/dept.shtml.*

JOHN BROWN UNIVERSITY
Siloam Springs, AR 72761

(479) 524-7150
(877) JBU-INFO; (479) 524-4196

Full-time: 800 men, 900 women	**Faculty:** IIB, --$
Part-time: 50 men, 40 women	**Ph.D.s:** n/av
Graduate: 140 men, 235 women	**Student/Faculty:** n/av
Year: semesters, summer session	**Tuition:** $17,800
Application Deadline: see profile	**Room & Board:** $7000
Freshman Class: n/av	
SAT or ACT: recommended	**VERY COMPETITIVE**

John Brown University, founded in 1919, is a private, interdenominational Christian university offering nearly 50 undergraduate degree programs, 3 degree completion programs, and 6 graduate degree programs. The figures in the above capsule and in this profile are approximate. In addition to regional accreditation, JBU has baccalaureate program accreditation with ABET, ACCE, and NCATE. The library contains 104,000 volumes, 67,000 microform items, and 3,000 audio/video tapes/CDs/DVDs. Computerized library services include interlibrary loans, database searching, and Internet access. Special learning facilities include a learning resource center, art gallery, radio station, TV station, and a wellness assessment laboratory. The 200-acre campus is in a small town 25 mile west of Rogers, Arkansas and 80 mile east of Tulsa, Oklahoma. Including any residence halls, there are 16 buildings.

Programs of Study: JBU confers B.A., B.S., B.Mus.Ed., B.S.E., and B.S.Eng. degrees. Associates and master's degrees are also awarded. Bachelor's degrees are awarded in BIOLOGICAL SCIENCE (biochemistry and biology/biological science), BUSINESS (accounting and business administration and management), COMMUNICATIONS AND THE ARTS (broadcasting, design, English, graphic design, illustration, journalism, music, public relations, and Spanish), COMPUTER AND PHYSICAL SCIENCE (chemistry, computer science, digital arts/technology, mathematics, and science), EDUCATION (early childhood education, elementary education, middle school education, music education, physical education, science education, and secondary education), ENGINEERING AND

ENVIRONMENTAL DESIGN (construction management, electrical/electronics engineering, engineering, and environmental science), HEALTH PROFESSIONS (community health work and sports medicine), SOCIAL SCIENCE (biblical studies, crosscultural studies, family and community services, history, interdisciplinary studies, international studies, ministries, political science/government, psychology, theological studies, and youth ministry). Engineering, teacher education, and business are the strongest academically. Business, digital media, and graphic design are the largest.

Special: Internships or field experiences are available in most majors. Study abroad in 15 countries, a Washington semester, work-study, and accelerated degree programs in business information systems, and organizational management, and early childhood education are offered. There is 1 national honor society, a freshman honors program, and 12 departmental honors programs.

Requirements: The SAT or ACT is recommended. In addition, applicants should have completed 14 high school units, including 4 in English, 3 in math, 2 each in science, social studies, and foreign language, and 1 in history. 2 references are required: 1 from a high school counselor or teacher, the other from a pastor or church leader. An essay and an interview are recommended. Applicants 21 years of age or older may be admitted without ACT or SAT scores. JBU requires applicants to be in the upper 50% of their class. A GPA of 2.5 is required. AP and CLEP credits are accepted.

Procedure: Freshmen are admitted fall and spring. Entrance exams should be taken during the spring of the junior year or fall of the senior year. There is a rolling admissions plan. Check with the school for current application deadlines. The application fee is $25. Applications are accepted on-line.

Financial Aid: The CSS/Profile, FAFSA, and FFS are required. Check with the school for current application deadlines.

Computers: Wireless access is available. Labs are available and all residence halls are wired for access and have computer labs. All students may access the system from 7:30 A.M. to 12 A.M. Monday through Thursday, 7:30 A.M. to 5 P.M. on Friday, 12 P.M. to 5 P.M. on Saturday and 3 P.M. to 11 P.M. on Sunday. There are no time limits and no fees.

JOHN CARROLL UNIVERSITY
University Heights, OH 44118   (216) 397-4294
                                          (888) 335-6800; (216) 397-4981

Full-time: 1420 men, 1475 women	**Faculty:** 212; IIA, -$
Part-time: 44 men, 37 women	**Ph.D.s:** 94%
Graduate: 252 men, 472 women	**Student/Faculty:** 14 to 1
Year: semesters, summer session	**Tuition:** $28,840
Application Deadline: February 1	**Room & Board:** $8330
Freshman Class: 3411 applied, 2763 accepted, 661 enrolled	
SAT CR/M/W: 534/534/529	**ACT:** 24 **VERY COMPETITIVE**

John Carroll University, founded in 1886, is a private Catholic institution operated by the Jesuits. It offers undergraduate degree programs in the arts, sciences, and business. There are 2 undergraduate schools and 2 graduate schools. In addition to regional accreditation, John Carroll has baccalaureate program accreditation with AACSB and NCATE. The library contains 710,403 microform items and 4880 audio/video tapes/CDs/DVDs, and subscribes to 1975 periodicals including electronic. Computerized library services include interlibrary loans and database searching. Special learning facilities include a learning resource center, radio station, and TV station. The 62-acre campus is in a suburban area 10 miles east of Cleveland. Including any residence halls, there are 26 buildings.

Programs of Study: John Carroll confers B.A., B.S., B.A.Classics, B.S.B.A., and B.S.Econ. degrees. Master's degrees are also awarded. Bachelor's degrees are awarded in BIOLOGICAL SCIENCE (biology/biological science), BUSINESS (accounting, banking and finance, business administration and management, and marketing/retailing/merchandising), COMMUNICATIONS AND THE ARTS (art history and appreciation, communications, English, French, German, Greek, Latin, literature, and Spanish), COMPUTER AND PHYSICAL SCIENCE (chemistry, computer science, mathematics, and physics), EDUCATION (early childhood education, elementary education, mathematics education, physical education, and secondary education), ENGINEERING AND ENVIRONMENTAL DESIGN (engineering physics), SOCIAL SCIENCE (economics, history, humanities, philosophy, political science/government, psychology, public administration, religion, and sociology). Accounting, biology, and chemistry are the strongest academically. Communications, biology, and marketing are the largest.

Special: Co-op programs are available, and cross-registration is offered with 9 area colleges, universities, and institutes. Study abroad is possible in 9 countries. Joint engineering degrees are offered with Case Western Reserve University, the University of Detroit Mercy, and Washington University. Work-study programs with local corporations, internships, a Washington semester, student-designed majors, dual majors, and some pass/fail options are available. There are 13 national honor societies and a freshman honors program.

Admissions: 81% of the 2009-2010 applicants were accepted. The SAT scores for the 2009-2010 freshman class were: Critical Reading--30% below 500, 51% between 500 and 599, 16% between 600 and 700, and 3% above 700; Math--35% below 500, 38% between 500 and 599, 25% between 600 and 700, and 1% above 700; Writing--33% below 500, 47% between 500 and 599, 18% between 600 and 700, and 2% above 700. The ACT scores were 23% below 21, 31% between 21 and 23, 24% between 24 and 26, 13% between 27 and 28, and 9% above 28. 50% of the current freshmen were in the top fifth of their class; 68% were in the top two fifths. 16 freshmen graduated first in their class.

Requirements: The SAT or ACT is required. In addition, applicants should be graduates of an accredited secondary school with a minimum of 16 academic credits, including 4 in English, 3 in math, 2 each in foreign language, lab science, and social studies, and 3 in electives. An essay is part of the application process, and an interview is highly encouraged for students concerned about admissions standards. John Carroll requires applicants to be in the upper 50% of their class. A GPA of 3.0 is required. AP and CLEP credits are accepted. Important factors in the admissions decision are advanced placement or honors courses, extracurricular activities record, and recommendations by school officials.

Procedure: Freshmen are admitted fall and spring. Entrance exams should be taken in the spring of the junior year or the fall of the senior year. There are deferred admissions and rolling admissions plans. Applications should be filed by February 1 for fall entry. Notification is sent on a rolling basis. Applications are accepted on-line.

Financial Aid: In 2009-2010, 97% of all full-time freshmen and 94% of continuing full-time students received some form of financial aid. 74% of all full-time freshmen and 60% of continuing full-time students received need-based aid. The average freshman award was $25,065. Need-based scholarships or need-based grants averaged $17,877 ($33,995 maximum); need-based self-help aid (loans and jobs) averaged $5716 ($9700 maximum); and other non-need-based awards and non-need-based scholarships averaged $1472 ($27,940 maximum). 30% of

undergraduate students work part-time. Average annual earnings from campus work are $2200. The average financial indebtedness of the 2009 graduate was $21,424. The FAFSA and the college's own financial statement are required. The priority date for freshman financial aid applications for fall entry is February 15.
Computers: Wireless access is available. There are more than 200 computers in labs across campus, including the library, academic buildings, and the student union. All students may access the system 24 hours a day. There are no time limits. The fee is $350. It is strongly recommended that all students have a personal computer.

JOHNS HOPKINS UNIVERSITY
Baltimore, MD 21218   (410) 516-8341; (410) 516-6025

Full-time: 2400 men, 2200 women	**Faculty:** 447
Part-time: 25 men, 5 women	**Ph.D.s:** 92%
Graduate: 1000 men, 600 women	**Student/Faculty:** n/av
Year: 4-1-4, summer session	**Tuition:** $39,150
Application Deadline: January 1	**Room & Board:** $12,040
Freshman Class: 16,123 applied, 4318 accepted	
SAT or ACT: required	**MOST COMPETITIVE**

The Johns Hopkins University, founded in 1876, is a private multicampus institution offering undergraduate degrees at the Homewood campus through the Zanvyl Krieger School of Arts and Sciences, the Whiting School of Engineering, and the Peabody Institute (music). Some figures in the above capsule and in this profile are approximate. There are 5 undergraduate schools and 8 graduate schools. In addition to regional accreditation, Johns Hopkins has baccalaureate program accreditation with ABET. The 4 libraries contain 2.6 million volumes, 4.1 million microform items, and 9707 audio/video tapes/CDs/DVDs, and subscribe to 30,120 periodicals including electronic. Computerized library services include interlibrary loans, database searching, Internet access, and laptop Internet portals. Special learning facilities include an art gallery, radio station, and Space Telescope Science Institute. The 140-acre campus is in a suburban area in a residential setting in northern Baltimore. Including any residence halls, there are 40 buildings.

Programs of Study: Johns Hopkins confers B.A. and B.S. degrees. Master's and doctoral degrees are also awarded. Bachelor's degrees are awarded in BIOLOGICAL SCIENCE (biology/biological science, biophysics, cell biology, molecular biology, and neurosciences), COMMUNICATIONS AND THE ARTS (art history and appreciation, classics, creative writing, English, French, German, Italian, media arts, romance languages and literature, and Spanish), COMPUTER AND PHYSICAL SCIENCE (applied mathematics, chemistry, computer science, earth science, mathematics, natural sciences, and physics), ENGINEERING AND ENVIRONMENTAL DESIGN (biomedical engineering, chemical engineering, civil engineering, computer engineering, electrical/electronics engineering, engineering, engineering mechanics, environmental engineering, environmental science, materials engineering, materials science, and mechanical engineering), SOCIAL SCIENCE (African studies, anthropology, cognitive science, East Asian studies, economics, history, history of science, humanities, interdisciplinary studies, international studies, Latin American studies, Near Eastern studies, philosophy, political science/government, psychology, social science, and sociology). International studies, public health studies, and biomedical engineering are the largest.

Special: Internships, dual majors in music and arts and sciences/engineering, cross-registration with Baltimore-area colleges and Johns Hopkins divisions, a cooperative double degree with Peabody Conservatory of Music, a student-designed semester at the Johns Hopkins School of International Studies in Washington, D.C., and various multidisciplinary programs are offered. Students may enroll at Johns Hopkins in Bologna, Italy, or Nanjing, China, or arrange programs in Europe, South America, the Far East, or Australia. Students may earn combined B.A.-B.S. degrees in physics, computer science, applied math, and statistics. There are 4 national honor societies, including Phi Beta Kappa, and 25 departmental honors programs.

Admissions: 24% of a recent year's applicants were accepted. 92% of a recent year's freshmen were in the top fifth of their class; 98% were in the top two fifths. 81 freshmen graduated first in their class in a recent year.

Requirements: The SAT or ACT with Writing is required. For those submitting SAT scores, Johns Hopkins recommends that applicants also submit 3 SAT Subject Tests. In addition, applicants should be graduates of an accredited secondary school or have the GED. The university recommends that secondary preparation include 4 years each of English and math, 2 (prefer 3) of social science or history and lab science, and 3 to 4 of a foreign language (2 for engineering majors). 2 personal essays are required, and an interview is recommended. AP credits are accepted. Important factors in the admissions decision are advanced placement or honors courses, extracurricular activities record, and personality/intangible qualities.

Procedure: Freshmen are admitted fall. Entrance exams should be taken by December for regular decision, or November for early decision. There are early decision and deferred admissions plans. Early decision applications should be filed by November 1; regular applications by January 1 for fall entry, along with a $70 fee. Notification for early decision is sent December 15; regular decision, April 1. Applications are accepted on-line.

Financial Aid: Johns Hopkins is a member of CSS. The CSS/Profile and FAFSA are required. The deadline for filing freshman financial aid applications for fall entry is March 1.

Computers: Wireless access is available. All students may access the system 24 hours a day, 7 days a week. There are no time limits and no fees.

JUILLIARD SCHOOL
New York, NY 10023-6588

(212) 799-5000, ext. 223
(212) 724-6420

Full-time: 270 men, 225 women	**Faculty:** n/av
Part-time: none	**Ph.D.s:** n/av
Graduate: 185 men, 165 women	**Student/Faculty:** n/av
Year: semesters	**Tuition:** $32,180
Application Deadline: December 1	**Room & Board:** $12,280
Freshman Class: n/av	**SPECIAL**

The Juilliard School, founded in 1905, is a private conservatory for dance, drama, and music. Figures in the above capsule and in this profile are approximate. The library contains 96,013 volumes, 1,399 microform items, and 25,960 audio/video tapes/CDs/DVDs, and subscribes to 230 periodicals including electronic. Computerized library services include interlibrary loans, database searching, Internet access, and laptop Internet portals. The campus is in an urban area at the Lincoln Center in New York City. Including any residence halls, there are 2 buildings.

Programs of Study: Juilliard confers B.Mus. and B.F.A. degrees. Master's and doctoral degrees are also awarded. Bachelor's degrees are awarded in COMMU-

NICATIONS AND THE ARTS (dance, dramatic arts, and music). Piano, voice, and violin are the largest.

Special: A joint program with Columbia College and Barnard College (at Columbia University) allows students to obtain a 5-year B.A.-B.-MM. degree. Internships are available with cultural organizations in New York City. There is study abroad in music academy in England. Work-study programs, accelerated degrees and dual majors in music.

Requirements: A high school diploma or GED is required. Students are accepted primarily on the basis of personal auditions rather than tests. Important factors in the admissions decision are evidence of special talent.

Procedure: Freshmen are admitted in the fall. Personal auditions should be completed in December for opera, January & February for drama; February & March for dance; March for music; February & March for jazz. Applications should be filed by December 1 for fall entry, along with a $100 fee. Notifications are sent April 1. Applications are accepted on-line. A waiting list is maintained.

Financial Aid: In a recent year, 92% of all full-time freshmen and 85% of continuing full-time students received some form of financial aid. 90% of all full-time freshmen and 77% of continuing full-time students received need-based aid. The average freshmen award was $26,745, with $20,877 ($35,460 maximum) from need-based scholarships or need-based grants; $6,577 ($11,000 maximum) from need-based self-help aid (loans and jobs); and $2,234 ($5,000 maximum) from other non-need-based awards and non-need-based scholarships. 61% of undergraduate students worked part-time. Average annual earnings from campus work were $1094. The average financial indebtedness of the 2009 graduate was $25,332. The FAFSA and the college's own financial statement are required. Check with the school for current application deadlines.

Computers: Wireless access is available. All students may access the system. Students are limited to during lab hours. There are no fees.

JUNIATA COLLEGE
Huntingdon, PA 16652

(814) 641-3420
(877) JUNIATA; (814) 641-3100

Full-time: 611 men, 788 women	**Faculty:** 102; IIB, av$
Part-time: 32 men, 37 women	**Ph.D.s:** 94%
Graduate: none	**Student/Faculty:** 14 to 1
Year: semesters, summer session	**Tuition:** $32,820
Application Deadline: March 15	**Room & Board:** $8980
Freshman Class: 1964 applied, 1410 accepted, 366 enrolled	
SAT CR/M: 590/600	**ACT:** 26 **HIGHLY COMPETITIVE**

Juniata College, founded in 1876, is an independent liberal arts college. In addition to regional accreditation, Juniata has baccalaureate program accreditation with CSWE. The library contains 350,000 volumes, 400 microform items, and 2,100 audio/video tapes/CDs/DVDs, and subscribes to 1,000 periodicals including electronic. Computerized library services include interlibrary loans, database searching, Internet access, and laptop Internet portals. Special learning facilities include a learning resource center, art gallery, radio station, an observatory, an environmental studies field station, a nature preserve, an early childhood education center, and a ceramics studio with an Anagama kiln. The 110-acre campus is in a small town 31 miles south of State College, in the heart of rural Pennsylvania. Including any residence halls, there are 43 buildings.

Programs of Study: Juniata confers B.A. and B.S. degrees. Bachelor's degrees are awarded in AGRICULTURE (environmental studies), BIOLOGICAL SCI-

ENCE (biochemistry, biology/biological science, botany, ecology, marine science, microbiology, molecular biology, and zoology), BUSINESS (accounting, banking and finance, business administration and management, human resources, international business management, and marketing/retailing/merchandising), COMMUNICATIONS AND THE ARTS (art history and appreciation, communications, digital communications, dramatic arts, English, French, German, Russian, Spanish, and studio art), COMPUTER AND PHYSICAL SCIENCE (chemistry, computer science, earth science, geology, information sciences and systems, mathematics, and physics), EDUCATION (early childhood education, elementary education, English education, foreign languages education, mathematics education, museum studies, science education, secondary education, social studies education, and special education), ENGINEERING AND ENVIRONMENTAL DESIGN (engineering physics and environmental science), HEALTH PROFESSIONS (chiropractic, physician's assistant, preallied health, predentistry, premedicine, preoptometry, prepharmacy, prepodiatry, and preveterinary science), SOCIAL SCIENCE (anthropology, criminal justice, economics, history, international studies, peace studies, philosophy, political science/government, prelaw, psychology, public administration, social work, sociology, and theological studies). Biology, chemistry, and psychology are the strongest academically. Biology, business, and education are the largest.

Special: Juniata offers cooperative programs in marine science, cytogenetics, cytotechnology, marine biology, biotechnology, nursing, medical technology, diagnostic imaging, occupational and physical therapy, dentistry, medicine, optometry, and podiatry. Internships, study abroad in 19 countries, Washington and Philadelphia semesters, and nondegree study are also offered. There are 3-2 engineering degrees with Columbia, Clarkson, Washington, and Pennsylvania State Universities, a 3-3 law program with Duquesne University, and various preprofessional programs, including optometry, chiropractic, medicine, dentistry, pharmacy, physician assistant, and podiatry. With the assistance of faculty advisers, most students design their own majors to meet their individual goals. There are 16 national honor societies, a freshman honors program, and 16 departmental honors programs.

Admissions: 72% of the 2009-2010 applicants were accepted. The SAT scores for the 2009-2010 freshman class were: Critical Reading--9% below 500, 44% between 500 and 599, 33% between 600 and 700, and 15% above 700; Math--7% below 500, 40% between 500 and 599, 41% between 600 and 700, and 12% above 700. 66% of the current freshmen were in the top fifth of their class; 92% were in the top two fifths. There were 4 National Merit finalists. 8 freshmen graduated first in their class.

Requirements: The SAT or ACT is recommended. In addition, candidates for admission should be graduates of an accredited secondary school and have completed 16 academic credits, including 4 in English, 2 in a foreign language, and a combination of 10 in math, social studies, and lab science. The GED is accepted, and home schoolers are encouraged to apply. An essay is required, and an interview is recommended. A GPA of 3.0 is required. AP credits are accepted. Important factors in the admissions decision are advanced placement or honors courses, leadership record, and recommendations by school officials.

Procedure: Freshmen are admitted fall and spring. Entrance exams should be taken by the January test date of the year of admission for fall entry. There are early decision, early admissions, deferred admissions, and rolling admissions plans. Early decision applications should be filed by December 1; regular applications, by March 15 for fall entry and December 1 for spring entry, along with a $30 fee. Notification of early decision is sent December 31; regular decision, sent on a rolling basis. Applications are accepted on-line. 87 applicants were on a recent waiting list, 4 were accepted.

Financial Aid: In 2009-2010, all full-time freshmen and all of continuing full-time students received some form of financial aid. 72% of all full-time freshmen and 71% of continuing full-time students received need-based aid. The average freshmen award was $26,119, with $13,609 ($38,030 maximum) from need-based scholarships or need-based grants and $5,226 ($6,000 maximum) from need-based self-help aid (loans and jobs). 51% of undergraduate students work part-time. Average annual earnings from campus work are $811. The average financial indebtedness of the 2009 graduate was $23,618. The FAFSA is required. The priority date for freshman financial aid applications for fall entry is March 1. The deadline for filing freshman financial aid applications for fall entry is May 1.

Computers: Wireless access is available. 5 major public computing areas provide students access to PC-based word processing, spreadsheet, presentations, statistics, and database software in addition to e-mail and Internet access. All classrooms are equipped with technology. In addition, the campus includes a network and telecommunications lab, an on-demand education resource and collaboration center, a foreign language/education lab, a graphics processing center, a telelearning and teleconferencing classroom, a computer imaging studio, a cybercafe, and the technology Solutions Center (digital video production). All students may access the system. There are no time limits and no fees. It is strongly recommended that all students have a personal computer. A Dell or Apple is recommended.

KALAMAZOO COLLEGE
Kalamazoo, MI 49006-3295　　　　　　　　　　**(269) 337-7166**
　　　　　　　　　　　　　　(800) 253-3602; (269) 337-7390

Full-time: 584 men, 772 women	**Faculty:** 93; IIB, -$
Part-time: none	**Ph.D.s:** 86%
Graduate: none	**Student/Faculty:** 14 to 1
Year: trimesters	**Tuition:** $32,643
Application Deadline: February 1	**Room & Board:** $7776
Freshman Class: 1806 applied, 1449 accepted, 391 enrolled	
SAT CR/M: 630/630	**ACT:** 28　**HIGHLY COMPETITIVE+**

Kalamazoo College is a liberal arts and sciences institution founded in 1833. There is 1 undergraduate school. The library contains 346,648 volumes, 54,055 microform items, and 8938 audio/video tapes/CDs/DVDs, and subscribes to 1250 periodicals including electronic. Computerized library services include interlibrary loans, database searching, Internet access, and laptop Internet portals. Special learning facilities include a learning resource center, art gallery, radio station, and TV station. The 60-acre campus is in a suburban area 140 miles from Detroit and Chicago. Including any residence halls, there are 30 buildings.

Programs of Study: Kalamazoo confers B.A. degrees. Bachelor's degrees are awarded in BIOLOGICAL SCIENCE (biology/biological science), BUSINESS (business economics), COMMUNICATIONS AND THE ARTS (art, art history and appreciation, dramatic arts, English, French, German, music, and Spanish), COMPUTER AND PHYSICAL SCIENCE (chemistry, computer science, mathematics, and physics), HEALTH PROFESSIONS (health science), SOCIAL SCIENCE (anthropology, classical/ancient civilization, economics, history, human development, interdisciplinary studies, international studies, philosophy, political science/government, psychology, religion, and sociology). Foreign languages, international studies and commerce, and health sciences are the strongest academically. Economics, English, and psychology are the largest.

Special: Students may study abroad in more than 25 countries and choose from among 900 career internships in the United States, Europe, Asia, and Africa. The school allows dual and interdisciplinary majors and has cross-registration with Western Michigan University. A 3-2 engineering degree is offered with Washington University and the University of Michigan. There are 3 national honor societies, including Phi Beta Kappa.

Admissions: 80% of the 2009-2010 applicants were accepted. The SAT scores for the 2009-2010 freshman class were: Critical Reading--12% below 500, 23% between 500 and 599, 42% between 600 and 700, and 23% above 700; Math--10% below 500, 23% between 500 and 599, 54% between 600 and 700, and 13% above 700; Writing--9% below 500, 36% between 500 and 599, 38% between 600 and 700, and 17% above 700. The ACT scores were 1% below 21, 9% between 21 and 23, 20% between 24 and 26, 26% between 27 and 28, and 43% above 28. 78% of the current freshmen were in the top fifth of their class; 96% were in the top two fifths. There were 14 National Merit finalists. 16 freshmen graduated first in their class.

Requirements: The SAT or ACT is required. The ACT Optional Writing test is also required. In addition, the college requires a high school transcript, an essay, and teacher and counselor recommendations; an interview is recommended. AP credits are accepted. Important factors in the admissions decision are recommendations by school officials, leadership record, and advanced placement or honors courses.

Procedure: Freshmen are admitted in fall. Entrance exams should be taken by December of the senior year. There are early decision, early admissions, and deferred admissions plans. Early decision applications should be filed by November 10; early action applications by November 20; and regular applications by February 1 for fall entry, along with a $40 fee. Notifications are sent April 1. 164 applicants were on the 2009 waiting list; 3 were admitted. Applications are accepted on-line only. The college is a Common Application exclusive user.

Financial Aid: In 2009-2010, 98% of all full-time freshmen and 98% of continuing full-time students received some form of financial aid. The FAFSA and the college's own financial statement are required. The priority date for freshman financial aid applications for fall entry is February 15.

Computers: Wireless access is available. High speed Internet access (wired and wireless) is available in all computer labs, academic buildings, and residence halls. All students may access the system. There are no time limits and no fees. It is strongly recommended that all students have a personal computer.

KANSAS CITY ART INSTITUTE

Kansas City, MO 64111   (816) 474-5224; (816) 802-3309

Full-time: 278 men, 393 women	**Faculty:** 46; IIB, --$
Part-time: 8 men, 11 women	**Ph.D.s:** 91%
Graduate: none	**Student/Faculty:** 15 to 1
Year: semesters, summer session	**Tuition:** $28,580
Application Deadline: February 1	**Room & Board:** $8710
Freshman Class: 387 applied, 376 accepted, 189 enrolled	
SAT CR/M/W: 535/525/500	**ACT:** 23 SPECIAL

The Kansas City Art Institute, founded in 1885, is an independent college of art and design. In addition to regional accreditation, KCAI has baccalaureate program accreditation with NASAD. The library contains 32,000 volumes, and 38 audio/video tapes/CDs/DVDs, and subscribes to 96 periodicals including electronic. Computerized library services include interlibrary loans, database searching, Internet access, and laptop Internet portals. Special learning facilities include a learning resource center and art gallery. The 15-acre campus is in an urban area in midtown Kansas City. Including any residence halls, there are 14 buildings.

Programs of Study: KCAI confers B.F.A. degrees. Bachelor's degrees are awarded in COMMUNICATIONS AND THE ARTS (animation, art history and appreciation, ceramic art and design, creative writing, design, digital communications, fiber/textiles/weaving, illustration, painting, photography, printmaking, and sculpture), COMPUTER AND PHYSICAL SCIENCE (digital arts/technology). Painting and graphic design are the largest.

Special: KCAI offers internships with major corporations such as Hallmark and Disney, independent study, work-study programs, study abroad in 7 countries, cross-registration, an exchange program, and nondegree study. There is also a Community Arts and Service Learning (CASL) certificate program.

Admissions: 97% of the 2009-2010 applicants were accepted. The SAT scores for the 2009-2010 freshman class were: Critical Reading--40% below 500, 33% between 500 and 599, 20% between 600 and 700; and 7% above 700; Math--37% below 500, 50% between 500 and 599, 10% between 600 and 700, and 3% above 700; Writing--47% below 500, 30% between 500 and 599, 20% between 600 and 700; and 3% above 700. The ACT scores were 23% below 21, 28% between 21 and 23, 23% between 24 and 26, 17% between 27 and 28, and 9% above 29. 33% of the current freshmen were in the top fifth of their class; 64% were in the top two fifths.

Requirements: The SAT or ACT is required. Applicants must submit a portfolio consisting of 10 to 20 pieces of artwork, 2 letters of recommendation, and high school transcripts. The GED is accepted. A statement of purpose and an interview are required. A GPA of 2.5 is required. AP and CLEP credits are accepted. Important factors in the admissions decision are evidence of special talent, advanced placement or honors courses, and recommendations by school officials.

Procedure: Freshmen are admitted fall and spring. Entrance exams should be taken in spring of the junior year or fall of the senior year. There are deferred admissions and rolling admissions plans. Applications should be filed by February 1 for fall entry, along with a $35 fee. Notification is sent on a rolling basis. Applications are accepted on-line.

Financial Aid: In 2009-2010, all full-time freshmen and 99% of continuing full-time students received some form of financial aid. 70% of all full-time freshmen and 69% of continuing full-time students received need-based aid. The average freshmen award was $22,582. Need-based scholarships or need-based grants averaged $18,537 ($25,680 maximum); need-based self-help aid (loans and jobs) averaged $4459 ($8500 maximum); and other non-need-based awards and non-need-based scholarships averaged $4588 ($25,680 maximum). 61% of undergraduate students work part-time. Average annual earnings from campus work are $1035. The average financial indebtedness of the 2009 graduate was $26,000. The FAFSA and student and parent IRS tax forms, if requested, are required. The priority date for freshman financial aid applications for fall entry is March 15. The deadline for filing freshman financial aid applications for fall entry is August 1.

Computers: Wireless access is available. All students may access the system. There are no time limits and no fees. It is strongly recommended that all students have a personal computer. Students enrolled in graphic design and animation majors must have a personal computer. A Mac is recommended.

KANSAS STATE UNIVERSITY

Manhattan, KS 66506　　　　　　　　**(785) 532-6250; (785) 532-6393**

Full-time: 8641 men, 7869 women	**Faculty:** 973; I, --$
Part-time: 1089 men, 1179 women	**Ph.D.s:** 84%
Graduate: 2016 men, 2787 women	**Student/Faculty:** 17 to 1
Year: semesters, summer session	**Tuition:** $6870 ($17,577)
Application Deadline: open	**Room & Board:** $6752
Freshman Class: 6906 applied, 4500 accepted, 3687 enrolled	
ACT: 24	**VERY COMPETITIVE**

Kansas State University, established in 1863, is a land-grant institution offering degree programs in agriculture, arts and sciences, business, engineering, human ecology, architecture, education, veterinary medicine, and technology. There are 9 undergraduate schools and 1 graduate school. In addition to regional accreditation, K-State has baccalaureate program accreditation with AACSB, ABET, ACCE, AHEA, CSWE, FIDER, NAAB, NASM, NCATE, and NRPA. The 5 libraries contain 1.9 million volumes, 2.7 million microform items, and 33,885 audio/video tapes/CDs/DVDs, and subscribe to 9529 periodicals including electronic. Computerized library services include interlibrary loans and database searching. Special learning facilities include a learning resource center, art gallery, planetarium, radio station, TV station, nuclear reactor, laser center, cancer research center, and telecommunications satellite teaching. The 668-acre campus is in a suburban area 125 miles west of Kansas City. Including any residence halls, there are 96 buildings.

Programs of Study: K-State confers B.A., B.S., B.Arch., B.F.A., B.Int.Arch., B.L.A., B.M., and B.M.E. degrees. Associate, master's, and doctoral degrees are also awarded. Bachelor's degrees are awarded in AGRICULTURE (agricultural business management, agricultural communications, agricultural economics, agronomy, animal science, fish and game management, horticulture, and wildlife management), BIOLOGICAL SCIENCE (biochemistry, biology/biological science, entomology, life science, microbiology, nutrition, and wildlife biology), BUSINESS (accounting, apparel and accessories marketing, banking and finance, business administration and management, entrepreneurial studies, hotel/motel and restaurant management, management information systems, and marketing/retailing/merchandising), COMMUNICATIONS AND THE ARTS (apparel design, applied music, art, communications, dramatic arts, English, journalism, modern language, and music), COMPUTER AND PHYSICAL SCIENCE (chemistry, computer science, geology, information sciences and systems, mathematics, physical sciences, physics, and statistics), EDUCATION (agricultural education, art education, athletic training, early childhood education, elementary education, music education, and secondary education), ENGINEERING AND ENVIRONMENTAL DESIGN (aeronautical technology, agricultural engineering, agricultural engineering technology, airline piloting and navigation, architectural engineering, architecture, chemical engineering, civil engineering, computer engineering, construction management, electrical/electronics engineering, electrical/electronics engineering technology, engineering management, engineering technology, industrial engineering, interior design, landscape architecture/design, manufacturing engineering, and mechanical engineering), HEALTH PROFESSIONS (exercise science and preveterinary science), SOCIAL SCIENCE (anthropology, dietetics, economics, ethnic studies, family and community services, family/consumer studies, food science, geography, history, humanities, parks and recreation management, philosophy, physical fitness/movement, political science/

government, psychology, social science, social work, sociology, textiles and clothing, and women's studies). Architecture, engineering, and accounting are the strongest academically. Journalism, elementary education, and mechanical engineering are the largest.

Special: K-State offers co-op programs, internships, and dual degrees and majors through most of its colleges. Cross-registration is available with Kansas State at Salina and Kansas Wesleyan University, as is study abroad in more than 100 countries. A 3-2 engineering degree program, nondegree study, and pass/fail options are also available. There are 78 national honor societies, including Phi Beta Kappa, a freshman honors program, and 7 departmental honors programs.

Admissions: 65% of the 2009-2010 applicants were accepted. The ACT scores were 19% below 21, 26% between 21 and 23, 26% between 24 and 26, 12% between 27 and 28, and 17% above 28. There were 17 National Merit finalists. 24 freshmen graduated first in their class.

Requirements: The ACT is recommended. In addition, applicants must meet 1 of these 3 criteria: an ACT score of 21 or above, class rank in the top third, or a 2.0 GPA in the Kansas core curriculum. It is recommended that students complete 4 units of English, 3 each of natural science, math, and social studies, and 1 of computer technology. The GED is accepted. AP and CLEP credits are accepted.

Procedure: Freshmen are admitted to all sessions. Entrance exams should be taken in the junior and senior years. There is a rolling admissions plan. Application deadlines are open. The fall 2009 application fee was $30. Notification is sent on a rolling basis. Applications are accepted on-line.

Financial Aid: In 2009-2010, 84% of all full-time freshmen and 73% of continuing full-time students received some form of financial aid. 42% of all full-time freshmen and 46% of continuing full-time students received need-based aid. Need-based scholarships or need-based grants averaged $4418 ($10,450 maximim); need-based self-help aid (loans and jobs) averaged $3925 ($8500 maximum); non-need-based athletic scholarships averaged $11,284 ($24,562 maximum); and other non-need-based awards, non-need-based scholarships, and parent PLUS loans averaged $7597 ($28,070 maximum). The average financial indebtedness of the 2009 graduate was $18,904. K-State is a member of CSS. The FAFSA is required. The priority date for freshman financial aid applications for fall entry is March 1.

Computers: Wireless access is available. All students may access the system 24 hours a day. There are no time limits. The fee is $11 per credit hour.

KENNESAW STATE UNIVERSITY

Kennesaw, GA 30144-5591	(770) 423-6300; (770) 423-6541
Full-time: 6446 men, 9062 women	Faculty: IIA, -$
Part-time: 1795 men, 3001 women	Ph.D.s: 75%
Graduate: 884 men, 1201 women	Student/Faculty: n/av
Year: semesters, summer session	Tuition: $5144 ($17,120)
Application Deadline: May 14	Room & Board: $10,445
Freshman Class: 7877 applied, 5010 accepted, 2749 enrolled	
SAT CR/M/W: 530/530/520	ACT: 22 COMPETITIVE

Kennesaw State University, founded in 1963, is a public college in the University System of Georgia. There are 7 undergraduate schools and 4 graduate schools. In addition to regional accreditation, Kennesaw State has baccalaureate program accreditation with AACSB, ABET, NASAD, NASM, NCATE, and NLN. The library contains 556,325 volumes, 1.8 million microform items, and 9,650 audio/

video tapes/CDs/DVDs, and subscribes to 42,000 periodicals including electronic. Computerized library services include interlibrary loans, database searching, Internet access, and laptop Internet portals. Special learning facilities include a learning resource center, art gallery, and radio station. The 384-acre campus is in a suburban area 25 miles north of Atlanta. Including any residence halls, there are 78 buildings.

Programs of Study: Kennesaw State confers B.A., B.S., B.B.A., B.F.A., and B.M. degrees. Master's and doctoral degrees are also awarded. Bachelor's degrees are awarded in BIOLOGICAL SCIENCE (biochemistry, biology/biological science, and biotechnology), BUSINESS (accounting, banking and finance, business economics, international business management, management science, marketing/retailing/merchandising, purchasing/inventory management, and sports management), COMMUNICATIONS AND THE ARTS (art, communications, dance, dramatic arts, English, modern language, music, and music performance), COMPUTER AND PHYSICAL SCIENCE (chemistry, computer science, computer security and information assurance, information sciences and systems, and mathematics), EDUCATION (art education, early childhood education, English education, health education, mathematics education, middle school education, music education, physical education, science education, and social studies education), HEALTH PROFESSIONS (exercise science and nursing), SOCIAL SCIENCE (African studies, anthropology, criminal justice, geographic information systems, geography, history, human services, interdisciplinary studies, international studies, political science/government, psychology, and sociology). Business, nursing, and education are the strongest academically. Elementary education, management, and nursing are the largest.

Special: Students may register for courses with any of the colleges in the University System of Georgia, study abroad in 37 countries, and participate in work-study programs and internships, some with pass/fail options. Dual majors, student-designed majors, and nondegree programs also are offered. There are 24 national honor societies, a freshman honors program, and 7 departmental honors programs.

Admissions: 64% of the 2009-2010 applicants were accepted. The SAT scores for the 2009-2010 freshman class were: Critical Reading--23% below 500, 59% between 500 and 599, 17% between 600 and 700, and 1% above 700; Math--26% below 500, 57% between 500 and 599, 16% between 600 and 700, and 1% above 700; Writing--36% below 500, 51% between 500 and 599, 12% between 600 and 700, and 1% above 700. The ACT scores were 28% below 21, 43% between 21 and 23, 21% between 24 and 26, 6% between 27 and 28, and 2% above 28.

Requirements: The SAT or ACT is required. In addition, applicants should be graduates of accredited secondary schools. Secondary preparation should include 4 units each of English and math, 3 each of social science and science, and 2 of a foreign language. A GPA of 2.5 is required. AP and CLEP credits are accepted.

Procedure: Freshmen are admitted fall, spring, and summer. Entrance exams should be taken before June 1. There is a rolling admissions plan. Applications should be filed by May 14 for fall entry, November 13 for spring entry, and April 9 for summer entry. The fall 2009 application fee was $40. Applications are accepted on-line.

Financial Aid: In 2009-2010, 89% of all full-time freshmen and 78% of continuing full-time students received some form of financial aid. 46% of all full-time freshmen and 49% of continuing full-time students received need-based aid. Need-based scholarships or need-based grants averaged $4286 ($8350 maximum); need-based self-help aid (loans and jobs) averaged $3370 ($7688 maximum); non-need-based athletic scholarships averaged $7640 ($18,586 maximum); and other non-need-based awards and non-need-based scholarships averaged $5944 ($22,283 maximum). The average financial indebtedness of the 2009 graduate was $18,805. The FAFSA is required. The priority date for freshman financial aid applications for fall entry is April 1.

Computers: Wireless access is available. All students may access the system 24 hours a day. There are no time limits and no fees.

KENT STATE UNIVERSITY
Kent, OH 44242-0001

(330) 672-2444
(800) 988-KENT; (330) 672-2499

Full-time: 6525 men, 9435 women	**Faculty:** I, --$
Part-time: 900 men, 1230 women	**Ph.D.s:** n/av
Graduate: 1500 men, 3230 women	**Student/Faculty:** n/av
Year: semesters, summer session	**Tuition:** $8730 ($16,420)
Application Deadline: see profile	**Room & Board:** $7940
Freshman Class: n/av	
SAT or ACT: required	**COMPETITIVE**

Kent State University, founded in 1910, is a public university offering degree programs in liberal and fine arts, business, health science, teacher and professional training, and aviation. Figures in the above capsule are approximate. There are 10 undergraduate schools and 8 graduate schools. In addition to regional accreditation, KSU has baccalaureate program accreditation with AACSB, ABET, ACB-SP, ACEJMC, ADA, FIDER, NAAB, NASAD, NASM, NCATE, and NLN. The 6 libraries contain 2.6 million volumes, 1.3 million microform items, and 10,400 audio/video tapes/CDs/DVDs, and subscribe to 12,000 periodicals including electronic. Computerized library services include interlibrary loans, database searching, Internet access, and laptop Internet portals. Special learning facilities include an art gallery, planetarium, radio station, TV station, fashion museum, and the Liquid Crystal Institute. The 866-acre campus is in a suburban area 45 miles southeast of Cleveland. Including any residence halls, there are 119 buildings.

Programs of Study: KSU confers B.A., B.S., B.A.R.C., B.B.A., B.F.A., B.G.S., B.M., B.R.I.T., B.S.E., and B.S.N. degrees. Associates, master's, and doctoral degrees are also awarded. Bachelor's degrees are awarded in AGRICULTURE (conservation and regulation), BIOLOGICAL SCIENCE (biology/biological science, biotechnology, botany, life science, nutrition, and zoology), BUSINESS (accounting, banking and finance, business administration and management, electronic business, fashion merchandising, marketing and distribution, marketing management, operations management, recreational facilities management, and sports management), COMMUNICATIONS AND THE ARTS (advertising, American Sign Language, art history and appreciation, classics, communications, crafts, dance, dramatic arts, English, French, German, Latin, music, photography, public relations, Spanish, visual and performing arts, and visual design), COMPUTER AND PHYSICAL SCIENCE (applied mathematics, chemistry, computer science, earth science, geology, mathematics, physical sciences, physics, and radiological technology), EDUCATION (art education, athletic training, early childhood education, middle school education, music education, physical education, social studies education, teaching English as a second/foreign language (TESOL/TEFOL), and trade and industrial education), ENGINEERING AND ENVIRONMENTAL DESIGN (aeronautical science, aeronautical technology, architecture, computer technology, industrial engineering technology, and interior design), HEALTH PROFESSIONS (community health work, medical laboratory technology, nursing, predentistry, premedicine, preosteopathy, preveterinary science, and speech pathology/audiology), SOCIAL SCIENCE (African studies, American studies, anthropology, Eastern European studies, economics, ethnic studies, fashion design and technology, geography, history, human development, international relations, Latin American studies, paralegal studies, philosophy, political science/government, psychology, Russian and Slavic studies, and sociology). Architecture, education, and fashion design and merchandising are the strongest academically. Business, psychology, and fashion merchandising are the largest.

Special: A co-op program is available with the School of Technology, and cross-registration is available with the University of Akron, Cleveland State University, and Northeastern Ohio University's College of Medicine (NEOUCOM). Work-study programs and internships are offered. Study abroad in 12 countries, a Washington semester, an accelerated medical degree program, B.A.-B.S. degrees, dual majors, a general studies degree, student-designed majors, credit for military education, nondegree study, and pass/fail options are also possible. The Honors College provides honors course work in all majors. Dual admission with Cuyahoga Community, Lakeland Community, NEOUCOM, and Lorain County Commmunity Colleges is available. Kent is a member of the national student exchange program. There are 15 national honor societies, including Phi Beta Kappa, and a freshman honors program.

Admissions: 38 freshmen graduated first in their class in a recent year.

Requirements: The SAT or ACT is required. Applicants most likely to be admitted with have at least a 2.5 cumulative GPA in a solid college-preparatory program and an ACT composite score of at least 21. A GPA of 2.5 is required. AP and CLEP credits are accepted.

Procedure: Freshmen are admitted fall, spring, and summer. Entrance exams should be taken in the spring of the junior year or the fall of the senior year. There is a rolling admissions plan. Check with the school for current application deadlines. The application fee is $30. Notification is sent on a rolling basis. Applications are accepted on-line. 560 applicants were on a recent waiting list, 399 were accepted.

Financial Aid: In a recent year, 81% of all full-time freshmen and 69% of continuing full-time students received some form of financial aid. 65% of all full-time freshmen and 59% of continuing full-time students received need-based aid. The average freshmen award was $8853. The average financial indebtedness of a recent graduate was $23,456. The FAFSA and the college's own financial statement are required. Check with the school for current application deadlines.

Computers: Wireless access is available in several labs and buildings. The wireless network allows students, faculty, and staff to work anywhere in a coverage area and still have access to all University computing resources. Students with departmental authorization may access the system 24 hours a day, 7 days a week. There are no time limits and no fees.

KENYON COLLEGE

Gambier, OH 43022-9623

(740) 427-5776
(800) 848-2468; (740) 427-5770

Full-time: 777 men, 841 women	**Faculty:** 156; IIB, +$
Part-time: 5 men, 10 women	**Ph.D.s:** 99%
Graduate: none	**Student/Faculty:** 11 to 1
Year: semesters	**Tuition:** $40,980
Application Deadline: January 15	**Room & Board:** $7260

Freshman Class: 3992 applied, 1538 accepted, 469 enrolled

SAT CR/M/W: 674/645/672 **ACT:** 29 **MOST COMPETITIVE**

Kenyon College is a private liberal arts and sciences undergraduate college founded in 1824 by Philander Chase, the first Episcopal Bishop of Ohio. Kenyon was historically an Episcopal institution, but is now non-denominational. There are no undergraduate schools. The library contains 889,142 volumes, 148,093 microform items, and 152,474 audio/video tapes/CDs/DVDs, and subscribes to 11,784 periodicals including electronic. Computerized library services include interlibrary loans, database searching, Internet access, and laptop Internet portals. Special learning facilities include a learning resource center, art gallery, radio station, an observatory, and an environmental center. The 1000-acre campus is in a rural area 50 miles northeast of Columbus, OH. Including any residence halls, there are 130 buildings.

Programs of Study: Kenyon confers B.A. degrees. Bachelor's degrees are awarded in BIOLOGICAL SCIENCE (biochemistry, biology/biological science, molecular biology, and neurosciences), COMMUNICATIONS AND THE ARTS (art history and appreciation, classics, dance, dramatic arts, English, French, German, Greek (classical), Latin, modern language, music, Spanish, and studio art), COMPUTER AND PHYSICAL SCIENCE (chemistry, mathematics, and physics), SOCIAL SCIENCE (American studies, anthropology, economics, history, international studies, philosophy, political science/government, psychology, religion, sociology, and women's studies).

Special: Students may study abroad in many countries. The college also offers dual and student-designed majors, pass/fail options, internships, winter and/or spring break externship programs, a Washington semester consisting of apprenticeships in any of several U.S. programs, and a 3-2 engineering degree with Case Western Reserve, Washington University in St. Louis, and Rensselaer Polytechnic Institute, as well as a 3-2 environmental studies program with Duke University. 3-2 or 4-1 master's (certification) programs with The Bank Street College of Education are also possible. Kenyon's Interdisciplinary Program in Humane Studies offers a tutorial-based concentration on the human predicament. There are 5 national honor societies and including Phi Beta Kappa.

Admissions: 39% of the 2009-2010 applicants were accepted. The SAT scores for the 2009-2010 freshman class were: Critical Reading--1% below 500, 13% between 500 and 599, 47% between 600 and 700, and 39% above 700; Math--1% below 500, 19% between 500 and 599, 62% between 600 and 700, and 17% above 700; Writing--1% below 500, 13% between 500 and 599, 47% between 600 and 700, and 39% above 700. The ACT scores were % below 21, 4% between 21 and 23, 13% between 24 and 26, 21% between 27 and 28, and 61% above 28. 84% of the current freshmen were in the top fifth of their class; 97% were in the top two fifths. There were 17 National Merit finalists. 15 freshmen graduated first in their class.

Requirements: The SAT or ACT is required. In addition, applicants should be graduates of an accredited secondary school. Kenyon recommends 4 units each of English, foreign language, and math, and 3 units history and 1 unit of social studies. Candidates are encouraged to exceed the minimum requirements, especially in math and science, and to take advance placement or honors work in at least 2 subjects. An essay and interview are important criteria in the admissions decision. Talent in music, theater, art, writing, and athletics is given extra consideration. AP credits are accepted. Important factors in the admissions decision are advanced placement or honors courses, evidence of special talent, and leadership record.

Procedure: Freshmen are admitted fall. Entrance exams should be taken in the fall of the senior year. There are early decision and deferred admissions plans. Early decision applications should be filed by November 15; regular applications, by January 15 for fall entry, along with a $45 fee. Notification of early decision is sent February 1; regular decision, April 1. 211 early decision candidates were accepted for the 2009-2010 class. 857 applicants were on the 2009 waiting list; 15 were admitted. Applications are accepted on-line.

Financial Aid: In 2009-2010, 55% of all full-time freshmen and 51% of continuing full-time students received some form of financial aid. 45% of all full-time freshmen and 41% of continuing full-time students received need-based aid. The average freshman award was $30,190. Need-based scholarships or need-based grants averaged $28,858 ; need-based self-help aid (loans and jobs) averaged $4,051; other non-need-based awards and non-need-based scholarships averaged $10,403; and $3,389 from other forms of aid. 44% of undergraduate students work part-time. Average annual earnings from campus work are $1255. The average financial indebtedness of the 2009 graduate was $19,934. Kenyon is a member of CSS. The CSS/Profile and FAFSA are required. The priority date for freshman financial aid applications for fall entry is February 15.

Computers: Wireless access is available. There are over 300 public computers in classrooms and labs. Wireless access is available in almost all campus buildings. All students may access the system. 24 hours a day. There are no time limits and no fees. It is strongly recommended that all students have a personal computer. A Windows XP or Windows Vista or any Apple running OSX or higher. is recommended.

KETTERING UNIVERSITY
Flint, MI 48504-4898

(810) 762-7865
(800) 955-4464; (810) 762-9837

Full-time: 1853 men, 325 women	**Faculty:** 125; IIB, +$
Part-time: none	**Ph.D.s:** 93%
Graduate: 352 men, 145 women	**Student/Faculty:** 17 to 1
Year: semesters, summer session	**Tuition:** $25,658
Application Deadline: see profile	**Room & Board:** $5,798
Freshman Class: n/av	**HIGHLY COMPETITIVE**

Kettering University is a private college founded in 1919. In the 4.5-year undergraduate program, students alternate 11-week terms of full-time classes with 12-week terms of full-time paid professional cooperative education (co-op) work experience in industry. Students typically begin co-op during their freshman year and co-op in 43 states and several countries. There are 3 undergraduate schools and one graduate school. In addition to regional accreditation, Kettering has baccalaureate program accreditation with ABET and ACBSP. The library contains 133,210 volumes, 35,000 microform items, 800 audio/video tapes/CDs/DVDs, and subscribes to 400 periodicals including electronic. Computerized library services include interlibrary loans, database searching, and Internet access. Special learning facilities include a learning resource center, art gallery, radio station, Industrial History Archives. The 85-acre campus is in a suburban area 60 miles north of Detroit. Including any residence halls, there are 10 buildings.

Programs of Study: Kettering confers B.S. degrees. Master's degrees are also awarded. Bachelor's degrees are awarded in BIOLOGICAL SCIENCE (biochemistry), COMPUTER AND PHYSICAL SCIENCE (applied mathematics, applied physics, chemistry, and computer science), ENGINEERING AND ENVIRONMENTAL DESIGN (computer engineering, electrical/electronics engineering, engineering physics, industrial engineering, and mechanical engineering). Mechanical, Electrical, and Computer Engineering are the largest.

Special: All undergraduate students participate in paid professional cooperative education work experience. Students may pursue a dual major in any degree combination. Accelerated degree programs in engineering are available in most majors, as is study abroad in 3 countries. There are 8 national honor societies.

Admissions: The SAT scores for the 2009-2010 freshman class were: Critical Reading--17% below 500, 47% between 500 and 599, 27% between 600 and 700, and 9% above 700; Math--6% below 500, 25% between 500 and 599, 51% between 600 and 700, and 18 above 700. The ACT scores were 3% below 21, 12% between 21 and 23, 40% between 24 and 26, 17% between 27 and 28, and 28% above 28. 64% of the current freshmen were in the top fifth of their class; 94% were in the top two fifths. 18 freshmen graduated first in their class.

Requirements: The SAT or ACT is required. In addition, applicants must graduate from an accredited secondary school with a minimum of 16 academic credits. Applicants must have completed 3 years of English, 3 1/2 years of math, including trigonometry, and 2 years of lab science, 1 of which must be chemistry or physics (both are strongly recommended). AP credits are accepted. Important factors in the admissions decision are leadership record, advanced placement or honors courses, and extracurricular activities record.

Procedure: Freshmen are admitted fall, winter, and summer. Entrance exams should be taken during the spring of the junior year and fall of the senior year. There are deferred admissions and rolling admissions plans. Application deadlines are open. Application fee is $35. Applications are accepted on-line.

Financial Aid: In 2009-2010, 89% of all full-time freshmen and 84% of continuing full-time students received some form of financial aid. 79% of all full-time freshmen and 67% of continuing full-time students received need-based aid. The average freshmen award was $18,078, with $3,672 ($4,700 maximum) from need-based self-help aid (loans and jobs). 18% of undergraduate students work part-time. Average annual earnings from campus work are $820. The average financial indebtedness of the 2009 graduate was $30,903. The FAFSA and the college's own financial statement are required. The priority date for freshman financial aid applications for fall entry is February 14.

Computers: Wireless access is available. There are various general use labs, library, student dorm and student lounge areas where PCs are available. Wireless is also available throughout the majority of the campus including many of the classrooms and common areas. All students may access the system. 24 hours per day, 7 days per week. There are no time limits and no fees. It is strongly recommended that all students have a personal computer.

KING COLLEGE

Bristol, TN 37620-2699

(423) 652-4861
(800) 362-0014; (423) 652-4727

Full-time: 430 men, 750 women	**Faculty:** IIB, --$
Part-time: 35 men, 55 women	**Ph.Ds:** 81%
Graduate: 90 men, 160 women	**Student/Faculty:** n/av
Year: semesters, summer session	**Tuition:** $22,900
Application Deadline: open	**Room & Board:** $7800
Freshman Class: n/av	
SAT or ACT: required	**VERY COMPETITIVE+**

King College, founded in 1867, is a private liberal arts college affiliated with the Presbyterian Church (U.S.A.). Figures in the above capsule are approximate. There are 5 undergraduate schools and 3 graduate schools. The library contains 110,000 volumes, 40,408 microform items, and 5832 audio/video tapes/CDs/DVDs, and subscribes to 389 periodicals including electronic. Computerized library services include interlibrary loans, database searching, Internet access, and laptop Internet portals. Special learning facilities include a learning resource center and an observatory. The 135-acre campus is in a small town 2 miles east of Bristol. Including any residence halls, there are 17 buildings.

Programs of Study: King confers B.A., B.S., B.B.A., B.Chem, B.S.Med.Tech., and B.S.N. degrees. Master's degrees are also awarded. Bachelor's degrees are awarded in BIOLOGICAL SCIENCE (biochemistry, biology/biological science, and neurosciences), BUSINESS (accounting, business administration and management, business economics, electronic business, international business management, management information systems, marketing management, and sports management), COMMUNICATIONS AND THE ARTS (English, French, modern language, Spanish, technical and business writing, and visual and performing arts), COMPUTER AND PHYSICAL SCIENCE (applied mathematics, applied science, chemistry, mathematics, and physics), EDUCATION (athletic training, elementary education, music education, physical education, and secondary education), ENGINEERING AND ENVIRONMENTAL DESIGN (engineering), HEALTH PROFESSIONS (health science, medical technology, nursing, and physical therapy), SOCIAL SCIENCE (American studies, biblical studies, economics, forensic studies, history, interdisciplinary studies, political science/government, psychology, and youth ministry). Business and economics, English, and natural sciences are the strongest academically. Business and economics, English, nursing, and social sciences are the largest.

Special: King offers co-op programs, cross-registration with Virginia Intermont College, internships, study abroad in approximately 50 countries, a Washington semester, and work-study programs. There are 3-2 engineering degrees available with Vanderbilt University and the University of Tennessee. Dual degrees in pharmacy, engineering, and physical therapy are offered. Nondegree study and pass/fail options for special students are available. There is 1 national honor society, a freshman honors program, and 1 departmental honors program.

Admissions: 6 freshmen graduated first in their class in a recent year.

Requirements: The SAT or ACT is required. In addition, graduation from an accredited or recognized secondary institution is required, with a minimum of 16 academic units, distributed as follows: 4 of English; 2 of algebra (algebra I and II); 1 of geometry; 2 of foreign language; 2 of history and social studies; 1 of natural science; and 4 of other academic electives. A GPA of 2.6 is required. AP and CLEP credits are accepted. Important factors in the admissions decision are advanced placement or honors courses, extracurricular activities record, and leadership record.

Procedure: Freshmen are admitted fall, spring, and summer. Entrance exams should be taken by May 1. There are deferred admissions and rolling admissions plans. Application deadlines are open. The fall 2009 application fee was $20. Applications are accepted on-line.

Financial Aid: In a recent year, 83% of all full-time freshmen and 69% of continuing full-time students received some form of financial aid. 80% of all full-time freshmen and 60% of continuing full-time students received need-based aid. The average freshmen award was $16,442. 30% of undergraduate students work part-time. Average annual earnings from campus work are $962. The average financial indebtedness of a recent graduate was $9998. King is a member of CSS. The FAFSA and the college's own financial statement are required. Check with the school for current application deadlines.

Computers: Wireless access is available. All students may access the system. There are no time limits and no fees. Students are provided labtops at campus check-in.

KNOX COLLEGE
Galesburg, IL 61401

(309) 341-7100
(800) 678-KNOX; (309) 341-7070

Full-time: 552 men, 832 women	**Faculty:** 103; IIB, -$
Part-time: 11 men, 12 women	**Ph.D.s:** 91%
Graduate: none	**Student/Faculty:** 13 to 1
Year: trimesters	**Tuition:** $31,911
Application Deadline: February 1	**Room & Board:** $7164
Freshman Class: 2427 applied, 1788 accepted, 359 enrolled	
SAT CR/M/W: 660/620/620	**ACT:** 29 **HIGHLY COMPETITIVE+**

Knox College, founded in 1837, is an independent liberal arts college. The 3 libraries contain 316,886 volumes, 98,728 microform items, and 9,179 audio/video tapes/CDs/DVDs, and subscribe to 15,781 periodicals including electronic. Computerized library services include interlibrary loans, database searching, and Internet access. Special learning facilities include a learning resource center, natural history museum, radio station, and a 760-acre biological field station near the campus. The 90-acre campus is in a small town 180 miles southwest of Chicago. Including any residence halls, there are 57 buildings.

Programs of Study: Knox confers B.A. degrees. Bachelor's degrees are awarded in BIOLOGICAL SCIENCE (biochemistry and biology/biological science), COMMUNICATIONS AND THE ARTS (art history and appreciation, classics, creative writing, dramatic arts, English literature, French, German, modern language, music, Spanish, and studio art), COMPUTER AND PHYSICAL SCIENCE (chemistry, computer science, mathematics, and physics), EDUCATION (elementary education and secondary education), ENGINEERING AND ENVIRONMENTAL DESIGN (environmental science), SOCIAL SCIENCE (African American studies, American studies, anthropology, Asian/Oriental studies, economics, history, international relations, philosophy, political science/government, psychology, sociology, and women's studies). Biology, chemistry, and math are the strongest academically. Creative writing, anthropology-sociology, and psychology are the largest.

Special: The normal academic load is 3 courses per term, with 3 terms per year. Cooperative programs are offered with Washington University in St.Louis in architecture and engineering; Columbia University in engineering and law; University of Illinois at Urbana-Champaign and Rensselaer Polytechnic Institute in engineering; Rush University in medicine, nursing, and medical technology; Duke University in forestry and environmental management; and University of Chicago in law and social work. Study abroad is available in 20 countries. Other programs include a Washington semester, an urban studies semester, science and library research programs, work-study programs, and numerous internships. Dual majors, student-designed majors, and pass/fail options are available. Early admission to George Washington University Medical School and Rush Medical College is possible. Nondegree study is possible. Knox College participates in the Kemper Scholars Program. There are 8 national honor societies, including Phi Beta Kappa, and 39 departmental honors programs.

Admissions: 74% of the 2009-2010 applicants were accepted. The SAT scores for the 2009-2010 freshman class were: Critical Reading--4% below 500, 21% between 500 and 599, 34% between 600 and 700, and 41% above 700; Math--6% below 500, 34% between 500 and 599, 38% between 600 and 700, and 22% above 700; Writing--7% below 500, 25% between 500 and 599, 43% between 600 and 700, and 25% above 700. The ACT scores were 1% below 21, 6% between 21 and 23, 18% between 24 and 26, 34% between 27 and 28, and 41% above 28. 65% of the current freshmen were in the top fifth of their class; 92% were in the top two fifths. There were 4 National Merit finalists. 9 freshmen graduated first in their class.

Requirements: An essay is required of all applicants. Applicants should be graduates of an accredited secondary school with a minimum of 15 academic credits (18-20 are recommended). An interview is strongly recommended. The submission of ACT/SAT scores is optional; scores will be considered if submitted. AP credits are accepted. Important factors in the admissions decision are advanced placement or honors courses, recommendations by school officials, and personality/intangible qualities.

Procedure: Freshmen are admitted in the fall. Entrance exams should be taken by December 15. There is a deferred admissions plan. Applications should be filed by February 1 for fall entry, November 1 for winter entry, and January 15 for spring entry, along with a $40 fee. Notifications are sent March 31. Applications are accepted on-line. 108 applicants were on a recent waiting list, 63 were accepted.

Financial Aid: In a recent year, 97% of all full-time freshmen and 98% of continuing full-time students received some form of financial aid. 71% of all full-time freshmen and 65% of continuing full-time students received need-based aid. The average freshman award was $20,346. Need-based scholarships or need-based grants averaged $17,736 ($35,478 maximum); need-based self-help aid (loans and jobs) averaged $4,852 ($9,250 maximum); and other non-need-based awards and non-need-based scholarships averaged $10,584 ($31,125 maximum). 60% of undergraduate students worked part-time. Average annual earnings from campus work were $1104. The average financial indebtedness of the 2009 graduate was $21,951. Knox is a member of CSS. The FAFSA, the college's own financial statement, and student and parent tax returns are required. Check with the school for current application deadlines.

Computers: Wireless access is available. The entire campus is in range of the wireless network, and all living units and academic buildings have hard wired Ethernet connections. Several campus labs exist, from which the network may also be accessed. All students may access the system. A large student computer lab is open 24 hours. Others are open until midnight. There are no time limits and no fees.

Easton, PA 18042   **(610) 330-5100; (610) 330-5355**

Full-time: 1226 men, 1123 women	**Faculty:** 208; IIB, ++$
Part-time: 28 men, 26 women	**Ph.D.s:** 100%
Graduate: none	**Student/Faculty:** 11 to 1
Year: semesters, summer session	**Tuition:** $38,490
Application Deadline: January 1	**Room & Board:** $11,799
Freshman Class: n/av	
SAT CR/M/W: 620/660/630	**ACT:** 28 **MOST COMPETITIVE**

Lafayette College, founded in 1826 is a highly selective, private institution emphasizing the liberal arts, sciences, and engineering. There are no undergraduate schools. In addition to regional accreditation, Lafayette has baccalaureate program accreditation with ABET. The 2 libraries contain 510,000 volumes, 120,000 microform items, and subscribe to 2,600 periodicals including electronic. Computerized library services include interlibrary loans and database searching. Special learning facilities include a learning resource center, art gallery, radio station, geological museum, foreign languages lab, and calculus lab. The 342-acre campus is in a suburban area 70 miles west of New York City. Including any residence halls, there are 65 buildings.

Programs of Study: Lafayette confers A.B., B.S., and B.S.Eng. degrees. Bachelor's degrees are awarded in BIOLOGICAL SCIENCE (biochemistry, biology/biological science, and neurosciences), BUSINESS (business economics and international economics), COMMUNICATIONS AND THE ARTS (art, English, French, German, music, and Spanish), COMPUTER AND PHYSICAL SCIENCE (chemistry, computer science, geology, mathematics, and physics), ENGINEERING AND ENVIRONMENTAL DESIGN (chemical engineering, civil engineering, electrical/electronics engineering, engineering, and mechanical engineering), SOCIAL SCIENCE (African studies, American studies, anthropology, Asian/Oriental studies, economics, history, interdisciplinary studies, international relations, philosophy, political science/government, prelaw, psychology, religion, Russian and Slavic studies, and sociology). Engineering, psychology, and English are the strongest academically. Economics, business, and engineering are the largest.

Special: Cross-registration is available through the Lehigh Valley Association of Independent Colleges, internships in all academic departments, study abroad in 3 countries as well as through other individually arranged plans, a Washington semester at American University, and work-study programs with area employers are possible. An accelerated degree plan in all majors, dual and student-designed majors, 5-year dual-degree programs, and pass/fail options in any nonmajor subject also are available. There are 12 national honor societies, including Phi Beta Kappa, and 24 departmental honors programs.

Admissions: The SAT scores for the 2009-2010 freshman class were: Critical Reading--4% below 500, 33% between 500 and 599, 49% between 600 and 700, and 14% above 700; Math--1% below 500, 20% between 500 and 599, 50% between 600 and 700, and 28% above 700; Writing--4% below 500, 28% between 500 and 599, 50% between 600 and 700, and 19% above 700.

Requirements: The SAT or ACT is required. The ACT Optional Writing test is also required. In addition, applicants should have taken 4 years of English, 3 of math (4 for science or engineering majors), 2 each of a foreign language and lab science (with physics and chemistry for science or engineering students), and at least an additional 5 units in academic subjects. An essay is required and an interview recommended. Evaluations from the secondary school counselor and a teacher are required. The GED is accepted. AP credits are accepted. Important factors in the admissions decision are advanced placement or honors courses, evidence of special talent, and personality/intangible qualities.

Procedure: Freshmen are admitted fall. Entrance exams should be taken by January of the senior year. There are early decision and deferred admissions plans. Early decision applications should be filed by January 1. Applications should be filed by January 1 for fall entry, along with a $60 fee. Notifications are sent in March. Applications are accepted on-line. 1449 applicants were on a recent waiting list, 80 were accepted.

Financial Aid: In 2009-2010, 42% of all full-time freshmen and 46% of continuing full-time students received some form of financial aid. 41% of all full-time freshmen and 45% of continuing full-time students received need-based aid. The average freshmen award was $31,097. 22% of undergraduate students work part-time. Average annual earnings from campus work was $2600. The average financial indebtedness of the 2009 graduate was $20,745. The CSS/Profile, FAFSA, and the college's own financial statement, and the Business/Farm supplement, and Divorce/Separation parent statement (if applicable) are required. are required. The deadline for filing freshman financial aid applications for fall entry is February 15.

Computers: Wireless access is available. All students may access the system. 24 hours per day. There are no time limits and no fees.

LAKE FOREST COLLEGE

Lake Forest, IL 60045-2399	(847) 735-5000
	(800) 828-4751; (847) 735-6271

Full-time: 565 men, 819 women	**Faculty:** 95; IIB, +$
Part-time: 5 men, 9 women	**Ph.D.s:** 98%
Graduate: 8 men, 9 women	**Student/Faculty:** n/av
Year: semesters, summer session	**Tuition:** $34206
Application Deadline: February 15	**Room & Board:** $8006
Freshman Class: 2026 applied, 1398 accepted, 355 enrolled	
	VERY COMPETITIVE

Lake Forest College, founded in 1857, is a private liberal arts institution affiliated by heritage with the Presbyterian Church (U.S.A.). There are no undergraduate schools. The library contains 281,079 volumes, 106,175 microform items, and 6,283 audio/video tapes/CDs/DVDs, and subscribes to 2,611 periodicals including electronic. Computerized library services include interlibrary loans, database searching, Internet access, and laptop Internet portals. Special learning facilities include a learning resource center, art gallery, radio station, a multimedia language lab, an electronic music studio with practice rooms, a technology resource center, equipped with high-end computing hardware and software. The 110-acre campus is in a suburban area 30 miles north of Chicago. Including any residence halls, there are 30 buildings.

Programs of Study: Lake Forest confers B.A. degrees. Master's degrees are also awarded. Bachelor's degrees are awarded in BIOLOGICAL SCIENCE (biology/biological science), BUSINESS (business economics), COMMUNICATIONS AND THE ARTS (art, communications, dramatic arts, English, French, music, and Spanish), COMPUTER AND PHYSICAL SCIENCE (chemistry, computer science, mathematics, and physics), EDUCATION (education), ENGINEERING AND ENVIRONMENTAL DESIGN (environmental science), SOCIAL SCIENCE (American studies, anthropology, area studies, Asian/Oriental studies, economics, history, international relations, Latin American studies, philosophy, political science/government, psychology, religion, and sociology). Business/economics, communications and psychology are the largest.

Special: Lake Forest offers cross-registration with Associated Colleges of the Midwest, an extensive internship program, through the Center for Chicago Programs, a student-designed Independent Scholar Program, and study abroad in 10 countries. Dual and interdisciplinary majors, including American studies, Asian studies, area studies, art (studio and art history), and environmental studies, are available. There is a Washington semester with American University and a work-study program. A 3-2 engineering degree with Washington University at St. Louis. Several minors and a pass/fail option are available. Several minors and a pass/fail option are available. There are 11 national honor societies, including Phi Beta Kappa, and a freshman honors program.

Admissions: 69% of the 2009-2010 applicants were accepted. 50% of the current freshmen were in the top fifth of their class; 77% were in the top two fifths.

Requirements: In addition, applicants are advised to complete a minimum of 16 academic credits, including 4 in English, 3 in math, 2 to 4 each in social and natural sciences, and study in 1 or more foreign languages. A GED is accepted. An interview is encouraged. AP credits are accepted. Important factors in the admissions decision are personality/intangible qualities, extracurricular activities record, and advanced placement or honors courses.

Procedure: Freshmen are admitted fall and spring. Entrance exams should be taken in the junior or senior year. There are early decision and deferred admissions plans. Early decision applications should be filed by December 1; regular applications, by February 15 for fall entry; and December 1 for spring entry, along with a $40 fee. Notification of early decision is sent December 21; regular decision, March 21. 25 applicants were on the 2009 waiting list; 18 were admitted. Applications are accepted on-line.

Financial Aid: In 2009-2010, 94% of all full-time freshmen and 94% of continuing full-time students received some form of financial aid. The average freshman award was $30,000. Need-based scholarships or need-based grants averaged $22,000 ($28,500 maximum); need-based self-help aid (loans and jobs) averaged $5,450 ($8,000 maximum); and other non-need-based awards and non-need-based scholarships averaged $13,600 ($18,000 maximum). 140% of undergraduate students work part-time. Average annual earnings from campus work are $2000. The average financial indebtedness of the 2009 graduate was $21,655. Lake Forest is a member of CSS. The FAFSA, and Federal Income Tax Return 1040 is required. The priority date for freshman financial aid applications for fall entry is February 15. The deadline for filing freshman financial aid applications for fall entry is May 1.

Computers: Wireless access is available. All students are given e-mail accounts, access to the college network, and 1.5 GB of network file storage, with additional network storage available by request. All residence hall rooms offer wired and wireless network access. All campus buildings, including each classroom, are wired for access to the network. Many academic buildings also offer wireless network access. There are more than 150 computers available for student use in the library, including 30 laptops which are available for checkout. 30 of these computers are available 24 hours a day, 7 days a week. There are approximately 40 additional computers available for student use in academic buildings on campus. All students may access the system. 24 hours a day, 7 days a week. There are no time limits and no fees. It is strongly recommended that all students have a personal computer.

LAWRENCE TECHNOLOGICAL UNIVERSITY

Southfield, MI 48075

(248) 204-3160
(800) CALL-LTU; (248) 204-3188

Full-time: 1212 men, 419 women	**Faculty:** 129
Part-time: 1238 men, 318 women	**Ph.D.s:** 72%
Graduate: 879 men, 452 women	**Student/Faculty:** 13 to 1
Year: semesters, summer session	**Tuition:** $23,008
Application Deadline: open	**Room & Board:** $9353
Freshman Class: 1698 applied, 845 accepted, 272 enrolled	
ACT: 24	**SAT:** recommended

VERY COMPETITIVE

Lawrence Technological University, founded in 1932 as Lawrence Institute of Technology, is a private institution housing colleges of engineering, management, arts and sciences, and architecture and design. There are 4 undergraduate schools and 4 graduate schools. In addition to regional accreditation, Lawrence Tech has baccalaureate program accreditation with ABET, ACBSP, FIDER, NAAB, and NASAD. The library contains 150,770 volumes, 29,650 microform items, and 490 audio/video tapes/CDs/DVDs, and subscribes to 69,400 periodicals including electronic. Computerized library services include interlibrary loans, database searching, and Internet access. Special learning facilities include a learning resource center, a Frank Lloyd Wright-designed home, used as academic resource, and the personal library of the late architect Albert Kahn and Acedemic Achievement Center. The 102-acre campus is in a suburban area 30 minutes north of downtown Detroit. Including any residence halls, there are 11 buildings.

Programs of Study: Lawrence Tech confers B.A., B.S., B.F.A., and B.F.M. degrees. Associate, master's, and doctoral degrees are also awarded. Bachelor's degrees are awarded in BIOLOGICAL SCIENCE (biochemistry and molecular biology), BUSINESS (business administration and management), COMMUNICATIONS AND THE ARTS (communications, English, illustration, and technical and business writing), COMPUTER AND PHYSICAL SCIENCE (chemistry, computer science, information sciences and systems, mathematics, and physics), ENGINEERING AND ENVIRONMENTAL DESIGN (architecture, biomedical engineering, civil engineering, computer engineering, construction management, electrical/electronics engineering, engineering technology, environmental science, interior design, mechanical engineering, and transportation engineering), SOCIAL SCIENCE (humanities and psychology). Mathematics, computer science, and engineering are the strongest academically. Engineering and architecture are the largest.

Special: There are co-op programs in a number of majors, internships, study abroad in 8 countries and dual majors available. There are 7 national honor societies and 6 departmental honors programs.

Admissions: 50% of the 2009-2010 applicants were accepted. The ACT scores were 25% below 21, 22% between 21 and 23, 24% between 24 and 26, 16% between 27 and 28, and 13% above 28. 48% of the current freshmen were in the top fifth of their class; 74% were in the top two fifths. 6 freshmen graduated first in their class.

Requirements: The ACT is required, the SAT is recommended. In addition, students must have a high school diploma and a GPA of no lower than 2.5, at least 2.0 in each subject area pertaining to their major. Applicants should have taken 4 years each of math, science, and English, and 3 years of social science. The

GED is accepted. An interview is recommended. A GPA of 2.5 is required. AP and CLEP credits are accepted. Important factors in the admissions decision are advanced placement or honors courses, personality/intangible qualities, and leadership record.

Procedure: Freshmen are admitted to all sessions. Entrance exams should be taken in the semester preceding entry. There are deferred admissions and rolling admissions plans. Application deadlines are open. The fall 2009 application fee was $30. Notification is sent on a rolling basis. Applications are accepted on-line.

Financial Aid: In 2009-2010, 89% of all full-time freshmen and 80% of continuing full-time students received some form of financial aid. 70% of all full-time freshmen and 60% of continuing full-time students received need-based aid. The average freshman award was $19,276. Need-based scholarships or need-based grants averaged $11,947 ($29,800 maximum); need-based self-help aid (loans and jobs) averaged $6,247 ($15,552 maximum); and other non-need based awards and non-need based scholarships averaged $10,387 ($25,000 maximum. 93% of undergraduate students work part-time. Average annual earnings from campus work are $2632. The average financial indebtedness of the 2009 graduate was $37,287. Lawrence Tech is a member of CSS. The FAFSA is required. The deadline for filing freshman financial aid applications for fall entry is April 1.

Computers: Wireless access is available. The LTU network is available to all students all day. There are 3500 PC systems on campus, each with network access, including Internet. Wireless service is available from any campus location. All students may access the system 24 hours daily. There are no time limits and no fees. All students are required to have a personal computer.

LAWRENCE UNIVERSITY
Appleton, WI 54912

(920) 832-6500
(800) 227-0982; (920) 832-6782

Full-time: 652 men, 755 women	**Faculty:** 157; IIB, av$
Part-time: 14 men, 12 women	**Ph.D.s:** 90%
Graduate: none	**Student/Faculty:** 9 to 1
Year: trimesters	**Tuition:** $34,596
Application Deadline: January 15	**Room & Board:** $7053
Freshman Class: 2516 applied, 1739 accepted, 352 enrolled	
SAT or ACT: not required	**HIGHLY COMPETITIVE+**

Lawrence University, founded in 1847, is a private liberal arts institution with a conservatory of music. There is one undergraduate school. In addition to regional accreditation, Lawrence has baccalaureate program accreditation with NASM. The library contains 403,347 volumes, 102,000 microform items, and 21,829 audio/video tapes/CDs/DVDs, and subscribes to 2,478 periodicals including electronic. Computerized library services include interlibrary loans, database searching, and Internet access. Special learning facilities include a learning resource center, art gallery, natural history museum, and radio station. The 84-acre campus is in an urban area 100 miles north of Milwaukee. Including any residence halls, there are 61 buildings.

Programs of Study: Lawrence confers B.A. and B.Mus. degrees. Bachelor's degrees are awarded in BIOLOGICAL SCIENCE (biochemistry, biology/biological science, and neurosciences), COMMUNICATIONS AND THE ARTS (art history and appreciation, Chinese, classics, dramatic arts, English, French, German, Japanese, linguistics, music performance, music theory and composition, Russian, Spanish, and studio art), COMPUTER AND PHYSICAL SCIENCE (chemistry, computer science, geology, mathematics, and physics), EDUCATION (art education, music education, and secondary education), ENGINEERING AND ENVIRONMENTAL DESIGN (environmental science), SOCIAL SCIENCE (anthropology, East Asian studies, economics, gender studies, history, international relations, philosophy, political science/government, psychology, and religion). Biology, music, and physics are the strongest academically.

Special: Lawrence offers Chicago-based programs in urban studies, urban education, and the arts, a humanities program at the Newberry Library, and a science internship at Oak Ridge National Laboratory. There are study-abroad programs in 26 countries, a Washington semester, limited pass/fail options, student-designed majors, and nondegree study. Students may take a 3-2 engineering degree with Columbia or Washington Universities, or Rensselaer Polytechnic Institute. Also available are 3-2 programs in forestry and environmental studies with Duke University, in occupational therapy with Washington University in St. Louis and in allied health sciences (nursing/medical technology) with Rush-Presbyterian-St. Luke's Medical Center in Chicago. A 5-year B.A.-B.Mus. degree is offered. There are 5 national honor societies and including Phi Beta Kappa.

Admissions: 69% of the 2009-2010 applicants were accepted. 63% of the current freshmen were in the top fifth of their class; 92% were in the top two fifths. There were 12 National Merit finalists. 10 freshmen graduated first in their class.

Requirements: In addition, Applicants should complete 16 high school academic credits. Lawrence requires an essay, reports from a teacher and counselor, and an audition for music majors. The school recommends an interview, and a portfolio for art majors. AP credits are accepted. Important factors in the admissions decision are advanced placement or honors courses, evidence of special talent, and extracurricular activities record.

Procedure: Freshmen are admitted fall. Entrance exams should be taken in the spring of the junior year or fall of the senior year. There are early decision, early admissions and deferred admissions plans. Early decision applications should be filed by November 15; regular applications, by January 15 for fall entry, along with a $40 fee. Notification of early decision is sent December 1; regular decision, April 1. Applications are accepted on-line. 175 applicants were on a recent waiting list, 27 were accepted.

Financial Aid: In 2009-2010, 92% of all full-time freshmen and 93% of continuing full-time students received some form of financial aid. 66% of all full-time freshmen and 68% of continuing full-time students received need-based aid. The average freshmen award was $27,500. 72% of undergraduate students work part-time. Average annual earnings from campus work are $1500. The average financial indebtedness of the 2009 graduate was $20,405. Lawrence is a member of CSS. The FAFSA and the college's own financial statement are required. The priority date for freshman financial aid applications for fall entry is March 15.

Computers: Wireless access is available. The campus network provides high-speed access to various servers as well as the Internet. Besides access to shared resources, students get their own work space on the network as well as an area for web development. All students receive an e-mail account. There are wired residence halls as well as computer labs in all major residence halls and academic facilities. Wireless access is available in all academic buildings, and limited wireless is available in residence halls. All students may access the system. 24 hours a day. There are no time limits and no fees. It is strongly recommended that all students have a personal computer.

Syracuse, NY 13214-1301

(315) 445-4300
(800) 333-4733; (315) 445-4711

Full-time: 915 men, 1417 women	**Faculty:** 156; IIA, av$
Part-time: 112 men, 340 women	**Ph.D.s:** 94%
Graduate: 252 men, 488 women	**Student/Faculty:** 15 to 1
Year: semesters, summer session	**Tuition:** $25,780
Application Deadline: February 1	**Room & Board:** $9990
Freshman Class: 4526 applied, 3023 accepted, 608 enrolled	
SAT CR/M: 540/560	**ACT:** 23 **VERY COMPETITIVE**

Le Moyne College, founded in 1946, is a private liberal arts and sciences institution affiliated with the Roman Catholic Society of Jesus (Jesuit) and offers undergraduate and graduate degrees in a variety of disciplines. In addition to regional accreditation, Le Moyne has baccalaureate program accreditation with AACSB and TEAC. The library contains 268,041 volumes, 614,968 microform items, and 10,502 audio/video tapes/CDs/DVDs, and subscribes to 57,437 periodicals including electronic. Computerized library services include interlibrary loans, database searching, Internet access, and laptop Internet portals. Special learning facilities include a learning resource center, art gallery, radio station, TV station, and W. Carroll Coyne Performing Arts Center. The 161-acre campus is in a suburban area on the eastern edge of Syracuse. Including any residence halls, there are 37 buildings.

Programs of Study: Le Moyne confers B.A. and B.S. degrees. Master's degrees are also awarded. Bachelor's degrees are awarded in BIOLOGICAL SCIENCE (biochemistry, biology/biological science, and ecology), BUSINESS (accounting, banking and finance, business administration and management, human resources, labor studies, management information systems, marketing management, operations management, and organizational leadership and management), COMMUNICATIONS AND THE ARTS (advertising, communications, creative writing, dramatic arts, English, film arts, French, journalism, literature, media arts, public relations, radio/television technology, and Spanish), COMPUTER AND PHYSICAL SCIENCE (actuarial science, applied mathematics, chemistry, computer science, information sciences and systems, mathematics, physical sciences, physics, science, and statistics), EDUCATION (elementary education, English education, foreign languages education, mathematics education, middle school education, science education, secondary education, social studies education, special education, and teaching English as a second/foreign language (TESOL/TEFOL)), ENGINEERING AND ENVIRONMENTAL DESIGN (environmental science), HEALTH PROFESSIONS (nursing, predentistry, premedicine, preoptometry, prepharmacy, prepodiatry, and preveterinary science), SOCIAL SCIENCE (anthropology, criminology, economics, forensic studies, history, human services, international studies, law enforcement and corrections, peace studies, philosophy, political science/government, prelaw, psychology, religion, and sociology). Biology, psychology, and accounting are the largest.

Special: Internships are available to students in all majors. A campus work-study program, study abroad in 10 countries, dual majors, and a Washington semester are offered. A 3-2 engineering degree is available with Manhattan College, Clarkson University, University of Detroit, and Syracuse University, and there are early assurance medical and dental programs. 3-3 and 3-4 dental, podiatry, and optometry programs are offered. Some pass/fail options are offered. There are 14 national honor societies, a freshman honors program, and 11 departmental honors programs.

Admissions: 67% of the 2009-2010 applicants were accepted. The SAT scores for the 2009-2010 freshman class were: Critical Reading--25% below 500, 51% between 500 and 599, 22% between 600 and 700, and 2% above 700; Math--18% below 500, 50% between 500 and 599, 30% between 600 and 700, and 2% above 700. The ACT scores were 23% below 21, 34% between 21 and 23, 25% between 24 and 26, 8% between 27 and 28, and 10% above 28. 45% of the current freshmen were in the top fifth of their class; 81% were in the top two-fifths. 1 freshman graduated first in the class.

Requirements: The SAT or ACT is required. In addition, students should graduate from an accredited high school having completed 17 academic units that include 4 in English and social studies, 3 to 4 each in math and science, and 3 in foreign language. A personal statement and letters of recommendation from a teacher and a counselor are required. AP and CLEP credits are accepted. Important factors in the admissions decision are recommendations by school officials, advanced placement or honors courses, and extracurricular activities record.

Procedure: Freshmen are admitted fall and spring. Entrance exams should be taken in the spring of the junior year or fall of the senior year. There are early decision, early admissions, deferred admissions, and rolling admissions plans. Early decision applications should be filed by December 1; regular applications, by February 1 for fall entry and December 1 for spring entry, along with a $35 fee. Notification of early decision is sent December 15; regular decision is sent on a rolling basis. Applications are accepted on-line. 95 applicants were on a recent waiting list, 7 were accepted.

Financial Aid: In 2009-2010, 94% of all full-time freshmen and 91% of continuing full-time students received some form of financial aid. 81% of all full-time freshmen and 76% of continuing full-time students received need-based aid. The average freshmen award was $20,230, with $11,013 ($33,400 maximum) from need-based scholarships or need-based grants; $4,152 ($5,029 maximum) from need-based self-help aid (loans and jobs); $6,652 ($35,239 maximum) from non-need-based athletic scholarships; and $10,399 ($19,500 maximum) from other non-need-based awards and non-need-based scholarships. 41% of undergraduate students work part-time. Average annual earnings from campus work are $833. The average financial indebtedness of the 2009 graduate was $27,668. Le Moyne is a member of CSS. The FAFSA and the college's own financial statement are required. The deadline for filing freshman financial aid applications for fall entry is February 1.

Computers: Wireless access is available. About 325 PCs and Macs are connected to the campus network in public and departmental labs across campus, providing access to the library system, the Internet, and Novell servers with a multitude of applications. There is access to personal space on these servers. Access from residence hall rooms includes the library system, personal space, and the Internet. Wireless is available throughout most of the campus, including all academic areas. Most residential halls also have wireless capability. All students may access the system 24 hours a day. There are no time limits and no fees.

Bethlehem, PA 18015　　　　**(610) 758-3100; (610) 758-4361**

Full-time: 2790 men, 1956 women	**Faculty:** 432; I, av$
Part-time: 31 men, 15 women	**Ph.D.s:** 99%
Graduate: 1164 men, 1023 women	**Student/Faculty:** 10 to 1
Year: semesters, summer session	**Tuition:** $38,630
Application Deadline: January 1	**Room & Board:** $10,200

Freshman Class: 11170 applied, 3662 accepted, 1193 enrolled
SAT CR/M/W: 630/670/630　　　　**ACT:** required

MOST COMPETITIVE

Lehigh University, founded in 1865, is a private research university offering both undergraduate and graduate programs in liberal arts, sciences, business, education, and engineering. Our students experience interesting, independent research, and work closely with faculty who offer their time and attention on hands-on projects, internships, and innovative studies. There are 3 undergraduate schools and 4 graduate schools. In addition to regional accreditation, Lehigh has baccalaureate program accreditation with AACSB, ABET, and NCATE. The 2 libraries contain 1.2 million volumes, 1.7 million microform items, and 21,500 audio/video tapes/CDs/DVDs, and subscribe to 0 periodicals including electronic. Computerized library services include interlibrary loans, database searching, Internet access, and laptop Internet portals. Special learning facilities include a learning resource center, art gallery, radio station, TV station, special collections/rare book reading room, digital media studio, financial services lab, and international multimedia resource center. The 1600-acre campus is in a suburban area 50 miles north of Philadelphia and 75 miles southwest of New York City. Including any residence halls, there are 153 buildings.

Programs of Study: Lehigh confers B.A., B.S., B.S.B.A., and B.S.E. degrees. Master's and doctoral degrees are also awarded. Bachelor's degrees are awarded in AGRICULTURE (environmental studies), BIOLOGICAL SCIENCE (biochemistry, biology/biological science, ecology, life science, and molecular biology), BUSINESS (accounting, banking and finance, business administration and management, business economics, business systems analysis, marketing/retailing/merchandising, and supply chain management), COMMUNICATIONS AND THE ARTS (art, art history and appreciation, classics, design, dramatic arts, English, French, German, journalism, music, music history and appreciation, music theory and composition, Spanish, and theater management), COMPUTER AND PHYSICAL SCIENCE (applied science, astronomy, astrophysics, chemistry, computer science, geology, information sciences and systems, mathematics, physics, science technology, and statistics), ENGINEERING AND ENVIRONMENTAL DESIGN (architectural history, architecture, bioengineering, chemical engineering, civil engineering, computer engineering, construction engineering, electrical/electronics engineering, engineering, engineering mechanics, engineering physics, environmental engineering, environmental science, industrial engineering, materials engineering, and mechanical engineering), HEALTH PROFESSIONS (predentistry, premedicine, and preoptometry), SOCIAL SCIENCE (African studies, American studies, anthropology, Asian/Oriental studies, behavioral science, classical/ancient civilization, cognitive science, economics, history, international relations, philosophy, political science/government, psychology, religion, sociology, and women's studies). Finance, mechanical engineering, and psychology are the largest.

Special: Lehigh offers many interdisciplinary programs including Integrated Product Development, Computer Science and Business, Integrated Business and Engineering, Integrated Degree in Engineering, Arts and Sciences, Global Citizenship, Lehigh Earth Observatory, and South Mountain College, Lehigh's residential academic program. The university offers co-op programs, cross-registration with the Lehigh Valley Association of Independent Colleges, many combinations of dual majors, study abroad programs in 40 countries, internships, a Washington semester, work-study, a 7-year BA/MD program with Drexel University College of Medicine, and a 7-year BA/OD program with SUNY Optometry. There are 18 national honor societies, including Phi Beta Kappa, and a freshman honors program.

Admissions: 33% of the 2009-2010 applicants were accepted. The SAT scores for the 2009-2010 freshman class were: Critical Reading--4% below 500, 25% between 500 and 599, 55% between 600 and 700, and 16% above 700; Math--1% below 500, 12% between 500 and 599, 54% between 600 and 700, and 33% above 700; Writing--5% below 500, 27% between 500 and 599, 53% between 600 and 700, and 16% above 700. 99% of the current freshmen were in the top fifth of their class; 100% were in the top two fifths. 1 freshman graduated first in the class.

Requirements: The SAT or ACT is required. The ACT Optional Writing test is also required. In addition, candidates for admission should have completed 4 years of English, 3 years of math and electives, and 2 years each of a foreign language, science, and social science. Most students present 4 years each of science, math, and English. An on-campus interview is recommended. AP credits are accepted. Important factors in the admissions decision are advanced placement or honors courses, evidence of special talent, and leadership record.

Procedure: Freshmen are admitted fall and spring. Entrance exams should be taken by the January test date. There is a early decision admissions plan. Early decision applications should be filed by November 15; regular applications, by January 1 for fall entry and November 15 for spring entry, along with a $70 fee. Notification of early decision is sent December 15; regular decision, April 1. Applications are accepted on-line. 1160 applicants were on a recent waiting list, 43 were accepted.

Financial Aid: In 2009-2010, 44% of all full-time freshmen and 45% of continuing full-time students received some form of financial aid. 45% of all full-time freshmen and 44% of continuing full-time students received need-based aid. The average freshmen award was $32,081, with $4,605 ($7,200 maximum) from need-based self-help aid (loans and jobs); $30,506 ($48,530 maximum) from non-need-based athletic scholarships; and $10,139 ($38,330 maximum) from other non-need-based awards and non-need-based scholarships. 26% of undergraduate students work part-time. Average annual earnings from campus work are $2337. The average financial indebtedness of the 2009 graduate was $31,123. Lehigh is a member of CSS. The CSS/Profile, FAFSA, and the college's own financial statement, and noncustodial profile, and business/farm supplement are required. The deadline for filing freshman financial aid applications for fall entry is February 15.

Computers: Wireless access is available. All students may access the system 24 hours per day, 7 days per week. There are no time limits and no fees.

LEWIS & CLARK COLLEGE

Portland, OR 97219-7899
(503) 768-7040
(800) 444-4111; (503) 768-7055

Full-time: 749 men, 1146 women	**Faculty:** 139
Part-time: 6 men, 4 women	**Ph.D.s:** n/av
Graduate: 584 men, 889 women	**Student/Faculty:** 14 to 1
Year: semesters, summer session	**Tuition:** $36,632
Application Deadline: February 1	**Room & Board:** $9,648
Freshman Class: 5343 applied, 3448 accepted, 498 enrolled	

VERY COMPETITIVE

Lewis & Clark College, founded in 1867, is a private, independent liberal arts and sciences institution with a global reach. There are 2 graduate schools. In addition to regional accreditation, L & C has baccalaureate program accreditation with NASM. The 2 libraries contain 532,749 volumes, 1.5 million microform items, and 21,403 audio/video tapes/CDs/DVDs, and subscribe to 6,942 periodicals including electronic. Computerized library services include interlibrary loans, database searching, Internet access, and laptop Internet portals. Special learning facilities include a learning resource center, art gallery, radio station, TV station, telescope, research astronomical observatory, language lab, greenhouse, and adaptive technology lab. The 137-acre campus is in a suburban area 6 miles south of downtown Portland. Including any residence halls, there are 58 buildings.

Programs of Study: L & C confers B.A. degrees. Master's and doctoral degrees are also awarded. Bachelor's degrees are awarded in AGRICULTURE (environmental studies), BIOLOGICAL SCIENCE (biochemistry and biology/biological science), COMMUNICATIONS AND THE ARTS (art history and appreciation, communications, dramatic arts, English, fine arts, languages, music, and studio art), COMPUTER AND PHYSICAL SCIENCE (chemistry, computer mathematics, computer science, mathematics, and physics), SOCIAL SCIENCE (anthropology, East Asian studies, economics, French studies, German area studies, Hispanic American studies, history, interdisciplinary studies, international relations, philosophy, political science/government, psychology, religion, and sociology). Biology/biochemistry, psychology, and international studies are the largest.

Special: L & C offers cross-registration with the Oregon Independent College Association, which includes Reed College and the University of Portland; internships; study-abroad programs in 60 countries; semesters in Washington and New York City; and dual and student-designed majors. A 3-2 engineering program is available with Columbia and Washington Universities, the University of Southern California, and the Oregon Graduate Institute. There are 5 national honor societies, including Phi Beta Kappa.

Admissions: 58% of the 2009-2010 applicants were accepted. 69% of the current freshmen were in the top fifth of their class; 96% were in the top two fifths. There were 12 National Merit finalists.

Requirements: A GED may be accepted. It is recommended that applicants have 4 years each of English and math, 3 to 4 years of science, 3 years each of history/social studies and foreign language, and 1 year of fine arts. An essay is required and an interview recommended. The college also admits exceptional students through the Portfolio Path option. Portfolios should include 4 samples of graded work from the junior or senior year: 2 writing, 1 quantitative, and 1 of the student's choice. A GPA of 2.0 is required. AP credits are accepted. Important factors in the admissions decision are advanced placement or honors courses, recommendations by school officials, and extracurricular activities record.

Procedure: Freshmen are admitted fall and spring. Entrance exams should be taken during spring of the junior year or fall of the senior year. There is a deferred admissions plan. Applications should be filed by February 1 for fall entry, December 1 for spring entry, and May 1 for summer entry, along with a $50 fee. Notifications are sent April 1. 234 applicants were on the 2009 waiting list; 33 were admitted. Applications are accepted on-line.

Financial Aid: In 2009-2010, 56% of all full-time freshmen and 54% of continuing full-time students received some form of financial aid. 55% of all full-time freshmen and 55% of continuing full-time students received need-based aid. The average freshman award was $27,150. Need-based scholarships or need-based grants averaged $21,303; need-based self-help (loans and jobs) averaged $4.435; other non-need based awards and non-need based scholarships averaged $11,010. 65% of undergraduate students work part-time. Average annual earnings from campus work are $969. The average financial indebtedness of the 2009 graduate was $17,084. The FAFSA is required. The priority date for freshman financial aid applications for fall entry is February 15. The deadline for filing freshman financial aid applications for fall entry is April 15.

Computers: Wireless access is available. Approximately 160 PCs are available to undergraduate students in open labs. In addition, wireless network access is available in the Boley Law Library, other student areas on the law campus, Watzek Library, the Dovecote Coffee house, and Maggie's Café. It is possible to access online reserves, read e-mail, and browse the Web from anywhere in the libraries. All students may access the system 24 hours a day. There are no time limits and no fees.

LINFIELD COLLEGE
McMinnville, OR 97128-6894

(503) 883-2213
(800) 640-2287; (503) 883-2472

Full-time: 686 men, 941 women	**Faculty:** 112; IIB, -$
Part-time: 31 men, 19 women	**Ph.D.s:** 96%
Graduate: none	**Student/Faculty:** 15 to 1
Year: 4-1-4, summer session	**Tuition:** $29,054
Application Deadline: February 15	**Room & Board:** $8280
Freshman Class: 1692 applied, 1381 accepted, 423 enrolled	
SAT CR/M/W: 540/540/520	**ACT:** 24 **VERY COMPETITIVE**

Linfield College, founded in 1858, is a private, comprehensive undergraduate institution with a broad liberal arts core. There are 3 undergraduate schools. In addition to regional accreditation, Linfield has baccalaureate program accreditation with NASM. The library contains 184,931 volumes, 17,473 microform items, and 36,434 audio/video tapes/CDs/DVDs, and subscribes to 958 periodicals including electronic. Computerized library services include interlibrary loans, database searching, Internet access, and laptop Internet portals. Special learning facilities include a learning resource center, art gallery, radio station, a writing center, psychology lab, computer lab, anthropology museum, multimedia studio, speaking center, and the Linfield Research Institute. The 193-acre campus is in a small town 40 miles southwest of Portland. Including any residence halls, there are 69 buildings.

Programs of Study: Linfield confers B.A., B.S., and B.S.N. degrees. Bachelor's degrees are awarded in AGRICULTURE (environmental studies), BIOLOGICAL SCIENCE (biology/biological science), BUSINESS (accounting, banking and finance, business administration and management, and international business management), COMMUNICATIONS AND THE ARTS (art, communications, creative writing, dramatic arts, English, French, German, Japanese, music, and Spanish), COMPUTER AND PHYSICAL SCIENCE (applied physics, chemistry, computer science, mathematics, physics, and science), EDUCATION (athletic training, elementary education, health education, music education, and physical education), HEALTH PROFESSIONS (exercise science, health science, and nursing), SOCIAL SCIENCE (anthropology, crosscultural studies, economics, French studies, German area studies, history, philosophy, political science/government, psychology, religion, and sociology). Business, elementary education, and nursing are the strongest academically.

Special: During the January term, academic classes are conducted in such areas as New York City, Hawaii, China, Japan, Ireland, Mexico, and Ghana. Linfield also has a Division of Continuing Education with majors offered on-line. Cross-registration with the Oregon Independent Colleges Association, internships, study-abroad for a semester in 11 countries, a Washington semester, work-study programs, B.A.-B.S. degrees, accelerated degrees, and student-designed majors are available. Also available is a 3-2 engineering degree with Oregon State and Washington State Universities and the University of Southern California. There are 18 national honor societies and 13 departmental honors programs.

Admissions: 82% of the 2009-2010 applicants were accepted. The SAT scores for the 2009-2010 freshman class were: Critical Reading--31% below 500, 40% between 500 and 599, 24% between 600 and 700, and 5% above 700; Math--29% below 500, 44% between 500 and 599, 22% between 600 and 700, and 5% above 700; Writing--38% below 500, 41% between 500 and 599, 18% between 600 and 700, and 2% above 700. The ACT scores were 16% below 21, 30% between 21 and 23, 24% between 24 and 26, 11% between 27 and 28, and 19% above 28. 60% of the current freshmen were in the top fifth of their class; 85% were in the top two fifths. 20 freshmen graduated first in their class.

Requirements: The SAT or ACT is required. In addition, applicants should have 4 years each of English and math, 3 to 4 years each of natural science and social studies, and 2 to 4 years of a foreign language. An essay is required, and an interview is recommended. The GED is accepted. AP and CLEP credits are accepted. Important factors in the admissions decision are advanced placement or honors courses, evidence of special talent, and recommendations by school officials.

Procedure: Freshmen are admitted fall and spring. Entrance exams should be taken during the fall of the senior year. There are early admissions and deferred admissions plans. Applications should be filed by February 15 for fall entry and December 1 for spring entry, along with a $40 fee. Notifications are sent April 1. Applications are accepted on-line. A waiting list is maintained.

Financial Aid: In 2009-2010, 99% of all full-time freshmen and 96% of continuing full-time students received some form of financial aid. 70% of all full-time freshmen and 65% of continuing full-time students received need-based aid. The average freshman award was $19,693. 100% of undergraduate students work part-time. Average annual earnings from campus work are $1800. The average financial indebtedness of the 2009 graduate was $27,750. Linfield is a member of CSS. The FAFSA and CSS Profile (for early action applicants only) are required. The priority date for freshman financial aid applications for fall entry is February 1.

Computers: The main campus has 228 computers in 8 public labs and 10 departmental labs for student use. Some labs are open 24 hours a day, 7 days per week. Approximately 45% of the computers are Macs. All residences have high-speed Internet access, and wireless network access is available in the library and many public and classroom areas. All students may access the system. There are no time limits and no fees.

LIPSCOMB UNIVERSITY
Nashville, TN 37204-3951

(615) 966-1776
(877) 582-4766; (615) 966-1804

Full-time: 988 men, 1323 women	**Faculty:** IIA, --$
Part-time: 78 men, 129 women	**Ph.D.s:** n/av
Graduate: 355 men, 545 women	**Student/Faculty:** n/av
Year: semesters, summer session	**Tuition:** $20,390
Application Deadline: open	**Room & Board:** $7850
Freshman Class: 2683 applied, 1783 accepted, 605 enrolled	
SAT CR/M: 551/554	**ACT:** 24 **VERY COMPETITIVE**

Lipscomb University, founded in 1891, is a Christian community of scholars whose principle of excellence in learning, leading, and serving is carried out through its service-learning program and numerous mission trips in the United States and abroad. More than 100 bachelor's degree programs in nearly 60 majors are offered, including majors in the liberal arts, business, biology/premed, computer science, education, and engineering; a nursing degree is offered through the Lipscomb/Vanderbilt nursing partnership. Master's degrees are offered in accounting, Bible, business, conflict management, education, psychology, and sustainability; a doctoral degree is offered in pharmacy. There are 5 undergraduate schools and 5 graduate schools. In addition to regional accreditation, Lipscomb has baccalaureate program accreditation with ABET, ACBSP, ACS, ADA, CAAHEP, CSWE, NASM, and NCATE. The library contains 253,398 volumes, 41,826 microform items, and 745 audio/video tapes/CDs/DVDs, and subscribes to 850 periodicals including electronic. Computerized library services include interlibrary loans, database searching, Internet access, and laptop Internet portals. Special learning facilities include a learning resource center and radio station. The 65-acre campus is in a suburban area 2 miles south of downtown Nashville. Including any residence halls, there are 18 buildings.

Programs of Study: Lipscomb confers B.A., B.S., B.B.A., B.M., B.S.N., and B.S.W. degrees. Master's and doctoral degrees are also awarded. Bachelor's degrees are awarded in BIOLOGICAL SCIENCE (biochemistry and biology/biological science), BUSINESS (accounting, banking and finance, business administration and management, fashion merchandising, and marketing management), COMMUNICATIONS AND THE ARTS (art, communications, English, French, German, journalism, music, music performance, Spanish, and visual and performing arts), COMPUTER AND PHYSICAL SCIENCE (chemistry, computer science, mathematics, and physics), EDUCATION (art education, athletic training, education, elementary education, English education, health education, mathematics education, music education, physical education, and special education), ENGINEERING AND ENVIRONMENTAL DESIGN (computer engineering, engineering, engineering mechanics, environmental science, and preengineering), HEALTH PROFESSIONS (exercise science, nursing, predentistry, premedicine, preoptometry, and prepharmacy), SOCIAL SCIENCE (American studies, biblical studies, dietetics, economics, family/consumer studies, food production/management/services, political science/government, prelaw, psychology, textiles and clothing, and urban studies). Biology and engineering are the strongest academically. Business, biology, and education are the largest.

Special: Some majors require an internship. There are study-abroad options on nearly all continents. A B.A.-B.S. degree is possible in music, nursing, and social work, and 3-2 engineering degrees are available. There is 1 national honor society and a freshman honors program.

Admissions: 66% of the 2009-2010 applicants were accepted. The SAT scores for the 2009-2010 freshman class were: Critical Reading--23% below 500, 46% between 500 and 599, 28% between 600 and 700, and 3% above 700; Math--27% below 500, 36% between 500 and 599, 28% between 600 and 700, and 8% above 700. The ACT scores were 23% below 21, 27% between 21 and 23, 23% between 24 and 26, 9% between 27 and 28, and 18% above 28. 32% of the current freshmen were in the top fifth of their class; 49% were in the top two fifths. 21 freshmen graduated first in their class.

Requirements: The SAT or ACT is required. In addition, candidates for admission should be graduates of accredited secondary schools. The GED is accepted. 14 academic units are required. Students should have completed 4 units of English and 2 units each of history, math, and science. 2 units of a foreign language are highly recommended. 2 additional units from the areas of English, foreign language, history, math, science, and social studies are also required. A GPA of 2.3 is required. AP and CLEP credits are accepted.

Procedure: Freshmen are admitted to all sessions. There is a rolling admissions plan. Application deadlines are open. Application fee is $25. Applications are accepted on-line.

Financial Aid: In 2009-2010, 70% of all full-time freshmen and 62% of continuing full-time students received some form of financial aid, including need-based aid. Need-based scholarships or need-based grants averaged $6128; need-based self-help aid (loans and jobs) averaged $3688; and non-need-based athletic scholarships averaged $13,416. The FAFSA is required. The priority date for freshman financial aid applications for fall entry is February 15.

Computers: Wireless access is available. There are several computer labs on campus, as well as in the dorms. Each building has wireless access. All students may access the system 24 hours per day, 7 days per week. There are no time limits and no fees. It is strongly recommended that all students have a personal computer.

LOUISIANA STATE UNIVERSITY AND AGRICULTURAL AND MECHANICAL COLLEGE

Baton Rouge, LA 70803　　　　　**(225) 578-1175; (225) 578-4433**

Full-time: 10,570 men, 10,969 women	**Faculty:** 1077; I, -$
Part-time: 762 men, 711 women	**Ph.D.s:** 87%
Graduate: 2742 men, 2889 women	**Student/Faculty:** 20 to 1
Year: semesters, summer session	**Tuition:** $5233 ($14,383)
Application Deadline: April 15	**Room & Board:** $7738
Freshman Class: 15,917 applied, 11,012 accepted, 4789 enrolled	
SAT CR/M/W: 580/595/552	**ACT:** 26　**VERY COMPETITIVE+**

Louisiana State University and Agricultural and Mechanical College, a public institution founded in 1860 and part of the Louisiana State University System, offers programs in agriculture, arts and sciences, basic sciences, business administration, coast and environment, art and design, education, engineering, music and dramatic arts, and mass communication. There are 11 undergraduate schools and 4 graduate schools. In addition to regional accreditation, LSU has baccalaureate program accreditation with AACSB, ABET, ACCE, ACEJMC, ADA, ASLA, CSWE, FIDER, NAAB, NASAD, NASM, NCATE, and SAF. The 2 libraries contain 4.1 million volumes, 9.0 million microform items, and 27,309 audio/video tapes/CDs/DVDs, and subscribe to 97,524 periodicals including electronic. Computerized library services include interlibrary loans, database searching, Internet access, and laptop Internet portals. Special learning facilities include a learning resource center, art gallery, natural history museum, radio station, TV station, 3 herbaria, and museums of natural science, natural history, geoscience, rural life, and art. The 2000-acre campus is in an urban area in Baton Rouge. Including any residence halls, there are 250 buildings.

Programs of Study: LSU confers B.A., B.S., B.A. in M.C., B.Arch., B.F.A., B.G.S., B.Int.Design, B.Land.Arch., B.M., B.M.Ed., B.S.B.E., B.S.C.E., B.S.Ch.E., B.S.Cons.M., B.S.E.E., B.S.Env.Engineering, B.S.F., B.S.I.E., B.S. in Coastal Environmental Science, and B.S. in Geol. degrees. Master's and doctoral degrees are also awarded. Bachelor's degrees are awarded in AGRICULTURE (agricultural business management, animal science, fish and game management, forestry and related sciences, natural resource management, plant science, and poultry science), BIOLOGICAL SCIENCE (biochemistry, biology/biological science, microbiology, and nutrition), BUSINESS (accounting, banking and finance, business administration and management, international economics, management science, marketing/retailing/merchandising, and sports management), COMMUNICATIONS AND THE ARTS (communications, dramatic arts, English, French, German, Latin, music, Spanish, and studio art), COMPUTER AND PHYSICAL SCIENCE (chemistry, computer science, geology, information sciences and systems, mathematics, and physics), EDUCATION (early childhood education, elementary education, music education, secondary education, and vocational education), ENGINEERING AND ENVIRONMENTAL DESIGN (architecture, bioengineering, chemical engineering, civil engineering, computer engineering, construction management, electrical/electronics engineering, environmental engineering, environmental science, industrial engineering, interior design, landscape architecture/design, mechanical engineering, and petroleum/natural gas engineering), HEALTH PROFESSIONS (speech pathology/audiology), SOCIAL SCIENCE (anthropology, child care/child and family studies, clothing and textiles management/production/services, economics, food science, gender studies, geography, history, international studies, liberal arts/general studies, philosophy, physical fitness/movement, political science/government, psychology, sociology, textiles and clothing, and women's studies). Biological sciences, mass communication, and kinesiology are the strongest academically. Biological sciences, chemistry, and civil and environmental engineering are the largest.

Special: Co-op programs in numerous majors, cross-registration with Southern University and Baton Rouge Community College, study abroad, and work-study programs are offered. B.A.-B.S. degrees, dual majors, a general studies degree, nondegree study, an evening school, a program of study for adult learners, and pass/fail options are available. There are 32 national honor societies, including Phi Beta Kappa, and a freshman honors program.

Admissions: 69% of the 2009-2010 applicants were accepted. The SAT scores for the 2009-2010 freshman class were: Critical Reading--17% below 500, 42% between 500 and 599, 33% between 600 and 700, and 9% above 700; Math--10% below 500, 41% between 500 and 599, 39% between 600 and 700, and 9% above 700; Writing--25% below 500, 44% between 500 and 599, 27% between 600 and 700, and 4% above 700. The ACT scores were 4% below 21, 27% between 21 and 23, 30% between 24 and 26, 19% between 27 and 28, and 19% above 28. 45% of the current freshmen were in the top fifth of their class; 73% were in the top two fifths. There were 37 National Merit finalists. 260 freshmen graduated first in their class.

Requirements: The SAT or ACT is required. In addition, applicants must be graduates of an accredited secondary school. GED certificates may be accepted in unusual circumstances. Students must have completed 18 units, including 4 credits in English, 3 each in specific math, science, and social studies courses, 2 credits in a foreign language, 1/2 credit in computer skills, and 2 1/2 additional credits from the above categories or certain courses in the visual and performing arts. A GPA of 3.0 is required. AP and CLEP credits are accepted. Important factors in the admissions decision are advanced placement or honors courses, extracurricular activities record, and evidence of special talent.

Procedure: Freshmen are admitted to all sessions. Entrance exams should be taken in spring of the junior year or fall of the senior year. There are early admissions and rolling admissions plans. Applications should be filed by April 15 for fall entry, December 1 for spring entry, and April 15 for summer entry, along with a $40 fee. Notification is sent on a rolling basis. Applications are accepted on-line.

Financial Aid: In 2008-2009, 95% of all full-time freshmen and 82% of all full-time students received some form of financial aid. 24% of all full-time freshmen and 27% of all full-time students received need-based aid. The average freshman award was $8600. Need-based scholarships or need-based grants averaged $6450; need-based self-help aid (loans and jobs) averaged $3200; non-need-based athletic scholarships averaged $15,100; and other non-need-based awards and non-need-based scholarships averaged $5300. 25% of undergraduate students work part-time. Average annual earnings from campus work are $2100. The average financial indebtedness of the 2008 graduate was $17,060. The FAFSA and the college's own financial statement are required. The deadline for filing freshman financial aid applications for fall entry is February 1.

Computers: Wireless access is available. There are 1500 computing devices available for student use across campus within the 3 main computing labs, the Information Commons, multimedia classrooms, residence hall computing rooms, and discipline-specific computing labs. In addition, there are 65 Internet kiosks located across campus and 70 mobile computing devices available free to students through the checkout program. With more than 2100 secure wireless access points across campus (indoor and outdoor) and Internet ports available in all campus residences in addition to full wireless coverage, students can access the Internet from any point on campus. All students may access the system. There are no time limits and no fees. It is strongly recommended that all students have a personal computer. Students enrolled in the College of Art & Design must have a personal computer.

LOYOLA MARYMOUNT UNIVERSITY

Los Angeles, CA 90045
(310) 338-2750
(800) LMU-INFO; (310) 338-2797

Full-time: 2302 men, 3211 women	**Faculty:** 498; IIA, ++$
Part-time: 83 men, 71 women	**Ph.D.s:** 98%
Graduate: 673 men, 1213 women	**Student/Faculty:** 11 to 1
Year: semesters, summer session	**Tuition:** n/av
Application Deadline: January 15	**Room & Board:** $12,025
Freshman Class: 9456 applied, 5594 accepted, 1385 enrolled	
SAT CR/M/W: 580/600/560	**ACT:** 26 **VERY COMPETITIVE+**

Loyola Marymount University, is a private institution founded in 1911 that is affiliated with the Roman Catholic Church. LMUS is the largest Catholic University on the West Coast and one of 28 Jesuit universities in the United States. LMU offers programs in liberal arts, business administration, fine arts, science, engineering, and law. There are 5 undergraduate schools and one graduate school. In addition to regional accreditation, LMU has baccalaureate program accreditation with AACSB, ABET, NASAD, NASDTEC, NASM, and NCATE. The 21 libraries contain 524,565 volumes, 143,738 microform items, 42,839 audio/video tapes/CDs/DVDs, and subscribe to 19,366 periodicals including electronic. Computerized library services include interlibrary loans, database searching, Internet access, and laptop Internet portals. Special learning facilities include a learning resource center, art gallery, radio station, TV station, the Burns Fine Arts Center, and the Little Theatre. The 142-acre campus is in a suburban area 15 miles southwest of downtown Los Angeles. Including any residence halls, there are 50 buildings.

Programs of Study: LMU confers B.A., B.S., B.B.A., B.S.A., and B.S.E. degrees. Master's degrees are also awarded. Bachelor's degrees are awarded in BIOLOGICAL SCIENCE (biochemistry and biology/biological science), BUSINESS (accounting and business administration and management), COMMUNICATIONS AND THE ARTS (art history and appreciation, classics, communications, dance, dramatic arts, English, French, Greek, Latin, media arts, music, Spanish, and studio art), COMPUTER AND PHYSICAL SCIENCE (chemistry, computer science, mathematics, natural sciences, and physics), ENGINEERING AND ENVIRONMENTAL DESIGN (civil engineering, computer graphics, electrical/electronics engineering, engineering physics, environmental science, and mechanical engineering), SOCIAL SCIENCE (African American studies, Asian/Oriental studies, classical/ancient civilization, economics, European studies, history, humanities, philosophy, political science/government, psychology, sociology, theological studies, urban studies, and women's studies). Communication arts, political science, and engineering are the strongest academically. Psychology, communication studies, and business administration are the largest.

Special: LMU offers internships and volunteer work experience with local firms, study abroad in Europe, Mexico, Japan, and China, a Washington semester, dual majors, work-study, student-designed and individualized studies majors, accelerated degree programs in all majors, a general studies degree, nondegree study, and pass/fail options for electives. There are 2 national honor societies and a freshman honors program.

Admissions: 59% of the 2009-2010 applicants were accepted. The SAT scores for the 2009-2010 freshman class were: Critical Reading--11% below 500, 47% between 500 and 599, 38% between 600 and 700, and 5 above 700; Math--10% below 500, 37% between 500 and 599, 47% between 600 and 700, and 7 above 700; Writing--19% below 500, 50% between 500 and 599, 29% between 600 and 700, and 2 above 700. The ACT scores were 5% below 21, 19% between 21 and 23, 33% between 24 and 26, 22% between 27 and 28, and 21% above 28.

Requirements: The SAT is required. In addition, prospective students must be graduates of an accredited secondary school and have completed 4 years of English, 3 each of a foreign language, math, and social studies, 2 of science, and 1 of an academic elective. A recommendation from an official of a previous school and essays are required. An interview is recommended. A GPA of 2.9 is required. AP credits are accepted. Important factors in the admissions decision are recommendations by school officials, advanced placement or honors courses, and evidence of special talent.

Procedure: Freshmen are admitted fall and spring. Entrance exams should be taken during the spring of the junior year or fall of the senior year. There are deferred admissions and rolling admissions plans. Applications should be filed by

January 15 for fall entry and December 1 for spring entry, along with a $50 fee. Applications are accepted on-line. A waiting list is maintained.

Financial Aid: In 2009-2010, 79% of all full-time freshmen and 76% of continuing full-time students received some form of financial aid. 58% of all full-time freshmen and 57% of continuing full-time students received need-based aid. The average freshmen award was $26,550, with $7,200 ($47,000 maximum) from need-based scholarships or need-based grants; $8,700 ($62,000 maximum) from need-based self-help aid (loans and jobs); $1,200 ($59,000 maximum) from non-need-based athletic scholarships; $2,300 ($52,000 maximum) from other non-need-based awards and non-need-based scholarships; and $1,300 from other forms of aid. 52% of undergraduate students work part-time. Average annual earnings from campus work are $1450. The average financial indebtedness of the 2009 graduate was $20,893. The CSS/Profile and FAFSA are required. The deadline for filing freshman financial aid applications for fall entry is February 15.

Computers: All students may access the system. Labs are available more than 60 hours per week. Students are limited to 2 hours for remote access. There are no fees. It is strongly recommended that all students have a personal computer.

LOYOLA UNIVERSITY CHICAGO

Chicago, IL 60660

(773) 508-3075
(800) 262-2373; (773) 508-8926

Full-time: 3332 men, 6016 women	**Faculty:** I, -$
Part-time: 238 men, 491 women	**Ph.D.s:** 97%
Graduate: 2158 men, 3644 women	**Student/Faculty:** n/av
Year: semesters, summer session	**Tuition:** $30,656
Application Deadline: April 1	**Room & Board:** $10,885
Freshman Class: 17,383 applied, 13,583 accepted, 2076 enrolled	
SAT CR/M/W: 600/590/590	**ACT:** 27 **VERY COMPETITIVE+**

Loyola University of Chicago, founded in 1870, is a private Roman Catholic (Jesuit) university offering undergraduate curricula in the arts and sciences, business, nursing, social work, and education. There are 7 undergraduate schools and 8 graduate schools. In addition to regional accreditation, Loyola has baccalaureate program accreditation with AACSB, CSWE, and NCATE. The 7 libraries contain 1.7 million volumes, 1.6 million microform items, and 15,174 audio/video tapes/CDs/DVDs, and subscribe to 54,309 periodicals including electronic. Computerized library services include interlibrary loans, database searching, Internet access, and laptop Internet portals. Special learning facilities include a learning resource center, art gallery, radio station, theater, mock trial room, labs for neuroscience, biodeisel, and nursing, computer resource center, and language learning resource center. The 105-acre campus is in an urban area in Chicago. Including any residence halls, there are 62 buildings.

Programs of Study: Loyola confers B.A., B.S., B.A.Classics, B.B.A., B.F.A., B.G., B.S.Ed., B.S.N, and B.S.W. degrees. Master's and doctoral degrees are also awarded. Bachelor's degrees are awarded in BIOLOGICAL SCIENCE (biochemistry, bioinformatics, biology/biological science, biophysics, and nutrition), BUSINESS (accounting, banking and finance, business administration and management, business economics, entrepreneurial studies, human resources, international business management, management information systems, marketing/retailing/merchandising, operations management, organizational leadership and management, and sports management), COMMUNICATIONS AND THE ARTS (advertising, communications, dramatic arts, English, fine arts, French, Greek, Italian, journalism, Latin, media arts, music, Spanish, studio art, and visual design), COMPUTER AND PHYSICAL SCIENCE (applied mathematics, chemistry, computer mathematics, computer science, computer security and information assurance, information sciences and systems, mathematics, physics, software engineering, and statistics), EDUCATION (bilingual/bicultural education, early childhood education, elementary education, mathematics education, science education, secondary education, and special education), ENGINEERING AND ENVIRONMENTAL DESIGN (environmental science), HEALTH PROFESSIONS (clinical science, dental hygiene, health care administration, hospital administration, nursing, and speech pathology/audiology), SOCIAL SCIENCE (African studies, anthropology, applied psychology, classical/ancient civilization, criminal justice, forensic studies, history, human services, interdisciplinary studies, international studies, philosophy, political science/government, psychology, religion, social work, sociology, theological studies, and women's studies). Biology, psychology, and nursing are the largest.

Special: Sophomores and juniors may study in 21 countries through 60 different programs. Dual majors in math education/secondary education and physics/engineering, a Washington semester, nondegree study, and pass/fail options are available. The school also offers a B.A.-B.S. degree in chemistry and a 2-3 engineering degree with Columbia and Washington Universities. There are 5-year programs and combination bachelor's/master's available. There is a chapter of Phi Beta Kappa and a freshman honors program.

Admissions: 78% of the 2009-2010 applicants were accepted. The SAT scores for the 2009-2010 freshman class were: Critical Reading--10% below 500, 40% between 500 and 599, 38% between 600 and 700, and 12% above 700; Math--14% below 500, 39% between 500 and 599, 39% between 600 and 700, and 8% above 700; Writing--12% below 500, 39% between 500 and 599, 42% between 600 and 700, and 6% above 700. The ACT scores were 3% below 21, 16% between 21 and 23, 32% between 24 and 26, 21% between 27 and 28, and 28% above 28. 55% of the current freshmen were in the top fifth of their class; 88% were in the top two fifths. There were 20 National Merit finalists. 24 freshmen graduated first in their class.

Requirements: The SAT or ACT is required. In addition, graduation from an accredited secondary school or satisfactory scores on the GED are required for admission. 15 academic credits are required. Secondary school courses should include 4 credits of English and 3 each of math, science, and social studies. An interview is recommended. AP and CLEP credits are accepted. Important factors in the admissions decision are advanced placement or honors courses, leadership record, and evidence of special talent.

Procedure: Freshmen are admitted to all sessions. Entrance exams should be taken as early as possible, normally in the spring of the junior year. There is a rolling admissions plan. Applications should be filed by April 1 for fall entry. None of the applicants on the 2009 waiting list were admitted. Applications are accepted on-line.

Financial Aid: In 2009-2010, 95% of all full-time freshmen and 89% of continuing full-time students received some form of financial aid. 72% of all full-time freshmen and 68% of continuing full-time students received need-based aid. The average freshman award was $26,274. Need-based scholarships or need-based grants averaged $12,503 ($42,821 maximum); need-based self-help aid (loans and jobs) averaged $8081 ($41,146 maximum); and non-need-based athletic scholarships averaged $20,183 ($39,748 maximum). 13% of undergraduate students work part-time. Average annual earnings from campus work are $1944. The average financial indebtedness of the 2009 graduate was $35,526. The FAF-

SA is required. The deadline for filing freshman financial aid applications for fall entry is March 1.

Computers: Wireless access is available. There are 1314 PCs available for student use in libraries, classrooms, and labs. All dorm rooms have connections. All students may access the system whenever facilities are open. There are no time limits and no fees.

LOYOLA UNIVERSITY IN MARYLAND
Loyola College in Maryland

Baltimore, MD 21210

(410) 617-5012
(800) 221-9107; (410) 617-2176

Full-time: 1507 men, 2212 women	**Faculty:** 331; IIA, +$
Part-time: 17 men, 21 women	**Ph.D.s:** 79%
Graduate: 830 men, 1391 women	**Student/Faculty:** 11 to 1
Year: semesters, summer session	**Tuition:** $37,775
Application Deadline: January 15	**Room & Board:** $10,200
Freshman Class: 9117 applied, 6008 accepted, 968 enrolled	
SAT or ACT: required	**VERY COMPETITIVE**

Loyola University, formerly Loyola College, founded in 1852, is a private liberal arts college affiliated with the Roman Catholic Church and the Jesuit tradition. It offers degree programs in arts and sciences, business, and management. There are 2 undergraduate schools and 2 graduate schools. In addition to regional accreditation, Loyola College has baccalaureate program accreditation with AACSB, ABET, CSAB, NASDTEC, and NCATE. The library contains 437,571 volumes, 338,337 microform items, and 39,422 audio/video tapes/CDs/DVDs, and subscribes to 14,901 periodicals including electronic. Computerized library services include interlibrary loans and database searching. Special learning facilities include an art gallery and radio station. The 89-acre campus is in an urban area 3 miles from downtown Baltimore. Including any residence halls, there are 29 buildings.

Programs of Study: Loyola College confers B.A., B.S., B.B.A., B.S.E.E., and B.S.E.S. degrees. Master's and doctoral degrees are also awarded. Bachelor's degrees are awarded in BIOLOGICAL SCIENCE (biology/biological science), BUSINESS (accounting and business administration and management), COMMUNICATIONS AND THE ARTS (communications, creative writing, English, fine arts, French, German, Latin, and Spanish), COMPUTER AND PHYSICAL SCIENCE (chemistry, computer science, mathematics, and physics), EDUCATION (elementary education), ENGINEERING AND ENVIRONMENTAL DESIGN (electrical/electronics engineering and engineering), HEALTH PROFESSIONS (speech pathology/audiology), SOCIAL SCIENCE (classical/ancient civilization, economics, history, philosophy, political science/government, psychology, sociology, and theological studies). General business, psychology, and communication are the largest.

Special: Loyola offers cross-registration with Johns Hopkins, Towson, and Morgan State Universities, Goucher College, the College of Notre Dame, Maryland Art Institute, and Peabody Conservatory. Credit-bearing internships are available in most majors and study abroad is possible in 36 countries. Work-study programs and dual majors are also offered. There are 23 national honor societies, including Phi Beta Kappa, a freshman honors program, and 1 departmental honors program.

Admissions: 66% of the 2009-2010 applicants were accepted. 65% of the current freshmen were in the top fifth of their class; 92% were in the top two fifths. 10 freshmen graduated first in their class.

Requirements: The SAT or ACT is required. In addition, applicants should have graduated from an accredited secondary school or have earned the GED. Secondary preparation should include 4 years of English, 4 each of math, foreign language, natural science, and classical or modern foreign language, and 2 to 3 of history. A personal essay is required; an interview is recommended. AP and CLEP credits are accepted. Important factors in the admissions decision are advanced placement or honors courses, recommendations by school officials, and extracurricular activities record.

Procedure: Freshmen are admitted fall, spring, and summer. Entrance exams should be taken by December of the senior year. There is a deferred admissions plan. Early action applications should be filed by November 15; regular applications, by January 15 for fall entry; and December 15 for spring entry, along with a $50 fee. Notification of early action is sent November 15; regular decision, April 1. 1079 applicants were on the 2009 waiting list; 917 were admitted. Applications are accepted on-line.

Financial Aid: In 2009-2010, at least 57% of all full-time freshmen and 46% of continuing full-time students received some form of financial aid. At least 53% of all full-time freshmen and 43% of continuing full-time students received need-based aid. The average freshman award was $26,345. Need-based scholarships or need-based grants averaged $18,750; need-based self-help aid (loans and jobs) averaged $7,595; non-need-based athletic scholarships averaged $32,280. Institutional awards averaged $12,530. 15% of undergraduate students work part-time. Average annual earnings from campus work are $1380. The average financial indebtedness of the 2009 graduate was $26,855. Loyola College is a member of CSS. The CSS/Profile, FAFSA, and if applicable, a noncustodial parent's statement and business/farm supplement are required. The deadline for filing freshman financial aid applications for fall entry is February 15.

Computers: All students may access the system. There are no time limits and no fees.

LOYOLA UNIVERSITY NEW ORLEANS
New Orleans, LA 70118-6195

(504) 865-3240
(800) 4-LOYOLA; (504) 865-3383

Full-time: 1082 men, 1381 women	**Faculty:** 235; IIA, +$
Part-time: 106 men, 195 women	**Ph.D.s:** 88%
Graduate: 670 men, 1280 women	**Student/Faculty:** 11 to 1
Year: semesters, summer session	**Tuition:** $31,504
Application Deadline: May 1	**Room & Board:** $10,388
Freshman Class: 4345 applied, 2538 accepted, 809 enrolled	
SAT or ACT: required	**HIGHLY COMPETITIVE**

Loyola University New Orleans, founded in 1912, is a private institution operated by the Society of Jesus and affiliated with the Roman Catholic Church. There are 4 undergraduate schools and 6 graduate schools. In addition to regional accreditation, Loyola has baccalaureate program accreditation with AACSB, NASM, and NLN. The 2 libraries contain 623,596 volumes, 1.1 million microform items, and 17,431 audio/video tapes/CDs/DVDs, and subscribe to 80,410 periodicals including electronic. Computerized library services include interlibrary loans, database searching, and Internet access. Special learning facilities include a learning resource center, art gallery, TV station, art gallery, humanities lab with Perseus

Project and TLG TV, multimedia classrooms graphic lab, visual arts lab, ad club communications lab, business computer lab, multi-media training center, and center for non-profit communication. The 26-acre campus is in an urban area 5 miles from downtown New Orleans. Including any residence halls, there are 24 buildings.

Programs of Study: Loyola confers B.A., B.S., B.Acc., B.A.Mus., B.A. Music, B.B.A., B.C.J., B.F.A., B.L.S., B.Mus., B.Mus.Ed., B.S.Mus. Industry, B.Mus. Therapy, and B.S.N. degrees. Master's and doctoral degrees are also awarded. Bachelor's degrees are awarded in BIOLOGICAL SCIENCE (biology/biological science), BUSINESS (accounting, banking and finance, business administration and management, international business management, management science, and marketing/retailing/merchandising), COMMUNICATIONS AND THE ARTS (communications, creative writing, dramatic arts, English literature, fine arts, French, graphic design, guitar, jazz, music, music business management, music performance, music theory and composition, piano/organ, Spanish, studio art, visual and performing arts, and voice), COMPUTER AND PHYSICAL SCIENCE (chemistry, mathematics, and physics), EDUCATION (music education), ENGINEERING AND ENVIRONMENTAL DESIGN (preengineering), HEALTH PROFESSIONS (music therapy, nursing, predentistry, premedicine, and preveterinary science), SOCIAL SCIENCE (anthropology, classical/ancient civilization, criminal justice, economics, forensic studies, history, Latin American studies, liberal arts/general studies, philosophy, political science/government, psychology, religion, religious education, social science, and sociology). Mass communication, psychology, and biology are the largest.

Special: Cross-registration is available with our Lady of Holy Cross, Xavier University, Notre Dame Seminary, the University of New Orleans, Tulane University, and Southern University of New Orleans. Internships with the New Orleans business community are also available. Study abroad in 8 countries, dual and student-designed majors, nondegree studies, an accelerated R.N. to M.S.N. program, and a general studies degree are offered. A Washington semester through American University and a 3-2 engineering degree with Tulane University and the University of New Orleans is also available. There are 13 national honor societies, a freshman honors program, and 9 departmental honors programs.

Admissions: 58% of the 2009-2010 applicants were accepted. The SAT scores for the 2009-2010 class were: Critical Reading--2% below 500, 31% between 500-599, 53% between 600-700, and 14% above 700: Math--5% below 500, 39% between 500-599, 45% between 600-700, and 10% above 700; Writing--5% below 500, 34% between 500-599, 49% between 600-700, and 12% above 700.

Requirements: The SAT or ACT is required. In addition, candidates for admission must be graduates of an accredited secondary school or have a GED. They should have completed 4 units in high school English and 3 each in math, science, and social sciences, along with 4 academic electives; 2 units in a foreign language are recommended. A portfolio is required for fine arts students; an audition for music majors. An interview is recommended for scholarship consideration. AP and CLEP credits are accepted. Important factors in the admissions decision are advanced placement or honors courses, evidence of special talent, extracurricular activities record, recommendations by school officials, parents or siblings attended your school, personality/intangible qualities, recommendations by alumni, and geographical diversity.

Procedure: Freshmen are admitted to all sessions. Entrance exams should be taken during the junior or senior year. There is a rolling admissions plan. Application deadlines are open. Application fee is $20. Applications are accepted on-line.

Financial Aid: In 2009-2010, 69% of all full-time freshmen and 64% of continuing full-time students received some form of financial aid. 69% of all full-time freshmen and 64% of continuing full-time students received need-based aid. The average freshmen award was $26,836. 27% of undergraduate students work part-time. Average annual earnings from campus work are $1920. The average financial indebtedness of the 2009 graduate was $22,320. The FAFSA is required. The priority date for freshman financial aid applications for fall entry is March 1. The deadline for filing freshman financial aid applications for fall entry is May 1.

Computers: Wireless access is available. Students may connect to the system via 2500 campus-wide Internet ports, 23 modem lines, 300 public workstation, and Internet-ready residence hall rooms. There is also wireless access in all outside open areas as well as inside the library , Danna Center, and all residence halls. All students may access the system at any time. There are no time limits. The fee is $225 (included in tuition and fees above.) It is strongly recommended that all students have a personal computer. A Dell or Macintosh, depending on the major is recommended.

LUTHER COLLEGE
Decorah, IA 52101

(563) 387-1287
(800) 458-8437; (563) 387-2159

Full-time: 1046 men, 1424 women	**Faculty:** 177; IIB, av$
Part-time: 24 men, 25 women	**Ph.D.s:** 92%
Graduate: none	**Student/Faculty:** n/av
Year: 4-1-4, summer session	**Tuition:** $32,290
Application Deadline: open	**Room & Board:** $5380
Freshman Class: 3445 applied, 2403 accepted, 657 enrolled	
SAT CR/M/W: 560/580/570	**ACT:** 25 **VERY COMPETITIVE**

Luther College, affiliated with the Evangelical Lutheran Church in America, is a private liberal arts institution founded in 1861. In addition to regional accreditation, Luther has baccalaureate program accreditation with CSWE, NASM, NCATE, and NLN. The library contains 329,949 volumes, 24,978 microform items, and 11,454 audio/video tapes/CDs/DVDs, and subscribes to 1828 periodicals including electronic. Computerized library services include interlibrary loans, database searching, and Internet access. Special learning facilities include a learning resource center, art gallery, natural history museum, planetarium, and radio station. The 200-acre campus is in a small town 70 miles south of Rochester, Minnesota. Including any residence halls, there are 35 buildings.

Programs of Study: Luther confers B.A. degrees. Bachelor's degrees are awarded in AGRICULTURE (environmental studies), BIOLOGICAL SCIENCE (biology/biological science), BUSINESS (accounting, management information systems, and management science), COMMUNICATIONS AND THE ARTS (art, classical languages, communications, dance, dramatic arts, English, French, German, music, Spanish, and speech/debate/rhetoric), COMPUTER AND PHYSICAL SCIENCE (chemistry, computer science, mathematics, physics, and statistics), EDUCATION (athletic training, elementary education, and physical education), HEALTH PROFESSIONS (health and nursing), SOCIAL SCIENCE (African American studies, anthropology, biblical languages, economics, history, philosophy, political science/government, psychology, religion, Scandinavian studies, social work, sociology, and women's studies). Biology, music, and English are the strongest academically. Biology, management, and music are the largest.

Special: Internships in most disciplines, work-study programs, a Washington semester, study-abroad plans in 40 countries, pass/fail options, student-designed and dual majors, and 3-2 engineering degrees with Washington University in St. Louis and the University of Minnesota are available. There are 13 national honor societies, including Phi Beta Kappa, and a freshman honors program.

Admissions: 70% of the 2009-2010 applicants were accepted. The SAT scores for the 2009-2010 freshman class were: Critical Reading--25% below 500, 35% between 500 and 599, 29% between 600 and 700, and 11% above 700; Math--15% below 500, 40% between 500 and 599, 28% between 600 and 700, and 17 above 700; Writing--27% below 500, 30% between 500 and 599, 33% between 600 and 700, and 10 above 700. The ACT scores were 7% below 21, 19% between 21 and 23, 24% between 24 and 26, 18% between 27 and 28, and 32% above 28. 55% of the current freshmen were in the top fifth of their class; 84% were in the top two-fifths. There were 4 National Merit finalists. 34 freshmen graduated first in their class.

Requirements: The SAT or ACT is required. In addition, applicants should be within 2 semesters of graduation from an accredited high school and have completed 4 years of English, which may include 1 year of speech, communications, or journalism; 3 years of math; 3 years of social science; 2 years of natural science, including 1 year of lab science; and 2 years of a foreign language. Applicants who do not meet these standards will be considered for admission if they submit above-average ACT or SAT scores. Luther requires applicants to be in the upper 50% of their class. A GPA of 2.5 is required. AP and CLEP credits are accepted. Important factors in the admissions decision are advanced placement or honors courses, evidence of special talent, and extracurricular activities record.

Procedure: Freshmen are admitted to all sessions. Entrance exams should be taken by the fall of the senior year. There is a deferred admissions plan. Application deadlines are open. Application fee is $25. Notification is sent November 1. Applications are accepted on-line.

Financial Aid: In 2009-2010, all students received some form of financial aid. 73% of all full-time freshmen and 68% of continuing full-time students received need-based aid. The average freshmen award was $26,727. 73% of undergraduate students work part-time. Average annual earnings from campus work are $1208. The average financial indebtedness of the 2009 graduate was $20,188. Luther is a member of CSS. The FAFSA, the college's own financial statement, and a family tax return are required. The priority date for freshman financial aid applications for fall entry is March 1.

Computers: Wireless access is available. The Luther College wireless initiative aims to provide wireless access to all academic and administrative buildings and to public spaces in residence halls when technically viable. The computer labs on campus are used by a variety of groups and individuals for a variety of purposes. The first priority for use of the labs is for classroom space. The next priority use of the labs is for individual student workstation space. Luther campus computer labs are expressly reserved for use by Luther students, faculty, and staff. All students may access the system anytime. There are no time limits and no fees.

Batesville, AR 72503-2317
(870) 307-7250
(800) 423-2542; (870) 307-7542

Full-time: 263 men, 317 women	**Faculty:** 41; IIB, --$
Part-time: 14 men, 20 women	**Ph.D.s:** 90%
Graduate: none	**Student/Faculty:** 14 to 1
Year: semesters, summer session	**Tuition:** $19,968
Application Deadline: August 1	**Room & Board:** $7340
Freshman Class: 1110 applied, 749 accepted, 217 enrolled	
SAT or ACT: required	**VERY COMPETITIVE**

Lyon College, founded in 1872, is a selective, private, residential, liberal arts college affiliated with the Presbyterian Church (U.S.A.). In addition to regional accreditation, Lyon has baccalaureate program accreditation with NCATE. The library contains 169,918 volumes, 2928 microform items, and 7020 audio/video tapes/CDs/DVDs, and subscribes to 21,991 periodicals including electronic. Computerized library services include interlibrary loans, database searching, Internet access, and laptop Internet portals. Special learning facilities include a learning resource center, art gallery, a language lab, and a computer lab. The 136-acre campus is in a small town 90 miles north of Little Rock. Including any residence halls, there are 30 buildings.

Programs of Study: Lyon confers B.A. and B.S. degrees. Bachelor's degrees are awarded in AGRICULTURE (environmental studies), BIOLOGICAL SCIENCE (biochemistry and biology/biological science), BUSINESS (accounting and business administration and management), COMMUNICATIONS AND THE ARTS (art, dramatic arts, English, music, and Spanish), COMPUTER AND PHYSICAL SCIENCE (chemistry, computer science, and mathematics), EDUCATION (early childhood education), SOCIAL SCIENCE (economics, history, political science/government, psychology, and religion). Business administration, biology, and psychology are the largest.

Special: Internships are offered as is cross-registration (for certain courses) with the University of Arkansas Community College at Batesville. A 2-2 engineering program is offered with the University of Missouri in Rolla, and a 3-2 program is offered with the University of Arkansas at Fayetteville. Work-study courses, study abroad in 4 countries, dual majors, student-designed majors, pass/fail options, a Washington semester, and credit for military experience are available. A 3-2 program is available with the University of Minnesota. There are 14 national honor societies.

Admissions: 67% of the 2009-2010 applicants were accepted. The ACT scores were 10% below 21, 32% between 21 and 23, 26% between 24 and 26, 16% between 27 and 28, and 16% above 28. 47% of the current freshmen were in the top fifth of their class; 77% were in the top two fifths. 13 freshmen graduated first in their class.

Requirements: The SAT or ACT is required. In addition, applicants should have completed a minimum of 16 high school units, including 4 in English, 3 each in science, math, and social sciences, and 2 in a foreign language. A letter of recommendation and an admission interview are recommended. AP credits are accepted.

Procedure: Freshmen are admitted fall and spring. Entrance exams should be taken in spring of the junior year and fall of the senior year. There are deferred admissions and rolling admissions plans. Applications should be filed by August

1 for fall entry; January 1 for spring entry. Application fee is $25. Notification is sent on a rolling basis. Applications are accepted on-line.

Financial Aid: In 2009-2010, all full-time freshmen and 99% of continuing full-time students received some form of financial aid. 58% of all full-time freshmen and 55% of continuing full-time students received need-based aid. The average freshman award was $15,934. Need-based scholarships or need-based grants averaged $4368; need-based self-help aid (loans and jobs) averaged $5496; non-need-based athletic scholarships averaged $12,011; and other non-need-based awards and non-need-based scholarships averaged $11,351. 23% of undergraduate students work part-time. Average annual earnings from campus work are $1225. The average financial indebtedness of the 2009 graduate was $18,134. The FAFSA is required. The priority date for freshman financial aid applications for fall entry is March 1.

Computers: Wireless access is available. All students may access the system. There are no time limits. The fee is $240.

MACALESTER COLLEGE
St. Paul, MN 55105

(651) 696-6357
(800) 231-7974; (651) 696-6724

Full-time: 832 men, 1126 women	**Faculty:** 163; IIB, +$
Part-time: 14 men, 24 women	**Ph.D.s:** 64%
Graduate: none	**Student/Faculty:** 12 to 1
Year: semesters	**Tuition:** $38,174
Application Deadline: January 15	**Room & Board:** $8768
Freshman Class: 4565 applied, 2109 accepted, 565 enrolled	
SAT CR/M/W: 720/720/690	**ACT:** 31 **MOST COMPETITIVE**

Macalester College, founded in 1874, is a nonsectarian liberal arts and sciences institution affiliated with the United Presbyterian Church. There is 1 undergraduate school. In addition to regional accreditation, Macalester has baccalaureate program accreditation with NASM. The library contains 434,215 volumes, 84,139 microform items, and 13,634 audio/video tapes/CDs/DVDs, and subscribes to 3387 periodicals including electronic. Computerized library services include interlibrary loans, database searching, Internet access, and laptop Internet portals. Special learning facilities include a learning resource center, art gallery, radio station, and a 280-acre natural history study area 25 miles from campus. The 53-acre campus is in an urban area midway between downtown St. Paul and Minneapolis. Including any residence halls, there are 39 buildings.

Programs of Study: Macalester confers B.A. degrees. Bachelor's degrees are awarded in AGRICULTURE (environmental studies), BIOLOGICAL SCIENCE (biology/biological science and neurosciences), COMMUNICATIONS AND THE ARTS (art, classics, dramatic arts, English, French, Japanese, linguistics, music, Russian, and Spanish), COMPUTER AND PHYSICAL SCIENCE (chemistry, computer science, geology, mathematics, and physics), EDUCATION (education), SOCIAL SCIENCE (American studies, anthropology, Asian/Oriental studies, economics, geography, German area studies, history, humanities, international studies, Latin American studies, philosophy, political science/government, psychology, religion, sociology, and women's studies). International studies, economics, and biology/chemistry are the strongest academically. Math and computer science, political science, and Hispanic and Latin American studies are the largest.

Special: Cross-registration at Minneapolis College of Art and Design is offered; in addition, the college belongs to several consortiums, including the Associated

Colleges of the Twin Cities. There also are cooperative programs in liberal arts and architecture with Washington University in St. Louis, and engineering with the same school and the University of Minnesota. Internships are available in government, financial services, law, medicine, research, the arts, and other fields. Students study abroad in more than 68 countries. Student-designed majors and pass/fail options for no more than 1 course per semester also are available. There are 13 national honor societies, including Phi Beta Kappa, and 30 departmental honors programs.

Admissions: 46% of the 2009-2010 applicants were accepted. The SAT scores for the 2009-2010 freshman class were: Critical Reading--1% below 500, 7% between 500 and 599, 38% between 600 and 700, and 53% above 700; Math--2% below 500, 13% between 500 and 599, 55% between 600 and 700, and 31% above 700; Writing--1% below 500, 8% between 500 and 599, 48% between 600 and 700, and 43% above 700. The ACT scores were 2% between 21 and 23, 9% between 24 and 26, 14% between 27 and 28, and 67% above 28. 89% of the current freshmen were in the top fifth of their class; 99% were in the top two fifths. There were 39 National Merit finalists. 53 freshmen graduated first in their class.

Requirements: The SAT or ACT is required. In addition, applicants should have earned at least 16 academic credits, including 4 years of English and 3 each in math, laboratory science, foreign language, and social studies/history. The college also expects applicants to have taken honors, AP, or IB courses where available. An essay is required, and an interview is recommended. AP credits are accepted. Important factors in the admissions decision are advanced placement or honors courses, extracurricular activities record, and recommendations by school officials.

Procedure: Freshmen are admitted in fall. Entrance exams should be taken in the fall of the senior year. There are early decision and deferred admissions plans. Early decision applications should be filed by November 15; regular applications by January 15 for fall entry, along with a $40 fee. Early decision notifications are sent December 15; regular decision, April 1. 128 early decision applicants were accepted for the 2009-2010 class. 242 applicants were on the 2009 waiting list; none were admitted. Applications are accepted on-line.

Financial Aid: In 2009-2010, 76% of all full-time freshmen and 72% of continuing full-time students received some form of financial aid. 71% of all full-time freshmen and 67% of continuing full-time students received need-based aid. The average freshman award was $32,533. Need-based scholarships and need-based grants averaged $28,280, and need-based self-help aid (loans and jobs) averaged $4564. 70% of undergraduate students work part-time. Average annual earnings from campus work are $1700. The average financial indebtedness of the 2009 graduate was $17,275. Macalester is a member of CSS. The CSS/Profile, FAFSA, parent's W-2 and tax forms, and student tax forms are required. The deadline for filing freshman financial aid applications for fall entry is March 1.

Computers: Wireless access is available. There is unrestricted access on campus. There are approximately 400 computers available for student use in residential and academic labs. Laser printing is available. All students may access the system 24 hours a day. There are no time limits and no fees. It is strongly recommended that all students have a personal computer.

Livonia, MI 48150-1173   **(734) 432-5341**
(800) 852-4951; (734) 432-5424

Full-time: 393 men, 1159 women	**Faculty:** 110; IIB, -$
Part-time: 372 men, 1094 women	**Ph.D.s:** 93%
Graduate: 180 men, 681 women	**Student/Faculty:** 14 to 1
Year: semesters, summer session	**Tuition:** $11,680
Application Deadline: open	**Room & Board:** $6,092
Freshman Class: 293 accepted, 182 enrolled	
ACT: 22	**VERY COMPETITIVE**

Madonna University, founded in 1947, is a liberal arts institution affiliated with the Roman Catholic Church. There are 8 undergraduate schools and one graduate school. In addition to regional accreditation, MU has baccalaureate program accreditation with ADA, CSWE, NCATE, and NLN. The library contains 110,000 volumes, 453,250 microform items, 1,000 audio/video tapes/CDs/DVDs, and subscribes to 18,666 periodicals including electronic. Computerized library services include inter-library loans, database searching, Internet access, and laptop Internet portals. Special learning facilities include a learning resource center, art gallery, radio station, TV station, writing lab, the Center for Personalized Instruction, Office of Disability Resources, and Office of Service Learning. The 49-acre campus is in a suburban area 25 miles west of Detroit. Including any residence halls, there are 4 buildings.

Programs of Study: MU confers B.A., B.S., B.A.S., BMus, B.S.N., and B.S.W. degrees. Associates and master's degrees are also awarded. Bachelor's degrees are awarded in BIOLOGICAL SCIENCE (biochemistry, biology/biological science, and nutrition), BUSINESS (accounting, business administration and management, hospitality management services, international business management, management science, marketing/retailing/merchandising, and sports management), COMMUNICATIONS AND THE ARTS (art, communications, English, fine arts, graphic design, journalism, language arts, music, Spanish, speech/debate/rhetoric, technical and business writing, and video), COMPUTER AND PHYSICAL SCIENCE (applied science, chemistry, computer science, information sciences and systems, mathematics, natural sciences, and science), EDUCATION (art education, music education, and secondary education), ENGINEERING AND ENVIRONMENTAL DESIGN (commercial art, environmental science, and occupational safety and health), HEALTH PROFESSIONS (allied health, hospice care, medical laboratory technology, and nursing), SOCIAL SCIENCE (child psychology/development, criminal justice, dietetics, family/consumer studies, fire science, food science, gerontology, history, interpreter for the deaf, Japanese studies, liberal arts/general studies, pastoral studies, psychology, religion, religious music, safety and security technology, social science, social work, and sociology). Nursing is the strongest academically. Nursing and criminal justice is the largest.

Special: MU offers cross-registration with Marygrove, Sacred Heart Seminary, and the University of Detroit Mercy. Students may pursue co-op programs in 30 majors, internships, and may receive credit for life, military, or work experience. Work-study at MU and study abroad in 17 countries are also possible. There are 10 national honor societies and 8 departmental honors programs.

Admissions: The ACT scores were 35% below 21, 36% between 21 and 23, 16% between 24 and 26, 7% between 27 and 28, and 6% above 28.

Requirements: The ACT is required. In addition, students should have completed 4 years of English, 3 of math, 2 of science, and 1 of history. The school accepts the GED. An essay is required. For some majors, students are asked to submit a portfolio or to appear for an interview or audition. A GPA of 2.8 is required. AP and CLEP credits are accepted. Important factors in the admissions decision are advanced placement or honors courses, recommendations by school officials, and leadership record.

Procedure: Freshmen are admitted to all sessions. Entrance exams should be taken during either the junior or senior year. There is a rolling admissions plan. Application deadlines are open. Application fee is $25. Notification is sent on a rolling basis. Applications are accepted on-line.

Financial Aid: In 2009-2010, 69% of all full-time freshmen and 76% of continuing full-time students received some form of financial aid. 40% of all full-time freshmen and 52% of continuing full-time students received need-based aid. The average freshmen award was $7,239, with $5,419 ($13,670 maximum) from need-based scholarships or need-based grants; $3,105 ($5,510 maximum) from need-based self-help aid (loans and jobs); $2,631 ($13,120 maximum) from non-need-based athletic scholarships; and $5,382 ($11,220 maximum) from other non-need-based awards and non-need-based scholarships. 29% of undergraduate students work part-time. The average financial indebtedness of the 2009 graduate was $22,629. The FAFSA is required. The deadline for filing freshman financial aid applications for fall entry is February 21.

Computers: Wireless access is available. Students have access to PCs in the Library and the Academic Computer Lab. There are a number of areas clearly labeled on campus in which students have wireless access to our network. All students may access the system. 8:30 A.M. to 10 P.M. Monday - Thursday, 8:30 A.M. to 5 P.M. Friday, 9 A.M. to 5 P.M. Saturday, and Sunday noon to 5 P.M. 1 hour per day if others are waiting. There are no fees.

MAHARISHI UNIVERSITY OF MANAGEMENT

Fairfield, IA 52557
(641) 472-1110
(800) 369-6480; (641) 472-1179

Full-time: 115 men, 80 women	**Faculty:** n/av
Part-time: 5 men, 10 women	**Ph.D.s:** 100%
Graduate: 605 men, 140 women	**Student/Faculty:** n/av
Year: semesters	**Tuition:** $24,430
Application Deadline: open	**Room & Board:** $6000
Freshman Class: n/av	
SAT or ACT: not required	**VERY COMPETITIVE**

Maharishi University of Management, established in 1971, is a private institution offering undergraduate and graduate programs in a broad range of disciplines. The University provides consciousness-based education and incorporates the group practice of the Maharishi Transcendental Meditation technique into a traditional academic program. Figures in the above capsule and this profile are approximate. There are 5 undergraduate schools and 5 graduate schools. The library contains 150,294 volumes, 59,851 microform items, and 21,291 audio/video tapes/CDs/DVDs, and subscribes to 23,345 periodicals including electronic. Computerized library services include interlibrary loans, database searching, and Internet access. Special learning facilities include a learning resource center, an art gallery, a radio station, psychophysiology, electronic engineering, visual technology, and physics labs, a scanning electron microscope, and domes for practicing the Transcendental Meditation Sidhi program. The 272-acre campus is in a small town 114 miles southeast of Des Moines and 60 miles southwest of Iowa City. Including any residence halls, there are 50 buildings.

Programs of Study: Maharishi confers B.A., B.S., and B.F.A. degrees. Master's and doctoral degrees are also awarded. Bachelor's degrees are awarded in BUSINESS (management science), COMMUNICATIONS AND THE ARTS (dramatic arts, fine arts, and literature), COMPUTER AND PHYSICAL SCIENCE (computer science and mathematics), EDUCATION (education). Sustainable living, Maharishi Vedic science, and business are the largest.

Special: Opportunities are provided for internships, study abroad, and nondegree study. Systematic programs are offered in the Science of Creative Intelligence, by which students apply knowledge to practical professional values. There are several 1-month blocks a year during which students may study, for example, art in Italy, literature in Switzerland, or business In China. There is a freshman honors program.

Requirements: Applicants must graduate from an accredited secondary school or have a GED. An essay and 2 personal recommendations are required. An interview is recommended. A GPA of 2.5 is required. AP and CLEP credits are accepted. Important factors in the admissions decision are personality/intangible qualities, recommendations by school officials, and leadership record.

Procedure: Freshmen are admitted fall and spring. Entrance exams should be taken in the fall of the senior year or spring of the junior year. There are early admissions, deferred admissions, and rolling admissions plans. Application deadlines are open. The application fee is $15. Applications are accepted on-line.

Financial Aid: In a recent year, 93% of all students received some form of financial aid, including need-based aid. The average freshman award was $23,963.Need-based scholarships or need-based grants averaged $14,080 ($21,000 maximum); need-based self-help aid (loans and jobs) averaged $8281 ($20,000 maximum); and other non-need-based awards and non-need-based scholarships averaged $1602 ($5000 maximum). 79% of undergraduate students work part-time. Average annual earnings from campus work are $1600. The average financial indebtedness of a recent graduate was $25,821. The FAFSA is required. Check with the school for current application deadlines.

Computers: All students may access the system daytime and evenings. There are no time limits and no fees. It is strongly recommended that all students have a personal computer.

MALONE UNIVERSITY
Canton, OH 44709
(330) 471-8156
(800) 521-1146; (330) 471-8149

Full-time: 782 men, 1075 women	**Faculty:** 106; IIA, --$
Part-time: 109 men, 225 women	**Ph.D.s:** 69%
Graduate: 145 men, 284 women	**Student/Faculty:** 18 to 1
Year: semesters, summer session	**Tuition:** $21,080
Application Deadline: July 1	**Room & Board:** $7100
Freshman Class: 1641 applied, 1157 accepted, 481 enrolled	
SAT CR/M: 540/540	**ACT:** 23 **VERY COMPETITIVE**

Malone University, formerly Malone College and founded in 1892, is a private Christian university for the arts, sciences, and professions in the liberal arts tradition. There are 6 undergraduate schools and 1 graduate school. In addition to regional accreditation, Malone has baccalaureate program accreditation with CCNE, CSWE, and IACBE. The library contains 181,000 volumes, 692,000 microform items, and 7310 audio/video tapes/CDs/DVDs, and subscribes to 49,458 periodicals including electronic. Computerized library services include interlibrary loans, database searching, and Internet access. Special learning facilities include a radio station, TV station, a writing lab, and subject area tutoring. The 87-acre campus is in a suburban area 56 miles southeast of Cleveland. Including any residence halls, there are 23 buildings.

Programs of Study: Malone confers B.A., B.S.Ed., and B.S.N. degrees. Master's degrees are also awarded. Bachelor's degrees are awarded in BIOLOGICAL SCIENCE (biology/biological science, life science, and zoology), BUSINESS (accounting, business administration and management, and sports management), COMMUNICATIONS AND THE ARTS (art, communications, English, language arts, music, music technology, and Spanish), COMPUTER AND PHYSICAL SCIENCE (chemistry, computer science, mathematics, and physical sciences), EDUCATION (art education, Christian education, early childhood education, foreign languages education, health education, middle school education, music education, physical education, science education, secondary education, social studies education, and special education), HEALTH PROFESSIONS (community health work, exercise science, medical laboratory technology, and nursing), SOCIAL SCIENCE (biblical studies, history, liberal arts/general studies, ministries, political science/government, psychology, religious music, social work, theological studies, and youth ministry). Biology, chemistry, and math are the strongest academically. Business administration, communication arts, and early childhood education are the largest.

Special: Students may participate in co-op programs and internships in many majors and may cross-register within the Christian College Consortium. Malone offers study abroad in England, China, Egypt, Australia, Uganda, and Kenya as well as Hollywood (film studies), Martha's Vineyard (contemporary music), or Washington semesters through the Council for Christian Colleges and Universities. A liberal arts degree, dual and student-designed majors, and credit for life, military, or work experience are also available. The Malone Management Program offers accelerated degree completion for students with 5 years of work experience and 40 to 88 transfer hours. There are 11 national honor societies and a freshman honors program.

Admissions: 71% of the 2009-2010 applicants were accepted. The SAT scores for the 2009-2010 freshman class were: Critical Reading--33% below 500, 42% between 500 and 599, 21% between 600 and 700, and 4% above 700; Math--34% below 500, 42% between 500 and 599, 22% between 600 and 700, and 2% above 700. The ACT scores were 32% below 21, 23% between 21 and 23, 26% between 24 and 26, 12% between 27 and 28, and 8% above 28. 41% of the current freshmen were in the top fifth of their class; 66% were in the top two fifths. 14 freshmen graduated first in their class.

Requirements: The ACT is required for traditional students. The ACT is preferred; the SAT is accepted. Applicants should be graduates of an accredited secondary school with a minimum GPA of 2.5. The GED is accepted. AP and CLEP credits are accepted. Important factors in the admissions decision are advanced placement or honors courses, leadership record, and extracurricular activities record.

Procedure: Freshmen are admitted fall, spring, and summer. Entrance exams should be taken in the junior year. There are early admissions, deferred admissions, and rolling admissions plans. Applications should be filed by July 1 for fall entry, along with a $20 fee (waived for on-line applications). Applications are accepted on-line.

Financial Aid: In 2009-2010, 99% of all full-time freshmen and 91% of continuing full-time students received some form of financial aid. 74% of all full-time

freshmen and 71% of continuing full-time students received need-based aid. The average freshman award was $22,618. Need-based scholarships or need-based grants averaged $7915 ($22,356 maximum); need-based self-help aid (loans and jobs) averaged $4964 ($9500 maximum); non-need-based athletic scholarships averaged $4368 ($15,000 maximum); other non-need-based awards and non-need-based scholarships averaged $11,253 ($29,500 maximum); and other forms of aid (parent loans) averaged $8039 ($21,000 maximum). 20% of undergraduate students work part-time. Average annual earnings from campus work are $2260. The average financial indebtedness of the 2009 graduate was $28,149. The FAF-SA and the verification worksheet and tax returns for students chosen for verification are required. The priority date for freshman financial aid applications for fall entry is March 1. The deadline for filing freshman financial aid applications for fall entry is July 31.

Computers: Wireless access is available. Students use the network for data storage, Internet access, online classes, and academic information. There are computers available in computer labs (155), residence halls (60), the library (28), and every classroom. Students have 24/7 access in the residence halls. Library and classroom computers are available all day during classes. Wireless is available 24/7 in most locations on campus. All students may access the system 24/7. There are no time limits and no fees.

MANHATTAN COLLEGE
Riverdale, NY 10471   (718) 862-7200
                                (800) 622-9235; (718) 862-8019

Full-time: 1310 men, 1410 women	**Faculty:** IIA,+$
Part-time: 105 men, 105 women	**Ph.D.s:** 94%
Graduate: 205 men, 205 women	**Student/Faculty:** n/avn
Year: semesters, summer session	**Tuition:** $24,000
Application Deadline: March 1	**Room & Board:** $9500
Freshman Class: n/av	
SAT: required	**VERY COMPETITIVE**

Manhattan College, founded in 1853, is a private institution affiliated with the Christian Brothers of the Catholic Church. It offers degree programs in the arts and sciences, education and human services, business, and engineering. The figures in the above capsule and in this profile are approximate. There are 5 undergraduate schools and 3 graduate schools. In addition to regional accreditation, Manhattan has baccalaureate program accreditation with ABET, AHEA, and CAHEA. The 4 libraries contain 193,100 volumes, 383,480 microform items, and 3,244 audio/video tapes/CDs/DVDs, and subscribe to 1,527 periodicals including electronic. Computerized library services include interlibrary loans and database searching. Special learning facilities include a learning resource center, radio station, nuclear reactor lab, and media center. The 26-acre campus is in an urban area 10 miles north of midtown Manhattan. Including any residence halls, there are 28 buildings.

Programs of Study: Manhattan confers B.A., B.S., and B.S.E. degrees. Master's degrees are also awarded. Bachelor's degrees are awarded in BIOLOGICAL SCIENCE (biochemistry and biology/biological science), BUSINESS (accounting, banking and finance, business economics, international business management, and marketing/retailing/merchandising), COMMUNICATIONS AND THE ARTS (communications, English, French, and Spanish), COMPUTER AND PHYSICAL SCIENCE (chemistry, computer science, information sciences and systems, mathematics, and physics), EDUCATION (early childhood education, elementary education, foreign languages education, health education, middle school education, physical education, science education, secondary education, and special education), ENGINEERING AND ENVIRONMENTAL DESIGN (chemical engineering, civil engineering, electrical/electronics engineering, environmental engineering, and mechanical engineering), HEALTH PROFESSIONS (predentistry, premedicine, and radiological science), SOCIAL SCIENCE (economics, history, peace studies, philosophy, political science/government, prelaw, psychology, religion, sociology, and urban studies). Engineering and business are the strongest academically. Arts, business, and education are the largest.

Special: Manhattan offers co-op programs in 11 majors, cross-registration with the College of Mount St. Vincent, and off-campus internships in business, industry, government, and social or cultural organizations. Students may study abroad in 10 countries and enter work-study programs with major U.S. corporations, health services, or in the arts. A general studies degree, a 3-2 engineering degree, a dual major in international business, credit by exam, and nondegree study are also available. There are 22 national honor societies, including Phi Beta Kappa, a freshman honors program, and 28 departmental honors programs.

Requirements: The SAT is required. In addition, applicants must graduate from an accredited secondary school or have earned a GED. 16 academic units are required, including 4 of English, 3 each of math and social studies, and 2 of foreign language, lab sciences, and electives. An essay is required and an interview is recommended. AP and CLEP credits are accepted. Important factors in the admissions decision are advanced placement or honors courses, leadership record, and recommendations by school officials.

Procedure: Freshmen are admitted fall and spring. Entrance exams should be taken in the spring of the junior year or the fall of the senior year. There are early decision, deferred admissions and rolling admissions plans. Early decision applications should be filed by November 15; regular applications, by March 1 for fall entry and December 1 for spring entry. The fall 2008 application fee was $40. Notification of early decision is sent December 1; regular decision, December 15. Applications are accepted on-line. A waiting list is maintained.

Financial Aid: In a recent year, 82% of all full-time freshmen and 71% of continuing full-time students received some form of financial aid. 73% of all full-time freshmen and 63% of continuing full-time students received need-based aid. The average freshmen award was $12,688. 15% of undergraduate students worked part-time. Average annual earnings from campus work were $600. The average financial indebtedness of the 2009 graduate was $12,100. The FAFSA and the college's own financial statement are required. Check with the school for current application deadlines.

Computers: All students may access the system 13 hours a day in the labs and 24 hours a day in residence halls or by modem. There are no time limits and no fees.

MANHATTANVILLE COLLEGE

Purchase, NY 10577

(914) 323-5464
(800) 32 VILLE; (914) 694-1732

Full-time: 588 men, 1129 women	**Faculty:** 102
Part-time: 48 men, 77 women	**Ph.D.s:** 99%
Graduate: 394 men, 745 women	**Student/Faculty:** 17 to 1
Year: semesters, summer session	**Tuition:** $32,760
Application Deadline: open	**Room & Board:** $13,500
Freshman Class: 4242 applied, 2240 accepted, 507 enrolled	
SAT CR/M: 530/540	**ACT:** 24 **VERY COMPETITIVE**

Manhattanville College, founded in 1841, is an independent liberal arts institution offering more than 45 undergraduate areas of study. There are 2 graduate schools. The library contains 250,209 volumes, 259,230 microform items, and 5,312 audio/video tapes/CDs/DVDs, and subscribes to 36,923 periodicals including electronic. Computerized library services include interlibrary loans, database searching, and Internet access. Special learning facilities include a learning resource center, art gallery, radio station, TV station, and an environmental sciences building. The 100-acre campus is in a suburban area 25 miles north of New York City. Including any residence halls, there are 18 buildings.

Programs of Study: M'ville confers B.A., B.S., B.F.A., and B.Mus. degrees. Master's degrees are also awarded. Bachelor's degrees are awarded in BIOLOGICAL SCIENCE (biochemistry and biology/biological science), BUSINESS (banking and finance and management science), COMMUNICATIONS AND THE ARTS (art, art history and appreciation, communications, dance, dramatic arts, English, French, music, and Spanish), COMPUTER AND PHYSICAL SCIENCE (chemistry, computer science, mathematics, and physics), EDUCATION (education), SOCIAL SCIENCE (American studies, Asian/Oriental studies, economics, history, international studies, philosophy, political science/government, psychology, religion, and sociology). English, art, and psychology are the strongest academically. Psychology, management, and history are the largest.

Special: Manhattanville offers cross-registration with SUNY Purchase, internships in all majors for credit, a Washington semester, and study abroad in 15 countries. Accelerated degree programs in behavioral studies, organizational management, and communications management are offered. Dual, student-designed, and interdisciplinary majors and pass/fail options are also available. Under the portfolio degree plan, students develop an individualized program combining both academic and nonacademic training. There is a freshman honors program and 16 departmental honors programs.

Admissions: 53% of the 2009-2010 applicants were accepted. The SAT scores for the 2009-2010 freshman class were: Critical Reading--5% below 500, 74% between 500 and 599, 20% between 600 and 700, and 1% above 700; Math--5% below 500, 67% between 500 and 599, 26% between 600 and 700, and 2% above 700. The ACT scores were 25% below 21, 33% between 21 and 23, 26% between 24 and 26, 8% between 27 and 28, and 8% above 28. 100 freshmen graduated first in their class.

Requirements: The SAT or ACT is required. In addition, applicants should graduate in the upper 50% of their class with 4 years of English, 3 each of history, math, and science, including 2 of lab science, and 1 half-year each of art and music. The GED is accepted. Interviews are strongly encouraged. Art applicants must submit a portfolio; music applicants must audition. A GPA of 2.0 is required. AP and CLEP credits are accepted. Important factors in the admissions decision are leadership record, recommendations by alumni, and recommendations by school officials.

Procedure: Freshmen are admitted fall and spring. Entrance exams should be taken in the spring of the junior year or fall of the senior year. There are early decision, early admissions, deferred admissions, and rolling admissions plans. Early decision applications should be filed by December 1; for regular applications, deadlines are open. Application fee is $70. Notification of early decision is sent December 31; regular decision, on a rolling basis. 146 early decision candidates were accepted for the 2009-2010 class. 100 applicants were on the 2009 waiting list; 20 were admitted. Applications are accepted on-line.

Financial Aid: In 2009-2010, 78% of all full-time freshmen and 76% of continuing full-time students received some form of financial aid. 63% of all full-time freshmen and 58% of continuing full-time students received need-based aid. The average freshmen award was $24,828. 33% of undergraduate students work part-time. Average annual earnings from campus work are $1750. The average financial indebtedness of the 2009 graduate was $23,294. The FAFSA, the state aid form, and the college's own financial statement are required. The deadline for filing freshman financial aid applications for fall entry is March 1.

Computers: Wireless access is available. All students may access the system. Internet and intranet are usable 24 hours per day, 7 days a week. Computer labs are open about 64 to 70 hours throughout the week. There are no time limits and no fees.

MARLBORO COLLEGE
Marlboro, VT 05344-0300　　　　　　　　　(802) 258-9261
　　　　　　　　　　　　　　　　　(800) 343-0049; (802) 258-9300

Full-time: 130 men, 200 women	**Faculty:** n/av
Part-time: 5 men, 5 women	**Ph.D.s:** 77%
Graduate: none	**Student/Faculty:** n/av
Year: semesters	**Tuition:** $35,000
Application Deadline: see profile	**Room & Board:** $9500
Freshman Class: n/av	
SAT or ACT: required	**VERY COMPETITIVE**

Marlboro College, established in 1946, is a small private institution offering degrees in the liberal and fine arts and humanities and employing self-designed programs of study. Figures in the above capsule and this profile are approximate. There is 1 graduate school. The library contains 65,216 volumes, 5799 microform items, and 2990 audio/video tapes/CDs/DVDs, and subscribes to 188 periodicals including electronic. Computerized library services include interlibrary loans, database searching, Internet access, and laptop Internet portals. Special learning facilities include a learning resource center, art gallery, planetarium, and observatory. The 366-acre campus is in a rural area 9 miles west of Brattleboro, 2 1/2 hours from Boston. Including any residence halls, there are 36 buildings.

Programs of Study: Marlboro confers B.A. and B.S. degrees. Master's degrees are also awarded. Bachelor's degrees are awarded in BIOLOGICAL SCIENCE (biochemistry, biology/biological science, botany, and microbiology), COMMUNICATIONS AND THE ARTS (creative writing, dance, dramatic arts, English, fine arts, French, German, Greek, Italian, Latin, linguistics, music, photography, Russian, and Spanish), COMPUTER AND PHYSICAL SCIENCE (chemistry, computer science, mathematics, and physics), HEALTH PROFESSIONS (premedicine), SOCIAL SCIENCE (anthropology, economics, history, interdisciplinary studies, international studies, philosophy, political science/government, prelaw, psychology, social science, and sociology). Sciences, humanities, and world studies are the strongest academically. Literature, biology, and sociology are the largest.

Special: Marlboro offers a variety of internships, cross-registration with Huron University in London, and study abroad in many countries. The World Studies Program combines liberal arts with international studies, including 5 to 8 months of internship work in another culture. Accelerated and B.A.-B.S. degree programs are available. Students may pursue dual majors. Majors reflect an integrated course of study designed by students and their faculty advisers during the junior year.

Requirements: The SAT or ACT is required. Applicants typically graduate from an accredited secondary school or have a GED. They are encouraged to earn 16 Carnegie units and complete 4 years of English and 3 years each of math, science, history, and a foreign language. Essays and interviews are required. AP and CLEP credits are accepted. Important factors in the admissions decision are advanced placement or honors courses, evidence of special talent, and extracurricular activities record.

Procedure: Freshmen are admitted fall and spring. Entrance exams should be taken by October before entry. There are early decision, early admissions and deferred admissions plans. Early decision applications should be filed by November 15; check with the school for other current application deadlines. Notification of early decision is sent December 15. The application fee is $50. Applications are accepted on-line.

Financial Aid: Marlboro is a member of CSS. The CSS/Profile and FAFSA are required. Check with the school for current application deadlines.

Computers: Wireless access is available. All students may access the system 24 hours a day. There are no time limits and no fees.

MARQUETTE UNIVERSITY
Milwaukee, WI 53201-1881

(414) 288-7302
(800) 222-6544; (414) 288-3764

Full- and part-time: 8000 men and women	**Faculty:** 512; I, --$
	Ph.D.s: 88%
Graduate: 3600 men and women	**Student/Faculty:** 15 to 1
Year: semesters, summer session	**Tuition:** $30,000
Application Deadline: see profile	**Room & Board:** $10,000
Freshman Class: n/av	
ACTor SAT: required	**HIGHLY COMPETITIVE+**

Marquette University, established in 1881, is a private Roman Catholic Jesuit institution. There are 7 undergraduate schools and 4 graduate schools. Figures in the above capsule and in this profile are approximate. In addition to regional accreditation, Marquette has baccalaureate program accreditation with AACSB, ABET, ACEJMC, ADA, APTA, ASLA, CSWE, NCATE, and NLN. The 2 libraries contain 1.3 million volumes, 1.5 million microform items, and 12,000 audio/video tapes/CDs/DVDs, and subscribe to 15,800 periodicals including electronic. Computerized library services include interlibrary loans, database searching, Internet access, and laptop Internet portals. Special learning facilities include a learning resource center, art gallery, radio station, and TV station. The 80-acre campus is in an urban area in the heart of Milwaukee. Including any residence halls, there are 60 buildings.

Programs of Study: Marquette confers B.A., B.S., and B.S.N. degrees. Associate, master's, and doctoral degrees are also awarded. Bachelor's degrees are awarded in BIOLOGICAL SCIENCE (biochemistry, biology/biological science, molecular biology, and physiology), BUSINESS (accounting, banking and finance, business administration and management, business economics, human resources, international business management, management information systems, and marketing/retailing/merchandising), COMMUNICATIONS AND THE ARTS (advertising, broadcasting, classical languages, classics, communications, dramatic arts, English, French, German, journalism, public relations, and Spanish), COMPUTER AND PHYSICAL SCIENCE (chemistry, computer science, information sciences and systems, mathematics, physics, and statistics), EDUCATION (secondary education), ENGINEERING AND ENVIRONMENTAL DESIGN (biomedical engineering, civil engineering, computer engineering, electrical/electronics engineering, engineering, environmental engineering, industrial engineering technology, and mechanical engineering), HEALTH PROFESSIONS (biomedical science, exercise science, medical laboratory science, nursing, premedicine, and speech pathology/audiology), SOCIAL SCIENCE (anthropology, criminology, economics, history, interdisciplinary studies, international relations, philosophy, political science/government, psychology, sociology, and theological studies). Biomedical engineering, nursing, and premedicine are the strongest academically. Business administration, nursing, and engineering are the largest.

Special: Marquette offers co-op programs in engineering, internships, study abroad in 16 countries, a Washington summer term, and work-study programs. Dual and student-designed majors, nondegree study, an accelerated degree program for predental and prelaw students, and pass/fail options are available. Cross-registration is possible with Milwaukee Institute of Art and Design, and there is a 2-2 engineering program with Waukesha County Technical College. The Freshman Frontier Program offers academic support for selected freshmen who do not meet regular admission requirements but show potential for success. The Educational Opportunity Program affords students from minority groups and low-income families the opportunity to attend the school. There are 8 national honor societies, including Phi Beta Kappa, a freshman honors program, and all departments have honors programs.

Admissions: 56% of the current freshmen were in the top fifth of their class; 84% were in the top two fifths.

Requirements: The SAT or ACT is required. In addition, applicants must be graduates of an accredited secondary school with a recommended 18 credits, including 4 years of English, 3 each of social studies and math, 2 each of sciences and foreign language, and 4 of additional academic subjects. Most students rank in the upper quarter of their high school class. The GED is accepted, with a minimum score of 225. Applicants must demonstrate ability, preparation, and motivation. An interview is recommended. AP and CLEP credits are accepted. Important factors in the admissions decision are advanced placement or honors courses, recommendations by school officials, and leadership record.

Procedure: Freshmen are admitted to all sessions. Entrance exams should be taken in the junior year and repeated early in the senior year if necessary. Check with the school for current application deadlines and fee. Applications are accepted on-line. 1516 applicants were on a recent waiting list, 334 were accepted.

Financial Aid: The FAFSA is required. Check with the school for current financial aid deadlines.

Computers: All rooms in university housing have high speed Internet access. Selected buildings (including the library) have wireless access, up to 3000 connections. The library also has wired connections and laptops available for 4-hour checkout. There are 1200 university-owned computers available for general student use all over campus including dorms, the student center, and the library. All students may access the system 24 hours a day. There are no time limits and no fees.

MARYLAND INSTITUTE COLLEGE OF ART
Baltimore, MD 21217   **(410) 225-2222; (410) 225-2337**

Full-time: 560 men, 1100 women	**Faculty:** n/av
Part-time: 10 men, 10 women	**Ph.Ds:** 82%
Graduate: 80 men, 160 women	**Student/Faculty:** n/av
Year: semesters, summer session	**Tuition:** $31,000
Application Deadline: see profile	**Room & Board:** $8500
Freshman Class: n/av	
SAT: required	**SPECIAL**

Maryland Institute College of Art, founded in 1826, is a private accredited institution offering undergraduate and graduate degrees in the fine arts. Figures in the above capsule and this profile are approximate. There are 9 graduate schools. In addition to regional accreditation, MICA has baccalaureate program accreditation with NASAD. The library contains 83,564 volumes and 5600 audio/video tapes/CDs/DVDs, and subscribes to 402 periodicals including electronic. Computerized library services include interlibrary loans, database searching, Internet access, and laptop Internet portals. Special learning facilities include a learning resource center, an art gallery, 12 large art galleries, open to the public year-round and featuring work by MICA faculty, students, and nationally and internationally known artists, a slide library containing 220,000 slides, and 8 other galleries for undergraduate and graduate exhibitions. The 13-acre campus is in an urban area. Including any residence halls, there are 25 buildings.

Programs of Study: MICA confers B.F.A. degrees. Master's degrees are also awarded. Bachelor's degrees are awarded in COMMUNICATIONS AND THE ARTS (animation, art history and appreciation, ceramic art and design, drawing, fiber/textiles/weaving, fine arts, graphic design, illustration, media arts, painting, photography, printmaking, sculpture, and video), ENGINEERING AND ENVIRONMENTAL DESIGN (environmental design). Painting, illustration, and general fine arts are the largest.

Special: Exchange programs are offered with Goucher College, Loyola and Notre Dame Colleges, Johns Hopkins University, the Peabody Conservatory of Music, the University of Baltimore, University of Maryland Baltimore County, Towson University, Morgan State University, and Baltimore Hebrew College. Cross-registration is possible with any member schools in the Alliance of Independent Colleges of Art and the East Coast Art Schools Consortium. A New York studio semester is available as well as a semester of study with any member schools in the Association of Independent Colleges of Art and Design. Study abroad is possible in the junior year in any of 45 schools in 24 countries.

Admissions: There were 2 National Merit finalists in a recent year.

Requirements: The SAT is required. Admission is based on a comprehensive set of criteria with the most emphasis placed on artistic ability as demonstrated in the portfolio and on academic achievement as demonstrated in test scores, GPA, and level of course work. Essays, recommendations, interview, and extracurricular activities are also considered. AP credits are accepted. Important factors in the admissions decision are evidence of special talent, advanced placement or honors courses, and extracurricular activities record.

Procedure: Freshmen are admitted fall and spring. Entrance exams should be taken in the spring of the junior year. There are early decisions, early admissions and deferred admissions plans. Check with the school for current application deadlines. The fall 2009 application fee was $50. A waiting list is maintained.

Financial Aid: In a recent year, 85% of all full-time students received some form of financial aid. 62% of all full-time freshmen and 65% of continuing full-time students received need-based aid. The average freshmen award was $17,006. 60% of undergraduate students work part-time. Average annual earnings from campus work are $1100. The average financial indebtedness of a recent graduate was $18,919. MICA is a member of CSS. The FAFSA and the college's own financial statement are required. Check with the school for current application deadlines.

Computers: Wireless access is available. More than 350 PCs are available in more than 30 classrooms, labs, and public areas. 60% of the campus has wireless access. Students can use the student portal, Web galleries, student blogs, e-mail, and blackboard e-learning. All students may access the system 24 hours a day. There are no time limits and no fees. It is strongly recommended that all students have a personal computer.

MARYMOUNT MANHATTAN COLLEGE

New York, NY 10021
(212) 517-0555
(800) 627-9668; (212) 517-0448

Full-time: 445 men, 1284 women	**Faculty:** IIB, av$
Part-time: 22 men, 228 women	**Ph.D.s:** 91%
Graduate: none	**Student/Faculty:** n/av
Year: semesters, summer session	**Tuition:** $22,656
Application Deadline: open	**Room & Board:** $12,874
Freshman Class: 3447 applied, 2419 accepted, 487 enrolled	
SAT or ACT: required	**VERY COMPETITIVE**

Marymount Manhattan College is an urban, independent liberal arts college, offering programs in the arts and sciences for all ages, as well as substantial preprofessional preparation. There is 1 undergraduate school. The library contains 75,000 volumes, 70 microform items, and 4,000 audio/video tapes/CDs/DVDs, and subscribes to 2,740 periodicals including electronic. Computerized library services include interlibrary loans, database searching, Internet access, and laptop Internet portals. Special learning facilities include a learning resource center, art gallery, radio station, TV station, and a communications arts multimedia suite featuring digital editing technology. The 1-acre campus is in an urban area in Manhattan. Including any residence halls, there are 3 buildings.

Programs of Study: MMC confers B.A., B.S., and B.F.A. degrees. Associate degrees are also awarded. Bachelor's degrees are awarded in BIOLOGICAL SCIENCE (biology/biological science), BUSINESS (accounting and business administration and management), COMMUNICATIONS AND THE ARTS (communications, dance, dramatic arts, English, and fine arts), COMPUTER AND PHYSICAL SCIENCE (information sciences and systems), EDUCATION (elementary education), HEALTH PROFESSIONS (premedicine and speech pathology/audiology), SOCIAL SCIENCE (history, international studies, liberal arts/general studies, philosophy and religion, political science/government, psychology, and sociology). Theater, communications, and business are the strongest academically.

Special: MMC offers study abroad, interdisciplinary courses, pass/fail options, nondegree study, credit for life experience, and some 250 internships in all majors. Cooperative programs in business and finance, dance, music, languages, nursing, and urban education are offered in conjunction with local colleges and institutes. There is a January mini-session, cross-registration with Hunter College, and the China Institute, and a 5-year masters in publishing with Pace University. There are 7 national honor societies and 5 departmental honors programs.

Admissions: 70% of the 2009-2010 applicants were accepted.

Requirements: The SAT or ACT is required. In addition, applicants should be graduates of an accredited secondary school or have a GED certificate. MMC recommends completion of 16 academic units, including 4 each in English and electives, and 3 each in language, math, social science, and science. Recommendations are required, and an interview is strongly advised. Applicants to the dance and acting programs must audition. A GPA of 2.5 is required. AP and CLEP credits are accepted. Important factors in the admissions decision are personality/intangible qualities, evidence of special talent, and leadership record.

Procedure: Freshmen are admitted to all sessions. Entrance exams should be taken as early as possible. There are deferred admissions and rolling admissions plans. Application deadlines are open. The fall 2009 application fee was $60. Notification is sent on a rolling basis. Applications are accepted on-line. A waiting list is maintained.

Financial Aid: In 2009-2010, at least 72% of all full-time freshmen and 75% of continuing full-time students received some form of financial aid. At least 70% of all full-time freshmen and 59% of continuing full-time students received need-based aid. The average freshman award was $14,025. Need-based scholarships or need-based grants averaged $11,158; need-based self-help aid (loans and jobs) averaged $3,686. Institutional awards averaged $5,263. 75% of undergraduate students work part-time. Average annual earnings from campus work are $2500. The average financial indebtedness of the 2009 graduate was $15,988. The FAFSA, and TAP for (New York state residents) is required. Check with the school for current application deadlines.

Computers: Wireless access is available. There are 2 PC labs with 22 stations each in the main building, and 1 PC lab for general use in the library. These are specialized computer labs for communications students and arts students. Wireless access is available in the library and in the Nugent building. There are 100 laptops in the library that can be used to access the Internet. All students may access the system. There are no time limits and no fees.

MARYVILLE COLLEGE
Maryville, TN 37804 (865) 981-8206
(800) 597-2687; (865) 981-8005

Full-time: 520 men, 645 women	**Faculty:** 78; IIB, -$
Part-time: 10 men, 5 women	**Ph.D.s:** 91%
Graduate: none	**Student/Faculty:** n/av
Year: 4-1-4, summer session	**Tuition:** $29,500
Application Deadline: see profile	**Room & Board:** $9000
Freshman Class: n/av	
SAT or ACT: required	**VERY COMPETITIVE**

Maryville College, founded in 1819, is a private liberal arts college affiliated with the Presbyterian Church (U.S.A.). Figures in the above capsule are approximate. In addition to regional accreditation, Maryville has baccalaureate program accreditation with NASM. The 2 libraries contain 133,686 volumes and 8263 microform items, and subscribe to 16,525 periodicals including electronic. Computerized library services include interlibrary loans, database searching, Internet access, and laptop Internet portals. Special learning facilities include a learning resource center, art gallery, greenhouse, and college woods. The 350-acre campus is in a suburban area 15 miles south of Knoxville. Including any residence halls, there are 22 buildings.

Programs of Study: Maryville confers B.A. and B.Mus. degrees. Bachelor's degrees are awarded in AGRICULTURE (environmental studies), BIOLOGICAL SCIENCE (biochemistry and biology/biological science), BUSINESS (business administration and management and recreation and leisure services), COMMUNICATIONS AND THE ARTS (American Sign Language, art, art history and appreciation, creative writing, dramatic arts, English, English as a second/foreign language, music, music performance, and Spanish), COMPUTER AND PHYSICAL SCIENCE (chemical physics, chemistry, computer science, and mathematics), EDUCATION (elementary education, music education, physical education, science education, and secondary education), ENGINEERING AND ENVIRONMENTAL DESIGN (engineering and preengineering), HEALTH PROFESSIONS (nursing, predentistry, and premedicine), SOCIAL SCIENCE (economics, history, international relations, interpreter for the deaf, political science/government, prelaw, psychology, religion, social science, and sociology). Biology, chemistry, and English are the strongest academically. Business, biology, and psychology are the largest.

Special: Maryville offers cross-registration with the University of Tennessee and Vanderbilt University, internships, study abroad in 9 countries, a Washington semester, accelerated degree programs, a B.A.-B.S. degree in engineering, and dual and student-designed majors. There are 3-2 engineering degrees offered with regional universities. Nondegree study and pass/fail options are possible. There are 6 national honor societies, a freshman honors program, and 100 departmental honors programs.

Admissions: 5 freshmen graduated first in their class in a recent year.

Requirements: The SAT or ACT is required. In addition, candidates should be graduates of accredited secondary schools or have the GED. They should also have 15 academic credits with 4 years of English, 3 each of math and science, 2 years of foreign language, and 2 of history or social studies. An essay, portfolio, audition, and interview are all recommended. A GPA of 2.5 is required. AP and CLEP credits are accepted. Important factors in the admissions decision are advanced placement or honors courses, extracurricular activities record, and leadership record.

Procedure: Freshmen are admitted fall, spring, and summer. Entrance exams should be taken by October of the senior year. There are early decisions, early admissions and deferred admissions plans. Early decision applications should be filed by November 15; check with the school for current application deadlines. Notification of early decision is sent December 1. The application fee is $25. Applications are accepted on-line.

Financial Aid: In a recent year, 100% of all full-time freshmen and 98% of continuing full-time students received some form of financial aid. 82% of all full-time freshmen and 79% of continuing full-time students received need-based aid. The average freshmen award was $26,518, with $17,728 ($36,610 maximum) from need-based scholarships or need-based grants; $2859 ($7500 maximum) from need-based self-help aid (loans and jobs); and $1947 ($23,000 maximum) from other non-need-based awards and non-need-based scholarships. 49% of undergraduate students work part-time. Average annual earnings from campus work are $1559. The average financial indebtedness of a recent graduate was $14,344. Maryville is a member of CSS. The FAFSA is required. Check with the school for current application deadlines.

Computers: All students may access the system 7 days a week, 16 hours a day. There are no time limits and no fees. It is strongly recommended that all students have a personal computer.

MARYVILLE UNIVERSITY OF SAINT LOUIS

St. Louis, MO 63141-7299 (314) 529-9350
(800) 627-9855; (314) 529-9927

Full-time: 457 men, 1212 women	**Faculty:** 88; IIA, --$
Part-time: 246 men, 1019 women	**Ph.D.s:** 86%
Graduate: 166 men, 434 women	**Student/Faculty:** 18 to 1
Year: semesters, summer session	**Tuition:** $20,994
Application Deadline: rolling	**Room & Board:** $8210
Freshman Class: 1154 applied, 764 accepted, 374 enrolled	
ACT: 24	**VERY COMPETITIVE**

Maryville University of Saint Louis, established in 1872, is an independent institution offering undergraduate programs in arts, sciences, business, education, and health-related fields and graduate programs in actuarial science, business administration, education, health administration, nursing, occupational therapy, physical therapy, and rehabilitation counseling. There are 4 undergraduate schools and 4 graduate schools. In addition to regional accreditation, Maryville has baccalaureate program accreditation with ACBSP, FIDER, NASAD, NASM, NCATE, and NLN. The library contains 158,930 volumes, 525,716 microform items, and 10,605 audio/video tapes/CDs/DVDs, and subscribes to 42,582 periodicals including electronic. Computerized library services include interlibrary loans, database searching, Internet access, and laptop Internet portals. Special learning facilities include a learning resource center, an observatory, a teaching lab, art and design labs, clinical labs for nursing, occupational therapy, physical therapy, a communications lab, video conferencing facilities on all campuses, 51 multimedia-ready classrooms, and residence hall computer labs. The 130-acre campus is in a suburban area 20 miles west of downtown St. Louis. Including any residence halls, there are 29 buildings.

Programs of Study: Maryville confers B.A., B.S., B.F.A., B.S.C.L.S., B.S.M.T., and B.S.N. degrees. Master's and doctoral degrees are also awarded. Bachelor's degrees are awarded in AGRICULTURE (environmental studies), BIOLOGICAL SCIENCE (biochemistry and biology/biological science), BUSINESS (accounting, business administration and management, electronic business, international business management, marketing/retailing/merchandising, organizational behavior, and sports management), COMMUNICATIONS AND THE ARTS (communications, English, graphic design, and studio art), COMPUTER AND PHYSICAL SCIENCE (actuarial science, chemistry, computer science, information sciences and systems, mathematics, and science), EDUCATION (art education, early childhood education, elementary education, middle school education, and secondary education), ENGINEERING AND ENVIRONMENTAL DESIGN (environmental science and interior design), HEALTH PROFESSIONS (clinical science, health care administration, health science, music therapy, nursing, and rehabilitation therapy), SOCIAL SCIENCE (criminology, history, international studies, liberal arts/general studies, paralegal studies, psychology, and sociology). Actuarial science, education, and physical therapy are the strongest academically. Nursing, business administration, and accounting are the largest.

Special: There is cross-registration with Missouri Baptist College and Fontbonne, Webster, and Lindenwood Universities. Students may choose internships in various fields, and cooperative programs are available with various employers. Other options include dual and student-designed majors, study abroad in Costa Rica, Italy, England, Spain, and other countries, a 3-2 engineering degree with Washington University, and a Washington semester. Accelerated degree programs are offered in actuarial science and nursing. A 3+4 B.S/O.D. optometry degree with the University of Missouri-St. Louis and a B.A. criminal justice/criminology degree in association with St. Louis County and Municipal Police Academy are possible. There are 6 national honor societies and a freshman honors program.

Admissions: 66% of the 2009-2010 applicants were accepted. The ACT scores were 11% below 21, 32% between 21 and 23, 32% between 24 and 26, 15% between 27 and 28, and 10% above 28. 47% of the current freshmen were in the top fifth of their class; 73% were in the top two-fifths. 16 freshmen graduated first in their class.

Requirements: The ACT is required. In addition, students must have graduated from an accredited secondary school with 22 academic credits or have the GED. Expected preparatory courses include 4 units of English, 3 of math, and 2 each of science and social studies, plus 3 additional units in any of the preceding areas or in a foreign language. Some majors have additional admission requirements. A GPA of 2.5 is required. AP and CLEP credits are accepted. Important factors in the admissions decision are recommendations by school officials, advanced placement or honors courses, and leadership record.

Procedure: Freshmen are admitted to all sessions. Entrance exams should be taken during the junior year. There is a rolling admissions plan. Check with the school for current application deadlines. The fall 2009 application fee was $30. Notification is sent on a rolling basis. Applications are accepted on-line.

Financial Aid: In 2009-2010, 95% of all full-time freshmen and 78% of continuing full-time students received some form of financial aid. 75% of all full-time freshmen and 63% of continuing full-time students received need-based aid. The average freshmen award was $19,994, Need-based scholarships or need-based grants averaged $13,040 ($28,500 maximum); need-based self-help aid (loans and jobs) averaged $4,235 ($20,500 maximum); non-need based athletic scholarships averaged $11,797 ($29,279 maximum); other non-need based awards and non-need based scholarships averaged $10,718 ($29,279 maximum); and parental loans averaged $13,068 ($19,900 maximum). 35% of undergraduate students work part-time. Average annual earnings from campus work are $1916. The average financial indebtedness of the 2009 graduate was $16,588. The FAFSA is required. The priority date for freshman financial aid applications for fall entry is March 1. The deadline for filing freshman financial aid applications for fall entry is April 1.

Computers: Wireless access is available. Wireless Internet access is available in all university facilities, including green spaces outside of buildings. High-speed Internet connections are available across campus in computer labs, classrooms, the library, and residence halls and apartments. All students may access the system. There are no time limits and no fees.

MASSACHUSETTS COLLEGE OF ART AND DESIGN

Boston, MA 02115   (617) 879-7221; (617) 879-7250

Full-time: 538 men, 1049 women	**Faculty:** 101
Part-time: 53 men, 132 women	**Ph.D.s:** 78%
Graduate: 60 men, 100 women	**Student/Faculty:** 16 to 1
Year: semesters, summer session	**Tuition:** $8400 ($24,400)
Application Deadline: February 1	**Room & Board:** $11,288
Freshman Class: 1631 applied, 837 accepted, 315 enrolled	
SAT CR/M/W: 560/540/540	**SPECIAL**

Massachusetts College of Art and Design, founded in 1873, is a public institution offering undergraduate and graduate programs in art, design, and education. There is 1 graduate school. In addition to regional accreditation, MassArt has baccalaureate program accreditation with NASAD. The library contains 231,586 volumes and 8700 microform items, and subscribes to 757 periodicals including electronic. Computerized library services include interlibrary loans, database searching, and Internet access. Special learning facilities include 7 art galleries, a foundry, glass furnaces, ceramic kilns, video and film studios, performance and studio spaces, and a Polaroid 20 x 24 camera. The 5-acre campus is in an urban area in Boston. Including any residence halls, there are 6 buildings.

Programs of Study: MassArt confers B.F.A. degrees. Master's degrees are also awarded. Bachelor's degrees are awarded in COMMUNICATIONS AND THE ARTS (animation, art history and appreciation, ceramic art and design, fiber/textiles/weaving, film arts, fine arts, glass, graphic design, illustration, industrial design, media arts, metal/jewelry, painting, photography, printmaking, sculpture, and studio art), EDUCATION (art education), ENGINEERING AND ENVIRONMENTAL DESIGN (architecture), SOCIAL SCIENCE (fashion design and technology). Painting, illustration, and graphic design are the largest.

Special: MassArt offers cross-registration with several consortiums, internships for advanced students, on- and off-campus work-study programs, study abroad and foreign-exchange programs, an open major for exceptional students, and dual majors in most combinations of concentrations.

Admissions: 51% of the 2009-2010 applicants were accepted. The SAT scores for the 2009-2010 freshman class were: Critical Reading--18% below 500, 47% between 500 and 599, 30% between 600 and 700; and 5% above 700; Math--26% below 500, 49% between 500 and 599, 22% between 600 and 700, and 3% above 700; Writing--23% below 500, 49% between 500 and 599, 24% between 600 and 700; and 3% above 700. 35% of the current freshmen were in the top fifth of their class; 72% were in the top two fifths.

Requirements: The SAT is required. In addition, applicants should be graduates of an accredited secondary school or have earned the GED. College preparatory studies should include as a minimum 4 years of English, 2 each of social studies, math, and science, 2 academic electives (1 math or science and 1 art elective), and a foreign language. A personal essay and portfolio are required, and an interview and letters of reference are recommended. A GPA of 3.0 is required. AP and CLEP credits are accepted. Important factors in the admissions decision are evidence of special talent, recommendations by school officials, and personality/intangible qualities.

Procedure: Freshmen are admitted fall and spring. Entrance exams should be taken in early fall of the senior year. There are deferred admissions and rolling admissions plans. Applications should be filed by February 1 for fall entry; November 1 for spring entry, along with an application fee of $30 (Massachusetts residents) or $65 (nonresidents). Notification is sent April 1. Applications are accepted on-line. 56 applicants were on a recent waiting list, 8 were accepted.

Financial Aid: In a recent year, 81% of all full-time freshmen and 76% of continuing full-time students received some form of financial aid. 60% of all full-time freshmen and 62% of continuing full-time students received need-based aid. The average freshman award was $8508. 84% of undergraduate students work part-time. Average annual earnings from campus work are $1000. The FAFSA is required. The priority deadline for filing freshman financial aid applications is March 1.

Computers: Wireless access is available. All students may access the system. There are no time limits. There is a fee.

MASSACHUSETTS COLLEGE OF PHARMACY AND HEALTH SCIENCES

Boston, MA 02115

(617) 732-2850
(800) 225-5506; (617) 732-2118

Full-time: 888 men, 1882 women	**Faculty:** 202
Part-time: 28 men, 85 women	**Ph.D.s:** 86%
Graduate: 447 men, 922 women	**Student/Faculty:** 21 to 1
Year: semesters, summer session	**Tuition:** $24,550
Application Deadline: February 1	**Room & Board:** $11,900
Freshman Class: 3194 applied, 1383 accepted, 764 enrolled	
SAT CR/M/W: 525/570/540	**ACT:** 24 SPECIAL

The Massachusetts College of Pharmacy and Health Sciences, established in 1823, is a private institution offering undergraduate programs in chemistry, the pharmaceutical sciences, and the health sciences. There are 5 undergraduate schools and 1 graduate school. In addition to regional accreditation, MCPHS has baccalaureate program accreditation with ACPE and ADA. The library contains 54,800 volumes, microform items, and audio/video tapes/CDs/DVDs, and subscribes to 32,800 periodicals including electronic. Computerized library services include interlibrary loans, database searching, Internet access, and laptop Internet portals. Special learning facilities include a learning resource center, pharmacy labs, dental hygiene clinic, and nursing labs. The 2-acre campus is in an urban area 1 mile from the center of Boston. Including any residence halls, there are 3 buildings.

Programs of Study: MCPHS confers B.S. and B.S.N. degrees. Master's and doctoral degrees are also awarded. Bachelor's degrees are awarded in COMPUTER AND PHYSICAL SCIENCE (chemistry and radiological technology), HEALTH PROFESSIONS (dental hygiene, health science, nuclear medical technology, nursing, pharmaceutical science, and premedicine). Pharmacy and nursing are the largest.

Special: MCPHS offers cross-registration with the other colleges of the Fenway Consortium and cooperative programs with several schools. Accelerated degrees and dual majors are available in some programs. There are 2 national honor societies.

Admissions: 43% of the 2009-2010 applicants were accepted. The SAT scores for the 2009-2010 freshman class were: Critical Reading--31% below 500, 55% between 500 and 599, 13% between 600 and 700, and 1% above 700; Math--16% below 500, 47% between 500 and 599, 34% between 600 and 700, and 4% above 700; Writing--26% below 500, 51% between 500 and 599, 22% between 600 and

700, and 1% above 700. The ACT scores were 20% below 21, 28% between 21 and 23, 34% between 24 and 26, 14% between 27 and 28, and 4% above 28.

Requirements: The SAT or ACT is required. In addition, applicants must graduate from an accredited secondary school with 16 units, including 4 of English, 3 of math, 2 of lab science, 1 of history, and 6 of other college-preparatory subjects. The college also advises advanced chemistry or physics with lab and an extra unit of math. Interviews are recommended. Letters of reference from a guidance counselor and a science or math teacher and 2 student essays are required. AP and CLEP credits are accepted. Important factors in the admissions decision are evidence of special talent, recommendations by school officials, and advanced placement or honors courses.

Procedure: Freshmen are admitted in fall. Entrance exams should be taken by December of the senior year. There are early admissions and deferred admissions plans. Applications should be filed by February 1 for fall entry. The fall 2009 application fee was $70. Notifications are sent April 1. Applications are accepted on-line.

Financial Aid: The average freshman award in 2009-2010 was $14,986. 20% of undergraduate students work part-time. Average annual earnings from campus work are $1200. MCPHS is a member of CSS. The FAFSA is required. The deadline for filing freshman financial aid applications for fall entry is March 15.

Computers: Wireless access is available. MPCHS provides Internet access in dorms, computer labs, hallway kiosks, and the library. There are more than 500 computers available to students. All students may access the system. There are no time limits and no fees. It is strongly recommended that all students have a personal computer.

MASSACHUSETTS INSTITUTE OF TECHNOLOGY

Cambridge, MA 02139   **(617) 253-3400; (617) 258-8304**

Full-time: 2300 men, 1901 women	**Faculty:** 1018; I, ++$
Part-time: 16 men, 15 women	**Ph.D.s:** 98%
Graduate: 4236 men, 1916 women	**Student/Faculty:** 4 to 1
Year: 4-1-4, summer session	**Tuition:** $37,782
Application Deadline: January 1	**Room & Board:** $11,360
Freshman Class: 15663 applied, 1676 accepted, 1072 enrolled	
SAT CR/M/W: 715/770/710	**ACT:** 33 **MOST COMPETITIVE**

Massachusetts Institute of Technology, founded in 1861, is a private, independent institution offering programs in architecture and planning, engineering, humanities, arts, and social sciences, management, science, and health sciences, and technology. There are 5 undergraduate schools and 6 graduate schools. In addition to regional accreditation, MIT has baccalaureate program accreditation with AACSB, ABET, and CSAB. The 7 libraries contain 3.1 million volumes, 2.4 million microform items, and 41,523 audio/video tapes/CDs/DVDs, and subscribe to 60,105 periodicals including electronic. Computerized library services include interlibrary loans, database searching, Internet access, and laptop Internet portals. Special learning facilities include an art gallery, radio station, TV station, and numerous labs and centers. The 168-acre campus is in an urban area 1 mile north of Boston. Including any residence halls, there are 142 buildings.

Programs of Study: MIT confers B.S. degrees. Master's and doctoral degrees are also awarded. Bachelor's degrees are awarded in BIOLOGICAL SCIENCE (biology/biological science and neurosciences), BUSINESS (management science), COMMUNICATIONS AND THE ARTS (creative writing, digital communications, linguistics, literature, media arts, and music), COMPUTER AND PHYSICAL SCIENCE (chemistry, computer science, earth science, mathematics, physics, and science technology), ENGINEERING AND ENVIRONMENTAL DESIGN (aeronautical engineering, aerospace studies, architecture, biomedical engineering, chemical engineering, civil engineering, electrical/electronics engineering, engineering, environmental engineering, materials engineering, materials science, mechanical engineering, nuclear engineering, and ocean engineering), SOCIAL SCIENCE (anthropology, archeology, cognitive science, economics, French studies, history, humanities, philosophy, political science/government, Spanish studies, and urban studies). Engineering is the largest.

Special: MIT offers cross-registration with Harvard, Wellesley, the Massachusetts College of Art and Design, and the School of the Museum of Fine Arts. Internships are offered in a number of programs. Study abroad is offered at the Cambridge University in England as part of the Cambridge-MIT Undergraduate Exchange. The Department of Aeronautics and Astronautics and Materials, Science, and Engineering have specific exchange programs. The Undergraduate Research Opportunities Program (UROP) offers students research work with faculty. There are 10 national honor societies, including Phi Beta Kappa.

Admissions: 11% of the 2009-2010 applicants were accepted. The SAT scores for the 2009-2010 freshman class were: Critical Reading--1% below 500, 5% between 500 and 599, 34% between 600 and 700, and 60% above 700; Math--12% between 600 and 700 and 88% above 700; Writing--6% between 500 and 599, 34% between 600 and 700, and 60% above 700. The ACT scores were 1% between 24 and 26, 4% between 27 and 28, and 95% above 28. All of the current freshmen were in the top fifth of their class. 232 freshmen graduated first in their class.

Requirements: The SAT or ACT is required. The ACT Optional Writing test is also required. In addition, 2 SAT Subject tests, including 1 math and 1 science, are required. 14 academic units are recommended, including 4 each of English, math, and science, 2 of social studies, and a foreign language. The GED is accepted. Essays, 2 teacher evaluations, an official transcript, and a guidance counselor report are required. An interview is strongly recommended. AP credits are accepted.

Procedure: Freshmen are admitted in the fall. Entrance exams should be taken by the January test date. There are early admissions and deferred admissions plans. Applications should be filed by January 1 for fall entry. The fall 2008 application fee was $75. Notifications are sent March 20. Applications are accepted on-line. 455 applicants were on a recent waiting list, 78 were accepted.

Financial Aid: In 2009-2010, 87% of all full-time freshmen and 76% of continuing full-time students received some form of financial aid. 67% of all full-time freshmen and 63% of continuing full-time students received need-based aid. The average freshman award was $32,430. Need-based scholarships or need-based grants averaged $35,271 ($57,389 maximum); need-based self-help aid (loans and jobs) averaged $3260 ($4750 maximum). 64% of undergraduate students work part-time. Average annual earnings from campus work are $2930. The average financial indebtedness of the 2009 graduate was $15,043. MIT is a member of CSS. The CSS/Profile, FAFSA, parent W-2s and 1040s, and the business tax form are required. The deadline for filing freshman financial aid applications for fall entry is February 15.

Computers: Wireless access is available. Students may use the wireless network with their own computers; students in dorms can access wireless as well as wired networks. All students have their own computers and/or loaners. In addition, there are more than 1000 public-access computers on campus. All students may access the system at all times. There are no time limits and no fees.

McDaniel College, founded in 1867 as Western Maryland College, is a private college offering programs in the liberal arts. Figures in the above capsule and this profile are approximate. There is 1 graduate school. In addition to regional accreditation, The Hill has baccalaureate program accreditation with CSWE and NCATE. The library contains 206,483 volumes, 1.4 million microform items, and 12,942 audio/video tapes/CDs/DVDs, and subscribes to 21,062 periodicals including electronic. Computerized library services include interlibrary loans, database searching, Internet access, and laptop Internet portals. Special learning facilities include an art gallery, radio station, TV station, physics observatory, and student research science labs. The 160-acre campus is in a suburban area 30 miles northwest of Baltimore. Including any residence halls, there are 62 buildings.

Programs of Study: The Hill confers B.A. degrees. Master's degrees are also awarded. Bachelor's degrees are awarded in BIOLOGICAL SCIENCE (biology/biological science), BUSINESS (business administration and management), COMMUNICATIONS AND THE ARTS (art history and appreciation, communications, dramatic arts, English, fine arts, French, German, music, and Spanish), COMPUTER AND PHYSICAL SCIENCE (chemistry, computer science, mathematics, and physics), EDUCATION (physical education), ENGINEERING AND ENVIRONMENTAL DESIGN (environmental science), SOCIAL SCIENCE (economics, history, philosophy, political science/government, psychology, religion, social work, and sociology). Business administration, psychology, and biology are the largest.

Special: Internships are available in all majors. Study abroad is available around the world including McDaniel's program in Budapest. There is a Washington semester in conjunction with American University and 3-2 engineering programs with Washington University and the University of Maryland. The college offers work-study programs, dual and student-designed majors, credit by exam (in foreign languages), and pass/fail options. McDaniel College has a 5-year deaf education program and offers certification in elementary and secondary education. The college also offers advanced standing for international baccalaureate recipients. There are 20 national honor societies, including Phi Beta Kappa, a freshman honors program, and 24 departmental honors programs.

Admissions: 8 freshmen graduated first in their class in a recent year.

Requirements: The SAT is required. In addition, applicants must be graduates of an accredited secondary school or have a GED. A minimum of 16 academic credits are required, including 4 years of English, 3 each of foreign language, math, and social studies, and 2 of a lab science. SAT Subject tests and an interview are recommended. An essay and academic recommendations are required.

The Hill requires applicants to be in the upper 50% of their class. A GPA of 2.5 is required. AP and CLEP credits are accepted. Important factors in the admissions decision are advanced placement or honors courses, leadership record, and evidence of special talent.

Procedure: Freshmen are admitted fall and spring. Entrance exams should be taken at the end of the junior year. There is a deferred admissions plan. Check with the school for current application deadlines. The fall 2009 application fee was $50. Applications are accepted on-line. 111 applicants were on a recent waiting list, 23 were accepted.

Financial Aid: In a recent year, 89% of all full-time freshmen and 83% of continuing full-time students received some form of financial aid. 71% of all full-time freshmen and 65% of continuing full-time students received need-based aid. The average freshman award was $23,294. 18% of undergraduate students work part-time. Average annual earnings from campus work are $866. The average financial indebtedness of a recent graduate was $22,753. The FAFSA and the college's own financial statement are required. Check with the school for current application deadlines.

Computers: Wireless access is available. All students may access the system. 1 lab is open 24 hours per day; other labs are open 8:30 A.M. to midnight daily. There are no time limits and no fees.

MERCER UNIVERSITY
Macon, GA 31207-0001

(478) 301-2650
(800) 840-8577; (478) 301-2828

Full-time: 1056 men, 1211 women	**Faculty:** 173; IIA, av$
Part-time: 21 men, 20 women	**Ph.D.s:** 88%
Graduate: 1279 men, 2262 women	**Student/Faculty:** 13 to 1
Year: semesters, summer session	**Tuition:** $29,540
Application Deadline: see profile	**Room & Board:** $8788
Freshman Class: n/av	
SAT or ACT: required	**VERY COMPETITIVE+**

Mercer University, founded in 1833, is a faith-based, private institution of higher learning that seeks to achieve excellence and scholarly discipline in the fields of liberal learning and professional knowledge. The university offers degree programs in liberal arts, music, business and economics, education, engineering, and professional studies. Mercer also offers a Great Books program as an alternative to the traditional core curriculum. There are 5 undergraduate schools and 8 graduate schools. In addition to regional accreditation, Mercer has baccalaureate program accreditation with AACSB, ABET, NASM, and NCATE. The 2 libraries contain 796,693 volumes, 3.0 million microform items, and 68,619 audio/video tapes/CDs/DVDs, and subscribe to 25,037 periodicals including electronic. Computerized library services include interlibrary loans, database searching, and Internet access. Special learning facilities include a learning resource center, radio station, TV station, and music building. The 130-acre campus is in a suburban area 85 miles south of Atlanta.

Programs of Study: Mercer confers B.A., B.S., B.B.A., B.M., B.M.E., B.S.E., B.S.E.D., B.S.M., and B.S.N. degrees. Master's and doctoral degrees are also awarded. Bachelor's degrees are awarded in BIOLOGICAL SCIENCE (biochemistry and biology/biological science), BUSINESS (business administration and management), COMMUNICATIONS AND THE ARTS (art, communications, dramatic arts, French, German, journalism, Latin, media arts, music, and Spanish), COMPUTER AND PHYSICAL SCIENCE (chemistry, computer science, earth science, information sciences and systems, mathematics, natural sciences, and physics), EDUCATION (early childhood education, elementary education, music education, secondary education, special education, and technical education), ENGINEERING AND ENVIRONMENTAL DESIGN (computational sciences, engineering, environmental science, and industrial administration/management), HEALTH PROFESSIONS (predentistry, premedicine, and prepharmacy), SOCIAL SCIENCE (African American studies, Christian studies, economics, gender studies, history, philosophy, political science/government, prelaw, psychology, religion, social science, sociology, and women's studies). Engineering, biology, and psychology are the largest.

Special: Mercer offers co-op programs in all majors, cross-registration with Wesleyan and Macon State Colleges, B.A.-B.S. degrees in various science and math fields, internships, student-designed majors, work-study programs, and satisfactory-unsatisfactory options for elective courses. Mercer offers a wide variety of study-abroad opportunities, including independent semester or year-long programs, faculty-led programs, or Mercer on Mission. There are 2 national honor societies, a freshman honors program, and 20 departmental honors programs.

Requirements: The SAT or ACT is required. In addition, applicants must be graduates of an accredited secondary school and have completed 16 academic units. Students should submit their transcript and class rank, a recommendation from a guidance counselor, and a list of extracurricular activities, including employment. A GPA of 3.0 is required. AP and CLEP credits are accepted.

Procedure: Freshmen are admitted fall, spring, and summer. Entrance exams should be taken in the spring of the junior year or fall of the senior year. There are deferred admissions and rolling admissions plans. Check with the school for current application deadlines. The fall 2009 application fee was $50. Notification is sent on a rolling basis.

Financial Aid: 77% of all full-time freshmen received need-based aid. The average financial indebtedness of the 2009 graduate was $29,065. The FAFSA and the college's own financial statement are required. The deadline for filing freshman financial aid applications for fall entry is April 1.

Computers: Wireless access is available. All students may access the system. 24 hours per day if they have dial-in access. There are no time limits and no fees. It is strongly recommended that all students have a personal computer.

MESSIAH COLLEGE
Grantham, PA 17027

(717) 691-6000
(800) 233-4220; (717) 796-5374

Full-time: 1025 men, 1750 women	**Faculty:** IIB, -$
Part-time: 25 men, 35 women	**Ph.D.s:** n/av
Graduate: none	**Student/Faculty:** 16 to 1
Year: semesters, summer session	**Tuition:** $26,700
Application Deadline: open	**Room & Board:** $7490
Freshman Class: n/av	
SAT or ACT: required	**VERY COMPETITIVE**

Messiah College, founded in 1909, is a private Christian college of the liberal and applied arts and sciences. The college is committed to the evangelical spirit rooted in the Anabaptist, Pietist, and Wesleyan traditions. There are 5 undergraduate schools. Enrollment figures in the above capsule and figures in this profile are approximate. In addition to regional accreditation, Messiah has baccalaureate program accreditation with ABET, ADA, CSWE, NASAD, and NASM. The library contains 297,257 volumes, 119,622 microform items, and 20,519 audio/

video tapes/CDs/DVDs, and subscribes to 27,958 periodicals including electronic. Computerized library services include interlibrary loans, database searching, and Internet access. Special learning facilities include a learning resource center, art gallery, natural history museum, and radio station. The 471-acre campus is in a small town 12 miles southwest of Harrisburg. Including any residence halls, there are 52 buildings.

Programs of Study: Messiah confers B.A., B.S., B.S.E., B.S.N., and B.S.W degrees. Bachelor's degrees are awarded in AGRICULTURE (environmental studies), BIOLOGICAL SCIENCE (biochemistry, biology/biological science, and nutrition), BUSINESS (accounting, business administration and management, entrepreneurial studies, international business management, management information systems, marketing/retailing/merchandising, personnel management, and sports management), COMMUNICATIONS AND THE ARTS (art history and appreciation, arts administration/management, broadcasting, communications, dramatic arts, English, French, German, journalism, music, Spanish, and studio art), COMPUTER AND PHYSICAL SCIENCE (chemistry, computer science, mathematics, and physics), EDUCATION (art education, athletic training, early childhood education, elementary education, English education, environmental education, foreign languages education, mathematics education, music education, physical education, recreation education, science education, and social studies education), ENGINEERING AND ENVIRONMENTAL DESIGN (engineering and environmental science), HEALTH PROFESSIONS (exercise science and nursing), SOCIAL SCIENCE (biopsychology, criminal justice, dietetics, economics, family/consumer studies, history, human development, humanities, interdisciplinary studies, ministries, philosophy, political science/government, psychology, social work, sociology, Spanish studies, and theological studies). Nursing, elementary education, and biology are the largest.

Special: Students may cross-register at Temple University in Philadelphia. Off-campus study is available through Brethren Colleges Abroad, at Jerusalem University College at Oxford University, in Thailand, and through Latin American, Central American, Middle East, and Russian studies programs, among others. Off-campus options within the United States include the American and Urban Studies programs, the AuSable Institute of Environmental Studies, Los Angeles Film Studies, Oregon Extension, and others. Students may also spend a semester or a year at any of 12 other Christian Consortium colleges in a student exchange program. Numerous internships, practicums, and ministry opportunities are available. There are 7 national honor societies, a freshman honors program, and 17 departmental honors programs.

Requirements: The SAT or ACT is required for some programs. Applicants graduating in the top 20% of their class have a scoreless option that requires an interview. Applicants must have graduated from an accredited high school or the equivalent. Secondary preparation of students who enroll usually includes 4 units in English, 3 or 4 in math, 3 each in natural science, social studies, and foreign languages, and 4 in academic electives. Students who enroll are usually in the top one third of their class and have a B average or better. A campus visit with an interview/information session is recommended. Potential music majors must audition. AP and CLEP credits are accepted. Important factors in the admissions decision are leadership record, recommendations by school officials, and advanced placement or honors courses.

Procedure: Freshmen are admitted fall and spring. Entrance exams should be taken in the spring of the junior year. There is a rolling admissions plan. Application deadlines are open. Application fee is $30. Notification is sent on a rolling basis. Applications are accepted on-line ($20 fee waived if received prior to November 15). A waiting list is maintained.

Financial Aid: In a recent year, 99% of all full-time freshmen and 96% of continuing full-time students received some form of financial aid. 71% of all full-time freshmen and 68% of continuing full-time students received need-based aid. The average freshmen award was $19,433. 58% of undergraduate students work part-time. Average annual earnings from campus work are $1898. The average financial indebtedness of a recent graduate was $33,283. Messiah is a member of CSS. The FAFSA is required. Check with the school for current deadlines.

Computers: Wireless access is available. All students may access the system 24 hours a day. There are no time limits and no fees.

METROPOLITAN COLLEGE OF NEW YORK
New York, NY 10013   (212) 343-1234, ext. 5001; (212) 343-8470

Full-time: 631 men and women	**Faculty:** n/av
Part-time: 45 men and women	**Ph.D.s:** 84%
Graduate: 409 men and women	**Student/Faculty:** n/av
Year: semesters, summer session	**Tuition:** $16,720
Application Deadline: open	**Room & Board:** n/app
Freshman Class: 650 applied, 330 accepted, 126 enrolled	

VERY COMPETITIVE

Metropolitan College of New York, founded in 1964, is a private commuter institution offering programs in human services and business management. All bachelor degree programs involve a combination of class work and field work and may be completed in 2 years and 8 months. Most master's degree programs can be completed in 1 year. There are 2 undergraduate schools and 2 graduate schools. The library contains 32,000 volumes and 1800 microform items, and subscribes to 3300 periodicals including electronic. Computerized library services include interlibrary loans, database searching, and Internet access. Special learning facilities include a learning resource center. The campus is in an urban area in New York City. There is 1 building.

Programs of Study: The college confers B.B.A. and B.P.S. degrees. Associate and master's degrees are also awarded. Bachelor's degrees are awarded in BUSINESS (business administration and management), EDUCATION (early childhood education), HEALTH PROFESSIONS (mental health/human services), SOCIAL SCIENCE (child care/child and family studies, community services, gerontology, human services, prelaw, psychology, and social work). Business management is the strongest academically. Human services is the largest.

Special: Internships include required weekly 14-hour field sites. Study abroad in 3 countries, work-study programs, B.A.-B.S. degrees, and accelerated degree programs in human services, business management, and American urban studies are offered, as well as credit by exam and credit for life experience.

Admissions: 51% of the 2009-2010 applicants were accepted.

Requirements: Students must take the ETS's Accuplacer Test in reading and math; recent high school graduates who have a satisfactory SAT score may present the SAT instead. Applicants must have graduated from an accredited secondary school. The GED is accepted. An essay and an interview are required. CLEP credits are accepted. Important factors in the admissions decision are evidence of special talent, leadership record, and personality/intangible qualities.

Procedure: Freshmen are admitted to all sessions. Entrance exams should be taken in the senior year. There are deferred admissions and rolling admissions plans.

Applications should be filed by December 1 for spring entry and April 1 for summer entry, along with a $30 fee. Applications are accepted on-line.

Financial Aid: In 2009-2010, 96% of all full-time freshmen and 90% of continuing full-time students received some form of financial aid. The average freshman award was $13,611. Need-based scholarships or need-based grants averaged $10,154; need-based self-help aid (loans and jobs) averaged $3517. The CSS/Profile, FAFSA, and the New York State Higher Education Financial Statement are required. The priority date for freshman financial aid applications for fall entry is March. The deadline for filing freshman financial aid applications for fall entry is August 15.

Computers: All students may access the system whenever the college is open. There are no time limits. The fee is $100. It is strongly recommended that all students have a personal computer.

METROPOLITAN STATE COLLEGE OF DENVER

Denver, CO 80217-3362	(303) 556-3058; (303) 556-6345
Full-time: 5875 men, 7035 women	**Faculty:** n/av
Part-time: 3705 men, 4845 women	**Ph.D.s:** n/av
Graduate: none	**Student/Faculty:** n/av
Year: semesters, summer session	**Tuition:** $4500 ($12,000)
Application Deadline: see profile	**Room & Board:** n/app
Freshman Class: n/av	
SAT or ACT: required	**LESS COMPETITIVE**

Metropolitan State College of Denver, founded in 1963, is a public commuter institution offering degree programs in the liberal arts and sciences, business, and professional studies, as well as individualized degree programs. Figures in the above capsule are approximate. There are 3 undergraduate schools. In addition to regional accreditation, Metro State has baccalaureate program accreditation with AACSB, ABET, CSWE, NASAD, NASM, NCATE, NLN, and NRPA. The library contains 692,677 volumes, 1.1 million microform items, and 16,975 audio/video tapes/CDs/DVDs, and subscribes to 4150 periodicals including electronic. Computerized library services include interlibrary loans and database searching. Special learning facilities include a learning resource center, art gallery, radio station, TV station, world indoor airport, writing center, and student support services. The 175-acre campus is in an urban area in Denver. There are 38 buildings.

Programs of Study: Metro State confers B.A., B.S., and B.F.A. degrees. Bachelor's degrees are awarded in BIOLOGICAL SCIENCE (biology/biological science), BUSINESS (accounting, banking and finance, hospitality management services, management science, marketing/retailing/merchandising, and recreation and leisure services), COMMUNICATIONS AND THE ARTS (art, communications, English, fine arts, industrial design, journalism, modern language, music performance, Spanish, and speech/debate/rhetoric), COMPUTER AND PHYSICAL SCIENCE (atmospheric sciences and meteorology, chemistry, computer management, computer science, information sciences and systems, mathematics, and physics), EDUCATION (music education and physical education), ENGINEERING AND ENVIRONMENTAL DESIGN (airline piloting and navigation, aviation administration/management, aviation computer technology, civil engineering technology, electrical/electronics engineering technology, environmental science, industrial administration/management, industrial engineering technology, land use management and reclamation, mechanical engineering technology, survey and mapping technology, and surveying engineering), HEALTH PROFESSIONS (health care administration and nursing), SOCIAL SCIENCE (African American studies, anthropology, behavioral science, criminal justice, economics, history, human services, Mexican-American/Chicano studies, philosophy, physical fitness/movement, political science/government, psychology, social work, sociology, and urban studies). Criminal justice, psychology, and management are the largest.

Special: Metro State offers co-op and service-learning programs in most majors and cross-registration with a consortium of state colleges and the University of Colorado at Denver. Internships, study abroad, work-study programs, dual majors, student-designed majors, an accelerated degree program in nursing, nondegree study, and pass/fail options are available. There are 9 national honor societies, a freshman honors program, and 10 departmental honors programs.

Requirements: The SAT or ACT is required. In addition, applicants should be graduates of an accredited secondary school, with 15 Carnegie units. The GED is accepted. AP and CLEP credits are accepted. Important factors in the admissions decision are recommendations by school officials, extracurricular activities record, and evidence of special talent.

Procedure: Freshmen are admitted to all sessions. Entrance exams should be taken prior to application. There is a rolling admissions plan. Check with the school for current application deadlines. The fall 2009 application fee was $25. Applications are accepted on-line.

Financial Aid: Metro State is a member of CSS. The FAFSA is required. Check with the school for current application deadlines.

Computers: All students may access the system. Labs are open 96 hours a week. There are no time limits.

METROPOLITAN STATE UNIVERSITY
St. Paul, MN 55106   (651) 793-1305; (651) 793-1310

Full-time: 900 men, 1200 women	**Faculty:** IIA, av$
Part-time: 1450 men, 2420 women	**Ph.D.s:** 81%
Graduate: 230 men, 325 women	**Student/Faculty:** n/av
Year: quarters, summer session	**Tuition:** $5610 ($11,160)
Application Deadline: see profile	**Room & Board:** n/app
Freshman Class: n/av	
SAT or ACT: recommended	**SPECIAL**

Metropolitan State University, founded in 1971, is a public institution primarily serving working adults through a variety of majors and individually designed degree programs. Figures in the above capsule and this profile are approximate. There are 6 undergraduate schools and 2 graduate schools. In addition to regional accreditation, Metro State has baccalaureate program accreditation with NLN. The 2 libraries contain 33,655 volumes and 5112 audio/video tapes/CDs/DVDs, and subscribe to 242 periodicals including electronic. Computerized library services include interlibrary loans, database searching, Internet access, and laptop Internet portals. Special learning facilities include a learning resource center and art gallery. The campus is composed of several small dispersed sites throughout the Twin Cities Metro area. There are 7 buildings.

Programs of Study: Metro State confers B.A., B.S., B.A.S., and B.S.N. degrees. Master's degrees are also awarded. Bachelor's degrees are awarded in BIOLOGICAL SCIENCE (biology/biological science), BUSINESS (accounting, banking and finance, business administration and management, hospitality management services, human resources, international business management, management in formation systems, marketing and distribution, marketing management, operations management, and trade and industrial supervision and management), COMMUNICATIONS AND THE ARTS (advertising, communications, dramatic arts, English, playwriting/screenwriting, and technical and business writing), COMPUTER AND PHYSICAL SCIENCE (applied mathematics, computer science, computer security and information assurance, and information sciences and systems), EDUCATION (early childhood education), HEALTH PROFESSIONS (nursing), SOCIAL SCIENCE (addiction studies, child psychology/development, criminal justice, developmental psychology, early childhood studies, economics, ethnic studies, food production/management/services, history, human services, law enforcement and corrections, liberal arts/general studies, philosophy, psychology, public administration, social science, social work, and women's studies). Nursing is the strongest academically. Accounting and business administration are the largest.

Special: Internships, co-op programs in many areas, study abroad, dual majors, and student-designed programs are offered. There is departmental honors program.

Requirements: The SAT or ACT is recommended. Metro State requires applicants to be in the upper 50% of their class or have ACT, PSAT, or SAT scores at or above the national median. Applicants not meeting these requirements will be considered in the alternative admissions process. The GED is accepted. AP and CLEP credits are accepted.

Procedure: Freshmen are admitted to all sessions. There is a deferred admissions plan. Check with the school for current application deadlines. The fall 2009 application fee was $20. Notification is sent on a rolling basis. Applications are accepted on-line.

Financial Aid: Metro State is a member of CSS. The FAFSA is required. Check with the school for current application deadlines.

Computers: Wireless access is available. All students may access the system. There are no time limits.

MIAMI UNIVERSITY
Oxford, OH 45056   **(513) 529-2531; (513) 529-1550**

Full-time: 6751 men, 7706 women	**Faculty:** 827; I, --$
Part-time: 120 men, 94 women	**Ph.D.s:** 89%
Graduate: 696 men, 1517 women	**Student/Faculty:** 17 to 1
Year: semesters, summer session	**Tuition:** $12,420 ($26,778)
Application Deadline: February 1	**Room & Board:** $9458
Freshman Class: 16772 applied, 13223 accepted, 3236 enrolled	
SAT CR/M: 580/610	**ACT:** 26 **VERY COMPETITIVE+**

Miami University, founded in 1809, is a public institution offering a variety of programs in the liberal arts and pre-professional-vocational training. There are 6 undergraduate schools and one graduate school. In addition to regional accreditation, has baccalaureate program accreditation with AACSB, ABET, ADA, CSWE, FIDER, NAAB, NASAD, NASM, NCATE, and NLN. The 4 libraries contain 2.7 million volumes, 3.0 million microform items, 26,468 audio/video tapes/CDs/DVDs, and subscribe to 13,710 periodicals including electronic. Computerized library services include interlibrary loans, database searching, Internet access, and laptop Internet portals. Special learning facilities include a learning resource center, art gallery, natural history museum, radio station, and TV station. The 1921-acre campus is in a small town 35 miles north of Cincinnati, OH. Including any residence halls, there are 162 buildings.

Programs of Study: Miami cfers B.A., B.S., B.E.D., B.F.A., B.Mus., and B.Phil. degrees. Associates, master's, and doctoral degrees are also awarded. Bachelor's degrees are awarded in BIOLOGICAL SCIENCE (biochemistry, biology/biological science, botany, microbiology, and zoology), BUSINESS (accounting, banking and finance, business administration and management, business economics, human resources, management information systems, management science, marketing/retailing/merchandising, operations research, organizational behavior, personnel management, purchasing/inventory management, and sports management), COMMUNICATIONS AND THE ARTS (art, art history and appreciation, broadcasting, communications, dramatic arts, English, fine arts, French, German, graphic design, Greek, Latin, linguistics, music, music performance, Russian, Spanish, speech/debate/rhetoric, and telecommunications), COMPUTER AND PHYSICAL SCIENCE (chemistry, computer science, geology, mathematics, physics, and statistics), EDUCATION (art education, athletic training, early childhood education, elementary education, foreign languages education, health education, middle school education, music education, physical education, science education, secondary education, and special education), ENGINEERING AND ENVIRONMENTAL DESIGN (architecture, electrical/electronics engineering, engineering, engineering management, engineering physics, engineering technology, environmental design, environmental science, interior design, manufacturing engineering, mechanical engineering, and paper and pulp science), HEALTH PROFESSIONS (exercise science, health, medical technology, nursing, premedicine, and speech pathology/audiology), SOCIAL SCIENCE (African American studies, American studies, anthropology, classical/ancient civilization, dietetics, economics, family/consumer studies, geography, history, interdisciplinary studies, international relations, international studies, philosophy, physical fitness/movement, political science/government, prelaw, psychology, public administration, religion, social science, social work, sociology, urban studies, and women's studies). Zoology, chemistry, and accountancy are the strongest academically. Marketing, finance, and zoology are the largest.

Special: The university offers cross-registration with Cincinnati area colleges, study abroad in 15 countries, co-op programs in the School of Applied Science, internships in health and sport studies and applied science, a 3-2 engineering degree with Case Western Reserve and Columbia Universities, and a 3-2 forestry degree with Duke University. Students may pursue student-designed majors through the Western Program or interdisciplinary majors, including decision sciences and history of art and architecture. There are 30 national honor societies, including Phi Beta Kappa, and a freshman honors program.

Admissions: 79% of the 2009-2010 applicants were accepted. The SAT scores for the 2009-2010 freshman class were: Critical Reading--11% below 500, 47% between 500 and 599, 35% between 600 and 700, and 7% above 700; Math--5% below 500, 36% between 500 and 599, 49% between 600 and 700, and 10% above 700. The ACT scores were 4% below 21, 20% between 21 and 23, 33% between 24 and 26, 18% between 27 and 28, and 25% above 28. 63% of the current freshmen were in the top fifth of their class; 92% were in the top two fifths.

Requirements: The SAT or ACT is required. The ACT Optional Writing test is also required. In addition, Applicants must complete either the ACT or the SAT. Candidates for admission must ordinarily be graduates of accredited secondary schools or hold the GED. Students should have completed 4 units of English, 3 each of math, science, and social studies/history, 2 of a foreign language, and 1 of fine arts. An audition, a portfolio, or an interview are required for direct admission to majors in the School of Fine Arts. AP and CLEP credits are accepted. Important factors in the admissions decision are advanced placement or honors courses, evidence of special talent, and extracurricular activities record.

Procedure: Freshmen are admitted to all sessions. Entrance exams should be taken by December of the senior year. There is an early decision addmission plan. Early decision applications should be filed by November 1; regular applications, by February 1 for fall entry and December 1 for spring entry, along with a $50 fee. Notification of early decision is sent December 15; regular decision, March 15. Applications are accepted on-line. 1024 applicants were on a recent waiting list, 802 were accepted.

Financial Aid: The FAFSA is required. The priority date for freshman financial aid applications for fall entry is February 15.

Computers: Wireless access is available. Approximately 1200 computers are available on campus for general use. The entire campus is equipped with a wireless campus network. All students may access the system. There are no time limits. The fee is $228. It is strongly recommended that all students have a personal computer.

MICHIGAN STATE UNIVERSITY
East Lansing, MI 48824   (517) 355-8332; (517) 353-1647

Full-time: 14855 men, 17345 women	**Faculty:** 2411; I, av$
Part-time: 1705 men, 1773 women	**Ph.Ds:** 90%
Graduate: 4017 men, 5471 women	**Student/Faculty:** 13 to 1
Year: semesters, summer session	**Tuition:** $7,945 ($19,697)
Application Deadline: July 25	**Room & Board:** $5,744
Freshman Class: 21844 applied, 16686 accepted, 7266 enrolled	
SAT: required	**ACT:** 24 **VERY COMPETITIVE**

Michigan State University, a pioneer land-grant institution, was founded in 1855. Its 14 colleges and more than 100 departments offer 200 undergraduate and 250 graduate fields of study. The university's Honors College offers students an alternative education program. There are 12 undergraduate schools and 13 graduate schools. In addition to regional accreditation, MSU has baccalaureate program accreditation with AACSB, ABET, ACEJMC, ADA, ASLA, CAHEA, CSWE, FIDER, NASM, NCATE, NLN, and SAF. The 10 libraries contain 4.5 million volumes, 5.6 million microform items, 299,287 audio/video tapes/CDs/DVDs, and subscribe to 33,760 periodicals including electronic. Computerized library services include inter-library loans, database searching, and Internet access. Special learning facilities include a learning resource center, art gallery, natural history museum, planetarium, radio station, TV station, a botanical garden, a superconducting cyclotron lab, environmental toxicology center, pesticide research center, a center for computer-aided and engineering and manufacturing. The 5239-acre campus is in a suburban area 80 miles northwest of Detroit. Including any residence halls, there are 564 buildings.

Programs of Study: MSU confers B.A., B.S., B.F.A., B.Land.Arch., B.Mus., and B.S. in Nursing degrees. Master's and doctoral degrees are also awarded. Bachelor's degrees are awarded in AGRICULTURE (agriculture, animal science, environmental studies, fishing and fisheries, forestry and related sciences, horticulture, natural resource management, soil science, and wildlife management), BIOLOGICAL SCIENCE (biochemistry, bioinformatics, biology/biological science, biotechnology, botany, entomology, environmental biology, microbiology, nutrition, physiology, plant pathology, and zoology), BUSINESS (accounting, banking and finance, business administration and management, hospitality management services, human resources, marketing management, marketing/retailing/

merchandising, personnel management, and tourism), COMMUNICATIONS AND THE ARTS (advertising, art history and appreciation, communications, dramatic arts, East Asian languages and literature, English, French, German, jazz, journalism, Latin, linguistics, music, music performance, music theory and composition, Russian, Spanish, studio art, and telecommunications), COMPUTER AND PHYSICAL SCIENCE (astrophysics, chemical physics, chemistry, computer science, earth science, geology, geophysics and seismology, geoscience, information sciences and systems, mathematics, physical sciences, physics, and statistics), EDUCATION (agricultural education, art education, education, music education, physical education, and special education), ENGINEERING AND ENVIRONMENTAL DESIGN (chemical engineering, city/community/regional planning, civil engineering, computational sciences, computer engineering, construction management, electrical/electronics engineering, engineering, engineering mechanics, interior design, landscape architecture/design, manufacturing engineering, materials engineering, mechanical engineering, textile technology, and urban planning technology), HEALTH PROFESSIONS (clinical science, medical laboratory technology, music therapy, nursing, speech pathology/audiology, and veterinary science), SOCIAL SCIENCE (American studies, anthropology, child psychology/development, classical/ancient civilization, criminal justice, dietetics, economics, family and community services, family/consumer resource management, family/consumer studies, food production/management/services, food science, geography, history, humanities, interdisciplinary studies, parks and recreation management, philosophy, political science/government, prelaw, psychology, public administration, religion, social science, social work, sociology, and women's studies). Engineering, education, and business are the strongest academically. Business, communications, and social science are the largest.

Special: Special academic programs include an engineering co-op program with business and industry; internships in business, education, political science, agriculture, and communication arts; study abroad in more than 62 countries; on-campus work-study programs; and a sea semester. An accelerated degree program in all majors and student-designed majors are offered at the Honors College. Non-degree study, pass/fail options in some courses, and dual majors are possible. Educationally disadvantaged students may avail themselves of the College Achievement Admissions Program (CAAP). Cross-registration with the Committee on Institutional Cooperation schools is available. There are 48 national honor societies, including Phi Beta Kappa, and a freshman honors program.

Admissions: 76% of the 2009-2010 applicants were accepted. The ACT scores were 14% below 21, 26% between 21 and 23, 32% between 24 and 26, 14% between 27 and 28, and 14% above 28. 52% of the current freshmen were in the top fifth of their class; 89% were in the top two fifths.

Requirements: The SAT or ACT is required. In addition, applicants must be graduates of an accredited secondary school and have completed 4 years of English, 3 years each of math and social studies, 2 years of science, and 2 years of a single foreign language. A personal statement is strongly recommended. The GED is accepted. Music majors must audition. AP and CLEP credits are accepted. Important factors in the admissions decision are advanced placement or honors courses, recommendations by school officials, and evidence of special talent.

Procedure: Freshmen are admitted fall, spring, and summer. Entrance exams should be taken during the junior year of high school. There are deferred admissions and rolling admissions plans. Applications should be filed by July 25 for fall entry, December 1 for spring entry, and April 15 for summer entry. The fall 2008 application fee was $35. Applications are accepted on-line. 1524 applicants were on a recent waiting list, 228 were accepted.

Financial Aid: In 2009-2010, 93% of all full-time freshmen and 68% of continuing full-time students received some form of financial aid. 28% of all full-time freshmen and 22% of continuing full-time students received need-based aid. The average freshmen award was $7,148. The average financial indebtedness of the 2009 graduate was $18,121. The FAFSA is required. The priority date for freshman financial aid applications for fall entry is March 1. The deadline for filing freshman financial aid applications for fall entry is June 30.

Computers: All students may access the system. 24 hours per day; 7 days per week. There are no time limits and no fees. All students are required to have a personal computer.

MICHIGAN TECHNOLOGICAL UNIVERSITY
Houghton, MI 49931-1295

(906) 487-2335
(888) MTU-1885; (906) 487-2125

Full-time: 4063 men, 1096 women	**Faculty:** 349; I, --$
Part-time: 323 men, 132 women	**Ph.D.s:** 83%
Graduate: 601 men, 295 women	**Student/Faculty:** 15 to 1
Year: semesters, summer session	**Tuition:** $8,194 ($19,390)
Application Deadline: open	**Room & Board:** $6,375
Freshman Class: 3928 applied, 3326 accepted, 1327 enrolled	
SAT: required	**ACT:** 25 **VERY COMPETITIVE**

Michigan Technological University, founded in 1885, is a state-supported institution offering degrees in engineering, liberal arts, sciences, forestry, business, and technology. There are 5 undergraduate schools and one graduate school. In addition to regional accreditation, Michigan Tech has baccalaureate program accreditation with AACSB, ABET, and SAF. The library contains 821,263 volumes, 546,199 microform items, 5,228 audio/video tapes/CDs/DVDs, and subscribes to 2,891 periodicals including electronic. Computerized library services include inter-library loans, database searching, Internet access, and laptop Internet portals. Special learning facilities include a learning resource center, radio station, the A.E. Seaman Mineral Museum, the Rozsa Center for the Performing Arts, the Ford Forestry Center and Researh Forest, cosmic ray observatory, x-ray fluorescence spectrometer, process simulation and control center, remote sensing institute, computer-aided engineering lab, microfabrication lab, and subsurface visualization lab. The 925-acre campus is in a small town 325 miles northwest of Milwaukee, Wisconsin. Including any residence halls, there are 42 buildings.

Programs of Study: Michigan Tech confers B.A. and B.S. degrees. Associates, master's, and doctoral degrees are also awarded. Bachelor's degrees are awarded in AGRICULTURE (forestry and related sciences and wildlife management), BIOLOGICAL SCIENCE (bioinformatics, biology/biological science, and ecology), BUSINESS (business administration and management), COMMUNICATIONS AND THE ARTS (audio technology, communications, technical and business writing, and theater design), COMPUTER AND PHYSICAL SCIENCE (applied physics, chemistry, computer science, geology, geophysics and seismology, mathematics, physics, and software engineering), ENGINEERING AND ENVIRONMENTAL DESIGN (biomedical engineering, chemical engineering, civil engineering, computer engineering, construction management, electrical/electronics engineering, electrical/electronics engineering technology, engineering, environmental engineering, geological engineering, materials engineering, mechanical engineering, mechanical engineering technology, and surveying engineering), HEALTH PROFESSIONS (clinical science), SOCIAL SCIENCE (economics, history, liberal arts/general studies, psychology, and social science). Engineering, forestry, and physical science are the strongest academically. Mechanical, civil, and electrical engineering are the largest.

Special: Michigan Tech offers co-op programs in almost all majors, internships in medical technology and secondary teacher education, work-study programs, study abroad in more than 100 countries, duel majors, and a B.A-B.S. degree in scientific and technical communication. There are inter-institutional programs with Northwestern Michigan, Gogebic Community, and Delta Colleges. A 3-2 engineering degree is possible in conjunction with the University of Wisconsin/Superior, the College of St. Scholastica, and Adrian, Albion, Augsburg, Northland, and Olivet Colleges. There are 16 national honor societies.

Admissions: 85% of the 2009-2010 applicants were accepted. The ACT scores were 12% below 21, 22% between 21 and 23, 29% between 24 and 26, 17% between 27 and 28, and 20% above 28. 47% of the current freshmen were in the top fifth of their class; 76% were in the top two fifths. There were 8 National Merit finalists. 50 freshmen graduated first in their class.

Requirements: The SAT or ACT is required. In addition, scores are used for admission and placement. Admissions requirements include graduation from an accredited secondary school, with 15 academic credits. These must include 3 credits in English, 1 credit of chemistry or physics, and 3 credits in math for engineering and science curricula; credits in social studies and foreign language are recommended. The GED is accepted. AP and CLEP credits are accepted. Important factors in the admissions decision are advanced placement or honors courses, leadership record, and recommendations by school officials.

Procedure: Freshmen are admitted to all sessions. Entrance exams should be taken in the junior year or fall of their senior year. There are deferred admissions and rolling admissions plans. Application deadlines are open. The fall 2008 application fee was $40. Notification is sent on a rolling basis. Applications are accepted on-line.

Financial Aid: In 2009-2010, 91% of all full-time freshmen and 83% of continuing full-time students received some form of financial aid. 53% of all full-time freshmen and 51% of continuing full-time students received need-based aid. The average freshmen award was $9,452, with $3,486 ($18,750 maximum) from need-based scholarships or need-based grants; $8,271 ($2,300 maximum) from need-based self-help aid (loans and jobs); $7,995 ($18,750 maximum) from non-need-based athletic scholarships; and $3,148 ($18,750 maximum) from other non-need-based awards and non-need-based scholarships. 25% of undergraduate students work part-time. Average annual earnings from campus work are $6292. The average financial indebtedness of the 2009 graduate was $13,344. Michigan Tech is a member of CSS. The FAFSA is required. The priority date for freshman financial aid applications for fall entry is February 21.

Computers: PC workstations are located in departmental labs, classrooms, the campus library, and the student union. Wireless hotspots are located throughout campus. Workstations and hotspots are accessible to any enrolled student provided that they have a valid network login. There are approximately 1,300 workstations on campus and all have access to the internet. All students may access the system. 24 hours a day. There are no time limits. The fee is $varies with major.

Murfreesboro, TN 37132　　　　　　　　　　　**(615) 898-2111**
　　　　　　　　　　　　　　　　　　　　(800) 433-MTSU; (615) 898-5478

Full-time: 9204 men, 9708 women	**Faculty:** IIA, -$
Part-time: 1577 men, 1810 women	**Ph.D.s:** 68%
Graduate: 963 men, 1926 women	**Student/Faculty:** n/av
Year: semesters, summer session	**Tuition:** $4000 ($11,900)
Application Deadline: July 1	**Room & Board:** $4650
Freshman Class: 9431 applied, 6616 accepted, 1758 enrolled	
ACT: 22	**SAT:** required　　**COMPETITIVE**

Middle Tennessee State University, founded in 1911, is a comprehensive public university that offers undergraduate and graduate programs reflecting an emphasis on research, creative arts, and public and professional service activities. The tuition figures in the above capsule are approximate. There are 6 undergraduate schools and one graduate school. In addition to regional accreditation, MTSU has baccalaureate program accreditation with AACSB, ABET, ACEJMC, ADA, CSAB, CSWE, FIDER, NASAD, NASM, NCATE, NLN, and NRPA. The library contains 702,764 volumes, 1.3 million microform items, and 0 audio/video tapes/CDs/DVDs, and subscribes to 3,798 periodicals including electronic. Computerized library services include interlibrary loans, database searching, and Internet access. Special learning facilities include a learning resource center, art gallery, planetarium, radio station, TV station, and numerous research centers. The 500-acre campus is in an urban area 32 miles southeast of Nashville, TN. Including any residence halls, there are 159 buildings.

Programs of Study: MTSU confers B.A., B.S., B.B.A., B.F.A., B.Mus., B.S.N., B.S.W., and B.U.S. degrees. Master's and doctoral degrees are also awarded. Bachelor's degrees are awarded in AGRICULTURE (agricultural business management, animal science, and plant science), BIOLOGICAL SCIENCE (biology/ biological science and nutrition), BUSINESS (accounting, banking and finance, business administration and management, entrepreneurial studies, marketing/ retailing/merchandising, office supervision and management, and recreation and leisure services), COMMUNICATIONS AND THE ARTS (communications, English, French, German, graphic design, music, music business management, public relations, Spanish, and studio art), COMPUTER AND PHYSICAL SCIENCE (chemistry, computer science, information sciences and systems, mathematics, physics, and science), EDUCATION (art education, athletic training, business education, early childhood education, health education, physical education, and special education), ENGINEERING AND ENVIRONMENTAL DESIGN (engineering technology, environmental science, industrial engineering technology, and interior design), HEALTH PROFESSIONS (health science and nursing), SOCIAL SCIENCE (anthropology, criminal justice, economics, family/ consumer studies, geography, history, interdisciplinary studies, international relations, philosophy, political science/government, prelaw, psychology, public administration, social work, sociology, and textiles and clothing). Nursing and science is the strongest academically. Recording industry is the largest.

Special: MTSU offers co-op programs in aerospace, computer science, math, engineering technology, and industrial studies, cross-registration with Tennessee State University, internships, study abroad, work-study, double majors, a general studies degree, student-designed majors, nondegree study, and pass/fail options. Credit for life, military, and work experience may be granted. There are 2 national honor societies, a freshman honors program, and 25 departmental honors programs.

Admissions: 70% of the 2009-2010 applicants were accepted. The ACT scores were 32% below 21, 35% between 21 and 23, 20% between 24 and 26, 7% between 27 and 28, and 5% above 28. There were 2 National Merit finalists. 31 freshmen graduated first in their class.

Requirements: The SAT or ACT is required. In addition, applicants must have a minimum composite score of 22 on the ACT if the GPA is less than 3.0. A high school diploma is required, the GED is accepted. The number of academic credits required is 14, including 4 years of English, 3 of math, 2 each of a foreign language and science, and 1 each of social studies, U.S. history, and visual and/or performance arts, with an additional unit of math, language, or art recommended. A GPA of 3.0 is required. AP and CLEP credits are accepted.

Procedure: Freshmen are admitted to all sessions. Entrance exams should be taken in the first half of the senior year. There are deferred admissions and rolling admissions plans. Applications should be filed by July 1 for fall entry, along with a $25 fee. Notification is sent on a rolling basis. Applications are accepted online.

Financial Aid: In 2009-2010, 35% of all full-time freshmen and 52% of continuing full-time students received some form of financial aid. 19% of all full-time freshmen and 29% of continuing full-time students received need-based aid. The average freshman award was $6,265. Need-based scholarships or need-based grants averaged $2,295 ($6,150 maximum); need-based self-help aid (loans and jobs) averaged $1,589 ($10,500 maximum); non-need-based athletic scholarships averaged $11,180 ($9,500 maximum); and other non-need-based awards and non-need-based scholarships averaged $4,057 ($5,000 maximum). 84% of undergraduate students work part-time. Average annual earnings from campus work are $3200. The average financial indebtedness of the 2009 graduate was $19,800. The FAFSA is required. Check with the school for current application deadlines.

Computers: All students may access the system 24 hours a day. There are no time limits and no fees.

MIDDLEBURY COLLEGE

Middlebury, VT 05753	(802) 443-3000; (802) 443-2065
Full-time: 1211 men, 1245 women	**Faculty:** 260; IIB, +$
Part-time: 11 men, 15 women	**Ph.D.s:** 95%
Graduate: none	**Student/Faculty:** 9 to 1
Year: 4-1-4	**Tuition:** $50,780
Application Deadline: December 15	**Room & Board:** n/av
Freshman Class: 6904 applied, 1413 accepted, 603 enrolled	
SAT or ACT: required	**MOST COMPETITIVE**

Middlebury College, founded in 1800, is a small, private liberal arts institution offering degree programs in languages, humanities, and social and natural sciences. There are 2 graduate schools. The 3 libraries contain 795,024 volumes, 377,283 microform items, and 43,599 audio/video tapes/CDs/DVDs, and subscribe to 38,000 periodicals including electronic. Computerized library services include interlibrary loans, database searching, and Internet access. Special learning facilities include a learning resource center, art gallery, planetarium, and radio station. The 355-acre campus is in a small town 35 miles south of Burlington. Including any residence halls, there are 96 buildings.

Programs of Study: Midd confers A.B. degrees. Master's and doctoral degrees are also awarded. Bachelor's degrees are awarded in BIOLOGICAL SCIENCE (biochemistry, biology/biological science, molecular biology, and neurosciences), BUSINESS (international economics), COMMUNICATIONS AND THE ARTS (American literature, Chinese, classics, dance, dramatic arts, English, film arts, French, German, Italian, Japanese, literature, music, Russian, Spanish, and studio art), COMPUTER AND PHYSICAL SCIENCE (chemistry, computer science, geology, mathematics, and physics), ENGINEERING AND ENVIRONMENTAL DESIGN (architectural history and environmental science), SOCIAL SCIENCE (African studies, American studies, anthropology, East Asian studies, economics, European studies, geography, history, international studies, Latin American studies, liberal arts/general studies, Middle Eastern studies, philosophy, political science/government, psychology, religion, Russian and Slavic studies, sociology, and women's studies). Foreign languages, international studies, and the sciences are the strongest academically. Economics, environmental studies and English and American literature are the largest.

Special: Off-campus opportunities include an international major program at one of the Middlebury College schools abroad; exchange programs with Berea, St. Mary's, and Swarthmore; a junior year abroad; study through the American Collegiate Consortium for East-West Cultural and Academic Exchange; a 1-year program at Lincoln and Worcester Colleges, Oxford; a Washington, D.C., semester; and a maritime studies program with Williams College at Mystic Seaport. Middlebury also offers an independent scholar program, joint and double majors, various professional programs, dual degrees in business management, forestry/environmental studies, engineering, and nursing, and an early assurance premed program with Dartmouth, Rochester, Tufts, and the Medical College of Pennsylvania, which assures medical school acceptance by the end of the sophomore year. There is a Phi Beta Kappa and 10 departmental honors programs.

Admissions: 20% of the 2009-2010 applicants were accepted. The SAT scores for the 2009-2010 freshman class were: Critical Reading--2% below 500, 12% between 500 and 599, 37% between 600 and 700, and 495 above 700; Math--1% below 500, 8% between 500 and 599, 42% between 600 and 700, and 495 above 700; Writing--2% below 500, 8% between 500 and 599, 38% between 600 and 700, and 525 above 700. The ACT scores were 2% between 18 and 23, 20% between 24 and 29, and 78% above 30. 95% of the current freshmen were in the top fifth of their class; 99% were in the top two fifths.

Requirements: The SAT or ACT is required. Students must submit scores from the SAT, or the ACT, or 3 SAT Subject Tests in different areas of study. Secondary school preparation should include 4 years each of English, math and/or computer science, and 1 foreign language, 3 or more years of lab science and history and social science, and some study of music, art, and/or drama. AP credits are accepted. Important factors in the admissions decision are advanced placement or honors courses, recommendations by school officials, and evidence of special talent.

Procedure: Freshmen are admitted fall and spring. Entrance exams should be taken by December of the senior year. There are early decision and deferred admissions plans. Early decision applications should be filed by November 15 and regular applications by December 15 for fall entry, along with a $65 fee. Notification of early decision is sent December 15; regular decision, April 1. Applications are accepted on-line. 1527 applicants were on a recent waiting list.

Financial Aid: In 2009-2010, 43% of all full-time freshmen and 49% of continuing full-time students received some form of financial aid. 43% of all full-time freshmen and 49% of continuing full-time students received need-based aid. The average freshman award was $35,197. Need-based scholarships or need-based grants averaged $34,362; need-based self-help aid (loans and jobs) averaged

$3,668. 60% of undergraduate students work part-time. Average annual earnings from campus work are $675. The average financial indebtedness of the 2009 graduate was $21,458. Midd is a member of CSS. The CSS/Profile, FAFSA, the college's own financial statement, and federal tax forms are required. The priority date for freshman financial aid applications for fall entry is November 1. The deadline for filing freshman financial aid applications for fall entry is February 1.

Computers: Wireless access is available. All students may access the system 24 hours a day. There are no time limits and no fees.

MILLS COLLEGE
Oakland, CA 94613

(510) 430-2135
(800) 87-MILLS; (510) 430-3314

Full-time: 870 women	**Faculty:** 93; IIA, ++$
Part-time: 51 women	**Ph.D.s:** 88%
Graduate: 111 men, 469 women	**Student/Faculty:** 9 to 1
Year: semesters	**Tuition:** $36,232
Application Deadline: February 1	**Room & Board:** $11,480
Freshman Class: 1519 applied, 862 accepted, 162 enrolled	
SAT CR/M/W: 600/550/580	**ACT:** 25 **VERY COMPETITIVE**

Mills College, founded in 1852, is a private women's college offering instruction in liberal and fine arts, sciences, and teacher preparation. Graduate programs are coed. The library contains 239,682 volumes, 28,265 microform items, and 11,883 audio/video tapes/CDs/DVDs, and subscribes to 42,009 periodicals including electronic. Computerized library services include interlibrary loans, database searching, Internet access, and laptop Internet portals. Special learning facilities include an art gallery, radio station, a children's school, a small book press, an electronic/computer music studio, a botanical garden, and a computer learning studio. The 135-acre campus is in an urban area 12 miles east of San Francisco and 8 miles from Berkeley. Including any residence halls, there are 85 buildings.

Programs of Study: Mills confers B.A. and B.S. degrees. Master's and doctoral degrees are also awarded. Bachelor's degrees are awarded in AGRICULTURE (environmental studies), BIOLOGICAL SCIENCE (biochemistry, biology/ biological science, and molecular biology), BUSINESS (business economics), COMMUNICATIONS AND THE ARTS (art history and appreciation, comparative literature, creative writing, dance, English, French, media arts, modern language, music, Spanish, and studio art), COMPUTER AND PHYSICAL SCIENCE (chemistry, computer science, and mathematics), ENGINEERING AND ENVIRONMENTAL DESIGN (environmental science), SOCIAL SCIENCE (American studies, anthropology, biopsychology, child psychology/development, economics, ethnic studies, Hispanic American studies, history, international relations, liberal arts/general studies, philosophy, political science/government, psychology, public administration, public affairs, sociology, and women's studies). English, psychology, and political, legal, and economic analysis are the strongest academically. Biology and child development are the largest.

Special: There is cross-registration with the University of California at Berkeley, California State University, and California College of the Arts, among others. Mills offers co-op programs, internships, study abroad, a Washington semester, work-study programs, dual majors, student-designed majors, and interdisciplinary majors, including political, legal, and economic analysis. Accelerated degree programs include 3-2 engineering, 4+1 M.B.A., 4+1 M.P.P., a 4+1 B.A./M.A. program in which students graduate in 5 years with a bachelor's degree in psychology and a master's in infant mental health, and a 4+1 program in which students earn a B.A., an M.A. in education, and complete a program qualifying them for a teaching credential. A general studies degree, credit by exam, and pass/fail options are also available. Mills also offers a a 3-2 engineering degree with USC and a prenursing program leading to a bachelor's degree in nursing at Samuel Merritt College. There are 5 national honor societies, including Phi Beta Kappa.

Admissions: 57% of the 2009-2010 applicants were accepted. The SAT scores for the 2009-2010 freshman class were: Critical Reading--9% below 500, 39% between 500 and 599, 39% between 600 and 700, and 12% above 700; Math--24% below 500, 48% between 500 and 599, 25% between 600 and 700, and 3% above 700; Writing--12% below 500, 45% between 500 and 599, 35% between 600 and 700, and 7% above 700. The ACT scores were 11% below 21, 26% between 21 and 23, 28% between 24 and 26, 16% between 27 and 28, and 18% above 28. 33% of the current freshmen were in the top fifth of their class; 55% were in the top two fifths. 7 freshmen graduated first in their class.

Requirements: The SAT or ACT is required. In addition, SAT Subject Tests are recommended. Applicants should graduate from an accredited secondary school or have a GED. An essay is required; an interview, recommended. AP and CLEP credits are accepted. Important factors in the admissions decision are advanced placement or honors courses, personality/intangible qualities, and recommendations by school officials.

Procedure: Freshmen are admitted fall and spring. Entrance exams should be taken at least 1 month prior to application. There are early decision and deferred admissions plans. Early decision applications should be filed by November 15; regular applications, by February 1 for fall entry and November 1 for spring entry, along with a $50 fee. Notification of early decision is sent December 20; regular decision, March 30. 225 early decision candidates were accepted for the 2009-2010 class. Applications are accepted on-line.

Financial Aid: In 2009-2010, 97% of all full-time students received some form of financial aid. 87% of all full-time freshmen and 83% of continuing full-time students received need-based aid. The average freshman award was $36,878. Need-based scholarships or need-based grants averaged $25,963 and need-based self-help aid (loans and jobs) averaged $6204. The average financial indebtedness of the 2009 graduate was $25,642. The FAFSA and the college's own financial statement are required. The priority date for freshman financial aid applications for fall entry is February 15.

Computers: Wireless access is available. Internet access is available remotely or on campus via 341 public computers. Wireless access is also available in all residence and administrative buildings. All students may access the system 24 hours a day, year-round. There are no time limits. The fee is $290. Students enrolled in computer science and book arts must have a personal computer. A Mac or Dell is recommended.

Jackson, MS 39210
(601) 974-1050
(800) 352-1050; (601) 974-1059

Full-time: 495 men, 503 women	**Faculty:** 96; IIB, av$
Part-time: 15 men, 4 women	**Ph.D.s:** 94%
Graduate: 61 men, 39 women	**Student/Faculty:** 10 to 1
Year: semesters, summer session	**Tuition:** $26,240
Application Deadline: rolling	**Room & Board:** $9252
Freshman Class: 1348 applied, 992 accepted, 283 enrolled	
SAT CR/M: 580/580	**ACT:** 26 **VERY COMPETITIVE+**

Millsaps College, founded in 1890, is an independent liberal arts institution affiliated with the United Methodist Church. Millsaps College is known for its academic strength, national-caliber faculty, small class size, and spirit of community service. There is 1 graduate school. In addition to regional accreditation, Millsaps has baccalaureate program accreditation with AACSB and NCATE. The library contains 196,277 volumes, 81,603 microform items, and 8779 audio/video tapes/CDs/DVDs, and subscribes to 877 periodicals including electronic. Computerized library services include interlibrary loans, database searching, Internet access, and laptop Internet portals. Special learning facilities include an art gallery, an observatory, a multi-disciplinary laboratory, and a moclecular biology/functional genomics research lab. The 100-acre campus is in an urban area in the capital city of Jackson. Including any residence halls, there are 33 buildings.

Programs of Study: Millsaps confers B.A., B.S., and B.B.A. degrees. Master's degrees are also awarded. Bachelor's degrees are awarded in BIOLOGICAL SCIENCE (biochemistry and biology/biological science), BUSINESS (accounting and business administration and management), COMMUNICATIONS AND THE ARTS (art history and appreciation, classics, communications, dramatic arts, English, French, music, Spanish, and studio art), COMPUTER AND PHYSICAL SCIENCE (applied mathematics, chemistry, computer science, geology, mathematics, and physics), EDUCATION (education), SOCIAL SCIENCE (anthropology, economics, European studies, history, Latin American studies, philosophy, political science/government, psychology, public administration, religion, and sociology). Biology/chemistry/premed, sociology/anthropology, and business/accounting are the strongest academically. Business administration, psychology, and biology are the largest.

Special: Millsaps sponsors international studies programs in Africa, Asia, Europe, and Latin America. Direct exchange options are offered in Japan and Ireland. Students may also participate in a wide variety of field research, honors, internship, fellowships, and service learning programs. There are 24 national honor societies, including Phi Beta Kappa, and 19 departmental honors programs.

Admissions: 74% of the 2009-2010 applicants were accepted. The SAT scores for the 2009-2010 freshman class were: Critical Reading--20% below 500, 42% between 500 and 599, 24% between 600 and 699, and 13% above 700; Math--15% below 500, 42% between 500 and 599, 32% between 600 and 699, and 11% above 700. The ACT scores were 36% below 24, 45% between 24 and 29, 19% between 30 and 36. 43% of the current freshmen were in the top fifth of their class; 66% were in the top two-fifths. There were 2 National Merit finalists. 8 freshmen graduated first in their class.

Requirements: The SAT or ACT is required. In addition, applicants should be graduates of an accredited secondary school or have a GED certificate, and have completed at least 14 academic units, including 4 in English, 3 in math, 2 in social studies, and 2 in history. An essay is required. A GPA of 2.5 is required. AP and CLEP credits are accepted. Important factors in the admissions decision are advanced placement or honors courses, extracurricular activities record, and recommendations by school officials.

Procedure: Freshmen are admitted fall and spring. Entrance exams should be taken in the spring of the junior year or fall of the senior year. There are nonbinding early action admissions, deferred admissions, and rolling admissions plans. Application deadlines are open. Notification is sent on a rolling basis. Applications are accepted on-line.

Financial Aid: In 2009-2010, 99% of all full-time freshmen and 97% of continuing full-time students received some form of financial aid. 66% of all full-time freshmen and 55% of continuing full-time students received need-based aid. The average freshmen award was $27,605, with $22,158 ($38,178 maximum) from need-based scholarships or need-based grants; $5,264 ($11,100 maximum) from need-based self-help aid (loans and jobs); and $14,372 ($38,178 maximum) from other non-need-based awards and non-need-based scholarships. 68% of undergraduate students work part-time. Average annual earnings from campus work are $170. The average financial indebtedness of the 2009 graduate was $31,304. The FAFSA is required. The priority date for freshman financial aid applications for fall entry is March 1.

Computers: Wireless access is available. Millsap provides wireless network in all college owned buildings. Students have access to 120 computers across campus. There are student residential on-site consultants who are trained in network connectivity, software support and troubleshooting, student workshops, training and access to multimedia facilities. All students may access the system at any time. There are no time limits and no fees. It is strongly recommended that all students have a personal computer. Millsaps partners with Dell to offer students a discount of 12-15% per year, a 4 year warranty, and extended customer support.

MILWAUKEE SCHOOL OF ENGINEERING
Milwaukee, WI 53202-3109

(414) 277-6765
(800) 332-6763; (414) 277-7475

Full-time: 1831 men, 415 women	**Faculty:** 129; IIB, +$
Part-time: 151 men, 41 women	**Ph.D.s:** 73%
Graduate: 155 men, 55 women	**Student/Faculty:** 17 to 1
Year: trimesters, summer session	**Tuition:** $28,665
Application Deadline: open	**Room & Board:** $7164
Freshman Class: 2126 applied, 1427 accepted, 534 enrolled	
SAT CR/M: 580/570	**ACT:** 26 **VERY COMPETITIVE+**

Milwaukee School of Engineering, established in 1903, is a private institution with programs in engineering, engineering technology, business, communication, and nursing. There are 5 undergraduate schools and 3 graduate schools. In addition to regional accreditation, MSOE has baccalaureate program accreditation with ABET and ACCE. The library contains 49,527 volumes, 80,654 microform items, and 1,518 audio/video tapes/CDs/DVDs, and subscribes to 389 periodicals including electronic. Computerized library services include interlibrary loans, database searching, Internet access, and laptop Internet portals. Special learning facilities include a learning resource center, art gallery, and radio station. The 15-acre campus is in an urban area in Milwaukee. Including any residence halls, there are 14 buildings.

Programs of Study: MSOE confers B.A. and B.S. degrees. Master's degrees are also awarded. Bachelor's degrees are awarded in BIOLOGICAL SCIENCE (molecular biology), BUSINESS (business administration and management, international business management, management information systems, and management science), COMMUNICATIONS AND THE ARTS (technical and business writing), COMPUTER AND PHYSICAL SCIENCE (software engineering), ENGINEERING AND ENVIRONMENTAL DESIGN (architectural engineering, biomedical engineering, computer engineering, construction management, electrical/electronics engineering, engineering, engineering technology, industrial engineering, and mechanical engineering), HEALTH PROFESSIONS (nursing). Biomedical engineering and computer engineering are the strongest academically. Architectural, mechanical, and electrical engineering are the largest.

Special: MSOE offers internships in the student's discipline, study-abroad in Germany, India, and Czech Republic, on-campus work-study programs, and non-degree study. A number of dual degrees along with a 5-year dual degree with a bachelor's in engineering and a master's in environmental engineering, are available. There are 5 national honor societies.

Admissions: 67% of the 2009-2010 applicants were accepted. The SAT scores for the 2009-2010 freshman class were: Critical Reading--13% below 500, 38% between 500 and 599, 45% between 600 and 700, and 2% above 700; Math--21% between 500 and 599, 53% between 600 and 700, and 26% above 700. The ACT scores were 4% below 21, 18% between 21 and 23, 32% between 24 and 26, 21% between 27 and 28, and 25% above 28.

Requirements: The ACT is required. The SAT is recommended and is acceptable. In addition, applicants must be graduates of an accredited secondary school, having completed 15 academic credits, including 4 units of English, 2 units each of science and math, and 1 unit each of social studies and history. More units in math, science, and English are strongly advised; 1 unit in computer science is recommended. The GED is accepted. An essay is required, and an interview is recommended. A GPA of 2.8 is required. AP and CLEP credits are accepted. Important factors in the admissions decision are advanced placement or honors courses, leadership record, and personality/intangible qualities.

Procedure: Freshmen are admitted to all sessions. Entrance exams should be taken during the junior year. There are deferred admissions and rolling admissions plans. Application deadlines are open. Application fee is $25. Applications are accepted on-line.

Financial Aid: In 2009-2010, all full-time freshmen and 98% of continuing full-time students received some form of financial aid. 81% of all full-time freshmen and 83% of continuing full-time students received need-based aid. The average freshman award was $26,472. Need-based scholarships or need-based grants averaged $6,584 ($14,085 maximum); need-based self-help aid (loans and jobs) averaged $2,839 ($5,500 maximum); other non-need based awards and non-need based scholarships averaged $10,340; and private loans, Plus loans, and unsubsidized Stafford loans averaged $6,546 ($29,969 maximum). 78% of undergraduate students work part-time. Average annual earnings from campus work are $1960. The average financial indebtedness of the 2009 graduate was $35,875. The FAFSA is required. The priority date for freshman financial aid applications for fall entry is March 15.

Computers: Wireless access is available. Students lease a laptop until graduation and after that, they own it. There are wireless networks or hard-line connections in every building. All students may access the system. There are no time limits and no fees. All students are required to have a personal computer. A Hewlett Packard HU-8240 is recommended.

Springfield, MO 65897

(417) 836-5000
(800) 492-7900; (417) 836-6334

Full-time: 5662 men, 7098 women	**Faculty:** IIA, --$
Part-time: 1516 men, 1979 women	**Ph.D.s:** 57%
Graduate: 1213 men, 1880 women	**Student/Faculty:** n/av
Year: semesters, summer session	**Tuition:** $5988 ($11,088)
Application Deadline: July 20	**Room & Board:** $5710
Freshman Class: 7216 applied, 5583 accepted, 2734 enrolled	
ACT: 24	**SAT:** required

VERY COMPETITIVE

Missouri State University, founded in 1905, is a public institution offering undergraduate programs in arts and letters, business administration, humanities and social sciences, education and psychology, health and applied sciences, and science and math. There are 7 undergraduate schools and one graduate school. In addition to regional accreditation, MSU has baccalaureate program accreditation with AACSB, ADA, AHEA, ASLA, CSAB, CSWE, NASM, NCATE, NLN, and NRPA. The library contains 900,738 volumes, 1.1 million microform items, and 37,400 audio/video tapes/CDs/DVDs, and subscribes to 30,534 periodicals including electronic. Computerized library services include interlibrary loans, database searching, and Internet access. Special learning facilities include a learning resource center, art gallery, and radio station. The 225-acre campus is in a suburban area 220 miles southwest of St. Louis. Including any residence halls, there are 66 buildings.

Programs of Study: MSU confers B.A., B.S., B.F.A., B.M., B.S.E., B.S.N., and B.S.W. degrees. Master's and doctoral degrees are also awarded. Bachelor's degrees are awarded in AGRICULTURE (agriculture, agronomy, animal science, conservation and regulation, horticulture, and wildlife management), BIOLOGICAL SCIENCE (biology/biological science, cell biology, and nutrition), BUSINESS (accounting, banking and finance, business administration and management, hotel/motel and restaurant management, institutional management, insurance, marketing/retailing/merchandising, and recreation and leisure services), COMMUNICATIONS AND THE ARTS (art, broadcasting, communications, dance, design, dramatic arts, English, film arts, French, German, journalism, Latin, media arts, music, music performance, performing arts, Spanish, speech/debate/rhetoric, technical and business writing, theater design, and theater management), COMPUTER AND PHYSICAL SCIENCE (chemistry, computer science, earth science, geology, information sciences and systems, mathematics, and physics), EDUCATION (agricultural education, art education, athletic training, business education, early childhood education, elementary education, English education, foreign languages education, health education, home economics education, industrial arts education, middle school education, music education, physical education, science education, secondary education, special education, and vocational education), ENGINEERING AND ENVIRONMENTAL DESIGN (cartography, construction management, drafting and design, electrical/electronics engineering technology, engineering physics, industrial administration/management, interior design, manufacturing technology, mechanical design technology, printing technology, technological management, and urban planning technology), HEALTH PROFESSIONS (medical laboratory technology, nursing, predentistry, radiograph medical technology, respiratory therapy, and speech pathology/audiology), SOCIAL SCIENCE (anthropology, child care/child and family studies, clothing and textiles management/production/services, criminology, dietetics, early childhood studies, economics, geography, gerontology, history, parks and recreation management, philosophy, political science/government, psychology, public administration, religion, social science, social work, and sociology). Business and education are the largest.

Special: MSU offers co-op programs, internships, study abroad in 40 countries, and work-study programs. Also available are B.A.-B.S. degrees in 12 majors, preprofessional programs in law and medicine, accelerated degree programs and student-designed and interdisciplinary majors, including antiquities, agriculture business and agriculture education, chemistry/biochemistry, communication management, and finance/real estate. A 3-2 engineering degree is available through the University of Missouri-Rolla. Credit for military experience and pass/not-pass options are offered. There are 31 national honor societies and a freshman honors program.

Admissions: 77% of the 2009-2010 applicants were accepted. The ACT scores were 16% below 21, 33% between 21 and 23, 26% between 24 and 26, 13% between 27 and 28, and 13% above 28. 39% of the current freshmen were in the top fifth of their class; 65% were in the top two fifths.

Requirements: The SAT or ACT is required; the ACT is preferred. Admission is based on a sliding scale of rank or GPA and test score. Freshmen must also have a 17-unit high school core curriculum, including 4 in English, 3 each in math and social studies, 3 in science, 1 in visual and performing arts, and 3 electives. AP and CLEP credits are accepted. Important factors in the admissions decision are advanced placement or honors courses, extracurricular activities record, and personality/intangible qualities.

Procedure: Freshmen are admitted to all sessions. Entrance exams should be taken as early as possible. There are deferred admissions and rolling admissions plans. Applications should be filed by July 20 for fall entry, along with a $35 fee. Notification is sent on a rolling basis. Applications are accepted on-line.

Financial Aid: In 2009-2010, 54% of all full-time freshmen and 61% of continuing full-time students received some form of financial aid. 40% of all full-time freshmen and 41% of continuing full-time students received need-based aid. The average freshman award was $6,093. Need-based scholarships or need-based grants averaged $4,437; need-based self-help aid (loans and jobs) averaged $3,795; non-need-based athletic scholarships averaged $9,193; and other non-need-based awards and non-need-based scholarships averaged $7,908. 51% of undergraduate students work part-time. Average annual earnings from campus work are $1500. The average financial indebtedness of the 2009 graduate was $16,003. MSU is a member of CSS. The FAFSA is required. The priority date for freshman financial aid applications for fall entry is March 30. The deadline for filing freshman financial aid applications for fall entry is rolling.

Computers: Wireless access is available. All students may access the system. There are no time limits and no fees.

MISSOURI UNIVERSITY OF SCIENCE AND TECHNOLOGY
University of Missouri at Rolla

Rolla, MO 65409

(573) 341-4164
(800) 522-0938; (573) 341-4082

Full-time: 3794 men, 1091 women	**Faculty:** 363; I, -$
Part-time: 251 men, 70 women	**Ph.D.s:** 79%
Graduate: 1285 men, 324 women	**Student/Faculty:** 13 to 1
Year: semesters, summer session	**Tuition:** $8498 ($19,589)
Application Deadline: July 1	**Room & Board:** $7595
Freshman Class: n/av	
SAT CR/M: 620/660	**ACT:** 28 **VERY COMPETITIVE+**

Missouri University of Science and Technology, founded in 1870, is part of the University of Missouri system. A public institution, it offers comprehensive undergraduate and graduate programs and confers degrees in arts and sciences, engineering, mines and metallurgy, and management and information systems. There is one undergraduate school. In addition to regional accreditation, Missouri S&T has baccalaureate program accreditation with ABET. The library contains 477,201 volumes, 573,058 microform items, and 8,041 audio/video tapes/CDs/DVDs, and subscribes to 2,593 periodicals including electronic. Computerized library services include interlibrary loans, database searching, Internet access, and laptop Internet portals. Special learning facilities include a learning resource center, radio station, a writing center, student design center, nuclear reactor, observatory, explosives testing labs, and underground mine. The 284-acre campus is in a small town 90 miles southwest of St. Louis. Including any residence halls, there are 71 buildings.

Programs of Study: Missouri S&T confers B.A. and B.S. degrees. Master's and doctoral degrees are also awarded. Bachelor's degrees are awarded in BIOLOGICAL SCIENCE (biology/biological science, environmental biology, and life science), BUSINESS (business administration and management and management information systems), COMMUNICATIONS AND THE ARTS (English and technical and business writing), COMPUTER AND PHYSICAL SCIENCE (applied mathematics, chemistry, computer science, geology, geophysics and seismology, information sciences and systems, mathematics, physics, and statistics), EDUCATION (secondary education), ENGINEERING AND ENVIRONMENTAL DESIGN (aeronautical engineering, architectural engineering, ceramic engineering, chemical engineering, civil engineering, computer engineering, electrical/electronics engineering, engineering management, engineering mechanics, environmental engineering, geological engineering, manufacturing engineering, materials engineering, mechanical engineering, metallurgical engineering, mining and mineral engineering, nuclear engineering, petroleum/natural gas engineering, and systems engineering), HEALTH PROFESSIONS (premedicine), SOCIAL SCIENCE (economics, history, philosophy, prelaw, and psychology). Engineering and science and technology are the strongest academically. Engineering, arts, sciences and mines, and metallurgy are the largest.

Special: MUS&T offers internships in business and government, co-op programs in which students work and attend school on alternating schedules, and study abroad in more than 40 countries. Accelerated degrees in science and engineering, dual majors, B.A.-B.S. degrees, a 3-2 engineering degree, work-study programs, credit for life/military/work experience, and pass/fail options in certain courses are also available. There are 26 national honor societies, a freshman honors program, and 25 departmental honors programs.

Admissions: The SAT scores for the 2009-2010 freshman class were: Critical Reading--15% below 500, 25% between 500 and 599, 46% between 600 and 700, and 14% above 700; Math--5% below 500, 18% between 500 and 599, 52% between 600 and 700, and 25% above 700. The ACT scores were 2% below 21, 10% between 21 and 23, 25% between 24 and 26, 21% between 27 and 28, and 42% above 28. 63% of the current freshmen were in the top fifth of their class; 87% were in the top two fifths. There were 13 National Merit finalists. 42 freshmen graduated first in their class.

Requirements: The SAT or ACT is required; the ACT is recommended. In addition, the sum of the high school student's class rank percentile and aptitude exam percentile must be 120 or higher. Candidates must be graduates of an accredited secondary school or have the GED. The applicant must have completed 16 academic credit units, including 4 each in English and math, 3 each in science and social studies, and 2 in a foreign language. AP and CLEP credits are accepted. Important factors in the admissions decision are leadership record, extracurricular activities record, and advanced placement or honors courses.

Procedure: Freshmen are admitted fall, winter, and summer. Entrance exams should be taken late in the junior year or early in the senior year. There is a rolling admissions plan. Applications should be filed by July 1 for fall entry, December 1 for spring entry, and May 1 for summer entry, along with a $45 fee. Applications are accepted on-line. A waiting list is maintained.

Financial Aid: Missouri S&T is a member of CSS. The FAFSA is required. The priority date for freshman financial aid applications for fall entry is March 1.

Computers: There are more than 4500 wired connections and there are wireless networks throughout campus buildings, library, and residence halls. Wireless can handle some 6000 users. All students may access the system. There are no time limits and no fees.

MONMOUTH UNIVERSITY
West Long Branch, NJ 07764-1898   (732) 571-3456
(800) 543-9671; (732) 263-5166

Full-time: 1867 men, 2439 women	**Faculty:** 212; IIA, av$
Part-time: 111 men, 264 women	**Ph.D.s:** 82%
Graduate: 500 men, 1318 women	**Student/Faculty:** 19 to 1
Year: semesters, , summer session	**Tuition:** $25,013
Application Deadline: March 1	**Room & Board:** $9,554
Freshman Class: 6738 applied, 4160 accepted, 998 enrolled	
SAT CR/M/W: 530/550/530	**ACT:** 23 **VERY COMPETITIVE**

Monmouth University, founded in 1933, is a private comprehensive institution offering both undergraduate and graduate programs in the arts and sciences, business, education, upper-level nursing, technology, and professional training. There are 7 undergraduate schools and one graduate school. In addition to regional accreditation, Monmouth has baccalaureate program accreditation with AACSB, ABET, CSWE, and NLN. The library contains 248,000 volumes, and subscribes to 22,500 periodicals including electronic. Computerized library services include interlibrary loans, database searching, Internet access, and laptop Internet portals. Special learning facilities include a learning resource center, art gallery, radio station, TV station, theater, and a greenhouse. The 156-acre campus is in a suburban area 60 miles south of New York City. Including any residence halls, there are 56 buildings.

Programs of Study: Monmouth confers B.A., B.S., B.F.A., B.S.N., and B.S.W. degrees. Associates and master's degrees are also awarded. Bachelor's degrees are awarded in BIOLOGICAL SCIENCE (biology/biological science and marine biology), BUSINESS (accounting, banking and finance, business administration and management, business economics, international business management, marketing management, and real estate), COMMUNICATIONS AND THE ARTS (art, art history and appreciation, communications, English, graphic design, modern language, music, music business management, and Spanish), COMPUTER AND PHYSICAL SCIENCE (chemistry, computer science, mathematics, and software engineering), EDUCATION (art education, English education, foreign languages education, health education, mathematics education, music education, physical education, science education, secondary education, and special education), ENGINEERING AND ENVIRONMENTAL DESIGN (computer graphics), HEALTH PROFESSIONS (clinical science, medical laboratory technology, nursing, and premedicine), SOCIAL SCIENCE (anthropology, criminal justice, history, political science/government, prelaw, psychology, social work, and sociology). Business, education, and communication are the largest.

Special: Students may study abroad. There are cooperative and internship programs and a Washington semester. Monmouth also offers work-study programs, dual majors, flexible studies programs, and credit for life experience. Nondegree study is possible. There are 22 national honor societies and a freshman honors program.

Admissions: 62% of the 2009-2010 applicants were accepted. The SAT scores for the 2009-2010 freshman class were: Critical Reading--28% below 500, 57% between 500 and 599, 14% between 600 and 700, and 1 above 700; Math--19% below 500, 55% between 500 and 599, 24% between 600 and 700, and 2 above 700; Writing--25% below 500, 58% between 500 and 599, 16% between 600 and 700, and 2 above 700. The ACT scores were 6% below 21, 47% between 21 and 23, 31% between 24 and 26, 11% between 27 and 28, and 5% above 28. 37% of the current freshmen were in the top fifth of their class; 71% were in the top two fifths.

Requirements: The SAT or ACT is required. The ACT Optional Writing test is also required. In addition, applicants must be graduates of accredited secondary schools or have earned a GED. The college requires 16 Carnegie units, based on 4 years of English, 3 of math, and 2 each of history and language, with the remaining 5 units in academic electives. An essay and an interview are also recommended. The personal statement is option. A GPA of 2.3 is required. AP and CLEP credits are accepted. Important factors in the admissions decision are advanced placement or honors courses, leadership record, and extracurricular activities record.

Procedure: Freshmen are admitted fall, spring, and summer. Entrance exams should be taken by December of the senior year. There is a deferred admissions plan. Applications should be filed by March 1 for fall entry and January 1 for spring entry, along with a $50 fee. Notifications are sent April 1. Applications are accepted on-line.

Financial Aid: In 2009-2010, 99% of all full-time freshmen and 97% of continuing full-time students received some form of financial aid. 30% of all full-time freshmen and 40% of continuing full-time students received need-based aid. Average annual earnings from campus work are $1500. The average financial indebtedness of the 2009 graduate was $25,000. The FAFSA is required. Check with the school for current application deadlines.

Computers: Wireless access is available. There are more than 670 computers available for students use in computer labs on campus in academic buildings, the library, the student center, and residence halls, and 2 of these labs are open 24 hours. There is wireless network service in the library, academic buildings, the student center, the resident dining hall, the administration building, and outside locations. Students are provided with campus-wide network connectivity, controlled Internet access, access to personal e-mail accounts, on campus, and access to netwrok servers. All students may access the system. 24 hours a day, 7 days a week. There are no time limits and no fees. A Pentium III, 80 GB hard drive, 256 MB RAM PC with CD is recommended.

MORAVIAN COLLEGE
Bethlehem, PA 18018

(610) 861-1320
(800) 441-3191; (610) 625-7930

Full-time: 663 men, 870 women	**Faculty:** IIB, av$
Part-time: 60 men, 135 women	**Ph.D.s:** n/av
Graduate: 45 men, 90 women	**Student/Faculty:** 11 to 1
Year: semesters, summer session	**Tuition:** $31,250
Application Deadline: see profile	**Room & Board:** $8728
Freshman Class: n/av	
SAT or ACT: required	**VERY COMPETITIVE**

Moravian College, established in 1742, is a private, liberal arts institution affiliated with the Moravian Church. There are 2 undergraduate schools and 1 graduate school. Enrollment figures in the above capsule and figures in this profile are approximate. In addition to regional accreditation, Moravian has baccalaureate program accreditation with CAHEA and NASM. The library contains 263,000 volumes, 11,000 microform items, and 5385 audio/video tapes/CDs/DVDs, and subscribes to 15,415 periodicals including electronic. Computerized library services include interlibrary loans, database searching, and Internet access. Special learning facilities include a learning resource center, art gallery, and radio station. The 80-acre campus is in a suburban area 60 miles north of Philadelphia and 90 miles west of New York City. Including any residence halls, there are 127 buildings.

Programs of Study: Moravian confers B.A., B.S., and B.Mus. degrees. Master's degrees are also awarded. Bachelor's degrees are awarded in BIOLOGICAL SCIENCE (biochemistry, biology/biological science, and neurosciences), BUSINESS (accounting, business administration and management, business economics, and international business management), COMMUNICATIONS AND THE ARTS (art history and appreciation, classics, dramatic arts, English, French, German, graphic design, music, Spanish, and studio art), COMPUTER AND PHYSICAL SCIENCE (chemistry, computer science, mathematics, and physics), EDUCATION (art education, elementary education, music education, and secondary education), HEALTH PROFESSIONS (nursing), SOCIAL SCIENCE (criminal justice, economics, German area studies, history, philosophy, political science/government, psychology, religion, social science, and sociology). Physics, chemistry, and computer science are the strongest academically. Psychology, management, and sociology are the largest.

Special: The college offers 3-2 engineering degrees in conjunction with Washington University and a 4-1 engineering program with Lehigh University. Moravian also offers cooperative programs in allied health, natural resource management, and geology with Lehigh, Duke, and Thomas Jefferson Universities. Cross-registration is available with Lehigh and DeSales Universities and Lafayette, Muhlenberg, and Cedar Crest Colleges. Internships, study abroad in many countries, a Washington semester, and student-designed majors may be pursued. There are 17 national honor societies and 30 departmental honors programs.

Requirements: The SAT or ACT is required. In addition, applicants must graduate from an accredited secondary school or have a GED. Moravian requires 16 Carnegie units, based on 4 years each of English and social science, 3 to 4 of math, and 2 each of lab science, a foreign language, and electives. Essays are required and interviews are recommended. For music students, auditions are required; for art students, portfolios are required. AP and CLEP credits are accepted. Important factors in the admissions decision are advanced placement or honors courses, recommendations by school officials, and leadership record.

Procedure: Freshmen are admitted fall and spring. Entrance exams should be taken with enough time to submit scores by the application deadline. There are early decision and deferred admissions plans. Early decision applications should be filed by February 1; check with the school for current application deadlines and fee. Notification of early decision is sent December 15. Applications are accepted on-line. 221 applicants were on a recent waiting list, 30 were accepted.

Financial Aid: In a recent year, 95% of all full-time freshmen and 93% of continuing full-time students received some form of financial aid. 72% of all full-time freshmen and 73% of continuing full-time students received need-based aid. The average freshmen award was $23,728. 43% of undergraduate students work part-time. Average annual earnings from campus work are $675. Moravian is a member of CSS. The CSS/Profile and FAFSA are required. Check with the school for current deadlines.

Computers: Wireless access is available in all academic buildings and common areas. All students may access the system 24 hours per day. There are no time limits and no fees.

MOUNT HOLYOKE COLLEGE
South Hadley, MA 01075 | **(413) 538-2023; (413) 538-2409**

Full-time: no men, 2224 women	**Faculty:** 224; IIB, ++$
Part-time: 5 men, 59 women	**Ph.Ds:** 95%
Graduate: 1 man, 15 women	**Student/Faculty:** 9 to 1
Year: semesters	**Tuition:** $39,126
Application Deadline: January 15	**Room & Board:** $11,450
Freshman Class: 3061 applied, 1771 accepted, 574 enrolled	
SAT CR/M/W: 660/660/670	**ACT:** 29 **HIGHLY COMPETITIVE+**

Mount Holyoke, founded in 1837, is an independent, liberal arts college and the oldest institution of higher learning for women in the United States. The 3 libraries contain 116,118 volumes, 24,173 microform items, and 9470 audio/video tapes/CDs/DVDs, and subscribe to 4119 periodicals including electronic. Computerized library services include interlibrary loans, database searching, Internet access, and laptop Internet portals. Special learning facilities include a learning resource center, art gallery, radio station, observatory, child study center, botanical garden and greenhouse, equestrian center, conference center, and centers for global initiatives, leadership, and the environment. The 800-acre campus is in a small town 90 miles west of Boston and 160 miles north of New York City. Including any residence halls, there are 62 buildings.

Programs of Study: Mount Holyoke confers A.B. degrees. Master's degrees are also awarded. Bachelor's degrees are awarded in AGRICULTURE (environmental studies), BIOLOGICAL SCIENCE (biochemistry, biology/biological science, and neurosciences), BUSINESS (organizational leadership and management), COMMUNICATIONS AND THE ARTS (art, art history and appreciation, classics, dance, dramatic arts, English, film arts, French, Greek, Italian, Latin, music, romance languages and literature, Russian, Russian languages and literature, Spanish, and studio art), COMPUTER AND PHYSICAL SCIENCE (astronomy, chemistry, computer science, geology, mathematics, physics, and statistics), EDUCATION (psychology education), ENGINEERING AND ENVIRONMENTAL DESIGN (architecture and engineering), SOCIAL SCIENCE (African American studies, American studies, anthropology, Asian/Oriental studies, classical/ancient civilization, economics, European studies, gender studies, geography, German area studies, history, international relations, Latin American studies, medieval studies, philosophy, political science/government, psychology, religion, social science, sociology, and women's studies). Sciences, social sciences, and international relations are the strongest academically. Biology, international relations, and English are the largest.

Special: Mount Holyoke offers students cross-registration through the Five College Consortium. Other opportunities include the 12 College Exchange Program, science and international studies internships, study abroad in 14 countries (semester or full-year), a Washington semester, work-study, student-designed majors, dual majors, a January program, accelerated degrees, nondegree study, and pass/fail options. A teacher licensure program is available. There are 2 national honor societies, including Phi Beta Kappa, and all departments have honors programs.

Admissions: 58% of the 2009-2010 applicants were accepted. The SAT scores for the 2009-2010 freshman class were: Critical Reading--1% below 500, 17% between 500 and 599, 46% between 600 and 700, and 36% above 700; Math--4% below 500, 18% between 500 and 599, 45% between 600 and 700, and 31% above 700; Writing--1% below 500, 13% between 500 and 599, 55% between 600 and 700, and 31% above 700. The ACT scores were 4% between 21 and 23, 13% between 24 and 26, 23% between 27 and 28, and 60% above 28. 82% of the current freshmen were in the top fifth of their class; 95% were in the top two fifths. 24 freshmen graduated first in their class.

Requirements: The school recommends that applicants have 4 years each of English and foreign language, 3 each of math and science, and 2 of social studies. An essay is required and an interview is strongly recommended. AP credits are accepted. Important factors in the admissions decision are recommendations by school officials, leadership record, and advanced placement or honors courses.

Procedure: Freshmen are admitted fall. Entrance exams should be taken before the application deadline. There are early decision and deferred admissions plans. Early decision applications should be filed by November 15; regular applications, by January 15 for fall entry, along with a $60 fee. Notification of early decision is sent December 31; regular decision, April 1. Applications are accepted on-line. 292 applicants were on a recent waiting list.

Financial Aid: In 2009-2010, 84% of all full-time freshmen and 76% of continuing full-time students received some form of financial aid. 72% of all full-time freshmen and 68% of continuing full-time students received need-based aid. The average freshmen award was $35,797. 95% of undergraduate students work part-time. Average annual earnings from campus work are $2100. The average financial indebtedness of the 2009 graduate was $23,008. Mount Holyoke is a member of CSS. The CSS/Profile, FAFSA, parent and student tax returns, and noncustodial parent form are required. The priority date for freshman financial aid applications for fall entry is February 15. The deadline for filing freshman financial aid applications for fall entry is March 1.

Computers: Wireless access is available. There are 586 publicly accessible computer workstations available for students on campus; students can access both the regular network and wireless system in the library, student center, and other locations throughout campus. All dorms, dining halls, libraries, and the student center are on a wireless network. All students may access the system. There are no time limits and no fees.

MUHLENBERG COLLEGE
Allentown, PA 18104　　　　　　　　　(484) 664-3200; (484) 664-3234

Full-time: 1001 men, 1351 women	**Faculty:** 166; IIB, av$
Part-time: 79 men, 86 women	**Ph.D.s:** 87%
Graduate: none	**Student/Faculty:** 14 to 1
Year: semesters, summer session	**Tuition:** $36,990
Application Deadline: February 15	**Room & Board:** $8440
Freshman Class: 4110 applied, 2002 accepted, 577 enrolled	
SAT CR/M/W: 610/610/610	**ACT:** 20　**HIGHLY COMPETITIVE**

Muhlenberg College, established in 1848, is a private liberal arts institution affiliated with the Lutheran Church. The library contains 233,410 volumes, 138,090 microform items, and 16,519 audio/video tapes/CDs/DVDs, and subscribes to 24,894 periodicals including electronic. Computerized library services include interlibrary loans, database searching, Internet access, and laptop Internet portals. Special learning facilities include a learning resource center, art gallery, natural history museum, radio station, TV station, and 2 environmental field stations. The 82-acre campus is in a suburban area 50 miles north of Philadelphia and 90 miles west of New York City. Including any residence halls, there are 91 buildings.

Programs of Study: Berg confers B.A. and B.S. degrees. Associates degrees are also awarded. Bachelor's degrees are awarded in BIOLOGICAL SCIENCE (biochemistry, biology/biological science, and neurosciences), BUSINESS (accounting, banking and finance, and business administration and management), COMMUNICATIONS AND THE ARTS (art, communications, dance, dramatic arts, English, film arts, French, German, music, and Spanish), COMPUTER AND PHYSICAL SCIENCE (chemistry, computer science, mathematics, natural sciences, physical sciences, and physics), ENGINEERING AND ENVIRONMENTAL DESIGN (environmental science), SOCIAL SCIENCE (American studies, anthropology, economics, German area studies, history, international studies, philosophy, political science/government, psychology, religion, Russian and Slavic studies, and sociology). Biology, theater, and psychology are the strongest academically. Biology, business administration, and communication are the largest.

Special: Students may cross-register with Lehigh, Lafayette, Cedar Crest, Moravian, and Allentown Colleges. Internships, work-study programs, B.A.-B.S. degrees, study abroad in Asia, Australia, Latin America, Russia, and Europe, and a Washington semester are available. Dual majors and student-designed majors may be pursued. A 3-2 engineering degree is available in cooperation with Columbia and Washington Universities, a 4-4 assured admission medical program with Drexel University College of Medicine, a 3-4 dental program with the University of Pennsylvania, and a 3-2 forestry degreewith Duke University. An army ROTC program is also available. Nondegree study and a pass/fail grading option are also offered. There are 14 national honor societies, including Phi Beta Kappa, a freshman honors program, and 8 departmental honors programs.

Admissions: 49% of the 2009-2010 applicants were accepted. The SAT scores for the 2009-2010 freshman class were: Critical Reading--9% below 500, 34% between 500 and 599, 45% between 600 and 700, and 13% above 700; Math--8% below 500, 35% between 500 and 599, 48% between 600 and 700, and 10%

above 700; Writing--7% below 500, 35% between 500 and 599, 42% between 600 and 700, and 15% above 700. The ACT scores were 2% below 21, 8% between 21 and 23, 33% between 24 and 26, 33% between 27 and 28, and 23% above 28. 84% of the current freshmen were in the top fifth of their class; 96% were in the top two fifths. 4 freshmen graduated first in their class in a recent year.

Requirements: Applicants must graduate from an accredited secondary school or have a GED. 16 Carnegie units are required, with 4 courses in English, 3 in math, and 2 each in history, science, and a foreign language. All students must submit essays. Interviews are recommended and are required for those who do not submit SAT scores. AP and CLEP credits are accepted. Important factors in the admissions decision are evidence of special talent, leadership record, and advanced placement or honors courses.

Procedure: Freshmen are admitted fall and spring. Entrance exams should be taken during the spring of the junior year or fall of the senior year. There are early decision, deferred admissions plan. Early decision applications should be filed by February 1; regular applications should be filed by February 15 for fall entry, along with a $50 fee. Notification of early decision is sent on a rolling basis; and sent March 15. Applications are accepted on-line. 354 applicants were on a recent waiting list, 21 were accepted.

Financial Aid: In a recent year, 72% of all full-time freshmen and 74% of continuing full-time students received some form of financial aid. 34% of all full-time freshmen and 38% of continuing full-time students received need-based aid. The average freshmen award was $21,653, with $19,426 ($35,580 maximum) from need-based scholarships or need-based grants; $4960 ($7800 maximum) from need-based self-help aid (loans and jobs); and $8319 ($21,500 maximum) from other non-need-based awards and non-need-based scholarships. 41% of undergraduate students work part-time. Average annual earnings from campus work are $1128. The average financial indebtedness of a recent graduate was $20,668. Berg is a member of CSS. The CSS/Profile, FAFSA, the college's own financial statement, and parent and student tax returns and W-2 forms are required. The deadline for filing freshman financial aid applications for fall entry is February 15.

Computers: Wireless access is available. There are student computers throughout campus and in residence halls. All students may access the system 24 hours a day. There are no time limits and no fees. It is strongly recommended that all students have a personal computer.

MURRAY STATE UNIVERSITY
Murray, KY 42071

(270) 809-3741
(800) 272-4678; (270) 809-3780

Full-time: 2883 men, 3983 women	**Faculty:** 386; IIA, --$
Part-time: 567 men, 859 women	**Ph.D.s:** 77%
Graduate: 564 men, 1265 women	**Student/Faculty:** 18 to 1
Year: semesters, summer session	**Tuition:** $5100 ($8000)
Application Deadline: August 1	**Room & Board:** $6560
Freshman Class: 1391 enrolled	
ACT: 23	**VERY COMPETITIVE**

Murray State University, founded in 1922, is a public institution offering degree programs in business, education, health sciences and human services, humanities and fine arts, engineering, technology and science, and agriculture. There are 6 undergraduate schools and 6 graduate schools. In addition to regional accreditation, MSU has baccalaureate program accreditation with AACSB, ABET, ACEJ-MC, ADA, ASLA, CSWE, NASAD, NASM, NCATE, and NLN. The 2 libraries contain 402,000 volumes, 210,000 microform items, and 5,000 audio/video tapes/CDs/DVDs, and subscribe to 2,500 periodicals including electronic. Computerized library services include interlibrary loans, database searching, Internet access, and laptop Internet portals. Special learning facilities include a learning resource center, art gallery, natural history museum, radio station, TV station, biological station, interactive telecommunications network, and web-based courses. The 253-acre campus is in a small town 130 miles northwest of Nashville. Including any residence halls, there are 102 buildings.

Programs of Study: MSU confers B.A., B.S., B.A.B., B.F.A., B.I.S., B.M., B.M.E., B.S.A., B.S.B., B.S.N., B.S.V.T.E., and B.S.W. degrees. Associates and master's degrees are also awarded. Bachelor's degrees are awarded in AGRICULTURE (agricultural mechanics, agriculture, animal science, fishing and fisheries, and horticulture), BIOLOGICAL SCIENCE (biochemistry, biology/biological science, and wildlife biology), BUSINESS (accounting, banking and finance, business administration and management, business economics, marketing/retailing/merchandising, personnel management, and recreation and leisure services), COMMUNICATIONS AND THE ARTS (advertising, broadcasting, communications, dramatic arts, English, fine arts, French, German, journalism, languages, music, public relations, Spanish, speech/debate/rhetoric, and telecommunications), COMPUTER AND PHYSICAL SCIENCE (chemistry, computer programming, computer science, earth science, geology, information sciences and systems, mathematics, and physics), EDUCATION (agricultural education, art education, business education, early childhood education, elementary education, foreign languages education, health education, home economics education, industrial arts education, middle school education, music education, secondary education, and special education), ENGINEERING AND ENVIRONMENTAL DESIGN (civil engineering technology, computer technology, construction technology, electrical/electronics engineering technology, engineering technology, occupational safety and health, and technological management), HEALTH PROFESSIONS (exercise science, nursing, predentistry, premedicine, speech pathology/audiology, and veterinary science), SOCIAL SCIENCE (criminal justice, crosscultural studies, dietetics, economics, geography, history, international studies, liberal arts/general studies, parks and recreation management, philosophy, political science/government, prelaw, psychology, social work, and sociology). Premedicine, engineering, and physics are the strongest academically. Business, communication, and education technologies are the largest.

Special: MSU offers cooperative programs in all majors, cross-registration through the National Student Exchange, internships, study abroad in 25 countries, work-study, dual majors, B.A.-B.S. degrees, and 3-2 engineering degrees with the University of Louisville and the University of Kentucky. Credit for life experience and a degree in independent studies are also offered. Nondegree study is possible. There are 25 national honor societies, including Phi Beta Kappa, a freshman honors program, and 20 departmental honors programs.

Admissions: The ACT scores were 20% below 21, 30% between 21 and 23, 30% between 24 and 26, 12% between 27 and 28, and 8% above 28. 56% of the current freshmen were in the top fifth of their class; 89% were in the top two fifths. 55 freshmen graduated first in their class.

Requirements: The ACT is required, with a minimum score of 18. Applicants must rank in the top half of their class or have a 3.0 GPA. Applicants should have completed 22 high school academic credits, including 4 units in English, 3 in math, 2 each in science and social studies, and 9 in electives; in addition, MSU strongly recommends a fourth year of math, 2 of foreign language, 1 in art appreciation, 1/2 in health, 1/2 in phys ed and 5 in electives. A portfolio or audition is required for art and music majors. An interview is recommended. MSU requires applicants to be in the upper 50% of their class. A GPA of 3.0 is required. AP and CLEP credits are accepted.

Procedure: Freshmen are admitted to all sessions. Entrance exams should be taken before January of the enrollment year. There are early admissions and rolling admissions plans. Applications should be filed by August 1 for fall entry, December 1 for spring entry, and May 1 for summer entry, along with a $30 fee. Applications are accepted on-line.

Financial Aid: In 2009-2010, 83% of all full-time freshmen and 75% of continuing full-time students received some form of financial aid. 72% of all full-time freshmen and 72% of continuing full-time students received need-based aid. The average freshmen award was $4,591. 21% of undergraduate students work part-time. Average annual earnings from campus work are $2700. The average financial indebtedness of the 2009 graduate was $18,000. The FAFSA and the college's own financial statement are required. The deadline for filing freshman financial aid applications for fall entry is April 1.

Computers: Wireless access is available in residential colleges, libraries, classrooms, and labs. All students may access the system. There are no time limits and no fees. It is strongly recommended that all students have a personal computer.

NATIONAL UNIVERSITY
La Jolla, CA 92037

800-NAT-UNIV
(800) NAT-UNIV; (858) 642-8709

Full-time: 670 men, 1000 women	**Faculty:** 11A,+$
Part-time: 2020 men, 2230 women	**Ph.D.s:** n/av
Graduate: 7700 men, 12275 women	**Student/Faculty:** n/av
Year: trimesters, summer session	**Tuition:** $8100
Application Deadline: open	**Room & Board:** n/app
Freshman Class: n/av	SPECIAL

National University is a private institution that makes lifelong learning opportunities accessible to nontraditional learners in 11 major cities. Courses are offered in an accelerated 1 course per month format. National also offers more than 30 degrees and 300 courses on-line. The figures given in the above capsule and in this profile are approximate. There are 6 undergraduate schools and 6 graduate schools. The library contains 250,916 volumes, and 7,459 audio/video tapes/CDs/DVDs, and subscribes to 14,111 periodicals including electronic. Computerized library services include interlibrary loans, database searching, Internet access, and laptop Internet portals. Special learning facilities include a learning resource center and TV station. The 15-acre campus is in an urban area 3 miles northeast of downtown San Diego.

Programs of Study: National confers B.A., B.S., B.B.A., and B.S.N. degrees. Associate and master's degrees are also awarded. Bachelor's degrees are awarded in BIOLOGICAL SCIENCE (life science), BUSINESS (accounting, banking and finance, management science, organizational behavior, and organizational leadership and management), COMMUNICATIONS AND THE ARTS (design, English, and multimedia), COMPUTER AND PHYSICAL SCIENCE (computer science, earth science, information sciences and systems, mathematics, and software engineering), ENGINEERING AND ENVIRONMENTAL DESIGN (construction engineering, construction management, and environmental science), HEALTH PROFESSIONS (allied health and nursing), SOCIAL SCIENCE (behavioral science, criminal justice, early childhood studies, history, interdisciplinary studies, international studies, liberal arts/general studies, prelaw, psychology, and sociology). Computer science, accounting, and psychology are the strongest academically. Criminal justice, psychology, and interdisciplinary studies are the largest.

Special: Cross-registration with California Community Colleges is possible. National offers all degree programs in an accelerated format of 1 course per month. There are 3 national honor societies.

Requirements: Graduation from an accredited secondary school or satisfactory scores on the GED are required for admission. A GPA of 2.0 is required. AP and CLEP credits are accepted.

Procedure: Freshmen are admitted to all sessions. There are deferred admissions and rolling admissions plans. Application deadlines are open. Application fee is $60. Applications are accepted on-line.

Financial Aid: The CSS/Profile, FAFSA, and the college's own financial statement are required. The deadline for filing freshman financial aid applications for fall entry is rolling.

Computers: Wireless access is available. 2500 computers are available to all students. Computer equipment and network access for student use is provided in the computer center, labs, and library. All students may access the system Monday through Friday, 8 A.M. to 9 P.M., and Saturday, 8 A.M. to 2 P.M. There are no time limits and no fees.

NAZARETH COLLEGE OF ROCHESTER
Rochester, NY 14618-3790

(585) 389-2860
(800) 462-3944; (585) 389-2826

Full-time: 500 men, 1500 women	**Faculty:** IIA, -$
Part-time: 50 men, 130 women	**Ph.D.s:** n/av
Graduate: 210 men, 830 women	**Student/Faculty:** n/av
Year: semesters, summer session	**Tuition:** $23,000
Application Deadline: February 15	**Room & Board:** $10,000
Freshman Class: n/av	**VERY COMPETITIVE**

Nazareth College of Rochester, founded in 1924, is an independent institution offering programs in the liberal arts and sciences and preprofessional areas. The figures in the above capsule and in this profile are approximate. There are 4 undergraduate schools and 4 graduate schools. In addition to regional accreditation, Nazareth has baccalaureate program accreditation with CSWE and NASM. The library contains 218,010 volumes, 460,199 microform items, and 12,417 audio/video tapes/CDs/DVDs, and subscribes to 1,432 periodicals including electronic. Computerized library services include interlibrary loans, database searching, and Internet access. Special learning facilities include a learning resource center, art gallery, and radio station. The 150-acre campus is in a suburban area 7 miles east of Rochester. Including any residence halls, there are 21 buildings.

Programs of Study: Nazareth confers B.A., B.S., and B.Mus. degrees. Master's and doctoral degrees are also awarded. Bachelor's degrees are awarded in BIOLOGICAL SCIENCE (biochemistry and biology/biological science), BUSINESS (accounting and business administration and management), COMMUNICATIONS AND THE ARTS (art, art history and appreciation, communications, dramatic arts, English, fine arts, French, German, Italian, music, music history and appreciation, music performance, Spanish, and speech/debate/rhetoric), COMPUTER AND PHYSICAL SCIENCE (chemistry, information sciences and systems, and mathematics), EDUCATION (art education, business education, elementary education, English education, foreign languages education, mathematics education, middle school education, music education, science education, social studies education, and special education), ENGINEERING AND ENVIRON-MENTAL DESIGN (environmental science), HEALTH PROFESSIONS (music therapy, nursing, physical therapy, and speech pathology/audiology), SOCIAL SCIENCE (American studies, anthropology, economics, history, international studies, peace studies, philosophy, political science/government, psychology, religion, social science, social work, and sociology). Physical therapy, math, and English are the strongest academically. Business, psychology, and art are the largest.

Special: There is cross-registration with members of the Rochester Area Colleges Consortium. Internships and a Washington semester are offered. There is study abroad in France, Spain, Italy, and Germany, and there are exchange programs in Australia, Japan, Italy, France, Peru, United Kingdom, Hungary, Wales. There are 20 national honor societies and 13 departmental honors programs.

Requirements: Applicants should graduate from an accredited secondary school or have a GED. A minimum of 16 academic credits is required, including 4 years of English and 3 each of social studies, foreign language, math, and science. An essay is required, as is an audition for music and theater students and a portfolio for art students. An interview is recommended. Nazareth requires applicants to be in the upper 50% of their class. A GPA of 2.8 is required. AP and CLEP credits are accepted. Important factors in the admissions decision are geographical diversity, advanced placement or honors courses, and evidence of special talent.

Procedure: Freshmen are admitted fall and spring. Entrance exams should be taken by December of the senior year. There are early decision, early admissions and deferred admissions plans. Early decision applications should be filed by November 15; regular applications, by February 15 for fall entry and November 15 for spring entry, along with a $40 fee. Notification of early decision is sent December 15; regular decision, March 1. Applications are accepted on-line. A waiting list is maintained.

Financial Aid: In a recent year, 98% of all full-time freshmen and 96% of continuing full-time students received some form of financial aid. 77% of all full-time freshmen and 73% of continuing full-time students received need-based aid. The average freshmen award was $16,446. 44% of undergraduate students worked part-time. Average annual earnings from campus work were $1421. The average financial indebtedness of the 2009 graduate was $26,795. Nazareth is a member of CSS. The FAFSA, and the CSS Profile are required for early decision applicants only. Check with the school for current application deadlines.

Computers: Wireless access is available. All students may access the system. There are no time limits and no fees.

NEW COLLEGE OF FLORIDA

Sarasota, FL 34243-2109	(941) 487-5000; (941) 487-5010
Full-time: 314 men, 511 women	**Faculty:** 71; IIB, av$
Part-time: none	**Ph.D.s:** 99%
Graduate: none	**Student/Faculty:** 11 to 1
Year: 4-1-4	**Tuition:** $4784 ($26,386)
Application Deadline: February 15	**Room & Board:** $7783
Freshman Class: 1294 applied, 739 accepted, 218 enrolled	
SAT CR/M/W: 684/637/644	**ACT:** 29 **HIGHLY COMPETITIVE+**

New College of Florida, established in 1960, is the honors college of the State University System of Florida. There is one undergraduate school. The library contains 297,525 volumes, 525,736 microform items, and 8,650 audio/video tapes/CDs/DVDs, and subscribes to 30,750 periodicals including electronic. Computerized library services include interlibrary loans, database searching, Internet access, and laptop Internet portals. Special learning facilities include a learning resource center, an art gallery,a media and educational technology center, writing resource center, math reading room, language resource center, marine biology research center, and a living ecosystem teaching and research aquarium. The 114-acre campus is in a suburban area 50 miles south of Tampa, on Sarasota Bay. Including any residence halls, there are 51 buildings.

Programs of Study: New College confers B.A. degrees. Bachelor's degrees are awarded in AGRICULTURE (environmental studies), BIOLOGICAL SCIENCE (biochemistry, biology/biological science, marine biology, and neurosciences), COMMUNICATIONS AND THE ARTS (art, art history and appreciation, Chinese, classics, English, French, Germanic languages and literature, literature, music, Russian languages and literature, and Spanish), COMPUTER AND PHYSICAL SCIENCE (applied mathematics, chemistry, mathematics, natural sciences, and physics), ENGINEERING AND ENVIRONMENTAL DESIGN (computational sciences), SOCIAL SCIENCE (anthropology, economics, French studies, gender studies, German area studies, history, humanities, international studies, Latin American studies, medieval studies, philosophy, political science/government, psychology, public affairs, religion, social science, sociology, Spanish studies, and urban studies). Economics,, biology, and anthropology are the largest.

Special: Domestic and international internships, study abroad in 39 countries, accelerated degree programs, student-designed interdisciplinary and dual majors, and independent study are available. There are a freshman honors program.

Admissions: 57% of the 2009-2010 applicants were accepted. The SAT scores for the 2009-2010 freshman class were: Critical Reading--12% between 500 and 599, 45% between 600 and 700, and 43% above 700; Math--1% below 500, 26% between 500 and 599, 56% between 600 and 700, and 17% above 700; Writing--22% between 500 and 599, 55% between 600 and 700, and 23% above 700. The ACT scores were 2% below 21, 6% between 21 and 23, 13% between 24 and 26, 18% between 27 and 28, and 61% above 28. 76% of the current freshmen were in the top fifth of their class; 95% were in the top two fifths. There were 12 National Merit finalists. 5 freshmen graduated first in their class.

Requirements: The SAT or ACT is required. The ACT Optional Writing test is also required (beginning with the fall 2011 class). In addition, Graduation from an accredited secondary school (preferred) or the GED. High school students should pursue at least 5 academic courses each year, at the most rigorous level available, with a minimum distribution of 4 years of English; 3 years each of math, sciences, and social sciences; 2 consecutive years of the same foreign language; and 3 other academic courses. Application essays must be submitted. A GPA of 3.0 is required. AP credits are accepted. Important factors in the admissions decision are advanced placement or honors courses, evidence of special talent, and recommendations by school officials.

Procedure: Freshmen are admitted fall and spring. Entrance exams should be taken by fall of the senior year. There is a deferred admissions plan. Applications should be filed by February 15 for fall entry and December 15 for spring entry, along with a $30 fee. Notifications are sent April 1. 243 applicants were on the 2009 waiting list; 2 were admitted. Applications are accepted on-line.

Financial Aid: In 2009-2010, 94% of all full-time freshmen and 96% of continuing full-time students received some form of financial aid. 94% of all full-time freshmen and 96% of continuing full-time students received need-based aid. The

average freshman award was $11,496, with $2,197 ($20,750 maximum) from need-based scholarships or need-based grants; $743 ($7,000 maximum) from need-based self-help aid (loans and jobs); and $7,870 ($32,535 maximum) from other non-need-based awards and non-need-based scholarships. 20% of undergraduate students work part-time. Average annual earnings from campus work are $2505. The average financial indebtedness of the 2009 graduate was $12,954. The FAFSA is required. The priority date for freshman financial aid applications for fall entry is February 15.

Computers: All students may use the network, either on-campus or through a proxy off-campus. Wireless is available in many locations on campus. There are PCs available in the library and in a computer lab. An Apple computer lab is also available to students. All students may access the system 24 hours a day. There are no time limits and no fees.

NEW JERSEY INSTITUTE OF TECHNOLOGY

Newark, NJ 07102-1982   **(973) 596-3300; (973) 596-6085**

Full-time: 3450 men, 910 women	**Faculty:** I, av$
Part-time: 1210 men, 310 women	**Ph.D.s:** n/av
Graduate: 2105 men, 1005 women	**Student/Faculty:** n/av
Year: semesters, summer session	**Tuition:** $9500 ($14,500)
Application Deadline: see profile	**Room & Board:** $9000
Freshman Class: n/av	
SAT: required	**VERY COMPETITIVE**

New Jersey Institute of Technology is a public research university providing instruction, research, and public service in engineering, computer science, management, architecture, engineering technology, applied sciences, and related fields. The figures in the above capsule and in this profile are approximate. There are 6 undergraduate schools and 1 graduate school. In addition to regional accreditation, NJIT has baccalaureate program accreditation with AACSB, ABET, and NAAB. The 2 libraries contain 220,000 volumes, 7,325 microform items, and 73,807 audio/video tapes/CDs/DVDs, and subscribe to 2,500 periodicals including electronic. Computerized library services include interlibrary loans and database searching. Special learning facilities include a learning resource center, art gallery, radio station, 3 TV studios. NJIT is home to many government- and industry-sponsored labs and research centers, including the EPA Northeast Hazardous Substance Research Center, the National Center for Transportation and Industrial Productivity, the Center for Manufacturing Systems, the Emission Reduction Research Center, the Microelectronics Research Center, the Center for Microwave and Lightwave Engineering, and the Multi-Lifecycle Engineering Center. The 45-acre campus is in an urban area 10 miles west of New York City. Including any residence halls, there are 25 buildings.

Programs of Study: NJIT confers B.A., B.S., and B.Arch. degrees. Master's and doctoral degrees are also awarded. Bachelor's degrees are awarded in BIOLOGICAL SCIENCE (biology/biological science), BUSINESS (management science), COMMUNICATIONS AND THE ARTS (communications and technical and business writing), COMPUTER AND PHYSICAL SCIENCE (applied mathematics, applied physics, chemistry, computer management, computer science, information sciences and systems, and mathematics), ENGINEERING AND ENVIRONMENTAL DESIGN (architecture, biomedical engineering, chemical engineering, civil engineering, computer engineering, computer technology, electrical/electronics engineering, engineering and applied science, engineering technology, environmental engineering, environmental science, geophysical engineering, industrial engineering, manufacturing engineering, mechanical engineering, technological management, and technology and public affairs), SOCIAL SCIENCE (history). Engineering, computer science, and architecture are the strongest academically. Engineering is the largest.

Special: Cross-registration is offered in conjunction with Essex County College, Rutgers University's Newark campus, and the University of Medicine and Dentistry of New Jersey. Cooperative programs, available in all majors, include two 6-month internships. There are 3-2 engineering degree programs with Stockton State College and Lincoln and Seton Hall Universities. NJIT also offers work-study programs, study abroad in 18 countries, dual and interdisciplinary majors, accelerated degree programs, distance learning, and nondegree study. There is 1 national honor society and a freshman honors program.

Requirements: The SAT is required. In addition, the SAT: Subject test in math I or II is also required. Applicants should have completed 16 secondary school units, including 4 each in English and math, 2 in a lab science, and 6 in a distribution of social studies, foreign language, math, and science courses. AP and CLEP credits are accepted. Important factors in the admissions decision are advanced placement or honors courses, recommendations by school officials, and geographical diversity.

Procedure: Freshmen are admitted fall and spring. Entrance exams should be taken in May of the junior year or November of the senior year. There is a rolling admissions plan. Applications should be filed by November 15 for spring entry, along with a $35 fee. Notifications are sent January 2. Applications are accepted on-line. A waiting list is maintained.

Financial Aid: The FAFSA and the college's own financial statement are required. Check with the school for current application deadlines.

Computers: All students may access the system. There are no time limits and no fees. All students are required to have a personal computer. All full-time freshmen are given a PC and a variety of software is recommended.

NEW MEXICO INSTITUTE OF MINING AND TECHNOLOGY

Socorro, NM 87801

(575) 835-5424
(800) 428-TECH; (575) 835-5989

Full-time: 801 men, 294 women	**Faculty:** n/av
Part-time: 37 men, 19 women	**Ph.D.s:** 97%
Graduate: 288 men, 148 women	**Student/Faculty:** n/av
Year: semesters, summer session	**Tuition:** $4607 ($13,568)
Application Deadline: August 1	**Room & Board:** $5702
Freshman Class: 445 applied, 353 accepted, 255 enrolled	
SAT: n/av	**ACT:** n/av **HIGHLY COMPETITIVE**

New Mexico Institute of Mining and Technology, founded in 1889 as the New Mexico School of Mines, is a science and engineering university. It has 4 research-associated divisions: the New Mexico Bureau of Geology and Mineral Resources, the Energetic Materials Research and Testing Center, the Petroleum Recovery Research Center, and the Langmuir Laboratory for Atmospheric Research. There is 1 graduate school. In addition to regional accreditation, New Mexico Tech has baccalaureate program accreditation with ABET. The library contains 321,829 volumes, 217,540 microform items, and 2526 audio/video tapes/CDs/DVDs, and subscribes to 884 periodicals including electronic. Computerized library services include interlibrary loans, database searching, Internet access, and laptop Internet portals. Special learning facilities include a radio station, a mineral museum, a seismic research mine, and a campus astronomical observatory. The 320-acre campus is in a small town 75 miles south of Albuquerque. Including any residence halls, there are 28 buildings.

Programs of Study: New Mexico Tech confers B.S. and B.G.S. degrees. Associate, master's, and doctoral degrees are also awarded. Bachelor's degrees are awarded in BIOLOGICAL SCIENCE (biology/biological science), BUSINESS (business administration and management), COMMUNICATIONS AND THE ARTS (technical and business writing), COMPUTER AND PHYSICAL SCIENCE (chemistry, computer science, earth science, information sciences and systems, mathematics, and physics), ENGINEERING AND ENVIRONMENTAL DESIGN (chemical engineering, civil engineering, electrical/electronics engineering, engineering mechanics, environmental engineering, environmental science, materials engineering, mechanical engineering, mining and mineral engineering, and petroleum/natural gas engineering), SOCIAL SCIENCE (liberal arts/general studies and psychology). Physics and electrical engineering are the strongest academically. Mechanical engineering, computer science, and electrical engineering are the largest.

Special: New Mexico Tech offers co-op programs in computer science and all engineering majors, internships in technical communications, and cross-registration with New Mexico State, University of New Mexico, and Los Alamos National Laboratories in the WERC consortium. Dual majors are offered in engineering, computer science, physics, and math. Work-study, student-designed majors in environmental science, general studies, and basic science, nondegree study, and pass/fail options are also available. There are 4 national honor societies.

Admissions: 41% of the 2009-2010 applicants were accepted. The SAT scores for the 2009-2010 freshman class were: Critical Reading--17% below 500, 31% between 500 and 599, 39% between 600 and 700, and 13% above 700; Math--11% below 500, 31% between 500 and 599, 46% between 600 and 700, and 12% above 700. The ACT scores were 7% below 21, 22% between 21 and 23, 22% between 24 and 26, 23% between 27 and 28, and 26% above 28. 51% of the current freshmen were in the top fifth of their class; 87% were in the top two fifths.

Requirements: The SAT or ACT is required, with a minimum score of 21 on the ACT. Applicants must be high school graduates or present a GED certificate. Students should have earned 15 academic credits, consisting of 4 units of English, 3 each of social science and math (2 beyond general math), 2 of lab science, and electives. A GPA of 2.5 is required. AP credits are accepted. Important factors in the admissions decision are advanced placement or honors courses, evidence of special talent, and extracurricular activities record.

Procedure: Freshmen are admitted to all sessions. Entrance exams should be taken by December of the senior year. There are early decision, early admissions, deferred admissions, and rolling admissions plans. Applications should be filed by August 1 for fall entry and December 1 for spring entry, along with a $15 fee. Notification is sent on a rolling basis beginning March 1.

Financial Aid: The FAFSA is required. The priority date for freshman financial aid applications for fall entry is March 1. The deadline for filing freshman financial aid applications for fall entry is June 1.

Computers: Wireless access is available. The New Mexico Tech wireless network serves wireless access services in all major academic locations and some of the open areas around campus. All students may access the system 16 1/2 hours a day on site; 24 hours a day via network. There are no time limits. The fee is $2 per semester. It is strongly recommended that all students have a personal computer.

Old Westbury, NY 11568-8000
(516) 686-7925
(800) 345-NYIT; (516) 686-7613

Full-time: 3235 men, 1910 women	**Faculty:** IIA,+$
Part-time: 1120 men, 635 women	**Ph.D.s:** n/av
Graduate: 2340 men, 1930 women	**Student/Faculty:** n/av
Year: semesters, summer session	**Tuition:** $21,600
Application Deadline: February 1	**Room & Board:** $10,500
Freshman Class: n/av	**VERY COMPETITIVE**

The New York Institute of Technology, founded in 1955, is a nonsectarian, institution of higher learning that provides undergraduate, graduate, and professional programs in allied health, architecture, art, business, culinary arts, communication, arts, education, engineering, hospitality management, and medicine and technology. Traditional and accelerated formats in day, evening, and weekend sessions are available, in addition to noncredit and personal enrichment programs and off-campus independent study. NYIT maintains additional campuses on Long Island and in Manhattan. NYIT'S on-line campus is an innovative virtual campus. Students can take courses or acquire a 4-year degree entirely through Web-based computer conferencing with no campus classes required. The figures in the above capsule and in this profile are approximate. There are 7 undergraduate schools and 8 graduate schools. In addition to regional accreditation, NYIT has baccalaureate program accreditation with ABET, ADA, FIDER, and NAAB. The 5 libraries contain 169,905 volumes, 805,375 microform items, and 43,860 audio/video tapes/CDs/DVDs, and subscribe to 1,245 periodicals including electronic. Computerized library services include interlibrary loans, database searching, Internet access, and laptop Internet portals. Special learning facilities include a learning resource center, art gallery, radio station, TV station, and TV studios. The 525-acre campus is in a suburban area 25 miles east of New York City, 10 miles from Queens. Including any residence halls, there are 57 buildings.

Programs of Study: NYIT confers B.A., B.S., B.Arch., B.F.A., B.P.S., and B.Tech. degrees. Associates, master's, and doctoral degrees are also awarded. Bachelor's degrees are awarded in BIOLOGICAL SCIENCE (biology/biological science, life science, and nutrition), BUSINESS (accounting, banking and finance, business administration and management, hospitality management services, marketing and distribution, and marketing/retailing/merchandising), COMMUNICATIONS AND THE ARTS (advertising, communications, English, fine arts, graphic design, technical and business writing, and telecommunications), COMPUTER AND PHYSICAL SCIENCE (chemistry, computer science, mathematics, and physics), EDUCATION (art education, business education, education, elementary education, health education, middle school education, science education, secondary education, technical education, and trade and industrial education), ENGINEERING AND ENVIRONMENTAL DESIGN (aeronautical engineering, architecture, biomedical engineering, computer engineering, computer graphics, electrical/electronics engineering, electrical/electronics engineering technology, engineering technology, environmental design, environmental engineering technology, industrial engineering, interior design, manufacturing engineering, mechanical engineering, and technological management), HEALTH PROFESSIONS (clinical science, nursing, occupational therapy, physical therapy, physician's assistant, and preosteopathy), SOCIAL SCIENCE (behavioral science, interdisciplinary studies, political science/government, prelaw, social studies, and sociology). Architecture, allied health programs, and engineering are the strongest academically. Computer science, business administration, and architectural technology are the largest.

Special: NYIT offers cooperative programs, summer study abroad, internships, student-designed majors, a B.A.-B.S. degree in interdisciplinary studies, accelerated degree programs in osteopathic medicine, mechanical engineering, physical therapy, occupational therapy, and criminal justice, and nondegree study. There are 7 national honor societies, a freshman honors program, and 2 departmental honors programs.

Requirements: All students must present evidence of completion of high school degree or an equivalence. Architecture, engineering, combined baccalaureate/doctor of osteopathic medicine, nursing, occupational therapy, physical therapy, and physician assistant programs requirements include interviews, essays, letters of recommendation, volunteer hours, and Regents units. Recommendations are required for education program applicants. Portfolios are required for fine arts applicants. AP and CLEP credits are accepted. Important factors in the admissions decision are advanced placement or honors courses, recommendations by school officials, and leadership record.

Procedure: Freshmen are admitted fall, spring, and summer. Entrance exams should be taken in spring for fall enrollment. There are deferred admissions and rolling admissions plans. Applications should be filed by February 1 for fall entry. The fall 2009 application fee was $50. Notification is sent on a rolling basis. Applications are accepted on-line.

Financial Aid: The FAFSA and NYS TAP form are required. Check with the school for current application deadlines.

Computers: Wireless access is available. All students may access the system. There are no time limits and no fees. All students are required to have a personal computer. Students enrolled in architecture, engineering, and technology majors must have a personal computer.

NEW YORK UNIVERSITY
New York, NY 10011   (212) 998-4500; (212) 995-4902

Full-time: 7929 men, 12352 women	**Faculty:** ; I, +$
Part-time: 565 men, 792 women	**Ph.D.s:** 92%
Graduate: 9365 men, 12401 women	**Student/Faculty:** n/av
Year: semesters, summer session	**Tuition:** $38,765
Application Deadline: January 1	**Room & Board:** $13,228
Freshman Class: 37462 applied, 14159 accepted, 5000 enrolled	
SAT CR/M/W: 658/672/664	**ACT:** 29 **MOST COMPETITIVE**

New York University, founded in 1831, is the largest private university in the United States. NYU, which is composed of 14 schools, colleges, and divisions, occupies 5 major centers in Manhattan and operates branch campus and research programs in other parts of the United States and abroad. There are 8 undergraduate schools and 11 graduate schools. In addition to regional accreditation, NYU has baccalaureate program accreditation with AACSB, ACEJMC, ADA, CSWE, and NLN. The 12 libraries contain 5.7 million volumes, 5.6 million microform items, and 1.6 million audio/video tapes/CDs/DVDs, and subscribe to 67,960 periodicals including electronic. Computerized library services include interlibrary loans, database searching, Internet access, and laptop Internet portals. Special learning facilities include a learning resource center, art gallery, radio station, TV station, speech/language/hearing clinic, center for students with disabilities, and Speaking Freely (free noncredit foreign language classes). The campus is in an urban area in New York City's Greenwich Village. Including any residence halls, there are 150 buildings.

Programs of Study: NYU confers B.A., B.S., B.F.A., B.S./B.E., and Mus.B. degrees. Associates, master's, and doctoral degrees are also awarded. Bachelor's degrees are awarded in BIOLOGICAL SCIENCE (biochemistry, biology/ biological science, neurosciences, and nutrition), BUSINESS (accounting, banking and finance, business administration and management, business economics, hotel/motel and restaurant management, international business management, management science, marketing/retailing/merchandising, operations research, organizational behavior, real estate, recreation and leisure services, and sports management), COMMUNICATIONS AND THE ARTS (American literature, art history and appreciation, classics, communications, communications technology, comparative literature, creative writing, dance, design, dramatic arts, English, English literature, film arts, fine arts, French, German, Germanic languages and literature, Greek, Greek (classical), Greek (modern), Hebrew, Italian, journalism, Latin, linguistics, media arts, music, music business management, music performance, music technology, music theory and composition, performing arts, photography, Portuguese, radio/television technology, romance languages and literature, Russian, Spanish, speech/debate/rhetoric, studio art, technical and business writing, theater management, and voice), COMPUTER AND PHYSICAL SCIENCE (actuarial science, chemistry, computer mathematics, computer science, digital arts/technology, earth science, information sciences and systems, mathematics, physics, and statistics), EDUCATION (art education, early childhood education, education, elementary education, English education, foreign languages education, mathematics education, music education, science education, secondary education, social studies education, special education, and speech correction), ENGINEERING AND ENVIRONMENTAL DESIGN (computer engineering, graphic arts technology, and urban design), HEALTH PROFESSIONS (dental hygiene, health care administration, nursing, predentistry, premedicine, and speech pathology/audiology), SOCIAL SCIENCE (African studies, African American studies, American studies, anthropology, applied psychology, area studies, Asian/American studies, classical/ancient civilization, early childhood studies, East Asian studies, economics, ethnic studies, European studies, gender studies, history, humanities, Iberian studies, international relations, Judaic studies, Latin American studies, Luso-Brazilian studies, medieval studies, Middle Eastern studies, philosophy, political science/government, psychology, public administration, religion, social science, social work, sociology, and urban studies). Theater, individualized studies, and finance are the largest.

Special: A vast array of internships is available, as well as study worldwide at NYU's 10 sites: Berlin, Buenos Aires, Florence, Ghana, London, Madrid, Paris, Prague, Shanghai, and Tel Aviv. B.A.-B.S. degree options, accelerated degrees in more than 230 majors, dual and student-designed majors, credit by exam, and pass/fail options are also available. A Washington semester is available to political science majors. There are exchange programs with several historically black colleges. There is a Phi Beta Kappa and a freshman honors program.

Admissions: 38% of the 2009-2010 applicants were accepted. The SAT scores for the 2009-2010 freshman class were: Critical Reading--1% below 500, 17% between 500 and 599, 51% between 600 and 700, and 31% above 700; Math--1% below 500, 14% between 500 and 599, 49% between 600 and 700, and 37 above 700; Writing--1% below 500, 15% between 500 and 599, 51% between 600 and 700, and 33% above 700. The ACT scores were 16% between 24 and 26, 21% between 27 and 28, and 63% above 28. 92% of the current freshmen were in the top fifth of their class; 99% were in the top two-fifths. 235 freshmen graduated first in their class in a recent year.

Requirements: The SAT or ACT is required. The ACT Optional Writing test is also required. In addition, applicants must graduate from an accredited secondary school.The GED is accepted. Students must present at least 16 Carnegie units, including 4 in English. Some majors require an audition or submission of a creative portfolio. All applicants must submit an essay and 2 letters of recommendation. Applicants can submit the SAT and 2 SAT: Subject tests; the ACT with Writing; the SAT and 2 Advanced Placement (AP) exam scores; 3 SAT: Subject tests (1 in literature or the humanities, 1 in math/science, and 1 in any non-language area); or 3 AP exam scores (1 in literature/humanities, 1 in math/science, and 1 in any nonlangue area). AP credits are accepted. Important factors in the admissions decision are advanced placement or honors courses, extracurricular activities record, and leadership record.

Procedure: Freshmen are admitted fall and spring. Entrance exams should be taken by November of the senior year. There is an early decision admissions plan. Early decision applications should be filed by November 1; regular applications should be filed by January 1 for fall entry, along with a $65 fee. Notification of early decision is sent December 15; regular decision, April 1. Applications are accepted on-line. 2626 applicants were on a recent waiting list, 298 were accepted.

Financial Aid: In 2009-2010, 52% of all full-time freshmen and 50% of continuing full-time students received some form of financial aid. 51% of all full-time freshmen and 47% of continuing full-time students received need-based aid. The average freshmen award was $26,287. 20% of undergraduate students work parttime. The average financial indebtedness of the 2009 graduate was $33,487. The FAFSA and the state aid form are required. The deadline for filing freshman financial aid applications for fall entry is February 15.

Computers: Wireless access is available. Facilities include Macs and PCs at 4 computer labs; more than 100 public terminals for walk-up access to e-mail and the Internet; laptop plug-in ports and circulating laptops at the library; modem connectors from home or while traveling; NYU Roam for wireless network access; and ResNet. All students may access the system 24 hours a day, 7 days a week. There are no time limits and no fees.

NORTH CAROLINA STATE UNIVERSITY
Raleigh, NC 27695-7103   **(919) 515-2434; (919) 515-5039**

Full-time: 11,700 men, 9030 women	**Faculty:** I, -$
Part-time: 1915 men, 1505 women	**Ph.D.s:** n/av
Graduate: 4120 men, 3540 women	**Student/Faculty:** n/av
Year: semesters, summer session	**Tuition:** $6500 ($19,000)
Application Deadline: see profile	**Room & Board:** $8200
Freshman Class: n/av	
SAT: required	**ACT:** required
	HIGHLY COMPETITIVE

North Carolina State University, founded in 1887, is a member of the University of North Carolina System. Its degree programs emphasize the arts and sciences, agriculture, business, education, engineering, and preprofessional training. Figures in the above capsule are approximate. There are 10 undergraduate schools and 9 graduate schools. In addition to regional accreditation, NC State has baccalaureate program accreditation with ABET, CSAB, CSWE, NAAB, NCATE, NRPA, and SAF. The 5 libraries contain 3.7 million volumes, 5.4 million microform items, and 4111 audio/video tapes/CDs/DVDs, and subscribe to 54,843 periodicals including electronic. Computerized library services include interlibrary loans, database searching, Internet access, and laptop Internet portals. Special learning facilities include a learning resource center, art gallery, radio station, TV station, nuclear reactor, phytotron, electron microscope facilities, Materials Research Center, Integrated Manufacturing Systems Engineering Institute, Japan Center, and Precision Engineering Center. The 2110-acre campus is in an urban area Raleigh. Including any residence halls, there are 150 buildings.

Programs of Study: NC State confers B.A., B.S., B.Arch., B.E.D.A., B.L.A., and B.S.W. degrees. Associates, master's, and doctoral degrees are also awarded. Bachelor's degrees are awarded in AGRICULTURE (agricultural business management, agricultural economics, agriculture, agronomy, animal science, conservation and regulation, fishing and fisheries, forestry and related sciences, horticulture, natural resource management, poultry science, soil science, and wood science), BIOLOGICAL SCIENCE (biochemistry, biology/biological science, botany, microbiology, and zoology), BUSINESS (accounting, business administration and management, business economics, and recreation and leisure services), COMMUNICATIONS AND THE ARTS (communications, design, English, French, graphic design, industrial design, and Spanish), COMPUTER AND PHYSICAL SCIENCE (atmospheric sciences and meteorology, chemistry, computer science, earth science, geology, mathematics, physics, and statistics), EDUCATION (agricultural education, education, foreign languages education, industrial arts education, marketing and distribution education, mathematics education, middle school education, science education, secondary education, social studies education, technical education, and vocational education), ENGINEERING AND ENVIRONMENTAL DESIGN (aeronautical engineering, agricultural engineering, architecture, chemical engineering, civil engineering, computer engineering, construction management, electrical/electronics engineering, engineering, environmental design, environmental engineering, environmental science, furniture design, industrial engineering, landscape architecture/design, materials science, mechanical engineering, nuclear engineering, paper and pulp science, and textile engineering), HEALTH PROFESSIONS (medical laboratory technology, predentistry, premedicine, preveterinary science, and speech pathology/audiology), SOCIAL SCIENCE (clothing and textiles management/production/services, criminal justice, economics, food science, history, interdisciplinary studies, parks and recreation management, philosophy, political science/government, prelaw, psychology, religion, social science, social work, sociology, and textiles and clothing). Electrical engineering, chemical engineering, and architecture are the strongest academically. Business management, mechanical engineering, and electrical engineering are the largest.

Special: NC State offers cross-registration within the Cooperating Raleigh Colleges network, study abroad in more than 90 countries, internships, work-study programs, an accelerated degree plan, dual majors within any program, a general studies degree in education, a 3-2 engineering degree with the University of North Carolina at Asheville, student-designed multidisciplinary studies majors, credit by examination, nondegree study, and pass/fail options. There are 15 national honor societies, including Phi Beta Kappa, a freshman honors program, and 44 departmental honors programs.

Requirements: The SAT or ACT is required. The ACT Optional Writing test is also required. In addition, the SAT Math test is recommended. Applicants must be graduates of an accredited secondary school or have a GED certificate. They must have completed 20 academic credits, including 4 units of English, 3 each of science and math (4 of math is advised), 2 each of social studies and foreign language, and 1 of history. An essay is recommended for all applicants. A portfolio and interview are required for the School of Design. AP and CLEP credits are accepted. Important factors in the admissions decision are advanced placement or honors courses, leadership record, and evidence of special talent.

Procedure: Freshmen are admitted to all sessions. Entrance exams should be taken in the spring of the junior year and the fall of the senior year. There is a deferred admissions plan. Check with the school for current application deadlines. The application fee is $70. Applications are accepted on-line. 775 applicants were on a recent waiting list, 25 were accepted.

Financial Aid: In a recent year, 98% of all full-time freshmen and 97% of continuing full-time students received some form of financial aid. 96% of all full-time freshmen and 94% of continuing full-time students received need-based aid. The average financial indebtedness of a recent graduate was $15,823. The FAFSA and the college's own financial statement are required. Check with the school for current application deadlines.

Computers: Wireless access is available. All students may access the system. Time limits vary by class. The fee is $100.

NORTH CENTRAL COLLEGE

Naperville, IL 60566

(630) 637-5800
(800) 411-1861; (630) 637-5819

Full-time: 993 men, 1340 women	**Faculty:** 118; IIA, -$
Part-time: 94 men, 95 women	**Ph.D.s:** 86%
Graduate: 124 men, 152 women	**Student/Faculty:** 18 to 1
Year: quarters, summer session	**Tuition:** $26,916
Application Deadline: open	**Room & Board:** $8379
Freshman Class: 2762 applied, 1854 accepted, 543 enrolled	
ACT: 24	**SAT:** required

VERY COMPETITIVE

North Central College, founded in 1861, is a private comprehensive liberal arts institution affiliated with the United Methodist Church. The college is highly selective, primarily residential, and primarily full-time undergraduate. The library contains 151,434 volumes, 155,661 microform items, and 4,140 audio/video tapes/CDs/DVDs, and subscribes to 14,286 periodicals including electronic. Computerized library services include interlibrary loans, database searching, and Internet access. Special learning facilities include a learning resource center, art gallery, radio station, a foreign language lab, support services center, and a writing center. The 60-acre campus is in a suburban area 30 miles west of Chicago. Including any residence halls, there are 42 buildings.

Programs of Study: North Central confers B.A. and B.S. degrees. Master's degrees are also awarded. Bachelor's degrees are awarded in BIOLOGICAL SCIENCE (biochemistry and biology/biological science), BUSINESS (accounting, banking and finance, business administration and management, international business management, and marketing/retailing/merchandising), COMMUNICATIONS AND THE ARTS (broadcasting, communications, English, fine arts, French, German, Japanese, music, Spanish, and speech/debate/rhetoric), COMPUTER AND PHYSICAL SCIENCE (actuarial science, applied mathematics, chemistry, computer science, mathematics, and physics), EDUCATION (elementary education and secondary education), ENGINEERING AND ENVIRONMENTAL DESIGN (preengineering), HEALTH PROFESSIONS (predentistry, premedicine, and preveterinary science), SOCIAL SCIENCE (anthropology, classical/ancient civilization, economics, history, philosophy, political science/

government, prelaw, psychology, religion, social science, and sociology). Business and education is the largest.

Special: North Central offers co-op programs in radiation therapy and nuclear medicine technology, cross-registration with Benedictine University and Aurora University, a Washington semester, and study abroad. Internships in most subject areas, a 3-2 engineering degree with the Universities of Minnesota and Illinios at Urbana-Champaign, experiential credit, and nondegree study are available. Dual majors, student-designed majors, and 5-year integrated Bachelor's/Master's degree programs are available. There are 14 national honor societies, a freshman honors program, and 12 departmental honors programs.

Admissions: 67% of the 2009-2010 applicants were accepted. The ACT scores were 15% below 21, 27% between 21 and 23, 28% between 24 and 26, 13% between 27 and 28, and 17% above 28. There was 1 National Merit finalist. 8 freshmen graduated first in their class.

Requirements: The SAT or ACT is required, with a minimum of 20 on the ACT or a satisfactory score on the SAT. Minimum requirements also include a GPA of at least 2.5 and involvement in school and/or community. An admission essay and/or admission interview may be recommended. The GED is accepted. The recommended secondary school courses are 4 years of English and 3 years each of math, science, social science, and foreign language. A GPA of 2.5 is required. AP and CLEP credits are accepted.

Procedure: Freshmen are admitted to all sessions. Entrance exams should be taken in the spring of the junior year or the fall of the senior year. There are deferred admissions and rolling admissions plans. Application deadlines are open. Application fee is $25. Applications are accepted on-line.

Financial Aid: In 2009-2010, all full-time freshmen and 96% of continuing full-time students received some form of financial aid. 64% of all full-time freshmen and 37% of continuing full-time students received need-based aid. The average freshmen award was $25,070, with $4,573 from other forms of aid. The average financial indebtedness of the 2009 graduate was $27,285. The FAFSA and the college's own financial statement are required. Check with the school for current application deadlines.

Computers: Every room in every building is cabled for Internet service as are residence halls. The library, MeileySwallow, Kaufman, BoilerHouse, and the student center are completely wireless as is the main spine of campus and the areas outside of residence halls. The remaining classroom buildings have a wireless access point. There are labs in 4 to 6 buildings. There are 240 PCs and 70 Macs available on campus. All students may access the system. 7 A.M. to midnight in the computer center or at any time from residence hall or wireless access points. There are no time limits and no fees.

NORTHEASTERN STATE UNIVERSITY
Tahlequah, OK 74464   (918) 456-5511, ext. 2200; (918) 458-2342

Full-time: 6134 men and women	**Faculty:** II A, --$
Part-time: 2057 men and women	**Ph.D.s:** 74%
Graduate: 1070 men and women	**Student/Faculty:** 21 to 1
Year: semesters, summer session	**Tuition:** $5000 ($11,000)
Application Deadline: se profile	**Room & Board:** $3500
Freshman Class: n/av	
ACT: required	**VERY COMPETITIVE**

Northeastern State University, founded in 1846, is a public institution offering programs in arts and sciences, professional training, teacher preparation, and business. There are 4 undergraduate schools and 5 graduate schools. Figures in this profile are approximate. In addition to regional accreditation, NSU has baccalaureate program accreditation with ACBSP, ADA, ASLA, CSWE, NASM, NCATE, and NLN. The library contains 400,000 volumes, 766,300 microform items, and 8659 audio/video tapes/CDs/DVDs, and subscribes to 15,000 periodicals including electronic. Computerized library services include interlibrary loans, database searching, Internet access, and laptop Internet portals. Special learning facilities include a learning resource center. The 200-acre campus is in a small town 70 miles from Tulsa. Including any residence halls, there are 51 buildings.

Programs of Study: NSU confers B.A., B.S., B.A.Ed., B.B.A., B.S.Ed., B.S.Sci.Ed., B.S.N., and B.S.W. degrees. Master's and doctoral degrees are also awarded. Bachelor's degrees are awarded in BIOLOGICAL SCIENCE (biology/ biological science), BUSINESS (accounting, banking and finance, business administration and management, and marketing/retailing/merchandising), COMMUNICATIONS AND THE ARTS (advertising, communications, English, fine arts, journalism, music, Spanish, and speech/debate/rhetoric), COMPUTER AND PHYSICAL SCIENCE (chemistry, computer science, information sciences and systems, and mathematics), EDUCATION (art education, early childhood education, elementary education, health education, industrial arts education, music education, science education, secondary education, and special education), HEALTH PROFESSIONS (medical laboratory technology and nursing), SOCIAL SCIENCE (criminal justice, geography, history, political science/government, social science, social work, and sociology).

Special: Internships are offered in business, mass communications, and education. There are 10 national honor societies, a freshman honors program, and 5 departmental honors programs.

Requirements: The ACT is required, with a minimum composite score on the ACT of 20. Applicants should be high school graduates or have a GED. Students should have completed 4 years of English, 3 of math, and 2 each of history and science. NSU requires applicants to be in the upper 50% of their class. A GPA of 2.7 is required. AP and CLEP credits are accepted.

Procedure: Freshmen are admitted to all sessions. There is a rolling admissions plan. Check with the school for current application deadlines and fee. Notification is sent on a rolling basis.

Financial Aid: The FAFSA and the college's own financial statement are required. Check with the school for current deadlines.

Computers: Wireless access is available. All students may access the system.

NORTHEASTERN UNIVERSITY

Boston, MA 02115   **(617) 373-2200; (617) 373-8780**

Full-time: 7751 men, 7948 women	**Faculty:** 984; I, av$
Part-time: none	**Ph.D.s:** 88%
Graduate: 3231 men, 3161 women	**Student/Faculty:** 16 to 1
Year: semesters, summer session	**Tuition:** $35,362
Application Deadline: January 15	**Room & Board:** $12,350
Freshman Class: 34,005 applied, 13,948 accepted, 2833 enrolled	
SAT CR/M/W: 630/660/630	**HIGHLY COMPETITIVE**

Northeastern University, founded in 1898, is a private research university. It offers an experiential learning program anchored in cooperative education. Students doing co-op in the United States and abroad alternate semesters of full-time study with semesters of full-time work in fields relevant to their professional interests and major. There are 6 undergraduate schools and 8 graduate schools. In addition to regional accreditation, Northeastern has baccalaureate program accreditation with AACSB, ABET, ACPE, APTA, CAHEA, CSAB, and NLN. The 3 libraries contain 966,923 volumes, 2.4 million microform items, and 17,953 audio/video tapes/CDs/DVDs, and subscribe to 31,331 periodicals including electronic. Computerized library services include interlibrary loans, database searching, Internet access, and laptop Internet portals. Special learning facilities include a learning resource center, art gallery, and radio station. The 73-acre campus is in an urban area in the heart of the Back Bay section of Boston. Including any residence halls, there are 88 buildings.

Programs of Study: Northeastern confers B.A., B.S., and B.F.A. degrees. Master's and doctoral degrees are also awarded. Bachelor's degrees are awarded in BIOLOGICAL SCIENCE (biochemistry, biology/biological science, neurosciences, and toxicology), BUSINESS (accounting, business administration and management, human resources, international business management, management information systems, and marketing/retailing/merchandising), COMMUNICATIONS AND THE ARTS (advertising, art, communications, dramatic arts, English, journalism, languages, linguistics, music, performing arts, and public relations), COMPUTER AND PHYSICAL SCIENCE (applied physics, chemistry, computer programming, computer science, geology, information sciences and systems, mathematics, and physics), EDUCATION (athletic training, early childhood education, and elementary education), ENGINEERING AND ENVIRONMENTAL DESIGN (architecture, chemical engineering, civil engineering, computer engineering, computer technology, electrical/electronics engineering, electrical/electronics engineering technology, engineering, engineering technology, industrial engineering, mechanical engineering, and mechanical engineering technology), HEALTH PROFESSIONS (health science, medical laboratory science, nursing, pharmacy, physical therapy, rehabilitation therapy, and speech pathology/audiology), SOCIAL SCIENCE (African American studies, anthropology, criminal justice, economics, history, human services, interdisciplinary studies, international relations, philosophy, physical fitness/movement, political science/government, psychology, and sociology). Arts and sciences and business administration are the strongest academically. Engineering and computer science are the largest.

Special: Northeastern offers paid professional internships with area companies in Boston, around the country, and throughout the world to integrate classroom instruction with professional experience. Cross-registration with the New England Conservatory of Music and Hebrew College, among other universities and colleges, study abroad in dozens of countries, a Washington semester, work-study through the university and in neighboring public and private agencies, dual majors, and student-designed majors in the arts and sciences are also offered. Nondegree adult and continuing education are available, as are programs and scholarships for racial minorities and women, and accelerated degrees in engineering, nursing, and arts and sciences. There are 11 national honor societies and a freshman honors program.

Admissions: 41% of the 2009-2010 applicants were accepted. The SAT scores for the 2009-2010 freshman class were: Critical Reading--5% below 500, 27% between 500 and 599, 53% between 600 and 700, and 15% above 700; Math--2% below 500, 14% between 500 and 599, 58% between 600 and 700, and 26% above 700; Writing--4% below 500, 27% between 500 and 599, 54% between 600 and 700, and 15% above 700. The ACT scores were 7% below 21, 55% between 24 and 26, and 38% above 28. 75% of the current freshmen were in the top fifth of their class; 94% were in the top two fifths. 38 freshmen graduated first in their class.

Requirements: The SAT or ACT with Writing component is required. In addition, Northeastern recommends that applicants have 17 academic units, including 4 in English, 3 each in math, science, and social studies, and 2 each in foreign language and history. Recommended are 4 units in math and science, and a foreign language. An essay is required. AP credits are accepted. Important factors in the admissions decision are advanced placement or honors courses, leadership record, evidence of special talent, and extracurricular activities record.

Procedure: Freshmen are admitted fall and spring. Entrance exams should be taken from May of the junior year through December of the senior year. There are early admissions and deferred admissions plans. Early decision applications should be filed by November 1; regular applications, by January 15 for fall entry and November 1 for winter entry. The fall 2009 application fee was $70. Notification of early decision is sent December 31; regular decision, April 1. 4790 applicants were on the 2009 waiting list; 167 were admitted. Applications are accepted on-line.

Financial Aid: The CSS/Profile and FAFSA are required. The deadline for filing freshman financial aid applications for fall entry is February 15.

Computers: Wireless access is available. 26,800 simultaneous users can be accommodated on the wireless network, and there are 663 open-wired network connections. All academic buildings, classrooms, offices, and one 1200-bed residence hall are 100% wireless. All other residential halls have wireless in the lobby, lounges, and laundry rooms. All students may access the system 24 hours daily. There are no time limits and no fees. Students in the School of Architecture should have a MacBook Pro.

NORTHERN MICHIGAN UNIVERSITY

Marquette, MI 49855

(906) 227-2650
(800) 682-9797; (906) 227-1747

Full-time: 3715 men, 4079 women	**Faculty:** 319; IIA, -$
Part-time: 332 men, 452 women	**Ph.D.s:** 80%
Graduate: 242 men, 438 women	**Student/Faculty:** 24 to 1
Year: semesters, summer session	**Tuition:** $7454 ($11,828)
Application Deadline: open	**Room & Board:** $7846
Freshman Class: 5955 applied, 4338 accepted, 945 enrolled	
ACT: 23	**VERY COMPETITIVE**

Northern Michigan University, founded in 1899, is a public institution offering undergraduate programs in the arts and sciences, business, education, health science, human services, nursing, and technology. There are 4 undergraduate schools and 1 graduate school. In addition to regional accreditation, NMU has baccalaureate program accreditation with AACSB, ADA, CSWE, NASM, NCATE, and NLN. The library contains 631,244 volumes, 344,002 microform items, and 7,718 audio/video tapes/CDs/DVDs, and subscribes to 20,657 periodicals including electronic. Computerized library services include interlibrary loans, database searching, Internet access, and laptop Internet portals. Special learning facilities include a learning resource center, art gallery, radio station, TV station, and an observatory. The 359-acre campus is in an urban area on the southern shores of Lake Superior. Including any residence halls, there are 55 buildings.

Programs of Study: NMU confers B.A., B.S., B.F.A., B.M.Ed., B.S.N., and B.S.W. degrees. Associate and master's degrees are also awarded. Bachelor's degrees are awarded in BIOLOGICAL SCIENCE (biochemistry, biology/biological science, botany, ecology, microbiology, physiology, and zoology), BUSINESS (accounting, banking and finance, business administration and management, entrepreneurial studies, and marketing/retailing/merchandising), COMMUNICATIONS AND THE ARTS (broadcasting, communications, design, dramatic arts, English, fine arts, French, language arts, music, public relations, Spanish, and speech/debate/rhetoric), COMPUTER AND PHYSICAL SCIENCE (chemistry, computer programming, computer science, earth science, information sciences and systems, mathematics, and physics), EDUCATION (art education, business education, computer education, education of the mentally handicapped, elementary education, health education, industrial arts education, music education, physical education, science education, and secondary education), ENGINEERING AND ENVIRONMENTAL DESIGN (architecture, construction management, electrical/electronics engineering technology, industrial engineering technology, and manufacturing technology), HEALTH PROFESSIONS (chiropractic, clinical science, cytotechnology, medical laboratory technology, nursing, physician's assistant, predentistry, premedicine, preveterinary science, and speech pathology/audiology), SOCIAL SCIENCE (criminal justice, economics, geography, history, international studies, parks and recreation management, philosophy, physical fitness/movement, political science/government, prelaw, psychology, public administration, social work, sociology, and water resources). Nursing, chemistry, and education are the strongest academically. Art and Design, education, and nursing are the largest.

Special: NMU offers internships, a co-op program in business, study abroad in a number of countries, a Washington semester, dual majors in computer information and accounting, and student-designed majors in individual studies and liberal arts. There are 8 national honor societies, a freshman honors program, and 1 departmental honors program.

Admissions: 73% of the 2009-2010 applicants were accepted. The ACT scores were 33% below 21, 30% between 21 and 23, 22% between 24 and 26, 8% between 27 and 28, and 7% above 28.

Requirements: The ACT is required, with a GPA of 2.25 and a satisfactory score for the SAT and 19 for the ACT. Applicants must be graduates of accredited secondary schools or have earned a GED. NMU requires 12 to 16 Carnegie units; recommended secondary school preparation includes 4 years of English, 3 each of math, history, social studies, foreign language, and science, 2 of fine arts or performing arts, and 1 of computer instruction. Students seeking art scholarships must submit a portfolio; those seeking music and theater scholarships must audition. A GPA of 2.3 is required. AP and CLEP credits are accepted. Important factors in the admissions decision are advanced placement or honors courses, evidence of special talent, and recommendations by school officials.

Procedure: Freshmen are admitted to all sessions. Entrance exams should be taken during the year prior to enrollment. There are deferred admissions and rolling admissions plans. Application deadlines are open. Application fee is $35. Notification is sent on a rolling basis. Applications are accepted on-line.

Financial Aid: In 2009-2010, 86% of all full-time freshmen and 85% of continuing full-time students received some form of financial aid. 40% of all full-time freshmen and 35% of continuing full-time students received need-based aid. Need-based scholarships or need-based grants averaged $3,940 ($17,434 maximum); need-based self-help aid (loans and jobs) averaged $3,190 ($9,250 maximum); non-need based athletic scholarships averaged $6,443 ($19,466 maximum); and other non-need based awards and non-need based scholarships averaged $3,160 ($21,586 maximum). 16% of undergraduate students work part-time. Average annual earnings from campus work are $2884. The average financial indebtedness of the 2009 graduate was $18,034. The FAFSA is required. The priority date for freshman financial aid applications for fall entry is March 1.

Computers: Wireless access is available. Students have free wireless connectivity off campus as well as anywhere on campus. All students may access the system. There are no time limits and no fees. All students are required to have a personal computer. An IBM ThinkPad or iBook is provided as part of tuition and fees.

NORTHWESTERN UNIVERSITY
Evanston, IL 60208 (847) 491-7271

Full-time: 3705 men, 4115 women	**Faculty:** I, ++$
Part-time: 95 men, 125 women	**Ph.D.s:** 100%
Graduate: 4005 men, 2895 women	**Student/Faculty:** n/av
Year: trimesters, summer session	**Tuition:** $38,088
Application Deadline: see profile	**Room & Board:** $9000
Freshman Class: n/av	
SAT or ACT: required	**MOST COMPETITIVE**

Northwestern University, founded in 1851, is an independent, nonprofit liberal arts institution offering undergraduate study in the arts and sciences, education and social policy, journalism, music, communication, and engineering and applied science.Figures in the above capsule and in this profile are approximate. There are 6 undergraduate schools and 7 graduate schools. In addition to regional accreditation, Northwestern has baccalaureate program accreditation with AACSB, ABET, ACEJMC, APTA, and NASM. The 3 libraries contain 4.3 million volumes, 4.2 million microform items, and 75,358 audio/video tapes/CDs/DVDs, and subscribe to 39,310 periodicals including electronic. Computerized library services include interlibrary loans, database searching, and Internet access. Special learning facilities include an art gallery, radio station, TV station, an observatory. The 231-acre campus is in a suburban area 12 miles north of Chicago on the shores of Lake Michigan. Including any residence halls, there are 180 buildings.

Programs of Study: Northwestern confers B.A., B.S., B.A.C.M.N., B.A.Mus., B.M.E., B.Mus., B.Ph., B.P.H.C., B.S.A.M., B.S.B.M., B.S.C.H., B.S.C.I., B.S.C.M.N., B.S.C.O., B.S.C.S., B.S.Ed., B.S.E.E., B.S.E.N., B.S.E.S., B.S.G.E., B.S.G.S., B.S.I.E., B.S.J., B.S.M., B.S.M.D., B.S.M.E., B.S.M.F., B.S.M.T., B.S.S.E., and B.S.S.P. degrees. Master's and doctoral degrees are also awarded. Bachelor's degrees are awarded in BIOLOGICAL SCIENCE (biology/biological science, ecology, molecular biology, and neuroscience), BUSINESS (organizational behavior), COMMUNICATIONS AND THE ARTS (art, art history and appreciation, classics, communications, communications technology, comparative literature, dance, dramatic arts, English, fine arts, French, German, Italian, jazz, journalism, linguistics, music, music performance, music technology, music theory and composition, percussion, performing arts, piano/organ, radio/television technology, Slavic languages, Spanish, strings, voice, and winds), COMPUTER AND PHYSICAL SCIENCE (applied mathematics, astronomy, chemistry, computer science, geology, information sciences and systems, mathematics, physics, and statistics), EDUCATION (education, mathematics education, music education, and secondary education), ENGINEERING AND ENVIRONMENTAL DESIGN (biomedical engineering, chemical engineering, civil engineering, computer engineering, electrical/electronics engineering, engineering, environmental engineering, environmental science, industrial engineering, manufacturing engineering, materials engineering, materials science, and mechanical engineering), HEALTH PROFESSIONS (premedicine and speech pathology/audiology), SOCIAL SCIENCE (African American studies, American studies, anthropology, cognitive science, economics, ethics, politics, and social policy, European studies, gender studies, geography, history, human development, international studies, philosophy, political science/government, psychology, religion, science and society, sociology, and urban studies). Journalism, communications, and physical and life sciences are the strongest academically. Economics, political science, and engineering are the largest.

Special: The university offers cooperative engineering programs throughout the country, many off-campus field studies and research opportunities, internships in the arts, journalism, and teaching, study abroad in 46 countries around the world, a Washington semester, and numerous work-study programs both on and off campus. There is an accelerated degree program in medical education, and B.A.-B.S. degrees in liberal arts and engineering, liberal arts and music, and music and engineering. An integrated science program, an interdisciplinary study in mathematical methods in social sciences and numerous other interdisciplinary majors, a variety of dual and student-designed majors, pass/fail options, and a teaching media program are also available. There are 23 national honor societies, including Phi Beta Kappa, a freshman honors program, and 40 departmental honors programs.

Requirements: The SAT or ACT is required. In addition, applicants must be graduates of an accredited secondary school or have a GED certificate, and have completed a minimum of 16 units, including 4 units of English, 3 of math, 2 or 3 each of a foreign language and history, and 2 of lab sciences. SAT II: Subject tests are required for the accelerated honors program in medical education and the integrated science program. Auditions are required for applicants to the School of Music. AP credits are accepted. Important factors in the admissions decision are advanced placement or honors courses, recommendations by school officials, and extracurricular activities record.

Procedure: Freshmen are admitted to all sessions. Entrance exams should be taken by December of the senior year. There is a early decision and deferred admissions plan. Early decision applications should be filed by November 1; regular applications by November 1 for winter entry, February 1 for spring entry, and May 1 for summer entry, along with a $65 fee. Notification of early decision is sent December 15; regular decision, April 15. Applications are accepted on-line. 330 applicants were on a recent waiting list, 102 were accepted.

Financial Aid: Northwestern is a member of CSS. The CSS/Profile and FAFSA, and tax returns under certain conditions are required. Check with the school for current application deadlines.

Computers: All students may access the system. 24 hours per day. There are no time limits and no fees. Students enrolled in engineering must have a personal computer.

Rochester, MI 48309-4401	**(248) 370-3360; (800) OAK-UNIV**
Full-time: 4486 men, 6849 women	Faculty: 476; I, --$
Part-time: 1510 men, 2430 women	Ph.D.s: 91%
Graduate: 1190 men, 2455 women	Student/Faculty: 24 to 1
Year: semesters, summer session	Tuition: $8783 ($20,498)
Application Deadline: see profile	Room & Board: $7350
Freshman Class: 10,070 applied, 6912 accepted, 2466 enrolled	
ACT: 22	**VERY COMPETITIVE**

Oakland University, established in 1957, is a comprehensive state-supported institution serving a primarily commuter student body. There are 6 undergraduate schools and one graduate school. In addition to regional accreditation, Oakland has baccalaureate program accreditation with AACSB, ABET, CSWE, NASM, and TEAC. The 2 libraries contain 856,760 volumes, 1.2 million microform items, and 21,323 audio/video tapes/CDs/DVDs, and subscribe to 20,490 periodicals including electronic. Computerized library services include interlibrary loans, database searching, Internet access, and laptop Internet portals. Special learning facilities include a learning resource center, art gallery, radio station, TV station, the Product Development and Manufacturing Center, the Historical House Museum, and the Lean-Learning Institute. The 1444-acre campus is in a suburban area 25 miles north of Detroit. Including any residence halls, there are 46 buildings.

Programs of Study: Oakland confers B.A., B.S., B.F.A., B.G.S., B.Mus., B.S.E., B.S.N., and B.S.W. degrees. Master's and doctoral degrees are also awarded. Bachelor's degrees are awarded in BIOLOGICAL SCIENCE (biochemistry and biology/biological science), BUSINESS (accounting, banking and finance, business administration and management, business economics, human resources, management information systems, marketing/retailing/merchandising, operations management, and personnel management), COMMUNICATIONS AND THE ARTS (art history and appreciation, Chinese, communications, dance, dramatic arts, English, film arts, French, German, Japanese, journalism, linguistics, music, performing arts, Spanish, and studio art), COMPUTER AND PHYSICAL SCIENCE (chemistry, computer science, information sciences and systems, mathematics, medical physics, physics, and statistics), EDUCATION (elementary education and music education), ENGINEERING AND ENVIRONMENTAL DESIGN (computer engineering, electrical/electronics engineering, engineering chemistry, engineering physics, environmental science, industrial engineering, mechanical engineering, and occupational safety and health), HEALTH PROFESSIONS (allied health, health science, medical laboratory science, nursing, and preventive/wellness health care), SOCIAL SCIENCE (African American studies, anthropology, East Asian studies, economics, history, international relations, Latin American studies, liberal arts/general studies, philosophy, political science/government, psychology, public administration, Russian and Slavic studies, social work, sociology, South Asian studies, and women's studies). Physical sciences, biological sciences, and engineering are the strongest academically. Psychology, elementary education, and communications are the largest.

Special: Special academic programs include internships, cooperative programs for most disciplines, and many work-study opportunities. There are organized programs for study abroad in 8 countries; independent programs can be arranged. Oakland also offers a B.A. or B.S. degree in biology and economics, a general studies program, dual majors, a student-designed major, cross-registration with

Macomb Community College, and preprofessional studies in medicine, dentistry, optometry, and veterinary medicine. There are 12 national honor societies and a freshman honors program.

Admissions: 69% of the 2009-2010 applicants were accepted. The ACT scores were 36% below 21, 38% between 21 and 23, 22% between 24 and 26, 8% between 27 and 28, and 7% above 28.

Requirements: The ACT is required. In addition, admissions requirements include graduation from an accredited secondary school and high school level college preparatory work, including 4 years of English and 3 years each of math, science, and social studies. 2 years of foreign language is recommended as well. Music and dance majors must audition. A GPA of 2.5 is required. AP and CLEP credits are accepted.

Procedure: Freshmen are admitted to all sessions. Entrance exams should be taken during the spring of the junior year or early fall of the senior year. There are deferred admissions and rolling admissions plans. Check with the school for current application deadlines. Notification is sent on a rolling basis. Applications are accepted on-line.

Financial Aid: The FAFSA is required. The deadline for filing freshman financial aid applications for fall entry is April 1.

Computers: Wireless access is available. All students may access the system. There are no time limits and no fees.

OBERLIN COLLEGE
Oberlin, OH 44074
(440) 775-8411
(800) 622-6243; (440) 775-6905

Full-time: 1268 men, 1574 women	**Faculty:** 285; IIB, +$
Part-time: 44 men, 24 women	**Ph.D.s:** 96%
Graduate: none	**Student/Faculty:** 9 to 1
Year: 4-1-4,	**Tuition:** $40,004
Application Deadline: January 15	**Room & Board:** $10,480
Freshman Class: 7227 applied, 2434 accepted, 809 enrolled	
SAT CR/M/W: 700/670/700	**ACT:** 30 **MOST COMPETITIVE**

Oberlin College, founded in 1833, is a private institution offering degree programs in the liberal arts and sciences, and music. There are 2 undergraduate schools. In addition to regional accreditation, Oberlin has baccalaureate program accreditation with NASM. The 4 libraries contain 1.4 million volumes, 356,864 microform items, 104,227 audio/video tapes/CDs/DVDs, and subscribe to 30,750 periodicals including electronic. Computerized library services include interlibrary loans, database searching, and Internet access. Special learning facilities include a learning resource center, art gallery, radio station, an observatory, art museum, art library, arboretum, a conservatory of music, and a music library. The 440-acre campus is in a small town 35 miles southwest of Cleveland, OH. Including any residence halls, there are 65 buildings.

Programs of Study: Oberlin confers B.A. and B.Mus. degrees. Master's degrees are also awarded. Bachelor's degrees are awarded in BIOLOGICAL SCIENCE (biochemistry, biology/biological science, and neurosciences), COMMUNICATIONS AND THE ARTS (art, classics, comparative literature, creative writing, dance, dramatic arts, English, film arts, fine arts, French, German, music, music history and appreciation, music performance, music theory and composition, romance languages and literature, Russian, and Spanish), COMPUTER AND PHYSICAL SCIENCE (astronomy, chemistry, computer science, geology, mathematics, and physics), EDUCATION (music education), ENGINEERING AND

ENVIRONMENTAL DESIGN (environmental science), SOCIAL SCIENCE (African American studies, American studies, anthropology, archeology, East Asian studies, economics, history, humanities, Judaic studies, Latin American studies, law, Near Eastern studies, philosophy, political science/government, psychology, religion, sociology, and women's studies). Sciences, art and humanities, and music are the strongest academically. English, biology, and history are the largest.

Special: Internships are available through the Business Initiatives Program. Students may study abroad in 38 countries. Moreover, about 40% of Oberlin students study abroad. The college offers independent and dual majors, 3-2 engineering programs with other institutions, non-degree study for special and visiting students, and a 5-year B.A.-B.Mus. double degree. Pass/no credit options are available to all students. There are 4 national honor societies, including Phi Beta Kappa, and 25 departmental honors programs.

Admissions: 34% of the 2009-2010 applicants were accepted. The SAT scores for the 2009-2010 freshman class were: Critical Reading--2% below 500, 8% between 500 and 599, 38% between 600 and 700, and 52% above 700; Math--2% below 500, 13% between 500 and 599, 50% between 600 and 700, and 35% above 700; Writing--2% below 500, 9% between 500 and 599, 44% between 600 and 700, and 45% above 700. 90% of the current freshmen were in the top fifth of their class; 99% were in the top two fifths. There were 55 National Merit finalists. 25 freshmen graduated first in their class.

Requirements: The SAT or ACT is required. In addition, candidates for admission should have completed 4 years each of English and math, and 3 each of science, social studies, and a foreign language. AP credits are accepted. Important factors in the admissions decision are advanced placement or honors courses, personality/intangible qualities, and leadership record.

Procedure: Freshmen are admitted fall. Entrance exams should be taken in the junior year or early in the senior year. There are early decision and deferred admissions plans. Early decision applications should be filed by November 15; regular applications, by January 15 for fall entry and November 15 for spring entry, along with a $35 fee. Notification of early decision is sent December 15; regular decision, April 1. Applications are accepted on-line. 995 applicants were on a recent waiting list, 15 were accepted.

Financial Aid: In 2009-2010, 88% of all full-time freshmen and 82% of continuing full-time students received some form of financial aid. 59% of all full-time freshmen and 56% of continuing full-time students received need-based aid. The average freshmen award was $30,403. 59% of undergraduate students work part-time. Average annual earnings from campus work are $1450. The average financial indebtedness of the 2009 graduate was $18,604. Oberlin is a member of CSS. The CSS/Profile, FAFSA, and the college's own financial statement are required. The deadline for filing freshman financial aid applications for fall entry is February 15.

Computers: Wireless access is available. All students may access the system. There are no time limits and no fees.

OCCIDENTAL COLLEGE

Los Angeles, CA 90041

(323) 259-2700
(800) 825-5262; (323) 341-4875

Full-time: 852 men, 1105 women	**Faculty:** 163; IIB, +$
Part-time: 9 men, 6 women	**Ph.D.s:** 94%
Graduate: 1 men, 16 women	**Student/Faculty:** 12 to 1
Year: semesters, summer session	**Tuition:** $38,922
Application Deadline: January 10	**Room & Board:** $10,780
Freshman Class: 6014 applied, 2583 accepted, 576 enrolled	
SAT CR/M/W: 650/650/660	**ACT:** 30 **MOST COMPETITIVE**

Occidental College, founded in 1887, is a private nonsectarian school of liberal arts and sciences. The library contains 443,780 volumes, 426,016 microform items, and 12,741 audio/video tapes/CDs/DVDs, and subscribes to 28,564 periodicals including electronic. Computerized library services include interlibrary loans, database searching, and Internet access. Special learning facilities include a learning resource center, art gallery, radio station, student newspaper, fully equipped theater, art studio, ornithology collection, and physics, plasma, and optic labs, green house, and geology collection. The 120-acre campus is in an urban area in Los Angeles. Including any residence halls, there are 44 buildings.

Programs of Study: Oxy confers A.B. degrees. Master's degrees are also awarded. Bachelor's degrees are awarded in BIOLOGICAL SCIENCE (biochemistry and biology/biological science), COMMUNICATIONS AND THE ARTS (art history and appreciation, comparative literature, dramatic arts, French, German, languages, music, and Spanish), COMPUTER AND PHYSICAL SCIENCE (chemistry, geochemistry, geology, geophysics and seismology, mathematics, and physics), SOCIAL SCIENCE (American studies, Asian/Oriental studies, cognitive science, economics, history, international relations, philosophy, physical fitness/movement, political science/government, psychobiology, psychology, religion, sociology, urban studies, and women's studies). Social sciences, biology, and chemistry are the strongest academically. Social sciences, English, and diplomacy and world affairs are the largest.

Special: Cross-registration is permitted with the California Institute of Technology and the Art Center College of Design. Students may study abroad in 41 countries in Europe, Asia, Africa, and Latin America. Opportunities are provided for internships, a Washington semester, a U.N. semester in New York City, dual and student-designed majors, a 3-2 engineering degree with the California Institute of Technology, a 3-3 law program with Columbia, a 4-2 biotech program with Keck, and an exchange program with Spelman and Morehouse. There are 8 national honor societies, including Phi Beta Kappa.

Admissions: 43% of the 2009-2010 applicants were accepted. The SAT scores for the 2009-2010 freshman class were: Critical Reading--3% below 500, 18% between 500 and 599, 53% between 600 and 700, and 26% above 700; Math--1% below 500, 21% between 500 and 599, 60% between 600 and 700, and 21% above 700; Writing--2% below 500, 18% between 500 and 599, 53% between 600 and 700, and 2% above 700. The ACT scores were 1% below 21, 3% between 21 and 23, 19% between 24 and 26, 24% between 27 and 28, and 53% above 28. 81% of the current freshmen were in the top fifth of their class; 98% were in the top two fifths. There was National Merit finalist. 15 freshmen graduated first in their class.

Requirements: The SAT or ACT is required. In addition, applicants should be high school graduates of high academic standing with 4 years of English, 4 of math, 3 each of foreign language and science, and 2 each of social studies and history. The GED is accepted. An essay is required and an interview is recommended. AP credits are accepted. Important factors in the admissions decision are extracurricular activities record, advanced placement or honors courses, and recommendations by school officials.

Procedure: Freshmen are admitted fall. Entrance exams should be taken no later than December of the senior year. There is an early decision and deferred admissions plans. Early decision applications should be filed by November 15; regular applications by January 10 for fall entry, along with a $50 fee. Notifications are sent December 15; regular decision, April 1. Applications are accepted on-line. A waiting list is maintained.

Financial Aid: In 2009-2010, 75% of continuing full-time students received some form of financial aid. 52% of all full-time freshmen and 53% of continuing full-time students received need-based aid. The average freshmen award was $34,171. 42% of undergraduate students work part-time. The average financial indebtedness of the 2009 graduate was $20,381. The CSS/Profile, FAFSA, and non-custodial parent's statement and business farm supplement are required. The deadline for filing freshman financial aid applications for fall entry is February 1.

Computers: Wireless access is available. Most of the campus is wireless. In addition, students have access to 300 PCs in residence halls, the library, and the computer center. All students are provided with an e-mail account and Internet access. Occidental supports Macs and PCs. All students may access the system at any time. There are no time limits and no fees.

OGLETHORPE UNIVERSITY
Atlanta, GA 30319-2797   (404) 364-8307
(800) 428-8491; (404) 364-8500

Full-time: 337 men, 513 women	**Faculty:** 46; IIB, -$
Part-time: 36 men, 57 women	**Ph.D.s:** 96%
Graduate: 3 men, 68 women	**Student/Faculty:** 18 to 1
Year: semesters, summer session	**Tuition:** $26,650
Application Deadline: open	**Room & Board:** $9990
Freshman Class: 4891 applied, 2040 accepted, 230 enrolled	
SAT CR/M/W: 600/570/565	**ACT:** 25 **VERY COMPETITIVE**

Oglethorpe University, founded in 1835, is an independent institution offering programs in the liberal arts and science, business, and preprofessional studies. There are 2 undergraduate schools and 1 graduate school. The library contains 155,000 volumes, 4189 microform items, and 6786 audio/video tapes/CDs/DVDs, and subscribes to 775 periodicals including electronic. Computerized library services include interlibrary loans, database searching, Internet access, and laptop Internet portals. Special learning facilities include a learning resource center, an art gallery, a radio station, an in-residence, professional theatre program, Georgia Shakespeare, and a Center for Civic Engagement. The 102-acre campus is in a suburban area 10 miles northeast of downtown Atlanta. Including any residence halls, there are 25 buildings.

Programs of Study: Oglethorpe confers B.A., B.S., B.A.L.S. and B.B.A. degrees. Master's degrees are also awarded. Bachelor's degrees are awarded in BIOLOGICAL SCIENCE (biology/biological science), BUSINESS (accounting and business administration and management), COMMUNICATIONS AND THE ARTS (art, art history and appreciation, communications, English, French, and Spanish), COMPUTER AND PHYSICAL SCIENCE (chemistry, mathematics, and physics), SOCIAL SCIENCE (American studies, behavioral science, biopsychology, economics, history, international studies, philosophy, political science/government, psychology, social work, and sociology). Accounting, biology, and English are the strongest academically. Business administration, biology, and communications and rhetoric are the largest.

Special: Oglethorpe offers co-op programs in all majors, cross-registration through the Atlanta Regional Consortium for Higher Education, international exchange agreements with several universities in Europe, Asia, and South America, and other study-abroad options. Internships are available in all areas of study for up to 15 credit hours for upperclassmen with a minimum 2.8 GPA, and a Washington semester offers internships with Georgia senators and others. There is a 3-2 engineering program with Georgia Institute of Technology, the Universities of Florida and Southern California, and Auburn University. Accelerated degrees, dual majors, student-designed majors, federal work-study programs, and nondegree study are offered. There are 7 national honor societies, a freshman honors program, and 99 departmental honors programs.

Admissions: 42% of the 2009-2010 applicants were accepted. The SAT scores for the 2009-2010 freshman class were: Critical Reading--9% below 500, 45% between 500 and 599, 32% between 600 and 700, and 14% above 700; Math--18% below 500, 45% between 500 and 599, 31% between 600 and 700, and 6% above 700; Writing--19% below 500, 41% between 500 and 599, 30% between 600 and 700, and 10% above 700. The ACT scores were 5% below 21, 29% between 21 and 23, 26% between 24 and 26, 32% between 27 and 28, and 8% above 28. 63% of the current freshmen were in the top fifth of their class; 87% were in the top two fifths.

Requirements: The SAT or ACT is required. In addition, students should graduate from an accredited high school or have a GED certificate. They should have completed 4 courses in English, 3 each in science and social studies, and a math sequence of algebra I and II and geometry. A counselor's or teacher's recommendation is required, and an essay is required for a scholarship. An interview is recommended. AP and CLEP credits are accepted. Important factors in the admissions decision are recommendations by school officials, extracurricular activities record, and advanced placement or honors courses.

Procedure: Freshmen are admitted to all sessions. Entrance exams should be taken late in the junior year or early in the senior year. There are early decision, early admissions, deferred admissions, and rolling admissions plans. Check with the school for current application deadlines. The application fee is $35. Notification is sent on a rolling basis. Applications are accepted on-line.

Financial Aid: In a recent year, 96% of all full-time freshmen and 85% of continuing full-time students received some form of financial aid. 69% of all full-time freshmen and 58% of continuing full-time students received need-based aid. The average financial indebtedness of a recent graduate was $16,250. Oglethorpe is a member of CSS. The FAFSA is required. Check with the school for current application deadlines.

Computers: Wireless access is available. Each resident student has a network portal in his or her room and there are several computer labs available on campus, including a 24-hour computer lab. All students are provided an e-mail address accessible from the network or from the Internet. All students may access the system. There are no time limits and no fees. It is strongly recommended that all students have a personal computer.

OHIO NORTHERN UNIVERSITY

Ada, OH 45810

(419) 772-2260
(800) 408-4668; (419) 772-2313

Full-time: 1185 men, 1050 women	**Faculty:** IIB, av$
Part-time: 35 men, 35 women	**Ph.D.s:** 82%
Graduate: 415 men, 575 women	**Student/Faculty:** n/av
Year: trimesters, summer session	**Tuition:** $33,000
Application Deadline: see profile	**Room & Board:** $9075
Freshman Class: n/av	
SAT or ACT: required	**VERY COMPETITIVE**

Ohio Northern University, founded in 1871, is a private institution affiliated with the United Methodist Church. Undergraduate programs are offered in arts and sciences, business administration, engineering, and pharmacy. Figures in the above capsule are approximate. There are 4 undergraduate schools and 1 graduate school. In addition to regional accreditation, ONU has baccalaureate program accreditation with ABET, ACPE, NASM, and NCATE. The 2 libraries contain 250,518 volumes, 72,067 microform items, and 10,815 audio/video tapes/CDs/DVDs, and subscribe to 1038 periodicals including electronic. Computerized library services include interlibrary loans and database searching. Special learning facilities include a learning resource center, art gallery, radio station, TV station, and pharmacy museum. The 285-acre campus is in a small town about 75 miles south of Toledo. Including any residence halls, there are 39 buildings.

Programs of Study: ONU confers B.A., B.S., B.F.A., B.M., B.S.B.A., B.S.C.E., B.S.C.P.E., B.S.E.E., B.S.M.E., B.S.M.T., and B.S.Ph. degrees. Doctoral degrees are also awarded. Bachelor's degrees are awarded in AGRICULTURE (environmental studies), BIOLOGICAL SCIENCE (biochemistry, biology/biological science, and molecular biology), BUSINESS (accounting, business administration and management, business economics, international business management, management science, and sports management), COMMUNICATIONS AND THE ARTS (broadcasting, ceramic art and design, communications, creative writing, dramatic arts, English, fine arts, French, graphic design, journalism, language arts, literature, music, music business management, music performance, music theory and composition, public relations, and Spanish), COMPUTER AND PHYSICAL SCIENCE (chemistry, computer science, mathematics, physics, and statistics), EDUCATION (athletic training, early childhood education, health education, middle school education, music education, and physical education), ENGINEERING AND ENVIRONMENTAL DESIGN (civil engineering, computer engineering, electrical/electronics engineering, mechanical engineering, and technological management), HEALTH PROFESSIONS (health, medical technology, and pharmacy), SOCIAL SCIENCE (criminal justice, history, international studies, philosophy, political science/government, psychology, religion, social studies, sociology, and youth ministry). Chemistry, engineering, and pharmacy are the strongest academically. Pharmacy, engineering, and biology are the largest.

Special: Co-op programs are available in civil, electrical, computer, and mechanical engineering and technology, computer science, and math. Students may take internships in pharmacy, engineering, and business and may study abroad in 15 countries. B.A.-B.S. degrees and dual majors are available in arts/engineering, arts/pharmacy, and arts/business. The university also offers pass/fail options and work-study programs. There are 38 national honor societies, a freshman honors program, and 21 departmental honors programs.

Requirements: The SAT or ACT is required. In addition, the preparatory program should include 4 years of English, 3 of math, and 2 each of science, social studies, art, history, and music; 2 years of foreign language are recommended. ONU requires applicants to be in the upper 50% of their class. A GPA of 2.5 is required. AP and CLEP credits are accepted. Important factors in the admissions decision are advanced placement or honors courses, leadership record, and extracurricular activities record.

Procedure: Freshmen are admitted to all sessions. Entrance exams should be taken in the spring of the junior year or the fall of the senior year. There are deferred admissions and rolling admissions plans. Check with the school for current application deadlines. The fall 2009 application fee was $30. Notification is sent on a rolling basis. Applications are accepted on-line.

Financial Aid: ONU is a member of CSS. The FAFSA and the college's own financial statement are required. Check with the school for current application deadlines.

Computers: All students may access the system during building hours and 24 hours a day via modem. There are no time limits and no fees.

OHIO STATE UNIVERSITY
Columbus, OH 43210-1200   (614) 292-3980; (614) 292-4818

Full-time: 20318 men, 17546 women	**Faculty:** I, av$
Part-time: 1847 men, 1637 women	**Ph.D.s:** 99%
Graduate: 6363 men, 7303 women	**Student/Faculty:** n/av
Year: varies, summer session	**Tuition:** $8706
Application Deadline: February 1	**Room & Board:** $8409
Freshman Class: 18256 applied, 13822 accepted, 6739 enrolled	
SAT CR/M/W: 600/640/590	**ACT:** 27 **HIGHLY COMPETITIVE**

The Ohio State University, founded in 1870, is a public land-grant institution offering programs in agriculture and natural resources, arts and sciences, business, education, architecture and engineering, nursing, pharmacy, social work, dental hygiene, and human ecology. There are 5 other campuses. There are 14 undergraduate schools and one graduate school. In addition to regional accreditation, Ohio State has baccalaureate program accreditation with AACSB, ABET, ACPE, ADA, APTA, ASLA, CSAB, FIDER, NASAD, NASM, NCATE, NLN, and SAF. The 13 libraries contain 6.2 million volumes, 6.1 million microform items, and 87,086 audio/video tapes/CDs/DVDs, and subscribe to 79,751 periodicals including electronic. Computerized library services include interlibrary loans, database searching, Internet access, and laptop Internet portals. Special learning facilities include a learning resource center, art gallery, planetarium, radio station, TV station, the Museum of Biological Diversity, the John Glenn Institute for Public Service and Public Policy, and the Cartoon Research Library. The 3469-acre campus is in an urban area 2 miles north of downtown Columbus, OH. Including any residence halls, there are 457 buildings.

Programs of Study: Ohio State confers B.A., B.S., B.A.E., B.F.A., B.Mus., and B.Mus.Ed. degrees. Associate, master's, and doctoral degrees are also awarded. Bachelor's degrees are awarded in AGRICULTURE (agricultural economics, animal science, fishing and fisheries, forestry and related sciences, natural resource management, and plant science), BIOLOGICAL SCIENCE (biochemistry, biology/biological science, entomology, evolutionary biology, microbiology, nutrition, plant physiology, and zoology), BUSINESS (accounting, banking and finance, business economics, hospitality management services, human resources, insurance and risk management, international business management, management information systems, marketing and distribution, real estate, and transportation management), COMMUNICATIONS AND THE ARTS (Arabic, art, Chinese, classics, communications, dance, English, French, German, Greek, Hebrew, industrial design, Italian, Japanese, jazz, journalism, linguistics, music, music history and appreciation, music performance, music theory and composition, Portuguese, Russian, and Spanish), COMPUTER AND PHYSICAL SCIENCE (actuarial science, astronomy, chemistry, computer science, geology, information sciences and systems, mathematics, and physics), EDUCATION (agricultural education, art education, dance education, environmental education, music education, and technical education), ENGINEERING AND ENVIRONMENTAL DESIGN (aeronautical engineering, architecture, ceramic engineering, chemical engineering, civil engineering, computer engineering, electrical/electronics engineering, engineering physics, environmental science, industrial engineering, interior design, landscape architecture/design, materials engineering, materials science, mechanical engineering, metallurgical engineering, and welding engineering), HEALTH PROFESSIONS (dental hygiene, medical technology, nursing, occupational therapy, physical therapy, radiograph medical technology, respiratory therapy, and speech pathology/audiology), SOCIAL SCIENCE (African American studies, anthropology, clothing and textiles management/production/services, criminology, economics, geography, history, human development, human ecology, industrial and organizational psychology, international studies, Islamic studies, Judaic studies, medieval studies, philosophy, political science/government, psychology, social work, sociology, and women's studies). Biology, finance, and political science are the largest.

Special: Students may cross-register with all central Ohio colleges. OSU offers internships, co-op programs, extensive study abroad in about 40 countries, work-study programs, dual and student-designed majors, a general degree, an accelerated degree, credit by exam, nondegree study, and pass/fail options. There are 39 national honor societies, including Phi Beta Kappa, a freshman honors program, and 16 departmental honors programs.

Admissions: 76% of the 2009-2010 applicants were accepted. The SAT scores for the 2009-2010 freshman class were: Critical Reading--10% below 500, 39% between 500 and 599, 41% between 600 and 700, and 10% above 700; Math--4% below 500, 26% between 500 and 599, 50% between 600 and 700, and 20% above 700; Writing--10% below 500, 42% between 500 and 599, 41% between 600 and 700, and 7% above 700. The ACT scores were 2% below 21, 7% between 21 and 23, 28% between 24 and 26, 27% between 27 and 28, and 36% above 28. 76% of the current freshmen were in the top fifth of their class; 96% were in the top two fifths. There were 117 National Merit finalists. 308 freshmen graduated first in their class.

Requirements: The SAT or ACT is required. In addition, applicants must complete high school with at least 18 academic credits, including 4 in English, 3 in math, 2 each in foreign language, science, and history or social studies, and 1 in art or music. The GED is accepted. AP and CLEP credits are accepted. Important factors in the admissions decision are advanced placement or honors courses, evidence of special talent, and extracurricular activities record.

Procedure: Freshmen are admitted to all sessions. Entrance exams should be taken by October of the senior year. There is a rolling admissions plan. Applications should be filed by February 1 for fall entry; November 1 for winter entry; February 1 for spring entry; and February 1 for summer entry, along with a $40 fee. Notifications are sent December 1. 661 applicants were on the 2009 waiting list; 10 were admitted. Applications are accepted on-line.

Financial Aid: In 2009-2010, 88% of all full-time freshmen and 80% of continuing full-time students received some form of financial aid. 49% of all full-time freshmen and 50% of continuing full-time students received need-based aid. The average freshman award was $13,840. Need-based scholarships or need-based grants averaged $7,385 ($26,737 maximum); need-based self-help aid (loans and jobs) averaged $3,843 ($10,500 maximum); non-need-based athletic scholarships averaged $16,142 ($45,030 maximum); and other non-need-based awards and non-need-based scholarships averaged $9,708 ($47,525 maximum). Average annual earnings from campus work are $2118. The average financial indebtedness of the 2009 graduate was $18,425. Ohio State is a member of CSS. The FAFSA is required. The priority date for freshman financial aid applications for fall entry is February 15.

Computers: Wireless access is available. Students may connect to the wireless system at student gathering places all over campus. 4000 Internet-connected computers are available in public student computing centers, libraries, and college computing labs throughout campus. Most centers, libraries, and labs also provide laptop hookup Internet access stations. All residence hall students have individual dedicated high-speed Internet access in their rooms. All students may access the system. 24 hours a day. There are no time limits and no fees. It is strongly recommended that all students have a personal computer. Students enrolled in Fisher College of Business Executive MBA program; all students in the Department of must have a personal computer.

OKLAHOMA BAPTIST UNIVERSITY
Shawnee, OK 74804

(405) 878-2033
(800) 654-3285; (405) 878-2068

Full-time: 550 men, 800 women	**Faculty:** n/av
Part-time: 160 men, 90 women	**Ph.D.s:** n/av
Graduate: 20 men, 15 women	**Student/Faculty:** n/av
Year: 4-1-4, summer session	**Tuition:** $18,670
Application Deadline: see profile	**Room & Board:** $5630
Freshman Class: n/av	
SAT or ACT: required	**VERY COMPETITIVE**

Oklahoma Baptist University, founded in 1910, is a liberal arts institution affiliated with the Southern Baptist Convention. OBU offers degrees in Christian service, business, nursing, fine arts, telecommunications, teacher education, and the traditional liberal arts areas. There are 5 undergraduate schools and 1 graduate school. Enrollment figures in the above capsule and figures in this profile are approximate. In addition to regional accreditation, OBU has baccalaureate program accreditation with ACBSP, NASM, NCATE, and NLN. The library contains 290,000 volumes, 230,000 microform items, and 1500 audio/video tapes/CDs/ DVDs, and subscribes to 600 periodicals including electronic. Computerized library services include interlibrary loans, database searching, Internet access, and laptop Internet portals. Special learning facilities include a learning resource center, art gallery, planetarium, TV station, a language lab, and a Biblical research library. The 189-acre campus is in a small town 30 miles east of Oklahoma City and 90 miles southwest of Tulsa. Including any residence halls, there are 54 buildings.

Programs of Study: OBU confers B.A., B.S., B.B.A., B.F.A., B.Hum., B.M., B.M.A., B.Mus.Ed., and B.S.E. degrees. Associates and master's degrees are also awarded. Bachelor's degrees are awarded in BIOLOGICAL SCIENCE (biology/ biological science), BUSINESS (accounting, banking and finance, business ad-

ministration and management, and marketing/retailing/merchandising), COM-
MUNICATIONS AND THE ARTS (broadcasting, communications, dramatic
arts, English, fine arts, French, German, journalism, music, Spanish, speech/
debate/rhetoric, and telecommunications), COMPUTER AND PHYSICAL SCI-
ENCE (chemistry, computer science, information sciences and systems, mathematics, and physics), EDUCATION (art education, early childhood education, elementary education, foreign languages education, music education, physical
education, science education, and secondary education), HEALTH PROFES-
SIONS (nursing, physical therapy, predentistry, and premedicine), SOCIAL SCI-
ENCE (history, political science/government, prelaw, psychology, religion, social
science, social work, and sociology). Teacher education, biology, and religion are
the strongest academically. Biology, elementary education, and nursing are the
largest.

Special: OBU offers co-op programs in business, and a 3-2 engineering degree
with Oklahoma State University. Students may study abroad in 15 countries in
Europe, Central and South America, Asia, and Africa. Internships in several
fields, student-designed majors, including an interdisciplinary program in humanities, and pass/fail options are available. There are 4 national honor societies and
a freshman honors program.

Requirements: The SAT or ACT is required. Admission is granted to students
with a 3.0 GPA and a composite scores of 950 on the SAT or 20 on the ACT.
Graduation from an accredited secondary school or satisfactory scores on the
GED are required for admission. High school courses should include 4 units of
English, 3 units of math, and 2 units each of social studies, lab science, and a foreign language. OBU requires applicants to be in the upper 50% of their class. AP
and CLEP credits are accepted. Important factors in the admissions decision are
advanced placement or honors courses, recommendations by school officials, and
leadership record.

Procedure: Freshmen are admitted to all sessions. Entrance exams should be tak-
en during the spring of the junior year. There are deferred admissions and rolling
admissions plans. Check with the school for current application deadlines and
fee. Applications are accepted on-line.

Financial Aid: In a recent year, 95% of all full-time freshmen and 92% of continuing full-time students received some form of financial aid. 52% of all full-
time freshmen and 50% of continuing full-time students received need-based aid.
The average freshmen award was $14,780. 95% of undergraduate students work
part-time. Average annual earnings from campus work are $1600. The average
financial indebtedness of a recent graduate was $14,000. The FAFSA is required.
Check with the school for current deadlines.

Computers: Wireless access is available. All students may access the system 75
hours per week. There are no time limits and no fees. It is strongly recommended
that all students have a personal computer.

Oklahoma City, OK 73106-1493   (405) 208-5050
(800) 633-7242; (405) 208-5916

Full-time: 745 men, 1141 women	**Faculty:** 168
Part-time: 166 men, 231 women	**Ph.D.s:** 80%
Graduate: 848 men, 679 women	**Student/Faculty:** 11 to 1
Year: semesters, summer session	**Tuition:** $23,400
Application Deadline: August 20	**Room & Board:** $7056
Freshman Class: 1185 applied, 931 accepted, 404 enrolled	
ACT: 25	**SAT:** required

VERY COMPETITIVE

Oklahoma City University, founded in 1904, is a private, comprehensive university affiliated with the United Methodist Church, offering undergraduate and graduate programs in arts and sciences, business, music and performing arts, religion and church vocations, nursing, and law. There are 8 undergraduate schools and 6 graduate schools. In addition to regional accreditation, OCU has baccalaureate program accreditation with ACBSP, NASM, and NLN. The 2 libraries contain 443,150 volumes, 1 million microform items, and 6,285 audio/video tapes/CDs/DVDs, and subscribe to 6,209 periodicals including electronic. Computerized library services include interlibrary loans, database searching, Internet access, and laptop Internet portals. Special learning facilities include a learning resource center, art gallery, TV station. The 78-acre campus is in an urban area within Oklahoma City. Including any residence halls, there are 34 buildings.

Programs of Study: OCU confers B.A., B.S., B.F.A., B.M., B.Perf.Arts, B.S.B., and B.S.N. degrees. Master's and doctoral degrees are also awarded. Bachelor's degrees are awarded in BIOLOGICAL SCIENCE (biochemistry, biology/biological science, and biophysics), BUSINESS (accounting, banking and finance, and business administration and management), COMMUNICATIONS AND THE ARTS (advertising, art, broadcasting, communications, dance, dramatic arts, English, French, German, graphic design, journalism, music, piano/organ, Spanish, and speech/debate/rhetoric), COMPUTER AND PHYSICAL SCIENCE (chemistry, computer management, computer science, mathematics, physics, and science), EDUCATION (early childhood education, elementary education, foreign languages education, music education, physical education, and science education), HEALTH PROFESSIONS (nursing and premedicine), SOCIAL SCIENCE (criminal justice, economics, history, humanities, philosophy, political science/government, prelaw, psychology, religion, and sociology). Business, performing arts, and sciences are the strongest academically. Sciences, performing arts, and liberal arts are the largest.

Special: OCU offers internships, a Washington semester, work-study programs, a general studies degree, dual and student-designed majors, credit for life experience, and study-abroad programs in 5 countries. B.A.-B.S. degrees and an accelerated degree program in nursing and law are also available. There are 9 national honor societies, a freshman honors program, and 10 departmental honors programs.

Admissions: 79% of the 2009-2010 applicants were accepted. The ACT scores were 11% below 21, 20% between 21 and 23, 34% between 24 and 26, 14% between 27 and 28, and 20% above 28. 59% of the current freshmen were in the top fifth of their class; 80% were in the top two fifths. 17 freshmen graduated first in their class.

Requirements: The SAT or ACT is required. In addition, with a satisfactory score on the SAT, or a minimum score of 20 on the ACT. Graduation from an accredited secondary school or satisfactory scores on the GED are also required for admission. High school courses must include 4 units of English, 3 units each of science, social studies, and math, and 2 units of a foreign language. Music and dance students are required to audition. OCU requires applicants to be in the upper 50% of their class. A GPA of 3.0 is required. AP and CLEP credits are accepted. Important factors in the admissions decision are evidence of special talent, advanced placement or honors courses, and leadership record.

Procedure: Freshmen are admitted to all sessions. Entrance exams should be taken by February of the senior year. There are deferred admissions and rolling admissions plans. Applications should be filed by August 20 for fall entry. The fall 2008 application fee was $35. Notification is sent on a rolling basis. Applications are accepted on-line.

Financial Aid: In 2009-2010, 91% of all full-time freshmen and 85% of continuing full-time students received some form of financial aid. 76% of all full-time freshmen and 53% of continuing full-time students received need-based aid. The average freshmen award was $15,115, with $12,240 ($12,695 maximum) from need-based scholarships or need-based grants; $4,604 ($8,480 maximum) from need-based self-help aid (loans and jobs); $5,446 ($15,005 maximum) from non-need-based athletic scholarships; and $13,143 ($32,670 maximum) from other non-need-based awards and non-need-based scholarships. 14% of undergraduate students work part-time. Average annual earnings from campus work are $2318. The average financial indebtedness of the 2009 graduate was $19,470. OCU is a member of CSS. The FAFSA and the college's own financial statement, and tax returns, if selected for verification are required. The priority date for freshman financial aid applications for fall entry is March 1. The deadline for filing freshman financial aid applications for fall entry is June 30.

Computers: Wireless access is available. PCs are located in 24/7 labs; a wireless system is available throughout all of the campus. All students may access the system 24 hours a day. There are no time limits. The fee is $305.

OKLAHOMA STATE UNIVERSITY
Stillwater, OK 74078
(405) 744-5358
(800) 223-5019, ext.1; (405) 744-7092

Full-time: 7921 men, 7375 women	**Faculty:** 777; I, --$
Part-time: 1265 men, 1288 women	**Ph.D.s:** 92%
Graduate: 2671 men, 2325 women	**Student/Faculty:** 20 to 1
Year: semesters, summer session	**Tuition:** $6202 ($16,556)
Application Deadline: open	**Room & Board:** $6402
Freshman Class: 7561 applied, 6537 accepted, 3148 enrolled	
SAT CR/M: 540/570	**ACT:** 24 **VERY COMPETITIVE**

Oklahoma State University, founded in 1890, is a publicly funded land-grant institution, offering undergraduate programs in agricultural sciences and natural resources, arts and sciences, business, education, engineering, architecture, technology, and human environmental resources. There are 6 undergraduate schools and 1 graduate school. In addition to regional accreditation, OSU has baccalaureate program accreditation with AACSB, ABET, ACEJMC, ADA, AHEA, ASLA, FIDER, NAAB, NASM, NCATE, NRPA, and SAF. The 5 libraries contain 2.8 million volumes, 44.9 million microform items, and 426,693 audio/video tapes/CDs/DVDs. Computerized library services include interlibrary loans, database searching, Internet access, and laptop Internet portals. Special learning facilities include a learning resource center, art gallery, and radio station. The 840-acre campus is in a small town 65 miles north of Oklahoma City.

Programs of Study: OSU confers B.A., B.S., B.Arch.,B.E.N., B.F.A., B.Land.Arch., B.M., B.S.A.E, B.S.A.G., B.S.B.A., B.S.B.E., B.S.C.H., B.S.C.P., B.S.C.V., B.S.E.E., B.S.E.T., B.S.I.E., B.S.M.E., and B.U.S. degrees. Master's and doctoral degrees are also awarded. Bachelor's degrees are awarded in AGRICULTURE (agricultural business management, agricultural communications, agricultural economics, animal science, horticulture, natural resource management, plant science, and soil science), BIOLOGICAL SCIENCE (biochemistry, biology/biological science, botany, cell biology, entomology, microbiology, molecular biology, nutrition, physiology, and zoology), BUSINESS (accounting, banking and finance, business administration and management, entrepreneurial studies, hotel/motel and restaurant management, international business management, management information systems, marketing/retailing/merchandising, and recreation and leisure services), COMMUNICATIONS AND THE ARTS (art, broadcasting, design, dramatic arts, English, French, German, journalism, music, Russian languages and literature, and Spanish), COMPUTER AND PHYSICAL SCIENCE (chemistry, computer science, geology, mathematics, physics, and statistics), EDUCATION (agricultural education, athletic training, education, elementary education, health education, music education, physical education, secondary education, and vocational education), ENGINEERING AND ENVIRONMENTAL DESIGN (aerospace studies, architectural engineering, architecture, bioengineering, chemical engineering, civil engineering, computer engineering, construction management, construction technology, electrical/electronics engineering, electrical/electronics engineering technology, environmental science, industrial administration/management, industrial engineering, landscape architecture/design, mechanical engineering, and mechanical engineering technology), HEALTH PROFESSIONS (speech pathology/audiology), SOCIAL SCIENCE (American studies, child care/child and family studies, economics, fire control and safety technology, food science, geography, history, human development, liberal arts/general studies, philosophy, political science/government, psychology, and sociology).

Special: OSU offers cross-registration with Northern Oklahoma College and Tulsa Community College, a Washington semester, and an internship program. A B.A.-B.S. degree, dual majors, an individualized university studies degree, multidisciplinary majors in biosystems engineering and in cell and molecular biology, nondegree study, and pass/fail options are available. Students may study abroad in several countries. The school also sponsors Semester at Sea, a 1-semester program of study on a ship traveling to ports throughout the world. There is a freshman honors program.

Admissions: 86% of the 2009-2010 applicants were accepted. The SAT scores for the 2009-2010 freshman class were: Critical Reading--29% below 500, 43% between 500 and 599, 23% between 600 and 700, and 5% above 700; Math--23% below 500, 37% between 500 and 599, 32% between 600 and 700, and 8% above 700. The ACT scores were 14% below 21, 26% between 21 and 23, 28% between 24 and 26, 13% between 27 and 28, and 19% above 28. 47% of the current freshmen were in the top fifth of their class; 76% were in the top two fifths. There were 11 National Merit finalists.

Requirements: The SAT or ACT is required. In addition, freshman applicants must have a cumulative high school GPA of 3.0 and rank in the upper third of their graduating class; or achieve at least a 24 composite score on the ACT or 1090 on the SAT; or have a 3.0 GPA in the required 15 curricular units, which include 4 years of English, 3 of math (algebra I and above), 2 each of history and lab science, 1 of citizenship skills, and 3 more from any of the above or computer science or foreign language, along with an ACT score of 21 or SAT 980. AP and CLEP credits are accepted. Important factors in the admissions decision are advanced placement or honors courses, evidence of special talent, and recommendations by school officials.

Procedure: Freshmen are admitted fall, spring, and summer. Entrance exams should be taken during the junior or senior year. There is a rolling admissions plan. Application deadlines are open. Application fee is $40. Applications are accepted on-line.

Financial Aid: The FAFSA and the college's own financial statement are required. The priority date for freshman financial aid applications for fall entry is February 1. The deadline for filing freshman financial aid applications for fall entry is rolling.

Computers: Wireless access is available. Students receive computer access, network data storage space, and e-mail upon enrollment. Students may use any of the 5 general campus labs (3 are open 24/7) and 24 departmental labs. Student technology resources are provided via an Ethernet-based network. All campus residences provide each resident and common living space with a dedicated connection to the Internet. Some areas provide wireless access for central campus. All students may access the system. There are no time limits. The fee is $9.40 per semester credit hour.

OTTAWA UNIVERSITY
Ottawa, KS 66067-3399

(785) 242-5200, ext. 5555
(800) 755-5200,; (785) 229-1008

Full-time: 300 men, 200 women	**Faculty:** 21; IIB, --$
Part-time: 10 men, 20 women	**Ph.D.s:** 54%
Graduate: none	**Student/Faculty:** 20 to 1
Year: semesters, summer session	**Tuition:** $19,100
Application Deadline: open	**Room & Board:** 6634
Freshman Class: n/av	
SAT or ACT: required	**VERY COMPETITIVE**

Ottawa University, founded in 1865 and affiliated with the American Baptist Churches, is a private institution offering programs through the divisions of arts and humanities, natural sciences, and social and behavioral sciences. Some figures in the above capsule and in this profile are approximate. The library contains 90,000 volumes, and subscribes to 400 periodicals including electronic. Computerized library services include interlibrary loans and database searching. Special learning facilities include a learning resource center, art gallery, and radio station. The 64-acre campus is in a small town 45 miles southwest of Kansas City. Including any residence halls, there are 15 buildings.

Programs of Study: OU confers B.A. degrees. Bachelor's degrees are awarded in BIOLOGICAL SCIENCE (biology/biological science), BUSINESS (accounting, business administration and management, and management information systems), COMMUNICATIONS AND THE ARTS (art, communications, dramatic arts, English, and music), COMPUTER AND PHYSICAL SCIENCE (chemistry, information sciences and systems, and mathematics), EDUCATION (elementary education and physical education), SOCIAL SCIENCE (history, human services, political science/government, psychology, religion, and sociology). English, business, and math are the strongest academically. Business, teacher education, and human services are the largest.

Special: Internships are available, especially in business, human services, and teacher education. Student-designed majors are an option. 3-2 engineering degrees with Kansas state and the University of Kansas, a 3+1 degree in medical technology, and preprofessional programs in premedicine, predentistry, prelaw, and preministry are available. Work-study programs are also offered. There are 2 national honor societies.

Requirements: The ACT or SAT is required. The GED is accepted. There are no specific high school courses required, but a sound college preparatory curriculum is highly recommended. A GPA of 2.5 is required. AP and CLEP credits are accepted. Important factors in the admissions decision are parents or siblings attended your school, recommendations by alumni, and recommendations by school officials.

Procedure: Freshmen are admitted to all sessions. Entrance exams should be taken as early as possible. There is a rolling admissions plan. Application deadlines are open. Check with the school for the current application fee.

Financial Aid: The FAFSA and the college's own financial statement are required. Check with the school for current application deadlines.

Computers: All students may access the system. There are no time limits and no fees.

OUACHITA BAPTIST UNIVERSITY
Arkadelphia, AR 71998-0001

(870) 245-5110
(800) 342-5628; (870) 245-5500

Full-time: 640 men, 800 women	**Faculty:** IIB, --$
Part-time: 30 men, 35 women	**Ph.D.s:** n/av
Graduate: none	**Student/Faculty:** n/av
Year: semesters, summer session	**Tuition:** $18,400
Application Deadline: open	**Room & Board:** $6000
Freshman Class: n/av	
SAT or ACT: required	**VERY COMPETITIVE**

Ouachita Baptist University, founded in 1886, is a private liberal arts institution affiliated with the Arkansas Baptist State Convention. The figures in the above capsule and in this profile are approximate. There are 7 undergraduate schools. In addition to regional accreditation, Ouachita has baccalaureate program accreditation with AACSB, ADA, NASM, and NCATE. The 2 libraries contain 117,517 volumes, 205,614 microform items, and 3,159 audio/video tapes/CDs/DVDs, and subscribe to 1,067 periodicals including electronic. Computerized library services include interlibrary loans and database searching. Special learning facilities include a learning resource center, art gallery, and planetarium. The 82-acre campus is in a small town 65 miles southwest of Little Rock. Including any residence halls, there are 33 buildings.

Programs of Study: Ouachita confers B.A., B.S., B.M., and B.M.E. degrees. Associates degrees are also awarded. Bachelor's degrees are awarded in BIOLOGICAL SCIENCE (biology/biological science), BUSINESS (accounting and business administration and management), COMMUNICATIONS AND THE ARTS (communications, dramatic arts, English, French, music, musical theater, Russian languages and literature, Spanish, and speech/debate/rhetoric), COMPUTER AND PHYSICAL SCIENCE (chemistry, computer science, mathematics, and physics), EDUCATION (art education, business education, early childhood education, elementary education, foreign languages education, health education, middle school education, music education, science education, and secondary education), HEALTH PROFESSIONS (predentistry, premedicine, and speech pathology/audiology), SOCIAL SCIENCE (biblical studies, dietetics, economics, history, ministries, philosophy, political science/government, prelaw, psychology, religion, sociology, and theological studies). Education, business, and religion are the largest.

Special: Ouachita offers cross-registration with Henderson State University, a Washington semester for political science majors, co-op programs for business majors, internships for business majors and some mass communications and Christian studies majors, B.A.-B.S. degrees, dual majors, pass/fail options, and nondegree study. Study-abroad opportunities are available in Germany, England, France, Italy, Russia, Japan, China, Hong Kong, Australia, Austria, Belize, Scotland, Spain, South Africa, Costa Rica, and Morocco. There are 8 national honor societies and a freshman honors program.

Requirements: The SAT or ACT is required. In addition, applicants should have completed 19 high school units, including 4 in English, 3 in social science, and 2 each in natural science and math; 2 in a foreign language and 1/2 in computer science are also recommended. A GPA of 2.8 is required. AP and CLEP credits are accepted.

Procedure: Freshmen are admitted to all sessions. Entrance exams should be taken in the junior year. There are deferred admissions and rolling admissions plans. Application deadlines are open. Application fee is $50. Applications are accepted on-line.

Financial Aid: In a recent year, 97% of all full-time freshmen and 95% of continuing full-time students received some form of financial aid. 50% of all full-time freshmen and 54% of continuing full-time students received need-based aid. The average freshmen award was $16,029. 50% of undergraduate students worked part-time. Average annual earnings from campus work were $1500. The average financial indebtedness of the 2009 graduate was $12,961. The FAFSA and the college's own financial statement are required. Check with the school for current application deadlines.

Computers: Wireless access is available. All campus housing rooms provide connections to the campus computer network (fiber optic or wireless), including Internet access. Network and Internet services also are available in 10 computer labs. All students may access the system. There are no time limits and no fees.

PACE UNIVERSITY

New York, NY 10038-1508	(212) 346-1225 or (914) 773-3321
(800) 874-PACE;	(212) 346-1040 or (914) 773-3851

Full-time: 2477 men, 4021 women	**Faculty:** 362; I, av$
Part-time: 714 men, 759 women	**Ph.D.s:** 89%
Graduate: 1902 men, 2833 women	**Student/Faculty:** 18 to 1
Year: semesters, summer session	**Tuition:** $32,626
Application Deadline: open	**Room & Board:** $11,560
Freshman Class: 8948 applied, 6613 accepted, 1672 enrolled	
SAT CR/M: 539/547	**ACT:** required
	VERY COMPETITIVE

Pace University, founded in 1906, is a private institution offering programs in arts and sciences, business, nursing, education, and computer and information science on 3 campuses, with undergraduate studies in New York City and Pleasantville and graduate studies in White Plains. There are 5 undergraduate schools and 6 graduate schools. In addition to regional accreditation, Pace has baccalaureate program accreditation with AACSB and ABET. The 3 libraries contain 619,687 volumes, 60,453 microform items, and 2794 audio/video tapes/CDs/

DVDs, and subscribe to 73,493 periodicals including electronic. Computerized library services include interlibrary loans and database searching. Special learning facilities include a learning resource center, radio station, TV station, 2 art galleries, a performing arts center, biological research labs, environmental center, language lab, and computer labs. The main campus is in an urban area in downtown New York City, and a 200-acre suburban campus is in Pleasantville/Briarcliff Manor. Including any residence halls, there are 65 buildings.

Programs of Study: Pace confers B.A., B.S., B.B.A., B.F.A., and B.S.N. degrees. Associate, master's, and doctoral degrees are also awarded. Bachelor's degrees are awarded in AGRICULTURE (environmental studies), BIOLOGICAL SCIENCE (biology/biological science), BUSINESS (accounting, banking and finance, business administration and management, business economics, entrepreneurial studies, hospitality management services, international business management, and marketing/retailing/merchandising), COMMUNICATIONS AND THE ARTS (art, art history and appreciation, communications, English, film arts, fine arts, modern language, Spanish, and theater design), COMPUTER AND PHYSICAL SCIENCE (chemistry, computer science, information sciences and systems, and mathematics), EDUCATION (elementary education), HEALTH PROFESSIONS (clinical science, nursing, and speech pathology/audiology), SOCIAL SCIENCE (American studies, biopsychology, criminal justice, economics, forensic studies, history, philosophy and religion, political science/government, psychology, social science, sociology, and women's studies). Accounting is the strongest academically. Business and finance are the largest.

Special: Internships, study abroad, and a cooperative education program in all majors are available. Pace also offers accelerated degree programs, B.A.-B.S. degrees, dual majors, general studies degrees, and 3-2 engineering degrees with Manhattan College and Rensselaer Polytechnic Institute. Credit for life, military, and work experience, nondegree study, and pass/fail options are available. There are 24 national honor societies, a freshman honors program, and 19 departmental honors programs.

Admissions: 74% of the 2009-2010 applicants were accepted. The SAT scores for the 2009-2010 freshman class were: Critical Reading--28% below 500, 49% between 500 and 599, 21% between 600 and 700, and 2% above 700; Math--24% below 500, 51% between 500 and 599, 24% between 600 and 700, and 1% above 700. The ACT scores were 19% below 21, 30% between 21 and 23, 32% between 24 and 26, 12% between 27 and 28, and 7% above 28.

Requirements: The SAT or ACT is required. In addition, applicants should be graduates of an accredited secondary school with at least 16 academic credits, including 4 in English, 3 to 4 each in math, science, and history, and 2 to 3 in foreign language. The GED is accepted. An essay and an interview are recommended. A GPA of 3.0 is required. AP and CLEP credits are accepted. Important factors in the admissions decision are advanced placement or honors courses, recommendations by school officials, and leadership record.

Procedure: Freshmen are admitted fall and spring. Entrance exams should be taken by December of the senior year. There are early admissions, deferred admissions, and rolling admissions plans. Application deadlines are open. The fall 2009 application fee was $45. Notifications are sent December 15. Applications are accepted on-line.

Financial Aid: In 2009-2010, 76% of all full-time freshmen and 71% of continuing full-time students received some form of financial aid. 76% of all full-time freshmen and 70% of continuing full-time students received need-based aid. The average freshman award was $27,024. Average annual earnings from campus work are $3633. The average financial indebtedness of the 2009 graduate was

$29,622. The FAFSA is required. The deadline for filing freshman financial aid applications for fall entry is February 15.

Computers: All students may access the system 24 hours a day. There are no time limits and no fees.

PACIFIC LUTHERAN UNIVERSITY
Tacoma, WA 98447

(253) 535-7151
(800) 274-6758; (253) 536-5136

Full-time: 1178 men, 1961 women	**Faculty:** 238; IIA, --$
Part-time: 79 men, 87 women	**Ph.D.s:** 82%
Graduate: 80 men, 196 women	**Student/Faculty:** 14 to 1
Year: 4-1-4, summer session	**Tuition:** $28,100
Application Deadline: open	**Room & Board:** $8600
Freshman Class: 2166 applied, 2014 accepted, 716 enrolled	
SAT CR/M/W: 551/556/539	**ACT:** 25 **VERY COMPETITIVE**

Pacific Lutheran University, founded in 1890, is a coeducational, independent institution affiliated with the Evangelical Lutheran Church in America. There are 7 undergraduate schools and 5 graduate schools. In addition to regional accreditation, PLU has baccalaureate program accreditation with AACSB, ABET, CSWE, NASM, and NCATE. The library contains 610,134 volumes, 236,411 microform items, and 13,521 audio/video tapes/CDs/DVDs, and subscribes to 474 periodicals including electronic. Computerized library services include interlibrary loans, database searching, Internet access, and laptop Internet portals. Special learning facilities include a learning resource center, art gallery, radio station, TV station, an herbarium, invertebrate and vertebrate museums, a biology field station, Northwest history collections, a Scandinavian history collection, and a language resource center. The 126-acre campus is in a suburban area 7 miles south of Tacoma. Including any residence halls, there are 41 buildings.

Programs of Study: PLU confers B.A., B.S., B.A.E., B.A.P.E., B.A.Rec., B.B.A., B.F.A., B.M., B.M.A., B.M.Ed., B.S.N., and B.S.P.E. degrees. Master's degrees are also awarded. Bachelor's degrees are awarded in BIOLOGICAL SCIENCE (biology/biological science), BUSINESS (business administration and management and recreation and leisure services), COMMUNICATIONS AND THE ARTS (art, classics, communications, English, fine arts, French, German, music, music performance, music theory and composition, piano/organ, Scandinavian languages, Spanish, and voice), COMPUTER AND PHYSICAL SCIENCE (applied physics, chemistry, computer programming, computer science, geoscience, mathematics, and physics), EDUCATION (education, music education, and physical education), ENGINEERING AND ENVIRONMENTAL DESIGN (computer engineering, engineering and applied science, and environmental science), HEALTH PROFESSIONS (nursing), SOCIAL SCIENCE (anthropology, Asian/Oriental studies, economics, history, international studies, philosophy, political science/government, psychology, religion, Scandinavian studies, social work, sociology, and women's studies). Business administration, education, and nursing are the largest.

Special: PLU offers 2 different bachelor's degrees simultaneously, 3-2 engineering degrees with Washington University in St. Louis and Columbia University, and accelerated degree programs in most majors. Dual majors and student-designed majors can be arranged. Extensive internships with local businesses and nonprofit organizations, work-study programs, non-degree study, and pass/fail options are also available. The Wang Center for International Programs supports the university's internationally focused academic programs. There are study-abroad programs in 28 countries. There are 6 national honor societies and a freshman honors program.

Admissions: 93% of the 2009-2010 applicants were accepted. The SAT scores for the 2009-2010 freshman class were: Critical Reading--25% below 500, 41% between 500 and 599, 24% between 600 and 700, and 6 above 700; Math--29% below 500, 42% between 500 and 599, 31% between 600 and 700, and 4 above 700; Writing--30% below 500, 42% between 500 and 599, 22% between 600 and 700, and 3 above 700. The ACT scores were 4% below 21, 24% between 21 and 23, 27% between 24 and 26, 15% between 27 and 28, and 18% above 28. 56% of the current freshmen were in the top fifth of their class; 90% were in the top two fifths. 9 freshmen graduated first in their class.

Requirements: The SAT or ACT is required. In addition, applicants should be graduates of accredited secondary schools, although GED certificates are accepted. PLU requires 2 years each of college preparatory math and a foreign language and recommends 4 years of English, 2 each of social studies and lab science, 1 of fine or performing arts, and 3 of electives. An essay is required. AP and CLEP credits are accepted. Important factors in the admissions decision are advanced placement or honors courses, leadership record, and evidence of special talent.

Procedure: Freshmen are admitted fall and spring. Entrance exams should be taken by January of the senior year. There are deferred admissions and rolling admissions plans. Application deadlines are open. Application fee is $40. Notification is sent on a rolling basis. Applications are accepted on-line.

Financial Aid: In 2009-2010, 97% of all full-time freshmen and 97% of continuing full-time students received some form of financial aid. 73% of all full-time freshmen and 70% of continuing full-time students received need-based aid. The average freshmen award was $22,366, with $6,807 ($22,666 maximum) from need-based scholarships or need-based grants; $3,608 ($10,739 maximum) from need-based self-help aid (loans and jobs); and $13,541 ($28,100 maximum) from other non-need-based awards and non-need-based scholarships. 47% of undergraduate students work part-time. Average annual earnings from campus work are $2375. The average financial indebtedness of the 2009 graduate was $24,639. The FAFSA is required. The priority date for freshman financial aid applications for fall entry is January 31.

Computers: Wireless access is available. Over 390 computers are available for general student use and 1200 ports are available. All students may access the system. There are no time limits and no fees.

PACIFIC UNION COLLEGE
Angwin, CA 94508-9707

(707) 965-6336
(800) 862-7080; (707) 965-6432

Full-time: 500 men, 575 women	**Faculty:** n/av
Part-time: 135 men, 165 women	**Ph.D.s:** n/av
Graduate: 1 woman	**Student/Faculty:** n/av
Year: trimesters, summer session	**Tuition:** $22,150
Application Deadline: open	**Room & Board:** $6000
Freshman Class: n/av	
SAT or ACT: recommended	**VERY COMPETITIVE**

Pacific Union College, founded in 1888, is a private college affiliated with the Seventh-day Adventist Church, offering programs in liberal arts, religion, business, health science, and teacher preparation, among others. The figures given in the above capsule and in this profile are approximate. There is 1 graduate school. In addition to regional accreditation, PUC has baccalaureate program accreditation with CSWE, NASM, and NLN. The library contains 148,218 volumes, 125,268 microform items, and 6,623 audio/video tapes/CDs/DVDs, and subscribes to 10,637 periodicals including electronic. Computerized library services include interlibrary loans, database searching, Internet access, and laptop Internet portals. Special learning facilities include a learning resource center, art gallery, natural history museum, radio station, a video production studio, an observatory, and a marine field station. The 1500-acre campus is in a rural area 70 miles north of San Francisco. Including any residence halls, there are 60 buildings.

Programs of Study: PUC confers B.A., B.S., B.B.A., B.Mus., and B.S.W. degrees. Associate and master's degrees are also awarded. Bachelor's degrees are awarded in BIOLOGICAL SCIENCE (biology/biological science and biophysics), BUSINESS (business administration and management), COMMUNICATIONS AND THE ARTS (communications, English, fine arts, French, graphic design, journalism, music, photography, public relations, radio/television technology, and Spanish), COMPUTER AND PHYSICAL SCIENCE (applied mathematics, chemistry, computer science, mathematics, natural sciences, and physics), EDUCATION (early childhood education and physical education), ENGINEERING AND ENVIRONMENTAL DESIGN (airline piloting and navigation and graphic arts technology), HEALTH PROFESSIONS (nursing), SOCIAL SCIENCE (history, psychology, religion, social studies, social work, and theological studies). Sciences and behavioral science are the strongest academically. Nursing and business administration are the largest.

Special: Students may study abroad in Austria, Spain, France, Argentina, and Italy, earn B.A.-B.S. degrees, take dual majors, and pursue a major in interdisciplinary studies. Internships, social work, education, ministerial field experiences, and accelerated degree programs in business management and early childhood education are also offered. The college offers nondegree study and credit for life, military, and work experience. There are 2 national honor societies and a freshman honors program.

Requirements: The SAT or ACT is recommended. Scores are used only for advising purposes. Candidates for admission should have completed 4 years of English, 2 of math, and 1 each of science and history. A GPA of 2.3 is required. AP and CLEP credits are accepted. Important factors in the admissions decision are recommendations by school officials, leadership record, and advanced placement or honors courses.

Procedure: Freshmen are admitted to all sessions. Entrance exams should be taken in the junior or senior year. There is a rolling admissions plan. Application deadlines are open. The 2008 application fee was $30. Applications are accepted on-line.

Financial Aid: In a recent year, all full-time freshmen and 99% of continuing full-time students received some form of financial aid. 95% of all full-time freshmen and 64% of continuing full-time students received need-based aid. The average freshman award was $15,899. 80% of undergraduate students worked part time. Average annual earnings from campus work were $1500. The average financial indebtedness of the 2009 graduate was $13,000. The FAFSA and the college's own financial statement are required. Check with the school for current application deadlines.

Computers: Wireless access is available. All dorms have an Ethernet port available. Wireless access is available in public areas such as dorm lobbies, dining commons, and the campus center. Labs providing Internet connectivity total approximately 175 computers. All students may access the system at any time. There are no time limits and no fees. It is strongly recommended that all students have a personal computer.

PARSONS NEW SCHOOL FOR DESIGN
Parsons School of Design

New York, NY 10011
(877) 528-3321
(877) 528-3324; (212) 229-5166

Full-time: 703 men, 2582 women	**Faculty:** 132
Part-time: 40 men, 212 women	**Ph.D.s:** n/av
Graduate: 137 men, 274 women	**Student/Faculty:** 25 to 1
Year: semesters, summer session	**Tuition:** $30,930
Application Deadline: open	**Room & Board:** $11,750
Freshman Class: n/av	
SAT or ACT required	**SPECIAL**

Parsons School of Design, founded in 1896, is a private professional art school and is part of the New School, a university. In addition to regional accreditation, Parsons has baccalaureate program accreditation with NAAB and NASAD. The 3 libraries contain 2.4 million volumes, 13,000 microform items, and 14,275 audio/video tapes/CDs/DVDs, and subscribe to 33,320 periodicals including electronic. Computerized library services include interlibrary loans, database searching, Internet access, and laptop Internet portals. Special learning facilities include an art gallery. The campus is in an urban area in Manhattan's Greenwich Village and in the Fashion District in Manhattan, on Seventh Avenue. Including any residence halls, there are 8 buildings.

Programs of Study: Parsons confers B.A.-B.F.A., B.B.A., and B.F.A. degrees. Associates and master's degrees are also awarded. Bachelor's degrees are awarded in BUSINESS (marketing/retailing/merchandising), COMMUNICATIONS AND THE ARTS (advertising, design, fine arts, graphic design, illustration, industrial design, photography, and studio art), COMPUTER AND PHYSICAL SCIENCE (digital arts/technology), ENGINEERING AND ENVIRONMENTAL DESIGN (architectural engineering and interior design), SOCIAL SCIENCE (fashion design and technology). Fashion design, communication design, and management are the largest.

Special: Students have increasing opportunities to enroll in courses offered by other divisions of the New School. Students may study abroad at the Parsons campus in Paris as well as several other programs. The 5-year combined B.A.-B.F.A. degree requires 180 credits for graduation.

Requirements: The SAT or ACT is required. In addition, applicants must be graduates of an accredited secondary school. The GED is accepted. Applicants should have completed 4 years each of art, English, history, and social studies. A portfolio and home exam are required, and an interview is recommended. A GPA of 3.0 is required. AP credits are accepted. Important factors in the admissions decision are personality/intangible qualities, advanced placement or honors courses, and evidence of special talent.

Procedure: Freshmen are admitted fall and spring. Entrance exams should be taken by spring of the junior year. There are deferred admissions and rolling admissions plans. Application deadlines are open. Application fee is $50. Notification is sent on a rolling basis. Applications are accepted on-line.

Financial Aid: In a recent year, 70% of all full-time freshmen and 71% of continuing full-time students received some form of financial aid. 70% of all full-time freshmen and 71% of continuing full-time students received need-based aid. The average freshmen award was $15,974, with $8,548 ($30,270 maximum) from need-based scholarships or need-based grants and $3,358 ($5,500 maximum) from need-based self-help aid (loans and jobs). Average annual earnings from campus work were $2000. The average financial indebtedness of the 2009 graduate was $17,339. Parsons is a member of CSS. The FAFSA, the state aid form, and the college's own financial statement are required. Check with the school for current application deadlines.

Computers: Wireless access is available. All students may access the system. There are no time limits and no fees. It is strongly recommended that all students have a personal computer.

PENN STATE UNIVERSITY/UNIVERSITY PARK CAMPUS

University Park, PA 16802	(814) 865-5471; (814) 863-7590
Full-time: 20484 men, 17001 women	**Faculty:** I, -$
Part-time: 694 men, 451 women	**Ph.D.s:** 75%
Graduate: 3596 men, 2959 women	**Student/Faculty:** n/av
Year: semesters, summer session	**Tuition:** $14,416 ($25,946)
Application Deadline: November 30	**Room & Board:** $8170
Freshman Class: 40714 applied, 21017 accepted, 6560 enrolled	
SAT CR/M/W: 580/620/590	**ACT:** required
	VERY COMPETITIVE

Penn State University/University Park Campus, founded in 1855, is a public institution that is the oldest and largest of 24 campuses in the Penn State system. The university offers undergraduate and graduate degrees in agricultural sciences, arts and architecture, business, earth and mineral sciences, education, engineering, health and human development, liberal arts, science, communications, and information sciences and technology. Penn State also offers graduate and first professional degrees in medicine and law. There are 15 undergraduate schools and one graduate school. In addition to regional accreditation, Penn State has baccalaureate program accreditation with AACSB, ABET, ACEJMC, APTA, ASLA, CSAB, NAAB, NASAD, NASM, NCATE, NLN, and SAF. The 14 libraries contain 5.2 million volumes, 5.4 million microform items, and 178,672 audio/video tapes/CDs/DVDs, and subscribe to 68,876 periodicals including electronic. Computerized library services include interlibrary loans, database searching, Internet access, and laptop Internet portals. Special learning facilities include a learning resource center, art gallery, planetarium, radio station, TV station, 5 major museums at University Park house, significant research and educational collections in the fields of agriculture, anthropology, entomology, earth and mineral sciences, and the fine arts. The 7264-acre campus is in a suburban area 90 miles west of Harrisburg, PA. Including any residence halls, there are 933 buildings.

Programs of Study: Penn State confers B.A., B.S., B.A.E, B.Arch., B.Des., B.Eled. B.F.A., B.Hum., B.L.A., B.M., B.M.A., B.M.E., B.Ph., and B.Sosc. degrees. Associates, master's, and doctoral degrees arc also awarded. Bachelor's degrees are awarded in AGRICULTURE (agricultural business management, agriculture, agronomy, animal science, forestry production and processing, forestry and related sciences, horticulture, natural resource management, and soil science), BIOLOGICAL SCIENCE (biochemistry, biology/biological science, biotechnology, ecology, microbiology, and nutrition), BUSINESS (accounting, banking and finance, business administration and management, hotel/motel and restaurant management, labor studies, management information systems, marketing/retailing/merchandising, and organizational behavior), COMMUNICATIONS AND THE ARTS (advertising, art, art history and appreciation, broadcasting, classics, communications, comparative literature, dramatic arts, English, film arts, French, German, graphic design, Italian, Japanese, journalism, music, music performance, Russian, Spanish, speech/debate/rhetoric, theater design, and visual and performing arts), COMPUTER AND PHYSICAL SCIENCE (actuarial science, astronomy, atmospheric sciences and meteorology, chemistry, computer science, earth science, geoscience, information sciences and systems, mathematics, physical sciences, physics, science, and statistics), EDUCATION (agricultural education, art education, elementary education, foreign languages education, health education, music education, secondary education, and special education), ENGINEERING AND ENVIRONMENTAL DESIGN (aeronautical engineering, agricultural engineering, architectural engineering, architecture, biomedical engineering, chemical engineering, civil engineering, computer engineering, electrical/electronics engineering, engineering, environmental science, industrial engineering, landscape architecture/design, materials science, mechanical engineering, mining and mineral engineering, nuclear engineering, and petroleum/natural gas engineering), HEALTH PROFESSIONS (biomedical science, exercise science, health care administration, nursing, premedicine, rehabilitation therapy, and speech pathology/audiology), SOCIAL SCIENCE (African American studies, American studies, anthropology, archeology, criminal justice, East Asian studies, economics, food science, geography, history, human development, international relations, Judaic studies, Latin American studies, liberal arts/general studies, medieval studies, parks and recreation management, philosophy, physical fitness/movement, political science/government, psychology, religion, sociology, and women's studies). Engineering, liberal arts, and business are the largest.

Special: Co-op programs, internships, study-abroad in more than 45 countries, and work-study programs are available. Dual majors and student-designed majors are possible. Accelerated degree programs, a Washington semester, and a 3-2 engineering degree are also offered. There are 34 national honor societies, including Phi Beta Kappa, and a freshman honors program.

Admissions: 52% of the 2009-2010 applicants were accepted. The SAT scores for the 2009-2010 freshman class were: Critical Reading--13% below 500, 44% between 500 and 599, 36% between 600 and 700, and 7% above 700; Math--8% below 500, 30% between 500 and 599, 47% between 600 and 700, and 15% above 700; Writing--11% below 500, 40% between 500 and 599, 41% between 600 and 700, and 8% above 700. The ACT scores were 25% below 21, 32% between 21 and 23, 23% between 24 and 26, 10% between 27 and 28, and 10% above 28.

Requirements: The SAT or ACT is required. In addition, applicants may submit an SAT or ACT scores. Admissions decisions for first-year students are made on the basis of several combined factors. Approximately two thirds of the decision for each student is based upon the high school GPA. The remaining one third of the decision is based on the factors, which may include standardized critical reading and math test scores, class rank, personal statement, and activities list. Weighted average or class rank for students who have taken AP/Honors courses are considered. AP and CLEP credits are accepted.

Procedure: Freshmen are admitted fall, spring, and summer. Entrance exams should be taken in the junior year. There are early admissions, deferred admissions, and rolling admissions plans. Applications should be filed by November 30 for fall entry, along with a $50 fee. Notification is sent on a rolling basis. Applications are accepted on-line. 1456 applicants were on a recent waiting list, 1455 were accepted.

Financial Aid: The average financial indebtedness of the 2009 graduate was $28,680. The FAFSA is required. The deadline for filing freshman financial aid applications for fall entry is February 15.

Computers: Wireless access is available. There are more than 50 computer labs and classrooms with about 2400 computers on the University Park campus. There are more than 1000 mobile computing ports that provide users with workstations and peripherals for Windows, Mac, and Unix platforms. The labs are equipped with printers and scanners, as well as more specialized hardware such as digital cameras and CD burners. All students may access the system. 24 hours a day, every day. There are no time limits. There is a fee. It is strongly recommended that all students have a personal computer. Students enrolled in The College of Education has a new notebook computer requirement for the Elementary must have a personal computer.

PEPPERDINE UNIVERSITY
Malibu, CA 90263-4392   (310) 506-4369; (310) 506-4861

Full-time: 1356 men, 1698 women	**Faculty:** IIA, ++$
Part-time: 203 men, 184 women	**Ph.D.s:** 100%
Graduate: 1810 men, 2484 women	**Student/Faculty:** n/av
Year: semesters, summer session	**Tuition:** $37,850
Application Deadline: January 15	**Room & Board:** $10,900
Freshman Class: 6426 applied, 2653 accepted, 797 enrolled	
SAT CR/M/W: 604/623/610	**ACT:** 29 **HIGHLY COMPETITIVE+**

Pepperdine University, founded in 1937, is a private liberal arts university affiliated with the Church of Christ. There are 4 graduate schools. In addition to regional accreditation, Pepperdine has baccalaureate program accreditation with AACSB and NCATE. The 3 libraries contain 324,174 volumes, 505,375 microform items, and 10,878 audio/video tapes/CDs/DVDs, and subscribe to 47,894 periodicals including electronic. Computerized library services include interlibrary loans, database searching, and Internet access. Special learning facilities include a learning resource center, art gallery, radio station, TV station, writing center, and Japanese tea ceremony room. The 830-acre campus is in a suburban area 35 miles northwest of Los Angeles, overlooking the Pacific Ocean. Including any residence halls, there are 76 buildings.

Programs of Study: Pepperdine confers B.A., B.S., and B.S.M. degrees. Master's and doctoral degrees are also awarded. Bachelor's degrees are awarded in BIOLOGICAL SCIENCE (biology/biological science and nutrition), BUSINESS (accounting, business administration and management, international business management, management science, and marketing management), COMMUNICATIONS AND THE ARTS (advertising, art, art history and appreciation, communications, creative writing, dramatic arts, English, film arts, French, German, Italian, journalism, media arts, music, public relations, Spanish, speech/debate/rhetoric, and telecommunications), COMPUTER AND PHYSICAL SCIENCE (chemistry, computer science, mathematics, natural sciences, and physics), EDUCATION (elementary education, mathematics education, physical education, and secondary education), ENGINEERING AND ENVIRONMENTAL DESIGN (engineering), HEALTH PROFESSIONS (sports medicine), SOCIAL SCIENCE (economics, Hispanic American studies, history, humanities, international studies, liberal arts/general studies, philosophy, political science/government, psychology, religion, social science, and sociology). Natural sciences (premed), sports medicine, and political science are the strongest academically. Communication and business are the largest.

Special: Students may earn 1 to 4 units for an internship, available in most majors, participate in a Washington semester, and study abroad in 8 countries. The school offers a 3-2 engineering degree with Washington University in St. Louis, the University of Southern California, and Boston University. There are dual majors in any discipline, student-designed contract majors, federal work-study programs, nondegree study, and pass/fail options. There are 16 national honor societies and 3 departmental honors programs.

Admissions: 41% of the 2009-2010 applicants were accepted. The SAT scores for the 2009-2010 freshman class were: Critical Reading--9% below 500, 39% between 500 and 599, 41% between 600 and 700, and 11% above 700; Math--8% below 500, 29% between 500 and 599, 45% between 600 and 700, and 18% above 700; Writing--6% below 500, 36% between 500 and 599, 48% between 600 and 700, and 10% above 700. The ACT scores were 6% below 21, 8% between 21 and 23, 19% between 24 and 26, 21% between 27 and 28, and 46% above 28. 68% of the current freshmen were in the top fifth of their class; 45% were in the top two fifths.

Requirements: The SAT or ACT is required. In addition, it is strongly recommended that candidates for admission present a college preparatory program that includes 4 years of English, 3 of math, 2 each of foreign language and science, and courses in speech communication, humanities, and social science. AP and CLEP credits are accepted. Important factors in the admissions decision are advanced placement or honors courses, recommendations by school officials, and evidence of special talent.

Procedure: Freshmen are admitted fall and spring. Entrance exams should be taken in the fall. There is a deferred admissions plan. Applications should be filed by January 15 for fall entry and October 15 for spring entry, along with a $65 fee. Notifications are sent April 1. 1319 applicants were on a recent waiting list.

Financial Aid: The FAFSA, the college's own financial statement, the federal income tax form, the state scholarship/grant form (California residents), and W-2 wage statements are required. The deadline for filing freshman financial aid applications for fall entry is February 15.

Computers: Wireless access is available. Students may access the system with permission from the faculty any time. Word processing labs are open to all students. There are no time limits and no fees.

PITZER COLLEGE

Claremont, CA 91711-6101

(909) 621-8129
(800) PITZER-1; (909) 621-8770

Full-time: 402 men, 584 women	**Faculty:** 73; IIB, +$
Part-time: 26 men, 31 women	**Ph.Ds:** 100%
Graduate: none	**Student/Faculty:** 14 to 1
Year: semesters, summer session	**Tuition:** $39,330
Application Deadline: January 1	**Room & Board:** $11,490
Freshman Class: 4081 applied, 828 accepted, 256 enrolled	
SAT or ACT: required	**MOST COMPETITIVE**

Pitzer College, founded in 1963, is a private liberal arts college that through an interdisciplinary approach emphasizes social justice, intercultural understanding, and environmental sensitivity. It is one of the Claremont Colleges. The library contains 250,000 volumes, 1.2 million microform items, and 17,000 audio/video tapes/CDs/DVDs, and subscribes to 35,000 periodicals including electronic. Computerized library services include interlibrary loans, database searching, Internet access, and laptop Internet portals. Special learning facilities include an art gallery, radio station, a social science lab, an arboretum, and a farm in Costa Rica. The 31-acre campus is in a suburban area 35 miles east of Los Angeles. Including any residence halls, there are 17 buildings.

Programs of Study: Pitzer confers B.A. degrees. Bachelor's degrees are awarded in BIOLOGICAL SCIENCE (biochemistry, biology/biological science, and neurosciences), BUSINESS (management engineering and organizational behavior), COMMUNICATIONS AND THE ARTS (art, classics, dance, dramatic arts, English, film arts, French, linguistics, media arts, music, and Spanish), COMPUTER AND PHYSICAL SCIENCE (chemistry, mathematics, physics, science, and science and management), ENGINEERING AND ENVIRONMENTAL DESIGN (environmental science), SOCIAL SCIENCE (African American studies, American studies, anthropology, Asian/American studies, Asian/Oriental studies, Caribbean studies, economics, European studies, history, international relations, Latin American studies, Mexican-American/Chicano studies, philosophy, political science/government, psychology, sociology, Third World studies, and women's studies). Social and behavioral sciences are the strongest academically and the largest.

Special: Students may cross-register at any of the other Claremont Colleges, or study abroad in 60 countries in Africa, Asia, Europe, Latin America, North America, or Oceania. There are co-op programs, work-study, internships, dual majors, student-designed majors, an extensive first-year seminar program, and interdisciplinary study offered in science and technology, and international or intercultural studies. Joint advanced degrees are offered in math, economics, M.I.S., psychology, and public policy, as is a 7-year B.A./D.O. program with the College of Western Health Sciences. There are independent study and limited pass/fail options. There is 1 national honor society and 18 departmental honors programs.

Admissions: 20% of the 2009-2010 applicants were accepted. The SAT scores for the 2009-2010 freshman class were: Critical Reading--3% below 500, 14% between 500 and 599, 58% between 600 and 700, and 25% above 700; Math--2% below 500, 24% between 500 and 599, 58% between 600 and 700, and 16% above 700. 89% of the current freshmen were in the top fifth of their class; 98% were in the top two fifths.

Requirements: Applicants must be graduates of an accredited secondary school or have earned the GED. Secondary school courses must include 4 years of English courses requiring extensive writing, and 3 years each of social and behavioral sciences including history, lab science, foreign language, and math. A personal essay is required and a personal interview is recommended. Students in the top 10% of their class or those with an unweighted GPA in academic subjects of 3.5 are not required to submit ACT or SAT scores. Students without these qualifications must submit either ACT or SAT scores, 2 SAT subject tests, 2 AP test scores of at least 4 (1 in English, 1 in math or science), 2 IB exams (English 1A and Mathematics Methods Standard Level or a higher-level course), or a recent analytical writing sample from a humanities or social science course and a math exam from a course at the algebra II level or higher, both including teacher's comments and grades. AP credits are accepted. Important factors in the admissions decision are advanced placement or honors courses, leadership record, and evidence of special talent.

Procedure: Freshmen are admitted fall and spring. Entrance exams should be taken by January 1. There are early decision and deferred admissions plans. Early decision applications should be filed by November 1; regular applications should be filed by January 1 for fall entry and October 15 for spring entry. The fall 2009 application fee was $50. Notifications are sent April 1. Applications are accepted on-line. A waiting list is maintained.

Financial Aid: In 2009-2010, 42% of all full-time freshmen and 40% of continuing full-time students received some form of financial aid. 42% of all full-time freshmen and 37% of continuing full-time students received need-based aid. The

average freshman award was $37,361. Pitzer is a member of CSS. The CSS/Profile, FAFSA, and the state aid form are required. The deadline for filing freshman financial aid applications for fall entry is February 1.

Computers: Wireless access is available. There are student computer labs and all residential-life rooms are hardwired. All students may access the system. There are no time limits and no fees.

POINT LOMA NAZARENE UNIVERSITY

San Diego, CA 92106-2899

(619) 849-2520
(800) 733-7770; (619) 849-2601

Full-time: 872 men, 1434 women	**Faculty:** IIB, +$
Part-time: 40 men, 41 women	**Ph.D.s:** 77%
Graduate: 293 men, 697 women	**Student/Faculty:** n/av
Year: semesters, summer session	**Tuition:** $25,300
Application Deadline: March 1	**Room & Board:** $8100
Freshman Class: 2490 applied, 1852 accepted, 535 enrolled	
SAT CR/M: 555/557	**ACT:** 25 **VERY COMPETITIVE**

Point Loma Nazarene University, founded in 1902, is a private liberal arts university affiliated with the Church of the Nazarene. There are 2 undergraduate schools and 5 graduate schools. In addition to regional accreditation, PLNU has baccalaureate program accreditation with ACBSP. The library contains 167,558 volumes, 129,478 microform items, and 4,995 audio/video tapes/CDs/DVDs, and subscribes to 6,600 periodicals including electronic. Computerized library services include interlibrary loans, database searching, and Internet access. Special learning facilities include a learning resource center, art gallery, radio station, and a lab preschool. The 90-acre campus is in a suburban area in San Diego. Including any residence halls, there are 51 buildings.

Programs of Study: PLNU confers B.A., B.S., B.Mus., and B.S.N. degrees. Master's degrees are also awarded. Bachelor's degrees are awarded in BIOLOGICAL SCIENCE (biology/biological science and nutrition), BUSINESS (accounting, business administration and management, and business communications), COMMUNICATIONS AND THE ARTS (broadcasting, communications, dramatic arts, graphic design, journalism, literature, media arts, music, music performance, music theory and composition, piano/organ, romance languages and literature, Spanish, visual and performing arts, and voice), COMPUTER AND PHYSICAL SCIENCE (chemistry, computer science, information sciences and systems, mathematics, and physics), EDUCATION (art education, athletic training, music education, and physical education), ENGINEERING AND ENVIRONMENTAL DESIGN (engineering physics and environmental science), HEALTH PROFESSIONS (exercise science and nursing), SOCIAL SCIENCE (biblical studies, child psychology/development, dietetics, family and community services, history, industrial and organizational psychology, international studies, liberal arts/general studies, ministries, philosophy, philosophy and religion, political science/government, psychology, religion, social science, social work, and sociology).

Special: PLNU offers internships in the church, in state and national governments, in journalism, in small business, and in the film industry. Students may study abroad in several world capitals and in more than 40 countries. There are Washington and United Nations semester programs. Various dual or interdepartmental majors are offered, including biology-chemistry, graphic communications, human environmental science-business, and church music-youth ministries. There are pre-professional programs in medicine/dentistry, law, and engineering.

470

A general studies degree in liberal studies is available, as is credit for life, military, and work experience for nursing students. There are 6 national honor societies, a freshman honors program, and 10 departmental honors programs.

Admissions: 74% of the 2009-2010 applicants were accepted. The SAT scores for the 2009-2010 freshman class were: Critical Reading--23% below 500, 47% between 500 and 599, 25% between 600 and 700, and 5% above 700; Math--26% below 500, 39% between 500 and 599, 30% between 600 and 700, and 5% above 700. The ACT scores were 17% below 21, 31% between 21 and 23, 26% between 24 and 26, 12% between 27 and 28, and 14% above 28. 55% of the current freshmen were in the top fifth of their class; 81% were in the top two fifths. 14 freshmen graduated first in their class.

Requirements: The SAT or ACT is required. In addition, candidates for admission should have completed 4 years of English, 3 of math, 2 each of a lab science and the same foreign language, and 1 of history. A GPA of 2.8 is required. AP and CLEP credits are accepted. Important factors in the admissions decision are personality/intangible qualities, leadership record, and advanced placement or honors courses.

Procedure: Freshmen are admitted fall and spring. Entrance exams should be taken in the junior year or early in the senior year. Applications should be filed by March 1 for fall entry, along with a $50 fee. Notifications are sent April 1. 246 applicants were on the 2009 waiting list; 109 were admitted. Applications are accepted on-line.

Financial Aid: PLNU is a member of CSS. The CSS/Profile, FAFSA, and the college's own financial statement are required. The priority date for freshman financial aid applications for fall entry is March 2.

Computers: All students may access the system when computer labs are open, wireless 24/7. There are no time limits and no fees. It is strongly recommended that all students have a personal computer. Students enrolled in business administration must have a personal computer. A Dell Latitude E6400 Laptop or Apple Macbook Pro 13 is recommended.

POLYTECHNIC INSTITUTE OF NEW YORK UNIVERSITY
Polytechnic University/Brooklyn

Brooklyn, NY 11201-3840	(718) 260-3100
	(800) 765-8324; (718) 260-3446

Full-time: 1155 men, 280 women	**Faculty:** I, -$
Part-time: 55 men, 15 women	**Ph.D.s:** n/av
Graduate: 1400 men, 435 women	**Student/Faculty:** n/av
Year: semesters, summer session	**Tuition:** $31,500
Application Deadline: see profile	**Room & Board:** $9000
Freshman Class: n/av	
SAT: required	**VERY COMPETITIVE**

Polytechnic University, founded in 1854, is a private, multi-campus university offering undergraduate and graduate programs through the divisions of arts and sciences, engineering, and management. The figures in the above capsule and in this profile are approximate. There are 2 graduate schools. In addition to regional accreditation, Brooklyn Poly has baccalaureate program accreditation with ABET and CSAB. The library contains 212,264 volumes, 60,106 microform items, and 337 audio/video tapes/CDs/DVDs, and subscribes to 1,621 periodicals including electronic. Computerized library services include interlibrary loans and database searching. Special learning facilities include a learning resource center and radio station. The 3-acre campus is in an urban area 5 minutes from downtown Manhattan. Including any residence halls, there are 6 buildings.

Programs of Study: Brooklyn Poly confers B.S. degrees. Master's and doctoral degrees are also awarded. Bachelor's degrees are awarded in BIOLOGICAL SCIENCE (molecular biology), BUSINESS (business administration and management), COMMUNICATIONS AND THE ARTS (technical and business writing), COMPUTER AND PHYSICAL SCIENCE (chemistry, computer science, information sciences and systems, mathematics, and physics), ENGINEERING AND ENVIRONMENTAL DESIGN (chemical engineering, civil engineering, computer engineering, construction management, electrical/electronics engineering, and mechanical engineering), SOCIAL SCIENCE (humanities, liberal arts/general studies, and social science). Engineering, management, and physical sciences are the strongest academically. Electrical engineering, computer engineering, and computer science are the largest.

Special: Cooperative programs are available in all majors. Opportunities are provided for internships, work-study programs, study abroad, accelerated degree programs in engineering and computer science, dual majors, student-designed majors, and nondegree study. There are 9 national honor societies, a freshman honors program, and 3 departmental honors programs.

Requirements: The SAT is required. In addition, graduation from an accredited secondary school is required; a GED will be accepted. Applicants must submit a minimum of 16 credit hours, including 4 each in English, math, and science and 1 each in foreign language, art, music, and social studies. An essay and an interview are recommended. AP credits are accepted. Important factors in the admissions decision are advanced placement or honors courses, leadership record, and evidence of special talent.

Procedure: Freshmen are admitted fall, spring, and summer. Entrance exams should be taken by November of the senior year. There are early admissions, deferred admissions, and rolling admissions plans. Application deadlines are open. The fall 2009 application fee was $50. Notification is sent on a rolling basis. Applications are accepted on-line.

Financial Aid: In a recent year, 98% of all full-time freshmen and 89% of continuing full-time students received some form of financial aid. 84% of all full-time freshmen and 82% of continuing full-time students received need-based aid. The average freshmen award was $21,685. 29% of undergraduate students worked part-time. Average annual earnings from campus work were $5720. The average financial indebtedness of the 2009 graduate was $22,332. Brooklyn Poly is a member of CSS. The FAFSA and the college's own financial statement are required. Check with the school for current application deadlines.

Computers: All students may access the system. 24-hour dial-up service is available. Computer labs are open 13 hours a day. There are no time limits and no fees. All students are required to have a personal computer.

POMONA COLLEGE

Claremont, CA 91711　　　　**(909) 621-8134; (909) 621-8952**

Full-time: 785 men, 755 women	**Faculty:** IIB, ++$
Part-time: 25 men, 20 women	**Ph.D.s:** n/av
Graduate: none	**Student/Faculty:** n/av
Year: semesters	**Tuition:** $36,170
Application Deadline: January 2	**Room & Board:** $12,600
Freshman Class: n/av	
SAT or ACT: required	**MOST COMPETITIVE**

Pomona College, the oldest and largest of the Claremont Colleges, (a consortium of colleges) is an independent, national liberal arts and sciences institution founded in 1887. Some of the figures given in the above capsule and in this profile are approximate. There are 5 undergraduate schools and 2 graduate schools. The 3 libraries contain 2 million volumes, 1.4 million microform items, and 777 audio/video tapes/CDs/DVDs, and subscribe to 6,624 periodicals including electronic. Computerized library services include interlibrary loans and database searching. Special learning facilities include an art gallery, radio station, observatory, and modern languages and international relations center. The 140-acre campus is in a suburban area 35 miles east of Los Angeles, and 20 miles east of Pasadena. Including any residence halls, there are 47 buildings.

Programs of Study: Pomona confers B.A. degrees. Bachelor's degrees are awarded in BIOLOGICAL SCIENCE (biology/biological science, molecular biology, and neurosciences), COMMUNICATIONS AND THE ARTS (art history and appreciation, Chinese, classics, dramatic arts, English, fine arts, French, German, Japanese, languages, linguistics, literature, media arts, music, Russian, Spanish, and studio art), COMPUTER AND PHYSICAL SCIENCE (chemistry, computer science, geology, mathematics, physics, and science), ENGINEERING AND ENVIRONMENTAL DESIGN (technology and public affairs), SOCIAL SCIENCE (African American studies, American studies, anthropology, Asian/Oriental studies, economics, German area studies, history, international relations, Latin American studies, philosophy, political science/government, psychology, public affairs, religion, sociology, and women's studies). Social sciences and sciences are the largest.

Special: Students may cross-register at any of the Claremont Colleges, study abroad in 22 countries, and spend a semester in Washington, D.C. Dual and student-designed majors, internships, and independent study are possible. A 3-2 engineering program is offered with California Institute of Technology or Washington University in St. Louis. Students may study for 1 semester at Colby, Smith, Spelman, or Swarthmore Colleges. There are pass/fail options. There are 9 national honor societies, including Phi Beta Kappa.

Requirements: The SAT or ACT is required. Although applicants need not be graduates of accredited high schools (some may be admitted after the junior year), most are, or have earned the GED. Secondary preparation must include 4 years of English, 3 years each of math and foreign languages, and 2 years each of lab and social sciences. An essay is required and an interview is strongly recommended. AP credits are accepted. Important factors in the admissions decision are recommendations by school officials, leadership record, and recommendations by alumni.

Procedure: Freshmen are admitted in the fall. Entrance exams should be taken before December of the senior year. There are early decision, early admissions, and deferred admissions plans. Early decision applications should be filed by November 15; regular applications, by January 2 for fall entry. The fall 2009 application fee was $55. Notification of early decision is sent December 15; regular decision, April 10. A waiting list is maintained.

Financial Aid: Pomona is a member of CSS. The CSS/Profile, FAFSA, and tax returns are required. Check with the school for current application deadlines.

Computers: All students may access the system. There are no time limits and no fees.

PRATT INSTITUTE
Brooklyn, NY 11205

(718) 636-3514
(800) 331-0834; (718) 636-3670

Full-time: 1057 men, 1762 women	**Faculty:** IIA, -$
Part-time: 74 men, 80 women	**Ph.D.s:** n/av
Graduate: 471 men, 1218 women	**Student/Faculty:** n/av
Year: semesters, summer session	**Tuition:** $31,080
Application Deadline: January 15	**Room & Board:** $8918
Freshman Class: 5471 applied, 2268 accepted, 625 enrolled	
SAT or ACT: required	**SPECIAL**

Pratt Institute, founded in 1887, is a private institution offering undergraduate and graduate programs in architecture, art and design education, art history, industrial, interior, and communication design, fine arts, design management, arts and cultural management, writing for publication, performance and media, and professional studies. The tuition figures in the above capsule are approximate. There are 2 undergraduate schools and 3 graduate schools. In addition to regional accreditation, Pratt has baccalaureate program accreditation with FIDER, NAAB, and NASAD. The library contains 208,000 volumes, 50,000 microform items, and 3,500 audio/video tapes/CDs/DVDs, and subscribes to 700 periodicals including electronic. Computerized library services include database searching and Internet access. Special learning facilities include a learning resource center, art gallery, radio station, bronze foundry, and metal forge. The 25-acre campus is in an urban area 3 miles east of downtown Manhattan. Including any residence halls, there are 23 buildings.

Programs of Study: Pratt confers B.Arch., B.F.A., B.I.D., and B.P.S. degrees. Associate and master's degrees are also awarded. Bachelor's degrees are awarded in COMMUNICATIONS AND THE ARTS (art history and appreciation, communications, creative writing, film arts, fine arts, industrial design, and photography), EDUCATION (art education), ENGINEERING AND ENVIRONMENTAL DESIGN (architecture, computer graphics, construction management, and interior design), SOCIAL SCIENCE (fashion design and technology). Fine arts, industrial design, and communications design are the strongest academically. Architecture and communications design are the largest.

Special: Pratt offers co-op programs with the East Coast Consortium (art and design schools) and cross-registration with St. John's College and Queen's College. Internships, study abroad in 4 countries, accelerated degree programs, work-study programs, dual majors, credit for work experience, nondegree study, and pass/fail options are available. There are 4 national honor societies.

Admissions: 41% of the 2009-2010 applicants were accepted.

Requirements: The SAT or ACT is required. In addition, SAT: Subject tests in writing and mathematics level I or II are recommended for architecture applicants. Applicants must be graduates of an accredited secondary school. The GED is accepted. Students should have completed 4 years of English, 4 of math, and 2 each of science and history, and 1 of social studies. A portfolio is required, as is an interview for all applicants who live within 100 miles of Pratt. A GPA of 2.8 is required. AP and CLEP credits are accepted. Important factors in the admissions decision are evidence of special talent, advanced placement or honors courses, and recommendations by school officials.

Procedure: Freshmen are admitted in the fall. Entrance exams should be taken by November of the senior year. There is a deferred admissions plan. Applications should be filed by January 15 for fall entry, along with a $50 fee. Notifications are sent April 1. 820 applicants were on the 2009 waiting list; 213 were admitted. Applications are accepted on-line.

Financial Aid: Pratt is a member of CSS. The CSS/Profile, FAFSA, the college's own financial statement, and the parents' and student's tax returns are required. Check with the school for current application deadlines.

Computers: All students may access the system 24 hours a day, 7 days a week. There are no time limits and no fees. It is strongly recommended that all students have a personal computer.

PRESBYTERIAN COLLEGE
Clinton, SC 29325

(864) 833-8230
(800) 960-7583; (864) 833-8195

Full-time: 591 men, 607 women	**Faculty:** 87; IIB, -$
Part-time: 8 men, 15 women	**Ph.D.s:** 92%
Graduate: none	**Student/Faculty:** 13 to 1
Year: semesters, summer session	**Tuition:** $28,880
Application Deadline: February 1	**Room & Board:** $8345
Freshman Class: 1455 applied, 1017 accepted, 364 enrolled	
SAT CR/M: 550/570	**ACT:** 24 **VERY COMPETITIVE**

Presbyterian College, founded in 1880, is a private liberal arts institution affiliated with the Presbyterian Church (U.S.A.). There is one undergraduate school. In addition to regional accreditation, PC has baccalaureate program accreditation with NCATE. The library contains 140,467 volumes, 1,072 microform items, and 12,117 audio/video tapes/CDs/DVDs, and subscribes to 8,094 periodicals including electronic. Computerized library services include interlibrary loans, database searching, Internet access, and laptop Internet portals. Special learning facilities include a learning resource center, art gallery, and radio station. The 240-acre campus is in a small town 40 miles south of Greenville. Including any residence halls, there are 74 buildings.

Programs of Study: PC confers B.A. and B.S. degrees. Bachelor's degrees are awarded in BIOLOGICAL SCIENCE (biology/biological science), BUSINESS (accounting, business administration and management, and business economics), COMMUNICATIONS AND THE ARTS (art, art history and appreciation, dramatic arts, English, fine arts, French, German, modern language, music, music performance, Spanish, and visual and performing arts), COMPUTER AND PHYSICAL SCIENCE (chemistry, computer science, mathematics, medical physics, and physics), EDUCATION (early childhood education, middle school education, music education, and special education), SOCIAL SCIENCE (economics, history, philosophy, political science/government, psychology, religion, religious education, religious music, and sociology). Business administration, biology, and history are the largest.

Special: Educational internships, study abroad in 25 countries, and a Washington semester are available. Dual majors, work-study programs, accelerated degree programs, B.A.-B.S. degrees, and a 3-2 engineering degree with Auburn, Clemson, and Vanderbilt Universities are offered. There is a forestry environmental studies program with Duke University. Credit for military experience, auditing courses, and pass/fail options are possible. There are 11 national honor societies, a freshman honors program, and 17 departmental honors programs.

Admissions: 70% of the 2009-2010 applicants were accepted. The SAT scores for the 2009-2010 freshman class were: Critical Reading--29% below 500, 40% between 500 and 599, 26% between 600 and 700, and 5% above 700; Math--20% below 500, 38% between 500 and 599, 36% between 600 and 700, and 6% above 700. The ACT scores were 20% below 21, 25% between 21 and 23, 26% between 24 and 26, 15% between 27 and 28, and 14% above 28. 59% of the current freshmen were in the top fifth of their class; 84% were in the top two fifths. 7 freshmen graduated first in their class.

Requirements: The SAT or ACT is required. In addition, applicants must be graduates of an accredited secondary school with 18 academic credits, including 4 years of English, 3 of math, and 2 or more each of foreign language, history, science, and social studies. The GED is accepted. An essay is required. For music scholarships, an audition is required. AP and CLEP credits are accepted. Important factors in the admissions decision are advanced placement or honors courses, recommendations by school officials, and leadership record.

Procedure: Freshmen are admitted to all sessions. Entrance exams should be taken during the spring of the junior year. There are early decision, early admissions, deferred admissions, and rolling admissions plans. Early decision applications should be filed by November 1; regular applications, by February 1 for fall entry and December 1 for spring entry, along with a $40 fee. Notification of early decision is sent December 1; regular decision, March 15. Applications are accepted on-line.

Financial Aid: In 2009-2010, 99% of all full-time freshmen and 98% of continuing full-time students received some form of financial aid. 72% of all full-time freshmen and 65% of continuing full-time students received need-based aid. 45% of undergraduate students work part-time. Average annual earnings from campus work are $800. PC is a member of CSS. The FAFSA and the college's own financial statement are required. The priority date for freshman financial aid applications for fall entry is June 30. The deadline for filing freshman financial aid applications for fall entry is March 15.

Computers: There are ports in every residence hall room that allow students to connect to the college network and the Internet, and there is wireless coverage from more than 95% of the open spaces on campus. There is also wireless coverage in the library and several academic buildings. There are numerous computers located in 3 labs, the library, and other smaller installations. All students may access the system. any time. There are no time limits and no fees. It is strongly recommended that all students have a personal computer.

PRINCETON UNIVERSITY

Princeton, NJ 08544-0430	(609) 258-3000; (609) 258-6743
Full-time: 2600 men, 2275 women	**Faculty:** I, ++$
Part-time: none	**Ph.D.s:** n/av
Graduate: 1410 men, 950 women	**Student/Faculty:** n/av
Year: semesters	**Tuition:** $35,000
Application Deadline: January 1	**Room & Board:** $12,000
Freshman Class: n/av	
SAT or ACT: required	**MOST COMPETITIVE**

Princeton University, established in 1746, is a private institution offering degrees in the liberal arts and sciences, engineering, applied science, architecture, public and international affairs, interdisciplinary and regional studies, and the creative arts. The figures in the above capsule and in this profile are approximate. There are 4 graduate schools. In addition to regional accreditation, Princeton has baccalaureate program accreditation with ABET and NAAB. The 16 libraries contain 6.2 million volumes, 6.3 million microform items, and 60,000 audio/video tapes/CDs/DVDs, and subscribe to 15,000 periodicals including electronic. Computerized library services include interlibrary loans and database searching. Special learning facilities include an art gallery, natural history museum, radio station, a music center, a visual and performing arts center, several theaters, an observatory, a plasma physics lab, and a center for environmental and energy studies. The 500-acre campus is in a small town 50 miles south of New York City. Including any residence halls, there are 160 buildings.

Programs of Study: Princeton confers A.B. and B.S.E. degrees. Master's and doctoral degrees are also awarded. Bachelor's degrees are awarded in BIOLOGICAL SCIENCE (ecology, evolutionary biology, and molecular biology), BUSINESS (operations research), COMMUNICATIONS AND THE ARTS (classics, comparative literature, English, French, German, Italian, music, Portuguese, Slavic languages, and Spanish), COMPUTER AND PHYSICAL SCIENCE (astrophysics, chemistry, computer science, geoscience, mathematics, and physics), ENGINEERING AND ENVIRONMENTAL DESIGN (aeronautical engineering, architectural engineering, architecture, chemical engineering, civil engineering, electrical/electronics engineering, and mechanical engineering), SOCIAL SCIENCE (anthropology, archeology, East Asian studies, economics, history, international relations, Near Eastern studies, philosophy, political science/government, psychology, religion, and sociology). Economics, politics, and history are the largest.

Special: Princeton offers independent study, accelerated degree programs, student-proposed courses and majors, field study, community-based learning course that enrich course work with related service projects, study abroad, freshman seminars, and independent work in the junior and senior year. They also offer a Program in Teacher Preparation. There are 2 national honor societies, including Phi Beta Kappa, and all departments have honors programs.

Requirements: The SAT or ACT is required. The ACT is accepted in lieu of SAT Reasoning test when every other school to which the student applies requires only the ACT. Three SAT Subject tests are also required for all applicants. Recommended college preparatory courses include 4 years each of English, math, science, and a foreign language; 2 years each of lab science and history; and some study of art and music. Essays are required as part of the application and an interview is recommended. Students with special talent in visual or performing arts may supplement tapes, CDs or DVDs. AP credits are accepted. Important factors in the admissions decision are personality/intangible qualities, recommendations by school officials, and advanced placement or honors courses.

Procedure: Freshmen are admitted in the fall. Entrance exams should be taken by January of the senior year at the latest. There are early admissions and deferred admissions plans. Applications should be filed by January 1 for fall entry, along with a $65 fee. Notifications are sent April 1. Applications are accepted online. A waiting list is maintained.

Financial Aid: In a recent year, 55% of all full-time freshmen and 51% of continuing full-time students received some form of financial aid. 55% of all full-time freshmen and 51% of continuing full-time students received need-based aid. The average freshmen award was $31,114. 67% of undergraduate students worked part-time. Average annual earnings from campus work were $1500. The average financial indebtedness of the 2009 graduate was $5,592. Princeton is a member of CSS. The FAFSA and the college's own financial statement are required. Check with the school for current application deadlines.

Computers: Wireless access is available. Students have access to a varied and powerful computing network at Princeton. High-speed data connections and wireless service are available in every undergraduate dorm room, and wireless service also is provided in many areas across campus. Additionally, students have access to more than 250 Windows-based and Macintosh computers in the two dozen computer clusters around campus. Most of the clusters are available 24 hours a day and also provide access to scanners and free printing. These resources allow students to take advantage of networked resources such as e-mail, central printing, online library systems, streaming video, and specialty course software. All students may access the system. There are no time limits and no fees. It is strongly recommended that all students have a personal computer.

PRINCIPIA COLLEGE
Elsah, IL 62028
(618) 374-5181
(800) 277-4648; (618) 374-4000

Full-time: 252 men, 274 women	**Faculty:** n/av
Part-time: none	**Ph.D.s:** 68%
Graduate: none	**Student/Faculty:** n/av
Year: quarters	**Tuition:** $22,950
Application Deadline: open	**Room & Board:** $8730
Freshman Class: 242 applied, 193 accepted, 148 enrolled	
SAT or ACT: required	**VERY COMPETITIVE**

Principia College, founded in 1910, is a private liberal arts and sciences college for Christian Scientists. It is the only college in the world strictly for Christian Scientists. In addition to regional accreditation, Prin has baccalaureate program accreditation with NCATE. The library contains 217,257 volumes, 115,665 microform items, and 4847 audio/video tapes/CDs/DVDs, and subscribes to 12,813 periodicals including electronic. Computerized library services include interlibrary loans, database searching, and Internet access. Special learning facilities include a learning resource center, art gallery, planetarium, radio station, and TV station. The 2600-acre campus is in a rural area 30 miles northeast of St. Louis. Including any residence halls, there are 33 buildings.

Programs of Study: Prin confers B.A. and B.S. degrees. Bachelor's degrees are awarded in BIOLOGICAL SCIENCE (biology/biological science), BUSINESS (business administration and management and sports management), COMMUNICATIONS AND THE ARTS (communications, dramatic arts, English, fine arts, French, languages, music, Spanish, and studio art), COMPUTER AND PHYSICAL SCIENCE (chemistry, computer science, mathematics, and physics), EDUCATION (elementary education), ENGINEERING AND ENVIRONMENTAL DESIGN (environmental science), SOCIAL SCIENCE (economics, history, international relations, philosophy, political science/government, religion, and sociology). Education, studio art, and biology are the strongest academically. Business administration, studio art, and education are the largest.

Special: Students may design their own majors, study abroad or in San Francisco, or pursue a B.A.-B.S. degree. Internships, student-planned with a professor, independent study, work-study, and an interdisciplinary major, global studies, are available. A 3-2 engineering program with Washington University in St. Louis, Southern Illinois University at Carbondale, the University of Southern California, or another university with approval is also possible. A San Francisco field program in business administration is offered. There is 1 national honor society, a freshman honors program, and 3 departmental honors programs.

Admissions: 80% of the 2009-2010 applicants were accepted.

Requirements: The SAT or ACT is required; the SAT is preferred. An essay is required. SAT Subject Tests in foreign language and math are recommended. High school preparation should include 4 years of English, 3 of math (including algebra II), 2 to 3 of a foreign language, 2 of natural sciences, history or social sciences, and electives. A GPA of 2.3 is required. AP and CLEP credits are accepted. Important factors in the admissions decision are advanced placement or honors courses, recommendations by school officials, and recommendations by alumni.

Procedure: Freshmen are admitted fall and winter. Entrance exams should be taken in the spring of the junior year and again in the fall of the senior year. There are deferred admissions and rolling admissions plans. Applications deadlines are open. Applications are accepted on-line.

Financial Aid: In 2009-2010, 93% of all full-time freshmen and 90% of continuing full-time students received some form of financial aid. 81% of all full-time freshmen and 72% of continuing full-time students received need-based aid. The average freshman award was $21,039. Need-based scholarships or need-based grants averaged $18,659 ($31,180 maximum); need-based self-help aid (loans and jobs) averaged $5304 ($17,802 maximum); and other non-need-based awards and non-need-based scholarships averaged $10,145 ($22,650 maximum). 52% of undergraduate students work part-time. Average annual earnings from campus work are $1368. The average financial indebtedness of the 2009 graduate was $15,784. Prin is a member of CSS. The CSS/Profile and the college's own financial statement are required. The priority date for freshman financial aid applications for fall entry is March 1. The deadline for filing freshman financial aid applications for fall entry is June 1.

Computers: Wireless access is available. All students may access the system 24 hours a day.

PROVIDENCE COLLEGE
Providence, RI 02918

(401) 865-2535
(800) 721-6444; (401) 865-2826

Full-time: 1750 men, 2200 women	**Faculty:** 291; IIA, +$
Part-time: 10 men, 5 women	**Ph.D.s:** 85%
Graduate: 300 men, 490 women	**Student/Faculty:** 14 to 1
Year: semesters, summer session	**Tuition:** $38,610
Application Deadline: January 15	**Room & Board:** $13,107
Freshman Class: n/av	
SAT or ACT: not required	**HIGHLY COMPETITIVE**

Providence College, founded in 1917, is a liberal arts and sciences institution operated by the Dominican Order of the Catholic Church. There is 1 undergraduate schools and 1 graduate school. Enrollment figures in the above capsule and figures in this profile are approximate. In addition to regional accreditation, Providence has baccalaureate program accreditation with CSWE. The library contains 369,251 volumes, 212,049 microform items, and subscribes to 31,367 periodicals including electronic. Computerized library services include interlibrary loans, database searching, Internet access, and laptop Internet portals. Special learning facilities include a learning resource center, art gallery, radio station, theater, arts center, science center, and computer and language labs. The 105-acre campus is in a suburban area 50 miles south of Boston. Including any residence halls, there are 45 buildings.

Programs of Study: Providence confers B.A. and B.S. degrees. Associates and master's degrees are also awarded. Bachelor's degrees are awarded in AGRICULTURE (wildlife management), BIOLOGICAL SCIENCE (biochemistry and biology/biological science), BUSINESS (accounting, banking and finance, business administration and management, business economics, and marketing management), COMMUNICATIONS AND THE ARTS (art history and appreciation, ceramic art and design, digital communications, dramatic arts, drawing, English, French, Italian, music, painting, photography, sculpture, Spanish, and studio art), COMPUTER AND PHYSICAL SCIENCE (applied physics, chemistry, computer science, and mathematics), EDUCATION (elementary education, English education, foreign languages education, mathematics education, music education, secondary education, social studies education, and special education), ENGINEERING AND ENVIRONMENTAL DESIGN (preengineering), HEALTH PROFESSIONS (health care administration), SOCIAL SCIENCE (American studies, community services, economics, fire science, history, humanities, international studies, liberal arts/general studies, philosophy, political science/government, psychology, social science, social work, sociology, theological studies, and women's studies). Biology, chemistry, and business are the strongest academically. Marketing, business administration, and management are the largest.

Special: Providence offers internships in politics, broadcasting, journalism, and business and study abroad in 6 countries. Other opportunities for study abroad are available through AIFS. Also available are dual and student-designed majors, a 3-2 engineering degree with Columbia University or Washington University in St. Louis, nondegree study, a Washington semester, work-study, B.A.-B.S. degrees, and pass/fail options. There are 18 national honor societies and a freshman honors program.

Requirements: Applicants must be graduates of an accredited secondary school. A GPA of 3.25 is recommended. High school preparation should include 4 years of English, 3 years of math, 3 years of 1 foreign language, 2 years of lab science, 2 years of history/social studies, and 2 other academic subjects. An essay and 2 academic letters of recommendation are required. SAT Subject tests in 2 areas of the applicant's choice are recommended. AP credits are accepted. Important factors in the admissions decision are advanced placement or honors courses, extracurricular activities record, and personality/intangible qualities.

Procedure: Freshmen are admitted fall and spring. Entrance exams should be taken in the junior or senior year. There are early admissions and deferred admissions plans. Applications should be filed by January 15 for fall entry and December 1 for spring entry. The application fee is $55. Notifications are sent April 1. Applications are accepted on-line. 2661 applicants were on a recent waiting list, 118 were accepted.

Financial Aid: In a recent year, 81% of all full-time freshmen and 74% of continuing full-time students received some form of financial aid. 66% of all full-time freshmen and 57% of continuing full-time students received need-based aid. The average freshmen award was $20,470, with $15,361 ($24,800 maximum) from need-based scholarships or need-based grants; $5511 ($5425 maximum) from need-based self-help aid (loans and jobs); $20,102 ($34,500 maximum) from non-need-based athletic scholarships; and $12,965 ($24,800 maximum) from other non-need-based awards and non-need-based scholarships. 30% of undergraduate students work part-time. Average annual earnings from campus work are $1400. The average financial indebtedness of a recent graduate is $35,216.

Providence is a member of CSS. The CSS/Profile and FAFSA are required. Check with the school for current deadlines.

Computers: Wireless access is available. Students use the college's network to access on-campus resources and the Internet. Every resident student has a network connection for a PC. There are a few wireless areas that students with laptops are able to access by the college network or Internet. All students may access the system. There are no time limits. The fee is $325.

PURDUE UNIVERSITY/WEST LAFAYETTE

West Lafayette, IN 47907 (765) 494-1776; (765) 494-0544

Full-time: 17352 men, 12499 women	**Faculty:** 2130; I, av$
Part-time: 577 men, 717 women	**Ph.D.s:** 80%
Graduate: 5037 men, 3515 women	**Student/Faculty:** 14 to 1
Year: semesters, summer session	**Tuition:** $8638 ($25,118)
Application Deadline: March 1	**Room & Board:** $8710
Freshman Class: 27213 applied, 19905 accepted, 6171 enrolled	
SAT CR/M/W: 555/606/547	**ACT:** 26 **VERY COMPETITIVE+**

Purdue University, founded in 1869, is a publicly supported institution offering degree programs with an emphasis on engineering, business, communications, arts, social sciences, and technology. There are 12 undergraduate schools and 1 graduate school. In addition to regional accreditation, Purdue has baccalaureate program accreditation with AACSB, ABET, ACCE, ACPE, ACS, ADA, APA, ASLA, AVMA, CACREP, CCNE, FIDER, NASM, NCATE, NLN, and SAF. The 12 libraries contain 2.5 million volumes, 3.1 million microform items, and 11,752 audio/video tapes/CDs/DVDs, and subscribe to 48,283 periodicals including electronic. Computerized library services include interlibrary loans, database searching, Internet access, and laptop Internet portals. Special learning facilities include a learning resource center, art gallery, and radio station. The 2552-acre campus is in a suburban area 65 miles northwest of Indianapolis. Including any residence halls, there are 375 buildings.

Programs of Study: Purdue confers B.A., B.S., B.S.A.A.E., B.S.A.B.E., B.S.B.M.E., B.S.C.E., B.S.Ch., B.S.Ch.E., B.S.C.M.P.E.,B.S.C.N.E., B.S.E., B.S.E.E., B.S.E.H., B.S.F.O.R., B.S.I.E., B.S.I.M., B.S.L.A., B.S.L.S.G.E., B.S.M.E., B.S.M.S.E., and B.S.N.E. degrees. Associate, master's, and doctoral degrees are also awarded. Bachelor's degrees are awarded in AGRICULTURE (agricultural business management, agricultural communications, agricultural economics, agriculture, agronomy, animal science, fishing and fisheries, forestry and related sciences, horticulture, natural resource management, plant protection (pest management), plant science, soil science, and wood science), BIOLOGICAL SCIENCE (biochemistry, biology/biological science, cell biology, ecology, entomology, genetics, microbiology, molecular biology, nutrition, plant genetics, plant physiology, and wildlife biology), BUSINESS (accounting, banking and finance, entrepreneurial studies, fashion merchandising, hospitality management services, human resources, marketing management, marketing/retailing/merchandising, organizational leadership and management, retailing, and tourism), COMMUNICATIONS AND THE ARTS (advertising, apparel design, art history and appreciation, audio technology, broadcasting, classics, communications, comparative literature, creative writing, dramatic arts, English, film arts, fine arts, French, German, graphic design, industrial design, Japanese, journalism, Latin, linguistics, photography, public relations, Russian, Spanish, and visual and performing arts), COMPUTER AND PHYSICAL SCIENCE (actuarial science, applied mathematics, applied physics, atmospheric sciences and meteorology, chemistry, computer science, earth science, geology, information sciences and systems, mathematics, physics, radiological technology, science, software engineering, and statistics), EDUCATION (agricultural education, art education, athletic training, early childhood education, education, elementary education, English education, foreign languages education, health education, mathematics education, science education, secondary education, social studies education, special education, and technical education), ENGINEERING AND ENVIRONMENTAL DESIGN (aeronautical engineering, aeronautical technology, agricultural engineering, air traffic control, airline piloting and navigation, aviation administration/management, aviation computer technology, bioengineering, biomedical engineering, chemical engineering, chemical engineering technology, civil engineering, computational sciences, computer engineering, computer graphics, computer technology, construction engineering, construction management, construction technology, electrical/electronics engineering, electrical/electronics engineering technology, engineering management, environmental science, food services technology, industrial administration/management, industrial engineering, industrial engineering technology, interior design, landscape architecture/design, manufacturing engineering, manufacturing technology, materials science, mechanical engineering, mechanical engineering technology, nuclear engineering, occupational safety and health, and surveying engineering), HEALTH PROFESSIONS (clinical science, environmental health science, exercise science, health science, medical laboratory technology, nursing, pharmaceutical science, radiological science, and speech pathology/audiology), SOCIAL SCIENCE (African American studies, anthropology, Asian/American studies, Asian/Oriental studies, behavioral science, criminal justice, dietetics, economics, family and community services, family/consumer studies, fashion design and technology, food production/management/services, food science, French studies, history, Italian studies, Japanese studies, Judaic studies, liberal arts/general studies, medieval studies, philosophy, physical fitness/movement, political science/government, psychology, religion, Russian and Slavic studies, social studies, social work, sociology, Spanish studies, and women's studies).

Special: Cooperative programs are available in engineering, technology, agriculture, science, and consumer and family sciences. Cross-registration with Purdue's regional campuses, numerous internships, study abroad in 44 countries, dual majors, student-designed majors, nondegree study, and pass/fail options are also offered. There are 14 national honor societies, including Phi Beta Kappa, a freshman honors program, and 10 departmental honors programs.

Admissions: 73% of the 2009-2010 applicants were accepted. The SAT scores for the 2009-2010 freshman class were: Critical Reading--24% below 500, 45% between 500 and 599, 25% between 600 and 700, and 6% above 700; Math--11% below 500, 33% between 500 and 599, 40% between 600 and 700, and 16% above 700; Writing--26% below 500, 46% between 500 and 599, 24% between 600 and 700, and 4% above 700. The ACT scores were 8% below 21, 20% between 21 and 23, 26% between 24 and 26, 18% between 27 and 28, and 28% above 28. 60% of the current freshmen were in the top fifth of their class; 89% were in the top two fifths. There were 87 National Merit finalists. 284 freshmen graduated first in their class.

Requirements: The SAT or ACT is required. The ACT Optional Writing test is also required. In addition, Purdue recommends that most students have 15 semester credits, including 4 years of English, 3 to 4 of math, and 2 to 4 of lab science, and 4 semesters of a foreign language. The GED is accepted. AP and CLEP credits are accepted. Important factors in the admissions decision are advanced placement or honors courses, extracurricular activities record, and geographical diversity.

Procedure: Freshmen are admitted to all sessions. Entrance exams should be taken at the end of the junior year. There is a rolling admissions plan. Applications should be filed by March 1 for fall entry, along with a $50 fee. Applications are accepted on-line.

Financial Aid: In 2009-2010, 44% of all full-time freshmen and 40% of continuing full-time students received some form of financial aid. 36% of all full-time students received need-based aid. The average freshman award was $9,990. Need-based scholarships or need-based grants averaged $8946; need-based self-help aid (loans and jobs) averaged $3208; non-need-based athletic scholarships averaged $17,039; and other non-need-based awards and non-need-based scholarships averaged $12,724. 12% of undergraduate students work part-time. Average annual earnings from campus work are $859. The average financial indebtedness of the 2009 graduate was $17,510. The FAFSA is required. The deadline for filing freshman financial aid applications for fall entry is March 1.

Computers: Wireless access is available. All students may access the system 24 hours daily. There are no time limits and no fees.

QUEENS UNIVERSITY OF CHARLOTTE

Charlotte, NC 28274

(704) 337-2212
(800) 849-0202; (704) 337-2403

Full-time: 340 men, 972 women	**Faculty:** 106
Part-time: 91 men, 509 women	**Ph.D.s:** 71%
Graduate: 206 men, 450 women	**Student/Faculty:** 14 to 1
Year: semesters, summer session	**Tuition:** $22,730
Application Deadline: rolling	**Room & Board:** $8236
Freshman Class: 1702 applied, 288 accepted, 315 enrolled	
SAT CR/M/W: 520/520/520	**ACT:** 22 **VERY COMPETITIVE+**

Queens University of Charlotte is a private, Presbyterian-affiliated liberal arts university offering undergraduate and graduate programs in arts and sciences, business, communication, education, and nursing. The Pauline Lewis Hayworth College offers undergraduate evening programs for working adults. There are 5 undergraduate schools and 1 graduate school. In addition to regional accreditation, Queens has baccalaureate program accreditation with AACSB, ACBSP, NASM, NCATE, and NLN. Computerized library services include interlibrary loans, database searching, and Internet access. Special learning facilities include a learning resource center, art gallery, rare books and archival collection, photographic lab, ceramics studio, and recital hall. The 30-acre campus is in a suburban area 2 miles south of uptown Charlotte. Including any residence halls, there are 37 buildings.

Programs of Study: Queens confers B.A., B.S., B.Mus., and B.S.N. degrees. Associate and master's degrees are also awarded. Bachelor's degrees are awarded in BIOLOGICAL SCIENCE (biochemistry and biology/biological science), BUSINESS (business administration and management), COMMUNICATIONS AND THE ARTS (art, communications, dramatic arts, English, fine arts, French, graphic design, music, and Spanish), COMPUTER AND PHYSICAL SCIENCE (chemistry, information sciences and systems, and mathematics), EDUCATION (elementary education and secondary education), ENGINEERING AND ENVIRONMENTAL DESIGN (environmental science and interior design), HEALTH PROFESSIONS (music therapy and nursing), SOCIAL SCIENCE (community services, history, human services, international studies, philosophy, political science/government, psychology, religion, and sociology). Liberal arts and sciences is the strongest academically. Business, nursing, and communications are the largest.

Special: Internships in all majors, cross-registration with colleges of the Charlotte Area Educational Consortium, dual majors, nondegree study, and pass/fail options are available. The school offers a Washington semester. Study tours in over 14 countries(included in the cost of tuition) may be arranged through the school's John Belk International Program. There are 5 national honor societies and a freshman honors program.

Admissions: 17% of the 2009-2010 applicants were accepted. The SAT scores for the 2009-2010 freshman class were: Critical Reading--38% below 500, 43% between 500 and 599, 17% between 600 and 700, and 2% above 700; Math--40% below 500, 40% between 500 and 599, 19% between 600 and 700, and 1% above 700; Writing--37% below 500, 44% between 500 and 599, 17% between 600 and 700, and 2% above 700. The ACT scores were 31% below 21, 30% between 21 and 23, 18% between 24 and 26, 15% between 27 and 28, and 5% above 28. 43% of the current freshmen were in the top fifth of their class; 73% were in the top two fifths. 2 freshmen graduated first in their class.

Requirements: The SAT or ACT is required. The ACT Optional Writing test is also required. In addition, applicants should have a college preparatory background in an accredited secondary school. The GED is accepted. High school courses should include 4 years of English, 3 of math, 2 each of history or social studies and a foreign language, and 2 years of science, including 1 of lab science. An interview is recommended. An audition or portfolio is recommended for art and music students. A GPA of 2.5 is required. AP and CLEP credits are accepted. Important factors in the admissions decision are recommendations by school officials, advanced placement or honors courses, and leadership record.

Procedure: Freshmen are admitted fall, spring, and summer. Entrance exams should be taken in the junior year or as early as possible in the senior year. There is a rolling admissions plan. Application deadlines are open. Application fee is $40. Applications are accepted on-line. A waiting list is maintained.

Financial Aid: In a recent year, 66% of all full-time freshmen received some form of financial aid. 63% of all full-time freshmen received need-based aid. The average freshmen award was $16,034. Average annual earnings from campus work are $1800. The average financial indebtedness of a recent graduate was $19,532. Queens is a member of CSS. The FAFSA is required. The priority date for freshman financial aid applications for fall entry is March 1.

Computers: Each student is issued an e-mail account and access to the university's network/wireless system. All residence halls have wireless access. Approximately 90% of campus is wireless capable. A 24-hour computer lab and numerous other labs are available across campus for student use. All students may access the system 24/7. There are no time limits and no fees.

Hamden, CT 06518　　　　　　　　**(203) 582-8600**
　　　　　　　　　　　　　(800) 462-1944; (203) 582-8906

Full-time: 2168 men, 3518 women	**Faculty:** IIA, ++$
Part-time: 112 men, 173 women	**Ph.D.s:** 86%
Graduate: 658 men, 1129 women	**Student/Faculty:** n/av
Year: semesters, summer session	**Tuition:** $32,400
Application Deadline: February 1	**Room & Board:** $12,380
Freshman Class: 13850 applied, 9619 accepted, 1587 enrolled	
SAT CR/M/W: 560/580/570	**ACT:** 25　**VERY COMPETITIVE**

Quinnipiac University, founded in 1929, is a private institution offering undergraduate and graduate degrees in health sciences, business, communications, liberal arts, education, and law. There are 4 undergraduate schools and 5 graduate schools. In addition to regional accreditation, Quinnipiac has baccalaureate program accreditation with AACSB, ABET, APTA, CAHEA, NCATE, and NLN. The 2 libraries contain 4,875 volumes, 9,100 microform items, and 1,890 audio/video tapes/CDs/DVDs, and subscribe to 4,000 periodicals including electronic. Computerized library services include interlibrary loans, database searching, Internet access, and laptop Internet portals. Special learning facilities include a learning resource center, art gallery, radio station, TV station, and an exhibit on the Irish famine. The 600-acre campus is in a suburban area 8 miles north of New Haven and 35 miles south of Hartford. Including any residence halls, there are 54 buildings.

Programs of Study: Quinnipiac confers B.A., B.S. degrees. Master's and doctoral degrees are also awarded. Bachelor's degrees are awarded in BIOLOGICAL SCIENCE (biochemistry, biology/biological science, biotechnology, and microbiology), BUSINESS (accounting, banking and finance, business administration and management, business economics, entrepreneurial studies, international business management, management science, and marketing/retailing/merchandising), COMMUNICATIONS AND THE ARTS (advertising, communications, dramatic arts, English, journalism, public relations, and Spanish), COMPUTER AND PHYSICAL SCIENCE (chemistry, computer science, digital arts/technology, and mathematics), HEALTH PROFESSIONS (health science, nursing, occupational therapy, predentistry, premedicine, and radiological science), SOCIAL SCIENCE (criminal justice, economics, gerontology, history, liberal arts/general studies, paralegal studies, political science/government, prelaw, psychobiology, psychology, social science, and sociology). Psychology, physical therapy, and nursing are the strongest academically. Communications, physical therapy, and management are the largest.

Special: Internships in all majors, study abroad in more than 25 countries, a Washington semester with American University, work-study programs, dual and student-designed majors, B.A.-B.S. degrees, credit for life experience, and nondegree study are available. A 6 1/2-year freshman entry-level doctorate in physical therapy and a 5 1/2 year freshman entry-level master's in occupational therapy are offered, as well as a 6-year BS in Health Sciences/MHS in a physician assistant master's program, and a 5-year master of arts in education for those interested in teaching at the elementary, or high school level. There are 20 national honor societies, a freshman honors program, and 20 departmental honors programs.

Admissions: 69% of the 2009-2010 applicants were accepted. 55% of the current freshmen were in the top fifth of their class; 90% were in the top two fifths. 45 freshmen graduated first in their class.

Requirements: The SAT or ACT is required. The ACT Optional Writing test is also required. A satisfactory score on the SAT (critical reading plus math) or 23 composite on the ACT is recommended. The scores are used for admission and scholarship purposes. All students must have completed 16 academic credits, including 4 in English, 3 in math, 2 each in science and social studies, and 5 in electives. The GED is accepted. An interview is recommended, and an essay and at least one letter of recommendation are required. For majors in the health sciences, 4 years each of math and science are required. Quinnipiac requires applicants to be in the upper 40% of their class. A GPA of 2.8 is required. AP and CLEP credits are accepted. Important factors in the admissions decision are advanced placement or honors courses, extracurricular activities record, and personality/intangible qualities.

Procedure: Freshmen are admitted fall and spring. Entrance exams should be taken in the junior year and early in the senior year. There are deferred admissions and rolling admissions plans. Applications should be filed by February 1 for fall entry and December 15 for spring entry, along with a $45 fee. Nursing, physical therapy, and physician assistant should file applications by November 1 for fall entry. Notifications are sent December 15. 1750 applicants were on the 2009 waiting list; 250 were admitted. Applications are accepted on-line.

Financial Aid: In 2009-2010, 74% of all full-time freshmen and 72% of continuing full-time students received some form of financial aid. 55% of all full-time freshmen and 55% of continuing full-time students received need-based aid. The average freshman award was $17,115. Need-based scholarships or need-based grants averaged $14,162. 28% of undergraduate students work part-time. Average annual earnings from campus work are $2100. The average financial indebtedness of the 2009 graduate was $37,000. Quinnipiac is a member of CSS. The FAFSA is required. The priority date for freshman financial aid applications for fall entry is March 1.

Computers: Wireless access is available. All students must purchase a university-recommended laptop when they enter Quinnipiac for classroom and residence hall use. All students may access the system 24 hours a day. There are no time limits and no fees. The current vendor is Dell.

RAMAPO COLLEGE OF NEW JERSEY

Mahwah, NJ 07430

(201) 684-7300
(800) 9-RAMAPO; (201) 684-7964

Full-time: 2196 men, 3028 women	**Faculty:** 213; IIB, +$
Part-time: 224 men, 328 women	**Ph.D.s:** 94%
Graduate: 60 men, 190 women	**Student/Faculty:** 18 to 1
Year: semesters, , summer session	**Tuition:** n/av
Application Deadline: March 1	**Room & Board:** $11,290
Freshman Class: 5556 applied, 2550 accepted, 880 enrolled	
SAT CR/M/W: 550/590/570	**HIGHLY COMPETITIVE**

Ramapo College, founded in 1969, is a public institution offering undergraduate programs in the arts and sciences, American and international studies, business administration, and human services. Personal interaction is incorporated throughout the curriculum as is an international and multicultural component including telecommunications and computer technology. There are 5 undergraduate schools and 3 graduate schools. In addition to regional accreditation, Ramapo has baccalaureate program accreditation with CSWE and TEAC. The library contains 176,128 volumes, 2,500 microform items, 9,663 audio/video tapes/CDs/DVDs, and subscribes to 950 periodicals including electronic. Computerized library services include inter-library loans, database searching, Internet access, and laptop Internet portals. Special learning facilities include a learning resource center, radio station, TV station, astronomical observatory, international telecommunications satellite center, the Marge Roukema Center for International Education and Entrepreneurship, a solar greenhouse center, a spirituality center, and a sustainability education center is under construction. The 314-acre campus is in a suburban area 25 miles northwest of New York City. Including any residence halls, there are 71 buildings.

Programs of Study: Ramapo confers B.A., B.S., B.S.N., and B.S.W. degrees. Master's degrees are also awarded. Bachelor's degrees are awarded in AGRICULTURE (environmental studies), BIOLOGICAL SCIENCE (biochemistry, bioinformatics, and biology/biological science), BUSINESS (accounting, business administration and management, and international business management), COMMUNICATIONS AND THE ARTS (art, communications, dramatic arts, literature, music, and visual and performing arts), COMPUTER AND PHYSICAL SCIENCE (chemistry, computer science, information sciences and systems, and mathematics), ENGINEERING AND ENVIRONMENTAL DESIGN (engineering physics and environmental science), HEALTH PROFESSIONS (allied health, clinical science, and nursing), SOCIAL SCIENCE (American studies, economics, history, international studies, law, liberal arts/general studies, political science/government, psychology, science and society, social science, social work, sociology, and Spanish studies). Physics, bioinformatics, and biology are the strongest academically. Psychology, business administration, and communication arts are the largest.

Special: Ramapo's curriculum emphasizes the interdependence of global society and includes an international dimension in all academic programs. Students may study abroad in many countries. Cooperative programs are available with various corporations and in foreign countries. Cross-registration is possible with local state colleges. Ramapo offers accelerated degree programs, dual and student-designed majors, credit for life experience, pass/fail options, internships, work-study programs, and certificate programs in gerontology and substance abuse. A teachers education program is offered. There are 20 national honor societies and a freshman honors program.

Admissions: 46% of the 2009-2010 applicants were accepted. The SAT scores for the 2009-2010 freshman class were: Critical Reading--10% below 500, 63% between 500 and 599, 23% between 600 and 700, and 4 above 700; Math--5% below 500, 51% between 500 and 599, 40% between 600 and 700, and 5 above 700; Writing--10% below 500, 56% between 500 and 599, 29% between 600 and 700, and 5 above 700. 51% of the current freshmen were in the top fifth of their class; 97% were in the top two fifths. 3 freshmen graduated first in their class.

Requirements: The SAT is required. In addition, applicants must be graduates of an accredited secondary schools or have earned a GED. The college requires 18 academic credits, including 4 in English, 3 each in math, science, and social studies, 2 in foreign language, and the remaining 3 in academic electives. Students must also submit an essay. An interview is recommended. A GPA of 3.0 is required. AP and CLEP credits are accepted. Important factors in the admissions decision are advanced placement or honors courses, recommendations by school officials, and evidence of special talent.

Procedure: Freshmen are admitted fall and spring. Entrance exams should be taken during the senior year. There are early admissions, deferred admissions, and rolling admissions plans. Applications should be filed by March 1 for fall entry and December 1 for spring entry. The fall 2008 application fee was $60. Notification is sent on a rolling basis. Applications are accepted on-line. 505 applicants were on a recent waiting list, 104 were accepted.

Financial Aid: In 2009-2010, 73% of all full-time freshmen and 71% of continuing full-time students received some form of financial aid. 47% of all full-time freshmen and 49% of continuing full-time students received need-based aid. The average freshmen award was $11,414, with $11,114 ($32,851 maximum) from need-based scholarships or need-based grants; $3,495 ($6,749 maximum) from need-based self-help aid (loans and jobs); and $13,539 ($25,480 maximum) from other non-need-based awards and non-need-based scholarships. 17% of undergraduate students work part-time. Average annual earnings from campus work are $2332. The average financial indebtedness of the 2009 graduate was $19,789. The FAFSA is required. The priority date for freshman financial aid applications for fall entry is March 1. The deadline for filing freshman financial aid applications for fall entry is March 15.

Computers: Wireless access is available. All residential halls are wired for Internet access. All students have access to computers on campus. There are approximately 908 PCs and 150 Mac computers networked in labs, academic cores, and the student center. All students may access the system according to posted schedules for lab times. There are no time limits and no fees.

RANDOLPH COLLEGE
Lynchburg, VA 24503

(434) 947-8100
(800) 745-7692; (434) 947-8996

Full-time: 73 men, 550 women	**Faculty:** 66; IIB, -$
Part-time: 4 men, 22 women	**Ph.D.s:** 92%
Graduate: 7 women	**Student/Faculty:** 9 to 1
Year: semesters, summer session	**Tuition:** $28,430
Application Deadline: April 1	**Room & Board:** $9715
Freshman Class: n/av	
SAT CR/M: 560/560	**ACT:** 24 **VERY COMPETITIVE**

Randolph College, founded in 1891, is an independent, coeducational, liberal arts institution. The college's curriculum offers the best feature of an honors education with a global outlook. Students are encouraged to travel, to take on real problems, to pursue and achieve a goal with personal meaning. Embedded within a student's education are opportunities to study abroad, both national and international internships, career guidance, leadership development, and one-on-one faculty advising. There is 1 graduate school. The enrollment figures in the above capsule are approximate. In addition to regional accreditation, Randolph has baccalaureate program accreditation with NASDTEC. The library contains 197,332 volumes, 187,000 microform items, and 3600 audio/video tapes/CDs/DVDs, and subscribes to 618 periodicals including electronic. Computerized library services include interlibrary loans and database searching. Special learning facilities include learning resource center, art gallery, radio station, observatory, collection of American art housed in the Maier Museum, 2 theaters, recital hall, organic garden, 100-acre equestrian center, and 3 nature preserves. The 100-acre campus is in a suburban area within minutes of the Blue Ridge Mountains, 1 hour south of Charlottesville. Including any residence halls, there are 18 buildings.

Programs of Study: Randolph confers B.A., B.S., and B.F.A. degrees. Master's degrees are also awarded. Bachelor's degrees are awarded in AGRICULTURE (environmental studies), BIOLOGICAL SCIENCE (biology/biological science),

COMMUNICATIONS AND THE ARTS (art, classics, communications, dance, dramatic arts, English, French, music, and Spanish), COMPUTER AND PHYSICAL SCIENCE (chemistry, mathematics, and physics), EDUCATION (business education), HEALTH PROFESSIONS (health science), SOCIAL SCIENCE (American studies, economics, history, international studies, philosophy, political science/government, psychology, religion, and sociology). Psychology, biology, and English are the largest.

Special: Randolph offers a spring semester American Culture Program, as well as study abroad in 11 countries, including its own program in England and internships. A Washington semester at American University is available, as is the Tri-College Consortium with Sweet Briar and Lynchburg Colleges, and the Seven-College Exchange Program with Hampden-Sydney, Hollins, Mary Baldwin, Randolph-Macon, and Sweet Briar Colleges, and Washington and Lee University. There is a 3-2 nursing program with Johns Hopkins University and a 3-2 engineering degree with several institutions. There are 9 national honor societies including Phi Beta Kappa.

Admissions: The SAT scores for the 2009-2010 freshman class were: Critical Reading--22% below 500, 41% between 500 and 599, 31% between 600 and 700, and 5 above 700; Math--23% below 500, 50% between 500 and 599, 25% between 600 and 700, and 2 above 700. 48% of the current freshmen were in the top fifth of their class; 80% were in the top two-fifths.

Requirements: The SAT or ACT is required. In addition, applicants must be graduates of an accredited secondary school with at least 16 academic credits, including 4 units in English, 3 to 4 in a foreign language, 3 in math, 2 in biology, chemistry, or physics with lab work, and 1 to 2 in electives from other academic study. An interview is strongly encouraged. AP and CLEP credits are accepted. Important factors in the admissions decision are advanced placement or honors courses, recommendations by school officials, and leadership record.

Procedure: Freshmen are admitted fall and spring. Entrance exams should be taken in the junior or senior year. There are early admissions, deferred admissions, and early action plans. Early action I applications should be filed by December 1; early action II by February 1; regular decision by April 1 for fall entry and December 1 for spring entry, along with a $35 fee. Early action I notification is sent December 15; early action II, February 15; regular decision, on a rolling basis. Applications are accepted on-line.

Financial Aid: In 2009-2010, 97% of all full-time freshmen and 98% of continuing full-time students received some form of financial aid. 76% of all full-time freshmen and 70% of continuing full-time students received need-based aid. The average freshmen award was $22,341, with $17,863 ($27,920 maximum) from need-based scholarships or need-based grants and $15,094 ($27,920 maximum) from other non-need-based awards and non-need-based scholarships. 66% of undergraduate students work part-time. Average annual earnings from campus work are $1100. The FAFSA and the state aid form are required. The priority date for freshman financial aid applications for fall entry is March 1.

Computers: Wireless access is available. Randolph College provides student access to 159 Dell computers with Internet access 24/7. The majority are located in a lab environment with scanner, printer, and overhead projector. Others are located in 38 classrooms and strategically placed throughout campus for ease of access and presentations. The campus has 6 different hot spots in common areas for students to use wireless. All students may access the system. There are no time limits and no fees.

REED COLLEGE

Portland, OR 97202-8199

(503) 777-7511
(800) 547-4750; (503) 777-7553

Full-time: 638 men, 768 women	**Faculty:** 121; IIB, +$
Part-time: 21 men, 25 women	**Ph.D.s:** 90%
Graduate: 15 men, 14 women	**Student/Faculty:** 10 to 1
Year: semesters	**Tuition:** $39,700
Application Deadline: January 15	**Room & Board:** $10,250
Freshman Class: 3161 applied, 1281 accepted, 368 enrolled	
SAT CR/M/W: 710/670/690	**ACT:** 31 **MOST COMPETITIVE**

Reed College, founded in 1908, is a private, nonsectarian institution offering programs in liberal arts and sciences, and emphasizing instruction through small conference-style classes. There is one graduate school. The library contains 600,697 volumes, 246,584 microform items, and 24,050 audio/video tapes/CDs/DVDs, and subscribes to 6,705 periodicals including electronic. Computerized library services include interlibrary loans, database searching, Internet access, and laptop Internet portals. Special learning facilities include a learning resource center, art gallery, radio station, a reactor, and centers for bio science, math, quantitative skills, science, and writing. The 116-acre campus is in an urban area in Portland. Including any residence halls, there are 43 buildings.

Programs of Study: Reed confers B.A. degrees. Master's degrees are also awarded. Bachelor's degrees are awarded in BIOLOGICAL SCIENCE (biology/biological science), COMMUNICATIONS AND THE ARTS (art, Chinese, classics, dramatic arts, English literature, Germanic languages and literature, linguistics, music, and Russian languages and literature), COMPUTER AND PHYSICAL SCIENCE (chemistry, mathematics, and physics), SOCIAL SCIENCE (anthropology, economics, French studies, history, philosophy, political science/government, psychology, religion, sociology, and Spanish studies). Biology, psychology, and physics are the largest.

Special: Cross-registration is available through the Oregon Independent Colleges organization and Pacific Northwest College of Art. Also available are 3-2 engineering degrees with California Institute of Technology, Columbia University, and Rensselaer Polytechnic Institute, combined 3-2 programs in science, and programs with the Pacific Northwest College of Art. Study abroad in 18 countries, a domestic exchange program with Howard University in Washington, D.C., Sarah Lawrence College, and Sea Education Association (SEA), accelerated degree programs, dual majors, student-designed majors, numerous interdisciplinary majors, nondegree study, and pass/fail options are also offered. There is a Phi Beta Kappa.

Admissions: 41% of the 2009-2010 applicants were accepted. The SAT scores for the 2009-2010 freshman class were: Critical Reading--6% between 500 and 599, 35% between 600 and 700, and 59% above 700; Math--1% below 500, 14% between 500 and 599, 52% between 600 and 700, and 34% above 700; Writing--1% below 500, 9% between 500 and 599, 43% between 600 and 700, and 47% above 700. The ACT scores were 2% between 21 and 23, 5% between 24 and 26, 15% between 27 and 28, and 78% above 28. 81% of the current freshmen were in the top fifth of their class; 97% were in the top two fifths. There were 6 National Merit finalists. 4 freshmen graduated first in their class.

Requirements: The SAT is required. Reed strongly recommends that applicants have 4 years of English, 3 each of math and science, and 2 each of foreign language, history, and social studies. An essay is required, and an interview is recommended. The GED is accepted. AP credits are accepted. Important factors in the admissions decision are advanced placement or honors courses, personality/ intangible qualities, and evidence of special talent.

Procedure: Freshmen are admitted fall and spring. There is an early decision and a deferred admissions plan. Early decision applications should be filed by November 15 and regular applications should be filed by January 15 for fall entry and November 15 for winter entry. The fall 2008 application fee was $50. Notification of early decision is sent December 15; regular decision, April 1. Applications are accepted on-line. 838 applicants were on a recent waiting list, 30 were accepted.

Financial Aid: In 2009-2010, 50% of all full-time freshmen and 53% of continuing full-time students received some form of financial aid. 43% of all full-time freshmen and 50% of continuing full-time students received need-based aid. The average freshman award was $33,161. Need-based scholarships or need-based grants averaged $33,181; need-based self-help aid (loans and jobs) averaged $4,000. 39% of undergraduate students work part-time. Average annual earnings from campus work are $710. The average financial indebtedness of the 2009 graduate was $20,750. Reed is a member of CSS. The CSS/Profile, FAFSA, the college's own financial statement, and parent and student federal tax forms are required. The deadline for filing freshman financial aid applications for fall entry is March 1.

Computers: Wireless access is available. High-speed networking is available in all residence hall rooms, classrooms, labs, and offices. All students may access the system 24 hours daily. There are no time limits and no fees.

RENSSELAER POLYTECHNIC INSTITUTE

Troy, NY 12180-3590

(518) 276-6216
(800) 448-6562; (518) 276-4072

Full-time: 4019 men, 1582 women	**Faculty:** 401; I, +$
Part-time: 41 men, 17 women	**Ph.D.s:** 92%
Graduate: 1482 men, 515 women	**Student/Faculty:** 14 to 1
Year: semesters, summer session	**Tuition:** $39,165
Application Deadline: January 15	**Room & Board:** $11,145
Freshman Class: 12350 applied, 5291 accepted, 1337 enrolled	
SAT CR/M/W: 650/700/630	**ACT:** 27 **MOST COMPETITIVE**

Rensselaer Polytechnic Institute, founded in 1824, is a private institution that offers bachelor's, master's and doctoral degrees in engineering, the sciences, information technology, architecture, management, and the humanities and social sciences. Institute programs serve undergraduates, graduate students, and working professionals around the world. There are 5 undergraduate schools and 5 graduate schools. In addition to regional accreditation, Rensselaer has baccalaureate program accreditation with AACSB, ABET, and NAAB. The 2 libraries contain 445,590 volumes, 173,901 microform items, and 6,439 audio/video tapes/CDs/ DVDs, and subscribe to 44,214 periodicals including electronic. Computerized library services include interlibrary loans, database searching, Internet access, and laptop Internet portals. Special learning facilities include a learning resource center, art gallery, radio station, TV station, and an observatory. The 276-acre campus is in a suburban area 10 miles north of Albany. Including any residence halls, there are 200 buildings.

Programs of Study: Rensselaer confers B.S. and B.Arch. degrees. Master's and doctoral degrees are also awarded. Bachelor's degrees are awarded in BIOLOGICAL SCIENCE (biochemistry, biology/biological science, and biophysics),

BUSINESS (management information systems, management science, and recreation and leisure services), COMMUNICATIONS AND THE ARTS (communications and media arts), COMPUTER AND PHYSICAL SCIENCE (applied physics, chemistry, computer science, geology, hydrogeology, mathematics, physics, and science technology), ENGINEERING AND ENVIRONMENTAL DESIGN (aeronautical engineering, architecture, biomedical engineering, chemical engineering, civil engineering, computer engineering, construction engineering, electrical/electronics engineering, engineering, engineering physics, environmental engineering, industrial engineering, materials engineering, mechanical engineering, and nuclear engineering), HEALTH PROFESSIONS (premedicine), SOCIAL SCIENCE (economics, interdisciplinary studies, philosophy, prelaw, and psychology). Engineering, sciences, and architecture are the strongest academically. General engineering, computer science, and management are the largest.

Special: Rensselaer offers co-op programs, internships, study abroad/exchange program, and pass/fail options are available. Students may pursue dual and student-designed majors, a 3-2 engineering degree with more than 40 universities, 2-2 agreements, an accelerated degree program in physician-scientist, law and MBA. There are 14 national honor societies and 8 departmental honors programs.

Admissions: 43% of the 2009-2010 applicants were accepted. The SAT scores for the 2009-2010 freshman class were: Critical Reading- 19% between 500 and 599, 54% between 600 and 700, and 27% above 700; Math- 5% between 500 and 599, 43% between 600 and 700, and 52% above 700; Writing--2% below 500, 27% between 500 and 599, 53% between 600 and 700, and 18% above 700. The ACT scores were 3% below 21, 11% between 21 and 23, 25% between 24 and 26, 25% between 27 and 28, and 36% above 28. 80% of the current freshmen were in the top fifth of their class; 96% were in the top two fifths. 46 freshmen graduated first in their class.

Requirements: The SAT or ACT is required. In addition, SAT subject tests in critical reading, math and science are required for accelerated-program applicants or ACT, which must include the optional writing component in lieu of SAT and SAT. AP credits are accepted. Important factors in the admissions decision are advanced placement or honors courses, recommendations by school officials, and leadership record.

Procedure: Freshmen are admitted fall and spring. Entrance exams should be taken in the junior or senior year. There arean early decision and deferred admissions plans. Early decision I applications should be filed by November 2; early decision II by December 15; accelerated programs by November 2; and regular applications should be filed by January 15 for fall entry; along with a $70 fee. Notifications are sent December 5 for early decision I; early April for accelerated programs; January 16 for early decision II; and March 13 for regular decision. 3799 applicants were on the 2009 waiting list; 276 were admitted. Applications are accepted on-line.

Financial Aid: In 2009-2010, all full-time freshmen and 97% of continuing full-time students received some form of financial aid. 66% of all full-time freshmen and 65% of continuing full-time students received need-based aid. The average freshman award was $27,793. Need-based scholarships or need-based grants averaged $22,418; need-based self-help aid (loans and jobs) averaged $7,750; non-need based athletic scholarships averaged $43,106; and other non-need based awards and non-need based scholarships averaged $13,043. 24% of undergraduate students work part-time. Average annual earnings from campus work are $2000. The average financial indebtedness of the 2009 graduate was $30,838. Rensselaer is a member of CSS. The CSS/Profile and FAFSA are required. The deadline for filing freshman financial aid applications for fall entry is February 15.

Computers: Wireless access is available. Services include support for interactive learning (including WebCT courses), electronic information-retrieval services by the libraries, and on-line student and administrative services. All students may access the system. There are no time limits and no fees. A laptop computer is required of all undergraduates. An Lenovo ThinkPad T61 is recommended.

RHODE ISLAND SCHOOL OF DESIGN

Providence, RI 02903

(401) 454-6300
(800) 364-7473; (401) 454-6309

Full-time: 640 men, 1240 women	**Faculty:** 144
Part-time: 155 men, 225 women	**Ph.D.s:** n/av
Graduate: 420 men and women	**Student/Faculty:** n/av
Year: 4-1-4	**Tuition:** $36,658
Application Deadline: see profile	**Room & Board:** $10,846
Freshman Class: n/av	
SAT or ACT: required	**SPECIAL**

Rhode Island School of Design, founded in 1877, is a private institution offering degree programs in fine arts, design, and architecture. There is 1 undergraduate school. Enrollment figures in the above capsule and figures in this profile are approximate. In addition to regional accreditation, RISD has baccalaureate program accreditation with NAAB and NASAD. The library contains 120,000 volumes, 1855 microform items, and 2100 audio/video tapes/CDs/DVDs, and subscribes to 400 periodicals including electronic. Computerized library services include interlibrary loans, database searching, and Internet access. Special learning facilities include an art gallery, art museum, nature lab, and writing center. The 13-acre campus is in an urban area 50 miles south of Boston. Including any residence halls, there are 42 buildings.

Programs of Study: RISD confers B.Arch., B.F.A., B.G.D., B.I.A., and B.I.D. degrees. Master's degrees are also awarded. Bachelor's degrees are awarded in COMMUNICATIONS AND THE ARTS (apparel design, ceramic art and design, film arts, glass, graphic design, illustration, industrial design, metal/jewelry, painting, photography, printmaking, and sculpture), ENGINEERING AND ENVIRONMENTAL DESIGN (architecture, furniture design, and interior design), SOCIAL SCIENCE (textiles and clothing). Illustration, graphic design, and architecture are the largest.

Special: RISD offers cross-registration with Brown University and through the AICAD mobility program, credit or noncredit summer programs, 6-week internships during the midyear winter session, and study abroad in 21 countries and through the senior-year European Honors Program in Rome. Students may also elect a liberal arts concentration in art/architectural history, literary studies, creative writing, or social sciences.

Requirements: The SAT is required; the ACT may be substituted. The ACT Optional Writing test is also required. In addition, applicants must be graduates of an accredited secondary school or have a GED. An essay, assigned drawings, a portfolio, and a statement of purpose are also required. Up to 3 letters of recommendation are recommended. AP credits are accepted. Important factors in the admissions decision are evidence of special talent, advanced placement or honors courses, and personality/intangible qualities.

Procedure: Freshmen are admitted fall and spring. Entrance exams should be taken at least 6 weeks before the application deadline. There are early admissions and deferred admissions plans. Check with the school for current deadlines. The application fee is $60. Applications are accepted on-line. A waiting list is maintained.

Financial Aid: RISD is a member of CSS. The CSS/Profile, FAFSA, and parents' income tax returns are required. Check with the school for current deadline.

Computers: Wireless access is available. All students may access the system. There are no time limits. The fee is $150. Students enrolled in industrial design, interior architecture, furniture design, graphic design, and architecture must have a personal computer.

RHODES COLLEGE

Memphis, TN 38112

(901) 843-3700
(800) 844-5969; (901) 843-3631

Full-time: 708 men, 945 women	**Faculty:** 161; IIB, av$
Part-time: 2 men, 4 women	**Ph.D.s:** 98%
Graduate: 4 men, 6 women	**Student/Faculty:** 10 to 1
Year: semesters	**Tuition:** $33,710
Application Deadline: January 15	**Room & Board:** $8314
Freshman Class: 5039 applied, 2113 accepted, 432 enrolled	
SAT CR/M/W: 630/640/620	**ACT:** 28 **MOST COMPETITIVE**

Rhodes College, founded in 1848, is a private liberal arts institution affiliated with the Presbyterian Church (U.S.A.). There 1 graduate school. The 2 libraries contain 278,392 volumes, 95,034 microform items, and 10,600 audio/video tapes/CDs/DVDs, and subscribe to 1,683 periodicals including electronic. Computerized library services include interlibrary loans, database searching, Internet access, and laptop Internet portals. Special learning facilities include an art gallery, 2 electron microscopes, a 0.8-meter infrared optimized telescope, a cell culture lab, and the Human Relations Area Files, containing 2 million pages of human behavior resources materials on microfiche. The 100-acre campus is in an urban area in Memphis. Including any residence halls, there are 44 buildings.

Programs of Study: Rhodes confers B.A. and B.S. degrees. Master's degrees are also awarded. Bachelor's degrees are awarded in BIOLOGICAL SCIENCE (biology/biological science), BUSINESS (business administration and management), COMMUNICATIONS AND THE ARTS (art, dramatic arts, English, French, German, music, and Spanish), COMPUTER AND PHYSICAL SCIENCE (chemistry, computer science, mathematics, and physics), SOCIAL SCIENCE (anthropology, classical/ancient civilization, economics, history, interdisciplinary studies, international studies, Latin American studies, philosophy, political science/government, psychology, religion, Russian and Slavic studies, sociology, and urban studies). Biology, English, and business administration are the strongest academically and have the largest enrollments.

Special: More than half of Rhodes students have an internship experience, in which off-campus work and significant academic work are combined for credit. Study abroad in 11 countries, a Washington semester, cross-registration with Memphis College of Art and Christian Brothers University, and a science semester at Oak Ridge National Laboratory are offered. A 3-2 engineering degree with Washington University is available. The B.A.-B.S. degree and dual majors are offered in any combination, and student-designed majors can be arranged. Nondegree study and pass/fail options are possible. There are 19 national honor societies, including Phi Beta Kappa, and all departs have honors programs.

Admissions: 42% of the 2009-2010 applicants were accepted. The SAT scores for the 2009-2010 freshman class were: Critical Reading--4% below 500, 31%

494

between 500 and 599, 48% between 600 and 700, and 19% above 700; Math--3% below 500, 27% between 500 and 599, 47% between 600 and 700, and 26% above 700; Writing--4% below 500, 31% between 500 and 599, 48% between 600 and 700, and 20% above 700. The ACT scores were % below 21, 5% between 21 and 23, 30% between 24 and 26, 20% between 27 and 28, and 45% above 28. 81% of the current freshmen were in the top fifth of their class; 96% were in the top two fifths.

Requirements: The SAT or ACT is required. Graduation from an accredited secondary school is required, with 16 or more academic credits, including 4 years of English, 3 of math, and 2 each of a foreign language, science, and social studies/history. The GED is accepted. An essay is required; an interview is recommended. AP credits are accepted. Important factors in the admissions decision are advanced placement or honors courses, recommendations by school officials, and extracurricular activities record.

Procedure: Freshmen are admitted fall and spring. Entrance exams should be taken prior to December of the senior year. There are early decision and deferred admissions plans. Early decision applications should be filed by November 1; regular applications, by January 15 for fall entry; and December 1 for spring entry. The fall 2009 application fee was $45. Notification of early decision is sent December 1; regular decision, April 1. 87 early decision candidates were accepted for the 2009-2010 class. 503 applicants were on the 2009 waiting list; 48 were admitted. Applications are accepted on-line. 503 applicants were on a recent waiting list, 48 were accepted.

Financial Aid: In 2009-2010, at least 48% of all full-time freshmen and 47% of continuing full-time students received some form of financial aid. At least 47% of all full-time freshmen and 45% of continuing full-time students received need-based aid. The average freshman award was $31,290. Need-based scholarships or need-based grants averaged $21,487; need-based self-help aid (loans and jobs) averaged $4,632. Institutional awards averaged $13,477. The average financial indebtedness of the 2009 graduate was $26,071. The CSS/Profile and FAFSA are required. Check with the school for current application deadlines.

Computers: Wireless access is available. More than 220 PCs are available for use by students. Wired Ethernet ports are available in each room for all students living in the residence halls. Wireless computing is available in selected locations in the residence halls and in many public locations on campus. The Barret Library provides wireless throughout. Access to the Internet is provided by a 48Mb link shared by the entire campus. All students may access the system 24 hours per day. There are no time limits and no fees. It is strongly recommended that all students have a personal computer.

RICE UNIVERSITY
Houston, TX 77251-1892

(713) 348-7423
(800) 527-OWLS; (713) 348-5952

Full-time: 1595 men, 1472 women	**Faculty:** 546; I, +$
Part-time: 22 men, 13 women	**Ph.D.s:** 97%
Graduate: 1429 men, 808 women	**Student/Faculty:** 6 to 1
Year: semesters, summer session	**Tuition:** $32,058
Application Deadline: see profile	**Room & Board:** $11,230
Freshman Class: 11,172 applied, 2495 accepted, 894 enrolled	
SAT CR/M/W: 650/670/640	**ACT:** 30 **MOST COMPETITIVE**

Rice University, founded in 1912, is a comprehensive research university offering undergraduate and graduate programs through its schools of Engineering,

Natural Sciences, Humanities, Social Sciences, Music, and Architecture; Rice's School of Business offers graduate degrees and an undergraduate minor. Enrollment figures in the above capsule are for fall 2008. There are 6 undergraduate schools and 7 graduate schools. In addition to regional accreditation, Rice has baccalaureate program accreditation with ABET and NAAB. The library contains 2.6 million volumes, 3.3 million microform items, and 62,279 audio/video tapes/CDs/DVDs, and subscribes to 72,352 periodicals including electronic. Computerized library services include interlibrary loans, database searching, Internet access, and laptop Internet portals. Special learning facilities include an art gallery, radio station, TV station, a media center, and an observatory. The 300-acre campus is in an urban area 3 miles southwest of downtown Houston. Including any residence halls, there are 75 buildings.

Programs of Study: Rice confers B.A., B.S., B.Arch., B.F.A., B.Mus., and B.S.E degrees. Master's and doctoral degrees are also awarded. Bachelor's degrees are awarded in BIOLOGICAL SCIENCE (biology/biological science), BUSINESS (management science), COMMUNICATIONS AND THE ARTS (art history and appreciation, classics, English, linguistics, music, music history and appreciation, music performance, music theory and composition, and visual and performing arts), COMPUTER AND PHYSICAL SCIENCE (applied mathematics, chemistry, computer science, earth science, geology, geophysics and seismology, mathematics, physics, and statistics), ENGINEERING AND ENVIRONMENTAL DESIGN (architectural engineering, architecture, bioengineering, chemical engineering, civil engineering, electrical/electronics engineering, environmental engineering, and mechanical engineering), HEALTH PROFESSIONS (exercise science), SOCIAL SCIENCE (anthropology, Asian/Oriental studies, classical/ancient civilization, cognitive science, economics, French studies, German area studies, Hispanic American studies, history, medieval studies, philosophy, political science/government, psychology, public affairs, religion, sociology, and women's studies). Biochemistry and cell biology, mechanical engineering, and political science are the largest.

Special: An 8-year guaranteed medical school program with the Baylor College of Medicine; a 5-year joint degree program for the B.S.E./M.S.E. in engineering; a 5-year joint degree for the B.S.E./M.B.A. in engineering and business; and a 3-2 engineering degree are possible, as are cross-registration, internships, study abroad, work-study, dual majors, and student-designed majors. There are 10 national honor societies, including Phi Beta Kappa, and 9 departmental honors programs.

Admissions: 22% of the 2009-2010 applicants were accepted. The SAT scores for the 2009-2010 freshman class were: Critical Reading--2% below 500, 9% between 500 and 599, 37% between 600 and 700, and 53% above 700; Math--9% between 500 and 599, 26% between 600 and 700, and 65% above 700; Writing--3% below 500, 9% between 500 and 599, 37% between 600 and 700, and 51% above 700. The ACT scores were 3% below 24, 18% between 24 and 29, and 79% between 30 and 36.

Requirements: The SAT or ACT is required. The ACT Optional Writing test is also required. In addition, official high school transcripts, 1 counselor recommendation, and 1 teacher recommendation are required. To satisfy the testing requirement, students must submit either (a) the SAT plus 2 SAT Subject Tests or (b) the ACT with the Writing Test. Music students must arrange an audition. Architecture students must submit a portfolio. An interview is recommended but not required. Candidates should have completed 16 college preparatory units, including 4 years of English, 3 of math, and 2 each of social studies, foreign language, and lab science. AP credits are accepted.

Procedure: Freshmen are admitted fall. Entrance exams should be taken no later than December of the senior year for regular decision and no later than November for early decision. Early decision applications should be filed by November 1; check with the school for current application deadlines for regular decision applications. The application fee is $65. Notification of early decision is sent December 15; regular decision, April 1. 220 early decision candidates were accepted for the 2009-2010 class. Applications are accepted on-line. A waiting list is maintained.

Financial Aid: In 2008-2009, 60% of all full-time students received some form of financial aid. 35% of all full-time freshmen and 37% of continuing full-time students received need-based aid. Need-based scholarships or need-based grants averaged $28,392; need-based self-help aid (loans and jobs) averaged $1624; non-need-based athletic scholarships averaged $16,276; and other non-need-based awards and non-need-based scholarships averaged $9589. The average financial indebtedness of the 2008 graduate was $11,108. Rice is a member of CSS. The CSS/Profile, the FAFSA, and parent and student tax returns are required. The deadline for filing freshman financial aid applications for fall entry is March 1.

Computers: Wireless access is available. All students may access the system. There are no time limits and no fees. It is strongly recommended that all students have a personal computer.

RICHARD STOCKTON COLLEGE OF NEW JERSEY

Pomona, NJ 08240-0195   **(609) 652-4261; (609) 748-5541**

Full-time: 2460 men, 3420 women	**Faculty:** IIB, +$
Part-time: 350 men, 560 women	**Ph.D.s:** n/av
Graduate: 160 men, 440 women	**Student/Faculty:** n/av
Year: semesters, summer session	**Tuition:** $10,000 ($14,500)
Application Deadline: see profile	**Room & Board:** $10,000
Freshman Class: n/av	
SAT or ACT: required	**VERY COMPETITIVE**

Richard Stockton College of New Jersey, founded in 1969, is a public liberal arts college with 28 undergraduate programs and 6 graduate specialty areas. The figures in the above capsule and in this profile are approximate. There is 1 graduate school. In addition to regional accreditation, Stockton has baccalaureate program accreditation with APTA, CSWE, NASDTEC, and NLN. The library contains 627,318 volumes, 1.1 million microform items, and 15,342 audio/video tapes/CDs/DVDs, and subscribes to 26,375 periodicals including electronic. Computerized library services include interlibrary loans, database searching, and Internet access. Special learning facilities include a learning resource center, art gallery, radio station, TV station, astronomical observatory, marine science field lab, marina with a fleet of small boats, Holocaust resource center, educational technology, training center, and performing arts center. The 1600-acre campus is in a suburban area 12 miles northwest of Atlantic City. Including any residence halls, there are 55 buildings.

Programs of Study: Stockton confers B.A., B.S., and B.S.N. degrees. Master's and doctoral degrees are also awarded. Bachelor's degrees are awarded in BIOLOGICAL SCIENCE (biochemistry, biology/biological science, and marine science), BUSINESS (accounting, banking and finance, business administration and management, and management science), COMMUNICATIONS AND THE ARTS (communications, dance, dramatic arts, fine arts, languages, literature, and music), COMPUTER AND PHYSICAL SCIENCE (chemistry, computer science, geology, information sciences and systems, mathematics, and physics), EDUCATION (education), ENGINEERING AND ENVIRONMENTAL DESIGN (computational sciences, environmental science, and preengineering), HEALTH PROFESSIONS (nursing, physical therapy, public health, and speech pathology/audiology), SOCIAL SCIENCE (anthropology, criminal justice, economics, history, liberal arts/general studies, philosophy, political science/government, psychology, and social work). Sciences is the strongest academically. Business, psychology, and criminal justice. are the largest.

Special: Stockton offers internships in all fields with a wide variety of companies, work-study with various government agencies and corporations, a Washington semester, independent study, and study abroad in 53 countries. Dual majors in all programs, student-designed majors, an accelerated degree in medicine and criminal justice, 3-2 engineering degrees with the New Jersey Institute of Technology and Rutgers University, and general studies degrees are also offered. Nondegree study, pass/fail options, and credit for life, military, and work experience are possible. There are 5 national honor societies and a freshman honors program.

Requirements: The SAT or ACT is required. In addition, applicants must be high school graduates; the GED is accepted. 16 academic credits are required, including 4 years in English, 3 each in math and social studies, 2 in science, and 4 additional years of any of the above or a foreign language, or both. An essay and an interview are recommended, and a portfolio or audition is necessary where appropriate. AP and CLEP credits are accepted. Important factors in the admissions decision are advanced placement or honors courses, leadership record, and evidence of special talent.

Procedure: Freshmen are admitted fall and spring. Entrance exams should be taken once in the junior year and again before January in the senior year. There is a rolling admissions plan. Applications should be filed by December 1 for spring entry. The fall 2009 application fee was $50. Notification is sent on a rolling basis. Applications are accepted on-line. A waiting list is maintained.

Financial Aid: In a recent year, 77% of all full-time freshmen and 90% of continuing full-time students received some form of financial aid. 40% of all full-time freshmen and 41% of continuing full-time students received need-based aid. The average freshmen award was $11,772, with $8,170 ($15,396 maximum) from need-based scholarships or need-based grants; $3,702 ($9,900 maximum) from need-based self-help aid (loans and jobs); and $3,602 ($23,555 maximum) from other non-need-based awards and non-need-based scholarships. 16% of undergraduate students worked part-time. Average annual earnings from campus work were $1394. The average financial indebtedness of the 2009 graduate was $15,624. The FAFSA is required. Check with the school for current application deadlines.

Computers: Wireless access is available. All students have access to the wireless network from their personally owned computers. All residential students have access to the campus network through a hard-wired Ethernet connection. All students have access to the network from 850 computers in 40 different computer labs. Three of these labs (64 computers) are open 24/7. The remaining labs are open 94 hours per week. All students may access the system 24 hours a day. There are no time limits and no fees.

ROCHESTER INSTITUTE OF TECHNOLOGY

Rochester, NY 14623   **(585) 475-6631; (585) 475-7424**

Full-time: 8125 men, 3800 women	**Faculty:** IIA, +$
Part-time: 1080 men, 500 women	**Ph.D.s:** n/avn
Graduate: 1630 men, 915 women	**Student/Faculty:** n/av
Year: trimesters, summer session	**Tuition:** $30,501
Application Deadline: March 1	**Room & Board:** $10,044
Freshman Class: n/av	
SAT or ACT: required	**VERY COMPETITIVE**

Rochester Institute of Technology, a private institution founded in 1829, offers programs in art and design, science, computer science, medical sciences, engineering, fine arts, business, hotel management, graphic arts, information technology, and photography, as well as liberal arts, and includes the National Technical Institute for the Deaf. Most programs include a cooperative education component, which provides full-time work experience to complement classroom studies. The figures in the above capsule and in this profile are approximate. There are 8 undergraduate schools and 8 graduate schools. In addition to regional accreditation, RIT has baccalaureate program accreditation with AACSB, ABET, ADA, CAHEA, CSAB, CSWE, FIDER, and NASAD. The library contains 422,281 volumes, 498,703 microform items, and 54,935 audio/video tapes/CDs/DVDs, and subscribes to 21,208 periodicals including electronic. Computerized library services include interlibrary loans, database searching, Internet access, and laptop Internet portals. Special learning facilities include a learning resource center, art gallery, radio station, TV station, a computer chip manufacturing facility, a student-operated restaurant, an electronic prepress lab, an imaging science facility, and an observatory. The 1300-acre campus is in a suburban area 5 miles south of Rochester. Including any residence halls, there are 195 buildings.

Programs of Study: RIT confers B.S. and B.F.A. degrees. Associates, master's, and doctoral degrees are also awarded. Bachelor's degrees are awarded in BIOLOGICAL SCIENCE (biochemistry, bioinformatics, biology/biological science, biotechnology, and nutrition), BUSINESS (accounting, banking and finance, business administration and management, business systems analysis, hotel/motel and restaurant management, international business management, management information systems, management science, marketing management, and tourism), COMMUNICATIONS AND THE ARTS (animation, applied art, ceramic art and design, communications, communications technology, crafts, design, film arts, fine arts, glass, graphic design, illustration, industrial design, metal/jewelry, painting, photography, publishing, sculpture, studio art, telecommunications, and video), COMPUTER AND PHYSICAL SCIENCE (applied mathematics, chemistry, computer mathematics, computer science, information sciences and systems, mathematics, physics, polymer science, software engineering, statistics, and systems analysis), EDUCATION (education of the deaf and hearing impaired), ENGINEERING AND ENVIRONMENTAL DESIGN (aerospace studies, biomedical engineering, civil engineering technology, computer engineering, computer graphics, computer technology, electrical/electronics engineering, electrical/electronics engineering technology, engineering, engineering technology, environmental engineering technology, environmental science, furniture design, graphic arts technology, graphic and printing production, industrial engineering, interior design, manufacturing engineering, manufacturing technology, materials science, mechanical engineering, mechanical engineering technology, military science, printing technology, and woodworking), HEALTH PROFESSIONS (allied health, physician's assistant, predentistry, premedicine, preveterinary science, and ultrasound technology), SOCIAL SCIENCE (criminal justice, dietetics, economics, experimental psychology, food production/management/services, interpreter for the deaf, prelaw, psychology, and public affairs). Mechanical engineering, computer science, and film and animation are the strongest academically. Engineering, information technology, and photography are the largest.

Special: RIT offers internships in social science and allied health majors, and cooperative education programs with 1900 co-op employers. Cooperative education is required or recommended in most programs and provides full-time paid work experience. Cross-registration with Rochester-area colleges is available. There are accelerated dual degree (BS/MS, BS/ME, BS/MBA) programs in science, engineering, public policy, math, computer science, materials science, imaging science, and business. Students may study abroad in 15 countries, and student-designed majors are permitted in applied arts and sciences. There is an Honors Program in general education and home colleges. There are 6 national honor societies, a freshman honors program, and 7 departmental honors programs.

Requirements: The SAT or ACT is required. In addition, applicants must be high school graduates or have a GED certificate. Applicants are required to submit an essay, and an interview is recommended. The School of Art and the School of Design emphasize a required portfolio of artwork. Required high school math and science credits vary by program, with 3 years in each area generally acceptable. RIT requires applicants to be in the upper 50% of their class. AP and CLEP credits are accepted. Important factors in the admissions decision are advanced placement or honors courses, recommendations by school officials, and extracurricular activities record.

Procedure: Freshmen are admitted to all sessions. Entrance exams should be taken during the junior or senior year. There are early decision and deferred admissions plans. Early decision applications should be filed by December 1; regular applications, by March 1 for fall entry, along with a $50 fee. Notification of early decision is sent January 15; regular decision, March 15. Applications are accepted on-line. A waiting list is maintained.

Financial Aid: In a recent year, 85% of all full-time freshmen and 75% of continuing full-time students received some form of financial aid. 73% of all full-time freshmen and 67% of continuing full-time students received need-based aid. The average freshmen award was $18,900. 70% of undergraduate students worked part-time. Average annual earnings from campus work were $2200. The average financial indebtedness of the 2009 graduate was $22,000. The FAFSA is required. Check with the school for current application deadlines.

Computers: Wireless access is available. More than 2,500 PCs are available for student use in university computer labs. All students may access the system 7 days per week, 24-hour access. There are no time limits and no fees.

ROLLINS COLLEGE

Winter Park, FL 32789 (407) 646-2161; (407) 646-1502

Full-time: 742 men, 1031 women	**Faculty:** 167; IIA, av$
Part-time: none	**Ph.D.s:** 93%
Graduate: 331 men, 382 women	**Student/Faculty:** 10 to 1
Year: semesters	**Tuition:** $36,220
Application Deadline: February 15	**Room & Board:** $11,320
Freshman Class: 2999 applied, 1847 accepted, 464 enrolled	
SAT CR/M: 610/611	**HIGHLY COMPETITIVE**

Rollins College, founded in 1885, is a private, liberal arts institution. There are 2 graduate schools. In addition to regional accreditation, Rollins has baccalaureate program accreditation with AACSB and NASM. The library contains 325,499 volumes, 897 microform items, and 6592 audio/video tapes/CDs/DVDs, and subscribes to 42,814 periodicals including electronic. Computerized library services include interlibrary loans, database searching, Internet access, and laptop Internet portals. Special learning facilities include a learning resource center, art gallery, radio station, TV station, art museum, theaters, writing center, and student resource center. The 70-acre campus is in a suburban area 5 miles north of Orlando. Including any residence halls, there are 70 buildings.

Programs of Study: Rollins confers A.B. degrees. Master's degrees are also awarded. Bachelor's degrees are awarded in BIOLOGICAL SCIENCE (biochemistry, biology/biological science, and marine biology), BUSINESS (international business management), COMMUNICATIONS AND THE ARTS (art history and appreciation, dramatic arts, English, French, media arts, music performance, Spanish, and studio art), COMPUTER AND PHYSICAL SCIENCE (chemistry, computer science, mathematics, and physics), EDUCATION (elementary education), ENGINEERING AND ENVIRONMENTAL DESIGN (environmental science), SOCIAL SCIENCE (anthropology, classical/ancient civilization, crosscultural studies, economics, history, international relations, Latin American studies, philosophy, political science/government, psychology, religion, and sociology). International business, psychology, and economics are the largest.

Special: Rollins offers cross-registration with the evening studies division and co-op programs with American University in Washington, D.C., and Duke University School of Forestry and Environmental Studies. Departmental and professional internships, study abroad in 9 countries, and a Washington semester are also options. Also available are an accelerated (3-2) M.B.A. program, a B.A.-B.S. degree in preengineering with Washington University (St. Louis), Auburn, and Columbia Universities, an interdepartmental biochemistry/molecular biology major, dual majors in any combination, and student-designed majors. Nondegree study and pass/fail options are possible. There are 5 national honor societies, a freshman honors program, and 28 departmental honors programs.

Admissions: 62% of the 2009-2010 applicants were accepted. The SAT scores for the 2009-2010 freshman class were: Critical Reading--7% below 500, 38% between 500 and 599, 43% between 600 and 700, and 12% above 700; Math--6% below 500, 41% between 500 and 599, 44% between 600 and 700, and 9% above 700. 65% of the current freshmen were in the top fifth of their class; 91% were in the top two fifths. 1 freshman graduated first in the class in a recent year. 99 were in the top 10% of their class.

Requirements: The SAT or ACT is required for some programs. Applicants must be graduates of an accredited secondary school or have a GED certificate and have completed 4 years of English, 3 of math, and 2 each of foreign language, science, and social studies. An essay is required. SAT Subject tests in writing, math, and foreign language and an interview are recommended. AP and CLEP credits are accepted. Important factors in the admissions decision are advanced placement or honors courses, evidence of special talent, and extracurricular activities record.

Procedure: Freshmen are admitted fall and spring. Entrance exams should be taken by the first semester of the senior year. There are early decision and deferred admissions plans. Early decision applications should be filed by January 15, regular applications, by February 15 for fall entry and December 1 for spring entry. The fall 2008 application fee was $40. Notification of early decision is sent February 1; regular decision, April 1. Applications are accepted on-line. 345 applicants were on a recent waiting list, 63 were accepted.

Financial Aid: In 2009-2010, 78% of all full-time freshmen and 77% of continuing full-time students received some form of financial aid. 52% of all full-time freshmen and 42% of continuing full-time students received need-based aid. The average freshman award was $29,800. Need-based scholarships or need-based grants averaged $24,274 ($47,540 maximum); need-based self-help aid (loans and jobs) averaged $5075 ($9200 maximum); non-need-based athletic scholarships averaged $21,929 ($47,450 maximum); and other non-need-based awards and non-need-based scholarships averaged $13,333 ($47,540 maximum). 21% of undergraduate students work part-time. Average annual earnings from campus work are $1377. The average financial indebtedness of the 2009 graduate was $21,789. Rollins is a member of CSS. The FAFSA and the college's own financial statement are required. The deadline for filing freshman financial aid applications for fall entry is March 1.

Computers: Wireless access is available. There are 8 computer labs on campus with 15 computers per lab. 30% of classrooms allow wire connectivity between student labtops and Internet, and 98% of classrooms allow wireless connectivity between labtops and Internet. Network access is available in dorm rooms and lounges. Rollins permits and provides student Web pages. Students can remotely access the Web and get their e-mail through the college's connection. Students can register for classes and perform additional administrative functions on-line. All students may access the system. There are no time limits and no fees. It is strongly recommended that all students have a personal computer.

ROOSEVELT UNIVERSITY

Chicago, IL 60605

(847) 619-8620
(877) APPLYRU; (847) 619-8636

Full-time: 685 men, 1185 women	**Faculty:** IIA, av$
Part-time: 750 men, 1700 women	**Ph.D.s:** 85%
Graduate: 1040 men, 2210 women	**Student/Faculty:** n/av
Year: semesters, summer session	**Tuition:** $21,250
Application Deadline: see profile	**Room & Board:** $11,094
Freshman Class: n/av	
SAT or ACT: required	**VERY COMPETITIVE**

Roosevelt University, founded in 1945, an independent, comprehensive university. Some information in the above capsule and in this profile is approximate. There are 5 undergraduate schools and 5 graduate schools. In addition to regional accreditation, Roosevelt has baccalaureate program accreditation with AACSB, NASM, and NCATE. The 2 libraries contain 405,022 volumes, 130,233 microform items, and 10,000 audio/video tapes/CDs/DVDs, and subscribe to 1,601 periodicals including electronic. Computerized library services include interlibrary loans and database searching. Special learning facilities include a learning resource center and radio station. The campus is in an urban area downtown Chicago. Including any residence halls, there are 2 buildings.

Programs of Study: Roosevelt confers B.A., B.S., B.A.Comp.Sci., B.A.Ed., B.F.A.Mus.Theater, B.G.S., B.M., B.S.B.A., B.S. in Hospitality Mgt., and B.S.Telecomm. degrees. Master's and doctoral degrees are also awarded. Bachelor's degrees are awarded in BIOLOGICAL SCIENCE (biology/biological science), BUSINESS (accounting, banking and finance, business administration and management, hotel/motel and restaurant management, insurance, insurance and risk management, management science, marketing/retailing/merchandising, and personnel management), COMMUNICATIONS AND THE ARTS (advertising, art history and appreciation, broadcasting, communications, dramatic arts, English, French, guitar, jazz, journalism, languages, literature, media arts, music, music history and appreciation, music performance, music theory and composition, musical theater, percussion, performing arts, piano/organ, public relations, Spanish, strings, telecommunications, theater design, theater management, voice, and winds), COMPUTER AND PHYSICAL SCIENCE (actuarial science, chemistry, computer science, information sciences and systems, mathematics, and statistics), EDUCATION (early childhood education, elementary education, music education, and secondary education), ENGINEERING AND ENVIRONMENTAL DESIGN (electrical/electronics engineering technology and environmental science), HEALTH PROFESSIONS (allied health, medical technology, nuclear medical technology, predentistry, premedicine, prepharmacy, and preveterinary science), SOCIAL SCIENCE (African American studies, American studies, economics, history, international studies, liberal arts/general studies, philosophy, political science/government, prelaw, psychology, public administration, social science, sociology, urban studies, and women's studies). Journalism, accounting, and psychology are the strongest academically.

Special: Roosevelt offers internships in approximately 20 subject areas, on-campus work-study, study abroad in 4 countries, dual and student-designed majors, pass/fail options, and noncredit courses. Adults older than 25 years of age may earn a Bachelor of General Studies through an accelerated degree program. Credit for life, military, and work experience is available in some majors through continuing education. The Roosevelt Scholars Program is offered. There are 4 national honor societies, a freshman honors program, and 20 departmental honors programs.

Requirements: The SAT or ACT is required. In addition, students must have completed 15 academic units, including 4 of English, 3 of math, 2 each of science, social studies, and foreign language, and 1 each of history and electives. An interview is recommended for all applicants, and an audition is required for music and theater candidates. A GPA of 2.3 is required. AP and CLEP credits are accepted. Important factors in the admissions decision are advanced placement or honors courses, evidence of special talent, and extracurricular activities record.

Procedure: Freshmen are admitted to all sessions. There are early decision, early admissions, deferred admissions, and rolling admissions plans. Application deadlines are open. The fall 2008 application fee was $25. Notifications are sent ongoing. Applications are accepted on-line.

Financial Aid: The FAFSA and the college's own financial statement are required. Check with the school for current application deadlines.

Computers: All students may access the system 1 hour when demand is great. There are no fees.

ROSE-HULMAN INSTITUTE OF TECHNOLOGY

Terre Haute, IN 47803
(812) 877-1511
(800) 248-7448; (812) 877-8941

Full-time: 1464 men, 370 women	**Faculty:** 168; IIB, +$
Part-time: 6 men, 2 women	**Ph.D.s:** 100%
Graduate: 95 men, 25 women	**Student/Faculty:** 12 to 1
Year: quarters, summer session	**Tuition:** $33900
Application Deadline: March 1	**Room & Board:** $9441
Freshman Class: 3554 applied, 2495 accepted, 465 enrolled	
SAT CR/M/W: 610/670/590	**ACT:** 29 **HIGHLY COMPETITIVE+**

Rose-Hulman Institute of Technology, founded in 1874, is a private college emphasizing engineering, science, and math. In addition to regional accreditation, Rose-Hulman has baccalaureate program accreditation with ABET. The library contains 80,902 volumes, 532 microform items, and 879 audio/video tapes/CDs/DVDs, and subscribes to 3,594 periodicals including electronic. Computerized library services include interlibrary loans, database searching, and Internet access. Special learning facilities include a learning resource center, art gallery, planetarium, and radio station. The 200-acre campus is in a suburban area on the east side of Terre Haute. Including any residence halls, there are 35 buildings.

Programs of Study: Rose-Hulman confers B.S. degrees. Master's degrees are also awarded. Bachelor's degrees are awarded in BIOLOGICAL SCIENCE (biochemistry and biology/biological science), COMPUTER AND PHYSICAL SCIENCE (chemistry, computer science, mathematics, physics, and software engineering), ENGINEERING AND ENVIRONMENTAL DESIGN (biomedical engineering, chemical engineering, civil engineering, computer engineering, electrical/electronics engineering, engineering physics, mechanical engineering, and optical engineering), SOCIAL SCIENCE (economics). Engineering, science, and mathematics are the strongest academically. Mechanical engineering, chemical engineering, and biomedical engineering are the largest.

Special: The institute offers co-op programs, independent study, cross-registration with Indiana State University and Saint Mary-of-the-Woods College, summer industrial internships, study abroad in 8 countries, and dual majors. Pass/fail options also are available. There are 7 national honor societies and 3 departmental honors programs.

Admissions: 70% of the 2009-2010 applicants were accepted. The SAT scores for the 2009-2010 freshman class were: Critical Reading--7% below 500, 37% between 500 and 599, 44% between 600 and 700, and 12% above 700; Math--11% between 500 and 599, 57% between 600 and 700, and 32% above 700; Writing--12% below 500, 40% between 500 and 599, 40% between 600 and 700, and 8% above 700. The ACT scores were 6% between 21 and 23, 19% between 24 and 26, 16% between 27 and 28, and 59% above 28. 83% of the current freshmen were in the top fifth of their class; 98% were in the top two fifths. There were 20 National Merit finalists. 39 freshmen graduated first in their class.

Requirements: The SAT or ACT is required. In addition, candidates should have at least 16 units of credit, including 4 in English, 2 in social sciences, and 1 each in math, chemistry, physics, and electives. An essay and interview are recommended. Rose-Hulman requires applicants to be in the upper 25% of their class. AP credits are accepted. Important factors in the admissions decision are advanced placement or honors courses, recommendations by school officials, and extracurricular activities record.

Procedure: Freshmen are admitted in the fall. Entrance exams should be taken in the fall of the senior year or spring of the junior year. There are deferred admissions and rolling admissions plans. Applications should be filed by March 1 for fall entry, along with a $40 fee. Applications are accepted on-line.

Financial Aid: In 2009-2010, 100% of all full-time freshmen and 98% of continuing full-time students received some form of financial aid. 72% of all full-time freshmen and 69% of continuing full-time students received need-based aid. The average freshman award was $26,168, with $21,882 ($33,900 maximum) from need-based scholarships or need-based grants; $10,216 ($41,176 maximum) from need-based self-help aid (loans and jobs); and $12,890 ($48,600 maximum) from other non-need-based awards and non-need-based scholarships. 67% of undergraduate students work part-time. Average annual earnings from campus work are $1660. The average financial indebtedness of the 2009 graduate was $35,261. Rose-Hulman is a member of CSS. The FAFSA is required. The priority date for freshman financial aid applications for fall entry is March 1.

Computers: Wireless access is available. There is ubiquitous access with more than 8,000 wired ports, including all classrooms, 2 ports per pillow in resident halls, and wireless 802.11a/b/g thoughout the academic complex. Free public printers are located throughout campus. All students may access the system. There are no time limits and no fees. All students are required to have a personal computer. A HP Compaq 8530 is recommended.

ROWAN UNIVERSITY
Glassboro, NJ 08028

(855) 256-4200
(800) 447-1165; (856) 256-4430

Full-time: 4114 men, 4221 women	**Faculty:** 380
Part-time: 469 men, 861 women	**Ph.D.s:** 82%
Graduate: 419 men, 922 women	**Student/Faculty:** 15 to 1
Year: semesters, summer session	**Tuition:** $11,234 ($18,308)
Application Deadline: n/av	**Room & Board:** $10,000
Freshman Class: n/av	
SAT: required	**VERY COMPETITIVE**

Rowan University was founded in 1923 as a public institution offering undergraduate programs in the arts and sciences, business administration, communication, education, fine and performing arts, and engineering. There are 6 undergraduate schools and one graduate school. In addition to regional accreditation, Rowan has baccalaureate program accreditation with AACSB, ABET, CSAB, NASAD, NASDTEC, NASM, and NCATE. The library contains 345,926 volumes, 497,842 microform items, 47,525 audio/video tapes/CDs/DVDs, and subscribes to 5,789 periodicals including electronic. Computerized library services include interlibrary loans, database searching, and Internet access. Special learning facilities include a learning resource center, art gallery, planetarium, radio station, TV station, an observatory. The 200-acre campus is in a suburban area 20 miles southeast of Philadelphia. Including any residence halls, there are 41 buildings.

Programs of Study: Rowan confers B.A., B.S., B.F.A., and B.M. degrees. Master's and doctoral degrees are also awarded. Bachelor's degrees are awarded in BIOLOGICAL SCIENCE (biology/biological science), BUSINESS (accounting, business administration and management, marketing/retailing/merchandising, personnel management, and small business management), COMMUNICATIONS AND THE ARTS (art, broadcasting, communications, dramatic arts, English, fine arts, journalism, music, Spanish, and speech/debate/rhetoric), COMPUTER

AND PHYSICAL SCIENCE (chemistry, computer science, mathematics, and physics), EDUCATION (early childhood education, elementary education, foreign languages education, music education, and science education), ENGINEERING AND ENVIRONMENTAL DESIGN (civil engineering and engineering), HEALTH PROFESSIONS (health), SOCIAL SCIENCE (criminal justice, economics, geography, history, liberal arts/general studies, political science/government, psychology, and sociology). Engineering, communications, and business administration are the strongest academically. Elementary education, communications, and business administration are the largest.

Special: Students may study abroad in 50 countries. Internships are available in all majors both with and without pay. Rowan also offers accelerated degree programs and 3-2 degrees in optometry, podiatry, and pharmacy. There are dual majors, pass/fail options, and credit for military experience. There are 12 national honor societies, a freshman honors program, and 100 departmental honors programs.

Admissions: n/av

Requirements: The SAT is required. In addition, students are required to score an 1080, or no less than 500 on either part. Students submitting ACT scores should have a minimum composite score of 23. Applicants must be graduates of accredited secondary schools or have earned a GED. Rowan requires 16 academic credits or Carnegie units, including 4 in English, 3 each in math and college preparatory electives, and 2 each in foreign language, history, and lab science. A portfolio or audition is required for specific majors. A GPA of 3.0 is required. AP and CLEP credits are accepted. Important factors in the admissions decision are advanced placement or honors courses, evidence of special talent, and leadership record.

Procedure: Freshmen are admitted fall and spring. Entrance exams should be taken by May or June of the junior year, or by December of the sen. There is a deferred admissions plan. Applications should be filed by November 1 for spring entry, along with a $50 fee. Notifications are sent April 15. Applications are accepted on-line. 100 applicants were on a waiting list, 40 were accepted.

Financial Aid: In 2009-2010, 70% of all full-time freshmen and 70% of continuing full-time students received some form of financial aid. 81% of all full-time freshmen and 81% of continuing full-time students received need-based aid. The average freshmen award was $8,793. 10% of undergraduate students work part-time. Average annual earnings from campus work are $1200. The FAFSA is required. The priority date for freshman financial aid applications for fall entry is January 1. The deadline for filing freshman financial aid applications for fall entry is March 15.

Computers: Wireless access is available. All students may access the system. 24 hours a day. There are no time limits and no fees. Students enrolled in engineering must have a personal computer.

RUTGERS, THE STATE UNIVERSITY OF NEW JERSEY/CAMDEN CAMPUS

Camden, NJ 08102-1461 (856) 225-6104

Full-time: 1568 men, 1769 women	**Faculty:** 252; IIA, ++$
Part-time: 271 men, 459 women	**Ph.D.s:** 99%
Graduate: 917 men, 743 women	**Student/Faculty:** 13 to 1
Year: semesters, summer session	**Tuition:** $11,698 ($22,330)
Application Deadline: open	**Room & Board:** $9788
Freshman Class: n/av	
SAT CR/M/W: 510/560/520	**ACT:** required

VERY COMPETITIVE

Rutgers, The State University of New Jersey/Camden Campus, founded in 1927, comprises 3 undergraduate, degree-granting schools: College of the Arts and Sciences, University College-Camden, and the School of Business-Camden. Each school has individual requirements, policies, and fees. There are also 3 graduate schools. In addition to regional accreditation, Camden has baccalaureate program accreditation with AACSB and CSWE. The 2 libraries contain 729,987 volumes, 974,491 microform items, and 591 audio/video tapes/CDs/DVDs, and subscribe to 12,325 periodicals including electronic. Computerized library services include interlibrary loans, database searching, and Internet access. Special learning facilities include a learning resource center, art gallery, and radio station. The 31-acre campus is in an urban area 1 mile east of Philadelphia. Including any residence halls, there are 34 buildings.

Programs of Study: Camden confers B.A., B.S., and B.H.M. degrees. Master's degrees are also awarded. Bachelor's degrees are awarded in BIOLOGICAL SCIENCE (biochemistry and biology/biological science), BUSINESS (accounting, banking and finance, hospitality management services, management science, and marketing/retailing/merchandising), COMMUNICATIONS AND THE ARTS (art, art history and appreciation, dramatic arts, English, French, German, music, and Spanish), COMPUTER AND PHYSICAL SCIENCE (chemistry, computer science, mathematics, physics, and science), HEALTH PROFESSIONS (medical laboratory technology and nursing), SOCIAL SCIENCE (African American studies, criminal justice, economics, history, liberal arts/general studies, philosophy, political science/government, psychology, religion, social work, sociology, and urban studies). Psychology, criminal justice, and biology are the largest.

Special: The university offers co-op programs, cross-registration, internships, accelerated degrees, student-designed majors, dual majors, nondegree study, and pass/fail options. Students may study abroad in 28 countries. There is an 8-year B.A./M.D. program with the University of Medicine and Dentistry of New Jersey and many combined bachelor's and master's programs. There are programs in distance learning, English as a Second Language, honors, and independent study. There is a freshman honors program.

Admissions: The SAT scores for the 2009-2010 freshman class were: Critical Reading--26% below 500, 49% between 500 and 599, 20% between 600 and 700, and 4% above 700; Math--20% below 500, 49% between 500 and 599, 26% between 600 and 700, and 5% above 700. 31% of the current freshmen were in the top fifth of their class; 63% were in the top two fifths.

Requirements: The SAT or ACT is required, except for students who have been out of high school for 2 years or more. SAT Subject tests are required of students without a high school diploma from an accredited high school and from some GED holders. A high school diploma is required; the GED is accepted. Students must have completed a general college-preparatory program, including 16 academic credits or Carnegie units, with 4 years of English, 3 years of math (4 recommended), and 2 years each of a foreign language and science, plus 5 in electives. AP and CLEP credits are accepted. Important factors in the admissions decision are advanced placement or honors courses, evidence of special talent, and leadership record.

Procedure: Freshmen are admitted in the fall. Entrance exams should be taken by December of senior year, but this is not required. There are early admissions and rolling admissions plans. Application deadlines are open. Application fee is $60. Notifications are sent March 1. Applications are accepted on-line. A waiting list is maintained.

Financial Aid: In 2009-2010, 93% of all full-time freshmen and 93% of continuing full-time students received some form of financial aid. 69% of all full-time freshmen and 73% of continuing full-time students received need-based aid. The average freshman award was $13,051. Need-based scholarships and need-based grants averaged $11,001; need-based self-help aid (loans and jobs) averaged $7453; and non-need-based awards and non-need-based scholarships averaged $8539. Average annual earnings from campus work are $1424. The average financial indebtedness of the 2009 graduate was $25,119. The FAFSA is required. The priority date for freshman financial aid applications for fall entry is March 15. The deadline for filing freshman financial aid applications for fall entry is open.

Computers: All students may access the system. Public labs are open whenever the building housing the lab is open. There are no time limits. The fee is $200.

RUTGERS, THE STATE UNIVERSITY OF NEW JERSEY/NEW BRUNSWICK/PISCATAWAY CAMPUS

Piscataway, NJ 08854   **(732) 932-4636; (732) 445-0237**

Full-time: 14,239 men, 13,349 women	**Faculty:** 1678; I, +$
Part-time: 757 men, 750 women	**Ph.D.s:** 99%
Graduate: 3155 men, 5114 women	**Student/Faculty:** 14 to 1
Year: semesters, summer session	**Tuition:** $11,886 ($22,518)
Application Deadline: open	**Room & Board:** $10,676
Freshman Class: 28,624 applied, 17,598 accepted, 5835 enrolled	
SAT CR/M/W: 580/620/590	**ACT:** required
	HIGHLY COMPETITIVE

Rutgers, The State University of New Jersey, New Brunswick Campus, founded in 1766, comprises 9 undergraduate units. Students in New Brunswick enroll in the School of Arts and Sciences, the liberal arts college, and/or in 1 of 8 professional schools: School of Environmental and Biological Sciences (formerly Cook College); Mason Gross School of the Arts; Rutgers Business School: Undergraduate-New Brunswick; School of Communication, Information, and Library Studies; School of Engineering; Edward J. Bloustein School of Planning and Public Policy; the School of Management and Labor Relations; or Ernest Mario School of Pharmacy. Each school within the New Brunswick campus has individual requirements, policies, and fees. There are also 10 graduate schools. In addition to regional accreditation, RU-New Brunswick has baccalaureate program accreditation with AACSB, ABET, ASLA, CSWE, and NASM. The 13 libraries contain 5.1 million volumes, 357,753 microform items, and 110,808 audio/video tapes/CDs/DVDs, and subscribe to 195,296 periodicals including electronic.

Computerized library services include interlibrary loans, database searching, and Internet access. Special learning facilities include a learning resource center, art gallery, radio station, TV station, geology museum, and various research centers. The 2683-acre campus is in a small town 33 miles south of New York City. Including any residence halls, there are 647 buildings.

Programs of Study: RU-New Brunswick confers B.A., B.S., B.F.A., and B.Mus. degrees. Master's and doctoral degrees are also awarded. Bachelor's degrees are awarded in AGRICULTURE (agriculture, animal science, natural resource management, and plant science), BIOLOGICAL SCIENCE (biochemistry, biology/biological science, biomathematics, biotechnology, botany, cell biology, ecology, evolutionary biology, genetics, marine science, microbiology, molecular biology, nutrition, and physiology), BUSINESS (accounting, banking and finance, business administration and management, labor studies, management information systems, management science, and marketing/retailing/merchandising), COMMUNICATIONS AND THE ARTS (art, art history and appreciation, Chinese, classics, communications, comparative literature, dance, dramatic arts, East Asian languages and literature, English, French, German, Italian, journalism, Latin, linguistics, music, Portuguese, Russian, Spanish, and visual and performing arts), COMPUTER AND PHYSICAL SCIENCE (astrophysics, chemistry, computer science, geology, information sciences and systems, mathematics, physics, and statistics), ENGINEERING AND ENVIRONMENTAL DESIGN (bioresource engineering, ceramic engineering, chemical engineering, civil engineering, electrical/electronics engineering, engineering and applied science, environmental science, industrial engineering, and mechanical engineering), HEALTH PROFESSIONS (biomedical science, exercise science, medical technology, pharmacy, and public health), SOCIAL SCIENCE (African American studies, American studies, anthropology, Asian/Oriental studies, criminal justice, economics, food science, geography, Hispanic American studies, history, humanities, Judaic studies, Latin American studies, medieval studies, Middle Eastern studies, philosophy, political science/government, psychology, religion, Russian and Slavic studies, social work, sociology, urban studies, and women's studies). Business, engineering, and biological sciences are the largest.

Special: The college offers co-op programs, cross registration, and study abroad in 28 countries. A Washington semester, work-study, accelerated degree programs, B.A.-B.S. degrees, student-designed majors, nondegree study, and pass/fail options are available. There is an 8-year B.A. or B.S./M.D. program with the University of Medicine and Dentistry New Jersey and several dual-degree (5-year and 6-year) programs. There are 2 national honor societies, including Phi Beta Kappa, and a freshman honors program.

Admissions: 61% of the 2009-2010 applicants were accepted. The SAT scores for the 2009-2010 freshman class were: Critical Reading--11% below 500, 49% between 500 and 599, 31% between 600 and 700, and 9% above 700; Math--6% below 500, 33% between 500 and 599, 42% between 600 and 700, and 19% above 700; Writing--17% below 500, 55% between 500 and 599, 22% between 600 and 700, and 6% above 700. 72% of the current freshmen were in the top fifth of their class; 95% were in the top two fifths.

Requirements: The SAT or ACT is required. In addition, a high school diploma is required. The GED is accepted. Students must have completed a general college-preparatory program, including 16 academic credits or Carnegie units, with 4 years of English, 3 years of math (4 recommended), including algebra I and II and geometry, 2 years each of a foreign language and science, and 5 in electives. Engineering students need 4 years of math and must take chemistry and physics; nursing and pharmacy students must take biology and chemistry. SAT Subject tests are required for students without a high school diploma from an accredited high school and from some GED holders. AP and CLEP credits are accepted. Important factors in the admissions decision are evidence of special talent, extracurricular activities record, and ability to finance college education.

Procedure: Freshmen are admitted in the fall. Entrance exams should be taken December of senior year but this is not required. There are early admissions and rolling admissions plans. Application deadlines are open. Application fee is $65. Notifications are sent March 1. Applications are accepted on-line. A waiting list is maintained.

Financial Aid: In 2009-2010, 88% of all full-time freshmen and 86% of continuing full-time students received some form of financial aid. 59% of all full-time freshmen and 60% of continuing full-time students received need-based aid. The average freshman award was $15,306. Need-based scholarships and need-based grants averaged $9882; need-based self-help aid (loans and jobs) averaged $6479; non-need-based athletic scholarships averaged $11,798; and other non-need-based awards and non-need-based scholarships averaged $6300. Average annual earnings from campus work are $1324. The average financial indebtedness of the 2009 graduate was $24,687. The FAFSA is required. The priority date for freshman financial aid applications for fall entry is March 15.

Computers: Wireless access is available. All students may access the system 24 hours per day. There are no time limits. The fee is $283.

RUTGERS, THE STATE UNIVERSITY OF NEW JERSEY/NEWARK CAMPUS

Newark, NJ 07102-1897	(973) 353-5205; (973) 353-1440
Full-time: 2705 men, 3049 women	**Faculty:** 447; I, +$
Part-time: 697 men, 856 women	**Ph.D.s:** 99%
Graduate: 2308 men, 1885 women	**Student/Faculty:** 13 to 1
Year: semesters, summer session	**Tuition:** $11,414 ($22,046)
Application Deadline: open	**Room & Board:** $11,155
Freshman Class: 12,462 applied, 7430 accepted, 872 enrolled	
SAT CR/M/W: 510/560/520	**ACT:** required
	VERY COMPETITIVE

Rutgers, The State University of New Jersey/Newark Campus, founded in 1930, comprises 4 undergraduate, degree-granting schools: Newark College of Arts and Sciences, University College-Newark, Rutgers Business School: Undergraduate-Newark, and College of Nursing. Each school has individual requirements, policies, and fees. There are also 4 graduate schools. In addition to regional accreditation, RU-Newark has baccalaureate program accreditation with AACSB, CSWE, and NASM. The 4 libraries contain 1 million volumes, 1.5 million microform items, and 42,504 audio/video tapes/CDs/DVDs, and subscribe to 23,731 periodicals including electronic. Computerized library services include interlibrary loans, database searching, and Internet access. Special learning facilities include a learning resource center, art gallery, radio station, molecular and behavioral neuroscience center, and institutes of jazz and animal behavior. The 348-acre campus is in an urban area 7 miles west of New York City. Including any residence halls, there are 33 buildings.

Programs of Study: RU-Newark confers B.A., B.S., and B.F.A. degrees. Master's and doctoral degrees are also awarded. Bachelor's degrees are awarded in BIOLOGICAL SCIENCE (biology/biological science, botany, and zoology), BUSINESS (accounting, banking and finance, business administration and management, management science, and marketing/retailing/merchandising), COM-

MUNICATIONS AND THE ARTS (art, dramatic arts, English, French, German, journalism, music, Portuguese, Spanish, and visual and performing arts), COMPUTER AND PHYSICAL SCIENCE (applied mathematics, applied physics, chemistry, computer science, geology, geoscience, information sciences and systems, mathematics, and physics), ENGINEERING AND ENVIRONMENTAL DESIGN (environmental science), HEALTH PROFESSIONS (allied health, clinical science, and nursing), SOCIAL SCIENCE (African American studies, American studies, anthropology, criminal justice, Eastern European studies, economics, history, medieval studies, philosophy, political science/government, psychology, Puerto Rican studies, science and society, social work, sociology, and women's studies). Accounting, biology, and nursing are the largest.

Special: Students may cross-register with the New Jersey Institute of Technology and the University of Medicine and Dentistry of New Jersey. Internships are available. The school offers study abroad in 28 countries, accelerated degree programs in business administration and criminal justice, co-op programs, independent study, distance learning, English as a second language, dual majors, student-designed majors, nondegree study, and pass/fail options. Contact the school for information on the Honors College. There are 12 national honor societies, including Phi Beta Kappa, and a freshman honors program.

Admissions: 60% of the 2009-2010 applicants were accepted. The SAT scores for the 2009-2010 freshman class were: Critical Reading--38% below 500, 45% between 500 and 599, 15% between 600 and 700, and 2% above 700; Math--20% below 500, 45% between 500 and 599, 31% between 600 and 700, and 4% above 700; Writing--36% below 500, 45% between 500 and 599, 16% between 600 and 700, and 3% above 700. 49% of the current freshmen were in the top fifth of their class; 78% were in the top two fifths.

Requirements: The SAT or ACT is required. In addition, a high school diploma is required; the GED is accepted. SAT Subject tests are required of students without a high school diploma from an accredited high school and from some GED holders. Students should have completed a general college-preparatory program, including 16 high school academic credits or Carnegie units, with 4 years of English, 3 years of math (4 recommended), 2 years each of science and foreign language, and 5 electives. Biology and chemistry are required for nursing students. AP and CLEP credits are accepted. Important factors in the admissions decision are advanced placement or honors courses, evidence of special talent, and leadership record.

Procedure: Freshmen are admitted in the fall. Entrance exams should be taken by December of senior year, but this is not required. There are early admissions and rolling admissions plans. Application deadlines are open. Application fee is $65. Notifications are sent March 1. Applications are accepted on-line. A waiting list is maintained.

Financial Aid: In 2009-2010, 85% of all full-time freshmen and 89% of continuing full-time students received some form of financial aid. 71% of all full-time freshmen and 83% of continuing full-time students received need-based aid. The average freshman award was $13,561. Need-based scholarships and need-based grants averaged $12,504; need-based self-help aid (loans and jobs) averaged $8457; non-need-based athletic scholarships averaged $7500; and other non-need-based awards and non-need-based scholarships averaged $3507. Average annual earnings from campus work are $1272. The average financial indebtedness of the 2009 graduate was $23,710. The FAFSA is required. The priority date for freshman financial aid applications for fall entry is March 15. The deadline for filing freshman financial aid applications for fall entry is open.

Computers: All students may access the system. There are no time limits. The fee is $283. All students are required to have a personal computer.

SAINT EDWARD'S UNIVERSITY

Austin, TX 78704
(512) 448-8500
(800) 555-0164; (512) 464-8877

Full-time: 1397 men, 2066 women	**Faculty:** 166; IIA, -$
Part-time: 384 men, 521 women	**Ph.D.s:** 90%
Graduate: 344 men, 581 women	**Student/Faculty:** 21 to 1
Year: semesters, summer session	**Tuition:** $24,440
Application Deadline: May 1	**Room & Board:** $8196
Freshman Class: 2981 applied, 1970 accepted, 757 enrolled	
SAT CR/M/W: 570/560/550	**ACT:** 24 **VERY COMPETITIVE**

Saint Edward's University, founded in 1885, is an independent Catholic liberal arts institution offering undergraduate courses in business, behavioral and social sciences, humanities, education, and natural sciences, and graduate courses in human service, business administration, counseling, liberal arts, computer information systems, teaching, college student development, organizational leadership and ethics. There are 6 undergraduate schools and 11 graduate schools. In addition to regional accreditation, SEU has baccalaureate program accreditation with CSWE. The library contains 201,930 volumes, 6,73 microform items, and 3934 audio/video tapes/CDs/DVDs, and subscribes to 1909 periodicals including electronic. Computerized library services include interlibrary loans, database searching, Internet access, and laptop Internet portals. Special learning facilities include a learning resource center, art gallery, and digital photography lab. The 160-acre campus is in an urban area in Austin. Including any residence halls, there are 58 buildings.

Programs of Study: SEU confers B.A., B.S., B.A.A.S., B.B.A., and B.L.S. degrees. Master's degrees are also awarded. Bachelor's degrees are awarded in BIOLOGICAL SCIENCE (biochemistry, bioinformatics, and biology/biological science), BUSINESS (accounting, banking and finance, business administration and management, entrepreneurial studies, international business management, and marketing management), COMMUNICATIONS AND THE ARTS (art, communications, creative writing, digital communications, dramatic arts, English literature, graphic design, photography, and Spanish), COMPUTER AND PHYSICAL SCIENCE (chemistry, computer science, information sciences and systems, and mathematics), EDUCATION (art education, drama education, English education, foreign languages education, mathematics education, physical education, science education, and social studies education), ENGINEERING AND ENVIRONMENTAL DESIGN (preengineering), HEALTH PROFESSIONS (predentistry and premedicine), SOCIAL SCIENCE (criminal justice, criminology, economics, forensic studies, history, interdisciplinary studies, international relations, Latin American studies, liberal arts/general studies, philosophy, physical fitness/movement, political science/government, prelaw, psychology, religion, religious education, social work, and sociology). Psychology, communication, and biology are the largest.

Special: Internships and study abroad in a variety of countries through the ISEP, SEU, and other university programs are available. Student-designed majors, credit for life experience, nondegree study, and pass/fail options also are possible. A flexible program for working adults is offered through New College. There are 10 national honor societies and a freshman honors program.

Admissions: 66% of the 2009-2010 applicants were accepted. The SAT scores for the 2009-2010 freshman class were: Critical Reading--17% below 500, 47% between 500 and 599, 31% between 600 and 700, and 5% above 700; Math--17% below 500, 51% between 500 and 599, 30% between 600 and 700, and 2% above 700; Writing--22% below 500, 46% between 500 and 599, 29% between 600 and 700, and 2% above 700. The ACT scores were 12% below 21, 28% between 21 and 23, 30% between 24 and 26, 21% between 27 and 28, and 9% above 28. 43% of the current freshmen were in the top fifth of their class; 77% were in the top two fifths. 9 freshmen graduated first in their class.

Requirements: The SAT or ACT is required. The ACT Optional Writing test is also required. If SAT Writing is taken also, ACT Writing is not required. Successful applicants should be in the top half of their graduating class with testing at or above a combined critical reading and math score of 1000 on the SAT, or a composite score, not including writing, of 21 on the ACT. The GED is accepted. An interview is recommended. An essay is required. AP and CLEP credits are accepted. Important factors in the admissions decision are advanced placement or honors courses, extracurricular activities record, and leadership record.

Procedure: Freshmen are admitted fall and spring. Entrance exams should be taken in spring of the junior year or in summer or fall of the senior year. There are deferred admissions and rolling admissions plans. Applications should be filed by May 1 for fall entry, November 15 for spring entry, and May 1 for summer entry, along with a $45 fee. Notification is sent on a rolling basis. 332 applicants were on the 2009 waiting list; 73 were admitted. Applications are accepted on-line. 332 applicants were on a recent waiting list, 73 were accepted.

Financial Aid: In 2009-2010, 92% of all full-time freshmen and 88% of continuing full-time students received some form of financial aid. 71% of all full-time freshmen and 63% of continuing full-time students received need-based aid. The average freshman award was $24,020. Need-based scholarships or need-based grants averaged $13,063 ($27,450 maximum); need-based self-help aid (loans and jobs) averaged $3683 ($7500 maximum); non-need-based athletic scholarships averaged $15,598 ($32,984 maximum); and other non-need-based awards and non-need-based scholarships averaged $7568 ($36,600 maximum). 21% of undergraduate students work part-time. Average annual earnings from campus work are $1836. The average financial indebtedness of the 2009 graduate was $29,810. SEU is a member of CSS. The FAFSA is required. The priority date for freshman financial aid applications for fall entry is March 1. The deadline for filing freshman financial aid applications for fall entry is April 15.

Computers: Wireless access is available. Students have access to 756 computers in classrooms, labs, and residence halls. Every residence hall room has an Ethernet network connection and wireless access. Wireless access is also available in all classrooms and public areas of every building. All students may access the system 24 hours every day. There are no time limits and no fees.

SAINT JOHN'S COLLEGE

Annapolis, MD 21404

(410) 626-2523
(800) 727-9238; (410) 269-7916

Full-time: 260 men, 230 women	**Faculty:** n/av
Part-time: none	**Ph.D.s:** 78%
Graduate: 50 men, 40 women	**Student/Faculty:** n/av
Year: semesters	**Tuition:** $37,000
Application Deadline: open	**Room & Board:** $9000
Freshman Class: n/av	
SAT or ACT: not required	**HIGHLY COMPETITIVE**

St. John's College, founded as King William's School in 1696 and chartered as St. John's in 1784, is a private institution that offers a single, all-required curriculum sometimes called the Great Books Program. Students and faculty work together in small discussion classes without lecture courses, written finals, or emphasis on grades. The program is a rigorous interdisciplinary curriculum based on the great works of literature, math, philosophy, theology, sciences, political theory, music, history, and economics. There is also a campus in Santa Fe, New Mexico. Figures in the above capsule and this profile are approximate. There is 1 graduate school. The 2 libraries contain 133,000 volumes, 2000 microform items, and 5000 audio/video tapes/CDs/DVDs, and subscribe to 240 periodicals including electronic. Computerized library services include interlibrary loans, database searching, Internet access, and laptop Internet portals. Special learning facilities include an art gallery and planetarium. The 36-acre campus is in a small town 35 miles east of Washington, D.C., and 32 miles south of Baltimore. Including any residence halls, there are 18 buildings.

Programs of Study: St. John's confers B.A. degrees. Master's degrees are also awarded. Bachelor's degrees are awarded in SOCIAL SCIENCE (liberal arts/general studies, Western European studies, and Western civilization/culture).

Special: St. John's offers summer internships and an informal study-abroad program.

Admissions: There were 4 National Merit finalists in a recent year.

Requirements: Applicants need not be high school graduates; some students are admitted before they complete high school. Test scores may be submitted but are not required. Secondary preparation should include 4 years of English, 3 years of math, and 2 years each of foreign language, science, and history. Applicants must submit written essays, which are critical to the admissions decision, and are strongly urged to visit. Important factors in the admissions decision are recommendations by school officials, advanced placement or honors courses, and personality/intangible qualities.

Procedure: Freshmen are admitted fall. There are early admissions, deferred admissions, and rolling admissions plans. Application deadlines are open. Notification is sent on a rolling basis. Applications are accepted on-line.

Financial Aid: In a recent year, 61% of all full-time freshmen and 68% of continuing full-time students received some form of financial aid. 57% of all full-time freshmen and 65% of continuing full-time students received need-based aid. The average freshman award was $30,545. 75% of undergraduate students work part-time. Average annual earnings from campus work are $2700. The average financial indebtedness of a recent graduate was $23,760. St. John's is a member of CSS. The CSS/Profile, the FAFSA, and parent and student federal tax returns are required. Check with the school for current application deadlines.

Computers: Wireless access is available. PCs are located in student computer labs and the library. Wireless access in some dorms and public areas. All students may access the system 24 hours a day. There are no time limits and no fees.

SAINT JOHN'S COLLEGE
Santa Fe, NM 87505

(505) 984-6060
(800) 331-5232; (505) 984-6162

Full-time: 265 men, 175 women	**Faculty:** n/av
Part-time: 5 men	**Ph.D.s:** n/av
Graduate: 75 men, 40 women	**Student/Faculty:** n/av
Year: semesters, summer session	**Tuition:** $37,000
Application Deadline: March 1	**Room & Board:** $9000
Freshman Class: n/av	
SAT: required	**HIGHLY COMPETITIVE**

St. John's College, founded in 1696, offers a curriculum based on the Great Books Program in which students and faculty work together in small discussion classes without lecture courses, written finals, or emphasis on grades. The program is a rigorous interdisciplinary curriculum based on great books -- literature, math, philosophy, theology, sciences, political theory, music, history, economics. The figures in the above capsule and in this profile are approximate. There is 1 graduate school. The library contains 65,000 volumes, and 8,205 audio/video tapes/CDs/DVDs, and subscribes to 135 periodicals including electronic. Computerized library services include interlibrary loans and database searching. Special learning facilities include an art gallery, a music library, a search and rescue headquarters, and music practice rooms. The 250-acre campus is in a suburban area in Santa Fe. Including any residence halls, there are 31 buildings.

Programs of Study: St. John's confers B.A. degrees. Master's degrees are also awarded. Bachelor's degrees are awarded in SOCIAL SCIENCE (liberal arts/general studies).

Special: Internships with alumni in a wide range of fields are available and students may transfer between the Santa Fe and Annapolis campuses. Work study programs are available with the state government, museums, galleries, Santa Fe Institute, businesses, and schools. Premedical studies at universities around the country and 4-1 teaching certification through the University of New Mexico are possible.

Requirements: The SAT is required. In addition, applicants must write 3 personal essays and submit 2 teacher references, a secondary school report including a reference from a school official, and transcripts of all academic work in high school and college. A campus visit and interview are recommended. 3 years of math and 2 years of foreign language are required; 4 years each of math, foreign language, English, and science are recommended. The GED is accepted for early admission candidates. The SAT or ACT is required of early admission candidates.

Procedure: Freshmen are admitted fall and spring. There are deferred admissions and rolling admissions plans. Application deadlines are open. Applications are accepted on-line. A waiting list is maintained.

Financial Aid: In a recent year, 56% of all full-time freshmen and 63% of continuing full-time students received some form of financial aid. 56% of all full-time freshmen and 63% of continuing full-time students received need-based aid. The average freshmen award was $23,160. 63% of undergraduate students worked part-time. Average annual earnings from campus work were $2400. The average financial indebtedness of the 2009 graduate was $17,829. The CSS/

Profile and FAFSA, and the Business/FARM Supplement and non-custodial parent statement are required. Check with the school for current application deadlines.

Computers: Wireless access is available. There is hi-speed Internet in all dorm rooms, 2 computer labs, and wireless in selected areas. All students may access the system. There are no time limits and no fees.

SAINT JOHN'S UNIVERSITY

Collegeville, MN 56321-7155

(320) 363-2196
(800) 544-1489; (320) 363-3206

Full-time: 1867 men	**Faculty:** 147; IIB, av$
Part-time: 48 men	**Ph.D.s:** 84%
Graduate: 55 men, 50 women	**Student/Faculty:** 13 to 1
Year: semesters	**Tuition:** $29,936
Application Deadline: open	**Room & Board:** $7714
Freshman Class: 1344 applied, 1125 accepted, 461 enrolled	
ACT: 25	**SAT:** required

VERY COMPETITIVE

St. John's University, founded in 1857, is a private Catholic Benedictine institution offering undergraduate liberal arts study for men in partnership with the College of Saint Benedict, a Catholic Benedictine institution for women. The coordinate institutions share an academic calendar, academic curriculum, and many combined extracurricular activities. There is 1 graduate school. In addition to regional accreditation, St. John's has baccalaureate program accreditation with ADA, CSWE, NASM, and NCATE. The 2 libraries contain 658,438 volumes, 121,244 microform items, and 40,637 audio/video tapes/CDs/DVDs, and subscribe to 71,720 periodicals including electronic. Computerized library services include interlibrary loans, database searching, Internet access, and laptop Internet portals. Special learning facilities include a learning resource center, art gallery, radio station, pottery studio, arboretum, observatory, greenhouse, herbarium, monastic manuscript library, and natural history museum. The 2500-acre campus is in a rural area 15 miles west of St. Cloud and 75 miles northwest of Minneapolis/St. Paul. Including any residence halls, there are 54 buildings.

Programs of Study: St. John's confers B.A. and B.S.N. degrees. Master's degrees are also awarded. Bachelor's degrees are awarded in AGRICULTURE (environmental studies), BIOLOGICAL SCIENCE (biochemistry, biology/biological science, and nutrition), BUSINESS (management science), COMMUNICATIONS AND THE ARTS (art, classics, communications, dramatic arts, English, French, German, music, and Spanish), COMPUTER AND PHYSICAL SCIENCE (chemistry, computer science, mathematics, natural sciences, and physics), EDUCATION (elementary education), ENGINEERING AND ENVIRONMENTAL DESIGN (preengineering), HEALTH PROFESSIONS (nursing, occupational therapy, predentistry, premedicine, preoptometry, prepharmacy, prephysical therapy, and preveterinary science), SOCIAL SCIENCE (dietetics, economics, gender studies, history, humanities, liberal arts/general studies, pastoral studies, peace studies, philosophy, political science/government, prelaw, psychology, social science, sociology, theological studies, and women's studies). Chemistry, economics, and biology are the strongest academically. Management, accounting, and biology are the largest.

Special: Students may cross-register with St. Cloud State University. There are study-abroad programs in Australia, Austria, Chile, China, England, France, Guatemala, Greece, Ireland, Italy, Japan, South Africa, and Spain. Internships, dual and student-designed majors, preprofessional programs, and liberal studies degrees may be pursued. A 3-2 engineering program is offered through the University of Minnesota, as is a 3-1 program in dentistry. Nondegree study and a pass/fail grading option are also available. There is a Phi Beta Kappa honors program and a freshman honors program.

Admissions: 84% of the 2009-2010 applicants were accepted. The SAT scores for the 2009-2010 freshman class were: Critical Reading--25% below 500, 27% between 500 and 599, 38% between 600 and 700, and 10% above 700; Math--20% below 500, 29% between 500 and 599, 30% between 600 and 700, and 21% above 700; Writing--29% below 500, 47% between 500 and 599, 15% between 600 and 700, and 9% above 700. The ACT scores were 9% below 21, 19% between 21 and 23, 30% between 24 and 26, 17% between 27 and 28, and 25% above 28. 46% of the current freshmen were in the top fifth of their class; 79% were in the top two fifths. There were 6 National Merit finalists. 7 freshmen graduated first in their class.

Requirements: The SAT or ACT is required. In addition, students should be graduates of an accredited secondary school. Academic preparation should include 15 units, including 4 of English, 3 of math, 2 each of a lab science and social studies, and 4 electives. A foreign language is recommended. The GED is accepted. An essay is required. Home-schooled applicants are not required to have a high school diploma but are required to provide appropriate documentation of college preparatory curriculum and standardized test scores. St. John's requires applicants to be in the upper 50% of their class. A GPA of 3.0 is required. AP and CLEP credits are accepted. Important factors in the admissions decision are advanced placement or honors courses, leadership record, and extracurricular activities record.

Procedure: Freshmen are admitted fall and spring. Entrance exams should be taken during the spring of the junior year or fall of the senior year. There is a deferred admissions plan. Application deadlines are open. Notification is sent April 1. Applications are accepted on-line. A waiting list is maintained.

Financial Aid: In 2009-2010, 91% of all full-time freshmen and 93% of continuing full-time students received some form of financial aid. 60% of all full-time freshmen and 59% of continuing full-time students received need-based aid. The average freshman award was $25,930. 60% of undergraduate students work part-time. Average annual earnings from campus work are $2600. St. John's is a member of CSS. The FAFSA, the college's own financial statement, and federal tax returns and W-2s are required. The priority date for freshman financial aid applications for fall entry is March 15. The deadline for filing freshman financial aid applications for fall entry is open.

Computers: Wireless access is available. Network connections are available for all students in residence halls. Students can also access computers in the computer labs, libraries, and student centers. All students may access the system 24 hours a day. There are no time limits. The fee is $220.

Philadelphia, PA 19131 (610) 660-1300
(888) BE-A-HAWK; (610) 660-1314

Full-time: 2215 men, 2312 women	**Faculty:** 284; IIA, +$
Part-time: 375 men, 502 women	**Ph.D.s:** 98%
Graduate: 1211 men, 1723 women	**Student/Faculty:** 16 to 1
Year: semesters, summer session	**Tuition:** $34,090
Application Deadline: February 1	**Room & Board:** $11,575
Freshman Class: 6520 applied, 5370 accepted, 1189 enrolled	
SAT CR/M: 550/570	**ACT:** 23 **VERY COMPETITIVE**

Saint Joseph's University, founded in 1851, is a Catholic, private college affiliated with the Jesuit order. It offers undergraduate programs in arts and sciences and business administration. There are 3 undergraduate schools and 2 graduate schools. In addition to regional accreditation, Saint Joseph's has baccalaureate program accreditation with AACSB. The 2 libraries contain 355,000 volumes, 868,000 microform items, and 5,100 audio/video tapes/CDs/DVDs, and subscribe to 29,000 periodicals including electronic. Computerized library services include interlibrary loans, database searching, and Internet access. Special learning facilities include a learning resource center, art gallery, radio station, instructional media center, foreign language labs, Mandeville Hall, Wall Street Trading Room, and Claver Honors House. The 103-acre campus is in a suburban area on the western edge of Philadelphia and eastern Montgomery County. Including any residence halls, there are 75 buildings.

Programs of Study: Saint Joseph's confers B.A., B.S., and B.B.A. degrees. Associate, master's, and doctoral degrees are also awarded. Bachelor's degrees are awarded in BIOLOGICAL SCIENCE (biology/biological science), BUSINESS (accounting, banking and finance, business administration and management, international business management, management information systems, and marketing/retailing/merchandising), COMMUNICATIONS AND THE ARTS (English, fine arts, French, German, Latin, and Spanish), COMPUTER AND PHYSICAL SCIENCE (actuarial science, chemistry, computer science, information sciences and systems, mathematics, and physics), EDUCATION (elementary education, secondary education, and special education), ENGINEERING AND ENVIRONMENTAL DESIGN (environmental science), HEALTH PROFESSIONS (health care administration), SOCIAL SCIENCE (criminal justice, economics, European studies, French studies, history, international relations, philosophy, political science/government, psychology, public administration, sociology, and theological studies). Biology and accounting are the strongest academically. Marketing, finance, and biology are the largest.

Special: The university offers internships, a Washington semester, advanced 5-year degrees in international marketing, psychology, and education, dual majors, minor concentrations, and study abroad in 16 countries. There are co-op programs for students majoring in accounting, finance, marketing, pharmaceutical marketing, decision/system sciences, management, food marketing, and international business and an interdisciplinary major in health services. There are 17 national honor societies, including Phi Beta Kappa, and a freshman honors program.

Admissions: 82% of the 2009-2010 applicants were accepted. The SAT scores for the 2009-2010 freshman class were: Critical Reading--19% below 500, 54% between 500 and 599, 24% between 600 and 700, and 3% above 700; Math--17% below 500, 48% between 500 and 599, 31% between 600 and 700, and 4% above

700; Writing--16% below 500, 55% between 500 and 599, 26% between 600 and 700, and 3% above 700. The ACT scores were 16% below 21, 34% between 21 and 23, 28% between 24 and 26, 11% between 27 and 28, and 11% above 28.

Requirements: The SAT or ACT is required. In addition, careful consideration is given to the applicant's GPA, the rigor of the high school record, the application essay, counselor or teacher recommendations, and character/personal qualities. Other factors include class rank, ACT/SAT scores, volunteer work, work experience, and alumni connections. A GPA of 3.0 is required. AP credits are accepted. Important factors in the admissions decision are advanced placement or honors courses, extracurricular activities record, and leadership record.

Procedure: Freshmen are admitted fall and spring. Entrance exams should be taken in the spring of the junior year and/or the fall of the senior year. There are early action and deferred admissions plans. Early action applications should be filed by November 15; regular applications should be filed by February 1 for fall entry, along with a $60 fee. Notifications are sent for early action by December 25; for regular decision by March 15. 234 applicants were on the 2009 waiting list, 114 were admitted. Applications are accepted on-line.

Financial Aid: Saint Joseph's is a member of CSS. The FAFSA is required. Check with the school for current application deadlines.

Computers: Wireless access is available. There are more than 80 technologically equipped classrooms, 60 computer lab/learning spaces, 15 classrooms with built in TV/VCR and DVD players, and 5 video-conferencing rooms. All university-owned housing is connected to the campus voice and data networks. In total, there are more than 7000 network connections points in classrooms, labs, offices, and residence halls. All students may access the system. There are no time limits and no fees. It is strongly recommended that all students have a personal computer. Students enrolled in Laptops for business school and psychology majors must have a personal computer. A Lenovo Thinkpad (business school); Apple (psychology majors) is recommended.

SAINT LAWRENCE UNIVERSITY
Canton, NY 13617

(315) 229-5261
(800) 285-1856; (315) 229-5818

Full-time: 1030 men, 1244 women	**Faculty:** 166; IIB, +$
Part-time: 10 men, 11 women	**Ph.D.s:** 98%
Graduate: 33 men, 73 women	**Student/Faculty:** 14 to 1
Year: semesters, summer session	**Tuition:** $39,765
Application Deadline: February 1	**Room & Board:** $10,160
Freshman Class: 4715 applied, 1848 accepted, 580 enrolled	
SAT CR/M/W: 603/610/600	**HIGHLY COMPETITIVE**

St. Lawrence University, established in 1856, is a private liberal arts institution. There is 1 graduate school. The 2 libraries contain 601,778 volumes, 599,249 microform items, and 7129 audio/video tapes/CDs/DVDs, and subscribe to 49,321 periodicals including electronic. Computerized library services include interlibrary loans, database searching, and Internet access. Special learning facilities include a learning resource center, art gallery, radio station, and science field station. The 1000-acre campus is in a rural area 80 miles south of Ottawa, Canada. Including any residence halls, there are 30 buildings.

Programs of Study: St. Lawrence confers B.A. and B.S. degrees. Master's degrees are also awarded. Bachelor's degrees are awarded in AGRICULTURE (conservation and regulation and environmental studies), BIOLOGICAL SCIENCE (biochemistry, biology/biological science, biophysics, and neurosciences),

BUSINESS (international economics), COMMUNICATIONS AND THE ARTS (art, art history and appreciation, communications, creative writing, dramatic arts, English, fine arts, French, German, languages, modern language, music, Spanish, studio art, and visual and performing arts), COMPUTER AND PHYSICAL SCIENCE (chemistry, computer science, geology, mathematics, and physics), ENGINEERING AND ENVIRONMENTAL DESIGN (environmental science), SOCIAL SCIENCE (African studies, anthropology, Asian/Oriental studies, Canadian studies, economics, history, interdisciplinary studies, international studies, philosophy, political science/government, psychology, religion, and sociology). Psychology, economics, and government are the largest.

Special: Students may cross-register with the Associated Colleges of the St. Lawrence Valley. Internships are available through the sociology, psychology, and English departments and through a service learning program. Study-abroad in 15 countries and a Washington semester are offered. Dual majors and student-designed majors can be arranged. Students may earn 3-2 engineering degrees in conjunction with 7 engineering schools. Nondegree study and pass/fail options are available. An Adirondack semester is also offered. There are 20 national honor societies, including Phi Beta Kappa, and 17 departmental honors programs.

Admissions: 39% of the 2009-2010 applicants were accepted. The SAT scores for the 2009-2010 freshman class were: Critical Reading--7% below 500, 35% between 500 and 599, 49% between 600 and 700, and 9% above 700; Math--5% below 500, 32% between 500 and 599, 54% between 600 and 700, and 9% above 700; Writing--5% below 500, 40% between 500 and 599, 48% between 600 and 700, and 6% above 700. 71% of the current freshmen were in the top fifth of their class; 92% were in the top two fifths. 13 freshmen graduated first in their class.

Requirements: Applicants must be graduates of an accredited high school. 16 or more academic credits are required, including 4 years of English and 3 years each of foreign languages, math, science, and social studies. Essays are required and interviews are recommended for all applicants. Submissions of standardized test scores is optional. AP credits are accepted. Important factors in the admissions decision are advanced placement or honors courses, extracurricular activities record, and recommendations by school officials.

Procedure: Freshmen are admitted fall and spring. Entrance exams should be taken during the spring of the junior year or the fall of the senior year. There are early decision and deferred admissions plans. Early decision applications should be filed by November 15 and January 15; regular applications, by February 1 for fall entry; and December 1 for spring entry, along with a $60 fee. Notification of early decision is sent December 15 and February 15; regular decision, March 30. 192 early decision candidates were accepted for the 2009-2010 class. 444 applicants were on the 2009 waiting list; 36 were admitted. Applications are accepted on-line.

Financial Aid: In 2009-2010, 85% of all full-time freshmen and 83% of continuing full-time students received some form of financial aid. 66% of all full-time students received need-based aid. The average freshman award was $36,029. Need-based scholarships or need-based grants averaged $27,822; need-based self-help aid (loans and jobs) averaged $4394; non-need-based athletic scholarships averaged $49,925; and other non-need-based awards and non-need-based scholarships averaged $11,344. 37% of undergraduate students work part-time. Average annual earnings from campus work are $1100. The average financial indebtedness of the 2009 graduate was $31,653. St. Lawrence is a member of CSS. The CSS/Profile, FAFSA, and the college's own financial statement are required. The deadline for filing freshman financial aid applications for fall entry is February 1.

Computers: Wireless access is available throughout the campus. There are 660 public access computers. All students may access the system 24 hours per day. There are no time limits and no fees.

SAINT LOUIS UNIVERSITY
St. Louis, MO 63103-2097
(314) 977-2500
(800) SLUFORU; (314) 977-7136

Full-time: 3092 men, 4215 women	**Faculty:** 541; I, --$
Part-time: 231 men, 581 women	**Ph.D.s:** 96%
Graduate: 2151 men, 3043 women	**Student/Faculty:** 14 to 1
Year: semesters, summer session	**Tuition:** $31,342
Application Deadline: December 1	**Room & Board:** $8900
Freshman Class: 10707 applied, 7616 accepted, 1597 enrolled	
ACT: 27	**VERY COMPETITIVE+**

Saint Louis University, founded in 1818, is a private institution affiliated with the Jesuit Order of the Roman Catholic Church. There are 9 undergraduate schools and 3 graduate schools. In addition to regional accreditation, SLU has baccalaureate program accreditation with AACSB, ABET, ADA, CSWE, and NCATE. The 3 libraries contain 1.8 million volumes, 2.7 million microform items, and 168,715 audio/video tapes/CDs/DVDs, and subscribe to 18,018 periodicals including electronic. Computerized library services include interlibrary loans, database searching, Internet access, and laptop Internet portals. Special learning facilities include a learning resource center, art gallery, radio station, TV station, biological station, entrepreneurial studies center, earthquake research center, performing arts center, supersonic wind tunnel, airport, sculpture/ceramics studio, physiology/gait research labs, demonstration clinics, and Vatican manuscripts microfilm library. The 235-acre campus is in an urban area in the midtown section of St. Louis, approximately 4 miles west of the Gateway Arch. Including any residence halls, there are 127 buildings.

Programs of Study: SLU confers B.A. and B.S. degrees. Master's and doctoral degrees are also awarded. Bachelor's degrees are awarded in BIOLOGICAL SCIENCE (biochemistry, biology/biological science, and nutrition), BUSINESS (business administration and management, entrepreneurial studies, human resources, management information systems, management science, marketing management, organizational behavior, and purchasing/inventory management), COMMUNICATIONS AND THE ARTS (art history and appreciation, classical languages, communications, dramatic arts, English, English literature, fine arts, French, Greek, music, Russian languages and literature, Spanish, and studio art), COMPUTER AND PHYSICAL SCIENCE (atmospheric sciences and meteorology, chemistry, computer programming, computer science, earth science, geology, geophysics and seismology, information sciences and systems, mathematics, and physics), EDUCATION (athletic training and education), ENGINEERING AND ENVIRONMENTAL DESIGN (aeronautical engineering, aerospace studies, airline piloting and navigation, aviation administration/management, biomedical engineering, civil engineering, computer engineering, computer technology, electrical/electronics engineering, engineering management, engineering physics, environmental science, industrial administration/management, and mechanical engineering), HEALTH PROFESSIONS (allied health, clinical science, cytotechnology, exercise science, medical laboratory science, medical records administration/services, medical technology, nuclear medical technology, nursing, occupational therapy, physical therapy, public health, radiation therapy, radiograph medical technology, and speech pathology/audiology), SOCIAL SCIENCE

(American studies, corrections, criminal justice, economics, German area studies, history, humanities, international relations, philosophy, political science/government, psychology, religion, social work, sociology, theological studies, urban studies, and women's studies). Psychology, physician's assistant, and physical therapy are the strongest academically. Biology, business administration, and nursing are the largest.

Special: Students may study abroad in 24 countries. Cross-registration with Washington University and the University of Missouri at St. Louis, internships, work-study programs on campus, an accelerated degree program in nursing, a 3-2 engineering degree program with Washington University in St. Louis, dual majors, student-designed majors, a Washington semester, and pass/fail options are also possible. Students may also participate in university-sponsored mission trips. There are 3 national honor societies, including Phi Beta Kappa, and a freshman honors program. In addition, SLU has an honors department that meets the needs of every department on campus.

Admissions: 71% of the 2009-2010 applicants were accepted. The SAT scores for the 2009-2010 freshman class were: Critical Reading--10% below 500, 38% between 500 and 599, 41% between 600 and 700, and 11% above 700; Math--11% below 500, 32% between 500 and 599, 41% between 600 and 700, and 16% above 700. The ACT scores were 4% below 21, 13% between 21 and 23, 26% between 24 and 26, 19% between 27 and 28, and 38% above 28. 62% of the current freshmen were in the top fifth of their class; 86% were in the top two fifths. There were 31 National Merit finalists.

Requirements: The ACT is required. In addition, a complete application is required, which consists of an application, an essay of the student's choice, a high school transcript, ACT or SAT test scores, and a secondary school report form from the high school counselor. A GPA of 2.5 is required. AP and CLEP credits are accepted. Important factors in the admissions decision are advanced placement or honors courses, leadership record, and recommendations by school officials.

Procedure: Freshmen are admitted fall, spring, and summer. Entrance exams should be taken in the junior or senior year. Junior is recommended. There are deferred admissions and rolling admissions plans. Applications should be filed by December 1 for fall entry; January 1 for spring entry, along with a $25 fee. Notification is sent on a rolling basis. Applications are accepted on-line.

Financial Aid: In 2009-2010, 98% of all full-time freshmen and 88% of continuing full-time students received some form of financial aid. 57% of all full-time freshmen and 55% of continuing full-time students received need-based aid. Need-based scholarships or need-based grants averaged $9869 ($29,940 maximum); need-based self-help aid (loans and jobs) averaged $3965 ($7500 maximum); non-need-based athletic scholarships averaged $14,761 ($40,560 maximum); and other non-need-based awards and scholarships averaged $16,821 ($45,000 maximum). The FAFSA and FFS are required. The priority date for freshman financial aid applications for fall entry is March 1.

Computers: Wireless access is available. The campus-wide network allows students to access their own information system on the student information system, enroll for classes, and access Web-based information provided by faculty, administrators, and other students. All students may access the system. There are no time limits and no fees. It is strongly recommended that all students have a personal computer. Students enrolled in MBA, law, and biology must have a personal computer. For the MBA, a PC is recommended; for biology and math, a Mac is recommended.

SAINT MARY'S COLLEGE

Notre Dame, IN 46556
(574) 284-4587
(800) 551-7621; (574) 284-4716

Full-time: 1641 women	**Faculty:** 146; IIB, av$
Part-time: 15 women	**Ph.D.s:** 84%
Graduate: none	**Student/Faculty:** 11 to 1
Year: semesters, summer session	**Tuition:** $29,616
Application Deadline: February 15	**Room & Board:** $9206
Freshman Class: 1357 applied, 1162 accepted, 435 enrolled	
SAT CR/M/W: 560/560/570	**ACT:** 25 **VERY COMPETITIVE**

Saint Mary's College, established in 1844, was founded and sponsored by the Congregation of the Sisters of the Holy Cross. It is a Catholic comprehensive college for women in the liberal arts tradition. In addition to regional accreditation, Saint Mary's has baccalaureate program accreditation with CSWE, NASAD, NASM, NCATE, and NLN. The library contains 271,161 volumes, 18,104 microform items, and 1,924 audio/video tapes/CDs/DVDs, and subscribes to 20,780 periodicals including electronic. Computerized library services include interlibrary loans, database searching, Internet access, and laptop Internet portals. Special learning facilities include an art gallery and TV station. The 275-acre campus is in a suburban area 90 miles east of Chicago. Including any residence halls, there are 20 buildings.

Programs of Study: Saint Mary's confers B.A., B.S., B.B.A., B.F.A., and B.Mus. degrees. Bachelor's degrees are awarded in BIOLOGICAL SCIENCE (biology/biological science), BUSINESS (accounting, business administration and management, and management information systems), COMMUNICATIONS AND THE ARTS (art, communications, creative writing, English literature, fine arts, French, Italian, music, Spanish, and visual and performing arts), COMPUTER AND PHYSICAL SCIENCE (chemistry, mathematics, and statistics), EDUCATION (elementary education), HEALTH PROFESSIONS (nursing and speech pathology/audiology), SOCIAL SCIENCE (economics, history, humanities, philosophy, political science/government, psychology, religion, social work, and sociology). Biology, nursing, and business are the strongest academically and the largest.

Special: Cross-registration is permitted with the University of Notre Dame and a consortium of 6 northern Indiana colleges. Opportunities are provided for internships, a Washington semester, an accelerated degree program in nursing, dual and student-designed majors, a 3-2 engineering degree with the University of Notre Dame, nondegree study, pass/fail options, and study abroad in 26 countries. There are 14 national honor societies.

Admissions: 86% of the 2009-2010 applicants were accepted. The SAT scores for the 2009-2010 freshman class were: Critical Reading--18% below 500, 48% between 500 and 599, 30% between 600 and 700, and 4% above 700; Math--20% below 500, 50% between 500 and 599, 27% between 600 and 700, and 3% above 700; Writing--20% below 500, 44% between 500 and 599, 31% between 600 and 700, and 5% above 700. The ACT scores were 8% below 21, 25% between 21 and 23, 33% between 24 and 26, 15% between 27 and 28, and 19% above 28. 58% of the current freshmen were in the top fifth of their class; 87% were in the top two fifths. 16 freshmen graduated first in their class.

Requirements: The SAT or ACT is required. The ACT Optional Writing test is also required. In addition, graduation from an accredited secondary school is required; a GED will be accepted. Applicants must have completed 16 academic credits, including 4 in English, 3 in math, and 2 each in a foreign language, history or social studies, and lab science with the remainder from college preparatory electives in the above areas. An essay is required. AP and CLEP credits are accepted. Important factors in the admissions decision are advanced placement or honors courses, evidence of special talent, and recommendations by school officials.

Procedure: Freshmen are admitted fall and spring. Entrance exams should be taken between March of the junior year and December of the senior year. There are early decision, deferred admissions and rolling admissions plans. Early decision applications should be filed by November 15; regular applications by February 15 for fall entry and November 15 for spring entry, along with a $30 fee. Notifications of early decision are sent December 15; regular decision, January 15. Applications are accepted on-line.

Financial Aid: In 2009-2010, 96% of all full-time freshmen and 94% of continuing full-time students received some form of financial aid. 68% of all full-time freshmen and 62% of continuing full-time students received need-based aid. 66% of undergraduate students work part-time. Average annual earnings from campus work are $1800. The average financial indebtedness of the 2009 graduate was $25,531. Saint Mary's is a member of CSS. The CSS/Profile and FAFSA are required. The deadline for filing freshman financial aid applications for fall entry is February 15.

Computers: Wireless access is available. The college provides network/Internet access to all of our students living on campus with a dedicated wired connection for each student. Students in some residence halls also have wireless/Internet from their rooms. Wireless network/Internet access is available from all of our academic buildings, library, and student center. The college provides over 250 computers for students' use in classrooms and clusters on campus. These computing areas are available in our academic buildings, library, student center, and residence halls, with some areas available 24/7. Printers are available in our academic buildings and library. All students may access the system 24 hours a day, 7 days a week. There are no time limits and no fees. It is strongly recommended that all students have a personal computer. A Dell or Apple product is recommended.

SAINT MARY'S COLLEGE OF MARYLAND

St. Marys City, MD 20686
(240) 895-5000
(800) 492-7181; (240) 895-5001

Full-time: 826 men, 1114 women	**Faculty:** 142; IIB
Part-time: 17 men, 21 women	**Ph.D.s:** 97%
Graduate: 8 men, 35 women	**Student/Faculty:** 12 to 1
Year: semesters, summer session	**Tuition:** $13,234 ($24,627)
Application Deadline: January 1	**Room & Board:** $9,950
Freshman Class: 2411 applied, 1381 accepted, 488 enrolled	
SAT CR/M/W: 640/610/620	**ACT:** 26 **HIGHLY COMPETITIVE**

St. Mary's College of Maryland, founded in 1840, is a small public liberal arts college designated by law as a Maryland honors college in 1992. There are no undergraduate schools and one graduate school. The library contains 1.7 million volumes, 40,602 microform items, 11,122 audio/video tapes/CDs/DVDs, and subscribes to 17,930 periodicals including electronic. Computerized library services include interlibrary loans, database searching, Internet access, and laptop Internet portals. Special learning facilities include a learning resource center, art gallery, radio station, TV station, historic archeological site, and estuarine research facilities. The 319-acre campus is in a rural area 70 miles southeast of Washington, D.C. Including any residence halls, there are 450 buildings.

Programs of Study: SMCM confers B.A. degrees. Master's degrees are also awarded. Bachelor's degrees are awarded in BIOLOGICAL SCIENCE (biochemistry and biology/biological science), COMMUNICATIONS AND THE ARTS (art, art history and appreciation, dramatic arts, English, film arts, languages, music, and visual and performing arts), COMPUTER AND PHYSICAL SCIENCE (chemistry, computer science, mathematics, natural sciences, and physics), SOCIAL SCIENCE (anthropology, Asian/Oriental studies, economics, history, human development, philosophy, political science/government, psychology, public affairs, religion, and sociology). Biology, psychology, and economics are the largest.

Special: St. Mary's offers internships, study abroad, national and international exchange programs, and work-study. Dual and student-designed majors and a 3-2 engineering degree with the University of Maryland, College Park, also are offered. Non-degree study and pass/fail options are possible. There are 8 national honor societies, including Phi Beta Kappa, and a freshman honors program.

Admissions: 57% of the 2009-2010 applicants were accepted. The SAT scores for the 2009-2010 freshman class were: Critical Reading--7% below 500, 24% between 500 and 599, 51% between 600 and 700, and 17% above 700; Math--12% below 500, 30% between 500 and 599, 52% between 600 and 700, and 6% above 700; Writing--9% below 500, 34% between 500 and 599, 48% between 600 and 700, and 9% above 700. The ACT scores were 7% below 21, 15% between 21 and 23, 30% between 24 and 26, 20% between 27 and 28, and 28% above 28. 71% of the current freshmen were in the top fifth of their class; 92% were in the top two fifths. 9 freshmen graduated first in their class.

Requirements: The SAT is required. In addition, applicants should have graduated from an accredited secondary school or earned the GED. Minimum high school preparation should include 4 units of English, 3 each of math, social studies, and science, and 7 electives. An essay, a resume of co-curricular activities, and 2 letters of recommendation are required. AP and CLEP credits are accepted. Important factors in the admissions decision are recommendations by school officials, extracurricular activities record, and advanced placement or honors courses.

Procedure: Freshmen are admitted fall. Entrance exams should be taken by the spring of their junior year. There is an early decision plan. Early decision applications should be filed by December 1; regular applications by January 1 for fall entry and November 1 for spring entry. The fall 2008 application fee was $50. Notification of early decision is sent January 1; regular decision, April 1. Applications are accepted on-line. 181 applicants were on a recent waiting list, 24 were accepted.

Financial Aid: In 2009-2010, 80% of all full-time freshmen and 71% of continuing full-time students received some form of financial aid. 60% of all full-time freshmen and 51% of continuing full-time students received need-based aid. The average freshmen award was $7,000, with $2,000 ($7,000 maximum) from need-based scholarships or need-based grants; $2,000 ($3,250 maximum) from need-based self-help aid (loans and jobs); and $3,000 ($7,000 maximum) from other non-need-based awards and non-need-based scholarships. 25% of undergraduate students work part-time. Average annual earnings from campus work are $1000. The average financial indebtedness of the 2009 graduate was $17,125. SMCM is a member of CSS. The FAFSA is required. The priority date for freshman financial aid applications for fall entry is February 15. The deadline for filing freshman financial aid applications for fall entry is March 1.

Computers: Wireless access is available. Throughout the campus, there are approximately 400 PCs in computer labs across campus, featuring Microsoft Windows XP and the Apple MacOS operating systems. These computer labs are available to all students for word processing, spreadsheet, and database work. There are also several smart classrooms and discipline-specific labs on campus. All of the computer labs have access to the library system, e-mail, and the Internet. There is also wireless access in all academic building areas of the campus for those who own wireless-ready laptop computers. All students may access the system. during all lab hours. There are no time limits and no fees.

SAINT MICHAEL'S COLLEGE
Colchester, VT 05439

(802) 654-3000
(800) 762-8000; (802) 654-2906

Full-time: 910 men, 990 women	**Faculty:** 151; IIB, +$
Part-time: 27 men, 23 women	**Ph.D.s:** 86%
Graduate: 145 men, 371 women	**Student/Faculty:** 16 to 1
Year: semesters, summer session	**Tuition:** $33,215
Application Deadline: February 1	**Room & Board:** $8280
Freshman Class: 3228 applied, 2613 accepted, 475 enrolled	
SAT CR/M/W: 570/570/560	**ACT:** 24 **VERY COMPETITIVE**

Saint Michael's College, founded in 1904 by the Society of Saint Edmund, is a residential, Catholic, liberal arts institution There is 1 graduate school. The library contains 267,650 volumes, 136,209 microform items, and 10,464 audio/video tapes/CDs/DVDs, and subscribes to 45,869 periodicals including electronic. Computerized library services include interlibrary loans, database searching, Internet access, and laptop Internet portals. Special learning facilities include a learning resource center, art gallery, radio station, an observatory. The 440-acre campus is in a suburban area 2 miles east of Burlington. Including any residence halls, there are 51 buildings.

Programs of Study: Saint Michael's confers B.A. and B.S. degrees. Master's degrees are also awarded. Bachelor's degrees are awarded in BIOLOGICAL SCIENCE (biochemistry and biology/biological science), BUSINESS (accounting and business administration and management), COMMUNICATIONS AND THE ARTS (dramatic arts, English, fine arts, French, journalism, music, and Spanish), COMPUTER AND PHYSICAL SCIENCE (chemistry, computer science, information sciences and systems, mathematics, physical sciences, and physics), EDUCATION (art education, elementary education, foreign languages education, science education, and secondary education), ENGINEERING AND ENVIRONMENTAL DESIGN (environmental science and preengineering), HEALTH PROFESSIONS (predentistry), SOCIAL SCIENCE (American studies, anthropology, economics, gender studies, history, philosophy, political science/government, prelaw, psychology, religion, and sociology). Business administration, psychology, and biology are the largest.

Special: A variety of internships and on-campus work-study are available. There is a Washington semester with American University and study abroad in 43 countries. Student-designed majors may be pursued. The college offers a 3-2 engineering degree program in cooperation with Clarkson University and the University of Vermont and a 4+1 graduate business program with Clarkson University. A B.S./Pharm.D. degree is also available with the Albany College of Pharmacy and Health Services. Nondegree study and pass/fail grading options are offered on a limited basis. Independent research opportunities are available through many departments. There are 11 national honor societies, including Phi Beta Kappa, a freshman honors program, and 1 departmental honors program.

Admissions: 81% of the 2009-2010 applicants were accepted. The SAT scores for the 2009-2010 freshman class were: Critical Reading--16% below 500, 46% between 500 and 599, 32% between 600 and 700, and 6% above 700; Math--16% below 500, 47% between 500 and 599, 32% between 600 and 700, and 5% above 700; Writing--13% below 500, 51% between 500 and 599, 32% between 600 and 700, and 4% above 700. The ACT scores were 14% below 21, 28% between 21 and 23, 31% between 24 and 26, 16% between 27 and 28, and 11% above 28. 48% of the current freshmen were in the top fifth of their class; 71% were in the top two fifths. 1 freshman graduated first in the class.

Requirements: The SAT or ACT is required. In addition, applicants must graduate from an accredited secondary school or have a GED. They must complete 16 Carnegie units. The college requires 4 credits in English, 3 to 4 credits in math and science, and 3 each in history (social studies) and a foreign language. An essay is required and an interview is recommended. AP and CLEP credits are accepted. Important factors in the admissions decision are advanced placement or honors courses, evidence of special talent, and recommendations by school officials.

Procedure: Freshmen are admitted fall and spring. Entrance exams should be taken in the fall of the senior year. There is a 1 and 2 early action and a deferred admissions plan. Early action applications should be filed by November 1 and December 1; regular applications should be filed by February 1 for fall entry and November 1 for spring entry, along with a $50 fee. Notifications are sent April 1. Applications are accepted on-line. 321 applicants were on a recent waiting list, 94 were accepted.

Financial Aid: In 2009-2010, 96% of all full-time freshmen and 90% of continuing full-time students received some form of financial aid. 67% of all full-time freshmen and 62% of continuing full-time students received need-based aid. The average freshman award was $21,500, Need-based scholarships or need-based grants averaged $17,779; need-based self-help aid (loans and jobs) averaged $6,275 ($11,500 maximum); non-need based athletic scholarships averaged $41,495 ($41,495 maximum); and other non-need based awards and non-need based scholarships averaged $9,195 ($41,495 maximum). 51% of undergraduate students work part-time. Average annual earnings from campus work are $1350. The average financial indebtedness of the 2009 graduate was $30,742. Saint Michael's is a member of CSS. The FAFSA, federal tax forms from both student and parents, and W-2 forms are required. The deadline for filing freshman financial aid applications for fall entry is February 15.

Computers: Wireless access is available. All enrolled students have access to the campus network, which provides connectivity to network resources, including full Internet access, e-mail, and network printing. Computing resources include 375 computers in labs and classrooms, 4 public computing labs, 10 computing labs in residence halls, 14 specialized computer labs, and 56 electronic classrooms. Wireless computing is available in about 90% of classrooms, the student center, and the library. All students may access the system. There are no time limits and no fees. It is strongly recommended that all students have a personal computer.

SAINT NORBERT COLLEGE

De Pere, WI 54115

(920) 403-3005
(800) 236-4878; (920) 403-4072

Full-time: 871 men, 1170 women	**Faculty:** 134; IIB, -$
Part-time: 27 men, 45 women	**Ph.D.s:** 87%
Graduate: 16 men, 45 women	**Student/Faculty:** 15 to 1
Year: semesters, summer session	**Tuition:** $26,972
Application Deadline: open	**Room & Board:** $7052
Freshman Class: 2024 applied, 1686 accepted, 545 enrolled	
SAT: recommended	**ACT:** 24 **VERY COMPETITIVE**

Saint Norbert College, founded in 1898, is a Catholic college in the Norbertine tradition of community offering bachelor's degrees in the arts, the sciences, and business administration. There are 3 graduate schools. The library contains 230,595 volumes, 30,464 microform items, and 7345 audio/video tapes/CDs/DVDs, and subscribes to 66,471 periodicals including electronic. Computerized library services include database searching, Internet access, and laptop Internet portals. Special learning facilities include a learning resource center, art gallery, radio station, TV station, language labs, media center with satellite hookup, observatory, 3 theaters, environmental sciences research craft, and international center. The 93-acre campus is in a suburban area 5 miles south of Green Bay. Including any residence halls, there are 41 buildings.

Programs of Study: St. Norbert confers B.A., B.S., B.B.A., and B.Mus. degrees. Master's degrees are also awarded. Bachelor's degrees are awarded in BIOLOGICAL SCIENCE (biology/biological science), BUSINESS (accounting, business administration and management, and international business management), COMMUNICATIONS AND THE ARTS (art, communications, dramatic arts, English, French, German, graphic design, music, and Spanish), COMPUTER AND PHYSICAL SCIENCE (chemistry, computer science, geology, mathematics, natural sciences, and physics), EDUCATION (elementary education and music education), ENGINEERING AND ENVIRONMENTAL DESIGN (commercial art and environmental science), SOCIAL SCIENCE (economics, history, humanities, international relations, philosophy, political science/government, psychology, religion, and sociology). Business administration, communications, and elementary education are the largest.

Special: A partnership program with Bellin College Nursing, cross-registration in Arabic courses with the University of Wisconsin-Green Bay, internships, study abroad in more than 31 countries, a Washington semester, and work-study programs are available. The college offers dual and student-designed majors, B.A.-B.S. degrees, nondegree study, and limited credit for military experience and work training. The Leadership and Service Program and leadership minor help students improve their leadership abilities through courses and activities. A 3-2 engineering degree is available with Michigan Tech University. There are 10 national honor societies and a freshman honors program.

Admissions: 83% of the 2009-2010 applicants were accepted. The ACT scores were 14% below 21, 33% between 21 and 23, 29% between 24 and 26, 11% between 27 and 28, and 12% above 28. 44% of the current freshmen were in the top fifth of their class; 77% were in the top two fifths. 12 freshmen graduated first in their class.

Requirements: The ACT is required; the SAT is recommended. In addition, admissions requirements are either graduation from an accredited secondary school with 16 units recommended, including 4 English, 3 math, 3 lab sciences, 2 foreign language 2 social studies, and 2 history, or a GED recommended score in the 55% range. AP and CLEP credits are accepted. Important factors in the admissions decision are advanced placement or honors courses, extracurricular activities record, and recommendations by school officials.

Procedure: Freshmen are admitted to all sessions. Entrance exams should be taken by the end of the junior year. There are early decision, deferred admissions and rolling admissions plans. Application deadlines are open. The application fee is $25. Notification of early decision is sent December 15; regular decision, sent on a rolling basis. Applications are accepted on-line.

Financial Aid: In a recent year, 90% of all full-time freshmen and 97% of continuing full-time students received some form of financial aid. 62% of all full-time freshmen and 64% of continuing full-time students received need-based aid. The average freshman award was $18,299. Need-based scholarships or need-based grants averaged $10,274; need-based self-help aid (loans and jobs) averaged $6127; and other non-need-based awards and non-need-based scholarships averaged $1898. 51% of undergraduate students worked part-time. Average annual earnings from campus work were $1334. The FAFSA is required. The priority date for freshman financial aid applications for fall entry is March 1.

Computers: Wireless access is available. St. Norbert provides access to the Internet from all residence hall rooms, classrooms, offices, and labs. The college has 271 PCs and Macs for student use in public labs, the library, and the campus center. Wireless computing is available in the library and campus center, as well as several instructional areas. All students may access the system during the semester as needed or as required by the instructor. There are no time limits and no fees.

SAINT OLAF COLLEGE
Northfield, MN 55057-1098

(507) 646-3025
(800) 800-3025; (507) 646-3832

Full-time: 1352 men, 1676 women	**Faculty:** 207; IIB, av$
Part-time: 32 men, 39 women	**Ph.D.s:** 90%
Graduate: none	**Student/Faculty:** 15 to 1
Year: 4-1-4, summer session	**Tuition:** $35,500
Application Deadline: January 15	**Room & Board:** $8200
Freshman Class: 3882 applied, 2230 accepted, 778 enrolled	
SAT CR/M: 660/640	**ACT:** 29 **HIGHLY COMPETITIVE+**

St. Olaf College, founded in 1874, is a private liberal arts institution affiliated with the Evangelical Lutheran Church in America. There is one undergraduate school. In addition to regional accreditation, St. Olaf has baccalaureate program accreditation with CSWE, NASM, and NCATE. The 4 libraries contain 751,464 volumes, 13,115 microform items, and 26,366 audio/video tapes/CDs/DVDs, and subscribe to 4,610 periodicals including electronic. Computerized library services include interlibrary loans, database searching, Internet access, and laptop Internet portals. Special learning facilities include a learning resource center, art gallery, radio station, TV station, and 700 acres of land dedicated to natural habitat, sustainable agriculture, and conventional agriculture. The 300-acre campus is in a small town 35 miles south of Minneapolis/St. Paul. Including any residence halls, there are 55 buildings.

Programs of Study: St. Olaf confers B.A., B.Mus. degrees. Bachelor's degrees are awarded in AGRICULTURE (environmental studies), BIOLOGICAL SCIENCE (biology/biological science), COMMUNICATIONS AND THE ARTS (art, art history and appreciation, classics, dance, dramatic arts, English, French,

German, Greek, Latin, music, music performance, music theory and composition, Norwegian, Russian, Spanish, and studio art), COMPUTER AND PHYSICAL SCIENCE (chemistry, computer science, mathematics, and physics), EDUCATION (music education and social studies education), HEALTH PROFESSIONS (exercise science and nursing), SOCIAL SCIENCE (American studies, Asian/American studies, classical/ancient civilization, economics, ethnic studies, Hispanic American studies, history, interdisciplinary studies, medieval studies, philosophy, political science/government, psychology, religion, religious music, Russian and Slavic studies, social work, sociology, and women's studies). English, biology, and mathematics are the largest.

Special: St. Olaf offers cross-registration with Carleton College, study abroad in 42 countries, a Washington semester, preprofessional programs, internships, and a 3-2 B.A.-B.S.E. degree in engineering with Washington University in St. Louis or the University of Minnesota. There are dual majors, nondegree study, on campus work study, and pass/fail options. The Center for Integrative Studies allows students to design individual majors with an emphasis on tutorials and seminars. There are 18 national honor societies, including Phi Beta Kappa.

Admissions: 57% of the 2009-2010 applicants were accepted. The SAT scores for the 2009-2010 freshman class were: Critical Reading--4% below 500, 18% between 500 and 599, 50% between 600 and 700, and 28% above 700; Math--3% below 500, 21% between 500 and 599, 55% between 600 and 700, and 21% above 700. The ACT scores were 6% between 21 and 23, 15% between 24 and 26, 20% between 27 and 28, and 58% above 28. 75% of the current freshmen were in the top fifth of their class; 95% were in the top two fifths. There were 37 National Merit finalists. 65 freshmen graduated first in their class.

Requirements: The SAT or ACT is required. In addition, it is recommended that applicants completed 4 years of English, 4 of math and social studies/history, 4 of science (2 labs), and 4 years of a foreign language. AP credits are accepted.

Procedure: Freshmen are admitted fall, winter, and spring. Entrance exams should be taken in the spring of the junior year or the fall of the senior year. There are early decision, early admissions and deferred admissions plans. Early decision applications should be filed by November 16; regular applications, by January 15 for fall entry. Notification of early decision is sent December 15; regular decision, March 19. Applications are accepted on-line. 759 applicants were on a recent waiting list, 18 were accepted.

Financial Aid: In 2009-2010, 85% of all full-time freshmen and 89% of continuing full-time students received some form of financial aid. 65% of all full-time freshmen and 65% of continuing full-time students received need-based aid. 70% of undergraduate students work part-time. Average annual earnings from campus work are $1100. The average financial indebtedness of the 2009 graduate was $24,125. St. Olaf is a member of CSS. The CSS/Profile or FAFSA, and St. Olaf noncustodial parent's statement are required. The priority date for freshman aid financial aid applications for fall entry is December 1. The deadline for filing freshman financial aid applications for fall entry is February 1.

Computers: St. Olaf students may access the college network, the Internet, and Internet 2 (a high-speed research network) from more than 900 student-accessible computers or from their own PCs in residence hall rooms. Students can also connect laptops to the campus wireless network at most locations on campus, including all residence halls, the library, student commons, and academic buildings. All students may access the system. There are no time limits and no fees.

Latrobe, PA 15650

(724) 537-4540
(800) SVC-5549; (724) 532-5069

Full-time: 800 men, 800 women	**Faculty:** IIB, -$
Part-time: 50 men, 50 women	**Ph.D.s:** n/av
Graduate: 90 men, 130 women	**Student/Faculty:** 18 to 1
Year: semesters, summer session	**Tuition:** $25,350
Application Deadline: see profile	**Room & Board:** $8082
Freshman Class: n/av	
SAT or ACT: required	**VERY COMPETITIVE**

Saint Vincent College, founded in 1846, is a private Catholic college of liberal arts and sciences sponsored by the Benedictine monks. There are 4 undergraduate schools and 3 graduate schools. Enrollment figures in the above capsule and figures in this profile are approximate. In addition to regional accreditation, Saint Vincent has baccalaureate program accreditation with ACBSP. The library contains 278,561 volumes, 91,144 microform items, and 5482 audio/video tapes/CDs/DVDs, and subscribes to 2500 periodicals including electronic. Computerized library services include interlibrary loans, database searching, and Internet access. Special learning facilities include a learning resource center, art gallery, planetarium, radio station, TV station, observatory, radio telescope, and small-business development center. The 200-acre campus is in a suburban area 35 miles east of Pittsburgh. Including any residence halls, there are 22 buildings.

Programs of Study: Saint Vincent confers B.A. and B.S. degrees. Master's degrees are also awarded. Bachelor's degrees are awarded in BIOLOGICAL SCIENCE (biochemistry, bioinformatics, and biology/biological science), BUSINESS (accounting, banking and finance, business administration and management, international business management, and marketing/retailing/merchandising), COMMUNICATIONS AND THE ARTS (art, art history and appreciation, arts administration/management, communications, English, fine arts, French, music, music performance, Spanish, studio art, and visual and performing arts), COMPUTER AND PHYSICAL SCIENCE (chemistry, computer science, information sciences and systems, mathematics, and physics), EDUCATION (art education, business education, elementary education, psychology education, and science education), ENGINEERING AND ENVIRONMENTAL DESIGN (environmental science), HEALTH PROFESSIONS (occupational therapy, physical therapy, physician's assistant, predentistry, premedicine, prepharmacy, and preveterinary science), SOCIAL SCIENCE (anthropology, economics, history, liberal arts/general studies, philosophy, political science/government, prelaw, psychology, public affairs, religious education, sociology, and theological studies). Biology, economics, and psychology are the strongest academically. Biology, psychology, and history are the largest.

Special: There is cross-registration with Seton Hill University, co-op programs, internships, study abroad in Europe and Asia, a Washington semester, a work-study program, dual majors, a general studies degree, credit by exam and for life/military/work experience, nondegree study, and pass/fail options. There is an accelerated degree engineering program and a 3-2 engineering option with Boston University, Pennsylvania state universities, the University of Pittsburgh, and the Catholic University of America. The college offers teacher certificate programs in early childhood, elementary, and secondary education. There are 11 national honor societies, a freshman honors program, and 100 departmental honors programs.

Requirements: The SAT or ACT is required. In addition, applicants must complete 15 academic credits, including 4 of English, 3 each of social studies and math, 2 of foreign language, and 1 of a lab science. Art students must submit a portfolio, and music and theater students must audition. An essay is required. A GED is accepted. A GPA of 3.2 is required. AP and CLEP credits are accepted. Important factors in the admissions decision are advanced placement or honors courses, evidence of special talent, and recommendations by school officials.

Procedure: Freshmen are admitted fall and spring. Entrance exams should be taken at the end of the junior year or the beginning of the senior year. There are early admissions, deferred admissions, and rolling admissions plans. Check with the school for current application deadlines. The application fee is $25. Applications are accepted on-line. 213 applicants were on a recent waiting list, 54 were accepted.

Financial Aid: In a recent year, 97% of all full-time freshmen and 93% of continuing full-time students received some form of financial aid. 79% of all full-time freshmen and 74% of continuing full-time students received need-based aid. The average freshmen award was $19,319, with $5533 ($15,500 maximum) from need-based scholarships or need-based grants; $3787 ($7800 maximum) from need-based self-help aid (loans and jobs); and $8890 ($31,356 maximum) from other non-need-based awards and non-need-based scholarships. 44% of undergraduate students work part-time. Average annual earnings from campus work are $1895. The average financial indebtedness of a recent graduate was $20,548. The FAFSA is required. Check with the school for current deadlines.

Computers: Wireless access is available. There are 286 public PCs in many locations on campus, network connections in all residence hall rooms, and wireless access in many campus locations, including the student center. All students may access the system during computer lab hours and 24 hours from dorm rooms. There are no time limits and no fees.

SALEM COLLEGE
Winston-Salem, NC 27101 (336) 721-2621
(800) 327-2536; (336) 917-5572

Full-time: 10 men, 695 women	**Faculty:** IIB, --$
Part-time: 15 men, 155 women	**Ph.D.s:** n/av
Graduate: 15 men, 225 women	**Student/Faculty:** n/av
Year: 4-1-4, summer session	**Tuition:** $21,600
Application Deadline: open	**Room & Board:** $11,500
Freshman Class: n/av	
ACT: required	**SAT:** required

VERY COMPETITIVE

Salem College was begun as a school for girls in 1772 by the Moravians, an early Protestant denomination. Today the private college, which retains a historical relationship with the church, offers a liberal arts education primarily for women. Figures in the above capsule are approximate. There is 1 graduate school. In addition to regional accreditation, Salem has baccalaureate program accreditation with NASM and NCATE. The 2 libraries contain 135,000 volumes, 302,534 microform items, and 13,553 audio/video tapes/CDs/DVDs, and subscribe to 15,000 periodicals including electronic. Computerized library services include interlibrary loans and database searching. Special learning facilities include a learning resource center, art gallery, radio station, and learning lab (computer lab with multimedia capability). The 64-acre campus is in an urban area in the center of

Old Salem, a restored 18th-century village. Including any residence halls, there are 17 buildings.

Programs of Study: Salem confers B.A., B.S., B.M., and B.S.B.A. degrees. Master's degrees are also awarded. Bachelor's degrees are awarded in BIOLOGICAL SCIENCE (biology/biological science), BUSINESS (accounting, business administration and management, and international business management), COMMUNICATIONS AND THE ARTS (art history and appreciation, arts administration/management, communications, English, French, German, music, Spanish, and studio art), COMPUTER AND PHYSICAL SCIENCE (chemistry and mathematics), ENGINEERING AND ENVIRONMENTAL DESIGN (interior design), HEALTH PROFESSIONS (medical laboratory technology), SOCIAL SCIENCE (American studies, economics, history, international relations, philosophy, psychology, religion, and sociology). Sociology, business, and communication are the largest.

Special: Salem offers an extensive internship program in all majors, cross-registration with Wake Forest University, and study abroad at various locations, including a summer program in Oxford, England. A Washington semester, student-designed and interdisciplinary majors, B.A.-B.S. degrees, nondegree study, and pass/fail options during the January term are available. A 3-2 engineering degree is available with Duke and Vanderbilt Universities. Students may participate in a model U.N. program directed by Drew University in Madison, New Jersey. Interdisciplinary majors are offered in American studies, arts management, and international relations. There are 9 national honor societies and a freshman honors program.

Requirements: The SAT or ACT is required. In addition, graduation from an accredited secondary school or the GED is required. Students must have 12 academic credits plus electives, including 4 years of high school English, 3 each of math and science, and 2 each of a foreign language and history. An essay is required for all students. Music students must audition. A GPA of 2.0 is also required. AP and CLEP credits are accepted. Important factors in the admissions decision are advanced placement or honors courses, leadership record, and evidence of special talent.

Procedure: Freshmen are admitted fall and spring. Entrance exams should be taken by January of the senior year. There are early admissions, deferred admissions, and rolling admissions plans. Application deadlines are open. The fall 2008 application fee was $30. Applications are accepted on-line.

Financial Aid: The FAFSA and the college's own financial statement are required. Check with the school for current application deadlines.

Computers: Wireless access is available in various locations on campus; computers are available in 2 labs and in the library. All residence hall rooms and classrooms have Internet access ports. All students may access the system 24 hours a day. There are no time limits and no fees.

SALVE REGINA UNIVERSITY

Newport, RI 02840-4192

(401) 341-2908
(888) GO-SALVE; (401) 848-2823

Full-time: 605 men, 1284 women	**Faculty:** 117; IIA, av$
Part-time: 17 men, 78 women	**Ph.D.s:** 78%
Graduate: 267 men, 327 women	**Student/Faculty:** 16 to 1
Year: semesters, summer session	**Tuition:** $30,000
Application Deadline: February 2	**Room & Board:** $10,950
Freshman Class: 5264 applied, 3385 accepted, 504 enrolled	
SAT CR/M/W: 540/550/540	**ACT:** 23 **VERY COMPETITIVE**

Salve Regina University, founded in 1934 and sponsored by the Sisters of Mercy, is an independent institution affiliated with the Roman Catholic Church. The university offers programs in liberal arts, business, health science, and professional training. There is 1 graduate school. In addition to regional accreditation, Salve has baccalaureate program accreditation with CSWE, NASAD, and NLN. The library contains 139,161 volumes, 43,146 microform items, and 19,420 audio/video tapes/CDs/DVDs, and subscribes to 1,041 periodicals including electronic. Computerized library services include interlibrary loans, database searching, Internet access, and laptop Internet portals. Special learning facilities include a learning resource center, art gallery, radio station, information systems and computer science labs. The 75-acre campus is in a suburban area on Newport's waterfront, 60 miles south of Boston. Including any residence halls, there are 50 buildings.

Programs of Study: Salve confers B.A., B.S., and B.A.S. degrees. Associate, master's, and doctoral degrees are also awarded. Bachelor's degrees are awarded in BIOLOGICAL SCIENCE (biology/biological science), BUSINESS (accounting, business administration and management, international business management, management science, and marketing and distribution), COMMUNICATIONS AND THE ARTS (art history and appreciation, communications, communications technology, dramatic arts, English, French, historic preservation, media arts, music, Spanish, and studio art), COMPUTER AND PHYSICAL SCIENCE (chemistry, information sciences and systems, and mathematics), EDUCATION (early childhood education, elementary education, secondary education, and special education), HEALTH PROFESSIONS (cytotechnology and nursing), SOCIAL SCIENCE (American studies, criminal justice, economics, history, international studies, philosophy, political science/government, psychology, religion, social work, and sociology). Psychology, social work, and accounting are the strongest academically. Business, administration of justice, and elementary education are the largest.

Special: Salve offers internships in most academic disciplines as well as work-study programs on campus. Study abroad in 18 countries, a Washington semester, B.A.-B.S. degrees in biology, business, and economics, dual majors in many programs, and accelerated degree programs in administration of justice, business, international relations, holistic counseling management, and rehabilitation counseling are available. A liberal studies degree, credit for life, military, and work experience, nondegree study, and pass/fail options are also offered. There are 15 national honor societies, a freshman honors program, and 10 departmental honors programs.

Admissions: 64% of the 2009-2010 applicants were accepted. The SAT scores for the 2009-2010 freshman class were: Critical Reading--22% below 500, 58% between 500 and 599, 20% between 600 and 700, and 2% above 700; Math--24%

below 500, 55% between 500 and 599, 21% between 6% above 700. The ACT scores were 6% below 21, 34% between 21 and 23, 42% between 24 and 26, 15% between 27 and 28, and 3% above 28. 48% of the current freshmen were in the top fifth of their class; 79% were in the top two fifths. 2 freshmen graduated first in their class.

Requirements: The SAT or ACT is required. In addition, applicants must be high school graduates or hold a GED. Students should have 16 Carnegie units, consisting of 4 each in English, 3 each in math including algebra and geometry, 2 each in science and foreign language, and 1 in history, and electives. An essay is required. A GPA of 2.7 is required. AP and CLEP credits are accepted. Important factors in the admissions decision are advanced placement or honors courses, recommendations by school officials, and leadership record.

Procedure: Freshmen are admitted fall and spring. Entrance exams should be taken as early as possible. There is a deferred admissions plan. Applications should be filed by February 2 for fall entry and December 15 for spring entry, along with a $50 fee. Notifications are sent April 1. 367 applicants were on the 2009 waiting list; 32 were admitted. Applications are accepted on-line. 367 applicants were on a recent waiting list, 32 were accepted.

Financial Aid: In 2009-2010, 87% of all full-time freshmen and 79% of continuing full-time students received some form of financial aid. 74% of all full-time freshmen and 65% of continuing full-time students received need-based aid. The average freshman award was $20,729. Need-based scholarships or need-based grants averaged $15,463 ($36,550 maximum); need-based self-help aid (loans and jobs) averaged $5,767; and other non-need based awards and non-need based scholarships averaged $6,573. 26% of undergraduate students work part-time. Average annual earnings from campus work are $891. Salve is a member of CSS. The CSS/Profile, FAFSA, and tax forms are required. The priority date for freshman financial aid applications for fall entry is March 1.

Computers: Wireless access is available. There are more than 1200 data connection points throughout the residence hall system; each resident student is provided a data connection point for Internet access. More than 130 general use computers are available in the university computer lab area and more than 45 general use computers are in the library for access to the Internet. Wireless access capabilities are present in various locations. All students may access the system 16 hours per day in labs and 24 hours per day by dial-in access to the Internet. There are no time limits and no fees. All students are required to have a personal computer. An HP Compaq nc6400 Notebook is provided through the university.

SAMFORD UNIVERSITY
Birmingham, AL 35229

(205) 726-2273
(800) 888-7218; (205) 726-2171

Full-time: 985 men, 1717 women	**Faculty:** 192
Part-time: 70 men, 136 women	**Ph.D.s:** 84%
Graduate: 822 men, 928 women	**Student/Faculty:** 12 to 1
Year: 4-1-4, summer session	**Tuition:** $20,220
Application Deadline: n/av	**Room & Board:** $6,624
Freshman Class: 2288 applied, 1911 accepted, 733 enrolled	
SAT CR/M: 580/570	**ACT:** 25 **VERY COMPETITIVE**

Samford University, founded in 1841, is a private, liberal arts institution that maintains a close relationship with the Alabama Baptist Convention. There are 5 undergraduate schools and 8 graduate schools. In addition to regional accreditation, Samford has baccalaureate program accreditation with AACSB, FIDER,

NASM, and NCATE. The 6 libraries contain 447,861 volumes, 1.3 million microform items, 11,408 audio/video tapes/CDs/DVDs, and subscribe to 202,238 periodicals including electronic. Computerized library services include interlibrary loans, database searching, Internet access, and laptop Internet portals. Special learning facilities include a learning resource center, art gallery, planetarium, radio station, TV station, a global center, drug information center, and a conservatory. The 180-acre campus is in a suburban area 4 miles south of Birmingham, AL. Including any residence halls, there are 64 buildings.

Programs of Study: Samford confers B.A., B.S., B.A.F., B.B.A., B.B.F., B.E.F., B.F.A., B.G.S., B.M., B.M.E., B.M.F., B.N.F., B.S.E., B.S.F., B.S.I., and B.S.N. degrees. Associates, master's, and doctoral degrees are also awarded. Bachelor's degrees are awarded in BIOLOGICAL SCIENCE (biochemistry, biology/biological science, marine science, and nutrition), BUSINESS (accounting and human resources), COMMUNICATIONS AND THE ARTS (art, classics, communications, English, English literature, French, German, graphic design, Greek, journalism, language arts, Latin, music, music performance, music theory and composition, musical theater, piano/organ, Spanish, and voice), COMPUTER AND PHYSICAL SCIENCE (chemistry, computer science, environmental geology, mathematics, physics, and science), EDUCATION (athletic training, early childhood education, education, elementary education, music education, physical education, and secondary education), ENGINEERING AND ENVIRONMENTAL DESIGN (engineering physics, environmental science, and interior design), HEALTH PROFESSIONS (exercise science, health, nursing, and sports medicine), SOCIAL SCIENCE (Asian/Oriental studies, community services, counseling/psychology, family/consumer studies, geography, history, international relations, Latin American studies, liberal arts/general studies, philosophy, political science/government, psychology, public administration, religion, religious music, social science, and sociology). Teacher education, business, and nursing are the strongest academically. Law, pharmacy, and nursing are the largest.

Special: A 3-2 engineering degree is available with Auburn, Mercer and the University of Alabama. The School of Arts and Sciences offers an interdisciplinary core curriculum with team teaching. Cross-registration with Birmingham-Southern College, the University of Alabama at Birmingham, the University of Montevallo, and Miles College, are available to students. Study abroad programs are offered in England and 8 other countries, additional major options, internships, credit for life experience, and pass/fail options are also offered. Accelerated degree programs are possible in some majors. There are a freshman honors program.

Admissions: 84% of the 2009-2010 applicants were accepted. The SAT scores for the 2009-2010 freshman class were: Critical Reading--14% below 500, 42% between 500 and 599, 35% between 600 and 700, and 9% above 700; Math--19% below 500, 38% between 500 and 599, 35% between 600 and 700, and 8% above 700. The ACT scores were 6% below 21, 24% between 21 and 23, 25% between 24 and 26, 15% between 27 and 28, and 29% above 28. 61% of the current freshmen were in the top fifth of their class; 84% were in the top two fifths. There were 15 National Merit finalists. 34 freshmen graduated first in their class.

Requirements: The SAT or ACT is required. In addition, applicants need 18 academic credits and 16 Carnegie units, including 4 in English, 3 each in math and science, and 2 each in social studies and history. In addition, 2 units in foreign language are recommended. An essay is required and an interview suggested. The GED is accepted. AP and CLEP credits are accepted. Important factors in the admissions decision are advanced placement or honors courses, leadership record, and recommendations by school officials.

Procedure: Freshmen are admitted fall, spring, and summer. Entrance exams should be taken in the junior year. There are early admissions, deferred admissions, and rolling admissions plans. Application deadlines are open. The fall 2008 application fee was $35. Applications are accepted on-line.

Financial Aid: In 2009-2010, 47% of all full-time freshmen and 42% of continuing full-time students received some form of financial aid. 44% of all full-time freshmen and 38% of continuing full-time students received need-based aid. 49% of undergraduate students work part-time. Average annual earnings from campus work are $1600. The average financial indebtedness of the 2009 graduate was $18,700. The FAFSA and the state aid form, and International Student's Certification of Finances are required. The priority date for freshman financial aid applications for fall entry is March 1.

Computers: Wireless access is available. There are 6 computer labs available for general academic and student use. Near the semester's end, hours of operation may be extended. PCs include Dell and Power Mac. There is a voice/data connection for every resident student. All students may access the system. There are no time limits and no fees.

SAN DIEGO STATE UNIVERSITY
San Diego, CA 92182-7455   **(619) 594-6336; (619) 594-1250**

Full-time: 9961 men, 13303 women	**Faculty:** IIA, +$
Part-time: 1813 men, 2460 women	**Ph.D.s:** n/av
Graduate: 2523 men, 3730 women	**Student/Faculty:** 22 to 1
Year: semesters, summer session	**Tuition:** $16062
Application Deadline: November 30	**Room & Board:** n/a
Freshman Class: 41986 applied, 15273 accepted, 1801 enrolled	
SAT CR/M: 520/540*	**ACT:** 22 **VERY COMPETITIVE**

San Diego State University, founded in 1897, is a public liberal arts university that is part of the California State University system. There are 8 undergraduate schools. In addition to regional accreditation, SDSU has baccalaureate program accreditation with AACSB, ABET, ACEJMC, ADA, ASLA, CSWE, FIDER, NASAD, NASM, NCATE, NLN, and NRPA. The library contains 1.7 million volumes, 4.5 million microform items, and 16,447 audio/video tapes/CDs/DVDs, and subscribes to 43,743 periodicals including electronic. Computerized library services include interlibrary loans and database searching. Special learning facilities include a learning resource center, art gallery, planetarium, radio station, TV station, a theater, and a recital hall. The 282-acre campus is in an urban area 8 miles east of downtown San Diego. Including any residence halls, there are 56 buildings.

Programs of Study: SDSU confers B.A., B.S., and B.M. degrees. Master's and doctoral degrees are also awarded. Bachelor's degrees are awarded in AGRICULTURE (agricultural business management and environmental studies), BIOLOGICAL SCIENCE (biology/biological science, microbiology, and nutrition), BUSINESS (accounting, banking and finance, business administration and management, hospitality management services, international business management, marketing/retailing/merchandising, and real estate), COMMUNICATIONS AND THE ARTS (advertising, art, art history and appreciation, broadcasting, classics, communications, comparative literature, dance, dramatic arts, English, film arts, fine arts, French, German, graphic design, Japanese, journalism, linguistics, multimedia, music, music performance, public relations, radio/television technology, Russian, Spanish, and studio art), COMPUTER AND PHYSICAL SCIENCE (applied mathematics, astronomy, chemical physics, chemistry, computer science, geology, information sciences and systems, mathematics, physical sciences, physics, and statistics), EDUCATION (music education, physical education, and vocational education), ENGINEERING AND ENVIRONMENTAL DESIGN (aeronautical engineering, civil engineering, computer engineering, construction engineering, electrical/electronics engineering, environmental engineering, interior design, and mechanical engineering), HEALTH PROFESSIONS (exercise science, health science, nursing, and speech pathology/audiology), SOCIAL SCIENCE (African American studies, American studies, anthropology, Asian/Oriental studies, child psychology/development, criminal justice, dietetics, economics, European studies, geography, gerontology, history, humanities, interdisciplinary studies, Judaic studies, Latin American studies, liberal arts/general studies, Mexican-American/Chicano studies, parks and recreation management, peace studies, philosophy, political science/government, psychology, public administration, religion, Russian and Slavic studies, social science, social work, sociology, urban studies, and women's studies). Business administration is the strongest academically and the largest.

Special: Students may study abroad in London and Paris and receive credit for life, military, and work experience. Cross-registration with the University of California, community colleges, and California State University, internships, dual majors, an interdisciplinary major, a political science internship in Sacramento or Washington, D.C., an off-campus public administration program, and a prelaw program in cooperation with California Western School of Law are available. There are 30 national honor societies, including Phi Beta Kappa, a freshman honors program, and 24 departmental honors programs.

Admissions: 36% of the 2009-2010 applicants were accepted. The SAT scores for the 2009-2010 freshman class were: Critical Reading--43% below 500, 41% between 500 and 599, 15% between 600 and 700, and 1% above 700; Math--37% below 500, 38% between 500 and 599, 23% between 600 and 700, and 2% above 700. The ACT scores were 14% below 21, 51% between 21 and 23, 34% between 24 and 26, % between 27 and 28, and 1% above 28.

Requirements: The SAT or ACT is required. In addition, applicants must have a qualifying CSU eligibility index, based on a combination of GPA and standardized test scores. Candidates for admission should have completed 4 years of English, 3 of math, 2 each of science and a foreign language, and 1 each of social studies, U.S. history, and visual and performing arts, and 1 of electives. A GPA of 2.5 is required.

Procedure: Freshmen are admitted fall and spring. Entrance exams should be taken by October of the senior year. Applications should be filed by November 30 for fall entry; August 31 for spring entry. The fall 2009 application fee was $55. Notifications are sent in March. Applications are accepted on-line.

Financial Aid: In 2009-2010, 42% of all full-time freshmen and 48% of continuing full-time students received some form of financial aid. 39% of all full-time freshmen and 45% of continuing full-time students received need-based aid. The average freshman award was $7,500. Need-based scholarships or need-based grants averaged $6,100 ; need-based self-help aid (loans and jobs) averaged $2,400; non-need-based athletic scholarships averaged $11,200; and other non-need-based awards and non-need-based scholarships averaged $2,100. The average financial indebtedness of the 2009 graduate was $14,500. SDSU is a member of CSS. The FAFSA and the state aid form are required. Check with the school for current application deadlines.

Computers: All students may access the system. There are no time limits and no fees.

SAN FRANCISCO STATE UNIVERSITY

San Francisco, CA 94132   (415) 338-2355; (415) 338-0903

Full-time: 8079 men, 11798 women	**Faculty:** IIA, +$
Part-time: 2263 men, 2861 women	**Ph.D.s:** 39%
Graduate: 1938 men, 3530 women	**Student/Faculty:** n/av
Year: semesters, summer session	**Tuition:** $4740 ($15,900)
Application Deadline: November 30	**Room & Board:** $10,904
Freshman Class: 28218 applied, 20465 accepted, 4032 enrolled	
SAT or ACT: recommended	**COMPETITIVE**

San Francisco State University, founded in 1899, is a public liberal arts institution offering graduate and undergraduate programs as part of the California State University system. There are 8 undergraduate schools and 8 graduate schools. In addition to regional accreditation, San Francisco State, SF State has baccalaureate program accreditation with AACSB, ACEJMC, ADA, AHEA, NASM, and NLN. The library contains 242,887 volumes, 2.6 million microform items, and 194,956 audio/video tapes/CDs/DVDs, and subscribes to 20,796 periodicals including electronic. Computerized library services include interlibrary loans, database searching, and Internet access. Special learning facilities include a learning resource center, art gallery, natural history museum, planetarium, radio station, TV station, a field campus, the Labor Archives and Research Center, a Media Access Center, and an anthropology museum. The 142-acre campus is in an urban area in San Francisco. Including any residence halls, there are 23 buildings.

Programs of Study: San Francisco State, SF State confers B.A., B.S., B.M. degrees. Master's and doctoral degrees are also awarded. Bachelor's degrees are awarded in AGRICULTURE (environmental studies and natural resource management), BIOLOGICAL SCIENCE (biochemistry, biology/biological science, botany, cell biology, ecology, marine biology, microbiology, physiology, and zoology), BUSINESS (accounting, banking and finance, business administration and management, electronic business, entrepreneurial studies, hospitality management services, hotel/motel and restaurant management, institutional management, international business management, labor studies, management science, marketing/retailing/merchandising, personnel management, and recreational facilities management), COMMUNICATIONS AND THE ARTS (apparel design, art, broadcasting, Chinese, classics, communications, comparative literature, creative writing, dance, design, dramatic arts, English, film arts, French, German, Italian, Japanese, journalism, languages, music, radio/television technology, Spanish, speech/debate/rhetoric, and visual design), COMPUTER AND PHYSICAL SCIENCE (applied mathematics, astronomy, astrophysics, atmospheric sciences and meteorology, chemistry, computer science, earth science, geology, information sciences and systems, mathematics, physics, and statistics), EDUCATION (elementary education, home economics education, industrial arts education, physical education, and recreation education), ENGINEERING AND ENVIRONMENTAL DESIGN (civil engineering, computer engineering, electrical/electronics engineering, industrial administration/management, industrial engineering technology, interior design, and mechanical engineering), HEALTH PROFESSIONS (clinical science, exercise science, health science, nursing, and speech pathology/audiology), SOCIAL SCIENCE (African studies, American studies, anthropology, Asian/American studies, clothing and textiles management/production/services, consumer services, criminal justice, dietetics, economics, family/consumer studies, geography, history, humanities, humanities and social science, interdisciplinary studies, international relations, Judaic studies, liberal arts/general studies, philosophy, political science/government, psychology, religion, social work, sociology, urban studies, and women's studies.

Special: Students may cross-register with the California College of Podiatric Medicine, the City College of San Francisco, Cogswell College of Engineering, and several other area universities. Study abroad in 23 countries, a Washington semester, campus work-study, a general studies degree, dual and student-designed majors, credit for life experience, nondegree study, and pass/fail options are also offered. There is a chapter of Phi Beta Kappa, a freshman honors program, and 1 departmental honors program.

Admissions: 73% of the 2009-2010 applicants were accepted.

Requirements: applicants should be graduates of an accredited secondary school with a minimum GPA of 2.0. The GED is accepted. The SAT or ACT are recommended. High school courses should include 4 years of English, 3 of math, 2 of foreign language, and 1 each of U.S. history or government, lab science, and visual and performing arts. A GPA of 2.0 is required. AP and CLEP credits are accepted.

Procedure: Freshmen are admitted fall and spring. There is a rolling admissions plan. Applications should be filed by November 30 for fall entry, along with a $55 fee. Notification is sent on a rolling basis. Applications are accepted on-line.

Financial Aid: San Francisco State is a member of CSS. The CSS/Profile and FFS are required. Check with the school for current application deadlines.

Computers: Wireless access is available. Campus-wide wireless connection requires SF State e-mail and password for log in. All students may access the syste 24 hours daily. There are no time limits and no fees. It is strongly recommended that all students have a personal computer.

SAN JOSE STATE UNIVERSITY
San Jose, CA 95192   (408) 924-2000; (408) 924-2050

Full-time: 7000 men, 7600 women	**Faculty:** IIA, +$
Part-time: 3450 men, 3400 women	**Ph.D.s:** 84%
Graduate: 2000 men, 3550 women	**Student/Faculty:** n/av
Year: semesters, summer session	**Tuition:** $4000 ($11,000)
Application Deadline: April 1	**Room & Board:** $9000
Freshman Class: n/av	
SAT or ACT: required	**COMPETITIVE**

San Jose State University, founded in 1857 and part of the California State University system, is a public institution offering undergraduate and graduate programs in applied arts and science, social science, and social work to a primarily commuter student body. There are 8 undergraduate schools and 8 graduate schools. In addition to regional accreditation, SJSU has baccalaureate program accreditation with AACSB, ABET, ACEJMC, ADA, ASLA, NASAD, NASM, NCATE, and NLN. The 2 libraries contain 1.1 million volumes, 1.6 million microform items, and 37,146 audio/video tapes/CDs/DVDs, and subscribe to 2,504 periodicals including electronic. Computerized library services include interlibrary loans and database searching. Special learning facilities include a learning resource center, art gallery, radio station, and TV station. The 104-acre campus is in an urban area in the center of San Jose. Including any residence halls, there are 55 buildings.

Programs of Study: SJSU confers B.A., B.S., B.F.A., and B.Mus. degrees. Master's degrees are also awarded. Bachelor's degrees are awarded in BIOLOGICAL SCIENCE (biochemistry, biology/biological science, botany, microbiology, and zoology), BUSINESS (accounting, banking and finance, business administration and management, international business management, and marketing/retailing/merchandising), COMMUNICATIONS AND THE ARTS (advertising, broadcasting, dance, design, dramatic arts, English, film arts, fine arts, French, German, journalism, music, Spanish, and speech/debate/rhetoric), COMPUTER AND PHYSICAL SCIENCE (chemistry, computer science, geology, mathematics, physics, and statistics), EDUCATION (early childhood education and teaching English as a second/foreign language (TESOL/TEFOL)), ENGINEERING AND ENVIRONMENTAL DESIGN (aeronautical engineering, chemical engineering, civil engineering, computer engineering, electrical/electronics engineering, engineering, industrial engineering, interior design, materials engineering, and mechanical engineering), HEALTH PROFESSIONS (nursing, occupational therapy, and speech pathology/audiology), SOCIAL SCIENCE (anthropology, criminal justice, economics, food science, geography, history, philosophy, political science/government, psychology, religion, social science, social work, and sociology). Accounting is the strongest academically. Accounting, electrical engineering, and management are the largest.

Special: SJSU has opportunities for cooperative programs in business, science, engineering, arts, and the humanities, work-study with many employers, internships (some required, some optional), study abroad in 16 countries, field experiences, and student teaching. An accelerated program is offered in nursing, and the B.A.-B.S. degree and dual majors are available in various areas of study. A general studies degree, student-designed majors, nondegree study, and credit/no-credit options are possible. There are 3 national honor societies and 18 departmental honors programs.

Requirements: The SAT or ACT is required. Scores are used to calculate an eligibility index rating, which determines qualification for admission. Graduation from an accredited secondary school is required; the GED is accepted. Applicants must have completed 4 years of English, 3 each of math and electives, 2 of a foreign language, and 1 each of history, science, and art. AP and CLEP credits are accepted. Important factors in the admissions decision are personality/intangible qualities, recommendations by alumni, and recommendations by school officials.

Procedure: Freshmen are admitted fall and spring. Entrance exams should be taken prior to the fall semester. There are early admissions, deferred admissions, and rolling admissions plans. Application deadlines are open. The fall 2008 application fee was $55.

Financial Aid: SJSU is a member of CSS. The FAFSA is required. Check with the school for current application deadlines.

Computers: All students may access the system 9 A.M. to 8 P.M. Monday through Friday and 9 A.M. to 5 P.M. Saturday. There are no time limits and no fees.

SANTA CLARA UNIVERSITY
Santa Clara, CA 95053   (408) 554-4700; (408) 554-5255

Full-time: 2375 men, 2810 women	**Faculty:** IIA, ++$
Part-time: 55 men, 45 women	**Ph.D.s:** n/av
Graduate: 1960 men, 1475 women	**Student/Faculty:** n/av
Year: trimesters, summer session	**Tuition:** $35,000
Application Deadline: January 7	**Room & Board:** $12,000
Freshman Class: n/av	
SAT or ACT: required	**HIGHLY COMPETITIVE**

Santa Clara University, founded in 1851 by Jesuit priests, is a private institution offering undergraduate and graduate degrees in arts and sciences, engineering, business law, education, and counseling. The figures given in the above capsule and in this profile are approximate. There are 3 undergraduate schools and 5 graduate schools. In addition to regional accreditation, has baccalaureate program accreditation with AACSB and ABET. The 2 libraries contain 970,803 volumes, 2 million microform items, and 15,497 audio/video tapes/CDs/DVDs, and subscribe to 8,795 periodicals including electronic. Computerized library services include interlibrary loans, database searching, Internet access, and laptop Internet portals. Special learning facilities include a learning resource center, art gallery, planetarium, radio station, TV station, and a California Mission (archeology lab). The 106-acre campus is in a suburban area 46 miles south of San Francisco. Including any residence halls, there are 49 buildings.

Programs of Study: Santa Clara confers B.A., B.S., and B.S.C. degrees. Master's and doctoral degrees are also awarded. Bachelor's degrees are awarded in AGRICULTURE (environmental studies), BIOLOGICAL SCIENCE (biochemistry and biology/biological science), BUSINESS (accounting, banking and finance, business administration and management, business economics, management information systems, and marketing/retailing/merchandising), COMMUNICATIONS AND THE ARTS (art history and appreciation, classical languages, classics, communications, dramatic arts, English, French, German, Greek, Italian, music, Spanish, and studio art), COMPUTER AND PHYSICAL SCIENCE (chemistry, computer science, information sciences and systems, mathematics, physics, and science), ENGINEERING AND ENVIRONMENTAL DESIGN (civil engineering, computer engineering, electrical/electronics engineering, engineering, engineering physics, environmental science, and mechanical engineering), SOCIAL SCIENCE (anthropology, classical/ancient civilization, economics, history, interdisciplinary studies, liberal arts/general studies, philosophy, political science/government, psychology, religion, sociology, and women's studies). Social sciences and engineering are the strongest academically. Social sciences and business are the largest.

Special: Study abroad in 48 countries at 167 sites is offered, as are international internship and volunteer opportunities. A co-op program in engineering, dual majors, internships in business, government, and nonprofit agencies, a general studies degree, student-designed majors, work-study, a Washington semester, and pass/fail options also are available. Minors are offered in environmental, retail, and international studies, and in international business. There are 26 national honor societies, including Phi Beta Kappa, a freshman honors program, and 4 departmental honors programs.

Requirements: The SAT or ACT is required. In addition, applicants should have 18 academic units, including 4 years each of English and math, 3 each of foreign language and science, 1 or 2 of which are a lab, 1 each in social studies and history, and 2 in electives. An essay is required. An audition is recommended for theater arts majors. The GED is not accepted. AP credits are accepted. Important factors in the admissions decision are advanced placement or honors courses, extracurricular activities record, and recommendations by school officials.

Procedure: Freshmen are admitted in the fall. Entrance exams should be taken by December 1. There are early admissions, deferred admissions, and rolling admissions plans. Applications should be filed by January 7 for fall entry, along with a $55 fee. Notification is sent on a rolling basis. Applications are accepted on-line. A waiting list is maintained.

Financial Aid: In a recent year, 77% of all full-time freshmen and 77% of continuing full-time students received some form of financial aid. 32% of all full-time freshmen and 41% of continuing full-time students received need-based aid. The average freshmen award was $21,409. 59% of undergraduate students worked part-time. Average annual earnings from campus work were $4140. The average financial indebtedness of the 2009 graduate was $23,773. Santa Clara is a member of CSS. The CSS/Profile and FAFSA are required. Check with the school for current application deadlines.

Computers: Wireless access is available. PCs are concentrated in 6 general-purpose computing labs and 21 discipline or college specific labs and are loaded with software for word processing, spreadsheet, database, presentation, programming, and discipline-specific use. There are more than 800 campus computer or kiosks. High-speed Ethernet access is available in residence hall rooms. Access to the network is monitored. Students may use their own computers to access the network. Wireless access is available in libraries, some classrooms, and campus common areas. All students may access the system. There are no time limits and no fees.

SARAH LAWRENCE COLLEGE
Bronxville, NY 10708 (914) 395-2510
(800) 888-2858; (914) 395-2515

Full-time: 325 men, 925 women	**Faculty:** IIB, ++$
Part-time: 15 men, 65 women	**Ph.D.s:** n/av
Graduate: 55 men, 310 women	**Student/Faculty:** n/av
Year: semesters	**Tuition:** $36,000
Application Deadline: see profile	**Room & Board:** $12,000
Freshman Class: n/av	**HIGHLY COMPETITIVE**

Sarah Lawrence College, established in 1926, is an independent institution conferring liberal arts degrees. The academic structure is based on the British don system. Students meet biweekly with professors in tutorials and are enrolled in small seminars. While there are no formal majors, students develop individual concentrations that are usually interdisciplinary. Figures in the above capsule and in this profile are approximate. There is 1 graduate school. The 3 libraries contain 282,676 volumes, 24,218 microform items, and 9,319 audio/video tapes/CDs/DVDs, and subscribe to 916 periodicals including electronic. Computerized library services include interlibrary loans, database searching, and Internet access. Special learning facilities include an art gallery, radio station, a slide library with 75,000 slides of art and architecture, early childhood center, electronic music studio; music library, student-run theater and student-run art gallery. The 41-acre campus is in a suburban area 15 miles north of midtown Manhattan. Including any residence halls, there are 50 buildings.

Programs of Study: Sarah Lawrence confers B.A. degrees. Master's degrees are also awarded. Bachelor's degrees are awarded in BIOLOGICAL SCIENCE (biology/biological science), COMMUNICATIONS AND THE ARTS (art history and appreciation, classics, creative writing, dance, dramatic arts, English, film arts, fine arts, French, German, Greek, Italian, Latin, literature, music, Russian, Spanish, and visual and performing arts), COMPUTER AND PHYSICAL SCIENCE (chemistry and mathematics), HEALTH PROFESSIONS (premedicine), SOCIAL SCIENCE (anthropology, Asian/Oriental studies, economics, history, liberal arts/general studies, philosophy, political science/government, psychology, religion, Russian and Slavic studies, sociology, and women's studies).

Special: Internships are available in a variety of fields, with the school offering proximity to New York City art galleries and agencies. Study abroad in many countries, work-study programs, dual concentrations, a 3-2 engineering degree with Columbia, and a general degree may be pursued. All concentrations are self-designed and can be combined.

Requirements: Important academic requirements are: secondary school record, teacher recommendation(s) and essay; class rank is considered. Nonacademic requirements include character and personality qualities; extracurricular activities, talent/ability, volunteer work, and work experience. Campus interview, alumnae relations, geographical residence, and minority status are considered. AP credits are accepted. Important factors in the admissions decision are recommendations by school officials, personality/intangible qualities, and extracurricular activities record.

Procedure: Freshmen are admitted in the fall. There are early decision, early admissions and deferred admissions plans. Early decision applications should be filed by November 15; regular applications, check with the school for current application deadlines. The fall 2009 application fee was $50. Notification of early decision is sent December 15; regular decision, April 1. Applications are accepted on-line. A waiting list is maintained.

Financial Aid: Sarah Lawrence is a member of CSS. The CSS/Profile, FAFSA, and non-custodial parent statement are required. Check with the school for current application deadlines.

Computers: All students may access the system 24 hours a day. There are no time limits and no fees.

SAVANNAH COLLEGE OF ART AND DESIGN

Savannah, GA 31401-3146

(912) 525-5100
(800) 869-7223; (912) 525-5995

Full-time: 2884 men, 4308 women	**Faculty:** 491
Part-time: 407 men, 589 women	**Ph.D.s:** 80%
Graduate: 707 men, 1011 women	**Student/Faculty:** 15 to 1
Year: quarters, summer session	**Tuition:** $28,265
Application Deadline: open	**Room & Board:** $10,780
Freshman Class: 8083 applied, 5491 accepted, 1678 enrolled	
SAT CR/M: 540/530	**ACT:** 23 **SPECIAL**

Savannah College of Art and Design, founded in 1978, is a private fine arts university emphasizing career preparation in the visual and performing arts, design, building arts, and the history of art and architecture. There are 7 undergraduate schools and 7 graduate schools. In addition to regional accreditation, SCAD has baccalaureate program accreditation with NAAB. The 2 libraries contain 203,002 volumes, 6,398 microform items, and 6,309 audio/video tapes/CDs/DVDs, and subscribe to 1,219 periodicals including electronic. Computerized library services include interlibrary loans, database searching, Internet access, and laptop Internet portals. Special learning facilities include a learning resource center, art gallery, radio station, TV station, international student center, writing center, Internet labs, and SCAD Museum of Art. The campus is in an urban area on the southeast coast of Georgia, midway between Charleston, SC and Jacksonville, FL. Including any residence halls, there are 79 buildings.

Programs of Study: SCAD confers B.A., B.F.A. degrees. Master's degrees are also awarded. Bachelor's degrees are awarded in AGRICULTURE (equine science), BUSINESS (fashion merchandising), COMMUNICATIONS AND THE ARTS (advertising, animation, art, art history and appreciation, audio technology, broadcasting, communications, creative writing, design, fiber/textiles/weaving, film arts, graphic design, historic preservation, illustration, industrial design, media arts, metal/jewelry, painting, performing arts, photography, printmaking, sculpture, and visual effects), COMPUTER AND PHYSICAL SCIENCE (digital arts/technology), ENGINEERING AND ENVIRONMENTAL DESIGN (architectural history, architecture, computer graphics, furniture design, and interior design), SOCIAL SCIENCE (fashion design and technology). Graphic design, animation, and fashion are the largest.

Special: The college offers study abroad in France and Italy, cross-registration with Atlanta Regional Council of Higher Education, on-campus work-study programs, dual majors in all disciplines, sessions for credit in New York and other domestic locations, and internships with artists, designers, museums, agencies, and architectural firms in the United States and abroad. There are 2 national honor societies.

Admissions: 68% of the 2009-2010 applicants were accepted. The SAT scores for the 2009-2010 freshman class were: Critical Reading--27% below 500, 45% between 500 and 599, 25% between 600 and 700, and 3% above 700; Math--37% below 500, 41% between 500 and 599, 20% between 600 and 700, and 2% above 700; Writing--36% below 500, 42% between 500 and 599, 20% between 600 and 700, and 2% above 700. The ACT scores were 27% below 21, 27% between 21 and 23, 27% between 24 and 26, 9% between 27 and 28, and 10% above 28.

Requirements: The SAT or ACT is required. In addition, students must submit a completed application and high school transcript indicating successful completion. Preference is given to students with a 3.0 GPA or above and to students whose SAT or ACT scores are above the national average (B.F.A. Architecture candidates with math scores below 540 or 23, respectively, may be admitted to architecture on a conditional basis); 3 letters of recommendation and a statement of purpose are required. An interview is recommended, and a portfolio is encouraged. AP and CLEP credits are accepted. Important factors in the admissions decision are recommendations by school officials, evidence of special talent, and leadership record.

Procedure: Freshmen are admitted to all sessions. Entrance exams should be taken by January of the senior year. There are early admissions and rolling admissions plans. Application deadlines are open. Application fee is $50 by mail, $25 electronic. Applications are accepted on-line.

Financial Aid: SCAD is a member of CSS. The FAFSA, the state aid form, and the college's own financial statement are required. The priority date for freshman financial aid applications for fall entry is April 1. The deadline for filing freshman financial aid applications for fall entry is September 1.

Computers: Wireless access is available. There are over 40 computer labs in 14 buildings. Wireless system is available in 33 buildings on the Savannah location and all Atlanta buildings. All students may access the system based on the hours of operation of specific buildings in which computer labs are housed. There are no fees. It is strongly recommended that all students have a personal computer.

SCHOOL OF THE ART INSTITUTE OF CHICAGO

Chicago, IL 60603	(312) 629-6100; (800) 232-7242
Full-time: 665 men, 1220 women	**Faculty:** n/av
Part-time: 35 men, 90 women	**Ph.D.s:** 87%
Graduate: 190 men, 390 women	**Student/Faculty:** n/av
Year: semesters, summer session	**Tuition:** $34,000
Application Deadline: see profile	**Room & Board:** $10,000
Freshman Class: n/av	
SAT or ACT: required	SPECIAL

The School of the Art Institute of Chicago, founded in 1866, offers a comprehensive college education centered in the visual and related arts. Figures in the above capsule and this profile are approximate. In addition to regional accreditation, SAIC has baccalaureate program accreditation with NASAD. The library contains 7100 volumes, 157 microform items, and 4000 audio/video tapes/CDs/DVDs, and subscribes to 350 periodicals including electronic. Computerized library services include interlibrary loans and database searching. Special learning facilities include a learning resource center, an art gallery, a TV station, the Gene Siskel Film Center, a video data bank, the Fashion Resource Center, student galleries, a poetry center, Free Radio SAIC, the Roger Brown Study Collection, the Joan Flasch Artists Book Collection, and the Collection of the Art Institute of Chicago. The campus is in an urban area in downtown Chicago. Including any residence halls, there are 5 buildings.

Programs of Study: SAIC confers B.A., B.F.A., and B.I.A. degrees. Master's degrees are also awarded. Bachelor's degrees are awarded in COMMUNICATIONS AND THE ARTS (art history and appreciation, audio technology, ceramic art and design, creative writing, design, drawing, fiber/textiles/weaving, film arts, painting, photography, printmaking, sculpture, video, and visual and performing arts), COMPUTER AND PHYSICAL SCIENCE (digital arts/technology), EDUCATION (art education), ENGINEERING AND ENVIRONMENTAL DESIGN (drafting and design technology and interior design), SOCIAL SCIENCE (fashion design and technology).

Special: The school offers internships, student-designed majors, a credit/no-credit grading system, visual arts co-op programs, cross-registration with Roosevelt University, and many cooperative work-study opportunities. Dual and student-designed majors, 6 undergraduate degrees, and study abroad in 20 countries with active exchange programs are possible.

Requirements: The SAT or ACT is required. In addition, applicants must be graduates of an accredited secondary school. The GED is accepted. All students must submit a portfolio and an essay. An interview is recommended. AP and CLEP credits are accepted. Important factors in the admissions decision are evidence of special talent, recommendations by school officials, and personality/intangible qualities.

Procedure: Freshmen are admitted fall and spring. There are early admissions, deferred admissions, and rolling admissions plans. Check with the school for current application deadlines. The application fee is $65. Notification is sent on a rolling basis.

Financial Aid: The FAFSA is required. Check with the school for current application deadlines.

Computers: Wireless access is available. All students may access the system. There are no time limits and no fees.

SCHOOL OF VISUAL ARTS

New York, NY 10010-3994

(212) 592-2100
(800) 436-4204; (212) 592-2116

Full-time: 1480 men, 1735 women	**Faculty:** n/av
Part-time: 50 men, 70 women	**Ph.D.s:** n/av
Graduate: 175 men, 160 women	**Student/Faculty:** n/av
Year: semesters, summer session	**Tuition:** $24,000
Application Deadline: February 1	**Room & Board:** $12,500
Freshman Class: n/av	
SAT or ACT: required	**SPECIAL**

The School of Visual Arts, established in 1947, is a private college of art and design conferring undergraduate and graduate degrees in fine and commercial arts.

The figures in the above capsule and in this profile are approximate. There is 1 graduate school. In addition to regional accreditation, SVA has baccalaureate program accreditation with FIDER and NASAD. The library contains 70,000 volumes, 1,070 microform items, and 3,168 audio/video tapes/CDs/DVDs, and subscribes to 307 periodicals including electronic. Computerized library services include database searching, Internet access, and laptop Internet portals. Special learning facilities include a learning resource center, art gallery, radio station, a design study center and archive, 5 student galleries, 3 media arts workshops, 3 film and 2 video studios, numerous editing facilities, animation studio with 3 pencil test facilities, digital audio room, tape transfer room, and multimedia facility with digital printing and editing systems. The campus is in an urban area in mid Manhattan. Including any residence halls, there are 14 buildings.

Programs of Study: SVA confers B.F.A. degrees. Master's degrees are also awarded. Bachelor's degrees are awarded in COMMUNICATIONS AND THE ARTS (advertising, animation, film arts, fine arts, graphic design, illustration, photography, video, and visual effects), ENGINEERING AND ENVIRONMENTAL DESIGN (computer graphics and interior design). Visual and critical studies; computer art; computer animation and special effects are the strongest academically. Graphic design; film/video and photography are the largest.

Special: SVA offers for-credit internships with more than 200 media-related, design, and advertising firms, including DC Comics, MTV, and Pentagram Design. A summer internship with Walt Disney Studios is possible for illustration/ cartooning majors. There are a freshman honors program.

Requirements: The SAT or ACT is required. In addition, applicants must graduate from an accredited secondary school or have a GED. A statement of intent is required of all students. A portfolio is also required. A personal interview and letters of recommendation are considered helpful. A GPA of 2.7 is required. AP and CLEP credits are accepted. Important factors in the admissions decision are personality/intangible qualities, extracurricular activities record, and evidence of special talent.

Procedure: Freshmen are admitted in the fall. There are early decision, deferred admissions and rolling admissions plans. Early decision applications should be filed by December 1; regular applications, by February 1 for fall entry. The fall 2009 application fee was $50. Notification of early decision is sent January 15. Applications are accepted on-line. 10 applicants were on a recent waiting list, 0 were accepted.

Financial Aid: In a recent year, 43% of all full-time freshmen and 40% of continuing full-time students received need-based aid. 7% of undergraduate students worked part-time. The average financial indebtedness of the 2009 graduate was $30,259. The FAFSA is required. Check with the school for current application deadlines.

Computers: Wireless access is available. Every student is given a log-in id to the College's internal network, including Web-based e-mail account; computer network can be accessed from off-campus; SVA has over 700 PCs and Macs available for student use, including in the library, public areas on campus, and the writing resource center. All students may access the system. during normal operating hours of the library and the writing resource center. There are no time limits and no fees. It is strongly recommended that all students have a personal computer. A Intel based Mac is recommended.

Claremont, CA 91711-3948 (909) 621-8149
(800) 770-1333; (909) 607-7508

Full-time: 902 women	**Faculty:** 81; IIB, ++$
Part-time: 1 man, 4 women	**Ph.D.s:** 97%
Graduate: 7 men, 8 women	**Student/Faculty:** 11 to 1
Year: semesters, summer session	**Tuition:** $38,700
Application Deadline: January 1	**Room & Board:** $11,850
Freshman Class: 2061 applied, 678 accepted, 203 enrolled	
SAT CR/M/W: 690/660/690	**ACT:** required

MOST COMPETITIVE

Scripps College, founded in 1926, is a private liberal arts institution for women. A member of the Claremont Colleges, Scripps emphasizes a challenging core curriculum based on interdisciplinary humanistic studies. The 4 libraries contain 2.6 million volumes, 1.5 million microform items, and 13,767 audio/video tapes/CDs/DVDs, and subscribe to 46,862 periodicals including electronic. Computerized library services include interlibrary loans, database searching, Internet access, and laptop Internet portals. Special learning facilities include an art gallery, radio station, TV station, humanities museum, and biological field station. The 37-acre campus is in a suburban area 35 miles east of Los Angeles. Including any residence halls, there are 27 buildings.

Programs of Study: Scripps confers B.A. degrees. Bachelor's degrees are awarded in AGRICULTURE (environmental studies), BIOLOGICAL SCIENCE (biology/biological science, molecular biology, and neurosciences), COMMUNICATIONS AND THE ARTS (art history and appreciation, Chinese, classical languages, communications, dance, dramatic arts, English, Germanic languages and literature, Italian, Japanese, languages, music, Russian, Spanish, and studio art), COMPUTER AND PHYSICAL SCIENCE (chemistry, computer science, geology, mathematics, physics, science and management, and science technology), ENGINEERING AND ENVIRONMENTAL DESIGN (environmental science and preengineering), SOCIAL SCIENCE (African American studies, American studies, anthropology, Asian/American studies, Asian/Oriental studies, classical/ancient civilization, economics, European studies, French studies, German area studies, Hispanic American studies, history, humanities, Italian studies, Judaic studies, Latin American studies, law, Mexican-American/Chicano studies, philosophy, political science/government, prelaw, psychology, religion, sociology, and women's studies). Psychology, English, and politics are the strongest academically. Art, biology, and psychology are the largest.

Special: Students may cross-register with any of the other Claremont Colleges. Scripps also offers study abroad in 36 countries, a Washington semester, and student-designed, dual, and interdisciplinary majors, including organizational studies and science, technology, and society. Many courses are offered as seminars. There are 4-1 accelerated degree programs in the arts and business administration. A 3-2 engineering program (B.A.-B.S.) is offered with Harvey Mudd College, USC, UC Berkeley, Columbia, Stanford, and Boston Universities, and others There are 5 national honor societies, including Phi Beta Kappa, and 29 departmental honors programs.

Admissions: 33% of the 2009-2010 applicants were accepted. The SAT scores for the 2009-2010 freshman class were: Critical Reading--13% between 500 and 599, 45% between 600 and 700, and 42% above 700; Math--2% below 500, 17% between 500 and 599, 55% between 600 and 700, and 26% above 700; Writing-

-1% below 500, 10% between 500 and 599, 46% between 600 and 700, and 43% above 700. The ACT scores were 5% between 21 and 23, 17% between 24 and 26, 18% between 27 and 28, and 60% above 28. 84% of the current freshmen were in the top fifth of their class; 99% were in the top two fifths. There were 10 National Merit finalists. 10 freshmen graduated first in their class.

Requirements: The SAT or ACT is required. In addition, applicants must have completed 4 units each of high school English and math, 3 each of lab science and social studies, and either 3 of a single foreign language or 2 each of 2 languages. SAT Subject Tests and an interview are recommended. An essay and a graded writing assignment from the junior or senior year are required. Scripps requires applicants to be in the upper 25% of their class. A GPA of 3.5 is required. AP and CLEP credits are accepted. Important factors in the admissions decision are advanced placement or honors courses, evidence of special talent, and leadership record.

Procedure: Freshmen are admitted fall and spring. Entrance exams should be taken by December of the senior year. There are early decision, early admissions, and deferred admissions plans. Early decision applications should be filed by November 1; regular applications, by January 1 for fall entry; and November 1 for spring entry, along with a $60 fee. Notification of early decision is sent December 15; regular decision, April 1. 68 early decision candidates were accepted for the 2009-2010 class. 519 applicants were on the 2009 waiting list; 26 were admitted. Applications are accepted on-line.

Financial Aid: In 2009-2010, 60% of all full-time freshmen and 56% of continuing full-time students received some form of financial aid. 51% of all full-time freshmen and 50% of continuing full-time students received need-based aid. The average freshman award was $33,879. Need-based scholarships or need-based grants averaged $30,601 ($47,050 maximum); need-based self-help aid (loans and jobs) averaged $3,367 ($5,300 maximum); and other non-need-based awards and non-need-based scholarships averaged $16,153 ($50,550 maximum). All undergraduate students work part-time. Average annual earnings from campus work are $1800. The average financial indebtedness of the 2009 graduate was $11,140. Scripps is a member of CSS. The CSS/Profile and FAFSA are required. The priority date for freshman financial aid applications for fall entry is February 1.

Computers: Wireless access is available. All students may access the system. There are no time limits and no fees.

SEATTLE UNIVERSITY
Seattle, WA 98122

(206) 296-2000
(800) 426-7123; (206) 296-5656

Full-time: 1510 men, 2325 women	**Faculty:** IIA, av$
Part-time: 110 men, 175 women	**Ph.D.s:** 85%
Graduate: 655 men, 1070 women	**Student/Faculty:** n/av
Year: trimesters, summer session	**Tuition:** $23,500
Application Deadline: see profile	**Room & Board:** $8000
Freshman Class: n/av	
SAT or ACT: required	**VERY COMPETITIVE**

Seattle University, founded in 1891, is a private, comprehensive institution affiliated with the Roman Catholic Church and operated by the Jesuit Fathers. The emphasis of the undergraduate and graduate programs is on the liberal arts and sciences, business, engineering, health science, teacher preparation, theological studies, and law. Figures in the above capsule and in this profile are approximate. There are 5 undergraduate schools and 7 graduate schools. In addition to regional accreditation, Seattle U has baccalaureate program accreditation with AACSB, ABET, CAHEA, NCATE, and NLN. The 2 libraries contain 234,978 volumes, 570,839 microform items, and 5,608 audio/video tapes/CDs/DVDs, and subscribe to 2,709 periodicals including electronic. Computerized library services include interlibrary loans, database searching, Internet access, and laptop Internet portals. Special learning facilities include a learning resource center, art gallery, planetarium, radio station, electron microscope, recording studio, and MRI. The 46-acre campus is in an urban area just east of downtown Seattle. Including any residence halls, there are 27 buildings.

Programs of Study: Seattle U confers B.A., B.S., B.A.B.A., B.A.E., B.A.H., B.C.J., B.P.A., B.S.B., B.S.B.C., B.S.C., B.S.C.E., B.S.C.S., B.S.D.U., B.S.E.E., B.S.G.S., B.S.M., B.S.M.E., B.S.M.T., B.S.N., and B.S.P. degrees. Master's and doctoral degrees are also awarded. Bachelor's degrees are awarded in BIOLOGICAL SCIENCE (biochemistry, biology/biological science, and ecology), BUSINESS (accounting, banking and finance, business administration and management, business economics, international business management, marketing/retailing/merchandising, and operations research), COMMUNICATIONS AND THE ARTS (communications, creative writing, dramatic arts, English, fine arts, French, German, journalism, and Spanish), COMPUTER AND PHYSICAL SCIENCE (chemistry, computer science, mathematics, physics, and science), ENGINEERING AND ENVIRONMENTAL DESIGN (civil engineering, electrical/electronics engineering, environmental engineering, manufacturing engineering, and mechanical engineering), HEALTH PROFESSIONS (medical technology, nursing, and ultrasound technology), SOCIAL SCIENCE (criminal justice, economics, history, humanities, international studies, liberal arts/general studies, philosophy, political science/government, psychology, public administration, religion, social work, and sociology). Engineering, accounting, and nursing are the strongest academically and have the largest enrollments.

Special: Special academic programs include internships in numerous disciplines, study abroad in 5 countries, and both on-and off-campus work-study through the Washington State Work-Study Program. A liberal studies degree and an accelerated degree program in business are offered. Pass/fail options, dual majors, and student-designed majors are possible. There is a freshman honors program and 8 departmental honors programs.

Requirements: The SAT or ACT is required. In addition, admissions requirements include graduation from an accredited secondary school, with 16 academic credits, including 4 years of English, 3 each of math and social studies, 2 of foreign language, 2 of lab science, and 2 academic electives; 4 years of math and lab physics and chemistry are required of science and engineering students; lab biology and chemistry are needed by nursing students. The GED is also accepted. A GPA of 2.8 is required. AP and CLEP credits are accepted. Important factors in the admissions decision are advanced placement or honors courses, recommendations by school officials, and extracurricular activities record.

Procedure: Freshmen are admitted to all sessions. Entrance exams should be taken during the fall of the senior year. There are early admissions, deferred admissions, and rolling admissions plans. Applications should be filed by February 1 for fall entry, November 1 for winter entry, February 1 for spring entry, and May 1 for summer entry, along with a $45 fee. Notification is sent on a rolling basis. 8 applicants are currently on a waiting list.

Financial Aid: In a recent year, 67% of all full-time freshmen and 67% of continuing full-time students received some form of financial aid. 64% of all full-time freshmen and 65% of continuing full-time students received need-based aid. The average freshmen award was $21,431. The average financial indebtedness of the 2009 graduate was $25,311. The FAFSA is required. Check with the school for current application deadlines.

Computers: All students may access the syste during posted hours or any time from networked residence hall rooms. There are no time limits and no fees.

SEWANEE: THE UNIVERSITY OF THE SOUTH
Sewanee, TN 37383-1000

(931) 598-1238
(800) 522-2234; (931) 538-3248

Full-time: 640 men, 760 women	**Faculty:** n/av
Part-time: 10 men, 12 women	**Ph.D.s:** 97%
Graduate: 62 men, 34 women	**Student/Faculty:** n/av
Year: semesters, summer session	**Tuition:** $34,000
Application Deadline: see profile	**Room & Board:** $9800
Freshman Class: n/av	
SAT or ACT: required	**HIGHLY COMPETITIVE**

Sewanee: The University of the South, formerly University of the South, was founded in 1857 and is an independent liberal arts institution affiliated with the Episcopal Church. Figures in the above capsule are approximate. There is 1 graduate school. The library contains 648,459 volumes, 328,090 microform items, and 72,964 audio/video tapes/CDs/DVDs, and subscribes to 3444 periodicals including electronic. Computerized library services include interlibrary loans, database searching, and Internet access. Special learning facilities include a learning resource center, art gallery, radio station, observatory, materials analysis lab with an electron scanning microscope, and rare books collection. The 10,000-acre campus is in a small town 45 miles west of Chattanooga. Including any residence halls, there are 43 buildings.

Programs of Study: Sewanee confers B.A. and B.S. degrees. Master's and doctoral degrees are also awarded. Bachelor's degrees are awarded in AGRICULTURE (environmental studies, forestry and related sciences, and natural resource management), BIOLOGICAL SCIENCE (biology/biological science), COMMUNICATIONS AND THE ARTS (art, art history and appreciation, dramatic arts, English, French, German, Greek, Latin, music, Russian, and Spanish), COMPUTER AND PHYSICAL SCIENCE (chemistry, computer science, geology, mathematics, and physics), SOCIAL SCIENCE (American studies, anthropology, Asian/Oriental studies, economics, French studies, German area studies, history, medieval studies, philosophy, political science/government, psychology, religion, Russian and Slavic studies, social science, and Third World studies). English and environmental studies are the strongest academically. English, economics, and history are the largest.

Special: Sewanee offers internships in economics and public affairs, study abroad in 13 countries, a Washington semester, and student-designed majors. Teacher certification and Peace Corps, medical, law, and veterinary preparation are available. A 3-2 engineering degree is offered with Columbia, Washington, and Vanderbilt Universities, Georgia Institute of Technology, and Rensselaer Polytechnic Institute. Pass/fail options are possible. There are 10 national honor societies, including Phi Beta Kappa, a freshman honors program, and 28 departmental honors programs.

Requirements: The SAT or ACT is required. In addition, candidates for admission should have 15 secondary school academic credits, including 4 years of English, 3 of math, and 2 each of lab science, a foreign language, and history or social science. An essay and recommendation are required and an interview is recommended. AP credits are accepted. Important factors in the admissions decision are advanced placement or honors courses, leadership record, and evidence of special talent.

Procedure: Freshmen are admitted fall. Entrance exams should be taken by December of the senior year. There are early decision, early admissions and deferred admissions plans. Early decision applications should be filed by November 15; check with the school for current application deadlines. Notification of early decision is sent December 15. The application fee is $25. Applications are accepted on-line. A waiting list is maintained.

Financial Aid: The FAFSA and the college's own financial statement are required. Check with the school for current application deadlines.

Computers: Wireless access is available. Students may access the network through a wired connection, which all rooms have, or through wireless hotspots across campus. All students may access the system 24 hours a day. There are no time limits and no fees.

SHIMER COLLEGE
Chicago, IL 60616

(312) 235-3500
(800) 215-7173; (312) 235-3501

Full-time: 49 men, 42 women	**Faculty:** 12
Part-time: 4 men, 9 women	**Ph.D.s:** 92%
Graduate: none	**Student/Faculty:** 10 to 1
Year: semesters, summer session	**Tuition:** $24,875
Application Deadline: July 31	**Room & Board:** $8000
Freshman Class: n/av	
SAT CR/M/W: 640/540/590	**ACT:** 27 **HIGHLY COMPETITIVE**

Shimer College, the Great Books College of Chicago, is a private liberal arts institution that shares space on the campus of the Illinois Institute of Technology. Founded in 1853 the College offers a curriculum based on original sources and a Socratic teaching method in discussion classes of 12 or fewer students. There are no undergraduate schools. The 3 libraries contain 20,500 volumes, 100 microform items, and 0 audio/video tapes/CDs/DVDs, and subscribe to 0 periodicals including electronic. Computerized library services include interlibrary loans, database searching, and Internet access. Special learning facilities include a learning resource center and radio station. The 120-acre campus is in an urban area Chicago. Including any residence halls, there are 40 buildings.

Programs of Study: Shimer confers B.A. and B.S. degrees. Bachelor's degrees are awarded in COMPUTER AND PHYSICAL SCIENCE (natural sciences), SOCIAL SCIENCE (humanities, liberal arts/general studies, and social science). Humanities and social science is the strongest academically. Humanities is the largest.

Special: Shimer offers internships in all areas of study and study abroad at Oxford in England. There is an accelerated degree program, a B.A.-B.S. degree, dual majors in all areas, student-designed majors, and a general studies degree. Non-degree study and pass/fail options are possible.

Admissions: The SAT scores for the 2009-2010 freshman class were: Critical Reading--% below 500, 33% between 500 and 599, 17% between 600 and 700, and 50% above 700; Math--17% below 500, 50% between 500 and 599, 33% between 600 and 700, and % above 700; Writing--% below 500, 50% between 500 and 599, 25% between 600 and 700, and 25% above 700. The ACT scores were % below 21, 14% between 21 and 23, 15% between 24 and 26, 42% between 27 and 28, and 29% above 28.

Requirements: In addition, applicants must submit essays, letters of recommendation, and an interview. The SAT or ACT required only of students who are applying for our Early Entrance program, a 55 year old program that offers full admission to high school age students - those who would be enrolling in their junior or senior years of high school, but prefer to matriculate early. Important factors in the admissions decision are evidence of special talent, personality/intangible qualities, and recommendations by school officials.

Procedure: Freshmen are admitted fall and spring. There are deferred admissions and rolling admissions plans. Applications should be filed by July 31 for fall entry; January 15 for spring entry, along with a $25 fee. Applications are accepted on-line.

Financial Aid: In 2009-2010, 87% of all full-time freshmen and 87% of continuing full-time students received some form of financial aid. 52% of undergraduate students work part-time. Average annual earnings from campus work are $1800. The average financial indebtedness of the 2009 graduate was $30,000. Shimer is a member of CSS. The FAFSA and the college's own financial statement are required. The priority date for freshman financial aid applications for fall entry is April 15. The deadline for filing freshman financial aid applications for fall entry is July 30.

Computers: Wireless access is available. Registered students are provided with a student ID card. They are then able to use the wireless network on campus on their own laptops. Desktops are available in PC labs across campus 24 hours a day. Portable memory devices are available to registered users. All students may access the system. 24 hours a day. There are no time limits and no fees.

SIENA COLLEGE
Loudonville, NY 12211-1462

(518) 783-2964
(888) AT SIENA; (518) 783-2436

Full-time: 1443 men, 1658 women	**Faculty:** 185; IIB, +$
Part-time: 80 men, 104 women	**Ph.D.s:** 89%
Graduate: 8 men, 12 women	**Student/Faculty:** 17 to 1
Year: semesters, summer session	**Tuition:** $25,285
Application Deadline: March 1	**Room & Board:** $9930
Freshman Class: 3889 accepted, 783 enrolled	
SAT CR/M: 559/583	**ACT:** 24 **VERY COMPETITIVE**

Siena College, founded in 1937, is a learning community advancing the ideals of a liberal arts education, rooted in its identity as a Franciscan and Catholic Institution. There are 3 undergraduate schools and 1 graduate school. In addition to regional accreditation, Siena has baccalaureate program accreditation with AACSB and CSWE. The library contains 354,963 volumes, 27,720 microform items, and 11,051 audio/video tapes/CDs/DVDs, and subscribes to 23,688 periodicals including electronic. Computerized library services include interlibrary loans, database searching, Internet access, and laptop Internet portals. Special learning facilities include an art gallery, radio station, and the Hickey Financial Technology Center, which features real-time capital market trading room with stock ticker, data screens, workstations, and access to financial information sources and accounting labs. The 166-acre campus is in a suburban area 2 miles north of Albany. Including any residence halls, there are 28 buildings.

Programs of Study: Siena confers B.A., B.S., and B.B.A. degrees. Bachelor's degrees are awarded in BIOLOGICAL SCIENCE (biochemistry and biology/biological science), BUSINESS (accounting, banking and finance, business administration and management, and marketing management), COMMUNICA-

TIONS AND THE ARTS (classics, English, French, Spanish, and visual and performing arts), COMPUTER AND PHYSICAL SCIENCE (actuarial science, chemistry, computer science, mathematics, and physics), ENGINEERING AND ENVIRONMENTAL DESIGN (environmental science), SOCIAL SCIENCE (American studies, economics, history, philosophy, political science/government, psychology, religion, social work, and sociology). Marketing/management, accounting, and biology are the largest.

Special: The college has opportunities for cooperative programs in business, environmental science, engineering, medical education, social work, elementary education, and dentistry. Cross-registration with the Hudson-Mohawk Association is offered. Domestic and international internships, study abroad in 23 countries, a Washington semester, and work-study programs are available. The college offers dual majors in different divisions and a B.A.-B.S. degree in math, economics, and biology as well as a 3-2 engineering degree with Rensselaer Polytechnic Institute, Catholic University, Clarkson University, Manhattan College, SUNY Binghamton, and Western New England College. A 4-4 medical program with Albany Medical College is also offered. There are 15 national honor societies, a freshman honors program, and 4 departmental honors programs.

Admissions: The SAT scores for the 2009-2010 freshman class were: Critical Reading--21% below 500, 48% between 500 and 599, 28% between 600 and 700, and 3% above 700; Math--13% below 500, 44% between 500 and 599, 39% between 600 and 700, and 4% above 700; Writing--23% below 500, 48% between 500 and 599, 26% between 600 and 700, and 2% above 700. The ACT scores were 18% below 21, 28% between 21 and 23, 39% between 24 and 26, 7% between 27 and 28, and 7% above 28. 49% of the current freshmen were in the top fifth of their class; 82% were in the top two fifths.

Requirements: The SAT or ACT is required. In addition, applicants must be graduates of an accredited secondary school or have a GED. 13 academic credits are required, including 4 years of English, and 3 to 4 years each of history/social studies, math, and science, and a recommended 3 years of foreign language study. All applicants must submit an essay; an interview is recommended. AP and CLEP credits are accepted. Important factors in the admissions decision are advanced placement or honors courses, personality/intangible qualities, and extracurricular activities record.

Procedure: Freshmen are admitted fall and spring. Entrance exams should be taken during spring of the junior year or fall of the senior year. There are early decision, early admissions and deferred admissions plans. Early decision applications should be filed by December 1, regular applications should be filed by March 1 for fall entry, December 1 for spring entry, and January 1 for summer entry. The fall 2009 application fee was $50. Early decision applications should be filed by January 15; regular decision, March 15. Applications are accepted online. 341 applicants were on a recent waiting list, 25 were accepted.

Financial Aid: The FAFSA and the state aid form are required. The priority date for freshman financial aid applications for fall entry is February 15. Check with the school for current application deadlines.

Computers: Wireless access is available. All students have accounts established for them prior to arrival. The campus network is currently available in most residences, the student union, parts of the library, and in some classrooms. Students may access more than 123 PCs, Macs, and terminals in more than a dozen locations, some of which are open 24 hours a day. Every residential space includes a network connection. A wireless system is available in the student union, parts of the library, and in some classrooms. A total of 215 wired network connections are available. All students may access the system 24 hours per day. There are no time limits and no fees.

SIERRA NEVADA COLLEGE

Incline Village, NV 89451

(775) 831-1314
(866) 412-4636; (775) 831-6223

Full-time: 70 men, 90 women	**Faculty:** n/av
Part-time: 25 men, 10 women	**Ph.D.s:** n/av
Graduate: 95 men, 245 women	**Student/Faculty:** n/av
Year: semesters, summer session	**Tuition:** $23,700
Application Deadline: February 15	**Room & Board:** $9000
Freshman Class: n/av	
ACT: required	**VERY COMPETITIVE**

Sierra Nevada College, founded in 1969, is a private institution offering programs in liberal arts, fine arts, business, hotel resort management, ski business management, environmental science, and teacher education. The figures in the above capsule and in this profile are approximate. There are 7 undergraduate schools. The library contains 20,000 volumes, 10,000 microform items, and subscribes to 100 periodicals including electronic. Computerized library services include interlibrary loans, database searching, Internet access, and laptop Internet portals. Special learning facilities include a learning resource center, art gallery, an observatory, and a recording studio. The 17-acre campus is in a rural area 25 miles west of Reno. Including any residence halls, there are 7 buildings.

Programs of Study: SNC confers B.A., B.S., and B.F.A. degrees. Bachelor's degrees are awarded in BUSINESS (business administration and management and recreational facilities management), COMMUNICATIONS AND THE ARTS (fine arts and music), COMPUTER AND PHYSICAL SCIENCE (science), ENGINEERING AND ENVIRONMENTAL DESIGN (environmental science), SOCIAL SCIENCE (humanities). Environmental science/ecology is the strongest academically. Business administration is the largest.

Special: Business administration concentrations are offered in ski business and resort management and in hotel, restaurant, and resort management. Student-designed majors, work-study programs, internships, credit for life experiences and volunteer community work, and nondegree study are available.

Requirements: The ACT is required. The ACT Optional Writing test is also required. All applicants are reviewed individually. Official transcripts, an essay, and 2 letters of recommendation are required, and an interview is recommended. AP and CLEP credits are accepted. Important factors in the admissions decision are advanced placement or honors courses, recommendations by school officials, and personality/intangible qualities.

Procedure: Freshmen are admitted to all sessions. Entrance exams should be taken in the spring of junior year or fall of senior year. There are early decision, early admissions, deferred admissions, and rolling admissions plans. Applications should be filed by February 15 for fall entry. Notification is sent on a rolling basis. Applications are accepted on-line.

Financial Aid: In a recent year, 80% of all full-time freshmen and 80% of continuing full-time students received some form of financial aid. 80% of all full-time freshmen and 80% of continuing full-time students received need-based aid. The average freshmen award was $15,000, with $7,000 ($16,000 maximum) from need-based scholarships or need-based grants; $3,800 ($7,500 maximum) from need-based self-help aid (loans and jobs); and $3,000 ($10,000 maximum) from other non-need-based awards and non-need-based scholarships. 37% of undergraduate students worked part-time. The FAFSA and the college's own financial statement are required. Check with the school for current application deadlines.

Computers: All students may access the system 8 A.M. to 9 P.M. daily. There are no time limits and no fees. It is strongly recommended that all students have a personal computer.

SIMMONS COLLEGE
Boston, MA 02115

(617) 521-2051
(800) 345-8468; (617) 521-3190

Full-time: 1746 women	**Faculty:** 188; IIA, av$
Part-time: 223 women	**Ph.Ds:** 65%
Graduate: 400 men, 2634 women	**Student/Faculty:** 9 to 1
Year: semesters, summer session	**Tuition:** $31,450
Application Deadline: April 1	**Room & Board:** $12,050
Freshman Class: 3522 applied, 2013 accepted, 357 enrolled	
SAT CR/M/W: 551/541/563	**ACT:** 24 **VERY COMPETITIVE**

Simmons College, founded in 1899, is a private institution with an undergraduate college for women that offers a comprehensive education combining the arts, sciences, and humanities with preprofessional training. All graduate programs are co-ed, with the exception of the women-only MBA program. There are 3 undergraduate schools and 5 graduate schools. In addition to regional accreditation, Simmons has baccalaureate program accreditation with ADA, APTA, CSWE, and NLN. The library contains 241,750 volumes, 13,515 microform items, and 7,867 audio/video tapes/CDs/DVDs, and subscribes to 1,873 periodicals including electronic. Computerized library services include interlibrary loans, database searching, Internet access, and laptop Internet portals. Special learning facilities include a learning resource center, art gallery, radio station, TV studio, modern language lab, physical therapy motion lab, nursing lab, and library science technology center. The 12-acre campus is in an urban area in Boston. Including any residence halls, there are 21 buildings.

Programs of Study: Simmons confers B.A. and B.S. degrees. Master's and doctoral degrees are also awarded. Bachelor's degrees are awarded in BIOLOGICAL SCIENCE (biochemistry, biology/biological science, and nutrition), BUSINESS (banking and finance, management information systems, and marketing/retailing/merchandising), COMMUNICATIONS AND THE ARTS (art, arts administration/management, communications, English, English as a second/foreign language, French, music, public relations, and Spanish), COMPUTER AND PHYSICAL SCIENCE (chemistry, computer science, and mathematics), EDUCATION (early childhood education, elementary education, secondary education, and special education), ENGINEERING AND ENVIRONMENTAL DESIGN (environmental science), HEALTH PROFESSIONS (nursing, physical therapy, and premedicine), SOCIAL SCIENCE (African American studies, dietetics, East Asian studies, economics, food science, history, human services, international relations, philosophy, political science/government, prelaw, psychobiology, psychology, sociology, and women's studies). Physical therapy, biology, and communication are the strongest academically. Nursing, communications, and psychology are the largest.

Special: Cross-registration is available with the New England Conservatory of Music, Hebrew, Emmanuel, and Wheelock Colleges, Massachusetts College of Art, Massachusetts College of Pharmacy and Health Sciences, and Wentworth Institute of Technology. Simmons offers study abroad in Europe through the Institute of European studies. A Washington semester at American University, accelerated degree programs, profit and nonprofit internship programs, a B.A.-B.S. degree, dual majors, interdisciplinary majors, student-designed majors, work-study programs, and pass/fail options are also offered. There is a dual-degree program in chemistry, pharmacy, and physician's assistant with Massachusetts College of Pharmacy. There are 3 national honor societies, a freshman honors program, and 23 departmental honors programs.

Admissions: 57% of the 2009-2010 applicants were accepted. The SAT scores for the 2009-2010 freshman class were: Critical Reading--25% below 500, 50% between 500 and 599, 21% between 600 and 700, and 3% above 700; Math--27% below 500, 47% between 500 and 599, 25% between 600 and 700, and 1% above 700; Writing--15% below 500, 53% between 500 and 599, 29% between 600 and 700, and 3% above 700. The ACT scores were 21% below 21, 30% between 21 and 23, 28% between 24 and 26, 16% between 27 and 28, and 6% above 28. 46% of the current freshmen were in the top fifth of their class; 78% were in the top two fifths.

Requirements: The SAT or ACT is required. In addition, Simmons recommends that applicants have 4 years of English, 3 each of math, science, and social studies, and 2 of foreign language. An essay is required, and an interview is strongly recommended. A GPA of 3.0 is required. AP and CLEP credits are accepted. Important factors in the admissions decision are advanced placement or honors courses, recommendations by school officials, and extracurricular activities record.

Procedure: Freshmen are admitted fall and spring. Entrance exams should be taken by February 1 of the senior year. There is a early decision, deferred admissions plan. Early decision applications should be filed by December 1; regular applications, by April 1 for fall entry and December 1 for spring entry, along with a $55 fee. Notification of early decision is sent January 20; regular decision, April 15. Applications are accepted on-line. A waiting list is maintained.

Financial Aid: In 2009-2010, 78% of all full-time freshmen and 67% of continuing full-time students received some form of financial aid. 74% of all full-time freshmen and 65% of continuing full-time students received need-based aid. The average freshman award was $21,501. Need-based scholarships or need-based grants averaged $6,569 ($21,250 maximum); and need-based self-help aid (loans and jobs) averaged $4,804 ($10,000 maximum). 34% of undergraduate students work part-time. Average annual earnings from campus work are $2500. The average financial indebtedness of the 2009 graduate was $42,174. Simmons is a member of CSS. The FAFSA and federal tax returns or W2 forms are required. The priority date for freshman financial aid applications for fall entry is February 1. The deadline for filing freshman financial aid applications for fall entry is March 1.

Computers: Wireless access is available. Students may use the college's network and/or wireless system for personal or academic reasons, including legal media file sharing, but not for commercial purposes. There are over 630 Macintosh and Windows computers on campus available for student use. All buildings on campus include Internet access, and many are covered by our wireless network as well. All students may access the system. There are no time limits and no fees. It is strongly recommended that all students have a personal computer.

SIMON'S ROCK COLLEGE OF BARD
Simon's Rock College of Bard

Great Barrington, MA 01230-9702　　　　**(413) 528-7355**
(800) 235-7186; (413) 528-7334

Full-time: 170 men, 233 women	**Faculty:** n/av
Part-time: 3 men, 2 women	**Ph.D.s:** n/av
Graduate: none	**Student/Faculty:** n/av
Year: semesters	**Tuition:** $37,130
Application Deadline: open	**Room & Board:** $9,730
Freshman Class: 333 applied, 296 accepted, 194 enrolled	
SAT CR/M: 662/587	**ACT:** 27　　**VERY COMPETITIVE+**

Bard College at Simon's Rock, formerly Simon's Rock College of Bard, founded in 1964, is a private liberal arts school especially designed to permit students who have completed the 10th or 11th grades to enroll for collegiate studies, earning either an associate's or a bachelor's degree. There are no undergraduate schools. The library contains 70,791 volumes, 7,550 microform items, 4,382 audio/video tapes/CDs/DVDs, and subscribes to 437 periodicals including electronic. Computerized library services include inter-library loans, database searching, and Internet access. Special learning facilities include a learning resource center, art gallery, radio station, TV station, language lab, greenhouse, and community garden. The 275-acre campus is in a small town 50 miles west of Springfield. Including any residence halls, there are 47 buildings.

Programs of Study: Simon's Rock confers B.A. degrees. Associates degrees are also awarded. Bachelor's degrees are awarded in BIOLOGICAL SCIENCE (biology/biological science and ecology), COMMUNICATIONS AND THE ARTS (art, art history and appreciation, creative writing, dance, dramatic arts, drawing, English literature, fine arts, French, German, Germanic languages and literature, literature, modern language, music history and appreciation, music performance, music theory and composition, painting, performing arts, photography, Spanish, studio art, and visual and performing arts), COMPUTER AND PHYSICAL SCIENCE (applied mathematics, chemistry, mathematics, natural sciences, physics, quantitative methods, and science), HEALTH PROFESSIONS (premedicine), SOCIAL SCIENCE (African American studies, American studies, Asian/Oriental studies, crosscultural studies, East Asian studies, Eastern European studies, ethics, politics, and social policy, European studies, French studies, German area studies, interdisciplinary studies, Latin American studies, philosophy, political science/government, psychology, and Russian and Slavic studies). Cross-cultural relations, psychology, and music are the strongest academically. Politics, law, and society are the largest.

Special: A major consists of selecting 2 concentrations from the 36 is available; one concentration may be self-designed. Independent study internships in many fields, study abroad, a cooperative program with Bard College, and a 3-2 engineering degree with Columbia University, Dartmouth College, or Washington University in St. Louis are available. Simon's Rock has an articulation agreement with Lincoln College and Oxford University that allows Simon's Rock students to spend their junior year in residence at Lincoln College. The Clark Early College Fellows Program is available.

Admissions: 89% of the 2009-2010 applicants were accepted. The SAT scores for the 2009-2010 freshman class were: Critical Reading--7% below 500, 32% between 500 and 599, 41% between 600 and 700, and 20 above 700; Math--16% below 500, 41% between 500 and 599, 30% between 600 and 700, and 13 above

700. The ACT scores were 6% below 21, 6% between 21 and 23, 63% between 24 and 26, % between 27 and 28, and 25% above 28.

Requirements: The ACT Optional Writing test is required. In addition, the admissions committee looks more toward the required interview, essay, recommendations, and special talent. The school recommends that prospective students finish 2 years each of English, foreign languages, history, math, science, and social studies. A GPA of 2.0 is required. AP credits are accepted. Important factors in the admissions decision are advanced placement or honors courses, recommendations by school officials, and evidence of special talent.

Procedure: Freshmen are admitted fall and spring. Entrance exams should be taken prior to June 10. There are deferred admissions and rolling admissions plans. Check with the school for current application deadlines. The application fee is $50. Notification is sent on a Rolling basis.

Financial Aid: In 2009-2010, 80% of all full-time freshmen and 84% of continuing full-time students received some form of financial aid. 67% of all full-time freshmen and 59% of continuing full-time students received need-based aid. The average freshmen award was $26,300, with $7,600 ($38,500 maximum) from need-based scholarships or need-based grants; $6,500 ($33,000 maximum) from need-based self-help aid (loans and jobs); $12,200 ($37,075 maximum) from other non-need-based awards and non-need-based scholarships; and $1,373 from other forms of aid. 20% of undergraduate students work part-time. Average annual earnings from campus work are $1500. The average financial indebtedness of the 2009 graduate was $13,525. Simon's Rock is a member of CSS. The CSS/Profile and FAFSA are required. The priority date for freshman financial aid applications for fall entry is April 15. The deadline for filing freshman financial aid applications for fall entry is May 31.

Computers: Wireless access is available. Secure wireless coverage is available throughout the academic buildings, classroom buildings, the Student Union and the campus library. Wireless coverage will be expanded to dormitories and other campus buildings. Ethernet outlets are located in all student rooms, classrooms and throughout the academic buildings on campus. Computers are available for student use in the library and in academic buildings; some computer labs are configured and reserved for particular academic departments. All students may access the system. There are no time limits and no fees. It is strongly recommended that all students have a personal computer.

SIMPSON COLLEGE
Indianola, IA 50125

(515) 961-1624
(800) 362-2454, ext. 1624; (515) 961-1870

Full-time: 645 men, 836 women	**Faculty:** 99; IIB, --$
Part-time: 213 men, 297 women	**Ph.D.s:** 90%
Graduate: 11 men, 19 women	**Student/Faculty:** 15 to 1
Year: see profile, summer session	**Tuition:** $25,733
Application Deadline:	**Room & Board:** $7261
Freshman Class: 1290 applied, 1142 accepted, 390 enrolled	
ACT: 24	**SAT:** recommended
	VERY COMPETITIVE

Simpson College, founded in 1860, is affiliated with the United Methodist Church. Simpson combines the best of a liberal arts education with outstanding career preparation and extracurricular programs. In addition to regional accreditation, Simpson has baccalaureate program accreditation with NASM. The library contains 162,197 volumes, 11,845 microform items, and 4,461 audio/video tapes/

CDs/DVDs, and subscribes to 28,663 periodicals including electronic. Computerized library services include interlibrary loans, database searching, Internet access, and laptop Internet portals. Special learning facilities include a learning resource center, art gallery, radio station, an extensive book collection from the antebellum era, the Iowa History Center, the John C. Culver Center for Public Policy Studies, an education lab, and a cadaver lab. The 85-acre campus is in a small town 12 miles south of Des Moines. Including any residence halls, there are 34 buildings.

Programs of Study: Simpson confers B.A. and B.Mus. degrees. Master's degrees are also awarded. Bachelor's degrees are awarded in AGRICULTURE (environmental studies), BIOLOGICAL SCIENCE (biochemistry and biology/biological science), BUSINESS (accounting, business administration and management, international business management, marketing management, and sports management), COMMUNICATIONS AND THE ARTS (art, communications, dramatic arts, English, French, German, journalism, music, music performance, and Spanish), COMPUTER AND PHYSICAL SCIENCE (chemistry, computer science, information sciences and systems, mathematics, and physics), EDUCATION (athletic training, elementary education, music education, physical education, and secondary education), ENGINEERING AND ENVIRONMENTAL DESIGN (preengineering), HEALTH PROFESSIONS (exercise science, predentistry, premedicine, preoptometry, prepharmacy, prephysical therapy, and preveterinary science), SOCIAL SCIENCE (criminal justice, economics, forensic studies, history, international relations, philosophy, political science/government, prelaw, psychology, public affairs, religion, social work, and sociology). Management, marketing, and communication studies are the largest.

Special: Internships, study abroad, a Washington semester, and work-study are all available. Dual and student-designed majors are possible. There is a preprofessional program in ministry, and 3-2 engineering degrees are offered with Washington University at St. Louis, Iowa State University, and Institute of Technology (University of Minnesota). There are 10 national honor societies, a freshman honors program, and 8 departmental honors programs.

Admissions: 89% of the 2009-2010 applicants were accepted. The ACT scores were 16% below 21, 30% between 21 and 23, 28% between 24 and 26, 15% between 27 and 28, and 12% above 28. 51% of the current freshmen were in the top fifth of their class; 79% were in the top two fifths. There was 1 National Merit finalist. 34 freshmen graduated first in their class.

Requirements: The ACT is required, the SAT is recommended. In addition, applicants must be graduates of an accredited secondary school; however, the GED is accepted. ACT or SAT test scores, counselor recommendations, GPA, college prep course grades, and class rank are all considered in a selective admissions process. The college strongly recommends that applicants complete 4 years of English and 3 each of math, lab science, social science, and a foreign language. AP and CLEP credits are accepted. Important factors in the admissions decision are advanced placement or honors courses, recommendations by school officials, and leadership record.

Procedure: Freshmen are admitted to all sessions. Entrance exams should be taken in the junior or senior year. There are deferred admissions and rolling admissions plans. Application deadlines are open. Notification is sent on a rolling basis. Applications are accepted on-line.

Financial Aid: In 2009-2010, all full-time freshmen and 99% of continuing full-time students received some form of financial aid. 87% of all full-time freshmen and 86% of continuing full-time students received need-based aid. The average freshman award was $26,269, with $20,180 ($34,868 maximum) from need-based scholarships or need-based grants. 34% of undergraduate students work part-time. Average annual earnings from campus work are $1000. The average financial indebtedness of the 2009 graduate was $30,339. The FAFSA is required. The deadline for filing freshman financial aid applications for fall entry is July 1.

Computers: Wireless access is available. The campus is equipped with 336 computers in various computer labs offering high-speed Internet access. The campus is completely wireless. All students may access the system 24 hours a day. There are no time limits and no fees.

SMITH COLLEGE

Northampton, MA 01063	(413) 585-2500; (413) 585-2527
Full-time: 2593 women	**Faculty:** 285; IIB, ++$
Part-time: 21 women	**Ph.D.s:** 98%
Graduate: 72 men, 435 women	**Student/Faculty:** 9 to 1
Year: semesters	**Tuition:** $37,758
Application Deadline: January 15	**Room & Board:** $12,622
Freshman Class: 4011 applied, 1904 accepted, 665 enrolled	
SAT CR/M/W: 660/640/660	**ACT:** 29 **MOST COMPETITIVE**

Smith College, founded in 1871, is the largest independent women's college in the United States and offers a liberal arts education. There is one undergraduate school and one graduate school. In addition to regional accreditation, Smith has baccalaureate program accreditation with ABET. The 4 libraries contain 1.4 million volumes, 149,174 microform items, and 75,525 audio/video tapes/CDs/DVDs, and subscribe to 40,000 periodicals including electronic. Computerized library services include interlibrary loans, database searching, Internet access, and laptop Internet portals. Special learning facilities include a learning resource center, art gallery, radio station, TV station, astronomy observatories, center for foreign languages and culture, digital design studio, plant and horticultural labs, art studios with casting, printmaking, and darkroom facilities, and specialized libraries for science, music, and art, and the Quantitative Learning Center, and the Jacobson Center for Writing, Teaching and Learning. The 147-acre campus is in a small town 90 miles west of Boston. Including any residence halls, there are 115 buildings.

Programs of Study: Smith confers A.B. and B.S.E.S degrees. Master's and doctoral degrees are also awarded. Bachelor's degrees are awarded in BIOLOGICAL SCIENCE (biochemistry, biology/biological science, and neurosciences), COMMUNICATIONS AND THE ARTS (art history and appreciation, classics, comparative literature, creative writing, dance, dramatic arts, East Asian languages and literature, English, film arts, French, Germanic languages and literature, Greek, Italian, Latin, music, Russian, Spanish, and studio art), COMPUTER AND PHYSICAL SCIENCE (astronomy, chemistry, computer science, geology, mathematics, and physics), EDUCATION (early childhood education, education, and elementary education), ENGINEERING AND ENVIRONMENTAL DESIGN (architecture and engineering), HEALTH PROFESSIONS (exercise science), SOCIAL SCIENCE (African studies, African American studies, American studies, anthropology, classical/ancient civilization, cognitive science, economics, ethics, politics, and social policy, European studies, French studies, history, international relations, Japanese studies, Judaic studies, Latin American studies, Luso-Brazilian studies, medieval studies, Middle Eastern studies, philosophy, political science/government, psychology, religion, Russian and Slavic studies, sociology, urban studies, and women's studies). Art, government, and psychology are the largest.

Special: Smith offers study abroad in more than 50 countries including the Smith College programs in Italy, France, Germany, and Switzerland, affiliated programs in India, Japan, Russia, China, South Africa, Peru, Brazil, and Spain, and many others. Other opportunities include cross-registration with 5 area colleges, a Washington semester, Smithsonian internships, exchanges with historically Black colleges and other liberal arts colleges, and at BioSphere2. A 3-2 engineering degree is offered with Dartmouth College. Support for nontraditional-age students and for international students is provided, and funding for a summer internship is available for every undergraduate. Accelerated degree programs, student-designed majors, dual majors, and non-degree study are offered. There are 3 national honor societies, including Phi Beta Kappa.

Admissions: 47% of the 2009-2010 applicants were accepted. The SAT scores for the 2009-2010 freshman class were: Critical Reading--2% below 500, 20% between 500 and 599, 46% between 600 and 700, and 33% above 700; Math--4% below 500, 24% between 500 and 599, 48% between 600 and 700, and 25% above 700; Writing--1% below 500, 19% between 500 and 599, 49% between 600 and 700, and 32% above 700. The ACT scores were 4% below 21, 6% between 21 and 23, 16% between 24 and 26, 26% between 27 and 28, and 48% above 28. 87% of the current freshmen were in the top fifth of their class; 98% were in the top two fifths. 28 freshmen graduated first in their class.

Requirements: Smith highly recommends that applicants have 4 years of English, 3 years each of math, science, and a foreign language, and 2 years of history. SAT and ACT are considered but not required. Interviews are recommended. The GED is accepted. AP credits are accepted.

Procedure: Freshmen are admitted in the fall. Entrance exams should be taken before January of the senior year. There are early decision, early admissions, and deferred admissions plans. Early decision applications should be filed by November 15, along with a $60 fee. Notification of early decision is sent December 15; regular decision, April 1. 166 early decision candidates were accepted for the 2009-2010 class. 578 applicants were on the 2009 waiting list; 96 were admitted. Applications are accepted on-line.

Financial Aid: In 2009-2010, 61% of all full-time freshmen and 63% of continuing full-time students received some form of financial aid. 57% of all full-time freshmen and 60% of continuing full-time students received need-based aid. The average freshman award was $33,269. Need-based scholarships or need-based grants averaged $31,980 ; and need-based self-help aid (loans and jobs) averaged $4,745. The average financial indebtedness of the 2009 graduate was $21,573. Smith is a member of CSS. The CSS/Profile, FAFSA, and the college's own financial statement are required. The deadline for filing freshman financial aid applications for fall entry is February 1.

Computers: Students can access the campus network and the Internet from over 500 college-owned personal computers located throughout the campus in the libraries, classrooms, labs, and the Campus Center or by using their own computer in their on-campus residence. Wireless access is available in the libraries, Campus Center, houses, and classrooms. All students may access the system. There are no time limits and no fees.

SOUTH DAKOTA SCHOOL OF MINES AND TECHNOLOGY

Rapid City, SD 57701-3995

(605) 394-2414
(877) 877-6044; (605) 394-1979

Full-time: 1173 men, 344 women	**Faculty:** 125; IIA, av$
Part-time: 181 men, 225 women	**Ph.D.s:** 87%
Graduate: 200 men, 64 women	**Student/Faculty:** 12 to 1
Year: semesters, summer session	**Tuition:** $6830 ($8210)
Application Deadline: August 15	**Room & Board:** $5080
Freshman Class: 975 applied, 801 accepted, 362 enrolled	
SAT CR/M: 590/600	**ACT:** 26 **VERY COMPETITIVE+**

South Dakota School of Mines and Technology, founded in 1885, is a public university offering undergraduate and graduate programs in engineering, science, and mathematics. There is 1 graduate school. In addition to regional accreditation, SDSM&T has baccalaureate program accreditation with ABET and CSAB. The library contains 17,252 volumes, 26,103 microform items, and 7903 audio/video tapes/CDs/DVDs, and subscribes to 15,149 periodicals including electronic. Computerized library services include interlibrary loans, database searching, Internet access, and laptop Internet portals. Special learning facilities include a learning resource center, art gallery, natural history museum, planetarium, and geology museum. The 120-acre campus is in a suburban area 350 miles northeast of Denver, Colorado. Including any residence halls, there are 18 buildings.

Programs of Study: SDSM&T confers B.S. degrees. Associate, master's, and doctoral degrees are also awarded. Bachelor's degrees are awarded in COMPUTER AND PHYSICAL SCIENCE (chemistry, computer science, geology, mathematics, and physics), ENGINEERING AND ENVIRONMENTAL DESIGN (chemical engineering, civil engineering, computer engineering, electrical/electronics engineering, environmental engineering, geological engineering, industrial engineering, mechanical engineering, metallurgical engineering, and mining and mineral engineering), SOCIAL SCIENCE (interdisciplinary studies). Engineering is the strongest academically. Mechanical engineering, civil engineering, and chemical engineering are the largest.

Special: Opportunities are provided for study abroad, co-op programs, internships, dual degrees, undergraduate research experiences, interdisciplinary design teams, credit by exam, and nondegree study. There are 5 national honor societies, including Phi Beta Kappa.

Admissions: 82% of the 2009-2010 applicants were accepted. The SAT scores for the 2009-2010 freshman class were: Critical Reading--23% below 500, 32% between 500 and 599, 39% between 600 and 700, and 5% above 700; Math--4% below 500, 39% between 500 and 599, 45% between 600 and 700, and 13% above 700. The ACT scores were 3% below 21, 18% between 21 and 23, 36% between 24 and 26, 19% between 27 and 28, and 24% above 28. 45% of the current freshmen were in the top fifth of their class; 78% were in the top two fifths. There was 1 National Merit finalist. 11 freshmen graduated first in their class.

Requirements: The SAT or ACT is required, with a minimum composite score of 920 (420 critical reading/writing and 500 math) on the SAT or a minimum composite score of 18 on the ACT. The ACT is preferred. Graduation from an accredited secondary school is required. A GED is accepted. Applicants must submit high school credits, distributed as follows: 4 years of English, 3 each of math, lab science, and social studies, and 1/2 year each of fine arts and computer science. A GPA of 2.8 is required. AP and CLEP credits are accepted.

Procedure: Freshmen are admitted fall, spring, and summer. Entrance exams should be taken in October and December. There is a rolling admissions plan. Applications should be filed by August 15 for fall entry and January 15 for spring entry. The fall 2009 application fee was $20. Notification is sent on a rolling basis. Applications are accepted on-line.

Financial Aid: In 2009-2010, 55% of all full-time freshmen and 54% of continuing full-time students received some form of financial aid. 41% of all full-time freshmen and 34% of continuing full-time students received need-based aid. The average freshman award was $8927. 8% of undergraduate students work part-time. Average annual earnings from campus work are $1887. The average financial indebtedness of the 2009 graduate was $18,296. The FAFSA is required. The deadline for filing freshman financial aid applications for fall entry is March 15.

Computers: Wireless access is available. All students are required to have a tablet PC, which they receive under the tablet program for a fee of $375 per semester, with an additional usage fee of $6 per credit hour. All students may access the system 24 hours per day. There are no time limits and no fees.

SOUTHERN METHODIST UNIVERSITY
Dallas, TX 75275-0181

(214) 768-4223
(800) 323-0672; (214) 768-0202

Full-time: 2793 men, 3128 women	**Faculty:** 660; I, av$
Part-time: 143 men, 164 women	**Ph.D.s:** 84%
Graduate: 2559 men, 2104 women	**Student/Faculty:** 9 to 1
Year: semesters, summer session	**Tuition:** $35,160
Application Deadline: January 15	**Room & Board:** $12,445
Freshman Class: 8356 applied, 4467 accepted, 1329 enrolled	
SAT CR/M/W: 610/630/610	**ACT:** 28 **HIGHLY COMPETITIVE+**

Southern Methodist University, founded in 1911, is a private nonsectarian institution affiliated with the United Methodist Church. SMU offers undergraduate and graduate programs in humanities and sciences, business, arts, engineering, and applied sciences. There are 5 undergraduate schools and 7 graduate schools. In addition to regional accreditation, SMU has baccalaureate program accreditation with AACSB, ABET, NASAD, and NASM. Computerized library services include interlibrary loans, database searching, Internet access, and laptop Internet portals. Special learning facilities include a learning resource center, art gallery, natural history museum, radio station, art museum, research labs, TV studio, and several performing arts theaters, including Classical Thrust Stage. The 231-acre campus is in a suburban area 5 miles north of downtown Dallas. Including any residence halls, there are 76 buildings.

Programs of Study: SMU confers B.A., B.S., B.B.A., B.F.A., B.Hum., B.M., B.S.Comp.Eng., B.S.E.E., B.S.Env.E., and B.S.M.E. degrees. Master's and doctoral degrees are also awarded. Bachelor's degrees are awarded in BIOLOGICAL SCIENCE (biochemistry and biology/biological science), BUSINESS (accounting, banking and finance, business administration and management, management information systems, management science, marketing/retailing/merchandising, organizational behavior, and real estate), COMMUNICATIONS AND THE ARTS (advertising, art history and appreciation, broadcasting, communications, communications technology, creative writing, dance, dramatic arts, English, film arts, French, German, journalism, languages, media arts, music performance, music theory and composition, piano/organ, performing arts, public relations, Russian, Spanish, studio art, telecommunications, and video), COMPUTER AND PHYSICAL SCIENCE (chemistry, computer science, environmental geology,

geology, geophysics and seismology, mathematics, physics, and statistics), EDUCATION (art education, dance education, elementary education, health education, music education, and physical education), ENGINEERING AND ENVIRONMENTAL DESIGN (civil engineering, computer engineering, electrical/electronics engineering, engineering management, environmental engineering, environmental science, and mechanical engineering), HEALTH PROFESSIONS (music therapy and speech pathology/audiology), SOCIAL SCIENCE (African American studies, anthropology, criminal justice, economics, German area studies, history, humanities, international studies, Italian studies, Latin American studies, liberal arts/general studies, medieval studies, Mexican-American/Chicano studies, philosophy, physical fitness/movement, political science/government, psychology, public affairs, religion, Russian and Slavic studies, social science, sociology, and Southwest American studies). Performing arts, life sciences, and history are the strongest academically. Business, communications, and psychology are the largest.

Special: SMU offers a co-op program in engineering, work-study programs, B.A.-B.S. degrees, study abroad in 48 countries with 145 programs, dual majors in any combination, student-designed majors, numerous internships, and interdisciplinary majors, including economics with finance applications and economics with systems analysis. A 3-2 advanced degree in business is available, as are evening degree programs in humanities and social sciences, and teacher certification programs. There are 26 national honor societies, including Phi Beta Kappa, and a freshman honors program. The majority of departments and majors have honors programs.

Admissions: 53% of the 2009-2010 applicants were accepted. The SAT scores for the 2009-2010 freshman class were: Critical Reading--8% below 500, 33% between 500 and 599, 44% between 600 and 700, and 14% above 700; Math--5% below 500, 31% between 500 and 599, 52% between 600 and 700, and 16% above 700; Writing--9% below 500, 33% between 500 and 599, 44% between 600 and 700, and 14% above 700. The ACT scores were 2% below 21, 5% between 21 and 23, 13% between 24 and 26, 12% between 27 and 28, and 22% above 28. 65% of the current freshmen were in the top fifth of their class; 87% were in the top two fifths.

Requirements: The SAT or ACT is recommended. In addition, applicants should graduate from an accredited high school with a minimum of 15 academic credits: 4 in English, 3 in higher math, including algebra I, II, and plane geometry, 3 each in natural science and social science, and 2 in a foreign language. Home School Certificate applicants may qualify with the SAT or ACT and 3 SAT Subject Tests in math, literature, and science. Performing arts majors must audition. AP and CLEP credits are accepted. Important factors in the admissions decision are advanced placement or honors courses, leadership record, and recommendations by school officials.

Procedure: Freshmen are admitted to all sessions. Entrance exams should be taken by December of the senior year. There are early decision admissions, deferred admissions, and rolling admissions plans. Early decision applications should be filed by November 1; regular applications by January 15 for fall entry and March 15 for spring entry, along with a $60 fee. Notification of early decision is sent December 31; regular decision, sent on a rolling basis. Applications are accepted on-line. 735 applicants were on a recent waiting list, 183 were accepted.

Financial Aid: In 2009-2010, 74% of all full-time freshmen and 70% of continuing full-time students received some form of financial aid. 40% of all full-time freshmen and 36% of continuing full-time students received need-based aid. The average freshman award was $33,921. Need-based scholarships or need-based

grants averaged $20,259; need-based self-help aid (loans and jobs) averaged $4,874; and non-need based athletic scholarships averaged $39,091. The average financial indebtedness of the 2009 graduate was $20,146. SMU is a member of CSS. The CSS/Profile and FAFSA are required. The priority date for freshman financial aid applications for fall entry is February 15.

Computers: Wireless access is available. All students may access the system 24 hours a day. There are no time limits and no fees.

SOUTHERN POLYTECHNIC STATE UNIVERSITY

Marietta, GA 30060-2896

(678) 915-7778
(800) 635-3204; (678) 915-7292

Full-time: 2690 men, 625 women	**Faculty:** 190; II A, --$
Part-time: 999 men, 249 women	**Ph.D.s:** 68%
Graduate: 391 men, 229 women	**Student/Faculty:** 18 to 1
Year: semesters, summer session	**Tuition:** $4498
Application Deadline: August 1	**Room & Board:** $6350
Freshman Class: 1250 applied, 935 accepted, 514 enrolled	
SAT CR/M/W: 550/580/510	**ACT:** 23 **VERY COMPETITIVE**

Southern Polytechnic State University, founded in 1948, is a member of the University System of Georgia. Through a fusion of technology with the liberal arts and sciences, SPSU creates a learning community that encourages thoughtful inquiry, diverse perspectives, and strong preparation of its graduates to be leaders in an increasingly technological world. The university offers degree programs in computer science, engineering, architecture, engineering technology, business, biology, construction, math, physics, chemistry, and communications. There are 4 undergraduate schools and 4 graduate schools. In addition to regional accreditation, Southern Polytechnic has baccalaureate program accreditation with ABET, ACBSP, ACCE, and NAAB. The library contains 125,636 volumes, 3,482 microform items, and 290 audio/video tapes/CDs/DVDs, and subscribes to 1,016 periodicals including electronic. Computerized library services include interlibrary loans, database searching, Internet access, and laptop Internet portals. Special learning facilities include a learning resource center and radio station. The 203-acre campus is in a suburban area 15 miles northwest of Atlanta. Including any residence halls, there are 44 buildings.

Programs of Study: Southern Polytechnic confers B.A., B.S., B.Arch., B.A.S., B.A.T., B.S.A., B.S.C.E., B.S.C.G.D.D., B.S. Eng., B.S.I.T., B.S.P., B.S.P.S., B.S.S.W.E., B.S.T.E.T., degrees. Associates and master's degrees are also awarded. Bachelor's degrees are awarded in BIOLOGICAL SCIENCE (biology/biological science), BUSINESS (accounting, business administration and management, and business communications), COMMUNICATIONS AND THE ARTS (apparel design, technical and business writing, and telecommunications), COMPUTER AND PHYSICAL SCIENCE (applied science, chemistry, computer science, information sciences and systems, mathematics, physics, and software engineering), ENGINEERING AND ENVIRONMENTAL DESIGN (architecture, civil engineering technology, computer engineering, construction engineering, construction management, electrical/electronics engineering technology, industrial engineering technology, manufacturing engineering, mechanical engineering technology, survey and mapping technology, and systems engineering), SOCIAL SCIENCE (clothing and textiles management/production/services, international studies, and psychology). Architecture, mechanical engineering technology, and civil engineering technology are the largest.

Special: Southern Polytechnic offers cross-registration through ARCHE cooperative programs, dual majors in all disciplines, internships, and study abroad in Germany and Mexico. There is 1 national honor society and a freshman honors program.

Admissions: 75% of the 2009-2010 applicants were accepted. The SAT scores for the 2009-2010 freshman class were: Critical Reading--21% below 500, 53% between 500 and 599, 23% between 600 and 700, and 3% above 700; Math--10% below 500, 51% between 500 and 599, 36% between 600 and 700, and 3% above 700; Writing--41% below 500, 46% between 500 and 599, 12% between 600 and 700, and 1% above 700. The ACT scores were 22% below 21, 37% between 21 and 23, 28% between 24 and 26, 8% between 27 and 28, and 5% above 28.

Requirements: The SAT or ACT is required. The ACT Optional Writing test is also required. In addition, applicants must be graduates of an accredited secondary school. Students should have completed 18 academic credits, including 4 years of English and math, 3 of science and social studies, and 2 of a foreign, plus 2 additional units. A GPA of 2.5 is required. AP and CLEP credits are accepted.

Procedure: Freshmen are admitted to all sessions. Entrance exams should be taken by the end of the junior year. There are early admissions and rolling admissions plans. Applications should be filed by August 1 for fall entry, December 1 for spring entry, and May 1 for summer entry, along with a $20 fee. Notification is sent on a rolling basis. Applications are accepted on-line.

Financial Aid: In 2009-2010, 51% of all full-time freshmen and 50% of continuing full-time students received some form of financial aid. The average financial indebtedness of the 2009 graduate was $8,300. Southern Polytechnic is a member of CSS. The FAFSA is required. The priority date for freshman financial aid applications for fall entry is April 1.

Computers: Wireless access is available. There are 25 computer labs with 850 workstations. All students may access the system. There are no time limits and no fees. Students enrolled in architecture must have a personal computer.

SOUTHWESTERN UNIVERSITY
Georgetown, TX 78626-6144 (512) 863-1200
(800) 252-3166; (512) 863-9601

Full-time: 495 men, 765 women	**Faculty:** IIB, av$
Part-time: 15 men, 10 women	**Ph.D.s:** 98%
Graduate: none	**Student/Faculty:** n/av
Year: semesters, summer session	**Tuition:** $31,600
Application Deadline: see profile	**Room & Board:** $9240
Freshman Class: n/av	
SAT or ACT: required	**HIGHLY COMPETITIVE**

Southwestern University, founded in 1840, is a private liberal arts institution affiliated with the United Methodist Church. Figures in the above capsule are approximate. There are 2 undergraduate schools. In addition to regional accreditation, Southwestern has baccalaureate program accreditation with NASM. The library contains 312,490 volumes, 56,531 microform items, and 12,186 audio/video tapes/CDs/DVDs, and subscribes to 1372 periodicals including electronic. Computerized library services include interlibrary loans and database searching. Special learning facilities include a learning resource center and art gallery. The 700-acre campus is in a suburban area 28 miles north of Austin. Including any residence halls, there are 31 buildings.

Programs of Study: Southwestern confers B.A., B.S., B.F.A., and B.Mus. degrees. Bachelor's degrees are awarded in AGRICULTURE (animal science and environmental studies), BIOLOGICAL SCIENCE (biology/biological science), BUSINESS (accounting and business administration and management), COMMUNICATIONS AND THE ARTS (art, classics, communications, dramatic arts, English, French, German, Latin, music, and Spanish), COMPUTER AND PHYSICAL SCIENCE (chemistry, computer science, mathematics, and physics), SOCIAL SCIENCE (American studies, early childhood studies, economics, history, international studies, philosophy, physical fitness/movement, political science/government, psychology, religion, sociology, and women's studies). Biology, sociology, and political science are the strongest academically. Psychology, biology, and business are the largest.

Special: Students may study abroad in England, France, Mexico, Korea, and other countries. The university offers a Washington semester; dual, student-designed, and independent majors; and internships in government, fine arts, psychology, sociology, science, and other fields in Texas, New York, and other states. A 3-2 engineering program may be arranged with Washington, Texas A&M, and Arizona State Universities and the University of Texas at Austin. Some pass/fail options are available, as are accelerated degrees in any field. There are 7 national honor societies, including Phi Beta Kappa, and 21 departmental honors programs.

Admissions: There were 5 National Merit finalists in a recent year. 7 freshmen graduated first in their class.

Requirements: The SAT or ACT is required. In addition, applicants should be graduates of an accredited high school or have the GED. Secondary preparation should include 4 years each of English and math, 3 each of science and social science or history, 2 of a foreign language, and 1 of an academic elective. An essay is required, and an interview is recommended. AP and CLEP credits are accepted. Important factors in the admissions decision are advanced placement or honors courses, recommendations by school officials, and leadership record.

Procedure: Freshmen are admitted fall and spring. Entrance exams should be taken in the fall of the senior year. There early decision and deferred admissions plans. Early decision applications should be filed by November 1; check with the school for current application deadlines. Notification of early decision is sent December 1. The application fee is $40. Applications are accepted on-line. 16 applicants were on a recent waiting list, 7 were accepted.

Financial Aid: In a recent year, 54% of all full-time freshmen and 49% of continuing full-time students received some form of financial aid. 54% of all full-time freshmen and 48% of continuing full-time students received need-based aid. The average freshmen award was $22,249. 59% of undergraduate students work part-time. Average annual earnings from campus work are $1083. The average financial indebtedness of a recent graduate was $22,652. Southwestern is a member of CSS. The FAFSA is required. Check with the school for current application deadlines.

Computers: All students may access the system at any time. There are no time limits and no fees.

SPELMAN COLLEGE

Atlanta, GA 30314
(404) 681-3643
(800) 982-2411; (404) 215-7788

Full-time: 25 men, 2205 women	**Faculty:** n/av
Part-time: 97 women	**Ph.D.s:** n/av
Graduate: none	**Student/Faculty:** n/av
Year: semesters	**Tuition:** $19,000
Application Deadline: February 1	**Room & Board:** $10,000
Freshman Class: n/av	
SAT or ACT: required	**VERY COMPETITIVE**

Spelman College, founded in 1881, is a private, nonsectarian, liberal arts college for black women. Some figures in the above capsule and in this profile are approximate. In addition to regional accreditation, Spelman has baccalaureate program accreditation with NASM and NCATE. The library contains 500,000 volumes, 385,538 microform items, and subscribes to 1,439 periodicals including electronic. Special learning facilities include a learning resource center, art gallery, a language lab, a media center, and music and art studios. The 32-acre campus is in an urban area 3 miles southwest of downtown Atlanta. Including any residence halls, there are 24 buildings.

Programs of Study: Spelman confers B.A. and B.S. degrees. Bachelor's degrees are awarded in BIOLOGICAL SCIENCE (biochemistry and biology/biological science), COMMUNICATIONS AND THE ARTS (art, dramatic arts, English, fine arts, French, music, and Spanish), COMPUTER AND PHYSICAL SCIENCE (chemistry, computer science, mathematics, natural sciences, and physics), EDUCATION (art education), ENGINEERING AND ENVIRONMENTAL DESIGN (engineering), SOCIAL SCIENCE (anthropology, child psychology/development, economics, history, philosophy, political science/government, psychology, religion, sociology, and women's studies). Biology and engineering are the strongest academically. Psychology, biology, and English are the largest.

Special: Students may cross-register with Atlanta University Center member institutions. Spelman offers internships, study abroad in several countries, student-designed majors, work-study programs at the school, B.A.-B.S. degrees, and dual majors, as well as a 3-2 engineering degree with Georgia Tech, Rochester Institute of Technology, University of Alabama at Huntsville, Auburn and Boston Universities, and North Carolina Agricultural and Technical State University. The college grants credit for life experience and permits nondegree study. There are 9 national honor societies, including Phi Beta Kappa, and a freshman honors program.

Requirements: The SAT or ACT is required, in addition applicants should be high school graduates or have a GED certificate. Students should have earned at least 12 academic credits, including 4 in English, 2 each in foreign language, math (algebra and geometry), social studies, and science (including a lab science). Students with additional years in math, science, and language and with AP and honors courses are considered more competitive. An essay is required. An audition or portfolio is recommended for art majors. A GPA of 2.0 is required. AP and CLEP credits are accepted. Important factors in the admissions decision are advanced placement or honors courses, leadership record, and recommendations by school officials.

Procedure: Freshmen are admitted fall. Entrance exams should be taken by December of the senior year. There are early decision, early admissions and deferred admissions plans. Early decision applications should be filed by November 15, regular applications by February 1 for fall entry, along with a $35 fee. Notifications of early decision are sent December 31; regular decision, April 1. A waiting list is maintained.

Financial Aid: Spelman is a member of CSS. The FAFSA and the college's own financial statement are required. Check with the school for current application deadlines.

Computers: All students may access the system. 24 hours a day. There are no time limits. There is a fee. It is strongly recommended that all students have a personal computer.

STANFORD UNIVERSITY
Stanford, CA 94305   (650) 725-5294; (650) 725-2846

Full-time: 3373 men, 3192 women	**Faculty:** 825; I, ++$
Part-time: 17 men, 20 women	**Ph.D.s:** 98%
Graduate: 7252 men, 4644 women	**Student/Faculty:** 8 to 1
Year: trimesters, summer session	**Tuition:** $37,881
Application Deadline: January 1	**Room & Board:** $11,463
Freshman Class: 30,429 applied, 2426 accepted, 1694 enrolled	
SAT or ACT: required	**MOST COMPETITIVE**

Stanford University, founded in 1885, is a private research-intensive university offering a broad curriculum in undergraduate liberal arts, graduate education, and professional training. There are 3 undergraduate schools and 7 graduate schools. In addition to regional accreditation, Stanford has baccalaureate program accreditation with AACSB and ABET. The 18 libraries contain 8.5 million volumes, 6 million microform items, and 1.5 million audio/video tapes/CDs/DVDs, and subscribe to 75,000 periodicals including electronic. Computerized library services include interlibrary loans, database searching, Internet access, and laptop Internet portals. Special learning facilities include a learning resource center, art gallery, radio station, TV station, an art museum, a biological preserve, and a linear accelerator. The 8180-acre campus is in a suburban area 30 miles south of San Francisco. Including any residence halls, there are 670 buildings.

Programs of Study: Stanford confers A.B., B.S., and B.A.S. degrees. Master's and doctoral degrees are also awarded. Bachelor's degrees are awarded in BIOLOGICAL SCIENCE (biology/biological science), COMMUNICATIONS AND THE ARTS (art, art history and appreciation, Chinese, classics, communications, comparative literature, dramatic arts, English, film arts, fine arts, French, Italian, Japanese, linguistics, music, Slavic languages, Spanish, and studio art), COMPUTER AND PHYSICAL SCIENCE (chemistry, computer science, earth science, geology, geophysics and seismology, geoscience, mathematics, physics, and statistics), ENGINEERING AND ENVIRONMENTAL DESIGN (aeronautical science, biomedical engineering, chemical engineering, chemical engineering technology, civil engineering, electrical/electronics engineering, energy management technology, engineering, engineering physics, environmental engineering, industrial engineering, materials science, mechanical engineering, petroleum/natural gas engineering, and systems engineering), SOCIAL SCIENCE (African American studies, American studies, anthropology, archeology, Asian/American studies, crosscultural studies, East Asian studies, economics, German area studies, Hispanic American studies, history, Iberian studies, international relations, Latin American studies, Native American studies, philosophy, political science/government, psychology, public administration, religion, sociology, systems science, urban studies, and women's studies). Biology, economics, and international relations are the largest.

Special: Internships, study abroad, a Washington semester, student-designed majors, dual majors, a B.A.-B.S. degree, pass/no credit options, and numerous research opportunities are offered, as well as honors programs, study at Stanford's marine station, and co-terminal bachelor's and master's programs. There is a Phi Beta Kappa honros program. Almost all departments have honors programs.

Admissions: 8% of the 2009-2010 applicants were accepted.

Requirements: The SAT or ACT is required; the SAT is preferred. The SAT writing test is used for admission; the ACT writing test is required. The university recommends that applicants have strong preparation in high school English, math, a foreign language, science, and social studies. SAT Subject tests are strongly recommended. AP credits are accepted. Important factors in the admissions decision are advanced placement or honors courses, personality/intangible qualities, and recommendations by school officials.

Procedure: Freshmen are admitted fall. Entrance exams should be taken so that scores arrive before January 1 for regular admission and November 1 for early action. There is a deferred admissions and an early action plan. Early action applications should be filed by November 1; regular applications, by January 1 for fall entry, along with a $90 fee. Notification of early decision is sent December 15; regular decision, April 1. 1354 applicants were on the 2009 waiting list; 127 were admitted. Applications are accepted on-line.

Financial Aid: In 2009-2010, 80% of all full-time students received some form of financial aid. 46% of all students received need-based aid. The average freshman award was $40,204. Need-based scholarships or need-based grants averaged $38,037; need-based self-help aid (loans and jobs) averaged $2123. The average financial indebtedness of the 2009 graduate was $16,219. The CSS/Profile and FAFSA are required. The priority date for freshman financial aid applications for fall entry is February 15.

Computers: Wireless access is available. Services include e-mail, web hosting, distributed file system, wireless and remote Internet access, courseware and research, and high-performance computing facilities. All students may access the system. There are no time limits and no fees.

STATE UNIVERSITY OF NEW YORK AT BINGHAMTON /BINGHAMTON UNIVERSITY

Binghamton, NY 13902-6000   **(607) 777-2171; (607) 777-4445**

Full-time: 5898 men, 5381 women	**Faculty:** 596; I, -$
Part-time: 251 men, 174 women	**Ph.D.s:** 91%
Graduate: 1558 men, 1449 women	**Student/Faculty:** 19 to 1
Year: semesters, summer session	**Tuition:** $6761 ($14,661)
Application Deadline: January 15	**Room & Board:** $10,614
Freshman Class: 29,062 applied, 9692 accepted, 2026 enrolled	
SAT CR/M: 630/660	**ACT:** 29 **HIGHLY COMPETITIVE+**

Part of the State University of New York (SUNY) system, Binghamton University was founded in 1946. The university offers programs in arts and sciences, education, nursing, management, engineering and applied science, and community and public affairs. There are 5 undergraduate schools and 1 graduate school. In addition to regional accreditation, Binghamton University has baccalaureate program accreditation with AACSB, ABET, CSWE, NASM, and TEAC. The 3 libraries contain 2.4 million volumes, 1.9 million microform items, and 125,656 audio/video tapes/CDs/DVDs, and subscribe to 81,959 periodicals including electronic. Computerized library services include interlibrary loans, database searching, Internet access, and laptop Internet portals. Special learning facilities include a learning resource center, art gallery, radio station, TV station, nature preserve, 4-climate greenhouse, performing arts center (5 theaters), art/dance studios, sculpture foundry, research centers, electron microscopy labs, geographic information systems core facility, public archeology facility, integrated electronics engineering center, institute for child development, and information commons. The 930-acre campus is in a suburban area 1 mile west of Binghamton. Including any residence halls, there are 107 buildings.

Programs of Study: Binghamton University confers B.A., B.S., and B.Mus. degrees. Master's and doctoral degrees are also awarded. Bachelor's degrees are awarded in BIOLOGICAL SCIENCE (biochemistry, biology/biological science, biophysics, cell biology, evolutionary biology, and molecular biology), BUSINESS (accounting, banking and finance, business administration and management, entrepreneurial studies, management information systems, management science, marketing management, operations management, and supply chain management), COMMUNICATIONS AND THE ARTS (Arabic, art, art history and appreciation, classics, comparative literature, creative writing, dance, dramatic arts, English, film arts, fine arts, French, German, Hebrew, Italian, Latin, linguistics, literature, music, music performance, Spanish, speech/debate/rhetoric, studio art, theater design, and visual and performing arts), COMPUTER AND PHYSICAL SCIENCE (actuarial science, applied physics, chemistry, computer science, environmental geology, geology, information sciences and systems, mathematics, and physics), ENGINEERING AND ENVIRONMENTAL DESIGN (bioengineering, computer engineering, electrical/electronics engineering, engineering, environmental science, industrial engineering, mechanical engineering, and systems engineering), HEALTH PROFESSIONS (nursing), SOCIAL SCIENCE (African American studies, anthropology, Asian/American studies, Caribbean studies, classical/ancient civilization, economics, geography, history, human development, interdisciplinary studies, international studies, Judaic studies, Latin American studies, medieval studies, philosophy, political science/government, psychobiology, psychology, and sociology). Management, political science, and biology are the strongest academically. Engineering, biology, and management are the largest.

Special: The university offers innovative study through the individualized major program (student-designed majors), internships, independent study, study abroad in more than 100 countries, a Washington semester through American University, on- and off-campus work-study programs, and B.A.-B.S. degrees in 28 departments. There are also dual and interdisciplinary majors such as philosophy, politics, and law and prehealth programs in medicine, denistry, optometry, veterinary medicine, podiatry, nutrition, physical and occupational therapy, and chiropractic. Early assurance programs guarantee graduate admission at partner SUNY schools. There are 23 national honor societies, including Phi Beta Kappa, a freshman honors program, and 32 departmental honors programs.

Admissions: 33% of the 2009-2010 applicants were accepted. The SAT scores for the 2009-2010 freshman class were: Critical Reading--3% below 500, 29% between 500 and 599, 52% between 600 and 700; and 15% above 700; Math--15% between 500 and 599, 57% between 600 and 700, and 28% above 700. The ACT scores were 6% between 21 and 23, 19% between 24 and 26, 23% between 27 and 28, and 52% above 29. 78% of the current freshmen were in the top fifth of their class; 94% were in the top two fifths.

Requirements: The SAT or ACT is required. The ACT Optional Writing test is also required. In addition, applicants must be graduates of an accredited secondary school or have a GED certificate and complete 16 academic credits. These include 4 units of English, 3 units of 1 foreign language or 2 units each of 2 foreign languages, 2 1/2 of math, and 2 each of science and social studies. Students may submit slides of artwork, request an audition for music, prepare a videotape for dance or theater, or share athletic achievements. An essay is required. AP and CLEP credits are accepted. Important factors in the admissions decision are advanced placement or honors courses, extracurricular activities record, and evidence of special talent.

Procedure: Freshmen are admitted fall and spring. Entrance exams should be taken in the spring of the junior year or the fall of the senior year. There are deferred admissions and rolling admissions plans. Applications should be filed by January 15 (priority date) for fall entry; November 15 for spring entry, along with a $40 fee. Notification is sent on a rolling basis beginning April 1. Applications are accepted on-line. 735 applicants were on a recent waiting list, 45 were accepted.

Financial Aid: In 2009-2010, 80% of all full-time freshmen and 87% of continuing full-time students received some form of financial aid. 60% of all full-time freshmen and 57% of continuing full-time students received need-based aid. The average freshmen award was $20,017. 8% of undergraduate students work part-time (not including work study). Average annual earnings from campus work are $1820. The average financial indebtedness of a 2008 graduate was $14,560. The FAFSA is required. The deadline for filing freshman financial aid applications for fall entry is February 1.

Computers: Wireless access is available. Every residence hall room has an ethernet port per resident. Wireless access is provided in all residential communities, throughout all academic buildings, in the Univesity Union and library, and in most outdoor spaces on the central campus. There are more than 1200 wireless access points. There are more than 620 computers in public computer rooms, classrooms, and labs, the largest of which is open nearly round-the-clock during the academic year. All students may access the system 24 hours per day. There are no time limits and no fees.

STATE UNIVERSITY OF NEW YORK AT FREDONIA

Fredonia, NY 14063

(716) 673-3251
(800) 252-1212; (716) 673-3249

Full-time: 2219 men, 2940 women	**Faculty:** 222; IIA, -$
Part-time: 98 men, 120 women	**Ph.D.s:** 81%
Graduate: 84 men, 296 women	**Student/Faculty:** 21 to 1
Year: semesters, summer session	**Tuition:** $6258 ($14,158)
Application Deadline: open	**Room & Board:** $9330
Freshman Class: 6632 applied, 3281 accepted, 1148 enrolled	
SAT CR/M: 550/560	**ACT:** 24 **VERY COMPETITIVE**

The State University of New York at Fredonia, established in 1826, is a public institution offering undergraduate programs in the arts and sciences, business and professional curricula, teacher preparation, and the fine and performing arts. There are 6 undergraduate schools and 1 graduate school. In addition to regional accreditation, Fredonia has baccalaureate program accreditation with CSWE, NASAD, NASM, and NCATE. The library contains 391,121 volumes, 1.1 million microform items, and 26,574 audio/video tapes/CDs/DVDs, and subscribes to 1983 periodicals including electronic. Computerized library services include interlibrary loans, database searching, and Internet access. Special learning facilities include a learning resource center, art gallery, radio station, TV station, greenhouse, daycare center, speech clinic, and arts center. The 266-acre campus is in a small town 50 miles south of Buffalo and 45 miles north of Erie, Pennsylvania. Including any residence halls, there are 25 buildings.

Programs of Study: Fredonia confers B.A., B.F.A., B.S., B.S.Ed., and B.Mus. degrees. Master's degrees are also awarded. Bachelor's degrees are awarded in BIOLOGICAL SCIENCE (biochemistry and biology/biological science), BUSINESS (accounting, business administration and management, business economics, and sports management), COMMUNICATIONS AND THE ARTS (audio technology, communications, dramatic arts, English, fine arts, French, graphic design, media arts, music, and Spanish), COMPUTER AND PHYSICAL SCIENCE (chemistry, computer science, earth science, geology, mathematics, and physics), EDUCATION (early childhood education, elementary education, foreign languages education, middle school education, music education, science education, and secondary education), HEALTH PROFESSIONS (health care administration, medical laboratory technology, predentistry, premedicine, and speech pathology/audiology), SOCIAL SCIENCE (history, interdisciplinary studies, philosophy, political science/government, psychology, social work, and sociology). Business, communication, and education are the largest.

Special: Cooperative programs are available with many other institutions. Students may cross-register with colleges in the Western New York Consortium. Fredonia offers a variety of internships, study-abroad programs in more than 50 countries, and a Washington semester. Accelerated degrees, a general studies degree, dual and student-designed majors, a 3-2 engineering degree program with 14 universities, nondegree study, and pass/fail grading options are available. There are 19 national honor societies, a freshman honors program, and 19 departmental honors programs.

Admissions: 49% of the 2009-2010 applicants were accepted. The SAT scores for the 2009-2010 freshman class were: Critical Reading--30% below 500, 51% between 500 and 599, 18% between 600 and 700, and 1% above 700; Math--23% below 500, 53% between 500 and 599, 23% between 600 and 700, and 1& above 700. The ACT scores were 21% below 21, 35% between 21 and 23, 30% between 24 and 26, 8% between 27 and 28, and 6% above 28. 37% of the current freshmen were in the top fifth of their class; 74% were in the top two fifths. 10 freshmen graduated first in their class.

Requirements: The SAT or ACT is required, with a satisfactory score on the SAT or 20 on the ACT. Applicants must possess a high school diploma or have a GED. 16 academic credits are recommended, including 4 credits each in English and social studies and 3 each in math, science, and a foreign language. 4 years of math and science are encouraged. Essays are required. Where applicable, an audition or portfolio is required. A GPA of 2.5 is required. AP and CLEP credits are accepted. Important factors in the admissions decision are advanced placement or honors courses and recommendations by school officials.

Procedure: Freshmen are admitted fall and spring. Entrance exams should be taken during the spring of the junior year or fall of the senior year. There are early decision, deferred admissions and rolling admissions plans. Early decision applications should be filed by November 1; check with the school for current application deadlines. The application fee is $40. Notification of early decision is sent November 25; regular decision, December 15. Applications are accepted online.

Financial Aid: In 2009-2010, 83% of all full-time freshmen and 77% of continuing full-time students received some form of financial aid. 68% of all students received need-based aid. The average financial indebtedness of the 2009 graduate was $23,452. The FAFSA, the state aid form, and the Express TAP Application

(ETA) are required. The priority date for freshman financial aid applications for fall entry is February 1.

Computers: Wireless access is available. All students may access the system. There are no time limits and no fees. It is strongly recommended that all students have a personal computer.

STATE UNIVERSITY OF NEW YORK AT OSWEGO

Oswego, NY 13126	(315) 312-2250; (315) 312-3260
Full-time: 3070 men, 3580 women	**Faculty:** IIA, -$
Part-time: 195 men, 280 women	**Ph.D.s:** n/av
Graduate: 345 men, 645 women	**Student/Faculty:** n/av
Year: semesters, summer session	**Tuition:** $6706 ($14,606)
Application Deadline: January 15	**Room & Board:** $9500
Freshman Class: n/av	
SAT or ACT: required	**VERY COMPETITIVE**

State University of New York at Oswego, founded in 1861, is a comprehensive institution offering more than 110 cooperative, preprofessional, and graduate programs in the arts and sciences, business, and education. The figures in the above capsule and in this profile are approximate. There are 3 undergraduate schools and 3 graduate schools. In addition to regional accreditation, Oswego has baccalaureate program accreditation with AACSB, NASM, and NCATE. The library contains 475,000 volumes, 2.1 million microform items, and 15,000 audio/video tapes/CDs/DVDs, and subscribes to 1,800 periodicals including electronic. Computerized library services include interlibrary loans, database searching, Internet access, and laptop Internet portals. Special learning facilities include a learning resource center, art gallery, planetarium, radio station, TV station, biological field station. The 696-acre campus is in a small town on the southeast shore of Lake Ontario, 35 miles northwest of Syracuse. Including any residence halls, there are 40 buildings.

Programs of Study: Oswego confers B.A., B.S., and B.F.A. degrees. Master's degrees are also awarded. Bachelor's degrees are awarded in BIOLOGICAL SCIENCE (biochemistry, biology/biological science, and zoology), BUSINESS (accounting, banking and finance, business administration and management, human resources, international economics, management science, marketing/retailing/merchandising, and recreational facilities management), COMMUNICATIONS AND THE ARTS (art, broadcasting, communications, creative writing, dramatic arts, English, film arts, French, German, graphic design, journalism, linguistics, music, public relations, and Spanish), COMPUTER AND PHYSICAL SCIENCE (applied mathematics, atmospheric sciences and meteorology, chemistry, computer science, geochemistry, geology, information sciences and systems, mathematics, and physics), EDUCATION (agricultural education, business education, elementary education, foreign languages education, secondary education, teaching English as a second/foreign language (TESOL/TEFOL), trade and industrial education, and vocational education), ENGINEERING AND ENVIRONMENTAL DESIGN (technological management), SOCIAL SCIENCE (American studies, anthropology, cognitive science, criminal justice, economics, history, human development, international studies, philosophy, political science/government, psychology, sociology, and women's studies). Chemistry, computer science, and accounting are the strongest academically. Elementary/secondary education, business administration, and communication studies are the largest.

Special: Oswego offers cross-registration with ACUSNY-Visiting Student Program. More than 1000 internships are available with business, social, cultural, and government agencies. The university also offers a Washington semester, study abroad in more than 40 programs, a 5-year accounting B.S./M.B.A. program, dual majors, B.A.-B.S. degrees in several sciences and a B.A.-B.F.A. in art, credit for military experience, nondegree study, and pass/fail options. A 3-2 engineering degree is offered with Clarkson University, SUNY at Binghamton, and Case Western Reserve University. A 3-4 degree in optometry with SUNY College of Optometry, a 3-2 degree in zoo technology with Santa Fe Community College and Niagara County Community College, and 2-2, 2-3, 3-3 and 4-3 degrees in health sciences with SUNY Health Sciences Center are also possible. There are 21 national honor societies, a freshman honors program, and 9 departmental honors programs.

Requirements: The SAT or ACT is required. In addition, applicants must be graduates of an accredited secondary school or have a GED certificate. 18 academic credits are required, including 4 years each of English and social studies, 3 each of math and science, and 2 of a foreign language. An essay and interview are recommended. A GPA of 82.0 is required. AP and CLEP credits are accepted. Important factors in the admissions decision are advanced placement or honors courses, extracurricular activities record, and evidence of special talent.

Procedure: Freshmen are admitted fall and spring. Entrance exams should be taken during the spring of the junior year and fall of the senior year. There are early decision, early admissions, deferred admissions, and rolling admissions plans. Early decision applications should be filed by November 15; regular applications, by January 15 for fall entry and November 15 for spring entry, along with a $40 fee. Notification of early decision is sent December 15; regular decision, January 1. Applications are accepted on-line.

Financial Aid: In a recent year, 82% of all full-time freshmen and 81% of continuing full-time students received some form of financial aid. 82% of all full-time freshmen and 81% of continuing full-time students received need-based aid. The average freshmen award was $7,132. 65% of undergraduate students worked part-time. Average annual earnings from campus work were $1500. The average financial indebtedness of the 2009 graduate was $18,606. Oswego is a member of CSS. The FAFSA and the state aid form are required. Check with the school for current application deadlines.

Computers: Wireless access is available. There are 11 open access labs and 40 departmental computer labs with more than 1000 computers available for student use. All residence halls are equipped with high speed Internet, and the library, the school of business, and several other academic buildings as well as all cafeterias have wireless Internet. The library is also accessible to all students through their Oswego accounts and offers rentals of laptop computers. All students may access the system anytime. There are no time limits and no fees. It is strongly recommended that all students have a personal computer. Students enrolled in School of Business majors must have a personal computer.

STATE UNIVERSITY OF NEW YORK/COLLEGE AT BROCKPORT

Brockport, NY 14420　　　　　(585) 395-2751; (585) 395-5452

Full-time: 2718 men, 3537 women	**Faculty:** IIA, -$
Part-time: 266 men, 371 women	**Ph.D.s:** n/av
Graduate: 462 men, 843 women	**Student/Faculty:** n/av
Year: semesters, summer session	**Tuition:** $6108 ($14,008)
Application Deadline: open	**Room & Board:** $9200
Freshman Class: 8522 applied, 3571 accepted, 1038 enrolled	
SAT CR/M/W: 560/540/520	**ACT:** 24　**VERY COMPETITIVE**

The State University of New York/College at Brockport, established in 1835, is a comprehensive public liberal arts college offering 42 undergraduate, 27 graduate (masters level), and 18 teacher certificate programs. There are 5 undergraduate schools and 1 graduate school. In addition to regional accreditation, SUNY Brockport has baccalaureate program accreditation with AACSB, ABET, CSAB, CSWE, NCATE, and NRPA. The library contains 521,649 volumes, 2.1 million microform items, and 10,481 audio/video tapes/CDs/DVDs, and subscribes to 31,857 periodicals including electronic. Computerized library services include interlibrary loans, database searching, Internet access, and laptop Internet portals. Special learning facilities include a learning resource center, art gallery, planetarium, radio station, TV station, aquaculture ponds, weather information system, high-resolution germanium detector, research vessel on Lake Ontario, electron microscope, low-temperature physics lab, vacuum deposition lab, computational physics lab, 2 supercomputers, Doppler Radar system, hydrotherapy room, student learning center, academic computing center, theaters, and ultramodern dance facilities, including green room. The 454-acre campus is in a small town 16 miles west of Rochester. Including any residence halls, there are 68 buildings.

Programs of Study: SUNY Brockport confers B.A., B.S., B.F.A., and B.S.N. degrees. Master's degrees are also awarded. Bachelor's degrees are awarded in BIOLOGICAL SCIENCE (biology/biological science), BUSINESS (accounting, business administration and management, international business management, and recreation and leisure services), COMMUNICATIONS AND THE ARTS (communications, dance, dramatic arts, English, French, journalism, Spanish, and studio art), COMPUTER AND PHYSICAL SCIENCE (atmospheric sciences and meteorology, chemistry, computer science, earth science, geology, mathematics, and physics), EDUCATION (physical education), ENGINEERING AND ENVIRONMENTAL DESIGN (computational sciences and environmental science), HEALTH PROFESSIONS (health science, medical technology, and nursing), SOCIAL SCIENCE (African studies, African American studies, anthropology, criminal justice, history, interdisciplinary studies, international studies, philosophy, political science/government, psychology, social work, sociology, water resources, and women's studies). Business administration, physical education, and criminal justice are the largest.

Special: Co-op programs, internships in most majors, and work-study programs in education are available. Brockport offers cross-registration with Rochester area colleges, a Washington semester, study abroad in 16 countries, accelerated degree programs, and an interdisciplinary major in arts for children, emphasizing art, dance, music, and theater. Credit for military and work experience, nondegree study, and pass/fail grading options are available. An alternative general education program, Delta College, is an interdisciplinary program that emphasizes global issues and provides opportunities for work or study in other countries, as well as locally, regionally, and nationally. There are 24 national honor societies, a freshman honors program, and 3 departmental honors programs.

Admissions: 42% of the 2009-2010 applicants were accepted. The SAT scores for the 2009-2010 freshman class were: Critical Reading--15% below 500, 56% between 500 and 599, 28% between 600 and 700, and 1% above 700; Math--24% below 500, 57% between 500 and 599, 18% between 600 and 700, and 1% above 700; Writing--36% below 500, 49% between 500 and 599, 14% between 600 and 700, and 1% above 700. The ACT scores were 11% below 21, 38% between 21 and 23, 37% between 24 and 26, 11% between 27 and 28, and 4% above 28. 45% of the current freshmen were in the top fifth of their class; 85% were in the top two fifths.

Requirements: The SAT or ACT is required. SUNY Brockport seeks students who have demonstrated academic success and who show persistence. Applicants must have a high school diploma (preferably from the New York State Regents Program) or have completed a minimum of 18 academic units: 4 each in English and social studies, 4 in academic electives, and 3 each in math and science (1 with lab). An essay and letters of recommendation are encouraged. An audition is required for dance and theater applicants. A GPA of 85.0 is required. AP and CLEP credits are accepted. Important factors in the admissions decision are advanced placement or honors courses, leadership record, and extracurricular activities record.

Procedure: Freshmen are admitted fall and spring. Entrance exams should be taken during the spring of the junior year and fall of the senior year. There are deferred admissions and rolling admissions plans. Application deadlines are open. Application fee is $40. Notification is sent on a rolling basis. Applications are accepted on-line.

Financial Aid: In a recent year, 90% of all full-time freshmen and 84% of continuing full-time students received some form of financial aid. 66% of all full-time freshmen and 68% of continuing full-time students received need-based aid. The average freshman award was $9332. Need-based scholarships or need-based grants averaged $4138 ($12,573 maximum); need-based self-help aid (loans and jobs) averaged $4367 ($8125 maximum); and non-need-based awards and non-need-based scholarships averaged $3860 ($15,216 maximum). 71% of undergraduate students work part-time. Average annual earnings from campus work are $1303. The average financial indebtedness of a recent graduate was $22,489. SUNY Brockport is a member of CSS. The FAFSA is required. The deadline for filing freshman financial aid applications for fall entry is February 15.

Computers: There are 650 PCs in public labs with full Internet access. The campus is wireless, including residence halls. All students may access the system 24 hours per day. There are no time limits. The fee is $234. It is strongly recommended that all students have a personal computer.

Full-time: 2301 men, 3093 women	**Faculty:** 251; IIA, -$
Part-time: 40 men, 60 women	**Ph.D.s:** 90%
Graduate: 26 men, 139 women	**Student/Faculty:** 21 to 1
Year: semesters, summer session	**Tuition:** $6326 ($14,226)
Application Deadline: January 1	**Room & Board:** $9550
Freshman Class: 10413 applied, 3630 accepted, 948 enrolled	
SAT CR/M: 670/670	**ACT:** 29 **MOST COMPETITIVE**

The State University of New York/College at Geneseo, founded in 1871, is a public institution offering liberal arts, business, and accounting programs, teaching certification, and training in communicative disorders and sciences. In addition to regional accreditation, Geneseo has baccalaureate program accreditation with AACSB and NCATE. The library contains 665,060 volumes, 848,654 microform items, and 25,474 audio/video tapes/CDs/DVDs, and subscribes to 62,691 periodicals including electronic. Computerized library services include interlibrary loans, database searching, Internet access, and laptop Internet portals. Special learning facilities include a learning resource center, art gallery, planetarium, radio station, TV station, and 4 theaters. The 220-acre campus is in a small town 30 miles south of Rochester. Including any residence halls, there are 54 buildings.

Programs of Study: Geneseo confers B.A., B.S., and B.S.Ed. degrees. Master's degrees are also awarded. Bachelor's degrees are awarded in BIOLOGICAL SCIENCE (biochemistry, biology/biological science, and biophysics), BUSINESS (accounting and business administration and management), COMMUNICATIONS AND THE ARTS (art history and appreciation, communications, comparative literature, English, French, music, musical theater, performing arts, Spanish, studio art, and theater design), COMPUTER AND PHYSICAL SCIENCE (applied physics, chemistry, computer science, geochemistry, geology, geophysics and seismology, mathematics, natural sciences, and physics), EDUCATION (early childhood education, elementary education, and special education), HEALTH PROFESSIONS (speech pathology/audiology), SOCIAL SCIENCE (African American studies, American studies, anthropology, economics, geography, history, international relations, philosophy, political science/government, psychology, and sociology). Education, biology, and business administration are the largest.

Special: The college offers a cooperative 3-2 engineering degree with Alfred, Case Western Reserve, Clarkson, Columbia, Penn State, and Syracuse Universities, SUNY at Binghamton and Buffalo, and the University of Rochester, as well as a 3-3 degree with Rochester Institute of Technology and Upstate Medical University. Cross-registration is available with the Rochester Area Colleges Consortium. Geneseo offers internships, study abroad, a Washington semester, dual majors, and work-study programs. There are 15 national honor societies, including Phi Beta Kappa, a freshman honors program, and 9 departmental honors programs.

Admissions: 35% of the 2009-2010 applicants were accepted. The SAT scores for the 2009-2010 freshman class were: Critical Reading--1% below 500, 7% between 500 and 599, 64% between 600 and 700, and 28% above 700; Math-- 4% between 500 and 599, 75% between 600 and 700, and 22% above 700. The ACT scores were 1% between 21 and 23, 5% between 24 and 26, 37% between 27 and

28, and 58% above 28. 84% of the current freshmen were in the top fifth of their class; 98% were in the top two fifths. 36 freshmen graduated first in their class.

Requirements: The SAT or ACT is required. In addition, applicants must be graduates of an accredited secondary school or have a GED certificate. The academic program must have included 4 years each of English, math, science, and social studies and 3 years of a foreign language. An essay is required. A portfolio or audition for certain programs and an interview are recommended. AP and CLEP credits are accepted. Important factors in the admissions decision are advanced placement or honors courses, leadership record, and ability to finance college education.

Procedure: Freshmen are admitted fall and spring. Entrance exams should be taken during the spring of the junior year. There are early decision and deferred admissions plans. Early decision applications should be filed by November 15; regular applications, by January 1 for fall entry and October 1 for spring entry, along with a $40 fee. Notification of early decision is sent December 15; regular decision, March 1. 780 applicants were on the 2009 waiting list. Applications are accepted on-line.

Financial Aid: In 2009-2010, 72% of all full-time freshmen and 76% of continuing full-time students received some form of financial aid. 62% of all full-time freshmen and 65% of continuing full-time students received need-based aid. The average freshman award was $10,631, with $3,846 ($9,850 maximum) from need-based scholarships or need-based grants; $4,837 ($7,000 maximum) from need-based self-help aid (loans and jobs); and $2,164 ($6,000 maximum) from other non-need-based awards and non-need-based scholarships. 16% of undergraduate students work part-time. Average annual earnings from campus work are $2490. The average financial indebtedness of the 2009 graduate was $19,000. Geneseo is a member of CSS. The FAFSA is required. The deadline for filing freshman financial aid applications for fall entry is February 15.

Computers: Geneseo provides almost 900 PCs for student use. Internet accessible PCs are provided in all academic buildings and residence halls. The college wireless network is partially present in all campus buildings, and full coverage is available in more than half of the buildings on campus. All students may access the system 24 hours a day. There are no time limits. The fee is $181. All students are required to have a personal computer.

STATE UNIVERSITY OF NEW YORK/COLLEGE AT ONEONTA

Oneonta, NY 13820-4015

(607) 436-2524
(800) 786-9123; (607) 436-3074

Full-time: 2372 men, 3208 women	**Faculty:** 259; IIA, --$
Part-time: 63 men, 68 women	**Ph.D.s:** 84%
Graduate: 41 men, 141 women	**Student/Faculty:** 17 to 1
Year: semesters, summer session	**Tuition:** $6185 ($14,085)
Application Deadline: open	**Room & Board:** $8900
Freshman Class: 12688 applied, 4972 accepted, 1109 enrolled	
SAT CR/M: 551/579	**ACT:** 24 **VERY COMPETITIVE**

The State University of New York/College at Oneonta, founded in 1889, offers undergraduate and graduate programs in the arts and sciences with a campus-wide emphasis on educational technology, student engagement, diversity, and community service. There is 1 graduate school. In addition to regional accreditation, SUNY Oneonta has baccalaureate program accreditation with ADA, NASM, and NCATE. The library contains 25,850 volumes, 1.2 million microform items, and 26,942 audio/video tapes/CDs/DVDs, and subscribes to 25,553 periodicals including electronic. Computerized library services include interlibrary loans, database searching, Internet access, and laptop Internet portals. Special learning facilities include a learning resource center, art gallery, planetarium, radio station, TV station, observatory, science discovery center, community service center, college camp, children's center, and off-campus biological field station. The 250-acre campus is in a rural area 75 miles southwest of Albany and 55 miles northeast of Binghamton. Including any residence halls, there are 36 buildings.

Programs of Study: SUNY Oneonta confers B.A. and B.S. degrees. Master's degrees are also awarded. Bachelor's degrees are awarded in BIOLOGICAL SCIENCE (biology/biological science), BUSINESS (accounting, business economics, and fashion merchandising), COMMUNICATIONS AND THE ARTS (art, communications, dramatic arts, English, fine arts, French, music, music business management, Spanish, and speech/debate/rhetoric), COMPUTER AND PHYSICAL SCIENCE (atmospheric sciences and meteorology, chemistry, computer science, earth science, geology, mathematics, physics, and statistics), EDUCATION (business education, elementary education, English education, foreign languages education, home economics education, mathematics education, science education, secondary education, and social science education), ENGINEERING AND ENVIRONMENTAL DESIGN (environmental science), HEALTH PROFESSIONS (predentistry and premedicine), SOCIAL SCIENCE (African studies, anthropology, child care/child and family studies, criminal justice, dietetics, economics, geography, gerontology, Hispanic American studies, history, home economics, interdisciplinary studies, international studies, philosophy, political science/government, prelaw, psychology, sociology, and water resources). Physical and natural sciences, business economics, and education are the strongest academically. Elementary education, music industry, and adolescent education are the largest.

Special: Oneonta offers limited cross-registration with Hartwick College, internships in most fields, study abroad in 400 countries, a Washington semester, work-study programs, and dual majors. A 3-2 engineering degree and other cooperative programs are offered. There are 14 national honor societies, a freshman honors program, and 10 departmental honors programs.

Admissions: 39% of the 2009-2010 applicants were accepted. The SAT scores for the 2009-2010 freshman class were: Critical Reading--13% below 500, 66% between 500 and 599, 20% between 600 and 700, and 1% above 700; Math--5% below 500, 56% between 500 and 599, 37% between 600 and 700, and 2% above 700. The ACT scores were 5% below 21, 29% between 21 and 23, 34% between 24 and 26, 20% between 27 and 28, and 12% above 28. 51% of the current freshmen were in the top fifth of their class; 96% were in the top two fifths.

Requirements: The SAT or ACT is required. In addition, applicants should be graduates of an accredited secondary school and have 16 academic credits, including 4 years each of English and history and 8 years combined of foreign language, math, and science, with at least 2 years in each of these 3 broad areas. The GED is accepted. A GPA of 2.0 is required. AP and CLEP credits are accepted. Important factors in the admissions decision are advanced placement or honors courses, evidence of special talent, and leadership record.

Procedure: Freshmen are admitted fall and spring. Entrance exams should be taken in the spring of the junior year or the fall of the senior year. There are deferred admissions and rolling admissions plans. Application deadlines are open. The application fee is $40. Notifications are sent December 1. 354 applicants were on the 2009 waiting list; 2 were admitted. Applications are accepted on-line.

Financial Aid: In 2009-2010, 54% of all full-time freshmen and 56% of continuing full-time students received some form of financial aid. 45% of all full-time freshmen and 46% of continuing full-time students received need-based aid. The average freshman award was $10,804. Need-based scholarships or need-based grants averaged $5131 ; need-based self-help aid (loans and jobs) averaged $3815; and other non-need-based awards and non-need-based scholarships averaged $1089. 36% of undergraduate students work part-time. Average annual earnings from campus work are $1003. The average financial indebtedness of the 2009 graduate was $12,527. The FAFSA and the state aid form are required. The priority date for freshman financial aid applications for fall entry is March 1. The deadline for filing freshman financial aid applications for fall entry is April 15.

Computers: Wireless access is available. Wireless and high-speed connections are available campus-wide; more than 700 computers are available in general, departmental, and residence hall labs. There is free dial-up access for off-campus students. All students may access the system anytime. There are no time limits and no fees. It is strongly recommended that all students have a personal computer. A network-ready PC or Mac is recommended.

STATE UNIVERSITY OF NEW YORK/COLLEGE OF ENVIRONMENTAL SCIENCE AND FORESTRY

Syracuse, NY 13210-2779 **(315) 470-6600; (315) 470-6933**

Full-time: 909 men, 618 women	**Faculty:** 140; I, --$
Part-time: 303 men, 347 women	**Ph.D.s:** 96%
Graduate: 315 men, 314 women	**Student/Faculty:** 13 to 1
Year: semesters	**Tuition:** $5891 ($13,791)
Application Deadline: n/av	**Room & Board:** $12,460
Freshman Class: 1678 applied, 723 accepted, 284 enrolled	
SAT CR/M: 584/600	**ACT:** 25 **HIGHLY COMPETITIVE**

The SUNY College of Environmental Science and Forestry, founded in 1911, is the nation's oldest and largest college focused exclusively on the science, design, engineering, and management of our environment and natural resources. The college offers 21 undergraduate and 28 graduate degree programs, including 8 Ph.D. programs. Students also benefit from a special partnership with Syracuse University (SU) that provides access to courses, housing, and student organizations. There is one undergraduate school and one graduate school. In addition to regional accreditation, ESF has baccalaureate program accreditation with ABET, ASLA, and SAF. The library contains 135,305 volumes, 200,090 microform items, and 1,118 audio/video tapes/CDs/DVDs, and subscribes to 2,001 periodicals including electronic. Computerized library services include interlibrary loans, database searching, Internet access, and laptop Internet portals. Special learning facilities include a learning resource center, art gallery, natural history museum, radio station, and TV station. The 12-acre campus is in an urban area in Syracuse with 25,000 additional acres in New York State used for teaching and research. Including any residence halls, there are 7 buildings.

Programs of Study: ESF confers B.S. and B.L.A. degrees. Associates, master's, and doctoral degrees are also awarded. Bachelor's degrees are awarded in AGRICULTURE (animal science, environmental studies, fishing and fisheries, forest engineering, forestry and related sciences, natural resource management, plant science, soil science, and wood science), BIOLOGICAL SCIENCE (biology/biological science, biotechnology, botany, ecology, entomology, environmental biology, microbiology, molecular biology, plant genetics, plant pathology, plant physiology, and wildlife biology), COMPUTER AND PHYSICAL SCIENCE (chemistry and polymer science), EDUCATION (environmental education and science education), ENGINEERING AND ENVIRONMENTAL DESIGN (chemical engineering, construction management, environmental design, environmental engineering, environmental science, landscape architecture/design, paper and pulp science, paper engineering, and survey and mapping technology), HEALTH PROFESSIONS (predentistry, premedicine, and prepharmacy), SOCIAL SCIENCE (prelaw). Engineering, chemistry, and biology are the strongest academically. Environmental and forest biology, landscape architecture, and environmental science are the largest.

Special: Cross-registration is offered with Syracuse University. Co-op programs, internships, and dual options in forest ecosystem science are available. Study abroad is available in landscape architecture and through Syracuse University. There is an honors program for outstanding students. There is 1 national honor society, a freshman honors program, and 8 departmental honors programs.

Admissions: 43% of the 2009-2010 applicants were accepted. The SAT scores for the 2009-2010 freshman class were: Critical Reading--7% below 500, 50% between 500 and 599, 37% between 600 and 700, and 6% above 700; Math--5% below 500, 44% between 500 and 599, 46% between 600 and 700, and 5% above 700. The ACT scores were 6% below 21, 29% between 21 and 23, 35% between 24 and 26, 21% between 27 and 28, and 9% above 28. 77% of the current freshmen were in the top fifth of their class; 96% were in the top two fifths. There was 1 National Merit finalist.

Requirements: The SAT or ACT is required. In addition, applicants are required to have a minimum of 3 years of math and science, including chemistry, in a college preparatory curriculum. A supplemental application form, essay and results of SAT or ACT exams are required. A campus visit, letters of recommendation, and a personal portfolio or resume are recommended. ESF requires applicants to be in the upper 50% of their class. A GPA of 85.0 is required. AP and CLEP credits are accepted. Important factors in the admissions decision are advanced placement or honors courses, leadership record, and extracurricular activities record.

Procedure: Freshmen are admitted fall and spring. Entrance exams should be taken by October of the senior year. There are early admissions, deferred admissions, and rolling admissions plans. Check with the school for current application deadlines. The application fee is $40. Notifications are sent March 1. Applications are accepted on-line. 70 applicants were on a recent waiting list, 20 were accepted.

Financial Aid: In 2009-2010, 85% of all full-time freshmen and 85% of continuing full-time students received some form of financial aid. 80% of all full-time freshmen and 80% of continuing full-time students received need-based aid. The average freshmen award was $7,200, with $1,500 ($3,000 maximum) from need-based scholarships or need-based grants; $4,250 ($5,500 maximum) from need-based self-help aid (loans and jobs); and $4,500 ($6,000 maximum) from other non-need-based awards and non-need-based scholarships. 75% of undergraduate students work part-time. Average annual earnings from campus work are $1400. The average financial indebtedness of the 2009 graduate was $21,125. ESF is a member of CSS. The FAFSA is required. The priority date for freshman financial aid applications for fall entry is March 1.

Computers: All ESF students are provided e-mail addresses. All student housing has wireless and Internet access. Wireless is accessible at several locations on campus. The college has over 120 computers available in 4 computing labs for student use. All students may access the system any time. There are no time limits and no fees. Students enrolled in landscape architecture must have a personal computer.

STATE UNIVERSITY OF NEW YORK/EMPIRE STATE COLLEGE

Saratoga Springs, NY 12866-4390   **(518) 587-2100, ext. 2214**
                                       (800) 847-3000; (518) 580-9759

Full-time: 1559 men, 3317 women	**Faculty:** 149; IIB, -$
Part-time: 3823 men, 4700 women	**Ph.D.s:** 96%
Graduate: 388 men, 538 women	**Student/Faculty:** 33 to 1
Year: trimesters, summer session	**Tuition:** $5195 ($13,095)
Application Deadline: June 1	**Room & Board:** n/app
Freshman Class: n/av	**SPECIAL**

Empire State College, founded in 1971, part of the State University of New York, offers degree programs in the arts and sciences through its statewide network of regional centers and units. It operates on a five-term calendar, with September, November, January, March, and May terms. The needs of adult learners are met through guided independent study, distance learning, study groups, cross-registration, and credit for lifelong learning. Computerized library services include interlibrary loans and database searching. Special learning facilities include a learning resource center and a technology building.

Programs of Study: Empire State College confers B.A., B.S., and B.P.S. degrees. Associates and master's degrees are also awarded. Bachelor's degrees are awarded in BUSINESS (business administration and management, labor studies, and management science), COMPUTER AND PHYSICAL SCIENCE (mathematics and science), EDUCATION (education), SOCIAL SCIENCE (community services, economics, history, human development, humanities and social science, interdisciplinary studies, liberal arts/general studies, and sociology). Business, management, and economics are the largest.

Special: Empire State College offers cross-registration with numerous consortiums and institutions in New York State, internships in government, business, nonprofits, and academia, and study abroad in Greece, Lebanon, Czech Republic, Albania, and Dominican Republic. Accelerated degrees and dual and student-designed majors are possible in all programs. Nondegree study, credit for life, military, and work experience is possible.

Requirements: Applicants must be high school graduates, have a GED, or show ability to succeed at the college level. Empire State College also considers the ability of a learning location to meet individual needs. AP and CLEP credits are accepted. Important factors in the admissions decision are recommendations by school officials and personality/intangible qualities.

Procedure: Freshmen are admitted to all sessions. Entrance exams should be taken. There is a rolling admissions plan. Applications should be filed by June 1 for fall entry, November 1 for winter entry, January 1 for spring entry, and March 1 for summer entry. Applications are accepted on-line.

Financial Aid: In 2009-2010, 50% of all full-time freshmen and 50% of continuing full-time students received some form of financial aid. 50% of all full-time freshmen and 50% of continuing full-time students received need-based aid. The average financial indebtedness of the 2009 graduate was $22,000. The FAFSA is required. Check with the school for current application deadlines.

Computers: Students can access college resources and their student records via the college Web site. All students may access the system. 24 hours a day. There are no time limits and no fees. It is strongly recommended that all students have a personal computer.

STATE UNIVERSITY OF NEW YORK/UNIVERSITY AT ALBANY

Albany, NY 12222   **(518) 442-5435; (518) 442-5383**

Full-time: 6353 men, 5966 women	**Faculty:** 520; I, av$
Part-time: 417 men, 378 women	**Ph.D.s:** 95%
Graduate: 1896 men, 3010 women	**Student/Faculty:** 24 to 1
Year: semesters, summer session	**Tuition:** $6748 ($14,648)
Application Deadline: March 1	**Room & Board:** $10,238
Freshman Class: 20,249 applied, 10,442 accepted, 2333 enrolled	
SAT CR/M: 560/590	**ACT:** 25 **VERY COMPETITIVE**

The State University of New York/University at Albany, established in 1844, is a public institution conferring undergraduate and graduate degrees in humanities and fine arts, science and math, social and behavioral sciences, business, public policy, education, and social welfare. There are 8 undergraduate schools and 9 graduate schools. In addition to regional accreditation, University at Albany has baccalaureate program accreditation with AACSB, CSWE, and TEAC. The 3 libraries contain 2.2 million volumes, 2.9 million microform items, and 18,088 audio/video tapes/CDs/DVDs, and subscribe to 29,247 periodicals including electronic. Computerized library services include interlibrary loans, database searching, Internet access, and laptop Internet portals. Special learning facilities include a learning resource center, art gallery, radio station, linear accelerator, sophisticated weather data system, national lightning detection system, interactive media center, extensive art studios, state-of-the-art electronic library, and the Northeast Regional Forensic Institute (NERFI). The 560-acre campus is in a suburban area about 5 miles west of downtown Albany. Including any residence halls, there are 166 buildings.

Programs of Study: University at Albany confers B.A. and B.S. degrees. Master's and doctoral degrees are also awarded. Bachelor's degrees are awarded in AGRICULTURE (environmental studies), BIOLOGICAL SCIENCE (biochemistry, biology/biological science, and molecular biology), BUSINESS (accounting and business administration and management), COMMUNICATIONS AND THE ARTS (art history and appreciation, Chinese, communications, dramatic arts, English, fine arts, French, Hebrew, Italian, Latin, linguistics, music, Russian, Spanish, and studio art), COMPUTER AND PHYSICAL SCIENCE (actuarial science, applied mathematics, atmospheric sciences and meteorology, chemistry, computer science, earth science, information sciences and systems, mathematics, and physics), ENGINEERING AND ENVIRONMENTAL DESIGN (materials engineering, materials science, and urban design), HEALTH PROFESSIONS (predentistry and premedicine), SOCIAL SCIENCE (African American studies, anthropology, Asian/Oriental studies, Caribbean studies, classical/ancient civilization, criminal justice, East Asian studies, Eastern European studies, economics, geography, Hispanic American studies, history, interdisciplinary studies, Latin American studies, medieval studies, philosophy, political science/government, prelaw, psychology, religion, Russian and Slavic studies, social work, sociology, and women's studies). Criminal justice, accounting, and public administration and policy are the strongest academically. Business, psychology, and communication and rhetoric are the largest.

Special: Cross-registration is available with Rensselaer Polytechnic Institute, Albany Law School, and Union, Siena, and Russell Sage Colleges. Internships may be arranged with state government agencies and private organizations. Study abroad in many countries, a Washington semester, B.A.-B.S. degrees, and work-study programs are offered. Dual and student-designed majors, nondegree study, and pass/fail grading options are available. There are accelerated 5-year bachelor's/master's programs in 40 fields; most arts and sciences fields may be combined with an accelerated M.B.A. A 3-2 engineering degree with 1 of 4 institutions is also possible. There are 15 national honor societies, including Phi Beta Kappa, a freshman honors program, and 30 departmental honors programs.

Admissions: 52% of the 2009-2010 applicants were accepted. The SAT scores for the 2009-2010 freshman class were: Critical Reading--10% below 500, 60% between 500 and 599, 27% between 600 and 700, and 3% above 700; Math--4% below 500, 51% between 500 and 599, 41% between 600 and 700, and 4% above 700. The ACT scores were 1% below 21, 29% between 21 and 23, 39% between 24 and 26, 21% between 27 and 28, and 10% above 28. 48% of the current freshmen were in the top fifth of their class; 87% were in the top two fifths.

Requirements: The SAT or ACT is required. In addition, applicants must be graduates of an accredited secondary school or have a GED. 18 academic credits are required, including 2 to 3 units of math, 2 units of lab sciences, and 1 unit of foreign language study. AP and CLEP credits are accepted. Important factors in the admissions decision are advanced placement or honors courses, personality/intangible qualities, and leadership record.

Procedure: Freshmen are admitted fall, spring, and summer. Entrance exams should be taken by November of the senior year. There are early decision, deferred admissions, and rolling admissions plans. Early decision applications should be filed by November 15; regular applications, by March 1 for fall entry, December 1 for spring entry, and May 1 for summer entry, along with a $40 fee. Notification of early decision is sent January 1. Applications are accepted on-line. A waiting list is maintained.

Financial Aid: In 2009-2010, 65% of all full-time freshmen and 62% of continuing full-time students received some form of financial aid. 54% of all full-time freshmen and 56% of continuing full-time students received need-based aid. The average freshman award was $9698. Need-based scholarships or need-based grants averaged $6331; need-based self-help aid (loans and jobs) averaged $4501; non-need-based athletic scholarships averaged $9764; and other non-need-based awards and non-need-based scholarships averaged $3445. 9% of undergraduate students work part-time. The FAFSA is required, and New York state residents should apply for TAP on-line at *http://www.tapweb.org*. The priority date for freshman financial aid applications for fall entry is March 15.

Computers: Wireless access is available. Wireless high-speed Internet connections are available in dorm rooms and in other select locations. Students without a wireless network interface card (NIC) can check one out at the circulation desk for use in the library. All students may access the system. There are no time limits and no fees.

STATE UNIVERSITY OF NEW YORK/UNIVERSITY AT STONY BROOK

Stony Brook, NY 11794 (631) 632-6868; 631) 632-9027

Full-time: 7883 men, 7241 women	**Faculty:** 949; I, av$
Part-time: 578 men, 693 women	**Ph.D.s:** 98%
Graduate: 3510 men, 4787 women	**Student/Faculty:** 16 to 1
Year: semesters, summer session	**Tuition:** $6488 ($14,388)
Application Deadline: March 1	**Room & Board:** $9590
Freshman Class: 28587 applied, 11411 accepted, 2806 enrolled	
SAT CR/M/W: 580/630/580	**ACT:** 26 **HIGHLY COMPETITIVE**

Stony Brook University, founded in 1957, and part of the State University of New York, is a public institution offering degree programs in arts and sciences, engineering and applied sciences, business, journalism, marine sciences and environmental studies, nursing, health technology and management, and social work. Professional programs in medicine are offered at the graduate level. There are 9 undergraduate schools and 10 graduate schools. In addition to regional accreditation, Stony Brook University has baccalaureate program accreditation with ABET, ADA, APTA, CAAHEP, CAHEA, CSWE, and NLN. The 7 libraries contain 2.5 million volumes, 3.8 million microform items, and 52,872 audio/video tapes/CDs/DVDs, and subscribe to 64,803 periodicals including electronic. Computerized library services include interlibrary loans, database searching, and Internet access. Special learning facilities include a learning resource center, art gallery, radio station, TV station, The Museum of Long Island Natural Sciences, and the Fine Arts Center, which has an 1100-seat main theater, a 400-seat recital hall, and 3 experimental theaters. The 1450-acre campus is in a suburban area on Long Island, 60 miles from New York City. Including any residence halls, there are 200 buildings.

Programs of Study: Stony Brook University confers B.A., B.S., and B.E. degrees. Master's and doctoral degrees are also awarded. Bachelor's degrees are awarded in AGRICULTURE (environmental studies), BIOLOGICAL SCIENCE (biochemistry, biology/biological science, ecology, and marine biology), BUSINESS (business administration and management), COMMUNICATIONS AND THE ARTS (art history and appreciation, comparative literature, dramatic arts, English, film arts, Germanic languages and literature, linguistics, music, Russian languages and literature, and studio art), COMPUTER AND PHYSICAL SCIENCE (applied mathematics, astronomy, atmospheric sciences and meteorology, chemistry, computer science, earth science, geology, information sciences and systems, mathematics, and physics), EDUCATION (athletic training), ENGINEERING AND ENVIRONMENTAL DESIGN (biomedical engineering, chemical engineering, computer engineering, electrical/electronics engineering, engineering and applied science, engineering chemistry, environmental design, environmental science, mechanical engineering, and technological management), HEALTH PROFESSIONS (clinical science, cytotechnology, health science, nursing, occupational therapy, pharmacology, physical therapy, and respiratory therapy), SOCIAL SCIENCE (African studies, American studies, anthropology, Asian/American studies, economics, ethnic studies, European studies, French studies, history, humanities, interdisciplinary studies, Italian studies, liberal arts/general studies, philosophy, political science/government, psychology, religion, social science, social work, sociology, Spanish studies, and women's studies). Biology, business management, and economics are the strongest academically. Psychology, history, and biochemistry are the largest.

Special: Cross-registration may be arranged through the Long Island Regional Advisory Council for Higher Education. The university offers a Washington semester and internships with a variety of government, legal, and social agencies, with hospitals and clinics, and in business and industry. The URECA Program allows undergraduates to work with faculty on research and creative projects. An accelerated degree program in nursing, dual majors, student-designed majors, a national student exchange program, and study abroad in 20 countries are available. Other academic opportunities include a scholars for medicine program, women in science, engineering program, and honors college. There are 6 national honor societies, including Phi Beta Kappa, a freshman honors program, and 30 departmental honors programs.

Admissions: 40% of the 2009-2010 applicants were accepted. The SAT scores for the 2009-2010 freshman class were: Critical Reading--17% below 500, 49% between 500 and 599, 38% between 600 and 700, and 5% above 700; Math--2% below 500, 25% between 500 and 599, 58% between 600 and 700, and 15% above 700; Writing--11% below 500, 46% between 500 and 599, 38% between 600 and 700, and 5% above 700. The ACT scores were 2% below 21, 12% between 21 and 23, 41% between 24 and 26, 21% between 27 and 28, and 24% above 28. 59% of the current freshmen were in the top fifth of their class; 86% were in the top two fifths. There were 2 National Merit finalists. 23 freshmen graduated first in their class.

Requirements: The SAT is required. In addition, applicants must be graduates of an accredited secondary school or have a GED certificate. 16 or 17 academic credits are required, including 4 years each of English and social studies, 3 or 4 of math, 3 of science (4 for engineering majors), and 2 or 3 of a foreign language. One letter of recommendation and supplemental application, including and essay, are required. 3 SAT Subject tests, an essay, and an interview are recommended. AP and CLEP credits are accepted. Important factors in the admissions decision are advanced placement or honors courses, extracurricular activities record, and evidence of special talent.

Procedure: Freshmen are admitted fall and spring. Entrance exams should be taken during the junior year or in the fall of the senior year. There are deferred admissions and rolling admissions plans. Applications should be filed by March 1 for fall entry and November 1 for spring entry. The fall 2009 application fee was $40. Notifications are sent March 1. 948 applicants were on the 2009 waiting list; 130 were admitted. Applications are accepted on-line.

Financial Aid: In 2009-2010, 74% of all full-time freshmen and 65% of continuing full-time students received some form of financial aid. 55% of all full-time freshmen and 53% of continuing full-time students received need-based aid. The average freshman award was $9,514, with $6,858 ($13,795 maximum) from need-based scholarships or need-based grants; $3,538 ($6,800 maximum) from need-based self-help aid (loans and jobs); $14,762 ($26,835 maximum) from non-need-based athletic scholarships; and $4,016 ($23,979 maximum) from other non-need-based awards and non-need-based scholarships. 13% of undergraduate students work part-time. Average annual earnings from campus work are $2208. The average financial indebtedness of the 2009 graduate was $17,524. Stony Brook University is a member of CSS. The FAFSA and the state aid form are required. The deadline for filing freshman financial aid applications for fall entry is March 1.

Computers: Wireless access is available. Network access is available in dorm rooms and lounges. All students may access the system 24 hours a day. There are no time limits and no fees.

STEPHENS COLLEGE

Columbia, MO 65215
(573) 876-7207
(800) 876-7207; (573) 876-7237

Full-time: 15 men, 560 women	**Faculty:** n/av
Part-time: 15 men, 170 women	**Ph.D.s:** 83%
Graduate: 11 men, 64 women	**Student/Faculty:** n/av
Year: semesters, summer session	**Tuition:** $25,500
Application Deadline: open	**Room & Board:** $9000
Freshman Class: n/av	
SAT or ACT: required	**VERY COMPETITIVE**

Stephens College, founded in 1833, is a private college primarily for women and offering undergraduate programs in the arts and sciences, business, education, and fine arts. Figures in the above capsule are approximate. There are 2 undergraduate schools and 2 graduate schools. The library contains 129,915 volumes, 11,322 microform items, and 1254 audio/video tapes/CDs/DVDs, and subscribes to 9836 periodicals including electronic. Computerized library services include interlibrary loans, database searching, and Internet access. Special learning facilities include a learning resource center, art gallery, radio station, and TV station. The 86-acre campus is in an urban area 120 miles west of St. Louis. Including any residence halls, there are 35 buildings.

Programs of Study: Stephens confers B.A., B.S., and B.F.A. degrees. Associates and master's degrees are also awarded. Bachelor's degrees are awarded in AGRICULTURE (equine science), BIOLOGICAL SCIENCE (biology/biological science), BUSINESS (accounting, business administration and management, and fashion merchandising), COMMUNICATIONS AND THE ARTS (creative writing, dance, dramatic arts, English, film arts, graphic design, public relations, and theater design), EDUCATION (early childhood education and elementary education), ENGINEERING AND ENVIRONMENTAL DESIGN (interior design), SOCIAL SCIENCE (fashion design and technology, liberal arts/general studies, and prelaw). Education and biology are the strongest academically. Performing arts, fashion, and biology are the largest.

Special: Students may study abroad in England, Italy, Mexico, France, Ecuador, South Korea, and Spain. Stephens also offers cross-registration with the Mid-Missouri Association of Colleges and Universities, many internships, a Washington semester, dual and student-designed majors, a 3-2 occupational therapy degree program with Washington University, accelerated degree programs in dance and theater arts, and pass/fail options for electives. There are 8 national honor societies and a freshman honors program.

Requirements: The SAT or ACT is required. In addition, applicants must be graduates of accredited secondary schools or have earned a GED. An essay is required, and an interview is recommended. A GPA of 2.5 is required. AP and CLEP credits are accepted. Important factors in the admissions decision are advanced placement or honors courses, leadership record, and recommendations by school officials.

Procedure: Freshmen are admitted fall and spring. There are deferred admissions and rolling admissions plans. Application deadlines are open. The application fee is $25. Applications are accepted on-line.

Financial Aid: The FAFSA is required. Check with the school for current application deadlines.

Computers: Wireless access is available. There are wireless computer labs, and wireless access is available in residence halls and academic buildings. All students may access the system. There are no time limits and no fees.

STETSON UNIVERSITY

DeLand, FL 32723
(386) 822-7100
(800) 688-0101; (386) 822-7112

Full-time: 892 men, 1187 women	**Faculty:** 173; IIA, +$
Part-time: 39 men, 44 women	**Ph.D.s:** 95%
Graduate: 183 men, 297 women	**Student/Faculty:** 12 to 1
Year: semesters, summer session	**Tuition:** $31,770
Application Deadline: March 15	**Room & Board:** $8934
Freshman Class: 4640 applied, 2479 accepted, 505 enrolled	
SAT CR/M/W: 558/550/542	**ACT:** 24 **VERY COMPETITIVE**

Stetson University, founded in 1883, is an independent institution offering undergraduate programs in liberal arts and sciences, music, and business administration and graduate programs. There are 3 undergraduate schools and 2 graduate schools. In addition to regional accreditation, Stetson has baccalaureate program accreditation with AACSB, NASM, and NCATE. The 3 libraries contain 404,061 volumes, 572,214 microform items, and 20,812 audio/video tapes/CDs/DVDs, and subscribe to 36,000 periodicals including electronic. Computerized library services include interlibrary loans, database searching, and Internet access. Special learning facilities include an art gallery and a museum of minerals. The 175-acre campus is in a small town 35 miles north of Orlando and 25 miles west of Daytona Beach. Including any residence halls, there are 80 buildings.

Programs of Study: Stetson confers B.A., B.S., B.B.A., B.M., and B.M.E. degrees. Master's degrees are also awarded. Bachelor's degrees are awarded in BIOLOGICAL SCIENCE (biochemistry, biology/biological science, marine biology, and molecular biology), BUSINESS (accounting, banking and finance, business administration and management, business economics, electronic business, international business management, management information systems, management science, marketing/retailing/merchandising, small business management, and sports management), COMMUNICATIONS AND THE ARTS (art, communications, dramatic arts, English, French, German, guitar, music, music performance, music theory and composition, piano/organ, Spanish, voice, and winds), COMPUTER AND PHYSICAL SCIENCE (chemistry, computer science, digital arts/technology, mathematics, and physics), EDUCATION (elementary education, music education, secondary education, and social science education), ENGINEERING AND ENVIRONMENTAL DESIGN (environmental science), HEALTH PROFESSIONS (health science, medical technology, and rehabilitation therapy), SOCIAL SCIENCE (American studies, economics, geography, history, humanities, international studies, Latin American studies, philosophy, political science/government, prelaw, psychology, religion, Russian and Slavic studies, social science, and sociology). Natural science, music, and business are the strongest academically. Business, psychology, and education are the largest.

Special: Stetson offers co-op programs in preengineering, prelaw, premedicine, forestry, environmental studies, internships in most disciplines, study abroad in France, Germany, Spain, Russia, Mexico, Hong Kong, Austria, and the United Kingdom, and a Washington semester at American University. B.A.-B.S. degrees, dual majors, student-designed majors through the honors programs, 3-2 engineering degrees with the University of Florida and Miami, a 3-3 law degree with Stetson College of Law, and pass/fail options are also offered. There is also the Leadership Development Program, the Roland George Investments Program, in which students manage an actual investment portfolio worth between $2.5 and $3 million, and the Family Business Center. There are 6 national honor societies, including Phi Beta Kappa, and a freshman honors program.

Admissions: 53% of the 2009-2010 applicants were accepted. The SAT scores for the 2009-2010 freshman class were: Critical Reading--20% below 500, 51% between 500 and 599, 25% between 600 and 700, and 4% above 700; Math--24% below 500, 47% between 500 and 599, 27% between 600 and 700, and 2% above 700; Writing--27% below 500, 51% between 500 and 599, 21% between 600 and 700, and 2% above 700. The ACT scores were 20% below 21, 34% between 21 and 23, 24% between 24 and 26, 14% between 27 and 28, and 9% above 28. 54% of the current freshmen were in the top fifth of their class; 84% were in the top two fifths. 3 freshmen graduated first in their class.

Requirements: The SAT or ACT is required. In addition, applicants must be graduates of an accredited secondary school or have a GED, and have completed 4 years of English, 3 of math and science, and 2 each of foreign language, social sciences, and electives. Auditions are required for music students. A GPA of 2.0 is required. AP and CLEP credits are accepted. Important factors in the admissions decision are advanced placement or honors courses, leadership record, and evidence of special talent.

Procedure: Freshmen are admitted in fall, spring, and summer. Entrance exams should be taken in the spring of the junior year or the fall of the senior year. There are early decision, deferred admissions, and rolling admissions plans. Application deadlines are open. Application fee is $40. Notification of early decision is sent November 1; regular decision, on a rolling basis. 20 early decision candidates were accepted for the 2009-2010 class. Applications are accepted on-line.

Financial Aid: In 2009-2010, 99% of all full-time freshmen and 97% of continuing full-time students received some form of financial aid. 61% of all full-time freshmen and 50% of continuing full-time students received need-based aid. The average freshman award was $30,914. Need-based scholarships or need-based grants averaged $23,625 ($43,742 maximum); need-based self-help aid (loans and jobs) averaged $8,624 ($23,589 maximum); non-need-based athletic scholarships averaged $21,823 ($41,693 maximum); and other non-need-based awards and non-need-based scholarships averaged $15,349 ($45,191 maximum). 45% of undergraduate students work part-time. Average annual earnings from campus work are $2672. The average financial indebtedness of the 2009 graduate was $30,914. Stetson is a member of CSS. The FAFSA is required. The priority date for freshman financial aid applications for fall entry is March 15.

Computers: Wireless access is available at many locations around the campus. All students may access the system. There are no time limits and no fees.

STEVENS INSTITUTE OF TECHNOLOGY

Hoboken, NJ 07030

(201) 216-5194
(800) 458-5323; (201) 216-8348

Full-time: 1654 men, 579 women	**Faculty:** 226; IIA, +$
Part-time: 1 man	**Ph.D.s:** 90%
Graduate: 2761 men, 867 women	**Student/Faculty:** 10 to 1
Year: semesters, summer session	**Tuition:** $37,980
Application Deadline: February 1	**Room & Board:** $12,150
Freshman Class: 3232 applied, 1609 accepted, 614 enrolled	
SAT CR/M/W: 600/670/600	**ACT:** 27 **HIGHLY COMPETITIVE**

Stevens Institute of Technology, founded in 1870, is a private institution offering programs of study in science, computer science, engineering, business, and humanities. There are 4 undergraduate schools and 3 graduate schools. In addition to regional accreditation, Stevens has baccalaureate program accreditation with ABET and CSAB. The library contains 123,063 volumes and subscribes to 39,500 periodicals including electronic. Computerized library services include interlibrary loans, database searching, Internet access, and laptop Internet portals. Special learning facilities include a radio station, TV station, a lab for ocean and coastal engineering, an environmental lab, a design and manufacturing institute, a technology center, a telecommunications institute, a computer vision lab, an ultrafast laser spectroscopy and high-speed communications lab, and a wireless network security center. The 55-acre campus is in an urban area on the banks of the Hudson River, overlooking the Manhattan skyline. Including any residence halls, there are 25 buildings.

Programs of Study: Stevens confers B.A., B.S., and B.E. degrees. Master's and doctoral degrees are also awarded. Bachelor's degrees are awarded in BIOLOGICAL SCIENCE (biochemistry and bioinformatics), BUSINESS (business administration and management), COMMUNICATIONS AND THE ARTS (literature and music technology), COMPUTER AND PHYSICAL SCIENCE (chemistry, computer science, computer security and information assurance, digital arts/technology, information sciences and systems, mathematics, physics, and science technology), ENGINEERING AND ENVIRONMENTAL DESIGN (biomedical engineering, chemical engineering, civil engineering, computational sciences, computer engineering, electrical/electronics engineering, engineering management, engineering physics, environmental engineering, mechanical engineering, naval architecture and marine engineering, and systems engineering), SOCIAL SCIENCE (history and philosophy). Engineering is the strongest academically. Mechanical engineering, civil engineering, and business are the largest.

Special: Stevens offers cross-registration and a 3-2 engineering degree with New York University, a work-study program within the school, co-op programs, corporate and research internships through the Undergraduate Projects in Technology and Medicine, study abroad in 7 countries, and pass/fail options for extra courses. Students may undertake dual majors as well as accelerated degree programs in medicine, dentistry, and law and can receive a B.A.-B.E. degree or a B.A.-B.S. degree in all majors. Undergraduates may take graduate courses. There are 9 national honor societies and a freshman honors program.

Admissions: 50% of the 2009-2010 applicants were accepted. The SAT scores for the 2009-2010 freshman class were: Critical Reading--9% below 500, 41% between 500 and 599, 41% between 600 and 700, and 9% above 700; Math--% below 500, 14% between 500 and 599, 58% between 600 and 700, and 28% above 700; Writing--11% below 500, 39% between 500 and 599, 41% between

600 and 700, and 9% above 700. The ACT scores were % below 21, 18% between 21 and 23, % between 24 and 26, 58% between 27 and 28, and 24% above 28. 78% of the current freshmen were in the top fifth of their class; 95% were in the top two fifths. 9 freshmen graduated first in their class.

Requirements: The SAT or ACT is required. In addition, applicants must provide official high school transcripts. Students should have taken 4 years of English, math, and science. An interview, essay, and 2 letters of recommendation are required. AP credits are accepted. Important factors in the admissions decision are advanced placement or honors courses, extracurricular activities record, and personality/intangible qualities.

Procedure: Freshmen are admitted in the fall. Entrance exams should be taken by February of the senior year. There are early decision and deferred admissions plans. Early decision applications should be filed by November 15; regular applications, by February 1 for fall entry and December 1 for spring entry, along with a $55 fee. Notification of early decision is sent December 15; regular decision, March 21. Applications are accepted on-line. 481 applicants were on a recent waiting list, 30 were accepted.

Financial Aid: In 2009-2010, 93% of all full-time freshmen and 90% of continuing full-time students received some form of financial aid. 84% of all full-time freshmen and 80% of continuing full-time students received need-based aid. The average freshman award was $24,380. Need-based scholarships or need-based grants averaged $15,021; need-based self-help aid (loans and jobs) averaged $4,613; and other non-need based awards and non-need based scholarships averaged $7,878. 24% of undergraduate students work part-time. Average annual earnings from campus work are $1202. The average financial indebtedness of the 2009 graduate was $1,587. Stevens is a member of CSS. The CSS/Profile and FAFSA are required. The priority date for freshman financial aid applications for fall entry is February 15.

Computers: Wireless access is available. All undergraduates receive a laptop as part of their admission to the institution. These laptops are all wireless enabled, and wireless access is available all over the campus. All students may access the system at all times. There are no time limits and no fees. All students are required to have a personal computer. Each student is provided with an HP 8530W with an Intel Core 2.

STONEHILL COLLEGE
Easton, MA 02357-0100 (508) 565-1373; (508) 565-1545

Full-time: 966 men, 1454 women	**Faculty:** 151; IIB, av$
Part-time: 20 men, 28 women	**Ph.D.s:** 83%
Graduate: none	**Student/Faculty:** 16 to 1
Year: semesters, summer session	**Tuition:** $31,210
Application Deadline: January 15	**Room & Board:** $12,240
Freshman Class: 5871 applied, 3313 accepted, 683 enrolled	
SAT CR/M: 590/610	**ACT:** 26 **HIGHLY COMPETITIVE**

Stonehill College, founded in 1948 by the Holy Cross Fathers, is a private Roman Catholic college offering undergraduate degrees in liberal arts and sciences, business, and other preprofessional disciplines. The library contains 246,055 volumes, 150,558 microform items, and 9296 audio/video tapes/CDs/DVDs, and subscribes to 13,488 periodicals including electronic. Computerized library services include interlibrary loans, database searching, Internet access, and laptop Internet portals. Special learning facilities include a learning resource center, art gallery, radio station, observatory, institute for the study of law and society, and several archives and special collections. The 375-acre campus is in a suburban area 20 miles south of Boston. Including any residence halls, there are 64 buildings.

Programs of Study: Stonehill confers B.A., B.S., and B.S.B.A. degrees. Bachelor's degrees are awarded in AGRICULTURE (environmental studies), BIOLOGICAL SCIENCE (biochemistry, biology/biological science, and neurosciences), BUSINESS (accounting, banking and finance, business administration and management, international business management, and marketing/retailing/merchandising), COMMUNICATIONS AND THE ARTS (art history and appreciation, communications, English, fine arts, French, and Spanish), COMPUTER AND PHYSICAL SCIENCE (chemistry, computer science, mathematics, and physics), EDUCATION (education), HEALTH PROFESSIONS (health care administration), SOCIAL SCIENCE (American studies, criminology, economics, gender studies, history, interdisciplinary studies, international studies, philosophy, political science/government, psychology, public administration, religion, and sociology). Business, biology, and psychology are the strongest academically.

Special: On-campus work-study, international and domestic internships, a Washington semester through the Washington Center, and a semester in New York City are available. Cross-registration with 8 other Massachusetts schools in the SACHEM consortium is also available. A 3-2 computer engineering degree is offered with the University of Notre Dame. Opportunities for study abroad include 120 programs in 35 countries. Nondegree, directed, and field study are available as well as a pass/fail option for upperclassmen. Programs in early childhood, elementary, and secondary education lead to the state's provisional teacher certification. Stonehill is also a member of the Marine Studies Consortium. Preprofessional preparation is available in medicine, dentistry, law, and theology. There are 19 national honor societies, a freshman honors program, and 15 departmental honors programs.

Admissions: 56% of the 2009-2010 applicants were accepted. The SAT scores for the 2009-2010 freshman class were: Critical Reading--4% below 500, 45% between 500 and 599, 46% between 600 and 700, and 5% above 700; Math--4% below 500, 32% between 500 and 599, 59% between 600 and 700, and 5% above 700. The ACT scores were 2% below 21, 12% between 21 and 23, 32% between 24 and 26, 28% between 27 and 28, and 26% above 28. 81% of the current freshmen were in the top fifth of their class; 98% were in the top two fifths. 10 freshmen graduated first in their class.

Requirements: Applicants should be graduates of an accredited high school or have earned the GED. Secondary preparation should include 4 units each of English and math, 3 units each of foreign language and science, and 3 combined units of history, political science, and social sciences plus 3 elective subjects. An essay, school report, 2 teacher evaluations, and a completed common application sent with a Stonehill Supplemental Information Form are required. AP credits are accepted. Important factors in the admissions decision are advanced placement or honors courses, leadership record, and extracurricular activities record.

Procedure: Freshmen are admitted fall and spring. There are early decision, early admissions, and deferred admissions plans. Early decision applications should be filed by November 1; regular applications, by January 15 for fall entry and November 1 for spring entry, along with a $60 fee. Notification of early decision is sent December 25; regular decision, April 1. 50 early decision candidates were accepted for the 2009-2010 class. 997 applicants were on the 2009 waiting list; 412 were admitted. Applications are accepted on-line.

Financial Aid: In 2009-2010, 97% of all full-time freshmen and 88% of continuing full-time students received some form of financial aid. 60% of all full-time freshmen and 57% of continuing full-time students received need-based aid. The average freshman award was $22,165. Need-based scholarships or need-based grants averaged $18,140 ($43,450 maximum); need-based self-help aid (loans and jobs) averaged $7700 ($9000 maximum); non-need-based athletic scholarships averaged $9126 ($43,450 maximum); and other non-need-based awards and non-need-based scholarships averaged $9001 ($31,210 maximum). 26% of undergraduate students work part-time. Average annual earnings from campus work are $1111. The average financial indebtedness of the 2009 graduate was $29,163. Stonehill is a member of CSS. The CSS/Profile, FAFSA, and noncustodial profile and business/farm supplement are required. The deadline for filing freshman financial aid applications for fall entry is February 1.

Computers: Wireless access is available. The college provides students with wired and wireless computing facilities including 10 multimedia labs with over 300 computers for classroom and student use. The software available includes extensive instructional packages, web page development tools, language programming, and database tools. Each lab is equipped with printers. All students may access the system 7 days a week, 24 hours a day. There are no time limits and no fees. It is strongly recommended that all students have a personal computer.

SUSQUEHANNA UNIVERSITY
Selinsgrove, PA 17870-1001

(570) 372-4260
(800) 326-9672; (570) 372-2722

Full-time: 910 men, 1050 women	**Faculty:** IIB, av$
Part-time: 10 men, 5 women	**Ph.D.s:** n/av
Graduate: none	**Student/Faculty:** 16 to 1
Year: semesters, summer session	**Tuition:** $34,070
Application Deadline: see profile	**Room & Board:** $9230
Freshman Class: n/av	
SAT or ACT: required	**VERY COMPETITIVE**

Susquehanna University, founded in 1858, is an independent, selective, residential institution affiliated with the Lutheran Church. It offers programs through schools of arts, humanities and communications, natural and social sciences, and business. There are 3 undergraduate schools. Enrollment figures in the above capsule and figures in this profile are approximate. In addition to regional accreditation, SU has baccalaureate program accreditation with AACSB and NASM. The library contains 341,020 volumes, 126,067 microform items, and 8681 audio/video tapes/CDs/DVDs, and subscribes to 16,480 periodicals including electronic. Computerized library services include interlibrary loans, database searching, Internet access, and laptop Internet portals. Special learning facilities include a learning resource center, radio station, multimedia classrooms, video studios, a campuswide telecommunications network, satellite dishes and distribution system for foreign-language broadcasts, video conferencing facility, ecological field station and observatory, child development center, and electronic music lab. The 220-acre campus is in a small town 50 miles north of Harrisburg. Including any residence halls, there are 52 buildings.

Programs of Study: SU confers B.A., B.S., and B.M. degrees. Associates degrees are also awarded. Bachelor's degrees are awarded in BIOLOGICAL SCIENCE (biochemistry, biology/biological science, and ecology), BUSINESS (accounting and business administration and management), COMMUNICATIONS AND THE ARTS (art history and appreciation, communications, English,

French, German, graphic design, music, music performance, Spanish, studio art, and visual and performing arts), COMPUTER AND PHYSICAL SCIENCE (chemistry, computer science, earth science, information sciences and systems, mathematics, and physics), EDUCATION (early childhood education, elementary education, and music education), ENGINEERING AND ENVIRONMENTAL DESIGN (environmental science), SOCIAL SCIENCE (economics, history, international studies, liberal arts/general studies, philosophy, political science/government, psychology, religion, and sociology). Biology, chemistry, and graphic design are the strongest academically. Business, elementary education, and creative writing are the largest.

Special: There is cross-registration with Bucknell University. Internships are offered in almost all majors and study abroad is available on 6 continents. The School of Business offers a semester in London for junior business majors. 2-week study seminars in Australia are available, as is a Boston semester, a Washington semester, a United Nations semester, and a work-and-study semester through the Philadelphia Center. The university offers dual and student-designed majors, work-study programs, credit by examination, nondegree study, and pass/fail options. The B.A.-B.S. degree is available in several majors, and there is a 3-2 program in forestry with Duke University, a 2-2 program in allied health with Thomas Jefferson University, and a 3-2 program in dentistry with Temple University. Highly motivated students have the option of earning their baccalaureate degree in 3 years. There are 19 national honor societies, a freshman honors program, and 16 departmental honors programs.

Requirements: The SAT or ACT is required. The ACT Optional Writing test is also required. Students with a cumulative class rank in the top 20% in a strong college preparatory program have the option of submitting either the SAT, ACT, or 2 graded writing samples. Students should be graduates of an accredited high school. Preparation should include 4 years of English and math, 3 to 4 years of science, and 2 to 3 years each of social studies and foreign language. In addition, 1 unit of art or music is recommended. An essay is required, as are, for relevant fields, a music audition or writing portfolio. An interview is strongly recommended. A GPA of 3.0 is required. AP and CLEP credits are accepted. Important factors in the admissions decision are advanced placement or honors courses, evidence of special talent, and recommendations by school officials.

Procedure: Freshmen are admitted fall and spring. Entrance exams should be taken by January of the senior year. There are early decision, deferred admissions and rolling admissions plans. Early decision applications should be filed by November 15; check with the school for current application deadlines. The application fee is $35. Notification of early decision is sent December 1. Applications are accepted on-line. 68 applicants were on a recent waiting list, 14 were accepted.

Financial Aid: In a recent year, 96% of all full-time freshmen and 96% of continuing full-time students received some form of financial aid. 66% of all full-time freshmen and 63% of continuing full-time students received need-based aid. 51% of undergraduate students work part-time. Average annual earnings from campus work are $839. SU is a member of CSS. The CSS/Profile, FAFSA, and prior year federal tax return for parents and students are required. Check with the school for current deadlines.

Computers: Wireless access is available. All students from their resident hall rooms have access to a high-speed broadband network connection that allows unrestricted access to the Internet. Students also have access to wireless Internet throughout most of the nonresidential campus buildings. More than 300 public computer labs and kiosks are available to students around the campus. Off-campus students have access to the same wireless and labs. All students may access the system 24 hours a day. There are no time limits and no fees. It is strongly recommended that all students have a personal computer.

SWARTHMORE COLLEGE
Swarthmore, PA 19081-1397

(800) 667-3110; (610) 328-8580

Full-time: 727 men, 783 women	**Faculty:** 175; IIB, ++$
Part-time: 3 men, 12 women	**Ph.D.s:** 100%
Graduate: none	**Student/Faculty:** 9 to 1
Year: semesters	**Tuition:** $37,860
Application Deadline: January 2	**Room & Board:** $11,740
Freshman Class: 5575 applied, 969 accepted, 394 enrolled	
SAT CR/M/W: 720/720/720	**ACT:** 32 **MOST COMPETITIVE**

Swarthmore College, established in 1864, is a private, nonprofit institution offering undergraduate courses in liberal arts and engineering. In addition to regional accreditation, Swarthmore has baccalaureate program accreditation with ABET. The 7 libraries contain 842,722 volumes, 142,530 microform items, and 28,048 audio/video tapes/CDs/DVDs, and subscribe to 16,142 periodicals including electronic. Computerized library services include interlibrary loans, database searching, Internet access, and laptop Internet portals. Special learning facilities include an art gallery, a radio station, a LEED-certified integrated science center with an observatory and robotics and solar energy labs, specialty libraries for the study of classical Jewish texts, the Friends Historical Library and Peace Collection, and the Lang Center for Civic and Social Responsibility. The 399-acre campus is in a suburban area 11 miles southwest of Philadelphia, approximately 20 minutes by commuter rail. Including any residence halls, there are 56 buildings.

Programs of Study: Swarthmore confers B.A. and B.S. degrees. Bachelor's degrees are awarded in BIOLOGICAL SCIENCE (biochemistry and biology/biological science), COMMUNICATIONS AND THE ARTS (art, art history and appreciation, Chinese, classics, comparative literature, dance, dramatic arts, English literature, film arts, French, German, Greek, Japanese, Latin, linguistics, literature, music, Russian, and Spanish), COMPUTER AND PHYSICAL SCIENCE (astronomy, astrophysics, chemical physics, chemistry, computer science, mathematics, and physics), EDUCATION (education), ENGINEERING AND ENVIRONMENTAL DESIGN (engineering), SOCIAL SCIENCE (anthropology, Asian/Oriental studies, classical/ancient civilization, economics, gender studies, German area studies, history, medieval studies, philosophy, political science/government, psychobiology, psychology, religion, and sociology). Economics, biology, and political science are the largest.

Special: Students may cross-register with Haverford and Bryn Mawr Colleges and the University of Pennsylvania. They may study abroad in their country of choice. Dual and student-designed majors and a B.A.-B.S. degree in engineering are available. Swarthmore's honors program features small groups of students working closely with faculty and peers, with an emphasis on independent learning and a final exam by outside scholars. There are 3 national honor societies, including Phi Beta Kappa, and 24 departmental honors programs.

Admissions: 17% of the 2009-2010 applicants were accepted. The SAT scores for the 2009-2010 freshman class were: Critical Reading--1% below 500, 7% between 500 and 599, 25% between 600 and 700, and 67% above 700; Math--5% between 500 and 599, 33% between 600 and 700, and 61% above 700; Writing--4% between 500 and 599, 30% between 600 and 700, and 65% above 700. The

597

ACT scores were 2% between 21 and 23, 7% between 24 and 26, 10% between 27 and 28, and 81% above 28. 97% of the current freshmen were in the top fifth of their class; 100% were in the top two fifths. 46 freshmen graduated first in their class.

Requirements: Applicants are required to submit scores for either the SAT and any 2 SAT Subject tests, the ACT with Writing, or the SAT and the ACT. Swarthmore does not require a specific high school curriculum but recommends the inclusion of 4 years of English, 3 years each of math, the sciences, and history and social studies, the study of 1 or 2 foreign languages, and course work in art and music. 2 essays are required, and interviews are recommended. AP credits are accepted.

Procedure: Freshmen are admitted fall. Entrance exams should be taken in spring of the junior year or fall of the senior year. There are early decison and deferred admissions plans. Early decision applications should be filed by November 15; regular applications, by January 2 for fall entry. The fall 2009 application fee was $60. Notification of early decision is sent December 15; regular decision, April 1. Applications are accepted on-line. A waiting list is maintained.

Financial Aid: In 2009-2010, 54% of all full-time freshmen and 49% of continuing full-time students received some form of financial aid, including need-based aid. The average freshman award was $36,008. 81% of undergraduate students work part-time. Average annual earnings from campus work are $1483. Swarthmore is a member of CSS. The CSS/Profile, FAFSA, the state aid form, the college's own financial statement, tax returns, W-2 statements, and year-end paycheck stubs are required. The deadline for filing freshman financial aid applications for fall entry is February 15.

Computers: There are more than 250 PCs and Macs available for student use in libraries, dorms, and classrooms. Course materials and academic software are available on-line for many courses. The Media Center may be used for audio, video, and graphics projects, and wireless networking is available in all campus buildings and most outdoor spaces. All students may access the system. There are no time limits and no fees.

SYRACUSE UNIVERSITY
Syracuse, NY 13244   **(315) 443-3611**

Full-time: 5255 men, 6476 women	**Faculty:** 911; I, -$
Part-time: 40 men, 25 women	**Ph.D.s:** 87%
Graduate: 2787 men, 3094 women	**Student/Faculty:** 14 to 1
Year: semesters, summer session	**Tuition:** $34,926
Application Deadline: January 1	**Room & Board:** $12,374
Freshman Class: 20951 applied, 12596 accepted, 3267 enrolled	
SAT or ACT: required	**HIGHLY COMPETITIVE**

Syracuse University, founded in 1870, is a private institution offering nearly 200 undergraduate programs in liberal arts, architecture, education, engineering and computer science, human ecology (including child and family studies, health and wellness, hospitality management, marriage and family therapy, nutrition sciences and dietetics, sport management, and social work); information management and technology; management; public communications; and visual and performing arts (including art, music, drama, and communication and rhetorical studies). SU is also noted for the quality of its internships, study abroad experiences, and partnerships. There are 9 undergraduate schools and 11 graduate schools. In addition to regional accreditation, Syracuse has baccalaureate program accreditation with ABET, ACEJMC, CSWE, FIDER, NAAB, NASAD,

NASM, and NCATE. The 6 libraries contain 3.2 million volumes, 7.5 million microform items, and 1.1 million audio/video tapes/CDs/DVDs, and subscribe to 39,703 periodicals including electronic. Computerized library services include interlibrary loans, database searching, Internet access, and laptop Internet portals. Special learning facilities include a learning resource center, art gallery, radio station, TV station, the Global Collaboratory connecting students via satellite to sites all over the world, media laboratories for Web-based news reporting and broadcast journalism and a digital convergence center, the Syracuse Center of Excellence in Environmental and Energy Systems, a life sciences complex for interdisciplinary research and education, an advanced flight simulator for students in aerospace engineering, the Ballentine Investment Institute in the Whitman School of Management, an art building with studios and film, video, photo, and computer graphic labs, a technology center, a professional Equity theater, the Mary Ann Shaw Center for Public Service, a child development laboratory school, an audio laboratory, a writing center, a math clinic, and a speech, language, and hearing clinic. The 200-acre campus is in an urban area approximately 280 miles northwest of New York City. Including any residence halls, there are 232 buildings.

Programs of Study: Syracuse confers B.A., B.S., B.Arch., B.F.A, B.I.D., B. Mus., and B.P.S. degrees. Associates, master's, and doctoral degrees are also awarded. Bachelor's degrees are awarded in BIOLOGICAL SCIENCE (biology/ biological science and nutrition), BUSINESS (banking and finance, business administration and management, entrepreneurial studies, hospitality management services, marketing management, real estate, retailing, sports management, and supply chain management), COMMUNICATIONS AND THE ARTS (advertising, art, art history and appreciation, broadcasting, ceramic art and design, classics, communications, comparative literature, dramatic arts, English, English literature, fiber/textiles/weaving, film arts, fine arts, French, Germanic languages and literature, graphic design, Greek, illustration, industrial design, journalism, linguistics, media arts, metal/jewelry, modern language, music, music business management, music history and appreciation, music performance, music theory and composition, musical theater, painting, percussion, photography, piano/ organ, printmaking, public relations, Russian, sculpture, Spanish, speech/debate/ rhetoric, strings, telecommunications, theater design, theater management, video, voice, and winds), COMPUTER AND PHYSICAL SCIENCE (chemistry, computer science, geology, information sciences and systems, mathematics, physics, and statistics), EDUCATION (art education, early childhood education, education, elementary education, English education, mathematics education, middle school education, music education, physical education, science education, social studies education, and special education), ENGINEERING AND ENVIRONMENTAL DESIGN (aeronautical engineering, architecture, bioengineering, chemical engineering, civil engineering, computer engineering, computer graphics, electrical/electronics engineering, engineering physics, environmental engineering, interior design, and mechanical engineering), HEALTH PROFESSIONS (health science, predentistry, premedicine, preveterinary science, public health, and speech pathology/audiology), SOCIAL SCIENCE (African American studies, American studies, anthropology, child care/child and family studies, classical/ancient civilization, economics, European studies, fashion design and technology, food production/management/services, geography, history, international relations, Italian studies, Latin American studies, Middle Eastern studies, philosophy, political science/government, prelaw, psychology, religion, Russian and Slavic studies, social work, sociology, and women's studies). Architecture, public communications, and life sciences are the strongest academically. Psychology, architecture, and information management are the largest.

Special: SU students are encouraged to undertake internships both during the academic year and during summers in the Syracuse community and across the nation, both for credit and not for credit. Cooperative education programs are available in engineering. Study abroad is available in 7 university-operated centers and through other special programs, and a Washington semester is offered through the International Relations Program. Work-study programs, dual majors, and student-designed majors are available. There are 9 national honor societies, including Phi Beta Kappa, and an honors program open to all undergraduates.

Admissions: 60% of the 2009-2010 applicants were accepted. The SAT scores for the 2009-2010 freshman class were: Critical Reading--18% below 500, 47% between 500 and 599, 29% between 600 and 700, and 6% above 700; Math--12% below 500, 37% between 500 and 599, 41% between 600 and 700, and 10% above 700. 62% of the current freshmen were in the top fifth of their class; 89% were in the top two fifths.

Requirements: The SAT or ACT is required. The ACT Optional Writing test is also required. In addition, applicants should have a strong college preparatory record from an accredited secondary school or have a GED equivalent. Essays are required. A portfolio is required for art and architecture majors, and an audition is required for music and drama majors. A secondary school counselor evaluation, or 2 academic recommendations, and a high school transcript, are also required. AP credits are accepted. Important factors in the admissions decision are advanced placement or honors courses, evidence of special talent, and leadership record.

Procedure: Freshmen are admitted fall and spring. Entrance exams should be taken before January of the senior year for regular decision and before November of the senior year for early decision. There are early decision, early admissions and deferred admissions plans. Early decision applications should be filed by November 15; regular applications, by January 1 for fall entry and November 15 for spring entry. The fall 2009 application fee was $70. Notification of early decision is sent in December; regular decision, mid-March. Applications are accepted online. 1,150 applicants were on a recent waiting list, 504 were accepted.

Financial Aid: In 2009-2010, 80% of all full-time freshmen and 80% of continuing full-time students received some form of financial aid. 60% of all full-time freshmen and 60% of continuing full-time students received need-based aid. The average freshmen award was $32,500. 40% of undergraduate students work part-time. Average annual earnings from campus work are $2500. The average financial indebtedness of the 2009 graduate was $28,358. Syracuse is a member of CSS. The CSS/Profile and FAFSA are required. The deadline for filing freshman financial aid applications for fall entry is February 1.

Computers: High-speed wired and wireless Internet access is available in residence halls, academic/administrative buildings and adjacent grounds on campus. There are more than 3400 computers available in over 100 specified computer labs, computer teaching labs/classrooms and collaborative spaces, as well as in 172 technology classrooms. All students may access the system 24 hours per day. There are no time limits and no fees. It is strongly recommended that all students have a personal computer.

Upland, IN 46989-1001

(765) 998-5134
(800) 882-3456; (765) 998-4925

Full-time: 855 men, 1040 women	**Faculty:** 129; IIB, --$
Part-time: 39 men, 58 women	**Ph.D.s:** 88%
Graduate: 71 men, 52 women	**Student/Faculty:** 15 to 1
Year: 4-1-4, summer session	**Tuition:** $25,396
Application Deadline: December 1	**Room & Board:** $6708
Freshman Class: 1975 applied, 1643 accepted, 486 enrolled	
SAT CR/M/W: 590/570/560	**ACT:** 27 **VERY COMPETITIVE+**

Taylor University, founded in 1846, is a private Christian interdenominational liberal arts institution. There is 1 graduate school. In addition to regional accreditation, Taylor has baccalaureate program accreditation with ABET, CSWE, NASM, and NCATE. The library contains 184,995 volumes, 14,661 microform items, and 10,356 audio/video tapes/CDs/DVDs. Computerized library services include interlibrary loans, database searching, Internet access, and laptop Internet portals. Special learning facilities include a learning resource center, art gallery, radio station, TV station, 65-acre arboretum, the C.S. Lewis Collection, and an observatory room. The 952-acre campus is in a rural area 70 miles north of Indianapolis. Including any residence halls, there are 36 buildings.

Programs of Study: Taylor confers B.A., B.B.A., B.Mus., and B.S. degrees. Associate and master's degrees are also awarded. Bachelor's degrees are awarded in BIOLOGICAL SCIENCE (biology/biological science and environmental biology), BUSINESS (accounting, banking and finance, international business management, management information systems, management science, marketing and distribution, recreation and leisure services, and sports management), COMMUNICATIONS AND THE ARTS (art, communications, dramatic arts, English, French, journalism, media arts, music, Spanish, and visual and performing arts), COMPUTER AND PHYSICAL SCIENCE (chemistry, computer science, environmental geology, mathematics, natural sciences, and physics), EDUCATION (art education, Christian education, early childhood education, elementary education, English education, foreign languages education, mathematics education, music education, physical education, science education, secondary education, and social studies education), ENGINEERING AND ENVIRONMENTAL DESIGN (computer engineering, computer graphics, engineering physics, environmental engineering, and environmental science), HEALTH PROFESSIONS (exercise science, health science, and premedicine), SOCIAL SCIENCE (biblical studies, economics, geography, history, international studies, philosophy, political science/government, psychology, social work, and sociology). Engineering physics and biology are the strongest academically. Business and education are the largest.

Special: Opportunities are provided for internships, cooperative programs, a Washington semester, study abroad in 28 countries, work-study programs, dual majors, student-designed majors, and B.A.-B.S. degrees. There is cross-registration with the other members of the Council for Christian Colleges and Universities and the Christian College Consortium. There are 7 national honor societies, including Phi Beta Kappa, a freshman honors program, and 23 departmental honors programs.

Admissions: 83% of the 2009-2010 applicants were accepted. 56% of the current freshmen were in the top fifth of their class; 83% were in the top two fifths. There were 6 National Merit finalists. 31 freshmen graduated first in their class.

Requirements: The SAT or ACT is required. The ACT Writing Test is recommended. In addition, graduation from an accredited secondary school is required; a GED will be accepted. It is recommended that applicants complete 4 years of English, 3 to 4 each of math and lab science, 2 each of social studies and a foreign language, and course work in computing, typing/keyboarding, and the arts. The application includes 1 essay. High school transcripts and recommendation forms from a guidance counselor and pastor are also required. An interview is recommended for all students, and an audition is required for music majors. Taylor requires applicants to be in the upper 40% of their class. A GPA of 2.8 is required. AP and CLEP credits are accepted. Important factors in the admissions decision are recommendations by school officials, extracurricular activities record, and leadership record.

Procedure: Freshmen are admitted fall, winter, and spring. Entrance exams should be taken during the spring of the junior year or fall of the senior year. There are early admissions and deferred admissions plans. Early decision applications should be filed by November 1; regular applications, by December 1 for fall entry; February 1 for winter entry; and April 1 for spring entry, along with a $25 fee. Notification of early decision is sent November 20; regular decision, December 20. Applications are accepted on-line. A waiting list is maintained.

Financial Aid: In 2009-2010, 96% of all full-time freshmen and 88% of continuing full-time students received some form of financial aid. 64% of all full-time freshmen and 59% of continuing full-time students received need-based aid. The average freshman award was $15,979. Need-based scholarships or need-based grants averaged $4069 ($15,000 maximum); need-based self-help aid (loans and jobs) averaged $3391 ($7400 maximum); non-need-based athletic scholarships averaged $983 ($25,164 maximum); and other non-need-based awards and non-need-based scholarships averaged $7536 ($12,500 maximum). 24% of undergraduate students work part-time. Average annual earnings from campus work are $1068. The average financial indebtedness of the 2009 graduate was $22,971. Taylor is a member of CSS. The FAFSA is required. The deadline for filing freshman financial aid applications for fall entry is March 10.

Computers: Wireless access is available. Wireless access is provided throughout the university. There are 60 computers in classrooms, 340 in labs, and 64 in student workstations. All students may access the system. There are no time limits and no fees. It is strongly recommended that all students have a personal computer.

TEMPLE UNIVERSITY
Philadelphia, PA 19122-1803   (215) 204-8556; (888) 340-2222

Full-time: 11,301 men, 12,811 women	**Faculty:** 1278; I, -$
Part-time: 1378 men, 1555 women	**Ph.D.s:** 76%
Graduate: 4270 men, 5190 women	**Student/Faculty:** 19 to 1
Year: semesters, summer session	**Tuition:** $11,764 ($21,044)
Application Deadline: March 1	**Room & Board:** $9198
Freshman Class: 23,584 applied, 15,626 accepted, 7104 enrolled	
SAT CR/M/W: 549/561/549	**ACT:** 22 **VERY COMPETITIVE**

Temple University, founded in 1888, is part of the Commonwealth System of Higher Education in Pennsylvania. It offers programs in the liberal arts and science and technology, health professions, education, engineering, art, business and management, communications and theater, architecture, landscape architecture and horticulture, music and dance, and social administration. Temple has 6 other campuses, including 1 in Rome and 1 in Tokyo. There are 17 undergraduate schools and 16 graduate schools. In addition to regional accreditation, Temple has baccalaureate program accreditation with AACSB, ABET, ACEJMC, ACPE, APTA, CAHEA, CAHIM, CAHME, CEPH, CSWE, NAAB, NASAD, NASM, NASSM, NATA, NRPA, and TEAC. The 11 libraries contain 3.2 million volumes, 3.3 million microform items, and 34,438 audio/video tapes/CDs/DVDs, and subscribe to 60,586 periodicals including electronic. Computerized library services include interlibrary loans, database searching, Internet access, and laptop Internet portals. Special learning facilities include a learning resource center, art gallery, planetarium, radio station, TV station, dance lab theater, media learning center for the study of critical languages, and multimedia lab for teacher education in music. The 330-acre campus is in an urban area approximately 1.5 miles from downtown Philadelphia. Including any residence halls, there are 142 buildings.

Programs of Study: Temple confers B.A., B.S., B.Ar., B.B.A., B.F.A., B.F.A./ Teaching Cert., B.M., B.S.Ar., B.S.A.T., B.S.C.E., B.S.Ed., B.S.E.E., B.S.E.T., B.S.M.E., B.S.N., and B.S.W. degrees. Associate, master's, and doctoral degrees are also awarded. Bachelor's degrees are awarded in AGRICULTURE (environmental studies and horticulture), BIOLOGICAL SCIENCE (biochemistry, biology/biological science, and biophysics), BUSINESS (accounting, banking and finance, business administration and management, entrepreneurial studies, insurance and risk management, international business management, management information systems, marketing/retailing/merchandising, real estate, sports management, and tourism), COMMUNICATIONS AND THE ARTS (advertising, art, art history and appreciation, broadcasting, ceramic art and design, classics, communications, dance, English, fiber/textiles/weaving, film arts, French, German, glass, graphic design, Hebrew, Italian, jazz, journalism, linguistics, metal/ jewelry, music, music history and appreciation, music performance, music theory and composition, painting, performing arts, photography, piano/organ, printmaking, public relations, Russian, sculpture, Spanish, speech/debate/rhetoric, telecommunications, theater design, and theater management), COMPUTER AND PHYSICAL SCIENCE (actuarial science, chemistry, computer science, geology, information sciences and systems, mathematics, and physics), EDUCATION (art education, education, elementary education, music education, physical education, secondary education, and technical education), ENGINEERING AND ENVIRONMENTAL DESIGN (architecture, city/community/regional planning, civil engineering, civil engineering technology, electrical/electronics engineering, engineering, engineering technology, environmental engineering technology, environmental science, landscape architecture/design, and mechanical engineering), HEALTH PROFESSIONS (music therapy, nursing, predentistry, premedicine, public health, and speech therapy), SOCIAL SCIENCE (African American studies, American studies, anthropology, Asian/Oriental studies, criminal justice, economics, geography, history, Latin American studies, philosophy, physical fitness/movement, political science/government, prelaw, psychology, religion, social science, social work, sociology, urban studies, and women's studies). Art, journalism, and business are the strongest academically. Biology, psychology, and elementary education are the largest.

Special: Temple offers co-op programs in business/marketing, computer/ information sciences, and engineering, cross-registration with Messiah College, internships, study abroad in 15 countries, an extern program in which participating students receive 2 or 3 academic credits, dual majors, student-designed majors, distance learning, dual enrollment, ESL, domestic exchange, independent study, and a teacher certification program. There are 3 national honor societies, including Phi Beta Kappa, and a freshman honors program.

Admissions: 66% of the 2009-2010 applicants were accepted. The SAT scores for the 2009-2010 freshman class were: Critical Reading--24% below 500, 47% between 500 and 599, 23% between 600 and 700, and 4% above 700; Math--18% below 500, 48% between 500 and 599, 28% between 600 and 700, and 4% above 700; Writing--22% below 500, 48% between 500 and 599, 24% between 600 and 700, and 4% above 700. The ACT scores were 8% below 21, 45% between 21 and 23, 23% between 24 and 26, 41% between 27 and 28, and 6% above 28. 41% of the current freshmen were in the top fifth of their class; 79% were in the top two fifths. 18 freshmen graduated first in their class.

Requirements: The SAT or ACT is required. In addition, applicants should complete 16 academic credits/Carnegie units, including 4 years of English, 3 of math, 2 each of social studies, foreign language, and science, including 1 of lab science, and 1 each of history and an academic elective. A GED is accepted. A portfolio and audition are required in relevant fields. AP and CLEP credits are accepted. Important factors in the admissions decision are advanced placement or honors courses, evidence of special talent, and recommendations by school officials.

Procedure: Freshmen are admitted fall and spring. Entrance exams should be taken by March of the junior year or April of the senior year. There is a rolling admissions plan. Applications should be filed by March 1 for fall entry and November 15 for spring entry. The fall 2008 application fee was $50. Notification is sent on a rolling basis. 1288 applicants were on the 2009 waiting list; 288 were admitted. Applications are accepted on-line.

Financial Aid: In 2009-2010, 65% of all full-time freshmen and 64% of continuing full-time students received some form of financial aid. 65% of all full-time freshmen and 64% of continuing full-time students received need-based aid. The average freshman award was $15,722. Need-based scholarships and need-based grants averaged $5804; need-based self-help aid (loans and jobs) averaged $3427; non-need-based athletic scholarships averaged $14,356; and other non-need-based awards and non-need-based scholarships averaged $8437. The average financial indebtedness of the 2009 graduate was $29,886. The FAFSA, the college's own financial statement, and the PHEAA (for Pennsylvania residents) are required. The priority date for freshman financial aid applications for fall entry is March 1.

Computers: Wireless access is available. From the outside, students may sign on to university systems using their assigned user ID and a secure password. They may also plug into the network in labs, dorms, and smart classrooms. Students have access to 3587 workstations. Wireless access is available in the student union, dining areas, library, and some classrooms, common areas, and dorms. Students need only register their computer to gain access. All students may access the system 24 hours per day. There are no time limits and no fees.

TEXAS A&M UNIVERSITY
College Station, TX 77843   **(979) 845-3741; (979) 847-8737**

Full-time: 17,840 men, 16,660 women	**Faculty:** I, -$
Part-time: 1590 men, 1270 women	**Ph.D.s:** 87%
Graduate: 5285 men, 3900 women	**Student/Faculty:** n/av
Year: semesters, summer session	**Tuition:** $8000 ($16,000)
Application Deadline: see profile	**Room & Board:** $7000
Freshman Class: n/av	
SAT or ACT: required	**HIGHLY COMPETITIVE**

Texas A&M University, founded in 1876, is part of the Texas A&M University system. Undergraduate degrees are offered in agriculture and life sciences, architecture, business administration, education, engineering, geosciences, liberal arts, science, and biomedical science. Figures in the above capsule are approximate. There are 9 undergraduate schools and 10 graduate schools. In addition to regional accreditation, Texas A&M has baccalaureate program accreditation with AACSB, ABET, ACCE, ACEJMC, ADA, ASLA, CSAB, NAAB, NCATE, and SAF. The 3 libraries contain 3.6 million volumes, 5.5 million microform items, and 45,412 audio/video tapes/CDs/DVDs, and subscribe to 45,806 periodicals including electronic. Computerized library services include interlibrary loans, database searching, Internet access, and laptop Internet portals. Special learning facilities include a learning resource center, art gallery, radio station, TV station, weather station, observatory, cyclotron, wind tunnel, visualization lab, nuclear reactor, ocean wave pool, and the Bush Museum and Library. The 8500-acre campus is in an urban area 90 miles northwest of Houston. Including any residence halls, there are 771 buildings.

Programs of Study: Texas A&M confers B.A., B.S., B.B.A., B.Ed., and B.L.A. degrees. Master's and doctoral degrees are also awarded. Bachelor's degrees are awarded in AGRICULTURE (agricultural business management, agricultural economics, animal science, dairy science, fish and game management, fishing and fisheries, forestry and related sciences, horticulture, poultry science, and range/farm management), BIOLOGICAL SCIENCE (biochemistry, biology/biological science, botany, entomology, genetics, microbiology, and zoology), BUSINESS (accounting, banking and finance, business systems analysis, management science, marketing/retailing/merchandising, and personnel management), COMMUNICATIONS AND THE ARTS (English, French, German, journalism, Russian, Spanish, and speech/debate/rhetoric), COMPUTER AND PHYSICAL SCIENCE (atmospheric sciences and meteorology, chemistry, computer science, geology, geophysics and seismology, mathematics, and physics), EDUCATION (elementary education, health education, physical education, and secondary education), ENGINEERING AND ENVIRONMENTAL DESIGN (aeronautical engineering, agricultural engineering, bioengineering, chemical engineering, civil engineering, computer engineering, construction engineering, electrical/electronics engineering, engineering technology, environmental design, environmental science, industrial engineering technology, landscape architecture/design, mechanical engineering, nuclear engineering, and petroleum/natural gas engineering), HEALTH PROFESSIONS (biomedical science), SOCIAL SCIENCE (anthropology, economics, history, international studies, parks and recreation management, philosophy, political science/government, psychology, and sociology). Biomedical science, business administration, and biology are the strongest academically.

Special: The university offers extensive opportunities through the Career Center and Study Abroad Office. B.A.- B.S. degrees, study abroad in 12 countries, internships, a Washington semester, credit for military experience, nondegree study, co-op programs, dual majors, and pass/fail options are available. A 5-year graduate business/liberal arts program is offered, as well as a 3-2 engineering degree with Sam Houston State University. There are 41 national honor societies, including Phi Beta Kappa, and a freshman honors program.

Admissions: There were 136 National Merit finalists in a recent year. 297 freshmen graduated first in their class.

Requirements: The SAT or ACT is required. The ACT Optional Writing test is also required. In addition, secondary school graduation is a condition of freshman admission. Required high school courses include 4 credits in English, 3 1/2 credits in math, 3 credits in science (2 from biology, chemistry, or physics), 2 credits of social studies and the same foreign language, and 1 of history. AP and CLEP

605

credits are accepted. Important factors in the admissions decision are leadership record, evidence of special talent, and extracurricular activities record.

Procedure: Freshmen are admitted fall, spring, and summer. Entrance exams should be taken during the spring of the junior year or by December of the senior year. There is a rolling admissions plan. Check with the school for current application deadlines. The fall 2009 application fee was $60. Applications are accepted on-line. A waiting list is maintained.

Financial Aid: In a recent year, 71% of all full-time freshmen and 61% of continuing full-time students received some form of financial aid. 38% of all full-time freshmen and 35% of continuing full-time students received need-based aid. The average freshmen award was $10,655. $9567 ($27,424 maximum) was from need-based scholarships or need-based grants; $4217 ($26,000 maximum) from need-based self-help aid (loans and jobs); $7281 ($19,043 maximum) from non-need-based athletic scholarships; and $4750 ($45,750 maximum) from other non-need-based awards and non-need-based scholarships. 20% of undergraduate students work part-time. Average annual earnings from campus work are $2049. The average financial indebtedness of a recent graduate was $19,981. The FAFSA is required. Check with the school for current application deadlines.

Computers: Wireless access is available. All students have full access to the Internet, e-mail, personal web pages, and computer labs. Wireless access is available in all libraries, dining facilities, and some academic departments and student common areas. All students may access the system at any time. There are no time limits. The fee in 2009 was $20.30 per credit hour ($304.50 maximum).

TEXAS CHRISTIAN UNIVERSITY
Fort Worth, TX 76129

(817) 257-7490
(800) TCU-FROG; (817) 257-7268

Full-time: 2958 men, 4368 women	**Faculty:** 506; I, --$
Part-time: 163 men, 151 women	**Ph.D.s:** 83%
Graduate: 574 men, 639 women	**Student/Faculty:** 15 to 1
Year: semesters, summer session	**Tuition:** $28,298
Application Deadline: February 15	**Room & Board:** $9810
Freshman Class: 11951 applied, 7081 accepted, 1821 enrolled	
SAT or ACT: recommended	**VERY COMPETITIVE**

Texas Christian University, founded in 1873, is a private university affiliated with the Christian Church (Disciples of Christ). TCU is a teaching and research institution offering undergraduate programs in arts, sciences, business, education, fine arts, communications, nursing, and engineering. There are 7 undergraduate schools and 7 graduate schools. In addition to regional accreditation, TCU has baccalaureate program accreditation with AACSB, ABET, ACEJMC, ADA, CSWE, FIDER, and NASM. The library contains 2.1 million volumes, 642,879 microform items, and 167,211 audio/video tapes/CDs/DVDs, and subscribes to 56,856 periodicals including electronic. Computerized library services include interlibrary loans, database searching, Internet access, and laptop Internet portals. Special learning facilities include a learning resource center, art gallery, natural history museum, radio station, TV station, observatory, and speech and hearing clinic. The 300-acre campus is in a suburban area 3 miles southwest of downtown Fort Worth. Including any residence halls, there are 109 buildings.

Programs of Study: TCU confers B.A., B.B.A., B.F.A., B.G.S., B.Med., B.Mus., B.S., B.S.Ed., B.S.N., and B.S.S.W. degrees. Master's and doctoral degrees are also awarded. Bachelor's degrees are awarded in AGRICULTURE (range/farm management), BIOLOGICAL SCIENCE (biochemistry, biology/

biological science, neurosciences, and nutrition), BUSINESS (accounting, banking and finance, business administration and management, business systems analysis, entrepreneurial studies, fashion merchandising, international business management, international economics, management science, marketing/retailing/merchandising, real estate, and supply chain management), COMMUNICATIONS AND THE ARTS (advertising, art history and appreciation, ballet, broadcasting, communications, creative writing, dance, digital communications, dramatic arts, English, film arts, French, German, graphic design, journalism, modern language, music, music performance, music theory and composition, musical theater, painting, performing arts, photography, piano/organ, printmaking, public relations, publishing, radio/television technology, Spanish, speech/debate/rhetoric, sports media, studio art, theater design, and voice), COMPUTER AND PHYSICAL SCIENCE (astronomy, chemistry, computer science, geology, information sciences and systems, mathematics, and physics), EDUCATION (art education, athletic training, bilingual/bicultural education, business education, early childhood education, education of the deaf and hearing impaired, education of the exceptional child, elementary education, English education, mathematics education, middle school education, music education, physical education, science education, secondary education, and social studies education), ENGINEERING AND ENVIRONMENTAL DESIGN (computer technology, engineering, environmental science, and interior design), HEALTH PROFESSIONS (exercise science, health, nursing, and speech pathology/audiology), SOCIAL SCIENCE (anthropology, criminal justice, dietetics, economics, food production/management/services, geography, history, international relations, liberal arts/general studies, philosophy, physical fitness/movement, political science/government, psychology, religion, religious music, social work, and sociology). Nursing, biology, and communication studies are the largest.

Special: A general studies degree and a combined B.A.-B.S. degree in numerous majors are offered. TCU also accepts credit by exam and credit for life, military, and work experience. 4-1 programs are available in education. Internships are available in almost all major areas. The university also offers a Washington semester, student exchange programs, and study abroad in 26 countries. TCU also offers study at its London Center and study through the American Airlines Leadership for the Americas program. An accelerated degree program in nursing is available. There are 4 national honor societies, including Phi Beta Kappa, a freshman honors program, and 38 departmental honors programs.

Admissions: 59% of the 2009-2010 applicants were accepted. 53% of the current freshmen were in the top fifth of their class; 84% were in the top two fifths.

Requirements: The SAT or ACT and ACT Writing Test are recommended. In addition, candidates should be graduates of an accredited secondary school and have completed 15 Carnegie units, including 4 years of English, 3 years each of math, science, and social studies, and 2 each of the same foreign language and of academic electives. TCU also requires an essay and counselor's recommendation. A personal interview is optional. AP and CLEP credits are accepted. Important factors in the admissions decision are advanced placement or honors courses, leadership record, and evidence of special talent.

Procedure: Freshmen are admitted to all sessions. Entrance exams should be taken during or before the fall semester of the senior year. There is a deferred admissions plan. Applications should be filed by February 15 for fall entry and December 1 for spring entry, along with a $40 fee. Notifications are sent April 1. Applications are accepted on-line. 400 applicants were on a recent waiting list, 300 were accepted.

Financial Aid: TCU is a member of CSS. The FAFSA is required. The deadline for filing freshman financial aid applications for fall entry is May 1.

Computers: Wireless access is available. All residence halls are wired for network access with multiple connections per room. All buildings, including residence halls, and most outdoor campus locations have wireless coverage. The university maintains more than 1400 lab computers in various building locations for student use. All students may access the system anytime. There are no time limits and no fees. It is strongly recommended that all students have a personal computer.

TEXAS STATE UNIVERSITY AT SAN MARCOS

San Marcos, TX 78666-4616	(512) 245-2364; (512) 245-8044
Full-time: 9566 men, 11649 women	**Faculty:** 1017; IIA, -$
Part-time: 2237 men, 2550 women	**Ph.D.s:** 77%
Graduate: 1781 men, 3020 women	**Student/Faculty:** 21 to 1
Year: semesters, summer session	**Tuition:** $7482 ($15,792)
Application Deadline: May 1	**Room & Board:** $6362
Freshman Class: 12172 applied, 9211 accepted, 3667 enrolled	
SAT CR/M/W: 520/540/500	**ACT:** 23 COMPETITIVE

Texas State University at San Marcos, was founded in 1899, is part of the Texas State University System and offers programs in general studies, applied arts and technology, business, education, fine arts, health professions, liberal arts, and science and engineering. There are 8 undergraduate schools and 1 graduate school. In addition to regional accreditation, Texas State has baccalaureate program accreditation with AACSB, ABET, ACCE, ADA, AHEA, ASLA, CSAB, CSWE, FIDER, NASM, and NRPA. The library contains 3.9 million volumes, 1.9 million microform items, and 280,818 audio/video tapes/CDs/DVDs, and subscribes to 22,846 periodicals including electronic. Computerized library services include interlibrary loans, database searching, Internet access, and laptop Internet portals. Special learning facilities include a learning resource center, art gallery, planetarium, radio station, a recording studio and a rivers and acquifer center. The 456-acre campus is in a suburban area 30 miles south of Austin and 45 miles northeast of San Antonio. Including any residence halls, there are 219 buildings.

Programs of Study: Texas State confers B.A., B.A.A.S., B.A.I.S., B.B.A., B.E.S.S., B.F.A., B.G.S., B.H.A., B.H.W.P., B.M., B.P.A., B.S., B.S.A.G., B.S.A.S., B.S.C.L.S., B.S.C.D., B.S.C.J., B.S.F.C.S., B.S.H.I.M., B.S.H.P., B.S.R.A., B.S.R.C., B.S.R.T., B.S.T., and B.S.W. degrees. Master's and doctoral degrees are also awarded. Bachelor's degrees are awarded in AGRICULTURE (agricultural business management, agriculture, and animal science), BIOLOGICAL SCIENCE (biochemistry, biology/biological science, botany, marine biology, microbiology, nutrition, physiology, wildlife biology, and zoology), BUSINESS (accounting, banking and finance, business administration and management, business economics, electronic business, fashion merchandising, marketing/retailing/merchandising, recreational facilities management, and tourism), COMMUNICATIONS AND THE ARTS (advertising, applied art, art, audio technology, broadcasting, communications, dance, dramatic arts, English, French, German, jazz, journalism, music, music performance, musical theater, photography, public relations, Spanish, and studio art), COMPUTER AND PHYSICAL SCIENCE (chemistry, computer science, computer security and information assurance, digital arts/technology, information sciences and systems, mathematics, and physics), EDUCATION (athletic training, early childhood education, elementary education, health education, physical education, and special education), ENGINEERING AND ENVIRONMENTAL DESIGN (cartography, city/community/regional planning, construction technology, electrical/electronics engineering, engineering technology, environmental science, industrial engineering technology, interior design, manufacturing engineering, manufacturing technology, urban planning technology, and water and waste water technology), HEALTH PROFESSIONS (clinical science, exercise science, health care administration, medical records administration/services, radiation therapy, respiratory therapy, and speech pathology/audiology), SOCIAL SCIENCE (American studies, anthropology, Asian/Oriental studies, child care/child and family studies, corrections, criminal justice, economics, European studies, family/consumer studies, geography, history, interdisciplinary studies, international relations, international studies, law enforcement and corrections, liberal arts/general studies, Middle Eastern studies, philosophy, political science/government, psychology, public administration, Russian and Slavic studies, social work, and sociology). Geography and education are the strongest academically. Education, business management, and marketing are the largest.

Special: Co-op programs in medicine, dentistry, engineering, architecture, law, pharmacy, nursing, occupational therapy, and veterinary medicine, internships in many departments, study abroad in 26 countries, and Washington semesters are available. Dual majors, credit for life experience, and nondegree study also are possible. 2 summer sessions are offered in most programs. A 3-2 engineering degree is possible with the University of Texas, Texas A&M, Texas Tech University, and University of Texas at San Antonio. There are 23 national honor societies, a freshman honors program, and 1 departmental honors program.

Admissions: 76% of the 2009-2010 applicants were accepted. The SAT scores for the 2009-2010 freshman class were: Critical Reading--35% below 500, 48% between 500 and 599, 15% between 600 and 700, and 2% above 700; Math--27% below 500, 52% between 500 and 599, 20% between 600 and 700, and 1% above 700; Writing--44% below 500, 45% between 500 and 599, and 10% between 600 and 700. The ACT scores were 17% below 21, 42% between 21 and 23, 27% between 24 and 26, 8% between 27 and 28, and 6% above 28. 39% of the current freshmen were in the top fifth of their class; 79% were in the top two fifths. 15 freshmen graduated first in their class.

Requirements: The SAT or ACT is required. The ACT Optional Writing test is also required. Minimum scores are determined by high school class rank. Applicants need 24 academic credits, including 4 units in English, 3.5 in social science and electives, 3 in math and science, 2 in foreign language, 1.5 in physical education, 1 in technology applications and fine arts and .5 in speech, economics, health education, 1 in fine arts, and 3.5 in electives The GED is accepted; applicants with a GED are treated as though they were in the 4th quarter of their graduating class. AP and CLEP credits are accepted. Important factors in the admissions decision are advanced placement or honors courses, leadership record, and extracurricular activities record.

Procedure: Freshmen are admitted to all sessions. Entrance exams should be taken at the end of the junior year. There is a rolling admissions plan. Applications should be filed by May 1 for fall entry, December 1 for spring entry, and May 1 for summer entry, along with a $60 fee. Applications are accepted on-line.

Financial Aid: In 2009-2010, 68% of all full-time freshmen and 62% of continuing full-time students received some form of financial aid. 52% of all full-time freshmen and 50% of continuing full-time students received need-based aid. The average freshman award was $5,452. Need-based scholarships or need-based grants averaged $5,286 ($9,120 maximum); need-based self-help aid (loans and jobs) averaged $4,796 ($12,729 maximum); non-need based athletic scholarships averaged $2,331 ($7,812 maximum); and other non-need based awards and non-need based scholarships averaged $3,567 ($34,500 maximum). 62% of undergraduate students work part-time. Average annual earnings from campus work are $6102. The average financial indebtedness of the 2009 graduate was $19,815. The FAFSA is required. The priority date for freshman financial aid applications for fall entry is April 1.

Computers: Wireless access is available. There are more than 1400 workstations with wireless access in the library, student center, and most academic buildings. All students may access the system 24 hours daily. There are no time limits. The fee is $15 per credit hour.

TEXAS TECH UNIVERSITY

Lubbock, TX 79409-5005   (806) 742-1480; (806) 742-0062

Full-time: 11,665 men, 9400 women	**Faculty:** I, --$
Part-time: 1175 men, 790 women	**Ph.D.s:** 92%
Graduate: 2755 men, 2485 women	**Student/Faculty:** n/av
Year: semesters, summer session	**Tuition:** $9700 ($17,000)
Application Deadline: see profile	**Room & Board:** $8000
Freshman Class: n/av	
SAT or ACT: required	**COMPETITIVE**

Texas Tech University, founded in 1923, is a large, comprehensive public university offering undergraduate and graduate programs in a variety of professional fields. Figures in the above capsule and this profile are approximate. There are 10 undergraduate schools and 1 graduate school. In addition to regional accreditation, Texas Tech has baccalaureate program accreditation with AACSB, ABET, ACEJMC, ASLA, CSWE, NAAB, NASAD, NASM, and NCATE. The 5 libraries contain 4.9 million volumes, 2.3 million microform items, and 85,909 audio/video tapes/CDs/DVDs, and subscribe to 22,717 periodicals including electronic. Computerized library services include interlibrary loans, database searching, Internet access, and laptop Internet portals. Special learning facilities include a learning resource center, art gallery, natural history museum, planetarium, radio station, TV station, ranching heritage center, international cultural center, international textile center, and Southwest collection. The 1839-acre campus is in an urban area in Lubbock. Including any residence halls, there are 138 buildings.

Programs of Study: Texas Tech confers B.A., B.S., B.F.A., B.G.S., B.I.D., B.Land.Arch., B.M., B.S.ARCH., B.S.C.E., B.S.Ch.E., B.S.E.E , B.S. Eng. Physics, B.S. Eng. Tech., B.S.Envir. Eng., B.S. in Family and Consumer Sciences, B.S. Home Eco., B.S. Indust. Eng., B.S. Int'l Eco., B.S. in Community, Family, and Addiction Services, B.S.M.E., B.S.P.E., and B.S.R.H.I.M degrees. Master's and doctoral degrees are also awarded. Bachelor's degrees are awarded in AGRICULTURE (agricultural business management, agricultural communications, agricultural economics, agronomy, animal science, conservation and regulation, fish and game management, horticulture, plant protection (pest management), range/farm management, and wildlife management), BIOLOGICAL SCIENCE (biochemistry, biology/biological science, cell biology, microbiology, molecular biology, nutrition, and zoology), BUSINESS (banking and finance, business administration and management, business economics, hotel/motel and restaurant management, international business management, international economics, management information systems, marketing and distribution, and retailing), COMMUNICATIONS AND THE ARTS (advertising, apparel design, art history and appreciation, broadcasting, classics, communications, dance, design, dramatic arts, English, French, German, journalism, music, music performance, music theory and composition, performing arts, photography, public relations, Spanish, studio art, telecommunications, theater design, and visual and performing arts), COMPUTER AND PHYSICAL SCIENCE (chemistry, computer science, geology, geophysics and seismology, geoscience, mathematics, and physics), EDUCATION (early childhood education, middle school education, and science education), ENGINEERING AND ENVIRONMENTAL DESIGN (architecture, chemical engineering, civil engineering, construction technology, electrical/electronics engineering, electrical/electronics engineering technology, energy management technology, engineering, engineering physics, engineering technology, environmental engineering, industrial engineering, interior design, landscape architecture/design, mechanical engineering, and mechanical engineering technology), HEALTH PROFESSIONS (exercise science and health), SOCIAL SCIENCE (addiction studies, anthropology, child psychology/development, clothing and textiles management/production/services, dietetics, economics, family/consumer resource management, family/consumer studies, food production/management/services, food science, geography, history, home economics, human development, Latin American studies, liberal arts/general studies, philosophy, political science/government, psychology, Russian and Slavic studies, social work, and sociology). Business, exercise and sports sciences, and mechanical engineering are the largest.

Special: Texas Tech offers many bachelor-to-masters accelerated degree programs, internships, study abroad, dual degrees, dual majors, extended studies, and pass/fail options. There are 20 national honor societies, including Phi Beta Kappa, and a freshman honors program.

Admissions: There were 11 National Merit finalists in a recent year. 23 freshmen graduated first in their class.

Requirements: The SAT or ACT is required. In addition, applicants should be graduates of an accredited high school or have the GED. The university requires 11 credits of academic work in high school, including 4 credits in English, 3 in math, 2 in lab sciences, and 2 in foreign language. AP and CLEP credits are accepted.

Procedure: Freshmen are admitted fall, spring, and summer. Entrance exams should be taken before registering for classes. There are early admissions and rolling admissions plans. Check with the school for current application deadlines. The application fee is $60. Notification is sent on a rolling basis. Applications are accepted on-line.

Financial Aid: In a recent year, 37% of all full-time freshmen and 40% of continuing full-time students received some form of financial aid, including need-based aid. 10% of undergraduate students work part-time. The average financial indebtedness of a recent graduate was $20,916. The FAFSA is required. Check with the school for current application deadlines.

Computers: Wireless access is available. PC and Macintosh computers are available for use by any student, faculty, or staff member with a valid eRaider username and paaword in the Advanced Technology Center and in academic departments. The dorms are wired for Internet use. All students may access the system 24 hours per day. There are no time limits and no fees. It is strongly recommended that all students have a personal computer.

THOMAS AQUINAS COLLEGE

Santa Paula, CA 93060   **(805) 634-9797**
                                    (800) 634-9797; (805) 421-5905

Full-time: 160 men, 185 women	**Faculty:** 28
Part-time: none	**Ph.D.s:** 61%
Graduate: none	**Student/Faculty:** 11 to 1
Year: semesters	**Tuition:** $22,400
Application Deadline: open	**Room & Board:** $7400

Freshman Class: 184 applied, 144 accepted, 102 enrolled
SAT CR/M/W: 670/610/640   **ACT:** 28 **HIGHLY COMPETITIVE+**

Thomas Aquinas College, founded in 1971 and affiliated with the Roman Catholic Church, is a private, liberal arts college offering an integrated studies curriculum based on the Great Books. All classes are conducted as conversations directed by teachers using the Socratic method. There is 1 undergraduate school. In addition to regional accreditation, TAC has baccalaureate program accreditation with AALE. The library contains 61,120 volumes and 5501 audio/video tapes/CDs/DVDs, and subscribes to 90 periodicals including electronic. Computerized library services include interlibrary loans, database searching, Internet access, and laptop Internet portals. Special learning facilities include a learning resource center. The 131-acre campus is in a rural area 60 miles northwest of Los Angeles. Including any residence halls, there are 19 buildings.

Programs of Study: TAC confers B.A. degrees. Bachelor's degrees are awarded in SOCIAL SCIENCE (liberal arts/general studies).

Admissions: 78% of the 2009-2010 applicants were accepted. The SAT scores for the 2009-2010 freshman class were: Critical Reading--20% between 500 and 599, 41% between 600 and 700, and 39% above 700; Math--4% below 500, 36% between 500 and 599, 51% between 600 and 700, and 9% above 700; Writing--5% below 500, 26% between 500 and 599, 47% between 600 and 700, and 22% above 700. The ACT scores were 3% below 21, 12% between 21 and 23, 29% between 24 and 26, 15% between 27 and 28, and 41% above 28.

Requirements: The SAT or ACT is required. In addition, candidates for admission should have completed 4 years of English, 3 years of math, and 2 years each of a foreign language, history, and science. Important factors in the admissions decision are personality/intangible qualities, advanced placement or honors courses, and recommendations by school officials.

Procedure: Freshmen are admitted fall. Entrance exams should be taken by November. There are deferred admissions and rolling admissions plans. Application deadlines are open. 2 applicants were on a recent waiting list, 1 was accepted.

Financial Aid: In 2009-2010, 88% of all full-time freshmen and 80% of continuing full-time students received some form of financial aid. 86% of all full-time freshmen and 77% of continuing full-time students received need-based aid. The average freshmen award was $20,327, with $13,527 ($21,159 maximum) from need-based scholarships or need-based grants; $6073 ($7636 maximum) from need-based self-help aid (loans and jobs); and $728 ($7800 maximum) from other non-need-based awards and non-need-based scholarships. 73% of undergraduate students work part-time. Average annual earnings from campus work are $3886. The average financial indebtedness of the 2009 graduate was $15,000. TAC is a member of CSS. The FAFSA, the college's own financial statement, and parent and student federal tax returns are required. The deadline for filing freshman financial aid applications for fall entry is March 2.

Computers: E-mail access is available in the library through the college PCs and laptop ports and in the career center. All students may access the system when available. There are no time limits and no fees.

TOWSON UNIVERSITY
Towson, MD 21252-0001

(410) 704-2113
(888) 4-TOWSON; (410) 704-3030

Full-time: 5540 men, 8645 women	**Faculty:** IIA, -$
Part-time: 940 men, 1105 women	**Ph.D.s:** 52%
Graduate: 890 men, 2655 women	**Student/Faculty:** n/av
Year: semesters, summer session	**Tuition:** $8000 ($17,500)
Application Deadline: see profile	**Room & Board:** $8000
Freshman Class: n/av	
SAT or ACT: required	**VERY COMPETITIVE**

Towson University, founded in 1866, is part of the University System of Maryland and offers undergraduate and graduate programs in liberal arts and sciences, allied health sciences, education, fine arts, communication, and business and economics. Figures in the above capsule and this profile are approximate. There are 7 undergraduate schools and 1 graduate school. In addition to regional accreditation, Towson has baccalaureate program accreditation with AACSB, CAHEA, NASDTEC, NASM, NCATE, and NLN. The library contains 364,468 volumes, 830,286 microform items, and 14,174 audio/video tapes/CDs/DVDs, and subscribes to 2164 periodicals including electronic. Computerized library services include interlibrary loans, database searching, and Internet access. Special learning facilities include a learning resource center, art gallery, planetarium, radio station, TV station, curriculum center, herbarium, animal museum, observatory, and greenhouse. The 328-acre campus is in a suburban area 2 miles north of Baltimore. Including any residence halls, there are 44 buildings.

Programs of Study: Towson confers B.A., B.S., B.F.A., and B.M. degrees. Master's and doctoral degrees are also awarded. Bachelor's degrees are awarded in BIOLOGICAL SCIENCE (biology/biological science and molecular biology), BUSINESS (accounting, business administration and management, and sports management), COMMUNICATIONS AND THE ARTS (art, communications, dance, English, French, German, media arts, music, Spanish, and theater design), COMPUTER AND PHYSICAL SCIENCE (chemistry, computer science, earth science, geology, geoscience, information sciences and systems, mathematics, and physics), EDUCATION (art education, athletic training, dance education, early childhood education, education, education of the deaf and hearing impaired, elementary education, music education, physical education, and special education), ENGINEERING AND ENVIRONMENTAL DESIGN (environmental science), HEALTH PROFESSIONS (exercise science, health care administration, health science, medical laboratory technology, nursing, occupational therapy, speech pathology/audiology, and sports medicine), SOCIAL SCIENCE (anthropology, crosscultural studies, economics, family/consumer studies, geography, gerontology, history, interdisciplinary studies, international studies, law, philosophy, political science/government, psychology, religion, social science, sociology, and women's studies). Fine arts, business, and education are the strongest academically. Business disciplines, mass communications, and psychology are the largest.

Special: Towson University offers cooperative programs with other institutions in the University System of Maryland and at Loyola College, the College of Notre Dame, and Johns Hopkins University, cross-registration at more than 80 colleges through the National Student Exchange, and study abroad. Students may pursue a dual major in physics and engineering, an interdisciplinary studies degree, which allows them to design their own majors, a 3-2 engineering program with the University of Maryland at College Park and Penn State, or nondegree study. There are pass/fail options, extensive evening offerings, and opportunities to earn credits between semesters. Internships are available in most majors, and work-study programs are offered both on and off campus. There are 20 national honor societies, a freshman honors program, and 12 departmental honors programs.

Admissions: 9 freshmen graduated first in their class in a recent year.

Requirements: The SAT or ACT is required. The ACT Optional Writing test is also required. In addition, applicants should have graduated from an accredited secondary school or earned the GED. Secondary preparation should include 4 years of English, 3 each of math, lab science, and social studies, and 2 of foreign language. Prospective music and dance majors must audition. A GPA of 3.1 is required. AP and CLEP credits are accepted. Important factors in the admissions decision are advanced placement or honors courses, recommendations by school officials, and leadership record.

Procedure: Freshmen are admitted fall and spring. Entrance exams should be taken in the junior or senior year. There are deferred admissions and rolling admissions plans. Check with the school for current application deadlines. The fall 2009 application fee was $45. Notification is sent on a rolling basis. Applications are accepted on-line. A waiting list is maintained.

Financial Aid: In a recent year, 70% of all full-time freshmen and 62% of continuing full-time students received some form of financial aid. 43% of all full-time freshmen and 39% of continuing full-time students received need-based aid. The average freshman award was $12,131. 72% of undergraduate students work part-time. Average annual earnings from campus work are $1185. The average financial indebtedness of a recent graduate was $14,085. The FAFSA is required. Check with the school for current application deadlines.

Computers: Wireless access is available. All students may access the system. Systems are accessible 24 hours daily except 5 P.M. to 9 P.M. Fridays. There are no time limits and no fees.

TRANSYLVANIA UNIVERSITY

Lexington, KY 40508-

(859) 233-8242
(800) 872-6798; (859) 233-8797

Full- and part-time: 1190 men and women	**Faculty:** 82; IIB, av$
Graduate: none	**Ph.D.s:** 97%
Year: 4-1-4, summer session	**Student/Faculty:** n/av
Application Deadline: see profile	**Tuition:** $25,280
Freshman Class: n/av	**Room & Board:** $7770
SAT or ACT: required	**VERY COMPETITIVE+**

Transylvania University, founded in 1780, is an independent liberal arts institution affiliated with the Christian Church (Disciples of Christ). Some figures in the above capsule and in this profile are approximate. In addition to regional accreditation, Transy has baccalaureate program accreditation with NCATE. The library contains 120,000 volumes, 50 microform items, and 2,400 audio/video tapes/CDs/DVDs, and subscribes to 12,000 periodicals including electronic. Computerized library services include interlibrary loans, database searching, Internet access, and laptop Internet portals. Special learning facilities include a learning resource center, art gallery, natural history museum, and radio station. The 48-acre campus is in an urban area 80 miles east of Louisville and 80 miles south of Cincinnati, Ohio. Including any residence halls, there are 24 buildings.

Programs of Study: Transy confers B.A. degrees. Bachelor's degrees are awarded in BIOLOGICAL SCIENCE (biology/biological science), BUSINESS (accounting and business administration and management), COMMUNICATIONS AND THE ARTS (dramatic arts, English, French, music, Spanish, and studio art), COMPUTER AND PHYSICAL SCIENCE (chemistry, computer science, mathematics, and physics), EDUCATION (elementary education and middle school education), HEALTH PROFESSIONS (exercise science), SOCIAL SCIENCE (anthropology, economics, history, philosophy, political science/government, psychology, religion, and sociology). Business, biology, and psychology are the largest.

Special: 3-2 engineering degrees with the University of Kentucky, Vanderbilt University, and Washington University in St. Louis are offered. Cross-registration with May Term Consortium schools, internships, study abroad in 17 countries, work-study programs, a Washington semester, dual majors, and student-designed majors are available. There are 9 national honor societies.

Admissions: The ACT scores for a recent year's freshman class were 6% below 21, 15% between 21 and 23, 27% between 24 and 26, 23% between 27 and 28, and 29% above 28. 76% of recent freshmen were in the top fifth of their class; 94% were in the top two fifths. There were 5 National Merit finalists. 24 freshmen graduated first in their class.

Requirements: The SAT or ACT is required. In addition, 1 essay and 2 recommendations are required. An interview is strongly recommended. Transy requires applicants to be in the upper 50% of their class. A GPA of 3.0 is required. AP credits are accepted. Important factors in the admissions decision are advanced placement or honors courses, recommendations by school officials, and extracurricular activities record.

Procedure: Freshmen are admitted fall and winter. Entrance exams should be taken during the junior year and no later than December of the senior year for scholarship consideration or February for general admission. There are early admissions and deferred admissions plans. Check with the school for current application deadlines and fee. Applications are accepted on-line. A waiting list is maintained.

Financial Aid: Transy is a member of CSS. The FAFSA is required. Check with the school for current financial aid deadlines.

Computers: There are 262 PCs in student labs. All residential rooms have access, and there are 30 wireless access points. All students may access the system 24 hours a day. There are no time limits and no fees. It is strongly recommended that all students have a personal computer. Any model capable of running Microsoft Windows XP is recommended.

TREVECCA NAZARENE UNIVERSITY

Nashville, TN 37210-2877

(615) 248-1320
(888) 210-4TNU; (615) 248-7406

Full-time: 506 men, 647 women	**Faculty:** 86; IIA, --$
Part-time: 65 men, 80 women	**Ph.D.s:** 81%
Graduate: 347 men, 831 women	**Student/Faculty:** 13 to 1
Year: semesters, summer session	**Tuition:** $16,876
Application Deadline: August 1	**Room & Board:** $7348
Freshman Class: 899 applied, 623 accepted, 244 enrolled	
SAT CR/M: 510/510	**ACT:** 22 **VERY COMPETITIVE**

Trevecca Nazarene offers programs in liberal arts and sciences and a number of professional content areas. The university also provides a variety of nontraditional continuing education professional programs at the undergraduate and graduate levels. There are 4 undergraduate schools and 4 graduate schools. In addition to regional accreditation, TNU has baccalaureate program accreditation with CAHEA, NASM, and NCATE. The library contains 82,792 volumes, 31,040 microform items, and 6,640 audio/video tapes/CDs/DVDs, and subscribes to 688 periodicals including electronic. Computerized library services include interlibrary loans, database searching, Internet access, and laptop Internet portals. Special learning facilities include a learning resource center, radio station, a curriculum library, Center for Learning, Calling, and Service. The 80-acre campus is in an urban area. Including any residence halls, there are 25 buildings.

Programs of Study: TNU confers B.A., B.S., B.B.A., and B.S.S.W. degrees. Associate, master's, and doctoral degrees are also awarded. Bachelor's degrees are awarded in BIOLOGICAL SCIENCE (biology/biological science), BUSINESS (accounting, business administration and management, electronic business, and marketing/retailing/merchandising), COMMUNICATIONS AND THE ARTS (communications, digital communications, dramatic arts, English, music, and music business management), COMPUTER AND PHYSICAL SCIENCE (chemistry, information sciences and systems, mathematics, physics, and science), EDUCATION (business education, drama education, education, English education, mathematics education, music education, physical education, and special education), HEALTH PROFESSIONS (medical laboratory technology and nursing), SOCIAL SCIENCE (behavioral science, criminal justice, history, political science/government, psychology, religion, social work, and sociology). Teacher education, business, and religion are the strongest academically. Management and human relations, religion, and education are the largest.

Special: There is cross-registration with other Nazarene colleges and universities in the United States, and work-study programs, internships, a Washington semester, and nondegree study are offered. Study abroad is possible. An evening program leads to the B.A. in management and human relations for adult learners over 23 with 62 semester hours of college work. A 3-2 nursing program is offered with Belmont University. There are preprofessional studies in physical therapy, medicine, dentistry, pharmacy, veterinary science, law, and engineering. There is 1 national honor society.

Admissions: 69% of the 2009-2010 applicants were accepted. The SAT scores for the 2009-2010 freshman class were: Critical Reading--45% below 500, 35% between 500 and 599, 18% between 600 and 700, and 2% above 700; Math--40% below 500, 41% between 500 and 599, 17% between 600 and 700, and 2% above 700. The ACT scores were 39% below 21, 25% between 21 and 23, 21% between 24 and 26, 7% between 27 and 28, and 8% above 28.

Requirements: The SAT or ACT is required, the ACT is preferred, with a composite score of at least 22. Candidates should have completed at least 15 academic secondary credits, including 4 units in English, 2 each in math, foreign language, and social science, and 1 in natural science. A GED of at least 45 is also accepted. The medical technology and teacher education programs have special admission requirements. A GPA of 2.5 is required. AP and CLEP credits are accepted.

Procedure: Freshmen are admitted fall, spring, and summer. Entrance exams should be taken in the junior or senior year. There are deferred admissions and rolling admissions plans. Applications should be filed by August 1 for fall entry and December 1 for spring entry, along with a $25 fee. Applications are accepted on-line.

Financial Aid: In 2009-2010, 94% of all full-time freshmen received some form of financial aid. The FAFSA is required. The priority date for freshman financial aid applications for fall entry is March 1.

Computers: Wireless access is available. All students may access the system from 8 A.M. to 11 P.M. every day, with residence hall labs open 24 hours. There are no time limits and no fees.

TRINITY COLLEGE
Hartford, CT 06106 (860) 297-2180; (860) 297-2287

Full-time: 1000 men, 1000 women	**Faculty:** IIB, +$
Part-time: 80 men, 110 women	**Ph.D.s:** 90%
Graduate: 100 men, 80 women	**Student/Faculty:** n/av
Year: semesters	**Tuition:** $37,000
Application Deadline: see profile	**Room & Board:** $9500
Freshman Class: n/av	
SAT or ACT: required	**HIGHLY COMPETITIVE**

Founded in 1823, Trinity College in Hartford is an independent, nonsectarian liberal arts college. Figures in the above capsule are approxiamte. There is 1 graduate school. In addition to regional accreditation, Trinity has baccalaureate program accreditation with ABET. The library contains 992,817 volumes, 399,394 microform items, and 225,477 audio/video tapes/CDs/DVDs, and subscribes to 2438 periodicals including electronic. Computerized library services include interlibrary loans, database searching, and Internet access. Special learning facilities include an art gallery and Connecticut Public Television and Radio. The 100-acre campus is in an urban area southwest of downtown Hartford. Including any residence halls, there are 78 buildings.

Programs of Study: Trinity confers B.A. and B.S. degrees. Master's degrees are also awarded. Bachelor's degrees are awarded in BIOLOGICAL SCIENCE (biochemistry, biology/biological science, and neurosciences), COMMUNICATIONS AND THE ARTS (art history and appreciation, classics, comparative literature, dance, dramatic arts, English, fine arts, French, German, Italian, modern language, music, Russian, Spanish, studio art, and theater management), COMPUTER AND PHYSICAL SCIENCE (chemistry, computer science, mathematics, and physics), EDUCATION (education), ENGINEERING AND ENVIRONMENTAL DESIGN (engineering and environmental science), SOCIAL SCIENCE (American studies, anthropology, classical/ancient civilization, economics, history, interdisciplinary studies, international studies, Judaic studies, philosophy, political science/government, psychology, public affairs, religion, sociology, and women's studies). Political science, economics, and English are the largest.

Special: Trinity offers special freshman programs for exceptional students, including interdisciplinary programs in the sciences and the humanities. There is an intensive study program under which students can devote a semester to 1 subject. Cross-registration through such programs as the Hartford Consortium and the Twelve-College Exchange Program, hundreds of internships (some with Connecticut Public Radio and TV on campus), study abroad in Rome, South Africa, Trinidad, Russia, Nepal, and other countries, a Washington semester, dual majors in all disciplines, student-designed majors, nondegree study, and pass/fail options also are offered. A 5-year advanced degree in electrical or mechanical engineering with Rensselaer Polytechnic Institute is available. There are 4 national honor societies, including Phi Beta Kappa.

Requirements: The SAT or ACT is required. Trinity strongly emphasizes individual character and personal qualities in admission. Consequently, an interview and essay are recommended. The college requires 4 years of English, 2 years each in foreign language and algebra, and 1 year each in geometry, history, and lab science. AP credits are accepted. Important factors in the admissions decision are advanced placement or honors courses, extracurricular activities record, and evidence of special talent.

Procedure: Freshmen are admitted fall. Entrance exams should be taken in the fall of the senior year. There are early decision and deferred admissions plan. Check with the school for current application deadlines. The application fee is $50. Applications are accepted on-line. A waiting list is maintained.

Financial Aid: Trinity is a member of CSS. The CSS/Profile and FAFSA are required. Check with the school for current application deadlines.

Computers: All students may access the system 24 hours a day. There are no time limits and no fees. It is strongly recommended that all students have a personal computer.

TRINITY UNIVERSITY
San Antonio, TX 78212-7200

(210) 999-7207
(800) TRINITY; (210) 999-8164

Full-time: 1075 men, 1255 women	**Faculty:** IIA, +$
Part-time: 20 men, 30 women	**Ph.D.s:** 97%
Graduate: 145 men, 85 women	**Student/Faculty:** n/av
Year: semesters, summer session	**Tuition:** $30,000
Application Deadline: see profile	**Room & Board:** $10,500
Freshman Class: n/av	
SAT or ACT: required	**HIGHLY COMPETITIVE+**

Trinity University, founded in 1869, is a private liberal arts university. Figures in the above capsule and this profile are approximate. There is 1 graduate school. In addition to regional accreditation, Trinity has baccalaureate program accreditation with AACSB, ABET, NASM, and NCATE. The library contains 927,349 volumes, 301,600 microform items, and 26,780 audio/video tapes/CDs/DVDs, and subscribes to 2135 periodicals including electronic. Computerized library services include interlibrary loans and database searching. Special learning facilities include an art gallery, radio station, and TV station. The 117-acre campus is in an urban area 3 miles north of downtown San Antonio. Including any residence halls, there are 45 buildings.

Programs of Study: Trinity confers B.A., B.S., and B.M. degrees. Master's degrees are also awarded. Bachelor's degrees are awarded in BIOLOGICAL SCIENCE (biochemistry and biology/biological science), BUSINESS (business administration and management), COMMUNICATIONS AND THE ARTS (art, art history and appreciation, Chinese, classics, communications, dramatic arts, English, French, German, Greek, Latin, music, Russian, Spanish, and speech/debate/rhetoric), COMPUTER AND PHYSICAL SCIENCE (chemistry, computer science, geoscience, mathematics, and physics), ENGINEERING AND ENVIRONMENTAL DESIGN (engineering and applied science), SOCIAL SCIENCE (anthropology, economics, history, international relations, philosophy, political science/government, psychology, religion, sociology, and urban studies). Business, communication, and modern languages and literatures are the largest.

Special: The university offers study abroad in 35 countries. A Washington semester, accelerated programs, dual majors, student-designed majors, and pass/fail options are also available, as well as teacher certification and a liberal arts/career combination. There are 5 national honor societies, including Phi Beta Kappa, and 14 departmental honors programs.

Requirements: The SAT or ACT is required. In addition, applicants should have completed 4 years of English, 3 1/2 of math, 3 each of lab science and social studies, and 2 of foreign language. A personal essay, an official high school transcript, a recommendation from a high school counselor, and a teacher's evaluation are also required. A campus visit and a visit with the university's counselor are recommended. AP credits are accepted. Important factors in the admissions decision are advanced placement or honors courses, recommendations by school officials, and extracurricular activities record.

Procedure: Freshmen are admitted fall, spring, and summer. Entrance exams should be taken late in the junior year or early in the senior year. There are early decision, early admissions and deferred admissions plans. Early decision applications should be filed by November 1; check with the school for current application deadlines. Notification of early decision is sent December 15. Applications are accepted on-line. 485 applicants were on a recent waiting list, 74 were accepted.

Financial Aid: In a recent year, 91% of all full-time freshmen and 86% of continuing full-time students received some form of financial aid. 37% of all full-time students received need-based aid. Average annual earnings from campus work are $1099. The FAFSA is required. Check with the school for current application deadlines.

Computers: Wireless access is available on the entire campus. There are several computer labs, and the library has a large information commons with more than 70 computers for student use. All students may access the system 24 hours per day. There are no time limits and no fees. It is strongly recommended that all students have a personal computer.

TRUMAN STATE UNIVERSITY

Kirksville, MO 63501 (660) 785-4114; (660) 785-7456

Full-time: 2233 men, 3126 women	**Faculty:** 339; IIA, --$
Part-time: 53 men, 56 women	**Ph.D.s:** 82%
Graduate: 87 men, 192 women	**Student/Faculty:** 16 to 1
Year: semesters, summer session	**Tuition:** $6,692 ($11,543)
Application Deadline: March 1	**Room & Board:** $6,854
Freshman Class: 4608 applied, 3333 accepted, 1342 enrolled	
SAT CR/M: 600/610	**ACT:** 27 **HIGHLY COMPETITIVE**

Truman State University, founded in 1867, is a public liberal arts institution offering undergraduate and graduate degree programs in business and accounting, arts and sciences, and education. There are 5 undergraduate schools and 5 graduate schools. In addition to regional accreditation, Truman has baccalaureate program accreditation with AACSB, NASM, and NCATE. The library contains 483,708 volumes, 1.5 million microform items, 37,797 audio/video tapes/CDs/DVDs, and subscribes to 3,942 periodicals including electronic. Computerized library services include interlibrary loans, database searching, Internet access, and laptop Internet portals. Special learning facilities include a learning resource center, art gallery, radio station, an independent learning center for nursing students, an observatory, a greenhouse chamber, a speech and hearing clinic, a broadcasting studio, language learning center, student success center, and various labs for science programs. The 140-acre campus is in a small town 170 miles northeast of Kansas City, MO and 200 miles north of St. Louis, MO. Including any residence halls, there are 35 buildings.

Programs of Study: Truman confers B.A., B.S., B.F.A., B.M., and B.S.N. degrees. Master's degrees are also awarded. Bachelor's degrees are awarded in AGRICULTURE (agricultural business management, agriculture, agronomy, animal science, equine science, and horticulture), BIOLOGICAL SCIENCE (biology/biological science), BUSINESS (accounting, business administration and management, and international business management), COMMUNICATIONS AND THE ARTS (art, art history and appreciation, classics, communications, dramatic arts, English, fine arts, French, German, journalism, linguistics, music, music performance, romance languages and literature, Russian, Spanish, studio art, and visual design), COMPUTER AND PHYSICAL SCIENCE (chemistry, computer science, mathematics, and physics), EDUCATION (athletic training and physical education), ENGINEERING AND ENVIRONMENTAL DESIGN (preengineering), HEALTH PROFESSIONS (clinical science, exercise science, health science, nursing, physical therapy, predentistry, premedicine, prepharmacy, preveterinary science, public health, and speech pathology/audiology), SOCIAL SCIENCE (anthropology, criminal justice, economics, history, interdisciplinary studies, philosophy, physical fitness/movement, political science/government, prelaw, psychology, religion, and sociology). Chemistry, political science, and accounting are the strongest academically. Business administration, biology, and English are the largest.

Special: Study abroad in 51 countries is offered through Truman's own programs and those of the College Consortium for International Studies, the Council on International Educational Exchange, and the International Student Exchange Program. The university requires internships in education and health and exercise science. Voluntary legislative internships are offered to all students at the state capitol, and internships through the Washington Center. There is a 3-2 engineering program with the University of Missouri-Rolla. Work-study programs, B.A.-B.S. degrees, dual majors, student-designed majors in health and exercise science, biology, history, and agricultural science, credit for military experience, pass/fail options for internships, and nondegree study are available. There are 18 national honor societies, including Phi Beta Kappa, a freshman honors program, and 19 departmental honors programs.

Admissions: 72% of the 2009-2010 applicants were accepted. The SAT scores for the 2009-2010 freshman class were: Critical Reading--12% below 500, 40% between 500 and 599, 34% between 600 and 700, and 14% above 700; Math--12% below 500, 28% between 500 and 599, 49% between 600 and 700, and 11 above 700. The ACT scores were 3% below 21, 14% between 21 and 23, 29% between 24 and 26, 16% between 27 and 28, and 38% above 28. 71% of the current freshmen were in the top fifth of their class; 94% were in the top two fifths. There were 19 National Merit finalists. 156 freshmen graduated first in their class.

Requirements: The ACT is required. In addition, Truman prefers the ACT, but accepts either the ACT or SAT. Applicants should have completed 4 units of English, 3 each of science and social studies, 2 of foreign language, and 1 of art or music. 4 units of math are strongly recommended. An essay is required and a visit is recommended. AP and CLEP credits are accepted. Important factors in the admissions decision are leadership record, advanced placement or honors courses, and extracurricular activities record.

Procedure: Freshmen are admitted to all sessions. Entrance exams should be taken during the spring or summer following the junior year. There are deferred admissions and rolling admissions plans. Applications should be filed by March 1 for fall entry, November 15 for spring entry, and March 1 for summer entry. Notification is sent on a rolling basis. Applications are accepted on-line.

Financial Aid: In 2009-2010, 94% of all full-time freshmen and 76% of continuing full-time students received some form of financial aid. 35% of all full-time freshmen and 30% of continuing full-time students received need-based aid. The average freshmen award was $8,875, with $3,821 ($7,960 maximum) from need-based scholarships or need-based grants; $3,391 ($11,000 maximum) from need-based self-help aid (loans and jobs); $2,585 ($17,772 maximum) from non-need-based athletic scholarships; and $4,926 ($21,700 maximum) from other non-need-based awards and non-need-based scholarships. 18% of undergraduate students work part-time. Average annual earnings from campus work are $1677. The average financial indebtedness of the 2009 graduate was $21,858. The FAFSA and the college's own financial statement are required. The priority date for freshman financial aid applications for fall entry is February 15. The deadline for filing freshman financial aid applications for fall entry is April 1.

Computers: Wireless access is available. Truman has 965 PCs and 116 Mac computers available for general student use in computer labs and classrooms in the residence halls, library, student union, and academic buildings. Truman's campus is completely wireless. All students may access the system. 24/7. There are no time limits and no fees.

TUFTS UNIVERSITY
Medford, MA 02155   (617) 627-3170; (617) 627-3860

Full-time: 2456 men, 2456 women	**Faculty:** 421; I, av$
Part-time: 22 men, 46 women	**Ph.D.s:** 95%
Graduate: 1215 men, 1808 women	**Student/Faculty:** 12 to 1
Year: semesters, summer session	**Tuition:** $36,700
Application Deadline: January 1	**Room & Board:** $10,160
Freshman Class: 15387 applied, 4231 accepted, 1373 enrolled	
	MOST COMPETITIVE

Tufts University, founded in 1852, is a private institution offering undergraduate programs in liberal arts and sciences, and engineering. There are 2 undergraduate schools and 8 graduate schools. In addition to regional accreditation, Tufts has baccalaureate program accreditation with ABET, ADA, and CAHEA. The 2 libraries contain 1.2 million volumes, 1.3 million microform items, 42,952 audio/video tapes/CDs/DVDs, and subscribe to 19,817 periodicals including electronic. Computerized library services include inter-library loans, database searching, Internet access, and laptop Internet portals. Special learning facilities include a learning resource center, art gallery, radio station, TV station, 300 seat recital hall and theater in the round. The 150-acre campus is in a suburban area 5 miles northwest of Boston. Including any residence halls, there are 170 buildings.

Programs of Study: Tufts confers B.A., B.S., B.S.C.E., B.S.Ch.E., B.S. Comp. Eng., B.S.E., B.S.E.E., B.S.E.S., B.S. Environmental Eng., B.S.M.E., B.S.B.M.E., and B.S.C.S degrees. Master's and doctoral degrees are also awarded. Bachelor's degrees are awarded in BIOLOGICAL SCIENCE (biochemistry, biology/biological science, and biotechnology), COMMUNICATIONS AND THE ARTS (art history and appreciation, Chinese, classics, dramatic arts, English, French, German, Greek, Italian, Japanese, Latin, music, Russian, and Spanish), COMPUTER AND PHYSICAL SCIENCE (applied physics, astrophysics, chemical physics, chemistry, computer science, geology, mathematics, and physics), ENGINEERING AND ENVIRONMENTAL DESIGN (architecture, biomedical engineering, chemical engineering, civil engineering, computer engineering, electrical/electronics engineering, engineering, engineering and applied science, engineering physics, environmental engineering, environmental science, and mechanical engineering), HEALTH PROFESSIONS (community health work), SOCIAL SCIENCE (American studies, anthropology, archeology, Asian/Oriental studies, biopsychology, child psychology/development, economics, German area studies, history, international relations, Judaic studies, Middle Eastern studies, peace studies, philosophy, political science/government, psychology, religion, Russian and Slavic studies, sociology, and women's studies). International relations, economics, and political science are the largest.

Special: The university offers cross-registration at Swarthmore College, Boston University, Boston College, and Brandeis University, a Washington semester, and study abroad in England, Spain, France, Chile, Japan, Ghana, China, Hong Kong, and Germany. Many internships are available. Double majors in the liberal arts are common; student-designed majors are possible. There is a 5-year B.A./M.A. or B.S./M.S. program in engineering or liberal arts, a B.A./B.F.A. program with the Museum School of Fine Arts, and a B.A./B.M. program with the New England Conservatory of Music. There are 4 national honor societies, including Phi Beta Kappa.

Admissions: 27% of the 2009-2010 applicants were accepted. 96% of the current freshmen were in the top fifth of their class; 99% were in the top two fifths. There were 41 National Merit finalists.

Requirements: In addition, the university accepts either the SAT Reasoning Test and the results of SAT Subject tests or the ACT. Liberal arts applicants should take the SAT Subject test of their choice; engineering applicants should take a math level I or II, and either physics or chemistry. In addition, all applicants should be high school graduates or hold the GED. Academic preparation is expected to include 4 years of English, 3 years each of humanities and a foreign language, 2 years each of social and natural sciences, and 1 year of history. AP credits are accepted. Important factors in the admissions decision are advanced placement or honors courses, recommendations by school officials, and extracurricular activities record.

Procedure: Freshmen are admitted in the fall. Entrance exams should be taken by January of the senior year. There is a deferred admissions plan. Applications should be filed by January 1 for fall entry, along with a $70 fee. Notifications are sent April 1. Applications are accepted on-line. A waiting list is maintained.

Financial Aid: In 2009-2010, 44% of all full-time freshmen and 50% of continuing full-time students received some form of financial aid. 45% of all full-time freshmen and 50% of continuing full-time students received need-based aid. The average freshmen award was $29,147. 40% of undergraduate students work part-time. The average financial indebtedness of the 2009 graduate was $14,190. Tufts is a member of CSS. The CSS/Profile and FAFSA, and parent and student federal income tax forms are required. The deadline for filing freshman financial aid applications for fall entry is February 15.

Computers: Wireless access is available. All students may access the system. 24 hours a day. There are no time limits and no fees.

TULANE UNIVERSITY

New Orleans, LA 70118

(504) 865-5731
(800) 873-9283; (504) 862-8715

Full-time: 2516 men, 2936 women	**Faculty:** 493; I, -$
Part-time: 700 men, 1058 women	**Ph.D.s:** 94%
Graduate: 2417 men, 2284 women	**Student/Faculty:** 11 to 1
Year: semesters, summer session	**Tuition:** $40,584
Application Deadline: January 15	**Room & Board:** $9606
Freshman Class: 39887 applied, 10563 accepted, 1502 enrolled	
SAT CR/M/W: 665/660/670	**ACT:** 31 **MOST COMPETITIVE**

Tulane University, founded in 1834, is a private institution offering degree programs in liberal arts and sciences, business, architecture, engineering, and social work. There are 6 undergraduate schools and 8 graduate schools. In addition to regional accreditation, Tulane has baccalaureate program accreditation with AACSB, ABET, CSAB, CSWE, and NAAB. The 9 libraries contain 3.2 million volumes, 2.3 million microform items, and 12,937 audio/video tapes/CDs/DVDs, and subscribe to 47,295 periodicals including electronic. Computerized library services include interlibrary loans, database searching, Internet access, and laptop Internet portals. Special learning facilities include a learning resource center, art gallery, natural history museum, radio station, TV station, an observatory, Middle American Research Institute, Amistad Research Center, Tulane Jazz Archives, Latin American Library, and Tulane Center for Research on Women. The 110-acre campus is in an urban area in uptown New Orleans. Including any residence halls, there are 70 buildings.

Programs of Study: Tulane confers B.A., B.S., B.A.R., B.B.S., B.F.A., B.P.H., B.S.E., B.S.M., M. Arch degrees. Associates, master's, and doctoral degrees are also awarded. Bachelor's degrees are awarded in BIOLOGICAL SCIENCE (biochemistry, cell biology, ecology, environmental biology, evolutionary biology, molecular biology, and neurosciences), BUSINESS (accounting, banking and finance, business administration and management, entrepreneurial studies, management science, and marketing management), COMMUNICATIONS AND THE ARTS (art history and appreciation, classics, communications, dance, dramatic arts, English, film arts, French, German, Greek (modern), Italian, jazz, journalism, linguistics, media arts, music, Portuguese, Russian, Spanish, studio art, and theater design), COMPUTER AND PHYSICAL SCIENCE (chemistry, earth science, geology, information sciences and systems, mathematics, physics, and science), EDUCATION (early childhood education and psychology education), ENGINEERING AND ENVIRONMENTAL DESIGN (architecture, biomedical engineering, chemical engineering, engineering physics, and environmental science), HEALTH PROFESSIONS (public health), SOCIAL SCIENCE (African studies, American studies, anthropology, Asian/Oriental studies, cognitive science, economics, gender studies, history, humanities, Judaic studies, Latin American studies, liberal arts/general studies, medieval studies, paralegal studies, philosophy, political science/government, psychology, religion, Russian and Slavic studies, social science, social studies, sociology, and women's studies). Environmental sciences, political economy, and preprofessional programs are the strongest academically. Business, English, and psychology are the largest.

Special: Students may pursue cross-registration with Loyola and Xavier Universities, numerous internships, study abroad in 23 countries, work-study programs, a Washington semester, and B.A.-B.S. degrees in liberal arts, engineering, and architecture. Tulane also offers accelerated joint degrees with its schools of medicine, law, business, and public health; student-designed, dual, and interdisciplinary majors, including art and biology, Greek and Latin, mathematical economics, political economy, and cognitive studies; a 3-2 engineering degree with Xavier University of Louisiana, joint graduate/professional programs, and 4+1 programs. There are 38 national honor societies, including Phi Beta Kappa, and a freshman honors program.

Admissions: 26% of the 2009-2010 applicants were accepted. The SAT scores for the 2009-2010 freshman class were: Critical Reading--4% below 500, 9% between 500 and 599, 43% between 600 and 700, and 44% above 700; Math--4% below 500, 25% between 500 and 599, 49% between 600 and 700, and 22% above 700; Writing--3% below 500, 21% between 500 and 599, 54% between 600 and 700, and 31% above 700. There were 38 National Merit finalists.

Requirements: AP credits are accepted. Important factors in the admissions decision are advanced placement or honors courses, recommendations by school officials, and extracurricular activities record.

Procedure: Freshmen are admitted fall and spring. Entrance exams should be taken during spring of the junior year or fall of the senior year. There is a deferred admissions plan. Applications should be filed by January 15 for fall entry and November 1 for spring entry. Notifications are sent April 1. Applications are accepted on-line. 2018 applicants were on a recent waiting list, 132 were accepted.

Financial Aid: 37% of all full-time freshmen received need-based aid. Average annual earnings from campus work are $2500. The average financial indebtedness of the 2009 graduate was $25,284. Tulane is a member of CSS. The CSS/Profile and FAFSA, and the Noncustodial Parents Statement and the Business/Farm Supplement (as applicable) are required. The deadline for filing freshman financial aid applications for fall entry is February 15.

Computers: Wireless access is available. The entire campus has wireless access. All students may access the system 24 hours a day. There are no time limits and no fees. It is strongly recommended that all students have a personal computer.

UNION COLLEGE
Lincoln, NE 68506

(402) 486-2504
(800) 228-4600; (402) 486-2895

Full-time: 284 men, 380 women	**Faculty:** 53
Part-time: 53 men, 69 women	**Ph.D.s:** 52%
Graduate: 21 men, 49 women	**Student/Faculty:** 15 to 1
Year: semesters, summer session	**Tuition:** $17,430
Application Deadline: open	**Room & Board:** $5840
Freshman Class: n/av	
ACT: 22	**VERY COMPETITIVE**

Union College, established in 1891, is a private liberal arts institution affiliated with the Seventh-Day Adventist Church. In addition to regional accreditation, Union has baccalaureate program accreditation with CSWE and NCATE. The library contains 161,728 volumes, 1938 microform items, and 2066 audio/video tapes/CDs/DVDs, and subscribes to 604 periodicals including electronic. Computerized library services include interlibrary loans, database searching, Internet access, and laptop Internet portals. Special learning facilities include a learning resource center, art gallery, and state-run natural arboretum. The 26-acre campus is in a suburban area in southeast Lincoln. Including any residence halls, there are 11 buildings.

Programs of Study: Union confers B.A., B.S., B.A.T., B.Ed., B.M., B.S.W., and B.T. degrees. Associates and master's degrees are also awarded. Bachelor's degrees are awarded in BIOLOGICAL SCIENCE (biology/biological science), BUSINESS (accounting, banking and finance, business administration and management, management science, marketing and distribution, and small business management), COMMUNICATIONS AND THE ARTS (communications, English, French, German, graphic design, journalism, literature, music, music performance, public relations, Spanish, and studio art), COMPUTER AND PHYSICAL SCIENCE (chemistry, computer science, mathematics, physics, and science), EDUCATION (art education, business education, computer education, elementary education, English education, mathematics education, music education, physical education, secondary education, and social science education), HEALTH PROFESSIONS (medical laboratory technology, nursing, and physician's assistant), SOCIAL SCIENCE (history, international public service, international studies, pastoral studies, physical fitness/movement, psychology, religion, religious education, social science, social work, and theological studies). Physician's assistant and physical science are the strongest academically. Nursing and international rescue and relief are the largest.

Special: Special academic programs include study abroad in 7 countries, co-op programs with 9 Adventist institutions abroad, and cross-registration with the University of Nebraska, Nebraska Wesleyan University, and Southeast Community College. Student-designed majors are available through the Personalized Bachelor's Degree Program. There are pass/fail options in electives for upperclassmen with a minimum cumulative GPA of 2.0. Some internships are available. There are a freshman honors program.

Admissions: 32% of the current freshmen were in the top fifth of their class; 69% were in the top two-fifths.

Requirements: The ACT is required. Freshmen with a high school GPA below 2.5 and/or an ACT composite score below the 20th percentile will be enrolled in the freshman development program. Applicants must have graduated from an accredited secondary school with 18 academic credits, including 3 units of English and 1 unit each of math, science, and history. For math and science programs, 2 units of algebra and 1 unit each of geometry and trigonometry are recommended. For majors in nursing, biology, chemistry, physics, or engineering, applicants should complete physics and chemistry courses. The GED is also accepted. An essay and interview are advised, and music students should audition. A GPA of 2.5 is required. AP and CLEP credits are accepted.

Procedure: Freshmen are admitted fall and spring. Entrance exams should be taken by fall of the senior year. There is a rolling admissions plan. Application deadlines are open.

Financial Aid: In a recent year, 99% of all full-time freshmen and 91% of continuing full-time students received some form of financial aid. 97% of all full-time freshmen and 79% of continuing full-time students received need-based aid. 54% of undergraduate students work part-time. Average annual earnings from campus work are $2400. The FAFSA is required. Check with the school for current application deadlines.

Computers: Wireless access is available. All students are assigned a user code and can access a variety of labs on campus with that code. They can also register their own computer and have the same access and services. All students may access the system. There are no time limits and no fees. It is strongly recommended that all students have a personal computer. Students enrolled in the physician's assistant program must have a personal computer.

UNION COLLEGE

Schenectady, NY 12308-2311

(518) 388-6112
(888) 843-6688; (518) 388-6986

Full-time: 1110 men, 1047 women	**Faculty:** 213; IIB, +$
Part-time: 16 men, 21 women	**Ph.D.s:** 96%
Graduate: none	**Student/Faculty:** 10 to 1
Year: trimesters	**Tuition:** $50,439
Application Deadline: January 15	**Room & Board:** n/av
Freshman Class: 4829 applied, 1987 accepted, 520 enrolled	
SAT CR/M/W: 630/660/630	**ACT:** 28 **HIGHLY COMPETITIVE+**

Union College, founded in 1795, is an independent liberal arts and engineering college. In addition to regional accreditation, Union has baccalaureate program accreditation with ABET. The library contains 634,183 volumes, 760,258 microform items, and 13,501 audio/video tapes/CDs/DVDs, and subscribes to 12,500 periodicals including electronic. Computerized library services include interlibrary loans, database searching, and Internet access. Special learning facilities include a radio station, a theater, a high-tech classroom, a lab center, a multimedia auditorium, a music center, and an art, science, and history gallery. The 12-acre campus is in an urban area 15 miles west of Albany. Including any residence halls, there are 100 buildings.

Programs of Study: Union confers B.A. and B.S degrees. Bachelor's degrees are awarded in AGRICULTURE (environmental studies), BIOLOGICAL SCIENCE (biochemistry, biology/biological science, and neurosciences), COMMUNICATIONS AND THE ARTS (classics, English, fine arts, modern language, and studio art), COMPUTER AND PHYSICAL SCIENCE (astronomy, chemistry, computer science, geology, mathematics, physics, and science), ENGINEERING AND ENVIRONMENTAL DESIGN (bioengineering, computer engineering, electrical/electronics engineering, environmental science, and mechanical engineering), SOCIAL SCIENCE (American studies, anthropology, Asian/Oriental studies, Caribbean studies, economics, French studies, German area studies, history, humanities, interdisciplinary studies, liberal arts/general studies, philosophy, political science/government, psychology, religion, social science, sociology, Spanish studies, and women's studies). Chemistry, history, and political science are the strongest academically. Political science, psychology, and economics are the largest.

Special: Cross-registration is permitted with the Hudson Mohawk Consortium. Opportunities are provided for legislative internships in Albany and Washington, D.C., pass/fail options, B.A.-B.S. degrees, dual and student-designed majors, accelerated degree programs in law and medicine, and study abroad in 22 countries. There are 14 national honor societies, including Phi Beta Kappa, a freshman honors program, and 19 departmental honors programs.

Admissions: 41% of the 2009-2010 applicants were accepted. The SAT scores for the 2009-2010 freshman class were: Critical Reading--2% below 500, 27% between 500 and 599, 58% between 600 and 700, and 13% above 700; Math--17% between 500 and 599, 55% between 600 and 700, and 28% above 700; Writing--2% below 500, 30% between 500 and 599, 52% between 600 and 700, and 16% above 700. The ACT scores were 6% between 21 and 23, 59% between 24 and 26, and 35% above 28. 77% of the current freshmen were in the top fifth of their class; 96% were in the top two fifths.

Requirements: Testing is optional except for combined programs. Applicants for the Leadership in Medicine and Law and Public Policy programs are required to submit the SAT and two SAT Subject tests. Graduation from an accredited secondary school is required. Applicants must submit a minimum of 16 full-year credits, distributed as follows: 4 years of English, 2 year of a foreign language, 2 1/2 to 3 1/2 years of math, 2 years each of science and social studies, and the remainder in college-preparatory courses. Engineering and math majors are expected to have completed additional math and science courses beyond the minimum requirements. An essay is also required, and an interview is recommended. AP credits are accepted. Important factors in the admissions decision are advanced placement or honors courses, recommendations by school officials, and extracurricular activities record.

Procedure: Freshmen are admitted fall. Entrance exams should be taken by January of the senior year (December for applicants to the Leadership in Medicine and Law and Public Policy programs). There are early decision and deferred admissions plan. Early decision applications should be filed by November 15; regular applications, by January 15 for fall entry, along with a $50 fee. Notification of early decision is sent December 15; regular decision, April 1. Applications are accepted on-line. 840 applicants were on a recent waiting list, 109 were accepted.

Financial Aid: In 2009-2010, 69% of all full-time freshmen and 67% of continuing full-time students received some form of financial aid. 57% of all full-time freshmen and 52% of continuing full-time students received need-based aid. The average freshmen award was $30,400, with $4500 ($7300 maximum) from need-based self-help aid (loans and jobs) and $10,000 ($12,500 maximum) from other non-need-based awards and non-need-based scholarships. 45% of undergraduate students work part-time. Average annual earnings from campus work are $1350. The average financial indebtedness of the 2009 graduate was $24,739. Union is a member of CSS. The CSS/Profile, the FAFSA, and the Noncustodial Profile and the Business/Farm Supplement are required. The deadline for filing freshman financial aid applications for fall entry is February 1.

Computers: Wireless access is available. There are more than 1500 personal computers and workstations on campus, including in classrooms, labs, offices, and public spaces. The college's network goes to every building on campus, and there are more than 2100 network connections in residence halls. All residence halls have wireless networking available in public and study areas. In addition, the college's wireless network extends to all public/study areas on campus, all classrooms, the library, and all academic buildings. There are also 37 electronic classrooms and 3 general-use computer labs. All students may access the system. at any time. There are no time limits and no fees.

UNITED STATES AIR FORCE ACADEMY
USAFA, CO 80840-5025

(719) 333-2520
(800) 443-9266; (719) 333-3012

Full-time: 3635 men, 835 women	**Faculty:** n/av
Part-time: none	**Ph.D.s:** 49%
Graduate: none	**Student/Faculty:** n/av
Year: semesters, summer session	**Tuition:** see profile
Application Deadline: see profile	**Room & Board:** see profile
Freshman Class: n/av	
SAT or ACT: required	**MOST COMPETITIVE**

The United States Air Force Academy was founded in 1954 and is a public institution. Graduates receive the B.S. degree and a second lieutenant's commission in the regular Air Force. All graduates are obligated to serve at least 5 years of active duty military service. Tuition, room, board, medical, and dental expenses are paid by the U.S. government. Each cadet receives a monthly salary from which to pay for uniforms, supplies, and personal expenses. Entering freshmen are required to deposit $2500 to defray the initial costs of uniforms and personal expenses incurred upon entry. Students who are unable to submit the full deposit will receive a reduced monthly cash allotment until prescribed levels are reached. Figures in the above capsule are approximate. In addition to regional accreditation, USAFA has baccalaureate program accreditation with ABET and CSAB. The 2 libraries contain 551,476 volumes, 729,880 microform items, and 3643 audio/video tapes/CDs/DVDs, and subscribe to 36,252 periodicals including electronic. Computerized library services include interlibrary loans, database searching, Internet access, and laptop Internet portals. Special learning facilities include a learning resource center, art gallery, planetarium, radio station, TV station, field engineering and readiness lab, and aeronautics lab/aeronautical research center. The 18,000-acre campus is in a suburban area 70 miles south of downtown Denver and 8 miles north of downtown Colorado Springs. Including any residence halls, there are 13 buildings.

Programs of Study: USAFA confers B.S. degrees. Bachelor's degrees are awarded in BIOLOGICAL SCIENCE (biology/biological science), BUSINESS (management science and operations research), COMMUNICATIONS AND THE ARTS (English), COMPUTER AND PHYSICAL SCIENCE (atmospheric sciences and meteorology, chemistry, computer science, mathematics, physics, and science), ENGINEERING AND ENVIRONMENTAL DESIGN (aeronautical engineering, aerospace studies, civil engineering, computer engineering, electrical/electronics engineering, engineering, engineering and applied science, engineering mechanics, environmental engineering, mechanical engineering, and military science), SOCIAL SCIENCE (behavioral science, economics, geography, history, humanities, international studies, law, political science/government, psychology, and social science). Engineering and basic sciences are the strongest academically. Engineering, management, and social sciences are the largest.

Special: All cadets receive orientation flights in Air Force aircraft and take aviation science courses. A semester exchange program is available with the French Air Force Academy and U.S. Army, Naval, and Coast Guard academies. Freshman classes start in June, and basic cadet training must be completed before academics begin in August. Work-study programs are available, and dual majors are possible in all areas. There is an interdisciplinary space operations major. There are 2 national honor societies and a freshman honors program.

Admissions: 45 freshmen graduated first in their class in a recent year.

Requirements: The SAT or ACT is required. In addition, candidates must be U.S. citizens between 17 and 22 years of age, unmarried with no dependents, and nominated from a legal source. Students should have completed 4 years each of English, math, and lab sciences and 2 years each of social sciences and foreign languages. A computer course is recommended. A personal interview is required, as is an essay and a drug and alcohol abuse certificate. A GPA of 2.0 is required. AP credits are accepted. Important factors in the admissions decision are advanced placement or honors courses, leadership record, and personality/intangible qualities.

Procedure: Freshmen are admitted summer. Entrance exams should be taken in the spring of the junior year. Check with the school for current application deadlines. Applications are accepted on-line.

Computers: Wireless access is available. Entering freshmen are issued a tablet computer, which they are required to use for almost all classes. Each student has full access to the USAFA network from dorm rooms and via wireless in the classrooms. All students may access the system 24 hours per day. There are no time limits and no fees.

The U.S. Coast Guard Academy, founded in 1876, is an Armed Forces Service Academy for men and women. Appointments are made solely on the basis of an annual nationwide competition. Except for an entrance fee of $3,000, the federal government covers all cadet expenses by providing a yearly allowance of $11,150. Figures in the above capsule are approximate. In addition to regional accreditation, USCGA has baccalaureate program accreditation with ABET. The library contains 150,000 volumes, 60,000 microform items, and 1500 audio/video tapes/CDs/DVDs, and subscribes to 850 periodicals including electronic. Computerized library services include interlibrary loans and database searching. The 110-acre campus is in a suburban area 45 miles southeast of Hartford. Including any residence halls, there are 25 buildings.

Programs of Study: USCGA confers B.S. degrees. Bachelor's degrees are awarded in BIOLOGICAL SCIENCE (marine science), BUSINESS (management science and operations research), ENGINEERING AND ENVIRONMENTAL DESIGN (civil engineering, electrical/electronics engineering, mechanical engineering, and naval architecture and marine engineering), SOCIAL SCIENCE (political science/government). Political science/government is the largest.

Special: Cross-registration with Connecticut College, summer cruises to foreign ports, 6-week internships with various government agencies and some engineering and science organizations, and a 1-semester exchange program with the 3 other military academies are available. All graduates are commissioned in the U.S. Coast Guard. There are 2 national honor societies, a freshman honors program, and 3 departmental honors programs.

Requirements: The SAT or ACT is required. The ACT Optional Writing test is also required. In addition, applicants must have reached the age of 17 but not the age of 23 by July 1 of the year of admission, be citizens of the United States, and be single at the time of appointment and remain single while attending the academy. Required secondary school courses include 4 years each of English and math.

Procedure: Freshmen are admitted fall. Entrance exams should be taken by January 31. There are early admissions and rolling admissions plans. Check with the school for current application deadlines. Notification is sent on a rolling basis. Applications are accepted on-line. A waiting list is maintained.

Computers: All students may access the system 24 hours a day. There are no time limits and no fees. All students are required to have a personal computer.

UNITED STATES MERCHANT MARINE ACADEMY

Kings Point, NY 11024-1699

(516) 773-5391
(866) 546-4778; (516) 773-5390

Full-time: 810 men, 120 women	**Faculty:** n/av
Part-time: none	**Ph.D.s:** n/av
Graduate: none	**Student/Faculty:** n/av
Year: varies	**Tuition:** $4000
Application Deadline: March 1	**Room & Board:** n/av
Freshman Class: n/av	
SAT or ACT: required	**HIGHLY COMPETITIVE**

The United States Merchant Marine Academy, founded in 1943, is a publicly supported institution offering maritime, military, and engineering programs for the purpose of training officers for the U.S. merchant marine, the maritime industry, and the armed forces. Students make no conventional tuition and room/board payments. Required fees for freshmen are approximately $7,020; costs in subsequent years are less. The figures in the above capsule and in this profile are approximate. In addition to regional accreditation, Kings Point has baccalaureate program accreditation with ABET. The library contains 202,567 volumes, 19,341 microform items, and 3,722 audio/video tapes/CDs/DVDs, and subscribes to 964 periodicals including electronic. Computerized library services include interlibrary loans, database searching, Internet access, and laptop Internet portals. Special learning facilities include a learning resource center, planetarium, and a maritime museum. The 82-acre campus is in a suburban area 19 miles east of midtown New York City. Including any residence halls, there are 28 buildings.

Programs of Study: Kings Point confers B.S. degrees. Master's degrees are also awarded. Bachelor's degrees are awarded in BUSINESS (logistics and transportation management), ENGINEERING AND ENVIRONMENTAL DESIGN (engineering, marine engineering, maritime science, naval architecture and marine engineering, and transportation technology). Marine engineering systems is the strongest academically. Logistics and intermodal transportation is the largest.

Special: The college offers internships in the maritime industry and work-study programs with U.S. shipping companies.

Requirements: The SAT or ACT is required. The ACT Optional Writing test is also required. In addition, candidates for admission to the academy must be nominated by a member of the U.S. Congress. They must be between the ages of 17 and 25, U.S. citizens (except by special arrangement), and in excellent physical condition. Applicants should be graduates of an accredited secondary school or have a GED equivalent. 18 academic credits are required, including 4 in English, 3 in math, 1 credit in physics or chemistry with a lab, and 10 in electives. An essay is required. AP credits are accepted. Important factors in the admissions decision are advanced placement or honors courses, leadership record, and extracurricular activities record.

Procedure: Freshmen are admitted in the fall. Entrance exams should be taken by the first test date of the year of entry. There are early decision and rolling admissions plans. Applications should be filed by March 1 for fall entry. Notifications are sent March 31. Applications are accepted on-line. A waiting list is maintained.

Financial Aid: In a recent year, 33% of all full-time freshmen received some form of financial aid. 37% of all full-time freshmen received need-based aid. The average freshmen award was $5,442, with $2,375 ($4,050 maximum) from need-based scholarships or need-based grants; $5,334 ($8,000 maximum) from need-based self-help aid (loans and jobs); and $967 ($2,000 maximum) from other non-need-based awards and non-need-based scholarships. The average financial indebtedness of the 2009 graduate was $9,221. The FAFSA is required. Check with the school for current application deadlines.

Computers: Wireless access is available. All students may access the system 24 hours per day. There are no time limits and no fees. All students are required to have a personal computer. A laptop computer is recommended.

UNITED STATES MILITARY ACADEMY
West Point, NY 10996   (845) 938-4041; (845) 938-8121

Full-time: 3535 men, 640 women	**Faculty:** n/av
Part-time: 0 men, 0 women	**Ph.D.s:** 39%
Graduate: none	**Student/Faculty:** n/av
Year: semesters, summer session	**Tuition:** see profile
Application Deadline: see profile	**Room & Board:** see profile
Freshman Class: n/av	
SAT or ACT: required	**MOST COMPETITIVE**

The United States Military Academy, founded in 1802, offers military, engineering, and comprehensive arts and sciences programs leading to a bachelor's degree and a commission as a second lieutenant in the U.S. Army, with a 5-year active duty service obligation. All students receive free tuition and room and board as well as an annual salary of $10,148. An initial deposit of $2900 is required. Figures in the above capsule are approximate. In addition to regional accreditation, West Point has baccalaureate program accreditation with ABET. The library contains 442,169 volumes, 748,443 microform items, and 12,378 audio/video tapes/CDs/DVDs, and subscribes to 1,963 periodicals including electronic. Computerized library services include interlibrary loans and database searching. Special learning facilities include a learning resource center, art gallery, radio station, TV station, and military museum. Cadets may conduct research in conjunction with the academic departments through the Operations Research Center, the Photonics Research Center, the Mechanical Engineering Research Center, and the Office of Artificial Intelligence, Analysis, and Evaluation. There is also a visiting artist program featuring painting, sculpture, and photography. The 16,080-acre campus is in a small town 56 miles north of New York City. Including any residence halls, there are 902 buildings.

Programs of Study: West Point confers B.S. degrees. Bachelor's degrees are awarded in BIOLOGICAL SCIENCE (life science), BUSINESS (management science and operations research), COMMUNICATIONS AND THE ARTS (languages and literature), COMPUTER AND PHYSICAL SCIENCE (chemistry, computer science, mathematics, and physics), ENGINEERING AND ENVIRONMENTAL DESIGN (civil engineering, electrical/electronics engineering, engineering management, engineering physics, environmental engineering, mechanical engineering, military science, nuclear engineering, and systems engineering), SOCIAL SCIENCE (behavioral science, economics, geography, history, international studies, law, philosophy, and political science/government). Engineering, behavioral sciences, and history are the largest.

Special: Junior and senior cadets may participate in 3-week summer educational experiences, including Operations Crossroads Africa, research work in technical areas throughout the country, medical internships at Walter Reed Medical Center, workfellow positions with federal and Department of Defense agencies, language training in foreign countries, and study at other military and civilian institutions.

There are 7 national honor societies, including Phi Beta Kappa, a freshman honors program, and 5 departmental honors programs.

Requirements: The SAT or ACT is required. In addition, applicants must be qualified academically, physically, and medically. Candidates must be nominated for admission by members of the U.S. Congress or executive sources. West Point recommends that applicants have 4 years each of English and math, 2 years each of foreign language and lab science, such as chemistry and physics, and 1 year of U.S. history. Courses in geography, government, and economics are also suggested. An essay is required, and an interview is recommended. The GED is accepted. Applicants must be 17 to 22 years old, a U.S. citizen at the time of enrollment (except by agreement with another country), unmarried, and not pregnant or legally obligated to support children. AP credits are accepted. Important factors in the admissions decision are leadership record, extracurricular activities record, and recommendations by school officials.

Procedure: Freshmen are admitted summer. Entrance exams should be taken in the spring of the junior year and not later than the fall of the senior year. There are early decision, early admissions and rolling admissions plans. Check with the school for current application deadlines. A waiting list is maintained.

Financial Aid: Check with the school for current application deadlines.

Computers: All students may access the system 24 hours daily. There are no time limits and no fees. All students are required to have a personal computer.

UNITED STATES NAVAL ACADEMY
Annapolis, MD 21402-5018

(410) 293-4361
(888) 249-7707; (410) 293-1815

Full-time: 3640 men, 928 women	**Faculty:** 525; IIB, ++$
Part-time: none	**Ph.D.s:** 64%
Graduate: none	**Student/Faculty:** 9 to 1
Year: semesters, summer session	**Tuition:** n/app
Application Deadline: January 31	**Room & Board:** n/app
Freshman Class: 4644 applied, 1464 accepted, 1251 enrolled	
SAT or ACT: required	**MOST COMPETITIVE**

The United States Naval Academy, founded in 1845, is a national military service college offering undergraduate degree programs and professional training in aviation, surface ships, submarines, and various military, maritime, and technical fields. The U.S. Navy pays tuition, room and board, medical and dental care, and a monthly stipend to all Naval Academy students. Graduates earn a Bachelor of Science degree and a commission in the United States Navy or the United States Marine Corp and have a five year obligation of active military service. In addition to regional accreditation, Annapolis has baccalaureate program accreditation with ABET and CSAB. The library contains 701,505 volumes, 201,854 microform items, and 7,317 audio/video tapes/CDs/DVDs, and subscribes to 1,979 periodicals including electronic. Computerized library services include interlibrary loans, database searching, Internet access, and laptop Internet portals. Special learning facilities include a learning resource center, planetarium, radio station, a propulsion lab, a nuclear reactor, an oceanographic research vessel, towing tanks, a flight simulator, and a naval history museum. The 329-acre campus is in a small town 30 miles southeast of Baltimore and 35 miles east of Washington, D.C. Including any residence halls, there are 75 buildings.

Programs of Study: Annapolis confers B.S. degrees. Bachelor's degrees are awarded in COMMUNICATIONS AND THE ARTS (Arabic, Chinese, and English), COMPUTER AND PHYSICAL SCIENCE (applied mathematics, chemistry, computer science, information sciences and systems, mathematics, oceanography, physics, and science), ENGINEERING AND ENVIRONMENTAL DESIGN (aeronautical engineering, aerospace studies, aerospace studies, electrical/electronics engineering technology, engineering, marine engineering, mechanical engineering, naval architecture and marine engineering, ocean engineering, and systems engineering), SOCIAL SCIENCE (economics, history, and political science/government). Political science, mechanical engineering, and systems engineering are the largest.

Special: A voluntary graduate program is available for those midshipmen who complete academic graduation requirements by the end of their seventh semester and wish to begin master's work at nearby universities, such as Georgetown, Johns Hopkins, or Maryland. Trident Scholars spend their senior year in independent research at the Naval Academy. Study abroad is available in 6 countries. There are 10 national honor societies and 5 departmental honors programs.

Admissions: 32% of the 2009-2010 applicants were accepted. The SAT scores for the 2009-2010 freshman class were: Critical Reading--8% below 500, 35% between 500 and 599, 41% between 600 and 700, and 16% above 700; Math--5% below 500, 25% between 500 and 599, 49% between 600 and 700, and 21% above 700. 76% of the current freshmen were in the top fifth of their class; 91% were in the top two fifths.

Requirements: The SAT or ACT is required. In addition, candidates must be unmarried with no dependents, U.S. citizens of good moral character, and between 17 and 23 years of age. Candidates should have a sound secondary school background, including 4 years each of English and math, 2 years of a foreign language, and 1 year each of U.S. history, world or European history, chemistry, physics, and computer literacy. Candidates must obtain an official nomination from congressional or military sources. An interview is conducted, and medical and physical exams must be passed to qualify for admission. AP credits are accepted.

Procedure: Freshmen are admitted in the summer. Entrance exams should be taken after December of the junior year. There are early admissions and rolling admissions plans. Applications should be filed by January 31 for fall entry. Notifications are sent April 15. Applications are accepted on-line. A waiting list is maintained.

Financial Aid: Check with the school for current application deadlines.

Computers: There are no time limits and no fees. All students are required to have a personal computer. A Each student is issued a standardized personal computer.

Buffalo, NY 14214   **(716) 645-6900**
(888) UB-ADMIT; (716) 645-6411

Full-time: 9500 men, 8035 women	**Faculty:** I, av$
Part-time: 640 men, 625 women	**Ph.D.s:** n/av
Graduate: 4430 men, 4855 women	**Student/Faculty:** n/avn
Year: semesters, summer session	**Tuition:** $7013 ($14,913)
Application Deadline: see profile	**Room & Board:** $9000
Freshman Class: n/av	
SAT: required	**VERY COMPETITIVE+**

The University at Buffalo, State University of New York at Buffalo, established in 1846, is a public institution offering more than 300 bachelor's, master's, and doctoral degree programs. UB is a comprehensive research-extensive university and the largest in the 64-campus State University of New York system. The figures in the above capsule and in this profile are approximate. There are 8 undergraduate schools and 13 graduate schools. In addition to regional accreditation, UB has baccalaureate program accreditation with AACSB, ABET, ACPE, ADA, APTA, CSWE, NAAB, and NASAD. The 10 libraries contain 3.5 million volumes, 5.5 million microform items, and 200,600 audio/video tapes/CDs/DVDs, and subscribe to 37,500 periodicals including electronic. Computerized library services include interlibrary loans, database searching, Internet access, and laptop Internet portals. Special learning facilities include a learning resource center, art gallery, radio station, TV station, an earthquake engineering research center, an arts center, a bio-informatics and life sciences center, a document analysis and Recognition center, a concert hall, an anthropology research center, a computational research center, a poetry and rare books collection, a virtual site museum, center for engineering design and industrial innovation, an electronic poetry center, and a archeological center. The 1350-acre campus is in a suburban area 3 miles north of Buffalo. Including any residence halls, there are 226 buildings.

Programs of Study: UB confers B.A., B.S., B.F.A., and Mus.B. degrees. Master's and doctoral degrees are also awarded. Bachelor's degrees are awarded in BIOLOGICAL SCIENCE (biochemistry, bioinformatics, biology/biological science, biophysics, and biotechnology), BUSINESS (business administration and management), COMMUNICATIONS AND THE ARTS (art history and appreciation, classics, communications, dance, English, film arts, fine arts, French, German, Italian, linguistics, media arts, music, music performance, musical theater, Spanish, studio art, and visual and performing arts), COMPUTER AND PHYSICAL SCIENCE (chemistry, computer science, geology, information sciences and systems, mathematics, and physics), ENGINEERING AND ENVIRONMENTAL DESIGN (aerospace studies, architecture, chemical engineering, civil engineering, computational sciences, computer engineering, electrical/electronics engineering, engineering physics, environmental design, environmental engineering, industrial engineering, and mechanical engineering), HEALTH PROFESSIONS (biomedical science, exercise science, medical technology, nuclear medical technology, nursing, occupational therapy, pharmaceutical science, pharmacology, pharmacy, physical therapy, and speech pathology/audiology), SOCIAL SCIENCE (African American studies, American studies, anthropology, Asian/Oriental studies, economics, geography, history, philosophy, political science/government, psychology, social science, sociology, and women's studies). Engineering, business administration, and psychology are the largest.

Special: Students may cross-register with the Western New York Consortium. Internships are available, and students may study abroad in 29 countries. UB offers a Washington semester, work-study programs, accelerated degree programs, B.A.-B.S. degrees, dual, student-designed, and interdisciplinary majors, and credit for military experience. A 3-2 engineering degree can be pursued. Students may choose a successful/unsuccessful (S/U) grading option for selected courses. There is an early assurance of admission program to medical school for undergraduate sophomore students who possess a minimum approximate overall and science GPA of 3.75 and complete particular science courses. There are 39 national honor societies, including Phi Beta Kappa, a freshman honors program, and all departments have honors programs.

Requirements: The SAT is required. Freshmen are evaluated based on secondary school performance, strength of curriculum, standardized test scores, and, in some cases, a supplemental application. A high school diploma is required and the GED is accepted. Music applicants must audition. AP and CLEP credits are accepted. Important factors in the admissions decision are advanced placement or honors courses, recommendations by school officials, and evidence of special talent.

Procedure: Freshmen are admitted fall and spring. Entrance exams should be taken during the spring of the junior year or the fall of the senior year. There are early decision and rolling admissions plans. Early decision applications should be filed by November 1; check with the school for current application deadlines. The fall 2009 application fee was $40. Notification of early decision is sent December 15; regular decision, sent in February. Applications are accepted on-line. A waiting list is maintained.

Financial Aid: In a recent year, 98% of all full-time freshmen and 98% of continuing full-time students received some form of financial aid. 63% of all full-time freshmen and 69% of continuing full-time students received need-based aid. The average freshmen award was $3,019, with $6,623 from other forms of aid. The average financial indebtedness of the 2009 graduate was $18,000. The FAFSA is required. Check with the school for current application deadlines.

Computers: Wireless access is available. Students have access to more than 2400 computers in labs that provides connectivity for mobile devices. Access to research networks, free mail, Microsoft productivity software for student PCs, and student web page hosting are provided. Many courses provide audio-or-video-streams of lectures which students can re-play on their portable devices. Learning spaces in the libraries and academic areas are equipped with technology to enable student group/team work and collaborative learning. A mobile campus initiative is underway to enable anywhere, anytime access to information and learning tools. All students may access the system any time. There are no time limits and no fees. It is strongly recommended that all students have a personal computer.

UNIVERSITY OF ALABAMA IN HUNTSVILLE

Huntsville, AL 35899

(256) 824-2773
(800) UAH-CALL; (256) 824-6073

Full-time: 2425 men, 2215 women	**Faculty:** 303; I, --$
Part-time: 819 men, 660 women	**Ph.D.s:** 90%
Graduate: 953 men, 609 women	**Student/Faculty:** 15 to 1
Year: semesters, summer session	**Tuition:** $6510 ($7208)
Application Deadline: August 15	**Room & Board:** $22,836
Freshman Class: 1924 applied, 1387 accepted, 802 enrolled	
SAT CR/M: 560/580	**ACT:** 25 **VERY COMPETITIVE**

The University of Alabama in Huntsville, founded in 1950 and part of the University of Alabama system, is a public institution offering programs in liberal arts and sciences, business, nursing, and engineering. There are 5 undergraduate schools and 1 graduate school. In addition to regional accreditation, UAH has baccalaureate program accreditation with AACSB, ABET, ACCE, CSAB, NASAD, NASDTEC, NASM, and NCATE. The library contains 358,530 volumes, 186,677 microform items, and 2,677 audio/video tapes/CDs/DVDs, and subscribes to 27,481 periodicals including electronic. Computerized library services include interlibrary loans, database searching, Internet access, and laptop Internet portals. Special learning facilities include a learning resource center, art gallery, radio station, and an observatory with a solar magnemeter. The 400-acre campus is in a suburban area 100 miles north of Birmingham and 90 miles south of Nashville. Including any residence halls, there are 55 buildings.

Programs of Study: UAH confers B.A., B.S., B.S.B.A., B.S.E., and B.S.N. degrees. Master's and doctoral degrees are also awarded. Bachelor's degrees are awarded in BIOLOGICAL SCIENCE (biology/biological science), BUSINESS (accounting, banking and finance, business administration and management, management information systems, and marketing/retailing/merchandising), COMMUNICATIONS AND THE ARTS (art, communications, English, languages, and music), COMPUTER AND PHYSICAL SCIENCE (chemistry, computer science, earth science, mathematics, and physics), EDUCATION (elementary education), ENGINEERING AND ENVIRONMENTAL DESIGN (chemical engineering, civil engineering, computer engineering, electrical/electronics engineering, industrial engineering, mechanical engineering, and optical engineering), HEALTH PROFESSIONS (nursing), SOCIAL SCIENCE (history, philosophy, political science/government, psychology, and sociology). Engineering, nursing, and biology are the largest.

Special: UAH offers co-op programs in all majors, cross-registration with Alabama Agricultural and Mechanical University, Athens State University, and Calhoun Community College, and internships in administrative science, communications, education, and political science. A 3-2 engineering degree is available with Oakwood College. Dual majors, B.A.-B.S. degrees in math and biology, study abroad in 11 countries, nondegree study, and a pass/fail option are also offered. There are 23 national honor societies, a freshman honors program, and 16 departmental honors programs.

Admissions: 72% of the 2009-2010 applicants were accepted. The SAT scores for the 2009-2010 freshman class were: Critical Reading--23% below 500, 47% between 500 and 599, 30% between 600 and 700, and 7$ above 700; Math--18% below 500, 36% between 500 and 599, 38% between 600 and 700, and 8% above 700. The ACT scores were 13% below 21, 22% between 21 and 23, 26% between 24 and 26, 16% between 27 and 28, and 23% above 28. 1% of the current freshmen were in the top fifth of their class; 77% were in the top two fifths. There were 7 National Merit finalists.

Requirements: The SAT or ACT is required. A sliding scale with the GPA determines the minimum test score needed. The GED is accepted. Students should present a minimum of 20 Carnegie units, including 4 years of English and social studies, and 3 each of math and science. A GPA of 2.0 is required. AP and CLEP credits are accepted.

Procedure: Freshmen are admitted fall, spring, and summer. Entrance exams should be taken during the junior year. There are early admissions, deferred admissions, and rolling admissions plans. Applications should be filed by August 15 for fall entry, December 15 for spring entry, and May 19 for summer entry, along with a $30 fee. Applications are accepted on-line.

Financial Aid: In 2009-2010, 84% of all full-time freshmen and 69% of continuing full-time students received some form of financial aid. 47% of all full-time freshmen and 50% of continuing full-time students received need-based aid. The average freshman award was $7,351. Need-based scholarships or need-based grants averaged $6,219 ($24.9323 maximum); need-based self-help aid (loans and jobs) averaged $5,448 (18,500 maximum); non-need-based athletic scholarships averaged $7,851 ($22,700 maximum); and other non-need-based awards; and non-need-based scholarships averaged $5442 ($21,128 maximum). 13% of undergraduate students work part-time. Average annual earnings from campus work are $3193. The average financial indebtedness of the 2009 graduate was $24,938. The FAFSA is required. The priority date for freshman financial aid applications for fall entry is April 1. The deadline for filing freshman financial aid applications for fall entry is July 31.

Computers: Wireless access is available. Students use the campus network in many ways as there are host/PC applications. Students without personal computers can access network resources from a number of department sponsored labs around campus. Wireless network is available from 107 access points om campus. All students may access the system 24 hours a day. There are no time limits and no fees. It is strongly recommended that all students have a personal computer.

UNIVERSITY OF ARIZONA
Tucson, AZ 85721-0040   (520) 621-3237; (520) 621-9799

Full-time: 12000 men, 13500 women	**Faculty:** I, -$
Part-time: 1800 men, 1850 women	**Ph.D.s:** n/av
Graduate: 4100 men, 5500 women	**Student/Faculty:** n/av
Year: semesters, summer session	**Tuition:** $5250 ($16,750)
Application Deadline: May 1	**Room & Board:** $7500
Freshman Class: n/av	
SAT or ACT: required	**COMPETITIVE**

The University of Arizona, founded in 1885, is a public land-grant institution controlled by the state of Arizona. Undergraduate programs are offered in agriculture, architecture, arts and sciences, business and public administration, education, engineering and mines, nursing, pharmacy, and other health-related professions. The figures in the above capsule and in is profile are approximate. There are 15 undergraduate schools and 114 graduate schools. In addition to regional accreditation, UA has baccalaureate program accreditation with AACSB, ABET, ACPE, ADA, ASLA, NAAB, NASAD, NASM, NCATE, and NLN. The 6 libraries contain 5.2 million volumes, 5.6 million microform items, and 63,547 audio/video tapes/CDs/DVDs, and subscribe to 62,143 periodicals including electronic. Computerized library services include interlibrary loans, database searching, Internet access, and laptop Internet portals. Special learning facilities include a learning resource center, art gallery, natural history museum, planetarium, radio station, TV station, the Ansel Adams Center for creative photography, and the Integrated Learning Center. The 387-acre campus is in an urban area in Tucson. Including any residence halls, there are 182 buildings.

Programs of Study: UA confers B.A., B.S., B.F.A., B.S.N., B.S.B., A.E.E., R.A.P., R.A.R., E.M.A., E.P.H., E.H.Y., B.E.S., G.E.E., B.H.S., M.N.E., B.S.E., B.E., C.H.E., C.V.E., C.O.E., B.S.P., B.A.E., E.L.E., E.B.A., E.M.G., I.N.E., M.S.E., B.S.C., M.E.E., B.M.U., O.S.E., S.Y.E. degrees. Master's and doctoral degrees are also awarded. Bachelor's degrees are awarded in AGRICULTURE (agricultural business management, agricultural economics, animal science, natural resource management, and plant science), BIOLOGICAL SCIENCE (biochemistry, biology/biological science, microbiology, and physiology), BUSINESS (accounting, business economics, entrepreneurial studies, management information systems, marketing/retailing/merchandising, and operations management), COMMUNICATIONS AND THE ARTS (classics, communications, creative writing, dance, English, fine arts, French, Italian, journalism, language arts, linguistics, media arts, music, musical theater, Russian, Spanish, and studio art), COMPUTER AND PHYSICAL SCIENCE (applied science, astronomy, chemistry, computer science, geoscience, mathematics, natural sciences, and physics), EDUCATION (agricultural education, art education, early childhood education, elementary education, health education, music education, physical education, science education, and secondary education), ENGINEERING AND ENVIRONMENTAL DESIGN (aerospace studies, agricultural engineering, agricultural engineering technology, architecture, chemical engineering, civil engineering, computer engineering, electrical/electronics engineering, engineering, engineering management, engineering physics, environmental science, geological engineering, industrial engineering, mechanical engineering, mining and mineral engineering, optical engineering, and systems engineering), HEALTH PROFESSIONS (nursing and veterinary science), SOCIAL SCIENCE (African American studies, anthropology, East Asian studies, economics, geography, German area studies, history, interdisciplinary studies, Judaic studies, Latin American studies, Mexican-American/Chicano studies, Near Eastern studies, philosophy, political science/government, psychology, social studies, sociology, and women's studies). Sciences, social sciences, and management information systems are the strongest academically. Social sciences and business are the largest.

Special: Co-op programs are available in almost all majors. B.A.-B.S. degrees, dual majors, interdisciplinary degrees such as engineering-math and theater arts-education, a 3-2 arts and sciences-business degree, and student designed majors are offered. Internships in almost all disciplines, a Washington semester, study abroad in numerous countries, work-study programs on campus, a general studies degree, and pass/fail options are offered. Nondegree study is possible. There are 27 national honor societies, including Phi Beta Kappa, and a freshman honors program.

Requirements: The SAT or ACT is required. In addition, applicants should have completed 4 years each in high school English and math, 3 in science, 2 of a foreign language, and 1 each in history, fine arts, and social studies. A GED may be considered in place of a high school diploma. Some fine arts programs require auditions prior to admission. A GPA of 2.0 is required. AP and CLEP credits are accepted. Important factors in the admissions decision are advanced placement or honors courses, leadership record, and extracurricular activities record.

Procedure: Freshmen are admitted to all sessions. Entrance exams should be taken during March of the junior year through December of the senior year. There is a rolling admissions plan. Applications should be filed by May 1 for fall entry, November 1 for spring entry, and May 1 for summer entry, along with a $25 fee. Notification is sent on a rolling basis. Applications are accepted on-line.

Financial Aid: In a recent year, 77% of all full-time freshmen and 68% of continuing full-time students received some form of financial aid. 37% of all full-time freshmen and 37% of continuing full-time students received need-based aid. The average freshmen award was $7,272. The average financial indebtedness of the 2009 graduate was $18,241. UA is a member of CSS. The FAFSA is required. Check with the school for current application deadlines.

Computers: Wireless access is available. All students may access the system 24 hours a day. There are no time limits and no fees.

UNIVERSITY OF ARKANSAS
Fayetteville, AR 72701

(479) 575-5346
(800) 377-8632; (479) 575-7515

Full-time: 6500 men, 6500 women	**Faculty:** I, --$
Part-time: 1200 men, 1200 women	**Ph.D.s:** n/av
Graduate: 3040 men, 3100 women	**Student/Faculty:** n/av
Year: semesters, summer session	**Tuition:** $8000 ($16,500)
Application Deadline: August 15	**Room & Board:** $8000
Freshman Class: n/av	
SAT or ACT: required	**VERY COMPETITIVE**

The University of Arkansas, founded in 1871, is a land-grant institution offering undergraduate and graduate programs in liberal arts and sciences, agricultural, food, social and natural sciences, life sciences, business administration, engineering, architecture, education, law, and human environmental sciences. The figures given the above capsule and in this profile are approximate. There are 8 undergraduate schools and 2 graduate schools. In addition to regional accreditation, U of A has baccalaureate program accreditation with AACSB, ABET, ACEJMC, ADA, ASLA, CSWE, FIDER, NAAB, NASM, NCATE, and NLN. The 4 libraries contain 1.8 million volumes, 5.5 million microform items, and 43,908 audio/video tapes/CDs/DVDs, and subscribe to 18,576 periodicals including electronic. Computerized library services include interlibrary loans, database searching, and Internet access. Special learning facilities include a planetarium, radio station, TV station, numerous research centers. The 412-acre campus is in an urban area 190 miles northwest of Little Rock. Including any residence halls, there are 177 buildings.

Programs of Study: U of A confers B.A., B.S., B.Arch., B.E.A., B.I.D., B.L.A., B.M., B.S.A., B.S.B.A., B.S.B.E., B.S.C.E., B.S.Ch.E., B.S.C.S.E., B.S.Cmp.E., B.S.E., B.S.E.E., B.S.H.E.S., B.S.I.B., B.S.I.E., B.S.M.E., B.S.N., and B.S.P.A. degrees. Master's and doctoral degrees are also awarded. Bachelor's degrees are awarded in AGRICULTURE (agricultural business management, animal science, horticulture, poultry science, and soil science), BIOLOGICAL SCIENCE (biology/biological science and nutrition), BUSINESS (accounting, apparel and accessories marketing, banking and finance, business administration and management, business economics, hospitality management services, human resources, international business management, marketing management, marketing/retailing/merchandising, and transportation management), COMMUNICATIONS AND THE ARTS (art, communications, dramatic arts, English, French, German, journalism, music, and Spanish), COMPUTER AND PHYSICAL SCIENCE (chemistry, computer science, earth science, geology, mathematics, and physics), EDU-CATION (agricultural education, early childhood education, elementary education, middle school education, music education, recreation education, and technical education), ENGINEERING AND ENVIRONMENTAL DESIGN (architecture, bioengineering, chemical engineering, civil engineering, computer engineering, electrical/electronics engineering, industrial engineering, interior design, landscape architecture/design, and mechanical engineering), HEALTH PROFESSIONS (exercise science, health science, and nursing), SOCIAL SCIENCE (American studies, anthropology, classical/ancient civilization, criminal justice, economics, food science, geography, history, human development, international relations, philosophy, political science/government, psychology, public administration, social work, and sociology). Business, chemical and electrical engineering, and computer science are the strongest academically. Nursing, kinesiology, and biology are the largest.

Special: Co-op programs and internships are available, as well as dual majors and B.A.-B.S. degrees in many majors, and study abroad in 47 countries. There are 3-2 engineering degrees with several universities, a combined medical/dental degree, and a 6-year B.S./J.D. degree for highly qualified students. Non-degree study is possible. There are 36 national honor societies, including Phi Beta Kappa, a freshman honors program, and 84 departmental honors programs.

Requirements: The SAT or ACT is required. In addition, U of A recommends 4 years of English and math and 3 years each of social science and natural science. AP and honors level courses will enhance the applicant's opportunity for admission. AP and CLEP credits are accepted. Important factors in the admissions decision are advanced placement or honors courses, leadership record, and evidence of special talent.

Procedure: Freshmen are admitted fall, spring, and summer. Entrance exams should be taken in the junior year or in October or December of the senior year. There are deferred admissions and rolling admissions plans. Applications should be filed by August 15 for fall entry and January 1 for spring entry. The fall 2009 application fee was $40. Notification is sent on a rolling basis. Applications are accepted on-line.

Financial Aid: In 2009-2010, 71% of all full-time freshmen and 66% of continuing full-time students received some form of financial aid. 31% of all full-time freshmen and 34% of continuing full-time students received need-based aid. The average freshmen award was $9,044, with $4,966 ($12,060 maximum) from need-based scholarships or need-based grants; $4,496 ($10,277 maximum) from need-based self-help aid (loans and jobs); $10,446 ($17,546 maximum) from non-need-based athletic scholarships; and $6,749 ($25,612 maximum) from other non-need-based awards and non-need-based scholarships. 5% of undergraduate students work part-time. Average annual earnings from campus work are $1301. The average financial indebtedness of the 2009 graduate was $22,689. The FAFSA is required. Check with the school for current application deadlines.

Computers: Wireless access is available. There are 5 general-access computer labs with a total of 296 PCs and 298 notebooks available for checkout. All students may access the system. 24 hours daily. There are no time limits and no fees.

UNIVERSITY OF CALIFORNIA AT BERKELEY

Berkeley, CA 94720-5800   **(510) 642-2316**

Full-time and part-time: 25,500 men and women	**Faculty:** I, +$
	Ph.D.s: 99%
Graduate: 10,300 men and women	**Student/Faculty:** n/av
Year: semesters, summer session	**Tuition:** $8938 ($31,665)
Application Deadline: November 30	**Room & Board:** $14,384
Freshman Class: 48650 applied, 10561 accepted, 4356 enrolled	
SAT CR/M/W: 660/700/670	**ACT:** 30 **MOST COMPETITIVE**

The University of California at Berkeley, founded in 1868, is a public institution offering a wide variety of programs in the social and physical sciences, liberal arts, and professional fields. It is the oldest campus of the University of California system. Enrollment figures in the above capsule are approximate. There are 7 undergraduate schools and 14 graduate schools. In addition to regional accreditation, Cal has baccalaureate program accreditation with AACSB, ABET, ADA, ASLA, and SAF. The 35 libraries contain 10.4 million volumes, 6.6 million microform items, and 46,162 audio/video tapes/CDs/DVDs, and subscribe to 82,151 periodicals including electronic. Computerized library services include interlibrary loans and database searching. Special learning facilities include a learning resource center, art gallery, natural history museum, radio station, TV station, botanical garden, anthropology museum, hall of science, seismographic station, herbaria, observatory, the University Art Museum and Pacific Film Archive, the Hall for the Performing Arts, and many off-campus facilities. The 1232-acre campus is in an urban area 10 miles east of San Francisco. Including any residence halls, there are 300 buildings.

Programs of Study: Cal confers A.B. and B.S. degrees. Master's and doctoral degrees are also awarded. Bachelor's degrees are awarded in AGRICULTURE (conservation and regulation and forestry and related sciences), BIOLOGICAL SCIENCE (biology/biological science, microbiology, molecular biology, nutrition, and plant genetics), BUSINESS (business administration and management, management science, and operations research), COMMUNICATIONS AND THE ARTS (art, art history and appreciation, Chinese, classical languages, communications, comparative literature, dance, dramatic arts, Dutch, English, film arts, French, German, Greek, Italian, Japanese, Latin, linguistics, music, Scandinavian languages, Slavic languages, Spanish, and speech/debate/rhetoric), COMPUTER AND PHYSICAL SCIENCE (applied mathematics, astrophysics, chemistry, computer science, earth science, mathematics, physical sciences, physics, and statistics), ENGINEERING AND ENVIRONMENTAL DESIGN (architecture, bioengineering, chemical engineering, civil engineering, computer engineering, electrical/electronics engineering, engineering and applied science, engineering physics, environmental engineering, environmental science, industrial engineering, landscape architecture/design, manufacturing engineering, materials engineering, materials science, mechanical engineering, and nuclear engineering), HEALTH PROFESSIONS (optometry and public health), SOCIAL SCIENCE (African American studies, American studies, anthropology, Asian/American studies, Asian/Oriental studies, Celtic studies, classical/ancient civilization, cognitive science, economics, ethnic studies, geography, Hispanic American studies, history, interdisciplinary studies, Latin American studies, law, Middle Eastern studies, Native American studies, Near Eastern studies, peace studies, political science/government, psychology, religion, social science, social work, sociology,

South Asian studies, urban studies, and women's studies). Electrical engineering and computer science, political science, and economics are the largest.

Special: Co-op programs, cross-registration with many area schools, internships, work-study programs, and study abroad in 35 countries are available. Interdisciplinary majors are also available, as are pass/fail options, independent study, an independent research and undergraduate research program, and a freshman seminar program, in which 15 to 25 students meet with professors to explore a wide range of majors. There is a 3-2 engineering program with the University of California, Santa Cruz. There is a Phi Beta Kappa honors program and a freshman honors program.

Admissions: 22% of the 2009-2010 applicants were accepted. The SAT scores for the 2009-2010 freshman class were: Critical Reading--8% below 500, 20% between 500 and 599, 43% between 600 and 700, and 29% above 700; Math--4% below 500, 14% between 500 and 599, 32% between 600 and 700, and 51% above 700; Writing--6% below 500, 18% between 500 and 599, 42% between 600 and 700, and 34% above 700.

Requirements: The SAT or ACT is required. In addition, applicants must submit scores from 2 SAT Subject Tests. Also required are 4 years of English, 3 of math (4 recommended), and 2 each of history/social sciences, lab science (3 recommended), foreign language (3 recommended), and college preparatory electives. AP credits are accepted. Important factors in the admissions decision are advanced placement or honors courses, evidence of special talent, and leadership record.

Procedure: Freshmen are admitted fall. Entrance exams should be taken no later than December test dates in the senior year. There is a deferred admissions plan. Applications should be filed by November 30 for fall entry, along with a $60 fee. Notifications are sent March 30. Applications are accepted on-line.

Financial Aid: In a recent year, 50% of all full-time freshmen and 49% of continuing full-time students received some form of financial aid. 48% of all full-time students received need-based aid. The average freshman award was $17,250. The average financial indebtedness of a recent graduate was $14,751. The FAFSA is required. The deadline for filing freshman financial aid applications for fall entry is March 2.

Computers: Wireless access is available. All students may access the system. There are no time limits and no fees. It is strongly recommended that all students have a personal computer.

UNIVERSITY OF CALIFORNIA AT DAVIS
Davis, CA 95616-8507 (530) 752-2971; (530) 752-1280

Full-time: 10,579 men, 13,573 women	**Faculty:** I, av$
Part-time: 154 men, 147 women	**Ph.D.s:** 98%
Graduate: 3179 men, 3413 women	**Student/Faculty:** n/av
Year: quarters, summer session	**Tuition:** $9364 ($31,385)
Application Deadline: November 30	**Room & Board:** $12,361
Freshman Class: 42,382 applied, 20,080 accepted, 4413 enrolled	
SAT CR/M/W: 580/630/580	**ACT:** 26 **HIGHLY COMPETITIVE**

University of California at Davis, founded in 1908, is a land-grant, comprehensive institution offering programs in arts and science, agricultural and environmental sciences, and engineering. There are 4 undergraduate schools and 5 graduate schools. In addition to regional accreditation, UC Davis has baccalaureate program accreditation with ABET, ADA, and ASLA. The 6 libraries contain 3.7 million volumes, 4.2 million microform items, and 17,238 audio/video tapes/

CDs/DVDs, and subscribe to 56,268 periodicals including electronic. Computerized library services include database searching. Special learning facilities include a learning resource center, art gallery, radio station, experimental farm, 150-acre arboretum, raptor center, equestrian center, primate research center, and the Crocker Nuclear Laboratory. The 5300-acre campus is in a suburban area 15 miles west of Sacramento and 72 miles northeast of San Francisco. Including any residence halls, there are 1186 buildings.

Programs of Study: UC Davis confers B.S., A.B., and B.A.S. degrees. Master's and doctoral degrees are also awarded. Bachelor's degrees are awarded in AGRICULTURE (agricultural business management, agricultural economics, animal science, international agriculture, plant science, range/farm management, and soil science), BIOLOGICAL SCIENCE (avian sciences, bacteriology, biochemistry, biology/biological science, botany, ecology, entomology, environmental biology, genetics, microbiology, nutrition, physiology, toxicology, wildlife biology, and zoology), BUSINESS (organizational behavior), COMMUNICATIONS AND THE ARTS (art history and appreciation, Chinese, communications, comparative literature, design, dramatic arts, English, fine arts, French, German, Greek, Italian, Japanese, Latin, linguistics, music, Russian, Spanish, speech/debate/rhetoric, and studio art), COMPUTER AND PHYSICAL SCIENCE (atmospheric sciences and meteorology, chemistry, computer science, geology, hydrology, mathematics, physics, polymer science, and statistics), EDUCATION (physical education), ENGINEERING AND ENVIRONMENTAL DESIGN (aeronautical engineering, agricultural engineering, bioengineering, chemical engineering, civil engineering, computer engineering, electrical/electronics engineering, environmental design, environmental science, landscape architecture/design, materials engineering, and mechanical engineering), HEALTH PROFESSIONS (community health work and environmental health science), SOCIAL SCIENCE (African studies, American studies, anthropology, behavioral science, classical/ancient civilization, dietetics, East Asian studies, economics, food science, geography, history, human development, human ecology, international relations, medieval studies, Mexican-American/Chicano studies, Native American studies, philosophy, political science/government, psychology, religion, social science, sociology, textiles and clothing, and women's studies). Agricultural, biological, and biotechnical sciences are the strongest academically. Biological science, biochemistry, and psychology are the largest.

Special: There are credit and noncredit internship programs. Study abroad in more than 32 countries and a Washington semester are offered. Students may participate in college work-study, federal work-study, and California work-study programs. Several A.B.-B.S. degrees are offered. Students may design their own majors, take dual majors, and elect pass/fail options. Interdisciplinary majors are offered in African American and African studies, American studies, Mexican American studies, comparative literature, East Asian studies, exercise science, international relations, linguistics, medieval studies, Native American studies, religious studies, and women's studies. There are 24 national honor societies, including Phi Beta Kappa, a freshman honors program, and 3 departmental honors programs.

Admissions: 47% of the 2009-2010 applicants were accepted. The SAT scores for the 2009-2010 freshman class were: Critical Reading--19% below 500, 39% between 500 and 599, 33% between 600 and 700, and 9% above 700; Math--12% below 500, 26% between 500 and 599, 45% between 600 and 700, and 18% above 700; Writing--18% below 500, 37% between 500 and 599, 36% between 600 and 700, and 9% above 700. 99% of the current freshmen were in the top fifth of their class; 99% were in the top two fifths.

Requirements: The SAT or ACT is required. The ACT Optional Writing test is also required. In addition, candidates for admission should have completed 4 units of English, 3 of math, and 2 each of foreign language, history/social science, lab science, and college preparatory electives, for a total of 15 units. 2 SAT Subject Tests are required in 2 different areas. A GPA of 3.0 is required. AP credits are accepted. Important factors in the admissions decision are advanced placement or honors courses, evidence of special talent, and leadership record.

Procedure: Freshmen are admitted fall, winter, and spring. Entrance exams should be taken by December of the senior year. There is a deferred admissions plan. Applications should be filed by November 30 for fall entry. The fall 2009 application fee was $60. Notifications are sent March 15. Applications are accepted on-line.

Financial Aid: In 2009-2010, 54% of all full-time freshmen received some form of financial aid. 51% of all full-time freshmen received need-based aid. The average freshman award was $15,811. Need-based scholarships or need-based grants averaged $12,361; need-based self-help aid (loans and jobs) averaged $5305; non-need-based athletic scholarships averaged $10,804; and other non-need-based awards and non-need-based scholarships averaged $4763. The average financial indebtedness of the 2009 graduate was $15,155. UC Davis is a member of CSS. The FAFSA is required. The deadline for filing freshman financial aid applications for fall entry is March 2.

Computers: Wireless access is available. All students may access the system. There are no time limits and no fees. It is strongly recommended that all students have a personal computer.

UNIVERSITY OF CALIFORNIA AT IRVINE

Irvine, CA 92697-1075   (949) 824-6703; (949) 824-2711

Full-time: 9500 men, 10,000 women	**Faculty:** I, +$
Part-time: 500 men, 350 women	**Ph.D.s:** n/av
Graduate: 2085 men, 1330 women	**Student/Faculty:** n/av
Year: trimesters, summer session	**Tuition:** $10,000 ($30,000)
Application Deadline: November 30	**Room & Board:** $11,000
Freshman Class: n/av	
SAT or ACT: required	**HIGHLY COMPETITIVE**

The University of California, Irvine, founded in 1965, is a public research university and part of the University of California System. The figures given in the above capsule and in this profile are approximate. There are 8 undergraduate schools and 3 graduate schools. In addition to regional accreditation, UCI has baccalaureate program accreditation with AACSB and ABET. The 3 libraries contain 2.6 million volumes, 2.6 million microform items, and 101,335 audio/video tapes/CDs/DVDs, and subscribe to 28,416 periodicals including electronic. Computerized library services include interlibrary loans and database searching. Special learning facilities include a learning resource center, art gallery, planetarium, radio station, a freshwater marsh reserve, an arboretum, a laser institute, and numerous research centers. The 1489-acre campus is in a suburban area 40 miles south of Los Angeles. Including any residence halls, there are 418 buildings.

Programs of Study: UCI confers B.A., B.S., B.F.A., and B.Mus. degrees. Master's and doctoral degrees are also awarded. Bachelor's degrees are awarded in BIOLOGICAL SCIENCE (biology/biological science and ecology), COMMUNICATIONS AND THE ARTS (art history and appreciation, Chinese, classics, comparative literature, dance, dramatic arts, English, film arts, French, German, Japanese, linguistics, music, Spanish, and studio art), COMPUTER AND PHYS-

ICAL SCIENCE (chemistry, information sciences and systems, mathematics, and physics), ENGINEERING AND ENVIRONMENTAL DESIGN (aeronautical engineering, chemical engineering, civil engineering, computer engineering, electrical/electronics engineering, engineering, environmental design, environmental engineering, and mechanical engineering), SOCIAL SCIENCE (anthropology, classical/ancient civilization, criminology, crosscultural studies, East Asian studies, economics, history, human ecology, humanities, international studies, philosophy, political science/government, psychology, social science, sociology, and women's studies). Biological sciences, political science, and economics are the strongest academically. Biological sciences, social ecology, and economics are the largest.

Special: Students may study abroad in Spain, England, India, Kenya, Sweden, and Egypt. UCI also offers internships, a Washington semester, work-study programs with the university, B.A.-B.S. degrees, dual majors, and pass/fail options. There are 3 national honor societies, including Phi Beta Kappa, a freshman honors program, and 14 departmental honors programs.

Requirements: The SAT or ACT is required, required minimum scores are determined by an eligibility index. In addition, SAT II: Subject tests in writing, math, and a third chosen from science, social science, foreign language, or English literature are required. Applicants need 15 academic credits, including 4 years of English, 3 in math, and 2 each in foreign language, history/social science, lab science, and electives. An additional year each in foreign language, math, and science is recommended. An essay also is needed. The GED is accepted. AP credits are accepted.

Procedure: Freshmen are admitted in the fall. Entrance exams should be taken no later than December of the senior year. Applications should be filed by November 30 for fall entry. The fall 2009 application fee was $40. Notifications are sent March 30. Applications are accepted on-line.

Financial Aid: UCI is a member of CSS. The FAFSA and GPA verification form to state agency is required. Check with the school for current application deadlines.

Computers: All students may access the system 24 hours a day. Students are limited to 2-hour sessions. There are no fees.

UNIVERSITY OF CALIFORNIA AT LOS ANGELES

Los Angeles, CA 90095 (310) 825-3101; (310) 206-1206

Full-time: 11,336 men, 14,420 women	**Faculty:** I, +$
Part-time: 513 men, 418 women	**Ph.D.s:** 98%
Graduate: 6962 men, 6335 women	**Student/Faculty:** n/av
Year: trimesters, summer session	**Tuition:** $8851 ($31,568)
Application Deadline: November 30	**Room & Board:** $13,314
Freshman Class: n/av	
SAT or ACT required	**MOST COMPETITIVE**

University of California at Los Angeles (UCLA), founded in 1919, is a public institution offering undergraduate and graduate degrees. Its disciplines include arts and sciences, engineering, applied science, health sciences, law, management, and theater, film, and television. Some of the figures in the above capsule and in this profile are approximate. There are 5 undergraduate schools and 12 graduate schools. In addition to regional accreditation, UCLA has baccalaureate program accreditation with AACSB, ABET, ADA, CSAB, CSWE, FIDER, NAAB, and NLN. The 13 libraries contain 9 million volumes, 6.2 million microform items, and 316,523 audio/video tapes/CDs/DVDs, and subscribe to 38,975 periodicals including electronic. Computerized library services include interlibrary loans, database searching, and Internet access. Special learning facilities include a learning resource center, art gallery, natural history museum, planetarium, radio station, and TV station. The 419-acre campus is in an urban area in Los Angeles. Including any residence halls, there are 174 buildings.

Programs of Study: UCLA confers B.A., B.S., and B.A.S degrees. Master's and doctoral degrees are also awarded. Bachelor's degrees are awarded in AGRI-CULTURE (environmental studies), BIOLOGICAL SCIENCE (biochemistry, biology/biological science, biophysics, cell biology, ecology, marine biology, microbiology, molecular biology, neurosciences, and physiology), BUSINESS (business economics), COMMUNICATIONS AND THE ARTS (American literature, Arabic, art, art history and appreciation, Chinese, classics, communications, dramatic arts, English, film arts, French, German, Greek, Hebrew, Italian, Japanese, Korean, Latin, linguistics, music, music history and appreciation, musicology/ethnomusicology, Portuguese, Russian languages and literature, Scandinavian languages, and Spanish), COMPUTER AND PHYSICAL SCIENCE (applied mathematics, astrophysics, atmospheric sciences and meteorology, chemistry, computer science, earth science, geology, geophysics and seismology, mathematics, physics, and statistics), EDUCATION (mathematics education), ENGINEERING AND ENVIRONMENTAL DESIGN (aeronautical engineering, aerospace studies, architecture, bioengineering, biomedical engineering, chemical engineering, civil engineering, computer engineering, electrical/electronics engineering, environmental science, geological engineering, materials engineering, materials science, and mechanical engineering), HEALTH PROFESSIONS (nursing), SOCIAL SCIENCE (African studies, African American studies, American Indian studies, anthropology, Asian/American studies, Asian/Oriental studies, classical/ancient civilization, cognitive science, East Asian studies, economics, European studies, French studies, geography, history, international studies, Italian studies, Judaic studies, Latin American studies, Mexican-American/Chicano studies, Middle Eastern studies, Near Eastern studies, philosophy, political science/government, psychobiology, psychology, religion, Russian and Slavic studies, sociology, South Asian studies, Spanish studies, and women's studies). Economics, psychology, and political science are the largest.

Special: Opportunities are provided for internships, work-study programs, study abroad in 33 countries, B.A.-B.S. degrees, student-designed majors, dual majors, and interdisciplinary majors, including chemistry and materials science, Chicana and Chicano studies, and math and engineering. There is a Washington, D.C., program for 20 to 30 students selected each fall and spring. There are 21 national honor societies, including Phi Beta Kappa, a freshman honors program, and all departments have honors programs.

Admissions: 22% of the 2009-2010 applicants were accepted. The SAT scores for the 2009-2010 freshman class were: Critical Reading--8% below 500, 28% between 500 and 599, 48% between 600 and 700, and 16% above 700; Math--4% below 500, 17% between 500 and 599, 42% between 600 and 700, and 37% above 700; Writing--6% below 500, 23% between 500 and 599, 43% between 600 and 700, and 28% above 700. The ACT scores were 8% below 21, 13% between 21 and 23, 18% between 24 and 26, 13% between 27 and 28, and 48% above 28.

Requirements: The SAT or ACT is required. The ACT Optional Writing test is also required. In addition, all applicants must take 2 SAT Subject tests in 2 different subject areas. (If a Math SAT Subject test is chosen, it must be the Math Level 2). Graduation from an accredited secondary school is required. Applicants must submit a challenging academic program, including honors and AP-level courses in English, math, a language other than English, science, and history and social science; most students complete at least 42 semester courses in these areas. An essay is required, and a portfolio and audition are required for all art, theater, and film and television majors. AP credits are accepted. Important factors in the admissions decision are advanced placement or honors courses, evidence of special talent, and leadership record.

Procedure: Freshmen are admitted in fall. Entrance exams should be taken preferably in the junior year, but no later than December of the senior year. Applications should be filed by November 30 for fall entry. The fall 2009 application fee was $60. Notifications are sent March 15. Applications are accepted on-line.

Financial Aid: In 2009-2010, 67% of all full-time freshmen and 64% of continuing full-time students received some form of financial aid. 49% of all full-time freshmen and 49% of continuing full-time students received need-based aid. The average freshman award was $16,568. Need-based scholarships or need-based grants averaged $13,643; need-based self-help aid (loans and jobs) averaged $5239; non-need-based athletic shcolarships averaged $15,726; and other non-need-based awards and non-need-based scholarships averaged $5026. 28% of undergraduate students work part-time. Average annual earnings from campus work are $3349. The average financial indebtedness of the 2009 graduate was $16,733. The FAFSA and the college's own financial statement are required. The deadline for filing freshman financial aid applications for fall entry is March 2.

Computers: Wireless access is available. All students may access the system 24 hours a day, 7 days a week. Time limits vary by individual department. There are no fees.

UNIVERSITY OF CALIFORNIA AT SAN DIEGO
La Jolla, CA 92093 (858) 534-4831

Full-time: 9775 men, 10700 women	**Faculty:** I, +$
Part-time: none	**Ph.D.s:** n/av
Graduate: 2160 men, 1475 women	**Student/Faculty:** n/av
Year: trimesters, summer session	**Tuition:** $9000 ($22,000)
Application Deadline: November 30	**Room & Board:** $12,000
Freshman Class: n/av	
SAT or ACT: required	**VERY COMPETITIVE**

University of California at San Diego, founded in 1960, is a public liberal arts institution. The figures given in the above capsule and in this profile are approximate. There are 6 undergraduate schools and 5 graduate schools. In addition to regional accreditation, UCSD has baccalaureate program accreditation with ABET. The 10 libraries contain 2.6 million volumes, 2.9 million microform items, and 87,625 audio/video tapes/CDs/DVDs, and subscribe to 24,986 periodicals including electronic. Computerized library services include interlibrary loans, database searching, and Internet access. Special learning facilities include an art gallery, radio station, TV station, aquarium-museum, supercomputer center, and theater. The 1976-acre campus is in a suburban area 12 miles north of downtown San Diego. Including any residence halls, there are 501 buildings.

Programs of Study: UCSD confers B.A. and B.S. degrees. Master's and doctoral degrees are also awarded. Bachelor's degrees are awarded in AGRICULTURE (animal science and environmental studies), BIOLOGICAL SCIENCE (biochemistry, bioinformatics, biology/biological science, biophysics, biotechnology, ecology, microbiology, molecular biology, and physiology), BUSINESS (management science), COMMUNICATIONS AND THE ARTS (art history and appreciation, Chinese, classics, communications, dance, dramatic arts, English literature, Germanic languages and literature, linguistics, literature, music, music history and appreciation, music technology, studio art, and visual and performing arts), COMPUTER AND PHYSICAL SCIENCE (applied mathematics, applied physics, chemistry, computer science, earth science, information sciences and systems, mathematics, physical chemistry, and physics), EDUCATION (mathematics education and science education), ENGINEERING AND ENVIRON-MENTAL DESIGN (aerospace studies, bioengineering, chemical engineering, computer engineering, electrical/electronics engineering, engineering, engineering physics, environmental engineering, environmental science, and mechanical engineering), SOCIAL SCIENCE (anthropology, cognitive science, economics, ethnic studies, French studies, gender studies, history, human development, international studies, Italian studies, Japanese studies, Judaic studies, Latin American studies, philosophy, political science/government, psychology, religion, Russian and Slavic studies, sociology, Spanish studies, Third World studies, and urban studies). Sciences, engineering, and the arts are the strongest academically. Biology, economics, and psychology are the largest.

Special: Internships in many fields, work-study, study abroad in more than 30 countries, and a Washington semester are offered. B.A.-B.S. degrees, an accelerated degree, dual majors, student-designed majors, and exchange programs with Dartmouth College, Spelman College, and Morehouse College are available. Nondegree study, credit for military experience, and pass/fail options are possible. There are 2 national honor societies, including Phi Beta Kappa, a freshman honors program, and 14 departmental honors programs.

Requirements: The SAT or ACT is required. In addition, the SAT Reasoning Test with critical reading, math and writing, or ACT Assesment plus Writing, and 2 SAT Subject Tests in two different areas: history/social science, literature, math (Level 2 only), science or language other than English, are required. Tests must be taken by December of senior year. A GPA of 2.8 is required. AP credits are accepted. Important factors in the admissions decision are advanced placement or honors courses, leadership record, and extracurricular activities record.

Procedure: Freshmen are admitted in the fall. Entrance exams should be taken by December of the senior year. Applications should be filed by November 30 for fall entry, along with a $55 fee. Notifications are sent March 30. Applications are accepted on-line.

Financial Aid: UCSD is a member of CSS. The FAFSA and the state aid form are required. Check with the school for current application deadlines.

Computers: All students may access the system 24 hours every day. There are no time limits and no fees. It is strongly recommended that all students have a personal computer.

UNIVERSITY OF CALIFORNIA AT SANTA BARBARA

Santa Barbara, CA 93106   (805) 893-2881; (805) 893-2676

Full-time: 8887 men, 10,420 women	**Faculty:** 919; I, +$
Part-time: 287 men, 202 women	**Ph.D.s:** 100%
Graduate: 1642 men, 1412 women	**Student/Faculty:** 20 to 1
Year: trimesters, summer session	**Tuition:** $9077 ($31,746)
Application Deadline: November 30	**Room & Board:** $12,405
Freshman Class: 44724 applied, 21540 accepted, 4587 enrolled	
SAT CR/M/W: 593/612/596	**ACT:** 27 **HIGHLY COMPETITIVE**

The University of California at Santa Barbara, founded in 1909, is a public liberal arts institution offering programs in creative studies, engineering, and letters and science. There are 3 undergraduate schools and 1 graduate school. In addition to regional accreditation, UCSB has baccalaureate program accreditation with ABET and CSAB. The library contains 3.4 million volumes, 3.8 million microform items, and 146,142 audio/video tapes/CDs/DVDs, and subscribes to 36,990 periodicals including electronic. Computerized library services include Internet access. Special learning facilities include a learning resource center, art gallery, radio station, language and learning lab, and numerous national and multicampus research institutes. The 1055-acre campus is in a suburban area 10 miles north of Santa Barbara. Including any residence halls, there are 300 buildings.

Programs of Study: UCSB confers B.A., B.F.A., B.M., and B.S. degrees. Master's and doctoral degrees are also awarded. Bachelor's degrees are awarded in BIOLOGICAL SCIENCE (biochemistry, biology/biological science, cell biology, ecology, evolutionary biology, marine biology, microbiology, molecular biology, physiology, and zoology), BUSINESS (business economics), COMMUNICATIONS AND THE ARTS (art, art history and appreciation, Chinese, classics, communications, comparative literature, dance, dramatic arts, English, film arts, French, German, Germanic languages and literature, Japanese, linguistics, literature, music, music performance, music theory and composition, Portuguese, Slavic languages, and Spanish), COMPUTER AND PHYSICAL SCIENCE (chemistry, computer science, earth science, geology, geophysics and seismology, hydrology, mathematics, physics, and statistics), ENGINEERING AND ENVIRONMENTAL DESIGN (chemical engineering, computer engineering, electrical/electronics engineering, environmental science, and mechanical engineering), HEALTH PROFESSIONS (pharmacy), SOCIAL SCIENCE (African American studies, anthropology, Asian/American studies, Asian/Oriental studies, biopsychology, economics, geography, history, interdisciplinary studies, international studies, Islamic studies, Italian studies, Latin American studies, medieval studies, Mexican-American/Chicano studies, Middle Eastern studies, philosophy, political science/government, psychology, religion, sociology, and women's studies). Business economics, biological science, and psychology are the largest.

Special: A Washington semester, internships, cross-registration with all University of California campuses, study abroad in 34 countries, work-study programs, dual majors, student-designed majors, the B.A.-B.S. degree, and an accelerated degree program in electrical engineering are offered. There are 3 national honor societies, including Phi Beta Kappa, and a freshman honors program.

Admissions: 48% of the 2009-2010 applicants were accepted. The SAT scores for the 2009-2010 freshman class were: Critical Reading--13% below 500, 37% between 500 and 599, 39% between 600 and 700, and 11% above 700; Math--12% below 500, 28% between 500 and 599, 45% between 600 and 700, and 15%

above 700; Writing--13% below 500, 34% between 500 and 599, 43% between 600 and 700, and 10% above 700. The ACT scores were 11% below 21, 13% between 21 and 23, 21% between 24 and 26, 18% between 27 and 28, and 37% above 28. 98% of the current freshmen were in the top fifth of their class; 100% were in the top two fifths. There were 3 National Merit finalists.

Requirements: The SAT is required, as well as SAT Subject tests in math and 1 other choice. The ACT is recommended. Candidates for admission must have completed 4 years of English, 3 of math, and 2 each of foreign language, lab science, history/social science, and college-preparatory electives. An additional year each in foreign language, math, and science is recommended. A GPA of 3.3 is required. AP credits are accepted.

Procedure: Freshmen are admitted fall. Entrance exams should be taken by December of the senior year. Applications should be filed by November 30 for fall entry, along with a $60 fee. Notifications are sent March 1. Applications are accepted on-line.

Financial Aid: In 2008-2009, 44% of continuing full-time students received some form of financial aid, including need-based aid. The average financial indebtedness of a 2008 graduate was $15,808. UCSB is a member of CSS. The FAFSA is required. The deadline for filing freshman financial aid applications for fall entry is March 2.

Computers: Wireless access is available. UCSB has more than 255 computers in 17 open access computing labs across campus for student use. All of the major buildings, including the student center and the library, have access to the wireless network. All of the residence halls have access to the residential life wireless network and several have computing labs. All students may access the system at any time, if they have their own computer and modem. There are no time limits and no fees.

UNIVERSITY OF CALIFORNIA AT SANTA CRUZ

Santa Cruz, CA 95064	(831) 459-4008; (831) 459-4452
Full-time: 6605 men, 7600 women	**Faculty:** I, av$
Part-time: 70 men, 110 women	**Ph.D.s:** 98%
Graduate: 705 men, 740 women	**Student/Faculty:** n/av
Year: varies, summer session	**Tuition:** $8000 ($27,500)
Application Deadline: see profile	**Room & Board:** $13,000
Freshman Class: n/av	
SAT or ACT: required	**VERY COMPETITIVE**

University of California, Santa Cruz, opened in 1965, is a public institution offering programs in the arts, engineering, humanities, physical and biological sciences, and social sciences. Figures in the above capsule are approximate. There are 10 undergraduate schools and 1 graduate school. In addition to regional accreditation, UCSC has baccalaureate program accreditation with ABET. The 2 libraries contain 1.5 million volumes, 729,698 microform items, and 63,002 audio/video tapes/CDs/DVDs, and subscribe to 28,264 periodicals including electronic. Computerized library services include interlibrary loans, database searching, and Internet access. Special learning facilities include a learning resource center, art gallery, natural history museum, radio station, TV station, agroecology program farm, arboretum, Long Marine Lab, and Lick Observatory on Mt. Hamilton. The 2000-acre campus is in a small town 30 miles southwest of San Jose and 75 miles south of San Francisco. Including any residence halls, there are 471 buildings.

Programs of Study: UCSC confers B.A., B.S., and B.M. degrees. Master's and doctoral degrees are also awarded. Bachelor's degrees are awarded in AGRICULTURE (environmental studies and plant science), BIOLOGICAL SCIENCE (biochemistry, bioinformatics, biology/biological science, cell biology, ecology, evolutionary biology, marine biology, molecular biology, and neurosciences), BUSINESS (business economics and international economics), COMMUNICATIONS AND THE ARTS (art, art history and appreciation, classical languages, dramatic arts, film arts, language arts, linguistics, literature, and music), COMPUTER AND PHYSICAL SCIENCE (chemistry, computer science, earth science, geology, information sciences and systems, mathematics, and physics), ENGINEERING AND ENVIRONMENTAL DESIGN (computer engineering and electrical/electronics engineering), HEALTH PROFESSIONS (health science), SOCIAL SCIENCE (American studies, anthropology, community services, economics, German area studies, history, Italian studies, Latin American studies, law, philosophy, political science/government, psychology, sociology, and women's studies). Psychology, business management economics, and art are the largest.

Special: Cross-registration is possible with other University of California campuses, Hampshire College, the University of New Hampshire, and the University of New Mexico. UCSC also offers work-study, a Washington semester, internships in many arenas, study abroad in 34 countries, student-designed majors, dual majors, and a B.A.-B.S. degree in earth sciences, chemistry, and computer science. There is a Phi Beta Kappa honors program and a freshman honors program.

Requirements: The SAT or ACT is required. The ACT Optional Writing test is also required. In addition, applicants must be graduates of an accredited secondary school or have a GED certificate. They should have completed 15 academic credits, including 4 years of English, 3 of math, and 2 each of foreign language, history, lab science, visual or performing arts, and college preparatory electives. Auditions are required for music majors, and portfolios are required for art majors. All students must submit a personal statement. Nonresidents must meet additional requirements. A GPA of 2.8 is required. AP credits are accepted. Important factors in the admissions decision are advanced placement or honors courses, evidence of special talent, and extracurricular activities record.

Procedure: Freshmen are admitted fall and winter. Entrance exams should be taken by December of the senior year. Check with the school for current application deadlines. The fall 2009 application fee was $55. Applications are accepted on-line.

Financial Aid: In a recent year, 47% of all full-time freshmen and 46% of continuing full-time students received some form of financial aid. 40% of all students received need-based aid. The FAFSA is required. Check with the school for current application deadlines.

Computers: Wireless access is available. Students have access to high-speed Internet in their rooms and at any one of 15 open-access computer labs throughout campus. All students may access the system. There are no time limits and no fees. It is strongly recommended that all students have a personal computer.

UNIVERSITY OF CENTRAL ARKANSAS

Conway, AR 72035-0001

(501) 450-3128
(800) 243-8245; (501) 450-5228

Full-time: 3810 men, 5215 women	**Faculty:** IIA, --$
Part-time: 975 men, 990 women	**Ph.D.s:** 58%
Graduate: 455 men, 1500 women	**Student/Faculty:** n/av
Year: semesters, summer session	**Tuition:** $6062 ($10,892)
Application Deadline: see profile	**Room & Board:** $4600
Freshman Class: n/av	
SAT or ACT: required	**VERY COMPETITIVE**

The University of Central Arkansas, established in 1907, is a comprehensive public institution offering undergraduate and graduate degrees in liberal arts, business, health-related sciences, and education. There are 7 undergraduate schools and 1 graduate school. In addition to regional accreditation, UCA has baccalaureate program accreditation with AACSB, ADA, APTA, CAHEA, NASAD, NASM, NCATE, and NLN. The library contains 440,376 volumes, 611,411 microform items, and 8,024 audio/video tapes/CDs/DVDs, and subscribes to 17,277 periodicals including electronic. Computerized library services include interlibrary loans, database searching, Internet access, and laptop Internet portals. Special learning facilities include a learning resource center, art gallery, planetarium, radio station, and TV station. The 262-acre campus is in a small town 29 miles north of Little Rock. Including any residence halls, there are 53 buildings.

Programs of Study: UCA confers B.A., B.S., B.S.E., B.P.S., B.B.A., B.F.A., B.M., and B.S.N. degrees. Associates, master's, and doctoral degrees are also awarded. Bachelor's degrees are awarded in BIOLOGICAL SCIENCE (biology/biological science), BUSINESS (accounting, banking and finance, business administration and management, business economics, insurance and risk management, and marketing/retailing/merchandising), COMMUNICATIONS AND THE ARTS (communications, English, French, journalism, music, Spanish, and speech/debate/rhetoric), COMPUTER AND PHYSICAL SCIENCE (chemistry, computer science, information sciences and systems, mathematics, and physics), EDUCATION (art education, athletic training, early childhood education, education of the exceptional child, elementary education, foreign languages education, guidance education, library science, middle school education, music education, physical education, science education, secondary education, and special education), ENGINEERING AND ENVIRONMENTAL DESIGN (environmental science, interior design, and preengineering), HEALTH PROFESSIONS (exercise science, health care administration, health science, medical technology, nuclear medical technology, nursing, occupational therapy, physical therapy, predentistry, premedicine, preoptometry, prepharmacy, preveterinary science, radiological science, and speech pathology/audiology), SOCIAL SCIENCE (dietetics, economics, family/consumer studies, geography, gerontology, history, philosophy, political science/government, psychology, public administration, religion, and sociology). Business, health-related sciences, and education are the strongest academically. Health professions and related sciences, business/marketing, and education are the largest.

Special: Study abroad, work-study programs, a B.S.-B.A. degree, a 3-2 engineering degree with the University of Arkansas at Fayetteville, dual majors, nondegree study, and pass/fail options are available. Co-op programs in business, computer science, and health sciences and internships in education are also possible.

There are 11 national honor societies, a freshman honors program, and 25 departmental honors programs.

Requirements: The SAT or ACT is required. AP and CLEP credits are accepted. Important factors in the admissions decision are advanced placement or honors courses, evidence of special talent, and recommendations by school officials.

Procedure: Freshmen are admitted to all sessions. There is a rolling admissions plan. Application deadlines are open. Applications are accepted on-line.

Financial Aid: The FAFSA is required. Check with the school for current application deadlines.

Computers: Wireless access is available. UCA's academic buildings are all wireless. For anyone to log in, they just need to know their student/staff/faculty user name and password. PCs are located all throughout campus with approximately 643 ready for general student use at all times. All students may access the system. There are no time limits and no fees. It is strongly recommended that all students have a personal computer.

UNIVERSITY OF CENTRAL FLORIDA
Orlando, FL 32816-0111 (407) 823-3000; (407) 823-3419

Full-time: 14,165 men, 16,890 women	**Faculty:** I, --$
Part-time: 4685 men, 5590 women	**Ph.D.s:** 79%
Graduate: 2965 men, 4220 women	**Student/Faculty:** n/av
Year: semesters, summer session	**Tuition:** $4000 ($18,000)
Application Deadline: see profile	**Room & Board:** $8500
Freshman Class: n/av	
SAT or ACT: required	**COMPETITIVE**

University of Central Florida, founded in 1963 and part of the State University System of Florida, offers programs in liberal and fine arts, business, engineering, health science, professional training, and teacher preparation and graduate and research programs in optics, biotechnology, simulation, computer science, and other areas. Figures in the above capsule and this profile are approximate. There are 10 undergraduate schools and 10 graduate schools. In addition to regional accreditation, UCF has baccalaureate program accreditation with AACSB, ABET, CSAB, CSWE, NASM, NCATE, and NLN. The library contains 1.7 million volumes, 2.6 million microform items, and 42,610 audio/video tapes/CDs/DVDs, and subscribes to 16,368 periodicals including electronic. Computerized library services include interlibrary loans, database searching, and Internet access. Special learning facilities include a learning resource center, art gallery, radio station, observatory, arboretum, center for research and education in optics and lasers, institute for simulation and training, the Florida Solar Energy Center, and the Biomolecular Science Center. The 1415-acre campus is in a suburban area 13 miles northeast of downtown Orlando. Including any residence halls, there are 147 buildings.

Programs of Study: UCF confers B.A., B.S., B.A.B.A., B.A.S., B.F.A., B.M., B.M.E., B.S.A.E., B.S.B.A., B.S.C.E., B.S.Con.E., B.S.Cp.E., B.S.E.E., B.S.E.E.T., B.S.Env.E., B.S.E.T., B.S.I.E., B.S.M.E., B.S.N., and B.S.W. degrees. Associates, master's, and doctoral degrees are also awarded. Bachelor's degrees are awarded in BIOLOGICAL SCIENCE (biology/biological science and microbiology), BUSINESS (accounting, banking and finance, business administration and management, hospitality management services, management information systems, management science, and marketing/retailing/merchandising), COMMUNICATIONS AND THE ARTS (advertising, art, broadcasting, communications, dramatic arts, English, film arts, fine arts, French, journalism, languages, music, public relations, and Spanish), COMPUTER AND PHYSICAL SCIENCE (chemistry, computer science, digital arts/technology, mathematics, physics, and statistics), EDUCATION (art education, business education, early childhood education, education of the exceptional child, elementary education, English education, foreign languages education, mathematics education, music education, physical education, science education, social science education, special education, and vocational education), ENGINEERING AND ENVIRONMENTAL DESIGN (aeronautical engineering, aerospace studies, civil engineering, computer engineering, electrical/electronics engineering, electrical/electronics engineering technology, engineering technology, environmental engineering, industrial engineering technology, and mechanical engineering), HEALTH PROFESSIONS (health care administration, health science, medical laboratory technology, nursing, radiological science, respiratory therapy, and speech pathology/audiology), SOCIAL SCIENCE (anthropology, criminal justice, economics, forensic studies, history, humanities, law, liberal arts/general studies, philosophy, political science/government, psychology, public administration, social science, social work, and sociology). Engineering, business administration, and computer science are the strongest academically. Business, education, and psychology are the largest.

Special: Internships are available in most majors through UCF's extensive partnerships with area businesses and industries such as NASA, Disney, Universal Studios, and AT&T. Students may participate in study abroad and co-op and work-study programs, earn B.A.-B.S. degrees or a liberal studies degree, or pursue dual majors. Nondegree study and pass/fail options are available. There is a 3-4 medical degree program with the University of South Florida. There are 42 national honor societies, a freshman honors program, and 47 departmental honors programs.

Admissions: There were 43 National Merit finalists in a recent year.

Requirements: The SAT or ACT is required. The ACT Optional Writing test is also required. GPA and standardized test scores are rated on a sliding scale. A high school diploma or GED is required. Applicants should have completed 4 units of English, 3 each of math, science (2 with labs), and social studies, and 2 of a foreign language, plus 3 of academic electives. A GPA of 2.0 is required. AP and CLEP credits are accepted. Important factors in the admissions decision are advanced placement or honors courses, evidence of special talent, and leadership record.

Procedure: Freshmen are admitted to all sessions. Entrance exams should be taken during the junior year or the first semester of the senior year. There is a rolling admissions plan. Check with the school for current application deadlines. The fall 2009 application fee was $30. Notification is sent on a rolling basis. Applications are accepted on-line. A waiting list is maintained.

Financial Aid: In a recent year, 95% of all full-time freshmen and 79% of continuing full-time students received some form of financial aid. 28% of all full-time freshmen and 38% of continuing full-time students received need-based aid. The average freshmen award was $5321. Need-based scholarships or need-based grants averaged $3592 ($10,110 maximum); need-based self-help aid (loans and jobs) averaged $2760 ($10,645 maximum); non-need-based athletic scholarships averaged $7879 ($12,307 maximum); and other non-need-based awards and non-need-based scholarships averaged $3990 ($31,349 maximum). 49% of undergraduate students work part-time. Average annual earnings from campus work are $5938. The average financial indebtedness of a recent graduate was $1623. The FAFSA is required. Check with the school for current application deadlines.

Computers: Wireless access is available. All UCF students have complete access to the university's wired and wireless network infrastructure and services. There is wireless network coverage in 100% of the interior spaces of all buildings, plus considerable outdoor wireless coverage. Students have access to the UCF network from 2926 personal computers located in public and departmental computer labs. In addition, all UCF residence halls have wireless network service. All students may access the system at all times. There are no time limits and no fees. It is strongly recommended that all students have a personal computer. Students enrolled in Digital Media must have a personal computer.

UNIVERSITY OF CHICAGO
Chicago, IL 60637   (773) 702-8650; (773) 702-4199

Full-time: 2562 men, 2513 women	**Faculty:** I, ++$
Part-time: 32 men, 27 women	**Ph.D.s:** 98%
Graduate: 5996 men, 4086 women	**Student/Faculty:** n/av
Year: trimesters, summer session	**Tuition:** $39,381
Application Deadline: January 2	**Room & Board:** $11,697
Freshman Class: 13,564 applied, 3708 accepted, 1335 enrolled	
SAT CR/M/W: 723/723/708	**ACT:** 30 **MOST COMPETITIVE**

The University of Chicago, founded in 1890, is a private liberal arts institution offering undergraduate and graduate programs with emphases on the biological and physical sciences, the humanities, and the social sciences. There are 11 graduate schools. In addition to regional accreditation, Chicago has baccalaureate program accreditation with NCATE. The 7 libraries contain 8.6 million volumes. Computerized library services include interlibrary loans, database searching, Internet access, and laptop Internet portals. Special learning facilities include a learning resource center, art gallery, radio station, film studies center, language labs, museum of Near Eastern antiquities, and Renaissance Society (contemporary art). The 211-acre campus is in an urban area in Chicago. Including any residence halls, there are 152 buildings.

Programs of Study: Chicago confers B.A. and B.S. degrees. Master's and doctoral degrees are also awarded. Bachelor's degrees are awarded in BIOLOGICAL SCIENCE (biochemistry and biology/biological science), COMMUNICATIONS AND THE ARTS (art history and appreciation, classics, comparative literature, East Asian languages and literature, English, film arts, German, linguistics, media arts, music, romance languages and literature, Russian, Slavic languages, and visual and performing arts), COMPUTER AND PHYSICAL SCIENCE (applied mathematics, chemistry, computer science, geoscience, mathematics, physics, and statistics), ENGINEERING AND ENVIRONMENTAL DESIGN (environmental science), SOCIAL SCIENCE (African American studies, anthropology, classical/ancient civilization, economics, gender studies, geography, history, humanities, interdisciplinary studies, international studies, Judaic studies, Latin American studies, law, medieval studies, Near Eastern studies, philosophy, political science/government, psychology, public affairs, religion, social science, sociology, and South Asian studies). Social sciences, biological and biomedical science, and foreign language are the largest.

Special: Special academic programs include cross-registration through the Committee on Institutional Cooperation, a summer internship in Washington, and study abroad in 18 countries. B.A.-B.S. and general studies degrees are offered, as are student-designed majors. Nondegree study and pass/fail options are possible. There are 2 national honor societies, including Phi Beta Kappa.

Admissions: 27% of the 2009-2010 applicants were accepted. The SAT scores for the 2009-2010 freshman class were: Critical Reading--7% between 500 and 599, 20% between 600 and 700; and 73% above 700; Math--1% below 500, 3% between 500 and 599, 26% between 600 and 700, and 70% above 700; Writing--1% below 500, 6% between 500 and 599, 30% between 600 and 700; and 63% above 700. The ACT scores were 5% between 21 and 23, 11% between 24 and 26, 17% between 27 and 28, and 67% above 29. 93% of the current freshmen were in the top fifth of their class. There were 137 National Merit finalists.

Requirements: The SAT or ACT is required. Other admissions criteria include a recommended secondary school curriculum of 4 years of English, 3 to 4 years each of history, social studies, math, and science, and 3 years of a foreign language. The GED is accepted. An essay must be submitted, and an interview is recommended. AP credits are accepted. Important factors in the admissions decision are advanced placement or honors courses, personality/intangible qualities, and extracurricular activities record.

Procedure: Freshmen are admitted in the fall. Entrance exams should be taken during the junior or senior year. There are early admissions and deferred admissions plans. Early decision applications should be filed by November 1; regular applications, by January 2 for fall entry, along with a $65 fee. Notification of early decision is sent December 15; regular decision, April 1. 2153 applicants were on the 2009 waiting list; 89 were admitted. Applications are accepted on-line.

Financial Aid: In 2009-2010, 48% of all full-time freshmen and 46% of continuing full-time students received some form of financial aid, including need-based aid. The average freshman award was $38,995. Chicago is a member of CSS. The CSS/Profile, FAFSA, and the college's own financial statement are required. The deadline for filing freshman financial aid applications for fall entry is February 1.

Computers: Wireless access is available. All students may access the system any time. There are no time limits and no fees.

UNIVERSITY OF CINCINNATI
Cincinnati, OH 45221-0127   (513) 556-1100; (513) 556-1105

Full-time: 9648 men, 8599 women	**Faculty:** 1187; I, --$
Part-time: 1200 men, 2437 women	**Ph.D.s:** 75%
Graduate: 3933 men, 5317 women	**Student/Faculty:** 15 to 1
Year: quarters, summer session	**Tuition:** $9399 ($23,922)
Application Deadline: July 31	**Room & Board:** $9702
Freshman Class: 15,270 applied, 11,413 accepted, 4301 enrolled	
SAT CR/M/W: 550/570/540	**ACT:** 24 COMPETITIVE+

The University of Cincinnati, founded in 1819, is a state-supported institution offering undergraduate programs in art and architecture, business, engineering, health science, liberal arts and sciences, music, and technical training. There are 12 undergraduate schools and 12 graduate schools. In addition to regional accreditation, UC has baccalaureate program accreditation with AACSB and NCATE. Computerized library services include interlibrary loans, database searching, and Internet access. Special learning facilities include a learning resource center, art gallery, and radio station. The 270-acre campus is in an urban area in downtown Cincinnati. Including any residence halls, there are 90 buildings.

Programs of Study: UC confers B.A., B.S., B.Arch., B.B.A., B.F.A., B.G.S., B.M., B.S.Des., B.S.E., B.S.I.M., B.S.N., B.S.Pharm., B.S.W, and B.U.P. degrees. Associate, master's, and doctoral degrees are also awarded. Bachelor's degrees are awarded in BIOLOGICAL SCIENCE (biochemistry and biology/

biological science), BUSINESS (accounting, banking and finance, business administration and management, management science, marketing/retailing/merchandising, and real estate), COMMUNICATIONS AND THE ARTS (broadcasting, communications, comparative literature, dance, design, digital communications, dramatic arts, English, fine arts, French, German, jazz, linguistics, music, music history and appreciation, music theory and composition, piano/organ, Spanish, theater design, and voice), COMPUTER AND PHYSICAL SCIENCE (chemical technology, chemistry, computer science, geology, information sciences and systems, mathematics, physics, and quantitative methods), EDUCATION (art education, business education, early childhood education, elementary education, foreign languages education, guidance education, health education, industrial arts education, middle school education, music education, nutrition education, science education, secondary education, and special education), ENGINEERING AND ENVIRONMENTAL DESIGN (aeronautical engineering, architectural engineering, architectural technology, chemical engineering, city/community/regional planning, civil engineering, computer engineering, construction management, electrical/electronics engineering, electrical/electronics engineering technology, engineering, engineering mechanics, engineering technology, industrial administration/management, industrial engineering technology, materials engineering, mechanical engineering, mechanical engineering technology, metallurgical engineering, and nuclear engineering), HEALTH PROFESSIONS (medical laboratory technology, nuclear medical technology, nursing, pharmacy, predentistry, premedicine, and speech pathology/audiology), SOCIAL SCIENCE (African American studies, anthropology, Asian/Oriental studies, classical/ancient civilization, criminal justice, economics, geography, history, international studies, Judaic studies, Latin American studies, liberal arts/general studies, philosophy, political science/government, prelaw, psychology, social science, social work, sociology, and urban studies). Architecture, music, and engineering are the strongest academically. Marketing, communications, and psychology are the largest.

Special: The Professional Practice Program, a 5-year cooperative plan offering alternate work in academic subjects and industry, is available for students in engineering, business, arts and sciences, design, architecture, and art. Study abroad is available in 29 countries. Nondegree study is possible. Honors programs include Phi Beta Kappa and a freshman honors program.

Admissions: 75% of the 2009-2010 applicants were accepted. The SAT scores for the 2009-2010 freshman class were: Critical Reading--26% below 500, 43% between 500 and 599, 26% between 600 and 700, and 5% above 700; Math--18% below 500, 41% between 500 and 599, 34% between 600 and 700, and 7% above 700; Writing--29% below 500, 46% between 500 and 599, 22% between 600 and 700, and 3% above 700. The ACT scores were 11% below 21, 29% between 21 and 23, 29% between 24 and 26, 14% between 27 and 28, and 17% above 28. 42% of the current freshmen were in the top fifth of their class; 68% were in the top two fifths. There were 28 National Merit finalists. 54 freshmen graduated first in their class.

Requirements: The SAT or ACT is required, with the ACT preferred. Applicants should be graduates of an accredited secondary school with 4 units of high school English, 3 of math, 2 each of science, social science, foreign language, and electives, and 1 of fine arts. A GPA of 2.0 is required. AP and CLEP credits are accepted.

Procedure: Freshmen are admitted to all sessions. Entrance exams should be taken in May of the junior year or January or March of the senior year. There is a rolling admissions plan. Applications should be filed by July 31 for fall entry, along with a $35 fee.

Financial Aid: In 2009-2010, 77% of all full-time freshmen and 72% of continuing full-time students received some form of financial aid. 45% of all full-time freshmen and 42% of continuing full-time students received need-based aid. The average freshman award was $8335. Need-based scholarships or need-based grants averaged $5889; need-based self-help aid (loans and jobs) averaged $1721; and non-need-based athletic scholarships averaged $18,097. The CSS/Profile and FAFSA are required. Check with the school for current application deadlines.

Computers: Wireless access is available. All students may access the system. There are no time limits and no fees.

UNIVERSITY OF COLORADO AT BOULDER

Boulder, CO 80309-0552	(303) 492-6301; (303) 492-7115
Full-time: 12,885 men, 11,864 women	**Faculty:** 1343; I, -$
Part-time: 994 men, 662 women	**Ph.D.s:** 90%
Graduate: 2786 men, 2145 women	**Student/Faculty:** 18 to 1
Year: semesters, summer session	**Tuition:** $7932 ($28,186)
Application Deadline: January 15	**Room & Board:** $10,378
Freshman Class: 19,649 applied, 16,514 accepted, 5555 enrolled	
SAT CR/M: 570/600	**ACT:** 26 **VERY COMPETITIVE+**

The University of Colorado at Boulder, established in 1876, is a public institution offering undergraduate and graduate programs in arts and sciences, business, engineering, architecture and planning, music, education, and journalism. There are 7 undergraduate schools and 3 graduate schools. In addition to regional accreditation, CU-Boulder has baccalaureate program accreditation with AACSB, ABET, ACEJMC, NASM, and NCATE. The 7 libraries contain 3.9 million volumes, 7.0 million microform items, and 1.1 million audio/video tapes/CDs/DVDs, and subscribe to 55,519 periodicals including electronic. Computerized library services include interlibrary loans, database searching, Internet access, and laptop Internet portals. Special learning facilities include a learning resource center, art gallery, natural history museum, planetarium, radio station, TV station, an interactive foreign language video center, a mountain research station, an integrated teaching and learning lab in engineering, and a multidisciplinary IT center in its own building in the center of campus. The 600-acre campus is in a suburban area 30 miles northwest of Denver. Including any residence halls, there are 200 buildings.

Programs of Study: CU-Boulder confers B.A., B.S., B.Env.D., B.F.A., B.A.Mus., B.Mus., and B.Mus.Ed. degrees. Master's and doctoral degrees are also awarded. Bachelor's degrees are awarded in BIOLOGICAL SCIENCE (biochemistry, ecology, and molecular biology), BUSINESS (accounting, banking and finance, business administration and management, management science, and marketing management), COMMUNICATIONS AND THE ARTS (advertising, art history and appreciation, broadcasting, Chinese, classics, communications, dance, dramatic arts, East Asian languages and literature, English, film arts, fine arts, French, Germanic languages and literature, Italian, Japanese, journalism, linguistics, music, Russian languages and literature, Spanish, and studio art), COMPUTER AND PHYSICAL SCIENCE (applied mathematics, astronomy, chemistry, computer science, geology, mathematics, and physics), EDUCATION (music education), ENGINEERING AND ENVIRONMENTAL DESIGN (aeronautical engineering, architectural engineering, bioengineering, chemical engineering, civil engineering, computer engineering, electrical/electronics engineering, engineering, engineering physics, environmental design, environmental engineering, environmental science, and mechanical engineering), HEALTH PROFESSIONS (exercise science and speech pathology/audiology), SOCIAL SCIENCE (anthropology, Asian/Oriental studies, ethnic studies, geography, history, humanities, international relations, philosophy, political science/government, psychology, religion, sociology, and women's studies). Physics, psychology, and integrative physiology are the strongest academically. Psychology, integrative physiology, and international affairs are the largest.

Special: 10 residential programs for freshmen and sophomores offer a small liberal arts college atmosphere while taking advantage of the resources of a major university. Student-designed and dual majors, internships, 5-year B.A.-M.A. degrees, and cooperative programs in engineering and computer science are available. Study abroad in more than 70 countries, work-study programs in federal labs, internships, a 3-2 engineering degree, and cross-registration with other University of Colorado campuses are offered. There are 26 national honor societies, including Phi Beta Kappa, and a freshman honors program. The journalism and engineering departments and all departments in arts and sciences have honors programs.

Admissions: 84% of the 2009-2010 applicants were accepted. The SAT scores for the 2009-2010 freshman class were: Critical Reading--15% below 500, 45% between 500 and 599, 36% between 600 and 700, and 5% above 700; Math--11% below 500, 38% between 500 and 599, 44% between 600 and 700, and 8% above 700. The ACT scores were 5% below 21, 19% between 21 and 23, 32% between 24 and 26, 20% between 27 and 28, and 24% above 28. 48% of the current freshmen were in the top fifth of their class; 82% were in the top two fifths. There were 13 National Merit finalists. 157 freshmen graduated first in their class.

Requirements: The SAT or ACT is required. In addition, applicants must have completed 17 credits of high school work as identified by the University of Colorado Minimum Academic Preparation Standards. Required application materials include 2 short-answer essay questions. Interviews are not used in the decision-making process. Auditions are required for consideration to the College of Music. Portfolios are discouraged. Students with a GED are considered on an individual basis and are encouraged to apply. A GPA of 2.0 is required. AP and CLEP credits are accepted.

Procedure: Freshmen are admitted fall, spring, and summer. Entrance exams should be taken no later than December of the senior year. There are early admissions and deferred admissions plans. Early notification applications should be filed by December 1; regular applications, by January 15 for fall entry, October 1 for spring entry, and January 15 for summer entry, along with a $50 fee. Early notification is December 2 to January 15; notification of regular decision is sent on or before April 1. Applications are accepted on-line. 926 applicants were on a recent waiting list, 81 were accepted.

Financial Aid: In 2009-2010, 86% of all full-time freshmen and 56% of continuing full-time students received some form of financial aid. 47% of all full-time freshmen and 38% of continuing full-time students received need-based aid. Need-based scholarships or need-based grants averaged $6930 ($50,465 maximum); need-based self-help aid (loans and jobs) averaged $5866 ($38,465 maximum); non-need-based athletic scholarships averaged $15,783 ($40,490 maximum); and other non-need-based awards and non-need-based scholarships averaged $4797 ($45,841 maximum). 24% of undergraduate students work part-time. Average annual earnings from campus work are $2490. The average financial indebtedness of the 2009 graduate was $14,354. The FAFSA and tax returns are required. Check with the school for current application deadlines.

Computers: Wireless access is available. There are about 70 PC labs and 150 kiosks throughout campus. Labs have either PCs or Macs and a variety of other hardware and software and high-speed access to the Internet. There is wireless network access in many of the public areas on campus and in some residence hall areas. Laptop checkout is available for students. All students may access the system 24 hours a day. There are no time limits and no fees. It is strongly recommended that all students have a personal computer.

UNIVERSITY OF COLORADO AT COLORADO SPRINGS

Colorado Springs, CO 80918   (719) 262-3383; (800) 990-8227

Full-time: 1850 men, 3000 women	**Faculty:** n/av
Part-time: 540 men, 780 women	**Ph.D.s:** 64%
Graduate: 595 men, 860 women	**Student/Faculty:** n/av
Year: semesters, summer session	**Tuition:** $5500 ($16,500)
Application Deadline: see profile	**Room & Board:** $8000
Freshman Class: n/av	
SAT or ACT: required	**VERY COMPETITIVE**

The University of Colorado at Colorado Springs, established in 1965, is a public institution, with programs in liberal arts, business, engineering, education, and nursing. Figures in the above capsule are approximate. There are 4 undergraduate schools and 5 graduate schools. In addition to regional accreditation, UCCS has baccalaureate program accreditation with AACSB, ABET, CSAB, NCATE, and NLN. The library contains 669,757 volumes, 432,872 microform items, and 5979 audio/video tapes/CDs/DVDs, and subscribes to 2247 periodicals including electronic. Computerized library services include interlibrary loans, database searching, and Internet access. Special learning facilities include a learning resource center, art gallery, center for excellence in oral communication, math learning center, science learning center, writing center, and language technology center. The 504-acre campus is in an urban area 70 miles south of Denver. Including any residence halls, there are 24 buildings.

Programs of Study: UCCS confers B.A. and B.S. degrees. Master's and doctoral degrees are also awarded. Bachelor's degrees are awarded in BIOLOGICAL SCIENCE (biology/biological science), BUSINESS (business administration and management), COMMUNICATIONS AND THE ARTS (communications, English, fine arts, and Spanish), COMPUTER AND PHYSICAL SCIENCE (chemistry, computer science, mathematics, and physics), ENGINEERING AND ENVIRONMENTAL DESIGN (electrical/electronics engineering), HEALTH PROFESSIONS (health care administration and nursing), SOCIAL SCIENCE (anthropology, economics, geography, history, philosophy, political science/government, psychology, and sociology). Business, engineering, and psychology are the strongest academically.

Special: The university offers work-study, dual majors, nondegree study, and pass/fail options. There are 3 national honor societies, including Phi Beta Kappa.

Requirements: The SAT or ACT is required. In addition, applicants must be graduates of an accredited secondary school. The GED is accepted. Secondary school courses must include 15 high school credits, including 4 years of English, 3 years each of math and science, 2 years each of foreign language and social studies, and 1 academic elective. AP and CLEP credits are accepted. Important factors in the admissions decision are advanced placement or honors courses, evidence of special talent, and recommendations by school officials.

Procedure: Freshmen are admitted to all sessions. Entrance exams should be taken during the senior year. There are deferred admissions and rolling admissions plans. Check with the school for current application deadlines. The application fee is $50. Applications are accepted on-line.

Financial Aid: The FAFSA is required. Check with the school for current application deadlines.

Computers: All students may access the system. There are no time limits and no fees. It is strongly recommended that all students have a personal computer.

UNIVERSITY OF CONNECTICUT
Storrs, CT 06269-3088   (860) 486-3137; (860) 486-1476

Full-time: 8170 men, 8166 women	**Faculty:** 1003; I, av$
Part-time: 390 men, 282 women	**Ph.D.s:** 94%
Graduate: 3851 men, 4170 women	**Student/Faculty:** 16 to 1
Year: semesters, summer session	**Tuition:** $10,416 ($26,880)
Application Deadline: February 1	**Room & Board:** $10,782
Freshman Class: 21,999 applied, 10,931 accepted, 3221 enrolled	
SAT CR/M/W: 600/630/600	**ACT:** 27 **HIGHLY COMPETITIVE**

The University of Connecticut, founded in 1881, is a public, land-grant, sea-grant, multicampus research institution offering degree programs in liberal arts and sciences and professional studies. There are 9 undergraduate schools and 5 graduate schools. In addition to regional accreditation, UConn has baccalaureate program accreditation with AACSB, ABET, ACPE, ADA, APTA, ASLA, CSAB, NASAD, NASM, NCATE, and NLN. The library contains 2.3 million volumes, 2.6 million microform items, and 5067 audio/video tapes/CDs/DVDs, and subscribes to 35,263 periodicals including electronic. Computerized library services include interlibrary loans, database searching, and Internet access. Special learning facilities include a learning resource center, art gallery, natural history museum, planetarium, radio station, and TV station. The 4108-acre campus is in a rural area 25 miles east of Hartford. Including any residence halls, there are 350 buildings.

Programs of Study: UConn confers B.A., B.S., B.F.A., B.G.S., B.Mus., B.S.E., B.S.N., and B.S.Pharm. degrees. Associate, master's, and doctoral degrees are also awarded. Bachelor's degrees are awarded in AGRICULTURE (agricultural economics, agriculture, agronomy, animal science, horticulture, and natural resource management), BIOLOGICAL SCIENCE (biology/biological science, biophysics, evolutionary biology, genetics, marine science, molecular biology, nutrition, and physiology), BUSINESS (accounting, banking and finance, business administration and management, insurance and risk management, management information systems, marketing/retailing/merchandising, and real estate), COMMUNICATIONS AND THE ARTS (art, art history and appreciation, classics, communications, dramatic arts, English, French, German, journalism, linguistics, music, Spanish, theater design, and visual and performing arts), COMPUTER AND PHYSICAL SCIENCE (chemistry, computer science, geology, mathematics, physics, and statistics), EDUCATION (agricultural education, athletic training, education, elementary education, English education, foreign languages education, mathematics education, music education, recreation education, science education, social studies education, and special education), ENGINEERING AND ENVIRONMENTAL DESIGN (biomedical engineering, chemical engineering, civil engineering, computer engineering, electrical/electronics engineering, environmental engineering, environmental science, landscape architecture/design, manufacturing engineering, materials engineering, and mechanical engineering), HEALTH PROFESSIONS (cytotechnology, exercise science, health care administration, medical laboratory technology, nursing, pharmacy, and physical therapy), SOCIAL SCIENCE (anthropology, dietetics, economics, geography, history, human development, Italian studies, Latin American studies, Middle Eastern studies, philosophy, political science/government, psychology, sociology, urban studies, and women's studies). Biological sciences, psychology, and political science are the largest.

Special: UConn offers co-op programs in most majors, internships, more than 200 study-abroad programs in 65 countries, dual majors, general studies degrees, student-designed majors, work-study programs, nondegree study, and pass/fail options. There are 31 national honor societies, including Phi Beta Kappa, a freshman honors program, and 8 departmental honors programs.

Admissions: 50% of the 2009-2010 applicants were accepted. The SAT scores for the 2009-2010 freshman class were: Critical Reading--5% below 500, 43% between 500 and 599, 45% between 600 and 700, and 7% above 700; Math--3% below 500, 29% between 500 and 599, 56% between 600 and 700, and 12% above 700; Writing--5% below 500, 38% between 500 and 599, 49% between 600 and 700, and 8% above 700. The ACT scores were 3% below 21, 11% between 21 and 23, 35% between 24 and 26, 25% between 27 and 28, and 26% above 28. 73% of the current freshmen were in the top fifth of their class; 96% were in the top two fifths. 49 freshmen graduated first in their class.

Requirements: The SAT or ACT is required. In addition, applicants must be graduates of an approved secondary school and should rank in the upper range of their class. The GED is accepted. Students must complete 16 high school academic units, including 4 years of English, 3 of math, 2 each of foreign language, science, and social studies, and 3 of electives. An essay is required. An audition is required for music and theater students and a portfolio for art students. AP credits are accepted. Important factors in the admissions decision are advanced placement or honors courses, evidence of special talent, and leadership record.

Procedure: Freshmen are admitted fall and spring. Entrance exams should be taken in the spring of the junior year or fall of the senior year. There are early action, deferred admissions, and rolling admissions plans. Early action applications should be filed by December 1; regular applications by February 1 for fall entry and October 15 for spring entry, along with a $70 fee. Notifications for early action are sent December through February; regular decision, late March through mid-April. 1668 applicants were on the 2009 waiting list; 434 were admitted. Applications are accepted on-line.

Financial Aid: 49% of undergraduate students work part-time. Average annual earnings from campus work are $2050. The FAFSA is required. The priority date for freshman financial aid applications for fall entry is March 1.

Computers: All students may access the system 24 hours weekdays and 8 A.M. to 12 P.M. weekends. There are no time limits and no fees.

Irving, TX 75062-4736

(972) 721-5266
(800) 628-6999; (972) 721-5017

Full-time: 550 men, 650 women	**Faculty:** IIA, --$
Part-time: 15 men, 20 women	**Ph.D.s:** 88%
Graduate: 1040 men, 705 women	**Student/Faculty:** n/av
Year: semesters, summer session	**Tuition:** $29,000
Application Deadline: see profile	**Room & Board:** $9000
Freshman Class: n/av	
SAT or ACT: required	**VERY COMPETITIVE+**

The University of Dallas, founded in 1955, is a private liberal arts institution affiliated with the Roman Catholic Church. Undergraduate programs are offered through the Constantin College of Liberal Arts, and the Braniff Graduate School has liberal arts and management divisions. Figures in the above capsule and this profile are approximate. There are 2 graduate schools. In addition to regional accreditation, UD has baccalaureate program accreditation with ACBSP. The library contains 223,350 volumes, 75,554 microform items, and 1636 audio/video tapes/CDs/DVDs, and subscribes to 583 periodicals including electronic. Computerized library services include interlibrary loans, database searching, and Internet access. Special learning facilities include a learning resource center, art gallery, radio station, 80-seat theater, and observatory. The 750-acre campus is in an urban area 12 miles west of Dallas. Including any residence halls, there are 26 buildings.

Programs of Study: UD confers B.A. and B.S. degrees. Master's and doctoral degrees are also awarded. Bachelor's degrees are awarded in BIOLOGICAL SCIENCE (biochemistry and biology/biological science), BUSINESS (business administration and management), COMMUNICATIONS AND THE ARTS (art history and appreciation, ceramic art and design, classics, dramatic arts, English, French, German, painting, printmaking, sculpture, and Spanish), COMPUTER AND PHYSICAL SCIENCE (chemistry, mathematics, and physics), EDUCATION (art education and elementary education), SOCIAL SCIENCE (economics, history, philosophy, political science/government, psychology, and theological studies). Classics, English, and politics are the strongest academically. English, biology, and business leadership are the largest.

Special: UD offers internships in field experience or an off-campus research semester, summer study abroad, on-campus work-study programs, B.A.-B.S. degrees, and double majors. There are 4 national honor societies, including Phi Beta Kappa.

Admissions: There were 9 National Merit finalists in a recent year. 9 freshmen graduated first in their class.

Requirements: The SAT or ACT is required. The ACT Optional Writing test is also required. The university seeks high school students who have pursued a curriculum of college preparatory courses including English, social science, math, science, and a foreign language. Applicants pursuing a discipline in the sciences should have 4 years of math. Depth in a foreign language is advised. Although the university is flexible in its admission requests, applicants should be in the upper third of their graduating class and should present satisfactory SAT or ACT scores. AP and CLEP credits are accepted. Important factors in the admissions decision are advanced placement or honors courses, leadership record, and extracurricular activities record.

Procedure: Freshmen are admitted fall and spring. Entrance exams should be taken during the junior year or by the fall of the senior year. There are early admissions, deferred admissions, and rolling admissions plans. Check with the school for current application deadlines. The application fee is $50. Notification is sent on a rolling basis. Applications are accepted on-line.

Financial Aid: In a recent year, 98% of all full-time freshmen and 95% of continuing full-time students received some form of financial aid. 86% of all full-time freshmen and 89% of continuing full-time students received need-based aid. The average freshmen award was $20,600. 40% of undergraduate students work part-time. Average annual earnings from campus work are $1900. The average financial indebtedness of the 2009 graduate was $21,700. The FAFSA is required. Check with the school for current application deadlines.

Computers: Wireless access is available. There are 4 computer labs with an average of 25 PCs per lab. All students may access the system. There are no time limits and no fees.

UNIVERSITY OF DAYTON
Dayton, OH 45469

(937) 229-4411
(800) 837-7433; (937) 229-4729

Full-time: 3514 men, 3386 women	**Faculty:** 414; IIA, av$
Part-time: 257 men, 249 women	**Ph.D.s:** 91%
Graduate: 1500 men, 2002 women	**Student/Faculty:** 17 to 1
Year: semesters, summer session	**Tuition:** $28,690
Application Deadline: open	**Room & Board:** $8280
Freshman Class: 12,212 applied, 8938 accepted, 1706 enrolled	
SAT CR/M: 560/580	**ACT:** 25 **VERY COMPETITIVE**

The University of Dayton, founded in 1850, is a nonprofit, private, comprehensive institution affiliated with the Roman Catholic Church. Part of the Southwestern Ohio Council for Higher Education, it has undergraduate and graduate programs emphasizing the arts and sciences, business administration, engineering, education, allied professions, and law. There are 4 undergraduate schools and 1 graduate school. In addition to regional accreditation, UD has baccalaureate program accreditation with AACSB, ABET, ADA, CADE, NASAD, NASM, and NCATE. The 3 libraries contain 937,000 volumes, 763,000 microform items, and 3512 audio/video tapes/CDs/DVDs, and subscribe to 23,000 periodicals including electronic. Computerized library services include interlibrary loans, database searching, and Internet access. Special learning facilities include a learning resource center, art gallery, radio station, TV station, UD Research Institute, Bombeck Family Learning Center, a learning teaching center, and Davis Center for Portfolio Management. The 372-acre campus is in a suburban area 2 miles south of downtown Dayton. Including any residence halls, there are 48 buildings.

Programs of Study: UD confers B.A., B.S., B.C.E., B.Ch.E., B.E.E., B.F.A., B.G.S., B.M.E., and B.Mus. degrees. Master's and doctoral degrees are also awarded. Bachelor's degrees are awarded in BIOLOGICAL SCIENCE (biochemistry, biology/biological science, environmental biology, and nutrition), BUSINESS (accounting, banking and finance, business economics, international business management, management information systems, management science, marketing/retailing/merchandising, operations research, and sports management), COMMUNICATIONS AND THE ARTS (art history and appreciation, broadcasting, communications, design, dramatic arts, English, fine arts, French, German, journalism, leadership, music, music performance, music theory and composition, photography, public relations, and Spanish), COMPUTER AND

PHYSICAL SCIENCE (chemistry, computer science, geology, information sciences and systems, mathematics, physical sciences, and physics), EDUCATION (art education, early childhood education, elementary education, music education, physical education, secondary education, and special education), ENGINEERING AND ENVIRONMENTAL DESIGN (chemical engineering, civil engineering, computer engineering, computer technology, electrical/electronics engineering, electrical/electronics engineering technology, engineering technology, industrial engineering technology, manufacturing technology, mechanical engineering, and mechanical engineering technology), HEALTH PROFESSIONS (exercise science, music therapy, predentistry, and premedicine), SOCIAL SCIENCE (American studies, criminal justice, dietetics, economics, history, international studies, liberal arts/general studies, philosophy, political science/government, prelaw, psychology, religion, sociology, and women's studies). Engineering, business, and education are the strongest academically. Business/marketing and engineering/engineering technologies are the largest.

Special: Traditional co-op programs are available in the School of Engineering; however, any student in any discipline may co-op, and qualification is determined on a case-by-case basis. Internships are available in all majors. Cross-registration is available with the Southwestern Ohio Council for Higher Education. Study abroad, work-study programs, a Washington semester, accelerated degree programs, and B.A.-B.S. degrees in chemistry, math, economics, and psychology are available. For students who wish to have a dual major, almost all programs may be combined. Student-designed majors include general studies and interdisciplinary studies. An engineering curriculum agreement exists with Sinclair Community College. There is a freshman honors program and a university-wide honors program.

Admissions: 73% of the 2009-2010 applicants were accepted. The SAT scores for the 2009-2010 freshman class were: Critical Reading--17% below 500, 48% between 500 and 599, 28% between 600 and 700, and 7% above 700; Math--16% below 500, 39% between 500 and 599, 34% between 600 and 700, and 10% above 700. The ACT scores were 3% below 21, 21% between 21 and 23, 34% between 24 and 26, 16% between 27 and 28, and 26% above 28. 48% of the current freshmen were in the top fifth of their class; 77% were in the top two fifths. There was 1 National Merit finalist. 41 freshmen graduated first in their class.

Requirements: The SAT or ACT is required. In addition, applicants should be graduates of an accredited secondary school with 16 units in English, math, science, social studies, and academic electives. 2 units of foreign language are required for admission to the College of Arts and Sciences. The GED is accepted. High school transcripts must be submitted. An essay or personal statement, a recommendation from the high school guidance counselor, and an interview are recommended. Music students must audition. AP and CLEP credits are accepted.

Procedure: Freshmen are admitted fall, winter, and summer. Entrance exams should be taken by December of the senior year. There are deferred admissions and rolling admissions plans. Application deadlines are open. Notification is sent on a rolling basis. 123 applicants were on the 2009 waiting list; 113 were admitted. Applications are accepted on-line.

Financial Aid: In 2009-2010, 89% of all full-time freshmen and 99% of continuing full-time students received some form of financial aid. 64% of all full-time freshmen and 60% of continuing full-time students received need-based aid. The average freshman award was $23,496. Need-based scholarships or need-based grants averaged $10,682 ($20,670 maximum); need-based self-help aid (loans and jobs) averaged $4288 ($9300 maximum); non-need-based athletic scholarships averaged $18,239 ($40,190 maximum); and other non-need-based awards and non-need-based scholarships averaged $11,626 ($40,190 maximum). The average financial indebtedness of the 2009 graduate was $32,862. UD is a member of CSS. The FAFSA is required. The priority date for freshman financial aid applications for fall entry is March 31.

Computers: Wireless access is available. All students may access the system 24 hours a day, 7 days a week. There are no time limits and no fees. All students are required to have a personal computer.

UNIVERSITY OF DELAWARE
Newark, DE 19716-6210   (302) 831-8123; (302) 831-6905

Full-time: 6363 men, 8679 women	**Faculty:** 1165; I, av$
Part-time: 313 men, 402 women	**Ph.D.s:** 85%
Graduate: 1745 men, 1889 women	**Student/Faculty:** 12 to 1
Year: 4-1-4, summer session	**Tuition:** $9486 ($23,186)
Application Deadline: January 15	**Room & Board:** $9,066
Freshman Class: 23005 applied, 14109 accepted, 4223 enrolled	
SAT CR/M/W: 580/600/580	**ACT:** required

VERY COMPETITIVE

The University of Delaware, founded in 1743 and chartered in 1833, is a state-assisted, Land-Grant, Sea-Grant, Space-Grant, Carnegie Research University offering programs in agriculture and natural resources, arts and sciences, business and economics, engineering, health sciences, and education and public policy. There are 7 undergraduate schools and 7 graduate schools. In addition to regional accreditation, Delaware has baccalaureate program accreditation with AACSB, ABET, ADA, APTA, CAHEA, NASM, NCATE, and NLN. The 5 libraries contain 2.8 million volumes, 3.4 million microform items, 600,000 audio/video tapes/CDs/DVDs, and subscribe to 30,000 periodicals including electronic. Computerized library services include interlibrary loans, database searching, Internet access, and laptop Internet portals. Special learning facilities include a learning resource center, art gallery, radio station, TV station, a preschool lab, development ice skating science center, computer-controlled greenhouse, nursing practice labs, physical therapy clinic, 400-acre agricultural research complex, exercise physiology biomechanics labs, foreign language media center, and composite materials center. The 969-acre campus is in a small town 12 miles southwest of Wilmington, DE. Including any residence halls, there are 347 buildings.

Programs of Study: Delaware confers B.A., B.S., B.A.E.S., B.A. Liberal Studies, B.C.E., B.Ch.E., B.C.P.E., B.E.E., B.En. E., B.F.A., B.M.E., B.Mus., B.R.N., B.S.Ed., and B.S.N. degrees. Associates, master's, and doctoral degrees are also awarded. Bachelor's degrees are awarded in AGRICULTURE (agricultural business management, agricultural economics, agriculture, animal science, natural resource management, plant science, soil science, and wildlife management), BIOLOGICAL SCIENCE (biochemistry, biology/biological science, biotechnology, entomology, nutrition, and plant pathology), BUSINESS (accounting, banking and finance, business administration and management, hotel/motel and restaurant management, management information systems, management science, marketing/retailing/merchandising, operations management, organizational leadership and management, and sports management), COMMUNICATIONS AND THE ARTS (apparel design, applied music, art, art history and appreciation, communications, comparative literature, English, fine arts, historic preservation, Italian, journalism, languages, music, music theory and composition, theater management, and visual design), COMPUTER AND PHYSICAL SCIENCE (astronomy, chemistry, computer science, geology, information sciences and systems, mathematics, physics, and statistics), EDUCATION (athletic training, early childhood education, education, elementary education, English education, foreign languages education, mathematics education, music education, physical education, psychology education, science education, secondary education, and special education), ENGINEERING AND ENVIRONMENTAL DESIGN (bioengineering, chemical engineering, civil engineering, computer engineering, electrical/electronics engineering, engineering, engineering technology, environmental engineering, environmental science, landscape architecture/design, and mechanical engineering), HEALTH PROFESSIONS (health, health science, medical laboratory technology, and nursing), SOCIAL SCIENCE (anthropology, criminal justice, dietetics, East Asian studies, economics, European studies, family and community services, fashion design and technology, food production/management/services, food science, geography, history, human development, human services, interdisciplinary studies, international relations, Latin American studies, liberal arts/general studies, philosophy, political science/government, psychology, sociology, and women's studies). Biological sciences, psychology, and nursing. are the largest.

Special: Students may participate in cooperative programs, internships, study abroad in 55 countries, a Washington semester, and work-study programs. The university offers accelerated degree programs, B.A.and B.S. degrees, dual majors, minors, student-designed majors (Bachelor of Arts in Liberal Studies), and pass/fail options. There are 4-1 degree programs in engineering, and hotel and restaurant management. Non-degree study is available through the Division of Continuing Education. There is an extensive undergraduate research program. Students may earn an enriched degree through the University Honors Program. There are 35 national honor societies, including Phi Beta Kappa, and a freshman honors program.

Admissions: 61% of the 2009-2010 applicants were accepted.

Requirements: The SAT or ACT is required. The ACT Optional Writing test is also required. In addition, applicants should be graduates of an accredited secondary school. The GED is accepted. Students should have completed a minimum of 18 high school academic units, including 4 units of English, 3 units of math, 3 units of science with 2 lab units, 2 units each of foreign language, history, and social studies, and 2 units of academic course electives. SAT Subject Tests are recommended, especially for honors program applicants. A writing sample and at least 1 letter of recommendation are required for all. AP credits are accepted. Important factors in the admissions decision are advanced placement or honors courses, recommendations by school officials, and personality/intangible qualities.

Procedure: Freshmen are admitted fall and spring. Entrance exams should be taken by their junior year or the beginning of the senior year. There are early admissions and deferred admissions plans. Applications should be filed by January 15 for fall entry and December 15 for spring entry, along with a $75 fee. Notifications are sent in mid-March. Applications are accepted on-line. 1488 applicants were on a recent waiting list, 288 were accepted.

Financial Aid: In 2009-2010, 36% of all full-time freshmen and 34% of continuing full-time students received some form of financial aid. 26% of all full-time freshmen and 24% of continuing full-time students received need-based aid. The average freshmen award was $9,706. The average financial indebtedness of the 2009 graduate was $17,200. The FAFSA is required. The priority date for freshman financial aid applications for fall entry is February 1. The deadline for filing freshman financial aid applications for fall entry is March 15.

Computers: Wireless access is available. All students may access the system. 24 hours a day. There are no time limits and no fees.

UNIVERSITY OF DENVER
Denver, CO 80208

(303) 871-2036
(800) 525-9495; (303) 871-3301

Full-time: 2232 men, 2661 women	**Faculty:** 468; I, -$
Part-time: 111 men, 372 women	**Ph.D.s:** 90%
Graduate: 2780 men, 3613 women	**Student/Faculty:** 11 to 1
Year: quarters, summer session	**Tuition:** $35,481
Application Deadline: January 15	**Room & Board:** $9495
Freshman Class: 8411 applied, 5935 accepted, 1210 enrolled	
SAT CR/M/W: 600/600/570	**ACT:** 27 **VERY COMPETITIVE+**

The University of Denver, established in 1864, is a private institution offering degrees in arts and sciences, fine arts, music, business, engineering, and education. There are 8 undergraduate schools and 10 graduate schools. In addition to regional accreditation, DU has baccalaureate program accreditation with AACSB, ABET, NASAD, and NASM. The 2 libraries contain 2.4 million volumes, 1.3 million microform items, and 23,992 audio/video tapes/CDs/DVDs, and subscribe to 250,934 periodicals including electronic. Computerized library services include interlibrary loans, database searching, Internet access, and laptop Internet portals. Special learning facilities include a learning resource center, art gallery, radio station, a high-altitude lab, an observatory, and an elementary and early learning center. The 125-acre campus is in an urban area 8 miles south of downtown Denver. Including any residence halls, there are 74 buildings.

Programs of Study: DU confers B.A., B.S., B.B.A., B.F.A., B.M., B.S.A.C.C., B.S.A.T., B.S.B.A., B.S.C.H., B.S.C.P.E., B.S.E.E., B.S.M.E. degrees. Master's and doctoral degrees are also awarded. Bachelor's degrees are awarded in AGRICULTURE (animal science), BIOLOGICAL SCIENCE (biochemistry and biology/biological science), BUSINESS (accounting, banking and finance, business administration and management, business economics, hospitality management services, international business management, marketing/retailing/merchandising, and real estate), COMMUNICATIONS AND THE ARTS (art, art history and appreciation, communications, dramatic arts, English, French, German, Italian, jazz, journalism, languages, music, music performance, and Spanish), COMPUTER AND PHYSICAL SCIENCE (astronomy, chemistry, computer science, digital arts/technology, information sciences and systems, mathematics, physics, science, and statistics), ENGINEERING AND ENVIRONMENTAL DESIGN (computer engineering, construction management, electrical/electronics engineering, environmental science, and mechanical engineering), SOCIAL SCIENCE (anthropology, Asian/American studies, cognitive science, economics, geography, history, international studies, philosophy, political science/government, psychology, public affairs, religion, Russian and Slavic studies, social science, sociology, and women's studies). Information technology studies, real estate and construction management, and accounting are the strongest academically. Management, biology, and general business are the largest.

Special: DU offers co-op programs, study abroad through more than 59 programs, internships across the country and internationally, a Washington quarter, work-study programs, accelerated degree programs, and dual majors. Nondegree study and pass/fail options are also available. There are 19 national honor societies, including Phi Beta Kappa, a freshman honors program, and all departments have honors programs.

Admissions: 71% of the 2009-2010 applicants were accepted. The SAT scores for the 2009-2010 freshman class were: Critical Reading--10% below 500, 40% between 500 and 599, 41% between 600 and 700, and 9% above 700; Math--9% below 500, 37% between 500 and 599, 45% between 600 and 700, and 9% above 700; Writing--14% below 500, 46% between 500 and 599, 35% between 600 and 700, and 5% above 700. The ACT scores were 5% below 21, 15% between 21 and 23, 27% between 24 and 26, 22% between 27 and 28, and 31% above 28. 67% of the current freshmen were in the top fifth of their class; 91% were in the top two fifths. 48 freshmen graduated first in their class.

Requirements: The SAT or ACT is required. In addition, applicants must be graduates of an accredited secondary school. The GED is accepted. DU recommends that applicants have 4 years in English, 3 to 4 in math, and 2 to 4 each in foreign language, social sciences, and natural sciences (2 with lab). An essay and a counselor recommendation are required, and a Hyde interview is strongly encouraged. AP and CLEP credits are accepted. Important factors in the admissions decision are advanced placement or honors courses, personality/intangible qualities, and evidence of special talent.

Procedure: Freshmen are admitted to all sessions. Entrance exams should be taken by January of the senior year. There are early decisions, early admissions and deferred admissions plans. Early decision applications should be filed by November 1, regular applications, January 15 for fall entry, December 1 for winter entry, February 15 for spring entry, and May 1 for summer entry, along with a $50 fee. Notification of early decisions is sent January 15, regular decision, March 15. 700 applicants were on the 2009 waiting list; 44 were admitted. Applications are accepted on-line.

Financial Aid: In 2009-2010, 86% of all full-time freshmen received some form of financial aid. 45% of all full-time freshmen received need-based aid. Average annual earnings from campus work are $3000. The average financial indebtedness of the 2009 graduate was $26,416. DU is a member of CSS. The CSS/Profile and FAFSA are required. The deadline for filing freshman financial aid applications for fall entry is March 1.

Computers: Wireless access is available. There are more than 24,000 Internet connections located in the library, the commons rooms, and every residence hall room. All buildings have smart classrooms. All students may access the system 24 hours a day. There are no time limits and no fees. All students are required to have a personal computer. An Apple, Dell, Toshiba, and Lenovo are recommended.

UNIVERSITY OF EVANSVILLE
Evansville, IN 47722

(812) 488-2468
(800) 423-8633; (812) 488-4076

Full-time: 1002 men, 1474 women	**Faculty:** 172; IIA, -$
Part-time: 33 men, 40 women	**Ph.D.s:** 87%
Graduate: 53 men, 115 women	**Student/Faculty:** 14 to 1
Year: semesters, summer session	**Tuition:** $26,756
Application Deadline: February 1	**Room & Board:** $8670
Freshman Class: 3012 applied, 2593 accepted, 701 enrolled	
SAT CR/M/W: 550/570/540	**ACT:** 25 **VERY COMPETITIVE**

The University of Evansville, founded in 1854, is a private institution affiliated with the United Methodist Church. The university offers undergraduate degree programs in arts and sciences, business administration, education and health sciences, engineering, and computer science. There are 4 undergraduate schools and

5 graduate schools. In addition to regional accreditation, UE has baccalaureate program accreditation with AACSB, ABET, APTA, CAATE, NASM, NCATE, and NLN. The library contains 277,330 volumes, 472,980 microform items, and 13,228 audio/video tapes/CDs/DVDs, and subscribes to 768 periodicals including electronic. Computerized library services include interlibrary loans, database searching, Internet access, and laptop Internet portals. Special learning facilities include a learning resource center, art gallery, and radio station. The 75-acre campus is in an urban area 180 miles southwest of Indianapolis, 170 miles east of St. Louis, and 120 miles west of Louisville. Including any residence halls, there are 49 buildings.

Programs of Study: UE confers B.A., B.S., B.F.A., and B.M. degrees. Associate, master's, and doctoral degrees are also awarded. Bachelor's degrees are awarded in BIOLOGICAL SCIENCE (biochemistry, biology/biological science, and neurosciences), BUSINESS (accounting, banking and finance, business administration and management, business economics, international business management, management information systems, marketing management, and sports management), COMMUNICATIONS AND THE ARTS (art, art history and appreciation, communications, creative writing, dramatic arts, French, German, literature, music, music business management, music performance, Spanish, and theater management), COMPUTER AND PHYSICAL SCIENCE (chemistry, computer science, mathematics, and physics), EDUCATION (art education, athletic training, drama education, elementary education, English education, foreign languages education, mathematics education, music education, physical education, science education, social studies education, and special education), ENGINEERING AND ENVIRONMENTAL DESIGN (civil engineering, computer engineering, electrical/electronics engineering, environmental science, and mechanical engineering), HEALTH PROFESSIONS (exercise science, health care administration, music therapy, nursing, predentistry, premedicine, preoptometry, prepharmacy, and preveterinary science), SOCIAL SCIENCE (archeology, biblical studies, classical/ancient civilization, cognitive science, economics, history, interdisciplinary studies, international studies, liberal arts/general studies, philosophy, political science/government, prelaw, psychology, sociology, and theological studies). Theater and engineering are the strongest academically. Business, exercise science, and nursing are the largest.

Special: Students may study abroad at the University of Evansville British campus, Harlaxton College, and more than 100 other sites. There is also an Italian archeological excavation program, a British Parliament internship, a U.S. Pentagon internship, an accelerated bachelor of science degree in global leadership, combined bachelor's/graduate degrees, cooperative education, dual enrollment of high school students, ESL, and teacher certification, as well as external degrees, honors, independent study programs, internships, and student-designed majors. There are 15 national honor societies and a freshman honors program.

Admissions: 86% of the 2009-2010 applicants were accepted. The SAT scores for the 2009-2010 freshman class were: Critical Reading--22% below 500, 46% between 500 and 599, 26% between 600 and 700, and 6% above 700; Math--21% below 500, 39% between 500 and 599, 35% between 600 and 700, and 5% above 700; Writing--27% below 500, 46% between 500 and 599, 23% between 600 and 700, and 4% above 700. The ACT scores were 13% below 21, 21% between 21 and 23, 26% between 24 and 26, 17% between 27 and 28, and 23% above 28. 60% of the current freshmen were in the top fifth of their class; 87% were in the top two fifths. There were 9 National Merit finalists. 59 freshmen graduated first in their class.

Requirements: The SAT or ACT is required. The ACT Optional Writing test is also required. To be competitive for admission, students should submit a minimum SAT composite score of 1500 (Math, Critical Reading, and Writing) or an ACT composite of 21. Applicants must be graduates of accredited secondary schools; applicants who have been homeschooled are also considered. The university requires completion of 4 years of college preparatory English, 3 years of math (algebra I and II, geometry) 2 years of lab science, and 1 year of history. 2 years of a foreign language; trigonometry, precalculus, or calculus; and physics are recommended. An interview is recommended but not required. AP and CLEP credits are accepted. Important factors in the admissions decision are advanced placement or honors courses, leadership record, and recommendations by school officials.

Procedure: Freshmen are admitted fall and spring. Entrance exams should be taken by the junior year of high school. There is a deferred admissions plan. Early decision applications should be filed by December 1; regular applications, by February 1 for fall entry, along with a $35 fee. Notification of early decision is sent December 15; regular decision, February 15. Applications are accepted online.

Financial Aid: In 2009-2010, all full-time freshmen and 96% of continuing full-time students received some form of financial aid. 79% of all full-time freshmen and 72% of continuing full-time students received need-based aid. The average freshman award was $25,709. Need-based scholarships or need-based grants averaged $22,648 ($32,660 maximum); need-based self-help aid (loans and jobs) averaged $4,213 ($11,200 maximum); and non-need-based athletic scholarships averaged $27,875 ($35,826 maximum). 16% of undergraduate students work part-time. Average annual earnings from campus work are $1700. The average financial indebtedness of the 2009 graduate was $21,726. UE is a member of CSS. The FAFSA is required. The deadline for filing freshman financial aid applications for fall entry is March 10.

Computers: Wireless access is available. Students access e-mail, daily university news, grades, and on-line class discussions using a personal account on the university Intranet. There is wireless network coverage across 100% of the campus. There are 7 public computer labs, several departmental computer clusters, and a small computer lab in each of the residence halls. All classrooms are wired for computer and projection systems for instructional use. All students may access the system at any time. There are no time limits and no fees. It is strongly recommended that all students have a personal computer. Students enrolled in engineering and computer science must have a personal computer.

UNIVERSITY OF FLORIDA
Gainesville, FL 32611-4000 (352) 392-1365

Full-time: 13934 men, 17370 women	**Faculty:** 1937; I, -$
Part-time: 1215 men, 1109 women	**Ph.D.s:** 93%
Graduate: 6283 men, 6323 women	**Student/Faculty:** n/av
Year: semesters, , summer session	**Tuition:** $4,400 ($23,800)
Application Deadline: November 1	**Room & Board:** $7500
Freshman Class: 10975 accepted, 6319 enrolled	
SAT: required	**ACT: 28 HIGHLY COMPETITIVE+**

The University of Florida, founded in 1853, is a public liberal arts institution that is part of the state university system of Florida. There are 16 undergraduate schools. In addition to regional accreditation, UF has baccalaureate program accreditation with AACSB, ABET, ACCE, ACEJMC, ACPE, ADA, AHEA,

671

APTA, ASLA, FIDER, NAAB, NASAD, NASM, NCATE, NLN, and SAF. The 15 libraries contain 4.3 million volumes, 7.9 million microform items, 68,102 audio/video tapes/CDs/DVDs, and subscribe to 71,336 periodicals including electronic. Computerized library services include interlibrary loans, database searching, Internet access, and laptop Internet portals. Special learning facilities include a learning resource center, art gallery, natural history museum, radio station, TV station, a performing arts center, and a teaching hospital. The 2000-acre campus is in a suburban area 75 miles from Jacksonville, FL. Including any residence halls, there are 976 buildings.

Programs of Study: UF confers B.A., B.S., B.A.E., B.F.A., B.H.S., B.M.E., B.Mus., B.S.A., B.S.B.A., B.S.F., B.S.N., and B.S.P. degrees. Master's and doctoral degrees are also awarded. Bachelor's degrees are awarded in AGRICULTURE (agricultural business management, agronomy, animal science, dairy science, forestry and related sciences, horticulture, natural resource management, plant science, and soil science), BIOLOGICAL SCIENCE (botany, entomology, microbiology, wildlife biology, and zoology), BUSINESS (accounting, banking and finance, business administration and management, human resources, insurance, management science, marketing/retailing/merchandising, and recreation and leisure services), COMMUNICATIONS AND THE ARTS (advertising, art, art history and appreciation, dance, East Asian languages and literature, English, French, German, graphic design, journalism, linguistics, music, performing arts, photography, Portuguese, public relations, Russian, Spanish, speech/debate/rhetoric, telecommunications, theater design, and visual and performing arts), COMPUTER AND PHYSICAL SCIENCE (astronomy, chemistry, computer science, earth science, geology, information sciences and systems, mathematics, physics, and statistics), EDUCATION (agricultural education, art education, elementary education, health education, and music education), ENGINEERING AND ENVIRONMENTAL DESIGN (aeronautical engineering, agricultural engineering, architecture, chemical engineering, civil engineering, computer engineering, construction engineering, electrical/electronics engineering, emergency/disaster science, engineering and applied science, environmental engineering, industrial engineering technology, interior design, landscape architecture/design, materials engineering, mechanical engineering, nuclear engineering, and nuclear engineering technology), HEALTH PROFESSIONS (allied health, exercise science, health science, nursing, occupational therapy, physical therapy, prepharmacy, rehabilitation therapy, and speech pathology/audiology), SOCIAL SCIENCE (American studies, anthropology, Asian/Oriental studies, classical/ancient civilization, criminology, economics, food science, geography, history, home economics, interdisciplinary studies, Judaic studies, philosophy, physical fitness/movement, political science/government, psychology, religion, and sociology). Psychology, finance, and political science are the strongest academically and the largest.

Special: There are including Phi Beta Kappa and a freshman honors program.

Admissions: The SAT scores for the 2009-2010 freshman class were: Critical Reading--8% below 500, 27% between 500 and 599, 48% between 600 and 700, and 17% above 700; Math--6% below 500, 21% between 500 and 599, 48% between 600 and 700, and 25% above 700. The ACT scores were 1% below 21, 10% between 21 and 23, 24% between 24 and 26, 27% between 27 and 28, and 38% above 28. 84% of the current freshmen were in the top fifth of their class; 97% were in the top two fifths. There were 205 National Merit finalists.

Requirements: The SAT or ACT is required. The ACT Optional Writing test is also required. In addition, a satisfactory score on the SAT and a minimum score of 19 on the ACT are required. Candidates should have graduated from an accredited secondary school or have a GED, and have completed 4 years of English, 3 years each of math, science, and social studies, 2 years of a foreign language, and 4 units of academic electives. AP and CLEP credits are accepted. Important factors in the admissions decision are advanced placement or honors courses, extracurricular activities record, and evidence of special talent.

Procedure: Freshmen are admitted to all sessions. Entrance exams should be taken in the junior year. There is an early decision plan. Applications should be filed by November 1 for fall entry, November 1 for spring entry, and November 1 for summer entry, along with a $30 fee. Notifications are sent February 12. Applications are accepted on-line.

Financial Aid: In 2009-2010, 39% of all full-time freshmen and 37% of continuing full-time students received some form of financial aid. 14% of all full-time freshmen and 22% of continuing full-time students received need-based aid. The average freshmen award was $11,060. 17% of undergraduate students work part-time. Average annual earnings from campus work are $1800. The average financial indebtedness of the 2009 graduate was $15,318. The FAFSA is required. The priority date for freshman financial aid applications for fall entry is March 15.

Computers: The Internet and wireless networks are available to students. University managed labs with PC's and access to the Internet are distributed across campus. Also, many colleges and department manage open computer labs. All students may access the system. There is a limit on the IBM systems, but no limit on the DEC cluster. There are no fees. All students are required to have a personal computer.

UNIVERSITY OF GEORGIA
Athens, GA 30602　　　　　　　　　　**(706) 542-8776; (706) 542-1466**

Full-time: 10386 men, 14284 women	**Faculty:** I, -$
Part-time: 718 men, 754 women	**Ph.D.s:** 83%
Graduate: 3611 men, 5132 women	**Student/Faculty:** n/av
Year: semesters, summer session	**Tuition:** $6288 ($21,964)
Application Deadline: January 15	**Room & Board:** $8046
Freshman Class: 17776 applied, 9557 accepted, 4684 enrolled	
SAT CR/M/W: 615/626/615	**ACT:** 28 **HIGHLY COMPETITIVE+**

The University of Georgia, chartered in 1785 and part of the University System of Georgia, offers degree programs in agricultural and environmental sciences, arts and sciences, business, education, environment and design, family and consumer sciences, forestry and natural resources, journalism and mass communication, law, pharmacy, public health, public and international affairs, social work and veterinary medicine. There are 15 undergraduate schools and 1 graduate school. In addition to regional accreditation, UGA has baccalaureate program accreditation with AACSB, ABET, ACEJMC, ACPE, ADA, ASLA, CSWE, FIDER, NASAD, NASM, NCATE, NRPA, and SAF. The 3 libraries contain 4.3 million volumes, 6.6 million microform items, and subscribe to 39,226 periodicals including electronic. Computerized library services include interlibrary loans, database searching, Internet access, and laptop Internet portals. Special learning facilities include a learning resource center, art gallery, natural history museum, radio station, bioscience learning center, rare book and manuscript library, performing arts center, broadcast newsroom, State Botanical Garden of Georgia, Peabody Awards Archives, Institute for Newspaper Management Studies, and Georgia Museum of Art. The 614-acre campus is in a small town 60 miles northeast of Atlanta. Including any residence halls, there are 379 buildings.

Programs of Study: UGA confers B.A.,B.S., A.B., A.B.J., B.B.A., B.F.A., B.L.A., B.Mus., B.S.A., B.S.A.B., B.S.A.E., B.S.B.E., B.S.C.S., B.S.Chem., B.S.Ed., B.S.E.H., B.S.E.S., B.S.F.R., B.S.H.P., and B.S.W. degrees. Master's and doctoral degrees are also awarded. Bachelor's degrees are awarded in AGRI-CULTURE (agricultural business management, agricultural communications, agricultural economics, animal science, dairy science, environmental studies, fishing and fisheries, forestry and related sciences, horticulture, natural resource management, plant science, poultry science, and wildlife management), BIO-LOGICAL SCIENCE (avian sciences, biochemistry, biology/biological science, biotechnology, cell biology, ecology, entomology, genetics, microbiology, nutrition, and zoology), BUSINESS (accounting, banking and finance, business administration and management, fashion merchandising, insurance and risk management, international business management, management information systems, management science, marketing/retailing/merchandising, real estate, and recreation and leisure services), COMMUNICATIONS AND THE ARTS (advertising, art, art history and appreciation, broadcasting, ceramic art and design, comparative literature, dance, design, digital communications, dramatic arts, drawing, English, fiber/textiles/weaving, film arts, French, German, Germanic languages and literature, Greek, illustration, Italian, journalism, Latin, linguistics, metal/ jewelry, music, music performance, music theory and composition, photography, printmaking, public relations, romance languages and literature, Russian, sculpture, Spanish, speech/debate/rhetoric, studio art, and telecommunications), COMPUTER AND PHYSICAL SCIENCE (astronomy, chemistry, computer science, geology, mathematics, physics, and statistics), EDUCATION (agricultural education, art education, business education, early childhood education, English education, foreign languages education, home economics education, marketing and distribution education, mathematics education, middle school education, music education, physical education, science education, social science education, special education, sports studies, and vocational education), ENGINEERING AND ENVIRONMENTAL DESIGN (agricultural engineering, bioengineering, environmental science, interior design, landscape architecture/design, preengineering, and technology and public affairs), HEALTH PROFESSIONS (environmental health science, exercise science, music therapy, premedicine, preveterinary science, and speech pathology/audiology), SOCIAL SCIENCE (African American studies, anthropology, child care/child and family studies, classical/ancient civilization, cognitive science, consumer services, criminal justice, dietetics, economics, family/consumer resource management, family/consumer studies, food science, geography, history, interdisciplinary studies, international relations, Japanese studies, philosophy, political science/government, psychology, religion, social work, sociology, water resources, and women's studies). Biology, psychology, and business are the largest.

Special: UGA offers cross-registration with University Center institutions in urban Atlanta. With the Governor's Intern Program, students may serve a full-time 10-week internship in a state government agency; many other internships are available within the departments, as well as work-study programs within the university and with many area businesses. A Washington semester, an accelerated degree program in business, a general studies degree, student-designed majors, dual degrees and double majors, and nondegree study are also available. There are 31 national honor societies, including Phi Beta Kappa, and a freshman honors program.

Admissions: 54% of the 2009-2010 applicants were accepted. The SAT scores for the 2009-2010 freshman class were: Critical Reading--5% below 500, 36% between 500 and 599, 45% between 600 and 700, and 13% above 700; Math--4%

below 500, 30% between 500 and 599, 51% between 600 and 700, and 14% above 700; Writing--6% below 500, 33% between 500 and 599, 49% between 600 and 700, and 12% above 700.

Requirements: The SAT or ACT is required. UGA admits freshmen primarily on the basis of high school curriculum, grades earned, and college admissions test scores. The university may consider qualitative information to determine a student's potential for success. Applicants should be high school graduates or present a GED certificate. Students should have taken 4 years of English, 3 each of math, science, and social studies, and 2 of a foreign language. Satisfactory scores are required on the SAT or ACT. An audition is required for music majors. AP and CLEP credits are accepted.

Procedure: Freshmen are admitted fall, spring, and summer. Entrance exams should be taken by January of the senior year. There is a deferred admissions plan. Applications should be filed by January 15 for fall entry, October 1 for spring entry, and January 15 for summer entry, along with a $60 fee. Notifications are sent April 1. Applications are accepted on-line. 863 applicants were on a recent waiting list, 724 were accepted.

Financial Aid: In 2009-2010, 35% of all full-time freshmen and 33% of continuing full-time students received some form of financial aid. 34% of all full-time freshmen and 29% of continuing full-time students received need-based aid. The average freshmen award was $11,122. Average annual earnings from campus work are $2523. The average financial indebtedness of the 2009 graduate was $14,766. UGA is a member of CSS. The FAFSA is required. The priority date for freshman financial aid applications for fall entry is March 1.

Computers: Wireless access is available. Computers and Internet access are available to students in the Student Learning Center and many departmental classrooms and labs. Wireless Internet access is available on most of the campus and part of the downtown area. All students may access the system. There is open access in computer center/labs, residence hall, library and student center. There are no time limits and no fees.

UNIVERSITY OF HAWAII AT MANOA
Honolulu, HI 96822
(808) 956-8975
(800) 823-9771; (808) 956-4148

Full-time: 5260 men, 6101 women	**Faculty:** 995; I, -$
Part-time: 1132 men, 1459 women	**Ph.D.s:** 89%
Graduate: 2707 men, 3776 women	**Student/Faculty:** 11 to 1
Year: semesters, summer session	**Tuition:** $7,170 ($19,220)
Application Deadline: May 1	**Room & Board:** $8490
Freshman Class: 7196 applied, 4837 accepted, 1992 enrolled	
SAT CR/M/W: 530/560/520	**ACT:** 23 **VERY COMPETITIVE**

The University of Hawaii at Manoa, founded in 1907, is a public research institution in the University of Hawaii system. The undergraduate programs offered include liberal arts and sciences, business, education, engineering, nursing, tropical agriculture, architecture, travel industry management, physical science, technology, Hawaiian, Asian-Pacific Studies, social work, and medicine. There are 14 undergraduate schools and 15 graduate schools. In addition to regional accreditation, UHM has baccalaureate program accreditation with AACSB, ABET, ADA, CSWE, NAAB, NASM, NCATE, and NLN. The 5 libraries contain 3.4 million volumes, 2.4 million microform items, 73,000 audio/video tapes/CDs/DVDs, and subscribe to 59,000 periodicals including electronic. Computerized library services include interlibrary loans, database searching, Internet access, and laptop

Internet portals. Special learning facilities include a learning resource center, art gallery, radio station, and TV station. The 304-acre campus is in an urban area in Honolulu. Including any residence halls, there are 255 buildings.

Programs of Study: UHM confers B.A., B.S., B.B.A., B.Ed., B.F.A., B.Mus., and B.S.W. degrees. Master's and doctoral degrees are also awarded. Bachelor's degrees are awarded in AGRICULTURE (animal science, natural resource management, plant protection (pest management), plant science, and soil science), BIOLOGICAL SCIENCE (biology/biological science, botany, marine biology, microbiology, and zoology), BUSINESS (accounting, banking and finance, business administration and management, human resources, international business management, management information systems, management science, marketing/retailing/merchandising, recreation and leisure services, and tourism), COMMUNICATIONS AND THE ARTS (apparel design, art, Chinese, classics, communications, dance, dramatic arts, English, English as a second/foreign language, French, German, Hawaiian, Japanese, journalism, Korean, linguistics, music, Russian, Spanish, and speech/debate/rhetoric), COMPUTER AND PHYSICAL SCIENCE (atmospheric sciences and meteorology, chemistry, computer science, geology, geophysics and seismology, information sciences and systems, mathematics, and physics), EDUCATION (elementary education, physical education, and secondary education), ENGINEERING AND ENVIRONMENTAL DESIGN (bioengineering, civil engineering, electrical/electronics engineering, environmental science, and mechanical engineering), HEALTH PROFESSIONS (dental hygiene, exercise science, medical laboratory technology, medical technology, nursing, and speech pathology/audiology), SOCIAL SCIENCE (American studies, anthropology, Asian/Oriental studies, economics, ethnic studies, family/consumer resource management, food science, geography, Hawaiian studies, history, interdisciplinary studies, Pacific area studies, peace studies, philosophy, political science/government, psychology, religion, social work, sociology, and women's studies). Biology, art, and business. are the largest.

Special: Internships are available with a variety of employers, including the state legislature, and through 55 different offices as well as academic departments via career services. Co-op and work-study programs, and internships are also offered. Dual majors, non-degree study, and pass/fail options are available. The liberal studies program offers student-designed majors. Students may study abroad in any one of 20 countries for a summer, a semester, or a year. There are 9 national honor societies, including Phi Beta Kappa, a freshman honors program, and 45 departmental honors programs.

Admissions: 67% of the 2009-2010 applicants were accepted. The SAT scores for the 2009-2010 freshman class were: Critical Reading--31% below 500, 49% between 500 and 599, 19% between 600 and 700, and 2% above 700; Math--19% below 500, 47% between 500 and 599, 31% between 600 and 700, and 4% above 700; Writing--35% below 500, 49% between 500 and 599, 15% between 600 and 700, and 1% above 700. The ACT scores were 25% below 21, 32% between 21 and 23, 26% between 24 and 26, 10% between 27 and 28, and 7% above 28. 51% of the current freshmen were in the top fifth of their class; 83% were in the top two fifths. 24 freshmen graduated first in their class.

Requirements: The SAT or ACT is required. The ACT Optional Writing test is also required. In addition, applicants must be graduates of an accredited secondary school, and have the minimum required score of 510 for each SAT section, or 22 on the ACT composite. The GED is also accepted. UHM requires 22 Carnegie units or 17 academic credits, including 4 units of English and 3 units each of math, science, and social studies, as well as 4 additional units of college preparatory courses and 5 electives. UHM requires applicants to be in the upper 40%

of their class. A GPA of 2.8 is required. AP and CLEP credits are accepted. Important factors in the admissions decision are advanced placement or honors courses, recommendations by school officials, and leadership record.

Procedure: Freshmen are admitted fall and spring. Entrance exams should be taken by December of the senior year for fall admission. There is a rolling admissions plan. Applications should be filed by May 1 for fall entry and October 1 for spring entry, along with a $70 fee. Notification is sent on a rolling basis. Applications are accepted on-line.

Financial Aid: In 2009-2010, 66% of all full-time freshmen and 59% of continuing full-time students received some form of financial aid. 38% of all full-time freshmen and 42% of continuing full-time students received need-based aid. The average freshmen award was $11,914, with $5,928 ($14,050 maximum) from need-based scholarships or need-based grants; $3,401 ($7,700 maximum) from need-based self-help aid (loans and jobs); $16,900 ($8,513 maximum) from non-need-based athletic scholarships; and $10,085 ($28,019 maximum) from other non-need-based awards and non-need-based scholarships. 27% of undergraduate students work part-time. Average annual earnings from campus work are $3211. The average financial indebtedness of the 2009 graduate was $14,835. The FAFSA and the college's own financial statement are required. The deadline for filing freshman financial aid applications for fall entry is March 1.

Computers: Wireless access is available. All students may access the system. There are no time limits and no fees. It is strongly recommended that all students have a personal computer. Students enrolled in architecture must have a personal computer.

UNIVERSITY OF HOUSTON
Houston, TX 77204-2018

(713) 743-1010; (800) 741-4449

Full-time: 10,330 men, 10,766 women	**Faculty:** 810; I, -$
Part-time: 4180 men, 4022 women	**Ph.D.s:** 88%
Graduate: 3789 men, 3913 women	**Student/Faculty:** 26 to 1
Year: semesters, summer session	**Tuition:** $6921 ($13,569)
Application Deadline: April 1	**Room & Board:** $7164
Freshman Class: 11,393 applied, 7941 accepted, 3295 enrolled	
SAT CR/M: 520/560	**ACT:** 22 **COMPETITIVE**

The University of Houston, established in 1927, is a public institution with programs in arts and sciences, business, education, engineering, law, and health professions. There are 9 undergraduate schools and 1 graduate school. In addition to regional accreditation, UH has baccalaureate program accreditation with AACSB, ABET, ACPE, ADA, CSWE, NAAB, NASM, and NCATE. The 6 libraries contain 2.7 million volumes, 6 million microform items, and 25,987 audio/video tapes/CDs/DVDs, and subscribe to 77,788 periodicals including electronic. Computerized library services include interlibrary loans, database searching, and Internet access. Special learning facilities include a learning resource center, art gallery, radio station, TV station, and observatory. The 667-acre campus is in an urban area 3 miles from downtown Houston. Including any residence halls, there are 114 buildings.

Programs of Study: UH confers B.A., B.S., B.Acc., B.A.C.Y., B.Arch., B.B.A., B.F.A., B.I.S.C.I., B.M., B.S.C.E., B.S.Ch.E, B.S.C.P.E., B.S.E.E., B.S.I.E., and B.S.M.E. degrees. Master's and doctoral degrees are also awarded. Bachelor's degrees are awarded in BIOLOGICAL SCIENCE (biochemistry, biology/biological science, biophysics, biotechnology, and nutrition), BUSINESS (accounting, banking and finance, business administration and management, entrepreneurial studies, hotel/motel and restaurant management, logistics, management information systems, marketing/retailing/merchandising, operations management, sports management, and supply chain management), COMMUNICATIONS AND THE ARTS (advertising, applied music, art, art history and appreciation, classics, communications, creative writing, dance, dramatic arts, English, French, German, graphic design, industrial design, journalism, linguistics, music, music theory and composition, painting, photography, printmaking, public relations, sculpture, Spanish, speech/debate/rhetoric, and studio art), COMPUTER AND PHYSICAL SCIENCE (chemistry, computer science, earth science, geology, geophysics and seismology, information sciences and systems, mathematics, physics, and statistics), EDUCATION (sports studies), ENGINEERING AND ENVIRONMENTAL DESIGN (architecture, biomedical engineering, chemical engineering, civil engineering, computer engineering, computer technology, construction management, construction technology, electrical/electronics engineering, electrical/electronics engineering technology, environmental design, environmental science, industrial engineering, interior design, mechanical engineering, mechanical engineering technology, occupational safety and health, survey and mapping technology, surveying engineering, and technological management), HEALTH PROFESSIONS (exercise science, health, medical technology, pharmaceutical science, and speech pathology/audiology), SOCIAL SCIENCE (anthropology, East Asian studies, economics, family/consumer studies, German area studies, history, human development, interdisciplinary studies, Italian studies, philosophy, political science/government, psychology, Russian and Slavic studies, and sociology). Business administration, biology/biological sciences, and psychology are the largest.

Special: There is cross-registration with the University of Texas and Rice, Baylor, and Texas Southern Universities. UH also offers internships and co-op programs in many majors, study abroad in 12 countries, work-study programs, and programs in Mexican American and African American studies. Also available are B.A.-B.S. degrees and dual majors in all areas of study. There are 8 national honor societies, a freshman honors program, and 40 departmental honors programs.

Admissions: 70% of the 2009-2010 applicants were accepted. The SAT scores for the 2009-2010 freshman class were: Critical Reading--38% below 500, 43% between 500 and 599, 16% between 600 and 700, and 3% above 700; Math--23% below 500, 44% between 500 and 599, 29% between 600 and 700, and 4% above 700. The ACT scores were 10% below 21, 54% between 21 and 23, 30% between 27 and 28, and 6% above 28. 29 freshmen graduated first in their class.

Requirements: The SAT or ACT is required. In addition, applicants must be graduates of an accredited secondary school or have the GED. Students that submit a complete admissions file by February 1 are automatically admitted if they are in the top 20% of their high school class, or if they are in the top 21-50% of high school class with an SAT score of 1000 or ACT of 21. Applicants that do not apply by February 1 or attended a nonaccredited high school will be considered for admission on an individual basis using a holistic review process. A GPA of 2.0 is required. AP and CLEP credits are accepted. Important factors in the admissions decision are evidence of special talent, advanced placement or honors courses, and recommendations by school officials.

Procedure: Freshmen are admitted to all sessions. Entrance exams should be taken no later than February of the senior year. There is a rolling admissions plan. Applications should be filed by April 1 for fall entry, December 1 for spring entry, and April 1 for summer entry, along with a $50 fee. Applications are accepted on-line.

Financial Aid: UH is a member of CSS. The FAFSA is required. Check with the school for current deadline.

Computers: Wireless access is available. Students may use the campus network, wired or wireless, to access the local area network, wide area network, or Internet. All students have access to computers through the many labs and computer kiosks located throughout campus. The campus has 7 major computer labs with a combined total of more than 1350 computers. All students may access the system. There are no time limits and no fees. Students enrolled in some programs, such as law, are required to have PCs with certain capabilities and software.

UNIVERSITY OF ILLINOIS AT CHICAGO

Chicago, IL 60680	(312) 996-4350; (312) 413-7628
Full-time: 7060 men, 7840 women	**Faculty:** I, -$
Part-time: 580 men, 570 women	**Ph.D.s:** 77%
Graduate: 4425 men, 6375 women	**Student/Faculty:** n/av
Year: semesters, summer session	**Tuition:** $12,000 ($24,500)
Application Deadline: see profile	**Room & Board:** $10,000
Freshman Class: n/av	
SAT or ACT: required	**VERY COMPETITIVE**

The University of Illinois at Chicago, founded in 1946, is a public institution with undergraduate and graduate programs in the liberal arts, art and fine arts, business, engineering, architecture, health sciences, music, teacher preparation, social work, and professional training in dentistry, medicine, and pharmacy. Figures in the above capsule and this profile are approximate. There are 8 undergraduate schools and 1 graduate school. In addition to regional accreditation, UIC has baccalaureate program accreditation with AACSB, ABET, ACPE, CSWE, NAAB, and NASAD. The 3 libraries contain 3.3 million volumes, 4.2 million microform items, and 16,198 audio/video tapes/CDs/DVDs, and subscribe to 66,350 periodicals including electronic. Computerized library services include interlibrary loans, database searching, Internet access, and laptop Internet portals. Special learning facilities include a learning resource center, art gallery, radio station, the Jane Addams Hull House, which is a restored settlement house, and the James Woodworth Prairie Reserve. The 240-acre campus is in an urban area just west of downtown Chicago. Including any residence halls, there are 122 buildings.

Programs of Study: UIC confers B.A., B.S., and B.F.A. degrees. Master's and doctoral degrees are also awarded. Bachelor's degrees are awarded in BIOLOGICAL SCIENCE (biochemistry, biology/biological science, neurosciences, and nutrition), BUSINESS (accounting, banking and finance, business administration and management, electronic business, entrepreneurial studies, management science, and marketing/retailing/merchandising), COMMUNICATIONS AND THE ARTS (art history and appreciation, communications, dramatic arts, English, film arts, French, German, graphic design, industrial design, Italian, music, photography, Polish, Russian, Spanish, and studio art), COMPUTER AND PHYSICAL SCIENCE (chemistry, computer mathematics, computer science, earth science, information sciences and systems, mathematics, physics, and statistics), EDUCATION (art education, elementary education, and health education), ENGINEERING AND ENVIRONMENTAL DESIGN (architecture, bioengineering, chemical engineering, civil engineering, computer engineering, electrical/electronics engineering, engineering management, engineering physics, industrial engineering technology, and mechanical engineering), HEALTH PROFESSIONS (dental hygiene and nursing), SOCIAL SCIENCE (African American studies, anthropology, classical/ancient civilization, criminal justice, criminology, economics, gender studies, German area studies, history, Latin American studies, philosophy, physical fitness/movement, political science/government, psychology, public affairs, sociology, urban studies, and women's studies). Math, health professions, and business and engineering are the strongest academically. Psychology, biological science, and accounting are the largest.

Special: Special academic programs include a wide variety of co-op and program internships, work-study with some 70 on- and off-campus employers, and study abroad opportunities at accredited foreign universities, as well as special programs in France, Italy, Canada, Austria, Spain, and Mexico. Interdisciplinary majors are offered in architectural studies, communications and theater, math and computer science, bioengineering, and information and decision sciences. Up to 4 semester hours of credit may be granted for military experience. Dual and student-designed majors, nondegree study, and pass/fail options are available. There are 10 national honor societies, including Phi Beta Kappa, a freshman honors program, and 90 departmental honors programs.

Requirements: The SAT or ACT is required. In addition, applicants should be graduates of an accredited secondary school; the GED is accepted. The recommended secondary school curriculum varies according to the college program chosen, but 15 high school credits are required as follows: English: 4; math: 3; science: 3; foreign language: 2; social studies. AP and CLEP credits are accepted.

Procedure: Freshmen are admitted fall. Entrance exams should be taken in the spring of the junior year or the fall of the senior year. There is a rolling admissions plan. Check with the school for current application deadlines. The fall 2009 application fee was $40 fee. Notification is sent on a rolling basis. Applications are accepted on-line.

Financial Aid: In 2009-2010, 75% of all full-time freshmen and 72% of continuing full-time students received some form of financial aid. 59% of all full-time freshmen received need-based aid. The average freshman award was $10,128. Need-based scholarships or need-based grants were $11,948; need-based self-help aid (loans and jobs) were $3,277; non-need based athletic scholarships were $19,721. The average financial indebtedness of a recent graduate was $15,576. UIC is a member of CSS. The FAFSA is required. The priority date for freshman financial aid applications is March 1.

Computers: Wireless access is available. The Academic Computing and Communications Center (ACCC) supports the educational and research needs of the UIC community by providing a variety of computing and communications resources. Student have ready access to both Unix systems and personal PCs. Through 1100 workstations, ACCC provides Internet connections in residence halls, libraries, and student centers. A wireless network in public areas on campus is also available. All students may access the system 24 hours daily. There are no time limits and no fees. It is strongly recommended that all students have a personal computer.

UNIVERSITY OF ILLINOIS AT URBANA-CHAMPAIGN

Urbana, IL 61801 (217) 244-4614

Full-time: 15,970 men, 14,235 women	**Faculty:** I, av$
Part-time: 420 men, 275 women	**Ph.D.s:** 92%
Graduate: 5915 men, 5515 women	**Student/Faculty:** n/av
Year: semesters, summer session	**Tuition:** $15,000 ($30,000)
Application Deadline: see profile	**Room & Board:** $9200
Freshman Class: n/av	
SAT or ACT: required	**HIGHLY COMPETITIVE**

The University of Illinois at Urbana-Champaign, founded in 1867, is the oldest and largest campus in the University of Illinois system, offering some 150 undergraduate and more than 100 graduate degree programs. Figures in the above capsule and this profile are approximate. There are 18 undergraduate schools. In addition to regional accreditation, Illinois has baccalaureate program accreditation with AACSB, AALE, ABET, ACEJMC, ADA, ASLA, CSAB, CSWE, NAAB, NASAD, NASM, NCATE, NRPA, and SAF. The 37 libraries contain 10.5 million volumes, 8.5 million microform items, and 932,128 audio/video tapes/CDs/DVDs, and subscribe to 133,488 periodicals including electronic. Computerized library services include interlibrary loans, database searching, Internet access, and laptop Internet portals. Special learning facilities include a learning resource center, radio station, TV station, language learning lab, performing arts center, graphic technologies lab, world history and cultural museum, rehabilitation-education center, center for American music, Japan House and gardens, and rare books and special collections libraries. The 4805-acre campus is in a small town 140 miles south of Chicago, 125 miles west of Indianapolis, and 180 miles northeast of St. Louis. Including any residence halls, there are 568 buildings.

Programs of Study: Illinois confers A.B., B.S., B.A.U.P., B.F.A., B.Land.Arch., B.Mus., B.S.Ed., B.S.J., B.S.W., and B.V.M. degrees. Master's and doctoral degrees are also awarded. Bachelor's degrees are awarded in AGRICULTURE (agricultural business management, agricultural communications, agricultural economics, agricultural mechanics, agronomy, animal science, forestry and related sciences, horticulture, natural resource management, range/farm management, and wildlife management), BIOLOGICAL SCIENCE (biology/biological science, biophysics, biotechnology, botany, cell biology, entomology, microbiology, molecular biology, nutrition, physiology, plant physiology, and wildlife biology), BUSINESS (accounting, banking and finance, entrepreneurial studies, hospitality management services, human resources, insurance, labor studies, logistics, management information systems, management science, marketing and distribution, marketing management, marketing/retailing/merchandising, operations research, organizational behavior, personnel management, purchasing/inventory management, real estate, and recreation and leisure services), COMMUNICATIONS AND THE ARTS (advertising, art history and appreciation, broadcasting, classics, communications, comparative literature, crafts, dance, dramatic arts, East Asian languages and literature, English, English literature, film arts, fine arts, French, Germanic languages and literature, graphic design, Hebrew, industrial design, Italian, journalism, linguistics, media arts, music, music history and appreciation, music performance, music theory and composition, painting, photography, Portuguese, Russian languages and literature, sculpture, Spanish, speech/debate/rhetoric, and voice), COMPUTER AND PHYSICAL SCIENCE (actuarial science, astronomy, chemistry, computer management, computer mathematics, computer programming, geology, mathematics, physics, and statistics), EDUCA-TION (agricultural education, art education, athletic training, computer education, early childhood education, education, education of the multiply handicapped, elementary education, English education, foreign languages education, mathematics education, music education, physical education, science education, secondary education, and vocational education), ENGINEERING AND ENVIRONMENTAL DESIGN (aeronautical engineering, agricultural engineering, airline piloting and navigation, architectural engineering, architecture, aviation administration/management, bioengineering, ceramic engineering, chemical engineering, city/community/regional planning, civil engineering, computational sciences, computer engineering, computer technology, electrical/electronics engineering, engineering, engineering mechanics, engineering physics, geological engineering, industrial administration/management, industrial engineering, landscape architecture/design, materials engineering, materials science, mechanical engineering, metallurgical engineering, nuclear engineering, and plastics engineering), HEALTH PROFESSIONS (biomedical science, community health work, exercise science, health care administration, preveterinary science, public health, and rehabilitation therapy), SOCIAL SCIENCE (anthropology, child psychology/development, dietetics, East Asian studies, economics, family/consumer studies, food production/management/services, food science, geography, history, human development, humanities, international studies, Latin American studies, liberal arts/general studies, parks and recreation management, philosophy, political science/government, prelaw, psychology, religion, Russian and Slavic studies, sociology, textiles and clothing, and women's studies). Engineering, computer science, and business are the strongest academically. Psychology, biology, and electrical and computer engineering are the largest.

Special: Illinois offers cooperative engineering programs with many Midwestern liberal arts colleges and summer, semester, and full-year programs abroad and numerous exchange opportunities. Unusual opportunities include a leisure studies semester in Scotland and a summer parliamentary internship in London. Dual degrees are offered, as well as student-designed majors and a 3-2 engineering program with numerous universities. Work-study and pass/fail options are possible. There are 89 national honor societies, including Phi Beta Kappa, a freshman honors program, and 99 departmental honors programs.

Admissions: There were 54 National Merit finalists in a recent year. 9 freshmen graduated first in their class.

Requirements: The SAT or ACT is required. The ACT Optional Writing test is also required. In addition, applicants should be graduates of accredited secondary schools or have the GED. Advanced placement tests are encouraged and accepted. High school preparation must include 4 years of English, 3 or more of math, 2 each of lab science and social studies, 2 of the same foreign language, and 2 of flexible academic units. A personal and professional essay is required. Visual arts applicants must submit a portfolio; performing arts applicants are required to audition. AP credits are accepted. Important factors in the admissions decision are advanced placement or honors courses, evidence of special talent, and geographical diversity.

Procedure: Freshmen are admitted fall. There are early decision, early admissions and deferred admissions plans. Check with the school for current application deadlines. The application fee is $40. Applications are accepted on-line. A waiting list is maintained.

Financial Aid: In a recent year, 42% of all full-time freshmen and 41% of continuing full-time students received some form of financial aid. 36% of all full-time freshmen and 40% of continuing full-time students received need-based aid.

The average freshman award was $10,418. 35% of undergraduate students work part-time. Average annual earnings from campus work are $1772. The average financial indebtedness of a recent graduate was $17,057. The FAFSA is required. Check with the school for current application deadlines.

Computers: Wireless access is available. All students may use the college network in residence halls, classrooms, computer labs, and public spaces on campus. There are 3507 general access computers in on-campus computer labs, residence hall labs, and libraries. There are approximately another 1000 computers accessible in various departmental labs. There are also e-mail kiosks around the campus, as well as wireless access all buildings across campus. All students may access the system 24 hours a day. Students are limited to 20 hours per week on dial-in access only; unlimited for DCL or wireless. There are no fees. It is strongly recommended that all students have a personal computer. Students enrolled in law school must have a personal computer.

UNIVERSITY OF IOWA
Iowa City, IA 52242-1396

(319) 335-3847
(800) 553-4692; (319) 335-1535

Full-time: 9048 men, 9428 women	**Faculty:** 1586; I, av$
Part-time: 886 men, 1212 women	**Ph.D.s:** 97%
Graduate: 4721 men, 5033 women	**Student/Faculty:** 12 to 1
Year: semesters, summer session	**Tuition:** $6824 ($22,198)
Application Deadline: April 1	**Room & Board:** $8004
Freshman Class: 15,060 applied, 12,503 accepted, 4063 enrolled	
SAT: required	**ACT:** 25 **VERY COMPETITIVE**

The University of Iowa, founded in 1847, is a comprehensive, public institution. Its undergraduate and graduate programs emphasize the liberal and fine arts, business, engineering, health science, and the professions. There are 6 undergraduate schools and 10 graduate schools. In addition to regional accreditation, Iowa has baccalaureate program accreditation with AACSB, ABET, ACEJMC, ACPE, ADA, AHEA, APTA, CAHEA, CSWE, NASM, NCATE, and NLN. The 13 libraries contain 4.6 million volumes, 718,946 microform items, and 60,603 audio/video tapes/CDs/DVDs, and subscribe to 51,374 periodicals including electronic. Computerized library services include interlibrary loans, database searching, and Internet access. Special learning facilities include an art gallery, natural history museum, radio station, UI hospitals and clinics, the Iowa Center for the Arts, Oakdale Research Center, Macbride Raptor Project, Iowa Lakeside lab, and a driving simulator. The 1900-acre campus is in a small town 110 miles east of Des Moines and 220 miles west of Chicago. Including any residence halls, there are 264 buildings.

Programs of Study: Iowa confers B.A., B.S., B.A.S., B.B.A., B.F.A., B.L.S., B.M., B.S.E., B.S.M., and B.S.N. degrees. Master's and doctoral degrees are also awarded. Bachelor's degrees are awarded in BIOLOGICAL SCIENCE (biochemistry, biology/biological science, and microbiology), BUSINESS (accounting, banking and finance, business administration and management, business economics, management science, marketing/retailing/merchandising, and recreation and leisure services), COMMUNICATIONS AND THE ARTS (art, art history and appreciation, classics, communications, comparative literature, dance, dramatic arts, English, film arts, fine arts, French, German, Greek, Italian, journalism, Latin, linguistics, music, Portuguese, Russian, Spanish, and speech/debate/rhetoric), COMPUTER AND PHYSICAL SCIENCE (actuarial science, astronomy, chemistry, computer science, geology, information sciences and systems, mathematics, physics, and statistics), EDUCATION (art education, elementary education, foreign languages education, health education, middle school education, music education, science education, and secondary education), ENGINEERING AND ENVIRONMENTAL DESIGN (biomedical engineering, chemical engineering, civil engineering, electrical/electronics engineering, engineering, environmental science, industrial administration/management, industrial engineering, and mechanical engineering), HEALTH PROFESSIONS (medical laboratory technology, nuclear medical technology, nursing, pharmacy, predentistry, premedicine, and speech pathology/audiology), SOCIAL SCIENCE (African American studies, American studies, anthropology, Asian/Oriental studies, classical/ancient civilization, economics, geography, history, liberal arts/general studies, parks and recreation management, philosophy, political science/government, prelaw, psychology, religion, Russian and Slavic studies, social science, social work, and sociology). English, communication studies, and business are the strongest academically. Business, engineering, and psychology are the largest.

Special: The University of Iowa offers cooperative education programs and internships in more than 70 academic departments, 6 joint-degree programs in computer science, engineering, German, linguistics, nursing, and urban and regional planning, and study abroad in 59 countries. Student-designed majors, B.A.-B.S. degrees, certificate programs including Native American studies, global studies, international business, and women's studies, credit for military experience, and pass/nonpass options are also available. There are 18 national honor societies, including Phi Beta Kappa, a freshman honors program, and 52 departmental honors programs.

Admissions: 83% of the 2009-2010 applicants were accepted. The SAT scores for the 2009-2010 freshman class were: Critical Reading--22% below 500, 35% between 500 and 599, 30% between 600 and 700, and 13% above 700; Math--11% below 500, 27% between 500 and 599, 38% between 600 and 700, and 24% above 700. The ACT scores were 8% below 21, 22% between 21 and 23, 32% between 24 and 26, 17% between 27 and 28, and 20% above 28. 44% of the current freshmen were in the top fifth of their class; 80% were in the top two fifths. There were 18 National Merit finalists. 101 freshmen graduated first in their class.

Requirements: The SAT or ACT is required. In addition, all applicants must have completed 4 years of high school English, 3 each of social studies, science, and math (including 2 years of algebra and 1 of geometry), and 2 of a single foreign language. Music students must audition. AP and CLEP credits are accepted.

Procedure: Freshmen are admitted to all sessions. Entrance exams should be taken in the junior year. There are deferred admissions and rolling admissions plans. Applications should be filed by April 1 for fall entry, November 15 for spring entry, and April 1 for summer entry, along with a $40 fee. Notification is sent on a rolling basis beginning September 20. Applications are accepted on-line. A waiting list is maintained.

Financial Aid: In a recent year, 80% of all full-time freshmen and 78% of continuing full-time students received some form of financial aid. 50% of all full-time freshmen and 51% of continuing full-time students received need-based aid. The average freshman award was $7,900. Need-based scholarships or need-based grants averaged $4500 ($17,000 maximum); need-based self-help aid (loans and jobs) averaged $3600 ($12,000 maximum); non-need-based athletic scholarships averaged $15,000 ($26,000 maximum); and other non-need-based awards and non-need-based scholarships averaged $1800 ($12,500 maximum). 95% of undergraduate students work part-time. Average annual earnings from campus work are $5220. The average financial indebtedness of the 2008 graduate was $22,615.

The FAFSA and the college's own financial statement are required. Check with the school for current application deadlines.

Computers: Wireless access is available. All residence halls have Internet access. Wireless is available at 40 campus locations. There are 26 computer centers on campus with more than 1200 PCs. All students may access the system 24 hours a day, 7 days a week. There are no time limits. There is a fee.

UNIVERSITY OF KANSAS
Lawrence, KS 66045 | **(785) 864-3911; (785) 864-5017**

Full-time: 9525 men, 9405 women	**Faculty:** 1221; I, av$
Part-time: 1033 men, 1103 women	**Ph.D.s:** 97%
Graduate: 3642 men, 4534 women	**Student/Faculty:** 16 to 1
Year: semesters, summer session	**Tuition:** $8206 ($20,175)
Application Deadline: April 1	**Room & Board:** $6802
Freshman Class: 10,653 applied, 9740 accepted, 3942 enrolled	
SAT: required	**ACT:** 25 **COMPETITIVE+**

The University of Kansas, founded in 1866, is a public, comprehensive institution. Its undergraduate and graduate programs emphasize the liberal arts, business, fine arts, music, teacher preparation, journalism, engineering, architecture, social welfare, law, and health science, including pharmacy. Its medical center campus is located in Kansas City. There are 11 undergraduate schools and 3 graduate schools. In addition to regional accreditation, KU has baccalaureate program accreditation with AACN, AACSB, ABET, ACEJMC, ACOTE, ACPE, AOTA, APTA, CAAHEP, CSWE, NAAB, NAACLS, NASAD, NASM, and NCATE. The 12 libraries contain 4.2 million volumes, 3.7 million microform items, and 63,062 audio/video tapes/CDs/DVDs, and subscribe to 62,016 periodicals including electronic. Computerized library services include interlibrary loans, database searching, Internet access, and laptop Internet portals. Special learning facilities include a learning resource center, radio station, TV station, observatory, film studio, space technology center, state-of-the-art performing arts center, art, natural history, classics, entomology, invertebrate paleontology museums, organ recital hall, Robert J. Dole Institute of Politics, and Hall Center for the Humanities. The 1100-acre campus is in a suburban area 30 miles west of Kansas City. Including any residence halls, there are more than 220 buildings.

Programs of Study: KU confers B.A., B.S., B.A.E., B.F.A., B.G.S., B.M., B.M.E., B.S.E., B.S.J., B.S.N., and B.S.W. degrees. Master's and doctoral degrees are also awarded. Bachelor's degrees are awarded in AGRICULTURE (environmental studies), BIOLOGICAL SCIENCE (biochemistry, biology/biological science, microbiology, and molecular biology), BUSINESS (accounting, banking and finance, business administration and management, marketing/retailing/merchandising, and supply chain management), COMMUNICATIONS AND THE ARTS (art, art history and appreciation, ceramic art and design, classical languages, dance, design, dramatic arts, East Asian languages and literature, English, film arts, French, German, Germanic languages and literature, industrial design, journalism, linguistics, metal/jewelry, music history and appreciation, music performance, music theory and composition, painting, printmaking, sculpture, Slavic languages, Spanish, speech/debate/rhetoric, theater design, and voice), COMPUTER AND PHYSICAL SCIENCE (astronomy, atmospheric sciences and meteorology, chemistry, computer science, geology, information sciences and systems, mathematics, and physics), EDUCATION (art education, athletic training, early childhood education, elementary education, health education, middle school education, music education, physical education, and secondary education), ENGINEERING AND ENVIRONMENTAL DESIGN (aeronautical engineering, architectural engineering, architecture, chemical engineering, civil engineering, computer engineering, electrical/electronics engineering, engineering physics, interior design, mechanical engineering, petroleum/natural gas engineering, and textile engineering), HEALTH PROFESSIONS (clinical science, community health work, cytotechnology, music therapy, nursing, occupational therapy, pharmacy, respiratory therapy, and sports medicine), SOCIAL SCIENCE (African studies, African American studies, American studies, anthropology, archeology, behavioral science, economics, European studies, geography, history, humanities, international studies, Latin American studies, philosophy, political science/government, psychology, public administration, religion, Russian and Slavic studies, social work, sociology, and women's studies). Business, pharmacy, and engineering are the strongest academically. Engineering, biological sciences, and business are the largest.

Special: Special academic programs include internships, study abroad in about 60 countries, a Washington semester, and work-study programs with the university. A cooperative program in engineering is offered, as are B.A.-B.S. degrees in many combinations, interdisciplinary majors, and dual majors in any approved combination. General studies degrees are available in many areas, and student-designed majors are possible. Nondegree study and pass/fail options are offered. There are 14 national honor societies, including Phi Beta Kappa, and a freshman honors program.

Admissions: 91% of the 2009-2010 applicants were accepted. The ACT scores were 13% below 21, 27% between 21 and 23, 29% between 24 and 26, 14% between 27 and 28, and 17% above 28. 54% of the current freshmen were in the top fifth of their class; 80% were in the top two fifths. There were 45 National Merit finalists.

Requirements: The SAT or ACT is required. In addition, Kansas resident applicants must have a minimum 2.0 GPA in the qualified admissions college preparatory curriculum; or have an ACT composite score of 21 or SAT combined score (Math and Critical Reading) of 980; or rank in the top third of their high school class. College preparatory curriculum includes 4 units of English, 3 of college preparatory math, 3 of natural science (1 must be chemistry or physics), and 3 of social sciences. 2 units of foreign language and 1 of fine or performing arts are recommended. Nonresidents have the same curriculum requirements, but they must have a minimum GPA of 2.5; or an ACT composite score of 24 or SAT combined score of 1090 with 2.0 GPA; or be in the top third of their high school class. AP and CLEP credits are accepted. Important factors in the admissions decision are advanced placement or honors courses, evidence of special talent, and recommendations by school officials.

Procedure: Freshmen are admitted to all sessions. Entrance exams should be taken by the end of the junior year. There is a rolling admissions plan. Applications should be filed by April 1 for fall entry, December 1 for spring entry, and February 1 for summer entry. The fall 2009 application fee was $30. Applications are accepted on-line.

Financial Aid: In 2009-2010, 60% of all full-time freshmen and 53% of continuing full-time students received some form of financial aid. 36% of all full-time freshmen and 39% of continuing full-time students received need-based aid. The average freshman award was $8,437. Need-based scholarships or need-based grants averaged $4709; need-based self-help aid (loans and jobs) averaged $2923; non-need-based athletic scholarships averaged $14,643; and other non-need-based awards and non-need-based scholarships averaged $3633. 15% of undergraduate students work part-time. Average annual earnings from campus work are \$4800. The average financial indebtedness of the 2009 graduate was \$22,478. The FAFSA is required. The deadline for filing freshman financial aid applications for fall entry is March 1.

Computers: Wireless access is available. All students may access the system 24 hours a day, 7 days a week. There are no time limits and no fees.

UNIVERSITY OF LOUISVILLE
Louisville, KY 40292

(502) 852-6531
(800) 334-8635; (502) 852-4476

Full-time: 5784 men, 6144 women	**Faculty:** ; I, --\$
Part-time: 1762 men, 1741 women	**Ph.D.s:** 86%
Graduate: 2438 men, 2913 women	**Student/Faculty:** n/av
Year: semesters, summer session	**Tuition:** \$7944 (\$19,272)
Application Deadline: August 21	**Room & Board:** \$5437
Freshman Class: 5712 applied, 4515 accepted, 2009 enrolled	
SAT: required	**ACT:** 20 **VERY COMPETITIVE**

The University of Louisville, founded in 1798, is a public institution offering a wide range of undergraduate and academic graduate programs. There are 7 undergraduate schools and 9 graduate schools. In addition to regional accreditation, U of L has baccalaureate program accreditation with AACSB, ABET, ACEJMC, ADA, ASLA, CAHEA, NAAB, NASM, NCATE, and NLN. The 6 libraries contain 2.1 million volumes, 2.2 million microform items, and 42,585 audio/video tapes/CDs/DVDs, and subscribe to 39,923 periodicals including electronic. Computerized library services include interlibrary loans and database searching. Special learning facilities include a learning resource center, art gallery, planetarium, and radio station. The 320-acre campus is in an urban area in Louisville. Including any residence halls, there are 72 buildings.

Programs of Study: U of L confers B.A., B.S., and B.F.A. degrees. Associates, master's, and doctoral degrees are also awarded. Bachelor's degrees are awarded in AGRICULTURE (equine science), BIOLOGICAL SCIENCE (biology/biological science), BUSINESS (accounting, banking and finance, business administration and management, business economics, management science, marketing/retailing/merchandising, and sports management), COMMUNICATIONS AND THE ARTS (art, art history and appreciation, communications, dramatic arts, English, French, linguistics, music, and Spanish), COMPUTER AND PHYSICAL SCIENCE (chemistry, computer science, information sciences and systems, mathematics, and physics), EDUCATION (art education, business education, early childhood education, elementary education, foreign languages education, middle school education, music education, physical education, science education, secondary education, and teaching English as a second/foreign language (TESOL/TEFOL)), ENGINEERING AND ENVIRONMENTAL DESIGN (chemical engineering, civil engineering, computer engineering, electrical/electronics engineering, engineering, engineering management, industrial engineering, and mechanical engineering), HEALTH PROFESSIONS (dental hygiene, health, medical laboratory technology, medical science, and nursing), SOCIAL SCIENCE (African studies, anthropology, criminal justice, geography, history, humanities, liberal arts/general studies, paralegal studies, philosophy, political science/government, psychology, sociology, and women's studies). Engineering, health professional, and business management are the strongest academically. The arts and sciences, business, and education are the largest.

Special: Cross-registration with other schools, study abroad in 5 countries (China, Panama, Portugal, Trinidad, Canada), work-study programs, and B.A.-B.S.

degrees are offered. A general studies degree, nondegree study, and pass/fail options are available. Co-op programs in engineering and business and internships are also possible. There are 20 national honor societies, a freshman honors program, and 1 departmental honors program.

Admissions: 79% of the 2009-2010 applicants were accepted. The ACT scores were 26% below 21, 30% between 21 and 23, 23% between 24 and 26, 10% between 27 and 28, and 12% above 28. There were 4 National Merit finalists.

Requirements: The SAT or ACT is required. In addition, applicants must be graduates from an accredited high school or have received a GED, must have completed a precollege curriculum with a GPA of 2.5, and must have at least 1 of the following: a composite ACT score of 20 or a satisfactory SAT score; completion of the U of L enhanced precollege curriculum (PCC) with a minimum GPA of 2.5; or a rank in the top 15% of the high school graduating class. A GPA of 2.5 is required. AP and CLEP credits are accepted.

Procedure: Freshmen are admitted fall, spring, and summer. Entrance exams should be taken in the spring or the summer of the junior year. There are early admissions, deferred admissions, and rolling admissions plans. Applications should be filed by August 21 for fall entry, along with a $30 fee. Applications are accepted on-line.

Financial Aid: In 2009-2010, 56% of all full-time freshmen and 50% of continuing full-time students received some form of financial aid. 30% of all full-time freshmen and 37% of continuing full-time students received need-based aid. The average freshmen award was $8229, with $5876 ($19,342 maximum) from need-based scholarships or need-based grants; $4086 ($22,641 maximum) from need-based self-help aid (loans and jobs); $14,846 ($22,329 maximum) from non-need-based athletic scholarships; and $5541 ($23,590 maximum) from other non-need-based awards and non-need-based scholarships. The average financial indebtedness of the 2009 graduate was $11,704. The FAFSA is required. The priority date for freshman financial aid applications for fall entry is March 15.

Computers: Wireless access is available. All students may access the system. There are no time limits and no fees.

UNIVERSITY OF MARY WASHINGTON
UMW

Fredericksburg, VA 22401-5300   (540) 654-2000
(800) 468-5614; (540) 654-1857

Full-time: 1305 men, 2416 women	**Faculty:** 219; IIB, av$
Part-time: 139 men, 236 women	**Ph.D.s:** 88%
Graduate: 40 men, 41 women	**Student/Faculty:** 17 to 1
Year: semesters, summer session	**Tuition:** $7212 ($18,940)
Application Deadline: February 1	**Room & Board:** $7462
Freshman Class: 4761 applied, 3541 accepted, 963 enrolled	
SAT or ACT: recommended	**VERY COMPETITIVE**

Mary Washington University, founded in 1908, is a public liberal arts and sciences institution. There is 1 graduate school. In addition to regional accreditation, UMW has baccalaureate program accreditation with NASM. The library contains 378,374 volumes, 667,330 microform items, and 3241 audio/video tapes/CDs/DVDs, and subscribes to 4586 periodicals including electronic. Computerized library services include interlibrary loans, database searching, Internet access, and laptop Internet portals. Special learning facilities include an art gallery, a radio station, the Center for Historic Preservation, the Leidecker Center for Asian Studies, and the James Farmer Multicultural Center. The 176-acre campus is in a suburban area 50 miles south of Washington, D.C., and 50 miles north of Richmond. Including any residence halls, there are 48 buildings.

Programs of Study: UMW confers B.A., B.S., and B.L.S. degrees. Master's degrees are also awarded. Bachelor's degrees are awarded in BIOLOGICAL SCIENCE (biology/biological science), BUSINESS (business administration and management), COMMUNICATIONS AND THE ARTS (art history and appreciation, classics, dramatic arts, English, French, German, historic preservation, music, Spanish, and studio art), COMPUTER AND PHYSICAL SCIENCE (chemistry, computer science, mathematics, and physics), ENGINEERING AND ENVIRONMENTAL DESIGN (environmental science), SOCIAL SCIENCE (American studies, anthropology, economics, geography, history, international relations, philosophy, political science/government, psychology, religion, and sociology). Historic preservation, history, political science, international affairs, English, biology, psychology, earth & environmental sciences are the strongest academically. Business administration, psychology, and biology are the largest.

Special: Study abroad anywhere in the world, a Washington semester, and credit for off-campus work experience are available. The university offers dual majors, work-study programs, student-designed majors, and pass/fail options. More than 500 internships for credit are also available. Teacher licensure preparation is offered for elementary and secondary education. Elementary education is a 5-year bachelor's-master's degree program. There are 25 national honor societies, including Phi Beta Kappa.

Admissions: 74% of the 2009-2010 applicants were accepted. The SAT scores for the 2009-2010 freshman class were: Critical Reading--10% below 500, 42% between 500 and 599, 37% between 600 and 700, and 10% above 700; Math--14% below 500, 47% between 500 and 599, 34% between 600 and 700, and 4% above 700; Writing--12% below 500, 45% between 500 and 599, 37% between 600 and 700, and 6% above 700. The ACT scores were 7% below 21, 24% between 21 and 23, 34% between 24 and 26, 18% between 27 and 28, and 17% above 28.

Requirements: The SAT or ACT and ACT Writing Test are recommended. In addition, applicants must be graduates of an accredited secondary school or hold the GED. The Admissions Committee recommends that applicants complete 4 years of each of math, English, foreign language, science, and social studies. A SAT: Subject test is strongly recommended. Application essays are required. A counselor or teacher recommendation is also required. AP and CLEP credits are accepted. Important factors in the admissions decision are advanced placement or honors courses, evidence of special talent, and recommendations by school officials.

Procedure: Freshmen are admitted fall and spring. Entrance exams should be taken by January of the senior year. There are early admissions and deferred admissions plans. Applications should be filed by February 1 for fall entry and November 1 for spring entry, along with a $50 fee. Notifications are sent April 1. Applications are accepted on-line. 300 applicants were on a recent waiting list, 150 were accepted.

Financial Aid: In 2009-2010, 62% of all full-time freshmen and 58% of continuing full-time students received some form of financial aid. 42% of all full-time freshmen and 50% of continuing full-time students received need-based aid. The average freshman award was $8000. Need-based scholarships or need-based grants averaged $6254 ($18,500 maximum); need-based self-help aid (loans and jobs) averaged $3980 ($5675 maximum); and other non-need-based awards and non-need-based scholarships averaged $4230 ($25,912 maximum). 25% of undergraduate students work part-time. Average annual earnings from campus work are $2100. The average financial indebtedness of the 2009 graduate was $14,800. The FAFSA and the college's own financial statement are required. The deadline for filing freshman financial aid applications for fall entry is March 1.

Computers: Wireless access is available. Students at UMW may use either our wired or wireless system to connect to the Internet. They use the networks to collaborate on course work, access documents and other information from their classes, and connect to proprietary databases and information services such as Lexis-Nexis, Project MUSE, and ARTstor. UMW provides general-access and program-specific labs on both campuses, and data ports on a "1 per pillow" basis in the residence halls. All students may access the system. There are no time limits and no fees. It is strongly recommended that all students have a personal computer. A Dell, Lenovo, Toshiba, or Apple is recommended.

UNIVERSITY OF MARYLAND/BALTIMORE COUNTY

Baltimore, MD 21250	(410) 455-2291; (410) 455-1094

Full-time: 4360 men, 3605 women	**Faculty:** I, -$
Part-time: 760 men, 745 women	**Ph.D.s:** 85%
Graduate: 1160 men, 1420 women	**Student/Faculty:** n/av
Year: 4-1-4, summer session	**Tuition:** $9000 ($18,000)
Application Deadline: see profile	**Room & Board:** $9000
Freshman Class: n/av	
SAT or ACT: required	**VERY COMPETITIVE**

UMBC, founded in 1966, is a public research university offering programs in liberal arts and sciences and engineering. There are 4 undergraduate schools and 3 graduate schools. Figures in the above capsule and this profile are approximate. In addition to regional accreditation, UMBC has baccalaureate program accreditation with ABET, CSWE, and NCATE. The library contains 1.0 million volumes, 1.1 million microform items, and 1.9 million audio/video tapes/CDs/DVDs, and subscribes to 4138 periodicals including electronic. Computerized library services include interlibrary loans, database searching, and Internet access. Special learning facilities include a learning resource center, an art gallery, a radio station, the Imaging Research Center, the Howard Hughes Medical Institute, and a telescope. The 530-acre campus is in a suburban area 5 miles southwest of Baltimore and 35 miles north of Washington, D.C. Including any residence halls, there are 50 buildings.

Programs of Study: UMBC confers B.A., B.S., B.F.A., and B.S.E. degrees. Master's and doctoral degrees are also awarded. Bachelor's degrees are awarded in AGRICULTURE (environmental studies), BIOLOGICAL SCIENCE (biochemistry, bioinformatics, and biology/biological science), COMMUNICATIONS AND THE ARTS (communications, dance, dramatic arts, English, fine arts, French, German, linguistics, modern language, music, Russian, Spanish, theater design, and visual and performing arts), COMPUTER AND PHYSICAL SCIENCE (chemistry, computer science, information sciences and systems, mathematics, physics, and statistics), ENGINEERING AND ENVIRONMENTAL DESIGN (chemical engineering, computer engineering, environmental science, and mechanical engineering), HEALTH PROFESSIONS (emergency medical technologies and health science), SOCIAL SCIENCE (African American studies, American studies, anthropology, classical/ancient civilization, economics, gender studies, geography, history, interdisciplinary studies, philosophy, political science/government, psychology, social work, sociology, and women's studies). Information systems, computer science, and biological sciences are the largest.

Special: Dual and student-designed majors, cooperative education programs in all majors, a Washington semester, the Sondheim Public Affairs Scholars Program, cross-registration with University of Maryland schools and Johns Hopkins University, internships, both paid and nonpaid, in public, private, and nonprofit organizations, study abroad in 19 countries, work-study programs, B.A.-B.S. degrees, pass/fail options, and nondegree study are available. UMBC also offers various opportunities in interdisciplinary studies and in such fields as artificial intelligence and optical communications. There are 15 national honor societies, including Phi Beta Kappa, a freshman honors program, and 17 departmental honors programs.

Requirements: The SAT or ACT is required. In addition, minimum high school preparation should include 4 years of English, 3 years each of social science/history and math, including algebra I and II and geometry, 3 years of lab sciences and 2 of a foreign language. An essay is required of all freshman applicants. A GPA of 3.0 is required. AP and CLEP credits are accepted. Important factors in the admissions decision are advanced placement or honors courses, recommendations by school officials, and leadership record.

Procedure: Freshmen are admitted to all sessions. Entrance exams should be taken by fall of the senior year. There is an early admissions plan. Check with the school for current application deadlines. The fall 2009 application fee was $50. Applications are accepted on-line. A waiting list is maintained.

Financial Aid: In a recent year, 46% of all full-time freshmen and 45% of continuing full-time students received some form of financial aid. 39% of all full-time freshmen and 43% of continuing full-time students received need-based aid. All undergraduate students work part-time. Average annual earnings from campus work are $1335. The average financial indebtedness of a recent graduate was $20,298. The FAFSA is required. Check with the school for current application deadlines.

Computers: There is wireless access throughout most academic buildings. There are 800 open, wired network connections available to students in the library, 107 in classrooms, 800 in computer labs, and 6000 elsewhere in the university. All college-owned and affiliated housing units are wired for high-speed Internet access. All students may access the system. For modem dial-up access, there is a 200 hour per month limit). All other access is unlimited. There are no fees. It is strongly recommended that all students have a personal computer.

UNIVERSITY OF MARYLAND/COLLEGE PARK

College Park, MD 20742   **(301) 314-8385**
       (800) 422-5867; (301) 314-9693

Full-time: 12,893 men, 11,724 women	**Faculty:** 1644; I, +$
Part-time: 1066 men, 859 women	**Ph.D.s:** n/av
Graduate: 5552 men, 5101 women	**Student/Faculty:** 15 to 1
Year: semesters, summer session	**Tuition:** $8052 ($23,989)
Application Deadline: January 20	**Room & Board:** $9375
Freshman Class: 28,443 applied, 11,976 accepted, 4202 enrolled	
SAT or ACT: required	**HIGHLY COMPETITIVE**

The University of Maryland/College Park, founded in 1856, is a land-grant institution and the flagship campus of the state's university system, offering undergraduate and graduate degrees. There are 11 undergraduate schools and 13 graduate schools. In addition to regional accreditation, Maryland has baccalaureate program accreditation with AACSB, ABET, ACEJMC, ASLA, NASM, and NCATE. The 7 libraries contain 3.8 million volumes, 5.8 million microform items, and 405,567 audio/video tapes/CDs/DVDs, and subscribe to 51,989 periodicals including electronic. Computerized library services include interlibrary loans, database searching, Internet access, and laptop Internet portals. Special learning facilities include a learning resource center, art gallery, radio station, TV station, and observatory. The 1250-acre campus is in a suburban area 3 miles northeast of Washington, D.C., and 35 miles south of Baltimore. Including any residence halls, there are 273 buildings.

Programs of Study: Maryland confers B.A., B.S., B.L.A., B.M., and B.M.E. degrees. Master's and doctoral degrees are also awarded. Bachelor's degrees are awarded in AGRICULTURE (agricultural business management, agricultural economics, agriculture, animal science, natural resource management, and plant science), BIOLOGICAL SCIENCE (biochemistry, biology/biological science, microbiology, and nutrition), BUSINESS (accounting, banking and finance, business administration and management, international business management, logistics, management information systems, marketing management, operations management, supply chain management, and transportation management), COMMUNICATIONS AND THE ARTS (art history and appreciation, Chinese, classics, communications, dance, dramatic arts, English, English literature, French, Germanic languages and literature, Japanese, journalism, linguistics, music, music performance, music theory and composition, romance languages and literature, Russian, Spanish, and studio art), COMPUTER AND PHYSICAL SCIENCE (astronomy, chemistry, computer science, geology, information sciences and systems, mathematics, natural sciences, physical sciences, and physics), EDUCATION (art education, drama education, early childhood education, education, elementary education, English education, foreign languages education, mathematics education, music education, physical education, science education, secondary education, social studies education, and special education), ENGINEERING AND ENVIRONMENTAL DESIGN (aeronautical engineering, architecture, bioresource engineering, chemical engineering, civil engineering, computer engineering, electrical/electronics engineering, engineering, environmental science, fire protection engineering, landscape architecture/design, materials engineering, and mechanical engineering), HEALTH PROFESSIONS (community health work, preveterinary science, speech pathology/audiology, and veterinary science), SOCIAL SCIENCE (African American studies, American studies, anthropology, criminal justice, criminology, dietetics, economics, family/consumer studies, food science, geography, history, Italian studies, Judaic studies, philosophy, political science/government, psychology, Russian and Slavic studies, sociology, and women's studies). Engineering, computer science, and business are the strongest academically. Economics, criminology and criminal justice, and government and politics are the largest.

Special: Each of the 11 undergraduate schools offers special programs, and there is a campus-wide co-op education program offering engineering and other majors. In addition, the university offers cross-registration with other colleges in the Consortium of Universities of the Washington Metropolitan Area, several living-learning programs for undergraduates, the B.A.-B.S. degree in most majors, dual and student-designed majors, nondegree study, an accelerated veterinary medicine program, varied study-abroad opportunities, work-study programs with government and nonprofit organizations, and internship opportunities with federal and state legislators, the local media, and various federal agencies. There are 53 national honor societies, including Phi Beta Kappa, a freshman honors program, and 39 departmental honors programs.

Admissions: 42% of the 2009-2010 applicants were accepted. The SAT scores for the 2009-2010 freshman class were: Critical Reading--4% below 500, 29% between 500 and 599, 49% between 600 and 700, and 18% above 700; Math--3% below 500, 15% between 500 and 599, 50% between 600 and 700, and 32% above 700.

Requirements: The SAT or ACT is required. The university evaluates exam scores along with GPA, curriculum, and other criteria. Applicants should be graduates of accredited secondary schools or have the GED. Secondary preparation should include 4 years of English, 3 of history or social sciences, 2 of algebra and 1 of plane geometry, and 2 of lab sciences. An essay and counselor recommendation are required. Music majors must also audition. AP and CLEP credits are accepted. Important factors in the admissions decision are advanced placement or honors courses, recommendations by school officials, and evidence of special talent.

Procedure: Freshmen are admitted fall, spring, and summer. Entrance exams should be taken at the end of the junior year or the beginning of the senior year. There are deferred admissions and rolling admissions plans. Applications should be filed by January 20 for fall entry and December 1 for spring entry. The fall 2008 application fee was $55. Notifications are sent April 1. Applications are accepted on-line.

Financial Aid: 19% of undergraduate students work part-time. Average annual earnings from campus work are $5789. The FAFSA is required. The priority date for freshman financial aid applications for fall entry is February 15.

Computers: Wireless access is available. There are 1800 computers provided for student use in computer labs throughout the campus; the wireless network is available in all college-owned housing, libraries, and classrooms as well as in many administration buildings across campus. All students may access the system 24 hours a day, 7 days a week. There are no time limits and no fees.

UNIVERSITY OF MARYLAND/UNIVERSITY COLLEGE

Adelphi, MD 20783

(249) 684-2101
(800) 888-8682; (240) 684-2153

Full-time: 1401 men, 2007 women	**Faculty:** 103
Part-time: 9311 men, 11565 women	**Ph.D.s:** 83%
Graduate: 5729 men, 7334 women	**Student/Faculty:** n/av
Year: semesters, summer session	**Tuition:** $5810
Application Deadline: open	**Room & Board:** n/a
Freshman Class: n/av	**SPECIAL**

University of Maryland University College, founded in 1947, serves the needs of the adult continuing education student, offering daytime, evening, weekend, and online programs in convenient locations in the Maryland, D.C. Metro, and Virginia areas. It There is one undergraduate school and one graduate school. The library contains 1,248 volumes and subscribes to 76,287 periodicals including electronic. Computerized library services include interlibrary loans, database searching, and Internet access. Special learning facilities include a learning resource center, art gallery, and TV station. The campus is in an urban area.

Programs of Study: UMUC confers B.A. and B.S. degrees. Associate, master's, and doctoral degrees are also awarded. Bachelor's degrees are awarded in BIOLOGICAL SCIENCE (biotechnology), BUSINESS (accounting, business administration and management, human resources, management information systems, management science, and marketing management), COMMUNICATIONS AND

THE ARTS (communications and English), COMPUTER AND PHYSICAL SCIENCE (computer science and information sciences and systems), ENGINEERING AND ENVIRONMENTAL DESIGN (computer technology, emergency/disaster science, and environmental science), SOCIAL SCIENCE (Asian/Oriental studies, criminal justice, fire science, gerontology, history, humanities, liberal arts/general studies, paralegal studies, political science/government, psychology, and social science).

Special: UMUC offers cooperative programs in several career programs. There are work-study programs with local employers. Credit by exam, credit for prior learning, 6 nondegree study, and pass/fail options are available. Through UMUC's open learning program, a number of independent learning courses are available. There are 64 national honor societies.

Requirements: Students should be graduates of an accredited secondary school or have a GED equivalent. AP and CLEP credits are accepted.

Procedure: Freshmen are admitted to all sessions. There is a rolling admissions plan. Application deadlines are open. Application fee is $50. Applications are accepted on-line.

Financial Aid: The FAFSA and SAR (for Pell grants) are required. Check with the school for current application deadlines.

Computers: Wireless access is available. All students may access the system. There are no time limits and no fees.

UNIVERSITY OF MASSACHUSETTS AMHERST

Amherst, MA 01003 (413) 545-0222; (413) 545-4312

Full-time: 9801 men, 9514 women	**Faculty:** 971; I, av$
Part-time: 669 men, 889 women	**Ph.D.s:** 93%
Graduate: 3053 men, 3090 women	**Student/Faculty:** 20 to 1
Year: semesters, summer session	**Tuition:** $11,732 ($23,229)
Application Deadline: January 15	**Room & Board:** $8276
Freshman Class: 29452 applied, 19703 accepted, 4124 enrolled	
SAT CR/M: 575/594	**ACT:** 25 **VERY COMPETITIVE**

Established in 1863, University of Massachusetts Amherst is a public research, land-grant institution offering nearly 100 academic majors. There are 8 undergraduate schools and 8 graduate schools. In addition to regional accreditation, UMass Amherst has baccalaureate program accreditation with AACSB, ABET, ASLA, FIDER, NASM, NCATE, NLN, and SAF. The 2 libraries contain 3.3 million volumes, 2.6 million microform items, and 25,230 audio/video tapes/CDs/DVDs, and subscribe to 57,233 periodicals including electronic. Computerized library services include interlibrary loans, database searching, Internet access, and laptop Internet portals. Special learning facilities include a learning resource center, art gallery, radio station, TV station, botanical gardens. The 1463-acre campus is in a small town 90 miles west of Boston and 60 miles north of Hartford, Connecticut. Including any residence halls, there are 344 buildings.

Programs of Study: UMass Amherst confers B.A., B.S., B.B.A., B.F.A., B.G.S., and B.Mus. degrees. Associate, master's, and doctoral degrees are also awarded. Bachelor's degrees are awarded in AGRICULTURE (agricultural economics, animal science, forestry and related sciences, natural resource management, plant science, soil science, wildlife management, and wood science), BIOLOGICAL SCIENCE (biochemistry, biology/biological science, microbiology, and nutrition), BUSINESS (accounting, banking and finance, business administration and management, hospitality management services, marketing management, and sports management), COMMUNICATIONS AND THE ARTS (art history and appreciation, Chinese, classics, communications, comparative literature, dance, design, dramatic arts, English, Germanic languages and literature, Japanese, journalism, linguistics, music, music performance, Portuguese, Spanish, and studio art), COMPUTER AND PHYSICAL SCIENCE (astronomy, chemistry, computer science, earth science, geology, mathematics, physics, and science), ENGINEERING AND ENVIRONMENTAL DESIGN (chemical engineering, civil engineering, computer engineering, electrical/electronics engineering, environmental design, environmental science, industrial engineering, landscape architecture/design, and mechanical engineering), HEALTH PROFESSIONS (exercise science, nursing, public health, and speech pathology/audiology), SOCIAL SCIENCE (African American studies, anthropology, economics, food science, French studies, gender studies, geography, history, interdisciplinary studies, Italian studies, Judaic studies, law, liberal arts/general studies, Middle Eastern studies, philosophy, political science/government, psychology, Russian and Slavic studies, sociology, and women's studies). Psychology, management, and biology are the largest.

Special: Cross-registration is possible with Smith, Mount Holyoke, Hampshire, and Amherst Colleges. Co-op programs, internships in every major, study abroad in more than 40 countries, a Washington semester, work-study programs, dual majors, and B.A.-B.S. degrees are available. The Bachelor's Degree with Individual Concentration (BDIC) is also available. The Commonwealth Honors College welcomes honor students who meet entrance requirements. There are also teacher certification, distance learning, independent study, and ESL programs. There are 30 national honor societies, including Phi Beta Kappa, a freshman honors program, and 74 departmental honors programs.

Admissions: 67% of the 2009-2010 applicants were accepted. The SAT scores for the 2009-2010 freshman class were: Math--10% below 500, 41% between 500 and 599, 41% between 600 and 700, and 9% above 700; Writing--14% below 500, 48% between 500 and 599, 31% between 600 and 700, and 7% above 700. The ACT scores were 9% below 21, 22% between 21 and 23, 32% between 24 and 26, 20% between 27 and 28, and 17% above 28. 54% of the current freshmen were in the top fifth of their class; 90% were in the top two fifths. 3 freshmen graduated first in their class.

Requirements: The SAT is required. In addition, applicants must be graduates of an accredited secondary school or have the GED. The university recommends that students complete 16 Carnegie units including 4 years of English, 3 years each of math, and science (including 2 years lab), and 2 years each of electives, foreign language, and social studies. 4 years of math are required for business, computer science, and engineering majors. Students must present a portfolio for admission to the art program and must audition for admission to music and dance. A GPA of 2.0 is required. AP and CLEP credits are accepted. Important factors in the admissions decision are advanced placement or honors courses, extracurricular activities record, and recommendations by school officials.

Procedure: Freshmen are admitted fall and spring. Entrance exams should be taken as soon as possible after admissions deadline. There are early admissions, deferred admissions, and rolling admissions plans. Early decision applications should be filed by November 1; regular applications, by January 15 for fall entry; and October 1 for spring entry, along with a $40 fee. Notifications are sent in March. 214 applicants were on the 2009 waiting list; 170 were admitted. Applications are accepted on-line.

Financial Aid: In 2009-2010, 84% of all full-time freshmen and 71% of continuing full-time students received some form of financial aid. 52% of all full-time

freshmen and 53% of continuing full-time students received need-based aid. The average freshman award was $9,590. Need-based scholarships or need-based grants averaged $8,892 ; need-based self-help aid (loans and jobs) averaged $4,232; non-need-based athletic scholarships averaged $15,623; and other non-need-based awards and non-need-based scholarships averaged $2,308. 19% of undergraduate students work part-time. Average annual earnings from campus work are $1400. The average financial indebtedness of the 2009 graduate was $23,847. UMass Amherst is a member of CSS. The FAFSA is required. The priority date for freshman financial aid applications for fall entry is February 14.

Computers: Wireless access is available. The university offers centralized computing services through the Office of Information Technologies. All students are required to have an account. This account provides students with access to numerous computers available for teaching and public use, a campuswide network accessible from residence halls, public buildings, and off campus, an e-mail account, the campus on-line course management system, and the campus wireless network, which is available at many on-campus locations. Registration, grades, and student information are available on-line. There is also an open learning space with computer terminals, work areas, printers, and support staff in the W.E.B. DuBois Library. All students may access the system. There are no time limits and no fees. It is strongly recommended that all students have a personal computer.

UNIVERSITY OF MIAMI
Coral Gables, FL 33124   (305) 284-4323; (305) 284-2507

Full-time: 4574 men, 4877 women	**Faculty:** I, av$
Part-time: 374 men, 545 women	**Ph.D.s:** 91%
Graduate: 626 men, 2633 women	**Student/Faculty:** n/av
Year: semesters, summer session	**Tuition:** $36,188
Application Deadline: January 15	**Room & Board:** $10,800
Freshman Class: 21845 applied, 9700 accepted, 2006 enrolled	
SAT CR/M/W: 630/650/620	**ACT:** 29 **MOST COMPETITIVE**

The University of Miami, founded in 1925, is a private not-for-profit university that offers 114 undergraduate, 104 master's, 53 doctoral, and 4 professional areas of study, including specializations. UM has been classified by the Carnegie Commission as a Very High Research University. There are 9 undergraduate schools and 3 graduate schools. In addition to regional accreditation, UM has baccalaureate program accreditation with AACSB, ABET, ACEJMC, APTA, NAAB, NASM, NCATE, and NLN. The 7 libraries contain 3.2 million volumes, 4 million microform items, and 76,869 audio/video tapes/CDs/DVDs, and subscribe to 48,610 periodicals including electronic. Computerized library services include interlibrary loans, database searching, Internet access, and laptop Internet portals. Special learning facilities include a learning resource center, art gallery, radio station, TV station, a state-of-the-art research vessel, a sound stage and film studios, a film theater, a performing arts theater, a concert hall, a wellness center, an arboretum, and a palmetum. The 230-acre campus is in a suburban area 6 miles south of Miami.

Programs of Study: UM confers B.A., B.S., B.A.M., B.A.M.A., B.Arch., B.B.A., B.F.A., B.G.S., B.L.A., B.M., B.S.A.E., B.S.A.S.E., B.S.B.A., B.S.B.E., B.S.C., B.S.C.E., B.S.Cp.E., B.S.Ed., B.S.E.E., B.S.E.S., B.S.En.E., B.S.H.S., B.S.I.E., B.S.I.T., B.S.M.A.S., B.S.M.E., B.S.N. degrees. Master's and doctoral degrees are also awarded. Bachelor's degrees are awarded in BIOLOGICAL SCIENCE (biochemistry, biology/biological science, marine science, microbiology, and neurosciences), BUSINESS (accounting, banking and finance, entrepreneurial studies, human resources, international business management, management information systems, management science, marketing/retailing/merchandising, real estate, and sports management), COMMUNICATIONS AND THE ARTS (advertising, art, art history and appreciation, audio technology, ceramic art and design, classics, communications, creative writing, English, film arts, fine arts, French, German, graphic design, jazz, journalism, media arts, music, music business management, music performance, music theory and composition, musical theater, painting, photography, printmaking, public relations, sculpture, Spanish, studio art, theater design, theater management, video, visual and performing arts, and voice), COMPUTER AND PHYSICAL SCIENCE (atmospheric sciences and meteorology, chemistry, computer science, geology, information sciences and systems, mathematics, physics, and software engineering), EDUCATION (athletic training, education, elementary education, music education, and special education), ENGINEERING AND ENVIRONMENTAL DESIGN (aeronautical engineering, architectural engineering, architecture, biomedical engineering, civil engineering, computer engineering, electrical/electronics engineering, engineering, environmental engineering, industrial engineering, manufacturing engineering, mechanical engineering, and occupational safety and health), HEALTH PROFESSIONS (exercise science, health science, music therapy, nursing, predentistry, premedicine, prepharmacy, prephysical therapy, and preveterinary science), SOCIAL SCIENCE (African American studies, American studies, anthropology, classical/ancient civilization, criminology, economics, geography, history, interdisciplinary studies, international studies, Judaic studies, Latin American studies, liberal arts/general studies, philosophy, political science/government, prelaw, psychology, public administration, religion, sociology, and women's studies). Biology, psychology, and business management and organization are the largest.

Special: UM offers co-op programs in engineering and internships in all disciplines. There is on- and off-campus work-study, and study abroad in 42 countries. There are accelerated degree programs in nursing, physical therapy, law, exercise physiology, Latin American, medicine, engineering, and marine geology. There is a Phi Beta Kappa and a freshman honors program.

Admissions: 44% of the 2009-2010 applicants were accepted. The SAT scores for the 2009-2010 freshman class were: Critical Reading--46% below 500, 29% between 500 and 599, 46% between 600 and 700, and 19% above 700; Math--3% below 500, 21% between 500 and 599, 51% between 600 and 700, and 26% above 700; Writing--8% below 500, 28% between 500 and 599, 49% between 600 and 700, and 15% above 700. The ACT scores were 7% between 21 and 23, 46% between 24 and 26, and 47% above 28. 81% of the current freshmen were in the top fifth of their class; 96% were in the top two fifths. There were 10 National Merit finalists. 46 freshmen graduated first in their class.

Requirements: The SAT or ACT is required. In addition, it is recommended that applicants have completed 4 years of English, 3 years of math, science, and social sciences, and 2 of foreign language. Also considered in the admissions decision are a recommendation from a high school counselor and an essay. The GED is accepted. AP and CLEP credits are accepted. Important factors in the admissions decision are advanced placement or honors courses, personality/intangible qualities, and recommendations by school officials.

Procedure: Freshmen are admitted fall and spring. Entrance exams should be taken in the fall of the senior year or earlier. There are early decision, early admissions and deferred admissions plans. Early admission applications should be filed by November 1, regular applications should be filed by January 15 for fall entry and November 1 for spring entry, along with a $65 fee. Notification of early decision are sent December 20, regular decision, April 15. Applications are accepted on-line. A waiting list is maintained.

Financial Aid: In 2009-2010, 80% of all full-time freshmen and 83% of continuing full-time students received some form of financial aid. 50% of all full-time freshmen and 49% of continuing full-time students received need-based aid. The average freshman award was $32,024. Need-based scholarships or need-based grants averaged $22,329 ($53,597 maximum); need-based self-help aid (loans and jobs) averaged $7,947 ($43,715 maximum); non-need based athletic scholarships averaged $23,764 ($52,294 maximum); other non-need based awards and non-need based scholarships averaged $17,665 ($55,072 maximum); and other awards, including tuition, remission, athletic scholarships and parent loans averaged $18,035 (48,242 maximum). 23% of undergraduate students work part-time. Average annual earnings from campus work are $2000. The average financial indebtedness of the 2009 graduate was $24,396. UM is a member of CSS. The FAFSA and the state aid form are required. The deadline for filing freshman financial aid applications for fall entry is February 1.

Computers: Wireless access is available. Computer labs are located in residential colleges, libraries, schools, and colleges. UM has a campus network, including network connections in each dorm room, with a gateway to national and international networks, the Internet, and Internet 2. All students may access the system 24 hours a day. There are no time limits and no fees.

UNIVERSITY OF MICHIGAN/ANN ARBOR
Ann Arbor, MI 48109   (734) 764-7433; (734) 936-0740

Full-time: 12848 men, 12494 women	**Faculty:** I, +$
Part-time: 463 men, 403 women	**Ph.D.s:** 98%
Graduate: 8519 men, 6947 women	**Student/Faculty:** n/av
Year: trimesters, summer session	**Tuition:** $13749
Application Deadline: February 1	**Room & Board:** $8,924

Freshman Class: 29965 applied, 14970 accepted, 6072 enrolled
SAT or ACT: required   **HIGHLY COMPETITIVE+**

The University of Michigan/Ann Arbor, founded in 1817, is the main campus of the University of Michigan. The public institution offers undergraduate programs in the arts and sciences, architecture, business administration, education, engineering, fine arts, kinesiology, natural resources, nursing, and professional studies, as well as a wide range of graduate and professional programs. There are 12 undergraduate schools and 18 graduate schools. In addition to regional accreditation, UM has baccalaureate program accreditation with AACSB, ABET, ACE-JMC, ACPE, ADA, ASLA, CSWE, NAAB, NASAD, NASM, NCATE, NLN, and SAF. The 27 libraries contain 9.6 million volumes, and 106,052 audio/video tapes/CDs/DVDs, and subscribe to 70,047 periodicals including electronic. Computerized library services include interlibrary loans, database searching, Internet access, and laptop Internet portals. Special learning facilities include a learning resource center, art gallery, natural history museum, planetarium, radio station, TV station, archeology museum, botanical gardens, two historical museums, electronics music studio, and Digital Media Commons. The 3245-acre campus is in a suburban area 38 miles west of Detroit. Including any residence halls, there are 538 buildings.

Programs of Study: UM confers B.A., B.S., A.B.Ed., B.B.A., B.D.A., B.F.A., B.G.S., B.Mus., B.Mus.A., B.S.Chem., B.S.E, B.S.Ed., and B.S.N. degrees. Master's and doctoral degrees are also awarded. Bachelor's degrees are awarded in

AGRICULTURE (environmental studies), BIOLOGICAL SCIENCE (biochemistry, biology/biological science, biophysics, botany, cell biology, ecology, evolutionary biology, microbiology, molecular biology, and neurosciences), BUSINESS (business administration and management, organizational behavior, and sports management), COMMUNICATIONS AND THE ARTS (Arabic, art, art history and appreciation, audio technology, ceramic art and design, classical languages, classics, communications, comparative literature, creative writing, dance, design, dramatic arts, drawing, English, English literature, fiber/textiles/weaving, film arts, French, German, Germanic languages and literature, graphic design, Greek, Greek (modern), Hebrew, historic preservation, illustration, industrial design, Italian, jazz, Latin, linguistics, literature, metal/jewelry, music, music history and appreciation, music performance, music technology, music theory and composition, musical theater, painting, performing arts, photography, printmaking, Russian, Russian languages and literature, sculpture, Spanish, speech/debate/rhetoric, theater design, video, and winds), COMPUTER AND PHYSICAL SCIENCE (astronomy, astrophysics, atmospheric sciences and meteorology, chemistry, computer science, earth science, environmental geology, geology, geoscience, mathematics, oceanography, physics, and statistics), EDUCATION (athletic training, elementary education, music education, and physical education), ENGINEERING AND ENVIRONMENTAL DESIGN (aeronautical engineering, aerospace studies, architecture, biomedical engineering, chemical engineering, civil engineering, computer engineering, electrical/electronics engineering, engineering, engineering physics, environmental engineering, geological engineering, geophysical engineering, industrial engineering, materials engineering, materials science, mechanical engineering, naval architecture and marine engineering, and nuclear engineering), HEALTH PROFESSIONS (dental hygiene, exercise science, nursing, pharmaceutical chemistry, pharmaceutical science, pharmacy, and radiological science), SOCIAL SCIENCE (African studies, African American studies, American studies, anthropology, archeology, Asian/Oriental studies, behavioral science, biblical studies, Caribbean studies, classical/ancient civilization, cognitive science, Eastern European studies, economics, European studies, Hispanic American studies, history, humanities, interdisciplinary studies, international studies, Islamic studies, Judaic studies, Latin American studies, liberal arts/general studies, medieval studies, Mexican-American/Chicano studies, Middle Eastern studies, Near Eastern studies, philosophy, physical fitness/movement, political science/government, psychology, public affairs, Puerto Rican studies, religion, Russian and Slavic studies, social science, sociology, Western European studies, and women's studies). All programs are equally strong. Psychology, engineering, and business administration are the largest.

Special: A co-op program in engineering and cross-registration with Big Ten institutions and the University of Chicago are available, as are internships, study abroad in approximately 36 countries, and a Washington semester. B.A.-B.S. degrees, dual and student-designed majors, and a 3-2 engineering degree with several colleges and universities are possible. Interdisciplinary majors are offered in anthropology and zoology, music and technology, natural resources and biometry, materials and metallurgical engineering, materials science and engineering, biopsychology and cognitive science, and social anthropology. Interdisciplinary liberal arts programs offering small group living/learning environments are available in the Residential College and the Lloyd Scholars Program. Also available are Honors College preferred admission to professional programs and a Women in Science Program. There are 22 national honor societies, including Phi Beta Kappa, and a freshman honors program.

Admissions: 50% of the 2009-2010 applicants were accepted. 98% of the current freshmen were in the top fifth of their class; 100% were in the top two fifths.

Requirements: The SAT or ACT is required. In addition, applicants must submit either SAT or ACT scores (or both). Applicants must be graduates of accredited secondary schools or have earned a GED. The university requires 16 Carnegie units, including 4 in English, 3 in math (4 for engineering majors), 3 in history and social studies, 2 in foreign language, and 3 in science. The following are recommended electives: 1 unit of hands-on computer study and 2 units of fine or performing arts. An essay is required for all applicants. Students applying to the School of Art must submit a portfolio; those applying to the School of Music must present an audition. AP and CLEP credits are accepted. Important factors in the admissions decision are advanced placement or honors courses, evidence of special talent, and geographical diversity.

Procedure: Freshmen are admitted to all sessions. Entrance exams should be taken by the end of the junior year or the beginning of the senior. There are deferred admissions and rolling admissions plans. Applications should be filed by February 1 for fall entry, October 1 for winter entry, February 1 for spring entry, and February 1 for summer entry. The fall 2008 application fee was $40. Notification is sent on a rolling basis. Applications are accepted on-line. 3440 applicants were on a recent waiting list, 100 were accepted.

Financial Aid: In 2009-2010, 90% of all full-time freshmen and 81% of continuing full-time students received some form of financial aid. 45% of all full-time freshmen and 47% of continuing full-time students received need-based aid. UM is a member of CSS. The FAFSA, and noncustodial profile and tax returns is required. The priority date for freshman financial aid applications for fall entry is April 29. The deadline for filing freshman financial aid applications for fall entry is May 30.

Computers: Wireless access is available in libraries, classroom buildings, labs, office buildings, and student unions. U of M provides an interactive map to help identify where wireless access is available. All students may access the system at any time. There are no time limits and no fees.

UNIVERSITY OF MICHIGAN/DEARBORN
Dearborn, MI 48128-1491   (313) 593-5100; (313) 436-9167

Full-time: 2100 men, 2140 women	**Faculty:** IIA, +$
Part-time: 1095 men, 1320 women	**Ph.D.s:** 88%
Graduate: 1080 men, 880 women	**Student/Faculty:** n/av
Year: semesters, summer session	**Tuition:** $10,000 ($23,000)
Application Deadline: open	**Room & Board:** n/app
Freshman Class: n/av	**VERY COMPETITIVE**

The University of Michigan/Dearborn, founded in 1959, is a public, comprehensive commuter institution that is part of the University of Michigan system. The emphasis of its degree programs is on the liberal arts, management, engineering, and education. Figures in the above capsule and this profile are approximate. There are 4 undergraduate schools and 4 graduate schools. In addition to regional accreditation, UM-Dearborn has baccalaureate program accreditation with AACSB, ABET, and NCATE. The library contains 334,620 volumes, 548,011 microform items, and 4593 audio/video tapes/CDs/DVDs, and subscribes to 1097 periodicals including electronic. Computerized library services include interlibrary loans, database searching, and Internet access. Special learning facilities include a learning resource center, art gallery, natural history museum, radio station, TV station, nature preserve, Armenian research center, child development center, engineering education and practice center, the Henry Ford Estate, a National Historic Landmark, and an astronomy dome. The 196-acre campus is in a suburban area 10 miles from Detroit. Including any residence halls, there are 20 buildings.

Programs of Study: UM-Dearborn confers B.A., B.S., B.B.A., B.G.S., B.S.A., and B.S.E. degrees. Master's degrees are also awarded. Bachelor's degrees are awarded in AGRICULTURE (environmental studies), BIOLOGICAL SCIENCE (biochemistry, biology/biological science, and microbiology), BUSINESS (accounting, business administration and management, management information systems, management science, and marketing management), COMMUNICATIONS AND THE ARTS (art history and appreciation, arts administration/management, communications, English, French, language arts, and music history and appreciation), COMPUTER AND PHYSICAL SCIENCE (chemistry, computer science, geology, mathematics, physics, science, and software engineering), EDUCATION (early childhood education, education, elementary education, mathematics education, science education, secondary education, social studies education, and special education), ENGINEERING AND ENVIRONMENTAL DESIGN (computer engineering, electrical/electronics engineering technology, engineering, environmental science, industrial engineering technology, manufacturing engineering, and mechanical engineering), HEALTH PROFESSIONS (health), SOCIAL SCIENCE (American studies, anthropology, behavioral science, criminal justice, economics, Hispanic American studies, history, humanities, international studies, liberal arts/general studies, philosophy, political science/government, psychology, social studies, sociology, urban studies, and women's studies). Electrical engineering and business administration are the strongest academically. Mechanical engineering, prebusiness, and business administration are the largest.

Special: UM-Dearborn offers internships, study abroad, work-study and accelerated degree programs, a general studies degree, a dual major in engineering math, student-designed majors, and co-op programs in engineering, business administration, and arts and sciences. Nondegree study and pass/fail options are possible. There is 1 national honor society, a freshman honors program, and 2 departmental honors programs.

Admissions: 5 freshmen graduated first in their class in a recent year.

Requirements: Admissions requirements normally include graduation from an accredited secondary school; recommended high school units include 4 years each in math, English, and history, 3 each in science and foreign language, and 1 each in art and information technology. The GED is accepted with a minimum score of 55. An essay and interview are recommended. A GPA of 3.0 is required. AP credits are accepted. Important factors in the admissions decision are advanced placement or honors courses, recommendations by school officials, and leadership record.

Procedure: Freshmen are admitted to all sessions. Entrance exams should be taken in the spring of the junior year or the fall of the senior year. There are deferred admissions and rolling admissions plans. Check with the school for current application deadlines. The fall 2009 application fee was $30. Notification is sent on a rolling basis. Applications are accepted on-line.

Financial Aid: The FAFSA is required. Check with the school for current application deadlines.

Computers: Wireless access is available. All students may access the system. There are no time limits and no fees.

UNIVERSITY OF MINNESOTA/MORRIS

Morris, MN 56267-2199

(320) 589-6035
(888) UMM-EDUC; (320) 589-1673

Full-time: 725 men, 1125 women	**Faculty:** IIB, -$
Part-time: none	**Ph.D.s:** 97%
Graduate: none	**Student/Faculty:** n/av
Year: semesters, summer session	**Tuition:** $11,150
Application Deadline: see profile	**Room & Board:** $6000
Freshman Class: n/av	
SAT or ACT: required	**VERY COMPETITIVE**

The University of Minnesota/Morris, founded in 1959, is a public liberal arts institution within the University of Minnesota system. Figures in the above capsule and this profile are approximate. In addition to regional accreditation, UMM has baccalaureate program accreditation with NCATE. The library contains 197,220 volumes, 221,216 microform items, and 2140 audio/video tapes/CDs/DVDs, and subscribes to 885 periodicals including electronic. Computerized library services include interlibrary loans and database searching. Special learning facilities include a learning resource center, art gallery, radio station, TV station, language lab, observatory, and agricultural experiment station. The 130-acre campus is in a small town 150 miles northwest of Minneapolis. Including any residence halls, there are 36 buildings.

Programs of Study: UMM confers B.A. degrees. Bachelor's degrees are awarded in BIOLOGICAL SCIENCE (biology/biological science), BUSINESS (management science), COMMUNICATIONS AND THE ARTS (art history and appreciation, dramatic arts, English, French, German, music, Spanish, speech/debate/rhetoric, and studio art), COMPUTER AND PHYSICAL SCIENCE (chemistry, computer science, geology, mathematics, physics, and statistics), EDUCATION (elementary education and secondary education), HEALTH PROFESSIONS (premedicine), SOCIAL SCIENCE (anthropology, economics, European studies, history, Latin American studies, liberal arts/general studies, philosophy, political science/government, prelaw, psychology, social science, sociology, and women's studies). Psychology and sciences are the strongest academically. Education, English, and biology are the largest.

Special: UMM offers work-study programs, internships, study abroad, dual majors, student-designed majors, nondegree study, pass/fail options, and credit for life, military, and work experience. There is a 3-2 engineering degree with the University of Minnesota at Twin Cities. A competitive, merit-based program that pairs students and professors to undertake creative projects is available. There is a freshman honors program and 100 departmental honors programs.

Requirements: The SAT or ACT is required. The ACT Optional Writing test is also required. In addition, applicants should be graduates of an accredited secondary school or have a GED certificate. They must have completed 4 years of English, 3 each of math and science, 2 of a single foreign language, and 1 each of social studies and American history. A GPA of 3.0 is required. AP and CLEP credits are accepted. Important factors in the admissions decision are leadership record, extracurricular activities record, and advanced placement or honors courses.

Procedure: Freshmen are admitted fall and spring. Entrance exams should be taken before December 1 of the senior year. There are deferred admissions and rolling admissions plans. Check with the school for current application deadlines. The fall 2009 application fee was $35. Applications are accepted on-line.

Financial Aid: The FAFSA is required. Check with the school for current application deadlines.

Computers: All students may access the system 24 hours per day. There are no time limits and no fees.

UNIVERSITY OF MINNESOTA/TWIN CITIES

Minneapolis, MN 55455
(612) 625-2008
(800) 752-1000; (612) 625-1693

Full-time: 13,212 men, 14,424 women	**Faculty:** I, av$
Part-time: 1140 men, 1145 women	**Ph.D.s:** 81%
Graduate: 9947 men, 8311 women	**Student/Faculty:** n/av
Year: semesters, summer session	**Tuition:** $11,293 ($15,293)
Application Deadline: open	**Room & Board:** $7280
Freshman Class: 33,910 applied, 16,960 admitted, 5400 enrolled	
SAT or ACT: required	**HIGHLY COMPETITIVE**

University of Minnesota/Twin Cities, founded in 1851, is a land-grant institution offering programs in liberal and fine arts, physical and biological sciences, health sciences, education, natural resources, human ecology, business, agriculture, and engineering and professional training in law, medicine, dentistry, pharmacy, and veterinary medicine. There are 16 undergraduate schools and 1 graduate school. In addition to regional accreditation, the university has baccalaureate program accreditation with AACSB, ABET, ABFSE, ACEJMC, ADA, APTA, ASLA, CSWE, FIDER, NAAB, NASM, NCATE, NLN, and SAF. The 14 libraries contain 6.2 million volumes, 5.4 million microform items, and 500,000 audio/video tapes/CDs/DVDs, and subscribe to 48,105 periodicals including electronic. Computerized library services include interlibrary loans and database searching. Special learning facilities include a learning resource center, art gallery, natural history museum, planetarium, radio station, and TV station. The 2000-acre campus is in an urban area within both Minneapolis and St. Paul. Including any residence halls, there are 205 buildings.

Programs of Study: The university confers B.A., B.S., B.A.E.M., B.C.E., B.S.Ch., B.Ch.E., B.Comp.Sci., B.E.E., B.F.A., B.G.E., B.I.S., B.Materials Sci.E., B.S. Mathematics, B.M.E., B.S.Bus., B.S.G., B.S. in Astrophysics, B.S. in Geophysics, B.S.N., B.S. Statistics., B.A.S., B.A.Sc., B.B.A.E., B.B.P.E., B.Bm.E., B.Comp.E., B.D.A., B.E.D., B.Mus., and B.S.Phys. degrees. Master's and doctoral degrees are also awarded. Bachelor's degrees are awarded in AGRICULTURE (agricultural business management, agricultural economics, fishing and fisheries, forestry production and processing, forestry and related sciences, and natural resource management), BIOLOGICAL SCIENCE (biochemistry, biology/biological science, botany, cell biology, ecology, evolutionary biology, genetics, microbiology, nutrition, physiology, and wildlife biology), BUSINESS (accounting, business administration and management, management science, marketing/retailing/merchandising, recreation and leisure services, recreational facilities management, and retailing), COMMUNICATIONS AND THE ARTS (art history and appreciation, Chinese, classical languages, dance, English, film arts, French, German, Greek, Hebrew, Italian, Japanese, languages, Latin, linguistics, music, Russian, Scandinavian languages, Spanish, speech/debate/rhetoric, and studio art), COMPUTER AND PHYSICAL SCIENCE (actuarial science, astronomy, astrophysics, chemistry, computer science, geology, geophysics and seismology, mathematics, physics, and statistics), EDUCATION (agricultural education, art education, bilingual/bicultural education, business education, early childhood education, elementary education, English education, home economics education, industrial arts education, mathematics education, music education, physical education, science education, social studies education, and teaching English as a second/foreign language (TESOL/TEFOL)), ENGINEERING AND ENVIRONMENTAL DESIGN (aeronautical engineering, agricultural engineering, architecture, chemical engineering, civil engineering, electrical/electronics engineering, environmental design, geological engineering, industrial engineering, interior design, landscape architecture/design, materials engineering, materials science, mechanical engineering, and metallurgical engineering), HEALTH PROFESSIONS (dental hygiene, medical laboratory technology, music therapy, nursing, occupational therapy, pharmacy, physical therapy, predentistry, premedicine, prepharmacy, preveterinary science, and speech pathology/audiology), SOCIAL SCIENCE (African studies, African American studies, American Indian studies, American studies, anthropology, child psychology/development, East Asian studies, economics, food science, geography, history, humanities, international relations, Mexican-American/Chicano studies, Middle Eastern studies, philosophy, political science/government, prelaw, psychology, Russian and Slavic studies, sociology, South Asian studies, textiles and clothing, urban studies, and women's studies). Engineering, psychology, economics are the strongest academically. Biology, engineering, and English/journalism are the largest.

Special: The university offers cooperative programs, cross-registration with the Minnesota Community College system, internships, study abroad in 65 countries, work-study programs both on and off campus, a B.A.-B.S. degree in all majors, a general studies degree, and dual and student-designed majors. Pass/fail options and credit for life, military, or work experience are available. There are 21 national honor societies, including Phi Beta Kappa, a freshman honors program, and 8 departmental honors programs.

Admissions: 50% of the 2009-2010 applicants were accepted.

Requirements: The SAT or ACT is required. The university uses a formula index in evaluating high school rank and ACT test scores. A portfolio is required for studio arts and architecture, an audition for music, and an interview for architecture and education. A high school diploma is required; the GED is accepted. AP and CLEP credits are accepted. Important factors in the admissions decision are advanced placement or honors courses, evidence of special talent, and leadership record.

Procedure: Freshmen are admitted to all sessions. Entrance exams should be taken by the end of the junior year or October/November/December of the senior year. There are early admissions, deferred admissions, and rolling admissions plans. Application deadlines are open. The application fee is $50. Notification is sent on a rolling basis. Applications are accepted on-line.

Financial Aid: In 2008-2009, 52% of all full-time freshmen and 53% of all full-time continuing students received some form of financial aid. The average freshman award was $12,984. Need-based scholarships or need-based grants averaged $8703. The average financial indebtedness of the 2009 graduate was $26,516. The FAFSA and the college's own financial statement are required. Check with the school for current application deadlines.

Computers: Wireless access is available. All students may access the system 24 hours a day, 7 days a week, 2 hours per session if there are others waiting or signed on. The fee is $45 per quarter. It is strongly recommended that all students have a personal computer.

UNIVERSITY OF MISSOURI/COLUMBIA

Columbia, MO 65211

(573) 882-7786
(800) 225-6075; (573) 882-7887

Full-time: 10,743 men, 11,639 women	**Faculty:** 1229; I, -$
Part-time: 714 men, 773 women	**Ph.D.s:** 91%
Graduate: 2549 men, 3745 women	**Student/Faculty:** 18 to 1
Year: semesters, summer session	**Tuition:** $8501 ($19,592)
Application Deadline: May 1	**Room & Board:** $8150
Freshman Class: n/av	
ACT: required	**VERY COMPETITIVE**

The University of Missouri/Columbia, established in 1839, offers a comprehensive array of undergraduate and graduate programs as well as professional training in law, medicine, and veterinary medicine. There are 20 undergraduate schools and 14 graduate schools. In addition to regional accreditation, Mizzou has baccalaureate program accreditation with AACSB, ABET, ACEJMC, ACOTE, ADA, APTA, CADE, CAHEA, CSWE, FIDER, NASM, NCATE, NRPA, and SAF. The 11 libraries contain 3.5 million volumes, 8.1 million microform items, and 32,523 audio/video tapes/CDs/DVDs, and subscribe to 46,543 periodicals including electronic. Computerized library services include interlibrary loans, database searching, Internet access, and laptop Internet portals. Special learning facilities include a learning resource center, art gallery, natural history museum, radio station, TV station, an astronomy observatory, a freedom of information center, an herbarium, State Historical Society of Missouri, Western Historical Manuscripts, and anthropology, fishery, and wildlife collections. The 1372-acre campus is in a suburban area 120 miles west of St. Louis and 120 miles east of Kansas City. Including any residence halls, there are 358 buildings.

Programs of Study: Mizzou confers B.A., B.S., B.E.S., B.F.A., B.G.S., B.H.S., B.J., B.M., B.S.Acc., B.S.B.A., B.S.B.E., B.S.ChE., B.S.CiE., B.S.CE., B.S.CoE., B.S.E.E., B.S.Ed., B.S.F., B.S.F.W., B.S.H.E.S., B.S.I.E., and B.S.M.E. degrees. Master's and doctoral degrees are also awarded. Bachelor's degrees are awarded in AGRICULTURE (agricultural business management, agricultural economics, agriculture, animal science, plant science, and soil science), BIOLOGICAL SCIENCE (biochemistry, biology/biological science, microbiology, and nutrition), BUSINESS (accounting, banking and finance, business administration and management, business economics, hotel/motel and restaurant management, marketing/retailing/merchandising, real estate, and tourism), COMMUNICATIONS AND THE ARTS (advertising, art history and appreciation, broadcasting, classics, communications, design, dramatic arts, English, French, German, journalism, linguistics, music, Russian, and Spanish), COMPUTER AND PHYSICAL SCIENCE (atmospheric sciences and meteorology, chemistry, computer science, geology, mathematics, physics, and statistics), EDUCATION (art education, early childhood education, education, elementary education, middle school education, music education, and secondary education), ENGINEERING AND ENVIRONMENTAL DESIGN (biomedical engineering, chemical engineering, civil engineering, computer engineering, electrical/electronics engineering, industrial engineering, and mechanical engineering), HEALTH PROFESSIONS (nursing, occupational therapy, physical therapy, radiological science, and respiratory therapy), SOCIAL SCIENCE (anthropology, archeology, economics, family/consumer resource management, food science, geography, history, human development, international studies, liberal arts/general studies, parks and recreation management, philosophy, political science/

government, psychology, religion, social science, social work, sociology, and textiles and clothing). Biological sciences, accounting, and journalism are the strongest academically. Business administration, journalism, and biological sciences are the largest.

Special: Available academic programs include co-op programs and cross-registration with other schools, internships, study abroad, a Washington semester, and work-study programs. Special degrees or studies include an accelerated degree, dual majors, a general studies degree, and student-designed majors. For highly motivated students, there is an honors college and the possibility of early admission to the schools of law and medicine. There are 25 national honor societies, including Phi Beta Kappa, a freshman honors program, and 34 departmental honors programs.

Admissions: The ACT scores were 7% below 21, 24% between 21 and 23, 32% between 24 and 26, 17% between 27 and 28, and 21% above 28. There were 19 National Merit finalists. 118 freshmen graduated first in their class.

Requirements: The ACT is required. In addition, students may gain probationary admission with sufficient GED scores. The usual requirements are completion of 17 Carnegie units, including 4 each in English and math, 3 each in social studies and science, 2 in a foreign language, and 1 in fine arts. Admission is determined by these units and a combination of class rank and ACT score. AP and CLEP credits are accepted. Important factors in the admissions decision are advanced placement or honors courses and evidence of special talent.

Procedure: Freshmen are admitted to all sessions. Entrance exams should be taken late in the junior year or in the senior year. There are deferred admissions and rolling admissions plans. Applications should be filed by May 1 for fall entry, along with a $45 fee. Notification is sent on a rolling basis. Applications are accepted on-line.

Financial Aid: In 2008-2009, 47% of all full-time freshmen and 44% of continuing full-time students received some form of financial aid. 42% of all full-time freshmen and 37% of continuing full-time students received need-based aid. Need-based scholarships or need-based grants averaged $7660; need-based self-help aid (loans and jobs) averaged $3766; and non-need-based athletic scholarships averaged $9342. The average financial indebtedness of the 2008 graduate was $20,814. The FAFSA is required. Check with the school for current application deadlines.

Computers: Wireless access is available. The majority of campus is wireless; residence hall rooms are wired for access as are numerous computer labs across campus. The network is easily accessible with user name and password, which students receive upon arriving. All students may access the system 24 hours daily by modem; lab hours vary, but labs are open 7 days a week. There are no time limits and no fees.

UNIVERSITY OF MISSOURI/KANSAS CITY

Kansas City, MO 64110 (816) 235-1111; (816) 235-5544

Full-time: 2000 men, 3100 women	**Faculty:** 1, --$
Part-time: 1700 men, 2400 women	**Ph.D.s:** 84%
Graduate: 2100 men, 3000 women	**Student/Faculty:** n/av
Year: semesters, summer session	**Tuition:** $8200 ($19,200)
Application Deadline: open	**Room & Board:** $8000
Freshman Class: n/av	
ACT: required	**VERY COMPETITIVE**

The University of Missouri/Kansas City, which opened in 1933, is a public institution offering undergraduate and graduate programs in the arts and sciences, engineering, business, education, health fields, preprofessional, and professional studies. Figures in the above capsule are approximate. There are 9 undergraduate schools and 13 graduate schools. In addition to regional accreditation, UMKC has baccalaureate program accreditation with AACSB, ABET, ACPE, ADA, NASM, NCATE, and NLN. The 4 libraries contain 1.3 million volumes, 2.4 million microform items, and 451,563 audio/video tapes/CDs/DVDs, and subscribe to 7222 periodicals including electronic. Computerized library services include interlibrary loans and database searching. Special learning facilities include a learning resource center, art gallery, natural history museum, planetarium, and radio station. The 262-acre campus is in an urban area in Kansas City. Including any residence halls, there are 42 buildings.

Programs of Study: UMKC confers B.A., B.S., B.B.A., B.F.A., B.I.T., B.L.A., B.M., B.M.E., B.S.C.I.E., B.S.D.H., B.S.E.E., B.S.M.E., and B.S.N. degrees. Master's and doctoral degrees are also awarded. Bachelor's degrees are awarded in BIOLOGICAL SCIENCE (biology/biological science), BUSINESS (accounting and business administration and management), COMMUNICATIONS AND THE ARTS (art, art history and appreciation, communications, dance, dramatic arts, English, fine arts, French, German, music, music performance, music theory and composition, performing arts, Spanish, speech/debate/rhetoric, and studio art), COMPUTER AND PHYSICAL SCIENCE (chemistry, computer science, geology, information sciences and systems, mathematics, and physics), EDUCATION (elementary education, health education, music education, physical education, and secondary education), ENGINEERING AND ENVIRONMENTAL DESIGN (civil engineering, electrical/electronics engineering, environmental science, and mechanical engineering), HEALTH PROFESSIONS (dental hygiene, medical technology, music therapy, and nursing), SOCIAL SCIENCE (American studies, criminal justice, economics, geography, history, Judaic studies, liberal arts/general studies, philosophy, political science/government, psychology, sociology, and urban studies). Health sciences and performing arts are the strongest academically. Liberal arts is the largest.

Special: Special academic programs include co-op programs and internships in several majors, study abroad in 8 countries, an accelerated degree program, dual majors, and numerous work-study opportunities in the Kansas City area. Special degrees include a B.A.-B.S. degree in the computer science program and a liberal arts degree offered by the adult program. The pass/fail option is available in some courses. Freshmen may enter 6-year medical and dental programs. There are 4 national honor societies, a freshman honors program, and 1 departmental honors program.

Requirements: The ACT is required. A combination of the student's test score and class rank determines admissibility; if the rank is 47 or below, the ACT score must be 24 or higher. Graduation from an accredited secondary school is a requirement for admission; the GED is also accepted. Required high school subjects include 4 units of English, 3 each of math and social studies, 2 of science, 1 of arts, and 3 more units selected from the above subjects or a foreign language. A portfolio is required for art majors, an audition for music majors, and an interview for only those students applying for the pharmacy degree or the 6-year medical and dental programs. AP and CLEP credits are accepted.

Procedure: Freshmen are admitted to all sessions. Entrance exams should be taken by March of the senior year. There is a rolling admissions plan. Application deadlines are open. The application fee is $50.

Financial Aid: The FAFSA is required. Check with the school for current application deadlines.

Computers: All students may access the system 24 hours, 7 days a week. There is no limit for lab use. There is a fee.

UNIVERSITY OF MISSOURI/ST. LOUIS

St. Louis, MO 63121-4400	(314) 516-UMSL; (314) 516-5310
Full-time: 2450 men, 3600 women	**Faculty:** I, --$
Part-time: 2525 men, 4210 women	**Ph.D.s:** n/av
Graduate: 1015 men, 1785 women	**Student/Faculty:** n/av
Year: semesters, summer session	**Tuition:** $8250 ($18,250)
Application Deadline: July 1	**Room & Board:** $8000
Freshman Class: n/av	
SAT or ACT: required	**VERY COMPETITIVE**

The University of Missouri/St. Louis, founded in 1963, is a public institution offering undergraduate and graduate programs and conferring degrees in arts and sciences, business, nursing, education, engineering, and optometry. The figures in the above capsule and in this profile are approximate. There are 7 undergraduate schools and 7 graduate schools. In addition to regional accreditation, UMSL has baccalaureate program accreditation with AACSB, ABET, CSWE, NASM, NCATE, and NLN. The 3 libraries contain 1.1 million volumes, 1.2 million microform items, and 3,902 audio/video tapes/CDs/DVDs, and subscribe to 3,199 periodicals including electronic. Computerized library services include interlibrary loans, database searching, Internet access, and laptop Internet portals. Special learning facilities include a learning resource center, art gallery, planetarium, and the Mercantile Library Collection is housed in the Thomas Jefferson Library. The 350-acre campus is in an urban area 10 miles north of downtown St. Louis. Including any residence halls, there are 44 buildings.

Programs of Study: UMSL confers B.A., B.S., B.F.A., B.G.S., B.L.S., B.M., B.M.E., B.S.Acc., B.S.B.A., B.S.C.I.E., B.S.Ed., B.S.E.E., B.S.M.E., B.S.MIS., B.E.S., B.S.N., B.S.P.P.A., and B.S.W. degrees. Master's and doctoral degrees are also awarded. Bachelor's degrees are awarded in BIOLOGICAL SCIENCE (biology/biological science), BUSINESS (accounting, business administration and management, and management information systems), COMMUNICATIONS AND THE ARTS (art history and appreciation, communications, dance, dramatic arts, English, French, German, music, Spanish, and studio art), COMPUTER AND PHYSICAL SCIENCE (chemistry, computer science, mathematics, and physics), EDUCATION (early childhood education, education, elementary education, music education, physical education, secondary education, and special education), ENGINEERING AND ENVIRONMENTAL DESIGN (civil engineering, electrical/electronics engineering, and mechanical engineering), HEALTH PROFESSIONS (nursing), SOCIAL SCIENCE (anthropology, criminal justice, economics, history, liberal arts/general studies, philosophy, political science/government, psychology, social work, and sociology). Business, chemistry, and education are the strongest academically. Business, education, and nursing are the largest.

Special: Cross-registration with Washington University, St. Louis University, and St. Louis Community College and cooperative programs in all majors are offered. Study abroad in 32 countries, including England, France, and Germany is available. Most degree programs are available through the Evening Courses. Some work-study is available. There is an accelerated nursing degree program and student-designed majors for the B.L.S. There are 24 national honor societies, a freshman honors program, and 16 departmental honors programs.

Requirements: The SAT or ACT is required. In addition, applicants are required to have a total of 17 units, including 4 each in English and math, 3 each in social studies and science, 2 in the same foreign language, and 1 in fine arts. Class rank and test scores are used to determine eligibility for admission. AP and CLEP credits are accepted.

Procedure: Freshmen are admitted fall, spring, and summer. Entrance exams should be taken in the junior year. There are early admissions and rolling admissions plans. Applications should be filed by July 1 for fall entry, December 1 for winter entry, and May 1 for summer entry, along with a $35 fee. Notification is sent on a rolling basis. Applications are accepted on-line.

Financial Aid: The FAFSA is required. Check with the school for current application deadlines.

Computers: Wireless access is available. There are more than 1,000 PCs on campus in classroom and open lab facilities for student usage. All students have access to the campus wireless network. Both types are accessed by student Single Sign On (SSO) ID and password. All students may access the system. There are no time limits. The fee is $11.00 per credit hour. It is strongly recommended that all students have a personal computer.

UNIVERSITY OF NEBRASKA AT LINCOLN
Lincoln, NE 68588-0417

(402) 472-2023
(800) 742-8800; (402) 472-0670

Full-time: 9000 men, 7765 women	**Faculty:** I, -$
Part-time: 740 men, 560 women	**Ph.D.s:** n/av
Graduate: 2345 men, 2590 women	**Student/Faculty:** n/av
Year: semesters, summer session	**Tuition:** $7000 ($17,000)
Application Deadline: June 30	**Room & Board:** $7000
Freshman Class: n/av	
SAT or ACT: recommended	**COMPETITIVE**

University of Nebraska-Lincoln, part of the University of Nebraska system, was founded in 1869 as a land-grant facility. The figures in the above capsule and in this profile are approximate. There are 8 undergraduate schools and 1 graduate school. In addition to regional accreditation, UNL has baccalaureate program accreditation with AACSB, ABET, ACCE, ACEJMC, ADA, FIDER, NAAB, NASAD, NASM, and NCATE. The 8 libraries contain 3.1 million volumes, 4.6 million microform items, and 37,222 audio/video tapes/CDs/DVDs, and subscribe to 53,466 periodicals including electronic. Computerized library services include interlibrary loans, database searching, Internet access, and laptop Internet portals. Special learning facilities include a learning resource center, art gallery, natural history museum, planetarium, radio station, TV station, a center for mass spectrometry, an observatory, the Buros Institute of Mental Measurements, an animal sciences complex, and a center for performing arts. The 617-acre campus is in an urban area 55 miles southwest of Omaha. Including any residence halls, there are 238 buildings.

Programs of Study: UNL confers B.A., B.S., B.A.Ed., B.B.A., B.F.A., B.F.A.Ed., B.J., B.M., B.M.Ed., B.S.A.E., B.S.Agr., B.S.Arch., B.S.B.A., B.S.B.S.E., B.S.C., B.S.C.E., B.S.C.M., B.S.C.S., B.S.Ch.E., B.S.E.E., B.S.E.T., B.S.Ed., B.S.H.E., B.S.H.R.E.S., B.S.I.C.E., B.S.I.E., B.S.I.T., B.S.M.E., and B.S.N.R. degrees. Associates, master's, and doctoral degrees are also awarded. Bachelor's degrees are awarded in AGRICULTURE (agricultural business management, agricultural communications, agricultural economics, agricultural mechanics, agriculture, agronomy, animal science, environmental studies, fish and game management, horticulture, natural resource management, plant protection (pest management), range/farm management, and soil science), BIOLOGICAL SCIENCE (biochemistry and biology/biological science), BUSINESS (accounting, banking and finance, business administration and management, business economics, international business management, management science, marketing/retailing/merchandising, and recreational facilities management), COMMUNICATIONS AND THE ARTS (advertising, art, art history and appreciation, broadcasting, classics, communications, dance, design, dramatic arts, English, English as a second/foreign language, film arts, fine arts, French, German, Greek, journalism, language arts, languages, Latin, music, Russian, Spanish, and speech/debate/rhetoric), COMPUTER AND PHYSICAL SCIENCE (actuarial science, atmospheric sciences and meteorology, chemistry, computer science, earth science, geology, information sciences and systems, mathematics, natural sciences, and physics), EDUCATION (agricultural education, art education, athletic training, business education, early childhood education, education, education of the deaf and hearing impaired, elementary education, foreign languages education, guidance education, health education, home economics education, industrial arts education, journalism education, middle school education, music education, nutrition education, physical education, reading education, science education, secondary education, special education, technical education, and trade and industrial education), ENGINEERING AND ENVIRONMENTAL DESIGN (agricultural engineering, architectural engineering, architecture, bioengineering, chemical engineering, civil engineering, computer engineering, construction management, construction technology, electrical/electronics engineering, electrical/electronics engineering technology, environmental design, environmental science, fire protection engineering, industrial engineering, industrial engineering technology, interior design, manufacturing technology, and mechanical engineering), HEALTH PROFESSIONS (community health work, exercise science, medical laboratory technology, predentistry, premedicine, prepharmacy, speech pathology/audiology, and veterinary science), SOCIAL SCIENCE (anthropology, area studies, dietetics, economics, ethnic studies, European studies, family/consumer studies, food science, geography, history, human development, interdisciplinary studies, international relations, international studies, Latin American studies, law, medieval studies, philosophy, political science/government, prelaw, psychology, religion, sociology, textiles and clothing, water resources, and women's studies). Biochemistry, engineering, and journalism are the strongest academically. Psychology, business administration, and education are the largest.

Special: There is cross-registration with many schools, and co-op programs are available in the Colleges of Engineering and Technology and Agriculture. Through membership in the International Student Exchange Program, the university can place students in more than 90 universities around the world. Internship opportunities abound, as do work-study programs. Accelerated degree programs, a Washington semester, B.A.-B.S. degrees, dual majors, combined pre-professional programs, student-designed majors, credit by exam, nondegree study, and pass/fail options are also available. There are 51 national honor societies, including Phi Beta Kappa, a freshman honors program, and 18 departmental honors programs.

Requirements: The SAT or ACT is recommended. In addition, applicants must be graduates of an accredited secondary school. The GED is accepted. Students must have completed 3 years of English, 2 years each of math, science, and social studies, and an additional year of language arts. UNL requires applicants to be in the upper 50% of their class. AP and CLEP credits are accepted. Important factors in the admissions decision are advanced placement or honors courses, recommendations by school officials, and evidence of special talent.

Procedure: Freshmen are admitted to all sessions. Entrance exams should be taken in April of the junior year. There is a rolling admissions plan. Applications should be filed by June 30 for fall entry and December 15 for spring entry, along with a $25 fee. Applications are accepted on-line.

Financial Aid: In a recent year 41% of all full-time freshmen and 36% of continuing full-time students received some form of financial aid. 36% of all full-time freshmen and 33% of continuing full-time students received need-based aid. The average freshmen award was $12,270. All of undergraduate students worked part-time. Average annual earnings from campus work were $1200. The average financial indebtedness of the 2009 graduate was $19,075. The FAFSA is required. Check with the school for current application deadlines.

Computers: Wireless access is available. There are 650 computer stations available. All students may access the system 24 hours a day, 7 days per week. There are no time limits and no fees. Students enrolled in architecture and community and regional planning must have a personal computer.

UNIVERSITY OF NEVADA, LAS VEGAS

Las Vegas, NV 89154-1021   (702) 774-UNLV; (702) 774-8008

Full-time: 7372 men, 9019 women	**Faculty:** 676; I, av$
Part-time: 3451 men, 2866 women	**Ph.D.s:** 95%
Graduate: 2201 men, 3355 women	**Student/Faculty:** 24 to 1
Year: semesters, summer session	**Tuition:** $4783 ($17,123)
Application Deadline: February 1	**Room & Board:** $12,250
Freshman Class: n/av	**COMPETITIVE**

University of Nevada, Las Vegas, established in 1957, is a state-supported institution offering undergraduate and graduate programs in business, education, health science, engineering, science and math, hotel administration, fine arts, liberal arts, urban affairs, and honors. There are 10 undergraduate schools and 1 graduate school. In addition to regional accreditation, UNLV has baccalaureate program accreditation with AACSB, ABET, ACCE, ADA, APTA, ASLA, CSAB, CSWE, FIDER, NAAB, NASAD, NASM, NCATE, and NLN. The 6 libraries contain 950,600 volumes, 1.8 million microform items, and 13,500 audio/video tapes/CDs/DVDs, and subscribe to 1759 periodicals including electronic. Computerized library services include interlibrary loans, database searching, Internet access, and laptop Internet portals. Special learning facilities include a learning resource center, art gallery, natural history museum, and radio station. The 353-acre campus is in an urban area on the southern tip of Nevada, just east of the Las Vegas strip. Including any residence halls, there are 90 buildings.

Programs of Study: UNLV confers B.A., B.S., and B.F.A. degrees. Master's and doctoral degrees are also awarded. Bachelor's degrees are awarded in BIO-

LOGICAL SCIENCE (biology/biological science), BUSINESS (accounting, banking and finance, hotel/motel and restaurant management, human resources, international business management, management information systems, management science, marketing/retailing/merchandising, real estate, and recreational facilities management), COMMUNICATIONS AND THE ARTS (art history and appreciation, communications, dance, dramatic arts, English, film arts, fine arts, French, German, music, romance languages and literature, and Spanish), COMPUTER AND PHYSICAL SCIENCE (applied physics, chemistry, computer science, earth science, geology, mathematics, physics, and radiological technology), EDUCATION (elementary education, health education, physical education, recreation education, secondary education, special education, and trade and industrial education), ENGINEERING AND ENVIRONMENTAL DESIGN (architectural engineering, civil engineering, computer engineering, construction management, electrical/electronics engineering, environmental science, interior design, landscape architecture/design, mechanical engineering, and urban planning technology), HEALTH PROFESSIONS (clinical science, exercise science, health care administration, nuclear medical technology, nursing, and sports medicine), SOCIAL SCIENCE (anthropology, criminal justice, economics, food production/management/services, history, interdisciplinary studies, philosophy, physical fitness/movement, political science/government, psychology, public administration, social science, social work, sociology, and women's studies). Hotel administration, fine arts, and engineering are the strongest academically.

Special: Opportunities are provided for internships, an accelerated degree program, B.A.-B.S. degrees, dual majors, credit by examination, credit for military service, nondegree study, pass/fail options, and study abroad in 25 countries. There are 16 national honor societies, including Phi Beta Kappa, a freshman honors program, and 11 departmental honors programs.

Admissions: The SAT scores for the 2009-2010 freshman class were: Critical Reading--50% below 500, 36% between 500 and 599, 13% between 600 and 700, and 1% above 700; Math--42% below 500, 38% between 500 and 599, 17% between 600 and 700, and 3% above 700. The ACT scores were 16% below 21, 52% between 21 and 23, 15% between 24 and 26, 14% between 27 and 28, and 3% above 28. 52% of the current freshmen were in the top fifth of their class; 85% were in the top two fifths. There were 3 National Merit finalists in a recent year.

Requirements: The SAT or ACT is required for some programs. In addition, graduation from an accredited secondary school is required. Applicants must also meet the academic core requirements, which include 4 credits in English and 3 each in history, social studies, math, and science. A GPA of 3.0 is required. AP and CLEP credits are accepted. Important factors in the admissions decision are recommendations by school officials, advanced placement or honors courses, and geographical diversity.

Procedure: Freshmen are admitted to all sessions. Entrance exams should be taken by February 1. There is a rolling admissions plan. Applications should be filed by February 1 for fall entry; October 1 for spring entry; and February 1 for summer entry, along with a $60 fee. Applications are accepted on-line.

Financial Aid: In a recent year, the average freshman award was $4711. Need-based scholarships or need-based grants averaged $3791, and need-based self-help aid (loans and jobs) averaged $3336. 75% of undergraduate students work part-time. UNLV is a member of CSS. The CCS/Profile, FAFSA, FFS, or SFS, and the college's own financial statement, and the Singlefile Form are required. The priority date for freshman financial aid applications for fall entry is February 1.

Computers: Wireless access is available. The UNLV wireless network is available to currently enrolled UNLV students, faculty, and staff. All students may access the system 24 hours a day, 7 days a week. There are no time limits and no fees.

UNIVERSITY OF NEW HAMPSHIRE
Durham, NH 03824 (603) 862-1360; (603) 862-0077

Full-time: 5045 men, 6513 women	**Faculty:** 610; I, av$
Part-time: 117 men, 137 women	**Ph.D.s:** 84%
Graduate: 1084 men, 1636 women	**Student/Faculty:** 19 to 1
Year: 4-1-4, summer session	**Tuition:** $12,743 ($26,713)
Application Deadline: February 1	**Room & Board:** $8874

Freshman Class: 15656 applied, 11145 accepted, 2837 enrolled
SAT CR/M: 553/570 **ACT:** required

VERY COMPETITIVE

The University of New Hampshire, founded in 1866, is part of the public university system of New Hampshire and offers degree programs in liberal arts, engineering, physical sciences, business, economics, life sciences, agriculture, and health and human services. There are 6 undergraduate schools and 1 graduate school. In addition to regional accreditation, UNH has baccalaureate program accreditation with AACSB, ABET, ADA, AHEA, CAHEA, CSAB, CSWE, NASM, NLN, NRPA, and SAF. The 5 libraries contain 2.4 million volumes, 3.0 million microform items, and 302,135 audio/video tapes/CDs/DVDs, and subscribe to 50,043 periodicals including electronic. Computerized library services include interlibrary loans, database searching, Internet access, and laptop Internet portals. Special learning facilities include a learning resource center, art gallery, radio station, TV station, optical observatory, marine research lab, experiential learning center, electron microscope, child development center, journalism lab, various agricultural and equine facilities, sawmill, language labs, performing arts center, and survey center. The 2600-acre campus is in a rural area 50 miles north of Boston. Including any residence halls, there are 183 buildings.

Programs of Study: UNH confers B.A., B.F.A., B.M., B.S., and B.S.F. degrees. Associates, master's, and doctoral degrees are also awarded. Bachelor's degrees are awarded in AGRICULTURE (animal science, dairy science, environmental studies, forestry and related sciences, horticulture, plant science, soil science, and wildlife management), BIOLOGICAL SCIENCE (biochemistry, biology/biological science, genetics, microbiology, molecular biology, neurosciences, nutrition, and zoology), BUSINESS (business administration and management, hospitality management services, hotel/motel and restaurant management, recreation and leisure services, and tourism), COMMUNICATIONS AND THE ARTS (classics, communications, English, English literature, fine arts, French, German, Greek, Latin, linguistics, music, music performance, music theory and composition, Russian, Spanish, studio art, and voice), COMPUTER AND PHYSICAL SCIENCE (chemistry, computer science, earth science, geology, information sciences and systems, mathematics, and physics), EDUCATION (athletic training, English education, environmental education, mathematics education, music education, physical education, recreation education, and science education), ENGINEERING AND ENVIRONMENTAL DESIGN (chemical engineering, city/community/regional planning, civil engineering, computer engineering, electrical/electronics engineering, environmental engineering, environmental science, and mechanical engineering), HEALTH PROFESSIONS (biomedical science, health care administration, health science, medical laboratory science, nursing, occupational therapy, preveterinary science, and speech pathology/audiology), SOCIAL SCIENCE (anthropology, economics, European studies, family/consumer studies, French studies, history, humanities, philosophy, physical fitness/movement, political science/government, psychology, social work, sociology, water resources, and women's studies). Business, engineering, and English are the strongest academically. Business, psychology, and English are the largest.

Special: Joint programs with Cornell University in marine science are available. Extensive cross-registration is possible through the New Hampshire College and University Council Consortium. There also is nationwide study through the National Student Exchange and worldwide study through the Center for International Education. Internships, study abroad throughout the world, a Washington semester, work-study, and B.A.-B.S. degrees, dual majors, a general studies degree, student-designed majors, extensive 3-2 B.S.-M.B.A. programs and other bachelor's-graduate degree plans, nondegree study, and pass/fail options are also available. A 3-2 engineering degree is offered with the New Hampshire Technical Institute, Vermont Technical College, Keene State College, and other institutions. There are 18 national honor societies, including Phi Beta Kappa, a freshman honors program, and 42 departmental honors programs.

Admissions: 71% of the 2009-2010 applicants were accepted. The SAT scores for the 2009-2010 freshman class were: Critical Reading--21% below 500, 51% between 500 and 599, 24% between 600 and 700, and 4% above 700; Math--16% below 500, 46% between 500 and 599, 34% between 600 and 700, and 4% above 700. 51% of the current freshmen were in the top fifth of their class; 90% were in the top two fifths. 62 freshmen graduated first in their class.

Requirements: The SAT or ACT is required. The ACT Optional Writing test is also required. In addition, applicants should have 18 academic credits, including 4 each in English and math, 3 each in science and foreign language, and 2 in social studies. An essay is required for all students. An audition is required for music students. AP and CLEP credits are accepted. Important factors in the admissions decision are advanced placement or honors courses, recommendations by school officials, and evidence of special talent.

Procedure: Freshmen are admitted fall and spring. Entrance exams should be taken before February 1 of the senior year. There are early decision, early admissions and deferred admissions plans. Early decision applications should be filed by November 15; regular applications by February 1 for fall entry and October 15 for spring entry. The application fee is $50 for New Hampshire residents and $60 for nonresidents. Notification of early decision is sent January 15; regular decision, April 15. Applications are accepted on-line.

Financial Aid: In 2009-2010, 84% of all full-time freshmen and 79% of continuing full-time students received some form of financial aid. 60% of all full-time freshmen and 59% of continuing full-time students received need-based aid. The average freshmen award was $18,637, with $7416 ($28,331 maximum) from need-based scholarships or need-based grants; $5275 ($10,000 maximum) from need-based self-help aid (loans and jobs); $24,504 ($33,832 maximum) from non-need-based athletic scholarships; and $10,123 ($35,000 maximum) from other non-need-based awards and non-need-based scholarships. 33% of undergraduate students work part-time. Average annual earnings from campus work are $3719. The average financial indebtedness of the 2009 graduate was $30,760. The FAFSA is required. The deadline for filing freshman financial aid applications for fall entry is March 1.

Computers: Wireless access is available. Students can access the system from residence halls, PC clusters, classrooms, and the library, as well as the student union and the front lawn of the main administrative building. All students may access the system. There are no time limits and no fees. It is strongly recommended that all students have a personal computer.

UNIVERSITY OF NEW MEXICO
Albuquerque, NM 87131-0001
(505) 277-2446
(800) 225-5866; (505) 277-6686

Full-time: 7011 men, 8386 women	**Faculty:** I, --$
Part-time: 2482 men, 3513 women	**Ph.D.s:** 84%
Graduate: 2555 men, 3357 women	**Student/Faculty:** n/av
Year: semesters, summer session	**Tuition:** $5101 ($17,254)
Application Deadline: June 15	**Room & Board:** $7746
Freshman Class: 10,743 applied, 6614 accepted,. 3409 enrolled	
SAT CR/M: 550/550	**ACT:** 22 **COMPETITIVE**

The University of New Mexico, founded in 1889, is a public university offering instruction in liberal and fine arts, business, engineering, health science, teacher preparation, law, and technology. In addition to the Albuquerque campus, there are 4 branch campuses. There are 9 undergraduate schools and 5 graduate schools. In addition to regional accreditation, UNM has baccalaureate program accreditation with AACSB, ABET, ACCE, ACEJMC, ACPE, ADA, CAHEA, CSAB, NAAB, NASM, and NCATE. The 8 libraries contain 3.1 million volumes, 4.7 million microform items, and 48,400 audio/video tapes/CDs/DVDs, and subscribe to 77,094 periodicals including electronic. Computerized library services include interlibrary loans, database searching, Internet access, and laptop Internet portals. Special learning facilities include a learning resource center, art gallery, planetarium, radio station, TV station, robotics lab, lithography and meteoritic institutes, observatory, arts lab, and museums of geology, anthropology, biology, and art. The 769-acre campus is in an urban area within the city of Albuquerque. Including any residence halls, there are 350 buildings.

Programs of Study: UNM confers B.A., B.S., B.A.A., B.A.E.P.D., B.A.Ed., B.A.F.A., B.B.A., B.F.A., B.M., B.M.E., B.S.C.E., B.S.Ch.E., B.S.Cp.E., B.S.Cn.E., B.S.C.S., B.S.D.H., B.S.E.E., B.S.Ed., B.S.M.E., B.S.M.L., B.S.N., B.S.D.H, B.S.N.E., and B.U.S. degrees. Associates, master's, and doctoral degrees are also awarded. Bachelor's degrees are awarded in BIOLOGICAL SCIENCE (biochemistry, biology/biological science, life science, and nutrition), BUSINESS (business administration and management), COMMUNICATIONS AND THE ARTS (American Sign Language, art, art history and appreciation, classics, communications, comparative literature, dance, English, fine arts, French, German, journalism, languages, linguistics, media arts, music, Portuguese, Russian, Spanish, studio art, and theater design), COMPUTER AND PHYSICAL SCIENCE (astrophysics, chemistry, computer science, digital arts/technology, earth science, mathematics, physics, and statistics), EDUCATION (art education, athletic training, drama education, early childhood education, elementary education, health education, music education, physical education, secondary education, and special education), ENGINEERING AND ENVIRONMENTAL DESIGN (architecture, chemical engineering, civil engineering, computer engineering, construction engineering, construction management, electrical/electronics engineering, environmental design, environmental science, mechanical engineering, nuclear engineering, and technological management), HEALTH PROFESSIONS (dental hygiene, emergency medical technologies, exercise science, health psychology, medical laboratory technology, nursing, physician's assistant, radiological science, and speech pathology/audiology), SOCIAL SCIENCE (African American studies, American studies, anthropology, Asian/

Oriental studies, child care/child and family studies, criminology, economics, European studies, family/consumer studies, geography, history, human development, human services, Latin American studies, Native American studies, philosophy, political science/government, psychology, religion, Russian and Slavic studies, sociology, and women's studies). Business administration, psychology, and biology are the largest.

Special: There is a 3-2 engineering program with the Anderson School of Management. Study abroad is available in 28 countries. The university offers cooperative programs in arts and sciences management, engineering, and fine arts, a Washington semester, work-study, dual and student-designed majors, a general studies degree, credit for military experience, nondegree study, and pass/fail options. There are 20 national honor societies, including Phi Beta Kappa, a freshman honors program, and 46 departmental honors programs.

Admissions: 62% of the 2009-2010 applicants were accepted. The SAT scores for the 2009-2010 freshman class were: Critical Reading--29% below 500, 38% between 500 and 599, 28% between 600 and 700; and 5% above 700; Math--32% below 500, 36% between 500 and 599, 29% between 600 and 700, and 3% above 700. The ACT scores were 38% below 21, 28% between 21 and 23, 20% between 24 and 26, 8% between 27 and 28, and 7% above 29. 37% of the current freshmen were in the top fifth of their class; 68% were in the top two fifths. 34 freshmen graduated first in their class.

Requirements: The SAT or ACT is required. A total of 13 academic credits is required, including 4 years of English, 3 years of math, and 2 years each of foreign language, natural science (1 lab), and social science (1 U.S. history). A GED is accepted. Freshman applicants must be graduates of a high school accredited by a regional accrediting association or by the state department of education and state university of the state in which the high school is located. The minimum GPA requirement for admission to bachelor degree programs is 2.25 (on a 4.00 scale) in all previous academic work from an accredited high school. Grades in all courses allowed toward high school graduation are computed in the average. A GPA of 2.3 is required. AP and CLEP credits are accepted.

Procedure: Freshmen are admitted fall, spring, and summer. Entrance exams should be taken the summer following the junior year. There are early admissions, deferred admissions, and rolling admissions plans. Applications should be filed by June 15 for fall entry, November 15 for spring entry, and May 1 for summer entry. The fall 2009 application fee was $20. Notification is sent on a rolling basis. Applications are accepted on-line.

Financial Aid: The FAFSA is required. The priority date for freshman financial aid applications for fall entry is March 1. The deadline for filing freshman financial aid applications for fall entry is June 30.

Computers: Wireless access is available. All students have access to 6 computer pods and 11 computer classrooms. Wireless access is available in most buildings and some outdoor areas. All students may access the system. There are no time limits and no fees.

Full-time: 3100 men, 3400 women
Part-time: 970 men, 1180 women
Graduate: 1100 men, 1600 women
Year: semesters, summer session
Application Deadline: July 1
Freshman Class: n/av
SAT or ACT: required

Faculty: n/av
Ph.D.s: n/av
Student/Faculty: n/av
Tuition: $4336 ($12,474)
Room & Board: $6570

VERY COMPETITIVE

University of New Orleans, founded in 1958, is a public liberal arts institution. There are 6 undergraduate schools. Some figures in the above capsule and in this profile are approximate. In addition to regional accreditation, UNO has baccalaureate program accreditation with AACSB, ABET, CACREP, NASM, NAST, and NCATE. The library contains 896,000 volumes, 12.4 million microform items, and 22,775 audio/video tapes/CDs/DVDs, and subscribes to 4950 periodicals including electronic. Computerized library services include interlibrary loans, database searching, and Internet access. Special learning facilities include a learning resource center, art gallery, and radio station. The 395-acre campus is in an urban area in a residential area of New Orleans. Including any residence halls, there are 34 buildings.

Programs of Study: UNO confers B.A., B.S., and B.G.S. degrees. Master's and doctoral degrees are also awarded. Bachelor's degrees are awarded in BIOLOGICAL SCIENCE (biology/biological science), BUSINESS (accounting, banking and finance, business administration and management, hotel/motel and restaurant management, marketing/retailing/merchandising, and tourism), COMMUNICATIONS AND THE ARTS (art, art history and appreciation, communications, dramatic arts, English, fine arts, French, music, Spanish, and studio art), COMPUTER AND PHYSICAL SCIENCE (chemistry, computer science, earth science, geology, geophysics and seismology, mathematics, and physics), EDUCATION (early childhood education, elementary education, English education, foreign languages education, mathematics education, music education, physical education, and secondary education), ENGINEERING AND ENVIRONMENTAL DESIGN (civil engineering, electrical/electronics engineering, environmental science, marine engineering, mechanical engineering, and naval architecture and marine engineering), HEALTH PROFESSIONS (health, medical technology, premedicine, and preveterinary science), SOCIAL SCIENCE (anthropology, economics, geography, history, international studies, philosophy, political science/government, psychology, sociology, and urban studies). Business administration, general studies, and film, theater, and communication arts are the largest.

Special: Students may participate in co-op programs and may cross-register with Southern University in New Orleans, Elaine P. Nunez Community College, and Delgado Community College. Internships are available, and work-study programs are available with various federal agencies and private companies. Students may study abroad in 14 countries or participate in a Washington semester. UNO also offers dual majors, B.A.-B.S. degrees, preprofessional programs in cardiopulmonary science, dental hygiene, dentistry, medical technology, medicine, nursing, occupational therapy, ophthalmic medical technology, pharmacy, physical therapy, physician's assistant, rehabilitation counseling, and veterinary medicine. 3-2 engineering degrees with Xavier University, Southern University in New Orleans, Loyola University New Orleans, and Dillard University are offered. There are 12 national honor societies, a freshman honors program, and 29 departmental honors programs.

Admissions: 81% of a recent year's applicants were accepted.

Requirements: The SAT or ACT is required. In addition, students who graduate from state-approved high schools must complete the Louisiana Board of Regents Core Curriculum and require no more than 1 developmental/remedial course (ACT of 19 or higher or equivalent SAT score of 460 or higher in Mathematics and ACT of 18 or higher or equivalent SAT score of 450 or higher in Critical Reading is nonremedial) AND 1 of the following: ACT composite score of 23 or greater (SAT 1060, Critical Reading and Math) OR high school cumulative GPA of 2.5 or greater and nonremedial in English and Math subscores OR high school graduation rank in top 25% of class. UNO requires applicants to be in the upper 25% of their class. A GPA of 2.5 is required. AP and CLEP credits are accepted. Important factors in the admissions decision are advanced placement or honors courses, recommendations by school officials, and evidence of special talent.

Procedure: Freshmen are admitted to all sessions. Entrance exams should be taken at least 6 months prior to enrollment. There are early admissions, deferred admissions, and rolling admissions plans. The priority application date for fall entry is July 1. Application fee is $40. Applications are accepted on-line.

Financial Aid: In a recent year, 71% of all full-time freshmen and 67% of continuing full-time students received some form of financial aid. 46% of all full-time freshmen and 45% of continuing full-time students received need-based aid. The average freshmen award was $6830. UNO is a member of CSS. The FAFSA is required. Check with the school for current application deadlines.

Computers: Wireless access is available. The campus network consists of an Ethernet-based backbone network connecting all main campus buildings and remote campus sites to provide data communications to meet academic and administrative needs. It provides support for more than 5000 wired and wireless clients, modem access, access to Internet1, and to the advanced research networks, Internet2 and the National LamdaRail. All students may access the system. There are no time limits and no fees.

UNIVERSITY OF NORTH CAROLINA AT ASHEVILLE

Asheville, NC 28804-8510

(828) 251-6481
(800) 531-9842; (828) 251-6482

Full-time: 1333 men, 1799 women	**Faculty:** 208; IIB, av$
Part-time: 336 men, 377 women	**Ph.D.s:** 85%
Graduate: 23 men, 29 women	**Student/Faculty:** 15 to 1
Year: semesters, summer session	**Tuition:** $4411 ($16,128)
Application Deadline: February 15	**Room & Board:** $6890
Freshman Class: 2510 applied, 1921 accepted, 641 enrolled	
SAT CR/M/W: 590/590/570	**ACT:** 25 **VERY COMPETITIVE**

The University of North Carolina at Asheville is the designated public liberal arts university in the 16-campus UNC system. There is 1 graduate school. In addition to regional accreditation, UNC Asheville has baccalaureate program accreditation with AACSB and NCATE. The library contains 269,044 volumes, 860,972 microform items, and 13,850 audio/video tapes/CDs/DVDs, and subscribes to 6943 periodicals including electronic. Computerized library services include interlibrary loans, database searching, Internet access, and laptop Internet portals. Special learning facilities include a learning resource center, art gallery, radio station, a distance learning facility, a center for creative retirement, an undergraduate research center, botanical gardens, a music recording center, the Key Center for Service Learning, and the National Environmental Modeling and Analysis Center. The 265-acre campus is in a suburban area. Including any residence halls, there are 33 buildings.

Programs of Study: UNC Asheville confers B.A., B.S., and B.F.A. degrees. Master's degrees are also awarded. Bachelor's degrees are awarded in BIOLOGICAL SCIENCE (biology/biological science), BUSINESS (accounting and business administration and management), COMMUNICATIONS AND THE ARTS (art, classics, communications, dramatic arts, French, German, literature, multimedia, music, music technology, and Spanish), COMPUTER AND PHYSICAL SCIENCE (atmospheric sciences and meteorology, chemistry, computer science, mathematics, and physics), ENGINEERING AND ENVIRONMENTAL DESIGN (engineering, environmental science, and industrial administration/management), HEALTH PROFESSIONS (health), SOCIAL SCIENCE (economics, history, liberal arts/general studies, philosophy, political science/government, psychology, religion, sociology, and women's studies). Psychology, literature, and environmental studies are the largest.

Special: UNC Asheville participates in a consortium with Warren Wilson and Mars Hill Colleges, and there is cross-registration with a number of North Carolina universities and colleges. Study-abroad programs are available in 46 countries. The school offers internships, dual majors, student-designed interdisciplinary majors, and a 2-2 engineering degree and joint engineering degree with North Carolina State University. Nondegree study is available. There are 13 national honor societies, a freshman honors program, and 11 departmental honors programs.

Admissions: 77% of the 2009-2010 applicants were accepted. The SAT scores for the 2009-2010 freshman class were: Critical Reading--11% below 500, 39% between 500 and 599, 42% between 600 and 700, and 8% above 700; Math--11% below 500, 44% between 500 and 599, 42% between 600 and 700, and 3% above 700; Writing--15% below 500, 45% between 500 and 599, 36% between 600 and 700, and 5% above 700. The ACT scores were 8% below 21, 28% between 21 and 23, 28% between 24 and 26, 21% between 27 and 28, and 15% above 28. 46% of the current freshmen were in the top fifth of their class; 84% were in the top two fifths. 4 freshmen graduated first in their class.

Requirements: The SAT or ACT is required. The ACT Optional Writing test is also required. In addition, graduation from an accredited secondary school is required. UNC Asheville requires a minimum of 16 high school academic units, including 4 of English, 4 of math (algebra I, geometry, algebra II, and a class beyond algebra II), 3 science (biology, physical science, and a lab course), 2 of social studies/history, and 2 of a foreign language. Applicants are evaluated primarily on their academic achievement record, extracurricular activities that support academic achievement, and SAT or ACT scores. AP and CLEP credits are accepted. Important factors in the admissions decision are advanced placement or honors courses, leadership record, and evidence of special talent.

Procedure: Freshmen are admitted fall and spring. Entrance exams should be taken at the end of the junior year or the beginning of the senior year. There are early admissions and deferred admissions plans. Applications should be filed by February 15 for fall entry and October 15 for spring entry. Application fee is $50. Notification is sent April 1. Applications are accepted on-line.

Financial Aid: In 2009-2010, 70% of all full-time freshmen and 66% of continuing full-time students received some form of financial aid. 50% of all full-time freshmen and 52% of continuing full-time students received need-based aid. The average freshman award was $8632. Need-based scholarships or need-based grants averaged $5916 ($15,019 maximum); need-based self-help aid (loans and jobs) averaged $2932 ($9,496 maximum); non-need-based athletic scholarships averaged $6859 ($11,975 maximum); and other non-need-based awards and non-need-based scholarships averaged $4014 ($12,600 maximum). 21% of undergraduate students work part-time. Average annual earnings from campus work are $1740. The average financial indebtedness of the 2009 graduate was $14,596. The FAFSA is required. The priority date for freshman financial aid applications for fall entry is March 1.

Computers: Wireless access is available. UNC Asheville students can access the college's network from more than 216 desktop computers located in computer labs, classrooms, library carrels, and dorm labs. All dorm rooms are wired with a high-speed Internet connection for each occupant. Wireless Internet access is available in the library, the student center, and some classroom buildings. Students can check out laptops for use in the library. All students may access the system 24 hours a day. There are no time limits and no fees.

UNIVERSITY OF NORTH CAROLINA AT CHAPEL HILL

Chapel Hill, NC 27599-2200   (919) 962-3621; (919) 962-3045

Full-time: 7053 men, 10130 women	**Faculty:** 1484; I, +$
Part-time: 324 men, 474 women	**Ph.D.s:** 84%
Graduate: 4448 men, 6457 women	**Student/Faculty:** 12 to 1
Year: semesters, summer session	**Tuition:** $5626 ($23,514)
Application Deadline: January 15	**Room & Board:** $8670
Freshman Class: 23224 applied, 7345 accepted, 3958 enrolled	
SAT CR/M/W: 640/660/630	**ACT:** 29 **MOST COMPETITIVE**

The University of North Carolina at Chapel Hill, chartered in 1789 and the nation's first public university, offers academic programs leading to 77 bachelor's, 107 master's, and 69 doctoral degrees, as well as 6 professional degrees. There are 9 undergraduate schools and 12 graduate schools. The 14 libraries contain 6.7 million volumes, 5.2 million microform items, and 382,214 audio/video tapes/CDs/DVDs, and subscribe to 80,132 periodicals including electronic. Computerized library services include interlibrary loans, database searching, Internet access, and laptop Internet portals. Special learning facilities include a learning resource center, art gallery, planetarium, radio station, TV station, botanical garden, and theater. The 729-acre campus is in a suburban area 25 miles west of Raleigh. Including any residence halls, there are 356 buildings.

Programs of Study: UNC-Chapel Hill confers A.B., B.S., A.B.E.D., A.B.J.M., B.F.A., B.Mus., B.S.A.S.C., B.S.B.A., B.S.BIO., B.S.C.H., B.S.C.L.S., B.S.C.S., B.S.D.H., B.S.E.N.S., B.S.Geo., B.S.Hum., B.S.I.S., B.S.Mat., B.S.M.D.S., B.S.N., B.S.P.H., B.S.Phy., and B.S.R.S. degrees. Master's and doctoral degrees are also awarded. Bachelor's degrees are awarded in AGRICULTURE (environmental studies), BIOLOGICAL SCIENCE (biology/biological science, biometrics and biostatistics, and nutrition), BUSINESS (business administration and management, management science, and recreational facilities management), COMMUNICATIONS AND THE ARTS (art history and appreciation, classics, communications, comparative literature, dramatic arts, English, German, journalism, linguistics, music, music performance, romance languages and literature, Russian, and studio art), COMPUTER AND PHYSICAL SCIENCE (applied mathematics, applied science, chemistry, computer science, geology, information sciences and systems, mathematics, and physics), EDUCATION (elementary education and middle school education), ENGINEERING AND ENVIRONMEN-

TAL DESIGN (environmental science), HEALTH PROFESSIONS (clinical science, dental hygiene, exercise science, health care administration, medical laboratory technology, nursing, pharmacology, and radiological science), SOCIAL SCIENCE (African American studies, American studies, anthropology, archeology, Asian/Oriental studies, child care/child and family studies, economics, European studies, geography, history, interdisciplinary studies, international studies, Latin American studies, peace studies, philosophy, political science/government, psychology, public affairs, religion, Russian and Slavic studies, sociology, and women's studies). Biology, business administration, psychology, and journalism are the largest.

Special: Students may participate in joint programs with Duke University and North Carolina State University. Internships, study abroad in 70 countries, B.A.-B.S. degrees, a Washington semester, and student-designed majors are available. There are pass/fail options and nondegree study. There are 10 national honor societies, including Phi Beta Kappa, a freshman honors program, and 54 departmental honors programs.

Admissions: 32% of the 2009-2010 applicants were accepted. The SAT scores for the 2009-2010 freshman class were: Critical Reading--3% below 500, 24% between 500 and 599, 47% between 600 and 700, and 27% above 700; Math--2% below 500, 15% between 500 and 599, 52% between 600 and 700, and 31% above 700; Writing--5% below 500, 27% between 500 and 599, 50% between 600 and 700, and 18% above 700. The ACT scores were 2% below 21, 7% between 21 and 23, 16% between 24 and 26, 19% between 27 and 28, and 56% above 28. 91% of the current freshmen were in the top fifth of their class; 98% were in the top two-fifths. There were 132 National Merit finalists. 223 freshmen graduated first in their class.

Requirements: The SAT or ACT is required. The ACT Optional Writing test is also required. In addition, applicants should present a minimum of 16 units of high school coursework within the 5 traditional academic areas (literature, math, physical and biological sciences, social sciences, and foreign languages), including 4 units of English, at least 4 units of college preparatory math (2 algebra, 1 geometry, and a higher level math course for which algebra II is a prerequisite), at least 2 units of a single foreign language, 3 units in science, including at least 1 unit in a life or biological science, at least 1 unit in a physical science, and at least 1 lab course, and 2 units of social science, including U.S. history. AP and CLEP credits are accepted.

Procedure: Freshmen are admitted in the fall. Entrance exams should be taken in the junior or senior year. There are early admissions and deferred admissions plans. Applications should be filed by January 15 for fall entry, along with a $70 fee. Notification is sent March 20. Applications are accepted on-line. 2500 applicants were on a recent waiting list.

Financial Aid: In 2009-2010, 63% of all full-time freshmen and 59% of continuing full-time students received some form of financial aid. 31% of all full-time freshmen and 32% of continuing full-time students received need-based aid. The average freshmen award was $10,996 ($37,663 maximum) from need-based scholarships or need-based grants; $2,759 ($12,173 maximum) from need-based self-help aid (loans and jobs); $10,706 ($27,730 maximum) from non-need-based athletic scholarships; and $4,646 ($37,662 maximum) from other non-need-based awards and non-need-based scholarships. 15% of undergraduate students work part-time. Average annual earnings from campus work are $3465. The average financial indebtedness of the 2009 graduate was $14,262. UNC-Chapel Hill is a member of CSS. The CSS/Profile and FAFSA are required. The priority date for freshman financial aid applications for fall entry is March 1.

Computers: Wireless access is available. All students may access the system 24 hours a day. There are no time limits and no fees. All students are required to have a personal computer. A Lenovo Thinkpad is recommended.

UNIVERSITY OF NORTH CAROLINA AT WILMINGTON

Wilmington, NC 28403-5904	(910) 962-3243; (910) 962-3038
Full-time: 4030 men, 5565 women	**Faculty:** IIA, av$
Part-time: 340 men, 655 women	**Ph.D.s:** n/av
Graduate: 380 men, 695 women	**Student/Faculty:** n/av
Year: semesters, summer session	**Tuition:** $4700 ($15,600)
Application Deadline: see profile	**Room & Board:** $7700
Freshman Class: n/av	
ACT: required	**SAT:** required
	VERY COMPETITIVE

The University of North Carolina at Wilmington, founded in 1947, is a publicly funded institution offering programs in the liberal arts and sciences, education, and business. It is a part of the University of North Carolina System. Figures in the above capsule are approximate. There are 4 undergraduate schools and 1 graduate school. In addition to regional accreditation, UNC at Wilmington has baccalaureate program accreditation with NCATE and NLN. The library contains 542,399 volumes, 230,800 microform items, and 69,682 audio/video tapes/CDs/DVDs, and subscribes to 13,683 periodicals including electronic. Computerized library services include interlibrary loans, database searching, Internet access, and laptop Internet portals. Special learning facilities include a radio station, TV station, wildflower preserve, nature preserve, museum of world cultures, and the research vessel Seahawk, used for a marine biology lab and for research. The 661-acre campus is in a suburban area 125 miles southeast of Raleigh. Including any residence halls, there are 84 buildings.

Programs of Study: UNC at Wilmington confers B.A., B.S., B.F.A., and B.S.W. degrees. Master's degrees are also awarded. Bachelor's degrees are awarded in BIOLOGICAL SCIENCE (biology/biological science, marine biology, and marine science), BUSINESS (accounting, banking and finance, business administration and management, business economics, business systems analysis, and marketing/retailing/merchandising), COMMUNICATIONS AND THE ARTS (art history and appreciation, creative writing, dramatic arts, English, film arts, French, music, music performance, Spanish, speech/debate/rhetoric, and studio art), COMPUTER AND PHYSICAL SCIENCE (chemistry, computer science, geology, mathematics, physics, and statistics), EDUCATION (athletic training, early childhood education, elementary education, middle school education, music education, physical education, secondary education, and special education), ENGINEERING AND ENVIRONMENTAL DESIGN (environmental science), HEALTH PROFESSIONS (clinical science and nursing), SOCIAL SCIENCE (anthropology, criminal justice, economics, geography, German area studies, history, parks and recreation management, philosophy, political science/government, psychology, religion, social work, sociology, and therapeutic riding). Psychology is the largest.

Special: UNCW offers short-term internships, study abroad in several countries, and work-study programs. Dual majors may be pursued if requirements are met, and credit is given for military experience. There are 13 national honor societies, a freshman honors program, and 31 departmental honors programs.

Requirements: The SAT or ACT is required; the SAT is preferred. The ACT Optional Writing test is also required. Graduation from an accredited secondary school or the GED is required for admission. High school courses must include 4 years of English, 4 years of math (algebra I, II, geometry, and a math beyond algebra II), 3 units of science (1 year each of biology, physical science, and a lab course), 2 years of social studies including 1 year of U.S. history, and 2 years of a foreign language. A GPA of 2.0 is required. AP and CLEP credits are accepted.

Procedure: Freshmen are admitted fall and summer. Entrance exams should be taken during the junior or senior year. There is an early admissions plan. Check with the school for current application deadlines. The application fee is $60. Applications are accepted on-line. A waiting list is maintained.

Financial Aid: Check with the school for current application deadlines.

Computers: Wireless access is available. UNCW has a laptop program that provides students with access to laptops equipped with wireless cards. Though provided by the centralized Information Technology Systems Division, these are available in distributed locations such as the library, the union, and the Technology Suppot Center. Students' personal computers are signed onto the network when they arrive on campus their freshman year. Students who live off-campus also have access to wireless and network services. All students may access the system from 8 A.M. to 11 P.M. at on-campus clusters and 24 hours daily via the Internet. There are no time limits and no fees. It is strongly recommended that all students have a personal computer. A Dell laptop is recommended.

UNIVERSITY OF NORTH DAKOTA
Grand Forks, ND 58202

(701) 777-4463
(800) 225-5863; (701) 777-2696

Full-time: 4775 men, 4025 women	**Faculty:** I, --$
Part-time: 755 men, 530 women	**Ph.D.s:** n/av
Graduate: 760 men, 1230 women	**Student/Faculty:** n/av
Year: semesters, summer session	**Tuition:** $6700 ($15,800)
Application Deadline: see profile	**Room & Board:** $5600
Freshman Class: n/av	
SAT or ACT: required	**VERY COMPETITIVE**

The University of North Dakota, established in 1883, is a state-supported comprehensive institution. Its undergraduate and graduate programs emphasize the liberal arts, fine arts, engineering, medicine, aerospace sciences, nursing, professional training, business and public administration, health science, teacher preparation, law, and computer science. Figures in the above capsule are approximate. There are 8 undergraduate schools and 3 graduate schools. In addition to regional accreditation, UND has baccalaureate program accreditation with AACSB, ABET, ACEJMC, ADA, APTA, CSAB, CSWE, NASAD, NASM, NCATE, and NLN. The 3 libraries contain 1.5 million volumes, 1.7 million microform items, and 17,972 audio/video tapes/CDs/DVDs, and subscribe to 41,565 periodicals including electronic. Computerized library services include interlibrary loans, database searching, Internet access, and laptop Internet portals. Special learning facilities include a learning resource center, art gallery, natural history museum, radio station, TV station, entrepreneur center, atmospherium, and art museum and gallery. The 549-acre campus is in an urban area 4 hours from Minneapolis/St. Paul and 2 hours from Winnipeg, Manitoba. Including any residence halls, there are 223 buildings.

Programs of Study: UND confers B.A., B.S., B.Acc., B.B.A., B.F.A., B.G.S., B.Mus., B.S.A., B.S.A.T., B.S.AtSc., B.S.C.E., B.S.Ch.E., B.S. Chem.,

B.S.C.J.S., B.S.C.L.S., B.S.C.N., B.S.C.S.C.I., B.S.Cyto., B.S.D., B.S.Ed., B.S.E.E., B.S.E.G., B.S.F.W.B., B.S.G.E., B.S.Geol., B.S.I.T., B.S.M.E., B.S.N., B.S.O.S.E.H., B.S.P.A., B.S.P.E., B.S.P.T., B.S.R.H.S., B.S.R.L.S., and B.S.S.W. degrees. Master's and doctoral degrees are also awarded. Bachelor's degrees are awarded in AGRICULTURE (fish and game management), BIOLOGICAL SCIENCE (biology/biological science), BUSINESS (accounting, banking and finance, business economics, entrepreneurial studies, management information systems, marketing/retailing/merchandising, and recreation and leisure services), COMMUNICATIONS AND THE ARTS (classical languages, communications, dramatic arts, English, French, German, graphic design, music, music performance, Norwegian, Spanish, and visual and performing arts), COMPUTER AND PHYSICAL SCIENCE (atmospheric sciences and meteorology, chemistry, computer science, geoenvironmental studies, geology, information sciences and systems, mathematics, and physics), EDUCATION (athletic training, business education, early childhood education, elementary education, marketing and distribution education, mathematics education, middle school education, music education, physical education, science education, and vocational education), ENGINEERING AND ENVIRONMENTAL DESIGN (air traffic control, airline piloting and navigation, aviation administration/management, aviation maintenance management, electrical/electronics engineering, environmental science, geological engineering, graphic arts technology, industrial engineering technology, mechanical engineering, and occupational safety and health), HEALTH PROFESSIONS (clinical science, community health work, cytotechnology, music therapy, nursing, physical therapy, and rehabilitation therapy), SOCIAL SCIENCE (anthropology, classical/ancient civilization, criminal justice, dietetics, economics, forensic studies, geography, history, interdisciplinary studies, international studies, philosophy, political science/government, psychology, public administration, social science, social work, and sociology). Health sciences, education, and foreign language are the strongest academically. Health sciences, business aviation, and engineering education are the largest.

Special: Special academic programs include cooperative programs, accelerated degree programs in most majors, internships in many majors, study abroad in at least 20 countries, work-study, and dual majors in all areas. Also offered are a general studies degree, honors programs, student-designed majors, B.A.-B.S. degrees, nondegree study, and pass/fail options. Alternative academic programs include the Division of Continuing Education's correspondence study, the Integrated Studies Program, which offers a means of fulfilling general education requirements by a semester of related course work, and study via telecommunications. Cross-registration with all North Dakota 2- and 4-year public institutions is possible. There are 28 national honor societies, including Phi Beta Kappa, a freshman honors program, and 1 departmental honors program.

Admissions: In a recent year, there were 9 National Merit finalists. 67 freshmen graduated first in their class.

Requirements: The SAT or ACT is required. The ACT is preferred, but the SAT will be accepted. Applicants must be graduates of an accredited secondary school or have passed the GED with an average of 50. A GPA of 2.5 is required. AP and CLEP credits are accepted.

Procedure: Freshmen are admitted to all sessions. Entrance exams should be taken in spring of the junior year or fall of the senior year. There are early decision and rolling admissions plans. Check with the school for current application deadlines. The application fee is $35. Notification is sent on a rolling basis.

Financial Aid: In a recent year, 82% of all full-time freshmen and 78% of continuing full-time students received some form of financial aid. 46% of all full-time freshmen and 45% of continuing full-time students received need-based aid. The average freshmen award was $4035, with $1543 ($2155 maximum) from need-based scholarships or need-based grants; $1929 ($3500 maximum) from need-based self-help aid (loans and jobs); $3097 ($20,376 maximum) from non-need-based athletic scholarships; and $2790 ($6000 maximum) from other non-need-based awards and non-need-based scholarships. 25% of undergraduate students work part-time. Average annual earnings from campus work are $2071. The average financial indebtedness of a recent graduate was $16,668. UND is a member of CSS. The FAFSA is required. Check with the school for current application deadlines.

Computers: Wireless access is available. The school provides e-mail accounts, web pages as permitted, and registration on-line. There is computer network access in computer centers/labs, residence halls, the library, and the student center. All students may access the system 24 hours a day. Students enrolled in aviation and medical must have a personal computer.

UNIVERSITY OF NORTH FLORIDA
Jacksonville, FL 32224   (904) 620-2624; (904) 620-2414

Full-time: 4541 men, 5905 women	**Faculty:** 392; II A, --$
Part-time: 1953 men, 2436 women	**Ph.D.s:** 86%
Graduate: 716 men, 1090 women	**Student/Faculty:** 42 to 1
Year: semesters, summer session	**Tuition:** $3774 ($15,823)
Application Deadline: November 13	**Room & Board:** $7872
Freshman Class: 6558 applied, 3428 accepted, 1108 enrolled	
SAT CR/M: 601/596	**ACT:** 24 **VERY COMPETITIVE**

The University of North Florida, founded in 1965, is a public university that is part of the state university system. There are 5 undergraduate schools and 5 graduate schools. In addition to regional accreditation, UNF has baccalaureate program accreditation with AACSB, ABET, ACCE, NASM, NCATE, and NLN. The library contains 817,643 volumes, 1.5 million microform items, and 27,447 audio/video tapes/CDs/DVDs, and subscribes to 35,225 periodicals including electronic. Computerized library services include interlibrary loans, database searching, Internet access, and laptop Internet portals. Special learning facilities include a learning resource center, art gallery, radio station, TV station, theater, auditorium, and nature preserve. The 1300-acre campus is in an urban area 12 miles southeast of downtown Jacksonville. Including any residence halls, there are 78 buildings.

Programs of Study: UNF confers B.A., B.S., B.A.E., B.B.A., B.F.A., B.M., B.S.E.E., B.S.H., and B.S.N. degrees. Associate, master's, and doctoral degrees are also awarded. Bachelor's degrees are awarded in BIOLOGICAL SCIENCE (biology/biological science), BUSINESS (accounting, banking and finance, business administration and management, business economics, marketing management, and transportation management), COMMUNICATIONS AND THE ARTS (art, communications, English, fine arts, jazz, music, music performance, and Spanish), COMPUTER AND PHYSICAL SCIENCE (chemistry, computer science, information sciences and systems, mathematics, physics, and statistics), EDUCATION (art education, athletic training, elementary education, mathematics education, middle school education, music education, physical education, science education, secondary education, social studies education, and special education), ENGINEERING AND ENVIRONMENTAL DESIGN (civil engineering, construction management, electrical/electronics engineering, and mechanical engineering), HEALTH PROFESSIONS (health science and nursing), SOCIAL

SCIENCE (anthropology, criminal justice, economics, history, philosophy, political science/government, psychology, and sociology). Nursing, fine arts, and elementary education are the strongest academically. Communication, psychology, and business are the largest.

Special: There are cooperative programs and internships in most majors and work-study programs with several Jacksonville businesses. Study abroad, a Washington semester, an accelerated degree program in nursing, B.A.-B.S. degrees in math, statistics, and psychology, dual majors, and student-designed majors also are available. Credit is given for military experience. There are 6 national honor societies, a freshman honors program, and 10 departmental honors programs.

Admissions: 52% of the 2009-2010 applicants were accepted. The SAT scores for the 2009-2010 freshman class were: Critical Reading--3% below 500, 44% between 500 and 599, 48% between 600 and 700, and 5% above 700; Math--4% below 500, 43% between 500 and 599, 49% between 600 and 700, and 4% above 700. The ACT scores were 5% below 21, 47% between 21 and 23, 35% between 24 and 26, 9% between 27 and 28, and 4% above 28. 44% of the current freshmen were in the top fifth of their class; 74% were in the top two fifths. 4 freshmen graduated first in their class.

Requirements: The SAT or ACT is required, with minimum acceptable composite scores of 970 on the SAT and 20 on the ACT. In addition, applicants must be graduates of an accredited secondary school or have a GED. A total of 15 academic credits plus 4 additional academic electives or 19 Carnegie units is required. Secondary school course work must include 4 years of English, 3 each of math, science, and social studies, and 2 of foreign language. This is the minimum to be considered. A GPA of 2.5 is required. AP and CLEP credits are accepted. Important factors in the admissions decision are advanced placement or honors courses, recommendations by school officials, and evidence of special talent.

Procedure: Freshmen are admitted to all sessions. Entrance exams should be taken during the spring of the junior year or the fall of the senior year. There are deferred admissions and rolling admissions plans. Applications should be filed by November 13 for fall entry and April 8 for summer entry. The fall 2008 application fee was $30. Notification is sent on a rolling basis. Applications are accepted on-line.

Financial Aid: In 2009-2010, 91% of all full-time freshmen and 78% of continuing full-time students received some form of financial aid. 39% of all full-time students received need-based aid. The average freshmen award was $1989. Need-based scholarships or need-based grants averaged $2147 ($9047 maximum); need-based self-help aid (loans and jobs) averaged $3097 ($4000 maximum); non-need-based athletic scholarships averaged $4867 ($10,257 maximum); and other non-need-based awards and non-need-based scholarships averaged $1826 ($24,147 maximum). 3% of undergraduate students work part-time. Average annual earnings from campus work are $6829. The average financial indebtedness of the 2009 graduate was $14,853. The FAFSA is required. The deadline for filing freshman financial aid applications for fall entry is April 1.

Computers: Wireless access is available. There are 300 public workstations in the library and 120 in the general computer lab. There are more than 150 wireless zones including the interior of buildings and dorms. All students may access the system. The general purpose labs are open more than 100 hours per week. There are no time limits and no fees. Students enrolled in building construction management must have a personal computer. A desktop or notebook with a minium 2.0ghz CPU, 1 gig RAM, and 80 GB is recommended.

UNIVERSITY OF NORTH TEXAS

Denton, TX 76203
(940) 565-2681
(800) UNT-8211; (940) 565-2408

Full-time: 9997 men, 12,143 women	**Faculty:** 613 I, --$
Part-time: 3053 men, 3281 women	**Ph.D.s:** 85%
Graduate: 2927 men, 4722 women	**Student/Faculty:** 36 to 1
Year: semesters, summer session	**Tuition:** $7301 ($15,611)
Application Deadline: August 1	**Room & Board:** $7301
Freshman Class: 12,833 applied, 8218 accepted, 3327 enrolled	
SAT or ACT: required	**COMPETITIVE**

The University of North Texas, founded in 1890, is a public institution offering programs through its schools of arts and sciences, education, business, engineering, public affairs and community service, information, music, merchandising and hospitality management, design and visual arts, honors, and journalism. There are 11 undergraduate schools and 1 graduate school. In addition to regional accreditation, UNT has baccalaureate program accreditation with AACSB, ABET, ACCE, ACEJMC, CSAB, CSWE, FIDER, NASM, NCATE, and NRPA. The 5 libraries contain 2.1 million volumes, 3.3 million microform items, and 218,285 audio/video tapes/CDs/DVDs, and subscribe to 37,380 periodicals including electronic. Computerized library services include interlibrary loans, database searching, Internet access, and laptop Internet portals. Special learning facilities include a learning resource center, art gallery, planetarium, radio station, observatory, and TV and film production unit. The 875-acre campus is in a suburban area 35 miles north of Dallas/Fort Worth. Including any residence halls, there are 160 buildings.

Programs of Study: UNT confers B.A., B.A.A.S., B.B.A., B.F.A., B.M., B.S., B.S.B.C., B.S.Bio., B.S.Chem., B.S.Eco., B.S.E.P., B.S.E.T., B.S.Math., B.S.M.T., B.S.Phy., and B.S.W. degrees. Master's and doctoral degrees are also awarded. Bachelor's degrees are awarded in BIOLOGICAL SCIENCE (biochemistry and biology/biological science), BUSINESS (accounting, banking and finance, business administration and management, electronic business, entrepreneurial studies, hospitality management services, human resources, insurance, investments and securities, logistics, management information systems, management science, marketing/retailing/merchandising, operations management, organizational behavior, organizational leadership and management, purchasing/inventory management, real estate, and recreation and leisure services), COMMUNICATIONS AND THE ARTS (applied art, art, art history and appreciation, broadcasting, choral music, communications, dance, design, dramatic arts, English, French, German, jazz, journalism, music, music history and appreciation, music performance, music theory and composition, musical theater, performing arts, radio/television technology, Spanish, studio art, telecommunications, theater design, theater management, and visual and performing arts), COMPUTER AND PHYSICAL SCIENCE (chemistry, computer science, information sciences and systems, mathematics, and physics), ENGINEERING AND ENVIRONMENTAL DESIGN (commercial art, computer engineering, construction engineering, electrical/electronics engineering, electrical/electronics engineering technology, emergency/disaster science, engineering physics, engineering technology, interior design, manufacturing engineering, mechanical engineering, mechanical engineering technology, and nuclear engineering technology), HEALTH PROFESSIONS (cytotechnology, health, medical laboratory technology, rehabilitation therapy, and speech pathology/audiology), SOCIAL SCIENCE (anthropology, applied psychology, child care/child and family studies, criminal justice, economics, fashion design and technology, geography, history, home furnishings and equipment management/production/services, human services, interdisciplinary studies, international studies, liberal arts/general studies, philosophy, physical fitness/movement, political science/government, psychology, social science, social work, and sociology). Accounting, jazz studies, and city management are the strongest academically. Biology, psychology, and interdisciplinary studies (teacher education department) are the largest.

Special: UNT offers co-op programs, internships, and work-study programs with the university. Students may study abroad in several locations. An accelerated degree program in math and science allows Texas high school students to obtain 2 years of college credit during their last 2 years in high school. Dual degrees, a general studies degree, and pass/fail options are also offered. There are 28 national honor societies and a freshman honors program.

Admissions: 64% of the 2009-2010 applicants were accepted. The SAT scores for the 2009-2010 freshman class were: Critical Reading--30% below 500, 45% between 500 and 599, 21% between 600 and 700; and 4% above 700; Math--26% below 500, 45% between 500 and 599, 24% between 600 and 700, and 5% above 700; Writing--44% below 500, 41% between 500 and 599, 14% between 600 and 700; and 2% above 700. The ACT scores were 59% below 21, 36% between 27 and 28, and 5% above 29.

Requirements: The SAT or ACT is required. In addition, applicants must be graduates of an accredited high school and submit a high school transcript. The required minimum score for entrance exams is determined by high school class rank. AP and CLEP credits are accepted.

Procedure: Freshmen are admitted fall, spring, and summer. Entrance exams should be taken at least 2 months before admissions deadlines. There are early admissions, deferred admissions, and rolling admissions plans. Applications should be filed by August 1 for fall entry, along with a $40 fee. Notification is sent on a rolling basis. Applications are accepted on-line.

Financial Aid: In 2009-2010, 53% of all full-time freshmen and 37% of continuing full-time students received some form of financial aid. 45% of all full-time freshmen and 29% of continuing full-time students received need-based aid. The average freshman award was $3800. 80% of undergraduate students work part-time. Average annual earnings from campus work are $2400. The average financial indebtedness of the 2009 graduate was $12,000. The FAFSA is required. The deadline for filing freshman financial aid applications for fall entry is June 1.

Computers: Wireless access is available across campus. All dorm rooms are wired for Internet. All students may access the system. Students are limited to 1 hour if labs are busy.

UNIVERSITY OF NOTRE DAME
Notre Dame, IN 46556   (574) 631-7505; (574) 631-8865

Full-time: 4491 men, 3865 women	**Faculty:** I, +$
Part-time: 10 men, 6 women	**Ph.D.s:** 95%
Graduate: 2085 men, 1359 women	**Student/Faculty:** n/av
Year: semesters, summer session	**Tuition:** $38,477
Application Deadline: December 31	**Room & Board:** $10,368
Freshman Class: 14357 applied, 4113 accepted, 2062 enrolled	
SAT or ACT: required	**MOST COMPETITIVE**

The University of Notre Dame, founded in 1842, is a private institution affiliated with the Roman Catholic Church offering undergraduate programs in architecture, arts and letters, business administration, engineering, and science. There are 5 undergraduate schools and 6 graduate schools. In addition to regional accreditation, Notre Dame has baccalaureate program accreditation with AACSB, ABET, APA-COA, and ATS. The 8 libraries contain 3.5 million volumes, 4.0 million microform items, and 43,368 audio/video tapes/CDs/DVDs, and subscribe to 88,352 periodicals including electronic. Computerized library services include interlibrary loans, database searching, Internet access, and laptop Internet portals. Special learning facilities include a learning resource center, art gallery, radio station, and art museum. The 1250-acre campus is in a suburban area 90 miles east of Chicago. Including any residence halls, there are 138 buildings.

Programs of Study: Notre Dame confers B.A., B.S., B.Arch., B.B.A., and B.F.A. degrees. Master's and doctoral degrees are also awarded. Bachelor's degrees are awarded in BIOLOGICAL SCIENCE (biochemistry and biology/biological science), BUSINESS (accounting, banking and finance, management information systems, management science, and marketing/retailing/merchandising), COMMUNICATIONS AND THE ARTS (Arabic, art history and appreciation, Chinese, design, English, film arts, French, German, Greek, Italian, Japanese, music, romance languages and literature, Russian, Spanish, and studio art), COMPUTER AND PHYSICAL SCIENCE (applied physics, chemistry, computer science, geoenvironmental studies, mathematics, medical physics, and physics), EDUCATION (science education), ENGINEERING AND ENVIRONMENTAL DESIGN (aeronautical engineering, architecture, chemical engineering, civil engineering, computer engineering, electrical/electronics engineering, environmental science, and mechanical engineering), HEALTH PROFESSIONS (predentistry and premedicine), SOCIAL SCIENCE (African studies, American studies, anthropology, classical/ancient civilization, economics, history, liberal arts/general studies, medieval studies, philosophy, philosophy and religion, political science/government, psychology, sociology, and theological studies). Engineering, theology, and business are the strongest academically. Finance, political science, and psychology are the largest.

Special: Cross-registration is offered with Saint Mary's College. Study abroad is possible in 20 countries. A 5-year arts and letters/engineering B.A.-B.S. degree is offered. There is a program of liberal studies, centered on the discussion of great books. Internships, an accelerated degree program, a Washington semester, dual majors, 3-2 engineering degrees, and pass/fail options are available. There are 10 national honor societies, including Phi Beta Kappa, and 2 departmental honors programs.

Admissions: 29% of the 2009-2010 applicants were accepted. The SAT scores for a recent freshman class were: Critical Reading--2% below 500, 10% between 500 and 599, 37% between 600 and 700, and 51% above 700; Math--1% below 500, 7% between 500 and 599, 34% between 600 and 700, and 58% above 700; Writing--2% below 500, 13% between 500 and 599, 42% between 600 and 700, and 43% above 700. The ACT scores were 2% between 21 and 23, 15% between 27 and 28, and 83% above 28. 96% of the current freshmen were in the top fifth of their class; all were in the top two fifths.

Requirements: The SAT or ACT is required. In addition, applicants should be graduates of an accredited secondary school with 16 Carnegie credits completed, including 4 years of English, 3 of math, and 2 each of science, foreign language, and history. The SAT subject test in a foreign language is recommended. An essay is required. An audition or a portfolio is recommended for some majors. AP credits are accepted.

Procedure: Freshmen are admitted in the fall. Entrance exams should be taken by fall of the senior year. There is a deferred admissions plan. Applications should be filed by December 31 for fall entry, along with a $65 fee. Notification is sent April 10. Applications are accepted on-line. 928 applicants were on a recent waiting list.

Financial Aid: Notre Dame is a member of CSS. The CSS/Profile, FAFSA, and federal income tax return are required. Check with the school for current application deadlines.

Computers: Wireless access is available. All students may access the system 24 hours a day. There are no time limits and no fees. It is strongly recommended that all students have a personal computer. Baseline configurations are specified each year; visit http://oit.nd.edu/policies/rup.shtml for policy details.

UNIVERSITY OF OKLAHOMA
Norman, OK 73019

(405) 325-2252
(800) 234-6868; (405) 325-7124

Full-time: 8442 men, 8581 women	**Faculty:** 1115; I, --$
Part-time: 1373 men, 1460 women	**Ph.D.s:** 76%
Graduate: 3417 men, 3383 women	**Student/Faculty:** 15 to 1
Year: semesters, summer session	**Tuition:** $6493 ($16,474)
Application Deadline: April 1	**Room & Board:** $7598
Freshman Class: 8951 applied, 8303 accepted, 3760 enrolled	
SAT CR/M: 570/590	**ACT:** 25 **VERY COMPETITIVE**

The University of Oklahoma, founded in 1890, is a comprehensive research university offering 163 areas for undergraduate study. There are 13 undergraduate schools and 12 graduate schools. In addition to regional accreditation, OU has baccalaureate program accreditation with AACSB, ABET, ACCE, ACEJMC, CSWE, FIDER, NAAB, NASM, and NCATE. The 9 libraries contain 5.4 million volumes, 4.5 million microform items, and 13,629 audio/video tapes/CDs/DVDs, and subscribe to 69,621 periodicals including electronic. Computerized library services include interlibrary loans, database searching, Internet access, and laptop Internet portals. Special learning facilities include an art gallery, natural history museum, radio station, TV station, and observatory. The 3910-acre campus is in a suburban area 18 miles south of Oklahoma City. Including any residence halls, there are 260 buildings.

Programs of Study: OU confers B.A., B.S., B.Arch., B.B.A., B.F.A., B.Int.Des., B.Lib.Studies, B.Mus.Arts, B.Mus.Ed., and B.Mus. degrees. Master's and doctoral degrees are also awarded. Bachelor's degrees are awarded in BIOLOGICAL SCIENCE (biochemistry, botany, microbiology, and zoology), BUSINESS (accounting, banking and finance, business administration and management, business economics, human resources, international business management, management information systems, and marketing/retailing/merchandising), COMMUNICATIONS AND THE ARTS (advertising, art, art history and appreciation, broadcasting, Chinese, classics, communications, comparative literature, dance, dramatic arts, English, film arts, French, German, journalism, language arts, languages, linguistics, music, musical theater, public relations, Russian, Spanish, and video), COMPUTER AND PHYSICAL SCIENCE (astronomy, astrophysics, atmospheric sciences and meteorology, chemistry, computer science, environmental geology, geology, geophysics and seismology, geoscience, information sciences and systems, mathematics, paleontology, and physics), EDUCATION (early childhood education, elementary education, foreign languages education, mathematics education, music education, science education, social studies education, and special education), ENGINEERING AND ENVIRONMENTAL DESIGN (aeronautical engineering, architectural engineering, architecture, aviation administration/management, chemical engineering, civil engineering, computer engineering, construction management, electrical/electronics engineering, engineering, engineering physics, environmental design, environmental engineering, environmental science, industrial engineering, interior design, land use management and reclamation, mechanical engineering, and petroleum/natural gas engineering), HEALTH PROFESSIONS (health science and medical laboratory technology), SOCIAL SCIENCE (African American studies, anthropology, area studies, Asian/Oriental studies, criminal justice, Eastern European studies, economics, European studies, geography, history, human development, interdisciplinary studies, international studies, Latin American studies, liberal arts/general studies, Native American studies, philosophy, political science/government, psychology, public affairs, religion, Russian and Slavic studies, social work, sociology, and women's studies). Meteorology, finance and accounting, and chemistry are the strongest academically. Management, journalism, and psychology are the largest.

Special: Co-op programs are available in arts and sciences, business, and engineering. A variety of voluntary and required internships are available in more than 50 fields of study. OU offers study abroad in 74 countries, work-study programs, a Washington semester, a general studies degree, dual and student-designed majors, nondegree study, pass/fail options, and credit for life experience. B.A.-B.S. degrees are offered in many subjects and an accelerated degree is offered in 15 majors. The interdisciplinary major in letters combines the classics, history, philosophy, and languages. A professional studies major is offered through the College of Continuing Education. There are 37 national honor societies, including Phi Beta Kappa, and a freshman honors program.

Admissions: 93% of the 2009-2010 applicants were accepted. The SAT scores for the 2009-2010 freshman class were: Critical Reading--20% below 500, 40% between 500 and 599, 28% between 600 and 700, and 12% above 700; Math--14% below 500, 38% between 500 and 599, 38% between 600 and 700, and 10% above 700. The ACT scores were 13% below 21, 14% between 21 and 23, 24% between 24 and 26, 13% between 27 and 28, and 36% above 28. 56% of the current freshmen were in the top fifth of their class; 86% were in the top two fifths. There were 196 National Merit finalists. 274 freshmen graduated first in their class.

Requirements: The SAT or ACT is required. Oklahoma residents performance requirements can be met by having a high school GPA of at least 3.00 and ranking in the upper 25% of their high school class, or by having a satisfactory score on the SAT, or 24 on the ACT, and a 3.00 GPA or ranking in the upper 50% of their high school class. With the same class ranking, minimum GPA 3.5 and scores of 1170 or 26 are required of nonresidents. Graduation from an accredited secondary school or a satisfactory score on the GED is required. Students must have a total of 15 curricular units, including 4 years of English, 3 of math, 2 each of history and lab science, 1 unit of citizenship skills, and 3 elective units from areas previously mentioned or computer science or foreign language. Some alternative admission opportunities are available, but are limited. OU requires applicants to be in the upper 50% of their class. A GPA of 3.0 is required. AP and CLEP credits are accepted.

Procedure: Freshmen are admitted to all sessions. Entrance exams should be taken during the junior year or the first part of the senior year. There is a rolling admissions plan. Applications should be filed by April 1 for fall entry, November 1 for spring entry, and April 1 for summer entry, along with a $40 fee. Notification is sent on a rolling basis. Applications are accepted on-line. 1707 applicants were on a recent waiting list, 1297 were accepted.

Financial Aid: In 2009-2010, 76% of all full-time freshmen and 70% of continuing full-time students received some form of financial aid. 48% of all full-time freshmen and 65% of continuing full-time students received need-based aid. The average freshmen award was $10,328, with $5,144 ($12,137 maximum) from need-based scholarships or need-based grants; $8,701 ($13,500 maximum) from need-based self-help aid (loans and jobs); and $5,028 ($29,190 maximum) from non-need-based athletic scholarships. 3% of undergraduate students work part-time. Average annual earnings from campus work are $2651. The average financial indebtedness of the 2009 graduate was $15,659. OU is a member of CSS. The FAFSA is required. The priority date for freshman financial aid applications for fall entry is March 1. The deadline for filing freshman financial aid applications for fall entry is June 1.

Computers: Wireless access is available. The university provides wired network connections in residence halls , classrooms, and many public areas for students to connect to the university network as well as Internet 1 and Internet 2. All students may access the system 24 hours per day. The fee is $15 per credit hour. It is strongly recommended that all students have a personal computer. Students enrolled in engineering programs must have a personal computer. A Dell or Apple is recommended.

UNIVERSITY OF OREGON

Eugene, OR 97403-1226

(541) 346-3201
(800) 232-3825; (541) 346-5815

Full-time: 8403 men, 8568 women	**Faculty:** 844; I, --$
Part-time: 766 men, 772 women	**Ph.D.s:** 96%
Graduate: 1787 men, 2039 women	**Student/Faculty:** 20 to 1
Year: quarters, summer session	**Tuition:** $7430 ($23,720)
Application Deadline: January 15	**Room & Board:** $8939
Freshman Class: 16780 applied, 13367 accepted, 3777 enrolled	
SAT or ACT: required	**VERY COMPETITIVE**

The University of Oregon, founded in 1876, is a public liberal arts institution within the Oregon University System. There are 6 undergraduate schools and 8 graduate schools. In addition to regional accreditation, UO has baccalaureate program accreditation with AACSB, ACEJMC, ASLA, FIDER, NAAB, NASM, and NRPA. The 5 libraries contain 3.1 million volumes, 4.2 million microform items, and 112,034 audio/video tapes/CDs/DVDs, and subscribe to 46,879 periodicals including electronic. Computerized library services include interlibrary loans, database searching, Internet access, and laptop Internet portals. Special learning facilities include a learning resource center, art gallery, natural history museum, radio station, an art museum, a natural and cultural history museum, centers for sports marketing, entrepreneurship, instrumentation, and computer music, a chemistry lab, and a longhouse. The 295-acre campus is in a suburban area 110 miles south of Portland. Including any residence halls, there are 107 buildings.

Programs of Study: UO confers B.A., B.S., B.Arch., B.Ed., B.F.A., B.I.Arch., B.L.A., and B.Mus. degrees. Master's and doctoral degrees are also awarded. Bachelor's degrees are awarded in AGRICULTURE (environmental studies), BIOLOGICAL SCIENCE (biochemistry, biology/biological science, marine biology, and physiology), BUSINESS (accounting and business administration and management), COMMUNICATIONS AND THE ARTS (advertising, art, art history and appreciation, ceramic art and design, Chinese, classics, communications, comparative literature, dance, design, digital communications, dramatic arts, English, fiber/textiles/weaving, fine arts, French, German, graphic design, Greek,

Italian, Japanese, jazz, journalism, Latin, linguistics, metal/jewelry, music, music performance, music theory and composition, painting, photography, printmaking, public relations, romance languages and literature, Russian, sculpture, and Spanish), COMPUTER AND PHYSICAL SCIENCE (chemistry, computer science, digital arts/technology, geology, mathematics, physics, and science), EDUCATION (education and music education), ENGINEERING AND ENVIRONMENTAL DESIGN (architecture, environmental science, interior design, and landscape architecture/design), HEALTH PROFESSIONS (speech pathology/audiology), SOCIAL SCIENCE (anthropology, Asian/Oriental studies, classical/ancient civilization, economics, ethnic studies, family and community services, geography, history, humanities, international studies, Judaic studies, Latin American studies, medieval studies, philosophy, political science/government, psychology, public administration, religion, sociology, and women's studies). Architecture, journalism, and biology are the strongest academically. Business, psychology, and journalism are the largest.

Special: UO offers cross-registration with other school in the Oregon University System, matriculation agreements with more than 25 Oregon and Washington community colleges, dual enrollment with Lane and Southwestern Oregon Community Colleges, study abroad in more than 90 countries, preengineering in conjunction with Lane Community College, and an engineering/physics program with Oregon State University. In addition, numerous internship opportunities, dual majors, a 3-2 engineering degree, and pass/fail options are available. There are 22 national honor societies, including Phi Beta Kappa, a freshman honors program, and 41 departmental honors programs.

Admissions: 80% of the 2009-2010 applicants were accepted. The SAT scores for the 2009-2010 freshman class were: Critical Reading--25% below 500, 44% between 500 and 599, 25% between 600 and 700, and 6% above 700; Math--25% below 500, 42% between 500 and 599, 28% between 600 and 700, and 5% above 700. 50% of the current freshmen were in the top fifth of their class; 83% were in the top two fifths. There were 13 National Merit finalists. 295 freshmen graduated first in their class.

Requirements: The SAT or ACT is required. The ACT Optional Writing test is also required. In addition, standard freshman admission requirements include a high school GPA of at least 3.0, graduation from a standard or regionally accredited high school, and C- or higher in 14 college preparatory courses. Applications are evaluated based on strength of academic course work, grade trends, class rank, standardized test scores, academic motivation as demonstrated in the application essay, special talents, extracurricular activities, including community service or the need to work to assist your family financially, and ability to enhance the diversity of the university. Applicants can earn automatic admission with a cumulative high school GPA of at least 3.4 and completion of at least 16 college preparatory units with grades of C- or better in each course. AP and CLEP credits are accepted.

Procedure: Freshmen are admitted to all sessions. Entrance exams should be taken after October 15 of the junior year and before March of the senior year. There is a rolling admissions plan. Applications should be filed by January 15 for fall entry, October 15 for winter entry, February 1 for spring entry, and March 1 for summer entry, along with a $50 fee. Notification is sent on a rolling basis beginning April 15. Applications are accepted on-line.

Financial Aid: In 2009-2010, 46% of all full-time freshmen and 43% of continuing full-time students received some form of financial aid. 16% of all full-time freshmen and 21% of continuing full-time students received need-based aid. The average freshman award was $8,112. Need-based scholarships or need-based

grants averaged $6114; need-based self-help aid (loans and jobs) averaged $4027; non-need-based athletic scholarships averaged $19,746; and other non-need-based awards and non-need-based scholarships averaged $2457. The average financial indebtedness of the 2009 graduate was $18,805. The FAFSA is required. The deadline for filing freshman financial aid applications for fall entry is March 1.

Computers: Wireless access is available. Access to the campus network and the Internet is provided via 40 computer labs with approximately 950 workstations for student use; approximately 5,000 Ethernet connections in student residences; and the campus wireless network, which covers the majority of the public space on campus. All students may access the system 24 hours a day. There are no time limits and no fees. It is strongly recommended that all students have a personal computer. Students enrolled in architecture and law must have a personal computer.

UNIVERSITY OF PENNSYLVANIA
Philadelphia, PA 19104 (215) 898-7507

Full-time: 5300 men, 5100 women	**Faculty:** I, ++$
Part-time: 175 men, 150 women	**Ph.D.s:** n/av
Graduate: 4500 men, 4800 women	**Student/Faculty:** 2 to 1
Year: semesters, summer session	**Tuition:** $36,208
Application Deadline: January 1	**Room & Board:** $11,430
Freshman Class: 22,718 applied, 34018 accepted, 2501 enrolled	
SAT or ACT: required	**MOST COMPETITIVE**

University of Pennsylvania, founded in 1740, is a private institution offering undergraduate and graduate degrees in arts and sciences, business, engineering and applied science, and nursing. There are 4 undergraduate schools and 12 graduate schools. Enrollment figures in the above capsule and figures in this profile are approximate. In addition to regional accreditation, Penn has baccalaureate program accreditation with AACSB, ABET, ADA, NAAB, NCATE, and NLN. The 15 libraries contain 5.8 million volumes, 4.1 million microform items, and 88,696 audio/video tapes/CDs/DVDs, and subscribe to 51,242 periodicals including electronic. Computerized library services include interlibrary loans, database searching, Internet access, and laptop Internet portals. Special learning facilities include a learning resource center, art gallery, planetarium, radio station, TV station, arboretum, animal research center, primate research center, language lab, center for performing arts, institute for contemporary art, wind tunnel, electron microscope, and museum of anthropology and archeology. The 269-acre campus is in an urban area in Philadelphia. Including any residence halls, there are 155 buildings.

Programs of Study: Penn confers B.A., B.S., B.Applied Sc., B.B.A., B.F.A., B.S.E., and B.S.N. degrees. Associates, master's, and doctoral degrees are also awarded. Bachelor's degrees are awarded in AGRICULTURE (environmental studies), BIOLOGICAL SCIENCE (biochemistry, biology/biological science, and biophysics), BUSINESS (accounting, business administration and management, entrepreneurial studies, human resources, insurance and risk management, logistics, management information systems, marketing/retailing/merchandising, operations management, real estate, retailing, and transportation management), COMMUNICATIONS AND THE ARTS (art history and appreciation, classics, communications, comparative literature, design, dramatic arts, English, fine arts, folklore and mythology, French, German, linguistics, music, Russian, and visual and performing arts), COMPUTER AND PHYSICAL SCIENCE (actuarial science, applied science, chemistry, computer science, digital arts/technology, geology, information sciences and systems, mathematics, physics, science technology, and statistics), EDUCATION (elementary education), ENGINEERING AND ENVIRONMENTAL DESIGN (architecture, bioengineering, chemical engineering, civil engineering, computer engineering, electrical/electronics engineering, and materials engineering), HEALTH PROFESSIONS (health, health care administration, and nursing), SOCIAL SCIENCE (African studies, African American studies, American studies, anthropology, Asian/Oriental studies, cognitive science, economics, gender studies, Hispanic American studies, history, history of science, international relations, international studies, Italian studies, Judaic studies, Latin American studies, law, Middle Eastern studies, Near Eastern studies, philosophy, political science/government, psychology, public administration, religion, sociology, South Asian studies, urban studies, and women's studies). Liberal arts, engineering, and management are the strongest academically. Finance, economics, and history are the largest.

Special: Cross-registration is permitted with Haverford, Swarthmore, and Bryn Mawr Colleges and through the Quaker Consortium. Opportunities are provided for internships, a Washington semester, accelerated degree programs, joint degree programs, preprofessional programs, B.A.-B.S. degrees, dual and student-designed majors, credit by exam, limited pass/fail options, and study abroad in 39 countries. Through the ''one university'' concept, students in 1 undergraduate school may study in any of the other 3. There are 11 national honor societies, a freshman honors program, and 27 departmental honors programs.

Admissions: 18% of the 2009-2010 applicants were accepted. 95.3% of freshmen were in the top 10% of their high school class.

Requirements: The SAT or ACT is required. Graduation from an accredited secondary school is not required. Recommended preparation includes 4 years of high school English, 3 or 4 each of a foreign language and math, and 3 each of history and social science. An essay is required. A portfolio is recommended for prospective art majors. AP credits are accepted. Important factors in the admissions decision are advanced placement or honors courses, recommendations by school officials, and evidence of special talent.

Procedure: Freshmen are admitted fall. Entrance exams should be taken by December of the senior year. There is a deferred admissions plan. Early decision applications should be filed by November 1; regular applications by January 1 for fall entry. Notification of early decision is sent December 15, regular decision, April 1. Check with the school for current application fee. Applications are accepted on-line. 1269 applicants were on a recent waiting list, 35 were accepted.

Financial Aid: In a recent year, 56% of all full-time freshmen and 58% of continuing full-time students received some form of financial aid. 38% of all full-time freshmen and 40% of continuing full-time students received need-based aid. The average freshmen award was $32,183, with $28,024 ($51,130 maximum) from need-based scholarships or need-based grants and $4159 ($9300 maximum) from need-based self-help aid (loans and jobs). All undergraduate students work part-time. Average annual earnings from campus work are $1834. The average financial indebtedness of a recent graduate was $18,800. Penn is a member of CSS. The CSS/Profile, FAFSA, the college's own financial statement, parents' and student's most recently filed federal income tax returns, and CSS Noncustodial Parent File are required. Check with the school for current deadlines.

Computers: Wireless Internet access is available in all campus residences, some Greek Houses, and most academic buildings, libraries, and public spaces. All campus buildings are also wired for Ethernet, and students residing in campus residences and in Greek houses have an Ethernet connection in their room, in addition to wireless access. They may also use the more than 1000 networked PCs in computer labs, libraries, and other locations on campus. All students may access the system. There are no time limits and no fees. It is strongly recommended that all students have a personal computer.

UNIVERSITY OF PITTSBURGH AT PITTSBURGH

Pittsburgh, PA 15260	**(412) 624-PITT; (412) 648-8815**
Full-time: 8244 men, 8475 women	**Faculty:** ; I, -$
Part-time: 600 men, 712 women	**Ph.D.s:** 90%
Graduate: 4601 men, 5696 women	**Student/Faculty:** n/av
Year: semesters, summer session	**Tuition:** $14,154 ($23,852)
Application Deadline: open	**Room & Board:** $8900
Freshman Class: 21737 applied, 12722 accepted, 3642 enrolled	
SAT CR/M/W: 620/640/610	**ACT:** 27 **HIGHLY COMPETITIVE**

The University of Pittsburgh, founded in 1787, is a state-related, public research university with programs in arts and sciences, education, engineering, law, social work, business, health science, information sciences, and public and international affairs. There are 10 undergraduate schools and 14 graduate schools. In addition to regional accreditation, Pitt has baccalaureate program accreditation with AACSB, ABET, ACPE, ADA, and CSWE. The 16 libraries contain 5.5 million volumes, 5.4 million microform items, and 1.1 million audio/video tapes/CDs/DVDs, and subscribe to 59,141 periodicals including electronic. Computerized library services include interlibrary loans, database searching, Internet access, and laptop Internet portals. Special learning facilities include a learning resource center, art gallery, radio station, international classrooms, located in the 42-story Cathedral of Learning, an observatory, and a music hall. The 132-acre campus is in an urban area 3 miles east of downtown Pittsburgh. Including any residence halls, there are 128 buildings.

Programs of Study: Pitt confers B.A., B.S., B.A.S.W., B.Phil., B.S.B.A., B.S.E., and B.S.N. degrees. Master's and doctoral degrees are also awarded. Bachelor's degrees are awarded in AGRICULTURE (environmental studies), BIOLOGICAL SCIENCE (bioinformatics, biology/biological science, ecology, evolutionary biology, microbiology, molecular biology, neurosciences, and nutrition), BUSINESS (accounting, banking and finance, business administration and management, business communications, international business management, management science, and marketing/retailing/merchandising), COMMUNICATIONS AND THE ARTS (art history and appreciation, Chinese, classics, communications, dramatic arts, English, English literature, film arts, French, German, Italian, Japanese, linguistics, music, Polish, Russian, Spanish, speech/debate/rhetoric, and studio art), COMPUTER AND PHYSICAL SCIENCE (actuarial science, applied mathematics, astronomy, chemistry, computer science, environmental geology, geology, information sciences and systems, mathematics, natural sciences, physics, and statistics), EDUCATION (athletic training and education), ENGINEERING AND ENVIRONMENTAL DESIGN (architecture, bioengineering, chemical engineering, civil engineering, computational sciences, computer engineering, electrical/electronics engineering, engineering physics, industrial engineering, materials engineering, materials science, and mechanical engineering), HEALTH PROFESSIONS (dental hygiene, emergency medical technologies, health, health care administration, nursing, occupational therapy, and rehabilitation therapy), SOCIAL SCIENCE (African studies, African American studies, anthropology, criminal justice, developmental psychology, dietetics, Eastern European studies, economics, history, history of science, humanities, interdisciplinary studies, international studies, liberal arts/general studies, philosophy, political science/government, prelaw, psychology, public administration, public affairs, religion, social science, social work, sociology, and urban studies). Engineering, psychology, and nursing are the strongest academically.

Special: Students may cross-register with 9 neighboring colleges and universities. Internships, unlimited study abroad, a Washington semester, work-study programs, a dual major in business and any other subject in arts and sciences, and student-designed majors are available. There are freshman seminars and a 5-year joint degree in arts and sciences/engineering. There are co-op programs in engineering, computer science, and chemistry. An accelerated second degree B.S.N. program is available as well as a 3-2 engineering degree. There are 17 national honor societies, including Phi Beta Kappa, and a freshman honors program.

Admissions: 59% of the 2009-2010 applicants were accepted. The SAT scores for the 2009-2010 freshman class were: Critical Reading--3% below 500, 36% between 500 and 599, 41% between 600 and 700, and 20% above 700; Math--2% below 500, 24% between 500 and 599, 54% between 600 and 700, and 20% above 700; Writing--5% below 500, 39% between 500 and 599, 44% between 600 and 700, and 12% above 700. The ACT scores were 2% below 21, 10% between 21 and 23, 31% between 24 and 26, 20% between 27 and 28, and 37% above 28. 78% of the current freshmen were in the top fifth of their class; 98% were in the top two-fifths. 105 freshmen graduated first in their class.

Requirements: The SAT or ACT is required. In addition, applicants for admission to the School of Arts and Sciences must be graduates of an accredited secondary school. Students must have 15 high school academic credits, including 4 units of English, 3 to 4 each of math and lab science, 1 of social studies, and 1 of history, plus 3 to 5 units in academic electives. Pitt recommends that the student have 3 or more years of a single foreign language. An essay is recommended if the student is seeking scholarship consideration, and music students must audition. AP and CLEP credits are accepted.

Procedure: Freshmen are admitted to all sessions. Entrance exams should be taken preferably by January for September admission. There are deferred admissions and rolling admissions plans. Application deadlines are open. Application fee is $45. Notification is sent on a rolling basis. Applications are accepted on-line. 911 applicants were on a recent waiting list, 22 were accepted.

Financial Aid: In a recent year, 64% of all full-time freshmen and 63% of continuing full-time students received some form of financial aid. 54% of all full-time freshmen and 55% of continuing full-time students received need-based aid. The average freshmen award was $9,309. The average financial indebtedness of a recent graduate was $15,331. The FAFSA and the college's own financial statement are required. The priority date for freshman financial aid applications for fall entry is March 1.

Computers: Wireless access is available. Students have access to the university's wired network from 7 campus computing labs and all university residence halls. Students may also access the wireless network service anywhere on the Pittsburgh campus. The university provides 650 PCs in the central campus computing labs. Students also have access to the Internet from approximately 500 additional PCs in departmental computing labs. Students bring their own computers to the residence halls and wireless network areas. All students may access the system 24 hours a day. There are no time limits and no fees.

UNIVERSITY OF PORTLAND

Portland, OR 97203
(503) 943-7147
(888) 627-5601; (503) 943-7315

Full-time: 2000 men, 1850 women	**Faculty:** IIA, -$
Part-time: 60 men, 40 women	**Ph.D.s:** n/av
Graduate: 520 men and women	**Student/Faculty:** 13 to 1
Year: semesters, summer session	**Tuition:** $30,800
Application Deadline: see profile	**Room & Board:** $9135
Freshman Class: n/av	
SAT or ACT: required	**VERY COMPETITIVE**

The University of Portland, founded in 1901, is an independent institution affiliated with the Roman Catholic Church. It offers degree programs in the arts and sciences, business administration, education, engineering, and nursing. There are 5 undergraduate schools and 1 graduate school. Figures in this profile are approximate. In addition to regional accreditation, UP has baccalaureate program accreditation with AACSB, ABET, NASM, NCATE, and NLN. The library contains 380,000 volumes, 545,904 microform items, and 14,190 audio/video tapes/CDs/DVDs, and subscribes to 1584 periodicals including electronic. Computerized library services include interlibrary loans, database searching, Internet access, and laptop Internet portals. Special learning facilities include a learning resource center, art gallery, radio station, and observatory. The 155-acre campus is in an urban area 4 miles north of downtown Portland. Including any residence halls, there are 30 buildings.

Programs of Study: UP confers B.A., B.S., B.A.Ed., B.B.A., B.M.Ed., B.S.C.E., B.S.E.E., B.S.E.M., B.S.E.S., B.S.M.E., and B.S.N. degrees. Master's degrees are also awarded. Bachelor's degrees are awarded in BIOLOGICAL SCIENCE (biology/biological science), BUSINESS (accounting, banking and finance, international business management, and marketing/retailing/merchandising), COMMUNICATIONS AND THE ARTS (communications, dramatic arts, English, music, Spanish, and theater management), COMPUTER AND PHYSICAL SCIENCE (chemistry, computer science, mathematics, and physics), EDUCATION (elementary education, music education, and secondary education), ENGINEERING AND ENVIRONMENTAL DESIGN (civil engineering, electrical/electronics engineering, engineering, engineering management, environmental science, and mechanical engineering), HEALTH PROFESSIONS (nursing), SOCIAL SCIENCE (criminal justice, French studies, German area studies, history, interdisciplinary studies, philosophy, political science/government, psychology, social work, sociology, and theological studies).

Special: UP offers internships through individual departments, cross-registration with members of the Oregon Independent College Association, dual and interdisciplinary majors, including engineering chemistry and organizational communications, work-study programs, and pass/fail options. Study abroad may be arranged in Japan, Mexico, Australia, Chile, and several European countries. There are 9 national honor societies and a freshman honors program.

Requirements: The SAT or ACT is required, with a minimum score of 550 on each section of the SAT or a composite of 19 on the ACT. Graduation from an accredited secondary school or satisfactory scores on the GED are required. The high school curriculum should include courses in English composition, math, social studies, science, and a foreign language. 2 essays are required, as is a letter of recommendation from the high school counselor or principal. UP requires applicants to be in the upper 50% of their class. A GPA of 3.0 is required. AP and CLEP credits are accepted.

Procedure: Freshmen are admitted to all sessions. Entrance exams should be taken preferably before February 1 but no later than June 1 of the senior year. There are deferred admissions and rolling admissions plans. Check with the school for current deadlines and fee. Notification is sent on a rolling basis. Applications are accepted on-line. A waiting list is maintained.

Financial Aid: The FAFSA and the college's own financial statement are required. Check with the school for current deadline.

Computers: Wireless access is available. There are 1900 open, wired network connections available to students including 350 PCs. Wireless network is available in libraries, some classrooms, computer labs, administrative/faculty offices, and college-owned housing. All students may access the system. There are no time limits and no fees. It is strongly recommended that all students have a personal computer.

UNIVERSITY OF PUGET SOUND
Tacoma, WA 98416
(253) 879-3211
(800) 396-7191; (253) 879-3993

Full-time: 1029 men, 1470 women	**Faculty:** 219; IIB, +$
Part-time: 20 men, 8 women	**Ph.D.s:** 93%
Graduate: 52 men, 183 women	**Student/Faculty:** 11 to 1
Year: semesters, summer session	**Tuition:** $35,800
Application Deadline: February 1	**Room & Board:** $9190
Freshman Class: 5263 applied, 3526 accepted, 728 enrolled	
SAT CR/M/W: 640/616/610	**ACT:** required
	HIGHLY COMPETITIVE

The University of Puget Sound, founded in 1888, is an independent, residential, undergraduate liberal arts and sciences college with selected graduate programs building effectively on a liberal arts foundation. There is one undergraduate school and 2 graduate schools. In addition to regional accreditation, Puget Sound has baccalaureate program accreditation with NASM. The library contains 545,378 volumes, 441,890 microform items, and 17,366 audio/video tapes/CDs/DVDs. Computerized library services include interlibrary loans, database searching, Internet access, and laptop Internet portals. Special learning facilities include a learning resource center, a radio station, student science labs, an observatory, turnaround computer classrooms, a media center, theater workshops, a concert hall, a center for writing, learning, and teaching, a bibliographic instruction room, a natural history museum, an electron microscopy facility, and a student theater. The 97-acre campus is in a suburban area 35 miles south of Seattle and 1 mile from Commencement Bay on Puget Sound. Including any residence halls, there are 40 buildings.

Programs of Study: Puget Sound confers B.A., B.M., and B.S. degrees. Master's and doctoral degrees are also awarded. Bachelor's degrees are awarded in BIOLOGICAL SCIENCE (biochemistry, biology/biological science, and molecular biology), BUSINESS (business administration and management and international economics), COMMUNICATIONS AND THE ARTS (art, classics, communications, dramatic arts, English, French, German, music, music performance, and Spanish), COMPUTER AND PHYSICAL SCIENCE (chemistry, computer science, geology, mathematics, natural sciences, and physics), EDUCATION (music education), HEALTH PROFESSIONS (exercise science), SOCIAL SCIENCE (economics, history, philosophy, political science/government, psychology, religion, science and society, and sociology). Asian studies, international studies, and biochemistry are the strongest academically. Business, psychology, and English are the largest.

Special: Special academic programs include on- and off-campus work study, paid and unpaid internships in the community in conjunction with an internship seminar, and study abroad in 50 countries. There are 3-2 engineering degrees with Washington University in St. Louis, Columbia and Duke Universities, and the University of Southern California. B.A.- B.S. degrees in chemistry, physics, economics, a special interdisciplinary major, and a B.A.- B.M. degree are available. Dual majors in foreign language and international affairs, music and business, and computer science and business as well as pass/fail options are possible. Special features of the curriculum include the intensive 4-year study of the classics of Western civilization and the Business Leadership Program, combining traditional business and liberal arts study. There are 15 national honor societies, including Phi Beta Kappa, a freshman honors program, and 13 departmental honors programs.

Admissions: 67% of the 2009-2010 applicants were accepted. The SAT scores for the 2009-2010 freshman class were: Critical Reading--5% below 500, 25% between 500 and 599, 46% between 600 and 700, and 24% above 700; Math--6% below 500, 35% between 500 and 599, 50% between 600 and 700, and 10% above 700; Writing--8% below 500, 34% between 500 and 599, 49% between 600 and 700, and 9% above 700. The ACT scores were 4% below 21, 11% between 21 and 23, 26% between 24 and 26, 23% between 27 and 28, and 37% above 28. 62% of the current freshmen were in the top fifth of their class; 89% were in the top two fifths. There were 15 National Merit finalists. 34 freshmen graduated first in their class.

Requirements: The SAT or ACT is required. Other admission requirements include graduation from an accredited secondary school with a recommended 4 years of English, 3 to 4 of math and natural or physical lab science, 3 of social studies or history, 2 to 3 of foreign language, and 1 of fine, visual, or performing arts. Also required are letters of personal recommendation from a teacher and counselor; 2 are preferred. An essay must be submitted, and an interview is recommended. It is recommended that art students present a portfolio and music students audition. The GED is also accepted. AP credits are accepted. Important factors in the admissions decision are advanced placement or honors courses, evidence of special talent, and personality/intangible qualities.

Procedure: Freshmen are admitted to all sessions. Entrance exams should be taken during the fall of the senior year. There are early decision, early admissions and deferred admissions plans. Early decision applications should be filed by November 15; regular applications should be filed by February 1 for fall entry and March 1 for summer entry, along with a $50 fee. Notification of early decision is sent December 15; regular decision, April 1. Applications are accepted on-line. 319 applicants were on a recent waiting list.

Financial Aid: In 2009-2010, 93% of all full-time freshmen and 91% of continuing full-time students received some form of financial aid. 65% of all full-time freshmen and 64% of continuing full-time students received need-based aid. The average freshmen award was $25,596, with $14,384 ($29,110 maximum) from need-based scholarships or need-based grants; $6575 ($9720 maximum) from need-based self-help aid (loans and jobs); and $8438 from other forms of aid. 44% of undergraduate students work part-time. Average annual earnings from campus work are $2175. The average financial indebtedness of the 2009 graduate was $21,179. Puget Sound is a member of CSS. The FAFSA is required. The

CSS/Profile is required of early decision candidates. The deadline for filing freshman financial aid applications for fall entry is February 1.

Computers: Wireless access is available throughout the campus. There are more than 400 wired computers across campus for general access in academic buildings, computer labs, classrooms, residence halls, and other spaces. All students may access the system. There are no time limits and no fees. It is strongly recommended that all students have a personal computer.

UNIVERSITY OF REDLANDS
Redlands, CA 92373-0999

(909) 335-4074
(800) 455-5064; (909) 335-4089

Full-time: 975 men, 1375 women	**Faculty:** IIA, av$
Part-time: 10 men, 15 women	**Ph.D.s:** 86%
Graduate: 30 men, 20 women	**Student/Faculty:** n/av
Year: 4-1-4	**Tuition:** $30,500
Application Deadline: see profile	**Room & Board:** $10,000
Freshman Class: n/av	
SAT or ACT: required	**VERY COMPETITIVE**

University of Redlands, founded in 1907, is a private institution that offers programs in liberal and fine arts, business, and teacher preparation. Figures in the above capsule are approximate. There are 2 undergraduate schools and 4 graduate schools. The library contains 421,219 volumes, 317,465 microform items, and 6091 audio/video tapes/CDs/DVDs, and subscribes to 12,800 periodicals including electronic. Computerized library services include interlibrary loans, database searching, and Internet access. Special learning facilities include an art gallery, radio station, language lab, computer center, and geographic information systems lab. The 160-acre campus is in a suburban area 60 miles east of Los Angeles. Including any residence halls, there are 86 buildings.

Programs of Study: Redlands confers B.A., B.S., and B.Mus. degrees. Master's degrees are also awarded. Bachelor's degrees are awarded in AGRICULTURE (environmental studies), BIOLOGICAL SCIENCE (biochemistry and biology/biological science), BUSINESS (accounting and business administration and management), COMMUNICATIONS AND THE ARTS (art, creative writing, dramatic arts, English, English literature, French, German, music, Spanish, and studio art), COMPUTER AND PHYSICAL SCIENCE (chemistry, computer science, information sciences and systems, mathematics, and physics), EDUCATION (music education), ENGINEERING AND ENVIRONMENTAL DESIGN (environmental science), SOCIAL SCIENCE (anthropology, Asian/Oriental studies, economics, history, interdisciplinary studies, international relations, liberal arts/general studies, philosophy, political science/government, psychology, religion, and sociology). Liberal arts is the strongest academically. Business is the largest.

Special: Cross-registration with sister colleges, various internships, and study abroad in 50 countries are offered. A Washington semester, a Sacramento program, various work-study programs, B.A.-B.S. degrees, a liberal studies degree, dual majors, and accelerated degree programs are available. Students may pursue nondegree study, take advantage of pass/fail options, and receive credit for life or work experience. At the Johnston Center for Integrative Studies, students design their own majors and courses of study. There are 4 national honor societies, including Phi Beta Kappa, a freshman honors program, and 23 departmental honors programs.

Requirements: The SAT or ACT is required. In addition, applicants should complete at least 16 credits in academic areas, including 4 years of English, 3 years of math, up to and including algebra II, and 2 to 3 years of foreign language, sciences, and social studies. AP and CLEP credits are accepted. Important factors in the admissions decision are advanced placement or honors courses, leadership record, and personality/intangible qualities.

Procedure: Freshmen are admitted fall and spring. Entrance exams should be taken prior to application. There are deferred admissions and rolling admissions plans. Check with the school for current application deadlines. The fall 2009 application fee was $45. Applications are accepted on-line. A waiting list is maintained.

Financial Aid: The FAFSA, the college's own financial statement, and the GPA verification form for California residents are required. Check with the school for current application deadlines.

Computers: Wireless access is available. Housed within the Fletcher Jones Center are labs/classrooms, a hands-on lab, and a faculty technology center. All labs/classrooms are available when not being used for class. All students may access the system. There are no time limits and no fees.

UNIVERSITY OF RICHMOND
University of Richmond, VA 23173 (804) 289-8640
(800) 700-1662; (804) 287-6003

Full-time: 1400 men, 1375 women	**Faculty:** IIB, +$
Part-time: 20 men, 15 women	**Ph.D.s:** 92%
Graduate: 85 men, 90 women	**Student/Faculty:** n/av
Year: semesters, summer session	**Tuition:** $42,000
Application Deadline: see profile	**Room & Board:** $9000
Freshman Class: n/av	
SAT or ACT: required	**MOST COMPETITIVE**

The University of Richmond, founded in 1830, is a private independent institution offering programs in arts and sciences, business, and leadership studies. Figures in the above capsule and this profile are approximate. There are 3 undergraduate schools and 3 graduate schools. In addition to regional accreditation, UR has baccalaureate program accreditation with AACSB and NASM. The 4 libraries contain 535,471 volumes, 90,484 microform items, and 43,590 audio/video tapes/CDs/DVDs, and subscribe to 159,301 periodicals including electronic. Computerized library services include interlibrary loans, database searching, Internet access, and laptop Internet portals. Special learning facilities include a learning resource center, art gallery, radio station, TV station, and the Lora Robins Gallery of Design from Nature. The 350-acre campus is in a suburban area 6 miles west of Richmond. Including any residence halls, there are 90 buildings.

Programs of Study: UR confers B.A., B.S., B.A.S., B.L.A., and B.S.B.A. degrees. Associate and master's degrees are also awarded. Bachelor's degrees are awarded in BIOLOGICAL SCIENCE (biochemistry, biology/biological science, and molecular biology), BUSINESS (accounting, business administration and management, and international business management), COMMUNICATIONS AND THE ARTS (art history and appreciation, communications, creative writing, dramatic arts, English, French, German, Greek, journalism, Latin, music, music performance, music theory and composition, Spanish, speech/debate/rhetoric, and studio art), COMPUTER AND PHYSICAL SCIENCE (chemistry, computer science, mathematics, and physics), ENGINEERING AND ENVIRONMENTAL DESIGN (environmental science and urban planning technology), SOCIAL SCIENCE (American studies, classical/ancient civilization, cognitive science, criminal justice, economics, history, interdisciplinary studies, international studies, medieval studies, philosophy, political science/government, psychology, religion, Russian and Slavic studies, sociology, urban studies, and women's studies). Business, biology, and political science are the largest.

Special: Internships in nearly every major, study abroad in 30 countries, and a Washington semester with American University are available. UR also offers work-study programs, B.A.-B.S. and B.S.-B.A. degrees, dual majors, student-designed majors, and a general studies degree through the School of Continuing Studies. There is a marine biology study option with the Marine Sciences Laboratory at Duke University. Also available are a 3-2 engineering degree with George Washington University, Virginia Tech, and Columbia University, a 3-1-1 degree with the University of Virginia, and a 4-1 degree with Virginia Commonwealth. There are 31 national honor societies, including Phi Beta Kappa, and 16 departmental honors programs.

Requirements: The SAT or ACT is required. In addition, applicants are encouraged to take the SAT Subject test or AP/IB test in a foreign language because it aids the language departments in determining placement. Applicants must be graduates of an accredited secondary school. The GED is accepted. Applicants must complete 16 high school academic credits, including 4 years of English, 3 of math, and at least 2 each of history, foreign language, and lab science. An essay, counselor recommendation, and auditions for music scholarships are required. AP and CLEP credits are accepted. Important factors in the admissions decision are advanced placement or honors courses, leadership record, and evidence of special talent.

Procedure: Freshmen are admitted in the fall. Entrance exams should be taken by February 1 of the senior year. There are early decision and deferred admissions plans. Early decision applications should be filed by November 15; check with the school for current application deadlines. The application fee is $50. Notification of early decision is sent December 15. Applications are accepted online. 1776 applicants were on a recent waiting list, 66 were accepted.

Financial Aid: The FAFSA and the college's own financial statement are required. Check with the school for current application deadlines

Computers: Wireless access is available. UR's high-speed wireless network allows students to register for classes, check their e-mail, access library databases, view their class Web sites, and access the Internet from nearly anywhere on campus. The wireless network, with approximately 560 wireless access points, allows access from all buildings on campus and many outdoor areas. In addition, UR, provides approximately 700 public computers spread across 14 computer labs, classrooms, and other public areas. All students may access the system. There are no time limits and no fees.

UNIVERSITY OF ROCHESTER

Rochester, NY 14627-0251

(585) 275-3221
(888) 822-2256; (585) 461-4595

Full-time: 2568 men, 2625 women	**Faculty:** I, av$
Part-time: 47 men, 207 women	**Ph.D.s:** 88%
Graduate: 2259 men, 2270 women	**Student/Faculty:** n/av
Year: semesters, summer session	**Tuition:** $38,690
Application Deadline: January 1	**Room & Board:** $11,200
Freshman Class: 12111 applied, 4686 accepted, 1087 enrolled	
SAT CR/M/W: 650/680/650	**ACT:** 30 **MOST COMPETITIVE**

The University of Rochester, founded in 1850, is a private institution offering programs in the arts and sciences, engineering and applied science, nursing, medicine and dentistry, business administration, music, and education. There are 4 undergraduate schools and 7 graduate schools. In addition to regional accreditation, UR has baccalaureate program accreditation with AACSB, ABET, ACPE, ADA, NASM, NCATE, and NLNAC. The 15 libraries contain 3.7 million volumes, 5.1 million microform items, and 110,495 audio/video tapes/CDs/DVDs, and subscribe to 27,240 periodicals including electronic. Computerized library services include interlibrary loans, database searching, and Internet access. Special learning facilities include a learning resource center, radio station, labs for nuclear structure research and laser energetics, a center for visual science, the Strong Memorial Hospital, an art center, an observatory, an institute of optics, a center for electronic imaging systems, and the National Science Foundation Center for Photoinduced Charge Transfer. The 655-acre campus is in a suburban area 2 miles south of downtown Rochester. Including any residence halls, there are 159 buildings.

Programs of Study: UR confers B.A., B.S., and B.M. degrees. Master's and doctoral degrees are also awarded. Bachelor's degrees are awarded in AGRICULTURE (environmental studies), BIOLOGICAL SCIENCE (biochemistry, biology/biological science, cell biology, ecology, microbiology, molecular biology, and neurosciences), BUSINESS (business economics), COMMUNICATIONS AND THE ARTS (American Sign Language, art history and appreciation, classics, comparative literature, English, film arts, French, German, Japanese, jazz, linguistics, media arts, music, music performance, music theory and composition, Russian, Spanish, and studio art), COMPUTER AND PHYSICAL SCIENCE (applied mathematics, astronomy, chemistry, computer science, geology, mathematics, optics, physics, and statistics), EDUCATION (music education), ENGINEERING AND ENVIRONMENTAL DESIGN (biomedical engineering, chemical engineering, electrical/electronics engineering, engineering and applied science, environmental science, geological engineering, and mechanical engineering), HEALTH PROFESSIONS (health, nursing, and public health), SOCIAL SCIENCE (African American studies, anthropology, archeology, cognitive science, economics, history, interdisciplinary studies, international relations, philosophy, political science/government, psychology, religion, Russian and Slavic studies, and women's studies). Biomedical engineering, optics, and political science are the strongest academically. Biology, economics, and engineering are the largest.

Special: Cross-registration is offered with Rochester Area Colleges. Selective programs for exceptional undergraduates in medicine (REMS), business (REBS), engineering (GEAR), and education (GRADE) guarantee admission to professional or graduate school upon completion of the bachelor's degree. The Take

Five Scholars Program allows students to stay tuition-free for a fifth year of study. Rochester offers 3-2 programs in business, engineering, human development, neuroscience, optics, physics and astronomy, and public health. Study abroad is possible in more than 30 countries. Internships, a Washington semester, B.A.-B.S. degrees, accelerated degree programs, dual and student-designed majors, nondegree study, and pass/fail options are available. There are 8 national honor societies, including Phi Beta Kappa, a freshman honors program, and 13 departmental honors programs.

Admissions: 39% of the 2009-2010 applicants were accepted. The SAT scores for the 2009-2010 freshman class were: Critical Reading--4% below 500, 26% between 500 and 599, 48% between 600 and 700, and 22% above 700; Math--2% below 500, 13% between 500 and 599, 48% between 600 and 700, and 37 above 700; Writing--3% below 500, 24% between 500 and 599, 52% between 600 and 700, and 21% above 700. The ACT scores were 2% between 21 and 23, 10% between 24 and 26, 19% between 27 and 28, and 69% above 28. 86% of the current freshmen were in the top fifth of their class; 99% were in the top two fifths. There were 21 National Merit finalists. 46 freshmen graduated first in their class.

Requirements: The SAT or ACT is required. In addition, applicants should be graduates of an accredited secondary school or have a GED equivalent. An essay or personal statement and recommendations are required. SAT Subject Tests and an interview are recommended. An audition is required for music majors. Applicants should complete the Common Application and the Rochester Supplement. AP credits are accepted. Important factors in the admissions decision are advanced placement or honors courses, personality/intangible qualities, and recommendations by school officials.

Procedure: Freshmen are admitted fall and spring. Entrance exams should be taken by December of the senior year. There are early decision and deferred admissions plan. Early decision applications should be filed by November 1; regular applications, by January 1 for fall entry and November 1 for spring entry, along with a $60 fee. Notification of early decision is sent December 15; regular decision, April 1. 300 early decision candidates were accepted for the 2009-2010 class. 1243 applicants were on the 2009 waiting list; 71 were admitted. Applications are accepted on-line.

Financial Aid: 60% of undergraduate students work part-time. Average annual earnings from campus work are $2500. UR is a member of CSS. The CSS/Profile, the FAFSA, and the state aid form are required. The deadline for filing freshman financial aid applications for fall entry is February 1.

Computers: Wireless access is available. There are 450 computers/terminals and 4,000 ports available on campus for general student use. High-speed Internet access is available in the residence halls. Wireless access is available in all academic areas. All students may access the system 24 hours daily. There are no time limits and no fees.

UNIVERSITY OF SAINT FRANCIS

Joliet, IL 60435

(815) 740-3400
(800) 735-7500; (815) 740-5032

Full-time: 389 men, 821 women	**Faculty:** 79; IIA, --$
Part-time: 26 men, 40 women	**Ph.D.s:** 68%
Graduate: 178 men, 703 women	**Student/Faculty:** 15 to 1
Year: semesters, , summer session	**Tuition:** $22,698
Application Deadline: August 1	**Room & Board:** $7,940
Freshman Class: 1274 applied, 632 accepted, 223 enrolled	
ACT: 23	**VERY COMPETITIVE**

The University of St. Francis, founded as a college in 1920, is a private liberal arts and professional institution affiliated with the Roman Catholic Church. There are 4 undergraduate schools and 4 graduate schools. In addition to regional accreditation, USF has baccalaureate program accreditation with ACBSP, CSWE, NCATE, and NRPA. The library contains 134,400 volumes, 1,767 microform items, 4,605 audio/video tapes/CDs/DVDs, and subscribes to 15,002 periodicals including electronic. Computerized library services include interlibrary loans, database searching, Internet access, and laptop Internet portals. Special learning facilities include a learning resource center, art gallery, radio station, TV station, greenhouse, wireless education classroom. SimLab for nursing students, P3 parking lot provides on campus research opportunities for undergraduate science students, multimedia classrooms, and the Rialto Square Theater. The 22-acre campus is in a suburban area 35 miles southwest of Chicago. Including any residence halls, there are 6 buildings.

Programs of Study: USF confers B.A., B.S., B.B.A., B.S.N and B.S.W. degrees. Master's and doctoral degrees are also awarded. Bachelor's degrees are awarded in BIOLOGICAL SCIENCE (biology/biological science), BUSINESS (accounting, banking and finance, business administration and management, management science, marketing/retailing/merchandising, and recreational facilities management), COMMUNICATIONS AND THE ARTS (communications, English, journalism, music, and visual and performing arts), COMPUTER AND PHYSICAL SCIENCE (computer programming, computer science, information sciences and systems, mathematics, and web technology), EDUCATION (elementary education, secondary education, and special education), ENGINEERING AND ENVIRONMENTAL DESIGN (computer technology and environmental science), HEALTH PROFESSIONS (allied health, health, medical technology, nuclear medical technology, nursing, predentistry, premedicine, preoptometry, prepharmacy, prephysical therapy, preveterinary science, radiation therapy, and radiograph medical technology), SOCIAL SCIENCE (criminal justice, history, liberal arts/general studies, political science/government, psychology, social work, and theological studies). Biology, education, and nursing are the strongest academically. Business, nursing, and education are the largest.

Special: Internships, on- and off-campus, paid and unpaid, are available in most majors. Dual and interdisciplinary majors, a pass/fail option, a Washington semester, study abroad, cross-registration with OCICU (Online Consortium of Independent Colleges and Universities), and credit for life, military, and work experience are available. There are 13 national honor societies and a freshman honors program.

Admissions: 50% of the 2009-2010 applicants were accepted. The ACT scores were 24% below 21, 32% between 21 and 23, 28% between 24 and 26, 9% between 27 and 28, and 8% above 28. 41% of the current freshmen were in the top fifth of their class; 78% were in the top two fifths.

Requirements: The ACT is required. In addition, applicants must take 4 years of English, 3 of either art, music, foreign language, or computer science, and 2 each of math, including geometry, science (1 lab), and social studies. USF requires applicants to be in the upper 50% of their class. A GPA of 2.5 is required. AP and CLEP credits are accepted. Important factors in the admissions decision are personality/intangible qualities, advanced placement or honors courses, and leadership record.

Procedure: Freshmen are admitted fall and spring. Entrance exams should be taken in the spring of the junior year or the fall of the senior year. There are deferred admissions and rolling admissions plans. Applications should be filed by August 1 for fall entry, along with a $30 fee. Notifications are sent September 1. Applications are accepted on-line.

Financial Aid: In 2009-2010, 100% of all full-time freshmen and 99% of continuing full-time students received some form of financial aid. 73% of all full-time freshmen and 70% of continuing full-time students received need-based aid. The average freshmen award was $24,153. 69% of undergraduate students work part-time. Average annual earnings from campus work are $2166. The average financial indebtedness of the 2009 graduate was $21,700. The FAFSA and the college's own financial statement are required. The priority date for freshman financial aid applications for fall entry is April 1.

Computers: Wireless access is available. There are over 275 computer workstations locations in classrooms, general student labs, science labs and specialized teaching classrooms that provide students full access to network services, programs and the Internet. The university library provides both wired and wireless access to the Internet and the institutional Intranet. There are 34 wired research stations for use and the entire building provides wireless access to the Internet and web based library services. In addition, the university residence halls have study rooms which provide 26 wired stations providing access to the campus intranet via the MyUSF portal. Wireless access to the Internet and the university Intranet is located in study rooms of residence halls, as wells as most areas of the main academic buildings on campus. All students may access the system. 24 hours a day. There are no time limits and no fees.

UNIVERSITY OF SAINT THOMAS
Houston, TX 77006-4696   **(713) 525-3500; (713) 525-3558**

Full-time: 490 men, 823 women	**Faculty:** 108; IIA, av$
Part-time: 234 men, 245 women	**Ph.D.s:** 92%
Graduate: 612 men, 830 women	**Student/Faculty:** 12 to 1
Year: semesters, summer session	**Tuition:** $21,830
Application Deadline: May 1	**Room & Board:** $7700
Freshman Class: 866 applied, 692 accepted, 287 enrolled	
SAT CR/M/W: 550/570/540	**ACT:** 24 **VERY COMPETITIVE**

The University of St. Thomas is a private institution committed to the liberal arts and to the religious, ethical, and intellectual tradition of Catholic higher education. There are 4 undergraduate schools and 4 graduate schools. In addition to regional accreditation, UST has baccalaureate program accreditation with ACBSP. The library contains 237,456 volumes, 603,356 microform items, and 6,107 audio/video tapes/CDs/DVDs. Computerized library services include interlibrary loans, database searching, and Internet access. Special learning facilities include a learning resource center, and archeology gallery. The 20-acre campus is in an urban area close to downtown Houston. Including any residence halls, there are 62 buildings.

Programs of Study: UST confers B.A., B.B.A., B.S., and B.A./B.F.A. degrees. Master's and doctoral degrees are also awarded. Bachelor's degrees are awarded in AGRICULTURE (environmental studies), BIOLOGICAL SCIENCE (biochemistry, bioinformatics, and biology/biological science), BUSINESS (accounting, banking and finance, business administration and management, and marketing/retailing/merchandising), COMMUNICATIONS AND THE ARTS (communications, dramatic arts, English, French, music, Spanish, and studio art), COMPUTER AND PHYSICAL SCIENCE (chemistry and mathematics), EDUCATION (education and music education), ENGINEERING AND ENVIRONMENTAL DESIGN (environmental science), SOCIAL SCIENCE (history, international studies, liberal arts/general studies, philosophy, political science/government, psychology, religion, and theological studies). Psychology, biology, and international studies are the largest.

Special: UST offers cross-registration with the University of Houston and a 3-2 engineering program with the University of Houston, Texas A&M University, and University of Notre Dame. Internships in the major field of study and study abroad in 11 countries are also available. Dual and joint majors and 5 year joint bachelor's and master's degree programs, combining BBA/MBA are available. There are 15 national honor societies and a freshman honors program.

Admissions: 80% of the 2009-2010 applicants were accepted. The SAT scores for the 2009-2010 freshman class were: Critical Reading--19% below 500, 50% between 500 and 599, 26% between 600 and 700, and 5% above 700; Math--19% below 500, 45% between 500 and 599, 31% between 600 and 700, and 5% above 700; Writing--24% below 500, 49% between 500 and 599, 23% between 600 and 700, and 4% above 700. The ACT scores were 23% below 21, 25% between 21 and 23, 29% between 24 and 26, 12% between 27 and 28, and 11% above 28. 49% of the current freshmen were in the top fifth of their class; 75% were in the top two fifths. 1 freshman graduated first in the class.

Requirements: The SAT or ACT is required. The ACT Optional Writing test is also required. In addition, applicants must graduate from an accredited secondary school, home school program or successfully complete the GED. Additionally, applicants should have competitive grades (mimimum high school GPA of 2.50 on a 4.0 scale) in a minimum of 18 college preparatory high school units: including 4 units of English, 3 units of social science, 3 units of mathematics, 3 units of science, 2 units of the same classical or modern language other than English, and 3 units of electives in college preparatory classes. Applicants should also have competitive official SAT or ACT scores and competitive class rank if high school ranks graduates. If appropriate, applicants should submit official transcripts of home school coursework. Home schooled students may also need to submit course descriptions, reading lists, or other information if requested. UST requires applicants to be in the upper 50% of their class. A GPA of 2.5 is required. AP and CLEP credits are accepted.

Procedure: Freshmen are admitted fall, spring, and summer. Entrance exams should be taken as early as possible. There is a deferred admissions plan. Applications should be filed by May 1 for fall entry, December 1 for spring entry, and May 1 for summer entry. The fall 2008 application fee was $25. Notification is sent on a rolling basis. Applications are accepted on-line.

Financial Aid: In 2009-2010, 90% of all full-time freshmen and 80% of continuing full-time students received some form of financial aid. 66% of all full-time freshmen and 58% of continuing full-time students received need-based aid. The average freshmen award was $16,133. The average financial indebtedness of the

2009 graduate was $22,857. The FAFSA is required. The priority date for freshman financial aid applications for fall entry is April 15.

Computers: Wireless access is available. Most areas of campus have wireless access. All students may access the system 24 hours a day, 7 days a week. There are no time limits and no fees.

UNIVERSITY OF SAN DIEGO
San Diego, CA 92110

(619) 260-4506
(800) 248-4873; (619) 260-6836

Full-time: 2101 men, 2795 women	**Faculty:** 273; I, av$
Part-time: 94 men, 121 women	**Ph.D.s:** 94%
Graduate: 1139 men, 1618 women	**Student/Faculty:** 18 to 1
Year: 4-1-4, summer session	**Tuition:** $36,292
Application Deadline: January 5	**Room & Board:** $12,602
Freshman Class: 11000 applied, 5434 accepted, 1082 enrolled	
SAT CR/M/W: 590/620/600	**ACT:** 27 **HIGHLY COMPETITIVE**

The University of San Diego, founded in 1949, is a private, Catholic liberal arts university. There are 4 undergraduate schools and 6 graduate schools. In addition to regional accreditation, USD has baccalaureate program accreditation with AACSB, ABET, and NCATE. The 2 libraries contain 704,887 volumes, 962,195 microform items, and 23,392 audio/video tapes/CDs/DVDs, and subscribe to 38,488 periodicals including electronic. Computerized library services include interlibrary loans, database searching, Internet access, and laptop Internet portals. Special learning facilities include a learning resource center, art gallery, radio station, TV station, a media center, and a child development center. The 180-acre campus is in an urban area 10 miles north of downtown San Diego. Including any residence halls, there are 85 buildings.

Programs of Study: USD confers B.A., B.A./B.S., B.Acc., B.B.A., and B.S.N. degrees. Master's and doctoral degrees are also awarded. Bachelor's degrees are awarded in BIOLOGICAL SCIENCE (biology/biological science and marine science), BUSINESS (accounting, business administration and management, and business economics), COMMUNICATIONS AND THE ARTS (communications, English, fine arts, French, music, and Spanish), COMPUTER AND PHYSICAL SCIENCE (chemistry, computer science, mathematics, oceanography, and physics), ENGINEERING AND ENVIRONMENTAL DESIGN (electrical/electronics engineering and industrial engineering), HEALTH PROFESSIONS (nursing), SOCIAL SCIENCE (anthropology, economics, history, humanities, international relations, liberal arts/general studies, philosophy, political science/government, psychology, religious education, and sociology). Business administration and communication studies are the largest.

Special: A B.A.-B.S. degree is offered in electrical, industrial and mechanical engineering. Internships in all disciplines, study abroad in 21 countries and work-study programs on campus are available. There are 15 national honor societies, including Phi Beta Kappa, and a freshman honors program.

Admissions: 49% of the 2009-2010 applicants were accepted. The SAT scores for the 2009-2010 freshman class were: Critical Reading--8% below 500, 43% between 500 and 599, 43% between 600 and 700, and 7% above 700; Math--6% below 500, 31% between 500 and 599, 52% between 600 and 700, and 11% above 700; Writing--8% below 500, 38% between 500 and 599, 46% between 600 and 700, and 8% above 700. The ACT scores were 2% below 21, 10% between 21 and 23, 31% between 24 and 26, 22% between 27 and 28, and 35%

above 28. 74% of the current freshmen were in the top fifth of their class; 94% were in the top two fifths. 40 freshmen graduated first in their class.

Requirements: The SAT is required. Admission is highly selective. Applicants should present a well-balanced secondary school program of college preparatory courses in English, foreign language, math, laboratory science, history, and social science. Both the content of the academic program as well as the quality of performance is considered. In addition, SAT / ACT results are used to broaden understanding of the applicant's potential. Participation in extracurricular activities at the school and in the community or church is taken into consideration in the admission decision. AP and CLEP credits are accepted. Important factors in the admissions decision are recommendations by school officials, extracurricular activities record, and advanced placement or honors courses.

Procedure: Freshmen are admitted fall, spring, and summer. Entrance exams should be taken before December 30 for early action and before March 1 for regular consideration. Applications should be filed by January 5 for fall entry and November 1 for spring entry, along with a $55 fee. Notifications are sent April 15. Applications are accepted on-line. 1600 applicants were on a recent waiting list, 387 were accepted.

Financial Aid: In 2009-2010, 71% of all full-time freshmen and 66% of continuing full-time students received some form of financial aid. The average freshman award was $26,809. Need-based scholarships or need-based grants averaged $21,255; need-based self-help aid (loans and jobs) averaged $5,818; non-need based athletic scholarships averaged $28,762; and other non-need based awards and non-need based scholarships averaged $13,952. 23% of undergraduate students work part-time. The average financial indebtedness of the 2009 graduate was $27,999. The FAFSA is required. The deadline for filing freshman financial aid applications for fall entry is March 2.

Computers: Wireless access is available. All students may access the system. There are no time limits and no fees. It is strongly recommended that all students have a personal computer.

UNIVERSITY OF SAN FRANCISCO

San Francisco, CA 94117-1080
(415) 422-6563
(800) CALL USF; (415) 422-2217

Full-time: 1910 men, 3270 women	**Faculty:** I, +$
Part-time: 100 men, 130 women	**Ph.D.s:** 93%
Graduate: 1320 men, 2000 women	**Student/Faculty:** n/av
Year: 4-1-4, summer session	**Tuition:** $31,500
Application Deadline: see profile	**Room & Board:** $11,000
Freshman Class: n/av	
SAT or ACT: required	**VERY COMPETITIVE**

The University of San Francisco, founded in 1855, is a private Roman Catholic institution run by the Jesuit Fathers and offering degree programs in the arts and sciences, business, education, nursing, and law. Figures in the above capsule are approximate. There are 5 undergraduate schools and 6 graduate schools. In addition to regional accreditation, USF has baccalaureate program accreditation with AACSB, CSAB, and NLN. The 2 libraries contain 1 million volumes, 900,000 microform items, and 6000 audio/video tapes/CDs/DVDs, and subscribe to 2500 periodicals including electronic. Computerized library services include interlibrary loans, database searching, Internet access, and laptop Internet portals. Special learning facilities include a learning resource center, art gallery, radio station, TV station, rare book room, the Institute for Chinese-Western Cultural History, and the Center for Pacific Rim Studies. The 55-acre campus is in an urban area in the heart of the city. Including any residence halls, there are 17 buildings.

Programs of Study: USF confers B.A., B.S., B.Arch., B.F.A., B.P.A., B.S.B.A., and B.S.N. degrees. Master's and doctoral degrees are also awarded. Bachelor's degrees are awarded in BIOLOGICAL SCIENCE (biology/biological science), BUSINESS (accounting, banking and finance, business administration and management, hospitality management services, hotel/motel and restaurant management, international business management, management information systems, marketing/retailing/merchandising, and organizational behavior), COMMUNICATIONS AND THE ARTS (art history and appreciation, arts administration/management, communications, drawing, English, fine arts, French, graphic design, illustration, media arts, painting, performing arts, Spanish, and visual and performing arts), COMPUTER AND PHYSICAL SCIENCE (chemistry, computer science, information sciences and systems, mathematics, and physics), EDUCATION (athletic training, elementary education, middle school education, and secondary education), ENGINEERING AND ENVIRONMENTAL DESIGN (architecture and environmental science), HEALTH PROFESSIONS (exercise science and nursing), SOCIAL SCIENCE (economics, history, Latin American studies, law enforcement and corrections, philosophy, political science/government, psychology, public administration, religion, sociology, and theological studies). Sciences and business are the strongest academically. Communications, nursing, and psychology are the largest.

Special: Cross-registration with the San Francisco Consortium, internships with local business, social services, and research opportunities are available. Study abroad in Europe and Japan, work-study programs on and off campus and with social service agencies, a B.A.-B.S. degree in exercise and sports science, dual majors in liberal arts and education, 3-2 engineering degrees with the University of Southern California, student-designed majors, nondegree study, and limited pass/fail options are also available. The College of Professional Studies is a degree completion program for working adults. There are 3 national honor societies, a freshman honors program, and 1 departmental honors program.

Requirements: The SAT or ACT is required. In addition, applicants are required to have 20 academic units, based on 6 years of academic electives, 4 of English, 3 each of math and social studies, and 2 each of foreign language and lab science. An essay is required. The GED is accepted. A GPA of 3.0 is required. AP and CLEP credits are accepted. Important factors in the admissions decision are extracurricular activities record, evidence of special talent, and leadership record.

Procedure: Freshmen are admitted fall and spring. Entrance exams should be taken during the first half of the senior year. There are deferred admissions and rolling admissions plans. Check with the school for current application deadlines. The fall 2009 application fee was $55. Notification is sent on a rolling basis. Applications are accepted on-line.

Financial Aid: The FAFSA is required. Check with the school for current application deadlines.

Computers: Wireless access is available. Students have wireless access in dorm rooms, the library, and most common areas. All students may access the system. There are no time limits and no fees.

UNIVERSITY OF SCIENCE AND ARTS OF OKLAHOMA

Chickasha, OK 73018-5322

(405) 574-1357
(800) 933-8726; (405) 574-1220

Full-time: 335 men, 592 women
Part-time: 47 men, 113 women
Graduate: none
Year: trimesters, summer session
Application Deadline: May 8
Freshman Class: 395 applied, 292 accepted, 187 enrolled
ACT: 22

Faculty: 55
Ph.D.s: 89%
Student/Faculty: 17 to 1
Tuition: $4440 ($10,560)
Room & Board: $4850

VERY COMPETITIVE

The University of Science and Arts of Oklahoma, founded in 1908, is Oklahoma's only publicly funded liberal arts college, providing interdisciplinary learning opportunities. In addition to regional accreditation, USAO has baccalaureate program accreditation with NASM and NCATE. The library contains 73,748 volumes, 114,515 microform items, and 3,690 audio/video tapes/CDs/DVDs, and subscribes to 110 periodicals including electronic. Computerized library services include interlibrary loans, database searching, and Internet access. Special learning facilities include a learning resource center, art gallery, a commercial art computer lab, a TV studio, a child development center, a herbarium, an art gallery, and a speech pathology clinic. The 75-acre campus is in a small town 40 miles southwest of Oklahoma City. Including any residence halls, there are 14 buildings.

Programs of Study: USAO confers B.A., B.S., and B.F.A. degrees. Bachelor's degrees are awarded in BIOLOGICAL SCIENCE (biology/biological science), BUSINESS (business administration and management), COMMUNICATIONS AND THE ARTS (art, communications, dramatic arts, English, fine arts, and music), COMPUTER AND PHYSICAL SCIENCE (chemistry, computer science, mathematics, natural sciences, and physics), EDUCATION (early childhood education, education of the deaf and hearing impaired, elementary education, and physical education), HEALTH PROFESSIONS (speech pathology/audiology), SOCIAL SCIENCE (American Indian studies, economics, history, political science/government, psychology, and sociology). Humanities and physical science are the strongest academically. Business administration, elementary education, and psychology are the largest.

Special: USAO offers dual majors, accelerated degree programs in all majors through year-round study, work-study programs, internship placement in community institutions, a Tutorial Scholars Program for student-designed majors, an interdisciplinary studies program, and a limited number of pass/fail options. There are 5 national honor societies, a freshman honors program, and 1 departmental honors program.

Admissions: 74% of the 2009-2010 applicants were accepted. The ACT scores were 33% below 21, 24% between 21 and 23, 26% between 24 and 26, 6% between 27 and 28, and 11% above 28. 44% of the current freshmen were in the top fifth of their class; 73% were in the top two fifths. 13 freshmen graduated first in their class.

Requirements: The ACT is required. In addition, applicants must meet one of the following 3 options: (1) have a minimum score of 24 on the ACT or a satisfactory on the SAT; (2) have a minimum high school GPA of 3.0 and be in the top 25% of their high school class; or (3) have a minimum GPA of 3.0 and a minimum score of 22 on the ACT or a satisfactory score on the SAT. They must be

graduates of an accredited secondary school or have a GED. 20 high school academic credits are recommended, including 4 years of English, 3 of math, and 2 each of lab science and history, 1 of which is American history. USAO requires applicants to be in the upper 33% of their class. A GPA of 3.0 is required. AP and CLEP credits are accepted. Important factors in the admissions decision are evidence of special talent, leadership record, and personality/intangible qualities.
Procedure: Freshmen are admitted to all sessions. Entrance exams should be taken by May of the preceding spring. There is a rolling admissions plan. Applications should be filed by May 8 for fall entry, along with a $25 fee. Notification is sent on a rolling basis. Applications are accepted on-line.

Financial Aid: In 2009-2010, 73% of all full-time freshmen and 61% of continuing full-time students received some form of financial aid. 71% of all full-time freshmen and 58% of continuing full-time students received need-based aid. The average freshman award was $9,208. 60% of undergraduate students work part-time. Average annual earnings from campus work are $2180. The average financial indebtedness of the 2009 graduate was $15,598. The FAFSA, the college's own financial statement, and Institution Information Sheet are required. The priority date for freshman financial aid applications for fall entry is March 15. The deadline for filing freshman financial aid applications for fall entry is rolling.

Computers: Wireless access is available. The entire campus has wireless coverage. Every academic building has at least 1 computer lab accessible by all students. Every dorm room and apartment has high-speed Internet access wired to the bedside. All students may access the system at any time. There are no time limits and no fees.

UNIVERSITY OF SCRANTON

Scranton, PA 18510-4699

(570) 941-7540
(888) SCRANTON; (570) 941-5928

Full-time: 1700 men, 2200 women	**Faculty:** 276; IIA, av$
Part-time: 103 men, 130 women	**Ph.D.s:** n/av
Graduate: 515 men, 1020 women	**Student/Faculty:** n/av
Year: semesters, summer session	**Tuition:** $32,824
Application Deadline: March 1	**Room & Board:** $11,301
Freshman Class: n/av	
SAT or ACT: required	**VERY COMPETITIVE**

The University of Scranton, founded in 1888, is a private institution operated by the Jesuit order of the Roman Catholic Church. It offers programs in business, behavioral sciences, education, health science, humanities, math, science, and social science. There are 4 undergraduate schools and 1 graduate school. Enrollment figures in the above capsule and figures in this profile are approximate. In addition to regional accreditation, the university has baccalaureate program accreditation with AACSB, APTA, CSAB, NCATE, and NLN. The library contains 486,718 volumes, 108,908 microform items, and 15,623 audio/video tapes/CDs/DVDs, and subscribes to 17,449 periodicals including electronic. Computerized library services include interlibrary loans, database searching, and Internet access. Special learning facilities include a learning resource center, art gallery, radio station, TV station, satellite dish for telecommunication reception, music center, language lab, and greenhouse. The 50-acre campus is in an urban area 125 miles north of Philadelphia. Including any residence halls, there are 69 buildings.
Programs of Study: The university confers B.A. and B.S. degrees. Associates, master's, and doctoral degrees are also awarded. Bachelor's degrees are awarded in BIOLOGICAL SCIENCE (biochemistry, biology/biological science, biophys-

ics, and neurosciences), BUSINESS (accounting, banking and finance, business administration and management, business economics, electronic business, human resources, international business management, marketing/retailing/ merchandising, and operations research), COMMUNICATIONS AND THE ARTS (communications, dramatic arts, English, French, German, Greek, Latin, and Spanish), COMPUTER AND PHYSICAL SCIENCE (chemistry, computer management, computer science, information sciences and systems, mathematics, and physics), EDUCATION (early childhood education, elementary education, science education, secondary education, and special education), ENGINEERING AND ENVIRONMENTAL DESIGN (electrical/electronics engineering and environmental science), HEALTH PROFESSIONS (exercise science, health care administration, medical laboratory technology, and nursing), SOCIAL SCIENCE (criminal justice, economics, gerontology, history, human services, international relations, philosophy, political science/government, psychology, sociology, and theological studies). Chemistry, biology, and nursing are the strongest academically. Biology, communication, and nursing are the largest.

Special: There are cooperative programs with the University of Detroit Mercy and cross-registration with 27 other Jesuit colleges. Internships are available in all career-oriented majors, and foreign study is offered in many countries. There is a Washington semester for history and political science majors. Students may earn a B.A.-B.S. degree in economics and accelerated degrees in history, chemistry, and biochemistry. The university also offers dual, student-designed, and interdisciplinary majors, including chemistry-business, chemistry-computers, electronics-business, and international language-business, credit by exam and for life/ military/work experience, work-study, nondegree study, and pass/fail options. There is also a special Jesuit-oriented general education program. There are 32 national honor societies.

Requirements: The SAT or ACT is required. In addition, applicants should be graduates of an accredited secondary school, though in some cases a GED may be accepted. They should complete 18 academic or Carnegie units, including 4 years of high school English, 3 each of math, science, history, and social studies, and 2 of foreign language. 2 letters of reference/recommendation are required. Essays are required. AP and CLEP credits are accepted. Important factors in the admissions decision are advanced placement or honors courses, leadership record, and extracurricular activities record.

Procedure: Freshmen are admitted fall and spring. Entrance exams should be taken by fall of the senior year. There are deferred admissions and rolling admissions plans. Check with the school for current application deadlines and fee. Applications are accepted on-line. 1207 applicants were on a recent waiting list, 21 were accepted.

Financial Aid: In a recent year, 85% of all full-time freshmen and 81% of continuing full-time students received some form of financial aid. 69% of all full-time freshmen and 66% of continuing full-time students received need-based aid. The average freshmen award was $17,509. 23% of undergraduate students work part-time. Average annual earnings from campus work are $1700. The average financial indebtedness of a recent graduate was $26,169. The university is a member of CSS. The FAFSA is required. Check with the school for current deadlines.

Computers: Wireless access is available. All students may access the system 24 hours a day. There are no time limits and no fees.

UNIVERSITY OF SOUTH CAROLINA AT COLUMBIA

Columbia, SC 29208

(803) 777-7700
(800) 868-5872; (803) 777-0101

Full-time: 8600 men, 10,379 women	**Faculty:** 829; I, --$
Part-time: 789 men, 726 women	**Ph.D.s:** 84%
Graduate: 3196 men, 4791 women	**Student/Faculty:** 23 to 1
Year: semesters, summer session	**Tuition:** $9156 ($23,732)
Application Deadline: December 1	**Room & Board:** $6986
Freshman Class: 17,694 applied, 11,262 accepted, 3917 enrolled	
SAT CR/M: 588/604	**ACT:** 26 **VERY COMPETITIVE+**

The University of South Carolina at Columbia, founded in 1801, is a publicly assisted institution serving the entire state of South Carolina. In addition to the main campus at Columbia, there are 3 senior campuses at Aiken, Beaufort, and Upstate, and 4 regional campuses at Lancaster, Salkehatchie, Sumter, and Union. There are 10 undergraduate schools and 14 graduate schools. In addition to regional accreditation, USC has baccalaureate program accreditation with AACSB, ABET, ACEJMC, ACPE, CSAB, NASM, NCATE, and NLN. The 7 libraries contain 3.3 million volumes, 5.1 million microform items, and 56,805 audio/video tapes/CDs/DVDs, and subscribe to 66,309 periodicals including electronic. Computerized library services include interlibrary loans and database searching. Special learning facilities include a learning resource center, art gallery, natural history museum, planetarium, and radio station. The 384-acre campus is in an urban area in the downtown area of Columbia. Including any residence halls, there are 167 buildings.

Programs of Study: USC confers B.A., B.S., B.A.I.S., B.A.J., B.A.P.E./B.S.P.E., B.A.R.S.C., B.F.A., B.M., B.M.A., B.S.B.A., B.S.Chem., B.S.C.S., B.S.E., B.S.I.S., and B.S.N. degrees. Master's and doctoral degrees are also awarded. Bachelor's degrees are awarded in BIOLOGICAL SCIENCE (biology/biological science and marine science), BUSINESS (accounting, banking and finance, business administration and management, business economics, hotel/motel and restaurant management, insurance, marketing/retailing/merchandising, office supervision and management, real estate, retailing, and sports management), COMMUNICATIONS AND THE ARTS (advertising, art history and appreciation, broadcasting, classics, communications, dance, dramatic arts, English, fine arts, French, German, Italian, journalism, media arts, music, public relations, Russian, Spanish, speech/debate/rhetoric, and studio art), COMPUTER AND PHYSICAL SCIENCE (chemistry, computer science, geology, geophysics and seismology, mathematics, physics, and statistics), EDUCATION (art education, music education, and physical education), ENGINEERING AND ENVIRONMENTAL DESIGN (chemical engineering, civil engineering, computer engineering, electrical/electronics engineering, and mechanical engineering), HEALTH PROFESSIONS (exercise science and nursing), SOCIAL SCIENCE (African American studies, anthropology, criminal justice, economics, European studies, geography, history, interdisciplinary studies, Latin American studies, philosophy, political science/government, psychology, religion, sociology, and women's studies). Biology, nursing, and experimental psychology are the largest.

Special: USC transmits live interactive televised instruction to more than 20 locations in the state. Cross-registration is offered with the National Technological University in Engineering and through the National Student Exchange. Internships in many fields, study abroad in many countries through the Byrnes International Center, co-op programs, and work-study programs are available. Double majors through the colleges of humanities and social sciences and science and math, student-designed majors, an interdisciplinary studies degree, and a 3-2 engineering degree with the College of Charleston are offered. Credit for military experience, nondegree study, and pass/fail options also are possible. There are 34 national honor societies, including Phi Beta Kappa, and a freshman honors program.

Admissions: 64% of the 2009-2010 applicants were accepted. The SAT scores for the 2009-2010 freshman class were: Critical Reading--9% below 500, 47% between 500 and 599, 35% between 600 and 700, and 9% above 700; Math--5% below 500, 40% between 500 and 599, 47% between 600 and 700, and 8% above 700. The ACT scores were 2% below 21, 20% between 21 and 23, 32% between 24 and 26, 20% between 27 and 28, and 27% above 28. 76% of the current freshmen were in the top fifth of their class; 99% were in the top two fifths. There were 48 National Merit finalists. 76 freshmen graduated first in their class.

Requirements: The SAT or ACT is required. Students are evaluated primarily on high school curriculum, grades on the required high school courses, and on SAT or ACT scores. A GPA of 2.0 is required. AP and CLEP credits are accepted. Important factors in the admissions decision are evidence of special talent and recommendations by school officials.

Procedure: Freshmen are admitted to all sessions. Entrance exams should be taken during spring of the junior year and fall of the senior year, if necessary. There are deferred admissions and rolling admissions plans. Applications should be filed by December 1 for fall entry, December 1 for spring entry, and May 15 for summer entry, along with a $50 fee. Applications are accepted on-line.

Financial Aid: In 2009-2010, 93% of all full-time freshmen and 86% of continuing full-time students received some form of financial aid. 39% of all full-time freshmen and 39% of continuing full-time students received need-based aid. The average freshman award was $12,927. Need-based scholarships or need-based grants averaged $7287 ($27,912 maximum). 14% of undergraduate students work part-time. Average annual earnings from campus work are $2858. The average financial indebtedness of the 2009 graduate was $21,755. USC is a member of CSS. The FAFSA is required. The deadline for filing freshman financial aid applications for fall entry is April 15.

Computers: Wireless access is available. Students can register, check grades, pay fees, search the Internet, and access the library and e-mail on the system. All students may access the system. There are no time limits and no fees. It is strongly recommended that all students have a personal computer.

UNIVERSITY OF SOUTH FLORIDA
Tampa, FL 33620   **(813) 974-3350; (813) 974-9689**

Full-time: 10,055 men, 14,545 women	**Faculty:** I, --$
Part-time: 4385 men, 5915 women	**Ph.D.s:** 90%
Graduate: 3620 men, 6360 women	**Student/Faculty:** n/av
Year: semesters, summer session	**Tuition:** $3500 ($16,200)
Application Deadline: see profile	**Room & Board:** $8000
Freshman Class: n/av	
SAT or ACT: required	**COMPETITIVE**

The University of South Florida, founded in 1956, is a comprehensive public institution and part of the Florida Division of Colleges and Universities, offering programs in liberal and fine arts, business, engineering, health science, and education. USF also maintains campuses at Lakeland, Sarasota, and St. Petersburg.

Figures in the above capsule and this profile are approximate. There are 6 undergraduate schools and 11 graduate schools. In addition to regional accreditation, USF has baccalaureate program accreditation with AACSB, ABET, ACEJMC, ASLA, CSAB, CSWE, NAAB, NASAD, NASM, NCATE, and NLN. The 5 libraries contain 2.3 million volumes, 4.4 million microform items, and 55,762 audio/video tapes/CDs/DVDs, and subscribe to 32,423 periodicals including electronic. Computerized library services include interlibrary loans, database searching, and Internet access. Special learning facilities include a learning resource center, art gallery, radio station, TV station, mock broadcasting studio, anthropology museum, and botanical gardens. The 1941-acre campus is in an urban area 10 miles northeast of downtown Tampa. Including any residence halls, there are 434 buildings.

Programs of Study: USF confers B.A., B.S., B.F.A., B.I.S., B.M., and B.S.W. degrees. Associate, master's, and doctoral degrees are also awarded. Bachelor's degrees are awarded in BIOLOGICAL SCIENCE (biology/biological science and microbiology), BUSINESS (accounting, banking and finance, business administration and management, business economics, management information systems, management science, and marketing/retailing/merchandising), COMMUNICATIONS AND THE ARTS (classics, communications, dance, dramatic arts, English literature, French, German, Italian, music, Russian, Spanish, and speech/debate/rhetoric), COMPUTER AND PHYSICAL SCIENCE (chemistry, geology, mathematics, physical sciences, and physics), EDUCATION (art education, business education, education, education of the emotionally handicapped, education of the mentally handicapped, elementary education, English education, foreign languages education, mathematics education, music education, physical education, science education, social studies education, special education, and specific learning disabilities), ENGINEERING AND ENVIRONMENTAL DESIGN (chemical engineering, civil engineering, computer engineering, electrical/electronics engineering, engineering, environmental science, industrial engineering, and mechanical engineering), HEALTH PROFESSIONS (medical technology and nursing), SOCIAL SCIENCE (African American studies, American studies, anthropology, criminology, economics, geography, gerontology, history, humanities, international relations, liberal arts/general studies, philosophy, political science/government, psychology, religion, social science, social work, and sociology). Education, business, and arts and sciences are the strongest academically. Business and education are the largest.

Special: USF offers co-op programs in business and engineering, study abroad, cross-registration, work-study programs, accelerated degree programs in public health and medicine, internships, a Washington semester, dual and student-designed majors, a liberal arts degree, nondegree study, and pass/fail options for some courses. There are 21 national honor societies, a freshman honors program, and 18 departmental honors programs.

Admissions: There were 12 National Merit finalists in a recent year.

Requirements: The SAT or ACT is required. In addition, candidates for admission should have completed 4 units each of English and academic electives, 3 each of math, science, and social studies, and 2 of a foreign language. The GED is accepted. Applicants who do not meet minimum requirements but have important attributes, special talents, or unique circumstances are considered for admission by an academic faculty committee. A GPA of 2.0 is required. AP and CLEP credits are accepted. Important factors in the admissions decision are advanced placement or honors courses, evidence of special talent, and recommendations by school officials.

Procedure: Freshmen are admitted to all sessions. Entrance exams should be taken at the end of the junior year or the beginning of the senior year. There is a rolling admissions plan. Check with the school for current application deadlines. The fall 2009 application fee was $30. Notification is sent on a rolling basis. Applications are accepted on-line.

Financial Aid: In a recent year, the average freshman award was $9230. 23% of undergraduate students work part-time. The average financial indebtedness of a recent graduate was $18,517. The FAFSA is required. Check with the school for current application deadlines.

Computers: Wireless access is available. All students may access the system. There are no time limits and no fees.

UNIVERSITY OF SOUTHERN CALIFORNIA
Los Angeles, CA 90089 — (213) 740-1111; (213) 740-6364

Full-time: 7986 men, 8110 women	Faculty: 1468; I, +$
Part-time: 361 men, 294 women	Ph.D.s: 89%
Graduate: 9605 men, 8468 women	Student/Faculty: 9 to 1
Year: semesters, summer session	Tuition: $39,184
Application Deadline: January 10	Room & Board: $11,458
Freshman Class: 35,753 applied, 8724 accepted, 2869 enrolled	
SAT: required	MOST COMPETITIVE

University of Southern California, founded in 1880, is a private institution offering undergraduate and graduate programs in liberal arts, fine arts, education, business, law, dentistry, engineering, communications, and health professions. There are 13 undergraduate schools and 18 graduate schools. In addition to regional accreditation, USC has baccalaureate program accreditation with AACSB, ABET, ACEJMC, ACPE, ADA, APTA, CSWE, NAAB, NASM, and NLN. The 21 libraries contain 4.1 million volumes, 6.4 million microform items, and 70,669 audio/video tapes/CDs/DVDs, and subscribe to 98,728 periodicals including electronic. Computerized library services include interlibrary loans, database searching, and Internet access. Special learning facilities include a learning resource center, art gallery, natural history museum, radio station, TV station, state-of-the-art cinema/film-making facilities, labs, wind tunnel, and marine science center. The 155-acre campus is in an urban area 3 miles south of the Los Angeles Civic Center. Including any residence halls, there are 166 buildings.

Programs of Study: USC confers B.A., B.S., B.Arch., B.F.A., B. Land. Arch., and B.M. degrees. Master's and doctoral degrees are also awarded. Bachelor's degrees are awarded in AGRICULTURE (environmental studies), BIOLOGICAL SCIENCE (biology/biological science, biophysics, and neurosciences), BUSINESS (accounting, business administration and management, and international business management), COMMUNICATIONS AND THE ARTS (art history and appreciation, broadcasting, classics, communications, comparative literature, creative writing, dramatic arts, East Asian languages and literature, English, English literature, film arts, fine arts, French, Italian, jazz, journalism, linguistics, music, music performance, playwriting/screenwriting, public relations, Russian, Spanish, studio art, theater design, theater management, video, and visual and performing arts), COMPUTER AND PHYSICAL SCIENCE (applied mathematics, astronomy, chemistry, computer science, geology, mathematics, physical sciences, and physics), ENGINEERING AND ENVIRONMENTAL DESIGN (aeronautical engineering, aerospace studies, architecture, biomedical engineering, chemical engineering, civil engineering, computer engineering, construction engineering, electrical/electronics engineering, environmental engineering, environmental science, industrial engineering, mechanical engineering, petroleum/natural gas engineering, and systems engineering), HEALTH PROFESSIONS (dental hygiene, exercise science, and occupational therapy), SOCIAL SCIENCE (African American studies, American studies, anthropology, Asian/American studies, classical/ancient civilization, East Asian studies, economics, ethics, politics, and social policy, geography, gerontology, history, international relations, Judaic studies, Latin American studies, philosophy, political science/government, psychology, religion, social science, sociology, and women's studies). Business, engineering, and communications are the largest.

Special: Cross-registration is permitted with Hebrew Union College and Howard University. Internships in various majors, a Washington semester, work-study programs, study abroad in 29 countries, dual majors, a general studies degree, student-designed majors, a 3-2 engineering degree, and pass/fail options are available. Students are encouraged to pursue interdisciplinary study linking core art and science disciplines to professional programs. There are 50 national honor societies, including Phi Beta Kappa, and a freshman honors program.

Admissions: 24% of the 2009-2010 applicants were accepted. The SAT scores for the 2009-2010 freshman class were: Critical Reading--1% below 500, 16% between 500 and 599, 50% between 600 and 700, and 33% above 700; Math--1% below 500, 9% between 500 and 599, 42% between 600 and 700, and 48% above 700; Writing--1% below 500, 9% between 500 and 599, 46% between 600 and 700, and 44% above 700. There were 232 National Merit finalists.

Requirements: The SAT is required. In addition, 3 SAT Subject tests are recommended. Graduation from an accredited secondary school is required. Applicants must have completed at least 13 year-long courses in English, humanities, math, natural sciences, social sciences, and foreign languages, plus 3 additional year-long courses in those areas or in computer science and, with some exceptions, theater, fine arts, journalism, music, or speech. AP credits are accepted. Important factors in the admissions decision are advanced placement or honors courses, recommendations by school officials, and evidence of special talent.

Procedure: Freshmen are admitted fall and spring. Entrance exams should be taken by November of the senior year for scholarship applicants; by December for all others. Applications should be filed by January 10 for fall entry, along with a $65 fee. Notifications are sent April 1. Applications are accepted on-line.

Financial Aid: In 2009-2010, 68% of all full-time freshmen and 62% of continuing full-time students received some form of financial aid. 43% of all full-time freshmen and 42% of continuing full-time students received need-based aid. The average freshman award was $35,653. Need-based scholarships and need-based grants averaged $25,657; need-based self-help aid (loans and jobs) averaged $5245; non-need-based athletic scholarships averaged $34,146; and other non-need-based awards and non-need-based scholarships averaged $15,726. The average financial indebtedness of the 2009 graduate was $30,097. USC is a member of CSS. The CSS/Profile, FAFSA, and parent and student federal income tax forms and all schedules are required. The priority date for freshman financial aid applications for fall entry is February 2.

Computers: Wireless access is available. All students may access the system. There are no time limits and no fees.

UNIVERSITY OF TENNESSEE AT KNOXVILLE

Knoxville, TN 37996-0230   **(865) 974-2184**

Full-time: 10119 men, 9655 women	**Faculty:** 1236; I, --$
Part-time: 675 men, 733 women	**Ph.D.s:** 82%
Graduate: 3957 men, 4795 women	**Student/Faculty:** 16 to 1
Year: semesters, summer session	**Tuition:** $6850 ($20,936)
Application Deadline: December 1	**Room & Board:** $6652
Freshman Class: 12234 applied, 8892 accepted, 3717 enrolled	
SAT CR/M: 577/586	**ACT:** 26 **VERY COMPETITIVE+**

The University of Tennessee, Knoxville, founded in 1794 and the original campus of the state university system, is now a large public institution offering more than 300 graduate and undergraduate programs. There are 11 undergraduate schools and 14 graduate schools. In addition to regional accreditation, UT Knoxville has baccalaureate program accreditation with AACSB, ABET, ACEJMC, ACPE, ADA, ASLA, CAHEA, CSWE, FIDER, NAAB, NASAD, NASM, NCATE, NLN, NRPA, and SAF. The 7 libraries contain 3.3 million volumes, 4.4 million microform items, and 45,363 audio/video tapes/CDs/DVDs, and subscribe to 39,913 periodicals including electronic. Computerized library services include interlibrary loans, database searching, Internet access, and laptop Internet portals. Special learning facilities include a learning resource center, art gallery, natural history museum, radio station, TV station, a science and engineering research facility, performance theaters, concert halls, and multifunctional indoor arena. The 550-acre campus is in an urban area adjacent to downtown Knoxville. Including any residence halls, there are 220 buildings.

Programs of Study: UT Knoxville confers B.A., B.S., B.Arch., B.F.A., B.M., and specialized B.S. degrees in 25 fields, including business administration, nursing, and social work. degrees. Master's and doctoral degrees are also awarded. Bachelor's degrees are awarded in AGRICULTURE (agricultural business management, agricultural economics, agriculture, animal science, fishing and fisheries, forestry and related sciences, horticulture, plant science, and soil science), BIOLOGICAL SCIENCE (biology/biological science and nutrition), BUSINESS (accounting, banking and finance, business administration and management, business economics, hotel/motel and restaurant management, human resources, logistics, management science, retailing, and sports management), COMMUNICATIONS AND THE ARTS (advertising, art, art history and appreciation, classics, communications, dramatic arts, English, French, German, graphic design, Italian, journalism, linguistics, music, public relations, Russian, Spanish, speech/debate/rhetoric, and studio art), COMPUTER AND PHYSICAL SCIENCE (chemistry, computer science, geology, mathematics, physics, and statistics), EDUCATION (agricultural education, art education, marketing and distribution education, music education, recreation education, and special education), ENGINEERING AND ENVIRONMENTAL DESIGN (aeronautical engineering, agricultural engineering, architecture, biomedical engineering, chemical engineering, civil engineering, computer engineering, electrical/electronics engineering, engineering physics, environmental science, industrial engineering, interior design, materials engineering, mechanical engineering, and nuclear engineering), HEALTH PROFESSIONS (clinical science, community health work, exercise science, nursing, predentistry, premedicine, prepharmacy, and preveterinary science), SOCIAL SCIENCE (anthropology, child care/child and family studies, economics, ethnic studies, food science, geography, history, interdisciplinary studies, philosophy, political science/government, psychology, public administration, religion, social work, and sociology). Engineering, physical sciences, and English are the strongest academically. Nursing and accounting are the largest.

Special: Cooperative programs are offered in engineering and business administration. Cross-registration is possible through the National Student Exchange and through the Academic Common Market, a Southern 14-state consortium in several majors and concentrations. Internships are available in agricultural sciences, architecture, arts and sciences, business, communication, education, engineering, and social work. Work-study programs are available on campus in many programs and offices. The 173 majors and concentrations, plus 85 minors offer many options for dual and student-designed academic programs, and accelerated study. Study abroad programs are offered in 59 countries. There are 51 national honor societies, including Phi Beta Kappa, a freshman honors program, and 23 departmental honors programs.

Admissions: 73% of the 2009-2010 applicants were accepted. The SAT scores for the 2009-2010 freshman class were: Critical Reading--17% below 500, 42% between 500 and 599, 31% between 600 and 700, and 10% above 700; Math--17% below 500, 42% between 500 and 599, 31% between 600 and 700, and 10% above 700. The ACT scores were 4% below 21, 16% between 21 and 23, 33% between 24 and 26, 19% between 27 and 28, and 28% above 28. 60% of the current freshmen were in the top fifth of their class; 85% were in the top two fifths. There were 40 National Merit finalists. 110 freshmen graduated first in their class.

Requirements: The SAT or ACT is required, in addition applicants should be high school graduates or have the GED. Required secondary school courses include 4 credits in English, 3 in math, 2 each in science and a single foreign language, 1 each in history and world history or world geography, and 1 unit of visual/performing arts. A GPA of 2.0 is required. AP and CLEP credits are accepted. Important factors in the admissions decision are advanced placement or honors courses, evidence of special talent, and extracurricular activities record.

Procedure: Freshmen are admitted to all sessions. Entrance exams should be taken in spring of the junior year or fall of the senior year. There is a deferred admissions plan. Applications should be filed by December 1 for fall entry, November 1 for spring entry, and December 1 for summer entry, along with a $30 fee. Applications are accepted on-line.

Financial Aid: The FAFSA is required. The priority date for freshman financial aid applications for fall entry is March 1.

Computers: Wireless access is available. All students have access to UTK's campus-wide network and wireless service is available throughout the entire campus. There are 600 computers available on campus for general student use. All students may access the system. There are no time limits and no fees.

UNIVERSITY OF TEXAS AT AUSTIN
Austin, TX 78712   (512) 475-7440; (512) 475-7475

Full-time: 16,500 men, 18,110 women	**Faculty:** I, av$
Part-time: 1480 men, 1375 women	**Ph.D.s:** 84%
Graduate: 5685 men, 5230 women	**Student/Faculty:** n/av
Year: semesters, summer session	**Tuition:** $9000 ($30,000)
Application Deadline: see profile	**Room & Board:** $10,000
Freshman Class: n/av	
SAT or ACT: required	**HIGHLY COMPETITIVE**

University of Texas at Austin, founded in 1883, is a major research institution within the University of Texas System and provides a broad range of degree programs. Figures in the above capsule and this profile are approximate. There are 12 undergraduate schools and 15 graduate schools. In addition to regional accreditation, UT has baccalaureate program accreditation with AACSB, ABET, ACEJ-MC, ACPE, ADA, CSWE, FIDER, NAAB, NASAD, and NASM. The 17 libraries contain 8.2 million volumes, 6.1 million microform items, and 991,469 audio/video tapes/CDs/DVDs, and subscribe to 50,014 periodicals including electronic. Computerized library services include interlibrary loans, database searching, Internet access, and laptop Internet portals. Special learning facilities include a learning resource center, art gallery, natural history museum, radio station, TV station, observatory, marine science institute, fusion reactor, and Lyndon Baines Johnson Library and Museum. The 350-acre campus is in an urban area near downtown Austin, just off the interstate. Including any residence halls, there are 120 buildings.

Programs of Study: UT confers B.A., B.S., B.Arch., B.B.A., B.F.A., B.M., B.J., and B.S.W. degrees. Master's and doctoral degrees are also awarded. Bachelor's degrees are awarded in BIOLOGICAL SCIENCE (biochemistry, biology/biological science, microbiology, molecular biology, and nutrition), BUSINESS (accounting, banking and finance, business administration and management, management information systems, management science, and marketing management), COMMUNICATIONS AND THE ARTS (advertising, applied music, Arabic, art history and appreciation, classics, dance, design, dramatic arts, English, film arts, French, German, Greek, Hebrew, Italian, journalism, Latin, linguistics, music, music theory and composition, Portuguese, public relations, Russian, Scandinavian languages, Slavic languages, Spanish, speech/debate/rhetoric, studio art, and visual and performing arts), COMPUTER AND PHYSICAL SCIENCE (astronomy, chemistry, computer science, geology, geophysics and seismology, mathematics, and physics), ENGINEERING AND ENVIRONMENTAL DESIGN (aerospace studies, architectural engineering, architecture, biomedical engineering, chemical engineering, civil engineering, electrical/electronics engineering, geophysical engineering, interior design, landscape architecture/design, mechanical engineering, and petroleum/natural gas engineering), HEALTH PROFESSIONS (medical technology, nursing, pharmacy, and speech pathology/audiology), SOCIAL SCIENCE (American studies, anthropology, archeology, Asian/Oriental studies, child care/child and family studies, classical/ancient civilization, dietetics, Eastern European studies, economics, ethnic studies, geography, history, human ecology, humanities, Islamic studies, Judaic studies, Latin American studies, liberal arts/general studies, Middle Eastern studies, philosophy, physical fitness/movement, political science/government, psychology, religion, Russian and Slavic studies, social work, sociology, textiles and clothing, and urban studies). Biological sciences, electrical and computer engineering, and government are the largest.

Special: Cooperative programs are available in most engineering courses, microbiology, chemistry, computer science, geology, and actuarial studies. Cross-registration is provided in pharmacy with the University of Texas at San Antonio. Internships, study abroad, B.A.-B.S. degrees, dual majors, student-designed majors for humanities students, and pass/fail options are offered. There are 45 national honor societies, including Phi Beta Kappa, a freshman honors program, and 50 departmental honors programs.

Requirements: The SAT or ACT is required. The ACT Optional Writing test is also required. In addition, all students graduating in the top 10% of their class from an accredited Texas high school are eligible for admission. Applicants not meeting that requirement are reviewed based on SAT or ACT scores, class rank, writing samples, and related factors; consideration may be given to socioeconomic and geographic information. In addition, applicants need 15 1/2 academic credits, including 4 in English, 3 each in math and social studies, 2 each in science and foreign language, and 1 1/2 in electives. An audition is required for applied music majors. The GED is accepted, with supportive information. Home-schooled students are required to submit the results of either the SAT: Subject tests or AP exams in English, math, and a third subject of the student's choosing. AP and CLEP credits are accepted. Important factors in the admissions decision are leadership record, evidence of special talent, and extracurricular activities record.

Procedure: Freshmen are admitted fall, spring, and summer. Entrance exams should be taken in the junior year or early in the senior year. There are deferred admissions and rolling admissions plans. Check with the school for current application deadlines. The application fee is $60. Applications are accepted on-line.

Financial Aid: In a recent year, 57% of all full-time freshmen and 51% of continuing full-time students received some form of financial aid, including need-based aid. The average freshman award was $9800. The average financial indebtedness of a recent graduate was $17,000. UT is a member of CSS. The FAFSA is required. Check with the school for current application deadlines.

Computers: Wireless access is available. Complete Internet access is available in every dorm room, all libraries, and a multitude of departmental computer labs and classrooms. Several public wireless sites exist. All students may access the system 24 hours a day. There are no time limits and no fees. Students enrolled in College of Education teacher preparation program must have a personal computer.

UNIVERSITY OF TEXAS AT DALLAS
Richardson, TX 75080   (972) 883-2270; (972) 883-2599

Full-time: 4118 men, 3208 women	**Faculty:** 345; I, +$
Part-time: 1246 men, 1229 women	**Ph.D.s:** 92%
Graduate: 3469 men, 2513 women	**Student/Faculty:** 21 to 1
Year: semesters, summer session	**Tuition:** $9510 ($20,340)
Application Deadline: August 1	**Room & Board:** $7733
Freshman Class: 5554 applied, 2870 accepted, 1342 enrolled	
SAT CR/M/W: 590/630/570	**ACT:** 27 **HIGHLY COMPETITIVE**

The University of Texas at Dallas, founded in 1969 as part of the University of Texas system, offers undergraduate and graduate programs in the liberal arts and sciences, business, engineering, computer science, cognitive science, and neuroscience. There are 7 undergraduate schools and 7 graduate schools. In addition to regional accreditation, UTD has baccalaureate program accreditation with AACSB and ABET. The library contains 1.6 million volumes, 2.8 million microform items, and 12,125 audio/video tapes/CDs/DVDs, and subscribes to 45,186 periodicals including electronic. Computerized library services include interlibrary loans, database searching, and Internet access. Special learning facilities include a learning resource center, art gallery, radio station, TV station, a center for communications disorders, a rare books library, and special library collections on aviation history, geophysics, philatelic research, and botanicals. The 500-acre campus is in a suburban area 18 miles north of downtown Dallas. Including any residence halls, there are 90 buildings.

Programs of Study: UTD confers B.A., B.S., B.S.E.E., B.S.T.E. degrees. Master's and doctoral degrees are also awarded. Bachelor's degrees are awarded in BIOLOGICAL SCIENCE (biochemistry, biology/biological science, molecular biology, and neurosciences), BUSINESS (accounting, banking and finance, and business administration and management), COMMUNICATIONS AND THE ARTS (fine arts, literature, telecommunications, and visual and performing arts), COMPUTER AND PHYSICAL SCIENCE (applied mathematics, chemistry, computer science, geoscience, mathematics, physics, software engineering, and statistics), ENGINEERING AND ENVIRONMENTAL DESIGN (computer technology, electrical/electronics engineering, and mechanical engineering), HEALTH PROFESSIONS (speech pathology/audiology), SOCIAL SCIENCE (American studies, cognitive science, criminology, economics, gender studies, geography, history, humanities, interdisciplinary studies, political science/government, psychology, public administration, and sociology). Electrical engineering, biology, and biochemistry are the strongest academically. Business administration, computer science, and electrical engineering are the largest.

Special: Cross-registration is available with other University of Texas campuses. Accelerated degree programs and B.A.-B.S. degrees are offered in several majors, as is a 3-2 engineering degree. Co-op programs, internships, work-study programs with several major corporations, and dual and student-designed majors are possible. Students may study abroad in Europe, Asia, Mexico, and New Zealand. There are 6 national honor societies, a freshman honors program, and 2 departmental honors programs.

Admissions: 52% of the 2009-2010 applicants were accepted. The SAT scores for the 2009-2010 freshman class were: Critical Reading--17% below 500, 36% between 500 and 599, 34% between 600 and 700, and 13% above 700; Math--9% below 500, 27% between 500 and 599, 44% between 600 and 700, and 21% above 700; Writing--19% below 500, 41% between 500 and 599, 30% between 600 and 700, and 9% above 700. The ACT scores were 9% below 21, 14% between 21 and 23, 24% between 24 and 26, 17% between 27 and 28, and 36% above 28. 62% of the current freshmen were in the top fifth of their class; 84% were in the top two fifths. There were 41 National Merit finalists. 21 freshmen graduated first in their class.

Requirements: The SAT or ACT is required. The ACT Optional Writing test is also required. In addition, applicants should be graduates of an accredited secondary school. In-state students who rank in the top 10% of their class gain automatic admission to UTD. Credentials for other students must include completion of 4 units of English, 3.5 of math, 3 each of social science and lab science, 2 of a foreign language, and course work in fine arts and electives, with health and phys ed courses recommended. AP and CLEP credits are accepted. Important factors in the admissions decision are advanced placement or honors courses, leadership record, and evidence of special talent.

Procedure: Freshmen are admitted to all sessions. Entrance exams should be taken at the end of the junior year or beginning of the senior year. There are deferred admissions and rolling admissions plans. Applications should be filed by August 1 for fall entry, December 1 for spring entry, and May 1 for summer entry, along with a $50 fee. Applications are accepted on-line.

Financial Aid: 5% of undergraduate students work part-time. Average annual earnings from campus work are $6541. The CSS/Profile, FAFSA, and the college's own financial statement are required. The priority date for freshman financial aid applications for fall entry is March 31. The deadline for filing freshman financial aid applications for fall entry is April 30.

Computers: Wireless access is available. There are several monitored computer labs for student use including PCs, Macs, PCs for visually impaired, scanners, and printers. There are approximately 120 computers for student use. Wireless LAN is part of UTD's network. All students may access the system 8 A.M. to midnight in most labs. There are no time limits and no fees. It is strongly recommended that all students have a personal computer. A computer with wireless connection capability is recommended.

UNIVERSITY OF TEXAS AT SAN ANTONIO

San Antonio, TX 78249
(210) 458-4536
(800) 669-0919; (210) 458-7857

Full-time: 9280 men, 9500 women	**Faculty:** IIA, +$
Part-time: 2720 men, 3210 women	**Ph.D.s:** 93%
Graduate: 1600 men, 2235 women	**Student/Faculty:** n/av
Year: semesters, summer session	**Tuition:** $8000 ($16,000)
Application Deadline: see profile	**Room & Board:** $9000
Freshman Class: n/av	
SAT or ACT: required	**LESS COMPETITIVE**

The University of Texas at San Antonio was established as part of the state university system in 1969 and is now a large, comprehensive institution offering undergraduate and graduate programs in arts, business, engineering, music, health science, and education. Figures in the above capsule and this profile are approximate. There are 8 undergraduate schools and 7 graduate schools. In addition to regional accreditation, UTSA has baccalaureate program accreditation with AACSB, ABET, CSWE, FIDER, NAAB, NASAD, and NASM. The 2 libraries contain 777,554 volumes, 3.2 million microform items, and 47,499 audio/video tapes/CDs/DVDs, and subscribe to 35,000 periodicals including electronic. Computerized library services include interlibrary loans, database searching, Internet access, and laptop Internet portals. Special learning facilities include a learning resource center, art gallery, and the Institute of Texan Cultures. The 600-acre campus is in a suburban area approximately 18 miles northwest of downtown San Antonio. Including any residence halls, there are 41 buildings.

Programs of Study: UTSA confers B.A., B.S., B.A.A.S., B.B.A., B.F.A., B.M., B.S.C.E., B.S.E.E., and B.S.M.E. degrees. Master's and doctoral degrees are also awarded. Bachelor's degrees are awarded in BIOLOGICAL SCIENCE (biology/biological science), BUSINESS (accounting, banking and finance, business administration and management, business economics, business statistics, entrepreneurial studies, human resources, international business management, management information systems, management science, marketing/retailing/merchandising, personnel management, small business management, and tourism), COMMUNICATIONS AND THE ARTS (art, art history and appreciation, classics, communications, English, fine arts, French, German, music, music business management, music performance, music theory and composition, and Spanish), COMPUTER AND PHYSICAL SCIENCE (actuarial science, applied physics, chemistry, computer science, computer security and information assurance, geology, information sciences and systems, mathematics, physics, science, and statistics), ENGINEERING AND ENVIRONMENTAL DESIGN (architecture, civil engineering, construction management, electrical/electronics engineering, environmental science, interior design, and mechanical engineering), HEALTH PROFESSIONS (clinical science, health, and occupational therapy), SOCIAL SCIENCE (American studies, anthropology, child care/child and family studies, classical/ancient civilization, criminal justice, early childhood studies, economics, family and community services, geography, history, humanities, interdisciplinary studies, Mexican-American/Chicano studies, philosophy, physical fitness/movement, political science/government, psychology, and sociology). Biology and interdisciplinary studies are the strongest academically. Psychology, architecture, and criminal justice are the largest.

Special: UTSA offers joint degrees in occupational therapy and clinical lab sciences with the University of Texas Health Science Center and study abroad in many countries. Internships, work-study, nondegree study, and pass/fail options are available. There are 38 national honor societies, a freshman honors program, and 17 departmental honors programs.

Admissions: 22 freshmen graduated first in their class in a recent year.

Requirements: The SAT or ACT is required. Admission is based on a formula derived from class rank and SAT or ACT scores. Applicants must be graduates of accredited high schools or have earned the GED. UTSA recommends that high school preparation include 4 units of English, at least 3 of math, at least 2 each of a foreign language, natural science, and social science, and at least 1 of fine arts. AP and CLEP credits are accepted.

Procedure: Freshmen are admitted to all sessions. Entrance exams should be taken in the spring of the junior year. There is a rolling admissions plan. Check with the school for current application deadlines. The fall 2009 application fee was $40. Notification is sent on a rolling basis. Applications are accepted on-line.

Financial Aid: In a recent year, 46% of all full-time freshmen and 53% of continuing full-time students received some form of financial aid. 45% of all full-time freshmen and 52% of continuing full-time students received need-based aid. The average freshman award was $8805. 4% of undergraduate students work part-time. Average annual earnings from campus work are $2551. The average financial indebtedness of a recent graduate was $18,687. The FAFSA and the college's own financial statement are required. Check with the school for current application deadlines.

Computers: Wireless access is available. Students may use any of the 3 general access labs, which offer a total of about 900 computer systems. Any registered student who pays the automated services fee will be given a lab user account, which also allows access to the wireless network. Students may purchase PCs through Gateway that are preconfigured by UTSA and have on-campus support. All students may access the system 24 hours a day. There are no time limits and no fees. It is strongly recommended that all students have a personal computer.

UNIVERSITY OF THE PACIFIC
Stockton, CA 95211-0197

(209) 946-2211
(800) 959-2867; (209) 946-2413

Full-time: 1537 men, 1847 women	**Faculty:** 310; IIA, +$
Part-time: 49 men, 68 women	**Ph.D.s:** 89%
Graduate: 1271 men, 1629 women	**Student/Faculty:** 13 to 1
Year: semesters, summer session	**Tuition:** $32,330
Application Deadline: January 15	**Room & Board:** $10,616
Freshman Class: 14970 applied, 6218 accepted, 894 enrolled	
SAT CR/M/W: 575/610/570	**ACT:** 27 **VERY COMPETITIVE+**

The University of the Pacific, founded in 1851, is a private institution that offers undergraduate and graduate programs in the arts and sciences, and professional programs in pharmacy, law, and dentistry. There are 8 undergraduate schools and one graduate school. In addition to regional accreditation, Pacific has baccalaureate program accreditation with AACSB, ABET, NASAD, NASM, and NCATE. The 2 libraries contain 376,012 volumes, 692,228 microform items, 11,211 audio/video tapes/CDs/DVDs, and subscribe to 1,781 periodicals including electronic. Computerized library services include interlibrary loans, database searching, and Internet access. Special learning facilities include a learning resource center, art gallery, radio station, the Brubeck Institute. The 175-acre campus is in a suburban area 80 miles east of San Francisco and 40 miles south of Sacramento. Including any residence halls, there are 68 buildings.

Programs of Study: Pacific confers B.A., B.S., B.F.A., B.M., B.S.B.A., B.S.B.E., B.S.C.E., B.S.E.E.., B.S.E.M., B.S.E.P., and B.S.M.E. degrees. Master's and doctoral degrees are also awarded. Bachelor's degrees are awarded in BIOLOGICAL SCIENCE (biochemistry and biology/biological science), BUSINESS (business administration and management), COMMUNICATIONS AND THE ARTS (art, communications, dramatic arts, English, French, German, graphic design, Japanese, music, music business management, music history and appreciation, music performance, music theory and composition, Spanish, and studio art), COMPUTER AND PHYSICAL SCIENCE (applied mathematics, chemistry, computer science, geology, geophysics and seismology, information sciences and systems, mathematics, and physics), EDUCATION (education, music education, and physical education), ENGINEERING AND ENVIRONMENTAL DESIGN (civil engineering, computer engineering, electrical/electronics engineering, engineering management, engineering physics, environmental science, and mechanical engineering), HEALTH PROFESSIONS (music therapy, prepharmacy, and speech pathology/audiology), SOCIAL SCIENCE (economics, history, international relations, international studies, liberal arts/general studies, philosophy, political science/government, psychology, religion, social science, and sociology). Natural sciences and the professions is the strongest academically. Arts and sciences, pharmacy, and business are the largest.

Special: The engineering school requires and guarantees a co-op program for specialized training in the field. Internships for credit or pay in all majors, more than 230 study-abroad programs in more than 80 countries, a Washington semester, and more than 20 work-study programs also are available. Student-designed majors, B.A./B.S. degrees, dual majors in most disciplines, and pass/fail options are possible. There are 18 national honor societies, a freshman honors program, and 42 departmental honors programs.

Admissions: 42% of the 2009-2010 applicants were accepted. The SAT scores for the 2009-2010 freshman class were: Critical Reading--18% below 500, 39% between 500 and 599, 36% between 600 and 700, and 7% above 700; Math--11% below 500, 31% between 500 and 599, 36% between 600 and 700, and 22% above 700; Writing--22% below 500, 37% between 500 and 599, 33% between 600 and 700, and 8% above 700. 61% of the current freshmen were in the top fifth of their class; 87% were in the top two fifths.

Requirements: The SAT or ACT is required. In addition, applicants must have 16 academic credits, including a recommended 4 years of high school English, 3 of math, 2 in the same foreign language, 2 of lab science, 1 of U.S history or government, 1 of fine or performing arts, and 4 additional academic courses. An essay is required and an interview is recommended. In addition, music students must audition. The GED is accepted plus one year of math and science for science and health related majors. A GPA of 2.5 is required. AP and CLEP credits are accepted. Important factors in the admissions decision are advanced placement or honors courses, leadership record, and extracurricular activities record.

Procedure: Freshmen are admitted fall and spring. Entrance exams should be taken in the spring of the junior year or fall of the senior year. There are early decision, early admissions, deferred admissions, and rolling admissions plans. Early decision applications should be filed by November 15; regular applications, by January 15 for fall entry and November 15 for spring entry. The fall 2008 application fee was $60. Notification of early decision is sent January 15; regular decision, March 15. Applications are accepted on-line. A waiting list is maintained.

Financial Aid: In 2009-2010, 75% of all full-time freshmen and 87% of continuing full-time students received some form of financial aid. 75% of all full-time freshmen and 69% of continuing full-time students received need-based aid. The average freshmen award was $25,147. 36% of undergraduate students work part-time. Average annual earnings from campus work are $1300. Pacific is a member of CSS. The FAFSA is required. The deadline for filing freshman financial aid applications for fall entry is February 15.

Computers: Wireless access is available. All students may access the system. any time. There are no time limits and no fees. Students enrolled in pharmacy must have a personal computer.

UNIVERSITY OF THE SCIENCES IN PHILADELPHIA

Philadelphia, PA 19104-4495　　　　　　　　　　**(215) 596-8815**
(888) 996-8747; (215) 596-8821

Full-time: 1014 men, 1544 women	**Faculty:** 157
Part-time: 22 men, 30 women	**Ph.D.s:** 78%
Graduate: 146 men, 218 women	**Student/Faculty:** 17 to 1
Year: semesters, summer session	**Tuition:** $29630
Application Deadline:	**Room & Board:** $11,582
Freshman Class: 4178 applied, 2591 accepted, 513 enrolled	
SAT CR/M/W: 560/600/570	**ACT:** 26　　**VERY COMPETITIVE**

University of the Sciences in Philadelphia, founded in 1821, is a private institution offering degree programs in the health sciences, pharmaceutical sciences, and arts and sciences. There are 4 undergraduate schools and 4 graduate schools. In addition to regional accreditation, USP has baccalaureate program accreditation with ACPE and APTA. The library contains 85,489 volumes, 19,679 microform items, and 1,726 audio/video tapes/CDs/DVDs, and subscribes to 13,827 periodicals including electronic. Computerized library services include interlibrary loans, database searching, Internet access, and laptop Internet portals. Special learning facilities include a learning resource center, a pharmaceutical history museum, the Center for Advanced Pharmacy Studies (CAPS), and the McNeil Science and Technology Center. The 35-acre campus is in an urban area Philadelphia. Including any residence halls, there are 17 buildings.

Programs of Study: USP confers B.S. and B.S.Ed. degrees. Master's and doctoral degrees are also awarded. Bachelor's degrees are awarded in BIOLOGICAL SCIENCE (biochemistry, bioinformatics, biology/biological science, microbiology, and toxicology), BUSINESS (marketing management and recreational facilities management), COMPUTER AND PHYSICAL SCIENCE (chemistry, computer science, and physics), ENGINEERING AND ENVIRONMENTAL DESIGN (environmental science), HEALTH PROFESSIONS (health science, medical technology, mental health/human services, occupational therapy, pharmaceutical chemistry, pharmaceutical science, pharmacology, pharmacy, physical therapy, and physician's assistant), SOCIAL SCIENCE (humanities and social science, interdisciplinary studies, and psychology). Pharmacy and physical therapy is the strongest academically. Pharmacy, physical therapy, and biology are the largest.

Special: USP offers 5- and 6-year integrated professional programs in occupational therapy, physical therapy, and physician's assistant studies. Internships are required in all health science disciplines. Study abroad is available in Asia, Africa, and Europe through the NYU Study Abroad program. A 1-year undeclared major program is offered, as is a program of curriculum and advisement to prepare students to enter medical school. Students may elect dual majors or a minor in communications, economics, psychology, sociology, math, physics, computer science, biochemistry, biology, chemistry, forensic science, humanities, math, microbiology, social sciences, and writing. There are 5 national honor societies.

Admissions: 62% of the 2009-2010 applicants were accepted. The SAT scores for the 2009-2010 freshman class were: Critical Reading--15% below 500, 59% between 500 and 599, 25% between 600 and 700, and 1% above 700; Math--3% below 500, 41% between 500 and 599, 49% between 600 and 700, and 7% above 700; Writing--13% below 500, 53% between 500 and 599, 31% between 600 and 700, and 3% above 700. The ACT scores were 6% below 21, 24% between 21 and 23, 37% between 24 and 26, 23% between 27 and 28, and 10% above 28. 70% of the current freshmen were in the top fifth of their class; 93% were in the top two fifths. 13 freshmen graduated first in their class.

Requirements: The SAT or ACT is required. In addition, applicants must be high school graduates or hold the GED. Minimum academic requirements include 4 credits in English, 1 credit each in American history and social science, and 4 credits in academic electives. Math requirements include 2 years of algebra and 1 year of geometry. The university strongly recommends an additional year of higher-level math, such as pre-calculus or calculus. In addition, 3 science credits are required, and the university strongly recommends that students have 1 credit each in biology, chemistry, and physics. A strong background in English, science, and math is recommended. USP requires applicants to be in the upper 50% of their class. AP and CLEP credits are accepted. Important factors in the admissions decision are extracurricular activities record, leadership record, and advanced placement or honors courses.

Procedure: Freshmen are admitted fall. Entrance exams should be taken by the end of the junior year or the fall of the senior year. There are deferred admissions and rolling admissions plans. Application deadlines are open. Application fee is $45. Notification is sent on a rolling basis. Applications are accepted on-line. 700 applicants were on a recent waiting list, 75 were accepted.

Financial Aid: In 2009-2010, 100% of all full-time freshmen and 100% of continuing full-time students received some form of financial aid. 86% of all full-time freshmen and 76% of continuing full-time students received need-based aid. 19% of undergraduate students work part-time. Average annual earnings from campus work are $565. The average financial indebtedness of the 2009 graduate was $103,544. The FAFSA is required. The priority date for freshman financial aid applications for fall entry is March 15.

Computers: Wireless access is available. There are 120 college-owned workstations in the dorms, library, computer center, and student center. All dorm rooms are wired for high-speed Internet connections and have access to the campus-wide network. All students may access the system. There are no time limits and no fees. It is strongly recommended that all students have a personal computer. A Windows operating systems is recommended.

Tulsa, OK 74104-3189

(918) 631-2307
(800) 331-3050; (918) 631-5003

Full-time: 1566 men, 1363 women	**Faculty:** 282; IIA, +$
Part-time: 85 men, 70 women	**Ph.D.s:** 96%
Graduate: 630 men, 473 women	**Student/Faculty:** 10 to 1
Year: semesters, summer session	**Tuition:** $26,812
Application Deadline: open	**Room & Board:** $8544
Freshman Class: 4698 applied, 2333 accepted, 690 enrolled	
SAT CR/M: 650/620	**ACT:** 28 **HIGHLY COMPETITIVE+**

The University of Tulsa, founded in 1894 and affiliated with the Presbyterian Church, is a private comprehensive institution offering 60 undergraduate major areas of study through its programs in liberal arts and sciences, engineering and natural sciences, and business administration. There are 3 undergraduate schools and 2 graduate schools. In addition to regional accreditation, TU has baccalaureate program accreditation with AACSB, ABET, CSAB, NASM, NCATE, and NLN. The 2 libraries contain 1.3 million volumes, 3.4 million microform items, and 21,144 audio/video tapes/CDs/DVDs, and subscribe to 34,278 periodicals including electronic. Computerized library services include interlibrary loans, database searching, Internet access, and laptop Internet portals. Special learning facilities include an art gallery, radio station, and TV station. The 209-acre campus is in an urban area in the city of Tulsa. Including any residence halls, there are 93 buildings.

Programs of Study: TU confers B.A., B.S., B.F.A., B.M., B.Mus.Ed., B.S.A.M., B.S.A.T., B.S.B., B.S.B.A., B.S.C., B.S.C.E., B.S.C.S., B.S.D.E., B.S.E., B.S.E.E., B.S.E.P., B.S.E.S.S., B.S.G.S., B.S.I.B.L., B.S.M.E., B.S.N., B.S.P.E., and B.S.S.P. degrees. Master's and doctoral degrees are also awarded. Bachelor's degrees are awarded in AGRICULTURE (environmental studies), BIOLOGICAL SCIENCE (biochemistry and biology/biological science), BUSINESS (accounting, banking and finance, international business management, management information systems, management science, marketing/retailing/merchandising, and sports management), COMMUNICATIONS AND THE ARTS (art, arts administration/management, communications, English, film arts, French, German, music, music performance, musical theater, piano/organ, Spanish, and voice), COMPUTER AND PHYSICAL SCIENCE (chemistry, computer science, geology, geoscience, information sciences and systems, mathematics, and physics), EDUCATION (athletic training, education, education of the deaf and hearing impaired, elementary education, and music education), ENGINEERING AND ENVIRONMENTAL DESIGN (chemical engineering, electrical/electronics engineering, engineering physics, mechanical engineering, and petroleum/natural gas engineering), HEALTH PROFESSIONS (exercise science, nursing, premedicine, and speech pathology/audiology), SOCIAL SCIENCE (anthropology, economics, history, philosophy, political science/government, prelaw, psychology, religion, Russian and Slavic studies, and sociology). Petroleum engineering, psychology, and English are the strongest academically. Petroleum engineering, mechanical engineering, and exercise and sports science are the largest.

Special: Internships are available in the Tulsa area during the school year and in cities throughout the United States during the summer. Students may participate in more than 40 study-abroad programs, most of them arranged through the Institute of European Studies. TU offers a Washington semester, B.A.-B.S. degrees, cross-registration with the 3 undergraduate schools, dual and student-designed majors, accelerated degree programs, nondegree study, work-study programs, and pass/fail options. There are 35 national honor societies, including Phi Beta Kappa, and a freshman honors program.

Admissions: 50% of the 2009-2010 applicants were accepted. The SAT scores for the 2009-2010 freshman class were: Critical Reading--8% below 500, 31% between 500 and 599, 37% between 600 and 700, and 24 above 700; Math--7% below 500, 25% between 500 and 599, 41% between 600 and 700, and 27 above 700. The ACT scores were 2% below 21, 14% between 21 and 23, 18% between 24 and 26, 19% between 27 and 28, and 47% above 28. 85% of the current freshmen were in the top fifth of their class; 94% were in the top two fifths. There were 74 National Merit finalists. 27 freshmen graduated first in their class.

Requirements: The SAT or ACT is required. In addition, Graduation from an accredited secondary school or satisfactory scores on the GED are also required for admission. The school recommends a minimum of 15 academic credits, including 4 years of English, 3 to 4 years each of math, science, and social studies (including history), and 2 years of a single foreign language. An essay and an interview are highly recommended. An audition or a portfolio is required for students applying for music, theater, or art scholarships. TU requires applicants to be in the upper 33% of their class. A GPA of 3.0 is required. AP credits are accepted. Important factors in the admissions decision are advanced placement or honors courses, leadership record, and extracurricular activities record.

Procedure: Freshmen are admitted fall, spring, and summer. Entrance exams should be taken during spring of the junior year or fall of the senior year. There are deferred admissions and rolling admissions plans. Application deadlines are open. Application fee is $35. Notification is sent on a rolling basis. Applications are accepted on-line. 317 applicants were on a recent waiting list, 191 were accepted.

Financial Aid: 23% of undergraduate students work part-time. Average annual earnings from campus work are $4100. The FAFSA and the college's own financial statement are required. The deadline for filing freshman financial aid applications for fall entry is April 1.

Computers: Wireless access is available. All students may access the system 24 hours per day. There are no time limits and no fees.

UNIVERSITY OF UTAH
Salt Lake City, UT 84112   (801) 581-7281; (801) 585-7864

Full-time: 8426 men, 6763 women	**Faculty:** 1290; I, -$
Part-time: 3782 men, 3178 women	**Ph.D.s:** 65%
Graduate: 4043 men, 3092 women	**Student/Faculty:** 12 to 1
Year: semesters, summer session	**Tuition:** $5742 ($18,132)
Application Deadline: April 1	**Room & Board:** $6240
Freshman Class: 7890 applied, 6318 accepted, 2688 enrolled	
SAT CR/M/W: 570/570/550	**ACT:** 24 **VERY COMPETITIVE**

The flagship of the Utah System of Higher Education, the University of Utah was founded in 1850 and offers graduate and undergraduate programs in various disciplines. There are 13 undergraduate schools and 15 graduate schools. In addition to regional accreditation, U of U has baccalaureate program accreditation with AACSB, ABET, ACEJMC, ACPE, APTA, CSWE, NAAB, NASM, and NLN. The 3 libraries contain 3.9 million volumes, 3.0 million microform items, and 86,321 audio/video tapes/CDs/DVDs, and subscribe to 64,843 periodicals including electronic. Computerized library services include interlibrary loans, database searching, Internet access, and laptop Internet portals. Special learning facilities include a learning resource center, art gallery, natural history museum, radio station, TV station, and arboretum. The 1535-acre campus is in an urban area in Salt Lake City. Including any residence halls, there are 301 buildings.

Programs of Study: U of U confers B.A., B.S., B.F.A., B.Mus., B.S.W., and B.U.S. degrees. Master's and doctoral degrees are also awarded. Bachelor's degrees are awarded in AGRICULTURE (environmental studies), BIOLOGICAL SCIENCE (biology/biological science), BUSINESS (accounting, banking and finance, business administration and management, business economics, entrepreneurial studies, management information systems, management science, marketing management, and marketing/retailing/merchandising), COMMUNICATIONS AND THE ARTS (art, art history and appreciation, ballet, Chinese, classics, communications, dance, dramatic arts, English, film arts, fine arts, French, German, Japanese, linguistics, media arts, music, Russian, Spanish, and visual and performing arts), COMPUTER AND PHYSICAL SCIENCE (atmospheric sciences and meteorology, chemistry, computer science, earth science, environmental geology, geology, geophysics and seismology, geoscience, information sciences and systems, mathematics, and physics), EDUCATION (art education, elementary education, English education, health education, social science education, special education, and teaching English as a second/foreign language (TESOL/TEFOL)), ENGINEERING AND ENVIRONMENTAL DESIGN (architecture, bioengineering, biomedical engineering, chemical engineering, civil engineering, computer engineering, electrical/electronics engineering, engineering, environmental engineering, geological engineering, materials engineering, materials science, mechanical engineering, metallurgical engineering, mining and mineral engineering, and urban planning technology), HEALTH PROFESSIONS (exercise science, medical laboratory science, medical laboratory technology, nursing, occupational therapy, pharmacy, physical therapy, public health, and speech pathology/audiology), SOCIAL SCIENCE (anthropology, Asian/Oriental studies, behavioral science, consumer services, economics, family/consumer studies, gender studies, geography, history, human development, humanities, international studies, Middle Eastern studies, parks and recreation management, philosophy, political science/government, psychology, social science, sociology, urban studies, and women's studies). Social and behavioral sciences and business are the largest.

Special: The university offers numerous opportunities for cooperative programs, cross-registration through the Western Undergraduate Exchange (WUC) as part of the Western Interstate Commission for Higher Education (WICHE), study abroad in more than 30 countries, internships, work-study and accelerated degree programs, and B.A.-B.S. degrees. Also available are the general studies degree, a Washington semester, student-designed and dual majors, credit for telecourses and military experience, nondegree study, and pass/fail options. There are 40 national honor societies, including Phi Beta Kappa, a freshman honors program, and 27 departmental honors programs.

Admissions: 80% of the 2009-2010 applicants were accepted. The SAT scores for the 2009-2010 freshman class were: Critical Reading--25% below 500, 40% between 500 and 599, 28% between 600 and 700, and 7% above 700; Math--22% below 500, 39% between 500 and 599, 31% between 600 and 700, and 8% above 700; Writing--28% below 500, 44% between 500 and 599, 24% between 600 and 700, and 4% above 700. The ACT scores were 21% below 21, 26% between 21 and 23, 24% between 24 and 26, 13% between 27 and 28, and 16% above 28. 45% of the current freshmen were in the top fifth of their class; 75% were in the top two fifths.

Requirements: The ACT is required. The SAT is accepted. In addition, applicants must be graduates of an accredited secondary school or have the GED. Academic credits required include 4 years each of English and electives, 2 years each of foreign language and math, 3 years of biological and/or physical science, and 1 year of history. A GPA of 2.6 is required. AP and CLEP credits are accepted. Important factors in the admissions decision are advanced placement or honors courses and leadership record.

Procedure: Freshmen are admitted fall, spring, and summer. Entrance exams should be taken in the junior year of high school. There is a rolling admissions plan. Applications should be filed by April 1 for fall entry, November 1 for spring entry, and March 15 for summer entry, along with a $45 fee. Notification is sent on a rolling basis. Applications are accepted on-line.

Financial Aid: In 2009-2010, 38% of all full-time freshmen and 41% of continuing full-time students received some form of financial aid. 31% of all full-time freshmen and 32% of continuing full-time students received need-based aid. The average freshmen award was $10,103, with $6070 ($36,470 maximum) from need-based scholarships or need-based grants; $4858 ($25,192 maximum) from need-based self-help aid (loans and jobs); $7479 ($60,000 maximum) from non-need-based athletic scholarships; and $6275 ($20,470 maximum) from other non-need-based awards and non-need-based scholarships. 3% of undergraduate students work part-time. Average annual earnings from campus work are $3300. The average financial indebtedness of the 2009 graduate was $15,201. The FAFSA and the college's own financial statement are required. The priority date for freshman financial aid applications for fall entry is March 15.

Computers: Wireless access is available. There are more than 20 computer labs on campus and a campuswide wireless network. All students may access the system 24 hours per day. There are no time limits and no fees.

UNIVERSITY OF VERMONT
Burlington, VT 05405   (802) 656-3370; (802) 656-8611

Full-time: 4531 men, 5503 women	**Faculty:** 597; I, --$
Part-time: 488 men, 682 women	**Ph.D.s:** 86%
Graduate: 634 men, 953 women	**Student/Faculty:** 17 to 1
Year: semesters, summer session	**Tuition:** $13,554 ($31,410)
Application Deadline: January 15	**Room & Board:** $8996
Freshman Class: 22365 applied, 15856 accepted, 2619 enrolled	
SAT CR/M/W: 590/590/580	**ACT:** 25 **VERY COMPETITIVE**

The University of Vermont, established in 1791, is a public, land-grant, comprehensive institution with a dual focus on teaching and research. Its undergraduate and graduate offerings include the liberal arts, business administration, engineering, math, natural resources, agricultural studies, fine arts, teacher preparation, social services, environmental studies, and health science, including nursing. There are 7 undergraduate schools and 2 graduate schools. In addition to regional accreditation, UVM has baccalaureate program accreditation with AACSB, ABET, APTA, ASLA, CAHEA, CSWE, and NCATE. The 3 libraries contain 258,659 volumes, 2.1 million microform items, and 42,873 audio/video tapes/CDs/DVDs, and subscribe to 21,060 periodicals including electronic. Computerized library services include interlibrary loans, database searching, and Internet access. Special learning facilities include a learning resource center, art gallery, radio station, TV station, a health care center, 4 research farms, the Fleming Museum, geology museum, 9 natural areas, lakeshore science center, and aquatic research vessel. The 460-acre campus is in a suburban area 90 miles south of Montreal, 200 miles north of Boston, on the shore of Lake Champlain. Including any residence halls, there are 118 buildings.

Programs of Study: UVM confers B.A., B.S., B.Mus., B.S.A.E., B.S.B.A., B.S.Ed., B.S.C.E., B.S.C.S., B.S.E.E., B.S.E.M., B.S.M., B.S.M.E., and B.S.M.S. degrees. Master's and doctoral degrees are also awarded. Bachelor's degrees are awarded in AGRICULTURE (agriculture, animal science, environmental studies, fishing and fisheries, forestry and related sciences, horticulture, natural resource management, and plant science), BIOLOGICAL SCIENCE (biochemistry, biology/biological science, botany, genetics, microbiology, molecular biology, nutrition, wildlife biology, and zoology), BUSINESS (business administration and management, entrepreneurial studies, and international economics), COMMUNICATIONS AND THE ARTS (art, art history and appreciation, Chinese, classics, dramatic arts, English, film arts, French, German, Greek, Japanese, Latin, music, Russian, and Spanish), COMPUTER AND PHYSICAL SCIENCE (chemistry, computer science, geology, information sciences and systems, mathematics, physics, and statistics), EDUCATION (art education, athletic training, early childhood education, education, elementary education, English education, foreign languages education, mathematics education, middle school education, music education, physical education, science education, secondary education, social studies education, and special education), ENGINEERING AND ENVIRONMENTAL DESIGN (civil engineering, electrical/electronics engineering, engineering, engineering management, environmental engineering, environmental science, landscape architecture/design, and mechanical engineering), HEALTH PROFESSIONS (biomedical science, exercise science, medical laboratory science, nuclear medical technology, nursing, radiation therapy, and speech pathology/audiology), SOCIAL SCIENCE (anthropology, Asian/Oriental studies, Canadian studies, dietetics, economics, European studies, food science, gender studies, geography, history, human development, Italian studies, Latin American studies, parks and recreation management, philosophy, political science/government, psychology, religion, Russian and Slavic studies, social work, and sociology). Business administration, psychology, and biology/biological science are the largest.

Special: Special academic programs include co-op programs, internships in every discipline, study abroad in 110 countries, a Washington semester, work-study, an accelerated degree program in computer science, secondary education, and public administration, RN-BS-MS, dual majors, and student-designed majors. In addition, a 3-4 veterinary medicine degree is offered with Tufts University. There are 25 national honor societies, including Phi Beta Kappa, a freshman honors program, and 14 departmental honors programs.

Admissions: 71% of the 2009-2010 applicants were accepted. The SAT scores for the 2009-2010 freshman class were: Critical Reading--11% below 500, 44% between 500 and 599, 37% between 600 and 700, and 8% above 700; Math--11% below 500, 44% between 500 and 599, 39% between 600 and 700, and 6% above 700; Writing--10% below 500, 46% between 500 and 599, 37% between 600 and 700, and 7% above 700. The ACT scores were 8% below 21, 23% between 21 and 23, 34% between 24 and 26, 16% between 27 and 28, and 19% above 28. 50% of the current freshmen were in the top fifth of their class; 88% were in the top two fifths. 27 freshmen graduated first in their class.

Requirements: The SAT or ACT is required. The ACT Optional Writing test is also required. In addition, other admissions requirements include graduation from an accredited secondary school with 16 Carnegie units. Required high school course work includes 4 years of English, 3 years each of social science and math, including algebra I and II and geometry, and 2 years each of the same foreign language and science (one of which must be a lab science). Some academic units require additional course work. An essay must be submitted. The GED is also accepted. AP and CLEP credits are accepted. Important factors in the admissions decision are advanced placement or honors courses, extracurricular activities record, and recommendations by school officials.

Procedure: Freshmen are admitted fall and spring. Entrance exams should be taken by November of the senior year. There are early admissions and deferred admissions plans. Early decision applications should be filed by November 1 and regular applications by January 15 for fall entry and November 1 for spring entry, along with a $55 fee. Notifications are sent March 15. Applications are accepted on-line. 1173 applicants were on a recent waiting list, 146 were accepted.

Financial Aid: In a recent year, 83% of all full-time freshmen and 73% of continuing full-time students received some form of financial aid. 57% of all full-time freshmen and 55% of continuing full-time students received need-based aid. The average freshman award was $18,611. Need-based scholarships or need-based grants averaged $11,723 ($34,100 maximum); need-based self-help aid (loans and jobs) averaged $6,269 ($14,325 maximum); non-need-based athletic scholarships averaged $19,602 (maximum $30,109); other non-need-based awards and non-need-based scholarships averaged $3,652 ($31,107 maximum). The average financial indebtedness of the 2009 graduate was $25,079. The FAFSA is required. Check with the school for current application deadlines.

Computers: Wireless access is available. All students may access the system at any time. There are no time limits and no fees. Students enrolled in business majors must have a personal computer. A IBM, Mac, or Dell is recommended.

UNIVERSITY OF VIRGINIA
Charlottesville, VA 22904-4160   (434) 982-3200; (434) 924-3587

Full-time: 6521 men, 8174 women	**Faculty:** 1083; I, +$
Part-time: 333 men, 436 women	**Ph.D.s:** 92%
Graduate: 3929 men, 4869 women	**Student/Faculty:** 16 to 1
Year: semesters, summer session	**Tuition:** $18,162
Application Deadline: January 1	**Room & Board:** $8290
Freshman Class: 21108 applied, 6768 accepted, 3246 enrolled	
SAT CR/M/W: 660/680/670	**ACT:** 30 **MOST COMPETITIVE**

The University of Virginia, founded in 1819, is a public institution with undergraduate programs in architecture, arts and sciences, commerce, education, engineering and applied science, and nursing. There are 6 undergraduate schools and 10 graduate schools. In addition to regional accreditation, UVA has baccalaureate program accreditation with AACSB, ABET, ASLA, NAAB, and TEAC. The 15 libraries contain 5.6 million volumes, 5.4 million microform items, and 126,800 audio/video tapes/CDs/DVDs, and subscribe to 172,057 periodicals including electronic. Computerized library services include interlibrary loans, database searching, Internet access, and laptop Internet portals. Special learning facilities include a learning resource center, art gallery, radio station, TV station, art museum, and observatory. The 1167-acre campus is in a suburban area 70 miles northwest of Richmond, VA. Including any residence halls, there are 537 buildings.

Programs of Study: UVA confers B.A., B.S., B.Ar.H., B.I.S., B.S.C., B.S.Ed., B.S.N. and B.U.E.P. degrees. Master's and doctoral degrees are also awarded. Bachelor's degrees are awarded in BIOLOGICAL SCIENCE (biology/biological science), BUSINESS (business administration and management), COMMUNICATIONS AND THE ARTS (art, classics, comparative literature, dramatic arts, English, French, German, Italian, music, Slavic languages, and Spanish), COMPUTER AND PHYSICAL SCIENCE (astronomy, chemistry, computer science, mathematics, and physics), EDUCATION (health education and physical education), ENGINEERING AND ENVIRONMENTAL DESIGN (aerospace studies, architectural history, architecture, biomedical engineering, chemical engineering, city/community/regional planning, civil engineering, computer engineering, electrical/electronics engineering, engineering and applied science, environmental science, mechanical engineering, and systems engineering), HEALTH PROFESSIONS (nursing and speech pathology/audiology), SOCIAL SCIENCE (African American studies, anthropology, area studies, economics, history, interdisciplinary studies, international relations, philosophy, political science/government, psychology, religion, and sociology). English, history, and biology are the strongest academically. Commerce, economics, and history are the largest.

Special: The college offers internships, study abroad, accelerated degree programs, B.A.-B.S. degrees in biology, environmental sciences, chemistry and physics, co-op programs in engineering, and nondegree study. Dual majors in most arts and sciences programs, student-designed majors, an interdisciplinary major and Echols, and Rodman Scholars program (invited students design own curricula with many requirements waived), and pass/fail options are available. There college has a chapter of Phi Beta Kappa, a freshman honors program, and 35 departmental honors programs.

Admissions: 32% of the 2009-2010 applicants were accepted. The SAT scores for the 2009-2010 freshman class were: Critical Reading--3% below 500, 19% between 500 and 599, 45% between 600 and 700, and 33% above 700; Math--3% below 500, 13% between 500 and 599, 44% between 600 and 700, and 40% above 700; Writing--3% below 500, 17% between 500 and 599, 45% between 600 and 700, and 35% above 700. The ACT scores were 2% below 21, 5% between 21 and 23, 12% between 24 and 26, 18% between 27 and 28, and 63% above 28. 96% of the current freshmen were in the top fifth of their class; 98% were in the top two fifths. 196 freshmen graduated first in their class.

Requirements: The SAT is required. In addition, applicants can substitute the ACT for the SAT if the optional ACT Writing Test is also taken. Two SAT subject tests of the student's choosing are strongly recommended. With few exceptions, candidates graduate from accredited secondary schools. While the GED is accepted, it is rare for candidates for first-year admission who have this credential to be competitive in the admissions process. Applicants should complete 16 high school academic courses, including 4 courses of English, 4 courses of math, 2 courses of physics, biology, or chemistry (3 if applying to engineering), 2 years of foreign language, and 1 course of social science. A letter of recommendation (preferably from the secondary school) is required; also, a teacher's recommendation is recommended. AP credits are accepted.

Procedure: Freshmen are admitted fall. Entrance exams should be taken by December of the senior year. There is a deferred admissions plan. Applications should be filed by January 1 for fall entry, along with a $60 fee. Notifications are sent April 1. Applications are accepted on-line. 4522 applicants were on a recent waiting list, 420 were accepted.

Financial Aid: In 2009-2010, 57% of all full-time freshmen and 44% of continuing full-time students received some form of financial aid. 32% of all full-time freshmen and 29% of continuing full-time students received need-based aid. The average freshmen award was $12,984. The average financial indebtedness of the 2009 graduate was $18,432. The FAFSA and the college's own financial statement are required. The deadline for filing freshman financial aid applications for fall entry is March 1.

Computers: Wireless access is available. Dormitories, libraries, and student centers have both wired and wireless access. Wireless access is available at about

80% of all buildings on campus. All students may access the system. 24 hours a day, 7 days a week. There are no time limits. The fee is $198. It is strongly recommended that all students have a personal computer.

UNIVERSITY OF WASHINGTON
Seattle, WA 98195 (206) 543-9686

Full-time: 11615 men, 12600 women	**Faculty:** I, av$
Part-time: 2145 men, 2225 women	**Ph.D.s:** 89%
Graduate: 5355 men, 6295 women	**Student/Faculty:** n/av
Year: trimesters, summer session	**Tuition:** $7762 ($24,367)
Application Deadline: see profile	**Room & Board:** $9000
Freshman Class: n/av	
SAT or ACT: required	**VERY COMPETITIVE**

The University of Washington, founded in 1861, is a public institution offering a broad range of degree programs. Figures in the above capsule and in this profile are approximate. There are 12 undergraduate schools and 1 graduate school. In addition to regional accreditation, UW has baccalaureate program accredita0 miction with AACSB, ABET, NCATE, and NLN. The 16 libraries contain 7.0 million volumes. Computerized library services include interlibrary loans, database searching, Internet access, and laptop Internet portals. Special learning facilities include a learning resource center, art gallery, natural history museum, planetarium, radio station, TV station, state museum, full teaching hospital, marine science lab, 200-acre arboretum, and field research forest. The 643-acre campus is in an urban area 5 miles from downtown Seattle. Including any residence halls, there are 279 buildings.

Programs of Study: UW confers B.A., B.S., B.A.B.A., B.C.H.S., B.L.Arch., B.Mus., B.S.A.&A., B.S.B.C., B.S.Cer.E., B.S.Comp.E., B.S.F., B.S.Fish., B.S.I.E., B.S.M.E., B.S.Med.Tech., B.S.Met.E., and B.S.Nur. degrees. Master's and doctoral degrees are also awarded. Bachelor's degrees are awarded in AGRICULTURE (fishing and fisheries, forest engineering, and forestry production and processing), BIOLOGICAL SCIENCE (biochemistry, biology/biological science, botany, microbiology, neurosciences, and zoology), BUSINESS (accounting, banking and finance, business administration and management, business economics, international business management, marketing/retailing/merchandising, and personnel management), COMMUNICATIONS AND THE ARTS (art history and appreciation, classics, communications, comparative literature, dance, dramatic arts, English, French, Germanic languages and literature, graphic design, Italian, Japanese, jazz, music history and appreciation, music performance, painting, photography, Scandinavian languages, sculpture, Slavic languages, Spanish, speech/debate/rhetoric, studio art, and technical and business writing), COMPUTER AND PHYSICAL SCIENCE (astronomy, atmospheric sciences and meteorology, computer science, geology, information sciences and systems, mathematics, oceanography, physics, quantitative methods, and statistics), EDUCATION (music education), ENGINEERING AND ENVIRONMENTAL DESIGN (aeronautical engineering, ceramic engineering, chemical engineering, civil engineering, computer engineering, construction engineering, electrical/ electronics engineering, engineering, landscape architecture/design, materials science, ocean engineering, and paper and pulp science), HEALTH PROFESSIONS (dental hygiene, environmental health science, health care administration, medical laboratory technology, nursing, and speech pathology/audiology), SOCIAL SCIENCE (African American studies, anthropology, Asian/American studies, Asian/Oriental studies, Canadian studies, economics, ethnic studies, food science, geography, history, international relations, Judaic studies, liberal arts/general studies, Near Eastern studies, philosophy, political science/government, psychology, religion, Russian and Slavic studies, social work, sociology, South Asian studies, and women's studies). Business, political science, and art are the largest.

Special: A wide variety of internships, including those for minority students in engineering, concurrent dual majors, study abroad in 60 countries, a Washington semester, a general studies degree, and co-op programs are available. Work-study programs, cross-registration with the National Student Exchange, credit/no credit options, student-designed majors, accelerated degree programs, nondegree study, and a 5-year B.A.-B.S. degree also are offered. There are 20 national honor societies, including Phi Beta Kappa, a freshman honors program, and 36 departmental honors programs.

Requirements: The SAT or ACT is required. The ACT Optional Writing test is also required. In addition, applicants must have completed 15 academic units, including 4 years of English, 3 each of math and social sciences, 2 each of foreign language and science, and 1/2 year each in fine/visual performing arts and electives. Admission is based on a comprehensive review. A GPA of 2.0 is required. AP credits are accepted.

Procedure: Freshmen are admitted to all sessions. Entrance exams should be taken by December of the senior year. Applications should be filed by September 15 for winter entry, December 15 for spring entry, and January 15 for summer entry, along with a $50 fee. Notifications are sent March 15. Applications are accepted on-line. 773 applicants were on a recent waiting list, 332 were accepted.

Financial Aid: In a recent year, 50% of all full-time freshmen and 45% of continuing full-time students received some form of financial aid. 32% of all full-time freshmen and 37% of continuing full-time students received need-based aid. The average financial indebtedness of the 2009 graduate was $16,116. Check with the school for application deadlines.

Computers: Wireless access is available. There are 9 computing labs across campus with hundreds of work stations available for student use. Wireless Internet access is available on nearly the entire campus and available by logging in with a student account. All students may access the system. 24 hours daily. There are no time limits and no fees.

UNIVERSITY OF WISCONSIN/EAU CLAIRE
Eau Claire, WI 54701

(715) 836-5415
(888) INFO-UWE; (715) 836-2409

Full-time: 4089 men, 5713 women	**Faculty:** 410; IIA, -$
Part-time: 267 men, 418 women	**Ph.D.s:** 81%
Graduate: 199 men, 360 women	**Student/Faculty:** 21 to 1
Year: semesters, summer session	**Tuition:** $6633
Application Deadline:	**Room & Board:** $5730
Freshman Class: 7404 applied, 4993 accepted, 2013 enrolled	
ACT: 24	**SAT:** recommended
	VERY COMPETITIVE

The University of Wisconsin/Eau Claire, founded in 1916, is a public institution offering programs in the liberal arts and sciences, business, teacher education, nursing, music, and the fine arts. There are 4 undergraduate schools. In addition to regional accreditation, UW-Eau Claire has baccalaureate program accreditation with AACSB, ACEJMC, CSWE, and NASM. The library contains 944,303 volumes, 1.1 million microform items, and 11,595 audio/video tapes/CDs/DVDs, and subscribes to 52,443 periodicals including electronic. Computerized library services include interlibrary loans, database searching, Internet access, and laptop Internet portals. Special learning facilities include a learning resource center, art gallery, planetarium, radio station, TV station, a human development center, natural preserve, ropes course, materials science center, college of nursing and health sciences clinical simulation/skills lab. The 333-acre campus is in an urban area 95 miles east of Minneapolis, Minnesota. Including any residence halls, there are 28 buildings.

Programs of Study: UW-Eau Claire confers B.A., B.S., B.B.A., B.F.A., B.L.S., B.M., B.M.E., B.S.E.Ph., B.S.H.C.A., B.S.N., and B.S.W. degrees. Associates and master's degrees are also awarded. Bachelor's degrees are awarded in BIOLOGICAL SCIENCE (biochemistry, biology/biological science, ecology, environmental biology, microbiology, and molecular biology), BUSINESS (accounting, banking and finance, business administration and management, business economics, business systems analysis, entrepreneurial studies, human resources, management information systems, marketing/retailing/merchandising, and operations management), COMMUNICATIONS AND THE ARTS (advertising, applied music, art, broadcasting, ceramic art and design, communications, creative writing, dramatic arts, drawing, English, English literature, fine arts, French, German, graphic design, illustration, journalism, linguistics, metal/jewelry, music, music history and appreciation, music theory and composition, painting, photography, piano/organ, printmaking, public relations, sculpture, Spanish, technical and business writing, and voice), COMPUTER AND PHYSICAL SCIENCE (actuarial science, applied mathematics, applied physics, chemistry, computer programming, computer science, earth science, environmental geology, geology, hydrology, information sciences and systems, mathematics, physical sciences, physics, planetary and space science, software engineering, statistics, and web services), EDUCATION (art education, athletic training, drama education, early childhood education, education, elementary education, English education, foreign languages education, mathematics education, middle school education, music education, physical education, science education, secondary education, social science education, social studies education, and special education), ENGINEERING AND ENVIRONMENTAL DESIGN (computer engineering, engineering physics, geological engineering, and materials science), HEALTH PROFESSIONS (exercise science, health care administration, music therapy, nursing, predentistry, premedicine, preoptometry, prepharmacy, prephysical therapy, preveterinary science, public health, and speech pathology/audiology), SOCIAL SCIENCE (American Indian studies, criminal justice, economics, geography, history, Latin American studies, liberal arts/general studies, philosophy, philosophy and religion, physical fitness/movement, political science/government, prelaw, psychology, religion, social science, social studies, social work, sociology, and women's studies). Elementary education, nursing, and biology are the largest.

Special: Numerous internships, work-study programs, and study abroad in 26 countries are offered. Dual majors and interdisciplinary majors are possible. Credit by examination, non-degree study, and pass/fail options are offered. There are 34 national honor societies, a freshman honors program, and 17 departmental honors programs.

Admissions: 67% of the 2009-2010 applicants were accepted. The ACT scores were 6% below 21, 33% between 21 and 23, 39% between 24 and 26, 13% between 27 and 28, and 9% above 28. 50% of the current freshmen were in the top fifth of their class; 88% were in the top two fifths. There were 4 National Merit finalists. 67 freshmen graduated first in their class.

Requirements: The ACT is required. The SAT is recommended. In addition, applicants should graduate from an accredited secondary school or present its equivalent, with 17 academic credits, including 4 in English, 3 each in social studies, college preparatory math, and science and 2 years of a single foreign language. Students must graduate in the upper 50% of their class or present a minimum composite score of 1090 on the SAT or 23 on the ACT. Probationary admission is sometimes offered for the spring semester. Music majors or minors must audition. AP and CLEP credits are accepted. Important factors in the admissions decision are advanced placement or honors courses, recommendations by school officials, and leadership record.

Procedure: Freshmen are admitted to all sessions. Entrance exams should be taken by December of the senior year. There are early admissions and rolling admissions plans. Application deadlines are open. The fall 2009 application fee was $44. Applications are accepted on-line. A waiting list is maintained.

Financial Aid: In 2009-2010, 70% of all full-time freshmen and 68% of continuing full-time students received some form of financial aid. 41% of all full-time freshmen and 44% of continuing full-time students received need-based aid. The average freshmen award was $7,621. 21% of undergraduate students work part-time. Average annual earnings from campus work are $1144. The average financial indebtedness of the 2009 graduate was $19,687. The FAFSA is required. The deadline for filing freshman financial aid applications for fall entry is April 15.

Computers: Wireless access is available. Students may use computer facilities for classroom assignments, research, network access to other resources, and mail. Terminals and PC are located across campus. There are 17 supported labs plus labs in housing and the library. Dial-in access is offered. All students may access the system. 24 hours a day, 7 days per week. There are no time limits and no fees.

UNIVERSITY OF WISCONSIN/LA CROSSE

La Crosse, WI 54601	(608) 785-8000; (608) 785-8940
Full-time: 3469 men, 4724 women	**Faculty:** IIA, --$
Part-time: 140 men, 160 women	**Ph.D.s:** 60%
Graduate: 343 men, 789 women	**Student/Faculty:** 21 to 1
Year: semesters, summer session	**Tuition:** $7509
Application Deadline:	**Room & Board:** $5630
Freshman Class: 6504 applied, 4492 accepted, 1103 enrolled	
ACT: 25	**SAT:** required
	VERY COMPETITIVE

The University of Wisconsin/La Crosse, founded in 1909, is a public institution offering undergraduate and graduate studies in arts and sciences, health and human services, business administration, education, phys ed and recreation, professional development, and educational administration. There are 6 undergraduate schools and one graduate school. In addition to regional accreditation, UW-L has baccalaureate program accreditation with AACSB, APTA, NASM, and NCATE. The library contains 666,883 volumes, 1.2 million microform items, and 2,027 audio/video tapes/CDs/DVDs, and subscribes to 1,603 periodicals including electronic. Computerized library services include interlibrary loans and database searching. Special learning facilities include a learning resource center, art gallery, planetarium, radio station, TV station, the River Studies Center and the Allied Health Center. The 121-acre campus is in a small town 140 miles west of Madison and 150 miles southeast of Minneapolis/St. Paul, WI. Including any residence halls, there are 32 buildings.

Programs of Study: UW-L confers B.A. and B.S. degrees. Associate and master's degrees are also awarded. Bachelor's degrees are awarded in BIOLOGICAL SCIENCE (biology/biological science and microbiology), BUSINESS (accounting, banking and finance, business administration and management, international business management, and marketing/retailing/merchandising), COMMUNICATIONS AND THE ARTS (art, communications, dramatic arts, English, fine arts, French, music, Spanish, and speech/debate/rhetoric), COMPUTER AND PHYSICAL SCIENCE (chemistry, computer science, information sciences and systems, mathematics, and physics), EDUCATION (athletic training, elementary education, health education, physical education, science education, secondary education, and social studies education), HEALTH PROFESSIONS (community health work, exercise science, medical laboratory technology, nuclear medical technology, occupational therapy, physician's assistant, radiation therapy, and recreation therapy), SOCIAL SCIENCE (archeology, economics, geography, German area studies, history, parks and recreation management, philosophy, political science/government, psychology, public administration, and sociology). Microbiology, nuclear medicine technology, and physics are the strongest academically. Business administration, elementary education, and biology are the largest.

Special: Cooperative programs and cross-registration are available with Viterbo College. There are study-abroad programs in 14 countries and an international student exchange program. UW-L also offers a 3-2 engineering degree with the University of Wisconsin/Madison, the University of Wisconsin/Milwaukee, Platteville, and the University of Minnesota, work-study programs, internships, non-degree study, credit by exam, and pass/fail options. There are 10 national honor societies, a freshman honors program, and 11 departmental honors programs.

Admissions: 69% of the 2009-2010 applicants were accepted. The ACT scores were 5% below 21, 28% between 21 and 23, 41% between 24 and 26, 17% between 27 and 28, and 9% above 28. 65% of the current freshmen were in the top fifth of their class; 94% were in the top two fifths. 49 freshmen graduated first in their class.

Requirements: The SAT or ACT is required. In addition, applicants must be graduates of an accredited secondary school or hold a GED certificate. They must have completed 17 academic credits, including 4 courses in English, 3 each in social studies, math, and science, 2 in algebra and 1 in geometry, and 4 other academic courses. Students completing rigorous courses, including in the senior year, will be stronger candidates for admission. Students must rank in the top 35% of their high school graduating class and score at least 22 on the ACT or the top 40% and score 25 on the ACT. UW-L requires applicants to be in the upper 40% of their class. A GPA of 2.0 is required. AP and CLEP credits are accepted. Important factors in the admissions decision are advanced placement or honors courses, leadership record, and recommendations by school officials.

Procedure: Freshmen are admitted to all sessions. Entrance exams should be taken by the junior year or at the beginning of the senior year. There are early admissions and rolling admissions plans. Application deadlines are open. Application fee is $35. Notification is sent on a rolling basis.

Financial Aid: In 2009-2010, 39% of all full-time freshmen and 41% of continuing full-time students received some form of financial aid. 18% of all full-time freshmen and 17% of continuing full-time students received need-based aid. The average freshman award was $4,906. Need-based scholarships or need-based grants averaged $4,937 ; need-based self-help aid (loans and jobs) averaged $2,993; and other non-need-based awards and non-need-based scholarships averaged $1,412. 79% of undergraduate students work part-time. Average annual earnings from campus work are $900. The average financial indebtedness of the 2009 graduate was $12,145. The FAFSA and the college's own financial statement are required. The priority date for freshman financial aid applications for fall entry is March 15.

Computers: All students may access the system. 7 A.M. to midnight. There are no time limits and no fees.

UNIVERSITY OF WISCONSIN/MADISON
Madison, WI 53706-1481   (608) 262-3961; (608) 262-7706

Full-time: 13,369 men, 14,434 women	**Faculty:** I, av$
Part-time: 1197 men, 1343 women	**Ph.D.s:** 91%
Graduate: 5719 men, 6037 women	**Student/Faculty:** n/av
Year: semesters, summer session	**Tuition:** $8314 ($23,063)
Application Deadline: February 1	**Room & Board:** $8040
Freshman Class: 24,855 applied, 14,228 accepted, 5680 enrolled	
SAT CR/M/W: 610/666/620	**ACT:** 28 **HIGHLY COMPETITIVE+**

The University of Wisconsin/Madison, founded in 1849, is a public, land-grant institution offering undergraduate and graduate study in almost every major field. There are 8 undergraduate schools and 13 graduate schools. In addition to regional accreditation, Wisconsin has baccalaureate program accreditation with AACSB, ABET, ACS, ADA, ASLA, CCNE, CSWE, FIDER, NASAD, NASM, NAST, and SAF. The 43 libraries contain 7.9 million volumes. Computerized library services include interlibrary loans, database searching, Internet access, and laptop Internet portals. Special learning facilities include a learning resource center, art gallery, natural history museum, planetarium, radio station, and TV station. The 935-acre campus is in an urban area 75 miles west of Milwaukee and 150 miles northwest of Chicago.

Programs of Study: Wisconsin confers B.A., B.S., B.B.A., B.F.A., B.M., and B.N.S. degrees. Master's and doctoral degrees are also awarded. Bachelor's degrees are awarded in AGRICULTURE (agricultural business management, agricultural economics, animal science, conservation and regulation, dairy science, forestry and related sciences, horticulture, poultry science, and soil science), BIOLOGICAL SCIENCE (bacteriology, biochemistry, biology/biological science, botany, entomology, genetics, microbiology, molecular biology, nutrition, plant pathology, toxicology, wildlife biology, and zoology), BUSINESS (accounting, banking and finance, insurance and risk management, marketing/retailing/merchandising, operations management, real estate, and retailing), COMMUNICATIONS AND THE ARTS (African languages, art, art history and appreciation, Chinese, classics, communications, comparative literature, dance, dramatic arts, English, French, German, Hebrew, Italian, Japanese, journalism, Latin, linguistics, music, Polish, Portuguese, Russian, and Spanish), COMPUTER AND PHYSICAL SCIENCE (actuarial science, applied mathematics, astronomy, atmospheric sciences and meteorology, chemistry, computer science, geology, information sciences and systems, mathematics, physics, and statistics), EDUCATION (agricultural education, art education, elementary education, physical education, and secondary education), ENGINEERING AND ENVIRONMENTAL DESIGN (bioengineering, biomedical engineering, cartography, chemical engineering, civil engineering, computer engineering, electrical/electronics engineering, engineering mechanics, engineering physics, geological engineering, industrial engineering, interior design, landscape architecture/design, materials science, mechanical engineering, naval architecture and marine engineering, nuclear engineering, and textile technology), HEALTH PROFESSIONS (medical laboratory technology, medical science, nursing, physician's assistant, and speech pathology/audiology), SOCIAL SCIENCE (African American studies, anthropology, Asian/Oriental studies, child care/child and family studies, consumer services, economics, family/consumer studies, food science, geography, history,

history of science, human ecology, international relations, Judaic studies, Latin American studies, law, philosophy, political science/government, psychology, religion, rural sociology, Scandinavian studies, social work, sociology, textiles and clothing, and women's studies). Political science, biology, and history are the largest.

Special: Co-op programs, internships, study abroad, work-study programs, and accelerated degrees in any major are available. B.A.-B.S. degrees and dual and student-designed majors also are available. There is a chapter of Phi Beta Kappa and a freshman honors program.

Admissions: 57% of the 2009-2010 applicants were accepted. The SAT scores for the 2009-2010 freshman class were: Critical Reading--10% below 500, 31% between 500 and 599, 42% between 600 and 700, and 17% above 700; Math--3% below 500, 15% between 500 and 599, 44% between 600 and 700, and 38% above 700; Writing--7% below 500, 28% between 500 and 599, 49% between 600 and 700, and 16% above 700. The ACT scores were 1% below 21, 6% between 21 and 23, 20% between 24 and 26, 25% between 27 and 28, and 48% above 28. 89% of the current freshmen were in the top fifth of their class; 99% were in the top two fifths.

Requirements: The SAT or ACT is required. The ACT Optional Writing test is also required. In addition, applicants must have completed the following number of units in high school (these are minimums; the number of units recommended is higher): 17 total units including 4 English, 3 each of math, science, and social studies, 2 foreign language, and 2 electives. Wisconsin requires applicants to be in the upper 50% of their class. AP and CLEP credits are accepted.

Procedure: Freshmen are admitted fall, spring, and summer. Entrance exams should be taken in the junior year. There are deferred admissions and rolling admissions plans. Applications should be filed by February 1 for fall entry, November 15 for spring entry, and February 1 for summer entry, along with a $44 fee. Notification is sent on a rolling basis. Applications are accepted on-line.

Financial Aid: Wisconsin is a member of CSS. The FAFSA, the college's own financial statement, and a federal income tax return are required. Check with the school for current application deadlines.

Computers: Wireless access is available. All students may access the system. There are no time limits and no fees.

UNIVERSITY OF WISCONSIN/MILWAUKEE
Milwaukee, WI 53201   **(414) 229-2222; (414) 229-6940**

Full-time: 10,406 men, 10,599 women	**Faculty:** I, --$
Part-time: 1897 men, 2302 women	**Ph.D.s:** n/av
Graduate: 2067 men, 3147 women	**Student/Faculty:** 21 to 1
Year: semesters, summer session	**Tuition:** $7702 ($17,431)
Application Deadline: July 1	**Room & Board:** $6838
Freshman Class: 9918 applied, 7881 accepted, 3635 enrolled	
SAT CR/M/W: 527/547/516	**ACT:** 22 **COMPETITIVE**

The University of Wisconsin/Milwaukee, founded in 1885, offers undergraduate and graduate degrees in arts and sciences, fine arts, business, education, engineering and applied sciences, architecture and urban planning, social welfare, and health fields. There are 10 undergraduate schools and 1 graduate school. In addition to regional accreditation, UWM has baccalaureate program accreditation with AACSB, ABET, ACEJMC, CAHEA, CSWE, NAAB, NASAD, NASM, NCATE, and NLN. The library contains 214,185 volumes, 1.7 million microform items, and 38,716 audio/video tapes/CDs/DVDs, and subscribes to 8757 periodicals including electronic. Computerized library services include interlibrary loans, database searching, and Internet access. Special learning facilities include a learning resource center, art gallery, planetarium, radio station, TV station, the American Geographical Society Library. The 93-acre campus is in an urban area in Milwaukee. Including any residence halls, there are 42 buildings.

Programs of Study: UWM confers B.A., B.S., B.B.A., B.F.A., B.S.Applied S., and B.S.E. degrees. Master's and doctoral degrees are also awarded. Bachelor's degrees are awarded in AGRICULTURE (conservation and regulation), BIOLOGICAL SCIENCE (biochemistry, biology/biological science, botany, microbiology, and zoology), BUSINESS (accounting, banking and finance, business administration and management, management information systems, marketing/retailing/merchandising, real estate, and recreation and leisure services), COMMUNICATIONS AND THE ARTS (art history and appreciation, classics, communications, comparative literature, dance, dramatic arts, English, film arts, fine arts, French, German, Hebrew, Italian, linguistics, music, Russian, and Spanish), COMPUTER AND PHYSICAL SCIENCE (applied mathematics, chemistry, computer science, geology, geoscience, mathematics, and physics), EDUCATION (art education, education, music education, and social science education), ENGINEERING AND ENVIRONMENTAL DESIGN (architecture, civil engineering, electrical/electronics engineering, engineering, industrial administration/management, industrial engineering, materials engineering, and mechanical engineering), HEALTH PROFESSIONS (clinical science, health care administration, health science, medical science, nursing, occupational therapy, predentistry, premedicine, and speech pathology/audiology), SOCIAL SCIENCE (African American studies, anthropology, criminal justice, economics, geography, history, law, philosophy, political science/government, prelaw, psychology, religion, social work, and sociology). Architecture and engineering are the strongest academically.

Special: UWM offers cooperative programs in engineering, cross-registration with UW/Parkside, study abroad in Europe and Asia, internships, a Washington semester, and work-study programs. Students may select an accelerated degree program, dual majors, a general studies degree, and student-designed majors. Credit/no credit options, nondegree study, credit by exam, and credit for life, military, and work experience are also available. There is 1 national honor society, including Phi Beta Kappa, a freshman honors program, and a departmental honors programs.

Admissions: 79% of the 2009-2010 applicants were accepted. The SAT scores for the 2009-2010 freshman class were: Critical Reading--33% below 500, 35% between 500 and 599, 27% between 600 and 700, and 6% above 700; Math--29% below 500, 33% between 500 and 599, 33% between 600 and 700, and 5% above 700; Writing--41% below 500, 36% between 500 and 599, 21% between 600 and 700, and 2% above 700. The ACT scores were 33% below 21, 33% between 21 and 23, 22% between 24 and 26, 7% between 27 and 28, and 5% above 28. 19% of the current freshmen were in the top fifth of their class; 50% were in the top two fifths.

Requirements: The SAT or ACT is required; the ACT is preferred, with a minimum score of 21 on the ACT required of all Wisconsin residents. Out-of-state students may substitute the SAT. Candidates must have graduated from an accredited secondary school with 17 Carnegie units, including at least 4 in English, 3 in history/social science, and 3 each in math and the natural sciences. A GED certificate is accepted. Music and theater majors must audition. For the School of Architecture and Urban Planning, higher rank and ACT requirements apply. AP and CLEP credits are accepted. Important factors in the admissions decision are advanced placement or honors courses, evidence of special talent, and leadership record.

Procedure: Freshmen are admitted to all sessions. Entrance exams should be taken in the spring of the junior year. There are deferred admissions and rolling admissions plans. Applications should be filed by July 1 for fall entry and December 1 for spring entry, along with a $44 fee. Application deadlines are earlier for some programs; check with the school. Notification is sent on a rolling basis. Applications are accepted on-line.

Financial Aid: In 2009-2010, 64% of all full-time freshmen and 61% of continuing full-time students received some form of financial aid. Need-based scholarships and need-based grants averaged $3605; need-based self-help aid (loans and jobs) averaged $3605; and non-need-based athletic scholarships averaged $823. 48% of all full-time freshmen and 52% of continuing full-time students received need-based aid. Check with the school for current application deadlines.

Computers: All students may access the system any time. There are no time limits and no fees.

UNIVERSITY OF WISCONSIN/SUPERIOR
Superior, WI 54880 (715) 394-8230; (715) 394-8407

Full-time: 951 men, 1132 women	**Faculty:** 110; IIA, --$
Part-time: 147 men, 345 women	**Ph.D.s:** 73%
Graduate: 69 men, 149 women	**Student/Faculty:** 19 to 1
Year: semesters, summer session	**Tuition:** $6736 ($14,308)
Application Deadline: open	**Room & Board:** $5600
Freshman Class: 965 applied, 655 accepted, 359 enrolled	
ACT: 22	**VERY COMPETITIVE**

The University of Wisconsin/Superior, founded in 1893, offers undergraduate programs in the liberal arts and sciences, business, education, fine arts, applied arts, and social sciences. There are 5 undergraduate schools and 1 graduate school. In addition to regional accreditation, UW/Superior has baccalaureate program accreditation with CSWE and NASM. The library contains 190,757 volumes, 1 million microform items, and 5304 audio/video tapes/CDs/DVDs, and subscribes to 785 periodicals including electronic. Computerized library services include interlibrary loans and database searching. Special learning facilities include a learning resource center, art gallery, planetarium, radio station, TV station, and aquatic lab. The 230-acre campus is in an urban area 150 miles north of Minneapolis/St. Paul. Including any residence halls, there are 17 buildings.

Programs of Study: UW/Superior confers B.A., B.S., B.F.A., B.M., and B.M.E. degrees. Associate and master's degrees are also awarded. Bachelor's degrees are awarded in BIOLOGICAL SCIENCE (biology/biological science), BUSINESS (accounting and business administration and management), COMMUNICATIONS AND THE ARTS (art history and appreciation, communications, dramatic arts, English, fine arts, music, music performance, speech/debate/rhetoric, and studio art), COMPUTER AND PHYSICAL SCIENCE (chemistry, computer science, information sciences and systems, and mathematics), EDUCATION (art education, elementary education, mathematics education, music education, physical education, science education, and secondary education), HEALTH PROFESSIONS (art therapy and community health work), SOCIAL SCIENCE (criminal justice, history, international studies, law, political science/government, psychology, public administration, social studies, social work, and sociology). Business, education, and aquatic biology are the strongest academically. Business and teacher education are the largest.

Special: UW/Superior offers work-study and co-op programs in business and internships in social work, business, mass communication, and criminal justice. There is a comprehensive program of student-designed majors, along with a cooperative program in marine studies with Texas A&M University, and 3-2 engineering and forestry programs with Michigan Technological University. Students may cross-register for 2 classes per semester at the University of Minnesota/Duluth or the College of St. Scholastica. An extended degree is offered. Credit for life experience and pass/fail options are available. There are 3 national honor societies.

Admissions: 68% of the 2009-2010 applicants were accepted. The ACT scores were 9% below 18, 59% between 18 and 23, 30% between 24 and 29, and 2% 30 and above. 33% of students were in the top fourth of their class; 75% were in the top half. 11% of freshmen graduated in the top 10% of their high school class.

Requirements: The ACT is required. Out-of-state residents may submit SAT scores instead. Applicants must graduate from an accredited secondary school or the equivalent. They must rank in the upper 50% of their graduating class or achieve a minimum composite score of 20 on the ACT. AP and CLEP credits are accepted.

Procedure: Freshmen are admitted fall, spring, and summer. Entrance exams should be taken in spring of the junior year or early fall of the senior year. There are deferred admissions and rolling admissions plans. Application deadlines are open. Application fee is $44. Notification is sent on a rolling basis. Applications are accepted on-line.

Financial Aid: In 2009-2010, 54% of all full-time freshmen and 58% of continuing full-time students received some form of financial aid. 21% of undergraduate students work part-time. Average annual earnings from campus work are $1200. The average financial indebtedness of the 2009 graduate was $20,803. The FAFSA is required. The priority date for freshman financial aid applications for fall entry is April 1.

Computers: Wireless access is available. All buildings have wired or wireless Internet access. The university provides 343 computers for student use. All students may access the system 24 hours a day. There are no time limits and no fees. It is strongly recommended that all students have a personal computer.

URSINUS COLLEGE

Collegeville, PA 19426   **(610) 409-3200; (610) 409-3662**

Full-time: 791 men, 923 women	**Faculty:** 125; IIB, +$
Part-time: 15 men, 19 women	**Ph.D.s:** 95%
Graduate: none	**Student/Faculty:** 11 to 1
Year: semesters	**Tuition:** $38,670
Application Deadline: February 15	**Room & Board:** $9250
Freshman Class: 6125 applied, 3471 accepted, 513 enrolled	
SAT CR/M/W: 630/620/600	**ACT:** 26 **VERY COMPETITIVE+**

Ursinus College, founded in 1869, is a private residential college offering programs in the liberal arts. The library contains 420,000 volumes, 201,995 microform items, and 32,000 audio/video tapes/CDs/DVDs, and subscribes to 25,883 periodicals including electronic. Computerized library services include interlibrary loans, database searching, Internet access, and laptop Internet portals. Special learning facilities include an art gallery, planetarium, radio station, TV station, and observatory. The 170-acre campus is in a suburban area 28 miles west of Philadelphia. Including any residence halls, there are 65 buildings.

Programs of Study: Ursinus confers B.A. and B.S. degrees. Bachelor's degrees are awarded in BIOLOGICAL SCIENCE (biochemistry, biology/biological science, and neurosciences), BUSINESS (business economics), COMMUNICATIONS AND THE ARTS (art, classics, communications, dance, dramatic arts, English, French, German, and Spanish), COMPUTER AND PHYSICAL SCIENCE (chemistry, computer science, mathematics, and physics), ENGINEERING AND ENVIRONMENTAL DESIGN (environmental science), HEALTH PROFESSIONS (exercise science), SOCIAL SCIENCE (American studies, anthropology, East Asian studies, history, international relations, philosophy, political science/government, psychology, and sociology). Biology, chemistry, and politics are the strongest academically. Economics, biology, and psychology are the largest.

Special: The college offers study abroad, student-designed majors, internships, a Washington semester, dual majors, and a 3-2 engineering degree with Columbia University and Washington University of St. Louis. Ursinus offers an international studies certificate in addition to a degree in international relations. There are 17 national honor societies, including Phi Beta Kappa, and 27 departmental honors programs.

Admissions: 57% of the 2009-2010 applicants were accepted. The SAT scores for the 2009-2010 freshman class were: Critical Reading--4% below 500, 31% between 500 and 599, 47% between 600 and 700, and 18% above 700; Math--5% below 500, 38% between 500 and 599, 48% between 600 and 700, and 12% above 700; Writing--10% below 500, 38% between 500 and 599, 42% between 600 and 700, and 11% above 700. The ACT scores were 13% below 21, 19% between 21 and 23, 28% between 24 and 26, 13% between 27 and 28, and 27% above 28. 72% of the current freshmen were in the top fifth of their class; 91% were in the top two-fifths. There were 42 National Merit finalists. 6 freshmen graduated first in their class.

Requirements: The SAT or ACT is required. In addition, SAT Subject Tests are recommended. Applicants should prepare with 16 academic credits, including 4 years of English, 3 of math, 2 of foreign language, and 1 each of science and social studies. An interview is recommended. Any student in the top 10% of his or her high school class may elect to waive the SAT/ACT requirement. A GPA of 2.0 is required. AP credits are accepted. Important factors in the admissions decision are advanced placement or honors courses, recommendations by school officials, and leadership record.

Procedure: Freshmen are admitted fall and spring. Entrance exams should be taken in the junior or senior year. There are early decision, early admissions, deferred admissions, and rolling admissions plans. Early decision applications should be filed by January 15; regular applications, by February 15 for fall entry and December 1 for spring entry. Notification of early decision is sent January 15; regular decision, April 1. Applications are accepted on-line. 519 applicants were on a recent waiting list, 72 were accepted.

Financial Aid: In 2009-2010, 94% of all full-time freshmen and 90% of continuing full-time students received some form of financial aid. 71% of all full-time freshmen and 69% of continuing full-time students received need-based aid. The average freshmen award was $29,150, with $25,580 ($32,000 maximum) from need-based scholarships or need-based grants; $4687 ($7000 maximum) from need-based self-help aid (loans and jobs); and $15,000 ($30,000 maximum) from other non-need-based awards and non-need-based scholarships. 69% of undergraduate students work part-time. Average annual earnings from campus work are $1404. The average financial indebtedness of the 2009 graduate was $32,593. Ursinus is a member of CSS. The CSS/Profile and FAFSA are required. The deadline for filing freshman financial aid applications for fall entry is February 15.

Computers: Wireless access is available. The campus is 95% wireless and there are additional wired connections in the classrooms and residence halls. In addition, there are 3 public computer labs on campus. All students may access the system. There are no time limits and no fees. The college provides all students with a Dell Latitude laptop.

VANDERBILT UNIVERSITY

Nashville, TN 37203-1700

(615) 322-2561
(800) 288-0432; (615) 343-7765

Full-time: 3218 men, 3511 women	**Faculty:** I, +$
Part-time: 26 men, 9 women	**Ph.D.s:** 97%
Graduate: 2525 men, 3187 women	**Student/Faculty:** n/av
Year: semesters, summer session	**Tuition:** $35,278
Application Deadline: January 3	**Room & Board:** $11,446
Freshman Class: 19353 applied, 3899 accepted, 783 enrolled	
SAT or ACT: required	**MOST COMPETITIVE**

Vanderbilt University, founded in 1873, is a private university offering programs in liberal and fine arts, business, engineering, health science, military science, religion, law, music, and teacher preparation. There are 4 undergraduate schools and 6 graduate schools. In addition to regional accreditation, Vanderbilt has baccalaureate program accreditation with AACSB, ABET, CAHEA, and NCATE. The 9 libraries contain 2.9 million volumes, 3.0 million microform items, and 63,403 audio/video tapes/CDs/DVDs, and subscribe to 29,173 periodicals including electronic. Computerized library services include interlibrary loans and database searching. Special learning facilities include a learning resource center, art gallery, radio station, TV station, two observatories, and a TV news archive. The 330-acre campus is in an urban area Nashville, TN. Including any residence halls, there are 217 buildings.

Programs of Study: Vanderbilt confers B.A. and B.S. degrees. Master's and doctoral degrees are also awarded. Bachelor's degrees are awarded in BIOLOGICAL SCIENCE (biology/biological science and molecular biology), COMMUNICATIONS AND THE ARTS (classical languages, classics, communications, English, fine arts, French, German, music history and appreciation, music performance, music theory and composition, Russian, Spanish, and theater design), COMPUTER AND PHYSICAL SCIENCE (chemistry, geology, mathematics, and physics), EDUCATION (early childhood education, education, elementary education, secondary education, and special education), ENGINEERING AND ENVIRONMENTAL DESIGN (bioengineering, chemical engineering, civil engineering, computer engineering, electrical/electronics engineering, engineering and applied science, and mechanical engineering), SOCIAL SCIENCE (African American studies, American studies, anthropology, child - psychology/development, cognitive science, East Asian studies, economics, European studies, history, human development, interdisciplinary studies, Latin American studies, philosophy, political science/government, psychology, public affairs, religion, sociology, and urban studies). Social science, engineering, and education are the largest.

Special: Vanderbilt offers cross-registration with Fisk and Howard Universities and Meharry Medical College, study abroad in 18 countries, a Washington semester, a work-study program, B.A.-B.S. degrees, dual and student-designed majors, accelerated degree programs, nondegree study, and pass/fail options. Internships, required for human development majors, are available in human service agencies, city and state government, and businesses. A 3-2 engineering degree is offered with Fisk University. The school belongs to NASA's Tennessee Space Grant Consortium, and the Intercollegiate Center for Classical Studies in Rome. There are 19 national honor societies, including Phi Beta Kappa, a freshman honors program, and 21 departmental honors programs.

Admissions: 20% of the 2009-2010 applicants were accepted. The SAT scores for the 2009-2010 freshman class were: Critical Reading--1% below 500, 6% between 500 and 599, 33% between 600 and 700, and 61% above 700; Math--% below 500, 4% between 500 and 599, 25% between 600 and 700, and 71% above 700; Writing--1% below 500, 6% between 500 and 599, 37% between 600 and 700, and 55% above 700. There were 149 National Merit finalists.

Requirements: The SAT or ACT is required. In addition, SAT Subject tests are recommended in math level I, II, or IIc, writing, and foreign language. Admission requirements vary by school. Candidates should be graduates of an accredited secondary school with a minimum of 15 academic credits. Most programs require 4 years of English, 3 of math, and 2 of a foreign language and recommend 2 of history and 1 of social studies. An essay is required. An audition is required for Blair School of Music. AP credits are accepted. Important factors in the admissions decision are advanced placement or honors courses and evidence of special talent.

Procedure: Freshmen are admitted fall. Entrance exams should be taken by spring of the junior year or the fall of the senior year. There are early decision and deferred admissions plans. Early decision applications should be filed by November 1; regular applications, by January 3 for fall entry, along with a $50 fee. Notification of early decision is sent December 15; regular decision, April 1. 1510 applicants were on the 2009 waiting list; 3 were admitted. Applications are accepted on-line. 1510 applicants were on a recent waiting list, 3 were accepted.

Financial Aid: In 2009-2010, 45% of all full-time freshmen and 41% of continuing full-time students received some form of financial aid. 68% of all full-time freshmen and 65% of continuing full-time students received need-based aid. The average freshman award was $36,399. Need-based scholarships or need-based grants averaged $28,838 ; need-based self-help aid (loans and jobs) averaged $4,573; non-need-based athletic scholarships averaged $30,446; and other non-need-based awards and non-need-based scholarships averaged $12,879. The average financial indebtedness of the 2009 graduate was $20,755. The CSS/Profile and FAFSA, and tax return information are required. The priority date for freshman financial aid applications for fall entry is February 1. The deadline for filing freshman financial aid applications for fall entry is January 3.

VASSAR COLLEGE
Poughkeepsie, NY 12604

(845) 437-7300
(800) 827-7270; (845) 437-7063

Full-time: 965 men, 1370 women	**Faculty:** IIB, +$
Part-time: 15 men, 40 women	**Ph.D.s:** 96%
Graduate: none	**Student/Faculty:** n/av
Year: semesters	**Tuition:** $41,930
Application Deadline: see profile	**Room & Board:** $9540
Freshman Class: n/av	
SAT or ACT: required	**MOST COMPETITIVE**

Vassar College, founded in 1861, is a private, independent college of the liberal arts and sciences. Figures in the above capsule are approximate. The 3 libraries contain 869,088 volumes, 611,076 microform items, and 23,590 audio/video tapes/CDs/DVDs, and subscribe to 4,001 periodicals including electronic. Computerized library services include interlibrary loans, database searching, Internet access, and laptop Internet portals. Special learning facilities include a learning resource center, art gallery, radio station, studio art building, geological museum, observatory, 3 theaters, concert hall, environmental field station, intercultural center, and research-oriented lab facilities for natural sciences. The 1000-acre campus is in a suburban area 75 miles north of New York City. Including any residence halls, there are 100 buildings.

Programs of Study: Vassar confers B.A. degrees. Master's degrees are also awarded. Bachelor's degrees are awarded in AGRICULTURE (environmental studies), BIOLOGICAL SCIENCE (biochemistry, biology/biological science, and neurosciences), COMMUNICATIONS AND THE ARTS (art, Chinese, dramatic arts, English, film arts, Japanese, languages, media arts, and music), COMPUTER AND PHYSICAL SCIENCE (astronomy, chemistry, computer science, geology, mathematics, and physics), EDUCATION (foreign languages education), ENGINEERING AND ENVIRONMENTAL DESIGN (technology and public affairs), HEALTH PROFESSIONS (premedicine), SOCIAL SCIENCE (African studies, American studies, anthropology, Asian/Oriental studies, biopsychology, classical/ancient civilization, cognitive science, economics, geography, history, international studies, Judaic studies, Latin American studies, medieval studies, philosophy, political science/government, prelaw, psychology, religion, social studies, sociology, Spanish studies, urban studies, Victorian studies, and women's studies). English, psychology, and political science are the largest.

Special: The school offers fieldwork in social agencies and schools, dual majors, independent majors, student-designed majors, cross-registration with the College Consortium, and nonrecorded grade options. Vassar runs study-abroad programs in 7 countries and students also may study in other approved programs around the world. A 3-2 engineering degree with Dartmouth College is offered. There is a Phi Beta Kappa honors society.

Requirements: The SAT is required. In addition, 2 SAT Subject tests, or the ACT, are required. Graduation from an accredited secondary school or satisfactory scores on the GED are required for admission. The high school program should typically include 4 years each of English, social studies, math, foreign language, and science. An essay and a writing sample are required. AP credits are accepted.

Procedure: Freshmen are admitted fall. Entrance exams should be taken as early as possible, but no later than December of the senior year. There are early decision and deferred admissions plans. Check with the school for current application deadlines. The application fee is $60. Applications are accepted on-line. A waiting list is maintained.

Financial Aid: Vassar is a member of CSS. The CSS/Profile, FAFSA, FFS, and the college's own financial statement are required. Check with the school for current application deadlines.

Computers: Wireless access is available. All students may access the system, 24 hours per day. There are no time limits and no fees.

Villanova, PA 19085-1672	(610) 519-4000; (610) 519-6450

Full-time: 6342 men and women	**Faculty:** 572; IIA, +$
Part-time: 350 men, 300 women	**Ph.D.s:** 90%
Graduate: 2228 men and women	**Student/Faculty:** 12 to 1
Year: semesters, summer session	**Tuition:** $37,725
Application Deadline: January 7	**Room & Board:** $10,340
Freshman Class: n/av	
SAT or ACT: required	**MOST COMPETITIVE**

Villanova University, founded in 1842 and affiliated with the Roman Catholic Church, offers undergraduate programs in liberal arts and sciences, commerce and finance, engineering, and nursing. There are 4 undergraduate schools and 5 graduate schools. Tuition figure in above capsule is an average; exact costs vary by college. Some figures in this profile are approximate. In addition to regional accreditation, Villanova has baccalaureate program accreditation with AACSB, ABET, and NLN. The 2 libraries contain 800,000 volumes, 1.8 million microform items, and 6500 audio/video tapes/CDs/DVDs, and subscribe to 12,000 periodicals including electronic. Computerized library services include interlibrary loans, database searching, Internet access, and laptop Internet portals. Special learning facilities include a learning resource center, art gallery, radio station, TV station, and 2 observatories. The 254-acre campus is in a suburban area 12 miles west of Philadelphia. Including any residence halls, there are 60 buildings.

Programs of Study: Villanova confers B.A., B.S., and B.S.N. degrees. Associates, master's, and doctoral degrees are also awarded. Bachelor's degrees are awarded in AGRICULTURE (environmental studies), BIOLOGICAL SCIENCE (biochemistry and biology/biological science), BUSINESS (accounting, banking and finance, business administration and management, business economics, international business management, management information systems, and marketing/retailing/merchandising), COMMUNICATIONS AND THE ARTS (art history and appreciation, classics, communications, English, French, German, Italian, and Spanish), COMPUTER AND PHYSICAL SCIENCE (astronomy, astrophysics, chemistry, computer science, information sciences and systems, mathematics, physics, and science), EDUCATION (elementary education and secondary education), ENGINEERING AND ENVIRONMENTAL DESIGN (chemical engineering, civil engineering, computer engineering, electrical/electronics engineering, environmental science, and mechanical engineering), HEALTH PROFESSIONS (nursing), SOCIAL SCIENCE (criminal justice, economics, geography, history, human services, humanities, interdisciplinary studies, liberal arts/general studies, philosophy, political science/government, psychology, religion, sociology, and theological studies). Liberal arts and business are the largest.

Special: Cross-registration is possible with Rosemont College. Internships are available for each college in the Philadelphia area as well as in New York City and Washington D.C. Students may study abroad worldwide. Villanova offers a Washington semester, an accelerated degree program in biology for allied health program, dual majors, a general studies degree, and credit by exam. There are 35 national honor societies, including Phi Beta Kappa, and a freshman honors program.

Requirements: The SAT or ACT is required. The ACT Optional Writing test is also required. In addition, applicants must be graduates of an accredited secondary school and should have completed 16 academic units. The specific courses required vary according to college. A GED is accepted. An essay is required. AP and CLEP credits are accepted. Important factors in the admissions decision are evidence of special talent, leadership record, and advanced placement or honors courses.

Procedure: Freshmen are admitted in fall. Entrance exams should be taken by December of the senior year. There is a deferred admissions plan. Applications should be filed by January 7 for fall entry, along with a $75 fee. Notifications are sent April 1. Applications are accepted on-line. 2077 applicants were on a recent waiting list, 210 were accepted.

Financial Aid: In a recent year, 71% of all full-time freshmen and 68% of continuing full-time students received some form of financial aid. 44% of all full-time freshmen and 40% of continuing full-time students received need-based aid. The average freshmen award was $24,905, with $13,709 ($34,360 maximum) from need-based scholarships or need-based grants; $4472 ($6625 maximum) from need-based self-help aid (loans and jobs); $1420 ($40,225 maximum) from non-need-based athletic scholarships; $623 ($43,940 maximum) from other non-need-based awards and non-need-based scholarships; and $2190 from other forms of aid. 35% of undergraduate students work part-time. Average annual earnings from campus work are $1215. The average financial indebtedness of a recent graduate was $28,107. The FAFSA, the college's own financial statement, and parent and student federal income tax return and W2s are required. Check with the school for current deadlines.

Computers: Wireless access is available. The university provides Dell laptops to students in Colleges of Commerce and Finance and Engineering as part of tuition. In all other colleges, a personal PC is recommended, although many computer labs are also available to all students. Students connect in their residence halls via Internet T1 lines. Most academic buildings and the student center are wireless. Students must purchase a network/wireless card(s). All students may access the system. There are no time limits and no fees.

VIRGINIA COMMONWEALTH UNIVERSITY
Richmond, VA 23284-2527
(804) 828-8476
(800) 841-3638; (804) 828-1899

Full-time: 8257 men, 10924 women	**Faculty:** I, --$
Part-time: 1699 men, 2269 women	**Ph.D.s:** n/av
Graduate: 3265 men, 6022 women	**Student/Faculty:** n/av
Year: semesters, summer session	**Tuition:** $7117 ($20,751)
Application Deadline: open	**Room & Board:** $10,960
Freshman Class: 14352 applied, 10055 accepted, 3665 enrolled	
SAT CR/M/W: 540/540/530	**ACT:** 22　　　**COMPETITIVE**

Virginia Commonwealth, founded in 1838, is a public research university. There are 12 undergraduate schools and 14 graduate schools. In addition to regional accreditation, VCU has baccalaureate program accreditation with AACSB, ABET, ACEJMC, ACPE, ADA, APTA, CSWE, FIDER, NASAD, NASDTEC, NASM, NCATE, NLN, and NRPA. The 7 libraries contain 2 million volumes, 3.3 million microform items, and 29,707 audio/video tapes/CDs/DVDs, and subscribe to 50,461 periodicals including electronic. Computerized library services include interlibrary loans, database searching, Internet access, and laptop Internet portals. Special learning facilities include a learning resource center, art gallery, radio station, and TV station. The 177-acre campus is in an urban area 2 miles west of downtown Richmond and 90 miles from Washington, D.C. Including any residence halls, there are 202 buildings.

Programs of Study: VCU confers B.A., B.S., B.I.S., B.M., and B.S.W. degrees. Master's and doctoral degrees are also awarded. Bachelor's degrees are awarded in AGRICULTURE (environmental studies), BIOLOGICAL SCIENCE (biology/biological science), BUSINESS (accounting, banking and finance, business administration and management, marketing/retailing/merchandising, and sports management), COMMUNICATIONS AND THE ARTS (art history and appreciation, communications, crafts, dance, dramatic arts, English, film arts, graphic design, languages, music, painting, photography, and sculpture), COMPUTER AND PHYSICAL SCIENCE (chemistry, computer science, information sciences and systems, mathematics, physics, and science), EDUCATION (art education, foreign languages education, and health education), ENGINEERING AND ENVIRONMENTAL DESIGN (biomedical engineering, chemical engineering, computer engineering, electrical/electronics engineering, interior design, and mechanical engineering), HEALTH PROFESSIONS (clinical science, dental hygiene, and nursing), SOCIAL SCIENCE (African American studies, anthropology, criminal justice, economics, fashion design and technology, forensic studies, geography, history, interdisciplinary studies, international studies, philosophy, political science/government, psychology, religion, safety science, social work, sociology, and urban studies). Biology, psychology, and mass communications are the largest.

Special: The college offers co-op programs in all majors, cross-registration with the University of Richmond, Virginia Union University, and Virginia State, internships, study abroad in 111 countries, work-study programs, and student-designed majors. There is a freshman honors program.

Admissions: 70% of the 2009-2010 applicants were accepted. The SAT scores for the 2009-2010 freshman class were: Critical Reading--27% below 500, 46% between 500 and 599, 22% between 600 and 700, and 5% above 700; Math--30% below 500, 45% between 500 and 599, 21% between 600 and 700, and 4% above 700; Writing--33% below 500, 46% between 500 and 599, 19% between 600 and 700, and 2% above 700. The ACT scores were 30% below 21, 34% between 21 and 23, 22% between 24 and 26, 6% between 27 and 28, and 8% above 28. 37% of the current freshmen were in the top fifth of their class; 73% were in the top two fifths. 25 freshmen graduated first in their class.

Requirements: The SAT or ACT is required. The ACT Optional Writing test is also required. In addition, a high school diploma is required and the GED is accepted. SAT or ACT scores must be received for fall term admission by March. AP and CLEP tests are used for placement. High school units required are: 4 in English, 3 each in math and science (at least 1 lab), 2 each in foreign language and history, 1 in social studies, and 5 in academic electives. A GPA of 2.0 is required. AP and CLEP credits are accepted.

Procedure: Freshmen are admitted fall and spring. Entrance exams should be taken SAT or ACT scores must be received for fall term admission by March. There are early admissions, deferred admissions, and rolling admissions plans. Check with the school for current application deadlines. The fall 2008 application fee was $40 online, $50 for paper. 1001 applicants were on the 2009 waiting list, 34 were accepted. Applications are accepted on-line. 1001 applicants were on a recent waiting list, 34 were accepted.

Financial Aid: In 2009-2010, 59% of all full-time freshmen and 59% of continuing full-time students received some form of financial aid. 45% of all full-time freshmen and 47% of continuing full-time students received need-based aid. Need-based scholarships or need-based grants averaged $5,344 ($14,981 maximum); need-based self-help aid (loans and jobs) averaged $3,584 ($10,472 maximum); non-need based athletic scholarships averaged $15,451 ($32,877 maximum); and other non-need based awards and non-need based scholarships averaged $2,853 ($21,984 maximum). The average financial indebtedness of the 2009 graduate was $21,982. The FAFSA is required. The priority date for freshman financial aid applications for fall entry is March 1.

Computers: Wireless access is available. VCU has nearly 59,088 network ports and 962 wireless access points in faculty and staff offices, residence halls, student service centers, libraries, and computer labs that connect to 24,800 personal computers and 2800 server and network support devices. All students may access the system. There are no time limits and no fees. It is strongly recommended that all students have a personal computer.

VIRGINIA POLYTECHNIC INSTITUTE AND STATE UNIVERSITY

Blacksburg, VA 24061 (540) 231-6267; (540) 231-3242

Full-time: 15886 men, 11992 women	**Faculty:** I, av$
Part-time: 1689 men, 1288 women	**Ph.D.s:** 90%
Graduate: 4086 men, 2853 women	**Student/Faculty:** n/av
Year: semesters, summer session	**Tuition:** $8605 ($21,878)
Application Deadline: January 15	**Room & Board:** $6024
Freshman Class: 21201 applied, 12947 accepted, 5177 enrolled	
SAT CR/M/W: 590/621/586	**ACT:** required

HIGHLY COMPETITIVE

Virginia Polytechnic Institute and State University, founded in 1872, is a public land-grant institution. It offers a cadet program within the larger, nonmilitary student body. There are 7 undergraduate schools and 2 graduate schools. In addition to regional accreditation, Virginia Tech has baccalaureate program accreditation with AACSB, ABET, ACCE, ADA, AHEA, ASLA, FIDER, NAAB, NCATE, and SAF. The 4 libraries contain 2.3 million volumes, 6.3 million microform items, and 27,574 audio/video tapes/CDs/DVDs, and subscribe to 35,596 periodicals including electronic. Computerized library services include interlibrary loans, database searching, and Internet access. Special learning facilities include a learning resource center, art gallery, natural history museum, radio station, TV station, airport, wind tunnels, agricultural stations, radio/visual observatories, satellite up-link station, multimedia, digital music, writing, CAD/CAM labs, math emporium, and CAVE (cave automatic virtual environment). The 2600-acre campus is in a rural area 40 miles southwest of Roanoke. Including any residence halls, there are 110 buildings.

Programs of Study: Virginia Tech confers B.A., B.S., B.Arch., B.F.A., B.Land.Arch., B.S.Bus., B.S.E., and B.S.Ed. degrees. Master's and doctoral degrees are also awarded. Bachelor's degrees are awarded in AGRICULTURE (agricultural economics, animal science, dairy science, forestry and related sciences, horticulture, poultry science, and soil science), BIOLOGICAL SCIENCE (biochemistry, biology/biological science, and nutrition), BUSINESS (accounting, apparel and accessories marketing, banking and finance, business economics, entrepreneurial studies, hotel/motel and restaurant management, management science, marketing management, and tourism), COMMUNICATIONS AND THE ARTS (art, communications, dramatic arts, English, French, German, industrial design, music, and Spanish), COMPUTER AND PHYSICAL SCIENCE (chemistry, computer science, geology, mathematics, physics, planetary and space science, and statistics), EDUCATION (agricultural education, business education, environmental education, foreign languages education, science education, and secondary education), ENGINEERING AND ENVIRONMENTAL DESIGN (aerospace studies, agricultural engineering, architecture, chemical engineering, civil engineering, computer engineering, construction engineering, construction management, electrical/electronics engineering, engineering mechanics, environmental science, industrial engineering, interior design, landscape architecture/design, materials engineering, mechanical engineering, mining and mineral engineering, and ocean engineering), HEALTH PROFESSIONS (physical therapy, predentistry, and premedicine), SOCIAL SCIENCE (dietetics, economics, food science, geography, history, human development, interdisciplinary studies, international studies, interpreter for the deaf, parks and recreation management, philosophy, physical fitness/movement, political science/government, prelaw, psychology, public affairs, sociology, and urban studies). Engineering, architecture, and business are the strongest academically. Engineering, computer science, and biology are the largest.

Special: Students may cross-register with Miami University in Ohio, Oxford Polytechnic Institute, California Polytechnic Institute, and Florida A & M. Study abroad in 36 countries, internships in nearly every major, a Washington semester, and a wide range of work-study programs are available, as well as co-ops in 48 majors. There are honors options for most majors, B.A.-B.S. degrees, dual and student-designed majors, credit for independent study or research, nondegree study, and pass/fail options. The Corps of Cadets, a militarily structured organization, is open to men and women. Undergraduate advising programs are available to students wishing to prepare for professional school in law, dentistry, medicine, pharmacy, physical therapy, or veterinary medicine. There are 13 national honor societies, including Phi Beta Kappa, and a freshman honors program.

Admissions: 61% of the 2009-2010 applicants were accepted. 82% of the current freshmen were in the top fifth of their class; 97% were in the top two fifths.

Requirements: The SAT or ACT is required. In addition, applicants must be graduates of an accredited secondary school, or the GED is accepted. Applicants should complete 18 high school academic credits, including 4 years of English, 3 of math, including algebra II and geometry, 2 of lab science, to be chosen from biology, chemistry, or physics, and 1 each of history and social studies. An additional 3 years from college preparatory courses and 4 from any credit course offerings are required. AP and CLEP credits are accepted. Important factors in the admissions decision are advanced placement or honors courses, evidence of special talent, and extracurricular activities record.

Procedure: Freshmen are admitted to all sessions. Entrance exams should be taken by January 1 of the senior year. There is a early decision and a deferred admissions plan. Applications should be filed for early decision by November 1, and for regular decision by January 15 for fall entry, October 1 for spring entry, and April 22 for summer entry, along with a $50 fee. Notification of early decision is sent December 15; regular decision, April 1. Applications are accepted on-line. 2919 applicants were on a recent waiting list, 308 were accepted.

Financial Aid: In 2008-2009, 36% of all full-time freshmen and 35% of continuing full-time students received some form of financial aid. 29% of all full-time freshmen and 28% of continuing full-time students received need-based aid. The average freshman award was $11,609. Need-based scholarships or need-based grants averaged $6,924; need-based self-help aid (loans and jobs) averaged $4,002 and other non-need based awards and non-need based scholarships averaged $2,562. The FAFSA is required. Check with the school for current application deadlines.

Computers: Wireless access is available. Each student brings a personal computer and has access to high-speed Ethernet connections in all residence halls, laboratories, and lecture rooms, as well as wireless access in all academic buildings.

There are 912 university-owned workstations available for general student use. All students may access the system any time. All students are required to have a personal computer. Requirements vary by major.

WABASH COLLEGE

Crawfordsville, IN 47933-0352   (765) 361-6253
                                                         (800) 345-5385; (765) 361-6437

Full-time: 874 men	**Faculty:** 90; IIB, +$
Part-time: 9 men	**Ph.D.s:** 98%
Graduate: none	**Student/Faculty:** 10 to 1
Year: semesters	**Tuition:** $29,750
Application Deadline: December 1	**Room & Board:** $8100
Freshman Class: 1588 applied, 775 accepted, 247 enrolled	
SAT CR/M/W: 554/596/536	**ACT:** 24 **VERY COMPETITIVE**

Wabash College, founded in 1832, is a private liberal arts men's college with a strong emphasis on preprofessional programs. In addition to regional accreditation, Wabash has baccalaureate program accreditation with NCATE. The library contains 431,942 volumes, 11,359 microform items, and 15,909 audio/video tapes/CDs/DVDs, and subscribes to 4776 periodicals including electronic. Computerized library services include interlibrary loans, database searching, Internet access, and laptop Internet portals. Special learning facilities include a learning resource center, art gallery, radio station, archival center, and research centers for the study of theology and religion and inquiry in the liberal arts. The 60-acre campus is in a small town 45 miles northwest of Indianapolis. Including any residence halls, there are 55 buildings.

Programs of Study: Wabash confers A.B. degrees. Bachelor's degrees are awarded in BIOLOGICAL SCIENCE (biology/biological science), COMMUNICATIONS AND THE ARTS (art, classics, dramatic arts, English, French, German, Greek, Latin, music, Spanish, and speech/debate/rhetoric), COMPUTER AND PHYSICAL SCIENCE (chemistry, mathematics, and physics), SOCIAL SCIENCE (economics, history, philosophy, political science/government, psychology, and religion). Preprofessional studies, economics, and religion are the strongest academically. English, philosophy, and religion are the largest.

Special: Wabash offers internships with off-campus organizations, study abroad in an unlimited number of countries, a Washington semester with American University, dual majors, a B.A.-B.S. degree in engineering, and both a 3-2 engineering program and a 3-3 law program with Columbia University and Washington University in St. Louis. A tuition-free Ninth Semester Teacher Education Program is also available. There are 9 national honor societies, including Phi Beta Kappa, and 7 departmental honors programs.

Admissions: 49% of the 2009-2010 applicants were accepted. The SAT scores for the 2009-2010 freshman class were: Critical Reading--24% below 500, 47% between 500 and 599, 22% between 600 and 700; and 7% above 700; Math--12% below 500, 35% between 500 and 599, 37% between 600 and 700, and 16% above 700; Writing--31% below 500, 41% between 500 and 599, 24% between 600 and 700; and 4% above 700. 70% of the current freshmen were in the top fifth of their class; 91% were in the top two fifths.

Requirements: The SAT or ACT is required. In addition, Wabash recommends applicants have 4 high school courses in English, 3 to 4 in math, and 2 each in foreign language, lab science, and social studies. An essay is required, and an interview is recommended. AP and CLEP credits are accepted. Important factors in the admissions decision are advanced placement or honors courses, leadership record, and extracurricular activities record.

Procedure: Freshmen are admitted fall and spring. Entrance exams should be taken by the spring of the junior year or fall of the senior year. There are early decision, early admissions, deferred admissions, and rolling admissions plans. Early decision applications should be filed by November 15; regular applications, by December 1 for fall entry and December 1 for spring entry, along with a $40 fee. Notification is sent on a rolling basis beginning November 15. Applications are accepted on-line. 33 applicants were on a recent waiting list, 4 were accepted.

Financial Aid: In 2009-2010, 82% of all full-time freshmen and 79% of continuing full-time students received some form of financial aid. 82% of all full-time freshmen and 79% of continuing full-time students received need-based aid. The average freshman award was $28,136. 75% of undergraduate students work part-time. Average annual earnings from campus work are $3000. The average financial indebtedness of the 2009 graduate was $28,383. Wabash is a member of CSS. The CSS/Profile, the FAFSA, and federal tax form with W-2 statements are required. The priority date for freshman financial aid applications for fall entry is February 15. The deadline for filing freshman financial aid applications for fall entry is March 1.

Computers: Wireless access is available. Every classroom building has publicly accessible computers, with more than 350 such computers on campus. There are 6 public computer labs, some open 24 hours a day. A wireless network is available in all buildings. Students have unlimited access to the Internet from their rooms. All students may access the system 24 hours per day or at designated times for specific computers. There are no time limits and no fees.

WAGNER COLLEGE
Staten Island, NY 10301

(718) 390-3411
(800) 221-1010; (718) 390-3105

Full-time: 664 men, 1135 women	**Faculty:** 99; IIA, -$
Part-time: 19 men, 52 women	**Ph.D.s:** 88%
Graduate: 136 men, 259 women	**Student/Faculty:** 18 to 1
Year: semesters, summer session	**Tuition:** $32,580
Application Deadline: February 15	**Room & Board:** $9700
Freshman Class: 2842 applied, 1873 accepted, 519 enrolled	
SAT CR/M/W: 560/540/530	**ACT:** 25 **VERY COMPETITIVE**

Wagner College, founded in 1883, is a private liberal arts institution. There is 1 graduate school. In addition to regional accreditation, Wagner has baccalaureate program accreditation with ACBSP, NCATE, and NLN. The library contains 175,344 volumes, 219 microform items, and 3695 audio/video tapes/CDs/DVDs, and subscribes to 20,600 periodicals including electronic. Computerized library services include interlibrary loans, database searching, and Internet access. Special learning facilities include an art gallery, planetarium, and radio station. The 105-acre campus is in a suburban area 10 miles from Manhattan. Including any residence halls, there are 18 buildings.

Programs of Study: Wagner confers B.A. and B.S. degrees. Master's degrees are also awarded. Bachelor's degrees are awarded in BIOLOGICAL SCIENCE (biology/biological science and microbiology), BUSINESS (accounting and business administration and management), COMMUNICATIONS AND THE ARTS (arts administration/management, dramatic arts, English, fine arts, and music), COMPUTER AND PHYSICAL SCIENCE (chemistry, computer science, mathematics, and physics), EDUCATION (elementary education, middle school education, and secondary education), HEALTH PROFESSIONS (nursing and physician's assistant), SOCIAL SCIENCE (anthropology, history, philosophy, political science/government, psychology, public administration, and sociology). Natural sciences and health professions is the strongest academically. Business, nursing, and psychology are the largest.

Special: Internships are required for business and English majors and are recommended for all majors. Students may earn B.A.-B.S. degrees in psychology. Student-designed and dual majors, credit for life experience, a Washington semester, nondegree study, and pass/fail options are available. Study abroad in 14 countries is possible. There are 11 national honor societies and a freshman honors program.

Admissions: 66% of the 2009-2010 applicants were accepted. The SAT scores for the 2009-2010 freshman class were: Critical Reading--6% below 700, 41% between 600 and 700, 42% between 500 and 599, and 11% below 500; Math--7% below 500, 43% between 500 and 599, 43% between 600 and 700, and 7 above 700; Writing--13% below 500, 41% between 500 and 599, 40% between 600 and 700, and 6 above 700. The ACT scores were 5% below 21, 28% between 21 and 23, 42% between 24 and 26, 17% between 27 and 28, and 8% above 28. 35% of the current freshmen were in the top fifth of their class; 86% were in the top two fifths. In a recent year, 8 freshmen graduated first in their class and 94 were in the top 10% of their class.

Requirements: The SAT or ACT is required. In addition, graduation from an accredited secondary school is required, with 18 academic credits or Carnegie units, including 4 years of English, 3 years each of history and math, 2 years each of foreign language, science, and social studies, and 1 year each of art and music. An essay is required, and an interview is strongly recommended. Auditions are required for music and theater applicants. An interview is required for the Physician Assistant Program. A GPA of 3.0 is required. AP and CLEP credits are accepted. Important factors in the admissions decision are advanced placement or honors courses, recommendations by school officials, and extracurricular activities record.

Procedure: Freshmen are admitted fall and spring. Entrance exams should be taken by December of the senior year. There are early decision and deferred admissions plans. Early decision applications should be filed by December 1; regular applications, by February 15 for fall entry, along with a $50 fee. Notification of early decision is sent February 15; regular decision, March 1. Applications are accepted on-line. A waiting list is maintained.

Financial Aid: In 2009-2010, 92% of all full-time freshmen and 90% of continuing full-time students received some form of financial aid. 68% of all full-time freshmen and 57% of continuing full-time students received need-based aid. The average freshmen award was $21,102. 25% of undergraduate students work part-time. Average annual earnings from campus work are $800. The average financial indebtedness of the 2009 graduate was $36,988. Wagner is a member of CSS. The FAFSA, the state aid form, and the college's own financial statement are required. The priority date for freshman financial aid applications for fall entry is February 15.

Computers: Wireless access is available. All students may access the system. There are no time limits and no fees. It is strongly recommended that all students have a personal computer.

WAKE FOREST UNIVERSITY

Winston-Salem, NC 27109-7305 (336) 758-5201

Full-time: 2201 men, 2313 women	**Faculty:** 417; IIA, ++$
Part-time: 36 men, 19 women	**Ph.D.s:** 90%
Graduate: 1370 men, 1140 women	**Student/Faculty:** 11 to 1
Year: semesters, summer session	**Tuition:** $38,306
Application Deadline: January 15	**Room & Board:** $10,410
Freshman Class: 10553 applied, 3959 accepted, 1200 enrolled	
SAT: required	**MOST COMPETITIVE**

Wake Forest University, established in 1834, is a private institution offering undergraduate programs in the liberal arts and sciences, education, and preprofessional fields. There are 2 undergraduate schools and 5 graduate schools. In addition to regional accreditation, Wake Forest has baccalaureate program accreditation with AACSB and NCATE. The 3 libraries contain 2.1 million volumes, 2.2 million microform items, and 38,265 audio/video tapes/CDs/DVDs, and subscribe to 51,262 periodicals including electronic. Computerized library services include interlibrary loans, database searching, Internet access, and laptop Internet portals. Special learning facilities include a learning resource center, art gallery, radio station, TV station, fine arts center, anthropology museum, and laser research facility. The 340-acre campus is in a suburban area 4 miles northwest of Winston-Salem. Including any residence halls, there are 43 buildings.

Programs of Study: Wake Forest confers B.A. and B.S. degrees. Master's and doctoral degrees are also awarded. Bachelor's degrees are awarded in BIOLOGICAL SCIENCE (biology/biological science), BUSINESS (accounting, banking and finance, and business administration and management), COMMUNICATIONS AND THE ARTS (art, Chinese, classics, communications, dramatic arts, English, French, German, Greek, Japanese, Latin, music, Russian, and Spanish), COMPUTER AND PHYSICAL SCIENCE (chemistry, computer science, mathematics, and physics), EDUCATION (education), HEALTH PROFESSIONS (exercise science), SOCIAL SCIENCE (anthropology, economics, history, philosophy, political science/government, psychology, religion, and sociology). Business, communication, and political science are the largest.

Special: Wake Forest offers cooperative programs in engineering with any other schools of engineering accredited by ABET; political science majors who minor in Latin American studies have the opportunity to pursue a 5-year cooperative B.A.-M.A. program with Georgetown University. Cross-registration with Salem College is available for full-time students. Wake Forest sponsors study-abroad semester programs in 16 countries. Other special opportunities include internships, work-study programs, dual majors, and a minor in entrepreneurship and social enterprise. Students can also be certified in Spanish language translation and interpreting. An accelerated degree program may be arranged in medical technology. Interdisciplinary honors courses and the Open Curriculum program are available for selected students. Wake Forest owns residences in London, Venice, and Vienna where students and professors attend semester-long courses in a variety of disciplines. A semester-long program in Washington, D.C., is also offered. There are 11 national honor societies, including Phi Beta Kappa, a freshman honors program, and 23 departmental honors programs.

Admissions: 38% of the 2009-2010 applicants were accepted. 86% of the current freshmen were in the top fifth of their class; 98% were in the top two fifths.

Requirements: The SAT is required. SAT Subject tests are considered if submitted. Graduation from an accredited secondary school or the GED is required. The school requires 16 academic credits, including 4 credits of English, 3 of math, 2 each of a foreign language, history, and social studies, and 1 of science. 1 credit each of art and music is recommended. All students must submit an essay. AP and CLEP credits are accepted. Important factors in the admissions decision are recommendations by school officials, leadership record, and advanced placement or honors courses.

Procedure: Freshmen are admitted fall and spring. There are early decision and deferred admissions plans. Early decision applications should be filed by November 15; regular applications, by January 15 for fall entry and November 15 for spring entry. The fall 2009 application fee was $50. Notification of early decision is sent December 15; regular decision, April 1. 337 early decision candidates were accepted for the 2009-2010 class. A waiting list is an active part of the admissions procedure. Applications are accepted on-line.

Financial Aid: In 2009-2010, 41% of all full-time freshmen and 36% of continuing full-time students received some form of financial aid. 39% of all full-time freshmen and 34% of continuing full-time students received need-based aid. The average freshman award was $33,285. Need-based scholarships or need-based grants averaged $28,085; need-based self-help aid (loans and jobs) averaged $10,486; non-need-based athletic scholarships averaged $36,849; and other non-need-based awards and non-need-based scholarships averaged $16,327. 26% of undergraduate students work part-time. Average annual earnings from campus work are $1844. The average financial indebtedness of the 2009 graduate was $24,561. Wake Forest is a member of CSS. The CSS/Profile, the FAFSA, the state aid form, and the noncustodial profile are required. The priority date for freshman financial aid applications for fall entry is February 15. The deadline for filing freshman financial aid applications for fall entry is March 1.

Computers: Wireless access is available. All new students receive a notebook computer. A service desk provides on-line, phone, and walk-in service. All students may access the system 24 hours per day. There are no time limits and no fees.

WARREN WILSON COLLEGE

Asheville, NC 28815-9000

(828) 771-2073
(800) 934-3536; (828) 298-1440

Full-time: 340 men, 525 women	**Faculty:** IIB, -_$
Part-time: 5 men, 5 women	**Ph.D.s:** n/av
Graduate: 25 men, 50 women	**Student/Faculty:** n/av
Year: semesters	**Tuition:** $25,600
Application Deadline: see profile	**Room & Board:** $4500
Freshman Class: n/av	
SAT or ACT: required	**VERY COMPETITIVE**

Warren Wilson College, founded in 1894, is a liberal arts institution affiliated with the Presbyterian Church (U.S.A.) and known for its triad of academics, work, and service. All students work 15 hours per week in jobs related to the operation and maintenance of the college. In exchange, room and board is provided at a low rate. Figures in the above capsule are approximate. There is 1 graduate school. In addition to regional accreditation, Warren Wilson College has baccalaureate program accreditation with CSWE and NCATE. The library contains 110,702 volumes, 34,046 microform items, and 3,338 audio/video tapes/CDs/DVDs, and subscribes to 11,076 periodicals including electronic. Computerized library services include interlibrary loans, database searching, and Internet access. Special learning facilities include a learning resource center, art gallery, radio station, and outdoor adventure learning lab. The 1135-acre campus is in a small town 5 miles east of Asheville. Including any residence halls, there are 62 buildings.

Programs of Study: confers B.A. and B.S. degrees. Master's degrees are also awarded. Bachelor's degrees are awarded in AGRICULTURE (environmental studies), BIOLOGICAL SCIENCE (biology/biological science), BUSINESS (business economics), COMMUNICATIONS AND THE ARTS (art, creative writing, English, and Spanish), COMPUTER AND PHYSICAL SCIENCE (chemistry and mathematics), EDUCATION (elementary education, English education, middle school education, and recreation education), SOCIAL SCIENCE (anthropology, behavioral science, history, humanities, international studies, philosophy, psychology, social work, sociology, and women's studies). Biology is the strongest academically. Environmental studies, biology, and English are the largest.

Special: Cross-registration is offered with Mars Hill College and the University of North Carolina at Asheville. Internships related to the major may be arranged. Study-abroad programs in South America, Europe, Japan, and India are available. The college offers an accelerated degree program in education, student-designed majors, nondegree study, and pass/fail options. There are dual majors in history/political science and English/theater arts. Cooperative programs are available in engineering with Washington University in St. Louis and with Duke University. There are 3 departmental honors programs.

Admissions: In a recent year, there were 5 National Merit finalists. 3 freshmen graduated first in their class.

Requirements: The SAT or ACT is required, with a score of 500 on each section of the SAT or a composite score of 21 on the ACT. Graduation from an accredited secondary school or the GED is required. Applicants should have a total of 12 academic credits. An essay and an interview are recommended. A GPA of 2.8 is required. AP credits are accepted. Important factors in the admissions decision are advanced placement or honors courses, evidence of special talent, and recommendations by school officials.

Procedure: Freshmen are admitted fall and winter. Entrance exams should be taken by January 20 of the senior year. There are early decision and deferred admissions plans. Early decision applications should be filed by November 15; check with the school for other current application deadlines. Notification of early decision is sent December 1. The application fee is $15.

Financial Aid: The FAFSA and the college's own financial statement are required. Check with the school for current application deadlines.

Computers: Wireless access is available. PCs are located in 1 30-seat lab and 4 smaller teaching labs. There is wireless access in 3 dorms, the library, and a computer lab. All students may access the system. There are no time limits and no fees. It is strongly recommended that all students have a personal computer.

WARTBURG COLLEGE

Waverly, IA 50677-0903

(319) 352-8264
(800) 772-2085; (319) 352-8579

Full-time: 800 men, 900 women	**Faculty:** 107; IIB, -$
Part-time: 30 men, 30 women	**Ph.D.s:** 96%
Graduate: none	**Student/Faculty:** 16 to 1
Year: see profile, summer session	**Tuition:** $28,220
Application Deadline: see profile	**Room & Board:** $7975
Freshman Class: n/av	
SAT or ACT: required	**VERY COMPETITIVE**

Wartburg College, established in 1852, is a private liberal arts institution affiliated with the Evangelical Lutheran Church in America. Some figures in the above capsule and in this profile are approximate. In addition to regional accreditation, Wartburg has baccalaureate program accreditation with CSWE, NASM, and NCATE. The library contains 164,363 volumes, 8,480 microform items, and 5,983 audio/video tapes/CDs/DVDs, and subscribes to 30,170 periodicals including electronic. Computerized library services include interlibrary loans, database searching, Internet access, and laptop Internet portals. Special learning facilities include a learning resource center, radio station, TV station, business center, classroom technology center, fine arts center, journalism lab, symbolic computation lab, music computer lab, the Center for Community Engagement, 6 acres of native grasses and prairie plants, and more than 100 acres of native timber used for field trips and research. The 118-acre campus is in a small town 15 miles north of Waterloo/Cedar Falls. Including any residence halls, there are 37 buildings.

Programs of Study: Wartburg confers B.A., B.A.A., B.A.S., B.M., and B.M.E. degrees. Bachelor's degrees are awarded in BIOLOGICAL SCIENCE (biochemistry and biology/biological science), BUSINESS (accounting, banking and finance, business administration and management, international business management, marketing/retailing/merchandising, and recreation and leisure services), COMMUNICATIONS AND THE ARTS (applied music, art, arts administration/management, broadcasting, communications, creative writing, dramatic arts, English, French, German, graphic design, journalism, music, music performance, music theory and composition, public relations, and Spanish), COMPUTER AND PHYSICAL SCIENCE (chemistry, computer science, information sciences and systems, mathematics, and physics), EDUCATION (art education, elementary education, English education, foreign languages education, journalism education, mathematics education, music education, physical education, science education, secondary education, and social studies education), ENGINEERING AND ENVIRONMENTAL DESIGN (engineering and applied science), HEALTH PROFESSIONS (medical laboratory technology, music therapy, and occupational therapy), SOCIAL SCIENCE (economics, French studies, German area studies, history, international relations, philosophy, political science/government, psychology, religion, religious music, social work, and sociology). Biology, music, and mathematics are the strongest academically. Business, biology, and communication arts are the largest.

Special: Special academic programs at Wartburg include those in leadership education and global and multicultural studies. Internships are available in all majors and there are internship programs in Denver, Washington, D.C., and abroad. Study abroad in 63 countries, on and off campus work-study, dual majors in any combination, and individualized majors are possible. 3-1 degrees are possible in medical technology and occupational therapy, as well as 3-1 and 2-2 degrees in nursing. A deferred admit program with the University of Iowa College of Dentistry is offered, as is an array of experiential learning opportunities. There are 12 national honor societies and a freshman honors program.

Admissions: 84% of a recent year's applicants were accepted. The SAT scores for a recent freshman class were: Critical Reading--21% below 500, 26% between 500 and 599, 47% between 600 and 700, and 5% above 700; Math--16% below 500, 53% between 500 and 599, 16% between 600 and 700, and 16% above 700; Writing--16% below 500, 32% between 500 and 599, 47% between 600 and 700, and 5% above 700. The ACT scores were 22% below 21, 27% between 21 and 23, 27% between 24 and 26, 13% between 27 and 28, and 11% above 28. 53% of recent freshmen were in the top fifth of their class; 76% were in the top two fifths. There was 1 National Merit finalist. 32 freshmen graduated first in their class.

Requirements: The SAT or ACT is required, and satisfactory scores are expected. Candidates for admission must be graduates of an accredited secondary school, having completed 4 years of English, 3 each of math and science, 2 each of social studies and foreign language, and 1 of introduction to computers. The GED is accepted, with an average of 50 or above. Wartburg requires applicants to be in the upper 50% of their class. A GPA of 2.2 is required. AP and CLEP credits are accepted. Important factors in the admissions decision are advanced placement or honors courses, recommendations by school officials, and leadership record.

Procedure: Freshmen are admitted fall and winter. Entrance exams should be taken before the senior year. There are early admissions and rolling admissions plans. Check with the school for current deadlines. Notification is sent on a rolling basis. Applications are accepted on-line.

Financial Aid: In a recent year, 99% of all full-time freshmen and 100% of continuing full-time students received some form of financial aid. 74% of all full-time freshmen and 66% of continuing full-time students received need-based aid. The average freshman award was $21,635. Need-based scholarships or need-based grants averaged $8,595 ($25,100 maximum); need-based self-help aid (loans and jobs) averaged $5,717 ($9,260 maximum); and non-need-based awards and non-need-based scholarships averaged $12,469 ($35,395 maximum). 63% of undergraduate students work part-time. Average annual earnings from campus work are $1135. The average financial indebtedness of a recent graduate was $15,813. The FAFSA is required. Check with the school for current deadlines.

Computers: Wireless access is available. Students access the Internet and the college network either by connecting (Ethernet cable or wireless card) with their own computer or by using a college-owned computer in one of the classrooms or one of the 200 college-owned computers in 10 computer labs on campus. Network jacks exist in every residence hall room, classroom, and gathering area. All students may access the system. There are no time limits and no fees.

Washington, PA 15301 (724) 223-6025
(888) 926-3529; (724) 223-6534

Full-time: 785 men, 711 women	**Faculty:** 116; IIB, av$
Part-time: 8 men, 10 women	**Ph.D.s:** 91%
Graduate: none	**Student/Faculty:** 12 to 1
Year: 4-1-4, summer session	**Tuition:** $32895
Application Deadline: March 1	**Room & Board:** $8925
Freshman Class: 6658 applied, 2777 accepted, 393 enrolled	
SAT CR/M: 550/570	**ACT:** 25 **VERY COMPETITIVE**

Washington & Jefferson College, founded in 1781, is a private liberal arts college. There are no undergraduate schools. The 3 libraries contain 123,517 volumes, 15,400 microform items, and 10,294 audio/video tapes/CDs/DVDs, and subscribe to 404 periodicals including electronic. Computerized library services include interlibrary loans, database searching, Internet access, and laptop Internet portals. Special learning facilities include a learning resource center, art gallery, radio station, and a biological field station. The 60-acre campus is in a small town 27 miles southwest of Pittsburgh, PA. Including any residence halls, there are 53 buildings.

Programs of Study: W & J confers B.A. degrees. Bachelor's degrees are awarded in AGRICULTURE (environmental studies), BIOLOGICAL SCIENCE (biochemistry, biology/biological science, biophysics, and cell biology), BUSINESS (accounting, business administration and management, and international business management), COMMUNICATIONS AND THE ARTS (art, dramatic arts, English, French, German, music, and Spanish), COMPUTER AND PHYSICAL SCIENCE (chemistry, information sciences and systems, mathematics, and physics), EDUCATION (art education and education), SOCIAL SCIENCE (economics, history, international studies, philosophy, political science/government, psychology, religion, and sociology). Biology, chemistry, and political science. are the strongest academically. Business/accounting, English, and political science are the largest.

Special: The college offers study abroad in 22 countries, internships in all majors, a Washington semester with American University, Hood Coastal Studies, dual and student-designed majors, credit by exam, and pass/fail options. There is a 3-2 engineering program with Case Western Reserve University, Washington University, and Columbia University. The college offers emphasis in data discovery, human resources management information systems, new media technologies, and neuroscience. Concentrations are offered in entrepreneurial and special programs are offered in education, engineering, pre-health professions, mind, brain, and behavior, pre-law, pre-physical therapy, pre-occupational therapy, and physician assistant programs. There is also a 3-4 podiatry program with the Pennsylvania and Ohio Colleges law program with Duquesne University School of Law and University of Pittsburgh School of Law. Students can take electives in Chineses, Arabic, earth and science, Japanese, physical education, Russian, and science. There are 21 national honor societies, including Phi Beta Kappa, and 17 departmental honors programs.

Admissions: 42% of the 2009-2010 applicants were accepted. The SAT scores for the 2009-2010 freshman class were: Critical Reading--20% below 500, 49% between 500 and 599, 25% between 600 and 700, and 6% above 700; Math--13% below 500, 48% between 500 and 599, 35% between 600 and 700, and 4% above 700. The ACT scores were 12% below 21, 26% between 21 and 23, 29% between

24 and 26, 16% between 27 and 28, and 18% above 28. 61% of the current freshmen were in the top fifth of their class; 90% were in the top two fifths. 17 freshmen graduated first in their class.

Requirements: In addition, a GED is accepted. Applicants must complete 15 academic credits or Carnegie units, including 3 credits of English and math, 2 of foreign language, and 1 of science. An essay is required and interviews are recommended. AP credits are accepted. Important factors in the admissions decision are advanced placement or honors courses, evidence of special talent, and personality/intangible qualities.

Procedure: Freshmen are admitted to all sessions. Entrance exams should be taken in the junior or senior year. There are early decision, early admissions, deferred admissions, and rolling admissions plans. Early decision applications should be filed by December 1; regular applications, by March 1 for fall entry, December 15 for winter entry, January 15 for spring entry, and April 30 for summer entry, along with a $25 fee. Notification of early decision is sent December 15; regular decision, April 1. Applications are accepted on-line. 52 applicants were on a recent waiting list.

Financial Aid: In 2009-2010, 100% of all full-time freshmen and 98% of continuing full-time students received some form of financial aid. 71% of all full-time freshmen and 70% of continuing full-time students received need-based aid. The average freshmen award was $24,773. 46% of undergraduate students work part-time. Average annual earnings from campus work are $1100. The average financial indebtedness of the 2009 graduate was $23,000. The FAFSA is required. The priority date for freshman financial aid applications for fall entry is February 1.

Computers: Wireless access is available. W & J supports wireless computing in and around many academic buildings and dormitories, including the library, the student center and dining halls, as well as most outdoor locations. Wired connections are available in all dormitories, all classrooms, and in public access areas such as study lounges, the library, dining areas, and meeting rooms. Open computing labs are available in several classroom buildings and the library. Some labs are open 24 hours a day for student use during the academic year. Through any point of connection on the college's network, students can access all services including Internet and the Web, email, home drives, Blackboard, and on-line financial and academic services via W & J Advisor. All students may access the system. any time. There are no time limits and no fees. It is strongly recommended that all students have a personal computer.

WASHINGTON AND LEE UNIVERSITY
Lexington, VA 24450-0303 (540) 458-8710; (540) 458-8062

Full-time: 876 men, 881 women	**Faculty:** 187; IIB, +$
Part-time: 1 woman	**Ph.D.s:** 96%
Graduate: 226 men, 168 women	**Student/Faculty:** 9 to 1
Year: see profile, 4-4-1	**Tuition:** $38,877
Application Deadline: January 15	**Room & Board:** $8410
Freshman Class: 6222 applied, 1181 accepted, 472 enrolled	
SAT CR/M/W: 690/690/690	**ACT:** 31 **MOST COMPETITIVE**

Washington and Lee University, established in 1749, is a private institution offering undergraduate liberal arts and sciences and preprofessional programs. There are 2 undergraduate schools and 1 graduate school. In addition to regional accreditation, Washington and Lee has baccalaureate program accreditation with AACSB, ACEJMC, and ACS. The 3 libraries contain 717,288 volumes, 17,839 microform items, and 14,277 audio/video tapes/CDs/DVDs, and subscribe to 6,113 periodicals including electronic. Computerized library services include interlibrary loans, database searching, Internet access, and laptop Internet portals. Special learning facilities include an art gallery, radio station, TV station, a performing arts center, a multimedia center, history, fine arts, and archeological museums, and special collections. The 322-acre campus is in a small town 50 miles northeast of Roanoke. Including any residence halls, there are 100 buildings.

Programs of Study: Washington and Lee confers B.A. and B.S. degrees. Master's and doctoral degrees are also awarded. Bachelor's degrees are awarded in BIOLOGICAL SCIENCE (biochemistry, biology/biological science, and neurosciences), BUSINESS (accounting and business administration and management), COMMUNICATIONS AND THE ARTS (art history and appreciation, classics, dramatic arts, English, French, German, Germanic languages and literature, journalism, music, romance languages and literature, Russian languages and literature, Spanish, and studio art), COMPUTER AND PHYSICAL SCIENCE (chemistry, computer science, geology, mathematics, natural sciences, and physics), ENGINEERING AND ENVIRONMENTAL DESIGN (chemical engineering, engineering physics, and environmental science), SOCIAL SCIENCE (anthropology, archeology, East Asian studies, economics, history, interdisciplinary studies, medieval studies, philosophy, political science/government, psychology, public affairs, religion, and sociology). Business administration, economics, English, and politics are the largest.

Special: There is cross-registration with area colleges, including VMI, and colleges in Georgia and Maine, and various internships are available. Study-abroad programs are offered in several countries. There is a 3-3 law program and a 3-2 engineering degree with Rensselaer Polytechnic Institute and Washington and Columbia Universities. Washington and Lee also offers B.A.-B.S. degrees, a Washington semester, and dual, interdisciplinary, and student-designed majors. There are 19 national honor societies, including Phi Beta Kappa, and 31 departmental honors programs.

Admissions: 19% of the 2009-2010 applicants were accepted. The SAT scores for the 2009-2010 freshman class were: Critical Reading--4% between 500 and 599, 48% between 600 and 700, and 48% above 700; Math--3% between 500 and 599, 48% between 600 and 700, and 49% above 700; Writing--4% between 500 and 599, 51% between 600 and 700, and 45% above 700. The ACT scores were 5% between 24 and 26, 12% between 27 and 28, and 83% above 28. 44% of the current freshmen were in the top fifth of their class; 99% were in the top two fifths. There were 23 National Merit finalists. 52 freshmen graduated first in their class.

Requirements: The SAT or ACT is required. In addition, 2 unrelated SAT Subject Tests are required. A high school diploma is not required. Applicants must earn 16 units, including 4 units in English, 3 in math, 2 in a foreign language, and 1 each in history and natural science. Course work in social sciences is also required. Essays, test scores, a transcript, and recommendation letters are needed to apply. An interview is recommended. AP credits are accepted. Important factors in the admissions decision are advanced placement or honors courses, leadership record, and recommendations by school officials.

Procedure: Freshmen are admitted fall. Entrance exams should be taken between March of the junior year and January of the senior year. There are early decision and deferred admissions plans. Early decision applications should be filed by November 15; regular applications, by January 15 for fall entry. The fall 2009 application fee was $50. Notification of early decision is sent December 22; regular decision, April 1. Applications are accepted on-line. 1870 applicants were on a recent waiting list, 97 were accepted.

Financial Aid: In 2008-2009, 36% of all full-time freshmen and 31% of continuing full-time students received some form of financial aid. 34% of all full-time freshmen and 32% of continuing full-time students received need-based aid. The average freshman award was $33,561. Need-based scholarships or need-based grants averaged $27,989; need-based self-help aid (loans and jobs) averaged $3814; and other non-need-based awards and non-need-based scholarships averaged $32,562. The average financial indebtedness of the 2009 graduate was $23,616. Washington and Lee is a member of CSS. The CSS/Profile or FAFSA, the noncustodial parent's statement, and the business/farm supplement are required. The deadline for filing freshman financial aid applications for fall entry is February 1.

Computers: Wireless access is available. All students have Internet access and e-mail accounts. Computer and network access are available in computer labs, residence halls, libraries, and the student center. There are 320 PCs and more than 1500 network connections available. It is recommended that students have a personal laptop. All students may access the system 24 hours a day, 7 days a week while classes are in session. There are no time limits. The fee is $250.

WASHINGTON COLLEGE
Chestertown, MD 21620-1197

(410) 778-7700
(800) 422-1782; (410) 778-7287

Full-time: 527 men, 758 women	**Faculty:** 98; IIB, +$
Part-time: 10 men, 19 women	**Ph.Ds:** 95%
Graduate: 23 men, 35 women	**Student/Faculty:** 13 to 1
Year: semesters	**Tuition:** $35,350
Application Deadline: March 1	**Room & Board:** $7460
Freshman Class: 4498 applied, 3240 accepted, 378 enrolled	
SAT CR/M: 560/570	**ACT:** required

VERY COMPETITIVE

Washington College, founded in 1782, is an independent college offering programs in the liberal arts and sciences, business management, and teacher preparation. There is 1 graduate school. The library contains 219,461 volumes, 100,635 microform items, and 8,701 audio/video tapes/CDs/DVDs, and subscribes to 28,222 periodicals including electronic. Computerized library services include interlibrary loans, database searching, Internet access, and laptop Internet portals. Special learning facilities include a learning resource center, art gallery, the Center for the American Experience, the Center for Environment and Society, and the Rose O'Neill Literary House. The 112-acre campus is in a small town 75 miles from Baltimore. Including any residence halls, there are 71 buildings.

Programs of Study: WC confers B.A. and B.S. degrees. Master's degrees are also awarded. Bachelor's degrees are awarded in BIOLOGICAL SCIENCE (biology/biological science), BUSINESS (business administration and management), COMMUNICATIONS AND THE ARTS (art, dramatic arts, English, fine arts, French, German, music, and Spanish), COMPUTER AND PHYSICAL SCIENCE (chemistry, computer science, mathematics, and physics), ENGINEERING AND ENVIRONMENTAL DESIGN (environmental science), SOCIAL SCIENCE (American studies, anthropology, economics, history, humanities, international studies, philosophy, political science/government, psychology, and sociology). English, psychology, and business management are the strongest academically.

Special: Internships are available in all majors. There is study abroad in 26 countries and a Washington semester. The college offers a 3-2 engineering degree with the University of Maryland at College Park as well as a 3-2 nursing program with Johns Hopkins University and student-designed majors. There are 7 national honor societies, including Phi Beta Kappa.

Admissions: 72% of the 2009-2010 applicants were accepted. The SAT scores for the 2009-2010 freshman class were: Critical Reading--12% below 500, 53% between 500 and 599, 28% between 600 and 700, and 7% above 700; Math--14% below 500, 52% between 500 and 599, 30% between 600 and 700, and 4% above 700. The ACT scores were 9% below 21, 30% between 21 and 23, 32% between 24 and 26, 18% between 27 and 28, and 11% above 28. 65% of the current freshmen were in the top fifth of their class; 81% were in the top two fifths. There were 3 National Merit finalists.

Requirements: The SAT or ACT is required. In addition, applicants must be graduates of an accredited secondary school or have a GED. 16 Carnegie units are required. Applicants should take high school courses in English, foreign language, history, math, science, and social studies. An essay is required, and an interview is recommended. A GPA of 2.5 is required. AP credits are accepted. Important factors in the admissions decision are advanced placement or honors courses, recommendations by school officials, and leadership record.

Procedure: Freshmen are admitted fall and spring. Entrance exams should be taken in the spring of the junior year or fall of the senior year. There are early decision, deferred admissions and rolling admissions plans. Early decision applications should be filed by November 1; regular applications, by March 1 for fall entry and December 1 for spring entry, along with a $55 fee. Notification is sent on a rolling basis. 45 early decision candidates were accepted for the 2009-2010 class. 400 applicants were on the 2009 waiting list; 100 were admitted. Applications are accepted on-line.

Financial Aid: In 2009-2010, 88% of all full-time freshmen and 82% of continuing full-time students received some form of financial aid. The average freshman award was $25,412. The average financial indebtedness of the 2009 graduate was $28,727. 40% of undergraduate students work part-time. Average annual earnings from campus work are $1000. WC is a member of CSS. The FAFSA, the college's own financial statement, and signed copies of the student's and parents' federal tax returns and W2s are required. The deadline for filing freshman financial aid applications for fall entry is February 15.

Computers: Wireless access is available. Students may use the college's network and/or wireless system for personal and academic use. There is a portal log-in for wireless use. All students may access the system. There are no time limits and no fees. It is strongly recommended that all students have a personal computer.

WASHINGTON UNIVERSITY IN SAINT LOUIS

St. Louis, MO 63130-4899

(314) 935-6000
(800) 638-0700; (314) 935-4290

Full-time: 3111 men, 3024 women	**Faculty:** 804; I, +$
Part-time: 330 men, 581 women	**Ph.D.s:** 98%
Graduate: 3254 men, 3275 women	**Student/Faculty:** 8 to 1
Year: semesters, summer session	**Tuition:** $37,800
Application Deadline: January 15	**Room & Board:** $12,465
Freshman Class: 23105 applied, 5128 accepted, 1510 enrolled	
SAT or ACT: required	**MOST COMPETITIVE**

Washington University, founded in 1853, is a private institution offering undergraduate and graduate programs in arts and sciences, business, architecture, engineering, art, and professional programs in law, medicine (including physical therapy and occupational therapy), and social work. There are 5 undergraduate schools and 8 graduate schools. In addition to regional accreditation, Washington U. has baccalaureate program accreditation with AACSB, ABET, and NASAD. The 14 libraries contain 4.3 million volumes, 3.5 million microform items, and 61,736 audio/video tapes/CDs/DVDs, and subscribe to 71,905 periodicals including electronic. Computerized library services include interlibrary loans, database searching, Internet access, and laptop Internet portals. Special learning facilities include a learning resource center, art gallery, planetarium, radio station, TV station, dance studio, professional theater, observatory, and studio theater. The 169-acre campus is in a suburban area 7 miles west of St. Louis, MS. Including any residence halls, there are 111 buildings.

Programs of Study: Washington U. confers B.A., B.S., B.F.A., B.M., B.S.B.A, B.S.B.M.E., B.S.C.E., B.S.Ch.E., B.S.C.S., B.S.Co.E., B.S.E.E., B.S.I.M., B.S.M.E., and B.S.S.S.E., degrees. Master's and doctoral degrees are also awarded. Bachelor's degrees are awarded in AGRICULTURE (environmental studies and plant science), BIOLOGICAL SCIENCE (biochemistry, bioinformatics, biology/biological science, biomathematics, biophysics, ecology, and neurosciences), BUSINESS (accounting, banking and finance, business administration and management, business economics, entrepreneurial studies, human resources, international business management, international economics, marketing management, marketing/retailing/merchandising, and trade and industrial supervision and management), COMMUNICATIONS AND THE ARTS (advertising, American literature, Arabic, art history and appreciation, ceramic art and design, Chinese, classical languages, classics, communications, comparative literature, creative writing, dance, design, dramatic arts, drawing, East Asian languages and literature, English, English literature, film arts, fine arts, French, German, Germanic languages and literature, graphic design, Greek (classical), Hebrew, illustration, Italian, Japanese, journalism, languages, Latin, linguistics, literature, music, music theory and composition, painting, performing arts, photography, printmaking, romance languages and literature, sculpture, Spanish, studio art, and visual and performing arts), COMPUTER AND PHYSICAL SCIENCE (applied mathematics, chemistry, computer programming, computer science, earth science, geology, information sciences and systems, mathematics, physical sciences, physics, and statistics), EDUCATION (art education, education, elementary education, foreign languages education, mathematics education, middle school education, science education, secondary education, social science education, and social studies education), ENGINEERING AND ENVIRONMENTAL DESIGN (architectural technology, architecture, bioengineering, biomedical engineering, chemical engineering, civil engineering, commercial art, computer engineering, electrical/electronics engineering, engineering, engineering mechanics, environmental science, mechanical engineering, systems engineering, and technology and public affairs), HEALTH PROFESSIONS (pharmacy, predentistry, premedicine, prepharmacy, and preveterinary science), SOCIAL SCIENCE (African studies, African American studies, American studies, anthropology, archeology, area studies, Asian/Oriental studies, biopsychology, East Asian studies, Eastern European studies, economics, ethnic studies, European studies, fashion design and technology, history, humanities, industrial and organizational psychology, interdisciplinary studies, international relations, international studies, Islamic studies, Judaic studies, Latin American studies, Middle Eastern studies, Near Eastern studies, philosophy, political science/government, psychology, religion, social science, South Asian studies, systems science, urban studies, Western European studies, and women's studies). Natural sciences and engineering is the strongest academically. Natural sciences, engineering, and business are the largest.

Special: Opportunities are provided for cooperative programs with other schools, internships, work-study programs, study abroad, a Washington (D.C.) semester, accelerated degree programs, a B.A.-B.S. engineering degree, credit by examination, nondegree study, pass/fail options, and dual and student-designed majors. There are 18 national honor societies, including Phi Beta Kappa.

Admissions: 22% of the 2009-2010 applicants were accepted. The SAT scores for the 2009-2010 freshman class were: Critical Reading--% below 500, 2% between 500 and 599, 32% between 600 and 700, and 66% above 700; Math--% below 500, % between 500 and 599, 18% between 600 and 700, and 82% above 700. The ACT scores were % below 21, % between 21 and 23, 1% between 24 and 26, 2% between 27 and 28, and 97% above 28.

Requirements: The SAT or ACT is required. In addition, an essay is required from all applicants. Fine arts students may submit portfolios. 4 years of English, math, science, and social science/history, and 2 of a foreign language are recommended. Also required are recommendations from a teacher and a counselor. SAT or ACT is requiresd. AP credits are accepted.

Procedure: Freshmen are admitted fall. Entrance exams should be taken by December of the senior year. There are early decision and deferred admissions plans. Early decision applications should be filed by November 15; regular applications, by January 15 for fall entry, along with a $55 fee. Notification of early decision is sent December 15; regular decision, April 1. Applications are accepted on-line. A waiting list is maintained.

Financial Aid: In 2009-2010, 55% of all full-time freshmen and 57% of continuing full-time students received some form of financial aid. 36% of all full-time freshmen and 42% of continuing full-time students received need-based aid. 50% of undergraduate students work part-time. Average annual earnings from campus work are $2000. Washington U. is a member of CSS. The CSS/Profile and FAFSA, and noncustodial parent's statement; student and parent 1040 tax return, or signed wavier if there is no tax return. are required. The deadline for filing freshman financial aid applications for fall entry is February 15.

Computers: Wireless access is available. Specialized computing resources are available to students. The Center for Engineering Computing provides access to about 100 computing stations accessible from the campus-wide network. The Olin Business School provides student labs and group rooms with more than 90 PCs. In addition, the residential network has 14 labs and 105 computers available throughout the residence halls, and printing is available in any of the labs 24x7. All rooms in the residence halls have Internet connections, and students now have wired and wireless access in the residential areas. The Olin Library provides wireless access to the Internet, e-mail, and a variety of other specialized software. All students may access the system. 24 hours per day, 7 days per week. There are no time limits and no fees.

WEBB INSTITUTE

Glen Cove, NY 11542	**(516) 671-2213; (516) 674-9838**
Full-time: 65 men, 20 women	**Faculty:** n/av
Part-time: none	**Ph.D.s:** 50%
Graduate: none	**Student/Faculty:** n/av
Year: semesters	**Tuition:** $8500
Application Deadline: see profile	**Room & Board:** n/app
Freshman Class: n/av	
SAT: required	**MOST COMPETITIVE**

Webb Institute, founded in 1889, is a private engineering school devoted to professional knowledge of ship construction, design, and motive power. All students receive 4-year, full-tuition scholarships. Figures in the above capsule are approximate. In addition to regional accreditation, Webb has baccalaureate program accreditation with ABET. The library contains 50,598 volumes, 1,633 microform items, and 1,851 audio/video tapes/CDs/DVDs, and subscribes to 267 periodicals including electronic. Computerized library services include interlibrary loans, database searching, and Internet access. The 26-acre campus is in a suburban area 24 miles east of New York City. Including any residence halls, there are 11 buildings.

Programs of Study: Webb confers B.S. degrees. Bachelor's degrees are awarded in ENGINEERING AND ENVIRONMENTAL DESIGN (naval architecture and marine engineering).

Special: All students are employed 2 months each year through co-op programs.

Requirements: The SAT is required, with a minimum satisfactory score. Applicants should be graduates of an accredited secondary school with 16 academic credits completed, including 4 each in English and math, 2 each in history and science, 1 in foreign language, and 3 in electives. 3 SAT Subject tests in writing, math level I or II, and physics or chemistry are required, as is an interview. Candidates must be U.S. citizens. Webb requires applicants to be in the upper 20% of their class. A GPA of 3.2 is required. Important factors in the admissions decision are advanced placement or honors courses, evidence of special talent, and personality/intangible qualities.

Procedure: Freshmen are admitted fall. Entrance exams should be taken by January of the senior year. There is an early decision admissions plan. Check with the school for current application deadlines. The application fee is $25.

Financial Aid: The CSS/Profile and the college's own financial statement are required. Check with the school for current application deadlines.

Computers: Wireless access is available. The school provides laptops for all students. All students may access the system 24 hours per day.

WELLESLEY COLLEGE

Wellesley, MA 02481   (781) 283-2270; (781) 283-3678

Full-time: 2185 women	**Faculty:** 259; IIB, ++$
Part-time: 83 women	**Ph.D.s:** 293%
Graduate: none	**Student/Faculty:** 8 to 1
Year: semesters	**Tuition:** $38,062
Application Deadline: January 15	**Room & Board:** $11,786
Freshman Class: 4156 applied, 1463 accepted, 589 enrolled	
SAT CR/M/W: 689/683/693	**ACT:** 30 **MOST COMPETITIVE**

Wellesley College, established in 1870, is a small, private, diverse liberal arts and sciences college for women. The 5 libraries contain 94,346 volumes, 536,499 microform items, and 36,439 audio/video tapes/CDs/DVDs, and subscribe to 1,945 periodicals including electronic. Computerized library services include interlibrary loans, database searching, and Internet access. Special learning facilities include a learning resource center, art gallery, radio station, a science center, a botanic greenhouse, an observatory, a center for developmental studies and services, centers for research on women and child study, and a media and technology center. The 500-acre campus is in a suburban area 12 miles west of Boston. Including any residence halls, there are 64 buildings.

Programs of Study: Wellesley confers B.A. degrees. Bachelor's degrees are awarded in AGRICULTURE (environmental studies), BIOLOGICAL SCIENCE (biochemistry, biology/biological science, and neurosciences), COMMUNICATIONS AND THE ARTS (art history and appreciation, Chinese, comparative literature, dramatic arts, English, film arts, French, German, Greek, Japanese, Latin, music, Russian, Russian languages and literature, Spanish, and studio art), COMPUTER AND PHYSICAL SCIENCE (astronomy, astrophysics, chemistry, computer science, geology, mathematics, and physics), ENGINEERING AND ENVIRONMENTAL DESIGN (architecture), SOCIAL SCIENCE (African American studies, American studies, anthropology, archeology, Asian/Oriental studies, classical/ancient civilization, cognitive science, economics, French studies, German area studies, history, international relations, Italian studies, Japanese studies, Judaic studies, Latin American studies, medieval studies, Middle Eastern studies, peace studies, philosophy, political science/government, psychology, religion, sociology, and women's studies). Psychology, English, and economics are the largest.

Special: Students may cross-register at MIT, Brandeis University, or Babson College. Exchange programs are available with Spelman College in Georgia and Mills College in California, with members of the Twelve College Exchange Program, with Williams College's maritime studies program, and with Connecticut College's National Theater Institute. Study abroad is possible through Wellesley-administered programs in France and Austria, exchange programs in Argentina, Japan, Korea, and the United Kingdom, and other programs in Italy, Japan, Spain, South Africa, and China. There are more than 150 approved study abroad programs available. There are summer internship programs in Boston and Washington, D.C. Dual majors, student-designed majors, nondegree study, and pass/fail options are possible. A 3-2 program with MIT, Dartmouth, and Columbia awards a B.A.-B.S. degree. There are 2 national honor societies, including Phi Beta Kappa, and 51 departmental honors programs.

Admissions: 35% of the 2009-2010 applicants were accepted. The SAT scores for the 2009-2010 freshman class were: Critical Reading-- 10% between 500 and 599, 38% between 600 and 700, and 52% above 700; Math-- 11% between 500 and 599, 45% between 600 and 700, and 43% above 700; Writing-- 8% between 500 and 599, 41% between 600 and 700, and 51% above 700. The ACT scores were 69% above 28. 96% of the current freshmen were in the top fifth of their class; All were in the top two fifths. 78 freshmen graduated first in their class.

Requirements: The SAT or ACT is required. The SAT Reasoning Test and 2 SAT subject tests, or the ACT with Writing are required. Wellesley College does not require a fixed plan of secondary school course preparation. Entering students normally have completed 4 years of college preparatory studies in secondary school that include training in clear and coherent writing and interpreting literature; history; principles of math (typically 4 years); competence in at least 1 foreign language, ancient or modern (usually 4 years of study); and experience in at least 2 lab sciences. An essay is required, and an interview is recommended. AP credits are accepted. Important factors in the admissions decision are advanced placement or honors courses, extracurricular activities record, and recommendations by school officials.

Procedure: Freshmen are admitted in the fall. Entrance exams should be taken during the spring of the junior year or fall of the senior year. December is the last month in which standaradized test should be taken. There are early decision and deferred admissions plans. Early decision applications should be filed by November 1; regular applications, by January 15 for fall entry. The fall 2008 application fee was $50. Notification of early decision is sent december 15; regular decision, April 1. Applications are accepted on-line and the application fee is waived. 543 applicants were on a recent waiting list, 30 were accepted.

Financial Aid: In 2009-2010, 56% of all full-time freshmen and 54% of continuing full-time students received some form of financial aid. 58% of all full-time freshmen and 58% of continuing full-time students received need-based aid. The average freshmen award was $36,064. Average annual earnings from campus work are $2000. The average financial indebtedness of the 2009 graduate was $13,324. Wellesley is a member of CSS. The CSS/Profile, FAFSA, and the college's own financial statement, and and the most recent income tax returns of parents and student. are required. The deadline for filing freshman financial aid applications for fall entry is January 15.

Computers: Wireless access is available. Computer terminals are available in the libraries. Wireless access is available in the libraries, academic buildings, and residence halls. All students may access the system. There are no time limits and no fees.

WELLS COLLEGE
Aurora, NY 13026

(315) 364-3264
(800) 952-9355; (315) 364-3227

Full-time: 125 men, 415 women	**Faculty:** 48; IIB, av$
Part-time: 5 men, 15 women	**Ph.D.s:** 100%
Graduate: none	**Student/Faculty:** 11 to 1
Year: semesters	**Tuition:** $29680
Application Deadline: see profile	**Room & Board:** $9000
Freshman Class: n/av	
SAT or ACT: required	**VERY COMPETITIVE**

Wells College is a private liberal arts instituion, founded in 1868. Historically a women's college, it became coeducational in 2005. Figures in the above capsule are approximate. The library contains 218,002 volumes, 14,882 microform items, and 1,154 audio/video tapes/CDs/DVDs, and subscribes to 371 periodicals including electronic. Computerized library services include interlibrary loans, database searching, Internet access, and laptop Internet portals. Special learning facilities include a learning resource center, art gallery, radio station, and the Book Arts Center. The 365-acre campus is in a small town on Cayuga Lake, 30 miles north of Ithaca. Including any residence halls, there are 22 buildings.

Programs of Study: Wells confers B.A. degrees. Bachelor's degrees are awarded in AGRICULTURE (environmental studies), BIOLOGICAL SCIENCE (biochemistry, biology/biological science, and molecular biology), BUSINESS (business administration and management), COMMUNICATIONS AND THE ARTS (dance, dramatic arts, English, fine arts, French, German, language arts, music, Spanish, and visual and performing arts), COMPUTER AND PHYSICAL SCIENCE (chemistry, computer science, mathematics, and physics), EDUCATION (elementary education), SOCIAL SCIENCE (American studies, anthropology, economics, ethics, politics, and social policy, history, international studies, philosophy, political science/government, psychology, public affairs, religion, sociology, and women's studies). Psychology, English, and biological and chemical sciences are the largest.

Special: Wells offers cross-registration with Cornell University, Cayuga Community College, and Ithaca College, a Washington semester with American University, internships, and accelerated degree programs in all majors. Study abroad in 13 countries is permitted. A 3-2 engineering degree is available with Columbia, Clarkson, and Cornell Universities. Students may also earn 3-2 degrees in business and community health with the University of Rochester and a 3-4 degree in veterinary medicine with Cornell University. Student-designed majors and pass-fail options are available. Work-study, B.A.-B.S. degrees, and dual majors are also available. There are 2 national honor societies, including Phi Beta Kappa.

Admissions: 3 freshmen graduated first in their class in a recent year.

Requirements: The SAT or ACT is required. In addition, graduation from an accredited secondary school should include 20 academic credits or Carnegie units. High school courses must include 4 years of English, 3 each of a foreign language and math, and 2 each of history and lab science. 2 teacher recommendations and an essay/personal statement are required, and an interview is strongly recommended. AP and CLEP credits are accepted. Important factors in the admissions decision are recommendations by school officials, extracurricular activities record, and advanced placement or honors courses.

Procedure: Freshmen are admitted fall. Entrance exams should be taken prior to application. There are early decision and deferred admissions plans. Check with the school for current application deadlines. The application fee is $40. Applications are accepted on-line.

Financial Aid: In a recent year, 91% of all full-time freshmen and 88% of continuing full-time students received some form of financial aid. 71% of all full-time freshmen and 76% of continuing full-time students received need-based aid. The average freshmen award was $18,505, with $13,645 ($21,320 maximum) from need-based scholarships or need-based grants; $4900 ($6600 maximum) from need-based self-help aid (loans and jobs); and $6850 ($10,500 maximum) from other non-need-based awards and non-need-based scholarships. 82% of undergraduate students work part-time. Average annual earnings from campus work are $1600. The average financial indebtedness of a recent graduate was $20,355. Wells is a member of CSS. The FAFSA is required. Early decision applicants must also submit the CSS Profile. Check with the school for current deadlines.

Computers: All residence hall rooms have Internet connectivity. All students may access the system. It is strongly recommended that all students have a personal computer.

WESLEYAN UNIVERSITY

Middletown, CT 06459-4890   (860) 685-3000; (860) 685-3001

Full-time: 1376 men, 1398 women	**Faculty:** 330; IIA, ++$
Part-time: 3 men, 10 women	**Ph.D.s:** 94%
Graduate: 178 men, 183 women	**Student/Faculty:** 9 to 1
Year: semesters	**Tuition:** $51,132
Application Deadline: January 1	**Room & Board:** $11,040
Freshman Class: 10068 applied, 2218 accepted, 745 enrolled	
SAT CR/M/W: 700/700/700	**ACT:** 32 **MOST COMPETITIVE**

Wesleyan University, founded in 1831, is a private institution offering programs in the liberal arts and sciences. There are no undergraduate schools and one graduate school. The 3 libraries contain 1.7 million volumes, 369,640 microform items, and 60,605 audio/video tapes/CDs/DVDs, and subscribe to 10,489 periodicals including electronic. Computerized library services include interlibrary loans, database searching, Internet access, and laptop Internet portals. Special learning facilities include a learning resource center, art gallery, radio station, and an observatory. The 340-acre campus is in a suburban area 15 miles south of Hartford, CN and 2 hours from both Boston and New York City. Including any residence halls, there are 316 buildings.

Programs of Study: Wesleyan confers B.A. degrees. Master's and doctoral degrees are also awarded. Bachelor's degrees are awarded in AGRICULTURE (environmental studies), BIOLOGICAL SCIENCE (biochemistry, biology/biological science, molecular biology, and neurosciences), COMMUNICATIONS AND THE ARTS (art history and appreciation, classics, dance, dramatic arts, English, film arts, Italian, music, romance languages and literature, Russian, Spanish, and studio art), COMPUTER AND PHYSICAL SCIENCE (astronomy, chemistry, computer science, earth science, mathematics, physics, and science technology), SOCIAL SCIENCE (African American studies, American studies, anthropology, archeology, classical/ancient civilization, East Asian studies, economics, French studies, gender studies, German area studies, history, Iberian studies, Latin American studies, medieval studies, philosophy, political science/government, psychology, religion, Russian and Slavic studies, and sociology). Sciences, economics, and history are the strongest academically. English, government, and psychology are the largest.

Special: Wesleyan offers exchange programs with 11 northeastern colleges, cross-registration with 2 area colleges, study abroad in 42 countries on 6 continents, internships, a Washington semester, dual and student-designed majors, and pass/fail options. 3-2 engineering programs with Cal Tech and Columbia University are also available. There are 2 national honor societies, including Phi Beta Kappa, and 40 departmental honors programs.

Admissions: 22% of the 2009-2010 applicants were accepted. The SAT scores for the 2009-2010 freshman class were: Critical Reading--1% below 500, 13% between 500 and 599, 34% between 600 and 700, and 52% above 700; Math--1% below 500, 10% between 500 and 599, 37% between 600 and 700, and 52% above 700; Writing--1% below 500, 10% between 500 and 599, 36% between 600 and 700, and 53% above 700. The ACT scores were % below 21, 2% between 21 and 23, 7% between 24 and 26, 13% between 27 and 28, and 78% above 28. 86% of the current freshmen were in the top fifth of their class.

Requirements: The SAT or ACT is required. In addition, applicants must submit the common application, transcript, recommendations, and either the ACT or SAT and 2 subject tests. Students should have a minimum of 20 academic credits, including 4 years each of English, foreign language, math, science, and social studies. AP credits are accepted. Important factors in the admissions decision are advanced placement or honors courses, recommendations by school officials, and leadership record.

Procedure: Freshmen are admitted fall. Entrance exams should be taken in the spring of the junior year or the fall of the senior year. There are early decision and deferred admissions plans. Early decision applications should be filed by November 15; regular decision, January 1 for fall entry, along with a $55 fee. Notification of early decision is sent December 15; regular decision, April 1. Applications are accepted on-line. 600 applicants were on a recent waiting list, 40 were accepted.

Financial Aid: In 2009-2010, 47% of all full-time freshmen and 46% of continuing full-time students received some form of financial aid. 47% of all full-time freshmen and 46% of continuing full-time students received need-based aid. The average freshmen award was $38,050. 75% of undergraduate students work part-time. Average annual earnings from campus work are $1431. The average financial indebtedness of the 2009 graduate was $19,769. Wesleyan is a member of CSS. The CSS/Profile and FAFSA are required. The deadline for filing freshman financial aid applications for fall entry is February 1.

Computers: Wireless access is available. Dorms and residence halls are connected to the campus network backbone. Students living in wood frame houses around campus are connected to the Internet through Comcast Cable modem. The campus has 290 wireless access points and provides close to 100% wireless coverage on campus. Each of the wood frame houses also has a wireless router. The campus network is connected to the Internet through the Connecticut Education Network. All students may access the system. There are no time limits and no fees. It is strongly recommended that all students have a personal computer.

WESTERN WASHINGTON UNIVERSITY

Bellingham, WA 98225-5996   (360) 650-3440; (360) 650-7369

Full-time: 5461 men, 6817 women	**Faculty:** 498; IIA, -$
Part-time: 479 men, 492 women	**Ph.D.s:** 86%
Graduate: 440 men, 739 women	**Student/Faculty:** 19 to 1
Year: quarters, summer session	**Tuition:** $6159 ($17,190)
Application Deadline: March 1	**Room & Board:** $8393
Freshman Class: 9620 applied, 6990 accepted, 2688 enrolled	
SAT CR/M/W: 560/560/540	**ACT:** 24 **VERY COMPETITIVE**

Western Washington University, founded in 1893, is a nonprofit, public institution whose emphasis is on the liberal arts and sciences, business and business administration, and economics, art, fine arts, and performing arts, music, teacher preparation, interdisciplinary learning, and environmental studies. There are 7 undergraduate schools and one graduate school. In addition to regional accreditation, WWU has baccalaureate program accreditation with AACSB, ABET, ASLA, NASM, NCATE, and NRPA. The 2 libraries contain 1.4 million volumes, 2.0 million microform items, and 48,672 audio/video tapes/CDs/DVDs, and subscribe to 11,500 periodicals including electronic. Computerized library services include interlibrary loans, database searching, Internet access, and laptop Internet portals. Special learning facilities include a learning resource center, art gallery, planetarium, radio station, marine lab, neutron generator lab, motor vehicle research lab, wind tunnel, air pollution lab, electronic music studio, and performing arts center. The 195-acre campus is in a small town 60 miles south of Vancouver,

British Columbia and 90 miles north of Seattle. Including any residence halls, there are 80 buildings.

Programs of Study: WWU confers B.A., B.S., B.A.E., B.F.A., and B.Mus. degrees. Master's degrees are also awarded. Bachelor's degrees are awarded in AGRICULTURE (environmental studies), BIOLOGICAL SCIENCE (biochemistry, biology/biological science, cell biology, ecology, life science, marine biology, marine science, and molecular biology), BUSINESS (accounting, business administration and management, fashion merchandising, human resources, international business management, international economics, management information systems, management science, marketing/retailing/merchandising, and operations management), COMMUNICATIONS AND THE ARTS (apparel design, art, ceramic art and design, classics, communications, creative writing, dance, design, dramatic arts, English, fine arts, French, German, Japanese, journalism, linguistics, multimedia, music, music history and appreciation, painting, photography, Russian, sculpture, Spanish, theater design, and visual and performing arts), COMPUTER AND PHYSICAL SCIENCE (applied mathematics, applied physics, chemistry, computer science, earth science, geology, mathematics, physics, and polymer science), EDUCATION (art education, early childhood education, education administration, elementary education, foreign languages education, health education, music education, physical education, reading education, recreation education, science education, secondary education, special education, and technical education), ENGINEERING AND ENVIRONMENTAL DESIGN (electrical/electronics engineering, electrical/electronics engineering technology, engineering technology, environmental science, industrial engineering technology, manufacturing technology, mechanical design technology, mechanical engineering technology, plastics engineering, and technology and public affairs), HEALTH PROFESSIONS (nursing, rehabilitation therapy, and speech pathology/audiology), SOCIAL SCIENCE (American studies, anthropology, behavioral science, Canadian studies, child psychology/development, East Asian studies, economics, geography, history, human services, interdisciplinary studies, parks and recreation management, philosophy, political science/government, psychology, public affairs, social studies, and sociology). Computer science, business, and technology are the strongest academically. Psychology, environmental studies, and education are the largest.

Special: Special academic programs include internships through various academic departments and study abroad in 75 countries. Dual majors are available through various departments. There is a general studies degree, and a B.A. in humanities. A 3-2 engineering degree is possible with the University of Washington. Student-designed majors are offered through the liberal studies department in the College of Arts and Sciences and through Fairhaven College, which affords an unusual degree of student involvement in the structure and content of their own programs and which uses faculty narrative for students' academic evaluations. In addition, Huxley College of Environmental Studies provides specialized education and research. Up to 30 credits of electives may be granted for military service, and nondegree study and pass/fail options are possible. There are 12 national honor societies, a freshman honors program, and 10 departmental honors programs.

Admissions: 73% of the 2009-2010 applicants were accepted. The SAT scores for the 2009-2010 freshman class were: Critical Reading--22% below 500, 43% between 500 and 599, 29% between 600 and 700, and 6% above 700; Math--20% below 500, 47% between 500 and 599, 30% between 600 and 700, and 3% above 700. 82% of the current freshmen were in the top fifth of their class; 92% were in the top two fifths.

Requirements: The SAT or ACT is required. In addition, Other admissions requirements include completion of 16 academic units, comprised of 4 years of college preparatory English composition and literature courses; 3 units of college preparatory math, including 2 years of algebra; 3 units of social studies/history; 2 units of science, including 1 unit of a chemistry or physics with an algebra prerequisite; 2 units of the same foreign language; 1 unit of fine and performing arts; and 1 semester in another academic field. Freshman applicants meeting minimum GPA and subject requirements are ranked by an index combining the GPA and a standardized test score. The GED is also accepted. Other factors taken into consideration include curricular rigor (level of difficulty of courses), grade trends, leadership, community involvement, special talent, multicultural experience, and personal hardship or circumstances. A GPA of 2.5 is required. AP credits are accepted. Important factors in the admissions decision are advanced placement or honors courses, leadership record, and personality/intangible qualities.

Procedure: Freshmen are admitted to all sessions. Entrance exams should be taken by fall of the senior year. Applications should be filed by March 1 for fall entry, October 15 for winter entry, January 15 for spring entry, and March 1 for summer entry. The fall 2009 application fee was $50. Notifications are sent March 15. Applications are accepted on-line. 774 applicants were on a recent waiting list, 354 were accepted.

Financial Aid: In 2009-2010, 41% of all full-time freshmen and 41% of continuing full-time students received some form of financial aid. 34% of all full-time freshmen and 31% of continuing full-time students received need-based aid. 10% of undergraduate students work part-time. Average annual earnings from campus work are $2540. The average financial indebtedness of the 2009 graduate was $15,929. The FAFSA is required. The priority date for freshman financial aid applications for fall entry is February 15. The deadline for filing freshman financial aid applications for fall entry is February 15.

Computers: Wireless access is available. There are 148 units in the library, 320 in classrooms, 1940 in computer labs and 390 elsewhere in the university. Wireless access is prevalent throughout the campus. All students may access the system. There are no time limits and no fees.

WESTMINSTER COLLEGE
Fulton, MO 65251

(573) 592-5251
(800) 475-3361; (573) 592-5255

Full-time: 597 men, 479 women	**Faculty:** 61; IIB, --$
Part-time: 3 men, 8 women	**Ph.D.s:** 78%
Graduate: none	**Student/Faculty:** 18 to 1
Year: semesters, summer session	**Tuition:** $18,700
Application Deadline: open	**Room & Board:** $7120
Freshman Class: 1356 applied, 1057 accepted, 311 enrolled	
SAT CR/M/W: 530/540/520	**ACT:** 25 **VERY COMPETITIVE**

Westminster College, founded in 1851, is a private liberal arts and sciences college affiliated with the Presbyterian Church (U.S.A.). The 2 libraries contain 98,840 volumes, 6,984 microform items, and 9,494 audio/video tapes/CDs/DVDs, and subscribe to 24,081 periodicals including electronic. Computerized library services include interlibrary loans, database searching, Internet access, and laptop Internet portals. Special learning facilities include a learning resource center, a cadaver lab, a photospectrometer lab, a multimedia language and learning lab, a multimedia classroom, and Winston Churchill Memorial Museum. The 87-

acre campus is in a small town 20 miles east of Columbia. Including any residence halls, there are 26 buildings.

Programs of Study: Westminster confers B.A. degrees. Bachelor's degrees are awarded in BIOLOGICAL SCIENCE (biochemistry and biology/biological science), BUSINESS (accounting, business administration and management, international business management, and management information systems), COMMUNICATIONS AND THE ARTS (English, French, and Spanish), COMPUTER AND PHYSICAL SCIENCE (chemistry, computer science, mathematics, and physics), EDUCATION (elementary education, middle school education, physical education, and secondary education), ENGINEERING AND ENVIRONMENTAL DESIGN (environmental science), SOCIAL SCIENCE (anthropology, economics, history, international studies, philosophy, political science/government, psychology, religion, and sociology). English, biology, and psychology are the strongest academically. Business administration, biology, and psychology are the largest.

Special: Westminster offers co-op programs with colleges of the Mid-Missouri Associated Colleges and Universities, cross-registration with William Woods University, internships in all areas, study abroad in 15 countries, a Washington semester, a United Nations semester, and an urban studies program in Chicago. Student-designed majors are available as well as a 3-2 engineering degree with Washington University in St. Louis. The pass/fail option and dual majors are available. There are 15 national honor societies, a freshman honors program, and 8 departmental honors programs.

Admissions: 78% of the 2009-2010 applicants were accepted. The SAT scores for the 2009-2010 freshman class were: Critical Reading--44% below 500, 26% between 500 and 599, 22% between 600 and 700, and 8% above 700; Math--36% below 500, 34% between 500 and 599, 24% between 600 and 700, and 6% above 700; Writing--48% below 500, 34% between 500 and 599, and 18% between 600 and 700. The ACT scores were 7% below 21, 27% between 21 and 23, 27% between 24 and 26, 27% between 27 and 28, and 12% above 28. 40% of the current freshmen were in the top fifth of their class; 71% were in the top two fifths. There were 2 National Merit finalists. 5 freshmen graduated first in their class.

Requirements: The ACT is required, the SAT is recommended. In addition, applicants must be graduates of an accredited secondary school. The GED is also accepted. Students must have completed 4 years each of social studies and English, 3 years each of math and science, and 2 years each of a foreign language and history. An essay is required and an interview is recommended. Westminster requires applicants to be in the upper 50% of their class. A GPA of 2.5 is required. AP and CLEP credits are accepted. Important factors in the admissions decision are advanced placement or honors courses, leadership record, and extracurricular activities record.

Procedure: Freshmen are admitted to all sessions. Entrance exams should be taken in the junior year of high school. There are early decision, deferred admissions and rolling admissions plans. Application deadlines are open. Applications are accepted on-line.

Financial Aid: In 2009-2010, 99% of all full-time freshmen and 99% of continuing full-time students received some form of financial aid. 53% of all full-time freshmen and 51% of continuing full-time students received need-based aid. The average freshman award was $18,906. Need-based scholarships or need-based grants averaged $14,707; need-based self-help aid (loans and jobs) averaged $4,797. 35% of undergraduate students work part-time. Average annual earnings from campus work are $2000. The average financial indebtedness of the 2009 graduate was $20,018. The FAFSA is required. The priority date for freshman financial aid applications for fall entry is February 15.

Computers: Wireless access is available. All students may access the system. There are no time limits and no fees. It is strongly recommended that all students have a personal computer.

WESTMINSTER COLLEGE

Salt Lake City, UT 84105

(801) 832-2200
(800) 748-4753; (801) 832-3101

Full-time: 900 men, 1135 women	**Faculty:** 136; IIB, av$
Part-time: 68 men, 69 women	**Ph.D.s:** 73%
Graduate: 490 men, 375 women	**Student/Faculty:** 15 to 1
Year: 4-1-4, summer session	**Tuition:** $24,996
Application Deadline: open	**Room & Board:** $7006
Freshman Class: 1625 applied, 1329 accepted, 469 enrolled	
SAT CR/M: 565/570	**ACT:** 25 **VERY COMPETITIVE**

Westminster College, founded in 1875, is a private, comprehensive, liberal arts institution offering undergraduate programs through the Bill and Vieve Gore School of Business, the St. Mark's Westminster School of Nursing and Health Sciences, the School of Arts and Sciences, and the School of Education. There are 4 undergraduate schools and 4 graduate schools. In addition to regional accreditation, Westminster has baccalaureate program accreditation with ACBSP and NLN. The library contains 168,573 volumes, 255,368 microform items, and 5,449 audio/video tapes/CDs/DVDs, and subscribes to 9,857 periodicals including electronic. Computerized library services include interlibrary loans, database searching, Internet access, and laptop Internet portals. Special learning facilities include a learning resource center, a multipurpose theater, networked classrooms, a flight simulation center, a center for financial analysis, and a health and wellness recreation center. The 27-acre campus is in an urban area 6 miles southeast of downtown Salt Lake City. Including any residence halls, there are 31 buildings.

Programs of Study: Westminster confers B.A., B.S., and B.F.A. degrees. Master's degrees are also awarded. Bachelor's degrees are awarded in AGRICULTURE (environmental studies), BIOLOGICAL SCIENCE (biology/biological science and neurosciences), BUSINESS (accounting, banking and finance, business administration and management, international business management, investments and securities, and marketing/retailing/merchandising), COMMUNICATIONS AND THE ARTS (art, arts administration/management, communications, dramatic arts, English, fine arts, and music), COMPUTER AND PHYSICAL SCIENCE (chemistry, computer science, information sciences and systems, mathematics, and physics), EDUCATION (early childhood education, elementary education, and special education), ENGINEERING AND ENVIRONMENTAL DESIGN (aviation administration/management and aviation computer technology), HEALTH PROFESSIONS (nursing), SOCIAL SCIENCE (criminal justice, economics, history, philosophy, political science/government, prelaw, psychology, social science, sociology, and Spanish studies). Nursing, biology, and English are the strongest academically. Business, nursing, and psychology are the largest.

Special: The college offers internships in every major, study abroad, dual and student-designed majors, an accelerated degree, co-op, work-study, independent study, weekend college, and freshman seminar courses. A 3-2 engineering degree with USC in Los Angeles or Washington University in St. Louis, Missouri, is also possible. There are 2 national honor societies, including Phi Beta Kappa, a freshman honors program, and 1 departmental honors program.

Admissions: 82% of the 2009-2010 applicants were accepted. The SAT scores for the 2009-2010 freshman class were: Critical Reading--20% below 500, 44% between 500 and 599, 29% between 600 and 700, and 7% above 700; Math--24% below 500, 38% between 500 and 599, 34% between 600 and 700, and 4% above 700. The ACT scores were 16% below 21, 23% between 21 and 23, 28% between 24 and 26, 17% between 27 and 28, and 16% above 28. 45% of the current freshmen were in the top fifth of their class; 81% were in the top two fifths. There were 10 National Merit finalists. 10 freshmen graduated first in their class.

Requirements: The SAT or ACT is required. In addition, applicants must be graduates of an accredited secondary school or have a GED certificate. College preparatory work should include 4 units of English, 3 of science, 2 each of math, foreign language, social studies, and electives, and 1 of history. An interview is recommended. AP and CLEP credits are accepted. Important factors in the admissions decision are evidence of special talent, extracurricular activities record, and advanced placement or honors courses.

Procedure: Freshmen are admitted to all sessions. Entrance exams should be taken in the junior or senior year of high school. There are deferred admissions and rolling admissions plans. Application deadlines are open. The fall 2009 application fee was $40. Applications are accepted on-line.

Financial Aid: In 2009-2010, 97% of all full-time freshmen and 93% of continuing full-time students received some form of financial aid. 60% of all full-time students received need-based aid. The average freshman award was $20,571. Need-based scholarships or need-based grants averaged $15,732 ($24,576 maximum); need-based self-help aid (loans and jobs) averaged $6029 ($9000 maximum); non-need-based athletic scholarships averaged $3357 ($5500 maximum); and other non-need-based awards and non-need-based scholarships averaged $6500 ($10,000 maximum). The average financial indebtedness of the 2009 graduate was $20,251. 70% of undergraduate students work part-time. Average annual earnings from campus work are $2500. Westminster is a member of CSS. The FAFSA is required. The priority date for freshman financial aid applications for fall entry is April 15. The deadline for filing freshman financial aid applications for fall entry is rolling.

Computers: Wireless access is available. There is wireless service in approximately 19 campus buildings. Every student has access to the Westminster network, including an e-mail account, 45 MB of storage space, and free on-campus Internet access. Students who bring PCs to the residence halls have access to the campus network and the Internet in their dorm rooms. In addition, each of the 5 residence halls has a 24/7 computer lab (up to 6 workstations), including access to printing. Several computer labs are available for student use around campus; the lab in Giovale Library has 50 workstations. All students may access the system. There are no time limits. The fee is $50 to $100 per semester. It is strongly recommended that all students have a personal computer.

WESTMONT COLLEGE

Santa Barbara, CA 93108

(805) 565-6005
(800) 777-9011; (805) 565-6234

Full-time: 515 men, 800 women	**Faculty:** IIB, +$
Part-time: 5 men, 20 women	**Ph.D.s:** 89%
Graduate: none	**Student/Faculty:** n/av
Year: semesters, summer session	**Tuition:** $31,500
Application Deadline: see profile	**Room & Board:** $10,000
Freshman Class: n/av	
SAT or ACT: required	**HIGHLY COMPETITIVE**

Westmont College, founded in 1937, is a private, nondenominational Christian institution offering undergraduate liberal arts degrees. Figures in the above capsule are approximate. The library contains 162,274 volumes, 20,687 microform items, and 7926 audio/video tapes/CDs/DVDs, and subscribes to 3211 periodicals including electronic. Computerized library services include interlibrary loans, database searching, and Internet access. Special learning facilities include a learning resource center, art gallery, radio station, observatory, science center with a premedical center, and physiology lab. The 111-acre campus is in a suburban area 90 miles north of Los Angeles. Including any residence halls, there are 30 buildings.

Programs of Study: Westmont confers B.A. and B.S. degrees. Bachelor's degrees are awarded in BIOLOGICAL SCIENCE (biology/biological science), BUSINESS (business economics), COMMUNICATIONS AND THE ARTS (art, communications, dramatic arts, English, French, modern language, music, and Spanish), COMPUTER AND PHYSICAL SCIENCE (chemistry, computer science, mathematics, and physics), EDUCATION (art education, English education, mathematics education, music education, and social science education), ENGINEERING AND ENVIRONMENTAL DESIGN (engineering physics), HEALTH PROFESSIONS (exercise science), SOCIAL SCIENCE (European studies, history, liberal arts/general studies, philosophy, political science/government, psychology, religion, social science, and sociology). Biology, communication studies, and economics/business are the largest.

Special: Westmont offers cross-registration with 12 Christian colleges in the Christian College Consortium, internships in local businesses and social agencies, study abroad in 11 countries, and semesters in Washington, D.C., San Francisco, and Los Angeles. B.A.-B.S. degrees, student-designed majors, work-study programs, a 3-2 engineering program with several California universities, the University of Washington, and Boston University, and pass/fail options are also available. There are preprofessional programs in sports medicine, dentistry, engineering, law, medicine, ministry/missions, optometry, pharmacology, physical therapy, teaching, and veterinary medicine. There are 8 national honor societies, a freshman honors program, and 9 departmental honors programs.

Requirements: The SAT or ACT is required. The ACT Optional Writing test is also required. In addition, applicants need 16 academic credits, including 4 years of high school English, 3 of math, 2 each of a foreign language, social science, and physical science, and 1 each of history and biological science. Interviews are recommended. Essays are required. The GED is accepted. AP and CLEP credits are accepted. Important factors in the admissions decision are advanced placement or honors courses, leadership record, and extracurricular activities record.

Procedure: Freshmen are admitted fall and spring. Entrance exams should be taken during the spring of the junior year or the beginning of the senior year.

Check with the school for current application deadlines. The fall 2009 application fee was $35. Applications are accepted on-line. A waiting list is maintained.

Financial Aid: In a recent year, 83% of all full-time freshmen and 85% of continuing full-time students received some form of financial aid, including need-based aid. The average freshmen award was $22,476. 54% of undergraduate students work part-time. Average annual earnings from campus work are $909. The average financial indebtedness of a recent graduate was $25,008. The FAFSA is required. Check with the school for current application deadlines.

Computers: Wireless access is available. High-speed Internet access is available in all dorms. All students may access the system. There are no time limits and no fees. It is strongly recommended that all students have a personal computer.

WHEATON COLLEGE
Wheaton, IL 60187-5593

(630) 752-5005
(800) 222-2419; (630) 752-5285

Full-time: 1115 men, 1117 women	**Faculty:** IIB, +$
Part-time: 35 men, 32 women	**Ph.D.s:** 95%
Graduate: 248 men, 273 women	**Student/Faculty:** n/av
Year: semesters, summer session	**Tuition:** $26,520
Application Deadline: January 10	**Room & Board:** $7770
Freshman Class: 1950 applied, 1390 accepted, 620 enrolled	
SAT CR/M/W: 660/650/650	**ACT:** 29 **HIGHLY COMPETITIVE+**

Wheaton College, founded in 1860, is a private nondenominational institution committed to providing students with a Christian education. A liberal arts school, it offers undergraduate programs in the sciences, business, the arts and fine arts, music, teacher preparation, and religious and Bible studies. There is one undergraduate school and one graduate school. In addition to regional accreditation, Wheaton has baccalaureate program accreditation with NASM and NCATE. The 2 libraries contain 1.1 million volumes, 608,584 microform items, and 12,260 audio/video tapes/CDs/DVDs, and subscribe to 132,311 periodicals including electronic. Computerized library services include interlibrary loans, database searching, Internet access, and laptop Internet portals. Special learning facilities include an art gallery, radio station, TV station, a communications resource center with TV and audio studios, a special collection of British authors' books and papers, an evangelical museum with document archives, and the Center for Applied Christian Ethics. The 80-acre campus is in a suburban area 25 miles west of Chicago. Including any residence halls, there are 65 buildings.

Programs of Study: Wheaton confers B.A., B.S., B.M., and B.M.E. degrees. Master's and doctoral degrees are also awarded. Bachelor's degrees are awarded in BIOLOGICAL SCIENCE (biology/biological science), BUSINESS (business economics), COMMUNICATIONS AND THE ARTS (art, classical languages, communications, English, French, German, music, and Spanish), COMPUTER AND PHYSICAL SCIENCE (chemistry, computer science, geology, mathematics, and physics), EDUCATION (Christian education, elementary education, music education, and secondary education), ENGINEERING AND ENVIRONMENTAL DESIGN (engineering and environmental science), HEALTH PROFESSIONS (health science and nursing), SOCIAL SCIENCE (anthropology, archeology, biblical studies, economics, history, interdisciplinary studies, international relations, philosophy, political science/government, psychology, social science, and sociology). Business economics, English, and psychology are the largest.

Special: There are 12 national honor societies and 15 departmental honors programs.

Admissions: 71% of the 2009-2010 applicants were accepted. The SAT scores for the 2009-2010 freshman class were: Critical Reading--2% below 500, 22% between 500 and 599, 50% between 600 and 700, and 27% above 700; Math--2% below 500, 21% between 500 and 599, 55% between 600 and 700, and 22% above 700; Writing--2% below 500, 23% between 500 and 599, 53% between 600 and 700, and 21% above 700. The ACT scores were 2% below 21, 6% between 21 and 23, 18% between 24 and 26, 23% between 27 and 28, and 51% above 28. 75% of the current freshmen were in the top fifth of their class; 91% were in the top two fifths. There were 27 National Merit finalists.

Requirements: The SAT or ACT is required. The ACT Optional Writing test is also required. In addition, a high school diploma is required and the GED is accepted. Wheaton requires a general college preparatory program of 18 units, including 4 of English, 3 to 4 of math, science, and social studies, and 2 to 3 of a foreign language. AP credits are accepted. Important factors in the admissions decision are recommendations by school officials, advanced placement or honors courses, and personality/intangible qualities.

Procedure: Freshmen are admitted in the fall. Entrance exams should be taken in October of the senior year (early action) and December. There are early admissions and deferred admissions plans. Applications should be filed by January 10 for fall entry, along with a $50 fee. Notifications are sent April 1. 438 applicants were on the 2009 waiting list; 51 were admitted.

Financial Aid: In 2009-2010, 47% of all full-time freshmen and 68% of continuing full-time students received some form of financial aid. 52% of all full-time freshmen and 51% of continuing full-time students received need-based aid. The average freshman award was $24,042, with $18,058 ($4,489 maximum) from need-based scholarships or need-based grants. 40% of undergraduate students work part-time. Average annual earnings from campus work are $1000. The average financial indebtedness of the 2009 graduate was $20,455. Wheaton is a member of CSS. The FAFSA and the college's own financial statement are required. The priority date for freshman financial aid applications for fall entry is February 15.

Computers: Wired access is available in all campus residences, the library, and student center. Wireless Internet is available in most campus locations, with the exception of classrooms. There are both general computer labs and discipline-specific computing clusters. All students may access the system 24 hours a day. There are no time limits and no fees. It is strongly recommended that all students have a personal computer. Students enrolled in the Conservatory of Music must have a personal computer.

WHEATON COLLEGE

Norton, MA 02766

(508) 286-8251
(800) 394-6003; (508) 286-8271

Full-time: 625 men, 1002 women	**Faculty:** 139; IIB, +$
Part-time: 1 man, 4 women	**Ph.D.s:** 88%
Graduate: none	**Student/Faculty:** 12 to 1
Year: semesters	**Tuition:** $39,850
Application Deadline: January 15	**Room & Board:** $9590
Freshman Class: 3304 applied, 1947 accepted, 424 enrolled	
SAT CR/M: 630/620	**ACT:** 29 **HIGHLY COMPETITIVE+**

Wheaton College, established in 1834, is an independent liberal arts institution. The library contains 376,616 volumes, 74,078 microform items, and 17,133 audio/video tapes/CDs/DVDs, and subscribes to 15,299 periodicals including electronic. Computerized library services include interlibrary loans, database searching, Internet access, and laptop Internet portals. Special learning facilities include a learning resource center, art gallery, planetarium, radio station, a greenhouse, and an observatory. The 400-acre campus is in a suburban area 35 miles south of Boston and 15 miles north of Providence. Including any residence halls, there are 92 buildings.

Programs of Study: Wheaton confers A.B. degrees. Bachelor's degrees are awarded in BIOLOGICAL SCIENCE (biochemistry, bioinformatics, and biology/biological science), COMMUNICATIONS AND THE ARTS (art history and appreciation, classics, creative writing, dramatic arts, English, fine arts, German, Greek, Latin, literature, music, Russian, and studio art), COMPUTER AND PHYSICAL SCIENCE (astronomy, chemistry, computer mathematics, computer science, mathematics, and physics), ENGINEERING AND ENVIRONMENTAL DESIGN (environmental science), SOCIAL SCIENCE (African studies, African American studies, American studies, anthropology, Asian/Oriental studies, classical/ancient civilization, economics, French studies, German area studies, Hispanic American studies, history, international relations, Italian studies, philosophy, political science/government, psychobiology, psychology, religion, Russian and Slavic studies, sociology, and women's studies). Arts and sciences are the strongest academically. Psychology, English, and economics are the largest.

Special: Students may cross-register with Brown University as well as with colleges in the Southeastern Association for Cooperation in Higher Education in Massachusetts and with schools participating in the 12 College Exchange Program. Wheaton offers study abroad in 54 countries, internship programs, nondegree study, dual majors, student-designed majors, a Washington semester at American University, and interdisciplinary majors, including math and economics, math and computer science, physics and astronomy, and theater and English dramatic literature. Dual-degree programs exist with the following institutions: Thayer School of Engineering, Dartmouth College (B.S. Engineering); Emerson College (M.A. Integrated Marketing Communication); Graduate School of Management, University of Rochester (M.B.A.); George Washington University (B.S. Engineering); School of the Museum of Fine Arts (B.F.A.); Andover-Newton Theological School (M.A. Religion); and New England School of Optometry (Doctor of Optometry). There are 8 national honor societies, including Phi Beta Kappa, and a freshman honors program. All departments have honors programs.

Admissions: 59% of the 2009-2010 applicants were accepted. The SAT scores for the 2009-2010 freshman class were: Critical Reading--6% below 500, 26% between 500 and 599, 46% between 600 and 700, and 22% above 700; Math--3%

below 500, 36% between 500 and 599, 45% between 600 and 700, and 16% above 700. The ACT scores were 2% below 21, 16% between 24 and 26, 35% between 27 and 28, and 47% above 28. 75% of the current freshmen were in the top fifth of their class; 92% were in the top two fifths. 6 freshmen graduated first in their class.

Requirements: Submission of SAT or ACT scores is optional. Applicants must be graduates of an accredited secondary school. Recommended courses include English with emphasis on composition skills, 4 years; foreign language and math, 4 years each; social studies, 3 years; and lab science, 2 to 3 years. Wheaton requires an essay and a graded writing sample and strongly recommends an interview. AP credits are accepted. Important factors in the admissions decision are advanced placement or honors courses, extracurricular activities record, and personality/intangible qualities.

Procedure: Freshmen are admitted fall and spring. Entrance exams should be taken in October and/or November. There are early decision and deferred admissions plans. Early decision applications should be filed by November 15; regular applications, by January 15 for fall entry and November 1 for spring entry, along with a $55 fee. Notification of early decision is sent December 15; regular decision, April 1. 140 early decision candidates were accepted for the 2009-2010 class. 380 applicants were on the 2009 waiting list; 18 were admitted. Applications are accepted on-line.

Financial Aid: In 2009-2010, 76% of all full-time freshmen and 66% of continuing full-time students received some form of financial aid.61% of all full-time freshmen and 54% of continuing full-time students received need-based aid. The average freshman award was $27,200. Need-based scholarships or need-based grants averaged $25,818 ($46,800 maximum); need-based self-help aid (loans and jobs) averaged $5,787 ($7,000 maximum); and other non-need-based awards and non-need-based scholarships averaged $11,250 ($15,000 maximum). The average financial indebtedness of the 2009 graduate was $25,540. 55% of undergraduate students work part-time. Average annual earnings from campus work are $1175. Wheaton is a member of CSS. The CSS/Profile or FAFSA and parents' and student's federal tax returns and if applicable, noncustodial profile and business/farm supplement are required. The deadline for filing freshman financial aid applications for fall entry is February 1.

Computers: The campus has both wireless and wired Internet access from every residence hall and college classroom. While nearly all students bring a computer with them to Wheaton, there are 375 computers available in public spaces, labs, and classrooms. Many faculty members use Moodle, a course management software system, to post documents such as syllabi and assignments, have electronic discussions, give quizzes, make announcements, and more. Services including registration and access to academic records and campus news and events are all available through the Internet. All students may access the system 24 hours a day, 7 days a week. There are no time limits. The fee is $120 per year. It is strongly recommended that all students have a personal computer.

WHITMAN COLLEGE

Walla Walla, WA 99362-2083

(509) 527-5176
(877) 462-9448; (509) 527-4967

Full-time: 628 men, 855 women	**Faculty:** 130; IIB, +$
Part-time: 13 men, 19 women	**Ph.D.s:** 95%
Graduate: none	**Student/Faculty:** 11 to 1
Year: semesters	**Tuition:** $36,940
Application Deadline: January 15	**Room & Board:** $9260
Freshman Class: 3290 applied, 1442 accepted, 396 enrolled	
SAT CR/M/W: 680/660/660	**ACT:** 30 **MOST COMPETITIVE**

Whitman College, founded in 1883, is a nonprofit, private, independent residential liberal arts and sciences college. There is 1 undergraduate school. The library contains 537,317 volumes and 7378 audio/video tapes/CDs/DVDs, and subscribes to 30,027 periodicals including electronic. Computerized library services include interlibrary loans, database searching, Internet access, and laptop Internet portals. Special learning facilities include a learning resource center, art gallery, natural history museum, radio station, electron microscope lab, indoor planetarium, off-campus observatory, on-campus astronomical telescopes, Asian art collection, video-conferencing center, outdoor sculpture walk, organic garden, and indoor and outdoor rock-climbing walls. The 117-acre campus is in a small town 150 miles south of Spokane, 260 miles southeast of Seattle, and 235 miles east of Portland, Oregon. Including any residence halls, there are 41 buildings.

Programs of Study: Whitman confers B.A. degrees. Bachelor's degrees are awarded in BIOLOGICAL SCIENCE (biology/biological science), COMMUNICATIONS AND THE ARTS (art history and appreciation, classics, dramatic arts, English, film arts, fine arts, French, German, music, Spanish, speech/debate/rhetoric, and studio art), COMPUTER AND PHYSICAL SCIENCE (astronomy, chemistry, geology, mathematics, and physics), ENGINEERING AND ENVIRONMENTAL DESIGN (environmental science), SOCIAL SCIENCE (anthropology, Asian/Oriental studies, economics, ethnic studies, history, Latin American studies, philosophy, political science/government, psychology, religion, and sociology). Biology, psychology, and politics are the largest.

Special: Special academic programs include more than 500 internships, study abroad in 43 countries, a Washington semester, and study programs in Chicago and Philadelphia. Dual majors are available in any area and student-designed majors are offered. There is a 3-2 environmental management and forestry program with Duke University and a 3-2 engineering program with Washington University in St. Louis, the California Institute of Technology and Applied Science, Columbia and Duke Universities, and the University of Washington. A 3-3 law program is offered through Columbia University. A 4-1 education program is available through Bank Street College of Education and the University of Puget Sound Cooperative. Certification is offered for elementary and secondary education. A pass-D-fail option is available. A 3-2 program is available with the Monterey Institute of International Studies. There are 3 national honor societies, including Phi Beta Kappa, and a freshman honors program. In addition, all departments have honors programs.

Admissions: 44% of the 2009-2010 applicants were accepted. The SAT scores for the 2009-2010 freshman class were: Critical Reading--1% below 500, 16% between 500 and 599, 43% between 600 and 700, and 41% above 700; Math--2% below 500, 15% between 500 and 599, 56% between 600 and 700, and 27% above 700; Writing--2% below 500, 19% between 500 and 599, 49% between

600 and 700, and 30% above 700. The ACT scores were 2% between 21 and 23, 10% between 24 and 26, 14% between 27 and 28, and 74% above 28. 91% of the current freshmen were in the top fifth of their class; 99% were in the top two fifths.

Requirements: The SAT or ACT is required. The GED is accepted. 3 essays must be submitted, and an interview is recommended. Credit by challenge examination is accepted. AP credits are accepted. Important factors in the admissions decision are advanced placement or honors courses, evidence of special talent, and extracurricular activities record.

Procedure: Freshmen are admitted fall and spring. Entrance exams should be taken by February of the senior year. There are early decision and deferred admissions plans. Early decision applications should be filed by November 15; regular applications, by January 15 for fall entry. The fall 2009 application fee was $45. Notification of early decision is sent December 15; regular decision, April 1. 137 early decision candidates were accepted for the 2009-2010 class. 551 applicants were on the 2009 waiting list; 10 were admitted. Applications are accepted on-line. 551 applicants were on a recent waiting list, 10 were accepted.

Financial Aid: In 2009-2010, 80% of all full-time freshmen and 73% of continuing full-time students received some form of financial aid. 49% of all full-time freshmen and 44% of continuing full-time students received need-based aid. The average freshman award was $15,583. Need-based scholarships or need-based grants averaged $24,366; need-based self-help aid (loans and jobs) averaged $5886; and other non-need-based awards and non-need-based scholarships averaged $10,686. The average financial indebtedness of the 2009 graduate was $15,811. Whitman is a member of CSS. The CSS/Profile and FAFSA are required. The priority date for freshman financial aid applications for fall entry is November 15. The deadline for filing freshman financial aid applications for fall entry is February 1.

Computers: Wireless access is available. There are 3 computer labs on campus and network ports in every residence hall room. Nearly all buildings on campus have wireless access. All students may access the system 24 hours a day. There are no time limits and no fees.

WILLAMETTE UNIVERSITY
Salem, OR 97301

(503) 370-6303
(877) 542-2787; (503) 375-5363

Full-time: 814 men, 999 women	**Faculty:** 155; IIA, +$
Part-time: 51 men, 68 women	**Ph.D.s:** 96%
Graduate: 398 men, 367 women	**Student/Faculty:** 12 to 1
Year: semesters	**Tuition:** $35,610
Application Deadline: February 1	**Room & Board:** $8350
Freshman Class: 5739 applied, 3416 accepted, 541 enrolled	
SAT CR/M/W: 620/610/600	**ACT:** 27 **VERY COMPETITIVE+**

Willamette University, founded in 1842, is an independent liberal arts institution affiliated with the Methodist Church. There are 3 graduate schools. In addition to regional accreditation, Willamette has baccalaureate program accreditation with NASM. The 2 libraries contain 428,173 volumes, 339,235 microform items, and 12,556 audio/video tapes/CDs/DVDs, and subscribe to 1,623 periodicals including electronic. Computerized library services include interlibrary loans, database searching, and Internet access. Special learning facilities include a learning resource center, art gallery, natural history museum, radio station, botanical and Japanese gardens, multimedia center, and "smart" classrooms. The 72-acre campus is in an urban area 50 minutes south of Portland. Including any residence halls, there are 45 buildings.

Programs of Study: Willamette confers B.A. and B.M. degrees. Master's and doctoral degrees are also awarded. Bachelor's degrees are awarded in BIOLOGICAL SCIENCE (biology/biological science), COMMUNICATIONS AND THE ARTS (art history and appreciation, comparative literature, dramatic arts, English, French, German, music, music performance, music theory and composition, Spanish, speech/debate/rhetoric, and studio art), COMPUTER AND PHYSICAL SCIENCE (chemistry, computer science, mathematics, physics, and science), EDUCATION (music education), ENGINEERING AND ENVIRONMENTAL DESIGN (environmental science), HEALTH PROFESSIONS (exercise science), SOCIAL SCIENCE (American studies, anthropology, Asian/Oriental studies, classical/ancient civilization, economics, history, humanities, international studies, Japanese studies, Latin American studies, philosophy, political science/government, psychology, religion, sociology, and women's studies). Social sciences, natural science, and humanities are the strongest academically. Psychology, politics, and biology are the largest.

Special: Willamette offers internships with the state and city governments, a Chicago semester, a Washington semester, and a 3-2 engineering degree with Washington University, University of Southern California, and Columbia University. Nondegree study, B.A.-B.S. degrees, dual majors, work-study programs with numerous employers in the Salem area and at the university, and credit/no-credit options are also available. Study abroad programs are available in 14 countries. There are 3-2 degrees in management, forestry, and computer science. There are 12 national honor societies including Phi Beta Kappa.

Admissions: 60% of the 2009-2010 applicants were accepted. The SAT scores for the 2009-2010 freshman class were: Critical Reading--6% below 500, 35% between 500 and 599, 43% between 600 and 700, and 16% above 700; Math--5% below 500, 34% between 500 and 599, 53% between 600 and 700, and 8% above 700; Writing--10% below 500, 39% between 500 and 599, 42% between 600 and 700, and 9% above 700. The ACT scores were 11% between 21 and 23, 26% between 24 and 26, 30% between 27 and 28, and 33% above 28. 64% of the current freshmen were in the top fifth of their class; 91% were in the top two fifths. 30 freshmen graduated first in their class.

Requirements: The SAT or ACT is required. The ACT Optional Writing test is also required. In addition, graduation from an accredited secondary school or satisfactory scores on the GED are required. Institutional preferences include 4 years each of English and math, and 3 years each of foreign language, lab science, and social studies or history. 2 essays are required, and an interview is recommended. Portfolios or auditions are recommended for art and music students. A GPA of 2.0 is required. AP credits are accepted. Important factors in the admissions decision are advanced placement or honors courses and recommendations by school officials.

Procedure: Freshmen are admitted fall and spring. Entrance exams should be taken December 1. There are early admissions and deferred admissions plans. Applications should be filed by February 1 for fall entry and November 1 for spring entry, along with a $50 fee. Notifications are sent April 1. Applications are accepted on-line. 97 applicants were on a recent waiting list, 11 were accepted.

Financial Aid: In 2009-2010, 97% of all full-time freshmen and 94% of continuing full-time students received some form of financial aid. 66% of all full-time freshmen and 61% of continuing full-time students received need-based aid. The average freshmen award was $25,216, with $4,561 ($10,500 maximum) from need-based self-help aid (loans and jobs). 55% of undergraduate students work part-time. Average annual earnings from campus work are $1303. The average financial indebtedness of the 2009 graduate was $23,534. Willamette is a member of CSS. The FAFSA is required. The priority date for freshman financial aid applications for fall entry is February 1.

Computers: Wireless access is available. Computers connected to the college's network are available at several different locations. There are 2 24-hour PC labs. Wireless Internet connection is available in all administrative buildings, the library, and student dorm lounges. All students may access the system 24 hours per day. There are no time limits and no fees.

WILLIAM JEWELL COLLEGE

Liberty, MO 64068
(816) 781-7700, ext. 5137
(800) 753-7009; (816) 415-5027

Full-time: 414 men, 616 women	**Faculty:** 70; IIB, --$
Part-time: none	**Ph.D.s:** 86%
Graduate: none	**Student/Faculty:** 15 to 1
Year: semesters, summer session	**Tuition:** $24,300
Application Deadline: August 15	**Room & Board:** $6700
Freshman Class: 2497 applied, 1374 accepted, 282 enrolled	
ACT: 26	**SAT:** required

VERY COMPETITIVE+

William Jewell College, founded in 1849, is an academically selective liberal arts college. It offers undergraduate programs in the arts and sciences, business, education, and nursing fields. In addition to regional accreditation, Jewell has baccalaureate program accreditation with NASM. The library contains 231,031 volumes, 1,050 microform items, and 11,232 audio/video tapes/CDs/DVDs, and subscribes to 500 periodicals including electronic. Computerized library services include interlibrary loans, database searching, and Internet access. Special learning facilities include a learning resource center, art gallery, planetarium, and radio station. The 200-acre campus is in a suburban area 15 miles northeast of Kansas City. Including any residence halls, there are 28 buildings.

Programs of Study: Jewell confers B.A. and B.S. degrees. Bachelor's degrees are awarded in BIOLOGICAL SCIENCE (biochemistry and biology/biological science), BUSINESS (accounting, business administration and management, business economics, and international business management), COMMUNICATIONS AND THE ARTS (art, communications, dramatic arts, English, French, music, and Spanish), COMPUTER AND PHYSICAL SCIENCE (chemistry, mathematics, and physics), EDUCATION (elementary education, music education, and secondary education), HEALTH PROFESSIONS (medical laboratory technology and nursing), SOCIAL SCIENCE (history, international relations, Japanese studies, philosophy, political science/government, psychology, and religion). Business is the largest.

Special: Internships for juniors or seniors, study abroad in Europe, Japan, Mexico, Australia, and Hong Kong, and a Washington semester are offered. B.A.-B.S. degrees, dual majors of any combination, internships, an accelerated degree in nursing, student-designed majors, and 3-2 engineering degrees with Washington University and the Universities of Missouri and Kansas are available. The Oxbridge Honors Program for major study is patterned after the teaching methods of Oxford and Cambridge and includes a year at either Oxford or Cambridge. Leadership and service learning programs are offered. There are 13 national honor societies, a freshman honors program, and 13 departmental honors programs.

Admissions: 55% of the 2009-2010 applicants were accepted. The SAT scores for the 2009-2010 freshman class were: Critical Reading--24% below 500, 30% between 500 and 599, 39% between 600 and 700, and 7% above 700; Math--21% below 500, 34% between 500 and 599, 39% between 600 and 700, and 11% above 700. The ACT scores were 9% below 21, 22% between 21 and 23, 25% between 24 and 26, 18% between 27 and 28, and 26% above 28. 68% of the current freshmen were in the top fifth of their class; 92% were in the top two fifths. 28 freshmen graduated first in their class.

Requirements: The SAT or ACT is required. In addition, students must be graduates of an accredited secondary school; the GED is also accepted. The college requires that applicants have taken 4 English courses and 4 academic electives, 3 courses each in math, social studies, and science; of these, 1 must be a lab, 2 in foreign language. An interview is recommended. An audition is advised for music applicants. AP and CLEP credits are accepted. Important factors in the admissions decision are advanced placement or honors courses, extracurricular activities record, and leadership record.

Procedure: Freshmen are admitted fall, spring, and summer. Entrance exams should be taken in the junior year. There are deferred admissions and rolling admissions plans. Applications should be filed by August 15 for fall entry, along with a $25 fee. Notification is sent on a rolling basis. Applications are accepted on-line.

Financial Aid: In 2009-2010, 99% of all full-time freshmen and 96% of continuing full-time students received some form of financial aid. 72% of all full-time freshmen and 69% of continuing full-time students received need-based aid. The average freshman award was $25,316. Need-based self-help aid (loans and jobs) averaged $6,783 ($16,500 maximum). The average financial indebtedness of the 2009 graduate was $24,102. Jewell is a member of CSS. The FAFSA is required. The priority date for freshman financial aid applications for fall entry is March 1.

Computers: Wireless access is available. All students may access the system. There are no time limits and no fees. It is strongly recommended that all students have a personal computer.

WILLIAMS COLLEGE
Williamstown, MA 01267 (413) 597-2211

Full-time: 987 men, 977 women	**Faculty:** 257; IIB, ++$
Part-time: 9 men, 24 women	**Ph.D.s:** 99%
Graduate: 18 men, 31 women	**Student/Faculty:** 8 to 1
Year: 4-1-4	**Tuition:** $35,670
Application Deadline: January 1	**Room & Board:** $9,470
Freshman Class: 6448 applied, 1194 accepted, 540 enrolled	
SAT CR/M: 720/710	**ACT:** 31 **MOST COMPETITIVE**

Williams College, founded in 1793, is a private institution offering undergraduate degrees in liberal arts and graduate degrees in art history and development economics. There are no undergraduate schools and 2 graduate schools. The 11 libraries contain 948,365 volumes, 492,374 microform items, 39,133 audio/video tapes/CDs/DVDs, and subscribe to 13,493 periodicals including electronic. Computerized library services include interlibrary loans, database searching, and Internet access. Special learning facilities include a learning resource center, art gallery, planetarium, radio station, a 2500-acre experimental forest, an environmental studies center, a center for foreign languages, literatures, and cultures, a rare book library, a studio art center, and a 3 stage center for the performing arts.

The 450-acre campus is in a small town 150 miles north of New York City. Including any residence halls, there are 97 buildings.

Programs of Study: Williams confers B.A. degrees. Master's degrees are also awarded. Bachelor's degrees are awarded in BIOLOGICAL SCIENCE (biology/ biological science), COMMUNICATIONS AND THE ARTS (art, art history and appreciation, classics, dramatic arts, English, fine arts, French, German, literature, music, Russian, and Spanish), COMPUTER AND PHYSICAL SCIENCE (astronomy, astrophysics, chemistry, computer science, geology, mathematics, and physics), SOCIAL SCIENCE (American studies, anthropology, Asian/ Oriental studies, economics, history, philosophy, political science/government, psychology, religion, sociology, and women's studies).

Special: Students may cross-register at Bennington or Massachusetts College of Liberal Arts and study abroad in Madrid, Oxford, Cairo, Beijing, and Kyoto, or any approved program with another college or university. Teaching and medical field experiences, dual and student-designed majors, internships, and a 3-2 engineering program with Columbia University and Washington University are offered. There are pass/fail options during the winter term. Each department offers at least 1 Oxford-model tutorial every year. There are 2 national honor societies, including Phi Beta Kappa.

Admissions: 19% of the 2009-2010 applicants were accepted. The SAT scores for the 2009-2010 freshman class were: Critical Reading--% below 500, 6% between 500 and 599, 28% between 600 and 700, and 66% above 700; Math--% below 500, 6% between 500 and 599, 32% between 600 and 700, and 61 above 700.

Requirements: The SAT is required. In addition, SAT: Subject tests in 3 subjects are required. Secondary preparation should include 4 years each of English and math, 3 to 4 years of foreign language, and at least 2 years each of science and social studies. A personal essay must be submitted. Williams accepts the Common Application AP credits are accepted. Important factors in the admissions decision are advanced placement or honors courses, recommendations by school officials, and evidence of special talent.

Procedure: Freshmen are admitted in the fall. There is a early decision and deferred admissions plans. Early decision applications should be filed by November 10; regular applications, by January 1 for fall entry. The fall 2008 application fee was $60. Applications are accepted on-line. 682 applicants were on a recent waiting list, 53 were accepted.

Financial Aid: In 2009-2010, 51% of all full-time freshmen and 45% of continuing full-time students received some form of financial aid. 51% of all full-time freshmen and 45% of continuing full-time students received need-based aid. The average freshmen award was $35,625. Average annual earnings from campus work are $800. The average financial indebtedness of the 2009 graduate was $9,727. The CSS/Profile, FAFSA, and the college's own financial statement are required. The deadline for filing freshman financial aid applications for fall entry is February 1.

Computers: Wireless access is available. Every student dorm room is wired for high-speed Internet access. Many public spaces on campus have wireless Internet availability. Numerous public computer terminals are located in the Computer Center and library as well as in other student spaces around campus. All students may access the system. There are no time limits and no fees.

WISCONSIN LUTHERAN COLLEGE

Milwaukee, WI 53226

(414) 443-8811
(888) 947-5884; (414) 443-8547

Full- and part-time: 780 men and women	**Faculty:** 47
Graduate: none	**Ph.D.s:** 70%
Year: semesters, summer session	**Student/Faculty:** 14 to 1
Application Deadline: see profile	**Tuition:** $21,200
Freshman Class: n/av	**Room & Board:** $7700
SAT or ACT: required	**VERY COMPETITIVE**

Wisconsin Lutheran College, founded in 1973 in affiliation with the Wisconsin Evangelical Lutheran Synod, offers higher education in the arts and sciences within a conservative Christian environment. Figures in the above capsule and in this profile are approximate. The library contains 72,600 volumes, 9,200 microform items, and 4,600 audio/video tapes/CDs/DVDs, and subscribes to 990 periodicals including electronic. Computerized library services include interlibrary loans, database searching, and Internet access. Special learning facilities include a learning resource center, art gallery, sound studio, electronic music lab, and language lab. The 21-acre campus is in a suburban area on the western edge of Milwaukee. Including any residence halls, there are 27 buildings.

Programs of Study: Wisconsin Lutheran confers B.A. and B.S. degrees. Bachelor's degrees are awarded in BIOLOGICAL SCIENCE (biology/biological science), BUSINESS (business economics), COMMUNICATIONS AND THE ARTS (art, communications, dramatic arts, English, music, and Spanish), COMPUTER AND PHYSICAL SCIENCE (chemistry and mathematics), EDUCATION (elementary education), SOCIAL SCIENCE (history, interdisciplinary studies, political science/government, psychology, social science, and theological studies). Chemistry, education, and biology are the strongest academically. Music, theology, and education are the largest.

Special: Student-designed majors and study abroad are offered. Internships are available in most departments.

Requirements: The ACT or SAT is required, with a minimum composite or combined score of 21 or 1000, respectively. Students should be graduates of an accredited high school or its equivalent with a minimum of 16 high school units, including 4 in English, 3 each in academic electives and math, and 2 each in science, foreign language, and social studies/history. Students must rank in the upper half of their graduating class or have a minimum GPA of 2.7. The Academic Recommendation Form must be submitted. A portfolio for art grants and an audition for music and drama grants are required. AP and CLEP credits are accepted. Important factors in the admissions decision are leadership record and personality/intangible qualities.

Procedure: Freshmen are admitted fall and spring. Entrance exams should be taken in the spring of the junior year. There is a rolling admissions plan. Check with the school for current application deadlines and fee. Notification is sent on a rolling basis. Applications are accepted on-line.

Financial Aid: The FAFSA and the college's own financial statement are required. The priority date for freshman financial aid applications for fall entry is March 1.

Computers: All students may access the system. There are no time limits and no fees. It is strongly recommended that all students have a personal computer.

WOFFORD COLLEGE

Spartanburg, SC 29303-3663   (864) 597-4130; (864) 597-4147

Full-time: 715 men, 705 women	**Faculty:** 117; IIB, av$
Part-time: 6 men, 3 women	**Ph.D.s:** 93%
Graduate: none	**Student/Faculty:** 12 to 1
Year: 4-1-4, summer session	**Tuition:** $30,280
Application Deadline: February 1	**Room & Board:** $8480
Freshman Class: 2442 applied, 1415 accepted, 392 enrolled	
SAT CR/M: 618/629	**ACT:** 26 **HIGHLY COMPETITIVE**

Wofford College, founded in 1854, is a private institution affiliated with the United Methodist Church, offering programs in liberal arts and preprofessional studies. In addition to regional accreditation, Wofford has baccalaureate program accreditation with NASDTEC. The library contains 197,725 volumes, 38,185 microform items, and 4,739 audio/video tapes/CDs/DVDs, and subscribes to 49,161 periodicals including electronic. Computerized library services include interlibrary loans, database searching, Internet access, and laptop Internet portals. Special learning facilities include a learning resource center, art gallery, foreign language center, international studies center with simultaneous translation capabilities, arboretum, greenhouse, and environmental center at Glendale Shoals. The 170-acre campus is in an urban area 65 miles southeast of Charlotte. Including any residence halls, there are 71 buildings.

Programs of Study: Wofford confers B.A. and B.S. degrees. Bachelor's degrees are awarded in AGRICULTURE (environmental studies), BIOLOGICAL SCIENCE (biology/biological science), BUSINESS (accounting, banking and finance, and business economics), COMMUNICATIONS AND THE ARTS (art history and appreciation, Chinese, dramatic arts, English, French, German, and Spanish), COMPUTER AND PHYSICAL SCIENCE (chemistry, computer science, mathematics, and physics), SOCIAL SCIENCE (crosscultural studies, economics, history, humanities, philosophy, political science/government, psychology, religion, and sociology). Biology, foreign languages, and finance/accounting are the strongest academically. Biology, business economics, and government are the largest.

Special: Special academic programs include study abroad in 59 countries, a Washington semester, and a concentration in Latin American and Caribbean studies. In addition, students can major or minor in multiple fields or complete interdisciplinary, humanities, or intercultural studies majors. Wofford participates in 3-2 programs in engineering with Clemson and Columbia Universities. The January interim allows students to concentrate on a single study project, internship, or travel experience. There are 9 national honor societies, including Phi Beta Kappa.

Admissions: 58% of the 2009-2010 applicants were accepted. The SAT scores for the 2009-2010 freshman class were: Critical Reading--9% below 500, 27% between 500 and 599, 46% between 600 and 700, and 18% above 700; Math--4% below 500, 27% between 500 and 599, 53% between 600 and 700, and 16% above 700; Writing--9% below 500, 31% between 500 and 599, 46% between 600 and 700, and 14% above 700. The ACT scores were 11% below 21, 26% between 21 and 23, 35% between 24 and 26, 19% between 27 and 28, and 9% above 28. 83% of the current freshmen were in the top fifth of their class; 97% were in the top two fifths. There were 4 National Merit finalists. 13 freshmen graduated first in their class.

Requirements: The SAT or ACT is required. In addition, applicants must be graduates of an accredited secondary school. The GED is accepted. Students should have completed 4 years each of high school English and math, 3 of lab science, and 3 each of a foreign language and social studies. An essay is required and an interview is strongly recommended. AP and CLEP credits are accepted. Important factors in the admissions decision are advanced placement or honors courses, leadership record, and personality/intangible qualities.

Procedure: Freshmen are admitted to all sessions. Entrance exams should be taken in the spring of the junior year or fall of the senior year. There are early decision and deferred admissions plans. Early decision applications should be filed by November 15; regular applications, by February 1 for fall entry, along with a $35 fee. Notification of early decision is sent December 5; regular decision, March 15. 47 applicants were on the 2009 waiting list; 22 were admitted. Applications are accepted on-line. 47 applicants were on a recent waiting list, 22 were accepted.

Financial Aid: In 2009-2010, 57% of all full-time freshmen and 56% of continuing full-time students received some form of financial aid. 52% of all full-time freshmen and 52% of continuing full-time students received need-based aid. The average freshman award was $29,406. The average financial indebtedness of the 2009 graduate was $22,199. The FAFSA is required. The deadline for filing freshman financial aid applications for fall entry is March 15.

Computers: Wireless access is available. All students may access the system 24 hours per day. There are no time limits and no fees. It is strongly recommended that all students have a personal computer. A PC/Windows is recommended.

WORCESTER POLYTECHNIC INSTITUTE
Worcester, MA 01609-2280 — (508) 831-5286; (508) 831-5875

Full-time: 2346 men, 927 women	**Faculty:** 263; IIA, +$
Part-time: 97 men, 21 women	**Ph.D.s:** 94%
Graduate: 847 men, 306 women	**Student/Faculty:** 12 to 1
Year: trimesters, summer session	**Tuition:** $37,440
Application Deadline: February 1	**Room & Board:** $11,360
Freshman Class: 6284 applied, 3989 accepted, 928 enrolled	
SAT CR/M/W: 610/670/600	**ACT:** 28 **HIGHLY COMPETITIVE+**

Worcester Polytechnic Institute, founded in 1865, is a private technological university offering degrees in the sciences, engineering, computer science, business management, and the liberal arts. The academic program emphasizes professional-level project work. There is 1 undergraduate school and 1 graduate school. In addition to regional accreditation, WPI has baccalaureate program accreditation with AACSB and ABET. The library contains 271,361 volumes, 111,000 microform items, and 1654 audio/video tapes/CDs/DVDs, and subscribes to 36,000 periodicals including electronic. Computerized library services include interlibrary loans, database searching, Internet access, and laptop Internet portals. Special learning facilities include a learning resource center, art gallery, radio station, TV station, robotics lab, wind tunnel, and greenhouse. The 80-acre campus is in a suburban area 40 miles west of Boston. Including any residence halls, there are 48 buildings.

Programs of Study: WPI confers B.A. and B.S. degrees. Master's and doctoral degrees are also awarded. Bachelor's degrees are awarded in AGRICULTURE (environmental studies), BIOLOGICAL SCIENCE (biochemistry and biotechnology), BUSINESS (business administration and management, management engineering, and management information systems), COMMUNICATIONS AND

THE ARTS (technical and business writing), COMPUTER AND PHYSICAL SCIENCE (actuarial science, chemistry, computer science, digital arts/technology, mathematics, and physics), ENGINEERING AND ENVIRONMENTAL DESIGN (aeronautical engineering, biomedical engineering, chemical engineering, civil engineering, computer graphics, electrical/electronics engineering, engineering physics, environmental engineering, industrial engineering, materials engineering, mechanical engineering, and technology and public affairs), SOCIAL SCIENCE (economics, fire protection, humanities, interdisciplinary studies, social science, and systems science). Engineering, biology, and computer science are the largest.

Special: Students may cross-register with 9 other colleges in the Colleges of Worcester Consortium. Co-op programs in all majors, internships, work-study programs, dual majors in every subject, student-designed majors, 3-2 engineering degrees, a Washington semester, nondegree study, and pass/fail options are all available. There are accelerated degree programs in fire protection engineering and math. There are 26 special project centers in 17 countries. There are 10 national honor societies.

Admissions: 63% of the 2009-2010 applicants were accepted. The SAT scores for the 2009-2010 freshman class were: Critical Reading--8% below 500, 35% between 500 and 599, 43% between 600 and 700, and 14% above 700; Math--% below 500, 12% between 500 and 599, 54% between 600 and 700, and 34% above 700; Writing--6% below 500, 28% between 500 and 599, 45% between 600 and 700, and 11% above 700. The ACT scores were 2% below 21, 9% between 21 and 23, 20% between 24 and 26, 25% between 27 and 28, and 44% above 28. 80% of the current freshmen were in the top fifth of their class; 96% were in the top two fifths. There were 6 National Merit finalists. 37 freshmen graduated first in their class.

Requirements: Applicants must have completed 4 years of math, including precalculus, 4 years of English, and 2 lab sciences. An essay is required as well as a letter of recommendation from either a math or science teacher and the guidance counselor. Those opting for Flex Path will submit academic work in place of the SAT or ACT. AP credits are accepted. Important factors in the admissions decision are advanced placement or honors courses, recommendations by school officials, and extracurricular activities record.

Procedure: Freshmen are admitted fall and spring. Entrance exams should be taken between April and January. There is a deferred admissions plan. Applications should be filed by February 1 for fall entry and November 15 for spring entry, along with a $60 fee. Notifications are sent April 1. 852 applicants were on the 2009 waiting list; 2 were admitted. Applications are accepted on-line.

Financial Aid: In 2009-2010, 99% of all full-time freshmen and 97% of continuing full-time students received some form of financial aid. 76% of all full-time freshmen and 64% of continuing full-time students received need-based aid. The average freshman award was $25,229. Need-based scholarships and need-based grants averaged $18,073; and need-based self-help aid (loans and jobs) averaged $7156. 19% of undergraduate students work part-time. Average annual earnings from campus work are $1322. The average financial indebtedness of the 2009 graduate was $44,340. WPI is a member of CSS. The CSS/Profile, FAFSA, CSS Noncustodial Profile, and WPI Upper-Class Application are required. The deadline for filing freshman financial aid applications for fall entry is February 1.

Computers: Wireless access is available. WPI has a state-of-the-art network infrastructure as well as wireless access in all academic and residential buildings. There are 28 computer labs/classrooms, including several with 24/7 card access. WPI students can also access network resources from off campus via our Virtual

Private Network. All students may access the system 24 hours daily. There are no time limits and no fees.

XAVIER UNIVERSITY
Cincinnati, OH 45207

(513) 745-3301
(877) 982-3648; (513) 745-4319

Full-time: 1709 men, 2020 women	**Faculty:** 304; IIA, -$
Part-time: 189 men, 310 women	**Ph.D.s:** 77%
Graduate: 1143 men, 1595 women	**Student/Faculty:** 12 to 1
Year: semesters, summer session	**Tuition:** $28,570
Application Deadline: February 1	**Room & Board:** $9250
Freshman Class: 7205 applied, 5272 accepted, 1178 enrolled	
SAT CR/M/W: 560/570/540	**ACT:** 25 **VERY COMPETITIVE**

Xavier University, founded in 1831, is a comprehensive Jesuit institution affiliated with the Roman Catholic Church. There are 3 undergraduate schools. In addition to regional accreditation, XU has baccalaureate program accreditation with AACSB, CSWE, NASM, and TEAC. The library contains 363,140 volumes, 751,271 microform items, and 11,029 audio/video tapes/CDs/DVDs, and subscribes to 54,264 periodicals including electronic. Computerized library services include interlibrary loans, database searching, Internet access, and laptop Internet portals. Special learning facilities include a learning resource center, art gallery, radio station, TV station, and observatory. The 148-acre campus is in an urban area 5 miles northeast of the center of Cincinnati in a residential area. Including any residence halls, there are 36 buildings.

Programs of Study: XU confers B.A., B.S., Honors A.B., B.F.A., B.L.A., B.S.B.A., B.S.N., and B.S.W. degrees. Associate, master's, and doctoral degrees are also awarded. Bachelor's degrees are awarded in BIOLOGICAL SCIENCE (biology/biological science), BUSINESS (accounting, banking and finance, business administration and management, business economics, entrepreneurial studies, human resources, international business management, management science, marketing/retailing/merchandising, and sports management), COMMUNICATIONS AND THE ARTS (advertising, art, classics, communications, English, fine arts, French, German, music, public relations, and Spanish), COMPUTER AND PHYSICAL SCIENCE (applied physics, chemistry, computer science, information sciences and systems, mathematics, natural sciences, and physics), EDUCATION (athletic training, early childhood education, education, middle school education, music education, science education, and special education), HEALTH PROFESSIONS (medical laboratory technology, nursing, and prepharmacy), SOCIAL SCIENCE (criminal justice, economics, history, international relations, liberal arts/general studies, philosophy, political science/government, psychology, social work, sociology, and theological studies). The philosophy, politics, and the public honors program and natural sciences are the strongest academically. Business, nursing, and liberal arts are the largest.

Special: Xavier offers internships related to some majors, cross-registration through the Greater Cincinnati Consortium, and co-op programs in business and computer science. Students may study abroad in 11 countries. A Washington semester and nondegree study are available. A 3-2 engineering degree is offered with the University of Cincinnati, and a 3-2 applied biology degree is offered with Duke University. A professional accountancy B.S.-B.A and M.B.A program is also offered. There are 10 national honor societies, including Phi Beta Kappa, a freshman honors program, and 1 departmental honors program.

Admissions: 73% of the 2009-2010 applicants were accepted. The SAT scores for the 2009-2010 freshman class were: Critical Reading--20% below 500, 48% between 500 and 599, 28% between 600 and 700, and 4% above 700; Math--20% below 500, 45% between 500 and 599, 32% between 600 and 700, and 3% above 700; Writing--23% below 500, 48% between 500 and 599, 26% between 600 and 700, and 3% above 700. The ACT scores were 11% below 21, 26% between 21 and 23, 28% between 24 and 26, 15% between 27 and 28, and 20% above 28. 49% of the current freshmen were in the top fifth of their class; 78% were in the top two fifths. There were 8 National Merit finalists. 20 freshmen graduated first in their class.

Requirements: The SAT or ACT is required. In addition, graduation from an accredited secondary school or satisfactory scores on the GED are required for admission. The school requires 21 academic credits, including 4 years of English, 3 each of math, social studies, and science, 2 of foreign language, and 1 of health/phys ed, plus 5 electives. AP and CLEP credits are accepted. Important factors in the admissions decision are advanced placement or honors courses, leadership record, and extracurricular activities record.

Procedure: Freshmen are admitted fall and spring. Entrance exams should be taken by fall of the senior year. There is a deferred admissions plan. Applications should be filed by February 1 for fall entry, along with a $35 fee. Notifications are sent March 15. Applications are accepted on-line. 71 applicants were on a recent waiting list.

Financial Aid: In 2009-2010, all full-time freshmen and 95% of continuing full-time students received some form of financial aid. 63% of all full-time freshmen and 56% of continuing full-time students received need-based aid. The average freshman award was $18,678. 21% of undergraduate students work part-time. Average annual earnings from campus work are $2000. The average financial indebtedness of the 2009 graduate was $22,769. XU is a member of CSS. The FAFSA is required. The priority date for freshman financial aid applications for fall entry is February 15.

Computers: Wireless access is available. There are more than 200 PCs for public use in labs. Wireless laptops may be checked out at the student center or library. Network connections for PCs are provided for all resident students as well as for students bringing wireless laptops to campus. Internet access is available at all locations. All students may access the system 24 hours a day, 7 days a week. There are no time limits and no fees.

YALE UNIVERSITY
New Haven, CT 06520-8234   (203) 432-9316; (203) 432-9392

Full-time: 5250 men and women	**Faculty:** I, ++$
Part-time: 15 men, 15 women	**Ph.D.s:** 85%
Graduate: 2320 men, 2440 women	**Student/Faculty:** n/av
Year: semesters, summer session	**Tuition:** $35,000
Application Deadline: see profile	**Room & Board:** $10,000
Freshman Class: n/av	
SAT or ACT: required	**MOST COMPETITIVE**

Yale University, founded in 1701, is a private liberal arts institution. Figures in the above capsule are approximate. There are 11 graduate schools. In addition to regional accreditation, Yale has baccalaureate program accreditation with AACSB, ABET, CAHEA, NAAB, NASM, NLN, and SAF. The 43 libraries contain 10.9 million volumes, 6.5 million microform items, and 15,554 audio/video tapes/CDs/DVDs, and subscribe to 69,664 periodicals including electronic. Computerized library services include interlibrary loans and database searching. Special learning facilities include an art gallery, natural history museum, planetarium, radio station, Beinecke Rare Books and Manuscript Library, Marsh Botanical Gardens and Yale Natural Preserves, and several research centers. The 200-acre campus is in an urban area 75 miles northeast of New York City. Including any residence halls, there are 200 buildings.

Programs of Study: Yale confers B.A., B.S., and B.L.S. degrees. Master's and doctoral degrees are also awarded. Bachelor's degrees are awarded in BIOLOGICAL SCIENCE (biochemistry, biology/biological science, and biophysics), COMMUNICATIONS AND THE ARTS (art, art history and appreciation, Chinese, classics, dramatic arts, English, film arts, French, German, Italian, Japanese, linguistics, literature, music, Portuguese, Russian, Spanish, and theater management), COMPUTER AND PHYSICAL SCIENCE (applied mathematics, astronomy, chemistry, computer science, geology, mathematics, and physics), ENGINEERING AND ENVIRONMENTAL DESIGN (architecture, biomedical engineering, chemical engineering, electrical/electronics engineering, engineering, engineering and applied science, and mechanical engineering), SOCIAL SCIENCE (African American studies, American studies, anthropology, archeology, classical/ancient civilization, East Asian studies, Eastern European studies, economics, ethics, politics, and social policy, ethnic studies, German area studies, history, history of science, humanities, Judaic studies, Latin American studies, Near Eastern studies, philosophy, political science/government, psychology, religion, sociology, and women's studies). History, political science, and economics are the largest.

Special: The university offers study abroad in several countries, including England, Russia, Germany, and Japan, and cooperates with other study-abroad opportunities. It also offers an accelerated degree program, B.A.-B.S. degrees, dual majors, and student-designed majors. Directed Studies, a special freshman program in the humanities, affords outstanding students the opportunity to survey the Western cultural tradition. Programs in the residential colleges allow students with special interests to pursue them in a more informal atmosphere. There is a Phi Beta Kappa honors program.

Requirements: The SAT or ACT is required. The ACT Optional Writing test is also required. Only those applicants submitting SAT scores must also take any 3 SAT Subject tests. Most successful applicants rank in the top 10% of their high school class. All students must have completed a rigorous high school program encompassing all academic disciplines. 2 essays are required, and an interview is recommended. AP credits are accepted. Important factors in the admissions decision are advanced placement or honors courses, leadership record, and extracurricular activities record.

Procedure: Freshmen are admitted fall. Entrance exams should be taken at any time up to and including the January test date in the year of application. There are early decision and deferred admissions plan. Check with the school for current application deadlines. The fall 2009 application fee was $75. Applications are accepted on-line. A waiting list is maintained.

Financial Aid: Yale is a member of CSS. The CSS/Profile, FAFSA, and student and parent tax returns, as well as the CSS Divorced/Separated Parents Statement and Business/Farm Supplement, if applicable, are required. Check with the school for current application deadlines.

Computers: All students may access the system 24 hours a day. There are no time limits and no fees. It is strongly recommended that all students have a personal computer.

New York, NY 10033-3201　　**(212) 960-5277; (212) 960-0086**

Full-time: 1305 men, 1010 women	**Faculty:** I, +$
Part-time: 40 men, 20 women	**Ph.D.s:** 79%
Graduate: 1300 men, 1700 women	**Student/Faculty:** n/av
Year: semesters, summer session	**Tuition:** $33,050
Application Deadline: see profile	**Room & Board:** $11,000
Freshman Class: n/av	
SAT or ACT: required	**VERY COMPETITIVE**

Yeshiva University, founded in 1886, is an independent liberal arts institution offering undergraduate programs through Yeshiva College, its undergraduate college for men, Stern College for Women, and Sy Syms School of Business. Figures in the above capsule are approximate. There are 7 graduate schools. In addition to regional accreditation, YU has baccalaureate program accreditation with CSWE. The 7 libraries contain 900,000 volumes, 759,000 microform items, and 980 audio/video tapes/CDs/DVDs, and subscribe to 7,790 periodicals including electronic. Computerized library services include interlibrary loans and database searching. Special learning facilities include an art gallery, radio station, and museum. The 26-acre campus is in an urban area.

Programs of Study: YU confers B.A. and B.S. degrees. Associates degrees are also awarded. Bachelor's degrees are awarded in BIOLOGICAL SCIENCE (biology/biological science), BUSINESS (accounting, business administration and management, and marketing/retailing/merchandising), COMMUNICATIONS AND THE ARTS (classical languages, communications, English, French, Hebrew, music, and speech/debate/rhetoric), COMPUTER AND PHYSICAL SCIENCE (chemistry, computer science, and mathematics), ENGINEERING AND ENVIRONMENTAL DESIGN (preengineering), HEALTH PROFESSIONS (health science), SOCIAL SCIENCE (economics, history, philosophy, political science/government, psychology, religion, and sociology). The dual program of liberal arts and Jewish studies is the strongest academically. Accounting, psychology, and economics are the largest.

Special: YU offers a 3-2 degree in occupational therapy with Columbia and New York Universities, a 3-4 degree in podiatry with the New York College of Podiatric Medicine, and a 3-2 or 4-2 degree in engineering with Columbia University. Stern College students may take courses in advertising, photography, and design at the Fashion Institute of Technology. Study-abroad programs may be arranged in Israel. The school offers independent study options and an optional pass/no credit system. There are 9 national honor societies and 20 departmental honors programs.

Requirements: The SAT or ACT is required. In addition, graduation from an accredited secondary school with 16 academic credits is required for admission. The GED is accepted under limited and specific circumstances. The SAT Subject test in Hebrew is recommended for placement purposes. An interview and an essay are required. A GPA of 3.3 is required. AP and CLEP credits are accepted. Important factors in the admissions decision are extracurricular activities record, personality/intangible qualities, and evidence of special talent.

Procedure: Freshmen are admitted to all sessions. There are early admissions, deferred admissions, and rolling admissions plans. Check with the school for current application deadlines. The application fee is $70. A waiting list is maintained.

Financial Aid: YU is a member of CSS. The CSS/Profile and the college's own financial statement are required. Check with the school for current application deadlines.

Computers: All students may access the system 24 hours per day via modem or when buildings are open. There are no time limits and no fees.

ALPHABETICAL INDEX

University of Science and Arts of Oklahoma, OK, **752**
University of Scranton, PA, **753**
University of South Carolina at Columbia, SC, **755**
University of South Florida, FL, **756**
University of Southern California, CA, **758**
University of Tennessee at Knoxville, TN, **760**
University of Texas at Austin, TX, **761**
University of Texas at Dallas, TX, **763**
University of Texas at San Antonio, TX, **765**
University of the Pacific, CA, **766**
University of the Sciences in Philadelphia, PA, **768**
University of Tulsa, OK, **770**
University of Utah, UT, **771**
University of Vermont, VT, **773**
University of Virginia, VA, **775**
University of Washington, WA, **777**
University of Wisconsin/Eau Claire, WI, **778**
University of Wisconsin/La Crosse, WI, **780**
University of Wisconsin/Madison, WI, **782**
University of Wisconsin/Milwaukee, WI, **783**
University of Wisconsin/Superior, WI, **785**
Ursinus College, PA, **786**
Vanderbilt University, TN, **788**
Vassar College, NY, **789**
Villanova University, PA, **791**
Virginia Commonwealth University, VA, **792**

Virginia Polytechnic Institute and State University, VA, **794**
Wabash College, IN, **796**
Wagner College, NY, **797**
Wake Forest University, NC, **799**
Warren Wilson College, NC, **800**
Wartburg College, IA, **802**
Washington and Jefferson College, PA, **804**
Washington and Lee University, VA, **805**
Washington College, MD, **807**
Washington University in Saint Louis, MO, **809**
Webb Institute, NY, **811**
Wellesley College, MA, **812**
Wells College, NY, **813**
Wesleyan University, CT, **815**
Western Washington University, WA, **816**
Westminster College, MO, **818**
Westminster College, UT, **820**
Westmont College, CA, **822**
Wheaton College, IL, **823**
Wheaton College, MA, **825**
Whitman College, WA, **827**
Willamette University, OR, **828**
William Jewell College, MO, **830**
Williams College, MA, **831**
Wisconsin Lutheran College, WI, **833**
Wofford College, SC, **834**
Worcester Polytechnic Institute, MA, **835**
Xavier University, OH, **837**
Yale University, CT, **838**
Yeshiva University, NY, **840**

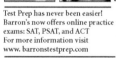